D0931583

NEW WORLD IMMIGRANTS

*A Consolidation of Ship Passenger Lists
and Associated Data
from Periodical Literature*

Edited by Michael Tepper

VOLUME II

Baltimore
GENEALOGICAL PUBLISHING CO., INC.
1980

© 1979
Genealogical Publishing Co., Inc.
Baltimore, Maryland
All Rights Reserved
First Printing 1979
Second Printing 1980
Library of Congress Catalogue Card Number 79-84392
International Standard Book Number: Volume II: 0-8063-0853-2
Set: 0-0863-0854-0
Made in the United States of America

CONTENTS

Germanic Immigrants Named in Early Pennsylvania Ship Lists, by Charles R. Roberts, *The Pennsylvania German Society Proceedings and Addresses*, XXXIX (1928), 5-20. — 1

Annotations to Strassburger and Hinke's Pennsylvania German Pioneers, by Friedrich Krebs, *The Pennsylvania Genealogical Magazine*, XXI (1960), 235-248. — 17

Palatines on the Ship "Thistle of Glasgow" (1730), by Fritz Braun, *The Pennsylvania Dutchman*, V (March 1954), 13. — 31

18th Century Palatine Emigrants from the Ludwigshafen Area, by Fritz Braun, *The Pennsylvania Dutchman*, V (March 1954), 13. — 32

Pennsylvania Dutch Pioneers, by Friedrich Krebs, *The Pennsylvania Dutchman*, VI (June 1954), 40, (September 1954), 37, (Winter 1954-1955), 39, (Spring 1955), 37-38; VII (Winter 1956), 38-39, (Spring 1956), 38-39; VIII (Summer 1956), 57-59. — 34

Pennsylvania Dutch Pioneers from South Palatine Parishes, by Fritz Braun and Friedrich Krebs, *The Pennsylvania Dutchman*, VIII (Spring 1957), 39-42. — 61

A List of the First Shipload of Georgia Settlers, by E. Merton Coulter, *Georgia Historical Quarterly*, XXXI (1947), 282-288. — 75

Purrysburgh, by Henry A. M. Smith, *The South Carolina Historical and Genealogical Magazine*, X (1909), 187-219. — 82

Early Highland Immigration to New York, by E. B. O'Callaghan, *The Historical Magazine and Notes and Queries Concerning the Antiquities, History and Biography of America*, V (1861), 301-304. — 115

Pioneers from Staudernheim, by Hugo Froehlich, *The Pennsylvania Dutchman*, VIII (Fall-Winter 1956-1957), 43-46. — 123

Augusta County Early Settlers, Importations, 1739-1740, by Mrs. W. W. King, *National Genealogical Society Quarterly*, XXV (1937), 46-48. — 133

A List of Convicts Transported to Maryland, by Frank F. White, Jr., *Maryland Historical Magazine*, XLIII (1948), 55-60.　136

Passengers on the "Loyal Judith" (1740), by Fritz Braun, *The Pennsylvania Dutchman*, V (March 1954), 12.　142

The Naturalization of Jews in the American Colonies Under the Act of 1740, by J. H. Hollander, *Publications of the American Jewish Historical Society*, No. 5 (1897), 103-117.　143

Naturalization of Jews in New York Under the Act of 1740, by Leon Hühner, *Publications of the American Jewish Historical Society*, No. 13 (1905), 1-6.　158

Some Saxe-Gothan Settlers, excerpted from "The German and German-Swiss Element in South Carolina," by Gilbert P. Voigt, *Bulletin of the University of South Carolina*, No. 113 (1922), 56-60.　164

Pennsylvania Pioneers from the Neckar Valley 1749-1750, by Friedrich Krebs, *The Pennsylvania Dutchman*, V (June 1953), 13.　169

Palatine Emigrants from the District of Neustadt—1750, by Friedrich Krebs, *The Pennsylvania Dutchman*, V (May 1953), 9.　172

18th Century Emigrants from Edenkoben in the Palatinate, by Friedrich Krebs, *The Pennsylvania Dutchman*, IV (January 1953), 9.　174

Emigrants from Baden-Durlach to Pennsylvania 1749-1755, by Friedrich Krebs, *National Genealogical Society Quarterly*, 45 (1957), 30-31.　176

Pennsylvania Dutch Pioneers from Baden-Durlach: 1752, by Friedrich Krebs, *The Pennsylvania Dutchman*, VIII (Summer-Fall 1957), 48.　178

More 18th Century Emigrants from the Palatinate, by Friedrich Krebs, *The Pennsylvania Dutchman*, V (March 1954), 12.　180

Moravian Pioneers in the Swatara Valley—1752, by William J. Hinke, *The Pennsylvania Dutchman*, II (December 1950), 6.　181

Moravian Bretheren in Heidelberg—1752, by William J. Hinke, *The Pennsylvania Dutchman*, II (January 1951), 6.　183

Records of Emigrants from England and Scotland to North Carolina, 1774-1775, by A. R. Newsome, *The North Carolina Historical Review*, XI (1934), 39-54, 129-143.   186

Scotch Emigrants to New York 1774-1775, by Wallace R. Freeman, *The Niagara Frontier Genealogical Magazine*, IV (1944), 89-90, 124-125, 136-137, 145.   217

A New Emigrant List, by Don Yoder, *The Pennsylvania Dutchman*, I (May 1949), 6.   224

French Immigrants to Louisiana 1796-1800, by L. Perez, *Publications of the Southern History Association*, XI (1907), 106-112.   226

Lehigh County Naturalization Records, by Don Yoder, *The Pennsylvania Dutchman*, I (May 1949), 6; II (January 1950), 6.   233

Naturalizations—During the Court Sessions of January, 1798, Washington Co., Maryland, by Kate Singer Curry, *National Genealogical Society Quarterly*, XXIII (1935), 111-113.   240

Early New York Naturalization Records in the Emmet Collection; with a List of Aliens Naturalized in New York 1802-1814, by Richard J. Wolfe, *Bulletin of The New York Public Library*, LXVII (1963), 211-217.   242

Abstracts of Naturalization Records, Circuit Court, District of Columbia, by Vivian Holland, *National Genealogical Society Quarterly*, XLI (1953), 41-44, 90-92, 130-131; XLII (1954), 22-24, 68-73, 149-150; XLIII (1955), 20-21, 146-147; 44 (1956), 16-19, 109-111, 147-149; 45 (1957), 21-26.   249

Early Irish Emigrants to America 1803-1806, *The Recorder; Bulletin of the American Irish Historical Society*, III (1926), 19-23.   289

American Passenger Lists, 1804-6, *Report of the Deputy Keeper of the Records for the Year 1929*, Northern Ireland, Public Record Office (1930), 15, 21-49.   295

List of German Passengers Arrived in the Port Philadelphia in the Ship Margaret, from Amsterdam . . . September 19th, 1804, *The Journal of the Lycoming Historical Society*, I (1956), 9-12.   325

Passenger Lists Published in "The Shamrock or Irish
Chronicle," 1811, by J. Dominick Hackett, *The Journal
of the American Irish Historical Society*, XXVIII
(1929-30), 65-82.   329

Passenger Lists from "The Shamrock or Irish Chronicle,"
1815-1816, by Charles Montague Early, *The Journal of
the American Irish Historical Society*, XXIX (1930-
31), 183-206.   347

"Restaurationen"—the Norse Mayflower, by Rasmus B.
Anderson, *The American-Scandinavian Review*, XIII
(1925), 348-360.   371

Four Immigrant Shiploads of 1836 and 1837, by Henry J.
Cadbury, *The Norwegian-American Historical Association Studies and Records*, II (1927), 20-52.   384

Passenger List of the "Sarah Sheaffe", May, 1836, by
Louis C. Cramton, *The Detroit Society for Genealogical
Research Magazine*, V (1942), 208.   417

An Immigrant Shipload of 1840, by C. A. Clausen,
Norwegian-American Studies and Records, XIV (1944),
54-77.   419

Ship List of the *Orient*, 19 May 1842, by Lucy Mary Kel-
logg, *The Detroit Society for Genealogical Research
Magazine*, XXVI (1962), 63-64.   443

State-Aided Emigration Schemes from Crown Estates in
Ireland c. 1850, by Eilish Ellis, *Analecta Hibernica*,
XXII (1960), 331-394.   448

Passenger List of Ship "Catherine" (August 14—September 19, 1850), excerpted from "Paulus den Bleyker:
Type and Prototype," by Timothy Rey, *Michigan Heritage*, II (1960), 15-16.   512

A Passenger List of Mennonite Immigrants from Russia
in 1878, *The Mennonite Quarterly Review*, XV (1941),
263-276.   514

Scraps & Splinters

Marriages of Emigrants to Virginia, by Winifred Lovering Holman, *The Virginia Magazine of History and
Biography*, XL (1932), 80.   529

Passengers on the *Griffin*, June 23, 1675, excerpted from "Fenwick, Adams, Hedge, and Champneys, of Salem, N.J.," by Lewis D. Cook, *The Genealogical Magazine of New Jersey*, XXXV (1960), 108.   530

Passengers on the *Griffin*, June 23, 1675, excerpted from "Memoir of John Fenwicke, Chief Proprietor of Salem Tenth, New Jersey," by Robert G. Johnson, *Proceedings of the New Jersey Historical Society*, IV (1849-1850), 61.   530

Passengers for New England, *The Essex Antiquarian*, XI (1907), 65.   531

Passengers from the Rhineland to Pennsylvania, by Harrold E. Gillingham, *Publications of the Genealogical Society of Pennsylvania*, XIV (1942), 79.   531

List of Convicts from Bristol to South Carolina [1728], excerpted from "The White Indentured Servants of South Carolina," by Theodore D. Jervey, *The South Carolina Historical and Genealogical Magazine*, XII (1911), 171.   532

Philadelphia Arrivals, 1738, by Harrold E. Gillingham, *Publications of the Genealogical Society of Pennsylvania*, XII (1934), 150.   533

Naturalization of Maryland Settlers in Pennsylvania, *Maryland Historical Magazine*, V (1910), 72.   533

List of Passengers and Crew on Board the Brigantine *Matty*, from Scotland to New York, May 19-July 22, 1774, excerpted from "Journal of Colonel Alexander Harvey of Scotland and Barnet, Vermont," *Proceedings of the Vermont Historical Society* (1921-1923), 204.   534

Index of Names   535

Index of Ships   601

NEW WORLD
IMMIGRANTS

VOLUME II

GERMANIC IMMIGRANTS NAMED IN EARLY PENNSYLVANIA SHIP LISTS

ETWEEN the years 1683 and 1727, how many persons of Germanic origin settled in Pennsylvania will probably never be known. Some writers have estimated the number as high as 50,000. The Crefeld colony under Pastorius came in 1683. In 1694 Johannes Kelpius came with his band of 40 pietists. Daniel Falkner and others arrived in 1704. In 1705 a number of German Reformed residing between Wolfenbuettel and Halberstadt, fled to Neuwied and then to Holland, and in 1707 sailed for New York. Their ship was carried into Delaware Bay and they eventually settled along the Musconetcong and the Passaic in New Jersey, in what is now known as the German Valley. In 1708 the Kocherthal colony came to New York, most of whom afterwards came to Pennsylvania. In 1709 a colony of Swiss, principally Mennonite, settled in Lancaster county.

In September, 1717, three ships arrived at Philadelphia with a total of 363 Palatines. In 1719 Jonathan Dickinson wrote, "We are daily expecting ships from London which bring over palatines, in number about six or seven thousand." On August 30, 1720, the ship Laurel arrived with 240 odd Palatines. Between the years 1708 and 1720, thousands arrived.

The Provincial Council, by a resolution adopted September 14, 1727, required shipmasters to make lists of all immigrants and that the immigrants sign an oath of allegiance to the King of England. The majority of these lists are preserved in the State Library at Harrisburg. It was on March 6, 1903, that I saw these original lists for the first time. They were in the library proper, as the Department of Public Records had not yet been established.

The first ship, record of whose passengers was kept by the Colonial Government, was the William and Sarah, which actually arrived about September 12, 1727, and not September 18th, and on September 21st not more than 51 of the 317 passengers, 109 of whom were men, signed the oath of allegiance. Rev. Dr. Hinke, in Volume 27, has shown us what errors there are in the published lists.

IMMIGRANTS NAMED IN SHIP LISTS

The leader of this band was Rev. George Michael Weiss, a Reformed clergyman, born in 1700 at Eppingen, in the Palatinate. Michael Diel, Rudolf Wellecker, George Kremer and Henrich Weller located in Philadelphia. Those who settled in Goshenhoppen, now Montgomery county, were John Frederick Hillegs, born in Alsace, Nov. 24, 1685, died Jan. 6, 1765; John George Welcker, born Feb. 6, 1697, died March 8, 1782; John Huth, who died suddenly in Philadelphia on Aug. 14, 1759. His funeral text was: "Mein Leben ist abgerissen

wie ein Weber spull." Michael Zimmerman and Benedict Strohm. David Schultz in his journal says that
Strohm's wife died in April, 1757, and on June 14, 1757,
he married again, at the age of 62, a girl of fifteen. John
George Bowman, Sebastian Smith and Ulrich Stephen
settled at Skippack and John George Schwab and
Leonard Seltenreich in the Conestoga valley.

John or John Michael Diffenderfer, the ancestor of
the founder, or one of the founders, of this society,
Frank Ried Diffenderfer, was born Jan. 10, 1695, at
Neresheim, near Heidelberg, in the Chur Pfalz, and died
in 1778 in Lancaster county. Alexander Diefenderfer,
an ancestor of the writer, died in 1768 in what is now
Lehigh county. They were the sons of John Duebendorffer, born Oct. 8, 1663. The family came from Due-
bendorf, six miles northeast of Zurich, Switzerland,
formerly Diebeldorf, anciently Tobelindorf. The family
is mentioned as early as 1130 and in 1229 Cuno von Diebendorf, Knight, is mentioned in a document of the
cloister at Zinckenburg as a witness.

Joseph Albright settled in Macungie township, now
Lehigh county, where he died in 1744. Some of his descendants removed to Northumberland county. Daniel
Levan settled in Maxatawny township, Berks county,
where he died in 1777.

On the ship Adventurer, October 2, 1727, was Ulrich
Rieser, born April 9, 1709, who died Sept. 9, 1784, in
Lower Milford township, now Lehigh county, and John
Dieter Bauman, who settled first in Marlbore township,
Philadelphia county, where he operated a grist mill and
about 1755 removed beyond the Blue Mountains, to
Towamensing township, now Carbon county, where he
died in 1762.

The ship Friendship, October 16, 1727, had among its
passengers Joseph Eberhard, a native of Switzerland,

who settled in Lower Milford township, now Lehigh
county, was one of the founders of the Great Swamp
church and at his death in 1760 left each of his six sons
a large farm. His brother, Michael Eberhard, settled
just over the county line in Milford township, Bucks
county, where he died in 1772.

On the ship Mortonhouse, August 24, 1728, was
Clement Dunkelberger, who died in 1782 in Berks
county. His son John removed to Mahanoy township,
Northumberland county. Also, Henrich Wilhelm Dillinger from Wurtemberg, who settled in Bucks, now Lehigh county.

On the ship James Goodwill, Sept. 11, 1728, came
Rev. John Caspar Stoever, Sr., a native of Franken-
berg, in Hesse, a Lutheran clergyman, who located in
Virginia, went to Europe in 1737, and died on board the
vessel on his attempted return to America, and Rev.
John Caspar Stoever, Jr., born at Luedorff, in Solinger
Amt, Duchy Berg, in the Palatinate, Dec. 21, 1707, and
died at Lebanon May 13, 1779.

Theobald Mechling, born (probably at Lambesheim
in Chur Pfaltz), who settled in Lower Milford, now Lehigh county, where a descendant, a member of this society, still owns the land he took up. He died in April,
1765. Four of his sons removed to Northumberland
county and many descendants reside in Western Pennsylvania and Ohio. His brother Jacob settled in Germantown.

Egidius Grim, from Wurtemberg, settled in Bucks
county, in what is now Macungie township, Lehigh
county, where he died in 1761.

Martin Moser settled in Montgomery county.

Philip Henry Seller settled in Philadelphia county,
was an elder of the Skippack church in 1734 and died

July 8, 1769. The town of Sellersville takes its name from the family.

Frederick Scholl settled first in Philadelphia county and in 1734 in Bucks county, where Hellertown, Northampton county, now is located. He was an elder of the Lower Saucon church and died in 1754.

On the Mortonhouse, Aug. 19, 1729, was Frederick Ludwig Marsteller, from Darmstadt. He settled on the Skippack creek in New Providence township, in Philadelphia, now Montgomery county. He was one of the founders and deacons of the Lutheran church at Trappe and his name appears in Latin over the door of this, the oldest Lutheran church building in America, erected in 1743. He was a warm friend of Rev. Henry Melchior Muhlenberg, who preached an English sermon at his funeral. He died October 14, 1753. His youngest son, Col. Philip Marsteller, was one of Washington's pallbearers.

Michael Weber and his wife Phillis were also passengers on this ship. He was born in the Palatinate in 1703 and settled in Bucks county, now Upper Saucon township, Lehigh county, where he died August 10, 1745, and was buried on his own land. His widow, Johanna Felicitas, subsequently married Anthony Wilhelm Boehm, eldest son of Rev. John Philip Boehm.

Wendel Wyandt, or Wieand, born July 14, 1709, at Frensheim in the Palatinate, settled in Upper Hanover township, Philadelphia county, and died there in 1787.

Michael Borst died near Lebanon in 1741. George Adam Weidel settled near Lebanon. Jacob Seller lived at Germantown.

On August 29, 1730, came the Thistle, with Peter Miller, born at Ober Amt Lautern, a graduate of Heidelberg University, and son of a Reformed minister, who, in 1735, went over to the Brethren at Ephrata, was called Brother Jabez, and died there Sept. 25, 1796.

Valentine Griesheimer, from Lampedheim, with his wife and four children, came with a passport given at Worms on April 28, 1730. He settled in Berks county and died in Hereford township about 1759.

Peter Fetterolf, born at Wachbach, March 20, 1699, settled in Berks county and died in Hereford township, Aug. 15, 1784. Descendants of his settled in Cameron township, Northumberland county.

Abraham Transue, born in Mutterstadt, in the Palatinate, also was on board and settled in Bucks county. Rudolph Drach also settled in Bucks county.

I have here a photostat of the original signatures of the passengers on the ship Brittania, which arrived Sept. 21, 1731. At the head of the list is the name Johannes Barthalomay Rieger, Hochteutscher Prediger. He was born at Oberingelheim, in the Palatinate, Jan. 23, 1707, and attended the universities of Heidelberg and Basel, became pastor at Philadelphia and Germantown and in New Jersey. He died at Lancaster in 1769.

Matthias Smeisser, born at Rugelbach in 1715, died in York county in 1778.

Leonard Steininger settled in Northampton county and died there in 1753.

Michael Stocker, John Eigender and John and Hubertus Bartsch settled in Bucks county.

The ship Snow Lowther arrived October 14, 1731, with Casper Peter, born in 1698 in Zell, Switzerland, whose three sons are the ancestors of the large Peters family of Lehigh county.

The ship Samuel came Aug. 11, 1732. On board were John Helfrich, born in 1699, who settled in Upper Milford township, Bucks county, now Lehigh, and died Feb. 27, 1764.

Christian and Benedict Gehman, Mennonites, settled

in Bucks county, as did also John George Kleinhantz.

Jacob Gochnaur and Oswald Hostetter settled in Lancaster county.

Anastasius Uhler, born in the Palatinate about 1710, settled in Lancaster county and died at Lebanon. He was constable of Lebanon township in 1769.

The ship Pennsylvania arrived Sept. 11, 1732, with 171 passengers. Paul Ritter, born in 1713, settled in Colebrookdale, Berks county, where he died Feb. 14, 1799. Henry Ritter settled in Lower Milford township, now Lehigh county, just west of the Great Swamp Church. A section of the log over the fireplace, with the date 1739, from a house built by him, is in the possession of the Lehigh County Historical Society. He removed to Salisbury township, where he died in January, 1797. Casper Ritter settled in Bethlehem township, Northampton county, where he built a mill and died in 1792.

Paul Linsen Bigler settled in Philadelphia county.

The ship Pink Johnson arrived Sept. 19, 1732. The archives gives 110 names, this photostat shows 112. There are many errors. Behn should be Bohn, Beer, Bey, Rouse, Rausch, Coplinger, Keplinger, etc. John Moessinger settled in Bucks county. With him was his son, Michael Messinger, born Nov. 10, 1719, who settled first in Bucks county and later in Forks township, Northampton county, where he had a grist mill, became prominent and was a member of the County Committee of Observation in the Revolution. He died October 24, 1791. He was the ancestor of one of the members of our Executive Committee and has many descendants in Northampton county.

Another passenger was Andreas Oberbeck, from Oberamt Neustadt in the Palatinate, born about 1690, settled first at Skippack, where he was elder of the Reformed Church from 1739 to 1744; removed to Bucks county, where he died in 1765.

The first name on the list is John Steiman. He was born in 1668 at Strassburg, the son of Peter Steinman, who was married June 18, 1645, to Sara Metzgar. She was born Feb. 3, 1623. With him was his son, John George Steinman, born March 18, 1703, who settled in Philadelphia county.

John George Sehm settled in Bucks county and John Dieter settled in what is now Northampton county, where he died in 1758.

The ship Adventurer came Sept. 23, 1732. On it came Mathias Riegel, born in 1709, who settled in Lower Saucon township, the present Northampton county, where he died in 1778. George Riegel, born in 1718, settled in Bucks county, and died May 17, 1798.

Tobias Moser, born 1702, settled in Bucks, now Lehigh county, and died in 1757.

George Breiner settled in Berks county.

Baltzer Bortner, born 1695, settled in Tulpehocken township, Lancaster county, and died in 1747. His son, Jacob, born in 1722, settled in 1761 in Northumberland county and died in 1792.

Mathias Wagner, born 1709, settled in Northampton county.

The ship Loyal Judith arrived Sept. 25, 1732, with Philip Jacob Acker, born 1696, who settled in Macungie township, now Lehigh county, and Henry Acker, born in 1700, who settled in Bucks county.

The ship Dragon arrived Sept. 30, 1732. Among its passengers were Peter Mattern, an ancestor of the writer, who settled in Bucks, now Lehigh county. Some descendants settled in Upper Mahanoy township, Northumberland county.

Felix Brunner settled in Lower Milford township of the present Lehigh county, where he died in 1760.

John Adam Romich, born Feb. 3, 1689, at Rueden-stein, in the Palatinate, a Lutheran and a deacon, in 1762 joined the Moravians in Lynn township, Lehigh county, and died there July 11, 1768.

Leonard Schlosser settled in Bucks, now Lehigh county.

Tobias Bahl settled in Upper Saucon township, Lehigh county, where he died in 1759.

Jacob Dubs, a gunsmith, born Aug. 31, 1710, in Aesch, parish of Birmensdorf, Canton of Zurich, Switzerland, settled in Lower Milford township, the present Lehigh county. He was the ancestor of Rev. Dr. Joseph H. Dubbs.

The ship Pink, John and William, arrived Oct. 17, 1732. On it were Sebastian Truckenmiller, born Aug. 1, 1715, died Feb. 1, 1795. He is buried in a field, formerly his own land, in Lehigh county. Some of his descendants settled in Northumberland county. Henry Keck, from Bavaria, is the ancestor of a large Lehigh county family.

On August 17, 1733, the ship Samuel arrived. The archives give 88 males over 16 on board, with one sick, which name Rupp gives, making 89. George Ruch. Senior's age is given as 48. His tombstone states he was born in Zitzendorf, Alsace, in 1664, making him 68. He died in Whitehall township, now Lehigh county, in 1769, aged 104 years and 11 months.

John Lichtenwalner, from Kreuth, in Kolmberg, in Brandenberg was a passenger. His passport, dated April 25, 1733, is still in existence. He settled in Bucks now Lehigh county.

Peter Troxell, from Switzerland, one of the founders

of the Egypt Church, Whitehall township, Lehigh county, and who is given as church censor in 1736.

Ulrich Flickinger, born 1702, died 1792, in Whitehall township.

Michael Brobst settled in Albany township, Berks county.

Peter Beisel, whose son Peter, aged 8, became a member of the Northampton County Revolutionary Committee of Observation.

Henry Roth, born in 1688, was one of the two men who gave the land for the Salisbury Church, near Allentown.

The ship Hope arrived August 28, 1733. I have here a photostat of the original list. Rupp says there are 83 over 16; he gives 81. The archives give 79. There are really 84, with some errors in the names.

David Deshler, born in 1711, died in 1792, settled in Germantown, and became a prominent merchant, noted for his honesty and integrity. "As honest as David Deshler" became a proverb. He built the Morris Mansion in 1774, which became the headquarters of Sir William Howe in the Revolution and the residence of President Washington in 1793.

Daniel Roth, a direct ancestor of the writer, born in Switzerland in 1703, died near Allentown in 1737. His son, Hon. Peter Rhoads, reared among Quakers, was a Revolutionary patriot and judge for 30 years.

Jacob Mueckli settled in Whitehall township, and died in 1769.

John Jacob Schreiber, born in Niederbronn, Alsace, in 1699, died in 1750 in Whitehall township.

Michale, Peter and Ulrich Witmer were among the passengers. Peter Witmer, born in 1737, in Hertzheim, Nassau-Dillenberg, Prussia, who in 1766 located near

Port Treverton, Snyder county, where he died in 1793, was probably a nephew of these Witmers.

Ulrich, Jacob and Ulrich Lonagcre, Jr., settled in Philadelphia county.

Henrich, Mathias and Bernard Fegley settled in Philadelphia, now Berks county. A member of our Executive Committee descends from one of these men.

Rudolph Schneebele, Christian and Peter Eschelman, John Snabley and Jacob Burki settled in Lancaster county.

On the Brigantine Richard and Elizabeth, Sept. 28, 1733, were John Nicholas Saeger, born 1694, at Reichenbach, Bavaria, who settled in Whitehall township, Bucks county, now Lehigh, and died there in 1762.

Ulrich Burkhalter, from Switzerland, born 1693, died in 1762, in Whitehall township.

On the ship St. Andrew, Sept. 12, 1734, came the important Schwenkfelder colony, which I will not mention in detail at this time. Also Jacob Wildfang, who located in Philadelphia. Descendants are in North Carolina.

On the ship Mercury, May 29, 1735, was a colony of Swiss, headed by Rev. Maurice Goetschy, from Saletz, Switzerland. Rev. Goetschy was sick when the ship arrived and died the following day. His son, John Henry, born March 8, 1718, was a student at the Latin school at Zurich and began to preach to the Reformed settlers at the age of 17, not only at Philadelphia, but at Skippack, Goshenhoppen, Great Swamp, Egypt, Saucon, Maxatawny, Moselem, Oley, Bern and Tulpehocken. He was licensed to preach in 1737 and ordained in 1741 and became a pastor in New Jersey.

John Conrad Wuertz, born Nov. 30, 1706, in the Canton of Zurich, Switzerland, married Anna, daughter of Rev. Maurice Goetschy. He became school teacher, began preaching in 1742, was ordained in 1752 and died at York Sept. 21, 1763.

Ulrich Arner, born in 1699 in Switzerland, settled in Bucks, now Lehigh county.

On the ship Harle, Sept. 1, 1736, was George Zeisloff, born 1709, who, with his wife and several children, was killed by Indians in Lynn township, Northampton county, now Lehigh, March 24, 1756, only two sons surviving. His house is still standing.

John Adam Schaus, born 1704, settled in Bucks county.

The ship Princess Augusta, Sept. 16, 1736, had as a passenger George Nicholas Gauger, born in 1718, who settled in Tulphehocken and whose son John Wilhelm settled in Northumberland county.

The ship Samuel, Aug. 30, 1737, brought John Troxell and his son John Peter Troxell, who was born April 3, 1719, in Switzerland, naturalized in 1748 and in 1756 built a large stone house, with a unique inscription, still standing, in which the Egypt Reformed congregation worshipped. In 1768 he sold his 410 acres and removed to Gwynedd township, Philadelphia county, where he owned a grist and a saw mill. In 1776 he removed to Maryland, where he died Jan. 25, 1799.

Frederick Eberhard, born 1697, died 1751, settled in Bucks county.

Philip Fenstermacher, born in the Palatinate Feb. 27, 1713, died in Longswamp township, Berks county, June 15, 1790.

This is the last ship list given in the Colonial Records.

The ship St. Andrew, Sept. 26, 1737, brought many who settled in Eastern Pennsylvania.

John Erdman, from Pfungstadt, Hesse Darmstadt, settled in Bucks county.

George Frederick Newhard, from Zweibruecken, born 1700, died Nov. 29, 1765, another ancestor of the writer, settled in Whitehall township, Bucks, now Lehigh county. His brother, Michael Newhard, born Feb. 9, 1713, died March 10, 1793, settled in the northern part of the same township, and George Newhard, born 1720, died 1800, settled in Allen township, Northampton county.

Balthazar Beil settled in Upper Saucon township, Bucks, now Lehigh county, as did also John Appel, from Pfungstadt.

George Kern settled in Whitehall township and Philip Seger settled in Lehigh township, Northampton county.

Martin Kocher, born at Holtzenhausen, Nassau Dillenberg, died about 1762, settled in what is now Lehigh county.

On the ship Winter Galley, Sept. 5, 1738, came Christopher Heller, born in 1688 in Petersheim, in the Palatinate. He settled in Northampton county, where he died in 1778. With him was his son Simon Heller, born June 18, 1721, died May 20, 1785, who settled in the same county.

On the ship Glasgow, Sept. 9, 1738, were the following:

Mathias Fenstermacher, born in 1678 in the Palatinate, who settled in Berks county.

Frantz Guildner, who settled in Bucks, now Lehigh county.

John Pontius, born in 1718 in Alsace, settled in Tulpehocken, Berks county. Several of his sons were pioneers in the Buffalo Valley.

September 11, 1738, came the ship Robert and Alice, with John Nicholas Schneider, who was evidently a well educated man, as he wrote a fine hand. He settled in what is now Lehigh county, where he was a Justice of the Peace in Colonial times, when still a part of Bucks county.

The ship Queen Elizabeth arrived Sept. 16, 1738. Here were Reinhard Laubach, aged 70, and his son Christian Laubach, born 1699, died Nov. 19, 1768, who settled in Lower Saucon township, Northampton county.

Anthony Lerch, born Sept. 20, 1720, died Aug. 28, 1793; his brother Pancratius Lerch, who died in 1794, and Peter Lerch, with their father, Andreas Lerch, aged 50, who all settled in Lower Saucon.

The Thistle, Sept. 19, 1738, brought Lorentz Guth, from Zweibruecken, who settled in Whitehall township, was the founder of the Jordan Reformed Church and died in 1770.

The ship Friendship came Sept. 20, 1738, with Jacob Folmer, born in the village of Rosswog, Wurtemberg in 1698, who settled in the Schoharie valley, New York, and later followed Conrad Weiser to Tulpehocken, where he died in 1762. His son Michael located on Limestone Run, in Northumberland county, in 1773, was the organizer of Follmer Lutheran Church in Turbot township, and died Sept. 29, 1793. He bequeathed £15 to the Dutch Lutheran Church, £10 to the school building and £10 towards teaching the poor children. His son, George Jacob Follmer, settled in 1773 in Turbot township, now Montour county. He was a member of the Assembly from Northumberland county in 1776 and 1777, re-elected in 1796, 1798, 1799, 1800 and 1801. In 1799 he received 3569 votes and Simon Snyder received 3047. Both were elected, as the two highest. In 1802 he was elected State Senator and died in office Aug. 24, 1804, and is buried at the Follmer Church. During one winter of the Assembly, two or three young lawyers, a little vain of their learning, interlarded their speeches with long quotations from Latin authors. This gave offense to Jacob Follmer, who in reply, remarked that as it was the fashion to make speeches in unknown tongues, he was to be excused if he spoke in the Delaware Indian dialect. This put an end to the Latin quotations.

On the ship Saint Andrew, Oct. 27, 1738, came John Rinehard Bene, who died in Northampton county in 1758. Michael Seider, born March 6, 1709, died Dec. 8, 1783, who settled in Upper Saucon township, then Bucks and now Lehigh county; John Nicholas Stahler, who died in September, 1794 in Northampton county, and George Bibighausen, born Sept. 3, 1708, in Elshof, in Wittgenstein.

The ship Bilander Thistle, Oct. 28, 1738, brought Conrad Merkam, who settled first in Berks county and later in Carbon county.

Peter Steckel, born 1719, settled in Whitehall township, where he died in 1784. His son, Daniel Steckel, died at Bath, Northampton county, aged 101 years and 17 days.

Samuel Eberhard Kopp, born in Lindenfingen, Wurtemberg, Jan. 8, 1700, settled in Bucks county, now Lehigh, where he died March 2, 1757.

On the ship Charming Nancy, Nov. 9, 1738, came Peter Butz, born in 1718, in Hertzogberg, Bavaria. He settled in Berks county and died March 18, 1780.

John Jacob Kuntz, born Feb. 19, 1692, at Niederbronn, Alsace, settled in Berks county. His son, Bernhard Kuntz, born Dec. 3, 1723, died July 14, 1807, settled in Northampton county. They are ancestors of one of our Executive Committee members.

On the ship Samuel, Aug. 27, 1739, came Joseph Biery, from the Canton of Bern, Switzerland, born 1703, who settled in Berks county and died in 1768. Also Casper Doll, born Feb. 2, 1724, died Feb. 4, 1793, in Plainfield township, Northampton county.

The ship Loyal Judith arrived Nov. 25, 1740, with Frederick Wilhelm Nagel, born in 1713, who settled in

Moore township, Northampton county, where he died Nov. 29, 1779.

These ship lists, up to the year 1775, if published and edited with notes as the example here given, would make a valuable addition to the history of the Pennsylvania Germans. At the July meeting of the Executive Committee I made the suggestion that this be done and that photostatic copies be made of all the lists. At the request of the Committee, I have therefore given the society this paper.

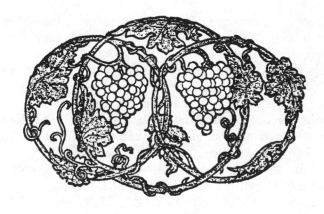

ANNOTATIONS TO STRASSBURGER AND HINKE'S PENNSYLVANIA GERMAN PIONEERS

By Friedrich Krebs

State Archives, Speyer on the Upper Rhine, West Germany

Editor's note—During the twenty-five years that have passed since the appearance of Strassburger and Hinke's valuable book, a number of German genealogists have spent time and effort in order to identify the European homes of those pioneers. Dr. Friedrich Krebs has been very active in that field. In 1953 he and Milton Rubicam, editor of the *National Genealogical Quarterly*, published *Emigrants from the Palatinate to the American Colonies in the 18th Century*, Pennsylvania German Soc'y., Norristown, Pa., 1953.

An article by Dr. Krebs, "Emigrants from Baden-Durlach 1749-55," appeared in the *National Genealogical Quarterly* of March 1957, pp. 30-31.

The following article is a composite of seven articles published in German genealogical magazines which the author has sent us for translation and publication.

R. D. O.

I

EARLY EMIGRATION from the COUNTY of HEIDELBERG, in the ELECTORAL PALATINATE, to AMERICA 1726-27.

Records deposited in the State Archives at Karlsruhe contain the following items:

1726-27

Permits to emigrate granted to

JACOB KIESSINGER—A poor resident of Sandhofen—to migrate to "the Island of Pennsylvania."

—————— BRECHT, widow of Johann Brecht, and her two sons Stephan and Johann from the village of Schriesheim.

MICHEL WEDEL, a resident of Dossenheim.

DANIEL LE VENT, a resident of Hockenheim.

MICHEL DIEL, a citizen of Mannheim-Seckenheim, upon payment of 36 florins, 55 kreuzers.

MICHEL BOETTLE (Bettle), citizen of Mannheim-Seckenheim, upon payment of 27 florins, 48 kreuzers, " to the new country." Diel and Boettle arrived in Philadelphia on the *William and Sarah* and took the oath of allegiance 21 Sept. 1727.

JOHANN JACOB CUNZ, resident of Walldorf, to " the island of Pennsylvania; " arrived on the *William and Sarah*, took the oath of allegiance 21 Sept. 1727.

CHRISTIAN MÜLLER, resident of Walldorf, " to the island of Pennsylvania." identical with either:

" CHRISTYAN MILLER," arriving on the ship *Molly*, oath of allegiance 30 Sept. 1727, or " CHRISTIAN MILLER," arriving on the ship *James Goodwill*, oath of allegiance 27 Sept. 1727.

JOHANN ALEXANDER DIEBENDOERFER, resident of Schriesheim; arrived on the *William and Sarah*, oath of allegiance 21 Sept. 1727.

ANNA MARIE WILL, resident of Schriesheim.

JACOB MUELLER, resident of Mannheim-Neckarau.
ANDREAS ZIMMERMANN, resident of Meckesheim.
JOHANN ANDREAS HILL, resident of Mannheim-Sandhofen.
CHRISTOPH WALTHER, resident of Dossenheim, undoubtedly identical with the Christopher Walther who arrive on the ship *William and Sarah* 18 Sept. 1727.

Original article " Zur Frü-auswanderung aus dem kurpfälzischen Oberamt Heidelberg nach Amerika (1726-27) " in *Sueddeutsche Blaetter für Familien- u. Wappenkunde,* June 1958, editor, Konrad v Alberti, Stuttgart-Sillenbach, West Germany.

II
Emigration from the County of Heidelberg 1741-1749

1741

The records of the county of Heidelberg on file in the General State Archives at Karlsruhe contain the following items:

VALENTIN ZWEISIG (ZWEISSIG), resident of Mauer, upon paying a fee of 3 florins, 30 kreuzers, was permitted to emigrate with his wife and four children " to the new land."
" VALDIN (VALENTIN) ZWEISIG " arrived in Philadelphia on the ship *Molly* 16 Oct. 1741.
MICHAEL MÜLLER, resident of Mauer, upon paying an emigration fee of 6 florins, was permitted to emigrate with his wife and five children.
" MICHAEL MILLER " arrived on the ship *Molly,* 16 Oct. 1741.
JOSEPH FABIAN, resident of Mauer.
" JOSEPH FABIAN " arrived in Philadelphia on the ship *Molly* 16 Oct. 1741.
JACOB HEZEL, resident of Schatthausen, made application for a permit, and presumably got it, but there seems to be no record of him as arriving in Philadelphia.
JACOB MUELLER—a cooper from Wiesloch, with the assistance of the town authorities, received permission to emigrate.

1742

CHRISTOPH GEISTER (GEISER?) of Eschelbronn was released from the status of a serf so that he might emigrate.
" CHRISTOF GEISER " arrived in Philadelphia 21 Sept. 1742.
Indigent brothers MICHAEL and DIETER DANNER of Walldorf were permitted to emigrate. They landed as Michael and Dietrich Danner on the ship *Robert and Alice;* took oath of allegiance 24 Sept 1742.

1743

CASPAR HAUCK, resident of Helmstadt, received a permit to migrate " to the island of Pennsylvania."
DIETRICH MUELLER, a baker, and
JACOB HOFFMANN, a shoemaker, both of Zuzenhausen, were permitted to leave without paying the usual fee because of their being poor. Jacob Hoffman arrived on the ship *Rosannah,* oath of allegiance 26 Sept. 1743.
ABRAHAM SCHWANN, from Schriesheim.
HIERONIMUS TRAUTMANN,

JOHANNES TRAUTMANN,
BERNHARD TUEBINGER (TIEBINGER)
GEORG HOFFSTAETTER all from Schriesheim, after paying the ten per cent tax on
the possessions they were taking out with them, received permits to emigrate.
" HYRONIMUS TRAUTTMANN and BERNHART DUEBINGER " arrived in Phila-
delphia on the ship *St. Andrew* 7 Oct. 1743.

1744

In the year 1744 permission to emigrate was given to JOHANN ESAIAS STEIN from
Zuzenhausen with wife, one stepson and three stepdaughters.
JOHANN ADAM KREHEBUEHL from Bammenthal with his wife and three children.
GEORG WELCKER from Spechbach with his wife and two children, and CONRAD
LANG, from Spechbach, with his wife and four children.
A group of persons from Zuzenhausen, namely ANNA MARIA (REGINA) HEYL-
MANN, single; GEORG KIRSCH and his wife and two small children; ANNA
DOROTHEA, widow of GEORG LICHT(N)ER and her 16 yr old son; two
single men JOHANN JACOB KIRSCH and CONRAD KIRSCH.

During the next few years the number of permits practically reached
the zero point. [The War of the Austrian Succession 1740-48 ended
with the treaty of Aix la Chapelle—Ed.]

In 1747 there was one permit granted, namely to a young man who had been exempted
from military service, CHRISTIAN RUPP, from Daudenzell. He was obliged to
pay his ten Pfennig tax amounting to 11 florins and an additional fee of two florins
40 kreuzers for an emergency locker. Christian Rupp arrived in Philadelphia on
the ship *Restauration,* oath of allegiance 9 Oct. 1747.
VEIT MEISTER, born at Bargen, son of Georg Bernhard Meister, married at Ort Hoffenheim, near Sinsheim, in 1744, and at that time paid 3 florins to receive a certificate of manumission. In 1787 the government of Dilsberg published a statement
that he and his wife and children had emigrated to America in 1751 arriving in
Philadelphia on the *Shirley* 5 Sept. 1751.

Beginning 1749 the number of permits for migration to America
from the county of Heidelberg increased rapidly.

Original article " Zur Amerika-auswanderung aus dem kurpfaelzischen Oberamt Heidelberg 1741-
1748 " in *Zeitschrift fuer die Geschichte des Ober-rheins,* Band 106, (Der neuen Folge 67, Band) pp.
485-86.

III

Emigration from County of Heidelberg 1737, 1738 1751, and 1754

The authorities of the County of Heidelberg, Electoral Paltinate, according to records now filed in the State Archives at Karlsruhe, granted
permission to a number of persons to emigrate to America, upon payment of manumission fees. Such a fee freed the subject from feudal
obligations to his landlord, the local petty nobleman.

Notable is the fact that of a considerable number of persons who received permission in 1751 relatively few can be identified in the lists of ships' passengers arriving in Philadelphia. There are two probable explanations: 1. not all ships from Holland or England came to Philadelphia; 2. some passengers died on board ship during the voyage.

Following are some emigrants:

1737

CHRISTIAN EWIG, resident of Wilhelmsfeld, upon payment of a manumission tax of 50 florins, received permission to migrate with his wife and three children to " the island of Pennsylvania." Arrived on the *Townshend*, took oath of allegiance Oct. 1737.

CASPAR WEDEL, resident of Wieblingen (modern Heidelberg-Wieblingen), upon payment of a manumission tax of 9 florins 54 kreuzers, received permission to emigrate to " the new land."

1738

JOHANN GEORG ARNOLD of Zuzenhausen, district of Sinsheim, upon payment of 10 florins as a manumission fee, was granted permission to emigrate with his wife and children, arrived Philadelphia on the *Elisabeth* 30 Oct. 1738.

JOHANN LEONHARD NOTZ, resident of Zuzenhausen, upon payment of 28 florins as a manumission fee, permitted to emigrate.

" LENHART NOTZ " arrived on the ship *Two Sisters*, took oath of allegiance Sept. 1738.

JOHANNES ROEHRER, a resident of Mauer, district of Heidelberg, upon payment of 10 florins as a manumission fee, permitted to emigrate to America with his wife and children.

" JOHANNES ROEHRER " (Johann Gottfried Rehrer) arrived on the ship *Robert and Alice* 11 Sept. 1738.

For the year 1751 there is an unusually large number of emigration permits:

PETER BENNINGER, a resident of Epfenbach, district of Sinsheim, with wife and four children, apparently without payment of the usual manumission fee.

HEINRICH BECK, a resident of Epfenbach, district of Sinsheim, with wife Anna Margaretha and son Johann Joerg. The latter was required to pay 11 florins for manumission and 10 florins for unpaid taxes.

ADAM BUCKLE (BICKLE), a schoolmaster of the Reformed Church at Spechbach, district of Heidelberg, permitted to emigrate with his wife and children gratis, because he was poor.

JOHANN GEORG ERNST, a resident of Lobenfeld, district of Heidelberg, permitted to emigrate.

BECKENBACH, ————, widow, a resident of Eiterbach, applied for a permit on behalf of herself and her children. After long negotiations, she paid 130 florins as a manumission fee and 177 florins and an additional 30 florins to satisfy the ten Pfenning tax on the value of what she took with her.

"CASPER BECKENBACH, GEORG ADAM BECKENBACH, GEORG LEON-HARDT BECKENBACH," all arrived on the ship *Janet* 7 Oct. 1751.

ELISABETH HILD, daughter of a citizen of Handschuhsheim (modern Heidelberg—Handschuhsheim) after paying a fee of five florins received a permit.

JOHANNES SCHILLING, a serf, residing at Richardshausen, district of Sinsheim, paid five florins as a manumission fee and thirteen florins for the ten Pfennig tax; arrived on the ship *Phoenix* Sept. 1751.

ANDREAS WETZSTEIN, resident of Gauangeloch, district of Heidelberg, paid ten florins as manumission fee and nine florins to satisfy the ten Pfennig tax. Permitted to emigrate with wife and two children.

SAMUEL SCHWEIGERT, (SCHWEIKERT), resident of Bargen, district of Sinsheim, after paying ten florins, received a permit.

LEONHARDT SCHEID, resident of Schriesheim, district of Mannheim, received a permit. At the same time Adam Heinrich Hoffmann, a former resident who had departed without paying his manumission fee, was declared free. (A relative may have paid it for him.)

JOHANN MICHAEL ROESCH, a day-laborer of Dossenheim, district of Heidelberg, permitted to emigrate with his wife and children without making any payment.

NICKLAS REINHARD, CASPAR HECKMANN, ADAM EISENHAUER, three day-laborers from Wilhelmsfeld, upon paying the usual fees, received permits to emigrate.

PETER LEYER, from Heiligenkreuzsreinach.

JACOB REICHERT, from Heddesbach, district of Heidelberg.

NICLAS ZIMMERMANN, from Altneudorf.

These three and their wives desired to emigrate. It is of interest that one of the three couples did not get the desired permit, because his wife was a Roman Catholic, and " in the land to which they plan to emigrate the exercise of the Catholic religion has not been introduced."

BALTHASAR KOENIG
JOERG HAPPES
JOHANNES WAGNER
JOERG LUECKER—four citizens of Schoenau, district of Heidelberg, permitted to depart without paying the usual fees because of their scant means.

"GEORG LICKER, BALZAR KOENIG, JOHANES WAGNER, and GEORGE HAPPES " arrived on the ship *Queen of Denmark* 4 Oct. 1751.

In 1753 there are two cases on record.

JOHANNES MUSSELMANN, an Anabaptist from Zuzenhausen, district of Sinsheim, secured a license to marry the daughter of Samuel Petzer, an Anabaptist, of Meckesheim, and also a permit to emigrate to America.

"HANS MUSSELMANN " arrived in Philadelphia on the ship *Patience* 17 Sept. 1753.

GEORG MARTIN, resident of Neunkirchen, district of Mosbach, received a permit for himself, his wife, and three children.

"JOERG MARTHIN " arrived in Philadelphia on the ship *Edinburgh* 14 Sept. 1753.

In 1754 the following were permitted to emigrate to America:

JOSEPH BUBIGKOFFER—an inhabitant, not a citizen, of Rohrhof, near Bruehl, district of Mannheim, received a permit gratis because of his poverty.
" JOSEF BUBIGKOFFER " arrived in Philadelphia on the ship *Brothers* 30 Sept. 1754.

NICLAUS FEDEROLFF, of Dossenheim, district of Heidelberg, received a permit to emigrate to South Carolina with his wife and three children.

JOHANNES KRAÜSS, day-laborer of Bruchhauserhof (modern Bruchhausen), Sandhausen, district of Heidelberg) was permitted to depart with wife and children without paying the usual fees.

PHILIPP LEYER, widower from Aglasterhausen, district of Mosbach, and his six children were permitted to emigrate without paying the usual fees, because of his having no means.

DAVID MUELLER, resident of Altneudorf, district of Heidelberg, was permitted to emigrate gratis.

JACOB SCHIFFERDECKER, resident of Neunkirchen, district of Mosbach, paid the usual fees and received a permit; arrived in Philadelphia on the ship *Henrietta* 22 Oct. 1754.

CATHARINA ZIMMERMANN of Moosbrunn, district of Heidelberg, secured both a license to be married and one to emigrate.

JOHANN STEPHAN MARTIN, son of a citizen in Neckarkatzenbach, district of Mosbach, received manumussion after having emigrated.
" HANS STEFFAN MARTHIN " arrived in Philadelphia on the ship *Shirley* 5 Sept. 1751.

Original article " Die Amerika-auswanderung aus dem kurpfaelzischen Oberamt Heidelberg in den Jahren 1737, 1738, 1751, und 1754." in *Badischische Heimat*, 338. Jahrg., 1958, Heft 3/4 pp. 303-304. Editor Prof. Dr. H. Schwarzweber, Freiburg i. Br.

IV

Emigrants from Wuerttemberg

A hasty examination of the records of the government of Wuerttemberg for 1749-50, now on file at State Archives in Ludwigsburg, revealed a number of entries concerning persons who had expressed the desire to emigrate to America, i.e., Pennsylvania. A few of them could be identified in the lists of Strassburger-Hinke:

ANDREAS HERTER, from Oberdigisheim, county of Balingen; arrived in Philadelphia on the ship *Osgood* 29 Sept. 1750.

GOTTLIEB MITTELBERGER, from Enzweihingen, county of Vaihingen. He " petitions that his divorce be hastened, so that he may be able to take a certificate of divorce with him to Pennsylvania." He made a round trip and published a book about it, *Gottlieb Mittelberger's Voyage to Pennsylvania in the Year 1750 and his return voyage to Germany in the year 1754.*" (Frankfurt/Main, and Leipzig, 1756, 110 pp).

HANS JERG FELBER, from Baach, county of Schondorf, petitioned that he be permitted to emigrate with his wife to Pennsylvania. Arrived on the ship *Elisabeth* 5 Sept. 1751.

JOHANNES ESE(N)WEIN, from Baltmannsweiler, county of Schondorf. Arrived on ship *Patience* 11 Aug. 1750.

HANSS MARTIN HERRE, from Zillhausen, county of Balingen, son of the local magistrate and tax collector Simon Herre. According to a record dated 6 May 1765 Hans Herre had married in 1743 Anna Maria Sassler. In 1749 they and three children " had emigrated to the American island of Pennsylvanai." "HANS MARTIN HERR" arrived in October 1749 on the ship *Fane;* oath of allegiance 17 Oct. 1749.

In 1765 Hans Herre re-visited his old home, to get his share in the settlement of an estate. For 100 florins he quit-claimed his share to the other heirs. When he was about to return to Pennsylvania, the Wuerttemberg government demanded an emigration fee of 43 florins, 65 Kreuzer, and 4½ Heller. He did not pay it. In the year 1770 he petitioned the government to cancel the charge, but it refused. Finally his relatives had to pay the charges.

Original article *"Einige Amerika-Auswanderer des 18. Jahrhunderts aus Wuerttemberg."* In *Suedwestdeutsche Blaetter fuer Familien- und Wappen-kunde.* (Stuttgart, February 1957, Series 9, no. 1, p. 442.) Editor, Reinhold Scholl, Stuttgart-Sillenbuch.

V

ADVERTISEMENTS for MISSING HEIRS

JOHANN GERLACH BORNHUETTER, of Daaderhuette (Daaden, a village in the district of Altenkirchen), Weserwald. He "left for America more than twenty years ago." Advertisement of government of Friedewald, Baden, 18 Feb. 1777; published in OPZ ("Oberpostamts Zeitung") 4 July 1777.
"JOHN GERLACH BORNHEKER," aged 29. Philadelphia 2 Oct. 1753; ship *Edinburgh.*

JOHANN WILHELM STRUNCK of Weitefeld, district of Altenkirchen, left there "thirteen years ago." Advertisement of government of Friedewald, Baden, 18 Feb. 1777, published in OPZ 4 July 1777. Cf. Strassburger-Hinke 249 C, 29 Nov. 1764.

EVA CATHARINA FATH, legitimate daughter of Georg Fath, deceased, of Offenbach, district of Landau, Palatinate, "left this village as a single woman more than twenty years ago, went to Pennsylvania, and has sent no word back since then." Advertisement of government of Landeck Klingenmuenster, Electoral Palatinate, 5 June 1778, published in OPZ 3 July and 9 Nov. 1778.

JACOB and ELISABETH HUTH, of Engelstadt, district of Bingen, left there about thirty years ago and, according to common report, went to Pennsylvania. Advertisement of government 13 Mch 1778; published in OPZ 12 May, 30 May, and 9 June 1778.
"JACOB HUTH," aged 29, *Loyal Judith* 2 Aug. 1743.

JOHANNES JUENGST, native of Grosskarben, district of Friedberg, Hessia "went to Pennsylvania twenty-six years ago." Advertisement of government of H. Burg Friedberg 13 July 1778, published in OPZ 24 Nov. 1778. Arrived on the ship *Edinburgh* 2 Oct. 1753.

HENRICH KRON, native of Essenheim, district of Mainz, "migrated as early as 1748 from there to America." Advertisement of County of Oppenheim, Palatinate, 19 Jan. 1776, published in OPZ 30 Aug. and 14 Dec. 1776.

" HEND^K CROWN " arrived on the ship *Hampshire* 7 Sept. 1748.

VEIT MEISTER, son of the deceased court employe at Bargen (district of Sinsheim, Baden) Georg Bernhard Meister " migrated as early as 1751 with wife and children from the village of Hoffenheim belonging to the Baron of Gemmingen, district of Sinsheim, to America. Advertisement of the government of Dilsberg, Electoral Palatinate 10 Dec. 1787, published in OPZ 8 Feb. 1788.

" VEIT MEISTER " arrived on ship *Shirley* 5 Sept. 1751.

GEORG THOMAS and MARIA BARBARA OSTERSTOCK, children of the deceased Johann Philipp Osterstock, subjects to and under the jurisdiction of Olnhausen (Wuerttemberg) 44 and 53 years old respectively, in 1751 went to America." Advertisement of the government of the Baron of Berlichingen at Jagsthausen 7 Dec. 1773, published in the Imperial *Official Post News* 10 Jan 1780.

" THOMAS OSTERSTOCK " on ship *St. Andrew* 14 Sept. 1751.

JOHANN DIETRICH REINER, born at Schwaigern, under the rule of the Count of Neipperg, Wuerttemberg, emigrated in April 1749 with his wife Maria Margaretha, nee Schleicher, and six children named Christian about 30 years old, Maria Magdalena 24 years old, Margaretha 22 years old, Sara 20 years old, Johannes 18 years old, Eberhardt about 16 years old, from their home to Pennsylvania. Announcement of the Council and state officials, also the Burgomaster and the court at Bonnigheim in the " Zabergau," Wuerttemberg, 27 Oct. 1777, published OPZ 16 March 1778.

The Lutheran churchbook at the Evangelical parsonage Meimsheim contains the following: Johann Dietrich Reiner, son of Friedrich Reiner, citizen and cooper at Schwaigern, was married 9 Oct. 1715 to Maria Margaretha Schleicher, daughter of the citizen and cobbler Schleicher. Their children, listed in the Evangelical churchbook, were: Johann Christian, b. 10 April 1718; Maria Magdalena, b. 21 Sept. 1720; Maria Margaretha, b. 12 Feb. 1723; Maria Sara, b. 2 Mai 1724; Georg Philipp, b. 30 Jan. 1727, d. 3 May 1729; Anna Maria, b. 9 June 1728, d. 8 June 1729; Johannes b. 13 July 1730; Eberharst Friedrich, b. 23 March 1733.

" JOHAN DIETRICH REINER " arrived on ship *Fane* 17 Oct. 1749.

Original article " Einige Amerika-Auswanderer des 18. Jahrhunderts " in *Senftnegger Monatsblatt fuer Genealogie und Heraldik, April 1958,* Karl Friedrich v. Frank, editor and publisher, Schloss Senftenegg, Post Ferschnitz, Niederoesterreich.

VI

Emigrants from Oppenheim 1742-49

The records of the county of Oppenheim, in the former Electoral Palatinate, which are now filed in the City Archives at Oppenheim on Rhine, contain information about a few persons who emigrated during the first half of the 18th century. They furnish evidence of permits granted, not of actual emigration.

The former county of Oppenheim included the present city of Oppenheim, the market place Nierstein, and the villages of Dexheim,

Schwabsburg, Oberingelheim, Niederingelheim, Daxweiler, Sauerschwabenheim, Gorsswinternheim, Wackernheim, Freinweinheim, Bubenheim, Elsheim, Stadtecken, and Essenheim. The many enigrants from Essenheim are not included in the following list, because they have been published. In order to avoid repetition we will list only the date of the permit, the name, the residence, the fees paid, the ship, and the date of arrival in Philadelphia.

1742

Permits and manumission certificates to the following residents of Stadtecken, namely, LORENTZ BLAESS, PETER WESTERBERGER, JOHANN KIEL, FRIEDERICH MENGEL, and JOHANNES DAUM, " to emigrate to Pennsylvania, where they have friends residing." On 3 Sept. 1742 on the ship *Loyal Judith* " LORENTZ PLACE, JOHANNES KUEHL, JOHANNES DOMIE, FRIETZ MENGEL, and PETER WASENBERGER."
Permits granted 17 April 1742, to FRIEDRICH PFEIL, JOHANN LEHN, residents of Gross-winternheim. They arrived 3 Sept. 1742 on the same ship.

In the same year a report to the county officials stated that certain residents of Oberingelheim, namely, Philip Odernheimer, Peter Weitzel, Ulrich Strassburger, and the widow of Nicolaus Doerr, had " recently sent their sons, whose names had been entered on the latest conscription list for military service, to the new land, and with the knowledge of the entire town, had given each of them 100 florins and some food for the voyage." The chief magistrate of the village of Oberingelheim was held responsible by the higher authorities. Johannes Odernheimer, Johann Paul Weytzel, Johann Heinrich Doerr, and Johann Andreas Strassburger arrived 3 Sept. 1742 on the *Loyal Judith*. The last named returned to Germany for a visit and came back to Philadelphia on the ship *Mercury* in October 1769.

25 February 1743 permit granted to PHILIP HARDT of Niederingelheim, upon payment of 10 Pfenning; permits to NICOLAUS RUNCKEL and NICOLAUS KELLER of Wackernheim. They arrived 2 Sept. 1743 on the *Loyal Judith*.
3 February 1748 permits " to migrate to the island of Pennsylvania " after paying 15 florins and 10 florins for manumission certificates and the usual 10 Pfenning fees, to FRIEDRICH PLATZ (PLOTZ) and ADAM IMHAEUSSER (IMMENHAUSER) of Stadtecken. They arrived on the ship *Hampshire* 7 Sept. 1748.
9 March 1748 permits to FRANZ GRAFF (GROVE), with wife and two children, BARTEL KRAEMER with wife and five children, ADAM WEISS with wife, all from Grosswinternheim, also WILHELM LAYMEISTER with wife and children from Schwabenheim, all upon paying the 10 Pfennig fee; to indigents WOLFGANG WOLF and —— HOSTERMANN from Grosswinternheim without such payment. They arrived 7 Sept. 1748 on the *Hampshire*. Their names are given as

FRANTZ GROVE, JOHANN WILHELM LEYMEISTER, WOLFGANG WULFF, HANS JACOB OSTERMANN, and JOHANN ADAM WEISS.

29 March 1748 permit to JOHANN BISCHOFF from Grosswinternheim," who was so in debt that he had to sell his property and did not know how he would be able to support himself." He arrived on the same ship, the *Hampshire* 7 Sept. 1748.

14 May 1748 permits to JOHANN JACOB RUNCKEL and FRIEDRICH HAMMER from Wackernheim. The former paid 40 florins, the latter 10 florins. Both arrived with the preceding on the *Hampshire*.

CHRISTIAN RAMB from Elsheim paid 43 florins for a permit. But his name has not been found in the ship's lists.

21 March 1749 permit to PHILIPP HABER with wife and three children from Sta-decken paid 54 florins for manumission and 54 florins for the 10 Pfenning tax; arrived 27 Sept. 1749 on the *Isaac*.

16 April 1749 permit to NICOLAUS REISINGER from Niederingelheim, upon paying the 10 Pfenning tax; arrived 26 Sept. 1749 on the *Dragon*.

29 April 1749 to three men from Oberingelheim, ADAM DOERR, upon payment of the 10 Pfenning tax, ANTON OSTER and WENDEL RUNCKEL, gratis, " all three being indigent and having bad records." Doerr arrived 9 Sept, 1749 on the *St. Andrew*. Oster arrived 26 Sept. on the *Dragon*. Runckel remained in Oberingel-heim, altho the authorities were anxious to get rid of him.

14 May 1749 permit to FRIEDRICH BOHR from Wackernheim, after paying ten florins, arrived 9 Sept. 1749 on the *St. Andrew*.

Christian Meckel from Elsheim had some difficulties. His oldest son was not emigrating with him. The authorities insisted that his share of his father's estate be retained and safely invested for him. Christian with wife and three younger children arrived 27 Sept. 1749 on the *Isaac*.

29 April 1749 PHILIPP MERZ, locksmith, from Nierstein, upon paying the 10 Pfenning tax, arrived 15 Sept. 1749 on the *Edinburgh*.

ULRICH JORDAN (JORDTE), an Anabaptist from Haxthaeuserhof near Ingelheim, also paid the 10 Pfenning tax. He arrived 9 Sept. 1749 on the *St. Andrew*.

The Roman Catholic widow CATHARINA PFEIFFER from Essenheim migrated " without permission of the authorities, secretly, to Pennsylvania." Therefore what-ever possessions she had left behind were confiscated. Johann Rooss and Abraham Schweickart from Niederingelheim also emigrated " secretly," and their property was confiscated.

Original article: " Amerika auswanderer aus dem Oberant Oppenheim 1742-49." in *Hessische Familien-kunde*, Band 3, (1955), Heft 6.

VII

Emigrants to America from the region now a part of the Palatinate and that of Nahe and Hunsrueck. The records are now filed in the Archives at Speyer.

JOHANN GEORG and CHRISTIAN, sons of CONRAD STRIBECK, citizen and woolspinner in Hornbach, district of Zweibruecken, by his first wife ELISABETHA SCHAEFFER, and their mother's brother together with their grandmother Elisabetha Schaeffer migrated as early as 1735 into the new land, with the knowledge and approval of His Highness. Since the grandparents were still living and the children had not received any inheritance from their mother, they were reported to have taken with them the portion derived from their grandmother. ELISABETH SHEVER, JERICH STREBECK, CHRISTIAN STREBECK, arrived on the ship *Pennsylvania Merchant* 18 Sept. 1733.

SAMUEL MAUSS, son of the official Friedrich Mauss of Hornbach and his wife SUSANNA MUELLER, former citizen of Zweibruecken, migrated to America " about 1754." He arrived 14 Sept. 1753 on the ship *Edinburgh*.

PHILIPP WILD, son of the citizen and tanner Nickel Wild of Hornbach and his wife ANNA MARIA, " about four years ago migrated to the new land with the knowledge, recognized and to be recognized, of the government. Before his departure he sold his . . . . inheritance to his brother Conrad Wild at Oberhausen." Deposition made 3 May 1760.

CATHARINA HENGE, daughter of the deceased citizen and tanner (" Rotgerber ") Samuel Mueller at Hornbach and his wife Maria Margaretha Mauss, had been married to Georg Henge and had had a son, named Philipp (now sixteen). She was divorced from her husband " pro adulterii." Later she went to America, where she after having made the necessary legal depositions was married to a man named Fischer. (Emigrated before 31 Jan. 1777.)

LUDWIG LEINER of Hornbach, " emigrated as a wool weaver." According to a deposition of his brother Georg Leiner he died in 1784 in America.

PHILIPP BLEY, son of the citizen and cooper Hanss Werner Bley of Hornbach and his wife Elisabeth Huber, " twenty-two years ago went into Alsace and married at Trachenbronn, from where he removed to America." Deposition made in 1770; (hence Philipp migrated about 1748).

DANIEL and BALTHASAR ZUTTER, sons of Benedikt Balthasar Zutter of Hornbach, woolspinner, " left secretly and migrated to America." (Deposition 7 June 1763.) Daniel and Balthasar Zutter arrived on ship *Chance* 1 Nov. 1763.

THEOBALD PFAFF " eight years ago ran away from Eisenbach, district of Kusel, and emigrated to America. He left nine children behind, of whom three are in the ducal orphanage at Homburg." (Deposition 29 Jan. 1777.)

THEOBALD PFAFF arrived 26 Oct. 1768 in ship *Betsy*.

Note: Pfaff could not have been born in Eisenbach, because the proof of his migration was filed in Hornbach.

PAUL HOCHSTRASER, son of the town official Samuel Hochstraser at Brenschelbach, district of Homburg, in the Saar, and his wife Elisabetha. He established himself as a tailor in Philadelphia. (Deposition 18 April 1761.) According to a power of attorney which Paul Hochstraser and his sister Catharina signed 23 Jan. 1764 at Albany, Province of New York, they were living there.

" PAUL HOCHSTRASER " arrived 14 Sept. 1753 in ship *Edinburg*.

In the year 1763 a Jacob Hochstraser emigrated to America, presumably he was a brother of Paul, for local records show that Paul had a brother of that name.

HEINRICH HALLER, son of the citizen and tailor Jacob Haller of Walshausen, district of Zweibruecken, and his first wife ELISABETH MOSER, " deserted from the old Ducal Guard and emigrated to Pennsylvania." He migrated about 1748 without having secured manumission. Therefore his property, i.e., an inheritance amounting to 102 florins was confiscated by the government of Zweibruecken. Presumably identical with Heinrich Haller, 18 Aug. 1750, in the ship *St. Andrew.*

ANNA APPOLONIA VOGELSANG, daughter of the citizen Nickel Gentes at Breit-furt, (district of Homburg, Saar), was married to Georg Vogelgesang, the younger, (apparently, also a resident of Breitfurt) living in America. (Deposition 6 May 1765.) Presumably " GEORG VOGELSANG " who arrived 21 Oct. 1761 in the *Snow Squirrel.*

GEORG NEU, inhabitant and citizen at Breitfurt (d. 18 July 1756) and his wife CHRISTINA MARGARETA GENTESS had the following children:

1. JOSEPH NEU, " who about 18 years ago migrated to America and is about 40 years old."
2. PETER NEU, " who also some five years ago removed to America and is about 30 years old." (Deposition, 8 Feb. 1758.)

ABRAHAM SCHMIDT, citizen and court employe ("Gerichtsmann") at Breitfurt, had:

1. MATTHEIS, " living in America."
2. GEORG, unmarried, 30 years old, in America. (Deposition, 7 Oct. 1760.)

JACOB WELKER, son of Wilhelm Welcker of Breitfurt, " who according to report has gone to America," emigrated before 4 Dec. 1777. Either " JACOB WELCKER," who arrived 26 Oct. 1768 in the ship *Crawford* or " JACOB WELCKER " who arrived 17 Sept. 1771 in the ship *Minerva.*

HEINRICH KUNZ of Boeckweiler (district of Homburg, Saar), " Heinrich Kunz, son of the deceased citizen ("Gemeindeman") of the same name, at Boeckweiler, left this land anno 1764 and, according to report, in defiance of the highest existing ordinance migrated to America." Notice in the *Frankfurter Kayserliche Reichs-Ober-Amtspost Zeitung* of 17 Sept. 1787 (literally " Imperial Higher Official Post News published in Frankfurt "). According to local records Heinrich Kunz had learned the trade of a wagon maker and had gone out in 1764 as a wandering jour-neyman. On 23 August 1768 he wrote a letter to Jonathan Heger from Canage-schick, Maryland, which was the last anyone in his home town received from him.

JOHANNES KELLER, son of Daniel Keller of Boeckweiler, was reported to be " estab-lished in the new land and married." He emigrated before 19 Oct. 1776.

" Children of WILHELM SCHUNK of Walsheim, district of Homburg, Saar, and his wife CATHARINA SCHWARTZ, namely: JOHANNES, CATHARINA, ELISA-BETH, MARIA, SIMON, have been in America the past nine or ten years." Rec-ord 18 Oct. 1781.

The following names of emigrants to America from the region of Nahe and Hunsrueck were copied from the Lutheran churchbooks at Hueffelsheim and Loetzbeuren and from the Reformed church books at Hundsbach.

JOHANN GEORG REITZEL (REUTZEL), a cobbler at Hueffelsheim, district of Kreuznach, and wife (ANNA) SYBILLA had children:

1. ANNA MARIA, b. 2 Aug. 1720. " This parish child migrated to the new land."
2. MARIA WILHELMINA, b. 2 Sept. 1734, " went with her father into the new land. 1741."

3. JOHANN PETER, b. 28 Oct. 1937. "went with his parents 1741 into the new land."
"JOHANN GEORG REUTZEL," arrived 17 Oct. 1741, aged 45 years.
JOHANNES WOLFFSKEHL, m. 19 Nov. 1730 at Hueffelsheim to ANNA MARIA VIEL; children born at Hueffelsheim:
1. ELISABETHA, b. 28 Dec. 1733.
2. ANNA MARGRETHA, b. 18 Nov. 1735.
3. MARIA AGNES, b. 27 Jan. 1738.
All three "went with their father into the new land 1742."
"JOHANNES WOLFFSKEHL," 3 Sept. 1742, ship *Loyal Judith.*
1. MARIA, 28 Feb. 1711 "to the new land 1742" (wife of J. Wolffskehl, cf. above).
2. JOHAN JACOB, b. 22 Nov. 1718 "went 17 May 1767 into the new land."
JOHANN MICHAEL RECH, b. 1 March 1751 at Hueffelsheim, son of JOHANN CONRAD RECH, and his wife ANNA MARGRETA. "Children and parents went to the new land."
CATHARINA ELISABETHA SCHNEE, b. 27 Aug. 1730 at Loetzbeuren, district of Zell, Mosel region, daughter of Johannes Schnee and his wife Maria Margretha. "Emigrated to Pennsylvania 1751."
MARIA CATHARINA HOFF. b. 26 May 1732 at Loetzbeuren, daughter of Johann Dieterich and his wife Susanna Elisabetha: "This person and her husband have gone to Pennsylvania."
JOHANN WILHELM LUTZ, b. 12 Sept. 1732 at Loetzbeuren, son of Matthes Luetz and his wife Elisabetha Catharina, "left for Pennsylvania 1751."
ANNA ELISABETHA FRANTZ, b. 25 March 1735 at Loetzbeuren, daughter of Johann Nicol Frantz and his wife Maria Elisabetha: "said to have migrated to Pennsylvania 1751."
ELISABETHA CATHARINA HEYL, b. 4 Jan. 1733 at Hundsbach, district of Kreuznach, "The father of this child has gone to Pennsylvania."

The following names of emigrants were found in "Akt Zweibruecken III No. 3358, "Act concerning dismissal . . . of subjects as well as the exporting of property acquired at marriage (Heirats gut), and the payment of the ten penny tax (1484-1792)," in the Archives at Speyer.

JOHANN NICKEL BEYER, b. at Kleinich, district of Bernkastel, son of Matthias Beyer
also JOHANN GEORG BARTGES, son of MATTHIAS BARTGES of the same place, both are permitted by the government of Sponheim to migrate from Trarbach to Pennsylvania "in order to perfect themselves in the trade they have learned. But if they do not return within three years, they will have to purchase their manumission, and in the mean time their prospective inheritance here is being held as a forfeit."
MICHAEL BARTGES, a tanner by trade, was permitted to depart for Pennsylvania on similar conditions.
"MICHAEL BARTJES," ship *Two Brothers,* 15 Sept. 1748.
JOHANN NICKEL NEU, son of Christoffel Neu, a weaver by trade, and JOHANN PETER VELTEN (FEHLTEN), son of Conrad Fehlten, a cobbler by trade, received permits to emigrate to America on similar conditions.

"PETER FELTE," ship *Two Brothers*, 15 Sept. 1748.

JOHANN CONRAD LAHM, a tailor by trade, son of Peter Lahm also JOHN MICHEL NEU, linen-weaver, son of Philipp Neu, also MATTHIAS BAYER, son of Matthias Bayer, Sr., all of Kleinich, were granted permission by the government of Trarbach 26 April 1741 to go to Pennsylvania, on condition that they either return within two years or pay their manumission fees.

That all of them emigrated is proved by the records. However, Matthias Bayer and Johann Michel Neu are said to have died soon after their arrival in America.

"JOHANN KONRADT LAHM," aged 22 years, arrived 20 Nov. 1741, in the ship *Europa*.

JOHANN PETER HEHN or HENN, son of Nicol Hehn of Horbruch, district of Bernkastel, according to a report of 11 March 1746 to the government at Trarbach, "emigrated anno 1741 to the so called new land."

MARIA CATHARINA LAHM and NICKEL LAHM, children of Matthias Lahm of Oberkleinich (district of Bernkastel) according to a report of the magistrate of Kleinich to the government at Trarbach 8 May 1741, "desire to migrate to the new land."

"JOHANN NICKLAUS LAHM" arrived 29 Sept. 1741, ship *Lydia*.

"This is to inform you that during the past year two young fellows under the pretext of completing their journeyman's stage (in learning their trade) emigrated to the so called new land. One, Johann Peter Lorentz, is a native of Hochscheid, the other, Johann Peter Lahm, is a native of Oberkleinich." Report of a local magistrate to the government at Sponheim 12 May 1741. An entry in the records of the government at Trarbach confirms that both had emigrated in 1740.

"PETER LORENTZ and PETER LAAM," 27 Sept. 1740 arrived in Philadelphia on ship *Lydia*.

Original article: "Amerika—Auswanderer des 18. Jahrhunderts aus der heutigen Pfalz und der Nahe- und Hunsrueck-gegend." In *Mitteilungen zur Wanderungs geschichte der Pfaelzer*, Supplement to *Pfaelzische Familien u Wappen-kunde*, Kaiserslautern, West Germany, 1954. Editor: Dr. Fritz Braun.

PALATINES ON THE SHIP "THISTLE OF GLASGOW" (1730)

By Dr. Fritz Braun
Kaiserslautern, Germany

On the Ship *Thistle of Glasgow*, which arrived in Philadelphia in August, 1730, there came 260 emigrants, listed as "Palatines," some of whose home villages were in the vicinity of Ludwigshafen. Those that can be positively identified are the following:

1. Hes, Jeremias—from Mutterstadt.
2. Grisimer (Griesheimer), Velde (Velten)—from "Lampedheim" (Lampertheim).
3. Schmitt, Johan Henrich—from Dannstadt.
4. Minigh, Hans—from Dannstadt.
5. Groscost (Grosskasten), Philipp—from Mutterstadt.
6. Buettner, Caspar—married in Maudach.
7. Cuntzer, Nickel—from Assweiler bei Nohfelden.
8. Transu, Abraham—from Mutterstadt.
9. Hoff, Lorentz—from Mutterstadt(?).
10. Trawiener, Peter—possibly from the neighborhood of Mutterstadt.
11. Federolf, Peter—from Wachbach, near Bad Mergentheim.
12. Mueller, Peter—from Alsenborn.
13. Thommas, Michel—from Schifferstadt.

From Fritz Braun, "Auswanderer aus der Umgebung von Ludwigshafen am Rhein auf dem Schiff 'Thistle of Glasgow' 1730," *Landsleute drinnen und draussen, Heimatstelle Pfalz—Mitteilungen zur Wanderungsgeschichte der Pfälzer*, 1953 Series 5, pp. 31-32.

18TH CENTURY PALATINE EMIGRANTS FROM THE LUDWIGSHAFEN AREA

By Dr. Fritz Braun

Kaiserslautern, Germany

Following our interest in determining the European homes of our Pennsylvania emigrant pioneers, we publish here a list of Palatine emigrants who came to Pennsylvania in the 18th Century, translated from Dr. Fritz Braun, "Auswanderung aus dem heutigen Stadtgebiet von Ludwigshafen am Rhein im 18. Jahrhundert," from *Landsleute drinnen und draussen— Heimatstelle Pfalz—Mitteilungen zur Wanderungsgeschichte der Pfälzer*, Series 5 (1953), pp. 25—31. We have not included in this list the emigrants who moved eastward into Eastern Europe into the German settlements in Galicia, the Banat, the Batschka, nor the few who came to French Guiana.— D.Y.

1. Bayer, Catharina, daughter of Adam and Marie Bayer of Oppau, married April 1729, Conrad Wetzel, born 1697 in "Waldsiefer," emigrated 1720 or earlier to Pennsylvania.

2. Beroth, Franz Ludwig, from Oppau, born *circa* 1699, died York County, Pennsylvania, August 1778, married before 1732, Susanna [—], Reformed, came to Pennsylvania on the Ship *Winter Galley*, September 5, 1738. The family were Moravians and lived for awhile at Bethlehem, Pa., with branches in York County and North Carolina.

3. Buettner (Bittner), (Johann) Caspar, Lutheran, married at Maudach, June 14, 1729, Maria Elisabetha Münch, daughter of Jean Noe Münch of Dannstadt and wife Johanna. Arrived at Philadelphia on the Ship *Thistle of Glasgow*, August 29, 1730. On the same ship was Johannes Munch (Hans Minigh), the father-in-law. In 1763—4 Peter Büttner of Maudach emigrated to Cayenne in French Guiana. From the Dannstadt Church Registers, furnished by Dr. Eyselein.

4. Eichert, Christian, from Oppau, a Mennonite, received permission gratis in 1752 to emigrate to Nova Scotia, with wife and two children. From the *Neustadter Oberamtsprotokolle* (Protocols of the District of Neustadt), Palatine State Archives, Speyer, furnished by Dr. Friedrich Krebs.

5. Glatz, Henrich, of Oppau, who appears in records of 1752 as wanting to go to Pennsylvania, was "manumitted gratis on account of his having no property." From the *Neustadter Oberamtsprotokolle*.

6. Herget (Hergedt), Johann Peter, citizen of Oggersheim, received in 1750 permission to emigrate to Pennsylvania, with his wife and children. This was granted upon payment of 60 florins tax plus 30 florins for his step-son, Christoph Braun. They arrived at Philadelphia on the Ship *Two*

Brothers, August 28, 1750. On the same ship was Balthasar Löffel (Löffler), q.v., also of Oggersheim. From the *Neustadter Oberamtsprotokolle*.

7. Joachim, Friedrich, and wife, of Edigheim, received permission in 1764, upon payment of the "Tenth Penny or Tithe," to emigrate to Pennsylvania, and arrived at Philadelphia on the Ship *Britannia*, September 26, 1764. From the *Neustadter Oberamtsprotokolle*.

8. Keppler, Simon, of Oggersheim, emigrated to America in 1754, arriving in Philadelphia on the Ship *Nancy*, September 14, 1754. In 1773 he petitions for the remittance of his inheritance, which was granted after paying a double portion of the Tithe. From the *Neustadter Oberamtsprotokolle*.

9. Loeffel (Loeffler), Balthasar, of Oggersheim, received permission in 1750 to emigrate to Pennsylvania, on paying 19 florins for the Tithe. He arrived at Philadelphia on the Ship *Two Brothers*, August 28, 1750, with Johann Peter Herget (q.v.). From the *Neustadter Oberamtsprotokolle*.

10. Niecke (Nick), Anna Regina, born at Rheingönnheim, April 22, 1737, died at Lititz, Pennsylvania, March 10, 1768. For seven years she was in service in the *Fenstermacher* Family (from Meisenheim) in Lititz, Pennsylvania.

11. Reuther, Anna Margaretha, of Oppau, daughter of Hans Jacob Reuther, married Abraham Reiber of Sandhofen, arrived at Philadelphia on the Ship *Dragon*, October 17, 1749. The Reiber Family settled in Goshenhoppen, Pennsylvania, in the house of Hans Bauer, and inquired after the family of Franz Ludwig Beroth (q.v.), according to Anita L. Eyster, "Notices by German Settlers in German Newspapers," *Pennsylvania German Folklore Society*, Volume III (Allentown, 1938). According to the *Oppauer Nahrungszettel* for June 12, 1718, Hans Jakob Reuther, aged 47, had the following family: (1) Mathes, aged 19; (2) Catharina, aged 15; (3) Susanne, aged 11; (4) Anna Margaretha, aged 9; and (5) Hans Stefan, aged 3, baptized January 27, 1715. Anna Margaretha was therefore 40 years old at the time of her emigration.

12. Sachs, Daniel, of Oggersheim, received permission in 1751 to emigrate to Pennsylvania, with wife and children, upon payment of a Tithe of 16 florins. From the *Neustadter Oberamtsprotokolle*.

PENNSYLVANIA DUTCH PIONEERS

By Dr. Friedrich Krebs

Palatine State Archives, Speyer, Germany

Translated by Don Yoder

The names of the following emigrants were culled from the collections of the State Archives of Coblenz. The names have been checked against Hinke's *Pennsylvania German Pioneers.*

From Niederbrombach (Kreis Birkenfeld)

1. PONTIUS, JOHANN DAVID, born March 3, 1738, and JOHANN PHILIPP, sons of Andreas Pontius of Niederbrombach and his wife Anna Marie. Both brothers "emigrated to America around 1767-68." [David Pontzius, *Pennsylvania Packet*, Oct. 3, 1768.]

2. APEL, JONAS of Niederbrombach went to America in 1768 after he had purchased freedom from serfdom. His wife and three children at first remained in Germany but followed in 1771. [Jonas Apel, *Pennsylvania Packet*, Oct. 3, 1768.]

From Birkenfeld

3. WART, BERNHARD, born Feb. 21, 1718 in Birkenfeld, tailor. "Is said to have gone to America in or about 1738." [Bern Warth, *Loyal Judith*, Sept. 3, 1739.]

From Ellenberg (Kreis Birkenfeld)

4. BRENER, PETER from Ellenberg emigrated in the year 1768 as a widower with his children to America and nothing was ever heard from him. [Frantz Peter Brenner, *Pennsylvania Packet*, Oct. 3, 1768.]

5. MAUS, GEORG JACOB and FRANZ CARL from Ellenberg set out for America around 1767. [Jacob Maus, *Pennsylvania Packet*, Oct. 10, 1768.]

From Sohren (Landkreis Zell, Mosel)

6. ALBERTTHAL, FRANZ NICLAUS and JOHANN NICLAUS, sons of Balthasar Alberthal and his wife Elisabeth Catharina, emigrated to New England, the former around 1765 and the latter around 1768. Since they left without manumission their property was seized and later also their inheritance, which after taxes was used for the Catholic church, for the poor, and the rest divided among relatives. [Nickellas Alberthal, *Tryal*, Dec. 12, 1764 and Johann Nickel Alberthal, *Sally*, Oct. 5, 1767. Franz Nikolaus Alberthal, farmer, and Johann Nicklaus Alberthal, tailor, according to documentation, lived in Hanover Township, Lancaster County.]

From Bockenau (Kreis Kreuznach)

7. GEIB, CONRAD from Bockenau left with his wife and three children for the new land. [Johann Conrad Geib, *Two Brothers*, Oct. 13, 1747.] Kreuznach Official Records 1751.

From Weinsheim (Kreis Kreuznach)

8. RUPPERTER, JOHANN LEONHARD from Weinsheim in 1752 applied for manumission from Pennsylvania where he married; granted after payment of fees in 1754. [Leonhard Rupperter, *Sandwich*, Nov. 30, 1750.]

From Ruedesheim (Kreis Kreuznach)

9. SUESS, CYRIACUS from Ruedesheim, according to Kreuznach official records of 1751, left for the New World.

From Buechenbeuren (Landkreis Zell, Mosel)

10. MAEURER, PHILIPP (JACOB) from Buechenbeuren around 1750 left as a "Schuhknecht" for the New World. [Phielib Jacob Maurer, *Patience*, Aug. 11, 1750.]

From Engelstadt (Kreis Bingen)

11. GRAFFERT, CHRISTOPH, PHILIPP PETER and JOHANN GERHARD, sons of Philipp Peter Graffert and his wife Anna Eva Finkenauer from Engelstadt left for the New World around 1749. [Christoffel Graffert, *Loyal Judith*, Sept. 2, 1743, and Philipp Peter Graffert, *Phoenix*, Oct. 20, 1744.]

The names of the following immigrants are from two sources: 1) *Oberamtsprotokolle* (bailiff minutes) of the city of Heidelberg, for 1741 and 1742, and 2) Lutheran Church Records of Woerrstadt. The names have been checked against Hinke's *Pennsylvania German Pioneers*.

From the Heidelberg Area

1. ZWEISIG, VALENTINE, from Mauer (Kreis Heidelberg) who has requested freedom from serfdom and permission to emigrate is set free, with wife and four children, upon payment of 3 Fl. and 30 Kr. Source: Oberamtsprotokolle of Heidelberg, 1741. [Valdin Zweisig, Ship *Molly*, Oct. 17, 1741.]

2. GEISER, CHRISTOPH, from Eschelbronn (Kreis Sinsheim, Baden) who wishes to emigrate is freed from serfdom. Source: Oberamtsprotokolle of Heidelberg, 1742. [Christof Geiser, Ship *Francis and Elizabeth*, Sept. 9, 1742.]

3. DANNER, MICHEL and DIETER, from Walldorf who wish to emigrate are relieved of emigration fees because the sum realized from the sale

of their properties was insufficient to cover their debts. Source: Oberamts-protokolle of Heidelberg, 1742. [Michel Danner, Dietrich Danner, Ship *Robert and Alice,* Sept. 24, 1742.]

From Woerrstadt (Kreis Alzey)

4. CHRISTIAN, PHILIP JACOB. "In 1743 Philip Jacob Christian, carpenter, and Elizabeth Margaretha, daughter of Joerg Emich Messer-schmid, cooper, were engaged on Easter Sunday; and their proclamation was read the following two Sundays. Several days later, however, the young man secretly left and finally went to England, from where he expects to sail to Pennsylvania. Whether he arrived there is not known as of this moment." [Fillip Christian, Ship *Loyal Judith*, Sept. 2, 1743.]

5. BAUSSMAN, MICHEL; WEISSKOPFF, ESAIAS; and BECKER, JACOB. "In 1748 Michel Baussmann and Esaias Weisskopff, both of them shoemakers and Protestants, and Jacob Becker, a Catholic, left with their families for Pennsylvania. They arrived safely according to reports from there." [Johann Michel Bausman, Johan Esaias Weiskob, Jacob Becker, Ship *Judith,* Sept. 15, 1748.]

6. SENDERLING, JOHANN NICLAUS; STUMP, JOHANN MICHEL; KRAEMER, JOHANN PETER; STEINBRECHER, JOHANN VALENTIN; KLEIN, JOHANN HEINRICH; CRAMER, JOHANN FRIEDRICH; SCHEDLA, JOHANN CHRISTIAN. "On May 22, 1749, Johann Niclaus Senderling, Johann Michel Stump, Johann Peter Kraemer, Johann Valentin Steinbrecher, Johann Heinrich Klein, Johann Friedrich Cramer, local residents and Johann Christian Schedla, single son of tailor Johann Heinrich Schedla, left for Pennsylvania, the former accompanied by their wives and children." [Johann Friedrich Cremer, Johann Vallentin Steinbrech, Johann Hennerich Klein, Johann Nickel Stump, Johann Nicolas Senderling, Ship *Isaac,* Sept. 9, 1749. Johann Peter Kraemer, Ship *Saint Andrew,* Sept. 9, 1749.]

7. SCHEDLA, JOHANN HEINRICH; GERHARDT, JOHANN DIETRICH; REUTER, JOHANN LORENTZ; KOCH, JOHANN CHRISTIAN. "In 1754 the following removed to Pennsylvania or rather into misfortune: Johann Heinrich Schedla with family, Johann Dietrich Gerhardt with wife and children, Johann Lorentz Reuter with wife and child, Johann Christian Koch with wife and children, along with others, in part single young men and women, approximately 40 in number. They had the misfortune of having to spend time in Cologne because the King of Prussia at first refused to grant them permission to pass through. This took a considerable period of time. The group consumed much of their little wealth and finally they had to travel by land to Rotterdam at great cost. I trust that the rest of the local citizenry remaining behind have lost the taste of the New World." [Dieter Gerhard, Lorents Rouyter, Henrich Schedler, Christian Koch, Ship *Phoenix,* Oct. 1, 1754.]

The following listings of Palatine emigrants to America in the eighteenth century are derived from several manuscript sources in German archives. Those from the Electoral Oberamt of Simmern, representing villages in the Hunsrueck area, come from the Census of the Electoral Oberamt of Simmern for the year 1750, in the State Archives of Coblenz (Abt. 4. Nr. 3319); those from Hueffelsheim from the Lutheran Church Register of Hueffelsheim; the remainder from various official acts in the Palatine State Archives at Speyer. The names have been checked against Strassburger and Hinke's *Pennsylvania German Pioneers*.

From the Electoral Oberamt of Simmern

1. JUNGKER, JOHANN NICKLAS—of Moerschbach (Kreis Simmern), "who has gone to the Island of Pensylphanien," pays in taxes two florins for the tithe.

2. MUEHLEISSEN, JOHANN JACOB—of Pleizenhausen (Kreis Simmern), "intends to go with wife and child to the New Land." He is, with his wife and child, freed from vassalage on payment of a manumission tax of 16 florins and a further tax of 15 florins for the tithe. [Jacob Muehleysen, Ship *Patience*, August 11, 1750.]

3. STIEHL, ABRAHAM—of Steinbach (Kreis Simmern), "has made up his mind to go to Pennsylvania"; is, with wife and four children, freed from vassalage on payment of 32 florins for manumission and 29 florins for the tithe. [Johann Abraham Stiehl, Ship *Patience*, August 11, 1750.]

4. DOERTER (DORTEN), JOHANN ANTON—of Laubach (Kreis Simmern), "who has gone to the Island of Pensylphania," pays, with wife and six children, 59 florins for manumission and 53 florins tithe.

5. BRACH, NICKEL—of Ravensbeuren (Kreis Zell, Mosel), "who went to Pensylphania," pays 20 florins for the tithe.

6. CUNTZ, NICKEL— of Unzenberg (Kreis Simmern), "who has gone to the Island of Pensylphania," pays 100 florins for the tithe. [Johann Nickel Cuntz, Ship *Patience*, August 11, 1750.]

From Hueffelsheim (Kreis Kreuznach)

7. WOLFFSKEHL, ANNA MARGRETHA—born 11-18-1735 at Hueffelsheim, daughter of Johannes Wolffskehl and wife Anna Maria, "went with her father to the New Land." ELISABETHA WOLFFSKEHL, born 12-28-1733 at Hueffelsheim to the same parents, "went with her father in 1742 to the New Land." MARIA AGNES WOLFFSKEHL, born 1-27-1738 of the same parents, "went with her father to the New Land." [Johannes Wolffskehl, Ship *Loyal Judith*, September 3, 1742.]

8. REITZEL, MARIA WILHELMINA—born 9-2-1734 at Hueffelsheim, daughter of the shoemaker Johann Georg Reitzel and wife Sybilla, "went with her father to the New Land in 1741." JOHANN PETER REITZEL, born at Hueffelsheim 10-28-1737 to the same parents, "went with his

parents to the New Land in 1741." [Johann Georg Reutzel, Ship *Molly*, 10-17-1741.]

From Eisenbach (Kreis Kusel)

9. PFAFF, THEOBALD—"who disappeared eight years ago from Eisenbach and emigrated to America, leaving nine children behind, of whom three are at present housed in the prince's orphanage at Homburg" (Document dated 1-29-1777). [Theobalt Pfaff, Ship *Betsy*, 10-26-1768.]

From Hornbach (Kreis Zweibruecken)

10. STRIBECK, JOHANN GEORG and CHRISTIAN—sons of Conrad Stribeck, citizen and woolspinner at Hornbach from his first marriage with Elisabetha Schaeffer, "who both after their mother's death went to the New Land in 1735 with their grandmother Elisabetha Schaeffer and their mother's brother, with the knowledge and permission of the most gracious authorities, and since the grandparents were still alive [and] said children consequently had nothing yet of their maternal inheritance, they have taken the grandmother's inheritance along." [Elizabeth Shever, Jerich Strebeck, Christian Strebeck, Ship *Pensilvania Merchant*, September 18, 1733.]

11. BLEY, PHILIPP—son of the citizen and master cooper, Werner Bley of Hornbach, "who married here (i.e., Hornbach), but ten years ago went to the District of Kleeburg in Alsace and later on, with the permission of the most gracious authorities, went to America." (The emigration to America took place around 1748-9.) Werner Bley's wife was Elisabetha Huber.

12. MAUS, SAMUEL—son of Friderich Maus, councilor at Hornbach and his wife Susanna Mueller, "went to America" around 1754. [Samuel Maus, Ship *Edinburg*, 9-14-1753.]

13. HENGE, CATHARINA—daughter of Samuel Mueller, citizen and tanner at Hornbach, and his wife Maria Margaretha Maus, "who was divorced on the grounds of adultery from her husband Georg Henge, to whom she had a son named Philipp, and afterwards went to America, where, according to a letter which reached here, she married a man named Fischer." (The emigration took place around 1766.) According to another document her son is also said to have gone to America.

14. LEINER, LUDWIG—of Hornbach, "went abroad as woolenweaver," and "is reported in 1784 to have died in America."

15. ZUTTER, DANIEL and BALTHASAR—sons of Benedict Baltzer Zutter, woolspinner at Hornbach, "secretly disappeared and went away to America" (Document dated 6-7-1763). [Daniel Zutter, Balthasar Zutter, Ship *Chance*, 12-1-1763.]

From Brenschelbach (Kreis Homburg, Saar)

16. HOCHSTRASER, PAUL—son of Samuel Hochstraser of Brenschelbach and his wife Elisabetha, "who has now established himself as master tailor in Philadelphia" (Document dated 4-18-1761). But according to a Letter of Attorney dated 1-23-1764, Paul Hochstraser, breeches maker, with his sister Catharina, was resident in the city of Albany, province of New York. [Paulus Hochstrasser, Ship *Edinburg*, 9-14-1753.] The Jacob Hochstrasser who emigrated in 1767 was perhaps a brother of Paul's since the latter had a brother by that name.

From Walsheim on the Blies (Kreis Homburg, Saar)

17. SCHUNK, JOHANNES, CATHARINA, ELISABETHA, MARIA, and SIMON—children of Wilhelm Schunk of Walsheim and wife Catharina Schwarz, "have been for nine or ten years in America" (Document dated 10-18-1781).

Albisheim (Kreis Kirchheimbolanden)

1. JOHANN ENGEL MORGENSTERN, born at Albisheim September 20, 1726—son of Johann Philipp Morgenstern and wife Maria Rosina—"residing in Pennsylvania." [Johann Engelbert Morgenstern, Ship *St. Andrew*, September 9, 1749.]

2. ABRAHAM BRUBACHER—son of Jacob Brubacher from his first marriage—"in Pennsylvania" (Document dated 1763). The Brubacher family, of Mennonite background, was in the 18th century located in the region of Albisheim, also in the Mennonite settlement of Ibersheim, near Worms.

Altenkirchen (Kreis Kusel)

3. JACOB BERG—son of Jacob Berg of Altenkirchen and wife Anna Margaretha Wagner—blacksmith by trade, went to Pennsylvania without manumission, along with JOHANN THEOBALD SCHRAMM—son of George Schramm of Altenkirchen—in the year 1769. The property of both of them, namely an inheritance which came to them later, was on that account confiscated by the Government of the Duchy of Zweibruecken, since they no longer intended to return to their homeland. Jacob Berg was referred to in the documents as a blacksmith at Middletown, near Frederick, Maryland, while of Theobald Schramm is known only that after his arrival in America he worked as a hostler in Philadelphia. [Jacob Berg, Theobald Schramm, Ship *Minerva*, October 13, 1769.]

Appenhofen (Kreis Bergzabern)

4. MARGRETHA and SIBILLA WINTZ—daughters of Georg Wintz of Appenhofen—"who are by this time living in the New Land" (Document

dated February 10, 1752). One of them was married to THOMAS SCHLEY of Frederick, Maryland.

5. MARGRETHA KUHN—daughter of Nicklaus Kuhn, citizen of Appenhofen, and his wife Elisabetha Nickler—was, according to official declarations, married at Billigheim to Friedrich WUERTHSBACHER (or WIRTHSBACHER), who was a physician born in the region of Heilbronn (Wuerttemberg), and went with him to America in 1764. [Friderich Wurtzbacher, Ship *Hero*, October 27, 1764.]

6. GEORG MICHEL BANZ, tailor by trade, and his sister CATHARINA BANZ, both from Appenhofen, the former single, the latter married to PETER BRUNNER of Klingen, went to Pennsylvania without issue about 1748. A letter still extant in the Speyer Archives describes Georg Michel Banz as settled in Frederick County, Maryland, Johann Peter Brunner in the neighborhood of the town of Frederick. [Peter Brunner, Ship *Albany*, September 2, 1749.]

Assenheim (Kreis Ludwigshafen)

7. FRANZ BALTHASAR SCHALTER—son of Johann Georg Schalter (died 1754) of Assenheim and his wife Elisabeth—went to Pennsylvania shortly after his father's death, in order to inherit here the property of a brother of his father, who had already been a long time resident of Pennsylvania. After the death of his uncle he stayed in Pennsylvania. On November 16, 1767, he wrote from Alsace Township, Berks County, to his relatives, that he renounced his share of the inheritance, which he would have had a claim on from home, and wishes only that a clock and a Bible be sent over to him. With him went JOHANN GEORG BOERSTLER, likewise from Assenheim, to America, but later returned home again. [Frantz Baltzer Schalter, Jorg Boerstler, Ship *Edinburgh*, September 30, 1754.]

8. JACOB NEFF—son of the Anabaptist (Mennonite) Peter Neff of Assenheim and his wife Veronika Roesch—"absent in America" (Document dated May 27, 1789). [Jacob Neff, Brig *Betsy*, October 15, 1785.]

Billigheim (Kreis Bergzabern)

9. BERNHARD KNEY—son of Philipp Kney of Billigheim and his wife Maria Margaretha Hutmacher—"who has gone to the so-called New Land" (Document dated May 10, 1755).

10. ANNA MARGARETHA DEGREIFF—daughter of the councilor Jacob Degreiff of Billigheim—"is married in the New Land" (Document dated May 12, 1755).

Boeckweiler (Kreis Homburg, Saar)

11. JOHANNES KELLER—son of Daniel Keller, of Boeckweiler—"established and married in the New Land" (Document dated October 19, 1776).

12. HENRICH KUNZ—"son of the deceased citizen of the same name, of Boeckweiler and wife Maria Margaretha Hock—removed himself from this country in 1764 and according to report that has reached here went to America without permission, contrary to the present governmental order" (Frankfurter Kayserl. Reichs-Ober-Amts-Postzeitung, 2-13-1787). According to the documents Henrich Kunz was a cartwright and from a letter dated August 21, 1768 we learn that he was living with Jonathan Heger in Canageschick in Maryland.

Breitfurt (Kreis Homburg, Saar)

13. JACOB WELKER—son of Wilhelm Welker of Breitfurt—"who according to report, has gone to America" (Document dated December 4, 1777). [Either Jacob Welcker, Ship *Minerva*, September 17, 1771, or Jacob Welcker, Ship *Crawford*, October 26, 1768.]

14. ANNA APPOLONIA VOGELGESANG—daughter of Nickel Gentes, magistrate and citizen of Breitfurt—"married to Georg Vogelgesang, Jr. (evidently also from Breitfurt), resident in America" (Document dated May 6, 1765). [Georg Vogelgesang, Ship *Squirrel*, October 21, 1761.]

15. MATHEISS and GEORG SCHMIDT—children of Abraham Schmidt, citizen and magistrate of Breitfurt—"in America" (Document dated October 7, 1760).

16. JOSEPH NEU—son of Georg Neu, resident of Breitfurt and his wife Christina Margaretha Gentess—"went to America" around 1740. His brother PETER NEU, "went to America" around 1753.

17. JOHANN OTTO NEU—son of Wilhelm Neu of Breitfurt and his wife Anna Margaretha—"now residing in the New Land" (Document of May 19, 1767). His brother JOHANN SIMON NEU, "also residing in the New Land" (Document of May 19, 1767).

Dannstadt (Kreis Ludwigshafen)

18. About the year 1748 RUDOLPH DRACH and his sister ANNA MARIA DRACH from Dannstadt, both single, went to America, where they married and had children. In the year 1788 they requested, through a power of attorney, the surrender of their property on payment of the tithe. Their property was, however, not surrendered, but confiscated according to the Emigration Edict of the Electoral Palatinate.

Edenkoben

19. PHILIPP CARL HAAS—son of Johann Georg Haas—intended in the year 1748, to go, with his wife and five children, to the New Land "on account of a better fortune." [Philipp Carel Haas, Ship *Patience*, September 16, 1748.]

20. ANNA ELISABETHA SEYFFERT—daughter of Johann Gottfried Seyffert of Edenkoben—"married to DAVID DELATER, who went to

Pennsylvania" (about 1740.) [David Delater, Ship *St. Andrew,* October 2, 1741.]

21. ANNA CATHARINA GLEICH—daughter of the master miller Henrich Gleich of Edenkoben—"went to Pennsylvania" (about 1756).

22. JOHANN GEORG CROISSANT and his sister ANNA CATHARINA CROISSANT—children of Jacob Croissant of Edenkoben—"who went to Pennsylvania" (about 1756).

Ellerstadt (Kreis Neustadt)

23. In a Property Inventory of Ellerstadt from the year 1781 it is reported of JOHANN CASPAR HUBER—son of Michael Huber of Ellerstadt and his wife Anna Barbara—"living in Philadelphia and 44 years old; he has been absent from here 18 years." [Casper Huber, Ship *Chance,* November 1, 1763.]

Elschbach (Kreis Kusel)

24. JOHANN GEORG JUNG—son of Hermann Jung of Elschbach and his wife Anna Margaretha—"living in the New Land" (Document dated 1754).

Freckenfeld (Kreis Germersheim)

25. JOHANN HAHN—son of Jacob Hahn of Freckenfeld and his wife Ottilia Eichenlaub—"went to the New Land." CONRAD HAHN, brother of the preceding, single, "to the New Land." JOHANN JACOB HAHN, brother of the two preceding emigrants, "in the New Land." The latter was baptized at Freckenfeld February 9, 1727. An Inventory of September 11, 1754, lists all three persons as emigrated before that date.

26. GEORG DIERWAECHTER, baptized at Freckenfeld, February 13, 1724, and JOHANN ERHARD DIERWAECHTER—sons of Peter Dierwaechter of Freckenfeld and his wife Anna Catharina Hummel—"who both went to the so-called New Land or Pennsylvania" (about 1751). [Ehrhardt Thuerwaechter, Ship *Janet,* October 7, 1751.

27. MARGARETHA APFEL—daughter of Georg Apfel of Freckenfeld and his wife Anna Catharina Gruber—"wife of MICHAEL HERRMAN, former citizen at Candel, who went to the New Land" (Document dated 1755). [Presumably Michel Hermann, Ship *Richard & Mary,* September 30, 1754.]

28. GEORG BAUR—son of the citizen and beadle Jacob Baur of Freckenfeld and his wife Anna Catharina Klein—"who went to the New Land" (Document dated June 10, 1761).

Freinsheim (Kreis Neustadt)

29. MICHEL REZER—son of the cooper Theobald Rezer of Freinsheim and his wife Anna Maria Held—"who went away in the year 1756 to Pennsylvania."

30. JOHANN NICLAUS BACH—son of Sebastian Bach, who died at Freinsheim in 1753—"who is now, however, in Pennsylvania" (Document dated June 25, 1768). Niclaus Bach was a resident of the city of New York, as appears from a letter written from there. [Possibly Nickel Bach, Ship *Adventure*, September 25, 1754.]

31. JOHANN PETER WEILBRENNER—son of Georg Daniel Weilbrenner, citizen and master butcher at Freinsheim and his wife Catharina Hilb—went to America in 1753 and settled at Boucherville near Montreal. In a document dated at Montreal, June 12, 1781, he renounced his share of the property that had fallen to him, in favor of his brothers and sisters. At the same time there was in Montreal JOHANN JACOB MAURER, born at Kriegsfeld in the Palatinate, Captain of the Second Battalion of the King's Royal Regiment, of New York. In a letter of his brother, from Heidelberg, he is "described as overseer of the Royal British ships in Canada."

Freisbach (Kreis Germersheim)

32. JOHANN THOMAS KERN, baptized at Freisbach,—September 19, 1700,—son of Peter Kern of Freisbach—"went to Pennsylvania"—married at Freisbach, February 17, 1733, Maria Margaretha—daughter of Michel Jopp of Ottersheim.
Children, born at Freisbach:
1. Johann Christoph, born January 25, 1736—"to Pennsylvania."
2. Anna Elisabeth, born November 20, 1733—"to Pennsylvania."
[Johann Thomas Kern, Ship *Samuel*, August 30, 1737.]

33. JACOB PETER MUENCH, born at Freisbach June 28, 1733—son of Peter Muench and wife Christina—"to Pennsylvania". JOHANN GEORG MUENCH, born at Freisbach September 27, 1731—son of the same parents—"to Pennsylvania." PHILIPP SIMON MUENCH, born August 25, 1728 at Freisbach—son of the same parents—"to Pennsylvania." [Presumably Hans Georg Muenig, Ship *Jacob*, October 2, 1749; Simon Minch, Ship *Brotherhood*, November 3, 1750.]

Grossbundenbach (Kreis Zweibruecken)

34. GEORG DELLER—son of Georg Deller of Grossbundenbach—"who went to the New Land" (Document dated April 4, 1761). [Johann Georg Deller, Ship *Dragon*, September 26, 1749.]

35. PETER LUGENBIEHL—son of Kilian Lugenbuehl of Grossbundenbach—"who emigrated to America in the year 1750." [Peter Lugenbuehl, Ship *Brotherhood*, November 3, 1750.]

36. GEORG PETER ECKEL—son of Michael Eckel of Grossbundenbach and his wife Anna Catharina Keller—"in America" (Document dated March 22, 1764). [Georg Peter Eckel, Ship *Richard & Mary*, September 26, 1752.]

37. JULIANA BACH—daughter of Albrecht Bach, Sr., of Alststadt— "who was married to JOHANN GEORG ECKEL at Grossbundenbach, who went to the New Land" (Inventory of 1756).

Hassloch (Kreis Neustadt)

JACOB TREIBELBISS from Hassloch, "went away to the New Land some thirty years ago" (Inventory of 1764). Johann Jacob Treibelbiss was born April 10, 1709, at Hassloch, son of the carpenter Jacob Treibelbiss and his wife Anna Margaretha. [Johann Jacob Dreibelbiss, Ship *Mary of London*, September 26, 1732.]

Hessheim (Kreis Frankenthal)

CARL LUDWIG BARDIER—son of Adam Bardier of Hessheim and his wife Sibilla—"at present in Pennsylvania" (Document dated June 26, 1772).

Heuchelheim (Kreis Bergzabern)

ANNA BARBARA DECKER—daughter of Philipp Strohschneider of Heuchelheim and his wife Anna Barbara—wife of GEORG DECKER from Wollmesheim, "now in the New Land" (Document dated March 11, 1754). [Johann Joerg Decker, Ship *Two Brothers*, September 21, 1751.]

MICHAEL ROEHMELL ("in the New Land") and GEORG ROEHMELL ("there too")—sons of Martin Roehmell of Heuchelheim and his wife Catharina Ullrich (Document dated June 12, 1756). [G. Michael and Hans George Rommigh, Ship *Two Brothers*, September 24, 1750?]

GEORG JACOB KAEUFER—son of Johannes Kaeufer of Heuchelheim and his wife Catharina Elisabetha—"in Pennsylvania" (Document dated May 4, 1757). Cf. the Weiss family, under Muehlhofen.

Horbruch (Kreis Bernkastel)

According to a report of the Village-Mayor of Irmenach, dated March 11, 1746, to the Government of Trarbach, JOHANN PETER HEHN (or HENN)—son of Nicol Hehn of Horbruch—had "gone away in the year 1741 to the so-called New Land."

Hornbach (near Zweibruecken)

SAMUEL MAUS—son of the councilor Friedrich Maus of Hornbach and his wife Susanna Mueller—"former citizen in Zweibruecken, but went ten years ago to America" (Inventory of 1763). [Samuel Maus, Ship *Edinburg*, September 14, 1753.] See *Dutchman*, Winter 1954.

Hueffelsheim (Kreis Kreuznach)

ANNA MARIA REUTZELE, born at Hueffelsheim August 2, 1720—daughter of the shoemaker Johann Georg Reutzele and wife Anna Sybilla—"This child of the parish has gone to the New Land."

JOHANN JACOB VIEL, born at Hueffelsheim November 22, 1718—son of Theobald Viel—"went on May 17, 1767, to the New Land."

MARIA WOLFFSKEHL, born at Hueffelsheim February 28, 1711—daughter of Theobald Viel and wife Anna Margaretha—married, at Hueffelsheim, November 19, 1730, JOHANNES WOLFFSKEHL, and "went to the New Land in 1742."

JOHANN MICHEL RECH, born at Hueffelsheim March 1, 1751—son of Johann Conrad Rech and wife Anna Margretha—"parents and children went to the New Land."

Hundsbach (Kreis Kreuznach)

ELISABETHA CATHARINA HEYL, born at Hundsbach January 4, 1733—daughter of Johann Peter Heyl, citizen at Hundsbach and wife Susanna Catharina—"this child's father has gone to Pennsylvania" (Reference in Lutheran Church Book of Hundsbach).

Ilbesheim (Kreis Landau)

CATHARINA MEDART—daughter of Johann Adam Medart of Ilbesheim and his wife Margaretha Kuntz—widow of GEORG CLEMENTZ of Ilbesheim, "who (the widow) went to the so-called New Land" (about 1753). CARL MEDART, her brother, "who also (about this same time) went to America"; VALENTIN MEDART, brother of the two preceding, "who also went to the New Land" (Document dated May 19, 1758).

JOHANN VALENTIN CLEMENTZ—son of Sebastian Clementz of Ilbesheim (died 1760)—"who went to the so-called New Land" (about 1754). [Valentine Clementz, Ship *Neptune*, September 30, 1754.]

BERNHARD and JOHANN ADAM WUERTENBECHER—sons of Johannes Wuertenbecher of Ilbesheim and his wife Anna Maria—"went to the so-called New Land" in May, 1753.

HANSS GEORG KAST—son of Hans Georg Kast of Ilbesheim and his wife Margaretha Doerner—"who traveled to America already in the year 1753." The Manumission Protocols of the Duchy of Zweibruecken give the year of emigration as 1749. However, the emigrant is presumably Hans Jerg Kast, Ship *Edinburgh*, September 16, 1751.

ANNA BARBARA KLUND—daughter of Johann Adam Klund, master shoemaker at Impflingen—"who went to the New Land" (about 1753).

ADAM HAHN, linenweaver, "who already in the year 1753 went to the so-called New Land." He was the son of Johann Niclaus Hahn and his wife Anna Catharina Heb.

JULIANA CLEMENTZ—daughter of Johann Adam Clementz of Ilbesheim and his wife Anna Maria Knoll—and wife of VALENTIN ZAHNEISSEN, "who went to the so-called New Land" (about 1754). According to the ship lists her husband came along: Vallentin Zaneichel, Ship *Barclay*, September 14, 1754.

MARIA CATHARINE DOERNER—daughter of Bernhard Doerner, citizen and master shoemaker of Ilbesheim and his wife Catharina Pfuster—"who was married to NICLAUS FASS and is in the New Land." [Nickel

Fass, Ship *Royal Union*, August 15, 1750.] JACOB DOERNER, her brother, "who likewise went to the so-called New Land." [Jacob Dorner, Ship *Phoenix*, November 2, 1752.]

PETER FRUTSCHY, of Ilbesheim, after the death of his wife Anna Regina Obert, went, with his daughter Elisabeth (born at Ilbesheim April 11, 1747), "secretly, and contrary to the governmental prohibition, to the New Land." [Johann Peter Frutzuy, Ship *Neptune*, October 7, 1755.]

WILHELM MICHAEL, master shoemaker of Ilbesheim, "went to the so-called New Land" (about 1754).

SEBASTIAN DOERR—son of Jacob Doerr of Ilbesheim and his wife Maria Catharina—"who learned the cooper trade and became a journeyman in the year 1749 and from here traveled to America."

Impflingen (Kreis Landau)

MARGARETHA BOSSERT—daughter of Johannes Bossert of Impflingen and his wife Margaretha—"who went from here (Impflingen) to America" (Document dated February 19, 1755).

Kandel (Kreis Germersheim)

LUDWIG EINSEL, baker, born at Kandel June 28, 1726, "at this time established in America, in the Province of New York, at Rhinebeck." [Johann Ludwig Einsel, Ship *Duke of Bedford*, September 14, 1751.]

JOHANN DIETHER BEYERLE—son of the blacksmith Simon Beyerle of Kandel and his wife Anna Catharina Einsel—"who has been now for some years in America" (Document of 1782). [Dieter Beyerle, Ship *Crawford*, October 14, 1769.]

GEORG LEONARD ZOLLER—son of Leonard Zoller, citizen of Kandel and his wife Maria Odilia Weiss—"now 19 years absent and in America" (Property Inventory of 1784). [Geo. Leonard Zoller, Ship *Hamilton*, October 6, 1767.]

FRIEDRICH BEYERLE—son of Johannes Beyerle of Kandel and his wife Anna Maria Stoll—"now (1789) 16 years absent and his residence unknown." This is presumably Frederick Beyerle, Ship *Union*, September 30, 1774.

ANNA ELISABETHA FAUBELL—daughter of Niclaus Bald, citizen of Kandel, and his wife Anna Maria Jooss—"wife of Johannes Faubell, former citizen here (at Kandel), who went together to the New Land" (Document dated May 17, 1756).

JOHANN DIETER ROEDEL—son of Georg Simon Roedel of Kandel and his wife Anna Apollonia—"now in America" (Document dated 1789). His brother GEORG FRIEDRICH ROEDEL was "also in America."

Of the six children of Jacob Burg, shoemaker at Kandel and his wife Apollonia Einsel, a document dated August 8, 1792, reports them all "absent in America." Their names were PHILIPP JACOB BURG, ELISABETHA MARGARETHA BURG, MARIA ELISABETHA BURG,

JOHANN GEORG BURG, MARIA CATHARINA BURG, and MARIA
MARGARETHA BURG.

Kleinbundenbach (Kreis Zweibruecken)

MARIA CATHARINA GERLINGER—daughter of Philipp Jacob
Gerlinger of Kleinbundenbach and his wife Agnes Kaercher—married to
ANDREAS GREINER (born at Diemeringen in Alsace), emigrated (before
1752) to America. Both were living in Whitemarsh Township, Philadelphia
County, Pennsylvania. [Andreas Creiner, Ship *Phoenix*, September 15,
1749.]

NICKEL KAERCHER of Kleinbundenbach, "has gone to America now
many years ago" (Document dated 1796). Presumably John Nicklas
Kargher, Ship *Richard & Mary*, September 26, 1752.

Kleinich (Kreis Bernkastel)

JOHANN NICKEL BEYER—son of Matthias Beyer of Kleinich—along
with JOHANN GEORG BAERTGES—son of Matthias Baertges from the
same place—are permitted by the Sponheim Government of Trarbach,
April 27, 1748, to go away to Pennsylvania, "in order to perfect themselves
in their chosen trade." Yet in case they do not return within three years,
they must buy themselves free of vassalage, toward which end their coming inheritance is sequestrated. Under the same conditions, with a permit
dated May 14, 1748, MICHAEL BAERTGES, brother of the above Georg
Baertges, tanner by trade, was able to emigrate to Pennsylvania. [Michael
Bartjes, Ship *Two Brothers*, September 15, 1748.]

On the same proviso, with permit dated March 18, 1748, JOHANN
NICKEL NEU—son of Christoffel Neu of Kleinich—weaver by trade; like-
wise JOHANN PETTER VELTEN (FEHLTEN)—son of Conrad Velten of
Kleinich—shoemaker by trade—were permitted to emigrate to America.
[Peter Felte, Ship *Two Brothers*, September 15, 1748.]

According to a permit from the Trarbach Government, dated April 26,
1741, JOHANN CONRAD LAHM, tailor—son of the turner Peter Lahm of
Kleinich; likewise the linenweaver JOHANN MICHEL NEU—son of Philps
Neu from the same place; and JOHANN MATTHIAS BAYER—son of the
mason Matthias Bayer of Kleinich, were permitted to emigrate to Pennsylvania. Yet in case they did not return in two years, their manumission
had to be paid (cf. above). The emigration of all three persons is docu-
mented in the official records. Matthias Bayer and Johann Michel Neu are
said, however, to have died soon after their arrival in America. [Johann
Konradt Lahm, Ship *Europa*, November 20, 1741.]

Klingen (Kreis Bergzabern)

ANDREAS FROHNHAEUSER—son of Mathes Frohnhaeuser and his
wife Maria Catharina Altschuh—"who has been in the New Land 25 years"
(Inventory of 1774).

MICHEL STUEBINGER—son of Andreas Stuebinger of Klingen—is "now in the so-called New Land" (Document dated September 15, 1756).

GEORG FISCHER—son of Philipp Fischer of Klingen and wife Anna Barbara Paul—"is in the New Land" (Document dated July 15, 1786).

Kuebelberg (Kreis Kusel)

JOHANN ADAM WAGNER—son of Theobald Wagner of Kuebelberg and wife Barbara—"married at Schmittweiler", is "in the New Land" (Document dated 1758).

Lachen (Kreis Neustadt)

JACOB TRUEB—son of David Trueb of Lachen and his wife Catharina Elisabetha Hammann—"residing in Pennsylvania" (Document dated September 29, 1772). ANNA BARBARA TRUEB, sister of Jacob, "likewise residing in Pennsylvania" (Document dated September 29, 1772).

MARIA CATHARINA THEOBALD of Lachen—daughter of Johannes Theobald of Lachen—widow of PETER HAMMANN, went to Pennsylvania in 1764 with her second husband JACOB SAUERHEBER from Hassloch and the children of her first marriage. Johann Jacob Sauerheber was a resident of Maiden Creek Township, Berks County, Pennsylvania. [Jacob Sauerheber, Ship *Hero*, October 27, 1764.]

MARIA ELISABETHA SCHUSTER, of Lachen, left her homeland unmarried at the age of 20 years—"now for thirty or more years away from Lachen and gone to America" (Property Inventory of 1784).

ANDREAS JAEGER went from Lachen to America in the year 1764 and took his niece CATHARINA KIRCHER (or KERCHER) with him. The latter married in America JOHANNES BRUNNER of Passyunck near Philadelphia. Andreas Jaeger lived in Upper Paxtang, Lancaster County. [Andreas Jaeger, Ship *Britannia*, September 26, 1764.]

Lambsborn (Kreis Zweibruecken)

MARIA EVA TRAUTMANN (married) and GEORG TRAUTMANN—children of Henrich Trautmann of Lambsborn and his wife Susanna Heinz of Langwieden—"have gone to the New Land" (Document dated April 9, 1749). [Hans George Drautman, Ship *Princess Augusta*, September 16, 1736.]

Lambsheim (Kreis Frankenthal)

JACOB HOENICH of Lambsheim, former resident (but non-citizen) of Lambsheim, who wants to go to Pennsylvania or to the New Land, is, on account to his meager property, manumitted gratis, likewise his stepdaughter ANNA MARIA HAUCK, yet the latter must pay 12 florins to buy her herself out of vassalage and 10 florins for the tithe (Protocols of the Oberamt of Neustadt, 1764). [Jacob Hoenick, Ship *Hero*, October 27, 1764.]

Limbach (Kreis Homburg, Saar)

JACOB LEIBROCK—son of Johann Georg Leibrock of Limbach—"who had resided at Bischweiler (Alsace), but has now gone to Pennsylvania" (Document dated March 13, 1752). [Jacob Leibrock, Ship *Patience*, September 9, 1751.]

PHILIPP CARL KOCH—son of the Reformed pastor Georg Friedrich Koch of Limbach—"who has learned the bookbinder's trade and has been about 14 years in America" (Inventory of 1790, which places his emigration therefore about 1776).

JOHANN HENRICH OBERKIRCHER—son of Wilhelm Oberkircher of Limbach and his wife Maria Margaretha Keller—"who about 12 years ago left his wife and children behind and secretly escaped from here" (Inventory of 1783). [Presumably Henrich Oberkircher, Ship *Sally*, October 31, 1774.]

Loetzbeuren (Kreis Zell, Mosel)

CATHARINA ELISABETHA SCHNEE, born at Loetzbeuren August 27, 1730—daughter of Johannes Schnee and wife Maria Margretha—"went away to Pennsylvania in 1751." (Reference in Lutheran Church Book of Loetzbeuren).

ANNA MARGRETHA DIETERICH, born at Loetzbeuren October 4, 1730—daughter of Johann Nicol Dieterich and wife Susanna Elisabetha—"this person has gone to Pennsylvania with her husband" (*Ibid*).

MARIA CATHARINA HOFF, born at Loetzbeuren May 26, 1732—daughter of Frantz Hoff and wife Anna Elisabetha—"went to Pennsylvania" (*Ibid*).

JOHANN WILLHELM LUETZ, born at Loetzbeuren September 12, 1732—son of Matthess Luetz and wife Elisabetha Catharina—"went away to Pennsylvania in 1751" (*Ibid.*).

ANNA ELISABETHA FRANTZ, born at Loetzbeuren March 25, 1735—daughter of Johann Nicol Frantz and wife Maria Elisabetha—"went to Pennsylvania in 1751" (*Ibid.*).

Mannweiler (Kreis Rockenhausen)

VALENTIN FROELLICH—son of Johann Henrich Froellich of Mannweiler and wife Anna Margaretha—"now absent and with his wife Apolonia nee Rapp as well as two children gone away to the New Land" (Document dated May 22, 1723).

Mauschbach (Kreis Zweibruecken)

DANIEL, GEORG and JACOB WEBER—sons of Philipp Weber of Mauschbach—"went to America" around the year 1750, "without previously being manumitted from vassalage by our most gracious authorities." [Possibly Johann Daniel Weber, Ship *Isaac*, September 27, 1749.]

Minderslachen (near Kandel)

ANNA BARBARA BOHLANDER—daughter of Georg Beyerle, citizen of Minderslachen, and his wife Anna Catharina Roth—married to JOHANN ADAM BOHLANDER of Minderslachen, "who went together to the New Land" (about 1755). [Johannes Bohlander, Ship *Good Intent*, October 3, 1754.]

JOSEPH FETSCH—son of Christian Fetsch of Minderslachen and his wife Barbara Himmler—"who is said actually to be residing in Philadelphia" (about 1774). [Joseph Foetsch, Ship *Union*, September 30, 1774.]

Minfeld (Kreis Germersheim)

GEORG MICHAEL GROSS, unmarried, and ANNA MARIA GROSS—children of Frantz Gross of Minfeld—"went to the New Land" (about 1751).

HANSS ERHARD FOSSELMANN—son of Ludwig Fosselman of Minfeld and wife Maria Margaretha Schaeffer—"who now thirty years ago went to the so-called New Land" (Inventory of 1762). [Hans Erhart Vosselman, Ship *John and William*, October 17, 1732.]

MARIA ELISABETHA KAUFFMANN, sister of Erhard Fosselmann, married to the mason JOHANNES KAUFFMANN, "who (about 1750) went to Zweibruecken and (about 1756) to America".

MARIA KOENIG and ABRAHAMB KOENIG—children of Frantz Koenig, farm-steward of the cloister at Minfeld, "went to the New Land" about 1752.

RACHELL BOUQUET—daughter of the citizen and farm-steward of the cloister at Minfeld, "who went off single to the West Indies." ROSINA BOUQUET, sister of Rachell, wife of HANSS GEORG HOFFMAN, "who likewise went to America." MATHEUS BOUQUET, brother of the two preceding, "who likewise went away, single, and in common with the above mentioned, to America". The emigration of all three is posited in a document dated February 26, 1762. JACOB HAEN of Minfeld, "went to the New Land" (Document dated 1761). [Jacob Haen, Snow *Ketty*, October 16, 1752.]

NICLAUS OTH—son of Michael Oth of Minfeld and wife Maria Margaretha Fosselmann—"in New England or America" (emigration about 1754). [Presumably Johann Nickolaus Ott, Ship *Phoenix*, November 2, 1752.]

Moersbach (Kreis Zweibruecken)

MICHAEL BINCKLE (BENCKLE)—son of Hanss Binckli of Moersbach —"went to America" (about 1734). The family was of Swiss origin—the official papers mention an aunt of the emigrant who died in Canton Berne. [Hans Michel Bingley, Ship *Oliver*, August 26, 1735.]

Muehlhofen (Kreis Bergzabern)

JOHANN ADAM TRAUB and JACOB TRAUB—sons of Heinrich Traub of Muehlhofen and his wife Maria Catharina Roeller—"who both went to the so-called New Land a year ago (1754)". [J. Adam Traub, Jacob Traub, Ship *Barclay*, September 14, 1754.]

VALENTIN JUNG—son of Peter Jung, citizen resident at Muehlhofen and his wife Magdalena Fine—"who went to the so-called New Land" (about 1736). [Valantine Young, Ship *Charming Nancy*, October 8, 1737.] JOHANN JACOB JUNG, brother of Valentin, "who also went there" (about 1749). MARIA CATHARINA, their sister, "married CASPAR BAER, and afterwards went there (i.e., America) with him" [Caspar Ber, Ship *Restauration*, October 9, 1747.] JOHANN ADAM JUNG, brother of the preceding, "who went there too" (Document dated September 15, 1756). [Johann Adam Jung, Ship *Two Brothers*, September 14, 1749.]

BENEDICT FORSTER—son of the citizen and master miller Ludwig Forster of Muehlhofen and his wife Anna Juditha Reuther—"to the New Land" (after 1746). [Benedict Forster, Ship *Neptune*, September 30, 1754.]

FRANTZ WEISS, ABRAHAM WEISS, HANSS PETER WEISS, and DANIEL WEISS—sons of Jacob Weiss of Muehlhofen and his wife Margaretha Kessler— "which four children went one after the other to America; news of them received now and then" (Property Inventory of March 16, 1763). According to official declarations of the end of April, 1750, ABRAHAM WEISS is said to have gone with wife and children to America, from Moerzheim, where he was working as a farmer. FRANTZ WEISS "is reported to have gone away, a single man, with his brother ABRAHAM WEISS, to America." According to the Acta he was born April 9, 1705, at Barbelroth in the Palatinate. For HANSS PETER WEISS (born May 5, 1712, at Barbelroth) the same emigration data apply as for his brother FRANTZ. [Johann Peter Weis, Ship *Anderson*, August 21, 1750.] DANIEL WEISS (born October 6, 1715, at Muehlhofen), "went to America from here (Muehlhofen) with his wife and four children in the year 1754". [Daniel Weiss, Ship *Barclay*, September 14, 1754.] MARGRETHA WEIS—daughter of Matheis Mans of Muehlhofen and his wife Eva—"wife of DANIEL WEIS, who went off the beginning of 1754 to New England." "Daniel Weis's wife, who left Muehlhofen in the year 1754 and went to America" (cf. DANIEL WEIS). CATHARINA WEISS (born October 10, 1709, at Barbelroth), "went to America with her husband (KAEUFER of Heuchelheim, q.v.) and FRANTZ and ABRAHAM WEISS to America.

BARBARA HAUSWIRTH—daughter of Adam Zimpelmann, assistant judge of Muehlhofen—"wife of CHRISTIAN HAUSWIRTH from here (Muehlhofen), who went with her husband to America in the year 1753." [Christian Hauswirth, Ship *John and Elizabeth*, November 7, 1754.]

JOHANN JACOB KOEHLER—son of the assistant judge and citizen Andreas Koehler at Muehlhofen and his wife Anna Catharine Zimmer—

"who now over fourteen years ago traveled to the so-called New Land" (Property Inventory of 1765). [Jacob Koehler, Ship *Phoenix*, September 25, 1751.]

ANNA ELISABETHA MEISTER—daughter of Peter Meister of Muehlhofen and his wife Anna Maria Kesseler—"went away single from Muehlhofen to America" (Document dated June 18, 1754).

Mutterstadt (Kreis Ludwigshafen)

BALTHASAR REYMER of Mutterstadt is permitted to go to the New Land with wife and children, but must pay the tithe on his property that he is taking out of the country (Protocols of the Oberamt of Neustadt, 1753). [Balthaser Reimer, Ship *Brothers*, September 30, 1754.]

Niederlustadt (Kreis Germersheim)

PETER ROCH—son of the blacksmith Peter Roch of Niederlustadt and his wife Maria Barbara Stadler—"who went to Pennsylvania in the year 1753 and left in this neighborhood at Offenbach his wife, Margaret nee Lutz, besides a little son, Friedrich Roch, aged eight years". [Johann Peter Roch, Ship *Rowand*, September 19, 1753.]

ANDREAS OTT—son of Georg Ott of Niederlustadt and his wife Catharina Groh—"went to the New Land" (about 1750).

Niedermiesau (today Miesau, Kreis Kusel)

GERTRUD FRANCK—daughter of Johannes Franck of Niedermiesau and his wife Anna Catharina Rheinberger of Otterberg—"married to Henrich Kohl in the New Land"; her sister ANNA MARIA was "married to Valentin HOFFMANN in the New Land" (Document dated April 1, 1762).

Oberkleinich (Kreis Bernkastel)

According to a report of the Village-Mayor of Kleinich to the Government of Trarbach, dated May 8, 1741, MARIA CATHARINA and NICKEL LAHM—children of Matthias Lahm of Oberkleinich—want "to go to the New Land." [Johann Nicklaus Lahm, Ship *Lydia*, September 29, 1741.] In a report to the Sponheim Government, dated May 12, 1741, the Village-Mayor of Irmenach wrote: "I wish herewith to report that in the past year, as I recently learned, two young apprentices have gone to the so-called New Land under the pretense of completing their apprenticeship. One of them, by the name of JOHANN PETER LORENTZ, was born in the village of Hoschidt (=Hochscheidt), the other, JOHAN PETTER LAHM, was a native of Oberkleinich." According to an entry of the Government of Trarbach, dated 1740, they were both described as actually emigrated "to the New Land". [Peter Lorentz, Peter Laam, Ship *Lydia*, September 27, 1740.]

Oberlustadt (Kreis Germersheim)

DANIEL HOFFMANN—son of Jacob Hoffman of Oberlustadt and Christina Brueckner, his second wife—"who went to the New Land" (Document dated August 30, 1758). [Either Daniel Hoffman, Ship *Neptune*, September 30, 1753, or Daniel Hoffman, Ship *Robert and Alice*, September 3, 1739.]

JOHANN JAKOB FAUTH—son of Bernhard Fauth of Oberlustadt and wife Katharina Haf—"went to America" (about 1765). [Jacob Faut, Ship *Polly*, August 24, 1765.] See next entry.

CATHARINA HEINTZ—daughter of Johann Adam Theiss of Oberlustadt and wife Magdalena Schmitt—"who married GEORG JAKOB HEINTZ of Roth (Rhodt u. Rietburg, Kreis Landau) and went with him to Pennsylvania." LOUISA, her sister, "married JACOB FAUTH from here and likewise went to Pennsylvania."

GEORG ADAM HORTER—son of Jacob Horter of Oberlustadt and Agnes Sohland his wife—"who now 12 years ago went to Pennsylvania" (Property Inventory of 1768, which places the date of emigration about 1756).

Basic to genealogical research in this country are the eighteenth century immigrant lists being assembled by scholars abroad. Dr. Friedrich Krebs, one of the principal researchers in Germany today, here concludes an article which was begun two issues back. The source materials are the state and municipal archives covering the areas from which so many thousands emigrated two centuries ago.

Oberlustadt (Kreis Germersheim)

BARBARA HORTER, "widow of GEORG HORTER, deceased citizen at Oberlustadt, left here about a year ago for the so-called New England with her son VELTEN HORTER. Also there was a son of hers by the name of GEORG JACOB HORTER who went to the above-mentioned New England several years ago" (Inventory of 1765). [Johann Valtin Horter, Ship *Britannia*, September 26, 1764.]

GEORG ADAM JAHRAUS—son of Andreas Jahraus of Oberlustadt and his wife Margaretha Schmid—"residing in America" (Document dated October 30, 1786).

ANNA ELISABETHA SCHMITT—daughter of Andreas Schmitt of Oberlustadt and his wife Catharina Jahraus—"wife of FRIEDRICH DOLL, inhabitant of Pennsylvania" (Document dated March 30, 1770).

ANNA APOLONIA SIGRIST—daughter of Martin Sigrist of Oberlustadt and wife Catharina Boehm—"went to Pennsylvania" (about 1744).

Obermiesau (Today Miesau, Kreis Kusel)

NICKEL LANG—son of Johannes Lang of Obermiesau and wife Anna Catharina—"went to the New Land" (about 1735) with wife and children, from Waldmohr, where he was then residing. His step-sister EVA ROSINA JACOBI—daughter of Martin Jacobi of Obermiesau—went to America at the same time, presumably with her brother, and was there married to FRIEDRICH STEFFINGER. Her sister CATHARINA JACOBI went "to the New Land" with her, along with her husband VALENTIN NEU. [Fallendin Neu, Nickel Lang, Ship *Harle*, September 1, 1736.]

CHRISTIAN HAMMEL—son of Bernhard Hammel of Obermiesau— "went to the New Land in 1734 as an apprentice butcher."

Obersuelzen (Kreis Frankenthal)

PAUL FRIED—son of the Anabaptist (Mennonite) Peter Fried of Obersuelzen—"went to the New Land" (Document dated June 6, 1747).

JOHANN JACOB FUCHS—son of Georg Henrich Fuchs of Obersuelzen —"who is in the New Land" (Document dated June 17, 1758).

LORENTZ BECK, of Obersuelzen, "in the New Land" (Document dated 1771). [Johan Loretz Beck, Ship *Hero*, November 27, 1764.]

Ottersheim (Kreis Kirchheimbolanden)

HENRICH LEBKUECHER—son of Johann Adam Lebkuecher of Ottersheim—"last summer (1753) for the second time went to the New Land, without paying the tithe." [Henrich Lebkucher, Ship *Lydia*, September 20, 1743.]

Ottersheim (Kreis Germersheim)

CONRAD DOLL—son of Georg Doll of Ottersheim and wife Anna Margaretha Weinheimer—"this man is in America" (Document dated March 21, 1753).

GEORG KUHN—son of Valentin Kuhn of Ottersheim—"is said to reside in the New Land, according to a letter written April 26, 1747 from 'Carlsdaun' (Charleston) in South Carolina."

Rohrbach (Kreis Bergzabern)

PHILIPP and ANDREAS BOUDMOND—sons of Philipp Boudmond, citizen of Rohrbach (died 1762)—"who both are in the New Land for the 12th year" (Inventory of 1762). [Andre Baudemont, Ship *Osgood*, September 29, 1750.]

PETER DORST—son of Peter Dorst of Rohrbach and his wife Maria Catharina—"who is in the New Land" (Document dated May 12, 1762).

HANSS GEORG HOFFMANN—son of Georg Bernhardt Hoffmann of Rohrbach and his wife Maria Elisabetha—"married in the New Land" (Document dated January 14, 1765).

ADAM BECKENHAUB—son of Jacob Beckenhaub of Rohrbach and wife Anna—"who went about 15 years ago to the New Land" (Property Inventory of 1766). [Hans Adam Beckenhaub, Ship *Neptune*, September 30, 1754.]

HANSS PETER HOFFMANN—son of Hans Georg Hoffmann of Rohrbach and wife Margaretha—"who now has been living in the New Land over nine years" (Inventory of 1742). [Presumably Johann Petter Hofman, Ship *Dragon,* September 30, 1732.]

Rumbach (Kreis Pirmasens)

MARGARETHA CATHARINA BLEY—daughter of Jacob Neuhard, assistant judge at Rumbach and his wife Anna Barbara—"married to ADAM BLEY, citizen here (at Rumbach) and in the Spring (1753) emigrated to America with her husband Adam Bley."

GEORG MICHAEL SCHAEFFER—son of Heinrich Schaeffer, citizen at Rumbach and his wife Anna Maria Schneider—"who has been a citizen here at Rumbach and emigrated secretly to America in the year 1766."

SUSANNA CATHARINA SCHAUB, HEINRICH SCHAUB, MARIA DOROTHEA SCHAUB—children of Balthasar Schaub of Rumbach—"emigrated to America" (Document dated June 23, 1770). [Henry Schaub, Ship *Sally,* November 10, 1767.] Of SUSANNA CATHARINA SCHAUB the records report, "now married to JACOB NEUHARD the blacksmith, citizen at Rumbach, and several years ago emigrated to America" (Document dated 1770). Of MARIA DOROTHEA: "Now married to GEORG MICHAEL SCHAEFFER, citizen here and likewise gone to America with the above mentioned."

St. Julian (Kreis Kusel)

JOHANN HENRICH ALLMANN, mason—son of Henrich Allmann of Sienhachenbach—married at St. Julian, January 18, 1746, to Maria Barbara Soffel, born at St. Julian October 5, 1723—daughter of Bernhardt Soffel of St. Julian and wife Maria Engel—"both emigrated to Pennsylvania with six children May 15, 1764."

Children, born at St. Julian:

1. Maria Sara, born July 6, 1747.
2. Anna Margretha, born November 20, 1749 ("died on the way to America in 1764").
3. Maria Elisabetha, born August 14, 1752.
4. Maria Catharina, born December 11, 1754.
5. Johann Nicol, born March 3, 1764 ("died on the way to America in the same year").
6. Anna Elisabetha, born August 27, 1760.

All references from the Lutheran Church Book of St. Julian.

JOHANN FRIEDRICH HIRSCHFELD(T), born at St. Julian October 12, 1728—son of Johann Philipp Hirschfeld and wife Maria Margretha—"turner by trade—emigrated to Pennsylvania with wife and three children [May 15,] 1764" (Reference in Lutheran Church Book of St. Julian). Friedrich Hirschfeld married at St. Julian, February 10, 1756, Maria Margretha Neu, born at Obereisenbach (Kreis Kusel), September 25, 1728—daughter of Johann Jacob Neu and wife Maria Elisabetha.

Children, born at St. Julian:
1. Maria Elisabetha, born December 22, 1756.
2. Johann Henrich, born June 13, 1759.
3. Maria Margaretha, born August 14, 1762.
[Henrich Allman, Friedrich Hirschfeldt, Ship *Richmond,* October 20, 1764.]

JOHANN JACOB JECKEL, born at St. Julian April 5, 1722—son of Johann Christoph Jeckel and wife Anna Maria—"emigrated to Pennsylvania April 24, 1752" (Reference in Lutheran Church Book of St. Julian).

GEORG ABRAHAM JACOB, blacksmith by trade, born at Eschenau (Kreis Kusel) December 31, 1723—son of Johann Peter Jacob of Eschenau and wife Anna Margretha—married at St. Julian, June 16, 1750, to Maria Dorothea Grill—born at St. Julian February 22, 1731—daughter of Johann Georg Grill of St. Julian—"both emigrated to Pennsylvania with five [four] children, May 15, 1764" (Reference in Lutheran Church Book of St. Julian).

Children, born at St. Julian:
1. Johann Georg, born March 11, 1760.
2. Maria Magdalena Elisabetha, born November 25, 1762.
3. Johann Peter, born November 10, 1757.
[Abraham Jacob, Ship *Richmond,* October 20, 1764].

JOHANN NICOL GRIMM, widower, married (1st) at St. Julian November 27, 1736, to Anna Elisabetha, widow of Adam Jeckel; married (2d) at St. Julian May 25, 1751, to Maria Magdalena, daughter of Johannes Dickes of Baumholder—"both migrated to Pennsylvania with [—] children, May 15, 1764" (Reference in Lutheran Church Book of St. Julian).

Children, born at St. Julian:
1. Friderich Jacob, born November 2, 1758—"died at Portsmouth in England on the way to America, 1764."
2. Maria Dorothea, born February 17, 1756.

Steinweiler *(Kreis Germersheim)*

JOHANNES LINGENFELDER—son of the master baker Peter Lingenfelder of Steinweiler—"who is staying in the so-called New Land" (emigrated about 1753).

Stetten *(Kreis Kirchheimbolanden)*

MICHEL NIEDERAUER—son of Jost Fritz Niederauer of Stetten—"who is in the New Land" (Document dated 1752). [Michel Niederauer, Ship *Two Brothers,* October 13, 1747.]

Waldmohr *(Kreis Kusel)*

JOHANNES HEILL—son of Michael Heill, resident and citizen at Waldmohr and his wife Maria Catharina Schaeffer—"went to the New Land" (Document dated March 10, 1745).

PHILIPP NICKEL BALBIERER—son of Henrich Balbierer of Waldmohr and his wife Maria Barbara—baptized March 22, 1712, at Kleinottweiler—went to America in 1750 with the family of FRANZ KUNZ. [Philliebs Balbirer, Ship *Edinburgh*, August 13, 1750.]

VALENTIN BLUM, blacksmith, "by trade a nailsmith, in the New Land," likewise his sister EVA ELISABETHA, who was married to NICKEL LANG (q.v.) of Waldmohr. Emigration about 1736.

Walshausen (Kreis Zweibruecken)

HEINRICH HALLER—son of the citizen and master tailor Jacob Haller of Walshausen, from his first marriage with Elisabetha Moser—"deserted from the old Ducal Body Guard and emigrated to Pennsylvania." This emigration took place around 1748. His property, specifically an inheritance which later fell to him, a sum of 102 florins 11 batzen and 6 pfennig, was therefore confiscated by the Zweibruecken authorities, since his emigration took place without manumission. [Henrich Haller, Ship *St. Andrew*, August 18, 1750.]

Weingarten (Kreis Germersheim)

PAUL BAUERSACHS, born September 29, 1744, at Weingarten—son of David Bauersachs, citizen of Weingarten and wife Anna Maria Damian of Boebingen—"who in the beginning settled himself as a citizen at Freisbach, but from there went away to America" (Document dated August 5, 1784). [Paulus Bauersachs, Brig *Betsey*, December 4, 1771.]

PETER BRUNNEMER, baptized at Weingarten April 28, 1726—son of Johannes Brunnemer and wife Anna Margaretha—"went away to Pennsylvania without previous permission" about 1749. According to a power of attorney authorized by him, dated August 15, 1766, Peter Brunnemer was settled in Augusta County in the Province of Virginia.

Weisenheim am Sand (Kreis Neustadt)

ANNA BARBARA REITENBACH—daughter of Jacob Reitenbach of Weisenheim am Sand and his wife Gertraud Keller—was taken along to America in the year 1764 by the brother of her father MICHEL REIDENBACH of Weisenheim. In America she married MICHEL LAUER. Michel Reidenbach's first emigration took place about 1744. In the year 1764 he returned to Weisenheim, to receive an inheritance for the two children of his brother JOHANN NICOLAUS REIDENBACH who had died in Pennsylvania. [Johann Nickel Reidenbach, Johann Michel Reidenbach, Ship *Lydia*, September 20, 1743; Michel Reidebach, Ship *Richmond*, October 20, 1764.]

LORENTZ and JOHANN CHRISTIAN LAUFFER, from Weisenheim am Sand, "went to the New Land" (about 1728).

JOHANNES QUAST of Weisenheim am Sand, "vassal, staying in Pennsylvania" (Document dated 1775). [Joh. Quast, Ship *Crawford*, October 16, 1772.]

Westheim (Kreis Germersheim)

VALENTIN BATTEIGER—son of Peter Batteiger of Westheim and wife Maria Eva—"absent, staying in America" (Document dated 1777). [Johann Valentin Batteiger, Ship *Minerva*, October 29, 1767.]

GEORG ADAM SCHWAB—son of Andreas Schwab of Westheim and wife Rosina Barbara—"residing in Pennsylvania" (Document dated March 17, 1765).

Wolfersheim (Kreis St. Ingbert, Saar)

CHRISTIAN BRENGEL—son of Kilian Brengel of Wolfersheim and wife Juliana—"having signified with the princely authorities his intention of returning, went to Maryland" (about 1754). His brother JACOB BRENGEL, "went under the same provision to America." [Christian Brengel, Jacob Brengel, Ship *Phoenix*, October 1, 1754.]

ANNA CATHARINA BRENGEL, sister of both, "followed her two brothers CHRISTIAN and JACOB BRENGEL to America" (about 1764). GEORG BRENGEL, brother of the above mentioned persons, "married in America, whither he went (about 1764) as an apprentice linenweaver."

Wolfstein (Kreis Kusel)

MARIA MARGARETHA FUCHS—daughter of Friedrich Fuchs of Wolfstein and wife Anna Maria—"wife of PETER DOERR of Rossbach (Kreis Kusel), who went with her husband to America" (Document dated 1781). [Peter Doerr, Ship *Prince of Wales*, November 5, 1764.]

JOHANN JACOB SCHMIDT—son of the master blacksmith Sebastian Schmidt of Wolfstein—went to America (before 1744). In a letter written October 17, 1753, from Bethel Township on the Little Swatara, in Berks County, Pennsylvania, he mentions that DEBALT WERNER from Wolfstein (emigrated 1744) and WILHELM DAUWER from Baumholder [Wilhelm Dauber, Ship [—], October 20, 1747] brought letters for him to America. His brother JOHANN HENRICH SCHMITT went to America in 1754. From him there is a letter from Philadelphia, received November 21, 1754, which describes the sea voyage and trip across to America.

Wollmesheim (Kreis Landau)

JOHANN MICHEL UNGERER—son of Stephan Ungerer of Wollmesheim and wife Anna Maria Sahner "living in the New Land" (Document dated October 26, 1759). [Johann Michel Ungerer, Ship *Beulah*, September 10, 1753.]

Zeiskam (Kreis Germersheim)

PHILIPP JACOB GEISS, farrier at Zeiskam—son of Henrich Geiss of Freisbach—married at Zeiskam, May 4, 1745, to Anna Appolonia Guenter —daughter of Andreas Guenter of Zeiskam—widow of the farrier Conrad Maylaender of Zeiskam.

Children, born at Zeiskam:

1. Agatha Geiss, born September 29, 1747.
2. Johann Georg Geiss, born December 27, 1748.
3. Maria Barbara, born October 5, 1750.

According to official records the family went to America about 1751 and according to a power of attorney of Philipp Jacob Geiss, dated May 28, 1763, was settled in Bern Township, Berks County, Pennsylvania. [Philipp Jacob Geis, Ship *Phoenix*, September 25, 1751.]

ANDREAS EBERHARDT, born at Zeiskam June 4, 1733—son of Friderich Eberhardt, master weaver, and his wife Elisabetha, at Zeiskam— "who has gone away to America" (Document dated June 22, 1772). [Presumably Andereas Ebehrth, Ship *Bannister*, October 21, 1754.]

Zeiskam (Kreis Germersheim)

LORENTZ SCHMITT, surgeon and barber—son of Mathes Schmitt, citizen at Billigheim—married at Zeiskam, May 14, 1748, Maria Helena Guth— daughter of Johannes Guth of Zeiskam. After his marriage Lorentz Schmitt was surgeon and barber at Zeiskam.

Children, born at Zeiskam:

1. Johann Jacob, born May 23, 1749—"has gone to the New Land".
2. Philipp Peter, born September 22, 1750.

Source: Reformed Church Book of Zeiskam. According to governmental records Maria Helena Schmitt, nee Guth, intended in 1751 to go with her husband and two children to the "New Land" and on that account had her inheritance paid out to her. According to another reference dated 1757 they had "gone away to America about six years ago." [Lorentz Schmitt, Ship *Phoenix*, September 25, 1751.]

JOHANN PETER ZWICKER, citizen at Zeiskam, married at Zeiskam August 9, 1753, Maria Magdalena Haffner.

Children, all born at Zeiskam:

1. Johann Peter, baptized May 24, 1736—"went to the New Land with his father and mother".
2. Magdalena, baptized August 4, 1739—same reference.
3. Georg Melchior, born November 9, 1743—same reference.
4. Johann Georg, born June 27, 1747—same reference.
5. Maria Barbara, born October 23, 1750—same reference.

Source: Reformed Church Book of Zeiskam.

SAMUEL SINN, master baker at Zeiskam—son of Peter Sinn, master baker at Zeiskam—married (at Zeiskam) January 31, 1747, Anna Barbara

Trauth—daughter of Johann Georg Trauth of Offenbach (Palatinate). Of their son, Johann Friedrich, born at Zeiskam, November 23, 1751, the Reformed Church Book of Zeiskam reports—"went with his father to the New Land."

PENNSYLVANIA DUTCH PIONEERS
from South Palatine Parishes*

By Fritz Braun and Friedrich Krebs §
Translated by Don Yoder

The number of Palatine church-registers with annotations on 18th century emigrants, is small. The following list is comprised of emigrants from villages in the southern part of the Palatinate: Bellheim, Freimersheim, Freisbach, Gommersheim, Minfeld, Niederlustadt, Oberlustadt, Otterheim, Weingarten, Westheim, and Zeiskam.*
The sources of the references to emigration are the Lutheran church-registers of Freimersheim, Freisbach, Gommersheim, Minfeld, Weingarten; the Reformed church-registers of Zeiskam and Oberlustadt, the latter serving for both Oberlustadt and Niederlustadt; the *Ausfautheiakten Germersheim;* the Electoral Palatine Archives (*Akten Kurpfalz*) for Westheim; and the Archives of the Johannite Order in the Palatine State Archives in Speyer; as well as materials in the *Heimatstelle Pfalz* in Kaiserslautern.

As far as possible, the birth or baptismal and marriage dates of the emigrants, and parents' and wives' names, were added to the basic emigration data, from the church-registers. In most cases, also, it was possible to locate the emigrants in the published ship-lists of arrivals at Philadelphia, the

---

*"*Amerika-Auswanderer des 18. Jahrhunderts aus südpfälzischen Gemeinden*," (Ludwigshafen am Rhein: Richard Louis Verlag, 1956), 20 pp., Volume 2 of the *Schriften zur Wanderungsgeschichte der Pfälzer,* edited by the *Heimatstelle Pfalz,* Kaiserslautern. Reprinted from *Mitteilungen zur Wanderungsgeschichte der Pfälzer,* Dr. Fritz Braun, editor, in *Pfälzische Familien—und Wappenkunde* 1956, Nos. 5-6.

§ Dr. Friedrich Krebs is a member of the staff of the Palatine State Archives at Speyer in the Palatinate; Dr. Fritz Braun is Director of the *Heimatstelle Pfalz,* in Kaiserslautern, Germany. American genealogists who have information on where these Palatine emigrants settled in America are asked to write to Dr. Braun at the above address.

*Readers should note that a few of the emigrants in this list from Minfeld were mentioned in Friedrich Krebs and Milton Rubincam, *Emigrants from the Palatinate to the American Colonies in the 18th Century* (Norristown, Pennsylvania: The Pennsylvania German Society, 1953); and several emigrants from Minfeld, Niederlustadt, Oberlustadt, Ottersheim, Weingarten, Westheim, and Zeiskam appear in Dr. Krebs' articles, "Pennsylvania Dutch Pioneers", in *The Pennsylvania Dutchman* for Spring 1956 and Summer 1956. In each case fuller information is given in the present article. Emigrants from Ottersheim are completely omitted in the translation because they have been covered completely in the *Dutchman*.

three-volume work, *Pennsylvania German Pioneers*, by Ralph Beaver Strassburger, edited by William J. Hinke (Norristown, Pennsylvania: The Pennsylvania German Society, 1934).

A word of thanks is due Pastor Dr. Kaul, who furnished the emigration data from the Lutheran church-register of Gommersheim.

The materials on the Bauersachs family, under Weingarten, are a good example of what can be done through the cooperation of Pennsylvania and Palatine genealogists.

The question of where the emigrants settled in American has in most cases been left open, pending receipt of definite materials from American genealogists.

BELLHEIM

1. WILL, ISAAC—born at Bellheim, April 19, 1724, son of the Reformed schoolmaster [Schuldiener] Wilhelm Will and wife Anna Eva Schlindwein; "at present living on the Island of Pennsylvania at Germantown, two hours from Philadelphia" ["dermahlen auff der Insel Pinsephania zu Germandon 2 Stund von Pilladelphia wohnhafft"] (Inventory of Wilhelm Will, April 29, 1748).

[Isaac Wille arrived at Philadelphia, September 30, 1743, on the Ship *Phoenix*.]

FREIMERSHEIM

2. ANDRES, GEORG MICHELL—son of the citizen Hanss Michell Andres (died 1711) of Freimersheim and wife Maria Juditha Wiedtemann; was, according to a conveyance of the widow Maria Juditha Wiedtemann dated April 18, 1733, "married, manumitted, and gone to the New Land" ("verheurathet, manumittiret, und inss neue Landt gezogen").

[A Michael Anderras arrived at Philadelphia, May 15, 1732, on the Ship *Norris*.]

3. BELERT (BOELERT), PHILIPP JACOB—born at Freimersheim, September 8, 1725, and ANNA MARGARETHA BELERT, born at Freimersheim, March 6, 1737, children of the citizen and town-councilor [Gemeindsmann] Johann Friderich Belert of Freimersheim and his wife Anna nee Müller of Freimersheim, "both children about 10 years ago gone away to the Island of Cajenne and since then nothing more heard of them" (Inventory of Widow Anna Müller, dated February 10, 1776).

The above-mentioned Philipp Jacob Böhlert married Maria Barbara Grehl, born at Freimersheim, June 12, 1725, daughter of the citizen and master-tailor Philipp Grehl (died about or before 1760) at Freimersheim and his wife Margaretha Zachelmeyer (Zagelmejer) (died in March 1770); wife and children "journeyed to Pennsylvania after obtaining manumission" ["nach erlangter Manumission nach Pennsylvanien peregriniret"] (Document of April 5, 1770).

Children, born at Freimersheim:
1. Eva Margaretha Belert, born November 14, 1753.
2. Johann Christoph Belert, born February 7, 1755.
3. Johann Michael Belert, born September 17, 1757.
4. Johann Adam Belert, born January 9, 1760.

FREISBACH

4. KERN, JOHANN THOMAS—born at Freisbach September 19, 1700, son of Peter Kern of Freisbach; married at Freisbach, February 17, 1733, to (Anna) Maria Margaretha Jopp, daughter of Michel Jopp of Ottersheim; "went to Pennsylvania."
Children born at Freisbach:
1. Anna Elisabeth Kern, born November 20, 1733; "in Pennsylvania."
2. Johann Christoph Kern, born January 25, 1736; "in Pennsylvania."
[Johann Thomas Kern, aged 36, arrived at Philadelphia, August 30, 1737, on the Ship *Samuel*. The family settled in Lancaster County, Pennsylvania.]
5. KERN, JOHANN JOST—born at Freisbach, 1746, is buried in the old graveyard of Hassinger's Church, between Middleburg and Paxtonville, Snyder County, Pennsylvania. In this cemetery many emigrants from the Upper Rhine country found their last resting place. On the tombstone of John Jost Kern his birthplace is given as "Freischbach, Germany" (i.e., Freisbach, Kreis Germersheim). Also members of the Bauersachs family (spelled Bowersox) are buried there. See Aaron Gern Gift, "The Hassinger Church," in *The Pennsylvania-German*, September, 1908.
[Jost Kern arrived at Philadelphia, October 13, 1766, on the Ship *Betsy*.]
One Johann Justus Kern was born at Freisbach, February 20, 1741, son of Philipp Jacob Kern and wife Sophie Margarethe. Since in the period concerned the Lutheran Church Register of Freisbach contains only the birth of this Johann Justus Kern, he may be identical with the emigrant.
6. MUENCH, JOHANN PETER—married at Freisbach, September 19, 1724, to Maria Christina Oster, daughter of Leonard Oster. Cf. below his brother, Johann Simon Münch, under Gommersheim.
Children, born at Freisbach:
1. Philipp Simon Münch, born August 25, 1728; "in Pennsylvania."
2. Johann Peter Münch, born January 13, 1730; in the Church Register there is no reference to his emigration and no death entry.
3. Johann Georg Münch, born September 27, 1731; "in Pennsylvania."
4. Jacob Peter Münch, born June 28, 1733; "in Pennsylvania."
[Peter Minech, aged 39, arrived at Philadelphia, August 30, 1737, on the Ship *Samuel*.]

GOMMERSHEIM

7. BERRY, ISAAK—shoemaker, died at Gommersheim, July 24, 1733; married at Gommersheim, February 4, 1723 to Anna Elisabeth Schwartz, born at Speyer in 1703, daughter of the cartwright Wendel Schwartz and wife Maria Francisca.
Children, born at Gommersheim:
1. Eva Christina Berry, born August 5, 1724; "in America."
2. Anna Eva Berry, born November 7, 1725; "in Georgia."
3. Maria Barbara Berry, born January 8, 1728; died at Gommersheim.
4. Johann Ludwig Berry, born December 24, 1729; "in Pennsylvania."
5. Anna Margaretha Berry, born March 27, 1732; "in Pennsylvania."

8. WALTHER, NICOLAUS—married at Gommersheim, February 21, 1735, to Anna Elisabeth Schwartz, widow of the abovementioned Isaak Berry, born at Speyer 1703.
Children, born at Gommersheim:
1. Anna Apollonia Walther, born February 5, 1736: died at Gommersheim.
[Nicholas Walter (Waller), aged 41, arrived at Philadelphia, September 5, 1738, on the Ship *Winter Galley*.]
The stepchildren (cf. Isaak Berry, above) would have emigrated with this couple.

9. BEYER (BAYER), JOHANN NIKOLAUS—born June, 1677, son of the Magistrate [Gerichtsmann] Christoph Beyer and wife Kunigunde; married Maria Elisabeth [_____]; "in Pennsylvania."
Children, born at Gommersheim:
1. Clara Elisabeth Beyer, born September 19, 1726; "in America."
2. Georg Jakob Beyer, born December 12, 1729; "in Pennsylvania."
3. Maria Magdalena Beyer, born February 1, 1732; "in Pennsylvania."
4. Johann Wendell Beyer, born May 30, 1734; "in Pennsylvania."
5. Anna Barbara Beyer, born January 27, 1739; "in Pennsylvania."

10. BEYER, JOHANN ANDREAS—born December, 1681, brother of the preceding, married Anna Apollonia [_____]; "in Pennsylvania."
Children, born at Gommersheim:
1. Thomas Beyer, born December 18, 1713.
2. Johann Philipp Beyer, born February 29, 1717.
3. Johann Martin Beyer, born June 23, 1720; "in Pennsylvania."
4. Eva Elisabeth Beyer, born September 27, 1725; "in Pennsylvania."
[Andres Beyer (Beier, Beir, Bayer), aged 57, Johann Philip Bayer and Martin Beyer, aged 18, arrived at Philadelphia, September 5, 1738, on the Ship *Winter Galley*. In the ship-list there is also listed another Johann Philipp Bayer.]

11. GIESLER, JOHANN ADAM—married at Gommersheim, May 6, 1732, to Maria Magdalena Rothmayer, daughter of Johannes Rothmayer.
Children, born at Gommersheim:
1. Maria Christina Giesler, born June 23, 1733; "in Pennsylvania."

2. Johann Michel Giesler, born February 27, 1737; "in Pennsylvania."
3. Anna Catharina Giesler, born February 23, 1739; "in Pennsylvania."
[Hans Adam Gissler (Geizler, Gesler) arrived at Philadelphia, September 11, 1738, on the Ship *Robert and Alice*. Perhaps this was the above-mentioned, who could have emigrated alone, letting wife and children follow later.]
12. HOCHLAENDER JOHANN MICHAEL—cowherd, married Juliana [_____]; "in Pennsylvania."
Children, born at Gommersheim:
1. Johann Adam Hochländer, born 1735, died at Gommersheim, January 25, 1738; Catholic.
2. Johannes Hochländer born August 14, 1737; "with the father in Pennsylvania."
[Hans Michael Hochlander (Hoglander, Slotsunder), aged 32, arrived at Philadelphia, September 5, 1738, on the Ship *Winter Galley*.]
13. KRIEG, MARGARETHA DOROTHEA—born at Gommersheim April 12, 1730, confirmed at Gommersheim 1745, daughter of Johann Philipp Krieg, cooper, and wife Anna Barbara; "in Pennsylvania."
14. MUENCH, JOHANN SIMON—weaver, son of the weaver Johann Philipp Münch, married at Gommersheim, August 17, 1728, to (Anna) Maria Katharina Schenk, daughter of the weaver Johann Jacob Schenk; "with children in Pennsylvania." Cf. above, Johann Peter Munch, under Freisbach.
Children, born at Gommersheim:
1. Maria Barbara Münch, born November 21, 1729; died at Gommersheim, March 17, 1736.
2. Maria Catharina Münch, born March 20, 1731; "in Pennsylvania."
3. Johann Nikolaus Münch, born June 22, 1732; "in Pennsylvania."
4. Johann Christoph Münch, born June 6, 1734; "in Pennsylvania."
5. Maria Apollonia Münch, born February 26, 1736; "in Pennsylvania."
[Simon Minech, aged 35, arrived at Philadelphia, August 30, 1737, on the Ship *Samuel*.]
John Simon Minich is buried at the Bernville Cemetery in Berks County, Pennsylvania. According to his tombstone he was born July 21, 1700, and died February 17, 1782; his wife Catharina was born in January, 1700, and died December 12, 1773. In the church-register of Gommersheim there are no birth-dates given for either the emigrant or his wife. In America the name is spelled Minnig, Muench, and Minnich. See Tombstone Inscriptions, Bernville, Pa." in *The Penn Germania*, 1913.
15. ROMETSCH, JOHANN CASPAR—born at Gommersheim, July 6, 1728 (after the death of his father), son of Caspar Rometsch (died at Gommersheim, May 22, 1728) and wife Anna Margaretha; "in Pennsylvania."
[Johann Caspar Rometsch (Rumetsch), aged 24, arrived at Philadelphia, September 24, 1753, on the Ship *Peggy*.]

16. SCHOPPING, ANNA BARBARA—born at Gommersheim, October 1705, daughter of the potter Johann Adam Schopping (died at Gommersheim, January 18, 1746, aged 72) and wife Magdalena; "went to Pennsylvania."

17. SCHREINER, JOHANN ADAM—born *circa* 1682, married Anna Margaretha [_____].
Children, born at Gommersheim:
1. Johann Michael Schreiner, born 1708; no reference to emigration in the Church Register.
2. Martin Schreiner, born January 3, 1716; no reference to emigration in the Church Register.
3. Anna Maria Schreiner, born December 7, 1718; died at Gommersheim, July 5, 1727.
4. Johann Philipp Schreiner, born September 9, 1721; "in Pennsylvania."
5. Johann Georg Heinrich Schreiner, born July 12, 1724; "in America."
6. Johann Valentin Schreiner, born December 16, 1728; "in Pennsylvania."
[Hans Adam Schreiner (Schreyner), aged 52, Johann Michael Schreiner, aged 28, and Martin Schreiner, aged 20, arrived at Philadelphia, September 5, 1738, on the Ship *Winter Galley*.]

18. WALTER, JOHANN JAKOB—born at Gommersheim, January 15, 1729, son of Johann Jakob Walther and wife Anna Maria Krieg; "in Pennsylvania."
[Johann Jacob Walther (Walter, Walder), aged 25, arrived at Philadelphia, September 24, 1753, on the Ship *Peggy*. Immediately before Johann Jacob in the same list appears the name of a Johannes (Hans) Walter, aged 35.]

19. WINGERTER, JOHANN DANIEL—citizen and butcher, son of David Wingerter from Kleinfischlingen; married at Gommersheim, August 18, 1733, to Anna Maria Schreiner, daughter of Johann Friedrich Schreiner.
Children, born at Gommersheim:
1. Anna Barbara Wingerter, born June 29, 1734; "in Pennsylvania."
2. Johann Jakob Wingerter, born August 20, 1736; "in Pennsylvania."
3. Anna Margaretha Wingerter, born March 8, 1738; "in Pennsylvania."
4. Maria Christina Wingerter, born September 24, 1740; "in Pennsylvania."

MINFELD

20. BOUQUET (BOCKE), MATHEUS—baptized at Minfeld, September 21, 1727, son of the citizen Abraham Bocke and wife Elisabeth, single, emigrated to America presumably with his sisters and his brother-in-law (Document dated February 26, 1762). Cf. below, his brother-in-law, Hanss Georg Hoffman.

21. BOUQUET (BOCKE), RACHELL (RAHEL)—baptized at Minfeld, October 11, 1722, sister of the preceding, emigrated as single woman to America ("West Indien") (Document of February 26, 1762).

22. DAUB, NISKLAUS—went to the New Land in 1752. Presumably he is identical with Nicklaus Daub, son of Ludwig Daub, married at Minfeld, February 7, 1741, to Anna Maria König, baptized at Minfeld, July 31, 1718, daughter of Frantz König and wife Rahel.

23. FOSSELMANN, HANSS ERHARD—baptized at Minfeld, September 25, 1701, son of Ludwig Fosselman in Minfeld and wife Maria Margaretha Schäffer; married at Minfeld, August 23, 1729, to Elisabetha Margaretha Probst, daughter of Christoph Probst; emigrated thirty years ago to the New Land (Document dated 1762). Cf. brother-in-law, Johannes Kauffmann.

24. GROSS, GEORG MICHAEL—baptized at Minfeld, December 3, 1719, son of Frantz Gross in Minfeld and wife Susanna nee Schäffer; emigrated as single man about 1751 to the New Land.

25. GROSS, ANNA MARIA—baptized at Minfeld, August 27, 1727, sister of the preceding; emigrated to the New Land about 1751.

26. HAEN (HAEHN), (JOHANN) JACOB—widower, married at Minfeld, July 2, 1749, in the parsonage there "on account of great poverty" ["Wegen grosser Armuth"], to Anna Barbara Egert, widow of Peter Egert, deceased farmer (Hoffmann) on the Rinkenbergerhof.

27. HEINTZ, MICHAEL—emigrated from Minfeld to America in 1753. Possibly he is identical with Johann Michael Heintz, son of Johann Michael Heintz, former citizen at Frechenfeld, and wife; married at Minfeld, February 11, 1749, to Johanna Ulm, baptized at Minfeld April 18, 1728, daughter of Johann Michael Ullm, citizen at Minfeld, and wife Anna Barbara nee Dudenhöfer.

28. HEINTZ, WENDELL—son of Michael Heintz (died 1752), citizen at Freckenfeld, and wife; married at Minfeld, October 30, 1752, to Eva Barbara Gross, daughter of Frantz Gross and wife Susanna nee Schäffer; went to the New Land in 1767.

[Wendel Heintz arrived at Philadelphia, October 6, 1767, on the Ship *Hamilton*.]

29. HOFFMAN, HANSS GEORG—son of Lorentz Hoffman (died 1749), former citizen at Rohrbach, and wife; married at Minfeld, April 8, 1749, to Rosina (Barbara) Bouquet (Bocke), baptized at Minfeld, January 20, 1726, daughter of the citizen Abraham Bouquet and wife, Elisabetha; emigrated to America presumably with his brother-in-law and sister-in-law to America (Document of February 26, 1762). Cf. above, his brother-in-law, Matheus Bouquet.

30. KAUFFMANN, JOHANNES—mason, baptized at Minfeld, April 23, 1696, son of Matheus Kauffmann, shoemaker at Minfeld, and wife Juliana; married at Minfeld, August 24, 1723, to Maria Elisabetha Fosselmann, baptized at Minfeld, May 25, 1704, daughter of (Johann) Ludwig Fosselmann in Minfeld and wife Maria Margaretha Schaeffer; went about 1750 to Zweibrücken and about 1765 emigrated from Gutenbrunnen (Kreis St. Ingbert) to America. Cf. brother-in-law, Hans Erhard Fosselmann.

Children, born at Minfeld:
1. Catharina Elisabetha Kauffmann, baptized July 9, 1724.
2. Maria Margaretha Kauffmann, baptized April 20, 1727.
3. Johann Jacob Kauffmann, baptized December 24, 1730.
4. Johannes Kauffmann, baptized December 7, 1732.
5. Johann Georg Kauffmann, baptized September 5, 1734.
6. Maria Apollonia Kauffmann, baptized April 18, 1737.
7. Anna Maria Kauffmann, baptized November 30, 1738.
8. Johanna Kauffmann, baptized September 24, 1740.
9. Anna Apollonia Kauffmann, baptized September 12, 1742.

[Johannes Kauffman arrived at Philadelphia, October 1, 1754, on the Ship *Phoenix*. With him in the same ship-list is named Johannes Kauffman, Jr.]

31. KOENIG, ABRAHAM—baptized at Minfeld, April 2, 1724, son of Frantz König and wife Rahel, married at Minfeld, January 7, 1751, to Maria Magdalena Kauffmann, baptized at Minfeld, March 12, 1730, daughter of the citizen and linen-weaver Christoph Kauffmann.

32. KOENIG, ANNA MARIA—baptized at Minfeld, July 31, 1718, sister of the preceding; married at Minfeld, February 7, 1741, to Nicklaus Daub; emigrated to the New Land about 1752. Cf. above. Nicklaus Daub.

33. OTH (OTT), NICLAUS—son of Johann Michael Ott; married January 30, 1725, to Maria Margaretha Fosselmann (Vosselmann), baptized at Minfeld, February 7, 1706, daughter of Ludwig Vosselmann and wife of Maria Margaretha; emigrated about 1754 to New England or America.

[A Johann Nickolaus Ott arrived at Philadelphia, November 2, 1752, on the ship *Phoenix*.]

NIEDERLUSTADT

34. OTT, JOHANN ANDREAS—born at Niederlustadt, September 20, 1728, son of Johann Georg Ott and wife Catharina Groh; "already gone to the New Land ten years ago" ["vor zehen Jahren allschon in das neue Land gezogen"] (Document of June 20, 1760). The emigration must have taken place around 1750.

[An Andreas Ott arrived at Philadelphia, September 22, 1752, on the Ship *Brothers*.]

35. ROCH, JOHANN PETER—born at Niederlustadt, August 24, 1724, son of Peter Roch, citizen and farrier at Niederlustadt, and wife Maria (Anna) Barbara Stadler; married Margaretha Lutz. See *The Dutchman*, Spring 1956, p. 39.

OBERLUSTADT

36. FAUTH, JOHANN JACOB—born at Oberlustadt, September 7, 1738, son of Bernhard Fauth (Church Register: Fäth), and wife Katharine Haf, "went away to America about 18 years ago" (Document of March 18, 1783); married Louisa Theiss, born at Oberlustadt, December 24, 1741,

daughter of Johann Adam Theiss of Oberlustadt and wife Magdalena Schmitt, "who married Jacob Fauth from here and likewise went to Pennsylvania" ["welche ahn Jacob Fauth von dahier verheurathet und ebenfalls in Pennsilvanien gezogen"] (Document of December 3, 1765). Cf. also his brother-in-law, Georg Jakob Heintz.

[Jacob Faut arrived at Philadelphia, August 24, 1765, on the Ship *Polly*.]

37. HAUSHALTER, GEORG SIMON—arrived in Philadelphia on the Ship *Polly*, August 24, 1765, with the brothers Christian and Johann Jakob Wunder as well as Johann Jacob Fauth. Since he wrote his name immediately after Fauth in the ship's list and the name Haushalter appears in Ober- and Niederlustadt in the period involved, we may assume that the emigrant is connected with the Haushalter family listed in the Church Register of Oberlustadt. The only point of uncertainty is whether the father Jörg Simon Haushalter emigrated with the family or whether the son Jörg Simon Haushalter emigrated alone.

Jörg Simon Haushalter, resident in Ober- or Niederlustadt, married Anna Maria. [_____], and had the following children, born at Ober- or Niederlustadt:

1. Jörg Simon Haushalter, born March 20, 1741.
2. Christian Haushalter, born December 3, 1743.
3. Eva Maria Haushalter, born September 5, 1746; died September 29, 1746.
4. Maria Eva Haushalter, born October 27, 1749.
5. Anna Margaretha Haushalter, born March 1, 1753.
6. Johann Jörg Haushalter, born September 28, 1757.

[Georg Simon Haushalter arrived at Philadelphia, August 24, 1765, on the Ship *Polly*.]

38. HEINTZ, GEORG JAKOB—from Rhodt under Rietburg, married Maria Catharina Theiss, born at Oberlustadt, February 20, 1736, daughter of Johann Adam Theiss of Oberlustadt and Magdalena Schmitt, "who married Georg Jakob Heintz from Roth and went with him to Pennsylvania" ["welche ahn Georg Jakob Heintz von Roth verheurathet und mit demselben in Pensilvanien gezogen"] (Document of December 3, 1765). Cf. above, his brother-in-law, Johann Jakob Fauth.

39. HOFFMANN, DANIEL—born at Oberlustadt, February 17, 1727, son of Johann Jacob Hoffmann and wife Susanna Christina Brückner; "who went to the New Land" (Document of August 30, 1758).

40. HORTER, GEORG ADAM—born at Oberlustadt, May 27, 1738, son of Jacob Horter and wife (Maria) Agnes Sohland, "already gone to Pennsylvania 12 years ago" (Document of April 20, 1768). The emigration must therefore have taken place around 1756.

41. HORTER, ANNA BARBARA—married before 1733 to Georg Horter, citizen and town councilor at Oberlustadt; died before 1764. "Whereas Barbara Horter, widow and relict of Georg Horter, deceased citizen and at Oberlustadt, went from here about one year ago to the so-called New England with her son Velten Horter, also a son of hers named Georg

Jacob Horter had gone there several years previously, so then both brothers and sisters and in-laws of hers still residing here, namely Jacob Wunder and his wife Anna Maria, and Jacob Sager, sent a manuscript letter asking her therein, since one of them had the desire to go to the above-mentioned New Land, if he should sell or convert into money the inheritance still coming to her here and bring it to her. Now since Jakob Wunder and his wife Anna Maria have likewise resolved to go to their respective mother and brothers and sisters and therefore have petitioned for permission, to convert into cash the properties of their inlaws still coming to them and take them to them," hence a complete inventory of the properties of Georg Jakob and Velten Horter was drawn up and the results of the sale given to the brother-in-law, Jacob Wunder, who emigrated in 1765 (Document of April 19, 1765).

Children, born at Oberlustadt:

1. Anna Maria Horter, born July 21, 1729, married Johann Jacob Wunder (q.v.)

2. Georg Jacob Horter, born July 9, 1733.

3. Johann Valentin Horter, born September 16, 1740.

[Johann Valtin Horter arrived at Philadelphia, September 26, 1764, on the Ship *Britannia.*]

42. JAHRAUS, GEORG ADAM—born at Oberlustadt, December 27, 1746, son of Andreas Jahraus and wife (Anna) Margaretha Schmid; "who resides in America" (Document of October 30, 1786).

43. SCHMITT, ANNA ELISABETHA—daughter of Andres Schmitt of Oberlustadt and wife Catharina Jahraus, "wife of Friedrich Doll, inhabitant of Pennsylvania" (Document of March 30, 1770).

44. SIGRIST, ANNA APOLLONIA—born at Oberlustadt, February 1, 1723, daughter of Martin Sigrist (Siegerist) and wife Catharina Böhm; "already gone to Pennsylvania 21 years ago" ["schon seith 21 Jahren in Pensilivanien gezogen"] (Document of October 3, 1765). She must therefore have emigrated around 1744.

45. TEIS, GEORG ADAM—arrived at Philadelphia with Georg Simon Haushalter (q.v.) on the Ship *Polly*, August 24, 1765, and his name is given in the ship's list immediately after Haushalter's. Perhaps he is identical with Jörg Adam Theiss, born at Ober- or Niederlustadt, February 9, 1739, son of Andreas Theiss and wife Magdalena.

46. WUNDER, JOHANN JAKOB—born at Oberlustadt, January 13, 1727, son of Sebastian Wunder and wife Anna Maria; married Anna Maria Horter, born at Oberlustadt, July 21, 1729, daughter of Georg Horter and wife Anna Barbara. Cf. Anna Barbara Horter, above.

Children, born at Oberlustadt:

1. Jörg Adam Wunder, born January 7, 1753.

2. Anna Maria Wunder, born August 22, 1755.

3. Valentin Wunder, born April 1, 1758.

4. Maria Barbara Wunder, born October 21, 1760.

5. Christoph Wunder, born January 5, 1764.

[Jacob Wunder arrived at Philadelphia, August 24, 1765, on the Ship *Polly.*]

47. WUNDER, CHRISTIAN, born at Oberlustadt, July 13, 1729, brother of the preceding, married Catharina [   ].

Children, born at Nieder- or Oberlustadt:

1. Maria Eva Wunder, born April 16, 1757.
2. Andreas Wunder, born October 18, 1751; died February 4, 1763.
3. Andreas Wunder, born December 27, 1763.

[Christian Wunder arrived at Philadelphia, August 24, 1765, on the Ship *Polly.*]

WEINGARTEN

48. BAUERSACHS, PAUL—born at Weingarten, September 29, 1744, son of Johann David Bauersachs and wife Anna Maria Damian of Böbingen, settled as citizen at Freisbach and from there went to America (Document of August 5, 1784).

[Paulus Bauersachs arrived at Philadelphia, December 4, 1771, on the Ship *Betsey.*]

The name Bauersachs (also spelled Bauersax in the Church Register of Weingarten) is spelled Bowersox in America. Paul Bowersox died March 8, 1806, in Center Township, now Snyder County, Pennsylvania, and is buried at the Hassinger Church Cemetery near Middleburg in Snyder County (cf. above, Johann Jost Kern of Freisbach). According to family tradition in Pennsylvania he had come to America before 1771, returned to Germany on a visit, and returned to Pennsylvania in 1771. For the children of Paul Bowersox, born in Pennsylvania, see Dr. Charles A. Fisher, *Early Pennsylvania Births*; see also Aaron Kern Gift, "The Hassinger Church," *The Pennsylvania German,* September 1908. Further information on the family can be had from the Reverend George E. Bowersox of McSherrystown, Pennsylvania.

49. BAUERSACHS, HANS NICKEL ("NICHEL")—arrived at Philadelphia, August 15, 1750, on the Ship *Royal Union.* It is probable that this emigrant belongs to the same family as the above Paul Bauersachs. However, there is in the Church Register of Weingarten no reference to the emigration of Hans Nickel Bauersachs, nor is his baptism recorded. Information from Pastor George E. Bowersox, McSherrystown, Pennsylvania, has cleared up the mystery:

Hans Nichol Bauersachs, son of the butcher Johann Bauersachs and wife Elisabetha "Itsgrund" (cf. below), was, according to an entry by Pastor H. M. Mühlenberg in the Old Goshenhoppen Church Register in Pennsylvania, born November 14, 1702, in "Memelsdorf" and baptized there November 15, 1702. His trade was given as "tailor". According to the same entry he went in the year 1727 to "Neider . . . stadt, 3 hours from Speyer", i.e., Niederlustadt, married there Maria Elisabetha Gothe, daughter of Velten Gothe and wife Eva Elisabeth, and emigrated in 1750 with wife and children to Pennsylvania.

Children, born at Oberstadt before the emigration:
1. Maria Elisabeth Bauersachs, born April 9, 1735; died before 1750.
2. Maria Barbara Bauersachs, born August 3, 1738; died June 9, 1740.
3. Johann Valentin Bauersachs, born July 7, 1741; confirmed at Old Goshenhoppen; married December 27, 1764, to Barbara [   ].
4. Jörg Adam Bauersachs, born February 26, 1744; confirmed at Old Goshenhoppen; married Magdalena Rauenzaner (Routzan).

Both sons served in the Revolutionary War, and after their release from service settled in Frederick County, Maryland. References to both families appear in the records of St. David's Lutheran Church near Hanover, Pennsylvania, on the Maryland border. The family of Georg Adam Bowersox is later named in the records of St. Mary's Lutheran Church, Silver Run, Maryland, where members of the family are buried. His own gravestone and that of his wife and his son Christian are at Uniontown, Maryland. Georg Adam Bowersox took the oath of citizenship to Maryland on June 19, 1779.

An inquiry to Memmelsdorf, Oberfranken, revealed that the name Bauersachs never appeared in the records there. In Memmelsdorf near Ebern in Unterfranken the relationship was proved through the researches of Pastor Löblein, from the Lutheran Church Register there: Johann (Hans) Bauersachs, widower, married at Memmelsdorf, November 22, 1698, to Anna Elisabetha Köhler of Memmelsdorf.

Their children, born at Memmelsdorf, included:
1. Johannes Bauersachs, baptized August 3, 1699.
2. Johann Nikolaus Bauersachs, baptized November 3, 1700.

Striking is the difference between the birth and baptismal dates in the Memmelsdorf and Goshenhoppen entries. But we must realize that the entry in Goshenhoppen was not made by Pastor Mühlenberg until after 1750. In Memmelsdorf for the period concerned there is no other entry to be found.

"*Itsgrund*": This word appears in the Goshenhoppen Church Register in connection with the reference to the parents of Johann Nickel Bauersachs, after the first name of the mother. Undoubtedly it is a place name, since the Itz, coming from Coburg, flows through the Memmelsdorf area and into the Main.

Through the entry in the Old Goshenhoppen Church Register in Pennsylvania we have learned where the Bauersachs Family of the Palatinate originated, and that Johann Nickel Bauersachs emigrated in 1750 from Niederlustadt to Pennsylvania.

Johannes Bauersachs, baptized at Memmelsdorf August 3, 1699, must likewise have settled in the Palatinate, for in the Lutheran Church Register of Weingarten, on June 9, 1716, is recorded his marriage to Anna Maria Hubin, native of Offenbach, single, and on November 27, 1718, the birth of the son Hans David Bauersachs, who married (1st) at Weingarten, February 9, 1740, Anna Maria Damian from Böbingen and after her death married (2nd) at Weingarten, January 25, 1757, to Anna Maria Luber

(Luwer) from Oberlustadt. Johannes Bauersachs was therefore the grand-father of the emigrant Paul(us) Bauersachs and a brother of the emigrant Johann Nikolaus Bauersachs.

50. BRUNNEMER, JOHANN PETER—born at Weingarten, April 28, 1726, son of Johannes Brunnemer and wife Anna Margaretha, had "already gone away to Pennsylvania 18 years ago, without receiving permission" ["bereits vor 18 J. in Pensilvanien ohne vorherige Erlaubnis abgezogen"] (Document of March 7, 1767). According to a Power of Attorney drawn up in Augusta County, Virginia, August 15, 1766, Johann Peter Brunnemer was residing there at the time.

51. KLINGLER, THEOBALD—born about 1714, married at Weingarten, November 26, 1737, to Maria Catharina Gölbert, daughter of the citizen and town-councilor Henrich Gelberth (Gölbert) (died about 1717) at Freimersheim and his wife Anna Rosina Geiss; according to a transfer of property of the widow Anna Rosina Geiss, dated April 19, 1746, "went to the New Land seven years ago."

[Debalt Klingler, age 24, arrived at Philadelphia September 20, 1738, on the Ship *Friendship.*]

WESTHEIM

52. BATTEIGER, JOHANN VALENTIN—born at Westheim, August 27, 1739, son of Johann Peter Batteiger and wife Anna Eva (in the acts Maria Eva): "Valentin 35 years old and absent in America" (Document of May 3, 1777).

[Johann Valentin Batteiger arrived at Philadelphia, October 29, 1767, on the Ship *Minerva.*]

53. SCHWAB, GEORG ADAM—born at Westheim, April 26, 1745, son of Andreas Schwab and wife Rosina Barbara; "resident in Pennsylvania" (Document of March 27, 1765).

ZEISKAM

54. GEISS, PHILIPP JACOB—farrier, born at Freisbach, April 12, 1712, son of Henrich Geiss, citizen and town-councilor of Freisbach, and wife Anna Catharina; married at Zeiskam and settled there as farrier and citizen. According to an official document of November 9, 1763, they had already gone 12 years ago to America, in the Province of Pennsylvania" ["allschon vor 12 Jahren nacher Americam in der Province Pinselpfanien"]. For additional information, see *Pennsylvania Dutchman*, Summer 1956, page 58.

55. SCHMITT, LORENZ—citizen, surgeon and barber at Billigheim, baptized at Billigheim, January 31, 1722, son of Matthes Schmitt, citizen and town-councilor at Billigheim, and wife Anna Maria Heckman; married at Zeiskam, May, 1748, to Maria Helena (Magdalena) Guth, daughter of Johannes Guth of Zeiskam. After his marriage he moved his residence to Zeiskam. According to the Germersheim records, Lorentz Schmitt's wife, because she wanted to go to the New Land with her husband and her two small sons, had her inheritance paid back in 1751. In an official document of February 4, 1757, it is said of Helena Schmitt nee Guth, that she "went

away to America about 6 years ago". The wife of Lorentz Schmitt appears as Maria Magdalena and as Maria Helena. In the Baptismal Register of Zeiskam is found only the baptism of a Maria Magdalena. At the marriage entry "Magdalena" is stricken out and "Helena" written above. At the entry of the birth of the first child the mother appears as "Maria Magdalena," at the second child's birth as "Maria Helena." For the children see *Pennsylvania Dutchman,* Summer 1956, page 59.

56. SINN (SIEN), SAMUEL—master-baker at Zeiskam, baptized at Zeiskam, August 28, 1710, son of Johann Peter Sinn, master-baker at Zeiskam, and wife Anna Agatha. For additional details, see *Pennsylvania Dutchman,* Summer 1956, page 59.

57. ZWICKER, JOHANN PETER—citizen and town-councilor at Zeiskam, baptized at Zeiskam, December 21, 1710, son of Samuel Zwicker and wife Susanna Barbara. For additional details, see *Pennsylvania Dutchman,* Summer 1956, page 59.

A List of the First Shipload of Georgia Settlers

Edited by E. MERTON COULTER

The original of the document which appears below is in the Egmont Manuscripts of the famous Phillipps Collection. John Percival (1683-1748), the first Earl of Egmont (a title which no longer exists), was one of the original trustees of Georgia and was as active in the establishment of the new colony as was Oglethorpe. Undoubtedly, many of the Egmont Manuscripts are in the Earl's handwriting and the others are either originals or contemporary copies made by others. These manuscripts, consisting of twenty-one volumes, were until recently a part of the immense collection of manuscripts made by Sir Thomas Phillipps, Bt., of Middle Hill, Worcestershire, and Thirlestaine House, Cheltenham. In 1946, the University of Georgia purchased the Egmont Manuscripts through the agency of Sotherby & Company, London. The document here presented is included in the volume (serial number 14207) entitled "Letters, papers, & Accts &c Sent to Georgia or post in England from 9 June 1732 to 9 June 1735" (pp. 61-63). Information on the subsequent career of these original settlers is given in another volume of the Egmont Manuscripts (serial number 14220) entitled "A List of Persons who went from Europe to Georgia On their own account, or at the Trustees charge, or who joyned the Colony, or were born in it distinguishing Such as had Grants there or were only Inmates." This information is included here in the footnotes, which amcompany the document.

As neither document is dated there is no way to determine with absolute certainty the time when each was written; but, of course, there is every reason to suggest that both were made in colonial times. It can be shown, however, that the second List was composed not earlier than 1752. In that year the calendar was changed to make the year begin on January 1, instead of March 25, which was the usage before that time. Subsequently, in referring to dates which came between January 1 and March 25 before the change, to prevent a misunderstanding as to whether it was Old Style or New Style reckoning, the simple devise of giving both years was used, as for instance "8 Feb. 1733-4", as is recorded in footnote 26.

A LIST OF THE PERSONS SENT TO GEORGIA ON THE CHARITY BY THE TRUSTEES FOR ESTABLISHING THE COLONY THERE. 16 Novbr. 1732.

By Capt. Thomas [of the *Anne*].

	No. of Persons
Paul Amatis[1] aged [blank space] understands the Nature & Production of Raw Silk	1.
Timothy Bowling[2] Aged 38. Potashmaker	1.
Wm Calvert[3] Trader of Goods aged 44, Mary[4] his Wife aged 42 Wm Greenfield[5] aged 19 & Charles Greenfield[6] aged 16 his [i. e. Calvert's] Nephews, Sarah Greenfield[7] aged 16 his Neice & Elizabeth Wallis[8] aged 19 his Servant	6.
Richard Cannon[,][9] Calendar & Carpenter aged 36, Mary[10] his Wife aged 33, his Sons Marmaduke[11] aged 9 & James[12] aged 7 months, his daughter Clementine[13] aged 2½ & His Servant Mary Hicks[14] aged [blank space]	6.
James Carwell[15] Peruke maker aged 35 & Margaret[16] his Wife aged 32	2.

1. "Italian silk man." "Brought from Piedmont to introduce silk in Georgia, but took a disgust and settled chiefly at Charleston, where he died [December, 1736]." His brother, Nicholas, was "brought from Piedmont for the same purpose, [arriving July 21, 1733] but proved an idle troublesome fellow & quitted the colony. In Aug. 1735, his Brother discharg'd him." These facts and all information in subsequent footnotes were taken from the volume of the Egmont Collection, entitled "A List of Persons who went from Europe to Georgia On their own account, or at the Trustees charge, or who joyned the Colony, or were born in it distinguishing Such as had Grants there or were only Inmates." The information about Amatis is on page 9. Hereafter, this volume will be cited as List
2. He died November 5, 1733. List, 19.
3. "Said to be a land holder at Fort Arguile, 16 Jan. 1737-8, but I don't find him in the list. Would have denyd a note of hand to Ja. Dormer. Acct was cast 7 July 1737." He received lot number 7 in Savannah. List, 29.
4. She died July 4, 1733. List, 29.
5. He settled at "Fort Arguile." List, 73.
6. The list gives nothing further about him. List, 73.
7. "Marry'd to Will Elbert 22 June 1734 and lived mostly in Carolina." List, 73.
8. "Became wife of Lawrence Cook." List, 229.
9. "He marry'd to his 2nd. wife the widow of Daniel Preston 24 Oct. 1734." He received lot 5 in Savannah. He died May 27, 1735. List, 31.
10. She died July 22, 1733. List, 31.
11. He afterwards became a servant to Thomas Causton. List, 31.
12. He died on shipboard on the way to Georgia. According to the record here he was 1 year old. List, 31.
13. According to the record she was 3 years old. List, 31.
14. "Discharged by consent and marry'd Fra. Wicks 17 April 1733." List, 85.
15. "Keeper of the Workhouse 1737 but of very bad character. In July 1739 Mr. Oglethorpe appointed him Provost Marshal and Jailer at Savannah wth. a sallary of 20 pounds." He received lot 4 in Savannah. List, 31.
16. She died September 7, 1733. List, 31.

Thomas Causton[,][17] Callicoe Printer aged 40........   1.
Thomas Christie [,][18] Merchant aged 32 & Robert
Johnson[Johnston,][19] his Servant aged 17..............   2.
Robert Clark [Clarke,][20] Taylor aged 37, Judith[21]
his Wife aged 29, & his Sons Charles[22] aged 11, John
aged 4, Peter[23] aged 3 and James[24] aged 9 months....   6.
Henry Close [,][25] Clothworker aged 42, Hannah[26]
his Wife aged 32 & Ann[27] his daughter aged under 2   3.
Joseph Coles [,][28] Miller & Baker aged 28, Anna[29]
his Wife aged 32, Anna[30] his daughter aged 13, &
Elias Ann Wellen[31] his Servant aged 18.................   4.
Joseph Cooper[,][32] Writer aged 37.....................   1.
Wm Cox [,][33] Surgeon aged 41, Frances[34] his Wife
aged 35, Wm. his Son aged above 12. Eunice[35] his
daughter aged 2¾ and Henry Lloyd [Loyd][36] his
Servant aged 21...   5.

17. "At first appointed 3d Bailif, then 2d & lastly 1st Bailif in 1735. He was also Publick Store-Keeper on Hughes death 30 Sept. 1733, but turn'd out of both Offices 1739 for abusing his Trust." He received lot 24 in Savannah. List, 31.
18. "Recorder of Savannah till made 1st Bailif in Hen. Parkers room 20 June 1739. But removed 25 March 1740 by letter from the Trustees, & likewise suspended from being Recorder till an acct. he had made with the stores be made up. He lives in open adultery wh. Turners wife & he is guilty of other faults. 26th April 1740 he left Georgia, & in June following came for England, where he proposed to stay, but returned." He received lot 19 in Savannah. List, 35.
19. "He marry'd Anne d. of Geo. Syms. His lot was granted him 20 Dec. 1733, and is supposed vacant." He received lot 13 in Savannah. He died July 23, 1734. List, 97.
20. He received lot 22 in Savannah. He died April 18, 1734. List, 33.
21. "Re-marry'd to Tho. Cross 29 June 1734 and quitted the colony with him [December, 1738]." List, 33.
22. He soon died but no date of his death is given. List, 33.
23. The records do not show anything further about these boys. List, 33.
24. He died on shipboard on the way to Georgia. The record here gives his age as 1 year. List, 33.
25. He received lot 40 in Savannah. "His lot was Swamp overflow'd." He died Dec. 14, 1734. List, 35.
26. "Re-marry'd to Ja. Smith a Carolinian 8 Feb. 1733-4 who lived here on her lot. Abt. May 1740 they both left the colony to settle in Scotland on an estate, and sold their lot to Capt. Thompson for 20£." List, 26.
27. She died April 2, 1734. List, 35.
28. He received lot 27 in Savannah. He died March 4, 1734-5. List, 35.
29. "Re-marry'd to Tho. Salter 9 Sept 1736 & lives with him on his lot 68." List, 35.
30. Nothing in this record about her.
31. "Sent back to England." List, 225.
32. He received lot 20 in Savannah. He died March 29, 1735. List, 37.
33. He received lot 6 in Savannah. He died April 6, 1733. List, 37.
34. "Re-marr'd to Ja. Watts Lieut. 1 June 1734 who died the same month. She afterwd. [1734] went to England wth. her two children." List, 35.
35. William and Eunice returned to England in 1734. List, 35.
36. "He bought out his time, & had lycense to keep a publick house 2 Dec. 1736. He marr'd Phobe—He went to Carolina to get work—His wife return'd to England wth. Capt. Thompson & arriv'd 2 May 1740." He received lot 171 in Savannah. He absconded February 6, 1738-9 but returned. List, 111.

Joseph Fitzwalter [,][37] Gardener Aged 31............... I.
Walter Fox [,][38] Turner aged 35.......................... I.
John Gready[39] understands Farming Aged 22......... .. I.
James Goddard [,][40] Carpenter & Joyner Aged 38,
Elizabeth[41] his Wife aged 42, John his Son aged
under 9 & Elizabeth[42] his Daur. aged 5.................... 4.
Peter Gordon [,][43] Upholsterer aged 34 & Kath-
erine[44] his Wife aged 28................................... 2.
Richard Hodges [,][45] Basketmaker aged 50, Mary[46]
his Wife aged 42, & his daughters Mary[47] aged 18,
Elizabeth[48] aged 16 & Sarah[49] aged 5.................... 5.
Joseph Hughes[50] in the Cyder Trade & understands
Writing & Accompts aged 28 & Elizabeth[51] his Wife
aged 22.. 2,
Noble Jones [,][52] Carpenter aged 32, Sarah[53] his
Wife aged 32, Noble[54] his Son aged 10 months

---

37. "He marry'd Molly an Indian d. of Capt Tukance [Tuscanee?] 8 Apr. 1735 who ran from him, a Rambler. He went over 1. Constable of Savannah. He was Publick gardiner till 1736. Mr Oglethorpe removed him for insufficiency [inefficiency?] 21 Oct. 1738." He received lot 8 in Savannah. List, 59.
38. "Made Tything Man 23 Nov. 1736. In all his time he only fell'd one acre of land." He received lot number 2 in Savannah. List, 61.
39. "Frequently in Carolina. Try'd & conv. [convicted] for breach of Covent. with Geo. Smith 9 July 1737." He received lot number 3 in Savannah. List, 73.
40. He received lot number 1 in Savannah. He died July 1, 1733. List, 71.
41. She died July 28, 1733. List, 71.
42. John and Elizabeth were servants to Thomas Christie. List, 71.
43. "Bailif of Savannah, but removed — 1738. He thereupon return'd & remaind with his wife in England, & by leave granted with his lot to the daughters of Major Will. Cook, 12 April 1738." He left Georgia April 12, 1738 and died in 1740. He received lot 23 in Savannah. List, 71.
44. Nothing in this record about her.
45. "He was 2d Bailif of Savannah : and succeeded by Tho. Causton 16 Oct. 1734." He received Lot 17 in Savannah. He died July 20, 1733. List, 85.
46. "In possession of the lot design'd her husband. She marry'd Edwd. Townsend 22 Feb. 1734-5. She was fyned 20 shill. for retailing liquours without lycence 2 Oct. 1734, a vile foul mouthed Malecontent, & fled the colony 21 July 1740 with her young daughter." She ran away July 29, 1740, to Carolina and there died. List, 85.
47. Nothing in this record about her.
48. "She marry'd Ri. [Richard] Lobb 8 May 1734." She died August 4, 1735. List, 85.
49. She ran away July 29, 1740. List, 85.
50. "Storekeeper to the Trust while he lived." He received lot 16 in Savannah. He died September 30, 1733. List, 87.
51. "Re-marry'd to Jo. West, and at both their desires this lot was granted to Danl. Prevost 31 May 1738. She marry'd John West 20 April 1734, who dying 1739 She lived with Will. Kelleway as wife with the character of a lewd woman." She died June 5, 1740. List, 87.
52. "Employ'd to Survey the peoples lots, but removed for negligence. He took possession of this lot 21 Dec. 1733, and afterwards improved land at some distance from the town. He was I think a Constable also, and Officer for executing the Rum act. He now resides mostly at his new plantation abt. 10 miles from Savannah. On 21 Oct 1738 Mr Oglethorp removed him from being Surveyor and first Constable, but afterward gave him the comand of the Narrows." He received lot 41 in Savannah. List, 97.
53. Nothing in this record about her.
54. He received lot 46 in Savannah. List, 97.

[years?], Mary[55] his daughter aged 3 & his Servants
Thomas Ellis[56] aged 17 & Mary Cormock[57] aged 11   6.
Wm Littell [Littel][58] understands Flax & Hemp
aged 31, Elizabeth[59] his Wife aged 31. his Son
Wm.[60] aged under 2 & Mary[61] his daughter aged 5...   4.
Thomas Millidge [,][62] Carpenter & Joyner aged 42,
Elizabeth[63] his Wife aged 40, his Sons John[64] aged
11, Richard[65] aged 8, & James[66] aged 1½ & his
daughters Sarah aged under 9 and Frances[67] aged 5...   7.
Francis Mugridge[68] Sawyer aged 39................   1.
James Muir [,][69] Peruke maker aged 38, Ellen[70] his
Wife aged 38, John[71] his Son aged 18 months &
Elizabeth Satchfield[72] his Servant aged 25...........   4.
Joshua Overend[73] aged 40........................   1.
Samuel Parker[74] a Heelmaker & understands Car-
penter's Work aged 33, Jane[75] his Wife aged 36, &
his Sons Samuel[76] aged 16 & Thomas[77] aged under 9   4.
John Penrose [,][78] Husbandman aged 35 & Eliza-

55. Nothing in this record about her.
56. "He had first lot 54, but exchanged it with Will. Mackay for this. Afterwards deserted the Colony. As late as 14 June 1737 he was a servant and consequently had then no lot." He received lot 55 in Savannah. He left Georgia
December 1738 but returned. List, 55.
57. Nothing in this record about her.
58. He received lot 37 in Savannah. He died July 12, 1733. List, 111.
59. "Re-marry'd to John West 28 Aug. 1733, and had possession of the lot
intended her husband Will. Littel 31 Dec. 1733." She died September 26, 1733.
List, 111.
60. The record here states that he was born in Georgia. List, 111.
61. She died July 12, 1733. List, 111.
62. He received lot 36 in Savannah. He died July 29, 1733. List, 119.
63. She died June, 2, 1734. List, 119.
64. He received lot 91 in Savannah. His age here is stated as twelve. List, 119.
65. Nothing in this record about him.
66. He died November 4, 1734. List, 119.
67. Nothing in this record about Sarah and Frances. List, 119.
68. "Possest of his lot 21 Dec. 1733. Doubted if he left not a Minor in England." He received lot number 12 in Savannah. He died July 1, 1735. List, 123.
69. "Possest of his lot 21 Dec. 1733. Re-marry'd to Mary Woodman 29 Dec.
1734. No cultivated of land. Ran to Carolina in 1739 and died there Sept. 1739."
He received lot 18 in Savannah. List, 123,
70. She died July 10, 1733. List, 123.
71. He left Georgia in March, 1733. List, 123.
72. Nothing in this record about her.
73. He was a mercer and received lot 11 in Savannah. "The Lot supposed
vacant Feb. 1738-9." He died June 23, 1733. List, 155.
74. "He lived not to take up his lot, which was possest by his widow. He
went over 2. Constable of Savannah." He received lot 38 in Savannah. He died
July 20, 1733. List, 159.
75. "She took possession of the lot intended her husband 21 Dec. 1733. Re-
marry'd to Sml. Mercer 6 May 1734." She died August 9, 1742. List, 159.
76. He was a smith, received lot 93 in Savannah, and died in 1741. List, 159.
77. Nothing in this record about him.
78. "Fyn'd thrice for retayling spirituous liquors with out lycence. And
twice for Assault and defamation. His lot swamp overflow'd. He went over 2d
Tything man of Savannah." He received lot 15 in Savannah. He ran away to
South Carolina in August, 1742. List, 161.

beth[79] his Wife aged 46.. 2.

Thomas Pratt[80] [occupation unknown] aged 21...... 1.

John Sammes [Samms,][81] Cordwainer aged 42........ 1.

Francis Scott[82] a reduced Military Officer aged 40
& his Servt John [Richard] Cameron[83] aged 35........ 2.

Joseph Stanly [Stanley,][84] Stockingmaker & can
draw & reel Silk aged 45, Elizabeth[85] his Wife aged
35, & John Mackoy [Mackay,][86] his Servant aged 25   3.

George Symes [,][87] Apothecary aged 55, Sarah[88]
his Wife aged 52, & Ann [Anne][89] his daughter
aged 21.. 3.

Daniel Thibaut[90] understands Vines aged 50, Mary[91]
his Wife aged 40, James[92] his Son aged under 12 &
Diana[93] his daughter aged under 7.............................. 4.

John Warrin [,][94] Flax & Hemp Dresser aged 34,
Elizabeth[95] his Wife aged 27, his Sons Wm.[96] aged
6, Richard[97] aged 4, John [98] aged 1½ & one to be
baptized aged 3 weeks & his daughter Elizabeth[99]
aged 3.. 7.

79. "Found guilty of the same things, and also of keeping a bawdy house 26 May 1736. Went to Carolina for fear of the Spaniards." She left Georgia in September, 1740. List, 161.
80. "Possest of his lot 21 Dec. 1733. His lot was given to Mrt. [Margaret?] Bovey, he forfeiting it By returning to England without leave 23 April 1735, contrary to Covenant." List, 163.
81. "Had possession of his lot 21 Dec. 1733." He received lot 9 in Savannah. He died August 21, 1733. List, 189.
82. He died January 2, 1734. List, 191.
83. Absconded at Palacholas. List, 29.
84. "Possest of his Lot 21 Dec. 1733, and had fell'd fenc'd & cleard 4 acres, which by his sickness were neglected: he left the Colony 29 July 1740 being superannuated and past labour." He received lot 21 in Savannah. He left Georgia in 1740. List, 197.
85. "Publick midwife of Savannah. She return'd to England to ly in Octbr. 1736." List, 197.
86. He died July 25, 1733. "He left neither wife nor child." List, 117.
87. "Possest of his Lot 21 Dec. 1733. Re-marry'd to Eliz. Gray 10 Mar. 1734-5. His lot was supposed vacant." He received lot 7 in Savannah. List, 197.
88. She died July 21, 1733. List, 197.
89. "Marry'd 1st to Robt. Johnston [Johnson]. 2dly. to Morgan Davis 26 Mar 1735." She died in 1739. List, 197.
90. He received lot 39 in Savannah. He died October 24, 1733. List, 213.
91. "Put in possession of the Lot designed her husband 21 Dec. 1733. She re-marry'd Jo. Cellier of Purysburg [S. C.] 17 March 1734-5 who lives with her on this lot." List, 213.
92. He became a servant to William Bradley. List, 213.
93. Nothing in this record about her.
94. "He landed with a child born on shipboard whose name I know not." He received lot 10 in Savannah. He died August 11, 1733. List, 223.
95. "She went to England on her husbands death in 1733-4 but married again to Jonathan Hood and return'd." List, 223.
96. He died September 5, 1733. List, 223.
97. "Went to England with his mother 1733 but his lot kept for him." List, 223.
98. He died June 12, 1733. According to this record he was two years old. List, 223.
99. Her name is not mentioned in this record.

Wm Waterland[100] late a Mercer aged 44...................   1.
John West [,][101] Smith aged 33, Elizabeth[102] his
Wife aged 33, & Richard[103] his Son aged 5.............   3.
James Wilson [,] [104] Sawyer aged 21....................   1.
John Wright [,][105] Vintner aged 33, Penelope[106] his
Wife aged 33, John his Son aged 13 & Elizabeth[107]
his daughter aged 11...   4.
Thomas Young [,][108] Wheelwright aged 45............   1.

16 Novr. 1732 Muster'd on board the Ann at
Gravesend.   Total...   114
The Freight of which Passengers amoted. to 91 Heads.[109]
     By Capt Smyter on board the Volant
Samuel Grey [,][110] Silk Throwster aged 30 & his
Apprentices Chetwin Furzer [Chetwyn Furzend,][111]
aged 16 & Cornelius Jones[112] aged 15......................   3.
John Vanderplank[113] bredd at Sea aged 48................   1.

                        Total   4.

---

100. "2nd Bailif of Savannah for a time but turned out 2 Aug. 1733 for misbehaviour, and afterwd went to Carolina & never returned. Brother to Dr. Waterland the Kings chaplain, who for his drunkenness would take no notice of him." He received lot 34 in Savannah. He left Georgia February 4, 1734. List, 223.
101. "Appointed 3d Bailif 13 Oct. 1733, which he some years later resign'd. On 7 Oct. 1735 he had a grant of 500 acres, and 11 May 1737 was permitted to alienate this lot. He marry'd Eliz. Little his 2. wife 28 Aug. 1733 and Eliz. Hughes his 3d wife 24 April 1734. In June 1739 he had leave to sell his Interest and quit the Colony by reason of ill health, but died of the consumption before he could set out. His wife remarry'd to Will. Kelleway." He received lot 31 in Savannah. He died in 1739. List, 225.
102. She died July 1, 1733. List, 225.
103. He died July 31, 1733. List, 225.
104. "Bound in recognizance for assaulting the guard on duty 30 July 1734. Convicted of extortion in selling flesh meet [meat] 14 July 1735. Fyn'd 5 shillings for wilfully destroying other mens hoggs 28 July 1735. m. Mildred d. of Robt. Moore 1 Feb. 1734-5." He received lot 32 in Savannah. He was absent for some years but returned in 1740. List, 227.
105. He received lot 30 in Savannah. "His lot swamp over-flow'd." He died in December, 1737. List, 227.
106. "Remarry'd to Joseph Fitzwalter, and lives on his lot No. 8." List, 227.
107. No information on John and Elizabeth in this record.
108. He received lot 26 in Savannah. "Possest of his lot 21 Dec. 1733. He marry'd the Widow Box of Abercorn July 1734." List, 235.
109. The remainder of this document refers to passengers arriving on another ship, who logically should not have been included in this list.
110. He was expelled from Georgia, June 17, 1733. List, 73.
111. "After discharge from his Service he took this lot, but went to Serve in the Scoutboat 1736." He received lot 152 in Savannah. He absconded in February 1736-7. List, 61.
112. "Apprentice to Saml. Grey. Discharged by his mother." List, 97.
113. "Made Naval Officer 7 Oct. 1735." He received lot 25 in Savannah. He died in 1737. List, 214.

PURRYSBURGH.

By Henry A. M. Smith.

The ancient town of Purrysburgh in South Carolina, which at the date of its settlement promised to be a rival of the nearby and nearly contemporaneously founded town of Savannah in Georgia, derived its name from Monsieur Jean Pierre Purry of Neufchatel in Switzerland. M. Purry is said to have been a Director-General of the French East India Company.[1] As early as June 1724 he addressed a memorial to the King proposing to procure to be transported to, and to settle, in South Carolina a number of poor Swiss protestants on condition that he should be granted four leagues square of land with the same rights and liberties to his settlers as were enjoyed by the other inhabitants of the Province; that the settlers should be formed into a Swiss regiment of which he should be made the Colonel, and that he should also be made a judge, and have the nomination of his own officers &c. and that his Majesty should transport the proposed settlers *gratis* from a port in England to one in Carolina.[2] The government of the Colony was then in the hands of the Crown, the Crown having assumed control after the upheaval of 1719-20. The Lords Proprietors however still claimed their charter rights and the ownership of the soil, and this me-

---

[1]Dalcho—p. 385.
[2]London MSS. in Off: Hist. Comm[n]. Vol. 11. pp. 13, 14, 127, 128, 132.

morial was referred to them.[3] M. Purry came to England in
1724 and came to an agreement with the Lords Proprietors
in pursuance of which they agreed to grant him 24000
acres for procuring 600 persons to settle, and also agreed
to pay the charges of their transportation from England to
Carolina; and on 27 April 1725 granted to Mons[r] Jean
Vatt of Watt in Switzerland the 24000 acres in trust to be
transferred to M. Purry when he should have fulfilled his
part of the agreement.[4]

M. Purry returned to Switzerland and evidently induced
quite a number to agree to emigrate to South Carolina
for M. Jean Vatt writes in October 1726 that a number had
repaired to Neufchatel for the purpose, but that in consequence of the failure of the Lords Proprietors to comply
with their agreement for their transportation to Carolina
the intending emigrants had been stranded in Neufchatel
to the great consequent misery of many who wandered up
and down the streets not knowing where to find a dinner
or a bed[5]: that Mon[r] Purry and the others associated with
him lacked even the £100 sterling that would have relieved the unfortunates, and had been forced to withdraw
from Neufchatel and leave the Swiss there to shift for
themselves[6]. M. Vatt stated also that 24 Swiss men women
and children had already lately gone from Switzerland to
South Carolina and petitioned that proper relief should be
given them.

With this unfortunate fiasco seems to have terminated
M. Purrys first attempt at his settlement.

In 1728 the Crown arrived at a settlement with the
Lords Proprietors and acquired all their interests in South
Carolina. Robert Johnson was appointed Governor in
1729 and by the 43[d] and 44th articles of the Instructions
issued to him on his appointment as Governor provision
was made for the laying out and settlement of eleven townships two of which were to be located on the Savannah

[3]Ibid; Vol. 11, p. 132.
[4]Ibid; Vol. 13, p. 77.
[5]Pub: Hist. Society of S. C., Vol. 1, p. 241.
[6]London MSS. in Off: Hist. Com[n]., Vol. 12, p. 190.

river. The specific instructions given him with regard to these townships were that a square of twenty thousand acres was to be first marked out for the township proper and in this square reservations were to be made for a town, a common for the use of the inhabitants of the town, and a glebe. Then the country surrounding this 20000 acres square for a distance of six miles in every direction from the outer line of the square was to be reserved for future settlers in the township.

In July 1730 M. Purry renewed his proposition to the Crown proposing to settle 600 Swiss protestants at their own expense within the space of 6 years provided they be placed on the same footing with the rest of his Majestys' subjects in the Province and that Purry be granted 12000 acres for himself free from all quit-rents[7]. This proposition was referred to Governor Robert Johnson who on 20 July 1730 wrote advising favourably as to the project and suggesting that the township for the settlers should be set out on the Savannah river near Palachuccola Fort[8].

This proposition of Purry's seems to have been accepted on the condition that the Swiss upon their arrival take the usual oath of allegiance, and that thereupon lands be assigned to them where they should dwell together in one or more townships as might be thought most convenient for the security of the Province, and that Purry be not entitled to his 12000 acres until he should have fully performed his agreement.[9]

Instructions to this effect were sent out to Governor Johnson and Purry with several other Swiss set out for South Carolina and seems to have arrived at Charles Town in the early part of 1731. The General Assembly of the Province in the Act for the imposition of certain duties on slaves &c, appropriated £5000 current money of the Province (about £715 sterling) out of all duties after the 25 March 1731 to be applied to laying out and survey-

[7]Ibid; Vol. 14, p. 112.
[8]Ibid; Vol. 14, p. 237.
[9]Pub: Hist. Soc. of S. C., Vol. 2, pp. 127-179-182.

ing Townships, and purchasing tools, provisions and other necessaries for poor protestants desiring to settle.[10]

In May 1731 Purry was in Charles Town for on 6th May Governor Johnson recemmends to the General Assembly to allow Col Purry £150. current money for his expenses to Savannah River to find a suitable spot for his Swiss settlement.[11]

From and after this date Purry is generally referred to as "Col" Purry or "Col" John Peter Purry this rank being apparently derived from the agreement that his settlers were to be formed into a regiment and that he was to be its colonel.

The General Assembly allowed the £150 which was paid on the 8th May 1731, and a letter was on that day sent to Capt Evans at the Palachocola Fort to meet Col Purry at Port Royal and attend him up the Savannah river and assist him in the location of a place for his settlement.[12]

Purry accordingly examined the banks of the Savannah river and finally selected a site on the north bank known as "Great Yamasee Bluff."[13] This was to be the site of the future town and Purry marked a tree where he desired the middle of his town to be.[14]

Under the instructions to the Governor the Township square of 20000 acres was to include this town site and then there was to be a circuit of six miles from the line of this Township reserved for the settlers in the Township.

The site having been selected Governor Johnson on 1st Septr 1731 issued a proclamation forbidding any one from procuring grants of lands within six miles of the proposed Township.[15]

Governor Johnson says that no survey was then made of the Township and the contiguous six-mile area, as the season was not propitious for surveying[16] and Purry seems then

---

[10]Stats. at Large, S. C., Vol. 3, p. 301.
[11]Council Journal, Vol. 5, p. 74.
[12]Ibid; p. 76.
[13]London MSS. Office Hist. Com., Vol. 16, p. 347.
[14]Ibid; Vol. 17, p. 174.
[15]Pub: Hist. Society, Vol. 3, p. 306—London MSS., Vol. 16, p. 318.
[16]London MSS. Off: Hist. Com., Vol. 17, p. 174.

to have returned to Europe to gather together his settlers. Whilst in South Carolina he seems to have effected an agreement with the General Assembly whereby he was personally to be allowed £600 sterling for every 100 effective men he procured to settle at Purrysburg.

Before his return however he drew up at Charles Town in September 1731 his "Proposals" for the encouragement of such Swiss Protestants as should agree to accompany him to Carolina to settle a new colony and also a description of the Province of South Carolina.[17]

According to these proposals persons could go as servants or on their own account. If they went as servants they would have to contract for service for three years, and their expenses, or certain of them were to be charged against their wages. Those who went on their own account were required to have each at least 50 crowns as their passage would cost from 20 to 25 crowns.

The alluring description of South Carolina covers too many pages to be reproduced here even in part No modern "boomer" of lands for sale could improve much upon Col Purry's rhetoric, and imaginative description. Of his proposed town he says:

"The Town of Purrysburg will be situated 30 miles "from the Sea, and about 7 miles from the highest tide; "the Land about it is a most delightful Plain and "the greatest part very good Soil especially for Pasturage "and the rest proper enough for some productions. It was "formerly called the great *Yamassee Port* and is esteemed "by the Inhabitants of the Province the best place in all "*Carolina.*"

And again:

"There are between 5 and 600 houses in *Charles* "*Town* the most of which are very costly; besides 5 hand-"some Churches *viz*: one for those of the Church of "*England* one for the Presbyterians, one for the Anabap-"tists, one for the Quakers and one for the *French*. If you "travel into the Country, you will see stately Buildings,

---

[17]Carrolls Hist. Coll[ns] of S. C., Vol. 2, p. 121.

"noble Castles and an infinite Number of all sorts of cattle,
"If it be ask'd what has produced all this? the Answer is:
" *'Tis only the rich Land of* Carolina."

Purry came with some others whom he styles a "small
company." The names signed to his proposals along with
his own are James Richard of Geneva Abraham Meuron of
St Sulpy and Henry Raymond of St Sulpy, all of whom subsequently were settlers in Purrysburg.

On his return to Europe Purry applied in March 1732 for
an increased allowance in land for his efforts in procuring
the settlement.[18] This was not unreasonable for as he
showed the mere cost of the passage of 600 persons from
England to South Carolina was about £2400 sterling.
His efforts were successful and in July 1732 an additional
instruction was sent over to Governor Johnson to the effect
that Col Purry or rather the "Sieur Jean Pierre Purry"
should have granted to him 48000 acres provided he should
have settled 600 Swiss protestants including men women
and children within 6 years from Christmas 1732[19]. This
48000 acres to be laid out in lands most contiguous to the
Township.[20]

At a meeting of the Trustees for Georgia held in London
on 22 July 1732 according to a letter published in
the South Carolina Gazette,[21]

"M[r] *Purry* Leader M[r] *Bingio* Minister & the Elders
"of the Swiss Protestants, who are going to establish
"a Town on the River *Savanah*; attended the Trustees
"in behalf of their Congregation, returned them
"Thanks for their Protection, and desired a Continu-
"ance of it. The Trustees ordered a Library of Books
"to be given the Minister, for the Use of him and
"his Successors, and a handsome sum of Money was
"raised by the Contributions of some of the Trustees
"then Present, in order to be put into the Hands of the
"Leaders and Elders of the Congregation for provid-

---

[18]London MSS. Off. Hist. Comm[n]. Vol. 15, p. 102.
[19]Ibid; Vol. 15, pp. 105-121, 113-125.
[20]Ibid; Vol. 16, p. 347.
[21]No. 47—Decr. 2 to Decr. 9, 1732.

"ing Refreshments for the Sick in their Passage and
"on their first Establishment."
Col Purry and his company must have sailed soon after.
The first notice we find in the South Carolina Gazette is
in the N° (42) for the Week from October 28 to Novr'
4, 1732 viz:
"On Wednesday last, a Ship arrived here in about
"12 Weeks from London, having above Sixty Switzers
"on Board, the Master of whom Reports that we may
"expect Col Purry with more every day."
In the next number for the week Novr' 4 to Novr 11,
1732 it is stated;
"Major James Richards" (presumably the same who
"signed the proposals with Purry) "is appointed Major
"and Capt. of the Company of Switzers lately arrived
"here."
The exact dates and numbers of the arrivals are stated
by Purry himself in an affidavit made at the time.[22]

"S° Carolina Customhouse Charles Town Coll° John
"Peter Purry being duly Sworn on the holy Evange-
"lists maketh Oath That he the said John Peter Purry
"hath here Landed and put on Shoar at Charles Town
"in this Province viz.
"Novem' 1st 1732 out of the
"Ship Peter and James Joseph Cornish Master Sixty
"one men Women and Children
"Decem' 13th. 1732 Out of the
"Ship Shoreham John Edwards Master Forty two
"men Women and Children.
"December 15th 1732 Out of the
"Ship Purrysburgh Joseph Fry master Forty nine men
"Women and Children who are all Come here on the
"footing of Switz Protestants.
"dated at Charles Town aforesaid this twelfth day of
"March 1732.
"Sworne to before us —   John Peter Purry

---

[22]Office Hist. Comⁿ, Book "Commissions Instruct^{ns} 1732-1742," p. 6.

"Wm Saxby Jur: & Comp:
"Tho: Gadsen Coll:
"Geo. Saxby
  "Nav. Officer"

The total stated in this affidavit is 152.

Governor Johnson in a letter to the Duke of Newcastle dated 15 December 1732 states that Mr Purry had arrived with 120 Swiss about 50 of whom are men, the rest women and children. For all of whom he had furnished provisions and necessaries at the expence of the Province.[23] In a later letter of Dec 21, 1732 he states that Mr Purry had arrived with 50 men and 70 women and children and that the 60 who had arrived before had gone to Purrysburgh.[24] Purry is likely however to have more accurately stated the total himself in his affidavit and as we have seen he puts it at 152.

The Provincial Council had on 6th Octr 1732 in anticipation of their arrival ordered Col Parris to provide such necessary tools as had been agreed by the General Assembly for the Swiss expected from Europe and also to hire "Perriagers" to transport them to "Purreesbourg" on Savano River with 3 months provisions for each of them, being computed to be about 150 Souls.[25]

On the 9th Octr 1732 the Council ordered delivered to Mr James Richard six small cannon at Port Royal and other tools nails &c for the use of the Swiss already arrived and to arrive;[26] and on the 16 Decr 1732 Col Parris was ordered to prepare his "Piragues" to transport Col Purry and his Swiss to Purrysburg.[27]

They left Charles Town according to the notice in the Gazette on Wednesday 20 Decr 1732.

"On Wednesday last Col John Peter Purry, set out, "in three Pettiaugus, with Eighty-Seven Switzers, in order "to settle a Colony on Savannah River in Granville County

---

[23]London MSS., Office Hist. Com^n, Vol. 16, p. 4.
[24]Pub: Hist. Soc. of S. C., Vol 1, p. 248.
[25]Council Journal No. 5, 1730-1734, p. 212.
[26]Ibid; p. 215.
[27]Ibid; p. 249.

"and was Saluted with Seven Guns from the Bastion at
"their Passing by.

"His Excellency our Governor has been pleased to appoint
"Mr Joseph Edward Flowers to be Captain; and Mr. John
"Savy to be Lieutenant under the said Col. Purry."

If Purry only at first carried 87 out of his 150 it is
probable that at the first occupation in winter of a wholly
bare and unsettled spot it was judged wiser to leave the
weaker members and the young children in Charles Town
until some suitable provision for their shelter could be made.

To each person above 12 years of age the Council allowed
as follows.

<blockquote>
8 Bushels corn and peas
300 Wght beef
50   "   Pork
200   "   rice
1   bushel salt
1   Axe
1   Broad and 1 Narrow hoe
</blockquote>

Also 1 cow 1 calf and 1 young sow for every 5 persons
with some powder and shot.[28]

The Council also on 21 Febry 1732 ordered M^r St: John
the Surveyor General to admeasure to each family of the
Switzers settled at Purrysburg one Town lot and fifty acres
of land additional and also to mark out 260 acres for a
common and 100 acres for a Glebe.[29]

Purry himself seems to have actually arrived on the ship
Purrysburgh on the 15th Decr' 1732 for on 14 Decr Govr
Johnson wrote to the Lower House of the Assembly that
there had arrived 43 Palatines[30] and on the next day Decr
15 he writes to correct this, saying that Col Purry had
arrived a few hours after his last letter and said that these
43 were of his party.[31]

Purry's party were not the only immigrants to South
Carolina arriving at that time for in the Gazette for the

[28]London MSS. Office Hist. Com^n. Vol. 17, p. 78.
[29]Council Journal, Vol. 5, 1730-1734, p. 277.
[30]Ibid; p. 341.
[31]Ibid; p. 342.

week Nov 25 - Dec 2. 1732 it is stated that there had just arrived a sloop in about eleven weeks from Barbadoes with 100 people on board who on the passage had been reduced to such extremity that they had but a pint of flour a day for 8 people for nigh three weeks.

The names of the first arrivals are no doubt those mentioned in the list set out later below of those who qualified before Governor Johnson on 22 and 23 December 1732. They only aggregate in number 93 and may therefore refer to the party who were carried to Purrysburgh in December 1732 as mentioned in the Gazette.

How long Col Purry remained with his infant settlement before returning to Europe for another contingent does not appear.

On 10th March 1732/3 the Provincial Council issued an order to pay Mr John Peter Purry £700 currency on account of £600 sterling to be paid him when he should have transported 100 effective men into the Province and another order to pay him on 1st July 1733 £700 currency on account of £400 sterling to be paid him when he should have transported 100 effective men into the Province.[32] On 31 Aug 1732 he petitioned the General Assembly to be allowed all of the next year to complete the number of people he was to bring over.[33]

On 6 Sept 1733 at the Council Meeting;

"The Honble William Bull Esqr laid before this Board
"a Plan of the Township of Purrysburgh and the re-
"served land thereto appertaining which was by him
"surveyed and run out.

"Which Plan having been examined by his Excy
"& His Majtie's Honble Council was allowed to be
"very regular & was approved of." * * "And also made
"an Order to pay Col Wm Bull £500 curr: for run-
"ning out & making a regular Plat of the Township of
"Purrysburgh & the reserved land thereto appertain-
"ing."[34]

---

[32]Council Journal, Vol. 5, 1730-1734, p. 396.
[33]Ibid; p. 514.
[34]Ibid; p. 514.

At the date this plat of Col Bull was approved of by Council Col Purry was in Charles Town or at least Governor Johnson so states in a letter the next year[35].

The settlement seems to have been definitely made whilst he was there. On 17 March 1732/3 Joseph Edward Flower appeared and took the oaths as Lieut: Col: of the Switz Regiment at Purrysburgh[36] and on 21 Sept[r] 1733, the Council ordered to be paid to M[r] Joseph Bignion the Swiss Minister the sum of £300 current money of the Province in consideration of his expense in coming over.[37]

When Purry effected his settlement he found an unexpected and disturbing condition of affairs.

Under the instructions to Gov[r] Johnson when the Township was determined upon, there was to be allotted for the Township first a square on the river containing 20,000 acres and then there was to be reserved for the use of the future settlers in the Township all the land within an area limited by a line six miles at every point from the outer line of the 20,000 acre original Township tract; this reserved area containing approximately 109500 acres, additional to the original 20,000. In 1731 when Purry selected his Town site Gov[r] Johnson issued a proclamation announcing the fact and notifying all persons not to take out grants within the six mile limit. Notwithstanding this a number of grants were taken out intruding within this limit one of the grants for 8000 acres being to no other than Gov[r] Robert Johnson himself. Purry must have communicated this fact to his friends at home for his son Charles Purry in May 1732 addressed a petition to the King on behalf of his father whom he stated had embarked with 150 Swiss for Carolina and was then settled upon part of the Township, and that Col Purry was apprehensive lest the remaining part of the Township should be taken up by indifferent persons before he could entitle himself to the 48000 acres to be granted to him in the reserved area, and praying therefore that a grant be at once made to him for so

---

[35]London MSS. Office Hist. Com[n]. Vol. 17, p. 174.
[36]Council Journal, Vol. 5, p. 294.
[37]Ibid; p. 505.

much of the 48000 acres as the proportion of the settlement already made by him would entitle him to.[38] This seemed reasonable to His Majestys Council and on 19 July 1733 an order was accordingly issued to Gov. Johnston to grant to Col Purry a proportional part of the 48000 acres according to the number of Swiss Protestants by him settled in the Province.[39]

Other settlers seemed to have come out to join Purrys settlement who did not come directly with his party; for in May 1733 the Duke of Newcastle wrote to Gov[r] Johnson recommending to him the bearer M[r] John Frederick Holzendorf a gentlemen of good family in Brandenbourg, who went to Carolina for the purpose of settling at the new town of Purysburg: that he desired a commission in the militia and as he carried over two servants (labourers) and necessary implements, desired an allotment of a proportionate quantity of land near that Town.[40]

Purry must have left Carolina in the autumn of 1733 or early in 1734; for in April 1734 he presented a petition to the King which went before the Privy Council stating that in 1731 Governor Johnson under His Majestys instructions had surveyed and set apart a Township on Savannah River since called Purrysburgh containing 20 000 acres and had issued a proclamation 1st Sept[r] 1731 forbidding persons to take up grants within six miles of the Township, the space included within which six miles limit was to be reserved for settlers in the Township. That a survey had been made of this area when it had been found that several persons had taken up grants on the South and East sides of the Township and within the six mile line which would defeat his Majestys intentions; that he had complained to Governor Johnson but the Governor did not regard himself authorized to remove these intruders; Purry therefore besought that these intruding grants be annulled and that his Majesty would order the six miles around the Township be surveyed and set apart for the settlers in the Town-

[38]London MSS. Office Hist. Com[n]., Vol. 16, p. 153.
[39]Ibid; p. 169.
[40]Ibid; p. 123.

ship; and that the most substantial settlers in the Township be allowed grants for additional land within this six mile limit, and that those whose lots were situated on the rivulet which ran through the Town should be allowed a double lot in the Town for their charges in cleaning and clearing the same.[41]   This petition was by Charles Purry as Agent for his father, but is was followed up by a list of the intruding grants furnished by Purry himself[42] viz — eight grants aggregating 47655 acres

Purry followed this list by a long letter dated 13 July 1733 stating his case, that he had borrowed from others the money to pay the expenses of making the settlement, that he had carried over and placed in Purrysburg 260 Swiss but that when his friends ascertained that persons claiming to be entitled to Grants from the Lords Proprietors had intruded upon and taken up lands within the reserved area, they refused to advance and assist him any more to complete his settlement.   This affected him Purry personally for the 48000 acres which was to be awarded him for carrying out the settlement was to be laid out in the lands in the six mile area most contiguous to the Township[43]

This petition of Purry was granted so far as related to allowing substantial settlers more land in the Township and reserved area, and also as to allowing the settlers along the rivulet double lots; the question as to the validity of the intruding grants was referred by the Committee on plantation affairs to the Board of Trade and by the Board to His Majesty's Attorney General and Solicitor General for an opinion and in the meantime Governor Johnson was written to for an explanation.   This explanation he gave fully in a letter dated 9 Novr 1734 in which he stated that as soon as Mr Purry had marked the tree where he designed the middle of his Town to be, he had issued a proclamation forbidding any person taking up lands within six miles of that place.   The Township and contiguous six miles were not surveyed at that time the season not being propitious

---

[41]London MSS. Office Hist. Commⁿ., Vol. 16, p. 318.
[42]Ibid; p. 343.
[43]London MSS: Office Hist. Comⁿ., Vol. 16, p. 347.

for surveying; that Col Bull had been sent to survey it as soon as possible and then found that several tracts had been laid out for intending grantees within the six mile limit; that Col Bull had reported the matter to the Provincial Council and gave it as his opinion that it would be better for the Township to replace the area thus lacking below the Town by an addition above, as the Township would then have a larger frontage on the river and that the Council had ordered Col. Bull accordingly to give a double quantity above the Town, that Mr Purry was at the time in Charles Town and made no objection. The mistake arose from the Township and six mile limit not being run out at the time when the spot was selected by Purry; that it was impossible to judge of distances in the woods.

Governor Johnson also gives an account of how the grant to himself (which he offers to surrender) came to be issued and adds that as soon as His Majestys orders came he would have a new survey made and thought that the people who had grants of whom there were not many would acquiesce.[44]

On 12 Aug 1734 the Attorney and Solicitor General gave in their opinion that the intruding grants were invalid[45] and instructions were issued accordingly but no direct action seems to have been taken and it was not until May 27 1738 that positive instructions were issued to Col Sam^1 Horsey just appointed Governor of South Carolina (he died without even reaching the Province) to resurvey the six mile area and remove the intruding claimants.[46]

Most of these intruding grants only invaded the reserved area for a portion of the grant, with the exception of the grant to Robert Thorpe for 12000 acres which was entirely within the six mile limit, and it appears in the other cases that as stated by Governor Johnson the trespass was due to mistake.

Whilst this controversy was going on Purry continued the completion of his settlement. He must have left Europe for South Carolina in the late summer or early

---

[44]Ibid; Vol. 17, p. 174.
[45]Ibid; Vol. 16, pp. 404-408.
[46]Ibid: Vol. 18, p. 224; Vol. 19, p. 170.

autumn of 1734 for on 8 Novr 1734 there is a letter from
Governor Johnson to the Council recommending that provision be made for subsisting Col Purrys people just arrived[47] and in his letter of the 9th Novr 1734 above referred
to he states that "M[r] Purry is arrived with about 280 souls.
"I ordered provisions to be ready against their arrival."

The Gazette for the week Nov 9 to Nov 16 1734 gives
the following account of this arrival:

> "Col *Purry* is lately arrived from England at *Purys-*
> "*burg* in the Ship *Simmon* Capt: *Cornish* with 260
> "Switzers Protestants and their minister M[r] Chiefelle;
> "one hundred and odd more are expected there every
> "day, who were ready to embark at the beginning of
> "October last, among those are 40 Persons of the per-
> "secuted Protestants in Piemont and a Collect has been
> "made for them in England, Where we hear that
> "James Oglethorpe Esq[r] has subscribed 40£ sterling
> "the Duc de Montague and several other Persons of
> "distinction have likewise handsomely subscribed—
> " 'Tis hoped the Province will be kind enough to afford
> "them the necessary Provisions, Tools, Cattle &c in
> "order to help forward an infant Colony which is now
> "almost two Years old"—

In the next number of the Gazette (16 Nov to 23 Novr
1734) the account is given

> "We hear that on Saturday last the Petition of Coll
> "Purry was read and exam[d] by the Hon: the Commons
> "House of Assembly wherein he demanded (1) that
> "the 200£ Sterl: due to him for having carried over
> "to *South Carolina* even a greater number of People
> "then he had engaged for, might be paid to him, 100
> "£ Sterl now and the other 100 in the Month of
> "March next (2) That the necessary Provisions be
> "given to the 260 Persons he brought over with him
> "last, the same as it was given to them that came over
> "before (3) And lastly that the debts made at Geor-

---

[47]Council Journal, Vol. 6, p. 2.

"gia by the Passengers that landed there for Purrys-
"burgh, for victuals and other necessaries, likewise for
"Periawgus to Carry them to the said Place might be
"paid. Both the Hon: Houses finding his demands
"very reasonable, readily granted them.

"To the petition of the Minister at Purysburg M^r
"Chiffelle, it was answered that the Pension of a Min-
"ister could not yet be allowed to him till the Town of
"*Purrysburg* should be erected into a Parish; in the
"meantime one hundred Pounds should be paid to him
"for defraying the Charges of his Voyage, and further
"care be taken to satisfy him.'

The record does not disclose whether Purry himself conducted any other band of settlers; nor does it show how
long he remained in South Carolina after his arrival in
November 1734.

The Gazette for the week 19th April to 26th April 1735
contains the following;

"By a Letter from *Purrysburg* of *April* 10 We are
"informed, that of the 200 Protestant Swiss who were
"to embark in *London* for that Place, 110 having been
"put a shore in *Georgia* by Capt *Thompson* were ar-
"rived there, that the King has given them out of his
"own Money 1200£ sterl. to pay their Passages on
"Condition that they should settle in Purrysburgh and
"no where else; That upon this Fund Notes were made
"amounting to the said Sum, payable in five Years
"with Interest, according to the Usage of *Carolina* to
"reckon from the Day of their Arrival, the Money
"accruing by the reimbursement of these Notes to be
"employed for the Use of that Town to fortifie it, and
"to render it more commodious to its Inhabitants."

And the Gazette for the next week following viz 26th Apl
to 3 May 1735 contains the item;

"On Monday arrived here the Scooner Dolphin
"*James Lusk* in 7 Weeks from *London* with about 30
"Swiss for Purrysburgh."

From the terms of Govr Johnsons Proclamation men-

tioned later Col Purry would certainly appear to have been
in Carolina in April 1735.

Purry seems to have early had trouble with his settlers.
The Gazette for the week 12th April to 19 April 1735 contains a proclamation by Gov[r] Robert Johnson reciting that
he had received information from Col. Peter Purry that
several persons at Purrysburgh had sold the lots and lands
in the Township of Purrysburg which they claimed, although they had obtained no grants to them, and notwithstanding they had received the benefits and bounty of the
Province in provisions &c &c. and that others had attempted
to sell their pretended lots in the Township although they
had never been to Purrysburgh, all of which was contrary
to the Kings intention in settling the Township, and a fraud
and imposition on the public as no grants would be issued
except to persons named in the warrants who were actual
settlers in the Township.

After his death his son and heir Charles Purry addressed
a petition dated 18 May 1738 to the King in which he
stated that his father had imported 600 Swiss and performed his part of the contract; and in the additional instructions to Governor Johnson dated 13 Febry 1734 it is
said that Col Purry had asked in his petition that as other
foreign protestants might desire to settle at Purrysburgh
all such should be credited to him in order to entitle him to
the 48000 acres.[48]

It is likely that settlers came over not directly in company with Purry but who as induced to come by his settlement he claimed to be entitled to the credit for.[note] There
was a petition addressed to the Lords Commissioners of
Trade in July 1735 by Daniel Vernezobre in which he
stated that about a year since he had given to a gentleman
who was about to settle at Purrysburgh several of his people
on condition that a proportion of the lands should be assigned over to him. That he had expended a considerable

---

[48]Office Hist. Com[n]. Vol. Commissions Instructions 1732-1742, p. 148.
Note. The Gazette for the week 12th July to 19th July, 1735, states
that 250 Switzers had arrived to settle a Township on the Edisto
River.

sum, above £1000 Stg, in the affair in transporting people tools implements ironwork trees negroes &c &c and desired that the lands granted should be put in his name. This petition was refused apparently on the grounds that none but an *inhabitant* could take up lands within the six mile limit; and Vernezohre seems later to have become an inhabitant.

The settlement was apparently a commercial venture on Purrys part. In which venture he seems to have induced others to aid and take part by advancing money &c &c. He was to receive the 48000 acres to be granted him by the King and the bonus or payment allowed by the Province viz £600 sterling for every 100 effective men. Some idea of the expense to which the Province was put is given by an estimate of the charges incurred at the time of the arrival of the first batch in 1732. The paper is headed "Estimate of the charge arriving by the encouraging Coll Purry to transport and settle Purysburg" [49]

	£	s.	d.
Expenses to locate T' ship	150.	0.	0
allowed Col Purry	2800.	0.	0
Survey	500.	0.	0
Provision for 250 persons over 12	4312.	10.	0
" " 50 Children under 12	405.	0.	0
Tools for 250 persons	1000.	0.	0
Sixty Cows & Calves	480.	0.	0
" Young Sows	180.	0.	0
Conveyance at £5. per head	1500.	0.	0
	11327.	10.	0

£11327.10.0 in current money was worth at the time about one seventh of the amount in sterling.

The expenses of the second batch of 260 or 280 who arrived in 1734 could scarcely have been less to the Province. How Purry and his friends came out of the venture can only be a matter of speculation now.

[49] London MSS. Office Hist. Com^n., Vol. 17, p. 78.

The following are the grants which on the record appear to have been made to Purry;

23 Febry 1732	100	acres
23 March 1733	12000	"
12 Nov' 1734	6650	"
16 Jany 1736	600	"
6 Octr 1733	One Town lot in Purrysburgh	

To Charles Purry there was granted on 9 Sept' 1736 town lot N° 56 in Purrysburgh and to John Rodolph Purry there was granted on 18 March 1735/6 300 acres and on 4 Novr 1736 a town lot in Purrysburgh.

The settlement was a large one for the time, say over 600 persons and composed in part at least of settlers of a very substantial character. Daniel Vernezobre as we have seen claims to have expended over £1000 stg a large sum for those days; Jean Baptiste Bourquin had been a surgeon in Marlborough's army;[note] John Frederick Holzendorff was of good family, Dr Daniel Brabant was a physician, and among the settlers was Hector Berenger de Beaufain, and also Henry de Saussure the ancestor of the family of that name. It has been spoken of as a French Huguenot settlement but this is an error. Many if not most of the settlers were French speaking Swiss but many were also German Swiss, and were Huguenots only in the sense of being protestants.

The settlement at the location at Purrysburg does not seem to have thriven. The site selected was an unfortunate one, not at a good point for navigation and in a very sickly and malarial locality. The circumstances that most tended to check its development was the settlement of Georgia and the near neighbourhood of the Town at Savannah. Many if not most of the settlers at Purrysburg appear to have drifted over into Georgia.

Note.
    S. C. Gazette for 30th Jany. 1784, states:
        "Died near Purrysburg Dr John B. Bourquin, aged 93 years—
        "He served nine years as a Surgeon in the Duke of Marl-
        "borough's army and settled at Purrysburgh in this State in
        "1732."

Others went elsewhere; Berenger de Beaufain lived in Charleston and others moved to Beaufort.

Very little is known of the subsequent history of the Town. The two ministers the Rev[d] M[r] Joseph Binion or Bignion or Bugnion and the Rev[d] M[r] Henry Chiffelle are said both to have been in orders in the Church of England.[note] The Rev[d] M[r] Binion is stated by Dalcho to have moved to the Parish of St. James Santee in 1734.

In 1746 the General Assembly passed an Act "for erecting the Township of Purrysburgh and parts adjacent into a separate and distinct Parish"[50]

This is the Act which creates the Parish of St Peter and it declares "That the church or chapel and the dwelling "house at Purrysburgh wherein the Rev M[r] Chiffelle hath "preached and dwelt for some years past shall be deemed "and taken and they are hereby declared to be the Parish "Church and parsonage house of the said Parish of St "Peter."

The Act further provided that the Minister or Rector should receive £100 currency yearly and that the Parish should have one representative in the Commons House of Assembly. The Church and parsonage had been built with public funds and were therefore by this Act only declared to be the Parish church and parsonage for the new Parish.[note]

In his petition in 1738 after the death of his father Charles Purry states that the not possessing the lands affected by the intruding grants surveyed to the Switzers, had occasioned their inability to support themselves after the provision for them was exhausted, whereby many had perished and more had been forced to disperse.

Note. Dalcho states that the Rev. M. Bugnion was ordained Priest by the Bp. of St. Davids 25 July 1732 and that the Rev. M[r] Chiffelle was a native of Switzerland ordained Priest by the Bp of London in 1734 and was sent out by the Society for the propagation of the Gospel in Foreign Parts—Dalcho, p. 386.

[50]Statutes at Large, Vol. 3, p. 668.

Note. The Tax Act for 1736-7 appropriates £200 for building a place for divine worship at Purrysburg—*Gen'l Stats. S. C., Vol. 3, p.* 484.

Dalcho states that in 1735 Purrysburgh contained near
100 dwellings.

Hewatt in his History, published in 1779, gives the account which has been followed by later writers—viz:

"On the other the poor Swiss emigrants began their
"labours with uncommon zeal and courage, highly ele-
"vated with the idea of possessing landed estates, and
"big with the hopes of future success. However, in
"a short time they felt the many inconveniences attend-
"ing a change of climate. Several of them sickened and
"died, and others found all the hardships of the first
"state of colonization falling heavily upon them. They
"became discontented with the provisions allowed them,
"and complained to Government of the persons em-
"ployed to distribute them; and to double their dis-
"tress, the period for receiving the bounty expired be-
"fore they had made such progress in cultivation as to
"raise sufficient provisions for themselves and fam-
"ilies."

The settlement continued however for many years.
Notwithstanding the depletion by withdrawals to Georgia,
to the healthier part of Beaufort now Hampton County, and
elsewhere, the Church at Purrysburgh continued as the
Parish Church of St Peters Parish for many years. The
Rev. Mr Chiffelle served until his death in 1758. He was
succeeded by the Rev. Abraham Imes who arrived in 1760
and continued until his death in 1766. Purrysburgh was
in 1779 the headquarters for some time of General Lincoln
and also of General Moultrie when they were facing Prevost
on the opposite side of the river but after the disastrous
rout of General Ash's command at Brier creek the Americans abandoned Purrysburgh, which place in April 1779
was occupied by the British Army under General Prevost
as the first step in the advance against Charles Town.

After that there is but little mention of Purrysburgh,
which apparently continued to dwindle until it practically
disappeared as a town settlement, altho in his "Statistics
of South Carolina" published in 1826, Mills enumerates it as
still one of the villages or towns of Beaufort County, com-

ing next to Beaufort and being situate on a high and pleasant bluff twenty miles north of the City of Savannah.

The following list is taken from a parchment bound volume in the office of the Historical Commission marked "Commissions Instructions 1732-1742," on p. 4. It appears to be a list of those Swiss who came over with Purry in the Autumn of 1732, or of such of them as went from Charles Town to Purrysburgh with him and qualified i. e. took the oath of allegiance.

"A List of the Germains and Switz Protestants under the "Command of Coll° Purry qualified before his Excellency "Robert Johnson Esquire Governour of this Province on "the 22 and 23 dayes of December 1732.

"David Huguenin agé de	60.
"Susanne Jacot sa femme	47.
"Dan¹ Huguenin son fils	14.
"David son fils	8.
"Abraham son fils	10.
"Marguerite sa fille	12.
"Josué Robert	56.
"Josué Robert son fils	21.
"Marie Madeleine sa fille	29.
"Anne Valleton Veuve de Pierre Jeanneret	49.
"Henry son fils	19.
"Jacques Abram son fils	17.
"Jean Pierre son fils	14.
"Marie sa fille age de	21.
"Rose Marie sa fille	9.
"François Buche	46.
"Margarette sa femme	50.
"Jean Pierre son fils	4.
"Dan¹ Henry son fils	1.
"Abram son fils	2.
"Susanne sa fille	8.
"Henry Girardin	32.
"Marguerite sa femme	32.
"David son fils	7.
"Henry son fils	4.

"Anne   sa fille .... 2.
"Francois Bachelois .... 46.
"Madeleine sa femme .... 36.
"Batiste   son fils .... 6.
"Francois   sa fille .... 3½.
"Marie   sa fille .... 1½.
"La veuve Breton .... 53.
"Jean Pierre breton son fils agé   de .... 17.
"Ulric bac   age de .... 50.
"Jacob Calame age de .... 56.
"Abram Marte age de .... 60.
"David Giroud age de .... 18.
"Jacob Henry Meuron   age de .... 19.
"Madame Varnod ....
"Abram Varnod son fils ....
"Francois son fils ....
"Frantions sa fille ....
"Mariane La   fille ....
"Andriane Richard ....
"Monsieur Purry ....
"Monsieur buttal ....
"Monsieur Flar ....

"Names of the Germains

"Jaque Winkler   15 de Lage ....
"Anna Catarina Winkler .... 43.
"Jaque Winkler .... 19.
"Nicholas Winkler .... 16.
"Son Jaque Winkler .... 9.
"Luis Winckler .... 6.
"Frederick Winckler .... 3.
"Eve Elizabeth .... 12.
"Theobald Küffer .... 49.
"Anna Margarita .... 40.
"Jaque Küffer .... 16.
"Theobald Küffer .... 13.
"Margaritt .... 14.
"Elissabeht Margaritt .... 11.

"Elizabeht Catarina .... 9.
"Maria Ottillia .... 4.
"Barbara .... 2.
"Luis Kohl .... 45.
"Anna Barbara .... 40.
"Son Nicolas .... 11.
"Son Jaquer .... 5.
"Nicolas .... 3.
"Margaritha .... 13.
"Anna Marill .... 8.
"Maria Margaritha .... 1.
"Nicolas Riger .... 46.
"Anna Barbara .... 36.
"Son Michael Riger .... 13.
"Janett Ottallia .... 18.
"Catarina Barbara .... 4.
"Henrich Cronenberger .... 40.
"Elizabeht .... 35.
"Nicolas Cronenberger .... 15.
"Gertrues .... 5.
"Anna Catharina .... 2.
"Sorg Mengersdorff .... 28.
"Anna Sibilla .... 26.
"Son Hendrick Mengersdorff .... 3.
"Elizabeht .... 2.
"Andrew Winckler .... 23.
"Anna Susan .... 23.
"Leonhards Franck .... 50.
"Anna Susana .... 48.
"Danl Franck .... 8.
"Christian Fuus .... 32.
"   La Sama .... 45."

In the following list of grants it is to be noted that there are non earlier than 4 December 1735. As the first settlers went to Purrysburgh in December 1732 it is somewhat strange that the earliest grants should be of a date three years later. Whether the lots were assigned but the actual grants were not issued until later; or what is more likely that the earliest volume of such grants has been lost, cannot now be stated with certainty. The earliest volume marked "Township Grants" in the office of the Secretary of State is numbered as vol. 41- 1734-1735. This number 41 does not bear any relation in numbering to the other volumes of grants and is only a designation or number placed on the volume many years later. The dates of the first warrants or orders to survey the land to be granted to Purry are 23 Febry and 27 Febry 1732 (1733 new style) and as no grants can be found of those dates it is likely that at first warrants were made out to survey and allot the lands to the several settlers and the formal grants were issued later.

The following list is made up from the volumes in the Secretary of States office denominated "Township Grants volumes numbered 41 and 42"

Grantee	No: Acres	Town Lot	Date
Peter Charmason	100	79	4 Decr 1735
Thomas Newall	400		,, ,, ,,
Anthony Ageron	200	80	,, ,, ,,
Anne Jenneret	250		17 Mch ,,
Henry Girardin	50		,, ,, ,,
Pierre Louis Recordon	150		,, ,, ,,
Andrew Winkler	100		,, ,, ,,
Henry De Roche	50		,, ,, ,,
Jacob Winkler	350		,, ,, ,,
Major James Richard	300		,, ,, ,,
Joseph Reymond	50		,, ,, ,,
Alexander La Croix	50		,, ,, ,,
Jeanne Urbaine Voyer	50		,, ,, ,,
Benjamin Henriond	200		,, ,, ,,
Heirs of Uhrich Bache	50		,, ,, ,,
Jean Delpont	50		,, ,, ,,
David Gantier	400		,, ,, ,,
Abraham Marthe	50		,, ,, ,,
Jean Henry Girardin	250		,, ,, ,,
Anthoine Thermin	100		,, ,, ,,
Jonas Spach	50		,, ,, ,,

Grantee	No : Acres	Town Lot	Date		
Rice Price	100		,,	,,	,,
Benjamin Calis	50		,,	,,	,,
Joseph Girardin	100		,,	,,	,,
Jean Baptist Bourquin	300		,,	,,	,,
Monsr Guill^o Brulott	50		,,	,,	,,
Abraham Muron	100		17	Mch	1735
Ann Barbara Frank	100		,,	,,	,,
David Ecolier	50		,,	,,	,,
Henry Francois Bourquin	300		,,	,,	,,
David Geroud	50		,,	,,	,,
George Minguers Dorff	100		,,	,,	,,
Augustus Bartoun	50		,,	,,	,,
Gabriel Francois Revout	50		,,	,,	,,
Jean Rudolph Netman	50		,,	,,	,,
Henry Grovenemberg	200		,,	,,	,,
Jean Pierre De Gallin	50		,,	,,	,,
Joseph Edwd Flower } Jemmett Cobley } Esq^{rs}	300		,,	,,	,,
Wallier Cuillatt	50		9	Apl	1736
Jacob Collume Dec^d	50		17	Mch	1735
Hector Berenger De Beaufin	800		10	Dec^r	1736
,, ,, ,, ,,	150		,,	,,	,,
,, ,, ,, ,,	200		,,	,,	,,
Samuel Montague	710		,,	,,	,,
Capt John Holdzendorf	200	60	,,	,,	,,
Mr John Chivillet	50	59	,,	,,	,,
Daniel Vernezobre	2000		29	June	1737
Abraham Elizard	800		,,	,,	,,
James De Las	300		,,	,,	,,
John Lewis Poyas	350		13	July	,,
Daniel & Francis Mongin	650		12	Aug	,,
John Fountain	150		6	Oct^r	1737
John Peter Brace	100		,,	,,	,,
Hector Berenger De Beaufin	800		1	June	,,
Col^o Samuel Montague	1100		,,	,,	1738
Hugh Rose	150		10	April	,,
John Kreeps	150		6	Sept^r	,,
George Talebach	250	272	16	,,	,,

Grantee	No : Acres	Town Lot	Date		
Gasper Myer	200	312	"	"	"
John Grabs	50		"	"	"
Jacob Tanner	300	67	"	"	"
Francis Buche	100		"	"	"
Abell Pinnell	150		"	"	"
Peter Abraham Devision	50		"	"	"
Abraham Fallet	400		"	"	"
Isaac Coste	150		"	"	"
Matthew La Pierre	50		"	"	"
Francis Vernays	50		"	"	"
John Redolph Netman ....⎫ Adam Cullet ....⎭	300		"	"	"
Joseph Banaki	250		"	"	"
David Buches	350	299	"	"	"
Andre Albatestier De Mon Clar	150		1 June		"
Francis Buech	200		16 Dec^r		"
John Linder	450	340	"	"	"
" "	150		"	"	"
Peter Laffite	150		3 Feby	1737	
Peter Laffite	450		3 Feby	1737	
Mary Masson	50	8	16 Sep^r	1738	
" "	50		"	"	"
Rodolff Purry	300		10 Apl		"
Charles Purry		56	"	"	"
John Chevelis	450		16 Sept^r		"
Henry Shaffele and Sister	100	58 & 115	"	"	"
Andre Verdier	500		"	"	"
Andelheith Grob	50		"	"	"
John Grenier	400		"	"	"
Elizabeth Grob	50		"	"	"
Stephen Vigneu	100		3 Feby	1737	
Henry Enderlin	290		16 Sept^r	1738	
Lewis Quinch		174	"	"	"
Levis Michel	50		"	"	"
Abraham Bonninger	200	186	"	"	"
Joseph Banaquier		265	"	"	"
Nicholas Riguer	250		"	"	"

Grantee	No : Acres	Town Lot	Date		
Christopher Brickell	200	193	,,	,,	,,
Abraham Chardonet	300		,,	,,	,,
Peter Masson	50		,,	,,	,,
John Peter Perrottet	100		,,	,,	,,
John Rodolff Lier	50		,,	,,	,,
Anna Maria Viller	300		,,	,,	,,
John Mog	150	397	,,	,,	,,
George Schonman Grober	50		,,	,,	,,
John Henry Mayerhoffer		244	16 Sep^r	1738	
Lewis Devill	50	98	,,	,,	,,
John Wunderlick	200	63	,,	,,	,,
Jonas Pelow		241	,,	,,	,,
John Dominick	50	266	,,	,,	,,
John Baptiste Bourquin	100		,,	,,	,,
Abraham Malkey (or Mattey)	200	140	,,	,,	,,
Henry Gasman	200	182	,,	,,	,,
Andrew Winkler	50		,,	,,	,,
Jacob Reck	50		,,	,,	,,
James Sterchis	250		,,	,,	,,
Anne Mary Viller	100		,,	,,	,,
John James Morr	200	184	,,	,,	,,
Theobald Kueffer	50		,,	,,	,,
Henry Bourquin	50		,,	,,	,,
Anna Inglerine	250	153	,,	,,	,,
Daniel Choupart	100	210	,,	,,	,,
John Grenier	400		,,	,,	,,
Andrew Winkler	50		,,	,,	,,
Anthony Pallons	200	176	,,	,,	,,
John Lagayes		231	,,	,,	,,
Benedict Bourquin	200	208	,,	,,	,,
Henry Desaussure	300		,,	,,	,,
Isaac Bonyoe	150		,,	,,	,,
David Sauce	50		,,	,,	,,
Anna Eunets Viller	300		,,	,,	,,
Charles Jacob Pichard	200		16 Sept^r	1738	
Daniel Merret	50		,,	,,	,,
John Philip Merret	150		,,	,,	,,

Grantee	No: Acres	Town Lot	Date		
David Huquin	100		"	"	"
Loudwick Khell	100		"	"	"
John Peter Perrotet		87	"	"	"
David Christians	250		"	"	"
Matthew Moore	150		"	"	"
John Labord		348	"	"	"
Mary Bourquin	100		"	"	"
Elias Bernard	100		"	"	"
" "	100		"	"	"
David Nichols	50		"	"	"
Capt Peter Laffite	450		4 Mch	1739	
John Bear	50	249	16 Sept^r	1738	
John Weffs	50		"	"	"
John Jacob Miller	100		"	"	"
Jaques Valours	200		23 Feby	"	
John Stranblar	300	108	16 Sept^r	"	
John Rodolph Pleir	50	246	"	"	"
Anthony Goliere	50	175	"	"	"
Major James Richards	400		12 Ap^l	1739	
Devall Kueffer	450		"	"	"
David Roberts	300		11 May	"	
David Faucounet	250		"	"	"
John Legare	100		7	"	
John Legare	50		11 May	1739	
Jane Lebray Widow ⎫					
Twinet Lebray ⎬	300		2 June	1739	
Fanshaw Lebray ⎭					
George Herchnecht	50	197	16 Sept^r	1738	
John Genbretz *alias* ⎫ Michael Gombze ⎭	200		"	"	"
Abraham Jindra	50	203	"	"	"
Daniel Pillet	100		11 May	1739	
John Jacob Roch	227		"	"	"
Robert Williams	1300		16 Sept^r	"	
Ludovick Kaill	300		14 Dec^r	"	
Gideon Mallett	550		"	"	"
Mary Henrie	50		"	"	"
John Labord	50		"	"	"

Grantee	No: Acres	Town Lot	Date
Anthony Jaton	50		,, ,, ,,
D' John Brabant (in Grant also styled D' Daniel Brabant)	500		,, ,, ,,
John Henry Mayorhotser	150		,, ,, ,,
John Ring	250		,, ,, ,,
Capt John Frederick Holzendorf	250		,, ,, ,,
Peter Sterchy	150		,, ,, ,,
John Francis Henry	50		,, ,, ,,
Peter De Pia	100		,, ,, ,,
John Francis Vanay	50		,, ,, ,,
Vincent Dalescale	50		,, ,, ,,
Jeremiah Remond	200		14 Dec[r] 1739
John Lewis Schetfley	450	119	3 Feby 1737
Peter Detscher	100		16 Sep[r] 1736
Joseph Laye	100		14 Dec[r] 1739
Abraham Donnatt	50		,, ,, ,,
David Zublier	600		,, ,, ,,
Daniel Jacob Ortellier	100		16 Sep[r] 1738
John Henry Derick	50		,, ,, ,,
John Henry D[e] Roch	50		,, Aug. 1741
Jacob Metsger	350	75	8 ,, ,,
Peter Ditmastre	400		29 Jany 1742
Henry Dessaure	50		9 Apl 1743
Henry Duberdosser	100		,, ,, ,,
David Ginger	300		,, ,, ,,
Francis Lewis Recorder	100		,, ,, ,,
Adam Cuillat	250		,, ,, ,,
Ann Marie Egnia	150		,, ,, ,,
John Henry Mayorholser	100		,, ,, ,,
John Michall	46.[51]		,, ,, ,,
John Labord	150		,, ,, ,,
Peter Detmestre	200		,, ,, ,,
George Mingersdorffe	50		,, ,, ,,
Peter Lutie	50		,, ,, ,,
John Martin Lasman	250		,, ,, ,,
Hans Ulrick Isoug	50		,, ,, ,,

Grantee	No: Acres	Town Lot	Date
Daniel Shipard	50		„ „ „
Anthony Jaton	50		9 Apl 1743
Savastian Zouberbukber	100		„ „ „
John Michall	30		„ „ „
Henry Mererhotfer	100		„ „ „
John Michall	22		„ „ „
Peter Maillier	200		„ „ „
Isaac Overy	200		„ „ „
Peter Latfitte	224.[24]		„ „ „
George Teleback	250		„ „ „
Henry Bourquin	100		24 Aug „
Hugh Rose	400		„ „ „
David Pierre Humber	200		„ „ „
Hugett Piarsh	50		„ „ „
Henry Chefeille	450		11 Nov^r „
Daniel Abraham David and Margaret Huguenium	200		„ „ „
John Rodolph Grand	350		8 Decr 1744
John Delagaye	250		24 May 1745
John Francis Henry	100		11 Novr 1743

In addition to the foregoing names the following appear as owners of lands bounding on the grants made but to whom no actual grants were found recorded viz

> Mr Sansober
> Pierre Galache
> David Saussy
> Francois Faure
> Widow Francoise Breton
> Francis Bachelor
> Revd Mr Bugnion
> Leonard Frank
> David Kuiffer
> Abraham Le Roy
> Jean Henry Pierre de Gallier
> Josua Roberts
> Urich Rachie

Louis Devall
Alles Voucher
Mr Vanderheyd
Samuel Augspourger
John Louis Shifle
Andrew Gender
Revd Mr Shiffle
Godfrey Detrevis
John Neef
Capt DeJeau
David Huginier
Pierre Malliet
Lewis Kehl
Francis Yanam
Sam : Delane
Godfrey Detrivirs
Jacob Stuly
Anna Ingler
Ulrich Buch
Capt John Perry felder
William Staples
James Turner
Peter Janett Vannerheid
John Jenbuck
Jacob Jannet

In the office of the Historical Commission there are several maps relating to Purrysburgh.

Two are of the Town proper. One of these is a plan of the Town, showing the glebe land and the commons as reserved and set out immediately contiguous to the Town. The other contains more lots : the lots are differently shaped in places, and there is no reservation for the glebe and commons. An examination of the plats annexed to the grants of the Town lots develops that these grants were made with reference to this last mentioned map, thus evidencing that it was the later and final map. Of the other two maps one is a map of the Township of 20,000 acres, exhibiting the space reserved for the Town proper, and the remainder cut

up into 50 acre subdivisions. The fourth map is a general
map, exhibiting the Township of 20,000 acres, and also the
entire area within the six mile limit, with the intruding
grants, and was made in 1735, by Hugh Bryan.

The Council, in February, 1732/3, ordered the Surveyor
General, M^r St. John, to admeasure to each family of the
Swiss settlers one town lot and 50 acres of land, and to lay
out a glebe and commons. In Sept^r, 1733, it is stated that
Col. William Bull laid before the Council a plan of the
township and the reserved land appertaining thereto. For
his survey and plat he was paid £500 currency of the Province. In the statement of the expense to which the Province had been put in settling the township this £500 is
also enumerated, but nothing is mentioned of any amount
paid to M^r St. John for any survey or map.

It would appear then that the older map of the Town
and the map of the Township subdivided into 50 acre plots
were the ones made by Col. Bull, as they both appear to
be in the same handwriting. Against this supposition is
that the minutes of the Council meeting state that Col.
Bull's map showed the "reserved" land appertaining, which
this map does not; if the word "reserved" was intended to
apply to the land within the six mile limit, but without the
Township proper, of 20,000 acres. The later map mentioned
as the fourth, made in 1735, was evidently the later map
made by order of Lieut. Governor Broughton, under the
later instructions he received, and was made by Hugh
Bryan.

The maps annexed to this article are copies of that map
of the Town, which appears to be the latest in date, and
which corresponds to the Grants, and also a reduced copy
of the Bryan map, of 1735, located on the map of the
Counties of Beaufort and Hampton, so as to show the position of the Township as originally designed and laid out.

EARLY HIGHLAND IMMIGRATION TO NEW YORK

In the year 1734, proposals were issued by the government of New York inviting settlers from Europe, to whom a certain quantity of wild land was to be granted on their arrival in this country. These proposals were repeated under the seal of the Province in 1736, and in 1738 Captain Lauchlin Campbell, of Isla, brought over a number of Scotch Highlanders, who were followed in 1739, 1740, and 1742 by others.

I have lately come across a list containing the names of these immigrants, and having arranged them in alphabetical order, for more easy reference, I send a copy for publication in the Historical Magazine, as it may interest the descendants of those people, if any there be, in America.

E. B. O'CALLAGHAN.

STATE-HALL, ALBANY.

N. B.—The date immediately following the name is that of the year of arrival.

William Adair, 1740; dead in 1763.

Mary Anderson, widow with two children; Duncan Liech and Mary Liech, 1740.

Patrick Anderson and Catharine McLean his wife, 1739.

Mary Bealton, 1738.

John Brady, 1740; dead in 1763. His son Hugh lived at Amboy.

Christian Brown, 1740; d. 1763, without issue.

John Caldwell and Mary Nutt his wife; Alexander and James, his sons, 1739.

James Cameron, 1739.

Alexander Campbell came in 1738; lived in Amboy in 1763.

Alexander Campbell (of the family of Lundie) came in 1740.

Alexander Campbell and Margaret his wife, and Merran, his daughter, came in 1740.

Anna Campbell, widow of Alexander McDuffie, and five children, 1739.

Anne Campbell, 1740.

Archibald Campbell, of Ardeatton, came in 1740.

Catharine Campbell came in 1739, from Isla.

Donald Campbell and Mary McKeay his wife came from Isla, in 1738, with four children, Robert, James, Peggy, and Isbell.

Dugald Campbell and his son John came in 1739, from Isla; both dead in 1763.

Duncan Campbell, of New York, and Sarah Frazer his wife, came in 1739.

Duncan Campbell (of the family of Dantroon) came in 1740.

Duncan Campbell (of the family of Dunn), 1740.

Duncan Campbell (Lochiell) came in 1740.

Duncan Campbell came in 1740; d. in 1763; his brother's daughter was named Mary Ann Campbell.

Duncan Campbell and Ann (Lenox) his wife, and one daughter, came in 1740.

George Campbell, merchant of the city of New York, sister's son of John Campbell, in Mubindrie, came over in pursuance of a letter, written by Capt. Campbell's orders, to him, dated 1742, offering him encouragement.

George Campbell, pedler, is his relative.

James Campbell and Anna McDougald his wife, of Isla, came in 1738, with four children, viz.: Archibald, Elisabeth, Lauchlin, and Janet his wife.

John Campbell and Anna his wife, from Ballanabie, came to New York, in 1738.

John Campbell, 1740.

Captain Lauglan Campbell, from Isla.

Malcolm Campbell came from Isla, in 1740.

Mary Campbell came in 1738, from Isla.

Neil Campbell came in 1739; lived in Jamaica in 1763; his mother married Alexander Montgomery.

Robert Campbell came in 1738, from Isla.

Ronald Campbell, from Isla, came in 1738; d. in 1763.

William Campbell, wheelwright, from Isla, came in 1738; died in 1763.

William Campbell, of Ardeatton, came in 1740.

William Campbell, joiner, from Isla, came in 1738; d. in 1763; family left in Scotland.

David Cargill, 1740.

Elizabeth Cargill, 1740.

James Cargill, 1740.

Jean Cargill, 1739.

John Cargill, 1740.

Margaret Cargill, 1740.

Donald Carmichael and Elizabeth McAlister his wife; John, Alexander, and Mary, their children, 1738.

Dugald Carmichael and Catharine McEuen his wife; Jennat, Mary, Neil, and Catharine, their children, 1739.

Alexander Christy, 1738; dead in 1763.

Angus Clark and Mary McCallum his wife; Catharine and Mary, their daughters, 1740.

William Clark, his wife, and son John, 1739.

Cornelius Collins, 1739.

John Cristy and Isbell McArthur his wife; and Hannah and Mary, their daughters, 1740.

Merran Culbreth, 1739; dead in 1763.

Donald Fergeson and Florence Shaw his wife; with one child of his own, and Catharin and Anna, his brother's children, 1739.

Jannet Forgison, 1738; dead in 1763; Alexander McDonald, ropemaker, N.Y., 1763, is her son.

Jennett Forgison, 1738.

Catherine Frazer, 1738; dead in 1763; left two grandchildren, viz.: Catherine Montgomery and Catherine Stevenson, of N.Y.

Catherine Frazer, 1739; dead in 1763; left one daughter.

Elizabeth Frazer, 1739.

Mary Frazer, 1739; married John McDonald, of N.Y.

Robert Frazer and Mary McLean his wife; Charles, Colin, Sarah, Catharine, Mary, and Isbell, their children, 1739.

Alexander Gillchrist, 1738.

Duncan Gillchrist and Florance McAllister his wife; Mary, their daughter, 1738.

John Gillchrist, 1738.

Margaret Gillchrist, 1740; alive in 1763.

Neil Gillespie and Mary McIllfeder his wife; Gilbert and Angus, their children, 1739.

Alexander Graham, 1738.

Angus Graham, 1740.

Archibald Graham, 1740.

Catharine Graham, 1740; died before 1763.

Edward Graham and Jean Frazer his wife, 1740.

Mary Graham, 1738; dead, 1763.

Peter Green, 1739.

Archibald Hamell, 1740; dead in 1763, without issue.

Mary Hamell, 1740.

Merran Hammell, 1738.

Murdoch Hamell, 1738.

Alexander Hunter and Anne Anderson his wife; William Alexander, and Jenat, their children, 1739.

Arch'd Johnston and Kirstine Johnston his wife, 1738.

Catherine Lesslie, 1738.

Donald Lindesay and Mary McQuore his wife; Richard, Duncan, Effie, and Christian, their children, 1739.

Donald Livingston and Isabell McCuag his wife; John and Duncan, their sons, 1739.

James Livingston, 1738.

Angus McAlister, 1738; living in South Carolina in 1763; his sister's daughter married Jacob Vandle, of New York.

Charles McAlister and Catharine McInnish his wife; John and Margaret, their children, 1739.

Duncan McAlister and Effie Keith his wife, 1739.

Margaret McAllister, 1740.

Robert McAlpine, 1740.

Alexander McArthur and Catharine Gillis his wife; Duncan and Flory, their children.

Alexander McArthur and Catharine McArthur his wife; John, Donald, Catharine, and Florence, their children, 1738.

Anna McArthur, 1740.

Charles McArthur, of N.Y., went in 1738 on board the ship with his wife and family, but, the vessel being too much crowded, was turned ashore; they then went to Ireland, where he took passage, and arrived in New York a fortnight before the ship in which he first engaged with Captain Campbell.

Duncan McArthur and Anna McQuin his wife; Anna, Mary, Margaret, and John, their children, 1738.

John McArthur; Neil and Christian, his children, 1740.

Margaret McArthur, wife to Arch'd McCollum, at New York; Anne and Mary, their daughters, 1740.

Neil McArthur and Mary Campbell his wife; Alexander, John, and Christian, their children, 1738.

Patrick McArthur and Mary McDugall his wife; Charles, Colin, and Jennet, their children, 1738.

Christian McAulla, 1739.

Dugald McCapine and Mary McPhaden his wife; Donald and Mary, their children, 1738.

Alexander McChristian, 1739.

Donald McCloud and Catharin Graham his wife; John and Duncan, their sons, 1738.

John McColl, 1738.

Arch'd McCollum and Merran McLean his wife: Donald, John, Margaret, Mary, and Allan, their children, 1739.

Archibald McCollum and Flory McEachoin his wife; Hugh and Duncan, their sons, 1740.

Duncan McCollum, 1740; dead in 1763, in N.Y.

Merrian McCollum; Donald and Mary, her children, 1740.

Archibald McCore, 1739; lives in Tappan.

John McCore, 1739; is married, and lives in the Highlands.

John McDonald, 1739; followed the sea in 1763.

Neil McDonald and Anne McDuffie his wife; Donald, Archibald, and Catharine, their children, 1738.

Allan McDougald and Eliz. Graham his wife; Margaret, Anna, and Hanna, their children, 1738.

Alexander McDuffie's widow (see Campbell); Archibald, Duncan, James, Mary, and Isbell, her children (McDuffie died at sea), 1739.

Arch'd McDuffie and Catharine Campbell his wife; John and Duncan, their sons, 1739.

Dudly McDuffie and Margaret Campbell his wife; Archibald, his son, 1738.

Malcom McDuffie and Rose Docherdy his wife; Margaret and Jenny, their daughters, 1738; Malcolm, dead in 1763.

Dudly McDuffy and Margaret McDugald his wife; Dugald and Mary, their children, 1740.

Angus McDugald, 1739.

Arch'd McDugald and Christian McIntire his wife; Alexander and John, their sons, 1738.

Duncan McDugald and Jenet Colder his wife; John, Alexander, Ronold, Dugald, and Margaret, their children, 1739.

Hugh McDugald, 1738.

Ronald McDugald and Betty his wife; John and Alexander, their sons, 1738.

John McDugall, 1739; died privateering in the last French war.

Arch'd McEachern and Jean McDonald his wife; and Catharine, their daughter, 1738.

Donald McEachern and Anne McDonald his wife; Catharine, their daughter, 1738.

Patrick McEachern and Mary McQuary, his wife, 1739.

Archibald McEuen and Jennat McDugald his wife, 1739.

Duncan, Janet, and Mary McEuen, children of Hugh McEuen, 1738.

James McEuen, Archibald's son, 1740.

John McEwen and Anna Johnston his wife; Malcolm, their son, 1739.

John McEuen, 1740.

Malcom McEuen, 1739.

Mary McEuen, daughter of John McEuen.

Merran McEuen, and her daughter.

John McGibbion, 1740 (went home).

William McGie, 1738; dead in 1763.

Margaret McGillchrist, 1740.

Archibald McGown; Duncan, John, and Margaret, his children, 1739.

John McGown and Anna McCuaige his wife; Malcom and Angus, their sons, 1739.

Malcom McGown and Anna McCuaige his wife; Patrick and Eachern (*alias* Hector), their children, 1739.

Archibald McIllfeder, 1739.

Catharine McIllfeder, 1739.

Effie McIlwry, 1740.

John McIlwrey and Catharine McDonald his wife; Hugh, Donald, Bridget, and Mary, their children, 1740.

Merran McIndiore, 1740.

Murdoch McInnish and Merran McKeay his wife; Catharine, Archibald, Neil, Anne, and Florence, their children, 1739.

Neil McInnish and Catharine McDonald his wife, 1739.

John McIntagert, 1738.

Donald McIntaylor, 1738; dead in 1763.

John McIntaylor, 1738; dead in 1763.

Angus McIntire, 1739.

Donald McIntire, 1738; dead in 1763; Malcom Graham, peruke-maker, of N.Y., his son.

John McIntire, 1740.

Nicolas McIntire and Margaret Patterson his wife; John and Catharine, their children, 1739.

Angus McIntosh, 1739.

Duncan McKay, 1740; dead in 1763.

Duncan McKeay, 1740.

Archibald McKellar and Janet Reid, his wife, 1738.

Charles McKellar and Florence McEachern his wife; Margaret, Catharine, and Mary, their daughters, 1738.

George McKenzie and Catharin McNiven his wife; Donald and Collin, their sons, 1738.

John McKenzie and Mary McVurich his wife; Archibald and Florence, their children, 1738.

Duncan McKinven, 1740.

Alexander McLean, 1738; died at Cuba.

John McLean, 1738; dead in 1763; left a cousin Archibald, in Albany.

Lauchlin McLean, 1740; dead in 1763.

Donald McMillan and Jenet Gillis his wife; Alexander, his son.

Donald McMillan, 1738; dead in 1763.

Donald McMillan and Mary McEachern his wife, 1738.

James McNaugh, 1740.

Alexander McNaught and Mary McDugall his wife; John, Moses, Jennat, and Florence, their children, 1738.

Anne McNeil, widow of Hugh McEuen; Alexander and Mary, her children, 1740.

Jean McNeil, 1740.

John McNeil, 1740.

Margaret McNeil, 1738.

Roger McNeil, 1740.

John McNeill and Eliz. Campbell his wife; Barbara, Peggy, Catharine, Betty, and Neil, their children, 1738.

John McNiven and Mary McArthur his wife; Elizabeth and Mary, their daughters, 1738.

Merran and Rachel McNiven, 1738.

Donald McPhaden, 1739.

Duncan McPhaden and Flory McCullum his wife; John and Duncan, their sons, 1740.

Neil McPhaden and Mary McDiarmid his wife; Dirvorgill and Margaret, their daughters, 1739.

John McPhail and Cristy Clark his wife; Gilbert, Flory, and Margaret, their children, 1739.

John McQuary and Anne McGuary his wife.

Duncan McQuore (*alias* Brown), and Effie McIllfeder his wife; Donald, John, Gilbert, and Christian, their children, 1739.

Archibald McVurich and Merran Shaw his wife, 1739.

Florence McVurich, 1739.

Lauchlin McVurich, 1738.

Lauchlin McVurich, 1739; dead in 1763.

Malcolm Martine and Florence Anderson his wife; Donald and Mary, their children, 1738.

Alexander Montgomery and Anna Sutherland his wife, 1738.

Hugh Montgomery, 1738.

Christian Munn, wife of Dan'l McIntire, 1740.

Anthony Murphy, 1740.

James Nutt and Rebecca Creighton his wife; Robert, John, and Elizabeth, their children, 1739.

Kirstin Peterson, 1738; dead in 1763.

Duncan Reid and Mary Semple his wife; Alexander, Nicklies, Angus, and Jeannie, their children.

John Reid and Margaret Hyman his wife; Donald, their son, 1739.

John Reid, 1740; went to Virginia; left Peter Reid, a relative, at Tappan.

Roger Reid, 1739.

Patrick Robertson, 1739; dead in 1763.

Peter Robertson, 1739; dead in 1763.

Jean Ross, 1738; dead in 1763; left one daughter.

Mary Ross, 1738.

Catharine Shaw, 1739.

Donald Shaw and Merran McInnish his wife, 1738.

Gustavus Shaw, 1739; dead in 1763.

John Shaw and Mary McNeil his wife; Neil and Duncan, their sons, 1739.

John Shaw and Merrian Brown his wife; Donald, Mary, and one infant, 1740.

Neil Shaw, 1739; ropemaker in New York, 1763; nephew of Gustavus S.

Neil Shaw and Florence McLauchlin his wife, 1739.

Duncan Smith, 1738.

James Stewart, 1738.

Elisbie Sutherland; James, Alexander, Duncan, Margaret, and Elizabeth Gillis, her children, 1738.

Duncan Taylor and Mary Gillis his wife; Mary, his daughter, 1738.

Mary Thompson, 1739; lived in Pennsylvania, in 1763; cousin of Duncan Reid, *supra.*

Allan Thomson, 1738; dead in 1763.

Elisbie Thomson, of Dunardree, 1738.

Dugald Thomson and Margaret McDuffie his wife; Archibald, Duncan, and Cristie, their children: also, Catharine, his brother Allan's daughter, 1739.

Rodger Thomson, 1740; died in the Provincial service; left a widow and one child at Amboy; Arch'd Gilchrist, of N.Y., guardian.

George Torry, 1739.

James Torry and Florrance McKeay his wife; Mary and Catharine, their children, 1739.

Jean Widron, 1740.

PIONEERS FROM STAUDERNHEIM

By Hugo Froehlich
Translated by Don Yoder

The Lutheran Church Register of the village of Staudernheim, in the Nahe Valley near Bad Kreuznach in the Northern Palatinate, belongs in the rare category of Palatine church books which contain a notable number of references to 18th century emigrants.

In the case of emigration, the minister—in the classical Latin of the clergy and the university—added a note to the record of his lost parishioner's baptism—*"Americanus factus"*—"became an American."

Emigration from 18th century Staudernheim involved three destinations—America, Prussia, and Poland. Some ninety persons left the village for America in the years 1738-1750, with the high point coming in the years 1739 and 1741, when entire families left together for Pennsylvania.

But there was also emigration into Prussia, sponsored by the Hohenzollerns in their attempt to build up Brandenburg and Pomerania. This movement (30 persons) took place in 1747 and 1748 and other unlisted years, and the pastor designated his loss with the Latin phrase *"Borussus factus"*—"became a Prussian"; for this emigration see Otto Gebhard, *Friederizianische Pfalzerkolonien in Brandenburg und Pommern* (Stettin, 1939).

Emigration to Poland (Galicia), involving fifteen persons from Staudernheim, took place around 1783 and 1784. It is significant that there are in this list some cases of one member of a family heading westward across the Atlantic to Pennsylvania, another turning up later in the German-speaking settlements of Eastern Europe.

The Latin and German phrases given in parentheses are quotations from the original church register; the materials in brackets giving arrivals in Philadelphia are, as usual in our emigrant lists, from the colonial ship-lists, as published in Strassburger and Hinke, *Pennsylvania German Pioneers* (Norristown, Pennsylvania: The Pennsylvania German Society. 1934)*

The materials have been translated from Hugo Fröhlich, *"Auswanderer im lutherischen Kirchenbuch von Staudernheim an der Nahe,"* which appeared in *Mitteilungen zur Wanderungsgeschichte der Pfalzer*, edited by Dr. Fritz Braun of the *Heimatstelle Pfalz*, Kaiserslautern, and published as a supplement to *Pfalzische Familien- und Wappenkunde*, 1954, to whose editorial board we are grateful for the privilege of reprinting these unusual materials.

---

*Readers should note also that the emigrants are arranged by family, and that in not every case did the head of a family emigrate.

BARTH, JOHANN NIKOLAUS—tailor, buried at Staundernheim, March 17, 1729, married at Staudernheim, January 23, 1714, Anna Maria Seiss, daughter of Michael Seiss and widow of Friedrich Lautenbach.
The following children, born at Staudernheim, emigrated:

1. Anna Christina Barth, baptized March 19, 1718; emigrated to Prussia with her illegitimate son, born at Staudernheim, Johann Nikolaus, baptized January 6, 1746 (Borussiana cum filio facta).
2. Johann Nikolaus Barth, baptized August 11, 1720 (Americanus factus).
3. Johannes Barth, baptized October 22, 1724 (Americanus factus). [Perhaps Johannes Barth, who arrived Philadelphia on the ship *Lydia*, October 19, 1749.]

BEIER, JOHANN FRIEDRICH—son of Johann Wilhelm Beier, married Anna Elisabeth Ebert, daughter of Johann George Ebert.
The following children, born at Staudernheim, emigrated to America:

1. Johann Kasimir Beier, baptized August 4, 1726 (anno 1741 Americanus factus).
2. Johann Nikolaus Beier, baptized January 4, 1730 (anno 1741 Americana (!) facta).
3. Johann Friedrich Beier, baptized December 15, 1732 (anno 1741 Americanus factus).
4. Anna Maria Beier, baptized January 27, 1737 (anno 1741 Americana facta).
5. Johann Andreas Beier, baptized February 6, 1739 (anno 1741 Americanus factus).

CHRISTIAN, JOHANN PETER—son of Johann Valentin Christian, linen-weaver, noted as dead at the confirmation of his son Philipp Jakob at Easter 1732, married at Staudernheim April 20, 1706, Maria Elisabeth Dorth, daughter of Johann Jakob Dorth at Pfalzisch-Weierbach.
Children, born at Staudernheim, emigrated:

1. Johann Georg Christian, baptized April 11, 1707, linen-weaver, emigrated to Pomerania (Borussus factus) with wife, Anna Barbara Kaul, daughter of Johannes Kaul at Hochstadten an der Alsenz (married at Staudernheim, November 13, 1736) and two children, (1) Johann Peter, baptized September 11, 1739 (cum parentibus Borussus factus); and (2) Daughter baptized June 19, 1746 (Pommerana cum parentibus facta.)
2. Philipp Jakob Christian, baptized May 13, 1717 (Americanus factus).

CONRADT, JOHANN NIKOLAUS—buried at Staudernheim June 1, 1736, married Anna Maria Wagner, daughter of Johann Sebastian Wagner at Gebroth; the widow married II. Simon Jakob Fey (q.v.).
Child, born at Staudernheim:

1. Johann Konrad Conradt, baptized October 21, 1728 (Americanus factus). [Perhaps Connrad Conrath, who arrived at Philadelphia on the Ship *Neptune*, October 25, 1746.]

CRON, SIMON JAKOB—baptized October 18, 1692, son of David Cron, married I. at Staudernheim, August 30, 1718, Anna Magdalena Rollauer, daughter of Ludwig Rollauer and widow of Johannes Schmidt, buried at Staudernheim, September 11, 1734; married II. at Staudernheim, January

17, 1736, Susanna Martha Sponheimer, daughter of Johann Wilhelm Sponheimer at Waldböckelheim.
Children born at Staudernheim—Nos. 1-4 of the first marriage, 5-6 of the second marriage:
1. Johann Konrad Cron, baptized February 5, 1722 (anno 1741 Americanus factus).
2. Johann Philipp Cron, baptized November 19, 1723 (anno 1741 Americanus factus).
3. Anna Christina Cron, baptized December 12, 1725 (anno 1741 Americana facta).
4. Anna Maria Cron, baptized September 14, 1730 (anno 1741 Americana facta).
5. Johann David Cron, baptized December 6, 1736 (anno 1741 Americanus factus).
6. Anna Margarethe Cron, baptized August 16, 1739 (anno 1741 Americana facta).
[Simon Jacob Cron (Croon), 48 years old, arrived at Philadelphia on the Ship *Friendship*, October 12, 1741.]
DIETZ, JOHANN MICHEL—son of Nikolaus Dietz, cartwright, buried February 9, 1727, married at Staudernheim, October 16, 1725, Maria Dorothea, daughter of Philipp Heinrich Cless, who possibly became the second wife of Johann Philipp Tesch (q.v.).
Child, born at Staudernheim:
1. Johann Jakob Dietz, baptized October 19, 1726 (anno 1741 Americanus factus).
[Possibly Johann Jacob Dietz (Ditts), 19 years old, who arrived at Philadelphia on the Ship *Marlborough*, September 23, 1741.]
EHRHARD, JOHANN PETER—son of Johannes Ehrhard, married at Staudernheim, February 3, 1708, Anna Margarethe Becker, daughter of Nikolaus Becker.
Children, born at Staudernheim:
1. Johann Heinrich Ehrhard, baptized November 19, 1713; according to the records arrived in America in 1739.
2. Maria Elisabeth Ehrhard, baptized November 30, 1716 (Americana facta).
3. Maria Christina Ehrhard, baptized August 17, 1721 (anno 1741 Americana facta).
[Johann Henrich Ehrhard (Erhart, Gerhard), 23 years old, arrived at Philadelphia on the Ship *Samuel*, August 27, 1739.]
EHRHARD, JOHANN PHILIPP—son of Johannes Ehrhard, married at Staudernheim November 30, 1717, Elisabeth Dorothea Jung, daughter of Johannes Jung at Huffelsheim.
Children, born at Staudernheim:
1. Anna Margarethe Ehrhard, baptized October 16, 1718 (anno 1742 Americana facta), married Johann Karl Schneider (q.v.).
2. Johannes Ehrhard, baptized August 11, 1720 (anno 1741 Americanus factus).

3. Anna Barbara Ehrhard, baptized April 29, 1723 (anno 1741 Americana facta).

4. Anna Maria Ehrhard, baptized May 9, 1726 (anno 1741 Americana facta).

[Johannes Ehrhard (Erhardt, Erhart), 21 years old, arrived at Philadelphia on the Ship *Friendship*, October 12, 1741; with him in the same ship list is Wilhelm Erhard, 20 years old.]

FEY, JOHANN LUDWIG—son of Johannes Fey, buried at Staudernheim September 9, 1759, married I. Anna Barbara, buried at Staudernheim January 26, 1735; married II. at Staudernheim, January 8, 1737, Anna Katharina Graff, daughter of Kaspar Graff at Huffelsheim, buried at Staudernheim November 25, 1787.

Children of the first marriage, born at Staudernheim:

1. Simon Jakob Fey, baptized January 22, 1708, buried at Staudernheim, March 22, 1787; married I. Staudernheim, November 13, 1736, Anna Maria, widow of Johann Nikolaus Conradt (q.v.); married II. Staudernheim, December 27, 1743, Maria Christina Kratzmann, daughter of Johann Nikolaus Kratzmann. His son Johann Peter Fey, of the second marriage, born 1755, married 1784 to Maria Magdalena Spiess, settled in Dornfeld, Galica, Poland; The emigrant's son Peter Fey was a schoolmaster at Reichenbach in Dornfeld.

2. Johann Tobias Fey, baptized July 6, 1724 (Americanus factus 1750.) [Tobias Fey arrived at Philadelphia on the Ship *Dragon*, September 26, 1749.]

FEY, JOHANN WILHELM—son of Johann Nikolaus Fay, cooper, baptized January 9, 1687 (Americanus factus), married at Staudernheim, November 26, 1715, Maria Barbara Dietz, daughter of Nikolaus Dietz.

Children, born at Staudernheim:

1. Anna Katharina Fey, baptized December 12, 1718 (anno 1741 Americana facta).

2. Anna Margarethe Fey, baptized January 15, 1723 (anno 1741 Americana facta).

3. Johann Michael Fey, baptized January 31, 1725 (anno 1741 (?) Americanus factus).

4. Johann Simon Fey, baptized January 6, 1727 (anno 1741 Americanus factus).

5. Susanna Barbara Fey, baptized September 28, 1730 (anno 1741 Americana facta).

6. Johann Nikolaus Fey, baptized September 23, 1734 (anno 1741 Americanus factus).

[Johann Wilhelm Fey, 53 years old, and Johann Michel Fey, 17 years old, arrived at Philadelphia on the *Snow Molly*, October 26, 1741.]

FINCK, HANS GEORG—son of Heinrich Finck, buried at Staudernheim, October 15, 1742, married I. Anna Maria, died at Staudernheim September 17, 1700; married II, at Staudernheim, April 5, 1701, Anna Maria Hoffmann, daughter of Konrad Hoffman at Abtweiler.

Child of the second marriage, born at Staudernheim:

1. Johann Nikolaus Finck, baptized February 13, 1707 (anno 1738 Americanus factus).

[Possibly Johann Nickel Finck, 33 years old, who arrived at Philadelphia on the Ship *Samuel*, August 30, 1737.]

FUCHS, JOHANN PETER—hired man on the Klosterhof, married Anna Margarethe.

Children, born at Staudernheim:

1. Elisabeth Katharina Fuchs, baptized March 31, 1730 (anno 1741 Americana facta).

2. Maria Magdalena Fuchs, baptized March 16, 1732 (anno 1741 Americana facta.)

3. Maria Margarethe Fuchs, baptized February 28, 1734 (anno 1741 Americana facta).

4. Johann Nikolaus Fuchs, baptized May 16, 1736 (anno 1741 Americanus factus).

5. Anna Katharina Fuchs, baptized September 28, 1738 (anno 1741 Americana facta).

6. Johann Jacob Fuchs, baptized July 22, 1740 (anno 1741 Americanus factus).

GRIMM, JOHANN PHILIPP—son of Johann Peter Grimm, married at Staudernheim, May 7, 1720, Anna Margarethe Weber, daughter of Sebastian Jakob Weber.

Children, born at Staudernheim:

1. Maria Elisabeth Grimm, baptized March 11, 1721 (anno 1739 Americana facta).

2. Johann Peter Grimm, baptized May 14, 1723 (anno 1739 cum patre America perfectus).

3. Johann Jakob Grimm, baptized August 23, 1726 (anno 1739 Americanus factus).

4. Anna Margarethe Grimm, baptized October 9, 1729 (anno 1739 Americana facta).

5. Johann David Grimm, baptized August 28, 1737 (anno 1739 Americanus factus).

HASPELHORN, JOHANN PETER—son of Hans Michael Haspelhorn, buried at Staudernheim February 10, 1762, married I. Sabina Katherina, buried at Staudernheim, September 25, 1748, Anna Barbara Janson, daughter of Johann Michael Janson at Neubamberg.

Children, born at Staudernheim:

1. Johann Ludwig Haspelhorn, baptized February 4, 1726 (Americanus factus).

2. Anna Sara Haspelhorn, baptized September 1, 1738; went to Poland in March of 1784.

[Ludwig Haspelhorn arrived in Philadelphia on the Ship *Dragon*, September 26, 1749.]

HEBLICH, CHRISTMANN—from Ebernburg, buried at Staudernheim, July 19, 1750, married at Staudernheim, November, 1708, Anna Christina, buried at Staudernheim, January 9, 1743.
Children, born at Staudernheim:
1. Anna Margarethe Heblich, baptized September 24, 1713 (Americana facta.)
2. Anna Elisabeth Heblich, baptized February 16, 1716 (Americana facta); married Johann Peter Kistner (q.v.).

KISTNER, JOHANN PETER—son of Johann Simon Kistner at Uberhochstetten, buried at Staudernheim, January 25, 1740, Anna Elisabeth Heblich (see above), who went to America with her son, born at Staudernheim: Simon Jakob Kistner, baptized January 27, 1743 (cum matre Americanus factus).

KLEIN, JOHANN GEORG—cabinet-maker, from Borrstadt on the other side of the Rhine in the territory of Idstein, buried at Staudernheim, July 20, 1770, married I. at Staudernheim, February 15, 1715, Maria Margarethe Schappert, daughter of Johannes Schappert, buried October 15, 1726; married II, at Staudernheim, after proclamation on the 20th, 21st, and 22nd Sundays after Trinity 1727, N.N.; married III, at Staudernheim around 1730 Anna Magdalena, buried at Staudernheim January 20, 1739; married IV, at Staudernheim, June 2, 1739, Anna Maria Kaul, daughter of Johann Peter Kaul at Waldböckelheim, buried September 25, 1781. (The marriage of 1739 is expressly designated as the fourth marriage. It is possible that the second and third marriages above are identical; in that case the first marriage would have taken place before 1715.)
Children, born at Staudernheim:
1. Johann Jakob Klein, baptized May 4, 1721 (anno Americanus factus).
2. Johann Peter Klein, baptized July 25, 1745 emigrated to Poland (den 25. August 1784 Polonius factus); cabinet-maker, married at Staudernheim, February 8, 1774, Anna Margarethe, widow of Philipp Freund at Kreuznach. Only one child appears to have been born at Staudernheim, Johann David Klein, born November 1, 1774, died September 11, 1781.
[Peter Klein of Staudernheim, farmer, two persons, appeared before the Hofkammer in Vienna, September 21, 1784, for settlement in Hungary; see Wilhelm and Kallbrunner, *Quelen zur deutschen Siedlungsgeschichte in Sudosteuropa*, p. 244.]
[Jacob Klein (Kleyn), 20 years old, arrived at Philadelphia, on the Ship *St. Andrew*, October 2, 1741.]

LAUTENBACH, JOHANNES—buried at Staudernheim May 16, 1736, married at Staudernheim, January 12, 1706, Anna Margarethe Gratzmann, daughter of Peter Gratzmann, buried at Staudernheim, February 27, 1746.
Children born in Staudernheim:
1. Maria Katharina Lautenbach, baptized December 4, 1712, emigrated to Pomerania with her husband. (Ist in Preussisch Bommern mit ihrem Mann Holtzapfel gezogen); married at Staudernheim, November 19, 1737,

Johann Nikolaus Holzapiel, son of Johann Martin Halzapfel at Kirn, shoemaker.

2. Johann David Lautenbach, baptized January 25, 1717 (anno 1739 Americanus factus).

3. Johannes Lautenbach, baptized February 17, 1724 (Americanus factus.)

[Johann David Lautenbagh (Laudenback, Loudinback), 23 years old, arrived at Philadelphia, on the Ship *Samuel*, August 27, 1739.]

LITZENBURGER, THEOBALD—son of Philipp Litzenburger, married at Staudernheim, May 10, 1718, Maria Barbara Seiberlein, daughter of Hans Konrad Seiberlein, School porter (Schuldiener) at Hennweiler.

Child, born at Staudernheim: Maria Christina, baptized July 28, 1720 (Americana facta).

MAURER, JOHANN JAKOB—son of Paul Maurer at Sobernheim, married Anna Elisabeth.

Children, born at Staudernheim:

1. Katharina Barbara Maurer, baptized December 6, 1730 (Americana cum patre).

2. Anna Eva Maurer, baptized October 29, 1736 (Americana cum patre).

[Jacob Maurer (Mower), 32 years old, arrived at Philadelphia on the Ship *Samuel*, December 3, 1740.]

OTTO, JOHANN FRIEDRICH—son of the village mayor (Schultheiss), dead before 1742, married at Staudernheim, February 23, 1706, Anna Katharina Schmidt, daughter of Johann Thielmann Schmidt, buried at Staudernheim, November 18, 1759.

Children, born at Staudernheim:

1. Maria Katharina Otto, baptized March 7, 1709; lived at Sobernheim, married Johannes Melchior and both came to America (Americani facti).

2. Johann Tobias Otto, baptized June 8, 1726 (anno 1741 Americanus factus).

[Johannes Melchior (Melchier), 28 years old, arrived at Philadelphia on the Ship *Friendship*, October 12, 1741.]

RITTER, JOHANN PETER—Village Mayor (Schultheiss), son of Matthias Ritter, married Maria Elisabeth.

Children, born at Staudernheim:

1. Johann Heinrich Ritter, baptized July 27, 1732 (Americanus cum patre factus).

2. Johann Michael Ritter, baptized September 8, 1734 (anno 1741 Americanus factus).

3. Johannes Ritter, baptized March 7, 1737 (anno 1741 Americanus factus).

ROLLARD, JOHANN PETER—son of Ludwig Rollard, buried at Staudernheim, March 4, 1733, married at Staudernheim, April 26, 1718, Anna Christina Muhlberger, daughter of George Muhlberger at Oberhausen, Oberamt Meisenheim; the widow married II, at Staudernheim, December 8, 1733, Matthias Wirth, son of Johann Philipp Wirth of Weiden.

Child, born at Staudernheim Johann Peter Rollard, baptized May 29, 1730 (Americanus factus).

[Johann Peter Roller (Rollar), arrived at Philadelphia on the Ship *Richard and Mary*, September 26, 1752.]

SCHAPPERT, JOHANN MICHAEL—son of Johannes Schappert, buried at Staudernheim, January 28, 1753, married I. at Kirschroth (Church Register Staudernheim), January 25, 1707, Anna Katharina Gutheil, daughter of Konrad Gutheil at Kirchroth, buried at Staudernheim, March 22, 1721; married II, at Staudernheim, February 3, 1722, Anna Katharina Grimm, daughter of Johann Simon Grimm, buried at Staudernheim, December 22, 1725; married III, at Staudernheim, January 8, 1732, Anna Barbara Seiss, daughter of Johannes Seiss.

Children, born at Staudernheim:

1. Anna Barbara Schappert, baptized November 28, 1725, emigrated to Prussia (Borussiana facta).

2. Johann Nikolaus Schappert, baptized September 21, 1746, was married in Switzerland, at Bern, and went from Switzerland to America (Ist in der Schweiz zu Bern verheiratet, aus der Schweiz in Amerika).

[Nicolaus Schapperdt arrived at Philadelphia on the Ship *Chance*, November 1, 1763. Before his name in the ship's list there appears the name of "Filb Schabbert". Possibly this was the brother of Johann Nikolaus Schappert, Johann Philipp Schappert, baptized at Staudernheim, February 25, 1739.]

SCHNEIDER, JOHANN KARL—stone-mason, son of Heinrich Schneider at "Fremersheim," married in Staudernheim, May 31, 1740, Anna Margarethe Ehrhard (q.v.).

Twins, born at Staudernheim:

1. Johannes Schneider

2. Anna Barbara Schneider, baptized March 3, 1741 (cum parentibus Americani facti).

[Carl Schneyder (Snyder), 23 years old, arrived at Philadelphia on the Ship *Friendship*, October 12, 1741.]

SEISS, JOHANN JAKOB—son of Matthias Seiss, musician, buried at Staudernheim, November 3, 1744, married I. Johannetta; married II. Maria Barbara, buried at Staudernheim, October 20, 1785.

Child of the first marriage, born at Staudernheim:

1. Johann Andreas Seiss, baptized December 15, 1720 (Americanus factus).

[Joh. Andreas Seysen arrived at Philadelphia on the Ship *Edinburgh*, August 13, 1750.]

SEISS, JOHANNES—son of Antonius Seiss, buried at Staudernheim, May 8, 1728, married I. Anna Elisabeth, died at Staudernheim, August 19, 1700; married II. at Staudernheim, June 7, 1701, Sabine Cron, daughter of Hans Simon Cron and widow of Johann Nikolaus Fey, buried at Staudernheim, June 4, 1751.

Child of the second marriage, born at Staudernheim:

1. Johann Adam Seiss, baptized August 18, 1710 (anno 1740 Americanus factus.)

[Possibly Johann Adam Syce (Seysen), 25 years old, who arrived at Philadelphia on the Ship *Friendship*, October 12, 1741.]

SPONHEIMER, JOHANN PETER—son of Johann Wilhelm Sponheimer, buried at Staudernheim, January 11, 1759, married I. at Staudernheim, May 14, 1706, Anna Christina Damgen, daughter of Christian Damgen at Sobernheim, buried at Staudernheim November 26, 1710; married II. at Staudernheim, November 17, 1711, Anna Maria Fey, daughter of Johannes Fey.

Children, of the first and second marriages, born at Staudernheim:

1. Anna Margarethe Sponheimer, baptized October 23, 1707 (anno 1741 Americana facta).

2. Johann Nikolaus Sponheimer, baptized September 4, 1712; served in Potsdam among King Frederick William's Giant Guards and was married there (dieser ist in Potsdam unter den grossen Granadieren und auch verheiratet).

TESCH, JOHANN PHILIPP—son of Paul Tesch, married I. at Staudernheim, April 30, 1726, Anna Christina Schappert, daughter of Johannes Schappert, buried at Staudernheim, January 4, 1733; married II. at Staudernheim, April 15, 1733, Maria Dorothea, widow.

Children of the first and second marriage, born at Staudernheim:

1. Johann Michel Tesch, baptized May 31, 1731 (anno 1741 Americanus factus).

2. Johann Peter Tesch, baptized December 20, 1733 (anno 1741 Americanus factus).

3. Simon Philipp Tesch, baptized July 25, 1737 (anno 1741 Americanus factus).

[Johann Philipp Desch (Tash), 40 years old, arrived at Philadelphia on the *Snow Molly*, October 26, 1741.]

TEXTOR, HIERONYMUS—gunsmith, married Anna Margarethe.

Child, born at Staudernheim:

1. Christina Elisabeth Textor—baptized August 8, 1748 (anno 1751 Americana cum parentibus facta).

[Hieronimus Textur arrived at Philadelphia on the Ship *Edinburgh*, September 16, 1751.]

WANDER, SIMON JAKOB—son of Johann Philipp Wander, died at Staudernheim, October 25, 1742 (reference in Baptismal Register), married Anna Maria.

Child, born at Staudernheim:

1. Anna Christina Wander, baptized October 29, 1717 (anno 1742 Americana facta).

WANDER, JOHANN TOBIAS—son of Heinrich Wander, buried at Staudernheim, September 22, 1735, married at Staudernheim, September

17, 1720, Anna Eva Seiss, daughter of Michel Seiss; the widow married II. at Staudernheim, April 3, 1736, Johann Nikolaus Lang.

Child, born at Staudernheim:

1. Johann Heinrich Wander, baptized October 28, 1723 (Americanus factus).

AUGUSTA COUNTY EARLY SETTLERS, IMPORTATIONS, 1739-1740*

By MRS. W. W. KING (Fannie Bayly), Staunton, Virginia

A List of Augusta County settlers who proved their importations from Great Britain at their own expense, in order to become entitled to enter public land. These proceedings were before the Orange County Court.

February 28, 1739

Ledgerwood, William: For himself & Agnes, Martha, Jane, Elener, William, James.

McCadden, Patrick: For himself & Samuel Givens.

McDowell, John: For himself & Magdalene, wife, Samuel, son & John Rutter.

McDowell, Robert: For himself & Martha, Jane, Margaret, William.

April 27, 1740

Carr, John: Also for Lucey, wife & Margaret & Matthew Glaspey.

May 22, 1740 (Wad. 38, 39)

Anderson, George: wife Elizabeth & children: William, Margaret, John & Frances.

Breckenridge, Alexander and John, George Robert, Smith and Letitia from Ireland to Philadelphia—see also elsewhere.

Brown, William and his children: Mary, Robert, Hugh & Margaret.

Caldwell, James & his children: Mary, Jean, Agnes, John, Sarah & Samuel.

Patterson, Robert, wife Grace & children: Thomas, Mary & Elizabeth.

Preston, John, came in with Breckenridge & others, but postponed proving his importation until 1746, when his appeared

---

*From a History of Rockbridge County, Staunton, Va. 1920, Oren F. Morton, Staunton, Va., 1920, Section XIII, Various Lists, p. 457, and Chalkley and Order Book.

before the Court of Augusta "to par-
take of his majesty's bounty, for taking
up lands."

Scott, Samuel, his wife Jane & son John.

Stephenson, John & his children: Sarah
& Mary.

Wilson, David, his wife Charity & son
James.

June 26, 1740

Anderson, John: For himself & Elizabeth,
wife, & William, Margaret, John,
Frances.

Bell, James: For himself & John, Margaret & Elizabeth Bell.

Campbell, Hugh and his children: Esther
& Sarah. (See also Owen F. Morton's
History of Rockbridge County).

Campbell, Patrick: For himself & Elizabeth, Charles, William, Patrick Jr.,
John, Mary, Elizabeth, Gennet.

Hays, John: For himself & Rebecca, Charles, Andrew, Barbara, Jane, Robert.

Hays, Patrick: For himself & Frances,
Jean, William, Margaret, Catherine,
Ruth.

Hutcheson, George: For himself & Elean-
or, wife, & Jennitt; also for Joseph
Carr.

Hutcheson, William: Also for John, Sr.,
John, Jr., Margaret, Mary.

Johnston, William: Also for Ann, Elizabeth, John, & for Samuel Crawford.

Logan, David: Also for Mary, wife &
William.

McClure, James: Also for Agnes, John,
Eleanor, Andrew, Jane, James Jr.

McCowen, Francis: For himself & Mary,
wife & Markham & Elizabeth.

Maxwell, John: For himself & Margaret,
John, Jr., Thomas, Mary, Alexander.

Mulhollen, John, Jane McAlegant, Agnes,
Reed, William & Elizabeth McCanlon.

O'Freiel, Morris: For himself & Catherine, wife.

Patterson, Robert: Also for Mary, wife, &
Thomas, Mary, Elizabeth.

Poague, Robert: Also for Elizabeth, wife,
& Margaret, John, Martha, Sarah,
George, Mary, Elizabeth, William, Rob-
ert.

Robinson, James: For himself & Jean,
William, George.

Smith, John: Also for Margaret, wife &
Abraham, Henry, Daniel, John, Joseph,
& for Robert McDowell.

Thompson, Moses: Also for Jane, William,

Robert, John & for Jane Cox.

Trimble John: For himself & Ann, Margaret, Mary.

Wilson, John: For himself & Martha,
Matthew, William, John, Sarah, Elizabeth.

Young, Robert: For himself & Agada,
Julia, Samuel, James.

July 24, 25, 1740

Crawford, Patrick: Also for Ann, James,
George, Margaret, Mary.

Davis, James: Also for Mary, Henry,
William, Samuel.

Davison, John: Also for James, George,
Thomas, William, Samuel.

Edmiston, David: For himself & Isabella,
Jesse, John, William, Rachel, David,
Moses; & for Jesse & James Daley.

Later Dates

Blair, John: Captain Hogg's Co. (Ch.
1, 215), (Proved May 18, 1780).

Bowyer, Michael: early settler (Wa. 130).
(Wa. 180). Father of Thos. &c.

Bowyer, Thomas: pre-revolutionary soldier (Ch. 1, 214), Mch. 24, 1780 proved
that in 1760 he was Lt. of Co. of Regu-
lars in Va. Co., Col. Byrd. Later served
in Regt. of Col. Hopkins, as subaltern.

Boyd Alexander: Paymaster Va. Regt.
(Ch. 3, 368).

Breckenridge, Alexander: came to Pa.
1728; to Augusta & proved in Court
1740 (Wa. 38, 39).

Breckenridge, Col. Robert, Sr.; appointed
trustee at incorporation of town of
Staunton, 1760, later moved to Bote-
tourt Co. & m. (1) daughter of Robert Poague, (2) Lettice Preston, D.
1772. (Wad. 199).

Brown, James: pre-revolutionary.

Bullett, Capt. Thomas, pre-revolutionary
soldier (Ch. 1, 475).

Burke, William: Capt. Peter Hogg's Co.,
Feb. 20, 1758. (Ch. 1, 483).

Burton, John: pre-revolutionary soldier
wounded in 1760. (Ch. 1, 251).

Carlyle, John, ranger (Ch. 1, 211).

Christian, Gilbert, landed at New Castle
1726 & almost at once came to Augusta
County.

Christian, Israel, came to Augusta 1740;
m. Elizabeth Stark; founded Fincastle

Note: **Gabriel James** was appointed prosecuting
attorney (King's atty.) for Augusta Co. April, 1746,
age 22 and was apparently the first attorney who
lived in that Co. In 1777 he was similarly appointed for Rockingham Co. (Wad. 81).

& Christiansburg. (Wad. 124).

Clark, John, with Boquet 1764. Proved August 17, 1779. (Ch. 1, 210).

Davis, David, with others "viewed and laid off a public road west of the Blue Ridge June, 1739" (Wad. 37).

Dennison, Daniel, early settler. (Wad. 39).

Doak, John, Muster Roll of 1742, Capt. John Christian's list. (Ch. 2, 509).

Dunlap, James, Ranger, Co. of Capt.

Hogg. (Ch. 1, 211).

Fearis, Robert, Co. of Capt. Hogg. (Ch. 1, 209).

Filbrick, Henry, with Capt. Thomas Bullitt. (Ch. 1, 475).

Gilkeson, Archibald; private in Capt. Martain's Co. & surveyor of highways 1767; m. Sarah ——. (McC. 209).

Gilkeson, Robert; founder of one Gilkeson family in Augusta Co. Will recorded in said Co. 1775. (McC: 209).

A LIST OF CONVICTS TRANSPORTED TO MARYLAND

By Frank F. White, Jr.

A list of one hundred fifteen convicts and felons transported by Andrew Reid [1] in 1740, a recent anonymous gift to the library of the Maryland Historical Society, is a document exceedingly rich in social and economic history. It sheds much light on the labor conditions of the eighteenth century when land, on the one hand, was plentiful, while labor, on the other, was notoriously scarce. One of the cheapest and most profitable methods to build up great estates and tremendous fortunes, therefore, was to import labor, white indentured servants in particular. [2]

Maryland received more convicts and felons than any other province in the eighteenth century. [3] Lodge and other writers maintain that Maryland received a greater proportion of convicts than any other province. [4] Scharf estimates that the total number of criminals sent to Maryland was about 20,000, with over six hundred a year coming in between the years 1737 and 1767. [5] In all probability, the majority of those so transported were not political offenders. [6] Clearly, then, Maryland became a dumping ground for the objectionable subjects of the realm.

Most of these " seven-year " criminals were the ordinary criminals of the British Isles. Those transported included both men and women of all ages and descriptions. Their crimes ranged from merely stealing a loaf of bread to armed robbery. The more serious offenders were not transported but were executed

---

[1] The contractor for the transportation of Newgate felons from April, 1739, to March, 1757. Abbot Smith, *Colonists in Bondage* (Chapel Hill, 1947), p. 114.
[2] See Basil Sollers, " Transported Convict Laborers in Maryland," *Maryland Historical Magazine*, II (1907), 17-47.
[3] Eugene I. McCormac, " White Servitude in Maryland, 1634-1820," *Johns Hopkins University Studies*, XXII, Nos. 3-4 (1904), 98.
[4] James Butler, " British Convicts Shipped to American Colonies," *American Historical Review*, II (October, 1896), 19; Henry Cabot Lodge, *A Short History of the English Colonies in America*. (Boston, 1882), pp. 124-125.
[5] John Thomas Scharf, *History of Maryland*, I (Baltimore, 1879), 371-372.
[6] Butler, *op. cit.*, 16.

shortly after their sentences were imposed. The Act of 1718 provided that persons who had been convicted of clergyable offenses such as burglary, robbery, perjury, or theft, be sent to America for seven years. James Went, for instance, one of those on the list, was guilty of robbing a house,[7] while John Wells,[8] William Snowd, and William Cardell, were charged with highway robbery.[9] Jarvis Hare, a mere lad of fourteen years, was sentenced for stealing a horse,[10] while Thomas Henning enlisted a man for the King of Prussia.[11] Sarah Kingman picked a pocket.[12] Thus, the British Government perceived the great need for " servants " who might improve the colonial plantations and at the same time make themselves more useful to His Majesty.

These felons and convicts frequently had to undergo great hardships before departing from England. Often they languished in the jails of the British Isles for long periods. Some of those on the following list had been confined in Newgate Prison for as much as nine months. James Went's sentence had been passed, for instance, in June, 1739, while Snowd and Wells were condemned in January, 1740.

Sheriffs were not allowed to deliver criminals to the transporters without license. The transporters themselves in turn had to give security that the felons would not return to England until their terms of banishment had expired. The captain of the ship had to swear that the people to be transported were received on board and would be effectually and immediately transported to America. This security had to be certified by a public official. Hence, Andrew Reid received a certificate of receipt from Anthony Bacon and Reid's oath in turn had to be certified by the Clerk of the Gaol Delivery for Middlesex County.

Because of the great demand for indentured servants, many of the transporters made tremendous wealth. Captain Anthony Bacon was but one of those who chose to earn his living in this manner. He appears to have been well-known to Marylanders, especially in the latter half of the eighteenth century as the owner of a prominent firm. Charles Carroll, Barrister, makes frequent

[7] *Gentleman's Magazine*, IX (June, 1739), 325.
[8] *Ibid.*, X (January, 1740), 34.
[9] *Ibid.*, IX (September, 1739), 404.
[10] *Ibid.*, IX (June, 1739), 325.
[11] *Ibid.*, IX (October, 1739), 551.
[12] *Ibid.*, IX (July, 1739), 383.

references to conducting business with the house of Bacon.[13] The
Bordley Papers in the Society's library contain many records of
Bacon's business transactions.

Marylanders tolerated the shipment of convicts simply because
they had to. They protested the intrusion of convicts, but were
unable to do much about it.[14] They imposed a duty on the numbers of convicts brought in and not infrequently kidnapped them
and spirited them away. The planter class appears to have been
the only group which from the first favored the importation of
convict labor. This group did, however, resent the King's making
Maryland the dumping ground for his objectionable subjects, but
were influential in forcing the passage of the 1728 Maryland law
which, among other things, made compulsory written testimonials
from each shipmaster as to the offense, the sentence, and the time
each convict had to serve.[15] Eventually, the agitation against convict labor became so great that the British Government were
forced to look elsewhere for the site of a penal colony. This
eventually became Botany Bay, Australia.

As previously suggested, the names of those to be transported
were chronicled in the British journals. *The Historical Register*
faithfully listed for many years the numbers of those to be transported, but none of those on the ship *York* could be traced
through this journal. *The Gentleman's Magazine* also chronicled
the names of those condemned, but usually these entries were in
the briefest possible form. Those to be transported seldom appeared in the latter journal, but their offenses were usually listed
with a remark such as " condemned and ordered to be transported
four men and three women."

The list follows.

Blackwall March 22nd 1739/40.

A List of One Hundred and Fifteen Felons & Convicts Shipped from
Newgate by Andrew Reid Esqr on board the York Capt Anthony Bacon
Commander, bound for Maryland, vizt:

1 James Wood	5 Mary Wood
2 Richard Merring	6 Daniel Sullivan
3 Myers Samuel	7 James Evans
4 Elizabeth Ward	8 Ann (Johanna) Price

[13] See particularly articles which appeared in the *Maryland Historical Magazine*,
XXXIII (1938), " Letters of Charles Carroll, Barrister."
[14] *Archives of Maryland*, II, 540-541.
[15] *Laws of Maryland*, 1728 Session, Chapter XXIII.

9 Thomas Watson
10 Richard Land
11 James Meredith
12 James Stuart
13 Elizabeth Jackson
14 Richard Mackloud
15 Benjamin Dunkersly
16 John Plummer
17 Thomas Ward
18 Thomas Deane
19 Ephraim Hubbard
20 John Cooke
21 Sarah Stanley
22 William Turner
23 Richard Underwood
24 William Maxwell
25 John Anderson
26 Cesar Franklin
27 John Brown
28 James Eakins
29 John Warren
30 John Myers
31 Mary Johnson
32 Samuel Peartree
33 Lucy Hughes
34 John Irving
35 Jacob Edmunds
36 James Bartley
37 Michael Smith
38 William Jones
39 Thomas Henning
40 William Cardell
41 Jarvis Hare
42 James Went
43 Sarah Kingman
44 Sarah Sumners
45 Margaret Betts
46 William Burchmore
47 John Hastings
48 William Green
49 John Matthews
50 Sarah Withers
51 John Morgan
52 Mary Hardcastle
53 Francis Smith
54 John Deacon
55 Sarah Jones
56 Samuel Powell
57 William Stewa.
58 Mary Castle
59 John Delane
60 John Duggen
61 Ann Groom
62 Elizabeth Price
63 Diana Cole
64 Elizabeth Fowles
65 James Brockwell
66 John Tizzard
67 Elizabeth Green
68 Alice Faulkner
69 John Patterson
70 Moses Beesely
71 Ann Stringer
72 William Shaw
73 Sarah Liddiard
74 Joshua Blackett
75 Henry Chapman
76 James Downes
77 Isaac Gaytes
78 Arnold Reynolds
79 Rebecca Peake
80 John Smith
81 John Mitchell
82 James Anderson
83 Hannah Thompson
84 William Graves
85 William Brown
86 Ann Wilson
87 Thomas Davis
88 James Stiles
89 John Patterson
90 William Berry
91 John Claxton
92 Charles Groom
93 Elianor Bolton
94 Elizabeth Smith
95 Martha Abbott
96 Margaret Ellis
97 Thomas Winter
98 John Wicks
99 Edward Groves
100 William Peake
101 John Blake
102 Marmaduke Bignoll
103 Richard Ford
104 Ann Williams

105 William Seale	111 William Kipps
106 Thomas Street	112 Mary Elliott
107 Francis Flack	113 George Vaughan
108 Mary Heckman	114 William Snowd
109 Benjamin Bellgrove (Dead)	115 Joseph Wells
110 John Potter	

Blackwall March 22d 1739/40.

I Anthony Bacon Master of the Ship York, now lying in the River of Thames & bound for Maryland in America do hereby humbly certify that the above named Persons being in Number One Hundred & Fifteen were this day all received on board my said Ship (except Benjamin Bellgrove who died in Newgate) by the Order of Andrew Reid Esqr. to be immediately & effectually transported to Maryland, one of His Majesty's Plantations in America, pursuant to the Acts of Parliament for that purpose made & provided.

Antho: Bacon

Witness
Jno Nicholls
John Davis

London I do hereby humbly certify that Andrew Reid of London Merchant hath given Security for the effectual Transportation of the Forty Three Felons first above named pursuant to the Orders of the Court of Goal Delivery of Newgate holden for the City of London at Justice Hall in the Old Bailey in the Suburbs of the same City on Wednesday the 16th day of January and Wednesday the Twenty Seventh day of February last past, which Security remains now in my hands. Dated the Third Day of April 1740.

Man [16]

(REVERSE)

Middx I do hereby humbly Certify that Andrew Reid of London Merchant hath given Security for the Effectual Transportation of the within last named Seventy two Felons pursuant to the orders of the Court of Gaole Delivery of Newgate holden for the County of Middx at Justicehall in the Old Bailey in the Suburbs of the City of London on Wednesday the 16th Day of January and Wednesday the 27th Day of February last past which Security remains now in my hands and that the within named Benjamin Bellgrove died in Newgate since the giving the said Security. Dated the 3rd Day of April 1740.

John Matthews Clerk of the Gaole Delivery
of Newgate for the County of Middx

---

[16] Man is unidentified, but is believed to be a minor official.

The mere presence of a name on the list does not mean that these criminals remained in Maryland. Many of them returned to England after their terms of banishment had expired. Without making extensive genealogical investigation, few traces of the one hundred fifteen could be found. In all probability, the stigma attached to the term convict caused many of them to change their names or to migrate to other provinces. At any rate, present day Marylanders need not be disturbed. If any on this list of convicts remained, they probably became, after a term of seven years with exacting masters, self-respecting, and possibly industrious and prosperous citizens.

PASSENGERS ON THE "LOYAL JUDITH" (1740)*

Dr. Fritz Braun

Dr. Fritz Braun, genealogist and historian of the Rhine Palatinate, whose wide knowledge of Pennsylvania family origins has helped our researchers here, offers new information on 18th Century emigrants and the places where they came from. In an article in Number 9/10 (November-December 1953) of the periodical issued by the *Nordpfälzer Geschichtsverein*, pp. 62-64, Dr. Braun lists all the heads of families or single persons who emigrated on the Ship *Loyal Judith*, arriving at Philadelphia, November 25, 1740. For as many of these as he was able to trace, he gives the name of the Palatine village from which they emigrated. His list includes the following names:

1. Keller, Anthony—from the village of *Lettweiler.*
2. Dielboen, Henrich (Thielbon), actually Henrich Thielemann Bohn—from the village of *Unkenbach.*
3. Haas (Hass), Johann Abraham—from the village of *Medard.*
4. Theobaldt, Johann Jacob—from the village of *Medard.*
5. Kickler (Kuechler), Joseph—from the village of *Callbach.*
6. Gerhard, Lenhart—from the village of *Lettweiler.*
7. Wolff, Johannes—from the village of *Gangloff.*
8. Sell (Zell), Johann Nikolaus—from the village of *Rehborn.*
9. Lindemann, Justus, Jacob, and Henrich—from the village of *Unkenbach.*
10. Krimm (Grimm?), Valentin and Jacob—from the village of *Unkenbach.*
11. Hartmann, Ulrich—from the village of *Unkenbach.*
12. Conradt, Georg—from the village of *Unkenbach.* Also Jacob Conrade, Jr.
13. Maurer, Adam—from the village of *Lettweiler.*
14. Mohr, Johann Peter—from the village of *Kellenbach (Simmern).*
15. Dietrich, Isaac—from the village of *Biesterschied.*
16. Esling, Johann Georg—"from the Palatinate."
17. Hype (Geib?), (Johann) Henrich—from the village of *Medard.* Some confusion exists over the identification.

---

*This brief article was apparently overlooked by Lancour, even though it appears on the same page of *The Pennsylvania Dutchman* as another article cited in his *Bibliography of Ship Passenger Lists.*

THE NATURALIZATION OF JEWS IN THE AMERICAN COLONIES UNDER THE ACT OF 1740.

By Dr. J. H. Hollander, *Johns Hopkins University, Baltimore, Md.*

At the first scientific meeting of the American Jewish Historical Society, held at Philadelphia, December 15, 1892, Hon. Simon W. Rosendale called attention to the act of 13 Geo. II, c. 7 (1740), permitting the naturalization of Jews in the American colonies. The text of this act was printed in full in No. I of the *Publications,* and the suggestion was made by Judge Rosendale, in an introductory note, that an examination of the records of the Commissioners for Trade and Plantations in London might result in the discovery of the names of Jewish colonists who had availed themselves of the benefit of the act. Accordingly, a year ago, the present writer, then planning to spend the summer in England, informed the secretary of the Society of his intention while in London to examine the archives of the Public Record Office, with this object in view. Soon after arriving, he learned incidentally that this had already been performed, at the suggestion of Hon. Oscar S. Straus, by the distinguished president of the Anglo-Jewish Historical Society, Mr. Lucien Wolf. Mr. Wolf generously placed the results of his search at the disposition of the present writer. It seemed best, however, to proceed independently, in order to permit collation and verification of results. This was actually done, and Mr. Wolf's list was found correct in almost every detail. To Mr. Wolf is thus due both the pleasure of priority and the credit of exact research.

It seems proper to add that ten years earlier (September 12, 1883), attention was called to the significance of this act of 1740 by Rev. Dr. B. Felsenthal of Chicago, in a letter addressed to Judge Charles P. Daly, LL. D., upon the occasion of the latter's address at the laying of the corner-stone of the Hebrew Orphan Asylum in New York City. The letter and the reply it elicited are appended by Mr. Max J. Kohler to his edition of Judge Daly's *The Settlement of the Jews in North America* (pp. 154–161), and will be referred to hereafter.

I.

Prior to the reign of James I, it was possible for a Jew to acquire civil status in Great Britain in the same manner as any other alien, viz. by naturalization by act of Parliament. The act of 7 James I, c. 2 (1610) directed against the Roman Catholics, had the collateral effect of excluding Jews from the privilege of naturalization, by providing that all persons thereafter to be naturalized should receive the sacrament within one month before the bill for their naturalization was exhibited. In 1675 this requirement was slightly relaxed by a statute which provided that any foreigner who should engage for three years in England, Wales, or Berwick, in hemp, flax or cotton cloth manufacture, should, upon taking the oaths of supremacy and allegiance before two justices of the peace, enjoy all privileges of natural-born subjects.

A statute of greater significance was the act of 13 George II, c. 7 (1740), with which we are here concerned. It was passed in the further interest of trade and colonization, and extended freedom of naturalization to foreigners residing seven years in the American colonies who should take the oath of abjuration, make the declaration of fidelity, and receive the sacrament. Neither special act of Parliament nor attendance in London was necessary. The person seeking naturalization merely took the required oath and paid to the secretary's office of the particular colony in which he resided a record fee of two shillings, in return for which he was granted a certificate which served as a complete naturalization paper. The secretary of each colony was required annually to transmit to the office of the Commissioners for Trade and Plantations in London a list of all persons who had entitled themselves to the benefit of the act. Such lists were to be "duly and regularly entered by the said Commissioners in a Book or Books to be had and kept for that Purpose in the said Office, for publick View and Inspection as Occasion shall require."

The provisions of particular significance for our purpose are contained in sections II and III of the statute. In the former of these, " such who profess the Jewish Religion " are specifically exempted from the necessity of receiving the sacrament as a qualification for naturalization ; in the latter the same persons are allowed to omit the phrase " upon the true faith of a Christian " in taking the oath of abjuration.

The bill when first proposed seems to have attracted little attention, and to have encountered no opposition from the public at large. This was doubtless in large part due to the fact that the word "Jews " did not appear in the title. Its legislative history was likewise uneventful. Pelham in 1753 declared that it "passed through both Houses without the least opposition." * The formal records show that leave to bring in the bill was granted in the Commons on November 30, 1739, *nemine contradicente*.† On January 29, 1740, it was sent to the Lords, where it seems to have been subjected to more careful discussion and to have received some slight amendments, to which the Commons assented. The measure passed on February 15, 1740, and received the royal assent on March 19, 1740.‡

The operation of the act occasioned as little opposition as its passage. In 1753, Pelham, in the speech already referred to, asserted that the act of 1740 " has now subsisted for several years without causing the least murmur among the

---

*Cobbett, *Parliamentary History*, vol. XV, p. 143.
†*Journal of House of Commons*, vol. XXIII, p. 394.
‡*Journal of House of Lords*, vol. XXV, pp. 453, 459, 461, 487.

people." Other testimony of the same character is available.* Not until 1753, and then only as an incident of the reaction which followed the passage of the "Jew Bill" of that year, was the act of 1740 threatened.

The popular hostility excited by the act of 1753, and judiciously nursed by the opposition, attained such dimensions† that soon after Parliament reconvened in the following year, a bill was passed repealing the naturalization act of 1753. Encouraged by the repeal of the act of 1753, an attempt was now made to effect the repeal of the earlier statute of 1740.‡

On November 19, 1753, Mr. George Cooke moved, after the reading of the Act of 1740, for an address to the Crown to cause lists to be laid before the House, of the names of persons professing the Jewish religion who had since June 1, 1740, entitled themselves to the benefit of that act.§ It was so ordered, and on November 22, Lord Dupplin, from the Commissioners for Trade and Plantations, presented to the House a copy of the names as ordered, compiled from the

* See Martin's speech, p. 107 below.

† The storm of popular disapproval which swept over all England upon the passage of the act of 1753 is graphically described by Walpole: "The whole nation found itself inflamed with a Christian zeal, which was thought happily extinguished with the ashes of Queen Anne and Sacheverel. Indeed, this holy spirit seized none but the populace, and the very lowest of the clergy. Yet all these grew suddenly so zealous for the honor of the prophecies that foretell calamity and eternal dispersion to the Jews, that they seemed to fear lest the completion of them should be defeated by Act of Parliament, and there wanted nothing to their ardor but to petition both Houses to enact the accomplishment. The little Curates preached against the Bishops for deserting the interests of the Gospel ; and aldermen grew drunk at county clubs in the cause of Jesus Christ, as they had used to do for the sake of King James "—Walpole, *Memoirs of George II* (ed. Holland), vol. I, pp. 357, 358.

‡ Cobbett, *Parliamentary History*, vol. XV, pp. 162, 163 ; Walpole, *Memoirs of George II*, vol. I, p. 364 *et seq.*; Coxe, *Memoirs of the Pelhams*, vol. II, p. 297 *et seq.*

§ *Journal of House of Commons*, vol. XXVI, p. 845.

lists transmitted by the secretaries of the several colonies. The copy was read by title and ordered to lie on the table "to be perused by members of the House."*

On December 4, Lord Harley and Sir James Dashwood moved for the formal repeal of the Act of 1740. Reports of the interesting debate which ensued have been preserved, and it seems worth while to append these in some fulness:

"Martin, the West Indian, opposed the motion in a speech of wit. He said this act had been made 13 years ago; had occasioned no clamor then, nor since. Foreigners would begin to think that there was no combustible material left in England but these poor Jews. One hundred and eighty-five have taken the benefit of the act. He had been so idle, he said, as to read all the pamphlets and papers on the late act, and must pronounce that no subject ever occasioned the spilling of so much nonsense. That America can only be peopled by foreigners, unless you would drain your own country, over and above those valuable colonists, the transported."

"Sir Roger Newdigate spoke for the last moved repeal. Nugent ridiculed it and said that if once the principle was admitted there would be no stopping. Why have 130 Jews been naturalized in Jamaica, and none in Barbadoes? Because three parts of the former are desert, and no part of the latter. Would you drive them out of the desert? Spanish Jews are the most proper because they can best support the climate. That noble pirate, the Knight of Malta, says, make perpetual war with perpetual enemies; so says the Inquisition—imitate them, and you will only have your Mediterranean trade. Then break with those who league with the enemies of your religion, as Spain does with Denmark. But no: you have done what you meant to do. Stop here: a Christian knows no perpetual enmity. The most prosperous, happy man here has the best chance for the

---

* *Journal of House of Commons*, vol. XXVI, p. 850.

next world. They who make these clamors now smile with us; if we gave way, would laugh at us."

"Sir John Bernard made a short, bad speech and went away."*

"Mr. Pelham said: 'To repeal the Plantation Act will be to tell the people we repeal this law not because it has made but because it ought to have made you uneasy. To part with those who hold our wealth will be to divest ourselves of our strength. To pay attention to mere clamor will produce the most serious consequences; but a repeal will revive the intolerant principles of the High Church, which have produced such pernicious effects, and encourage that spirit, which can only be gratified while it is thundering for its essential anathemas.'"

"Mr. Pitt spoke with still more energy than Mr. Pelham. 'I did not expect,' he observed, 'that this would have been the first return for the recent condescension of parliament. A stand must be made or our authority is at an end. I consider the recent clamor to be a little election art which has been judiciously humored. The bill was not a toleration, but a preference given to Jews over other sects. My maxim is, not to grant more consideration to the church than it actually enjoys; for if a High Church spirit should revive, the fate which threatens the Jews to-day will menace the Presbyterian to-morrow, and the country will be agitated by a septennial church clamor. We are not to be influenced by laws passed before the Reformation. Our ancestors would have said, "A Lollard has no right to inherit lands." We, on the contrary, do not fear to indulge Jews. They are not likely to become great purchasers of land, for they love their money and can employ it to much better advantage in trade.'"†

At the conclusion of debate the question was put, on the same day, December 4, 1753. A division of the House

---

* Walpole, *Memoirs of George II*, vol. I, pp. 364–366.

† Coxe, *Memoirs of Pelham*, vol. II, pp. 297, 298; cf. also Walpole, *Memoirs of George II*, vol. I, pp. 366, 367.

resulted in 88 in favor of repeal and 208 against.* This decisive verdict placed a quietus upon all further agitation, and the act continued in operation until the course of historic events rendered unnecessary the British naturalization of American colonists.

During the period of its operation, the Act of 1740 thus afforded an easy means of complete naturalization to Jews resident for a period of seven years or more in the American colonies. A distinguished writer on American Jewish history, Hon. Charles P. Daly, has stated that under the provisions of this act " naturalization could only be obtained by applying for an Act of Parliament."† This view would certainly seem to be erroneous. Not only is the text of the statute explicit, but the actual operation of the measure makes it certain that no special Act of Parliament was necessary. Judge Daly cites Smollett's *History of England* in verification or illustration of his contention. It seems hardly necessary to add that Smollett is a secondary source, and that his narrative is here inexact and garbled.

II.

The names transmitted by the colonial secretaries to the Commissioners of Trade and Plantations in London, as the persons naturalized under the provisions of the Act of 1740, are contained in two quarto vellum bound volumes of some two hundred and sixty pages each (of vol. II only 14 pages are filled), lettered " Names of Persons Naturalized in His Majesty's Plantations in America." The volumes are preserved in the Public Record Office, and are indexed : " Colonial Office Records, (Board of Trade) Plantation Journal, Vol. 59, 60."

As contemplated by the act, three classes of persons were naturalized under its provisions—(1) Jews, (2) Quakers and (3) other aliens. The first two classes were exempted from the

* *Journal of House of Commons*, vol. XXVI, p. 861.
† *The Settlement of the Jews in North America* (ed. Kohler), p. 157.

necessity of receiving the sacrament. Pennsylvania Germans furnished the largest quota of the third class, and indeed aggregate probably several times as many as all the other names together. Almost all the entries from Jamaica are of Jews. The total number of Jews recorded is 184. These are specifically described as " Jews " or " persons professing the Jewish religion," or bear distinctively Jewish names. To this number might be tentatively added 5 names, the correctness of including which in this category is uncertain. The aggregate of 189 names is distributed as follows :

Jamaica...... ..... 151, of which 1 is doubtful.
New York.......... 24,
Pennsylvania....... 9, of which 1 is doubtful.
Maryland .... 4, " " 3 are "
South Carolina...... 1,

Total .... 189, of which 5 are doubtful.

We have no means of ascertaining to what extent, if any, persons were naturalized under the act in the colonies without the fact thereof being transmitted to the commissioners in London. Possible error in the selection of Jewish names from the Commissioners' record would perhaps be avoided by comparison with the list laid before the Commons in 1753, referred to above. It has, however, been impossible to discover this list. The Journal of the House of Commons † records that "the said copy is preserved amongst the other papers of this session," but it is not contained in the printed sessional papers. Mr. Lucien Wolf speaks confidently of having seen it, but was unable to recall in what particular connection. Search and inquiry by the present writer in the British Museum, the Public Record Office and the Journal Office of the House of Commons were unattended with success.

In the debate upon the repeal of the act in 1753, Martin spoke of 185 Jews having availed themselves of its benefits,

† Vol. XXVI, p. 850.

and Sir Roger Newdigate added that 130 of these were from
Jamaica. These statements were of course based upon the
list of names then before the House. Bearing in mind that
persons were naturalized after 1753, these statements indicate a substantial but not entire agreement of the earlier
compilation with that here appended.

Of the one hundred and eighty-nine entries, one hundred
and eight are dated between 1740 and 1743, and one hundred and forty-four between 1740 and 1746. Few names,
Jewish or other, occur in the volumes after 1761, and this
fact, together with their occurrence in non-chronological
order, throws a possible doubt upon the correctness of the
dating of the 9 names ascribed to Jamaica in 1762. The
precise distribution in time of the one hundred and eighty-
nine names is as follows:

1740	53	1748	8
1741	19	1749	14
1742	6	1750	6
1743	30	1752	2
1744	7	1755	2
1745	11	1757	1
1746	18	1762	9
1747	2	Undated	1

III.

A LIST OF PERSONS THAT HAVE INTITULED THEMSELVES ^{Extract of Jew-ish names.} TO THE BENEFIT OF THE ACT (13 GEO. II) FOR NAT-
URALIZING SUCH FOREIGN PROTESTANTS AND OTHERS
THEREIN MENTIONED AS ARE SETTLED OR THAT SHALL
SETTLE IN ANY OF HIS MAJESTYS COLONIES IN AMERICA.

JAMAICA.

Tuesday the 25th Day of November, 1740. Persons professing Vol. I, fol. 21.
the Jewish Religion.

Jacob Mendes Gutteres   Isaac Fuertado
Benjamin Bravo   Moses Martius

Abraham Ribiero   D^{el} M^z Da Costa
Moses Lopes Heneriques   Isaac Ramalho
Jacob Pinto Brandon   Moses Cohen Delarha
David Bravo   Aaron Lamera

Thursday the 26th Day of February, 1740.   *Persons professing the Jewish Religion.*

Elias Fernandes Corche   Jacob Da Silva
Moses Alvares Corche   Ab^m Laguna
Aron Dias Fernandes   Jacob Fernandes Mesquitta
Jacob De la Penha   Benjn Rodrigues Gabriel
Jacob Gutteres Penha   Joseph Abrathar
Solomon Mendes   Daniel Dovalle
Jacob Lyon   Isaac Henriques Sequira
David Torres   Is^1 de la Penha
Henriq. Israel   Moses Rodrigues
Isaac Henriques Campos   Isaac Fernandes, Pr^{ll} [*Portu-*
David Salom   Rap^l Mendes   *gal*]

Vol. I, fol. 22.   *Tuesday the 2d Day of March,* 1740.

Rachaell Cardosa . . . A person professing the Christian Religion

Tuesday the 26th Day of May, 1741.   *Persons professing the Jewish Religion.*

Abraham Henriques Sequira   Abraham Lopez Henriques
Solomon Curiel   Jacob Lopez De Crasto

Tuesday the 25th Day of August, 1741.   *Persons professing the Jewish Religion.*

Isaac Nunez Da Costa   Phinelias Mattos
Daniel Alves Fernandes   Isaac Devalle
Isaac Lopes Prette   Jacob Nunez Da Costa

Tuesday the 24th Day of November, 1741.

Jacob Brandon   Leah Soares
Joseph Soares   Rebecca Pennea
Monashe Ribas

Wednesday the 24th *Day of February*, 1741.

Moses Alvares

Wednesday the 26th *Day of May* 1742.

David Mendez   Joshua Gomez Silva

Wednesday the 1st *Day of September*, 1742. *Persons professing* Vol. I, fol. 23.
the Jewish Religion.

Rodriques Moeda

Wednesday the 1st *Day of December*, 1742.

Daniel Da Silva   Daniel Cardoza

Wednesday the 23rd *Day of February*, 1762.

Jacob Pereira Mendes   Rachael Da Costa Alvaringa
Esther Pereira Mendes   Sarah Sanches
Esther Da Costa Alvaringa   Moses Ladesma
Leah Ramalho   Isaac Gomes Silva
Rachael Alvaringa

Friday the 31st *Day of May*, 1743.

Abraham Nunez Da Costa   Rachael Henriques
Leah Martins   Moses Alvares Correa
Sarah Cardoza   Jacob Laguna, Junr
Leah Cardoza   Moses Levy
Rachael Oroibo Furtado   Isaac Henriques Cuna
Sarah Nunez

Thursday the 30th *Day of August*, 1743. *Persons professing* Vol. I, fol. 24.
the Jewish Religion.

Moses Nunez da Costa   Jacob Lopes Henriques
Isaac Campos Almeyda   Hannah Lopes Riz

Tuesday the 29th *Day of November*, 1743.

Isaac Mendes Cunha   Rachael Cordoso
David Fernandes   Joshua Nunez
Joseph Alvares Corche   Abigail Mendes
Jacob Cordoso

Tuesday the 28th *Day of February,* 1743.

Sime Mendes   Henry Levy
Rebecca Laguna   Rema Torres
Sarah Lopes Henriques   Abraham Dovall Saldana
Rachael Lopes Henriques

Friday the 1st *Day of June,* 1744.

David Valentia   Abigall Valentia

Tuesday the 27th *Day of November,* 1744.   *Persons professing
the Jewish Religion.*

David Da Silva Fles

Tuesday the 26th *Day of February,* 1744.   *Persons professing
the Jewish Religion.*

Jacob Nunes Henriques   Abigail Fernandez
Ab^m Roiz Cardozo   Abram De Campos, Senr

Tuesday the 27th *Day of August,* 1745.   *Persons professing
the Jewish Religion.*

Moses Nunes Henriques   Esther Salom
Esther Lopes Pereira   Isaac Rodriques Miranda
Judith Orobio Furtudo   Elias Lazares
Rice Vega   Esther Pinto Brandon
Rachel Henriques   Rica Campos Almeyda

Thursday the 27th *Day of February,* 1745.   *Persons professing
the Jewish Religion.*

Solomon Abrahams

Thursday the 27th *Day of May,* 1746.

Moses Aguilar   Solomon Saldana

Tuesday the 26th *Day of August,* 1746.   *Persons professing
the Jewish Religion.*

Abraham Sanches   Esther Mendes
Moses Roderiques   Judica Da Silva

Benjamin Sanches	Rica Da Silva
Gabriel Mendes	Rachel Mendes
Moses Per^a Da Costa	Judith Mendes
Rachel Fernandes Pereira	Esther Mendes

Wednesday the 26th Day of November, 1746.
Rachel Lopez Depais

Tuesday the 24th Day of February, 1746.   *Persons professing* Vol. I, fol. 26.
the *Jewish Religion*.

Abraham Surzedas	Rachael Surzedas

Tuesday the 23rd Day of February, 1747.   *Persons professing*
the *Jewish Religion*.

Rebecca Nunez Vizea	Ester Henriques Furtado

Wednesday the 31st Day of August, 1748.

Abraham Pereira Mendes	Daniel Lopes Barrios
Ben. Dias Fernandes	David Nunes Trois
Sam^{ll} Pr^a Mendes	Abraham Carille

Tuesday the 28th November, 1749.   *Persons professing the*   Vol. I, fol. 27.
Jewish Religion.

Ester Nunes Trois	Ester Dias Fernandes
Judith Henriques Campos	Rachel Henriques Cunha

Tuesday the 27th February, 1749.

Abraham of Benjamin Pereira	Daniel Albuquerques
Mendes	Moses Mesquita, Senr
Jacob Nunez De Lara	Joshua Aboab

Tuesday the 29th May, 1750.
Alexander Nathane

Wednesday the 28th November, 1750.

Abigail Lopez	Isaac Henriques Furtado
Moses Dias Fernandes	

Tuesday the 26*th February,* 1750.

Isaac Rodriques Nunes　　　Jacob Mendes Seixas

SOUTH CAROLINA.

Vol. I, fol. 68.　Tobias Joseph, a Jew.　Certificate recorded 11th December, 1741.

MARYLAND.

Vol. I, fol. 89.　*Between the* 1*st of June,* 1742, *and the* 1*st of June,* 1743.

Phineas Alferino.

Between the 1*st of June,* 1743, *and the* 1*st of June,* 1744.

Jacob Stern.

April Assize, 1749.

Jacob Frank, of Frederick County.

Vol. I, fol. 90.　　　　　　　*September Term,* 1757.

Ansel Israells

PENNSYLVANIA.

Vol. I, fol. 125.　Moses Heyman, a Jew :　Philadelphia county.

NEW YORK.

Vol. I, fol. 137.　　*Between the* 1*st June,* 1740, *and the* 1*st June,* 1741.

Jews :

David Gomez

Mordecai Gomez

Daniel Gomez

Jacob Ferro, Jun[r]

Samuel Myers Cohen

Abraham Myers Cohen

Abraham Isaacs

Isaac Levy

Solomon Myers

Joseph Simson

Solomon Bares

David Huy

Abr[m] Rodrigues de Rivieres

Dan[ll] Rodrigues Vinera

Moses Lopez

Judah Hayes

Levy Samuel

Solo[n] Hart, Jun[r]

Vol. I, fol. 138.

October 23*rd*, 1741.
Isaac Nunes Henriques, Jew
Abraham De Leas, Do.

April 19*th*, 1743.
Moses Levy, Jew.

Vol. I, fol. 140.

January 21*st*, 1746.
Jacob Rodrigues Revera, Jew

April 26*th*, 1748.
Isaac Hays, Jew

October 18*th*, 1748.
Moses Benjn Franks, Jew.

PENNSYLVANIA.

Vol. I, fol. 227.

March 25, 1749.

Jos. Simon, a Jew ; Lancaster County.
Joseph Solomon, Lancaster ; a Jew sworn on the Old Vol. I, fol. 230.
Testament.
Mathias Bush, a Jew; Philadelphia City, sworn on the
Old Testament only.

September 20, 1752. *Jews sworn on the Old Testament only.* Vol. I, fol. 233.

Solomon Heim Bonn, of the city of Philadelphia.
Midrach Israel, of the city of Philadelphia.

Vol. 1, fol. 239.

March 31, 1755.

H. B. Franks [of] Yorktown, York County ; a Jew.

April 8, 1755.
Jacob Isaac.

NATURALIZATION OF JEWS IN NEW YORK UNDER THE ACT OF 1740.

By Leon Hühner, A. M., L.L.B., *New York City.*

At the first meeting of this Society, the Hon. Simon W. Rosendale presented a copy of the Act of 1740, allowing naturalization of Jews in the American colonies.[1] He called particular attention to Section 5 thereof, which required "the Secretary of every colony to send to the offices of the Commissioners for Trade and Plantations, to be kept in the City of London or Westminster, a true and perfect list of the names of all and every person and persons who have entitled themselves to the benefit of the Act, which lists so transmitted were required to be regularly entered by the Commissioners in a book to be kept for that purpose."

On that occasion Judge Rosendale recommended that these European lists be looked up with a view of identifying some of the early Jewish settlers in America.

Following this suggestion, a very valuable paper was submitted at the meeting of 1896 by Dr. J. H. Hollander, in which a complete history of the Act was given, as well as an account of the ineffective movement for its repeal in 1753. It appeared that Mr. Lucien Wolf, of London, had previously examined the archives of the Public Record Office and made a list of the names to be found in the offices of the Commissioners referred to. This list was verified by Dr. Hollander

---

[1] Simon W. Rosendale, " An Act Allowing Naturalization of Jews in the Colonies," *American Jewish Historical Society Publications*, No. 1, p. 93.

by independent research and appeared in No. 5 of the Society's Publications.[2]

The present paper is devoted to another line of research
heretofore untouched, namely, the original official lists made
in America, from which the English lists were prepared.

Investigation shows that the lists examined by Dr. Hollander are neither conclusive nor absolutely correct. Errors
naturally crept in, due partly to the clerks in America who
transcribed the names, and partly no doubt to the clerks in
England when making their entries. Furthermore, after
some years the London officials seem to have grown careless
in making entries; thus, while in New York, for instance, the
colonial officials continued to send home lists of naturalizations pursuant to statute as late as 1770, the last entry relating to New York found by Dr. Hollander in England is dated
October, 1748.

Through the courtesy of Mr. Eames, and Mr. Palsits, of the
Lenox Library, the present writer had the privilege last summer of examining a mass of original manuscripts relating to
New York, belonging to that institution. He there found a
large folio manuscript book belonging to the Emmett collection
which turned out to be the original book of entry for naturalizations in New York under the Act mentioned.

This volume adds to our knowledge of the Act and also of
the persons who took advantage thereof. In point of numbers
it adds at least ten names to the list of New York Jews not
included in the English transcript. From it we learn also
the exact date of naturalization in each instance and the
spelling of some of the names is corrected. The English list
in some cases had substituted an entirely different name from
that in the original entry. Thus, for instance, in Dr. Hollander's list a name is given as Solomon Bares; the original

---

[2] J. H. Hollander, " The Naturalization of Jews in the American
Colonies under the Act of 1740," *American Jewish Historical
Society Publications*, No. 5, p. 105.

entry in New York shows the name of the person to have been Solomon Nare.

The manuscript at the Lenox Library is entitled as follows: " The Severall Persons hereafter named took the Oaths made repeated the Declaration as Directed by an Act of Parliament made in the thirteenth year of the Reign of King George the Second—Entituled 'An Act for Naturalizing such foreign Protestants and others therein mentioned as are settled or shall settle in any of His Majesty's Colonies in America.' "

The book is marked off in parallel columns toward the binding so that the names run along over both pages, one under the other. The headings of these columns are as follows:

Names of the Persons naturalized.
Their religious Profession.
Their Temporall Profession and Place of Abode.
Minister Certifying receiving the Sacrament.
The witnesses names to the Certificate.
The day of the month.

No witnesses appear in connection with any of the Jewish names, while in the case of all other applicants the names of witnesses are given. This fact is fully explained by the provisions of the Statute. Article II provides that with the exception of Quakers and Jews " No one shall be naturalized by virtue of this Act, unless such person shall have received the Sacrament of the Lord's Supper in some Protestant and Reformed Congregation within this Kingdom of Great Britain or within some of the said Colonies in America within three months next before taking and subscribing the said oaths and making, repeating and subscribing the said Declaration, and shall at the time of his taking and subscribing the said oaths and making, repeating and subscribing the said Declaration, produce a certificate signed by the person Administering the Said Sacrament and attested by two credible Witnesses, whereof an entry shall be made in the Secretary's Office of the Colony," etc.

As the Statute provided that naturalization might take place in open court before the Chief Judge or other Judge of the Colony wherein the person resides, and that an entry be made in a book to be kept in court for the purpose, it is likely that there were several books in the different courts. These were ultimately transcribed by the Secretary of the Colony in a special book kept by him. The book at the Lenox Library is evidently the Secretary's book, whose duty it was to transmit the names to England, for it shows such transmission from time to time.

Although the statute required the names to be transmitted yearly, this provision does not seem to have been observed after 1741. Following an entry April 27, 1741, appears the following note:

" So far Sent Home in May 1741, according to the Statute."

No similar entry appears for years afterward, the last being July, 1770, followed by the remark, " Hitherto lists sent to the Board Trade." The last Jewish naturalization bears date January, 1766.

The book contains 34 Jewish names in all, each particularly described as " Jew." All are described as of the " City of New York, merchant," with the following exceptions:

Isaac Hays, Tallow chandler.
Isaac Adolphus, Trader.
Hyam Myers, Butcher.
Manuel Myers, Trader.
Isaac Elizer, Rhode Island, Merchant.
Levy Hart, of the Colony of New York, Merchant.
Jonas Solomons,　　　"　　　　"　　　　"
Joseph Jesurum Pinto, Minister of Jewish Congregaton.

The last-named was naturalized January 22, 1766, and his is the last Jewish name on the list.

While discussing this list with my friend Mr. Kohler, he suggested that the Rhode Island name may have been that of a Jew who was refused naturalization in his own colony. Investigation led to the following interesting result:

In 1762, Aaron Lopez and Isaac Elizar, both of Newport, applied for naturalization, which was refused.

The decision of the court was based in part upon the fact that the applicants were Jews. In order to give it some color of logic, however, the following far-fetched construction was put upon the Act of 1740: The Naturalization Act, it was argued, " was designed for increasing the number of inhabitants, but as the colony was already full, it could not be the intention of the Act that any more should be naturalized." On this episode, Arnold the historian suggests what is probably the truth, that the decision was not due to religious prejudice, but was simply a political expedient to prevent any increase in the voting population during the struggle then going on between Chief Justice Ward and Governor Hopkins.[3] In a paper on the " Jews of New England Prior to 1800," presented at the last meeting, the present writer called attention to the fact that Lopez promptly went to Massachusetts and obtained naturalization at Boston.[4] The original New York record now shows that Elizar at about the same time came to New York and there obtained the benefits of the Act.

It is not unreasonable to suppose that similar manuscripts have been preserved in the rest of the thirteen colonies. If the present paper serves to stimulate research in that direction and thereby to bring to light names of early Jewish settlers, its object will have been amply fulfilled.

[3] Charles P. Daly, " The Settlement of the Jews in North America," New York, 1893, pp. 82-84. See also Arnold's " History of Rhode Island," p. 496.

[4] " The Jews of New England (other than Rhode Island) prior to 1800," *American Jewish Historical Society Publications*, No. 11, p. 81. See also *Collections of the Massachusetts Historical Society*, 1858-1860, Vol. IV, p. 342.

APPENDIX. (SHOWING ARRANGEMENT IN ORIGINAL RECORD.)

Names of the Persons Naturalized.	Their Religious Profession.	Their Temporall Profession and Place of Abode.	Minister Certifying Receiving of Sacrament.	The Witnesses Names to the Certificate.	The Day of the Month.
David Gomez	Jew.	City of New York. Merchant.	.....	.....	Jan'y 24, 1740.
Mordecai Gomez	Jew.	Do.			
Daniel Gomez	Do.	Do.			
Jacob Ferro, Jur	Do.	Do.			
Samuel Levy	Do.	Do.			
Samuel Myers Cohen	Do.	Do.			
Abraham Myers Cohen	Do.	Do.			
Abraham Isaacs	Do.	Do.			
Isaac Levy	Do.	Do.			
Solomon Myers	Do.	Do.			
Joseph Simson	Do.	Do.			
Solomon Nare	Do.	.....			
David Hay	Do.	.....			
Abm. Rodrigues De Rivera	Do.	.....			
Dan'l Rodrigues Vinera	Do.	.....			
Moses Lopez	Do.	City of New York. Merchant.	.....	.....	April 27, 1741.
Judah Hay	Do.	Do.			Do.
Levy Samuel	Do.	Do.			
Solomon Hart, Jur	Do.	Do.	.....	.....	Do.

SO FAR SENT HOME IN MAY 1741 ACCORDING TO THE STATUTE.

Names of the Persons Naturalized.	Their Religious Profession.	Their Temporall Profession and Place of Abode.	Minister Certifying Receiving the Sacrament.	The Names of the Witnesses to the Certificate.	The Month & Year.
Isaac Nunes Henriques	Jew.	.....	.....	.....	Oct. 23, 1741.
Abraham De Leas	Do.	of the City of New York. Merchant.			April 19, 1743.
Moses Levy	Jew.	of the City of New York. Merchant.			Novr 4, 1745
Isaac Seixas	Do.	of the Same City. Merchant.			Jan. 21, 1746.
Jacob Rodrigues Rivera	Jew.	of the Same City. Tallow Chandler.			April 26, 1748.
Isaac Hays	Jew.	of the Same City.			Octr 18, 1748.
Moses Benjamin Franks	Jew.	Do. Trader.			July 27, 1758.
Isaac Adolphus	Jew.	Do. Butcher.			Jan'y 16, 1759.
Hyam Myers	Do.	Do. Trader.			Jan'y 16, 1759.
Manuel Myers	Jew.	Rhode Island. Merchant.			July 23, 1765.
Isaac Elizer	Jew.	Colony of New York. Merchant.			Octobr 27, 1763.
Levy Hart	Do.	Do.			Octobr 27, 1763.
Jonas Solomons	Do.	City of New York. Merchant.			April 27, 1764.
Napthaly Hart Meyers	Jew.	Do.			Jan'y 22d 1766.
Joseph Jesurum Pinto	Jew.	Do. Minister of Jewish Congn.	.....	.....	

HITHERTO LIST SENT TO THE BOARD TRADE.

There are no other Jewish names though the other entries continue to July 1770.

Some Saxe-Gothan Settlers.[*]

The following list of German and German Swiss settlers at Saxe-Gotha, or Congaree, is only a partial one. In some instances the origin of the settler is given. There were two distinct elements, the German-Swiss (Reformed) and the German (Lutheran).

DATE OF GRANT	NAME	ORIGIN
June 3, 1742.	Jno. Theyler	(Switzer)
" " "	Jac. Theiler	(Switzer)
" " "	Jac. Remensperger (Riemensperger)	(Switzer)
" " "	Ulrich Shillig	
" " "	Jno. Liver (Lever)	
" " "	Chas. Kansler (or Kanster)	
" " "	Hans Buss	
" " "	Henry Weiber	
" " "	Abram Giger (Geiger)	
" " "	Herman Gyger (Geiger)	
" " "	Hans Jac. Gyger (Geiger)	
" " "	Jno. Landriker (?)	
" " "	Henry Boume	
" " "	Casper Frey (Fry)	(Switzer)
" " "	Julius Credy	
" " "	John Gallasper	
" " "	Martin Fridig (Friday)	
" " "	Gasper Hanstear	
Sept. 7, 1742.	John Frasher	
March 2, 1743.	Jac. Spenler	
June 8, 1743.	Jacob Young (Jung)	
April 14, 1744.	Jno. Wessingher	
Oct. 5, 1744.	Philip Pool	
Nov. 29, 1744.	John Mathys (Mathias?) (near Saxe-Gotha).	
Nov. 30, 1744.	Rudolph Buchter	
Dec. 8, 1744.	Hanna Maria Stolea	
Dec. 8, 1744.	Jno. Shillig	
Dec. 8, 1744.	Michael Long	(Berne)

*Excerpted from "The German and German-Swiss Element in South Carolina, 1732-1752," by Gilbert P. Voigt, in *Bulletin of the University of South Carolina*, No. 113 (1922), 56-60.

Jan. 18, 1745. Andrew Buck.............................
Jan. 18, 1745. Melchior Sower (Sauer)..................
Jan. 31, 1745. Ulrick Bachman (Additional Grant).........
Mar. 14, 1745. J. J. Fridig (opposite SaxeGotha. Additional grant.)
Mar. 16, 1745. Jacob Drafts..........................
Mar. 18, 1745. Mich'l Craft (Croft).......(Wuerttemberg)
Mar. 19, 1745. John Rester..............(Wuerttemberg)
Apr. 22, 1745. Jno. Christian Hauser.....................
June 6, 1747. Godfrey Trayor (Dreher?)..................
Aug. 14, 1747. Solomon Ade (Addy).......(from Georgia)
Nov. 6, 1747. Christian Kotiler (via Philadelphia).........
Nov. 6, 1747. Lawrence Wetzel.........................
Nov. 6, 1745. Jac. Stackley (opposite Saxe-Gotha)..........
Nov. 6, 1747. Antony Cottler (Kotiler?).................
Nov. 6, 1747. Jno. Blewer (via Havana).................
Nov. 10, 1747. Jno. Abraham Schwerdafeger.....(Prussia)
Nov. 12, 1747. Hans Eric Scheffer (German Protestant)...
Nov. 18, 1747. Jno. Teller...................(Switzer ?)
Nov. 20, 1747. Henry Ton (had arrived about 1737).......
Jan. 13, 1748. Conrad Scheis...........................
Jan. 13, 1748. David Amstutz (Berne. Had previous grant in Orangeburg)
Jan. 22, 1748. Casper Fry (had arrived in 1737)..........
Jan. 28, 1748. Catherine Croft (Kraft)..................
Jan. 28, 1748. Abraham Eichler.......................
Mar. 4, 1748. Geo. Ackerman..........................
Mar. 9, 1748. Jacob Weaver. Arrived some time before....
Mar. 9, 1748. Jno. Geger (near Saxe-Gotha. Arrived some years before).
Apr. 30, 1748. Henry Fiesler..........................
   "   "   " Conrad Scheis..........................
   "   "   " John Friday...........................
   "   "   " Anna Baumgart......................
May 19, 1748. Mich'l Reais (From Georgia)..............
July 19, 1748. Barbary Appeal (?) ....
   "   "   " Martin Hassemager.....................
   "   "   " Christian Kohla (Kotiler?) (Near Saxe-Gotha)
   "   "   " Magdalen Appeal.......................

July 19, 1748. Jacob Burchland......................
"   "   "   Barbary Husar.......................
"   "   "   Henry Metz (Near Saxe-Gotha) ....
Dec. 20, 1748. Conrade Myer (Meyer)..........(Switzer)
"   "   "   Jacob Warle............................
"   "   "   Mary Magdalen Millner..................
Jan. 6, 1749. Christian Bendeker (Congrees or Waterees.
              Captured en route.
Jan. 12,1749. Valentine Door.........................
Jan. 19, 1749. Geo. Hind..............................
"   "   "   Maria Reyn............................
"   "   "   Jno. Bokman...........................
"   "   "   Henry Crody...........................
"   "   "   Jno. Hendrich Hillman..................
Jan. 24, 1749. Margaret Swart (From Pennsylvania).......
Feb. 2, 1749. Gilbert Guilder.........................
"   "   "   John Gable.............................
Feb. 3, 1749. Mary Ann Seaman (?).....................
"   "   "   Jno. Walder............................
Aug. 2, 1749. Hans Bother (or Bothen).................
"   "   "   John Struck............................
"   "   "   John Struck, Jr........................
"   "   "   Christian Rottlesperger (Rodelsperger).....
Sept. 6, 1749. Baletis Affray.........................

Oct. 17, 1749.	Joh. Kuller	
" " "	Mich'l Calfiel	
" " "	Geo. Ludovick Finch	
" " "	Geo. Hipp	
" " "	Hans Mich'l Swagert	
" " "	Joh. Rich	
" " "	Joh. Circus	
" " "	Joh. Jac Leitzeit	
" " "	Chris'r Saltzer	
" " "	Joh. Freyer	
" " "	Fred'k Mack	
" " "	Andreas Emmesk	
" " "	Andreas Cranmer	
" " "	Jno. Geo. Watchter	
" " "	Jno. Geo. Buckheart	
" " "	Andreas Schwachlerback	
" " "	Conrad Beck	Arived 1749.
" " "	Jno. Titerly	Palatines.
" " "	Conrad Burkmeier	
" " "	Joh. Curner	
" " "	Verner Ulmer	
" " "	Jno. Geo. Lapp	
" " "	Mich'l Looser	
" " "	Geo. Gottlieb	
" " "	Jno. Adam Epting	
" " "	Nich. Prester	
" " "	Nich. Dirr	
" " "	Chris'r Ramenstein	
" " "	Marg't Burkmayer	
" " "	Jos. Vorsner	
" " "	Chris'r Henry Hoppold	
" " "	Andreas Rift	
" " "	Clemens Fromm	
" " "	Evea Knoll	

Nov. 24, 1749.	Jno. David Mercle (German. Arrived "lately")	
" " "	Jos. Meyer	" " "
" " "	Joh. Herman	" " "
" " "	Jac. Hoffner	" " "
" " "	Peter Herr	" " "
" " "	Peter Hummel	" " "
" " "	Conrad Shirer	" " "
" " "	Michael Bucks	" " "
" " "	Jacob Bollmann	" " "
Dec. 17, 1749.	Frederick Schmebile.. (Above Saxe-Gotha)	
Dec. 15, 1749.	Abraham Pflining	" " "
" " "	Hans Geo. Franz	" (Switzer)
" " "	Hans Jacob Hogheim	" (German)
" " "	Phil. Jac. Schuller	" " "
" " "	Anna Maria Ruffin (Ruff)	" "

PENNSYLVANIA PIONEERS FROM THE
NECKAR VALLEY 1749–1750

By Dr. Friedrich Krebs

Palatine State Archives
Speyer, Germany

Again we turn to the local government records of Germany for information on eighteenth-century emigrants to Pennsylvania. The source of the present emigrant list is the Protocols of the Districts (*Oberämter*) of Heidelberg and Mosbach, which in the eighteenth century were part of the dominions of the Electors of the Palatinate, but today form part of the state of Württemberg-Baden.

These emigrants from the Electoral Palatinate had to pay a fee for their manumission from vassalage, besides the additional tax of the "Tenth Penny" or Tithe, (*Zehnten Pfennig*)–the tenth part of their property. Those without property were however manumitted gratis.

We have included in this List persons whose destination was not expressly stated as "America," if their names could be found in the Pennsylvania Ship Lists of the particular year involved. As far as the names of the emigrants could be identified in these Ship Lists—the Strassburger-Hinke *Pennsylvania German Pioneers* (Norristown, Pa.: The Pennsylvania German Society, 1934)—they have been added in brackets. The List has been published in German in *Badische Heimat* (Freiburg, May, 1953).

District of Heidelberg (1749)

Johannes Euler, citizen and master blacksmith at Hohensachsen (Kr. Mannheim), is manumitted upon payment of 10 florins (gulden) for the Tenth Penny. [Johannes Eulers, Ship *Patience*, September 19, 1749.]

Leon[h]ard Eberle, of Eiterbach (Kr. Heidelberg), may go to the "New Land" [*ins Neue Land*] with his wife and three children, with the permission of the Electoral government, upon payment of 4 florins to buy himself out of vassalage, and 40 florins for the additional tax.

Jacob Grauss [Krauss], inhabitant of Daisbach (Kr. Sinsheim), is, on account of his poverty and propertyless state, manumitted gratis in order to go to the New Land with his wife and children. [Jacob Krauss, Ship *Dragon*, September 26, 1749.]

Philipp Georg Mueller, of Meckesheim (Kr. Heidelberg), is permitted to go to the New Land with wife and two children, upon payment of 10 florins for the additional tax. [Pips Georg Müller, Ship *Chesterfield*, September 2, 1749.]

Johann Michael Mueller, of Meckesheim (Kr. Heidelberg), leaving behind the Tenth Penny on his Property, may go to Pennsylvania in the hope of better luck [*"in Hoffnung besseren Glücks"*]. [Johann Michael Müller, Ship *Speedwell*, September 26, 1749.]

Jacob Frey, of Wieblingen (today part of Heidelberg), may go free upon payment of the Tenth Penny. [Jacob Frey, Ship *Dragon*, September 26, 1749.]

George Linz, Philipp Brenner, and Georg Kumpff, from Asbach (Kr. Mosbach), receive permission to emigrate to the New Land, upon payment of the Tenth Penny. Georg Linz must also pay 10 florins for his manumission. [Jerg Lintz, Hans Philipp Brenner, Ship *Patience*, September 19, 1749.]

District of Mosbach (1749)

Whilhelm Besch, from Mittelschefflenz (Kr. Mosbach) may go to Pennsylvania.

Jacob Behr and Martin Treibel, from Eberbach (Kr. Heidelberg), may go to [New] England upon payment of the Tenth Penny. [Johann Jacob Behr, Martin Treibel, Ship *Jacob*, October 2, 1749.]

Peter Ehret, from Mittelschefflenz, may emigrate to New England upon payment of the Tenth Penny.

Adam Ludwig and Jacob Bender, from Burcken (Neckarburken), receive permission to emigrate to New England. [Hans Adam Ludwig, Ship *Patience*, September 19, 1749.]

Peter Spohn, from Schollbronn (Schollbrunn, Kr. Mosbach), may go to New England upon payment of 14 florins for manumission from vassalage and 14 florins for the Tenth Penny. [Petter Spohn, Ship *Patience*, September 19, 1749.]

Michel Zilling, from Mittelschefflenz, wants to emigrate to New England. [Michel Zilling, Ship *Patience*, September 19, 1749.]

District of Heidelberg (1750)

Johann Battenfeld, from Michelbach (Kr. Mosbach), receives permission to go with his wife, two sons and three daughters, to the New Land, upon payment of the Tenth Penny at 30 florins. [Johannes Battefeldt, Ship *Two Brothers*, August 28, 1750.]

Johann Adam Eberle, from Eiterbach (Kr. Heidelberg), is manumitted upon payment of 10 florins for manumission and 9 florins additional tax. [Adam Eberle, Ship *Brothers*, Aug. 24, 1750.]

Johann Georg Gansshorn, from Bammental (Kr. Heidelberg), baker, may emigrate gratis. [Hans Jörg Ganshorn, Ship *Two Brothers*, August 24, 1750.]

Johann Mathias Gerner, of Helmstadt (Kr. Sinsheim) wants to go to the so-called New Land. [Johan Matthes Gerner, Ship *Two Brothers*, August 28, 1750.]

Johann Georg Koberstein and Johann Georg Ludwig, of Zuzenhausen (Kr. Sinsheim), are permitted to go to the so-called New Land with their wives, Anna Catharina and Maria Margaretha; yet the former must pay 3 florins, the latter 2 florins 36 kreuzer Manumission Tax. [Hans Gorg Koberstein, Johan George Ludwig, Ship *Osgood*, September 29, 1750.]

Johann Friedrich Mueller, of Meckesheim (Kr. Heidelberg), is permitted to go to the so-called New Land, upon payment of 2 florins on his property of 20 florins.

Johann Adam Wollfarth, an orphaned citizen's son from Spechbach (Kr. Heidelberg), is released from vassalage upon payment of 20 florins and granted the right of emigration on payment of 18 florins additional tax. [Johann Adam Wolfart, Ship *Brothers*, August 24, 1750.]

PALATINE EMIGRANTS FROM THE DISTRICT OF NEUSTADT–1750

By Dr. Friedrich Krebs

Palatine State Archives

Speyer, Germany

This short new list of Palatine emigrants of the eighteenth century is derived from an extract from the Protocols of the District of Neustadt in the Electoral Palatinate for the year 1750. Since these government protocols contain only the record of permission to emigrate, and, strictly speaking, do not prove emigration itself, it is quite necessary for the historian and genealogist to search the respective church registers, to determine whether the supposed "emigrant" actually left the community or not.

In the present instance this further research has been omitted, since most of the persons who applied for permission to emigrate actually do appear in the ships' lists of emigrants landing at Philadelphia. Our references to ships and dates appended in brackets after almost every item, are naturally from Strassburger-Hinke, *Pennsylvania German Pioneers* (Norristown, Pa.: The Pennsylvania German Society, 1934).

The few persons whose names do not appear in these official lists, can be assumed also to have emigrated, yet the cautionary statement is always necessary. The Protocols of the District of Neustadt are part of the holdings of the *Palatine State Archives* at Speyer.—F.K.

1. Jacob Ackermann, citizen at Weidenthal, is permitted, along with his wife and three children, and upon payment of 10 florins for the "Tenth Penny" [Zehnten Pfennig], to go to Pennsylvania. [Jacob Ackermahnn, Ship *Anderson*, August 21, 1750.]

2. Peter Franck and Jacob Brickert, inhabitants of Lachen, are permitted along with their wives and children, and upon payment of the "Tenth Penny"—which amounts to 27 florins for the former and 5 florins 30 kreuzer for the latter, to go to Pennsylvania. [Jacob Bricker, Ship *Sandwich*, November 30, 1750.]

3. Mathias Brickert, of Lachen, is permitted to go to Pennsylvania gratis. [Matthäus Brückert, Ship *Brotherhood*, November 3, 1750.]

4. Philipp Rheinhard Gassmann, the citizen of Winzingen [today part of the City of Neustadt], is permitted, along with his wife and three children, to go to Pennsylvania. [Philipp Gassmann, Ship *Sandwich*, November 30, 1750.]

5. Johannes Guschwa, of Weidenthal, is permitted, along with his wife and two children, to go to Pennsylvania gratis.

6. Peter Herget, the citizen of Oggersheim, is permitted, along with his wife and children, upon payment of 60 florins supplementary tax and 30

florins for his stepson Christoph Braun, to go to Pennsylvania. [Petter Hergedt, Ship *Two Brothers*, August 28, 1750.]

7. Balthasar Loeffel, of Oggersheim, is permitted, upon payment of 19 florins for the "Tenth Penny," to emigrate with his wife to Pennsylvania. [Balsazar Löffler, Ship *Two Brothers*, August 28, 1750.]

8. Andreas Muehlschlaegel, the Reformed schoolmaster [Schuldiener] of Weidenthal, is permitted to go to Pennsylvania, but must first pay the supplementary tax (Tenth Penny) upon his property of 300 florins. [Johann Andreas Mühlschlägel, Ship *Patience*, August 11, 1750.]

9. David Schmitt, of Weidenthal, is permitted, upon payment of 5 florins supplementary tax (Tenth Penny), to emigrate with his wife and three daughters to Pennsylvania. [David Smith, Ship *Patience*, August 11, 1750.]

10. Johann Adam Wetzel, of Weidenthal, is permitted, upon payment of 8 florins 30 kreuzer for the "Tenth Penny," to go to Pennsylvania. [Possibly Johann Adam Wentzell, Ship *Patience*, August 11, 1750.]

11. Lorentz Laxgang, of Dannstadt, is granted free permission to leave for Pennsylvania, along with his wife and stepchildren.

12. Jacob Koerner, of Edenkoben, who wants to go to Pennsylvania, is, along with his wife, released gratis from serfdom. [This is possibly Jacob Karner, Ship *Royal Union*, August 15, 1750.]

13. Maria Catharine Hammann, of Lachen, is permitted to emigrate to Pennsylvania gratis.

18TH CENTURY EMIGRANTS FROM EDENKOBEN IN THE PALATINATE

By Dr. Friedrich Krebs

Palatine State Archives, Speyer

[Pennsylvania's genealogists are always glad when a new list of German emigrants to Pennsylvania or other American colonies turns up in 18th Century sources. During our 1952 Tour of the Palatinate, in connection with our formal visit to the "wine-happy" town of Edenkoben in the Palatinate, the *Geschäfts Anzeiger* (Edenkoben, August 2, 1952) published the following article by Dr. Krebs, Archivist in Speyer, who has unearthed other names of Pennsylvania Dutch emigrant pioneers which will be published in the forthcoming *Yearbook of the Pennsylvania German Folklore Society*. The present article was translated by the Editor.—D.Y.]

That the longing for the "Land of Unlimited Possibilities" has not abated up until the present day, is proved by a report of Dr. Friedrich Krebs, of the State Archives in Speyer, which throws light on the difficulties faced by the Palatine serfs of the 18th Century when it came to emigration.

In many respects, the emigrants of those earlier times had, even from the side of the authorities, to struggle with much greater difficulties than the emigrants of the present day, whose departure is rather encouraged by the state. For their release from bondage as subjects and their manumission from serfdom, a special duty had to be paid, besides the so-called "Tenth Penny," a sum to the extent of 10% of the emigrant's property. Yet emigrants with no means were "manumitted" anyway. But for secret emigration, the penalty was mostly the confiscation of the property. There are these facts to be noticed in the following.

From Edenkoben, then under the rule of the Electoral Palatinate, there emigrated in the 18th Century, according to the Protocols of the Bailiwick of Neustadt, a comparatively large number of persons. Actually the number may have been still higher, due to secret emigration. Many of these emigrants' names can be located in the Pennsylvania Ship Lists.

For instance, in 1750 Jacob Körner of Edenkoben, who was going to Pennsylvania with his wife, was released from serfdom gratis, likewise in 1751 George Krauss, with wife and two children. In 1752 Niclas Leonhard, who had secretly emigrated around 1749, requested manumission so that his inheritance could be handed over to him. His request was granted, yet he had to pay 35 florins (guldens) for his manumission, for the "Tenth Penny" 31 florins, and for the Military Treasury, in lieu of military service unrendered, 7 florins. His brother Wilhelm Leonhard, who later also wanted to emigrate, was described as an "ill-behaved and dissolute petitioner" (*ohnartiger und liederlicher Supplicant*), so that his request for emigration could be granted with no difficulties at all.

In 1752 Martin Grün, Heinrich Schenkel, and Christoph Müller went to "Pennsylvanien." They had to pay all the aforementioned duties, except Martin Grün who, because of his having no property, was manumitted without charge. But the request for emigration met with great difficulties in the case of the three stepdaughters of Martin Grün—Anna Barbara, Maria Elisabetha, and Maria Catharina Frank—who were such good workers, at the best age for working, and so plainly valued by the Electoral Government that they received manumission reluctantly and only after long struggles.

For the same year, 1752, a great emigration year, Philipp Carl Schenkel and Jacob Welde of Edenkoben also went as emigrants to North America, all manumitted gratis on account of their poverty. Likewise in 1752 came the departure from Edenkoben of Jacob Schuster and the wife of Johann Philipp Schenkel, both serfs of the Zweibrücken Government, with the husband of the latter. The departure of other persons, Abraham Sonntag and Jacob Schenkel, occasioned serious apprehensions on the part of the Electoral Government, on account of the competition with Pfalz-Zweibrücken, which also possessed serfs in Edenkoben.

But when the Mayor of Edenkoben reported that the Electoral Palatinate possessed 315 men and 377 women as serfs in Edenkoben, while Zweibrücken could muster only 36 men and 40 women, the right of departure was granted the petitioners for the payment of a small duty, or even gratis, "because they have so little property and cannot make a good living in Edenkoben."

Johann Adam Hartmann took the shortest road—he left the land very suddenly, for he had killed a stag on the government preserves and faced a heavy penalty! In 1764 he sailed under a false name on the Ship *Boston*, and so after his landing in Philadelphia, escaped legal prosecution!

EMIGRANTS FROM BADEN-DURLACH TO PENNSYLVANIA
1749-1755
By Dr. FRIEDRICH KREBS, Archivist, Speyer, Germany

During the years 1749-1755, emigration from southwestern Germany was at its height, as is evident from the number of ships which arrived in the harbor of Philadelphia (see Hinke-Strassburger: "Pennsylvania Pioneers," Vol. I, p. xxix). A considerable number of persons must have migrated to the "New Land" at this time from the tiny district of Baden-Durlach, judging by the great number of petitions for permits to depart that are preserved in the court archives. These petitions were first taken up by the Court Council, then passed on to the Revenue Office, which made a formal proclamation of the manumission of the parties concerned and fixed the amount of tax to be paid. The council and revenue records of Baden-Durlach are, for this reason, the chief source for research into the emigration from the region at that time.

In the list below, whenever the emigrant can be identified in the Hinke-Strassburger ship lists from the port of Philadelphia, this is indicated in a following parenthesis.

HUNOLD, Matthäus, Reformed, charcoal-burner, from Weiler bei Pforzheim, permitted to go to Pennsylvania with wife and child (Ship "Two Brothers", Sept. 21, 1751).

LOBLE, Georg, aged 70, from Wössingen, permitted to travel with his wife to join his four children already settled in Pennsylvania.

WINTHER, Samuel, also from Wössingen, to Pennsylvania with wife and children.

SCHICKLE, Georg, the younger, from Bauschlott, with wife and four children.

ROSSLE, Gabriel, from Wössingen, with wife and three children ("Shirley," Sept. 5, 1751.)

DURR, Johann Georg, from Nöttingen, cooper, unmarried ("*Duke of Wirtenberg*", Oct. 16, 1751).

SCHMELZLE, Rudolph, from Obermutschelbach.

WILDEMANN, Jacob, also from Obermutschelbach.

MEYER, Hanss Jerg, from Obermutschelbach, with wife and four children. (The last two on "Duke of Wirtenberg", Oct. 16, 1751).

WORLICH, Michael, nail-maker at Stein.

HEYD, Jacob, from Grötzingen.

FRANTZ, Jacob, also from Grötzingen, single.

NAGEL, Sebastian, from Blankenloch.

HEMPERL, Elisabetha, from Blankenloch.
(Nagel, Frantz and Heyd on ship "*Brothers*", Sept. 16, 1751).

GRONER or KRONER, Jacob, a youth from Bauschlott.

AUGENSTEIN, Christian, Anna Maria, Caspar and Hannss Georg, four unmarried children of Abraham Augenstein, widower, a citizen of Auerbach (See "*Two Brothers*", Sept. 21, 1751, and "*Duke of Wirtenberg*", Oct. 16, 1751.)

HAUER, Bernhardt and Christoph, from Blankenloch, destination not recorded. ("*Brothers*", Sept. 16, 1751.)

REICH, Mattheus, a citizen of Singen, to go to Pennsylvania "*Duke of Wirtenberg*", Oct. 16, 1751).

NAGEL, Joachim, a former grenadier, born at Blankenloch, requested manumission for himself and wife to go to Pennsylvania. ("*Brothers*", Sept. 16, 1751).

BOSSERT, Michael, unmarried, from Bauschlott.

KAUCHER, Michael, unmarried, from Göbrichen. (Both above on "*Phoenix*", Sept. 25, 1751.)

KAUCHER, Jacob the younger, of Göbrichen, manumitted with wife and children.

WORNER, Philipp Jacob, a citizen of Wössingen ("*Duke of Wirtenberg*", Oct. 16, 1751)

HAUSS, Michael of Knielingen, manumitted with his wife. ("*Brothers*", Sept. 16, 1751)

HAUSS, Johannes of Knielingen, wife and children. Found only in the council records. ("*Anderson*", Aug. 25, 1751).

SCHLICKERS, Ludwig of Knielingen, with wife and stepson.

MUSSGNUNG, D a v i d, of Grötzingen. ("*Brothers*", Sept. 16, 1751).

DECKER, Johann Jacob, unmarried, from Weissenstein ("*Kitty*", Oct. 16, 1752)

DILLMANN, Georg of Teutscheneureuth, with wife and two children

MEINZER, Martin of Knielingen, with wife and two children ("*Brothers*", Sept. 16, 1751—both the foregoing).

GRAF (GRAVIN), Barbara, unmarried, from Ispringen.

MEINZER, Johannes ,from Hagsfelden, with wife and two children ("*Brothers*", Sept. 16, 1751).

SCHWARZ, Matthias, from Auerbach.

MAYER, Michael, from Bauschlott.

BINDER, Jacob, from Bauschlott, with wife and children.

LOFFLER, Dieterich, from Grötzingen, with wife and 4 children, a tenant farmer. ("*Phoenix*", Sept. 25, 1751).

———

PENNSYLVANIA DUTCH PIONEERS
FROM BADEN–DURLACH: 1752

By Dr. Friedrich Krebs

Palatine State Archives
Speyer, Germany

Translated by Don Yoder

The Protocols of the Council and Revenue Chamber of Baden-Durlach, preserved in the General State Archives of Baden, at Karlsruhe, are the source for the present list of persons who received permission to emigrate.

The petitions for emigration were handled in the sessions of the Council and then referred to the Revenue Chamber, which formally pronounced the manumission and fixed the emigration taxes.

As far as the identity of the emigrants cited in the protocols is established with certainty, or probability, the dates of their arrival in Philadelphia have been noted from the ship lists published by Hinke and Strassburger and the number of the relevant list cited in parentheses under the abbreviation HS.

1. ARMBRUSTER, JACOB—from Söllingen, with wife and three children (Pr. 853 Nr. 936, Pr. 1336 Nr. 1058), September 27, 1752 (HS 186 C).

2. BERTSCH, GEORG—citizen at Königsbach, went to the "New Land" with his second wife and the youngest child of his first marriage, on account of continual quarreling with the children of the first marriage (Pr. 854 Nr. 1198), September 25, 1751 (HS 173 C).

3. BIETIGHOFFER, PHILIPP—From Söllingen, without specifying goal of emigration (Pr. 854 No. 1303, Pr. 1336 Nr. 1670), September 27, 1752 (HS 186 C).

4. CAMMERER, JOSEPH—of Stein, with wife and children (Pr. 853 Nr. 576, Pr. 1335 No. 769).

5. DAHLINGER, CASPAR—from Weiler, had the Tithe (Tenth Penny) to pay (Pr. 1336 Nr. 1522).

6. EURICH, HANSS (GEORG), of Königsbach, manumitted on account of poverty, goal of emigration: Pennsylvania (Pr. 854 No. 1196, Pr. 1336 No. 1427).

7. FINCK, FRIEDRICH—of Königsbach, goal of emigration: Carolina (Pr. 854 No. 1197, Pr. 1336 No. 1428).

8. GRAEB[N]ER, EMANUEL—of Königsbach, goal of emigration: Carolina (Pr. 854 No. 1194, Pr. 1336 No. 1430).

9. HAUSHALTER, LORENTZ—of Söllingen, without specifying goal of emigration (Pr. 1335 No. 956), October 23, 1752 (HS 191 C).

10. MUSSGNUG, JACOB—of Sollingen, with wife and 4 children, without specifying goal of emigration (Pr. 853 No. 996, Pr. 1336 No. 1084), September 27, 1752 (HS 186 C).

11. REISER (REISTER?), JACOB—day-laborer, of Stein, had the Tithe to pay, goal of emigration: Carolina (Pr. 853 Nr. 1, Pr. 1335 Nr. 258), September 27, 1752 (HS 184 C).

12. SCHNEIDEMANN, GEORG FRIEDRICH—day-laborer, of Stein, had the Tithe to pay, goal of emigration: Carolina (Pr. 853 Nr. 2, Pr. 1335 Nr. 259).

13. SEIZ, JOHANNES—from Russheim, with wife and 3 children to Pennsylvania, had to pay no emigration taxes, "on account of their extreme poverty [*"um deren äusserster Armut willen"*] and "since they are leaving the country really as beggars" [*"da sie als pure Bettler aus dem Lande ziehen"*] (Pr. 853 Nr. 951, Pr. 1336 Nr. 1054), October 23, 1752 (HS 191 C).

14. SPATZ, GEORG MICHAEL—of Sollingen, was with his family manumitted without payment of taxes for emigration to America, "on account of great poverty" [*"um grosser Armut willen"*] (Pr. 854 Nr. 1200, Pr. 1336 Nr. 1434), September 27, 1752 (HS 186 C).

15. STEINWENDER, DANIEL—of Stein (Pr. 853 Nr. 577, Pr. 1335 Nr. 770).

16. TIEFENBACH, MRS.—the wife of CASPAR TIEFENBACH, who has already gone from Graben to America (August 13, 1750, HS 184 C), with her children, who were so poor, that the community declared itself ready to advance the travel money (Pr. 853, Nr. 952, Pr. 1336 Nr. 1055).

17. VETTER, ADAM of Königsbach, manumitted gratis on account of poverty, goal of emigration: Carolina (Pr. 854 Nr. 1195, Pr. 1336 Nr. 1429).

18. WEISS, CONRAD—of Sollingen, without specifying goal of emigration (Pr. 1336 Nr. 1670), September 27, 1752 (HS 186 C).

19. WOESSINGER, MATTHEUS—of Darmsbach, with wife and 4 children (Pr. 853 No. 575, Pr. 1335 Nr. 823), October 20, 1752 (HS 190 C: WESSENER).

20. XANDER, DAVID—of Sollingen, with wife and children (Pr. 853 Nr. 935, Pr. 1336 Nr. 1059), September 27, 1752 (HS 186 C).

21. ZIMMERMANN, DAVID—of Berghausen, with wife and 5 children, without specifying goal of emigration (Pr. 1336 Nr. 1081), November 22, 1752 (HS 195 C).

---

§ Translated from *"Amerika-Auswanderer aus Baden-Durlach im Jahre 1752,"* by Friedrich Krebs, columns 289-292, *Senftenegger Monatsblatt für Genealogie und Heraldik,* ed. Karl Friedrich v. Frank (Schloss Senftenegg, Post Ferschnitz, Niederösterreich), III. Band. 9-10 Heft, March/April 1956.

MORE 18TH CENTURY EMIGRANTS FROM THE PALATINATE

By Dr. Friedrich Krebs

Palatine State Archives

Speyer-am-Rhein, Germany

From the *Oberamtsprotokollen von Neustadt an der Weinstrasse (Pfalz) 1754-68* [Protocols of the District of Neustadt on the Weinstrasse (Palatinate) 1754-68], come the following new names of Pennsylvania pioneers of the 18th century:

1. Renner, Johann Jacob—of Mutterstadt, permitted in 1754 to emigrate to the "New Land" with wife and children, but had to pay the tithe on property which he took out of the country. Jacob Renner is listed on the Ship *Edinburgh*, arriving at Philadelphia, September 30, 1754.

2. Moerschheimer, Henrich (Merschheimer)—citizen of Lambsheim, permitted 1764 to go to Pennsylvania, in return for the Tithe on the property he was taking with him. Henrich Morschheimer, Ship *Britannia*, September 26, 1764.

3. Wernz, Jacob, with Jacob Braun and Andres Matheis—all of Ellerstadt—"because they are not in condition to be able further to support themselves there, they ask permission to go to the New Land." Were granted permission to leave without further ado, in case none of their property remains after satisfying their creditors, otherwise an account is to be rendered. In the Ship Lists only the name of Jacob Werns appears, on the Ship, *Jeneffer*, November 5, 1764.

4. Hirschberger, Henrich—of Eppstein, Mennonite (*Wiedertäufer*), is permitted to go to the Province of Pennsylvania, upon payment of 30 florins for the Tithe. He was also permitted to take along the property which is coming to his three brothers (obviously also in America), upon payment of 156 florins. Henrich Herschberger, Ship *Crawford*, October 26, 1768.

From the *Protocols of the District of Heidelberg* (1751) we hear of other emigrants from the Odenwald: The following citizens and residents of Schoenau near Heidelberg, in the Odenwald, were, on account of their poverty, manumitted gratis: Balthasar Koenig, Joerg Happes, Johann Wagner, and Joerg Luecker. All four arrived in Philadelphia on the Ship *Queen of Denmark*, October 4, 1751: George Licker, Balzer Konig, Johanes Wagner, George Happes.

MORAVIAN PIONEERS IN THE SWATARA VALLEY—1752

Transcribed by William J. Hinke

Undoubtedly the Moravians were the best record-keepers of all the Pennsylvania Dutch church groups. For when they established a congregation, they prepared family registers of all their members, giving vital statistics of parents and children, and, most valuable of all, telling where in the old homeland the emigrant had come from.

We print here one of these lists, the *Catalogus der Geschwister in Swatara den 25. Oct. 1752* (Catalogue of the Brethren and Sisters in Swatara, October 25, 1752). It was painstakingly transcribed from the original document in the Moravian Archives at Bethlehem by the late Rev. Dr. William J. Hinke.—D.Y.

1) Ludwig Born, a tailor, from Rimschweyler in Zweybruecken, b. 1702, Reformed. Wife: Anna Marie, from Wuenschberg, b. 1705, Reformed. Husband received into Moravian membership, 1749; wife, 1750. Children: (a) Johann Daniel, b. September 18, 1726; (b) Maria Barbara, b. December 15, 1731; (c) Anna Catharina, b. 1735; (d) Christina Margaretha, b. 1738; (e) Anna Maria, b. January 28, 1741; (f) Johannes, b. March 28, 1747; and (g) Samuel, b. December 7, 1749.

2) Johannes Spittler, from Pennwihl, born December 7, 1690, Reformed. Wife: Catharina, from Ebding, Basel, born 1700, Reformed. Husband received into Moravian membership, 1749. Children: (a) Johannes, b. September 24, 1717; (b) Verona, b. November 3, 1720; (c) Jacob, b. August 30, 1722; and (d) Barbara, b. April 4, 1728.

3) Friedrich Weiser, from Schohari, born November 3, 1714, Lutheran. Wife: Anna Catharina, from Hagenburg, born February 26, 1718, Reformed. Husband received into Moravian membership, 1750. Children: (a) Friedrich, b. May 21, 1740; (b) Jacob, b. August 5, 1742; (c) Rebecca, b. April 5, 1748; and (d) Philippus, b. August 21, 1750.

4) Robert Laer, from London, born 1697, Anglican. Wife: Margaretha, from Erthon in Ireland, born 1699, Catholic. Husband received into membership, 1749. Children: (a) Henrich, b. March, 1725; (b) Robert, b. July, 1728; (c) Thomas, b. August 19, 1731; and (d) Joseph, b. March 1, 1743.

5) Casper Corr, from Nassau, born 1725, Lutheran. Wife: Barbara, from Siegen, born 1728, Reformed. Husband received into Moravian membership, 1750. Children: (a) Christian, b. January 7, 1747.

6) Philip Mies, a cabinetmaker, from Altenhausen in Wittgenstein, born 1712, Reformed. Wife: Louisa, from Kiselberg in Freudenberg, born 1721, Reformed. Husband received into Moravian membership, 1749. Children: (a) Johann Georg, b. February 7, 1740; (b) Christiana, b. November, 1742; (c) Anna Barbara, b. August 26, 1745; (d) Casper, b. June 7, 1748; and Philippus, b. September, 1750.

*8) Christian Ohrendorf, widower, from Kiselberg in Freudenberg, born 1692, Reformed. Received into Moravian membership, 1749. Children: (a) Louisa, b. 1721; (b) Anna Margaretha, b. 1724; (c) Johann Christian, b. 1727; (d) Barbara, b. 1728; (e) Magdalena, b. 1731; and Johann Heinrich, b. 1733.

9) Georg Miss, from Berghausen, born 1704, Reformed. Wife: Anna Juliana, from Ambthausen in Wittgenstein, born 1714, Reformed. Husband received into Moravian membership, 1750. Children: (a) Maria Christina, b. December 16, 1736; (b) Johann Georg, b. September 28, 1739; (c) Catharina, b. May 10, 1749; (d) Johann Gerhard, b. November, 1747; and (e) Johann Heinrich, b. January 24, 1752.

10) Christian Birme, from Guggisberg in Schwartzenburg, Reformed. Wife: Maria Sara, from Tulpehocken in Pennsylvania, born 1724, Lutheran. Both received into Moravian membership, 1751. Children: (a) Anna Maria, b. January 9, 1746; (b) Anna Barbara, b. March 22, 1749; and (c) Christian, b. April 23, 1751.

*Note: The original article jumps from number 6 to number 8. Number 7 may have been accidently omitted, or there may have been a fault in the numbering.

MORAVIAN BRETHREN IN HEIDELBERG – 1752

Transcribed by William J. Hinke

The following list of emigrant pioneers comes from the *"Catalogus der Geschwister in Heidelberg Oct. 1752"* (List of the Brethren and Sisters in Heidelberg, October, 1752). This transcription is from the William J. Hinke Collection in the Historical Society of the Evangelical and Reformed Church, at Franklin and Marshall College, Lancaster, Pa., and was made from the original in the Moravian Archives at Bethlehem, Pa.—D.Y.

1) Tobias Boeckel, from Kallstadt in the County of Leningen, born November, 1711, Lutheran. Wife: Christiana, from Muckstein (?), born May, 1714, Reformed. Husband received into Moravian membership, 1745. Children: (a) Johann Nicolaus, b. October 20, 1741; (b) Friedrich, b. November 9, 1743; (c) Maria, b. November 19, 1745; (d) Johannes, b. March 26, 1750; and (e) Magdalena, b. April 28, 1752.

2) George Brendel on the Muddy Creek, from Lorraine, born April 18, 1713, Lutheran. Wife: Eva Catharina, from Lorraine, born September 11, 1717, Lutheran. Children: (a) Anna Maria, b. August, 1741; (b) Johann Georg, b. August 12, 1743; (c) Eva Catharina, b. February 20, 1745; (d) Johannes, b. June 22, 1746; (e) Heinrich, b. March 3, 1748; (f) Elisabeth, b. January 31, 1750; and (g) Maria Barbara, b. February 19, 1752.

3) Jacob Conrad, from Miedesheim [Miekesheim?] in Alsace, born February 3, 1717, Lutheran. Wife: Maria Catharina, from Behl near Landau in the Palatinate, Reformed. Husband received into Moravian membership, 1746. Children: (a) Christian, b. December 13, 1744; (b) Johannes, b. January 15, 1747; and (c) Johan Jacob, b. September 7, 1751.

4) Johannes Fischer, from Eckartshausen, born December, 1693, Reformed. Second wife: Anna Sybilla, from Creuznach, born 1701, Lutheran. Both received into Moravian membership, 1745. Children: (a) [---]; (b) Catharina Barbara, b. September 22, 1740; and (c) Anna Maria, b. February 10, 1742.

5) Peter Foltz, a cooper, from Guntershofen in Alsace, born July 25, 1726, Lutheran. Wife: Eva Elisabeth, from the same place, Lutheran. Husband received into Moravian membership, 1752. Children: (a) Johann Stephan, b. March 25, 1747; (b) Johann Peter, b. April 1, 1749; and (c) Andreas, b. March 6, 1751.

6) Peter Frey, from Wingan in Sickingen, born September 27, 1689, Lutheran. Wife: Anna Barbara, from same place, born April 5, 1696, Lutheran. Children: (a) Maria Margaretha, b. November 20, 1716; (b) Anna Eva, b. December 30, 1718; (c) Johann Valentin, b. March 9, 1721; (d) Anna Barbara, b. September 7, 1723; (e) Johann Peter, b. November 13, 1729; (f) Christian, b. December 31, 1731; (g) Anna Maria, b. April 7, 1726; (h) Juliana, b. February, 1735; and (i) Johann Georg, b. December, 1740.

7) Friedrich Gerhardt, from Langen Selbolt in Ysenburg, born March 26, 1715. Reformed. Second wife: Barbara, from Birken in Basel, born 1718, Reformed. Both received into Moravian membership, 1745. Children: (a) Peter, b. October 28, 1737; (b) Conrad, b. November 11, 1740, baptized by Rieger; (c) Elisabeth, b. September 27, 1742; (d) Friedrich, b. September 12, 1744; (e) Johannes, b. February 1, 1749; (f) Anna Maria, b. June 2, 1749; and (g) Jacob, b. December 21, 1751.

8) Nicolaus Glat, from Waltersbach in Alsace, born November, 1713, Lutheran. Second wife: Elisabeth, from Bischweiler in Alsace, born March 25, 1720, Lutheran. Husband received into Moravian membership, 1745; wife, 1750. Children: (a) Elisabeth, b. October 27, 1742; (b) Anna Maria, b. December 14, 1744, baptized by Lischy; (c) Georg, b. November 4, 1746; and (d) Maria Catharina, b. November 14, 1751.

9) Jacob Groeter, from Gumbartshofen in Alsace, born 1708, Lutheran. Second wife: Barbara, from Breuschdorf in Alsace, born May 18, 1703, Lutheran. Both received into Moravian membership, 1745. Children: (a) Johann Georg, b. September 22, 1739; and (b) Abraham, b. January 22, 1745.

10) Johannes Keller, from Switzerland, born 1711, Reformed. Second wife: Elisabetha Eva, from Neustadt on the Hardt, Reformed. Husband received into Moravian membership, 1745; wife, 1746. Children: (a) Johannes, b. September 21, 1743.

11) Johannes Meyer, from Duerckheim on the Hardt, born June 29, 1715, Lutheran. Wife: Maria Margaretha, from Kallstadt in Alsace, born September, 1714, Reformed. Both received into Moravian membership, 1745. Children: (a) Anna Catharina, b. November 30, 1738, baptized by Schmidt; (b) Tobias, b. September 21, 1740; (c) Johannes, b. August 2, 1742; (d) Christina, b. June 19, 1745; (d) Anna Maria, b. October 17, 1747; and (e) Johann Philip, b. November 1, 1749.

12) Jacob Mueller, from Erbach in Zweybruecken, born 1708, Mennonite. Wife: Anna Elisabeth, from Gumbiller in Zweybruecken, born 1718, Reformed. Husband received into Moravian membership, 1748; wife, 1749. Children: (a) Johannes, b. July 24, 1741; (b) Salome, b. February 12, 1743; (c) Joseph, b. August 21, 1747; (d) Catharina, b. April 10, 1749; and (e) Friedrich, b. February 22, 1741.

13) Casper Ried, from Wallborn in the Westrich, born 1707, Lutheran. Wife: Anna Margareth, from Zuzenhausen in the Palatinate, born 1707, Reformed. Both received into Moravian membership, 1748. Children: (a) Johann Georg, (b) Johann Michael, (c) Elisabetha Catharina, (d) Maria Barbara, (e) Johann Casper, (f) Maria Margaretha, b. May 20, 1747; (g) Johann Philip; (h) Christina, b. 1749; and (i) Friedrich, b. October 28, 1751.

14) Heinrich Schuchart, from Eckartshausen, born 1695, Reformed. Wife: Anna Catharina, from Istlinhoffen. Husband received into Moravian membership, 1745; wife, 1748. Children: (a) Johann Jost, b. February 7, 1731; (b) Johannes, b. August, 1733; (c) Anna Maria, b. March 9, 1735;

(d) Margaretha Catharina, b. May 9, 1736; (e) Maria Christina, b. 1737; (f) Johan Heinrich, b. September 4, 1741; (g) Carl, b. 1744; (h) Tobias, b. February 8, 1747; and (i) Anna Elisabeth, b. December 4, 1749.

15) Heinrich Stoehr, shoemaker, from Langen Sulzbach in Alsace, born January 11, 1715, Lutheran. Wife: Maria Barbara, from same place, born June 16, 1715, Lutheran. Both received into Moravian membership, 1745. Children: (a) Anna Margaretha, b. August 2, 1740; (b) Philip, b. August 26, 1742; (c) Anna Maria, b. July 11, 1744; (d) Heinrich, November 25, 1746; and (e) Johannes.

16) Philip Stoehr, from Langen Sulzbach in Alsace, born February 18, 1716, Lutheran. Wife: Anna Maria, from Umckstein (?), born 1725, Lutheran. Both received into Moravian membership, 1747. Children: (a) Maria Barbara, b. August 31, 1743; (b) Anna Elisabeth, b. August 17, 1745; and (c) Maria Magdalena, b. September 11, 1751.

17) Heinrich Schmit, from Wingen in Alsace, born December 19, 1688, Lutheran. Second wife: Anna Maria, also married for the second time, from Preuschdorf in Alsace, Lutheran. Both received into Moravian membership, 1745. Children: (a) Johann Friedrich, b. April 11, 1722; (b) Balthasar, b. 1730; (c) Maria Eva, b. August 29, 1719; (d) Johann Jacob, b. June 15, 1736; and (e) Maria Dorothea, b. August, 1743.

18) Christoph Weiser, from Grossen Asbach, born February, 1699, born Lutheran, but of late a "Presbyterian" [Reformed]. Wife: Elisabeth, from Neuwiek [Neuwied?], born 1702, born Lutheran, then "Presbyterian." Husband recieved into Moravian membership, August, 1746; wife, October, 1750. Children: (a) Johann Conrad, b. September 19, 1725; (b) Margaretha, b. September 28, 1728; (c) Elisabeth, b. April 19, 1730; (d) Christoph, b. November 18, 1731; (e) Jacob, b. September 22, 1736; (f) Anna, b. April 5, 1738; (g) Benjamin, b. March 8, 1740; (h) Jabez, b. August 4, 1742; and (i) Georg Friedrich, b. May 22, 1746.

RECORDS OF EMIGRANTS FROM ENGLAND AND SCOTLAND TO NORTH CAROLINA, 1774-1775

Edited by A. R. Newsome

I

INTRODUCTION

Pursuant to a letter from John Robinson, secretary of the Treasury, December 8, 1773, customs officials in England and Scotland supplied lists of persons who took passage on ships leaving Great Britain during the years 1773-1776, giving names, ages, quality, occupation, employment, former residence, reasons for emigrating, and the name of the vessel and master. These records, somewhat incomplete as now preserved in the Public Record Office of Great Britain under the classification Treasury Class 47, Bundles 9-12, contain many thousands of names and important information on a remarkable population movement which was of great significance to America and of arresting attention to the landed and manufacturing interests and the government of Great Britain.[1] They have been printed in part in *The New England Historical and Genealogical Register* (1908-1911).

The largest group consisted of indented servants bound for New York, Pennsylvania, Maryland, and Virginia; and the next largest, of emigrants sailing from ports in northern England to Nova Scotia, Virginia, and New York. The emigration practically ceased after September, 1775. The movement from Scotland was due chiefly to the oppressive rent policy of the Highland proprietors and middlemen of the region extending from Ayr County to the Shetland Islands. A traveler on an emigrant ship in 1774 wrote: "It is needless to make any comment on the conduct of our Highland and Island proprietors. It is self-evident what consequences must be produced in time from such numbers of subjects being driven from the country. Should levies be again necessary, the recruiting drum may long be at a loss to procure such soldiers as are now aboard this vessel."[2]

---

[1] *Acts of the Privy Council of England, Colonial Series*, V, 340.
[2] Charles M. Andrews, *Guide to the Materials for American History, to 1783, in the Public Record Office of Great Britain*, II, 224-5.

However, in the war which began a year later between England and the American colonies, many of the Highlanders were loyal to England and from them was recruited the Royal Highland Regiment. Economic conditions were of paramount importance in driving the emigrants from England and Scotland and in luring them to the New World.

With less attractive economic conditions, North Carolina did not receive so large a share of the new settlers, particularly those from England, as did Virginia, Maryland, Pennsylvania, or New York. The mass movement to North Carolina was more pronounced among the Scotch Highlanders, due partly to the fact that since about 1739 many of their kinsmen had already settled on the Cape Fear in the counties of Cumberland, Bladen, and Anson. In 1770 the General Assembly, in behalf of about sixteen hundred Highlanders who had landed in the province during the past three years, passed an act exempting settlers who came direct from Europe from the payment of all taxes for a term of four years.[3] At the outbreak of the Revolution, the estimated number of Scotch Highlanders in North Carolina was 15,000.[4]

The compilation here printed is from transcripts in the North Carolina Historical Commission of the selected records of those emigrants whose destination was North Carolina.

The list of emigrants from England to North Carolina contains about one hundred names. There are nearly three times as many males as females, and the average recorded age of the entire group is twenty-five years. Twenty-three are listed as indented servants, of whom three are women, nine are indented for four years, and two for two years. The chief group consists of artisans from the cities of England. Several pleasure-seekers and six family groups are noted.

Nearly five hundred names are in the lists from Scotland. There are nearly one hundred family groups. The males exceed the females in the ratio of about three to two, and there are seventy children without sex designation. The average recorded age is twenty-five years. The majority consists of farmers and laborers from the Highland counties of Argyle, Sutherland, and

---

3 *Acts of the Privy Council of England, Colonial Series,* V. 340.
4 R. D. W. Connor, *Race Elements in the White Population of North Carolina,* 57.

Caithness. Low wages, high rents, low prices of cattle, high prices of bread due to distilling, the conversion of farm lands into sheep pastures, and the exactions of landlords at home, added to the reputation of Carolina for high wages, cheap land, and plentiful provisions, account largely for the emigration.

RECORDS OF EMIGRANTS FROM ENGLAND[5]

An Account of all Persons who have taken their passage on Board any Ship or Vessel, to go out of this Kingdom from any Port in England, with a description of their Age, Quality, Occupation or Employment, former residence, to what Port, or place they propose to go, & on what Account, & for what purposes they leave the Country[6]

FROM JANUARY 15 TO JANUARY 23, 1774

Embarked from the Port of London

William Wilson, 38, Planter, London, Carolina, Carolina, Jn⁰. Besnard, as a planter.

Benjamin Blackburn, 28, Clergyman, London, Carolina, Carolina, Jn⁰. Besnard, to settle there.

Robert Rose, 20, Planter, London, Carolina, Carolina, Jn⁰. Besnard, as a planter.

George Ogier, 15, Planter, London, Carolina, Carolina, Jn⁰. Besnard, as a planter.

Robᵗ. Knight, 26, Planter, London, Carolina, Carolina, Jn⁰. Besnard, as a planter.

Henry Chapman, 30, Jeweller, London, Carolina, Carolina, Jn⁰. Besnard, to work at his Business.

Henry Maskal, 19, Clerk, London, Carolina, Carolina, Jn⁰. Besnard, as a Clerk.

John Williams, 30, Cabinet Maker, London, Carolina, Carolina, Jn⁰. Besnard, for Employment.

Thomas Vernan, 22, Silk Throwster, London, Carolina, Carolina, Jn⁰. Besnard, for Employment.

Embarked from the Port of Falmouth[7]

Colin Campbell, ..., ..., Carolina, Le De Spencer (Packet Boat), Capt. Pond, no further Account.

Custom House London, 15ᵗʰ February 1774. Exᵈ. Jn⁰. Tomkyns.[8]

[5] These records are compiled from transcripts in the North Carolina Historical Commission of selections from emigration lists in Treasury Class 47, Bundle 9, in the Public Record Office of Great Britain.
[6] The information concerning each emigrant, in the order given, is classified in the original reports under the following headings: names; age; quality, occupation or employment; former residence; to what port or place bound; by what ship or vessel; master's name; for what purposes they leave the country.
[7] A port in Cornwall in southwest England.
[8] Endorsed: "Sixth Week Account of the Emigration."

From February 20 to February 27, 1774

Embarked from the Port of London

William Scott, 21, Malster, Scotland, North Carolina, Margaret & Mary, Sam[l]. Tzatt, for Employment.

Margaret Scott, 16, Spinster, Scotland, North Carolina, Margaret & Mary, Sam[l]. Tzatt, for Employment.

William Sim, 24, Husbandman, Scotland, North Carolina, Margaret & Mary, Sam[l]. Tzatt, for Employment.

Jane Sim, 24, Wife to William Sim, Scotland, North Carolina, Margaret & Mary, Sam[l]. Tzatt, for Employment.

David Marshal, 24, Clerk, Scotland, North Carolina, Margaret & Mary, Sam[l]. Tzatt, as a Clerk.

James Blakswik, 21, Clerk, Scotland, North Carolina, Margaret & Mary, Sam[l]. Tzatt, as a Clerk.

David Wilson, 38, Merchant, London, Carolina, Union, W[m]. Combs, on Business.

John Macklin, 24, Gentleman, Oxford, Carolina, Union, W[m]. Combs, to Settle.

Mary Macklin, 23, Wife to John Macklin, Oxford, Carolina, Union, W[m]. Combs, to Settle.

Lewis Ogier, 47, Weaver, London, Carolina, Union, W[m]. Combs, to Settle.

Catherine Ogier, 40, Wife to the above, London, Carolina, Union, W[m]. Combs, to Settle.

Thomas Ogier, 20, Silk Throwster, London, Carolina, Union, W[m]. Combs, to Settle.

Lewis Ogier, 19, Silk Throwster, London, Carolina, Union, W[m]. Combs, to Settle.

Catherine Ogier, 16, Spinster, London, Carolina, Union, W[m]. Combs, to Settle.

Lucy Ogier, 13, Spinster, London, Carolina, Union, W[m]. Combs, to Settle.

Charlotte Ogier, 9, Spinster, London, Carolina, Union, W[m]. Combs, to Settle.

John Ogier, 8, School Boy, London, Carolina, Union, W[m]. Combs, to Settle.

Mary Ogier, 6, Spinster, London, Carolina, Union, W[m]. Combs, to Settle.

Peter Ogier, 5, School Boy, London, Carolina, Union, W[m]. Combs, to Settle.

Custom House London, 22[d] April 1774. Ex[d]. Jn[o]. Tomkyns.[9]

---

9 Endorsed: "The Eleventh Week's Emigration Account."

FROM MARCH 21 TO MARCH 28, 1774

Embarked from the Port of Liverpool

John Edward, 26, Farmer, Cheshire, South Carolina, Polly, ...,
To Farm.

Jane Edward, 27, his Wife, Cheshire, South Carolina, Polly,
............., going with her Husband.

William Simpson, 43, Cooper, B Lincolnshire, South Carolina,
Polly, ..., To Trade.

James Wilson, 18, Sadler, Bedfordshire, South Carolina, Polly,
............., To Trade.

James Clark, 42, Butcher, Middlesex, South Carolina, Polly,
............., To Trade.

William Walker, 37, Merchant, Yorkshire, South Carolina, Polly,
............., To Trade.

Custom Ho: London, 28th May 1774. Exd. Jno. Tomkyns.[10]

FROM APRIL 19 TO APRIL 26, 1774

Embarked from the Port of London

Janet Belton, 20, Spinster, London, Carolina, Magna Charta, Rd.
Maitland, going to her Friends.

Tobiah Blackett, 25, Spinster, London, Carolina, Magna Charta,
Rd. Maitland, going to her Friends.

Custom H. London, 22d. June 1774. Exd. Jno. Tomkyns.[11]

FROM MAY 10 TO MAY 17, 1774

Embarked from the Port of London

John Grafton, 25, Drawing Master, London, Carolina, Briton,
Alexr. Urquhart, on Business.

Nathaniel Worker, 25, Gentleman, London, Carolina, Briton,
Alexr. Urquhart, on Pleasure.

Custom Ho. London, 5th July 1774. Exd. Jno. Tomkyns.[12]

FROM MAY 17 TO MAY 24, 1774

Embarked from the Port of London

Mary Bands, 35, Widow, Herts, North Carolina, Friendship, John
Smith, Indented Servant for Four Years.

Mary Kenneday, 21, Spinster, Scotland, North Carolina, Friendship, John Smith, Indented Servant for Four Years.

John Brown, 21, Book keeper, Birmingham, North Carolina,
Friendship, John Smith, Indented Servant for Four Years.

George Taverner, 21, Groom, Southwark, North Carolina, Friendship, John Smith, Indented Servant for Four Years.

---

[10] Endorsed: "The Fifteenth Week of the Emigration Account."
[11] Endorsed: "The Nineteenth Week of the Emigration Account."
[12] Endorsed: "The Twenty-Second Week of the Emigration Account."

FROM MAY 17 TO MAY 24, 1774—*continued*

Embarked from the Port of London

Edward Gilks, 22, Leather dresser, Coventry, North Carolina, Friendship, John Smith, Indented Servant for Four Years.

John Forster, 24, Printer, London, North Carolina, Friendship, John Smith, Indented Servant for Four Years.

Thomas Winship, 26, Clockmaker, Reading, North Carolina, Friendship, John Smith, Indented Servant for Four Years.

John Darby, 40, Baker, London, North Carolina, Friendship, John Smith, Indented Servant for Four Years.

William Andrews, 31, Carpenter, Surry, North Carolina, Friendship, John Smith, Indented Servant for Four Years.

Custom H°. London, 13 July 1774. Ex^d. Jn°. Tomkyns.[13]

FROM MAY 24 TO MAY 31, 1774

Embarked from the Port of London

Miss Tong, 16, Spinster, London, Carolina, Pallas, J. Turner, going on Pleasure.

M^r. Ginnings, 25, Clerk, London, Carolina, Pallas, J. Turner, as Clerk to a Merchant.

M^rs. Molley, 30, ..., London, Carolina, Pallas, J. Turner, going to her Husband.

Custom H°. London, 13th. July 1774. Ex^d. Jn°. Tomkyns.[14]

FROM JULY 10 TO JULY 17, 1774

Embarked from the Port of London

Sarah White, 56, Merchant, London, Carolina, Carolina, Jn°. Besnard, going on Business.

John Detlaf, 30, Taylor, London, Carolina, Carolina, Jn°. Besnard, going to Settle.

Sarah Detlaf, 25, Wife of John Detlaf, London, Carolina, Carolina, Jn°. Besnard, going to Settle.

Custom H°. London, 15 August 1774. Ex^d. Jn°. Tomkyns Assist: Insp^r. Genl.[15]

FROM JULY 31 TO AUGUST 7, 1774

Embarked from the Port of London

John Butler, 25, Gentleman, London, Carolina, Carolina Packet, John White, going to Settle.

Ann Butler, 25, Wife of John Butler, London, Carolina, Carolina Packet, John White, going to Settle.

---

[13] Endorsed: "The Twenty-Third Week of the Emigration Account."
[14] Endorsed: "The Twenty-Fourth Week of the Emigration Account."
[15] Endorsed: "The Thirty-First Week of the Emigration Account."

FROM JULY 31 TO AUGUST 7, 1774—*continued*

Embarked from the Port of London

Thomas Andrews, 35, Potter, London, Carolina, Carolina Packet, John White, going to Settle.

William Templeman, 28, Jeweller, London, Carolina, Carolina Packet, John White, going to Settle.

John Smith, 22, Cabinet Maker, London, Carolina, Carolina Packet, John White, going to Settle.

Custom Hº. London, 31ˢᵗ. August 1774. Exᵈ. Jnº. Tomkyns, Assist: Inspʳ. Genˡ.[16]

FROM AUGUST 14 TO AUGUST 21, 1774

Embarked from the Port of London

David Adkins, 22, Cooper, Lincoln, Carolina, William, Philip Wescott, Indented Servant.

James Nichols, 24, Silver Caster, London, Carolina, William, Philip Wescott, Indented Servant.

Thomas Winter, 21, Husbandman, Leicester, Carolina, William, Philip Wescott, Indented Servant.

John Rixon, 22, Brazier & Copper Smith, Birmingham, Carolina, William, Philip Wescott, Indented Servant.

Benjamin Evans, 22, Sail Cloth Weaver, Cornwall, Carolina, William, Philip Wescott, Indented Servant.

John Anthony, 21, Baker, Middlesex, Carolina, William, Philip Wescott, Indented Servant.

James Smith, 21, Painter & Glazier, Nottingham, Carolina, William, Philip Wescott, Indented Servant.

Michael Delancy, 21, Husbandman, Ireland, Carolina, William, Philip Wescott, Indented Servant.

Custom House London, 24ᵗʰ Octob- 1774. Exᵈ. Jnº. Tomkyns Assist: Inspʳ. Genˡ.[17]

FROM OCTOBER 3 TO OCTOBER 10, 1774

Embarked from the Port of London

Rachael L'Fabuere, 40, Lady, London, ... Curling, going for Pleasure.

Jane Bignell, 47, Servant of Rachael L'Fabuere, London, Carolina, London, ... Curling, going with Mʳˢ L'Fabeure.

Ann Bowie, 36, Servant of Rachael L'Fabeure, London, Carolina, London, ... Curling, going with Mʳˢ L'Fabeure.

Elizᵃ. Batty, 16, a native of Carolina, London, Carolina, London, ... Curling, going home.

Ann Weston, 30, Lady, London, Carolina, London, ... Curling, going for pleasure.

---

[16] Endorsed: "The Thirty-Fourth Week of the Emigration Account."
[17] Endorsed: "Emigration Account. No. 36."

FROM OCTOBER 3 TO OCTOBER 10, 1774—*continued*

Embarked from the Port of London

John West, 28, Gentleman, London, Carolina, London, ...
Curling, going for pleasure.
John Auldjo, 15, Gentleman, London, Carolina, London, ...
Curling, going for pleasure.
Alex[r]. Auldjo, 16, Gentleman, London, Carolina, London, ...
Curling, going for pleasure.
Robert Dee, 33, Gentleman, London, Carolina, London, ...
Curling, going for pleasure.
Henry Houseman, 35, Gentleman, London, Carolina, London,
.... Curling, going for pleasure.

Embarked from the Port of Newcastle

Thomas Stead, 17, Butcher, Hull, Cape Fear, Rockingham, Richard Hopper, going to his Father, who lives there.
Custom H[o]. London, 10th Novemb. 1774. Ex[d]. Jn[o]. Tomkyns Assist: Insp[r]. Gen[l].[18]

FROM OCTOBER 17 TO OCTOBER 24, 1774

Embarked from the Port of London

Stephen Eglin, 25, Draper, London, Carolina, Newmarket, Gilbert Wilson, going to settle.
Jasper Scouler, 30, Carpenter, London, Carolina, Newmarket, Gilbert Wilson, going to settle.
Rob[t]. Maxwell, 18, Clerk, Scotland, Carolina, James, Isaac Thompson, going to settle.
Willson Dabzall, 25, Jeweller, Scotland, Carolina, James, Isaac Thompson, going to settle.
Bezabeer Forsyth, 22, Gentleman, Scotland, Carolina, James, Isaac Thompson, going to settle.
Sarah Eastwood, 16, Spinster, London, South Carolina, Lowther, Tho[s]. Cowman, Indented Servant.
Joseph Dyer, 21, Waiter, London, South Carolina, Lowther, Tho[s]. Cowman, Indented Servant.
William Kenneday, 25, Peruke Maker, London, South Carolina, Lowther, Tho[s]. Cowman, Indented Servant.
Ralph Richardson, 35, Gardener, Surry, South Carolina, Lowther, Tho[s]. Cowman, Indented Servant.
Custom H[o]. London, 5th Decemb. 1774. Ex[d]. Jn[o]. Tomkyns. Assist: Insp[r]. Gen[l].[19]

---

[18] Endorsed: "Emigration Account. No. 43."
[19] Endorsed: "Emigration Account. No. 45."

From November 7 to November 14, 1774

Embarked from the Port of London

William Ripley, 22, Farmer, York, Carolina, Mary & Hannah, Henry Dixon, going to Settle.

John Sanderson, 45, Farmer, York, Carolina, Mary & Hannah, Henry Dixon, going to Settle.

John Blythe, 32, Gentleman, London, Carolina, Mary & Hannah, Henry Dixon, on Pleasure.

James Flatt, 25, Taylor, London, Carolina, Mary & Hannah, Henry Dixon, Indented Servant for two years.

James Trenham, 22, Butcher, York, Carolina, Mary & Hannah, Henry Dixon, Indented Servant for two years.

Custom Hᵒ. London, 5ᵗʰ December 1774. Exᵈ. Jnᵒ. Tomkyns Assist: Inspʳ. Genˡ.[20]

From November 28 to December 6, 1774

Embarked from the Port of London

John Mackenzie, 16, Clerk & Bookkeeper, Scotland, Carolina, Briton, Alexʳ. Urquhart, going to settle.

Alexander Douglas, 22, Husbandman, Scotland, Carolina, Briton, Alexʳ. Urquhart, going to settle.

Christopher Smith, 49, Husbandman, Switzerland, Carolina, Briton, Alexʳ. Urquhart, going to settle.

Esther Smith, 35, Wife to the above, Switzerland, Carolina, Briton, Alexʳ. Urquhart, going to settle.

Andrew Milborn, 7, Child, Switzerland, Carolina, Briton, Alexʳ. Urquhart, going to settle.

Christopher Milborn, 2, Child, Switzerland, Carolina, Briton, Alexʳ. Urquhart, going to settle.

Custom Hᵒ. London, 13ᵗʰ Janry 1775. Exᵈ. Jnᵒ. Tomkyns Assist: Inspʳ. Genˡ.[21]

---

[20] Endorsed: "Emigration Account. No. 48."
[21] Endorsed: "Emigration Account. No. 51."

RECORDS OF EMIGRANTS FROM SCOTLAND[22]

R. E. Philips to John Robinson

Sir

In obedience to your Letter of the 8th. of December 1773, I am directed to enclose to You, Lists of Persons, who have taken their Passage from the Ports of Port Glasgow[23] and Kirkaldy,[24] for North America on board the Ships Commerce and Jamaica Packet, for the Information of the Right Honorable the Lords Commissioners of His Majesty's Treasury.

Customhouse Edinburgh   R. E. Philips
20th. June 1775

Port Kirkaldy An Account of Emigration from this Port and precinct to America or other Foreign Ports from the 5th. of June 1775, to the 11th. d°. both inclusive.

Emigrants on board the Jamaica Packet of Burntisland[25] Thomas Smith master for Brunswick North Carolina.

Miss Elizabeth Mills & her servant going to reside in S°. Carolina from Dundee.[26]

John Durmmond & John Marshall Coopers from Leith,[27] goes out because they get Wages than in their own Country.

John Douglas Labourer from Dundee, goes out for the above Occasion John Mills and Thomas Hill Joiners from D°. go to settle in S°. Carolina.

Andrew Williamson, James Jamaison & William Mitchell Farmers & Fishermen from Schetland[28] with their Wives & seven Children.

Farmers and Fishermen go abroad because the Landholders in Schetland have raised their rents so high that they could not live without sinking the little matter they had left. Total 20 Passengers.

N.B. no other Emigration from this Port or precinct in the Course of this week.

Signed   { Robert Whyt Coll[r]:
             { Philip Paton Comp[r]:

---

22 These records are compiled from transcripts in the North Carolina Historical Commission of selections from emigration lists in Treasury Class 47, Bundle 12, in the Public Record Office of Great Britain, under the title, "Lists of Emigrants from Scotland to America with letters from Comers. of Customs in Scotland touching the sailing of the Emigrant Ships, 1774-5."
23 In Renfrew County on the River Clyde.
24 In Fife County across the Firth of Forth from Edinburgh.
25 Near Kirkcaldy.
26 In Forfar County on the eastern coast.
27 Near Edinburgh.
28 The Shetland Islands off the northern coast of Scotland.

Port Stranraer,[29] An Account of Emigrants shipped at Stranraer the
31st May 1775 on board the Jackie of Glasgow James Morris Master
for New York in North America, with a Description of their Age,
Quality, Occupation, Employment, Former Residence, On what Account and for what purposes they leave the Country.[30]

25, Jas. Matheson, 38, Labourer, New Luce,[31] North Carolina,
In hopes of good Employment.

26, Jean McQuiston, 27, ..., New Luce, North Carolina,
....

27, Margt. Matheson, 4, ..., New Luce, North Carolina,
....

28, Jno. McQuiston, 46, Labourer, Inch,[31] North Carolina, In
hopes of better Employmt.

29, Cathr: Walker, 46, ..., New Luce, North Carolina, For a
better way of doing.

36, Jas. McBride, 38, Farmer, New Luce, North Carolina, The
High rent of Land.

37, Janet McMiken, 39, ..., New Luce, North Carolina,
....

38, Archd. McBride, 7, ..., New Luce, North Carolina, ...

39, Eliz: McBride, 5, ..., New Luce, North Carolina, ...

40, Jenny McBride, 4, ..., New Luce, North Carolina, ...

61, Jas. Steven, 27, Farmer, Inch, No. Carolina, In hopes of
better Bread.

62, Chrn. Steven, 23, ..., Inch, No. Carolina, with her
Brother.

63, Sarah Steven, 16, ..., Inch, No. Carolina, with her
Brother.

64, Thos. Steven, 11, ..., Inch, No. Carolina, with his
Brother.

65, Jno. Dalrymple, 40, Farmer, New Luce, No. Carolina, The
High Rent of Land.

66, Marg. Gordon, 39, ..., New Luce, No. Carolina, ...

67, Mary Dalrymple, 19, ..., New Luce, No. Carolina, ...

68, Jn. Dalrymple, 17, ..., New Luce, No. Carolina, ...

69, Archd. Dalrymple, 15, ..., New Luce, No. Carolina, ...

70, Jas. Dalrymple, 11, ..., New Luce, No. Carolina, ...

71, Ann Dalrymple, 9, ..., New Luce, No. Carolina, ...

72, Janet Dalrymple, 7, ..., New Luce, No. Carolina, ...

73, Jean Dalrymple, 5, ..., New Luce, No. Carolina, ...

74, Wm. Dalrymple, 2, ..., New Luce, No. Carolina, ...

---

[29] On Loch Ryan in Wigtown County in southwestern Scotland.
[30] In the order here given, the information is classified in the original report under the
following headings: number, emigrants' names, ages years, occupation or employment,
former residence, to what port or place bound, on what account and for what purposes they
leave the country.
[31] Near Stranraer.

Port Stranraer—*continued*
75, Alex^r. McBride, 22, Labourer, New Luce, N°. Carolina, In hopes of better Employment.
78, John Duff, 20, A Herdsman, New Luce, N°. Carolina, In hopes of good Employ^t.
79, Wm Eckles, 40, Shoemaker, Inch, N°. Carolina, In hopes of good Business.
80, Martha McKenzie, 45, ..., Inch, N°. Carolina, ...
81, John Eckles, 12, ..., Inch, N°. Carolina, ...

Customh°. Stranraer 5 June 1775.

N.B. As all the Married Women follow their Husbands and the Children their parents, We have inserted no Reason, for their leaving the Country, after their Names.

John Clugston Collr.
Polk McIntire
Comp.

R. E. Philips to John Robinson

Sir,
In obedience to your Letter of the 8th. of December 1773, I am directed to inclose to you, a List of Persons who have taken their Passage from the Port of Greenock,^{32} for North America, on board the Ship Christy Hugh Rellie Master bound to New York, and Georgia, and the Ship Ulysses James Wilson Master bound for North Carolina, for the Information of the Right Honorable the Lords Commissioners of His Majestys Treasury.

Customhouse Edinburgh, 8th May 1775.   R. E. Philips

Port Greenock List of Passengers from the 28th April 1775, Inc^l. to the 5 May 1775 Exclusive, [by the Ulysses James Wilson Master for North Carolina].^{33}

Math. Lyon, 49, Weaver, Glasgow,^{34} Want of Employ.
Mary Lyon, his spouse, 50, ..., Glasgow, ...
James Lyon, 21, Weaver, Glasgow, Want of employ.
John Kennburgh, 24, Labourer, Glasgow, Want of employ.
James Kennburgh, 27, Labourer, Glasgow, Want of employ.
John McNabb, 24, Labourer, Argyleshire,^{35} Want of employ.
Jean Campbell his Spouse, 19, ..., Argyleshire, ...
Tebby McNabb, 20, to get a husband, Argyleshire, ...
Doug. McVey, 30, Labourer, Argyleshire, Want of employ.
James Buges, 27, Merchant, Edinb., to follow his business.
Marg. Hog his spouse, 25, to comfort her husband, Edinb., ...

Ed. Penman D Coll^r
John McVicar D Comp

---

32 In Renfrew County near Port Glasgow.
33 The information in the order given here is classified in the original report under the headings: names, age, occupation, former place of residence, reasons for emigration.
34 In Lanark County on the River Clyde.
35 On the western coast of Scotland.

R. E. Philips to John Robinson

Sir

In obedience to your Letter of the 8th of December 1773, I am directed to inclose to you, a List of Persons who have taken their Passage from the Port of Greenock, for North America, on board the Ship Monimia Edward Morrison Master, bound for New York, and the Ajax Robert Cunningham Master for North Carolina, for the Information of the Right Honorable the Lords Commissioners of His Majestys Treasury.

Custom house Edinburgh
8th June 1775

R. E. Philips

List of Passengers from the 26th of May 1775 Inclusive to the 2[d] June 1775 Exclusive.[36]

Walter Mcfarlane, 20, Gentleman, To be a Merchant, North Carolina, In the Ajax Robert Cunningham Master.

Mary Menzies, 25, Lady, Going to her Husband, ..., In the Ajax Robert Cunningham Master.

Signed $\left\{\begin{array}{l}\text{Edward Penman D. Collector} \\ \text{John McVicar D. Comp}^r \\ \text{John Dunlop Tide Surveyor}\end{array}\right.$

Commissioners of the Customs in Scotland to John Robinson

Sir,

The inclosed Paper is a List of Persons lately sailed as Emigrants, to Wilmington in North Carolina, from the Port of Greenock, which We transmit to you Sir, for the Information of the Right Honorable the Lords Commissioners of the Treasury.

Charterhouse Edinburgh, 22 August 1774. $\left\{\begin{array}{l}\text{Arch}^d \text{ Menzies} \\ \text{George Clerk Maxwell} \\ \text{Basil Cochrane}\end{array}\right.$

List of Passengers on board the Ship Ulysses James Chalmers Mas[r] for Wilmington in North Carolina.[37]

Robe[t] McNicol, 30, Glenurcha,[38] Gent[n], High Rents and oppression.
Jean Campbell, 24, Glenurcha, his wife, ...
Annapel McNicol their Daug., 8, Glenurcha, ...
Abram Hunter, 28, Greenock, Shipmas., To Build.
Thomas Young, 21, Glasgow, Surgeon, To follow his Trade.
John McNicol, 24, Glenurcha, Workman, High rents & oppression.

----

[36] The information in the order given is classified in the original report under the headings: names, age, occupation, on what account and for what purpose they go, to what place bound, in what ship they take their passage.
[37] The information in the order given is classified in the original report under the headings: passengers' names, age, former place of residence, business, reasons for emigrating.
[38] In Argyle County on the western coast of Scotland.

Angus Galbreath, 30, Glenurcha, Workman, Poverty Occasioned by want of work.

Katrine Brown his wife, 26, ..., ..., Poverty Occasioned by want of work.

Angus Fletcher, 40, Glenurcha, Farmer, High rents & Oppression.

Katrine McIntyre his wife, 40, Glenurcha, ..., High rents & Oppression.

Euphame Fletcher, 10, Glenurcha, their child, High rents & Oppression.

Mary Fletcher, 6, Glenurcha, their child, High rents & Oppression.

Nancy Fletcher, 3, their child, High rents & Oppression.

John McIntyre, 45, Glenurcha, Farmer, High rents & Oppression.

Mary Downie, 35, Glenurcha, his wife, High rents & Oppression.

Nancy McIntyre, 11, Glenurcha, their child, High rents & Oppression.

Don^d McIntyre, 8, Glenurcha, their child, High rents & Oppression.

Christy McIntyre, 5, Glenurcha, their child, High rents & Oppression.

John McIntyre, 4, Glenurcha, their child, High rents & Oppression.

Duncan McIntyre, 40, Glenurcha, Farmer, High rents & Oppression.

Katrine McIntyre, 28, Glenurcha, his wife, High rents & Oppression.

John Sinclair, 32, Glenurcha, Farmer, High rents & Oppression.

Mary Sinclair, 32, Glenurcha, his wife, High rents & Oppression.

Donald McIntyre, 28, Glenurcha, Farmer, High rents & Oppression.

Mary McIntyre, 25, Glenurcha, his wife, High rents & Oppression.

Don^d McFarlane, 26, Glenurcha, Farmer, High rents & Oppression.

Don^d McFarlane, 6, Glenurcha, his son, High rents & Oppression.

Duncan Sinclair, 24, Glenurcha, Farmer, High rents & Oppression.

Isobel McIntyre, 24, Glenurcha, his wife, High rents & Oppression.

John McIntyre, 35, Glenurcha, Farmer, High rents & Oppression.

Marg^t. McIntyre, 30, Glenurcha, his wife, High rents & Oppression.

Malcolm McPherson, 40, Glenurcha, Farmer, High rents & Oppression.

Christ^n Downie, 30, Glenurcha, his wife, High rents & Oppression.

Janet McPherson, 10, Glenurcha, their child, High rents & Oppression.

Willm. McPherson, 9, Glenurcha, their child, High rents & Oppression.

Willm. Picken, 32, Glenurcha, Farmer, High rents & Oppression.

Martha Huie, 26, Glenurcha, his wife, High rents & Oppression.

Robt Howie, 18, Glenurcha, Workman, Poverty Occasion'd by want of work.

Arc^d McMillan, 58, Glenurcha, Farmer, High rents & Oppression.

Mary Taylor, 40, Glenurcha, his wife, High rents & Oppression.

Barbra McMillan, 20, Glenurcha, their Daug^r, High rents & Oppression.

John Greenlees, 25, Kintyre,[39] Farmer, High rents & Oppression.
Mary Howie, 25, Kintyre, his wife, High rents & Oppression.
Peter McArthur, 58, Kintyre, Farmer, High rents & Oppression.
Chirs^t Bride, 52, Kintyre, his wife, High rents & Oppression.
John McArthur, 16, Kintyre, their child, ...
Ann McArthur, 38, Kintyre, their child, ...
Jean McArthur, 20, Kintyre, their child, ...
John McArthur, 28, Kintyre, their child, ...
Danl Calewell, 18, Kintyre, Shoemaker, Poverty Occasion'd by want of work.
Robt Mitchell, 26, Kintyre, Taylor, Poverty Ocasion'd by want of work.
Ann Campbell, 19, Kintyre, his wife, Poverty Ocasion'd by want of work.
Alex^r Allan, 22, Kintyre, Workman, Poverty Ocasion'd by want of work.
Iver McMillan, 26, Kintyre, Farmer, High rents & Opression.
Jean Huie, 23, Kintyre, his wife, High rents & Opression.
John Ferguson, 19, Kintyre, Workman, Poverty Occasiond by want of work.
Rob McKichan, 32, Kintyre, Farmer, High rents & Opression.
Janet McKendrick, 24, Kintyre, his wife, High rents & Opression.
Neil McKichan, 5, Kintyre, their son, High rents & Opression.
Mal^m McMullan, 58, Kintyre, Farmer, High rents & Opression.
Cath^n McArthur, 58, ..., his wife, ...
Daniel McMillan, 24, ..., Farmer their child, High rents & Opression.
Arch^d McMillan, 16, ..., their child, High rents & Opression.
Gelb^t McMillan, 8, ..., their child, ...
Don^d McKay, 20, ..., Taylor, High rents & Opression.
Danl Campbell, 25, ..., Farmer, High rents & Opression.
And^w Hyndman, 46, ..., Farmer, High rents & Opression.
Cath^n Campbell, 46, ..., his wife, High rents & Opression.
Mary Hindman, 18, ..., their child, High rents & Opression.
Marg^t Hyndman, 14, ..., their child, High rents & Opression.
Angus Gilchrist, 25, ..., their child, High rents & Opression.
Mal^m Smith, 64, ..., Farmer, High rents & Opression.
Mary McAlester, 64, ..., his wife, High rents & Opression.
Peter Smith, 23, ..., their child, High rents & Opression.
Mary Smith, 19, ..., their child, High rents & Opression.
Duncan McAllum, 22, ..., Shoemaker, High rents & Opression.
Cath^n McAlester, 30, ..., his wife, High rents & Opression.
Neil Thomson, 23, ..., Farmer, High rents & Opression.
David Beaton, 28, ..., Farmer, High rents & Opression.

---

[39] In Argyle County on the western coast.

Flora Bride, 29, ..., his Wife, High rents & Opression.
John Gilchrist, 25, ..., Cooper, High rents & Opression.
Marion Taylor, 21, ..., his wife, High rents & Opression.
Neil McNeil, 64, ..., Farmer, High rents & Opression.
Isobel Simpson, 64, ..., his wife, High rents & Opression.
Dan¹ McNeil, 28, ..., their child, High rents & Opression.
Hector McNeil, 24, ..., their child, High rents & Opression.
Peter McNeil, 22, ..., their child, High rents & Opression.
Neil McNeil, 18, ..., their child, High rents & Opression.
Willm McNeil, 15, ..., their child, ...
Mary McNeil, 9, ..., their child, ...
Allan Cameron, 28, ..., Farmer, High rents & Opression.
Angus Cameron, 18, ..., Farmer, High rents & Opression.
Katrine Cameron, 21, ..., his wife, High rents & Opression.

Alex Campbell D Com^r   Jo Clerk D. Coll^r
P^t Greenock   John Dunlop T S

The above List of Passengers is from the 12th August 1774 Inc¹. to
the 18th Augt 1774 Inc¹.

RECORDS OF EMIGRANTS FROM ENGLAND AND SCOTLAND TO NORTH CAROLINA, 1774-1775

Edited by A. R. Newsome

II

RECORDS OF EMIGRANTS FROM SCOTLAND

Commissioners of the Customs in Scotland to John Robinson

Sir

We have herewith transmitted a Copy of a Letter from the principal Officers of the Customs at Campbelton,[40] giving an Account of a Ship touching there, from Greenock, with Emigrants taken on board in the Island of Isla,[41] which, if judged requisite, you will be pleased to lay before the Lords Commissioners of His Majestys Treasury.

Customh°. Edinb^g
3^d. Jany 1775

M Cardonnel
George Clerk Maxwell
Basil Cochrane

Ronald Campbell and Archibald Buchanan to Commissioners of Customs in Scotland

Customhouse Campbelton
12th December 1774

Honourable Sirs,

In obedience to your Letter of the 15th of December 1773, We beg leave to acquaint your Honours that the Brigantine Carolina Packet Malcolm McNeil Master, with Goods from Greenock for Cape Fair in North Carolina, was put into this Harbour by a contrary wind on the 2^d. and sailed on the 7th. instant, having on board sixty two Passengers, of whom thirty were men, fifteen Women, and seventeen Children; This Ship after sailing from Greenock, called at Lochindale in Isla, where the Passengers were taken on board, part of whom belonged to the Island of Isla, and part to the Island of Mull[42] who had come to Isla, to take their Passage.

By the best accounts we could get, only five of these Passengers were People of any consequence the rest were of a lower class, Servants of these Gentlemen, or Labourers who could pay for their Passage. We are &c^a.

Signed ⎰ Ronald Campbell
⎱ Arch^d Buchanan

---

40 In Argyle County, near Kintyre.
41 Islay Island in Argyle County.
42 In Argyle County, north of Islay Island.

Commissioners of the Customs in Scotland to John Robinson

Sir

The Officers of the Customs in the Islands of Schetland in consequence of the Instructions received from hence, having particularly examined sundry Emigrants for America, put into Schetland by Distress of Weather; We have inclosed the said Examinations, (Copies of them) as containing apparently the genuine Causes of many Persons leaving the Country, and going to America, desiring you will lay the same before the Lords Commissioners of the Treasury for their Information.

Customh⁰. Eding., 30th May 1774.

Archd Menzies
George Clerk Maxwell
Basil Cochrane

Port Lerwick[43]

Report of the Examination of the Emigrants from the Counties of Caithness and Sutherland[44] on board the Ship Bachelor of Leith bound to Wilmington in North Carolina.

William Gordon saith that he is aged sixty and upwards, by Trade a Farmer, married, hath six children, who Emigrate with him, with the Wives and Children of his two sons John & Alexander Gordon. Resided last at Wymore in the Parish of Clyne in the County of Sutherland, upon Lands belonging to William Baillie of Rosehall. That having two sons already settled in Carolina, who wrote him encouraging him to come there, and finding the Rents of Lands raised in so much that a Possession for which his Grandfather paid only Eight Merks Scots he himself at last paid Sixty, he was induced to emigrate for the greater benefit of his children being himself an Old Man and lame so that it was indifferent to him in what Country he died. That his Circumstances were greatly reduced not only by the rise of Rents but by the loss of Cattle, particularly in the severe Winter 1771. That the lands on which he lived have often changed Masters, and that the Rents have been raised on every Change; and when Mr Baillie bought them they were farmed with the rest of his purchase to one Tacksman[45] at a very high Rent, who must also have his profits out of them. All these things concurring induced him to leave his own country in hopes that his Children would earn their Bread more comfortably elsewhere. That one of his sons is a Weaver and another a Shoe Maker, and he hopes they may get bread for themselves and be a help to support him.

William McKay, aged Thirty, by Trade a Farmer, married, hath three children from Eight to two years Old, besides one dead since he left his own country, resided last at —————— in the Parish of Farr in the County of Strathnaver upon the Estate of the Countess of Sutherland. Intends to go to Wilmington in North Carolina, because his stock

---

[43] In the Shetland Islands.
[44] Caithness and Sutherland counties constitute the northern end of Scotland.
[45] A middleman who leased a large piece of land from the owner and sublet it in small farms.

being small, Crops failing, and bread excessively dear, and the price of Cattle low, he found he could not have bread for his Family at home, and was encouraged to emigrate by the Accounts received from his Countrymen who had gone to America before him, assuring him that he might procure a Comfortable Subsistence in that country. That the land he possessed was a Wadset of the Family of Sutherland to Mr Charles Gordon of Skelpick, lying in the height of the country of Strathnaver, the Rents were not raised.

W^m. Sutherland, aged Forty, a Farmer, married, hath five children from 19 to 9 years old, lived last at Strathalidale in the Parish of Rea, in the County of Caithness, upon the Estate of the late Colonel McKay of Bighouse; Intends to go to North Carolina; left his own country because the Rents were raised, as Soldiers returning upon the peace with a little money had offered higher Rents; and longer Fines or Grassums,[46] besides the Services were oppressive in the highest degree. That from his Farm which paid 60 Merks Scots, he was obliged to find two Horses and two Servants from the middle of July to the end of Harvest solely at his own Expence, besides plowing, Cutting Turf, making middings,[47] mixing Dung and leading it out in Seed time, and besides cutting, winning, leading and stacking 10 Fathoms of Peats yearly, all done without so much as a bit of bread or a drink to his Servants.

John Catanoch, aged Fifty Years, by Trade a Farmer, married, hath 4 Children from 19 to 7 years old; resided last at Chabster in the Parish of Rae, in the County of Caithness, upon the Estate of M^r. Alex^r. Nicolson, Minister at Thurso, Intends to go to Wilmington North Carolina; left his own Country because crops failed, Bread became dear, the Rents of his Possession were raised from Two to Five Pounds Sterling, besides his Pasture or Common Grounds were taken up by placing new Tennants thereon, especially the grounds adjacent to his Farm, which were the only grounds on which his Cattle pastured. That this method of parking and placing Tenants on the pasture Grounds rendered his Farm useless, his Cattle died for want of Grass, and his Corn Farm was unfit to support his Family, after paying the Extravagant Tack duty. That beside the rise of Rents and Scarcity of bread, the Landlord exacted arbitrary and oppressive Services, such as obliging the Declarant to labour up his ground, cart, win, lead and stack his Peats, Mow, win and lead his Hay, and cut his Corn and lead it in the yard which took up about 30 or 40 days of his servants and Horses each year, without the least Acknowledgement for it, and without Victuals, save the men that mowed the Hay who got their Dinner only. That he was induced to Emigrate by Advices received from his Friends in America, that Provisions are extremely plenty & cheap, and the price of labour very high, so that People who are temperate and laborious have

---

46 A premium paid to a feudal superior on entering upon the holding.
47 Manure heaps.

every Chance of bettering their circumstances- Adds that the price of Bread in the Country he hath left is greatly Enhanced by distilling, that being for so long a time so scarce and dear, and the price of Cattle at the same time reduced full one half while the Rents of lands have been raised nearly in the same proportion, all the smaller Farms must inevitably be ruined.

Eliz: McDonald, Aged 29, unmarried, servant to James Duncan in Mointle in the Parish of Farr in the County of Sutherland, Intends to go to Wilmington in North Carolina; left her own country because several of her Friends having gone to Carolina before her, had assured her that she would get much better service and greater Encouragement in Carolina than in her own Country.

Donald McDonald, Aged 29 years, by Trade a Farmer and Taylor, married, hath One Child six years Old. Resided last at Chapter in the Parish of Rae in the County of Caithness upon the Estate of Mr Alex^r Nicolson Minister at Thurso, intends to go to Carolina; left his own Country for the reasons assigned by John Catanoch, as he resided in the same Town and was subjected to the same Hardships with the other. Complains as he doth of the advanced price of Corn, owing in a great measure to the consumption of it in Distilling.

John McBeath Aged 37, by Trade a Farmer and Shoe maker, Married, hath 5 children from 13 years to 9 months old. Resided last in Mault in the Parish of Kildonnan in the County of Sutherland, upon the Estate of Sutherland. Intends to go to Wilmington in North Carolina; left his own country because Crops failed, he lost his Cattle, the Rent of his Possession was raised, and bread had been long dear; he could get no Employment at home, whereby he could support himself and Family, being unable to buy Bread at the prices the Factors on the Estate of Sutherland & neighboring Estates exacted from him. That he was Encouraged to emigrate by the Accounts received from his own and his Wife's Friends already in America, assuring him that he would procure comfortable subsistence in that country for his Wife and Children, and that the price of labour was very high. He also assigns for the Cause of Bread being dear in his Country that it is owing to the great quantities of Corn consumed in brewing Risquebah.

James Duncan, Aged twenty seven years, by Trade a Farmer, married, hath two Children, one five years the other 9 Months old. Resided last at Mondle in the Parish of Farr in the Shire of Sutherland, upon the Estate of Sutherland, Intends to go to Wilmington in North Carolina; left his own Country because Crops failed him for several years, and among the last years of his labouring he scarce reaped any Crop; Bread became dear and the price of Cattle so much reduced that One Cows price could only buy a Boll[48] of Meal. That the People on the Estate of Sutherland were often supplied with meal from

---

[48] A measure of 6 bushels generally in Scotland.

Caithness, but the Farmers there had of late stopt the sale of their Meal, because it rendered them a much greater Profit by Distilling. That he could find no Employment at home whereby he could support his Family. That he has very promising Prospects by the Advices from his Friends in Carolina, as they have bettered their circumstances greatly since they went there by their labours. Lands being cheap and good Provisions plenty, and the price of Labour very encouraging.

Hector Mcdonald, Aged 75, Married, a Farmer, hath three sons who emigrate with him, John Alexander & George from 27 to 22 years old, also two Grand Children Hector Campbell aged 16, and Alex^r Campbell aged 12, who go to their Mother already in Carolina. Resided last at Langwall in the Parish of Rogart in the County of Sutherland, upon the Estate of Sutherland. Intends to go to North Carolina, Left his own Country because the Rents of his possession had been raised from One pound seven shillings to Four pounds, while the price of the Cattle raised upon it fell more than One half, and not being in a Corn Country the price of Bread was so far advanced, that a Cow formerly worth from 50sh. to £ 3 - could only purchase a Boll of Meal. He suffered much by the death of Cattle, and still more by oppressive Services exacted by the factor, being obliged to work with his People & Cattle for 40 days and more Each year, without a bit of Bread. That falling into reduced Circumstances he was assured by some of his children already in America that his Family might subsist more comfortably there, and in all events they can scarce be worse. Ascribes the excessive price of corn to the consumption of it in distilling.

William McDonald, Aged 71, by Trade a Farmer married hath 3 children from 7 to 5 years Old, who emigrate with him. Resided last at little Savall in the Parish of Lairg in the county of Sutherland, upon the Estate of Hugh Monro of Achanny. Intends to go to Wilmington in North Carolina; left his own Country because Crops failed, Bread became dear, the Rents of his possession were raised, but not so high as the Lands belonging to the neighboring Heritors, by which and the excessive price of Meal, the lowness of the price of Cattle, and still further by a Cautionary[49] by which he lost 30 £ Sterling, his Circumstances were much straightened, so that he could no longer support his Family at Home, tho' M^r. Monro used him with great humanity. That his Friends already in Carolina, have given him assurance of bettering his condition, as the price of labour is high and Provisions very cheap. Ascribes the high price of Corn to the Consumption of it in Distilling.

Hugh Matheson, Aged 32, married, hath 3 children from 8 to 2 years Old, also a Sister Kathrine Matheson aged 16, who emigrate with him, was a Farmer last at Rimsdale in the Parish of Kildonan in the County of Sutherland, Leaves his Country and goes to Carolina, be-

---

49 Personal security.

cause upon the rise of the price of Cattle some years ago the Rent of his Possession was raised from £ 2.16.0 to £ 5.10.0. But the price of Cattle has been of late so low, and that of Bread so high, that the Factor who was also a Drover would give no more than a Boll of Meal for a Cow, which was formerly worth from 50 sh to 3 £ and obliged the Tenants to give him their Cattle at his own price. That in these grassing Counties little Corn can be raised, and for some years past the little they had was in a great measure blighted and rendered useless by the frost which is common in the beginning of Autumn in the Inland parts of the Country. That in such Circumstances it seems impossible for Farmers to avoid Ruin, and their distresses heighten'd by the consumption of corn in distilling in a Grassing Country where little can be raised. That encouraged by his Friends already in America, he hath good hopes of bettering his Condition in that Country.

Willm. McKay, Aged 26, Married, a Farmer last at Craigie in the Parish of Rae and County of Caithness, upon the Estate of George McRay Island handy;[50] Goes to Carolina because the Rent of his Possession was raised to double at the same time that the price of Cattle was reduced one half, and even lower as he was obliged to sell them to the Factor at what price he pleased; at the same time his Crope was destroyed by bad Harvests, and Bread became excessive dear, owing in a great measure to the Consumption by distilling. That the Services were oppressive, being unlimited and arbitrary, at the pleasure of the Factor, and when by reason of sickness the Declarant could not perform them he was charged at the rate of one shilling p day. He had Assurances from his Friends in America that the high price of labour and cheapness of Provisions would enable him to support himself in that Country.

Alex. Sinclair, Aged 36, Married, hath 3 children from 18 to 2 years Old, a Farmer last at Dollochcagy in the Parish of Rae and County of Caithness, upon the Estate of Sir John Sinclair of Murkle. Left his own Country and goes to Carolina, because the Tacksman of Sr John Sinclair's Estate, demanded an advanced Rent and Arbitrary Services, which in the present Distresses of the Country could not be complied with without ruin. That he is encouraged by his Friends in America to hope to better his Circumstances there.

George Grant, Aged twenty, Married, a Farmer last at Aschog in the Parish of Kildonan in the County of Sutherland on the Estate of ————— Intends to go to North Carolina, because Crops failed so that he was obliged to buy four months Provisions in a year, and at the same time the price of Cattle was reduced more than One half. That his Brothers in Law, already in America have assured him that from the Cheapness of Provisions, and the high price of labour, he may better his Circumstances in that Country.

---

50 Handa Island off the western coast of Sutherland County.

William Bain, Aged 37, a Widower, by Trade a Shopkeeper, resided last in Wick in the County of Caithness. Intends to go to Carolina. Left his own Country because he could not get bread in his Employment, the Poverty of the Common People with whom he dealt disabling them to pay their debts. Hopes to better his Condition in America, but in what business he cannot determine till he comes there.

George Morgan, Aged 37, Married, hath two children. One 7 the other One year Old, a Farmer last at Chabster in the Parish of Rae, and County of Caithness, upon lands belonging to M^r. Alex^r. Nicolson Minister at Thurso. Goes to Carolina leaving his country for the same reasons and upon the same Motives assigned by John Catanoch, who was his Neighbour. See Pages 3^d & 4th of this Report.

Willm Monro, Aged thirty four, Married, Emigrates with his Wife, a servant maid, and a servant Boy, by Trade a Shoemaker, resided last at Borgymore in the Parish of Tongue, and County of Sutherland. Left his own Country as his Employment was little and he had no hopes of bettering his Circumstances in it, which he expects to do in America.

Patrick Ross, Aged thirty five Unmarried, lately Schoolmaster in the Parish of Farr, in the County of Sutherland. Goes to America on the Assurance of some of his Friends already in that Country of procuring a more profitable School for him.

Alex^r. Morison, Aged Sixty, Married, hath One Son and a Servant Maid, who emigrate with him; resided last at Kinside in the Parish of Tongue and County of Sutherland, on the Estate of Sutherland, by Occupation a Farmer. Left his Country as the Rents of his Possession were near doubled, the price of Cattle low, and little being raised in that Country, what they bought was excessive dear, beside the Tenans were in various ways opprest by Lord Raes Factors; and by the Reports from America he is in hopes of bettering his Circumstances in that Country.

George McKay, Aged 40, Married, hath one Child, a year old, by Trade a Taylor and Farmer, last at Strathoolie in the Parish of Kildonan and County of Sutherland, upon that part of the Estate of Sutherland set in Tack to George Gordon by whom his rent was augmented, and great Services demanded, vizt 12 days work yearly over and above what he paid to the Family of Sutherland. That the price of Cattle on which he chiefly depended was greatly reduced, and the little Corn raised in the Country almost totally blighted by Frost for two years past, by which the Farmers in general were brought into great distress. In these Circumstances he had no resource but to follow his Countrymen to America as the condition can scarce be worse.

Donald Gun, Aged thirty three, married, hath three Children from 8 years to 5 weeks old, by Trade a Taylor, resided last at Achinnaris in the Parish of Halerick in the County of Caithness. Finding he cannot make bread in his own Country, intends to go to America in hopes of doing it better there.

John Ross, Aged 47, a Widower hath six Children, from 20 to 5 years Old, who emigrate with him, by Trade a Farmer, last at Kabel in the Parish of Farr and County of Sutherland, upon the Estate of Sutherland. Goes to Carolina, because the rent of his Possession was greatly Advanced the price of Cattle which must pay that Rent reduced more than one half, and bread which they must always buy excessively dear. The evil is the greater that the Estate being parcelled out to different Factors and Tacksmen, these must oppress the subtenants, in order to raise a profit to themselves, particularly on the Article of Cattle, which they never fail to take at their own prices, lately at 20/ or 20 Merks, and seldom or never higher than 30/ tho' the same Cattle have been sold in the Country from 50 to 55 sh. By these means reduced in his circumstances, And encouraged by his Friends already in America, he hopes to live more comfortably in that Country.

James Sinclair, Aged twenty one years, a Farmer, married, hath no Children, resided last at Forsenain in the Parish of Rea, and County of Caithness, upon the Estate of Bighouse now possest by George McRay of Islandhanda, upon a Farm, paying 8 £ Sterling Rent, that he left his own Country because Crops of Corn had, and Bread was very dear; he had lost great part of his Cattle two years ago, the rearing Cattle being his principal business, the prices of Cattle were reduced one half while the Rents were nevertheless kept up and in many places advanced. In such Circumstances it was not possible for people of small stock to evite ruin. His Father, Mother and Sisters and some other Friends go along with him to Carolina, where he is informed land and Provisions are cheap, labour dear, and Crops seldom fail. What employment he shall follow there he hath not yet determined, but thinks it will be Husbandry.

Aeneas McLeod, Aged sixty, a Farmer, married, hath one Daughter 15 years Old. Resided last in the Parish of Tongue in the County of Sutherland upon the Estate of Lord Rae. Goes to Wilmington in North Carolina, where he proposes to live by day labour, being informed that one days Wages will support him a week. Left his own Country because upon the rise of the price of Cattle some years ago, the Rent of his Possession was raised from 28/ to 38/ a year, but thereafter when the price of Cattle was reduced one half the Rent was nevertheless still kept up. Moreover being near the house of Tongue, He was harrassed and oppressed with arbitrary Services daily called for without Wages or Maintenance.

Aeneas Mackay, Aged twenty, single, resided last with his Father in the Parish of Tongue and county of Sutherland; hath been taught to read, write and cypher, and goes to Carolina in hopes of being employed either as a Teacher or as a Clerk; He has several Relations and Acquaintances there already, who inform him he may get from 60 to 70 £ a year in this way, which is much better than he had any reason to expect at home.

Donald Campbell, Aged 50, a Farmer, married, has one Son 12 years Old, resided last in the Parish of Adrahoolish, in the County of Sutherland on the Estate of Rea. Intends to go to Carolina because the small Farm he possest could not keep a Plough, and he could not raise so much Corn by delving as maintain his Family and pay his Rent, which was advanced from 21/ to 30/. Has hopes of meeting an Uncle in America who will be able to put him in a way of gaining his Bread.

W^m McRay, Aged 37, a Farmer, married, has four Children from 8 years to 18 Months old; and one man Servant, who emigrate with him; resided last at Shathaledale in the Parish of Rea, and County of Caithness upon the Estate of George McRay of Bighouse. Left his Country because the Rent of his Possession was raised from 30 to 80 £ Scots, while at the same time the price of Cattle upon which his subsistence and the payment of his Rent chiefly depended had fallen in the last Seven years at least one half. In the year 1772 he lost of the little Crop his Farm produced and in Cattle to the value of 40 £ Sterling – under these loses and discouragements, he had assurances from a Brother and Sister already in Carolina, that a sober industrious man could not fail of living comfortably, Lands could be rented cheap, and Grounds not cleared purchased for 6 ^d. an Acre, that the soil was fertile, and if a man could bring a small Sum of Money with him he might make rich very fast. He proposes to follow Agriculture but has not yet determined, whether he will purchase or rent a Possession.

Willm McLeod, Aged twenty six, a Farmer, married, has one Son two years old; resided last in the Parish of Adrachoolish, in the County of Sutherland, upon the Estate of Bighouse; intends to go to Wilmington in North Carolina, where he has a Brother settled who wrote him to come out assuring him that he would find a better Farm for him than he possest at home (the rent of which was considerably raised upon him) for One fourth of the Money, and that he will live more comfortably in every respect.

Hugh Monro, Aged twenty-six, a Shoemaker, married, hath no children. Resided last in the Parish of Tongue and County of Sutherland. Goes to Carolina upon assurance that Tradesmen of all kinds will find large Encouragement.

Willm. Sutherland Aged twenty four, married, left an only Child at home. Resided last in the Parish of Latheron and County of Caithness, upon the Estate of John Sutherland of Forse. Goes to Carolina because he lost his Cattle in 1772, and for a farm of 40/ Rent, was obliged to perform with his Family and his Horses so many and so arbitrary services to his Landlord at all times of the year, but especially in Seed time & Harvest, that he could not in two years he possest it, raise as much Corn as serve his Family for six months That his little Stock daily decreasing, he was encouraged to go to Carolina, by the Assurances of the fertility of the land, which yields three Crops a year, by which means Provisions are extremely cheap, Wheat being sold at 3 shill^s. a Boll, Potatoes at 1 Sh so that one Mans labour will maintain a Family of Twenty Persons. He has no Money, therefore proposes to employ himself as a Day labourer, his Wife can spin & Sew, and he has heard of many going out in the same way who are now substantial Farmers. At any rate he comforts himself in the hopes that he cannot be worse than he has been at home.

James McKay, Aged 60, a shoemaker, married, has one child, Resided last on Lord Raes Estate in Strathnaver. Left his own country, being exceeding poor, and assured by his Friends who contributed among them the money required to pay for his Passage, that he would find better employment in Carolina.

This and the 20 preceding Pages contain the Examination of the Emigrants on board the Ship Batchelor of Leith, Alex^r Ramage Master, taken by the officers at the Port of Lerwick.

15th April 1774.

A List of Passengers or Emigrants on Board the Ship Jupiter of Larne Samuel Brown Master for Wilmington in North Carolina, their Names, Ages, Occupations or Employments and former Residence.[51]

1, John Stewart, 48, Clothier, Glenurchy.
2, Elizabeth, 46, his wife, Glenurchy.
3, John Stewart, 15, their son, Glenurchy.
4, Margaret, 13, their Daughter, Glenurchy.
5, Janet, 12, their Daughter, Glenurchy.
6, Patrick Stewart, 6, their son, Glenurchy.
7, Elizabeth, 3, their Daughter, Glenurchy.
8, Donald MacIntire, 54, Labourer, Glenurchy.
9, Katherine, 41, His Wife, Glenurchy.
10, Mary, 12, their Daughter, Glenurchy.
11, Margaret, 9, their Daughter, Glenurchy.
12, John McIntire, 6, their son, Glenurchy.
13, Duncan McIntire, 5, their son, Glenurchy.
14, William Campbell, 28, Labourer, Glenurchy.
15, Katherine, 32, His Wife, Glenurchy.
16, Robert Campbell, 2, His Son, Glenurchy.
17, Duncan Campbell, ————, His Son an Infant, Glenurchy.
18, Donald Mac Nichol, 40, Labourer, Glenurchy.

---

[51] The information in the order given is classified in the original report under the headings: number, names, ages, occupation or employment, former residence.

19, Katherine, 33, His Wife, Glenurchy.
20, John McNicol, 6, their son, Glenurchy.
21, Nicol McNicol, 4, their son, Glenurchy.
22, Archibald McNicol, 2, their son, Glenurchy.
23, Mary, —————, their daughter an Infant, Glenurchy.
24, John McIntire, 35, Labourer, Glenurchy.
25, Ann, 32, His Wife, Glenurchy.
26, Margaret, 6, their Daughter, Glenurchy.
27, Archibald McIntire, 4, their Son, Glenurchy.
28, John McIntire, —————, their Son an Infant, Glenurchy.
29, Archibald Stewart, 30, Shoemaker, Glenurchy.
30, Ann Sinclair, 65, Spinster, Glenurchy.
31, Margarit her Daugh^r., 25, Spinster, Glenurchy.
32, Ann McIntire, 60, Spinster, Glenurchy.
33, Christian Downy, 25, Spinster, Glenurchy.
34, Katherine McVane, 30, Spinster, Glennurchy.
35, Mary Downie, 4, her daughter, Glennurchy.
36, Joseph Downie an Infant, —————, her son, Glennurchy.
37, Dugal McCole, 38, Labourer, Glennurchy.
38, Ann, 38, his Wife, Glennurchy.
39, Marget, 10, their Daughter, Glennurchy.
40, Mary, 8, their Daughter, Glennurchy.
41, Sarah, 2, their Daughter, Glennurchy.
42, An Infant, —————, —————, Glennurchy.
43, Angus McNicol, 30, Labourer, Glennurchy.
44, Ann, 20, His Wife, Glennurchy.
45, Dougald Stewart, 40, Labourer, Glenurchy.
46, His Wife, 40, Labourer, Glenurchy.
47, John Stewart, 16, their son, Glenurchy.
48, James Stewart, 10, their son, Glenurchy.
49, Thomas Stewart, 6, their son, Glenurchy.
50, Alexander Stewart, 4, their son, Glenurchy.
51, Allan Stewart, 44, Late Lieut^t. in Frasers Regiment, Apine.[52]
52, Donald Carmichail, 22, His servant, Apine.
53, Lilly Stewart, 7, his natural Daugh^r., Apine.
54, Alexander Stewart, 35, Gentleman Farmer, Apine.
55, Charles Stewart, 15, His Son, Apine.
56, John McCole, 49, Labourer, Apine.
57, Mildred McCole, 40, His Wife, Apine.
58, John McCole, 16, their son, Apine.
59, Samuel McCole, 15, their son, Apine.
60, Donald McCole, 12, their son, Apine.
61, Dougald McCole, 8, their son, Apine.
62, Alexander McCole, 4, their son, Apine.

---

[52] In Argyle County.

63, Katherine, 2, their Daughter, Apine.
64, Evan Carmichael, 40, Labourer, Apine.
65, Margaret, 38, His Wife, Apine.
66, Archibald Carmichael, 14, their Son, Apine.
67, Allan Carmichael, 12, their Son, Apine.
68, Katherine, 3, their Daughter, Apine.
69, Duncan McCole, 35, Farmer, Apine.
70, Christian, 35, His Wife, Apine.
71, Dugald McCole, 20, Their son, Apine.
72, Christian, 2, their Daughter, Apine.
73, Katherine, 3, their Daughter, Apine.
74, Malcolm McInish, 40, Labourer, Apine.
75, Jannet, 36, His Wife, Apine.
76, John McInish, 20, Their son, Apine.
77, Ann, 15, Their Daughter, Apine.
78, Catherine, 11, Their Daughter, Apine.
79, Donald McInish, 8, their Son, Apine.
80, Archibald McInish, 4, their Son, Apine.
81, Kenneth Stewart, 40, late Ship Master, Apine.
82, Isobel, 30, His Wife, Apine.
83, Alexander Stewart, 14, their Son, Apine.
84, John Stewart, 5, their Son, Apine.
85, Banco Stewart, 3, their Son, Apine.
86, Christian, 3, their Daughter, Apine.
87, William an Infant, ————, their son, Apine.
88, Mary Black, 16, their Servant, Apine.
89, Christian Carmichael, 14, their Servant, Apine.
90, John Black, 14, their Servant, Apine.
91, Dugald Carmichael, 55, Farmer, Apine.
92, Mary, 55, His Wife, Apine.
93, Archibald Colquhoun, 22, her Son, Apine.
94, Ann Colquhoun, 20, her Daughter, Apine.
95, Donald McCole, 34, Labourer, Apine.
96, Katherine, 40, his Wife, Apine.
97, Evan McCole, 6, their son, Apine.
98, John McIntire, 32, Taylor, Alpine.
99, Katherine, 30, his Wife, Alpine.
100, Donald McIntire, 3, their son, Alpine.
101, John McIntire, 1, their son, Alpine.
102, Gilbert McIntire, 34, Taylor, Alpine.
103, Ann, 36, his Wife, Alpine.
104, Charles McIntire, 11, their Son, Alpine.
105, Margaret, 9, their Daughter, Alpine.
106, Evan McIntyre, 5, their Son, Alpine.
107, Malcolm McIntire, 1, their Son, Alpine.
108, Duncan McCole, 45, Farmer, Alpine.

109, Christian, 40, His Wife, Alpine.
110, Duncan McCole, 21, His son, Alpine.
111, Mary, 18, their Daughter, Alpine.
112, Sarah, 15, their Daughter, Alpine.
113, Christian, 10, their Daughter, Alpine.
114, Mildred, 6, their Daughter, Alpine.
115, Ann, 3, their Daughter, Alpine.
116, Donald Black, 45, Labourer, Lismore.[53]
117, Jannet, 34, His Wife, Lismore.
118, Christian, 8, his Daughter, Lismore.
119, Ann, 4, his Daughter, Lismore.
120, Ewen, 4, their Son, Lismore.
121, Duncan, 1¾, their Son, Lismore.
122, Archibald Carmichael, 26, Labourer, Lismore.
123, Mary, 26, His Wife, Lismore.
124, Catherine, 7, their Daughter, Lismore.
125, Lachlan McLaren, 25, Labourer, Apine.
126, Lawrine McLarine, 20, Joiner, Apine.
127, Donald McLaren, 12, Labourer, Apine.
128, Duncan McLaren, 30, Labourer, Apine.
129, David McCole, 30, Labourer, Apine.
130, Duncan McIntire, 55, Labourer, Apine.
131, Katherine, 55, His Wife, Apine.
132, May, 24, Their Daughter, Apine.
133, Katherine, 17, Their Daughter, Apine.
134, Elizabeth, 14, Their Daughter, Apine.
135, Miss Christy McDonald, 25, Symstress, Apine.
136, Duncan McCallum, 30, Labourer, Apine.

Reasons assigned by the Persons named on this and ye three preceeding Pages of this List for their Emigrating follows Viz^t. The Farmers and Labourers who are taking their Passage in this Ship Unanimously declare that they never would have thought of leaving their native Country, could they have Supplied their Families in it. But such of them as were Farmers were obliged to quit their Lands either on account of the advanced Rent or to make room for Sheepherds. Those in particular from Apine say that out of one hundred Mark Land that formerly was occupied by Tennants who made their Rents by rearing Cattle and raising Grain, Thirty three Mark Land of it is now turned into Sheep Walks and they seem to think in a few years more, Two thirds of that Country, at least will be in the same State so of course the greatest part of the Inhabitants will be obliged to leave it. The Labourers Declare they could not Support their families on the Wages they earned and that it is not from any other motive but the dread of want that they quit a Country which above all others they would wish

---

[53] In Argyle County.

to live in. Captain Allan Stewart formerly a Lieutenant in Frasers Regiment goes with an Intention of settling in the Lands granted him by the Government at the End of last War. But should the Troubles continue in America he is Determined to make the Best of his way to Boston and Offer his Services to General Gage.

The Tradesmen have a prospect of getting better Wages but their principal reason seems to be that their relations are going and rather than part with them they chuse to go along.

September 4th. 1775. Signed { Duncan Campbell Collector
Neil Campbell Comptroller

Port Greenock List of Passengers from this Port from the 8th September 1774 inclusive, to the 15th September 1774 exclusive, [in the Diana, Dugald Ruthven for North Carolina].[54]

William McDonald, Kintyre, Farmer, 40, Wilmington North Carolina, For High Rents & better Encouragement.

Isobel Wright, Kintyre, ————, 36, Wilmington North Carolina, For High Rents & better Encouragement.

Mary McDonald, Kintyre, ————, 4, Wilmington North Carolina, For High Rents & better Encouragement.

Jessy McDonald, Kintyre, ————, 2, Wilmington North Carolina, For High Rents & better Encouragement.

Archibald Campbell, Kintyre, Farmer, 38, Wilmington North Carolina, For High Rents & better Encouragement.

Jean McNeil, Kintyre, ————, 32, Wilmington North Carolina, For High Rents & better Encouragement.

Mary Campbell, Kintyre, ————, 7, Wilmington North Carolina, For High Rents & better Encouragement.

Lachlan Campbell, Kintyre, ————, 2, Wilmington North Carolina, For High Rents & better Encouragement.

Girzie Campbell, Kintyre, ————, 6, Wilmington North Carolina, For High Rents & better Encouragement.

Finlay Murchie, Kintyre, Farmer, 45, Wilmington, North Carolina, For High Rents & better Encouragement.

Catherine Hendry, Kintyre, ————, 35, Wilmington North Carolina, For High Rents & better Encouragement.

Archd McMurchy, Kintyre, ————, 10, Wilmington North Carolina, For High Rents & better Encouragement.

Charles McMurchy, Kintyre, ————, 5, Wilmington North Carolina, For High Rents & better Encouragement.

Neil McMurchy, Kintyre, ————, 3, Wilmington North Carolina, For High Rents & better Encouragement.

---

[54] The information in the order given is classified in the original report under the headings: names, former residence, occupation or employment, age, to what port or place bound, on what account and for what purpose.

Barbara McMurchy, Kintyre, ————, ½, Wilmington North Carolina, For High Rents & better Encouragement.

Duncan McRob, Kintyre, Taylor, 26, Wilmington North Carolina, For High Rents & better Encouragement.

Elizabeth McMurchy, Kintyre, ————, 8, Wilmington North Carolina, For High Rents & better Encouragement.

Hugh Sillar, Kintyre, Farmer, 55, Wilmington, North Carolina, For High Rents & better Encouragement.

Catharine Currie, Kintyre, ————, 62, Wilmington North Carolina, For High Rents & better Encouragement.

Mary Sillar, Kintyre, ————, 27, Wilmington North Carolina, For High Rents & better Encouragement.

Catharine Sillar, Kintyre, ————, 23, Wilmington North Carolina, For High Rents & better Encouragement.

Gilbert McKenzie, Kintyre, Farmer, 34, Wilmington North Carolina, For High Rents & better Encouragement.

Mary McKenzie, Kintyre, ————, 27, Wilmington North Carolina, For High Rents & better Encouragement.

Arch^d. McMillan, Kintyre, Farmer, ——, Wilmington North Carolina, For High Rents & better Encouragement.

Patrick McMurchie, Kintyre, Farmer, 17, Wilmington North Carolina, For High Rents & better Encouragement.

Elizabeth Kelso, Kintyre, ————, 50, Wilmington North Carolina, For High Rents & better Encouragement.

Hugh McMurchie, Kintyre, Farmer, 46, Wilmington North Carolina, For High Rents & better Encouragement.

Arch^d McMurchie, Kintyre, Farmer, 21, Wilmington North Carolina, For High Rents & better Encouragement.

Mary McMurchie, Kintyre, ————, 17, Wilmington North Carolina, For High Rents & better Encouragement.

Elizabeth McMurchie, Kintyre, ————, 14, Wilmington North Carolina, For High Rents & better Encouragement.

Robert McMurchie, Kintyre, ————, 9, Wilmington North Carolina, For High Rents & better Encouragement.

Neil Hendry, Kintyre, Taylor, 27, Wilmington North Carolina, For High Rents & better Encouragement.

Coll McAlester, Kintyre, Taylor, 24, Wilmington North Carolina, For High Rents & better Encouragement.

Mary McAlester, Kintyre, ————, 31, Wilmington North Carolina, For High Rents & better Encouragement.

John McVicar, Glasgow, Taylor, 36, Wilmington North Carolina, For High Rents & better Encouragement.

Alexander Speir, Glasgow, Clerk, 19, Wilmington North Carolina, For High Rents & better Encouragement.

Signed { Jo Clerk D Coll^r
{ Alex^r. Campbell D Compt^r

SCOTCH EMIGRANTS TO NEW YORK 1774 – 1775

Contributed by Wallace R. Freeman

(Copied from mss. in New York Public Library, Fifth Avenue and 42nd Street, New York City, entitled "Emigrants from Scotland, 1774-1775" by Viola Root Cameron, who copied them from the originals in Scotland. These emigrants shipped at Stranraer, on May 16, 1774 on board the "Gale" of Whithaven, bound for New York. Henry Jefferson was Master.)

Name		Age	Occupation	Remarks
Alexander,	Hugh	45	Carpenter	of Galloway
"	Agnes	30	his wife	" "
"	John	10	his child	" "
"	Ann	10	" "	" "
"	Hugh	7	" "	" "
"	Alexander	5	" "	" "
"	James	3	" "	" "
"	Robert	1	" "	" "
Agnew,	Alexander	40	Farmer	" "
"	Janet	40	his wife	" "
"	Forbes	18	laborer	" "
"	William	15	"	" "
Adair,	Patrick	50	Farmer	" Glenluce
"	Agnes	25	(cannot find a husband)	" "
"	Jean	25	ditto	" "
"	William	17	laborer	" "
"	Ann	26	a wife (prob. of Pat.)	" "
Alexander,	Robert	25	Carpenter	" Dailly
Angus,	William	40	laborer	" Galloway
Beatty,	William	40	"	" "
"	Agnes	40	his wife	" "
"	Mary	16	" child	" "
Buchanan,	John	58	Farmer	" " (from curiosity)
Biggam,	Thomas	40	Weaver	of Galloway
"	Mary	33	his wife	" "
"	Andrew	9	" child	" "
"	Jean	4	" "	" "
Boyd,	James	32	Merchant	" " (no business)

	Name	Age	Occupation	Remarks
Boyd,	Jean	22	his wife	of Galloway
Bruce,	Robert	22	Gardener	,, ,,
Biggam,	William	40	Farmer	,, ,,
Blane,	Patrick	34	,,	,, ,,
,,	Eliza	30	his wife	,, ,,
,,	Jenny	2	,, child	,, ,,
,,	Jean	8	,, ,,	,, ,,
Campbell,	Jean	20	--------------	,, ,,
Cummings,	John	26	Tailor	,, Air
Campbell,	Andrew	34	Shoemaker	,, Galloway
,,	Agnes	33	his wife	,, ,,
,,	Jean	4	,, child	,, ,,
,,	Mary Ann	1	,, ,,	,, ,,
,,	John	22	Tailor	,, ,,
Clarke,	James	—	Waiter	,, ,,
Ell,	John	40	laborer	,, Gavin
Ell,	William	15	,,	,, ,,
Ganley,	Jean	25	a wife	--------------
Galloway,	John	22	Joiner	of Galloway
,,	Sarah	20	his wife	,, ,,
Gibson,	John	19	Farmer	,, ,,
Kelley,	Robert	38	,,	,, ,,
,,	Mary	38	his wife	,, ,,
,,	Margaret	9	,, child	,, ,,
,,	James	6	,, ,,	,, ,,
,,	Jean	3	,, ,,	,, ,,
,,	Peter	26	Laborer	of Glenluce
,,	Jean	10	—	,, ,,
,,	Alexander	8	—	,, ,,
,,	Elizabeth	5	—	,, ,,
,,	Alexander	22	Laborer	,, Galloway
Linn,	William	21	,,	,, ,,
Long,	Henry	—	,,	,, ,,
McHaig,	John	36	Farmer	,, ,,
,,	Grizzel	26	his wife	,, ,,
,,	Ann	4	,, child	,, ,,
,,	Margaret	2	,, ,,	,, ,,
Mikine,	John (McKine?)	40	Joiner	,, ,,
,,	Rosanna	36	his wife	,, ,,
,,	Rosina	9	,, child	,, ,,
,,	Agnes	7	,, ,,	,, ,,
,,	Mary	6	,, ,,	,, ,,
,,	Jean	5	,, ,,	,, ,,

Name		Age	Occupation	Remarks	
Mikine,	Nanny	1	his child	of Galloway	
McKissack,	Janet	56	----------	,,	,,
McMasters,	Robert	24	Merchant	,,	,,
Millroy,	John	30	Shoemaker	,,	,,
,,	Sarah	26	his wife	,,	,,
McMasters,	John	20	Housewright	,,	,,
McTaggart,	James	20	Laborer	,,	,,
McClumpha,	Jean	22	----------	,,	,,
,,	John	2	----------	,,	,,
,,	Thomas	26	Farmer	,,	,,
McDougal,	Alexander	21	Gardener	,,	,,
McComb,	Alexander	21	,,	,,	,,
Millroy,	John	40	Farmer	,,	,,
,,	Eliza	38	his wife	,,	,,
,,	Mary	12	,, child	,,	,,
,,	Janet	10	,, ,,	,,	,,
,,	Eliza	8	,, ,,	,,	,,
,,	Anthony	7	,, ,,	,,	,,
,,	John	6	,, ,,	,,	,,
,,	Agnes	4	,, ,,	,,	,,
McWilliams,	James	24	Mason	,,	,,
McKackey,	John	25	Smith	,,	,,
McKinley,	Michael	40	Farmer	,,	,,
,,	Jean	26	----------	,,	,,
McMiking,	John	21	Farmer	,,	,,
,,	Thomas	24	,,	,,	,,
Millwane,	Thomas	17	,,	,,	,,
Maxwell,	Jean	32	----------	,,	,,
,,	John	2	----------	,,	,,
McMicken,	James	4	----------	,,	,,
,,	William	2	----------	,,	,,
McWilliams	Janet	27	----------	,,	,,
Millroy,	Anthony	—	Laborer	,,	,,
McCrae,	Hugh	—	,,	,,	,,
Maxwell,	David	34	Tailor	,,	,,
McGarvin,	Jean	34	a wife	,,	,,
Maxwell,	Marion	8	----------	,,	,,
McWilliams,	James	23	Farmer	,,	,,
McMillan,	Margaret	25	a wife	,,	,,
McMicken,	Alexander	23	Farmer	,, Glenluce	
McComb,	Alexander	21	,,	,,	,,
McAwan?,	Agnes	23	a wife	,,	,,
McQueen,	William	25	Farmer	,,	,,

	Name	Age	Occupation	Remarks
McDonall,	Alexander	40	Laborer	of Galloway
McWilliams,	Elizabeth	35	a wife	" "
McDowall,	Edward	9	----------	" "
"	Robert	7	----------	" "
McKissack,	Thomas	26	Farmer	" Girvan
McMicken,	William	25	Laborer	" Galloway
McQuestion,	Anthony	18	Baker	" "
McMasters,	Eliza	21	----------	" "
"	Elianora	25	----------	" "
McMicken,	Janet	21	----------	" "
McKie,	Samuel	26	Weaver	" "
"	Margaret	26	his wife	" "
McWilliams,	George	25	Farmer	" "
McCann,	William	35	Weaver	" "
"	Jean	27	his wife	" "
"	Sarah	8	" child	" "
"	John	6	" "	" "
"	Janet	4	" "	" "
Millwane,	Mary	26	----------	" "
Mean,	William	21	Tailor	" Air (?)
McMiking,	James	16	Farmer	" Galloway
Ross,	Alexander	32	Carpenter	" "
"	Jean	30	his wife	" "
"	Margaret	8	" child	" "
"	Isabella	4	" "	" "
"	Jean	2	" "	" "
Stewart,	William	22	Housewright	" "
Shaw,	John	23	Blacksmith	" "
Torburn,	Andrew	7	----------	" Glenluce
Kennedy,	John (OMITTED)	22	Laborer	" Galloway

The following from Broad Albion, Perthshire, shipped from Port Greenock, July 9, 1775, in Brigantine "Commerce" bound for New York. John Mathie, Master.

	Name	Age	Occupation	Remarks
Allen,	David	24	Wright	(All of Broad
"	Janet Stewart	19	Wife	Albion Perths)
Cameron,	Angus	47	Farmer	
"	Katherine McDonald	32	Wife	
"	Mary	16	Child	

	Name	Age	Occupation	Remarks
Cameron	John	14	Child	
"	Alexander	13	"	
"	Duncan	11	"	
Cromery,	James	29	Wright	
Campbell,	Colin	27	Smith	
Dunn,	James	29	Farmer	
"	Catherine	30	Wife	
"	John	26	Tidler (?)	
Ferguson,	James	32	Farmer	
"	Jean McGregor	29	Wife	
"	Mary	21	Child	
"	Robert	13	"	
"	Helen	11	"	
"	Ann	7	"	
Kennedy,	Angus	26	Farmer	
Kay,	Alexander	26	Piper	
Korest,	Mary	18	Servant (McKorest?)	
Littlejohn,	Duncan	38	Wright	
McIsaac,	Malcom	29	Smith	
McArthur,	Duncan	52	Farmer	
"	Eliza McEwen	47	Wife	
"	John	20	Mason	
"	Donald	15	Tailor	
"	Peter	12	Child	
"	John	11	"	
"	Donald	2	"	
Murray,	William	44	Farmer	
"	Margaret McDougal	41	Wife	
"	John	22	Mason	
"	Alexander	18	Tailor	
"	Archibald	17	Shoemaker	
"	Christian	12	Child	
"	Katherine	8	"	
"	James	1	"	
McIntyre,	Donald	43	Schoolmaster	
"	Ann Walker	36	Wife	
"	Catherine	19	Servant	
"	Archibald	8	Child	
McLeran,	Hugh	34	Farmer (McLaren?)	
McNaughton,	John	38	Farmer	
"	Janet Anderson	30	Wife	
"	Christian	14	Child	

Name		Age	Occupation	Remarks
McNaughton,	Katherine	11	Child	
”	Duncan	7	”	
”	Katherine (sic)	3	”	
”	John	3	”	
”	Elizabeth	2	”	
”	Daniel	1	”	
”	Peter	½	”	
”	Angus	¼	” ????	
Mattock,	Isobel	18	Servant	
McLaren,	James	32	Tailor	
McArthur,	Donald	59	Farmer	
McNaughton,	Katherine	46	— (wife of Donald McArthur)	
McArthur,	John	22	Mason	
”	Donald	17	Tailor	
”	Catherine	14	Child	
”	Archibald	8	”	
”	Duncan	20	Weaver	
McDiarmed,	Mary	21	Servant	
”	Eliza	17	”	
”	Katherine	14	Child	
”	John	3	”	
”	Jean	3	” (prob. twin of John)	
McMartin,	Peter	21	Smith	
McVurah,	Peter	19	Founder	
McNaughton,	John	24	Farmer	
”	Christian	20	Servant	
McVain,	Sarah	17	”	
”	Mary	21	”	
McIntyre,	Duncan	47	Farmer	
”	Helen McNab	42	Wife	
”	John	13	Child	
”	Alexander	20	Farmer	
”	Duncan	15	Child	
”	Margaret	10	”	
McCullum,	Peter	27	Farmer	
McGregor,	Hugh	42	”	
”	Jean McNaughton	38	Wife	
”	Donald	14	Child	
”	Katherine	12	”	
McNaughton,	Donald	19	Farmer	
”	Angus	29	”	

Name		Age	Occupation	Remarks
McNaughton,	Katherine Robertson	24	Wife	
"	John	6	Child	
"	Jean	4	"	
McMartine,	Duncan	63	Farmer	
"	Isabel McGregor	59	Wife	
"	Margaret	24	Servant	
"	Hugh	21	"	
"	Donald	20	Wright	
Thomson,	Alexander	48	Farmer	
"	Janet Korest	33	Wife	
"	William	14	Child	
"	Katherine	11	"	
"	Betty	9	"	
"	Henry	1	"	
Thompson,	George	41	Farmer	
"	Janet Wilson	40	Wife	
"	Peter	18	Farmer	
Walker,	Eliza	18	Servant	
"	David	18	Piper	
"	Donald	13	Tailor	

NOTE: Causes of Emigration — Farmers—High rental; Smiths, etc.—No work; Children—With parents; Older children—Poverty, no work.

A NEW EMIGRANT LIST

If you are tracing your family history, any information on the European birthplaces of your emigrant ancestors, is welcome news. In recent years several important lists of Pennsylvania Dutch emigrants of the eighteenth century have come to light. The following list includes the names of some emigrant pioneers who came to this country during and after the American Revolution. Some of them served with the British troops, but pleased by the fertile farms and busy towns of the Dutchland, decided to become Americans! The list appears, in German, in the early Allentown weekly newspaper, *Der Friedens-Bothe* ("The Messenger of Peace"), for June 17, 1825.

Where Are These People?

The following persons are herewith strongly urged as soon as possible to let us know their present place of residence, since we have important news concerning them from their Fatherland.

If any of them should no longer be alive, then fuller particulars about them, as well as about the state of any property left behind by them, and a legally certified Death Certificate, in return for the costs incurred thereby, will be gratefully received by the GERMAN EUROPEAN COMMISSION AND FORWARDING OFFICE in Philadelphia:

1) Jacob Fetherolff and Johann Georg Fetherolff, from Wuerttemberg, went to America in the year 1777 or 1778.

2) [----] Meyer, from Frankfurt-am-Main, formerly a member of the firm of Meyer and Parker in Philadelphia.

3) Anna Maria Jacobi, nee Stolze, widow, who formerly lived in Calcutta, but 13 or 14 years ago came to Philadelphia and lived in a country house near this city.

4) Friedrich Sebastian Goetz, from Oberliederbach near Frankfurt-am-Main, a miller by trade, who went to Philadelphia in the year 1775 or 1776, and is said to have owned a grist and powder mill near this city, and whose three children, left behind in Germany, are at present living in dire need.

5) Johann Heinrich Breitenbach and Friedrich Breitenbach, in America since the year 1780 or 1783.

6) Philipp Lohr, tailor, from Langen near Frankfurt-am-Main, was living in the year 1809 in New York, Water Street Number 350.

7) Georg Adam Trautman, from Schernan, went to America in the year 1776.

8) Conrad Eckert, of Grasreuth, went to America in year 1781.

9) Frantz Xaver Baumann, butcher.

10) Johann Peter Weber, from Badenhausen, went to America in the year 1776.

11) George Michael Goetz, from Herlsheim.

12) Friedrich Kreutzer, from Herlsheim, wagonmaker, went to America about 40 years ago.

13) Nicholas Gullerin, from Harrenhausen, went to America as a soldier in the year 1776.

14) Johann Matthaeus Claas, from Unnau, went to America in the year 1801.

15) Joseph Kaiser, from Limburg, shoemaker, went to America in the year 1797.

16) Philipp Heinrich Haxel, Johann Adam Haxel, and Johann Friedrich Haxel, three brothers, from Marienfels.

17) Philipp Koebel, from Oberwoellstadt.

18) Jacob Erle, from Heidelberg.

19) Johann Daniel Geisemer, from Frankfurt-am-Main.

20) Johann Philipp Fischer, from Coburg, went to America in the year 1803, lodged with Mr. H. L. Ras, Philadelphia.

21) [----] Lucius, preacher, formerly in Charlestown, S. C.

22) Georg Ludwig Gail, from Worms, is said to have died as a baker in Charlestown, S. C., in the year 1781 or 1782, and left a property of $11,000.

23) Christoph Heinrich Essig, of Stuttgart, went to America with the Hessians in the year 1776.

24) Jacob Bricker, from Flonheim, is said to have died on September 3, 1793, in Fredericktown, Maryland.

25) Friedrich Weibel, from Oppenheim.

26) Heinrich Bruch, baker, from Frankfurt-am-Main, is said to have died of the yellow fever in New Orleans in the year 1822 or 1823.

27) Nicolaus Kuhn, from Wabern, went to America with the Hessians.

28) Simon Isaak Levy, who went nine years ago to Baltimore, but of whom nothing has been heard for six years.

FRENCH IMMIGRANTS TO LOUISIANA 1796-1800.

Settlements of Bastrop and Morehouse in the District of Ouachita. Condensed Documentary History.

[This brief account of an early movement of French settlers to southern United States is extracted from the original sources by Mr. L. Perez, Washington, D. C. A list of names follows.]

Memorial of the Baron de Bastrop to the Baron de Carondelet. New Orleans, June 20, 1796. Certified copy. 3 pages.

Concession of governor Carondelet, New Orleans, June 21, 1796. Certified copy. 2 pages.

The project and concession embraced (1) a grant of about twelve square leagues, in the district of Ouachita including the Bayu Liard; (2) free lands to the immigrant families (no one to receive over four hundred square arpanes); (3) permission to export the flour produced in Ouachita directly to Havana, without selling at New Orleans; (4) liberty of conscience to non-Catholics, etc. The originals were given to U. S. Consul Trist in 1835, as appears from a receipt which is among the papers.

Other documents in the *expediente* are the following: "List des familles arrivées par M. le Baron de Bastrop le 19 Avril 1797.—en vertu de son Contract." Fort Miró, May 8, 1797. Sixty-four persons; names given.

"Etat des familles arrivées á ce Poste des Etats Unis le 7e May 1797—par le voye de la N^lle Madrid et de le Natchez, sous la conduite de Mr. de Breard, en vertu du Contract passé avec Mr. le Baron de Bastrop." Fort Miró, May 10, 1797. Thirty-five persons; names given.

Letter of the Baron de Carondelet to the Intendant Morales in support of the project of the Baron de Bastrop, dwelling upon the advantages which would accrue to the province from it, stating the needs of the colony and the policy of his administration. New Orleans, June 11, 1797. 16 pages.

The Intendant Morales to the secretary of finance, D. Pedro Varela y Ulloa, expressing his disapproval of the concession on the ground that the settlers were Americans, English and Protestants imbued with maxims of liberty, and were too close to the Mexican border. New Orleans, June 30, 1797.

Memorial of Abraham Morehouse to the Marquis de Casa-Calvo. New Orleans, December 11, 1799. Original. 7 pages. Request that his right to the Baron de Bastrop's privileges and properties, sold to him by Bastrop, should be duly confirmed, and that permission be given h'm to erect flour-mills, to introduce laborers and machinerv for the extraction of iron ore and coal, etc.

Letter of the Marquis de Casa-Calvo to the Intendant Morales in recommendation of Morehouse's proposals. New Orleans, Dec. 12, 1799.

Decision of the acting Comptroller General and Fiscal of the Royal Treasury, Don Gilberto Leonard, on Morehouse's proposals, stating that the concession to Bastrop had not received the royal sanction; that it had become void on account of non-fulfillment on the part of Bastrop; that the ambitions of the U. S. made it unwise to allow American sellers within the territory, especially at a point so contiguous to New Spain; etc. New Orleans, January 18, 1800. 4 pages.

Letter of the commander of Ouachita, Filhiol, to the intendant stating that the project of settlement had proved a failure and reporting unfavorably on the character of the immigrants. Ouachita, March 26, 1800. Spanish translation. 4 pages.

Letter of Don Ramón López y Angulo to the Secretary

of State asking him not to sanction the grants to Bastrop or Morgan or any others recommended by the marquis de Casa-Calvo. New Orleans, September 25, 1800, 2 pages.

Letter of Don Ramón López y Angulo to the Secretary of State reviewing the subject of the concession to Bastrop and the project of Morehouse, expressing views adverse to the whole proceeding. New Orleans, July 13, 1801. 12 pages. Expedientes de intendencia, Legajo 595. Cf. *American State Papers.. Public Lands.* V. 2, pp. 772-773.

Etat des Familles arrivées par M^r. le Baron de Bastrop le 19e. Avril 1797.—en vertu de Son Contract.

Samüel Curswel, ... age de	35	ans
Sa Femme, ...	34	"
Jeanne Sa Fille, ...	10	"
Robert Son Fils, ...	5	"
Mathiew, do., ...	3	"

5 têttes

Jean de Hart, ...	43	ans
Sa Femme, ...	43	"
Abraham Son Fils, ...	14	"
Jean, Idem, ...	12	"
Winton, Idem, ...	10	"
Jeannette Sa Fille, ...	7	"
Jacob Son Fils, ...	2	"

7 têttes

Samuel Brown, ...	31	ans
Sa Femme, ...	31	"
Charles Son Fils, ...	4	"
Sali Sa Fille, ...	6	"
Charles Son Fille, ...	4	"
Elisabeth Sa Fille, ...	3	"
Rachel ditto, ...	2	"

7 têttes

Charles Gim, ... 27 ans ⎫
    Sa Femme, ... 25 " ⎬ 4 têttes
    Jean Son Fils, ... 1 " ⎬
    Henriette Hardy, Opheline, ... 9 " ⎭

Jacques MacCalester, ... 32 ans ⎫
    Sa Femme, ... 25 " ⎬ 4 têttes
    Elisabeth Sa Fille, ... 9 " ⎬
    Jacques Son Fils, ... 5 " ⎭

Jean Kurter, ... 36 ans ⎫
    Sa Femme, ... 32 " ⎬
    William, Son Fils, ... 7 " ⎬
    Mathieu, ditto, ... 6 " ⎬ 6 têttes
    Hamilton, do., ... 4 " ⎬
    Jeannette, Sa Fille, ... 1 " ⎭

Joseph Seggers, ... 46 ans ⎫
    Sa Femme, ... 36 " ⎬
    Jean, Son Fils, ... 12 " ⎬
    Sali, Sa Fille, ... 11 " ⎬
    Joseph, Son Fils, ... 10 " ⎬ 8 têttes
    Faderie, Idem, ... 8 " ⎬
    Marie, Sa Fille, ... 4 " ⎬
    Elisabeth, do., ... 2 " ⎭

Jacques MacMahan, ... 25 ans ⎫
    Sa Femme, ... 23 " ⎬ 4 têttes
    Elisabeth, Sa Fille, ... 4 " ⎬
    Maria, ditto, ... 2 " ⎭

Jean Kugel, ... 22 ans ⎫
　　Sa Femme, ... 19 " ⎪
　　Elisie, Son Fils [sic], ... 3 " ⎬ 4 têttes
　　Marthe, Idem, ... 1 " ⎭

Guillaume Stuart, ... 53 ans ⎫
　　Sa Femme, ... 37 " ⎪
　　George, Son Fils, ... 18 " ⎪
　　Michel, ditto, ... 12 " ⎪
　　Salli, Sa Fille, ... 10 " ⎬ 8 têttes
　　David, Son Fils, ... 8 " ⎪
　　Rachel, Sa Fille, ... 6 " ⎪
　　Mary, ditto, ... 2 " ⎭

Joseph Boëñ, ... Garcon, ... 23 ans ⎫
Isaac Och, ... do., ... 21 " ⎪
Bernard Jochs, ... do., ... 19 " ⎪
George Cimbers, ... do., ... 24 " ⎬ 7 têttes
Silvain Baskem, ... do., ... 22 " ⎪
Michel Rotscher, ... do., ... 23 " ⎪
André Wilhe, ... do., ... 22 " ⎭

　　　　Total des Individus, ... 64 têttes
Au Fort Miro le 8ᵉ, May 1797 ./.
　　............　　　　　Fithiol.

Etat des familles arrivées á ce Poste, des Etats Unis, le 7ᵉ, May 1797—par la voye de la Nˡˡᵉ Madrid et de le Natchés, sous la conduite du Mʳ. de Bréard en Vertu du contract passé avec Mʳ. le Baron de Bastrop.

William Burney, ...age de 58 ans ⎫
    Sa Femme, ... 46 "   ⎪
    Elisabeth Arrie, Ophéline, ... 1 "   ⎬ 4 têttes
    Datis Négrisse *da dit* Burney,.. 11 " ⎭

William Burney, Fils, ... 28 ans ⎫
    Sa Femme, ... 25 " ⎪
    Jean, Son Fils, ... 8 "   ⎬ 5 têttes
    Jacques, Idem, ... 6 "   ⎪
    Gillaume, Idem, ... 1 "   ⎭

Latrie Power, ... 43 ans ⎫
    Sa Femme, ... 30 " ⎪
    Catherine, Sa Fille, ... 10 " ⎪
    Nancy, ditto, ... 8 "   ⎪
    Thomas, Son Fils, ... 7 "   ⎬ 8 têttes
    Folli, Sa Fille, ... 5 "   ⎪
    Margareite, do., ... 4 "   ⎪
    Martha, do., ... $2\frac{1}{2}$ " ⎭

Henry Kurter, ... 28 ans ⎫
    Sa Femme, ... 26 " ⎪
    Catherine Sa Fille, ... 5 "   ⎬ 4 têttes
    Joseph, Son Fils, ... $3\frac{1}{2}$ " ⎭

Abraham Kurter Frere *da sus dit?*.... 22 ans ⎫
Joseph Kurter, Idem, ... 21 "   ⎬ 2 têttes

Christoffer Offen, ...	49 ans	
Sa Femme, ...	50 "	
Jean, Son Fils, ...	20 "	
Joseph, Idem, ...	18 "	6 têttes
Maria, Sa Fille, ...	14 "	
Margareite, do., ...	8 "	

Y^{ve} Qacharie, Champagne, ...	50 ans	2 têttes
[or Vve] Nice, Sa Negrisse, ...	15 "	

Charles Onil, ...	35 ans	
Michel Silvain, ...	35 "	4 têttes
Caleb Husted [?]	21 "	
Guill. Miller, ...	21 "	

En tout, ... 35 têttes

Au Fort Miro le 10 May, 1797 ./.

    ————   Fithiol.

LEHIGH COUNTY NATURALIZATION RECORDS

Transcribed by Don Yoder

In the editor's search for the European origins of our Pennsylvania German pioneers, he has turned to a rich and hitherto untapped source—the Naturalization Papers of Aliens, preserved at the County Courthouses in accordance with a federal law of 1798.

The immigrant alien who settled in Pennsylvania after the formation of the United States Government under the Constitution had to file several papers with the Court of Common Pleas of the County in which he had taken up residence. The first of these papers was the "Declaration of Intention to Become a Citizen," the second was the "Petition for Naturalization," which was acted upon by the court, resulting in favorable cases in the naturalization of the petitioner.

The value of such papers for those interested in Pennsylvania Dutch genealogy, is that for the most part, they give us the name of the village, or at least the province of Germany, from which the emigrant came. This first article in a lengthy series of "Naturalization Records" which the Editor plans to publish, comes from information copied from the original papers in the Prothonotary's Office of the Lehigh County Courthouse in Allentown.

Not all these immigrants landed on our shores before 1808—the traditional and arbitrary date after which no immigrant is considered "Pennsylvania German" by the Membership Committee of the Pennsylvania German Society. However, I have included all German immigrants who petitioned for naturalization up to the year 1820. Most of them settled among the Pennsylvania Dutch, intermarried with them, and their descendants are indistinguishable from the mass of descendants of the Eighteenth Century Pennsylvania German Pioneers.

1) JOHANN FRIEDRICH HUEBENER (D1), on December 22, 1812, filed the following "Affidavit & Declaration of John F. Hubner—Intention to Become a Citizen of the United States": "STATE OF PENNSYLVANIA, LEHIGH COUNTY SS. JOHN F. HUBNER of the age of thirty eight years and upwards, a subject of the IMPERIAL CITY OF HAMBURG, in [the] empire of GERMANY, now residing within the COUNTY of LEHIGH af[ore]s[ai]d under the Jurisdiction of the United States, doth upon his oath administered according to law declare that it is bona fide his Intention to become a citizen of these United States and to renounce forever all allegiance and fidelity to any foreign prince Potentate State or Sovereignity whatsoever and particularly to the Government of the Imperial City of Hamburg aforesaid to whom he is a subject and also all orders & letters of Nobility to which he may be entitled. Sworn & Declared in open Court, Dec. 22, 1812. Signed: JOH FRID HUEBENER."

2) DAVID THIM (D2), on December 22, 1812, filed a Declaration of Intention, stating that he was "of the age of thirty seven years & upwards a subject of WEST PRUSSIA in the EMPIRE of GERMANY, now residing within the COUNTY OF LEHIGH."

3) SAMUEL HEILNER (D3), on December 22, 1812, filed a Declaration of Intention, stating that he was "of the age of twenty four years or thereabouts a Subject of the PRINCIPALITY of WERTZBURG [WUERZ-BURG] in the EMPIRE of GERMANY," now resident in Lehigh County.

4) JOHANN CHRISTOPH ZAENGLEIN (D4), on February 24, 1813, filed a Declaration of Intention, stating that he was "of the age of thirty seven years & upwards, a subject of PRUSSIAN KONINGSBERG in the EMPIRE of GERMANY," now resident in Lehigh County. Sworn in open court, August 31, 1813.

5) NICHOLAS DICK (D5), on February 24, 1813, filed a Declaration of Intention, stating that he is "of the age of twenty seven years or thereabouts formerly inhabitant of WEST PRUSSIA in the EMPIRE of GER-MANY," now resident in Lehigh County, and offers to renounce his allegiance to Frederick IV, King of Prussia.

6) JACOB GUELICH (D8), on February 2, 1814, filed a Declaration of Intention, stating that he was "born in the year of our Lord one thousand seven hundred & eighty four—in HAMBURG in the EMPIRE of GER-MANY—whence he migrated in the year of our Lord one thousand eight hundred & seven and has selected the Commonwealth of Pennsylvania, as the place of his intended settlement." The Prothonotary spelled his name "GILLICH."

7) MICHAEL HERLEIN (D10), on May 3, 1814, filed a Declaration of Intention, stating that he was "born in the year of our Lord one thousand seven hundred & fifty seven—in the COUNTY or CIRCLE of FRANCO-NIA in the KINGDOM of BAVARIA in GERMANY whence he migrated in the year of our Lord one thousand eight hundred and five." He offers to renounce the sovereignty of the King of Bavaria.

8) DAVID TREXLER (D11), on August 29, 1814, filed a Declaration of Intention, stating that he was "born in the year one thousand seven hundred and eighty three, in the KINGDOM of WIRTEMBERG [WUERT—TEMBERG], whence he migrated in the year A.D. 1805." He offers to renounce the King of Wuerttemberg. The alien signed his name in German, "DAVID DREXLER."

9) JAKOB WILHELM DECHANT (P9), on February 2, 1814, filed the following Petition for Naturalization. This immigrant is of especial interest in that he was a Reformed minister in Pennsylvania and Ohio for many years. "To the honorable Robert Porter Esquire, President and his Associates Judges of the Court of Common Pleas of the County of Lehigh. The Petition of JACOB WILLIAM DECHANT a native of OPPENHEIM in the ELECTORATE of MENTZ [MAINZ] in the EMPIRE of GERMANY, respectfully sheweth, That your petitioner on the twenty second day of January in the year of our Lord one thousand eight hundred and ten, filed

a declaration in the Court of Common Pleas of NORTHAMPTON COUNTY in the State of Pennsylvania, stating on oath, that he was then of the age of twenty seven years and a native of OPPENHEIM in the ELECTORATE of MENTZ [MAINZ] in the EMPIRE of GERMANY, but then residing in the township of UPPER SAUCON in the COUNTY of NORTHAMPTON & State aforesaid, & that it was bona fide his Intention to become a citizen of the United States & to renounce forever all allegiance & fidelity to any foreign prince, potentate state of sovereignty whatever & particularly to the ELECTOR of MENTZ to whom he is now subject. That more than three years are elapsed since the making and filing [of] the above declaration. That your petitioner hath never borne any hereditary title or been of any of the orders of nobility, and if any such should by means unexpected descend to him, he doth absolutely and entirely renounce the same; that he hath never been heretofore proscribed by any state, or been legally convicted of having joined the Army of Great Britain during the late [revolutionary] war. That he is now ready and desirous to take the necessary Oath required by the Act of Congress in such Cases provided. Your petitioner therefore prays your honorable Court to admit him to become a citizen of the United States & of the Commonwealth of Pennsylvania. And he will pray, &c. JK. WM. DECHANT, February 2d. 1814."

In another document he swears he will support the Constitution and renounce allegiance to the ELECTOR of MENTZ and to NAPOLEON, EMPEROR of FRANCE and PROTECTOR TO THE RHENISH CONFEDERATION. He was resident in the United States on September 2, 1805.

An affidavit of DANIEL COOPER declares that the petitioner has "behaved as a man of Good moral character attached to the principles of the Constitution of the United States."

LEHIGH COUNTY NATURALIZATION RECORDS

Any of your ancestors in this list? We continue from The DUTCHMAN for May 5, 1949, the list of German and Swiss emigrants who applied for naturalization before the courts of Lehigh County, Pennsylvania, up to the year 1830. If you recognize any of your forefathers among them, write us. We would like further information on all of these families—D.Y.

1) HENRY HEINEN (P12), on December 7, 1815, filed a Petition for Naturalization, stating that he was "a native of EAST FRIESLAND, in GERMANY." On November 18, 1812, he had filed his first papers in the Court of Common Pleas of Northampton County. He renounces the King of Prussia, and denies having been in the British Army in the late revolutionary war. He further states that he was resident in the United States on or about July 30, 1804, and for nine years past has lived in Pennsylvania. He renounces the King of Prussia and the King of Hanover, "to whose Dominion East: Friesland has lately been annexed." JOHN MARX or MARCK testifies as to his good moral character. According to Preston Laury, *The History of the Allentown Conference of the Ministerium of Pennsylvania* (Kutztown: Kutztown Publishing Company, 1926), this immigrant was the Reverend HEINRICH HEINE, who from 1808-1817 served the Zionsville-Western Salisbury Parish, later removing to Gettysburg. The Prothonotary's Index refers to these papers under the name "Rev. HENRY HEINEN."

2) ANSEL ARNOLD (D13), on September 3, 1817, filed a Declaration of Intention, stating that he was born March 2, 1797, in EBENHOUSEN in the KINGDOM of WIRTEMBERG [WUERTTEMBERG] in GERMANY, whence he migrated on March 18, 1816, to the United States, selecting Pennsylvania as his home. Intends to renounce his allegiance to Frederick II, King of Wuerttemberg. A second paper (DR13) a Report Preparatory to the Declaration of Intention, states he now resides in BERKS COUNTY. He arrived at BALTIMORE on or about July 28, 1816. He has no parents, guardian, master or mistress.

3) DANIEL ZACHARIAS (DR45), in May Term 1818, filed a Report Preparatory to Filing a Declaration of Intention, stating that he was born in WITGENSTEIN now in the PRINCIPALITY of DARMSTADT in the EMPIRE of GERMANY, on April 22, 1783, and owes allegiance to Francis II, Emperor of Germany. He emigrated from Wittgenstein, May 22, 1805, arriving at Philadelphia, November 28, 1805. With no parents, etc., he chooses Lehigh County, Pennsylvania, as his home. In May Term 1818 he also filed his Declaration of Intention (D15), stating the same information. On September 1, 1823, he filed his Petition for Naturalization, renouncing the Emperor of Austria "of whom I was born a subject." The printer, CHARLES L. HUTTER, vouches for his good character.

4) HENRY DETWEILER (D16), on May 6, 1818, filed his Declaration of Intention, stating that he was born December 18, 1795, in LANGEN-BRUK, in the CANTON of BASEL, in SWITZERLAND, whence he migrated April 2, 1817, to the United States. He signs his name "DR. HENRY DETWILLER." He was therefore the Allentown physician, famous in the annals of homeopathic medicine in America. His Report (DR16), filed at the same time, states that he arrived at Philadelphia, July 20, 1817, and having no parents, etc., has settled in Lehigh County. In September Term, 1823, "HENRY DETWILLER, M.D." filed his Petition for Naturalization (P42), and renounced the government of the Canton of Basel in the Republic of Switzerland. JOHN BAHL vouches for his good character.

5) CARL FRIEDRICH SCHAEFFLE (D17), on May 6, 1819, filed his Declaration of Intention, stating that he "is a subject of the King of WIRTEMBERG in Europe, that he belongs to the WIRTEMBERG NATION, that he was born" August 29, 1796, "in the town of DURRMENZ in the COUNTY of MAULBRUNN and KINGDOM of WIRTEMBERG afores'd, whence he migrated on" April 12, 1818, landing at Philadelphia, August 28, 1818. He is now 22 years, 8 months, and 7 days old, and intends to make Pennsylvania his residence. In his Report (DR17), filed at the same time, May Term, 1819, he offers to renounce his allegiance to William I, King of Wuerttemberg.

6) CHRISTOPH GOTTLIEB RETTICH (D18), in May Term, 1819, filed his Declaration of Intention, stating that he was born July 13, 1796, in the town of MAEHRINGEN in the COUNTY of TUEBINGEN, in the KINGDOM of WIRTEMBERG, whence he migrated May 29, 1817, landing at Philadelphia on October 10, 1817. His age is 22 years, 9 months, and 23 days. In his Report (DR18) he offers to renounce William I, King of Wuerttemberg.

7) JOHN CASPAR PFEIFFER (D19), on September 6, 1820, filed his Declaration of Intention, stating that he was born at KLEIN SACHSEN-HEIM, in the COUNTY or OBERAMBT of VAYHINGEN, in the KINGDOM of WIRTEMBERG. His age is 34 years, and he intends to make his home in Heidelberg Township, Lehigh County.

8) THOMAS MEYER (D20) on September 4, 1820, filed his Declaration of Intention, stating that he was born at NEUSYLINGEN or NESLYNGEN in the KINGDOM of BAVARIA. His age is 48 years, and he intends to settle in the Borough of Northampton [i.e., Allentown].

9) GEORGE ISING (P21), on December 9, 1820, filed his Petition for Naturalization, stating that he landed in the United States in September, 1786, and has resided for the last seven years in Lehigh County. The foreign sovereignty which he renounces in particular is that of the KING of DENMARK. CASPAR MAYER vouches for his good character.

10) JACOB MONHEIMER (D26), on December 2, 1818, filed his Declaration of Intention, stating that he was born in the year 1786 in the COUNTY of RETZATKREIS in the KINGDOM of BAVARIA, whence he

migrated in 1818. He offers to renounce his allegiance to Joseph Maxmilian, King of Bavaria.

11) GIDEON IBACH (D35), on September 6, 1816, filed his Declaration of Intention, stating that he was born in the DUKEDOM of BERG in the CIRCLE of WESTPHALIA, in the year 1785, whence he emigrated in 1796 and made his home in Pennsylvania. Offers to renounce the sovereignty of the Emperor of Austria. In September Term, 1823, he filed his Petition for Naturalization (P34), at which time GUSTAVUS IBACH of the Borough of Northampton vouches for his good character, having known him from infancy; JOHANNES SMITH of the Borough of Northampton likewise vouches for him.

12) GUSTAVUS IBACH (D39), on September 7, 1816, filed his Declaration of Intention, stating that he was born in the DUKEDOM of BERG in the CIRCLE of WESTPHALIA, whence he emigrated in the year 1796. Offers to renounce the sovereignty of the Emperor of Austria. In September Term, 1823, he filed his Petition for Naturalization (P40), in which he gives the year of his birth as 1791. GIDEON IBACH of South Whitehall Township vouches for his good character, as does JOHANNES J. SCHMIDT of the Borough of Northampton.

13) HENRICH [HEYMAN] WOOLF (D36), on August 31, 1818, filed his Declaration of Intention, stating that he was born April 15, 1787, in OBERDORF, in the KINGDOM of WIRDENBERG [WUERTTEMBERG], whence he migrated, May 8, 1817, to the United States. Offers to renounce the sovereignty of Frederich II, King of Wuerttemberg. Signs his name in German: HEYMAN WOOLFF. In his Report (DR36), filed at the same time, his name appears as "HAYMAN WOOLFF," and he states that he landed at Philadelphia, December 20, 1817; has no parents, etc. In September Term, 1823, "HENRY WOLF otherwise called HAYMAN WOLF," filed his Petition for Naturalization (P37), in which he signs himself in German: HENRICH WOOLF. PETER GROSS vouches for his good character.

14) DANIEL ALBRECHT (P54), on May 3, 1825, filed his Petition for Naturalization, which states that "DANIEL ALBRIGHT, a native of the PALATINATE of WURTEMBERG [*sic*] in GERMANY, now resident in the Township of Upper Milford in the said County" of Lehigh, was resident in the United States between June 18, 1796, and April 14, 1802, and has continued to reside there ever since, having also lived in Pennsylvania for more than one year last past. Signs his name: DANIEL ALBRECHT. Renounces the sovereignty of the *Duke* of Wurttemberg [Evidently he did not know that little Wuerttemberg had become a Kingdom!]. His good character is vouched for by GEORGE KEMMERER.

15) JOHN T. HOLLMANN (P85), on September 5, 1829, filed his Petition for Naturalization, stating that he is a native of BREMEN, and was resident in the United States between April 14, 1802, and June 18, 1812, and has continued to reside here. Signs his name in English: JOHN T. HOLLMANN. Renounces the sovereignty of the Government of Bremen

and the Emperor of Austria. JOHN F. HALBACH and HENRY JARRETT vouch for his good character.

16) JACOB AGSTER (P86), on September 8, 1829, filed his Petition for Naturalization, in which he states he is a native of ILSFELD in the KINGDOM of WURTEMBERG, and was resident in the United States between April 14, 1802, and June 18, 1812, and has continued to reside here. Renounces the sovereignty of the King of Wuerttemberg. Signs his name in German: JACOB AGSTER. HENRY JARRETT and CONRAD NEYMEYER vouch for his good character.

NATURALIZATIONS—DURING THE COURT SESSIONS OF JANUARY, 1798, WASHINGTON CO., MARYLAND

By Miss Kate Singer Curry, Washington, D. C.

Henry Adam of Hagerstown, a German and formerly a subject of Prince of Hesse.

Michael Beard, native of Germany.

Conrad Bleutlingers, of Hagerstown, native of Switzerland.

Henry Bowser, of Salisbury District, Washington Co. Md. Native of Switzerland.

Frederick Clinch, laborer, of Hagerstown. Native of Germany.

Daniel Cline of Funkstown, formerly a subject of the Emperor of Germany.

Henry Cline, butcher, of Hagerstown, formerly subject of the Emperor of Germany.

George Creager, of Hagerstown, a German & formerly a subject of Prince of Hanover.

Henry Delman, weaver of Hagerstown, native of Holland.

Christian Fightig, shoemaker of Funkstown, formerly subject of Emperor of Germany.

Francis Garmyer, shoemaker near Antietam, formerly subject of Emperor of Germany.

George Crisman, butcher of Hagerstown.   Native of Germany.

John Goll, near Hagerstown, German, formerly subject of Prince of Landgrave.

Henry Hickroat, of Williamsport, German, formerly subject of Prince of Hesse.

Charles Holbrick, blacksmith, Antietam Hundred.   Native of Germany.

John Johnson, farmer near Gilbert's Mills.   Native of Ireland.

Gregorius Kempff, clock maker of Hagerstown.   Native of Germany.

John Leight, of Hagerstown, tinner, formerly subject of Emperor of Germany.

John Longemon, residence Washington Co. Md.   Native of Germany.

John Miller, baker, of Hagerstown, formerly a subject of Emperor of Germany.

John Neitzell, of Williamsport, cooper.   Native of Germany.

Conrad Null, of Hagerstown, a German, formerly subject of the Prince of Hesse.

Ralph Ormston near Booth's Mills, farmer.   Native of Great Britain.

Vendel Oyer, near Williamsport, laborer.   Formerly subject of Emperor of Germany.

Samuel Ross, shoemaker, Williamsport.   An Irishman.

William Seagler, of Marsh Hundred, Washington Co., Md.   Native of Germany and formerly a subject of the Prince of Hesse.

Henry Schrader, of Marsh Hundred, formerly subject of King of Prussia.

Charles Seltzer, of Hagerstown, and formerly a subject of the Prince of Hesse.

Conrad Shafer, of Boonsberry, Washington Co., Md., formerly a subject of the Prince of Hesse.

Conrad Shane, of Hagerstown, whitesmith, formerly a subject of the Emperor of Germany.

William Shiker, rear Hagerstown, formerly subject of the King of Prussia.

Matthias Shold, tailor near Antietam.   Native of Germany.

John Smith, of Hagerstown, bricklayer & stonemason.   Native of Ireland.

Adam Smotz (?), farmer Lower Antietam.   Native of Germany.

Henry Snyder, farmer near Hagerstown.   Native of Germany.

Christian Stemple, of Hagerstown, a German & formerly subject of Prince of Wurtemburg.

Christian Stinebrenner, of Hagerstown.   Native of Germany.

Henry Strouse, stone cutter.   Native of Germany.

Christopher Swope, of Hagerstown, formerly subject of Emperor of Germany.

Edward Augustus Thomas, surveyor, near Booth's Mills.   Native of England.

John Wagenor, native of France.

Jacob Weber, laborer of Hagerstown.   Native of Germany.

Adam Weller, native of Germany, residing in Washington Co., Md.

John Jacob Werner, bookbinder of Hagerstown.   Native of Germany.

James Wilson, of Boonsberry, carpenter.   Native of Ireland.

Early New York Naturalization Records in the Emmet Collection

With a List of Aliens Naturalized in New York 1802–1814

By RICHARD J. WOLFE
The New York Public Library

AMONG the 2,500 miscellaneous pieces accompanying the Emmet Collection upon its presentation to The New York Public Library in 1896 were two manuscript lists of immigrants naturalized in New York Colony and New York State between 1740–1769 and 1802–1814 respectively.[1] A transcript of the earlier of these lists, forwarded by the Secretary of the Colony of New York to the office of the Commissioners for Trade and Plantations in London pursuant to Act 13 George II (1739) and now among the records of the Colonial Office at the Public Record Office, was used as a prime source for M. S. Giuseppi's *Naturalization of Foreign Protestants in the American and West Indian Colonies*.[2] The later list, containing the names of 115 aliens naturalized in New York City between 29 October 1802 and 10 March 1814, has remained unpublished over the years.

Both lists came to my attention in the course of work on a revision of Harold Lancour's *Passenger Lists of Ships Coming to North America, 1607–1825*, a bibliography originally published by the Library in May 1937 and to be reissued in a revised and enlarged form this spring.[3] In view of the

---

[1] The Manuscripts of the Emmett Collection number about 10,800, and they include one or more autographs of almost every man at all distinguished in American affairs during the Revolution as well as a number of earlier colonial documents and letters of more recent date. The collection was presented to The New York Public Library in 1896 by John S. Kennedy. The Library published a calendar of the Collection in 1900; this was reissued in facsimile in 1959. Some Emmet manuscripts of historical interest not described in the published calendar can be found listed in "Manuscript Collections . . . in the Lenox Building," *Bulletin of The New York Public Library* v (1901) 306–336 (the present documents on 323).

The Library classification for the two documents in question is: New York, *Colony and State*. Naturalization statistics, giving names, etc., of persons naturalized, 1740–1769; also a list giving names, etc., of immigrants, 1802–1814. 24 pp. N. Y. F°.

[2] Volume 24 of *The Publications of The Huguenot Society of London* (Manchester 1921) p 30–40. The list was printed there in a rearranged form and frequently omits essential information such as occupations and names of witnesses present on the Emmet MS. Because of this and obvious errors of spelling and transcription, plans are under way to republish the 1740–1769 list based on the Emmet MS in an appropriate genealogical magazine.

[3] In spite of its delimiting title, the Lancour bibliography is not restricted to passenger lists alone. In reality, it contains citations to all known published lists of immigrants to North America before 1825 found in a variety of sources, including naturalization records, ration lists, records of indenture, parish registers, "protocols" (visa permits) of foreign lands, lists of entry kept at American ports, and oaths of allegiance and abjuration, as well as passenger lists.

obvious importance of such source records to genealogists and historians alike and because of the desirability of indexing the 1802–1814 list in the Lancour revision, it is published here.

This list was undoubtedly compiled in consequence of the act passed on 14 April 1802 (2 Stat. L., 153) which repealed the stringent naturalization law of 1798 (1 Stat. L., 566) and reenacted the main provisions of the law of 1795 (1 Stat. L., 414), the second naturalization law of the United States. The conditions required for naturalization under this statute were fourfold: (1) that the alien declare under oath before the Supreme Court, a district or circuit court, or a court of one of the states or territories his intention to become a citizen and renounce all allegiance to a foreign power; (2) that he swear to support the Constitution of the United States; (3) that he renounce any hereditary title or orders of nobility in the kingdom or state from which he came; (4) that the court admitting the alien be satisfied that he had resided in the United States for at least five years and within the state or territory where such court was held for a period of at least one year. The act also prescribed a few simple modes and forms for registering aliens applying for naturalization. The law remained in force for one hundred and four years. It was modified in 1804 (2 Stat. L., 292), in 1816 (3 Stat. L., 258) and in 1824 (4 Stat. L., 69) and amended in 1813. The act passed on 30 July 1813 (3 Stat. L., 53) permitted naturalization of persons who were living in this country prior to 18 June 1812 and who had made declarations of intention or were otherwise entitled to naturalization, though according to existing law they were alien enemies at the time. There was no federal supervision of naturalization under these laws. Each court administered the law according to its own interpretation and even designed its own form for records it was charged to keep. The law of 1802 specified that such records were to contain birthplace, age, nation, and allegiance of each alien, together with the country from which he or she migrated and the place of his or her intended settlement. It was not until the passage of the Naturalization Act of 29 June 1906 (34 Stat. L., 596), setting up the Bureau of Immigration and Naturalization, that Congress enacted uniform rules and forms for the naturalization of aliens throughout the United States.

ALIENS NATURALIZED IN NEW YORK 1802–1814

(Manuscript Division, The New York Public Library)

NAME	PLACE OF BIRTH	AGE	NATION	ALLEGIANCE	COUNTRY WHENCE HE EMIGRATED	PLACE OF INTENDED SETTLEMENT	TIME OF FILING REPORT
[page 1]							
George Cumings	Newry	34 years	Ireland	King of Great Britain & Ireland	Hamburgh	New York State	29th October 1802
Joseph Cuthbert	Belfast	40	Ireland	Do	Do	Do	30th October 1802
William Kernan	Cavan	21	Ireland	Do	Ireland	Do	December 23d 1802
Robert Mayhew	Southampton	35	England	Do	London	Do	June 1st 1803
William Read	Dublin	41	Ireland	Do	Ireland	Do	November 10th 1803
Joseph Sproull	Tyrone	46	Ireland	Do	Ireland	Do	February 8th 1804
John Blackburn	Cork	24	Ireland	Do	Ireland	Georgia	June 5th 1804
Alexander Orr	Belfast	25	Ireland	Do	Ireland	New York State	June 28th 1804
Henry Dudley	Cork	19	Ireland	Do	Ireland	Do	June 28th 1804
John Thomas Netterville	Cavan	34	Ireland	Do	Ireland	Do	October 27th 1804
John Morris	Kings County	40	Ireland	Do	London	Do	August 29th 1804
William Higgins	Dublin	32	Ireland	Do	London	Do	August 29th 1804
William R. Williams	Surrey	63	England	Do	London	Do	August 29th 1804
Thomas Addis Emmet	Cork	41	Ireland	Do	Bordeaux, France	Do	November 14th 1804
Jonas Lander	Cork	28	Ireland	Do	Ireland	Do	November 15th 1804
Robert Hunter	Galway	45	Scotland	Do	England	Do	November 19th 1804
[page 2]							
James Lougheed	Sligo	21	Ireland	Do	Ireland	Do	November 21st 1804
James Joseph McDonnell	Mayo	40	Ireland	Do	France	Do	June 7th 1805
Richard Whyte Thompson	Dublin	25	Ireland	Do	Ireland	Do	June 12th 1805
William James McNevan	Galway	35	Ireland	Do	France	Do	July 5th 1805
Henry Casimar Rham	Yverdon	21	Switzerland	Republic of Switzerland	Switzerland	Do	November 14th 1805

NAME	PLACE OF BIRTH	AGE	NATION	ALLEGIANCE	COUNTRY WHENCE HE EMIGRATED	PLACE OF INTENDED SETTLEMENT	TIME OF FILING REPORT
[page 2, continued]							
Armand John James Delessert	Aubonne	26	Switzerland	Do	Switzerland	Do	November 14th 1805
John Swiney	Cork	29	Ireland	King of Great Britain & Ireland	France	Do	December 18th 1805
Dennis James Conroy	Cork	35	Ireland	Do	Ireland	Do	January 9th 1806
Bernard Redmond	Wexford	58	Ireland	Do	Ireland	Do	February 10th 1806
Hugh O Neil	Derry	35	Ireland	Do	Ireland	Do	March 22d 1806
Dennis O Connor	Dublin	30	Ireland	Do	Ireland	Do	March 22d 1806
John Chambers	Dublin	51	Ireland	Do	Ireland	Do	May 12th 1806
Charles Chambers	Dublin	24	Ireland	Do	Ireland	Do	May 12th 1806
George Mills	Dublin	32	Ireland	Do	Ireland	Do	May 16th 1806
William Sampson	Londonderry	41	Ireland	Do	England	Do	July 12th 1806
Augustus Claudius	Lippstadt	39	Germany	King of Prussia	England	Do	August 13th 1806
John Bailie	Madras	19	West Indies	King of Great Britain & Ireland	England	Do	March 20th 1807
Owen Keveny	Sligo	20	Ireland	Do	Ireland	Do	May 10th 1807
John Te Kamp	Crefeld	29	France	King of Prussia	Prussia	Do	June 6th 1807
John Sweetman	Dublin	50	Ireland	King of Great Britain & Ireland	Ireland	Do	June 25th 1807
William Swan	Armagh	22	Ireland	Do	Ireland	Do	July 10th 1807
[page 3]							
George McBride	Armagh	26	Ireland	King of Great Britain & Ireland	Ireland	New York State	July 10th 1807
Peter Grantham	Dublin	28	Ireland	Do	Ireland	Do	October 30th 1807
Stephen Rickard	Dublin	27	Ireland	Do	Ireland	Do	November 17th 1807
Anthony D. Duff	Chatham	26	England	Do	Portugal	Do	November 30th 1807
William Stubbs	Meath	50	Ireland	Do	Ireland	Do	December 31st 1807
Edward Stubbs	Dublin	22	Ireland	Do	Ireland	Do	December 31st 1807
Valentine Derry	Down	41	Ireland	Do	France	Do	May 21st 1808

NAME	PLACE OF BIRTH	AGE	NATION	ALLEGIANCE	COUNTRY WHENCE HE EMIGRATED	PLACE OF INTENDED SETTLEMENT	TIME OF FILING REPORT
[page 3, continued]							
James Horrica	Sligo	32	Ireland	Do	Ireland	Do	June 14th 1808
Alexander Crofts	Dublin	27	Ireland	Do	Ireland	Do	July 1st 1808
Ferben Lange	Frederxberg	39	Denmark	King of Denmark	Isle of France	Do	September 19th 1808
Bernard Dornin	Dublin	40	Ireland	King of Great Britain & Ireland	Ireland	Do	October 11th 1808
Mark Evans	Queens County	35	Ireland	Do	Ireland	Do	November 16th 1808
Pierce Aylward	Wicklow	25	Ireland	Do	Ireland	Do	April 17th 1809
Israel H. Lewis	Norwich	17	England	Do	England	Do	June 12th 1809
James Wallace	Kilkenny	28	Ireland	Do	Ireland	Do	July 24th 1809
Hugh McKenna	Ireland	20	Ireland	Do	Ireland	Do	August 18th 1809
Nicholas Gray	Wexford	33	Ireland	Do	Ireland	Do	October 25th 1809
[page 4]							
Hugh Henderson	Monaghan	21	Ireland	Do	Ireland	Do	October 31st 1809
Wheaton Bradish	Dublin	22	Ireland	Do	Ireland	Do	November 8th 1809
Edward Stephens	Dublin	26	Ireland	Do	Ireland	Do	November 9th 1809
Samuel Jamison	Coleraine	21	Ireland	Do	Ireland	Do	December 18th 1809
Thomas Smith	Scotland	33	Scotland	Do	Scotland	Do	December 26th 1809
John William Schmidt	Wunsiedel	28	Germany	King of Prussia	Germany	Do	January 3d 1810
Lawrence Bracken	Westmeath	31	Ireland	King of Great Britain & Ireland	Ireland	Do	April 9th 1810
Hamilton Biggam	Down	27	Ireland	Do	Ireland	Do	April 11th 1810
Charles Moony	Antrim	28	Ireland	Do	Ireland	Do	April 23d 1810
Pierre Francois Gentil	Caudebec	32	France	Emperor of French	Martinique	Do	April 24th 1810
Antony Vas	Lisbon	37	Portugal	Prince Regent of Portugal	Havanna	Do	May 2d 1810
Luke Branman	Ireland	33	Ireland	King of Great Britain & Ireland	England	Do	June 16th 1810
John Brennan	Clare	27	Ireland	Do	Ireland	Do	June 20th 1810

NAME	PLACE OF BIRTH	AGE	NATION	ALLEGIANCE	COUNTRY WHENCE HE EMIGRATED	PLACE OF INTENDED SETTLEMENT	TIME OF FILING REPORT
[page 4, continued]							
Harmann Friedrich Van Lengerke	Bremen	20	Germany	Republic of Bremen	Germany	Do	October 10th 1810
Grace Sampson	Antrim	40	Ireland	King of Great Britain	Ireland	Do	October 29th 1810
John Curran Sampson	Antrim	16	Ireland	Do	Ireland	Do	October 29th 1810
Catharine Anne Sampson	Antrim	14	Ireland	Do	Ireland	Do	October 29th 1810
John Swanton	Cork	35	Ireland	Do	France	Do	September 1st 1810
[page 5]							
Francis Dempsey	Wicklow	45	Ireland	King of Great Britain & Ireland	Ireland	New York State	September 18th 1810
Mary Dempsey	Wexford	50	Ireland	Do	Ireland	Do	September 18th 1810
Edward Dempsey	Wicklow	12	Ireland	Do	Ireland	Do	September 18th 1810
Mary Dempsey	Wexford	14	Ireland	Do	Ireland	Do	September 18th 1810
John B. Montgomery	Down	25	Ireland	Do	Ireland	Do	September 28th 1810
Charles Del Vecchio	Como	23	Italy	King of Italy	Ireland	Do	December 4th 1810
Francis Kernan	Cavan	28	Ireland	King of Great Britain & Ireland	Ireland	Do	February 18th 1811
William Brown	Belfast	21	Ireland	Do	Ireland	Do	April 4th 1811
Robert Boston	Kelso	32	Scotland	Do	England	Do	April 17th 1811
Pierce N Dillon	Dublin	17	Ireland	Do	Ireland	Do	June 3d 1811
Arthur Daly	Kildare	50	Ireland	Do	Ireland	Do	June 12th 1811
Peter MacGregor	Greenock	23	Scotland	Do	England	Do	June 15th 1811
Henry Calam	Bath	25	England	Do	England	Do	July 10th 1811
John Clarke	Montreal	30	Canada	Do	Canada	Do	October 15th 1811
Robert Hutchison	St Ninians	28	Scotland	Do	Scotland	Do	November 2d 1811
Thomas Rhodes	Roserea	27	Ireland	Do	Ireland	Do	January 4th 1812
James Reynolds	Roserea	32	Ireland	Do	Ireland	Do	January 28th 1812
James Delaney O Donnell	Dublin	22	Ireland	Do	Ireland	Do	April 2d 1812
William Montgomery	Comber	17	Ireland	Do	Ireland	Do	April 6th 1812

NAME	PLACE OF BIRTH	AGE	NATION	ALLEGIANCE	COUNTRY WHENCE HE EMIGRATED	PLACE OF INTENDED SETTLEMENT	TIME OF FILING REPORT
[page 6]							
David Wylie	Gallaugh	27	Ireland	Do	Ireland	Do	March 4th 1812
Edward Campbell	Tyrone	39	Ireland	Do	England	Do	May 15th 1813
William Morgan	Pembroke	42	Wales	Do	Nova Scotia	Do	June 15th 1812
James Coghlan	Clonlyon	39	Ireland	Do	Ireland	Do	June 22d 1812
Francis Farrell	Dublin	43	Ireland	Do	Ireland	Do	June 22d 1812
Charles Mahon	Dublin	26	Ireland	Do	Ireland	Do	June 22d 1812
Arthur Calloway	Dublin	30	Ireland	Do	Ireland	Do	June 22d 1812
John French Armstrong	Ireland	19	Ireland	Do	Ireland	Do	June 23d 1812
Benjamin F. Ferrand	Nottingham	25	England	Do	England	Do	June 25th 1812
Gilbert Smissaert	Utrecht	32	Holland	Gov't of Holland	Holland	Do	June 26th 1812
Peter Duffy	Dublin	50	Ireland	King of Great Britain & Ireland	Ireland	Do	June 29th 1812
Jacob Calloway	Dublin	26	Ireland		Ireland	Do	June 29th 1812
Charles Pindar	Constadt	27	Russia	Emperor of Russia	Russia	Do	July 20th 1812
David Graham	Ballyrock	29	Ireland	King of Great Britain & Ireland	England	Do	July 24th 1812
George Chown	London	24	England	Do	England	Do	July 25th 1812
George Newport	Waterford	30	Ireland		Ireland	Do	July 17th 1812
Adrian Stephen Delessert	Aubonne	23	Switzerland	Republic of Switzerland	France	Do	November 18th 1812
James McCall	Armagh	22	Ireland	King of Great Britain & Ireland	Ireland	Do	March 22d 1813
John McCall	Monaghan	18	Ireland	Do	Ireland	Do	June 16th 1813
[page 7]							
Charles A. Geldermersher	Bremen	25	Germany	Emperor of French	France	New York State	August 19th 1813
Michael Keegan	Manchester	21	England	King UK of Great Britain & Ireland	Liverpool	Do	November 13th 1813
James Jackson	Surrey	37	England	Do	London	Do	20th
Nicholas Campbell		34	Ireland	Do	Dublin	Do	March 10, 1814

ABSTRACTS OF NATURALIZATION RECORDS, CIRCUIT COURT, DISTRICT OF COLUMBIA

PETITIONS RECEIVED, 1802-1820

Compiled by VIVIAN HOLLAND, Washington, D. C.

Six of the original thirteen states, Delaware, Massachusetts, New York, South Carolina, Virginia and Maryland already had general naturalization laws when the Constitution, providing for Federal naturalization, was adopted.

Maryland was encouraging immigration and in July 1779 passed a law (Statute Ch. VI, an Act of Naturalization), which promised all newcomers two years' exemption from taxes and to those who were "tradesmen, artificers or manufacturers," a term of four years' exemption from taxation, requiring in return only an oath of allegiance to Maryland.

The Constitution gave Congress the power to "establish an uniform rule of naturalization." The first law required only one year's residence. It met with much opposition expecially from James Madison. An act amending this first bill was passed 26 March 1790 (1 Stat. L., 103), and extended the term of residence to two years, one year to be spent in the state of intended residence. This act empowered any common-law court of record to admit to citizenship "any free, white alien of good moral character" who would forswear allegiance to any other sovereign or state and swear to support the U. S. Constitution. Naturalization of a parent gave citizenship to his minor children.

The second naturalization law, introduced by Madison as chairman of the committee which framed it, was passed by Congress 29 January 1795 (1 Stat. L., 414). It was a sound law. Its principles are incorporated in the naturalization laws that are in effect today. There were six requirements: (1) must forswear allegiance to every other sovereignty; (2) must have lived in the United States for five years and in the state where application was made for at least one year before naturalization; (3) must have "good moral character" and be "attached to the principles of the Constitution of the United States"; (4) must take oath of allegiance to the United States; (5) must renounce title, if any; (6) must have made a declaration of intention at least three years before admission to citizenship. For the benefit of people who had lived in this country prior to 1795, permission was granted to secure naturalization after two years' residence under the act of 26 March 1790. Also any person "proscribed by the legislature" of any state and convicted of having fought with the British army during the Revolution was not admitted to citizenship without the consent of that legislature.

The first two laws became effective during the administration of George Washington.

Growing political uncertainties, both here and abroad, were reflected in the third law, act of June 1798 (1 Stat. L., 566), passed during Adam's term of office and remained in force for four years. It had the severest requirements of any naturalization law ever passed in this country and grew out of the agitation which also created the alien and sedition laws. Every "free, white alien" was required to register; the term of residence was extended to fourteen years with at least five years spent in the state where application was made; the declaration of intention had to be made at least five years before naturalization. Aliens already in this country prior to 1795 were allowed to secure naturalization within one year after enactment of the law and, if they had already made a declaration of intention, they were granted citizenship if they met the requirements of the previous law of 1795. Citizens of a country with which we might be at war were not allowed to apply for citizenship. Clerks of Courts were required to make abstracts of both declarations of intention and naturalization records and send them to the Secretary of State. This was the only law with such a stipulation until the passage of the act of 29 June 1906.

On 14 April 1802, an act sponsored by Thomas Jefferson was passed which repealed the strict law of 1798 and reenacted the chief features of the previous law of

1795. It remained in force for one hundred and four years. An act passed 26 March 1804 modified it to the extent of admitting persons who had lived in the United States between 18 June 1798 and 14 April 1802 but who had not made a declaration of intention; and by granting naturalization to the widow and minor children, upon taking the prescribed oath, of applicants who died after making a declaration of intention but before naturalization had been granted. An amendment to the law, imposed by the act of 13 March 1813, required a continuous term of five years' residence, no absences allowed, and it remained in force until repeated by the act of 26 June 1848.

An act passed 30 June 1813 permitted naturalization of persons who were living in this country prior to 18 June 1812 and had made declarations of intention, or were otherwise entitled to naturalization though according to existing law they were enemy aliens.

There is nothing consistent in the information furnished in these naturalization records. There was no federal supervision and procedures varied widely. Each court administered the law according to its own interpretation and even designed its own form of records. There were considerable differences within the same court, the wealth or dearth of information depending upon the interest and efficiency of the presiding officials.

Old naturalization records, if they still exist, are the property of the court which granted them and are kept within their offices or in some other suitable repository in the community. In the District of Columbia the old naturalization records (1802 to 1926) of the Circuit Court which was abolished in 1911, and of its successor, the District Court, are kept in the National Archives as the most suitable repository in the District of Columbia.

A few of the many records available at National Archives that are of special interest to genealogists are the Population Census Schedules 1790 to 1870, inclusive; (immigration) passenger lists from 1819; records of original entry in Public Lands States; military service records 1775 to 1912; pension records; industrial records; government service records; and genealogical publications.

A few quick references reveal that George HADFIELD, the first to apply for citizenship in the new Federal City, was an architect and designed some of the famous buildings of his adopted city; that Pishie THOMPSON established a bookstore on Pennsylvania Avenue; that Thomas LAW married Eliza CUSTIS, the granddaughter of Martha WASHINGTON; that John SESSFORD, the printer (who remained nameless in the naturalization records for twenty years) published an annual report on the City of Washington; that Dr. John LOGAN traveled to Missouri, then to Illinois where he established his home and became the father of John A. LOGAN, General of the Civil War and later Senator from Illinois. Far from being dry-as-dust statistics, each naturalization record is a potential key to a biography or a link in a family genealogy.

The following are abstracts made from the Naturalization Records of the Circuit Court of the District of Columbia, presumably complete—petitions received 1802 to 1820. The few discrepancies are listed as they appear.

ANDREI, John (William); age 45 in 1817; nativity, Carara, Tuscany, Italy; emigrated from Leghorn, Italy; arrived at Baltimore, Md., 31 Jan. 1806; Declaration of Intention, 6 Dec. 1817; Proof of Residence, June 1820; no witnesses listed; naturalization granted 24 Apr. 1821.

ARNEY, Joseph; confectioner; age 26 in 1813; nativity, Switzerland; Declaration of Intention, 12 Jan. 1813; Proof of Residence, June 1818; witnesses: Frederick Vieller (?), Frederick D. Tschiffely; naturalization granted June 1818.

ARNOTT, John; nativity, England; in U. S. since Dec. 1795, 12 years in Virginia; Declaration of Intention, 27 Dec. 1813; Proof of Residence, 27 Dec. 1813; witness, John Sessford; naturalization granted 27 Dec. 1813.

BACHUS, John; age 23 in 1813; nativity, England; Declaration of Intention, 7 Jan. 1813; Proof of Residence, 26 Dec. 1815; witness, John McPherson; naturalization granted 26 Dec. 1815.

BARNARD, Robert; age 33 in 1819; nativity, Boston, England; emigrated from Liverpool, Eng.; arrived at New York, 18 Oct. 1819; Declaration of Intention, 27 Dec. 1819; Proof of Residence, 28 Dec. 1824; witnesses: Thos. Corcoran, Jr., Jas. Wharton; naturalization granted 28 Dec. 1824.

BLANCHARD, William; nativity, England; in U. S. since 1 Jan. 1806, Washington, D. C., "upwards of two years"; Declaration of Intention, 13 Jan. 1808; Proof of Residence, 17 Jan. 1811; witness, William Cocking; naturalization granted 17 Jan. 1811.

BOND, Isaac; nativity, Great Britain; in U. S. "about 20 yrs.", in Georgetown "about 15 or 17 yrs.;" Declaration of Intention, 6 June 1811; Proof of Residence, 6 June 1811; witness, Thomas Beall; naturalization granted 6 June 1811.

BOND, Samuel; in U. S. "before 14th day of April 1802;" Proof of Residence, 5 Jan. 1814; witness, Peter Howard; naturalization granted 5 Jan. 1814.

BOPP, Frederick; blacksmith; age 34 in 1812; nativity, near Frankfort-on-the-Maine, Germany; former allegiance, Prince of Braumfels; emigrated from Hamburg, Germany; arrived at Baltimore, Md., 28 Mar. 1805; Declaration of Intention, 20 June 1812; Proof of Residence, 21 May 1824; witnesses: John Waters, Henry Smith; naturalization granted 21 May 1824.

BRADY, Peter; age 26 in 1819; nativity, Longford County, Ireland; emigrated from Liverpool, England; arrived at New York, 9 Nov. 1815; Declaration of Intention, 7 July 1819; Proof of Residence, 8 Jan. 1825; witnesses: John Dumphey, Thomas M u r r a y; naturalization granted 8 Jan. 1825.

BRANNAN, John; age 36 in 1820; nativity, city of Exeter, England; emigrated from London, England; arrived at Baltimore, Md., 6 Nov.

1818; Declaration of Intention, 14 Jan. 1820; Proof of Residence, 18 Jan. 1825; witnesses: Thomas Holliday, James Martin; naturalization granted 18 Jan. 1825.

BRERTON, Samuel; age 35 in 1819; Former allegiance, Great Britain; emigrated from Liverpool, England; arrived at Alexandria, Va., 29 Aug. 1818; Declaration of Intention, 18 May 1819; Proof of Residence, 28 May 1824; witnesses: John McClelland, Hania (?) Cassaway; another document also dated 28 May 1824, additional signatures only: Wm. Grintor (or Guntor), Wm. Waters, Henry Stoneby, Thos. G. Waters, Moses Poor (?), Charles Fowler, Lowry Griffith Coombe, Truman Tyler, Jacob Noyes, John M. Mc C l e l l a n d; naturalization granted 28 May 1824.

BROADBACK (Brodback), Jacob; age 37 in 1810; former allegiance, Republic of Helvetia; emigrated from Amsterdam, Holland; arrived at Philadelphia, Pa., Nov. 1802; Declaration of Intention, 9 July 1810; Proof of Residence, 11 June 1824; witnesses: Tench Ringgold, Thomas Cook; naturalization granted 11 June 1824.

BROOKS, Francis; age 45 in 1820; nativity, Down County, Ireland; emigrated from Nuery; arrived at New York, 14 May 1812; Declaration of Intention, 20 Jan. 1820; Proof of Residence, 3 June 1826; witnesses: George Sweeney, A. T. F. Bill; naturalization granted 3 June 1826.

BROUER, Frederick; in U. S. 18 June 1798; Proof of Residence, 1 Nov. 1819; witnesses: John Knoblock, G e o r g e Stuiger; naturalization granted 1 Nov. 1819.

BUCKLEY, Christian; age 26 in 1819; nativity, Canton Grison, Switzerland; emigrated from Tonniagen; arrived at Philadelphia, Pa., 20 Nov. 1810; Declaration of Intention, 12 June 1819; Proof of Residence, 19 Apr. 1824; witnesses: Benjamin M. Belt, John Duckworth; a second Proof of Residence type document dated 1 June 1824, witnesses: Hezekiah Lenglay, John McLaughlin; naturalization granted 19 Apr. 1824.

BURNES (Burns), Charles; age 28 in 1817; nativity, County of Queens, Ireland; emigrated from Cork, Ireland; arrived at Alexandria, Va., 16 Sept. 1816; Declaration of Intention, 4 Jan. 1817; Proof of Residence, 21 Jan. 1824; witnesses: James Scallion, Nicholas Cassaday; naturalization granted 21 Jan. 1824.

BURNS, John; in U. S. since 1800 "inlisted as a seaman in the service of the U. S.," in Washington, D. C. "four years last passed"; Proof of Residence, 31 Oct. 1811; witness: James B. Potts; naturalization granted 1 Nov. 1811.

BURTON, Charles; artist; age 36 in 1818; nativity, London, England; emigrated from Liverpool, Eng.; a document dated 16 June 1818 called "Report of ———, an alien made to the Clerk of the Court of Common Pleas called the Mayor's Court of the City of New York"; Declaration of Intention, 16 June 1818; Proof of Residence, 9 May 1825, made in Albemarle County, Va.; witnesses: Thomas Phoebus, William Young; the Index to the Minutes of the Court state that naturalization was granted 16 June 1818 (but should it be the date of the Proof of Residence document dated 9 May 1825?).

CALLAN, Nicholas; nativity, Ireland; in U. S. from 18 June 1798; Declaration of Intention undated; Proof of Residence, 6 June 1809; witnesses, Patrick Callan; naturalization granted 6 June 1809.

CAMPBELL, Dan; nativity, Dundee, Scotland; Declaration of Intention, (District of Columbia, County of Alexandria), 25 July 1812; Proof of Residence, 13 June 1817, witnesses, Joseph Huddleston, Greenberry Gaither; naturalization granted 13 June 1817.

CARROLL, Daniel, age 38 in 1821; nativity, County of Tipperary, Ireland; emigrated from London, England; arrived at New York, 21 June 1819; Declaration of Intention, 8 Apr. 1821; Proof of Residence, 8 May 1826; witnesses: Walter Clarke, Edward Berry; naturalization granted 8 May 1826.

CARUSO (Carusi), Gaetano; age "51 years and upwards" in 1817; nativity, Naples, Italy; Declaration of Intention, (Court of Common Pleas, Philadelphia), 24 Jan. 1817; Proof of Residence, 30 Dec. 1824; witnesses: Felice Pulizzi, Venenando (Benenando) Pulizzi; naturalization granted 30 Dec. 1824.

CASHELL, Randall; age 36 in 1813; nativity, England; Proof of Residence, 19 June 1813, witnesses: Nathl. Bigsby, Archo Lee, Wm. Moore, Jerh. Mudd, Clemt. Newton, Jos. Clarke, Jeremiah Perkins, Tho. Reynolds, James Wharton, Robt. Clarke, George St. Clair, Igni. Boone; naturalization granted 21 June 1813.

CATON, John; nativity, Ireland; in U. S. from 18 June 1798; Proof of Residence, 9 June 1809; witness, Mathias Kyne; naturalization granted 9 June 1809.

CLARK, Joseph; in U. S. since 18 June 1798; Proof of Residence, 29 Nov. 1826; witnesses: Richard Spalding, James Birth; naturalization granted 29 Nov. 1826.

CLARKE, Francis; former allegiance, Great Britain; Declaration of Intention, undated, made in County Court, Frederick County, Maryland, term beginning "first Monday of Feb. 1803"; Proof of Residence, 17 Apr. 1810; witness: Charles Glover; naturalization granted 18 Apr. 1810.

CLARKE, William; nativity, Great Britain; in U. S. "before 14 April 1802"; Proof of Residence, 12 Jan. 1814; witness, James C. King; naturalization granted 12 Jan. 1814.

ABSTRACTS OF NATURALIZATION RECORDS, CIRCUIT COURT
DISTRICT OF COLUMBIA
PETITIONS RECEIVED, 1802-1820

Compiled by VIVIAN HOLLAND JEWETT,[1] Washington, D. C.

CONNELLY, Francis; age 23 in 1819; nativity, Down, Ireland; emigrated from Dublin, Ireland; arrived at Philadelphia, Pa., 16 July 1817; Declaration of Intention, 7 Jan. 1819; Proof of Residence, 5 June 1824; witnesses: Nicholas Callon, William Ottridge; naturalization granted 5 June 1824.

COOK, David; former allegiance, "King of Great Britain and Ireland"; in U. S. "on or about the year 1798," in District of Columbia since 1800; Declaration of Intention, undated; Proof of Residence, 2 documents both dated 4 June 1817; one witnessed by John Wimsett (?), the other by Joseph Johnson; naturalization granted 15 June 1817.

COSTIGAN, Joseph; nativity, Ireland; in U. S. since 1 Dec. 1801; Declaration of Intention undated; Proof of Residence, 20 June 1809, witness, Richard Spalding; naturalization granted 20 June 1809.

COUMBA, William; age 26 in 1819; nativity, County of Cornwall, England; emigrated from St. Johns, New Brunswick; arrived at Boston, Mass., 2 June 1818; Declaration of Intention, 2 July 1819; Proof of Residence, 11 Jan. 1825; witnesses: John Hoover, Michael Hoover; naturalization granted 11 Jan. 1825.

COURTENAY, John; age 26 in 1820; nativity, Borough of Mitchell, Cornwall, England; emigrated from Plymouth, England; arrived at Boston, Mass., Sept. 1819; Declaration of Intention, 28 March 1820; Proof of Residence, 1 June 1821; witnesses: Robert Keyworth, Solomon Drew; naturalization granted 1 June 1826.

CROPLEY, George; age 20 in 1819; nativity, City of Norwick, County of Norfolk, England; emigrated from Liverpool, Eng.; arrived at Phila-

delphia, Pa., 2 Nov. 1819; Declaration of Intention, 24 Dec. 1819; Proof of Residence, 12 May 1825; witnesses: John Lutz, George W. Haller; naturalization granted 12 May 1825.

CROPLEY, Richard; age 45 in 1819; nativity, County Norfolk, England; emigrated from Liverpool, Eng.; arrived at Philadelphia, Pa., 2 Nov. 1819; Declaration of Intention, 4 Dec. 1819; Proof of Residence, 28 Dec. 1824, witnesses: Thomas Corcoran, Jr., James Wharton; naturalization granted 28 Dec. 1824.

CROWLEY, Timothy; in U. S. "previous to 14 April 1802"; Proof of Residence, 3 June 1817; witnesses: Benjamin Fhiny, John Horner; naturalization granted 3 June 1817.

CUMMINS, Christopher; age 32 in 1820; nativity, Dublin, Ireland; emigrated from Londonderry, Ireland; arrived at New York 4 July 1819; Declaration of Intention, 3 Aug. 1820; Proof of Residence, 26 Dec. 1825; witnesses: F r e d e r i c k St—ger (St—ges), Robert Miller; naturalization granted 26 Dec. 1825.

DAVIS, Edward; nativity, England; in U. S. since Dec. 1806; Declaration of Intention, 30 June 1809; Proof of Residence, 20 June 1812; witness: Thomas C. Wright; naturalization granted 2 Nov. 1813.

DAVIS, Edward; nativity, Great Britain; Declaration of Intention, 30 June 1809; "Declaration of Naturalization," 30 June 1809; naturalization granted 30 June 1809.

DEVLIN, John; nativity, Ireland; emigrated from Belfast, Ireland; arrived at Quebec, Canada in 1819, thence to U. S. in same year; Declaration of Intention, dated "first Monday of March 1821," Rockville, Md., Montgomery Co.; another document similar to the preceding one

[1]Mrs. Jewett's surname was unfortunately omitted in the June issue

dated 31 May 1821, Montgomery County Court, State of Maryland; Proof of Residence, 5 May 1825; witnesses: John Waters, Benedict L. Adams; naturalization granted 25 May 1825 (?).

DIX, John; age 29 in 1820; nativity, Staffordshire, E n g l a n d; emigrated from London, England; arrived at Alexandria, Va., 1 Dec. 1810; Declaration of Intention, 12 June 1820; Proof of Residence, 30 May 1825; witnesses: Anthony Holmead, Isaac C. Caske (?); naturalization granted 30 May 1826.

DONOUGHUA, Patrick; nativity, Ireland; in U. S. since 18 June 1798; Proof of Residence, 10 June 1809; witness: John C. Clayton; naturalization granted 10 June 1809.

DOUGHERTY, Joseph; nativity, Ireland in U. S. since 1 Dec. 1801; Proof of Residence, 29 June 1809; witness: Clotworthy Stephenson; naturalization granted 29 June 1809.

DREW, Solomon; Proof of Residence, 4 June 1825; witnesses: Nicholas Blasdell, Jonathan Wallace; naturalization granted 4 June 1825.

DUFIEF (Duffief), Cheruibin; in U. S. since 1794; f o r m e r allegiance, France; a document dated 16 June 1813, at Philadelphia, by Mathew Carey, stating Dufief was "bound apprentice to him about the year 1794 and served him for six years or thereabouts;" another document dated 17 June 1813, Philadelphia, by James Black, stating Dufief "was bound apprentice to him by Mathew Carey in the year 1800;" Declaration of Intention, undated but apparently the same date as the Proof of Residence, judging from the writing and the paper upon which written; Proof of Residence, 24 June 1813; witness, Alexr. L. Joncherez; naturalization granted 24 June 1813.

DULANY, Patrick; nativity, Ireland; emigrated from Dublin, Ireland; arrived at Alexandria "in the District of Columbia," 17 June 1819; Declaration of Intention, 27 June 1820; Proof of Residence, 2 documents; one dated 1 June 1824; witnesses:

Grover Miller, Jacob Dixon; and the second, dated 20 Dec. 1825; witnesses: Thomas Robinson, Jesse Fox; naturalization granted 20 Dec. 1825.

DUMPH (Dumphey) John; age 30 in 1822; nativity, Kilkenny County, Ireland; emigrated from Dublin, Ireland; arrived at New York, 8 Oct. 1816; Declaration of Intention, 8 June 1822; Proof of Residence, 1 June 1824, witnesses, Thomas Parsons, George P. Maxwell, naturalization granted 1 June 1824.

ECLOFF (Eckloff), Christian; age 35 in 1819; former allegiance "King of Prussia"; emigrated from Amsterdam, Holland; arrived at Philadelphia, Pa., 3 July 1817; Declaration of Intention, 10 June 1819; Proof of Residence, 2 documents, the earlier one dated 1 June 1824, witnessed by George Cover is crossed out with a large X, the second one dated 12 June 1824, witnesses, Robert Miller, Henry C. Neals; naturalization granted 12 June 1824.

ELLIOTT (Elliot), Johnathan; printer; age 28 in 1813; nativity, England; Declaration of Intention, 30 Jan. 1813; Proof of Residence, 6 June 1818, witnesses, Richard Wallack, T h o m a s Dunn; naturalization granted 6 June 1818.

EPINETTE, Peter (Rev.); in U. S. since 5 Nov. 1806, in Washington, D. C. "more than one year last past"; Proof of Residence, 2 Nov. 1811, witness, Rev'd. Francis Neale, naturalization granted 2 Nov. 1811.

ERSKINE, John; nativity, Ireland; in U. S. since 18 June 1803, "eight years last past" within the County of Washington; Proof of Residence, 13 June 1814, witness, Clotworthy Stephenson; naturalization granted 14 June 1814.

ESCHBACK, John; age 25 in 1825; nativity, Germany; emigrated from Amsterdam, Holland; arrived at Annapolis, Md., Jan. 1817 "being three years and more before he attained the age of twenty-one years."; Declaration of Intention and Proof of Residence, 4 Feb.

1825, witnesses, Henry Bernard, Ernest Guttschride; naturalization granted 4 Feb. 1825.

FALLON, Edward; nativity, Ireland; arrived in Philadelphia, Pa., 1795, to Baltimore in 1777 (1797?), to Washington, D. C., in 1799; Declaration of Intention and Proof of Residence, 11 Jan. 1814, witness, Clotworthy Stephenson; naturalization granted 11 Jan. 1814.

FLINN, Lawrence; age 28 in 1819; nativity, Ireland; emigrated from Newfoundland; arrived at Boston, Mass., 20 April 1818; Declaration of Intention, 1 Jan. 1819; Proof of Residence, 2 June 1824, witnesses, William Joice, George Joice; naturalization granted 2 June 1824.

GANNON, James; nativity, Ireland; in U. S. since 18 June 1798; Proof of Residence, 18 April 1814, witness, Charles G l o v e r; naturalization granted 18 April 1814.

GERARD, William G.; Merchant; in New York 1798; deposition dated 5 March 1813 stating that he had lived in New York since 1798; Proof of Residence, 31 Dec. 1813, witness, Thomas Greeves; naturalization granted 5 Jan. 1814.

GOODALL, Thomas; age 26 in 1820; nativity, Ireland; emigrated from Portsmouth, England; arrived at Baltimore, Md., 20 April 1819; Declaration of Intention, 14 Jan. 1820; Proof of Residence, 18 Jan. 1825, witnesses, Thomas Holiday, J a m e s M a r t i n; naturalization granted 18 Jan. 1825.

GRACE, William; age 28 in 1818; nativity, Capaheaden, Ireland; emigrated from Capaheaden, Ireland; arrived at Alexandria, Va., 20 July 1817; Declaration of Intention, 26 June 1818; Proof of Residence, 8 May 1826, witnesses, George King, John B. Gorman; (Note: "Admitted 9 Aug. 1826") but the Index Book to the Minutes of the Circuit Court says naturalization was granted 8 May 1826.

GRAMMER, Gottlieb Christopher; age 27 in 1814; nativity, Wertemburgh, Germany; emigrated from Amster-

dam, Holland; arrived at Philadelphia, Pa., 2 Dec. 1807; Declaration of Intention, 7 June 1814; Proof of Residence, 10 June 1824, witnesses, Richard Wallach, Esq., Peter Lenox; naturalization 10 June 1824.

GRAMMER, Gottlieb Christopher; in U. S. since 1809; Proof of Residence undated but enclosed in envelope date 1814, witness, Seth Hayatt; naturalization granted 7 June 1814.

GRASSI (Grossi), Rev. John; age 35 in 1810; nativity, Venice, Italy; arrived at Baltimore, Md., 20 Oct. 1810; Declaration of Intention, 20 Dec. 1810; Proof of Residence, 27 Dec. 1815, witness, James Wallace; naturalization g r a n t e d 27 Dec. 1815.

GREER, James; in U. S. "for five years last past", "one year at least last past in Georgetown"; Proof of Residence, 9 July 1814, witness, Joseph J o h n s o n; naturalization granted 9 July 1814.

GUEGAN, Louis Henry; age 27 in 1820; nativity, Guemene, France; "he resides in the City of Baltimore"; Declaration of Intention, 2 documents both dated 14 Sept. 1820; Proof of Residence, 17 Jan. 1825, witnesses, Thomas Carbery, Alexander Kerr; naturalization granted 17 Jan. 1826 (?).

GUTTSLICK (Guttschlick), Ernest; age 37 in 1819; nativity, Prussia; emigrated from Amsterdam, Holland; arrived at Annapolis, Md., 2 Feb. 1817; Declaration of Intention, 16 June 1819; Proof of Residence, 27 Jan. 1825, witnesses, A. T. F. Bill, L e w i s Magruder; naturalization granted 27 Jan. 1825.

HADFIELD (Hatfield), George; architect; age 36 in 1802; former allegiance, Great Britain; in U. S. "upwards of five years" and in "County of Washington upwards of two years"; only one document, without signature, serving, apparently, for both Declaration of Intention and Proof of Residence, dated 14 Aug. 1802; naturalization granted 14 Aug. 1802.

ABSTRACTS OF NATURALIZATION RECORDS, CIRCUIT COURT
DISTRICT OF COLUMBIA
PETITIONS RECEIVED, 1802-1820
Compiled by VIVIAN HOLLAND JEWETT, Washington, D. C.

HARPER, Walter; age 18 in 1821; nativity, County Wexford, Ireland; emigrated from Dublin, Ireland; arrived at New York month of Sept. 1817; Declaration of Intention, 27 Aug. 1821; Proof of Residence, 27 Dec. 1826, w i t n e s s e s, William Corme, Samuel Stettinius (sworn 28 Dec. 1826); naturalization granted 27 Dec. 1826.

HARRINGTON, Robert; age 21 in 1819; nativity, County Kerry, Ireland; emigrated from City of Cork, Ireland; arrived at Alexandria, Va., 1 Sept. 1818; Declaration of Intention, 4 Jan. 1819; another document marked "void" lists name of Florence McCarthy as w i t n e s s; Proof of Residence, 28 Jan. 1825, witnesses, Ambrose Moriarty, Charles Byrne; naturalization granted 28 Jan. 1825.

HART, John; in U. S. since 18 June 1798 (1794); Proof of Residence, 29 Dec. 1813, witness, Abner Ritchie, who "adds with pleasure that" (torn spot—John Hart ?) "was under his command in the Western Reg." (torn spot) "of 1794 and behaved himself well—Col. Carlisles Regt. 2nd Compy of Inty"; naturalization granted 30 Dec. 1813.

HAYRE, John; taylor; age 45 in 1812; nativity, Ireland; in U. S. "about 7 years", in District of Columbia "about 6 years"; Declaration of Intention, 2 petitions dated 19 June 1812 and 10 June 1814; Proof of Residence, 15 June 1814, witness, Wm. H. P. Tuckfield; naturalization granted 15 June 1814.

HOLLARAN, William; age 35 in 1821; nativity, Queens County, Ireland; emigrated from Waterford, Ireland; arrived at New York, 4 Aug. 1816; Declaration of Intention, 23 April 1821; Proof of Residence, 17 May 1826, witnesses, Nicholas Callan, Thomas Murray; naturalization granted 17 May 1826.

HOLROYD, Joseph; age 32 in 1820; nativity, Yorkshire, England; emigrated from Liverpool, England; arrived at Alexandria, Va., 8 July 1819; Declaration of Intention, 13 Jan. 1820; Proof of Residence, 18 Jan. 1825; witnesses, Thomas Holiday, James Martin; naturalization granted 18 Jan. 1825.

HUTCHINSON, Samuel; in U. S. since 18 June 1798; spent seven months abroad on business latter part of 1810 and following spring, family remained here; Proof of Residence, 29 Dec. 1813, witness, Sam Brook; naturalization granted 30 Dec. 1813.

JOHNSTON, James; in U. S. since 18 June 1798, one year within the District of Columbia; Proof of Residence, 25 May 1825, witnesses, Henry Tims, George Thompson; naturalization granted 25 May 1825.

JOYCE (Joice), George; age 34 in 1818; nativity, City of Cork, Ireland; emigrated from Cork, Ireland; arrived at Alexandria, Va., 1 Nov. 1817; Declaration of Intention, 20 June 1818; Proof of Residence, 21 May 1824, witnesses, Thomas McIntosh, John Hollihorn; naturalization granted 21 May 1824.

JOYCE (Joice), William; age 40 in 1818; nativity, Ireland; emigrated from City of Cork, Ireland; arrived at Alexandria, Va., 1 Nov. 1817; Declaration of Intention, 20 June 1818; Proof of Residence, 29 May 1824, witnesses, George Joice, John Hollihan; naturalization granted 29 May 1824.

KEOGH, Mathew (Mathias)

(KEOGLE, Matthias); in U. S. "previous to month of Jan. 1795", in Virginia and Alexandria, "about the month of Jan. 1811" in Washington County; Proof of Residence, 1 Jan. 1814 witness, Sarah McCarthys; naturalization granted 3 Jan. 1814.

KIERNAN, Hugh; age 24 in 1818; nativity, Killesandia; emigrated from Liverpool, England; arrived at New York, 22 July 1817; Declaration of Intention, 26 June 1818; naturalization granted 2 June 1828.

KINCAID, J a m e s; nativity, Glasgow, Scotland; arrived at Alexandria in the ship William and John, Capt. Woodhouse, in 1807; Declaration of Intention, 30 Apr. 1816; Proof of Residence, 29 Jan. 1820, witnesses, John Laird, John Murdoch; naturalization granted 31 Jan. 1820.

KINCHEY, Paul; age 34 in 1819; nativity, Switzerland; emigrated from Haver de Grace; arrived at New York, 10 May 1817; Declaration of Intention, 16 June 1819; Proof of Residence, 12 Jan. 1826, witnesses, Benjamin M. Belt, Solomon Drew; naturalization granted 12 Jan. 1826.

KNELLER (Kueller), George; in U. S. "5 years at least", in District of Columbia "1 year at least"; Declaration of Intention, 26 Jan. 1809; Proof of Residence, 1 Feb. 1812, witness, Samuel Stettinius; naturalization granted 12 Feb. 1812.

KOLMAN, Rev. Anthony; age 37 in 1808; nativity, Kaiserburg, Alsatia; emigrated from Russia; Declaration of Intention, 9 June 1808; Proof of Residence, 3 June 1818, witnesses, Rev. Benedict Fenwick, Joseph Carberry; naturalization granted 3 June 1818.

KYNE, Mathias; nativity, Ireland; in U. S. from 18 June 1798; Proof of Residence, 9 June 1809, witness John Caton; naturalization granted 10 June 1809.

LAKE, George; nativity, Great Britain; in U. S. "since 1793", in District of Columbia "since 1804"; Declaration of Intention undated; Proof of Residence, 6 June 1811, witness, Edward Bland; naturalization granted 6 June 1811.

LAMBRIGHT, George; nativity, Hesse, Germany; in U. S. since 1798; Declaration of Intention, 22 June 1809 (Georgetown); Proof of Residence, 22 June 1809, witnesses, James Calder, James Melvin; naturalization granted 22 June 1809.

LAURIE, James; clergyman; age 30 in 1812; nativity, Scotland; in U. S. "since 1802"; Declaration of Intention, 21 July 1812; Proof of Residence undated but enclosed in envelope dated 1813, witness, Joseph Nourse; naturalization granted 28 Dec. 1813.

LAW, Thomas, Esqr.; nativity, England; in U.S. since Aug. 1794 (for 15 months, Aug. 1802 to Nov. 1803, in Europe on business), "other occasional absences" but "his domicile is in this district"; Declaration of Intention undated; Proof of Residence, 10 Jan. 1814, witness, James D. Barry; naturalization granted 14 Jan. 1815.

LEIDICKS (Leidick), Francis; mason; age 44 in 1813; nativity, Darmstedt, Germany; Declaration of Intention, 25 Apr. 1813; Proof of Residence, 8 June 1824, witnesses, Tench Ringgold, Henry Smith; naturalization granted 8 June 1824.

LITTLE, Robert; age 47 in 1819; nativity, London, England; emigrated from Liverpool, England; arrived at Baltimore, Md., 3 Oct. 1819; Declaration of Intention, 27 Dec. 1819; Proof of Residence, 30 Dec. 1824, witnesses, Richard Wallach, Alexdr. McWilliams; naturalization granted 30 Dec. 1824.

LOGAN, John; age 27 in 1818; nativity, Ayrshire, Scotland; emigrated from Liverpool, E n g l a n d (and Nova Scotia); arrived at Philadelphia, Pa., Dec. 1816; Declaration of Intention, 24 June 1818; Proof of Residence, 5 June 1824, witnesses, Thomas Hughes, D a v i d Apples (Applen or Appler); naturalization granted 5 June 1824.

MAGNIER, Thomas; age 27 in 1818; nativity, County Cork, Ireland; emigrated from Cork, Ireland; arrived at New York, Aug. 1816; Declaration of Intention, 23 Feb. 1818 (note "Report made in Court 30 Jan. 1818") document on back has signatures blotted out; Proof of Residence, 24 May 1824, witnesses, Thomas Parsons, Timothy Bean; naturalization granted 24 M a y 1824.

ABSTRACTS OF NATURALIZATION RECORDS, CIRCUIT COURT
DISTRICT OF COLUMBIA

PETITIONS RECEIVED, 1802-1820

Compiled by VIVIAN HOLLAND JEWETT, Washington, D. C.

MAGRATH (McGrath), Thomas; nativity, Ireland; in U. S. since 18 June 1798; Declaration of Intention, undated; Proof of Residence, June 1815, witness, John Travers; naturalization granted 8 June 1815.

MATHEWSON, John Jr.; in U. S. since 18 June 1798; Proof of Residence, 5 Nov. 1813, witness, Abraham Lynch; naturalization granted 5 Nov. 1813.

MATHEWSON, John Sr.; in U. S. since 18 June 1798; Proof of Residence 5 Nov. 1813, witness, Thomas Murray; naturalization granted 5 Nov. 1813.

McCORMICK, Michael; in U. S. "13 years at least", in District of Columbia "7 years last past"; Proof of Residence, 9 July 1814, witness, Joseph Johnson; naturalization granted 9 July 1814.

McDONALD, John; painter; nativity, Great Gritain; in U. S. "on or before 14 April 1802"; on 20 May 1813, was drafted in the D. C. Militia "and served 3 months in actual service of the U. S."; Proof of Residence, 19 June 1812, witness, Benjamin Bryan; document dated 10 Jan. 1814, called petition for citizenship after Militia Service; Proof of Residence, 10 Jan. 1814, witness, William Prime; naturalization granted 10 Jan. 1814.

McELROY, Rev. John; age 33 in 1816; nativity, Ireland; emigrated from Londonderry, Ireland; arrived at Baltimore, Md., 26 Aug. 1803; Declaration of Intention, 9 Jan. 1816; Proof of Residence, 1 Jan. 1819, witnesses, Charles King, Thomas Mulledy (Mullidy); naturalization granted 11 Jan. 1819.

McINTOSH, Thomas; age 30 in 1815; nativity, Scotland; emigrated from "thence"; arrived at Philadelphia, Pa., 23 Aug. 1803; Declaration of Intention, 7 June 1815; Proof of Residence, 20 June 1818, witnesses, George Henderson, George Blagden (Blagsen); naturalization granted 27 June 1818.

MEYER, Henry; in U. S. "at least five years", in Washington "one year at least"; Proof of Residence, 1 Feb. 1812, witness, John F. Keller; naturalization granted 1 Feb. 1812.

MOFFET (Moffit), John; mariner; age 22 in 1815; nativity, Ireland; in U. S. "before 18 June 1812"; Declaration of Intention, 22 Nov. 1815 made in Philadelphia, District Court of United States, Eastern District of Pennsylvania; Proof of Residence, 15 June 1819, witnesses, Robert Moffit, Mary Moffit; naturalization granted 15 June 1819.

MOORE, James; nativity, Scotland; in U. S. "in the year 1786", resided in Georgetown and Washington; Declaration of Intention, 10 Jan. 1814; Proof of Residence, 10 Jan. 1814, witness, Clotworthy Stephenson; naturalization granted 10 Jan. 1814.

MURPHY, Edward; age 33 in 1819; nativity, Ireland; emigrated from Cork, Ireland; arrived at Philadelphia, Pa., 22 Nov. 1816 (?); Declaration of Intention, 26 June 1819; Proof of Residence, 27 May 1826, witnesses, Wm. H. Stewart, Josiah Epex; naturalization granted 27 May 1826.

MURRAY, Michael; age 30 in 1821; nativity, Roscommon, Ireland; emigrated from Roscommon, Ireland; arrived at New York 19 May 1818; Declaration of Intention, 5 May 1821; Proof of Residence, 25 May 1826, witnesses, Thomas Murray, Patrick Delany; naturalization granted 25 May 1826.

OGLEBY, David; stonecutter; age 30 in 1802; nativity, Scotland; in "City of Washington from the year

1793"; Proof of Residence, 14 Aug. 1802, witness, Thomas Machen; naturalization g r a n t e d 14 Aug. 1802.

ORR, John; nativity, Ireland; in U. S. since 1800; Declaration of Intention, 30 Dec. 1813; Proof of Residence, 30 Dec. 1813, witness, Ambrose M o r i a t t a; naturalization granted 31 Dec. 1813.

OTTRIDGE, William; age 40 in 1819; nativity, Ireland; emigrated from the City of Cork, Ireland; arrived at Norfolk, Va., 10 April 1817; Declaration of Intention, (13) 15 Jan. 1819; Proof of Residence, 4 June 1824, witnesses, Thomas Murray, William Pancoast; naturalization granted 4 June 1824.

OULD, Henry; teacher; age 19 in 1818; nativity, England; arrived at "City Point in Virginia" 12 Nov. 1811; Declaration of Intention, 19 June 1818; Proof of Residence, 20 June 1818, witnesses, James A. Magruder, John Wiley; naturalization granted 20 June 1818.

PAIRO, Thomas W.; nativity, Germany; in U. S. "about 8 years", in District of Columbia "about 7 years last past"; Declaration of Intention, 11 June 1811; Proof of Residence, 11 June 1811, witness, Damie Rennoi; naturalization granted 9 Jan. 1816.

PHILIPS, George; age 31 in 1818; nativity, Edinburgh, Scotland; emigrated from Kirkaldie, Scotland; arrived at Norfolk, Va., 20 July 1817; Declaration of Intention, 20 June 1818; Proof of Residence, 21 May 1824, witnesses, Thomas McIntosh, John Hoolhand; naturalization granted 21 May 1824.

PLUNKETT, Rev'd Robt.; in U. S. since 1790; Proof of Residence, 20 Nov. 1811, witness, Rev'd Francis Neale; naturalization g r a n t e d 2 Nov. 1811. (?)

PRESTON, William; age 26 in 1817; nativity, Ireland; emigrated from Sileby, Leicestershire, England; arrived at New York 7 Aug. 1816; Proof of Residence, 27 Dec. 1817, witnesses, John Wiseman, William

Rider; naturalization granted 29 May 1824.

PRIME, William; nativity, Great Britain; in U. S. "constantly since 28 Nov. 1803" and a note in the Proof of Residence states that he was in the U. S. "before the 14th day of April 1802"; Declaration of Intention, 10 Jan. 1814; Proof of Residence, 11 Jan. 1814, witness, Zipporah C o r n i n g; naturalization granted 11 Jan. 1814.

SCALLAM, James; age 27 in 1812; nativity, Ireland; in U. S. at least 6 or 7 years prior to 1816; Declaration of Intention, 18 June 1812; Proof of Residence, 6 Jan. 1816, witness, Thomas Howard; naturalization granted 6 Jan. 1816.

SCALLAN (Scallon), Robert; age 21 in 1818; nativity, County Wexford, Ireland; emigrated from Liverpool, England; arrived at Norfolk, Va., 24 Sept. 1817; Declaration of Intention, 11 Nov. 1818; Proof of Residence, 3 June 1824, witnesses, Sam'l Smoot, Wm Fletcher; naturalization granted 3 June 1824.

SCHNELLER, Joseph; age 21 in 1818; nativity, town of Tyrol, Germany; former allegiance, Emperor of Austria; emigrated from Kiel, Denmark; arrived at Philadelphia, Pa., 3 April 1812; Declaration of Intention, 25 June 1818; Proof of Residence, 20 May 1824, witnesses, Thomas Carbery, Lewis Johnson; naturalization granted 21 May 1824.

SCHWARZ, Conrad; age 24 in 1818; nativity, Hamburg, Germany; emigrated from Amsterdam, Holland; arrived at Baltimore, Md., Jan. 1803; Declaration of Intention, 4 June 1818; Proof of Residence, 13 April 1824; witnesses, Philip Munro, William Cooper, naturalization granted 13 April 1824.

——— (Sessford), John; printer; age 26 in 1802; former allegiance, Great Britain; arrived in U. S. 5 Dec. 1795, in Washington, D. C., Oct. 1800; document d a t e d "Circuit Court, July term 1802"; document dated 9 July (?) 1826; oath dated

9 June 1826, petitioner states that he is the John ———— of the 1802 document; another oath dated 10 June 1826, w i t n e s s e d by Wm Cranch (Crauch); naturalization granted (two dates given) 14 Aug. 1802 and 5 June 1826.

SHAEFFTER (Schaefter — Schaeffter), George Frederich; age 36 in 1819; nativity, Spyeim, Germany; emigrated from Hamburgh, Germany; arrived at Philadelphia, Pa., 26 Sept. 1803; Declaration of Intention, 17 June 1819; Proof of Residence, 13 Jan. 1826, witnesses, John Queen, John Holohan; naturalization granted 13 Jan. 1826.

SIOUSA, John; age 35 in 1815; nativity, Paris, France; arrived at New York May 1806; Declaration of Intention, 8 June 1815; Proof of Residence, 10 June 1819, witnesses, Worthington Sutherland, Thomas J. Sutherland; naturalization granted 10 June 1819.

SMITH, John; age 45 in 1820; nativity, Lincolnshire, England; emigrated from London, England; arrived at Hampton Roads, Va., 13 Sept. 1819; Declaration of Intention, 5 Jan. 1820; Proof of Residence, 1 June 1826; witnesses, Robert Heyworth, S o l o m o n Drew; naturalization granted 1 June 1826.

SPRATT, Thomas; age 29 in 1820; nativity, Ireland; emigrated from Waterford, Ireland; arrived at New London, Conn., 1 June 1812; Declaration of Intention, 19 June 1820; Proof of Residence, 27 Dec. 1825, witnesses, James Gettys, John Hollohon; naturalization granted 27 Dec. 1825.

STEPHENS, Edward; age 32 in 1815; nativity, Ireland; in U. S. since 1809, in Washington "2 years last past"; Declaration of Intention, 7 June 1815; Proof of Residence, 7 June 1815, witness, George Andrews; naturalization granted 7 June 1815.

SULLIVAN, Jeremiah; age 26 in 1821; nativity, Ireland; emigrated from Cork, Ireland; arrived at Baltimore, Md., 29 July 1817; Declaration of

Intention, 16 April 1821; Proof of Residence, 10 May 1826, witnesses, John Hallohan, Danl. C a r r o l l; naturalization granted 10 May 1826.

TASTET (Tastel), Nicholas; age 29 in 1819; nativity, Madrid, Spain; emigrated from St. Sebastian, Spain; arrived at Boston, Mass., 6 Jan. 1814; Declaration of Intention, 23 June 1819; Proof of Residence, 21 Dec. 1824, w i t n e s s e s, Michael Shaules, Walter Clarke; naturalization granted 20 Dec. 1824.

THOMPSON, Pishey; age 34 in 1819; nativity, Lincolnshire, E n g l a n d; emigrated from Liverpool, England; arrived at New York 27 Oct. 1819; Declaration of Intention, 27 Dec. 1819; Proof of Residence, 25 May 1825, witnesses, Joseph Gales, Jr., Nathaniel P. Poor; naturalization granted 25 May 1825.

TSCHIFFELY, Frederick D.; nativity, Bern, Switzerland; in U. S. "nearly 9 years last past"; Proof of Residence, 6 June 1814, witness, Joseph Nourse; another document is a letter to the Court from Mr. Tschiffely enclosing the Proof of Residence; naturalization granted 6 June 1814.

TUCKER, James; age 33 in 1820; nativity, Plymouth, England; emigrated from Plymouth, England; arrived at Baltimore, Md., 19 July 1819; Declaration of Intention, 11 Jan. 1820; Proof of Residence, 18 Jan. 1825, witnesses, Benjamin King, A n d r e w Forrest; naturalization granted 18 Jan. 1825.

TUCKFIELD, Wm H. P.; nativity, Great Britain; in U. S. since April 1801; Declaration of Intention, 29 Jan. 1810; Proof of Residence, 30 Jan. 1810; w i t n e s s, William Smith; naturalization granted 30 Jan. 1810.

WALKER, David; nativity, Ireland; in U. S. "before 14 April 1802"; Proof of Residence, 31 Dec. 1813, witness, Barney Dolan (?); naturalization granted 31 Dec. 1813.

WALKER, William; in U. S. 29 Jan. 1795; Proof of Residence, 3 Nov. 1813, witness, Samuel Eliot, Jr.; naturalization granted 4 Nov. 1813.

ABSTRACTS OF NATURALIZATION RECORDS, CIRCUIT COURT, DISTRICT OF COLUMBIA

PETITIONS RECEIVED 1802 THROUGH 1820

Compiled by VIVIAN HOLLAND JEWETT

WALLACE, James; note: Rev. Mr. Wallace; age 28 in 1809; nativity, Kilkenny, Ireland; document "Report of ——— an alien" dated 24 July 1809, "Supreme Court, State and City of New York"; affadavit, 2 April 1814, Court of Common Pleas, Mayor's Court of the City of New York, witness, Dewitt Clinton, Esq., mayor of New York; naturalization granted in Circuit Court, District of Columbia, 7 Nov. 1814.

WILLIAMS, Thomas; nativity, Ireland; in U. S. 18 June 1798; Proof of Residence, 30 Dec. 1813, witness, Thomas McCutchen; naturalization granted 30 Dec. 1813.

WILLIAMS, Thomas Hollaway; age 33 in 1820; nativity, Plymouth, England; emigrated from Plymouth, England; arrived at Philadelphia, Pa., 26 July 1818; Declaration of Intention, 14 Jan. 1820; Proof of Residence, 2 Feb. 1825, witnesses, James Scallun, P h i l i p Crewer; naturalization granted 2 Feb. 1825.

WILMOTT (Willmott), Samuel Devonshire; age 53 in 1819; nativity, County of Somerset, England; Declaration of Intention, 8 March 1819 in Court of Common Pleas, Burlington County, New Jersey; note: No papers were to be found showing the date Mr. Wilmott appeared in Court in Washington, D. C. The Index to the Minute Books gives the naturalization date as 8 March 1819 which is obviously erroneous.

WINTER, Samuel; nativity, England; in U. S. since 1785; Declaration of Intention, undated; Proof of Residence, 29 Dec. 1814, witness, Ronald Donaldson; naturalization granted 28 Dec. 1814. (?)

PETITIONS RECEIVED, 1821-1850

ABBOT, Joseph; age 40 in 1829; nativity, Plymouth, E n g l a n d; emigrated from Plymouth, England; arrived at Norfolk, Va., 21 Sept. 1819; Declaration of Intention, 7 July 1829; Proof of Residence, 4 Dec. 1833, witnesses, Charles W. Boteler and Jonah Bosworth; naturalization granted, 4 Dec. 1833.

ADAMS, Thomas; nativity, Ireland; in U. S. prior to 14 April 1802; Proof of Residence, 25 May 1832, witnesses, George Sweeny and Thomas Hyde; naturalization granted, 28 May 1832.

ADIE, James; age 30 in 1838; nativity, Scotland; emigrated from Glasgow, Scotland; arrived at New York, 29 April 1829; Declaration of Intention, 6 Dec. 1838; Proof of Residence, 8 Dec. 1840, witnesses, Robert Brown and John Douglas; naturalization granted, 8 Dec. 1840.

ADLER, Morris (Moses) ; age 22 in 1821; nativity, Hesse Cassel; emigrated from Amsterdam; arrived at Philadelphia, 3 Nov. 1816; Declaration of Intention, 11 April 1821; Proof of Residence, 19 May 1827, witnesses, John Baker and Samuel Mickum; naturalization granted, 19 May 1827.

AGG, John; age 39 in 1823; nativity, Evesham, County of Worcester, England; emigrated f r o m Evesham; arrived at Philadelphia, 22 May 1818; Declaration of Intention dated, State of New Jersey, County of Burlington, 25 June 1818; another Declaration of Intention dated Washington, D. C., 13 Dec. 1823; Proof of Residence, 29 Oct. 1827, witnesses, Richard Coxe and Richard Wallack; naturalization granted, 29 Oct. 1827.

AHMEY, Frederick; nativity, Prussia; Declaration of Intention, District Court, Alexandria, 11 Nov. 1844; Proof of Residence, District Court, Alexandria, 5 June 1848, witness, Charley Schussler; naturalization, granted 5 June 1848.

AIGLER, Jacob; age 24 in 1842; nativity, Germany; emigrated from Bremen; arrived at Baltimore, 29 June 1841; Declaration of Intention, 4 Oct. 1842; Proof of Residence, District Court, 5 June 1848, witness, George Willner; naturalization granted, 5 June 1848.

AILER, George; age 36 in 1833; nativity, Germany; emigrated f r o m Germany; arrived at Baltimore, 9 Nov. 1816; Declaration of Intention, 26 April 1833; Proof of Residence, 9 Dec. 1836, witnesses, Geo. Lambright and Jonah Essex; naturalization granted, 9 Dec. 1836.

ALEXANDER, Charles P.; age 39 in 1822; nativity, Paris, France; emigrated from Bordeaux, France; arrived at New York, 6 May 1817; Declaration of Intention, 4 June 1822; Proof of Residence, 24 March 1835, witnesses, Jonas P. Keller and Louis Labrille; naturalization granted, 24 March 1835.

ALEXANDER, William; age 50 in 1840; nativity, Ireland; emigrated from Liverpool, England; a r r i v e d at Georgetown, D. C., 5 Sept. 1837; Declaration of Intention, 7 Sept. 1840; Proof of Residence, 29 Dec. 1842, witnesses, William H. Edes and Walter Smoot; naturalization granted, 29 Dec. 1842.

ARCHER, William; age about 32 in 1818; nativity, Scotland; emigrated from Greenwich, England; arrived at New York, 25 Sept. 1815; Declaration of Intention, 6 Jan. 1818; Proof of Residence, 3 May 1821, witnesses, Tench Ringgold a n d Thomas T a y l o r; naturalization granted, 3 May 1821.

ARTESER, John; age 26 in 1841; nativity, Switzerland; emigrated from Havre de Grasse; arrived at New York, 4 Oct. 1837; Declaration of Intention, 13 Jan. 1841; Proof of Residence, 31 March 1845, witness, N i c h o l a s Hopp; naturalization granted, 29 March 1845.

BAKER, Conrad; age 26 in 1845; nativity, Germany; emigrated from Bremen, Germany; arrived at Baltimore, 1 Oct. 1839; Declaration of Intention, 17 March 1845; Proof of Residence, District Court, 5 June 1848, witness, Henry Ebeling; naturalization granted, 5 June 1848.

BARCROFT, John; nativity, Ireland; in U. S. prior to 14 April 1802; Proof of Residence, 24 March 1830, witness, Charles Litle; naturalization granted, 26 March 1830.

BARKER, Jacob; age 35 in 1844; nativity, Germany; emigrated from Bremen, Germany; arrived at Baltimore, 1 May 1840; Declaration of Intention, 9 April 1844; Proof of Residence, 4 June 1849, witness,

Charles H. Willberger (Wiltberger); naturalization g r a n t e d, 4 June 1849.

BARR, Thomas; age 45 in 1845; nativity, Ireland; emigrated from Londonderry, Ireland; arrived at Alexandria, D. C., 12 Aug. 1818; Declaration of Intention 13 Sept. 1845; Proof of Residence 12 April 1848, witness Thomas Plumpsell; naturalization granted, 12 April 1848.

BARRY, Francis; nativity, Ireland; in U. S .prior to 14 April 1802; Proof of Residence, 27 May 1836, witnesses, Richard Barry and William Spieden; naturalization granted, 29 May 1836.

BARRY, James; age 21 in 1823; nativity Ireland; emigrated from County Cork; arrived at Boston, 18 May 1819; Declaration of Intention, 19 April 1823; Proof of Residence, 22 May 1828, witnesses Jacob Bender and Thos. Magnier (M a g u i r e); naturalization granted, 22 May 1828.

BARRY, Richard; age 28 in 1833; nativity, Ireland; emigrated from Dublin, Ireland; arrived at Philadelphia, May 1811; Declaration of Intention, 19 April 1833; Proof of Residence, 19 April 1833, witnesses, William Spieden and Robert T. Barry; naturalization granted, 19 April 1833.

BATES, Thomas; age 39 in 1823; nativity, England; emigrated from Liverpool, England; arrived at Baltimore, 11 Dec. 1818; Declaration of Intention, 25 April 1823; Proof of Residence, 24 June 1829, witnesses, Philip Munro (Manro) and William Nedin; naturalization granted, 24 June 1829.

BAXTER, Revd. Roger; occupation, minister; age about 25 in 1818; nativity, Lancashire, England; emigrated from England; arrived at Baltimore, 5 Jan. 1817; Declaration of Intention, 5 Jan. 1818; Proof of Residence, 7 April 1822, witnesses, Revd. Enoch Fenwick and Stephen H. Gough; naturalization granted, 11 April 1822.

BEARDSLEY, Joseph; age 52 in 1832; nativity, Derbyshire, England; emigrated from Liverpool, England; arrived at Baltimore, 16 June 1819; Declaration of Intention, 29 May 1832; Proof of Residence, 30 May 1835, witnesses, Gregory Ennis and Wm. Service (Serren); naturalization granted, 30 May 1835.

BEARDSLEY, Joseph, Jr.; nativity, England; emigrated from Liverpool, England; arrived at Philadelphia in 1821; Declaration of Intention, 20 May 1835; Proof of Residence, 20 May 1835, witnesses, Richard Wright and Levi W a s h b o u r n (Washburn); naturalization granted, 30 May 1835.

BEASLEY, George; age 28 in 1848; nativity, England; emigrated from Liverpool, England; arrived at New York, 1 Feb. 1841; Declaration of Intention, 27 May 1848; Proof of Residence, 27 May 1850, witness, Michael P. Mohnn; naturalization granted, 27 May 1850.

BEDE, George; age 50 in 1846; nativity, Ireland; emigrated from Liverpool, England; arrived at New York, 10 March 1818; Declaration of Intention, 15 June 1846; Proof of Residence, 4 June 1849, witness, Charles McNamee; naturalization granted, 4 June 1849.

BERGEMANN, Henry; age 29 in 1840; nativity, Germany; emigrated from Bremen, Germany; arrived at Baltimore, 1 August 1837; Declaration of Intention, Hamilton County, Ohio, 22 June 1840; Proof of Residence, Washington, D. C., 29 May 1850, witness, E. L. Kuse; naturalization granted, 29 May 1950.

BERGER, William; nativity, Germany; Declaration of Intention, 27 May 1850; Proof of Residence, 27 May 1850, witness, Henry Ebeling; naturalization granted, 27 May 1850.

BERGMAN, J. H. C.; age about 40 in 1849 (?); nativity, Germany; Declaration of Intention, Philadelphia, 19 Jan. 1841; Proof of Residence, District Court, Washington, D. C., 4 June 1849, witness, Charles Willberger (Wiltberger); naturalization granted, 4 June 1849.

BERST, Anthony; age 27 in 1842; nativity, France; emigrated from Havre; arrived at New York in 1826 or 1827; Declaration o f Intention, March term 1842; Proof of Residence, 16 April 1842, witnesses, Benjamin F. Haddock and Samuel Wilkinson; naturalization granted, 16 April 1842.

BETTNER, Godfrey; age 35 in 1834; nativity, Gotha, Saxony; emigrated from Bremen, Germany; arrived at Baltimore, 5 June 1833; Declaration of Intention, 2 Dec. 1834; Proof of Residence, 28 June 1838, witnesses, Lewis Beeler and E. Guttschlick; naturalization granted, 28 June 1838.

BIONDI, Antonio; age 29 in 1850 (?); nativity, "Scicely"; in U. S. since 1836; Declaration of Intention, 19 Aug. 1850; Proof of Residence, 19 Aug. 1850, witness, Antonio Catalano; naturalization granted, 19 Aug. 1850 (?).

BISHOP, Henry; in U. S. before 12 June 1812, residing in Mass. and N. J. also in District about 10 years; Proof of Residence, Commonwealth of Mass., Essex County, 12 May 1831, witnesses, George W. Raddin and John Hall; Proof of Residence, Washington, D. C., 3 June 1831, witnesses, Thomas Hyde and Edmund J. Brown; Proof of Residence, Washington, D. C., 7 June 1831, witnesses, Daniel Brown and Phebe Brown; naturalization granted, 8 June 1831.

BLACKBURN, Robt.; occupation, fancy chair maker; age 36 in Feb. 1816; nativity, Rothwell, near Leeds, England; emigrated from Liverpool, England; Declaration of Intention, New York, 19 (28?) Feb. 1816; Proof of Residence, Washington, D. C., 2 May 1823, witnesses, John Espey (Esbey) and John Coussins; naturalization granted, 2 May 1823.

BOHLAYER, John C.; age 24 in 1836; nativity, Wertemburgh; emigrated from Havre de Grasse; arrived at New York, 17 Oct. 1833; Declaration of Intention, 16 June 1836;

Proof of Residence, 8 March 1844, witnesses, John Maguire and Frederick S c h n e i d e r; naturalization granted, 8 March 1844.

BOHLEYER, John; age 31 in 1825; nativity, Wirtemburg; emigrated from Rotterdam; arrived at Boston, 22 March 1821; Declaration of Intention, 19 May 1825; Proof of Residence, 25 May 1830, witnesses, Edward Simms and Morris March; naturalization granted, 25 May 1830.

BORLAND, Alexander; age 34 in 1823; nativity, Ireland; emigrated from Londonderry, Ireland; arrived at New York, 17 July 1815; Declaration of Intention, 31 Dec. 1823; Proof of Residence, 27 May 1831, witnessess, W i l l i a m Jones and Nicholas C a l l a n; naturalization granted, 27 May 1831.

BOULANGER, Jean Joseph Paschale; age 43 in 1831; nativity, Leige; emigrated from Portsmouth, England; arrived at Annapolis, 14 Aug. 1825; Declaration of Intention, 2 April 1831; Proof of Residence, 13 June 1836, witnesses, Charles W. Gouldsborough and Edmund Hanly; naturalization granted, 13 June 1836.

BOUTHRON, John; age 30 in 1819; nativity, Fifeshire, Scotland; emigrated from Fifeshire; arrived at Philadelphia, 22 (2) April 1817; Declaration of Intention, 13 Jan. 1819; Proof of Residence, 2 June 1828, witnesses, James Ewell and Alexander McCormick; naturalization granted, 2 June 1828.

BOYLE, Christopher; age 30 in 1848; nativity, Ireland; emigrated from Dublin, Ireland; arrived at New York, 15 Sept. 1844; Declaration of Intention, 15 Feb. 1848; Proof of Residence, 27 May 1850, witness, John Foy; naturalization granted, 27 May 1850.

BRADY, Thomas; age 30 in 1840; nativity, Ireland; Declaration of Intention, Philadelphia, 12 Oct. 1840; Proof of Residence, Washington, D. C., 10 Dec. 1844, witnesses, Gregory Ennis and John B. Gray; naturalization granted, 10 Dec. 1844.

BRECKINRIDGE, William D u n l o p; "Florist at Institute"; age 32 in 1842; nativity, Scotland; Declaration of Intention, Philadelphia, 10 Aug. 1842; Proof of Residence, District Court, Washington, D. C., 5 June 1848, witness, John A. Smith; naturalization granted, 5 June 1848.

BRIT, James; age 33 in 1838; nativity, Ireland; emigrated from Dublin, Ireland; arrived at New York, Aug. 1830; Declaration of Intention, 24 Dec. 1838; Proof of Residence, 2 Sept. 1844, witnesses, John Carroll and Peter O'Donoghue; naturalization granted, 3 Sept. 1844.

BRODBECK, Jacob; age 29 in 1847 (?); nativity, Switzerland; emigrated from Havre; arrived at New York, 2 Nov. 1835; Declaration of Intention, undated (1847); Proof of Residence, undated (1847?), witnesses, G e o r g e T. McGlue and Frederick Schneider; naturalization granted, Oct. 1847.

BRODERICK, Thomas; age about 24 in 1818; nativity, Dublin, Ireland; emigrated from Cork, Ireland; arrived at Norfolk, Va., about 4 March 1816; Declaration of Intention, 20 June 1818; Proof of Residence, 2 June 1823, witnesses, Neil McNauty (Mc Nantz) and John H. Downs (?), naturalization granted, 11 June 1823.

BROWN, David; age 27 in 1845; nativity, St. Johns, New Brunswick; emigrated from St. Andrews; arrived at Eastport, Maine in 1836; Declaration of Intentoin, 20 Feb. 1845; Proof of Residence, 9 April 1847, witness, Amaziah Tucker; naturalization granted, 9 April 1847.

BROWN, Robert; occupation, stonecutter; age about 32 in 1818; nativity, Scotland; emigrated from Scotland; arrived at New York "latter end Sept. 1810"; Declaration of Intention, 8 Jan. 1818; Proof of Residence, 13 Dec. 1823, witnesses, Peter Lenox and William Archer; naturalization granted, 13 Dec. 1823.

BROWN, Thomas; age 25 in 1837; nativity, Liestershire, England; emigrated from Liverpool, England; arrived at Baltimore, 7 June 1830; Declaration of Intention, 5 Dec. 1837; Proof of Residence, 14 Dec. 1839, witnesses, William I. Sibley and Benjamin Jackson; naturalization granted, 14 Dec. 1839.

BROWN, William; nativity, England; Declaration of Intention, New York, 25 Nov. 1844; Proof of Residence, District Court, Washington, D. C., 5 June 1848, witness, Samuel Dorah; naturalization granted, 5 June 1848.

ABSTRACTS OF NATURALIZATION RECORDS, CIRCUIT COURT,
DISTRICT OF COLUMBIA

PETITIONS RECEIVED 1821 THROUGH 1850

Compiled by VIVIAN HOLLAND JEWETT

Bruning, John H.; age 26 in 1849; nativity, Germany; emigrated from Bremen, Germany; arrived at Baltimore, Md., "about last of May 1841"; Declaration of Intention, 14 April 1849; Proof of Residence, same, witness, Charles Schussler; naturalization granted 14 April 1849.

Bryan (Brien), Bernard; age 23 in 1821; nativity, Tyrone, Ireland; emigrated from Londonderry, Ireland; arrived at Philadelphia, Pa., 14 August 1816; Declaration of Intention, 18 April 1821; Proof of Residence, 5 May 1829, witnesses, Lewis Carbery and Nicholas Hedges; naturalization granted 5 May 1829.

Buckley, Timothy K.; age 29 in 1846; nativity, Ireland; emigrated from Cork, Ireland; arrived at New York, June 1842; Declaration of Intention, 12 February 1846; Proof of Residence, 24 May 1850, witness, William Greason; naturalization granted 24 May 1850.

Buist, David; age 24 in 1841; nativity, Scotland; emigrated from Liverpool, England; arrived at New York, 15 March 1833; Declaration of Intention, 21 January 1841; Proof of Residence, same, witnesses, Watson Kirkham and William Buist; naturalization granted 21 January 1841.

Buist, William; age 26 in 1837; nativity, Scotland; emigrated from Liverpool, England; arrived at Philadelphia, Pa., 27 April 1832; Declaration of Intention, Philadelphia, 27 September 1837; Proof of Residence, Washington, D. C., 20 January 1841, witnesses, James L. Gunnell and Watson Kirkham; naturalization granted 20 January 1841.

Bulger, Patrick; age 30 in 1826; nativity, County of Wexford, Ireland; emigrated from Waterford, Ireland; arrived at Baltimore, 20 August 1825; Declaration of Intention, 13 June 1826; Proof of Residence, 28 May

1834, witnesses, Gregory Ennis and James Lawrence; naturalization granted 28 May 1834.

Burrows, John; occupation, mariner; age "born 1791"; nativity, Liverpool, England; arrived at New York, 1807; Declaration of Intention, District Court, Boston, Mass., 2 (or 22) March 1822, while he was residing in Salem, Mass.; Proof of Residence, Alexandria County, District of Columbia, 6 May 1826, witnesses, Oliver Lapham and Thomas Mount; a second Proof of Residence is filed, 11 May 1827, Alexandria County, District of Columbia, witnesses, Daniel Wright and Oliver Lapham; naturalization granted 12 May 1827.

Buthmann, John H.; age 38 in 1844; nativity, Germany; emigrated from Amsterdam; arrived at New York, July 1825; Declaration of Intention, 25 April 1844; Proof of Residence, 22 October 1847, witness, Charles McNamee; naturalization granted 22 October 1847.

Butler, Abraham; age 39 in 1834; nativity, England; emigrated from Liverpool, England; arrived at Alexandria, D. C., 8 July 1819; Declaration of Intention, 4 April 1834; Proof of Residence, 18 May 1837, witnesses Richard Wright and Louis F. Joncherez; naturalization granted 18 May 1837.

Byrne, James; age 27 in 1843; nativity, County Louthe, Ireland; emigrated from Liverpool, England; arrived at Baltimore, 14 June 1840; Declaration of Intention, 28 June 1843; Proof of Residence, Dist. Court, Washington, D.C., 5 June 1848; witness, Nicholas Callan; naturalization granted 5 June 1848.

Caden, James; age 44 (or 22) in 1822; nativity, Monaghan County, Ireland; emigrated from Ireland; arrived at Philadelphia, Pa., 3 August 1817; Declaration of Intention, Alexandria, D. C., 14 June 1822; Proof of Residence, 6 June 1831, witnesses, John B. Gormans and Edward Dyer; naturalization granted 6 June 1831.

Callan, Patrick; age 40 in 1838; nativity, Ireland; emigrated from Liverpool, England; arrived at Baltimore, 19 June 1837; Declaration of Intention, 14 December 1838; Proof of Residence, 28 December 1842, witnesses, Nicholas Callan, Sr., Nicholas Callan, Jr.; naturalization granted 28 December 1842.

Calvert, Charles; age 38 in 1832; nativity, England; emigrated from Hull, England; arrived at Whitehall, N. Y., 25 August 1818; Declaration of Intention, 6 June 1832; Proof of Residence, 6 June 1834, witnesses, J. H. Hook (Cook) and Charles G. Wilcox; naturalization granted 6 June 1834.

Carmack (Cammack), Christopher; age 33 in 1830; nativity, England; emigrated from Liverpool, England; arrived at New York, 18 November 1816; Declaration of Intention, 28 December 1830; Proof of Residence, 28 December 1833, witnesses, Nicholas Callan and Edwd Dyer; naturalization granted 28 December 1833.

Carmack (Cammack), William; age 38 in 1839; nativity, Lincolnshire, England; emigrated from Liverpool, England; arrived at New York, 17 November 1816; Declaration of Intention, 11 January 1839; Proof of Residence, same, witnesses, Clement T. Coote

and Christopher C a r m a c k (Cammack); naturalization granted 11 January 1839.

Carroll, John; age 30 in 1836; nativity, Tipperary, Ireland; emigrated from Waterford, Ireland; arrived at Baltimore, 28 June 1825; Declaration of Intention, 27 June 1836; Proof of Residence, 27 November 1839, witnesses, Henry B. Robertson and Thomas Lloyd; naturalization granted 27 November 1839.

Carter, James; age 23 in 1830; nativity, Plymouth, England; emigrated from Havre; arrived at· New York Aug. 1817; Declaration of Intention, 6 January 1830; Proof of Residence, 6 January 1830, witnesses, Moses Poor and Alfred Elliot; naturalization granted 6 January 1830.

Carusi, Augustus; age 26 in 1842; nativity, "Sicilia"; emigrated from Palevino, Sicilia; arrived at Boston, 10 May 1836; Declaration of Intention, 17 October 1842; Proof of Residence, 4 November 1848, w i t n e s s, Lewis Carusi; naturalization granted 4 November 1848.

Casparis, James; age 28 in 1841; nativity, Switzerland; emigrated from Havre; arrived at New York, 14 September 1839; Declaration of Intention, 30 December 1841; Proof of Residence, 20 December 1844, w i t n e s s, John Hitz; naturalization granted 20 December 1844.

ABSTRACTS OF NATURALIZATION RECORDS, CIRCUIT COURT, DISTRICT OF COLUMBIA

PETITIONS RECEIVED 1821 THROUGH 1850
Compiled by VIVIAN HOLLAND JEWETT

Catalano, Salvadore; age "about 48" in 1812; nativity, Island of Sicily (Syracuse); emigrated from Syracuse; arrived at City of Washington, November 1805; Declaration of Intention, 22 June 1812; Proof of Residence, 16 June 1823, witnesses, Richard Spaulding and Tench Ringgold; naturalization granted 16 June 1823.

Choppin, William; age 38 in 1846; nativity, Great Britain; emigrated from Liverpool, England; arrived at New York, 21 September 1830; Declaration of Intention, 21 April 1846; Proof of Residence, 2 May 1848, witness, Henry Trunnel; naturalization granted 2 May 1848.

Chutkowski, Ignatius; age "about 28" in 1842; nativity, Poland; Declaration of Intention, New York, 29 May 1840; Proof of R e s i d e n c e, Washington, D. C., 12 August 1842, witnesses,

Julian K. Rosynkowski and Joseph H. Bradley; naturalization granted 12 August 1842. (Mr. Chutkowski was a First Sgt. of Capt. Henry W. Fowler's Company, 2nd Regiment of U. S. Dragoons. He enlisted 11 April 1837 and was honorably discharged at Fort Heileman E. Florida, signed by Col. D. E. Twiggs.)

Clark, James A.; nativity, Scotland; lived in Mount Clemens, Michigan, since latter part of 1818 until 1826, in Washington, D. C. since (3) 23 December 1826; Declaration of Intention, Territory of Michigan, County of Macomb, 3 February 1824. Proof of Residence, Territory of Michigan, County of Macomb, 5 February 1829, witnesses, Associate Justices of Macomb County Court, Christian Clemens and Erskine (Ezekiel) Allen; another Proof of Residence, Washington, D. C., 30 March 1829, witnesses, Richard Davis and William Hughes, naturalization granted 29 March 1829.

Clark (Clarke), William; age 32 in 1846; Nativity, England; emigrated from London; arrived at New York 5 June 1843; Declaration of Intention, 7 October 1846; Proof of Residence, 19 February 1849, witness, John Oliphant; naturalization granted 19 February 1849.

Clarke, John; age 26 in 1842; nativity, England; emigrated from Liverpool, England; arrived at New York, September 1828; Declaration of Intention, 25 June 1842; Proof of Residence, 5 June 1848, witness, Thomas Goodall; naturalization granted 5 June 1848.

Claveloux, Mark; age 28 in 1840; nativity, France; emigrated from Havre, France; arrived at Philadelphia, 15 June 1827; Declaration of Intention, 6 June 1840; Proof of Residence, 5 January 1843, witnesses, Thomas Goodal and James O'Neale; naturalization granted 5 January 1843.

Clephane, James; age 25 in 1818; nativity, Scotland; emigrated from Cacalden, Fifeshire, Scotland; arrived at Norfolk, Va., 20 July 1817; Declaration of Intention, 19 January 1818; Proof of Residence, 10 December 1833, witnesses, Richard Wallach and Wm. Redin; naturalization granted 10 December 1833.

Clitsh, Henry Christian Frederick; age 35 in 1839; nativity, Clausthal, Hanover, Germany; emigrated from Bremen, Germany; arrived at Baltimore, Md., 5 September 1837; Declaration of Intention, 5 June 1839; Proof of Residence, 20 May 1845, witness, Charles McNamee; naturalization granted 20 May 1845.

Coleman, Charles; age 25 in 1838; nativity, Hanover, Germany; emigrated from Bremen, Germany; arrived at Baltimore, 12 July 1837; Declaration of Intention, 6 June 1838; Proof of Residence, 29 May 1846, witness, William C. Goddard; naturalization granted 29 May 1846.

Collins, George C.; occupation, school teacher; age 19 in 1834; nativity, Ireland; emigrated from ——, England; arrived in this country, 1832; Declaration of Intention, St. Lawrence County, New York, 13 July 1834; Proof of Residence, Washington, D. C., 10 December 1844, witnesses, Nicholas Callan and John and Sylvanus Holmes; naturalization granted 10 December 1844.

Collins, Thomas; occupation, laborer; birthdate, 6 May 1808; nativity, Castlehyde County, Cork, Ireland; arrived at Boston, Mass., 3 November 1832; Declaration of Intention, Boston, Mass., 6 January 1834; Proof of Residence, Washington, D. C., 7 April 1838, witnesses, John Foy and Thomas Lloyd; another Proof of Residence, Boston, Mass., 9 April 1838, witnesses, John Lynch, John Dillon and Samuel A. Elliot, Mayor of Boston; naturalization granted in Washington, D. C., 7 April 1838.

Columbus, Charles; age 40 in 1845; nativity, Leghorn, Italy; emigrated from Leghorn, Italy; arrived at Baltimore, November 1816; Declaration of Intention, 31 May 1845; Proof of Residence 31 May 1845, witness, Leonard Harbaugh; naturalization granted 31 May 1845.

Conlon, Peter; nativity, United Kingdom; Declaration of Intention, New York, N. Y., 26 July 1836; Proof of Residence, Washington, D. C., 31 December 1840, witnesses, Harry Ellis and John Doyle; naturalization granted 31 December 1840.

Conly (Connelly), Thomas Y.; age 26 in 1835; nativity, County of Armagh, Ireland; emigrated from Belfast, Ireland; arrived at Baltimore, Md., 26 July 1825; Declaration of Intention, 2 May 1835; Proof of Residence, 2 May 1835, witnesses (S) L. M. Wilson and William Onne (Orme); naturalization granted 2 April (?) 1835.

Connelly, Owen; nativity, Ireland; emigrated from Sligo; arrived at Alexandria, Va., 15 September 1823; Declaration of Intention, Baltimore, Md., 1 October 1830; Proof of Residence, Washington, D. C., 30 December 1836, witnesses, John Ward and Philip H. Minors (Miner, Minor); naturalization granted 30 December 1836.

ABSTRACTS OF NATURALIZATION RECORDS, CIRCUIT COURT,
DISTRICT OF COLUMBIA

PETITIONS RECEIVED 1821 THROUGH 1850

Compiled by VIVIAN HOLLAND JEWETT

Conroy, Dominick; age 55 in 1846; nativity, Ire.; emigrated from county Wexford, Ire.; arrived at New York, August 1832; Declaration of Intention, 23 March 1846; Proof of Residence, 4 June 1849, witness, Jacob Barker; naturalization g r a n t e d 4 June 1849.

Conway, James; nativity, Parish of Tullaho, County of Kilkenny, Ire.; Declaration of Intention, 28 March 1829, at Dauphin County, Penn.; Proof of Residence, 6 April 1846, at Washington, D. C., witness, John Carroll; naturalization granted 6 April 1846.

Cooper, Joseph; age 36 in 1827; nativity, Derbyshire, Eng.; emigrated from Liverpool, Eng.; arrived at Annapolis, Md., 26 September 1819; Declaration of Intention, 31 May 1827; Proof of Residence, 31 May 1832, witnesses, Alexander McIntire and T h o m a s Woodward; naturalization granted 31 May 1827.

Cooper, William, Jr., age 36 in 1834; nativity, Great Britain; emigrated from London; arrived at Philadelphia 4 June 1805; Declaration of Intention, 29 May 1834; Proof of Residence, 29 May 1834, witnesses, Thomas Munroe and John H. Reily; naturalization granted 29 May 1834.

Coote, Clement T.; age 34 in 1819; nativity, England; emigrated from Cambridgeshire, Eng.; arrived at Philadelphia, 29 August 1817; Declaration of Intention, 15 June 1819; Proof of Residence, 18 October 1822, witnesses, Richard Eno and Thomas Eno; naturalization granted 19 October 1822.

Cowan, Hugh; nativity, Ireland; Declaration of Intention, Chester County, Penn., 16 December 1839; Proof of Residence, Washington, D. C., 5 June 1848, witness, Elkansh W. Denham; naturalization granted 5 June 1848.

Creaser (Creasor), Thomas; age 28 in 1837; nativity, England; emigrated from Hull, Eng.; arrived at New York, 21 May 1831; Declaration of Intention, 27 November 1837; Proof of Residence, 9 December 1839, witnesses, Isaac Ross and Joseph B. Ford; naturalization granted 9 December 1839.

Creutzfeldt, William; age 32 in 1843; nativity, Germany; emigrated from Stockholm, Sweden; arrived at Alexandria, D. C., 1 October 1840; Declaration of Intention, 1 October 1843; Proof of Residence, 27 October 1845, witness, William Uttermuhle; naturalization granted 27 October 1847 (?).

Croggan (Croggon), Henry B.; age 25 in 1837; nativity, England; emigrated from Plymouth, Eng.; arrived at Alexandria, D. C., 1 July 1818; Declaration of Intention, 20 December 1837; Proof of Residence, 20 December 1837, witnesses, James Mankin and Isaac N. J. Croggan; naturalization granted 20 December 1837.

Cropley, Edward S.; age 28 in 1832; nativity, England; emigrated from Liverpool, Eng.; arrived at New York October 1827; Declaration of Intention, 16 June 1832; Proof of Residence, 19 December 1835, witnesses, William Woodward and William Phillips; naturalization granted 19 December 1835.

Crotty, Patrick; age 40 in 1839; nativity, Ireland; emigrated from Limerick, Ire.; arrived at New York, 12 June 1831; Declaration of Intention, 5 March 1839; Proof of Residence, 12 December 1844, witness, Charles McNamee; naturalization granted 12 December 1844.

Cruit, Robert; age 29 in 1824; nativity, Devonshire, Eng.; emigrated from Plymouth, Eng.; arrived at Philadelphia, 15 June 1819; Declaration of Intention, 3 June 1824; Proof of Residence, 27 May 1835, witnesses, Thomas Woodward and Randolph Spalding; naturalization granted 27 May 1835.

Cull, John; age 37 in 1846; nativity, England; emigrated from Guernsey; arrived at Baltimore, 29 June 1818; Declaration of Intention, 27 March 1846; Proof of Residence, 27 March 1846, witness, Andrew Coyle; naturalization granted 27 March 1846.

Cummings, James; age 26 in 1840; nativity, Ireland; emigrated from Liverpool, Eng.; arrived in New York 20 August 1836; Declaration of Intention, 14 December 1840; Proof of Residence 24 March 1847, witness, Lewis Carbery; naturalization granted 25 March 1847.

Cummings, Patrick; age 24 in 1840; nativity Ireland; emigrated from Liverpool, Eng.; arrived at New York, 5 August 1837; Declaration of Intention, 12 December 1840; Proof of Residence, 24 March 1847, witness, Lewis Carberry; naturalization granted 25 March 1847.

Cunningham, Samuel; age 22 in 1820; nativity, County of Armagh, Ire.; arrived at New York, 12 July 1817; Declaration of Intention, Hagerstown, Md., 20 November 1820; Proof of Residence, Washington, D. C., 1 December 1837, witnesses, Henry B. Robertson, Owen Connelly; naturalization granted 1 December 1837.

Cunnington, Michael; age 28 in 1842; nativity, Ireland; emigrated from Liverpool, Eng.; arrived at New York, 24 July 1832; Declaration of Intention, 1 March 1844; Proof of Residence, 10 December 1844, witnesses, Gregory Ennis and John B. Gray; naturalization granted 10 December 1844.

Curley, James; age 25 in 1822; nativity, County of Roscommon, Ire.; emigrated from Dublin, Ire.; arrived at Philadelphia; Declaration of Intention, Frederick Town, Md., 9 March 1822; Proof of Residence, Washington, D. C., 21 December 1832, witnesses, Thomas Meade and George King; naturalization granted 21 December 1832.

Cuvillier, Joseph; age 33 in 1839; nativity, France; emigrated from Gibralter; arrived at New York, 27 January 1824; Declaration of Intention, 27 May 1839; Proof of Residence, 27 May 1839, witnesses, Edward W. Clarke and Venerando Pulizzi; naturalizaton granted 27 May 1839.

Daily, John; age 26 in 1836; nativity, Ireland; arrived in this country, 1816; Declaration of Intention, 4 January 1836; Proof of Residence, 4 January 1836, witnesses, Gregory Ennis and Jeremiah S u l l i v a n; naturalization granted 4 June 1836 (?).

Davidson, John; age 37 in 1846; nativity, Ireland; emigrated from Belfast, Ire.; arrived at Baltimore 12 September 1827; Declaration of Intention, 27 May 1846; Proof of Residence, 5 June 1848, witness, Valentine Harbaugh; naturalization granted 5 June 1848.

Dawes, Frederick Dawes, (wife, Charlotte Maria); aged 25 in 1819; nativity, England; emigrated from Liverpool, Eng. 1 December 1818; arrived at New York 5 February 1819 with wife, Charlotte Maria Dawes, age 25 years; Declaration of Intention, Montgomery County, Maryland, 13 November 1826; another Declaration of Intention, County of Washington, 16 November 1819; Proof of Residence, Washington, D. C., 2 June 1832, witnesses, Clement T. Coote and Peter Brady; naturalization granted 2 June 1832.

Develin, John S.; age 21 in 1824; nativity, Ireland; emigrated from Montreal; arrived at Plattsburgh, N. Y., 2 April 1820; Declaration of Intention, Washington, D. C., 12 April 1824; Proof of Residence, 26 May 1829, witnesses, V. Pulitizi and Mathew Wright; naturalization granted 26 May 1829.

Deveraux, William; age 30 in 1838; nativity, Ireland; Declaration of Intention, Philadelphia, 6 November 1838; Proof of Residence, Washington, D. C., 1 December 1846, witness, Sylvanus Holmes; naturalization granted 1 December 1846.

ABSTRACTS OF NATURALIZATION RECORDS, CIRCUIT COURT, DISTRICT OF COLUMBIA

PETITIONS RECEIVED 1821 THROUGH 1850

Compiled by VIVIAN HOLLAND JEWETT

Dewdney, John; age 27 in 1832; nativity, Kent County, England; emigrated from Brest, France; arrived at Norfolk, Virginia, 2 August 1823; Declaration of Intention, 2 June 1832; Proof of Residence, 2 June 1832, witnesses, John Barcroft, Leonard Ashton, Thomas Conner; naturalization granted 2 June 1832.

Dickson, John; age 4 1in 1838; nativity, Ireland; emigrated from Portiferry; arrived at Newberryport, Massachusetts, May 1818; Declaration of Intention, 29 November 1838; note says, "A d m i t t e d—Certificate given 23 March 1841", naturalization granted 23 March 1841.

Dillon, William; age 25 in 1848; nativity, England; emigrated from Liverpool; arrived at New York, 18 June 1841; Declaration of Intention, 28 January 1848; Proof of Residence, 28 May 1850, witness, Charles A. Davis; naturalization granted 28 May 1850.

Dixon, James; age 40 in 1936; nativity, Lanarkshire, S c o t l a n d; emigrated from Port Glasgo (w); arrived at New York, 3 June 1827; Declaration of Intention, 7 June 1836; Proof of Residence, 4 January 1839, witnesses, Nicholas Callan and W. McNamee; naturalization g r anted 4 January 1839.

Dodds, James; age 45 in 1824; nativity, Northumberland C o u n t y, England; emigrated from Port of Leath, Scotland; arrived at New York, 1 September 1816; Declaration of Intention, 9 June 1824; Proof of Residence, 30 June 1836, witnesses, Thomas Magnier and Archibald Thompson naturalization granted 30 June 1836.

Doermer, Charles; age 25 in 1842; nativity, Germany; emigrated from Bremen; arrived at Baltimore, 7 September 1839; Declaration of Intention, 21 May 1842; Proof of Residence, 19

October 1848, witness, Charles Coleman; naturalization granted 19 February 1849.

Donnoghue, John; age 24 in 1825; nativity. County Cork, Ireland; emigrated from Liverpool; arrived at Alexandria, July 1822; Declaration of Intention, 19 December 1825; Proof of Residence, 30 June 1832, witnesses, Thomas Orme and Thomas Hyde; naturalization granted 30 June 1832.

Donovan (Donivan), James; age 32 in 1842; nativity, Ireland; emigrated from Cork; arrived at New York, 29 August 1834; Declaration of Intention, 29 March 1842; Proof of Residence, 10 April 1844, witnesses, William McDermott and John Lynch; naturalization granted 10 April 1844.

Donovan, John; age 32 in 1847; nativity, Ireland; emigrated from Cork; arrived at Philadelphia, 10 June 1828; Declaration of Intention, 1 June 1847; Proof of Residence, 1 June 1847, witness, William Powers; naturalization granted 1 June 1847.

Donovan (Donavan), Michael; nativity, Great Britain; Declaration of Intention, New York, 8 April 1844; Proof of Residence, Washington, D. C., 10 May 1850, witness, James Fitzgerald; naturalization granted 10 May 1850.

Dooley, Michael; age 31 in 1836; nativity, Kilkenny, Ireland; emigrated from Liverpool; arrived at New York, 20 August 1832; Declaration of Intention, 21 (31) May 1836; Proof of dence, 6 December 1839, witnesses, Charles M. McNamee and James Maher; naturalization granted 6 December 1839.

Douglass, John; age 29 in 1828; nativity, Scotland; emigrated from Island Jamacia (?) (Jamorcia?); arrived at Boston, November 1816; Declaration of Intention, 11 December 1828; Proof of Residence 11 December 1828, witnesses, Cadwallader Evans and Thomas M. Abbott; naturalization granted 11 December 1828.

Dowling, William; age 37 in 1824; nativity, Ireland; emigrated from Dublin; arrived at Baltimore, 17 October 1817; Declaration of Intention, 5 June 1824; Proof of Residence, (?) 17 May 1830, witnesses, George Miller and Patrick

Delaney; naturalization granted 17 May 1830.

Doyle, John; Declaration of Intention, New York, 9 February 1835; Proof of Residence, Washington, D. C., 4 December 1840, witnesses, John Fry and James Maher; naturalization granted 4 December 1840.

Doyle, Michael; age 28 in 1846; nativity, Ireland; emigrated from Liverpool; arrived at New York, 15 July 1839; Declaration of Intention, 25 March 1846; Proof of Residence, 4 June 1849, witness, John H. Gibbs; naturalization granted 4 June 1849.

Draine, Charles; age 30 in 1829; nativity, Ireland; emigrated from Belfast; arrived at Eastport, Maine, 7 September 1822; Declaration of Intention, 27 May 1829; Proof of Residence, 24 June 1834, witnesses, John Simon and Samuel Rumy (Rury); naturalization granted 24 June 1834.

Dreisch, Michael; nativity, Bavaria; Declaration of Intention, Baltimore, Md., 9 November 1840; Proof of Residence, Washington, D. C., 14 April 1848, witness, Zachariah M. Offutt; naturalization granted 14 April 1848.

Dubant, Marc; age 48 in 1841; nativity, France; emigrated from Bordeaux; arrived at Philadelphia, 15 April 1816; Declaration of Intention, 23 March 1841; Proof of Residence, 2 June 1845, witness, James F. Holliday (Halliday); naturalization granted 2 June 1845.

Dubuisson (Duboisson), Revd. Stephen Langaudelle; occupation, minister; age about 29 in 1816; nativity, France; emigrated from France; arrived at New York, 21 November 1815; Declaration of Intention, 17 June 1816; a paper dated Leonardtown, Md., 22 April 1822, mentions a Proof of Residence, but does not include an enclosure, signed W. J. Brooke; naturalization granted 29 April 1822.

Duffey, James; age 27 in 1846; nativity, Ireland; emigrated from Liverpool; arrived at New York, 29 September 1842; Declaration of Intention, 15 January 1846; Proof of Residence, 5 June 1848, witness, William S. Burch; naturalization granted 5 June 1848.

Drumphey, Thomas; age 26 in 1842; nativity, Ireland; emigrated f r o m Waterford; a r r i v e d at Baltimore, July 1820; Declaration of Intention, March Term 1842; Proof of Residence, March Term 1842, witnesses, John A. Donlin and Robert Ball; naturalization granted March Term 1842.

Dunn, John; Proof of Residence, 17 December 1823, witnesses, James Scallon and Nicholas Cassidy; naturalization granted 17 December 1823.

Dzierozynski, Francis; age 43 in 1822; nativity, Orsani, Poland; emigrated from Orsani, Poland, 12 November 1821; Declaration of Intention, County of Alexandria, District of Columbia, 14 June 1822; Proof of Residence, Washington, D. C., 12 May 1828, witnesses, Joohue Millard and James Neale; naturalization granted 12 May 1828.

Earl, Robert; age 37 in 1837; nativity, Cambridgeshire, England; emigrated from Liverpool; arrived at Alexandria, Virginia, 9 August 1820; Declaration of Intention, 13 April 1837; Proof of Residence, 10 December 1839, witnesses, James Williams and John Dove; naturalization granted 10 December 1839.

Ebeleng, Henry; age 26 in 1848; nativity, Germany; emigrated from Bremen; arrived at Baltimore, 31 May 1839; Declaration of Intention, 5 June 1848; Proof of Residence, same, witness, C h a r l e s Schussler; naturalization granted 5 June 1848.

Ebeling, Frederick; nativity, Germany; Declaration of Intention, 27 May 1850; Proof of Residence, same, witness, Henry Ebeling; naturalization granted 27 May 1850.

Eberback, Henry; age 30 in 1837; nativity, Germany; emigrated from Rotterdam; arrived at Baltimore, 23 August 1832; Declaration of Intention, 15 August 1837; Proof of Residence, 12 December 1840, witnesses, Edward Simms and Charles Miller; naturalization granted 12 December 1840.

Eckardt, Henry; age 39 in 1825; nativity, Wirtemberg; emigrated from Amsterdam; arrived at Baltimore, 19 February 1820; Declaration of Intention, 10 May 1825; Proof of Residence, 18 May 1830, witnesses, David Appler and Frederick Stringer; naturalization granted 18 May 1830.

Eckloff, Godfrey; age 39 in 1823 (born 14 January 1784); nativity, Prussia; emigrated from Amsterdam; arrived at Philadelphia, 2 August 1817; Declaration of Intention, Philadelphia, 11 October 1823; Proof of Residence, Washington, D. C., 3 May 1836, witnesses, Christian Eckloff and Lewis Beelers; naturalization granted 3 May 1836.

Egan, William; age 45 in 1838; nativity, Ireland; emigrated from Scotland; arrived at New York, March 1818; Declaration of Intention, 5 December 1838; Proof of Residence, 10 December 1840, witnesses, Joseph S. Clarke and Anthony Holmeade; naturalization granted 10 December 1840.

Eigler, Jacob (filed under Aigler in Index to Naturalization); age 24 in 1842; nativity, Germany; emigrated from Bremen; arrived at Baltimore, 29 June 1841; Declaration of Intention, 4 October 1842; Proof of Residence, 5 June 1848, witness, George Willner; naturalization granted 5 June 1848.

Einbroet, John David; age 43 in 1840; nativity, Germany; emigrated from Bremen; arrived at Baltimore, 26 June 1837; Declaration of Intention, 12 October 1840; Proof of Residence 21 December 1846, witness, Frederick Stuotz (?); naturalization granted 21 December 1846.

Ellis, Henry; nativity, Great Britain; Declaration of Intention, New York, 26 September 1836 (a note says 7 August 1832); Proof of Residence Washington, D. C., 4 December 1840, witnesses, John Fry and James Maher; naturalization granted 4 December 1840.

Elvans, Richard; age 41 in 1821; nativity, England; emigrated from Guernsey; arrived at Baltimore, 20 October 1818; Declaration of Intention, 16 April 1821; Proof of Residence, 23 June 1829, witnesses, Robert Barnard and Morris Adler; naturalization granted 23 June 1829.

Emmerick, John; age 45 in 1833; nativity, Hesse, Darmstatt, Germany; emigrated from Bremen; arrived at Baltimore, 2 January 1833; Declaration of Intention, 24 September 1833; Proof of Residence, 2 January 1838, witnesses, Nichlas Burr and E. Guttschlick; naturalization granted 2 January 1838.

ABSTRACTS OF NATURALIZATION RECORDS, CIRCUIT COURT
DISTRICT OF COLUMBIA

PETITIONS RECEIVED, 1802-1820

Compiled by VIVIAN HOLLAND JEWETT, San Diego, California

Emmert, Henry; age 35 in 1845; nativity, Germany; emigrated from Bremen; arrived at Baltimore, 31 August 1839; Declaration of Intention, 26 May 1845; Proof of Residence, 31 May 1850, witness, Benedict Yost; naturalization granted 31 May 1850.

Emmert, William; age 30 in 1833; nativity, Germany but claimed former allegiance to the King of Denmark; emigrated from Hamburg; arrived at Baltimore, 9 September 1832; Declaration of Intention, 28 November 1833; Proof of Residence, 5 December 1837, witnesses, Louis Beeler and Godfrey Eckloff; naturalization granted 5 December 1837.

Ennis, Gregory; age 30 in 1822; nativity, Ireland; emigrated from Newfoundland; arrived at Boston, 4 May 1816; Declaration of Intention, 3 June 1822; Proof of Residence, 29 May 1832, witnesses, Jeremiah Sullivan and Mich¹ Connelly; naturalization granted 30 May 1832.

Ennis, Philip; age 36 in 1824; nativity, Ireland; emigrated from County of Wexford; arrived at Baltimore, 9 April 1819; Declaration of Intention, 15 January 1824; Proof of Residence, 6 July 1829, witnesses, Joseph S. Clark and George Sweeny; naturalization granted 6 July 1829.

Erb, Charles; age 30 in 1834; nativity, Darmstadt, Germany; emigrated from Bremen; arrived at Baltimore, 4 June 1831; Declaration of Intention, 2 December 1834; Proof of Residence, 4 June 1842, witnesses, John Lynch and Sebastian Kleinduist; naturalization granted 4 June 1842.

Evans, Evan; age 25 in 1838; nativity, Cardingshire, S. Wales; emigrated from Aberystwith, Wales; arrived at Alexandria, D. C., 17 September 1832; Declaration of Intention, 22 May 1838; Proof of Residence, 1

April 1843, witnesses, Charles H. James and Abraham Butler; naturalization granted 1 April 1843.

Farrar, John Morgan; Age 35 in 1825; nativity, County of Dublin, Ireland; emigrated from London; arrived at Baltimore, 21 October 1817; Declaration of Intention, 8 January 1825; Proof of Residence, 25 May 1830, witnesses, Edward Simmes (Semmes) and Morris March; naturalization granted 25 May 1830.

Feeney, William; age 20 in 1839; nativity, Ireland; emigrated from Dublin; arrived at Baltimore, 15 October 1828; Declaration of Intention, 4 December 1839; Proof of Residence, 26 May 1850; witness, Leonidas Bowen; naturalization granted 26 May 1850.

Feiner, William; age 29 in 1822; nativity, Munster; emigrated from Munster 22 May 1812; Declaration of Intention dated Alexandria, District of Columbia, 14 June 1822; Proof of Residence dated Washington, D. C., 12 May 1828, witnesses, Joshua Millard and James Neale; naturalization granted 12 May 1828.

Ferguson, William; age 25 in 1838; nativity, Scotland; emigrated from Greenock, Scotland; arrived at New York, 23 April 1837; Declaration of Intention, 25 December 1838; Proof of Residence, 27 May 1842, witnesses, Samuel Walker and Henry Ellis; naturalization granted 27 May 1842.

Ferrity, Nicholas; age 32 in 1842; nativity, Ireland; emigrated from Tralee; arrived at Philadelphia, 20 October 1828; Declaration of Intention, 15 January 1842; Proof of Residence, 2 June 1846, witness, Charles McNamee; naturalization granted 2 June 1846.

Fill, John; age 29 in 1834; nativity County of Norfolk, England; emigrated from Liverpool; arrived at Philadelphia, 4 September 1832; Declaration of Intention, 4 January 1834; Proof of Residence, 29 December 1837; witnesses, Clement Coote and Charles McNamee; naturalization granted 29 December 1837.

Finkman, Conrad; age 31 in 1845; nativity, Germany; emigrated from Bremen; arrived at Baltimore, 2 December 1839; Declaration of Intention, 26 May 1845; Proof of Residence, 25 October 1847, witnesses, Godfrey Eckloff and William G. Bitner; naturalization granted 25 October 1847.

Fischer, George Andrew; age 28 in 1844; nativity, Germany; emigrated from Rotterdam; arrived at Baltimore, 15 July 1840; Declaration of Intention, 22 May 1844; Proof of Residence, 6 April 1850, witness, Jacob Eigler; naturalization granted 6 April 1850.

Fister, John; age 30 in 1837; nativity, Switzerland; emigrated from Amsterdam; arrived at Philadelphia, 15 October 1816; Declaration of Intention, 18 May 1837; Proof of Residence, 22 April 1841, witnesses, Robert Connel alnd Jacob Kengla; naturalization granted 22 April 1841.

Fitzgerald, David; age 28 in 1845; nativity, Ireland; emigrated from Liverpool; arrived at Philadelphia, 22 June 1841; Declaration of Intention, 6 February 1845; Proof of Residence, District Court, 5 June 1848, witness, Peter Coulan; naturalization granted 5 June 1848.

Fitzgerald, James; age 34 in 1833; nativity, County of Waterford, Ireland; emigrated from Town of Waterford, Ireland; arrived at New York, November 1825; Declaration of Intention, 27 November 1833; Proof of Residence, 30 March 1836, witnesses, John H. Baker and Michael McCarty; naturalization granted 23 May 1836.

Fitzgerald, John; age 36 in 1832; nativity, Ireland; emigrated from Cork; arrived at Albany, N. Y., 24 December 1826; Declaration of Intention, 20 March 1832; Proof of Residence, 4 June 1836, witnesses, Gregory Ennis and Philip Mohun; naturalization granted 4 June 1836.

Fitzgerald, John; age 33 in 1845; nativity, Ireland; emigrated from Liverpool; arrived at New York, 28 June 1842; Declaration of Intention, 21 June 1845; Proof of Residence, District Court, 5 June 1848, witness, Peter Coulan; naturalization granted 5 June 1848.

Fitzpatrick, James; age 25 in 1829; nativity, County of Cavan, Ireland; emigrated from Belfast; arrived at Baltimore, 19 August 1827; Declaration of Intention, 3 June 1829; Proof of Residence, 30 March 1833, witnesses, John B. (?) Gorman and Philip Ennis; naturalization granted 30 March 1833.

Flaherty, John; age 31 in 1848; nativity, Ireland; emigrated from Galway; arrived at Baltimore, June 1818; Declaration of Intention, District Court, 5 June 1848; Proof of Residence, same, witness, William Flaherty; naturalization granted 5 June 1848.

Flaherty, William; age 25 in 1839; nativity, Ireland; emigrated from Galway; arrived at New York, 2 June 1836; Declaration of Intention, 1 April 1839; Proof of Residence, 25 March, witness, William Bond; naturalization granted 25 March 1845.

Flannigan, Michael; age 39 in 1824; nativity, Ireland; emigrated from Cork, Ireland; arrived at Baltimore, 29 September 1818; Declaration of Intention, 2 June 1824; Proof of Residence, 5 April 1830, witnesses, Thomas Magnier and Francis Conly, naturalization granted 5 April 1830.

Fleming, John; age 29 in 1823; nativity, County of Cork, Ireland; emigrated from Quebec; arrived at Alexandria, 1 November 1818; Declaration of Intention, 17 April 1823; Proof of Residence, 16 May 1828, witnesses, George McCormick and Martin Larner; naturalization granted 16 May 1828.

Forrestil (Forrestel), James; age 35 in 1844; nativity, Ireland; emigrated from Dublin; arrived at New York, 10 May 1842; Declaration of Intention 11 December 1844; Proof of Residence, 27 May 1847, witness, John

Mockabee; naturalization granted 27 May 1847.

Foy, John; occupation, gardener; nativity, United Kingdom; in U. S. "many years before the 18th day of June 1812"; Declaration of Intention, June Term 1817 Fayette Circuit Court, Kentucky; Proof of Residence, Washington, D. C., 11 May 1821, witnesses, Alex McWilliams and Thomas Claxton; naturalization granted 12 May 1821.

Foy, John; age 30 in 1829; nativity, Roscommon, Ireland; emigrated from Liverpool; arrived at Alexandria, 3 May 1829; Declaration of intention, 29 June 1829; Proof of Residence, 27 May 1834, witnesses, Phillip Ennis and Michael McDermott; naturalization granted 27 May 1834.

Foy, Mordecai; age 36 in 1827; nativity, Roscommon, Ireland; emigrated from Liverpool; a r r i v e d at Portland, Maine, 22 August 1827; Declaration of Intention, 17 January 1827; Proof of Residence, 30 March 1832, witnesses, Gregory Ennis and Jeremiah Sullivan; naturalization granted 30 May 1832.

Francis, John; birthdate, 10 June 1806; nativity, County K e r r y, Ireland; emigrated from County Kerry, 12 June 1825; arrived at Albany, N. Y., 13 August 1825; Declaration of Intention, Cambria County, Pennsylvania, 3 October 1832; Proof of Residence, Washington, D. C., 12 December 1840, witnesses, Philip Ennis and Owen Connelly; naturalization granted 14 December 1840.

Francis, Richard; age 23 in 1848; nativity, Maderia; emigrated from Maderia; arrived at Alexandria, D. C., 1 February 1841; Declaration of Intention, 28 March 1848; Proof of Residence, same; w i t n e s s David Aker; naturalization g r a n t e d 28 March 1848.

Franklin, William; nativity, Great Briton; Declaration of Intention, New York, 29 September 1834; Proof of Residence, Washington, D. C., 26 March 1849, witness, Michael P. Williams; naturalization g r a n t e d 26 March 1849.

Fraser, James; age 42 in 1824; nativity, England; emigrated from Liverpool; arrived at Alexandria, 24 May 1817; Declaration of Intention dated Supreme Court, County of Fairfax, 25 May 1818; a second Declaration of Intention is dated Washington, D. C., 3 June 1824; Proof of Residence, Washington, D. C., 3 June 1824, witness, Cornelius Wells; there is, also, a second Proof of Residence dated Dist of Columbia, 4 June 1827, witnesses, Cornelius Wells and Robert G. Lanphier; naturalization granted 4 June 1827.

Frere, Barrow; age 45 in 1833; nativity, England; emigrated from Bristol; arrived at New York, 24 August 1832; Declaration of Intention, 25 November 1833; Proof of Residence, 1 June 1850, witness, James Mahar; naturalization granted 1 June 1850.

Frere, James B.; age 43 in 1825; nativity, Hereford County, England; emigrated from Cadiz, Spain; arrived at Boston, June 1815; Declaration of Intention, 16 April 1825; Proof of Residence, 29 November 1837, witnesses, James Gettys and Henry B. Robertson; naturalization granted 30 November 1837.

Fullalove, James; age 42 in 1832; nativity, England; emigrated from Liverpool; arrived at Baltimore, October 1817; Declaration of Intention, 25 June 1832; Proof of Residence, 21 April 1841, witnesses, James Gettys and Francis Goss (?); naturalization granted 21 April 1841.

Gaddis, Adam; age 25 in 1822; nativity, Ireland; emigrated from New Brunswick; arrived at Alexandria, 21 August 1820; Declaration of Intention, 29 October 1822; Proof of Residence, 5 June 1831, witnesses, Morris D. C. Marsh and John Judge; naturalization granted 6 June 1831.

Gahan, William; age 51 in 1833; nativity, Ireland; emigrated from Engcorthy (?), Ireland; arrived at Boston, 8 June 1818; Declaration of Intention, 27 May 1833; Proof of Residence, 21 May 1836, witnesses, Gregory Ennis and John F. Callan; naturalization granted 31 May 1836.

ABSTRACTS OF NATURALIZATION RECORDS, CIRCUIT COURT, DISTRICT OF COLUMBIA

PETITIONS RECEIVED, 1802-1820

Compiled by VIVIAN HOLLAND JEWETT

Galabrun (Gallibrun), Louis Jean; age 35 in 1937; nativity, France; emigrated from Havre; arrived at New York, January 1834; Declaration of Intention, 9 January 1837; Proof of Residence, 20 May 1845, witness, J o n a s P. Keller; naturalization granted 20 May 1845.

Gallant, William; in U. S. prior to 1802; Proof of Residence, 31 May 1830, witnesses, David Glenn and Thomas Connolly; naturalization granted 31 May 1830.

Gautier, Charles; age 35 in 1844; nativity, France; emigrated from Havre; arrived at New York, 20 December 1838; Declaration of Intention, 5 October 1844; Proof of Residence, 13 April 1850, witness, William Morrow; naturalization granted 13 April 1850.

Gerdes, Ferdinand H.; age 33 in 1843; nativity, Germany; emigrated from Bremen; arrived at New York, 27 May 1836; Declaration of Intention, 9 December 1843; Proof of Residence, 19 October 1846, witness, John F. Ennis; naturalization granted October Term 1846.

Geffers, William Joseph, age 29 in 1844; nativity, England; emigrated from London; arrived at Boston, 4 March 1841; Declaration of Intention, 8 October 1844; Proof of Residence, 2 November 1848, witness, Jacob Curtis; naturalization granted 2 November 1848.

Gillott, Joseph; age 30 in 1845; nativity, England; emigrated from Liverpool; arrived at New York, fall of 1830; Declaration of Intention, 2 June 1845; Proof of Residence, 2 June 1845; witness, John L. Wirt; naturalization granted 2 June 1845.

Giveny, Bernard; age 41 in 1831; nativity, County of Cavan, Ireland; emigrated from Dublin; arrived at Philadelphia, 19 October 1819; Declaration of Intention, 11 October 1831;

Proof of Residence, 2 May 1835, witnesses, William Dowling and John Goinor; naturalization granted 2 May 1835.

Gonzalez, Ambrozio I.; age 29 in 1849; nativity, Cuba; emigrated from Cuba to U. S. in 1828; Declaration of Intention, 26 March 1849; Proof of Residence, same, witness, George A. Gardiner; naturalization granted 26 March 1849.

Gordon, James; age 63 in 1845; nativity, Ireland; emigrated from Liverpool; arrived at Boston, 23 May 1809; Declaration of Intention, 1 July 1845; Proof of Residence, Dist. Court, 5 June 1848, witness, Gustavus A. Clarke; naturalization granted 5 June 1848.

Gormlay, Philip; age 21 in 1828; nativity, Ireland; emigrated from Dublin; arrived at New York, 8 May 1827; Declaration of Intention, 10 June 1828; Proof of Residence, 4 January 1836, witnesses, Gregory Ennis and James F. ?; naturalization granted 4 January 1836.

Gould, John; age 48 in 1848; nativity, England; emigrated from London; arrived in U. S. 1816; Declaration of Intention, 1 November 1848; Proof of Residence, same, witnesss, Gustavus A. Clarke; naturalization granted 1 November 1848.

Greason, William; age 22 in 1840; nativity, Ireland; emigrated from Liverpool; arrived at Baltimore, 31 May 1837; Declaration of Intention, 23 April 1840; Proof of Residence, 3 June 1843, witnesses, Michl McDermott and Patrick Moran; naturalization granted 3 June 1843.

Green, James; nativity, Great Britain; Declaration of Intention, New York, 11 November 1845; Proof of Residence, Washington, D. C., 15 December 1849, witness, Owen Green; naturalization granted 15 December 1849.

Green, Owen; Declaration of Intention, New York, 15 April 1845; Proof of Residence, Washington, D. C., 28 November 1847, witness, Thomas Mc-Naney; naturalization granted 23 November 1847.

Green, Patrick; age 54 in 1848; nativity, Ireland; emigrated from Dublin; arrived at Alexandria, D. C., 1 June 1819; Declaration of Intention, 3 June 1848; Proof of Residence, 3 June 1850, witness, Charles Kiernan; naturalization granted 3 June 1850.

Grey, C y r i l Vernon; nativity, Great Britain and Ireland; Declaration of Intention, New York, 29 October 1842; Proof of Residence, New York, 10 December 1846, witnesses, William J. Cochran, 261 Bleeker St., N. Y. and William Lee, Senior, 59 Reade St., N. Y.; another Proof of Residence dated Washington, D. C., 21 December 1846, witness, John Heart; naturalization granted 21 December 1846.

Grimes, Guy; age 46 in 1837; nativity, County Down, Ireland; emigrated from Belfast; arrived at Baltimore, 12 July 1818; Declaration of Intention, 17 January 1837; Proof of Residence, 9 December 1840, witnesses, Robert Cunningham a n d William Douglass; naturalization granted 9 December 1840.

Grupe, William; age 32 in 1844; nativity, Germany; emigrated from Bremen; arrived at Baltimore, 8 July 1841; Declaration of Intention, 13 August 1844; Proof of Residence, 24 March 1847, witness, Anthony Best; naturalization granted 24 March 1847.

Gunton, Thomas, Junior; age about 33 in 1817; nativity, County of Norfolk, England; emigrated from England; arrived at Baltimore about last of June 1816; Declaration of Intention, 7 November 1817; Proof of Residence, 9 November 1822, witnesses, Richard Wallach and William Gunton; naturalization granted 9 November 1822.

Guttensohn, John; age 32 in 1843; nativity, Wertembourg, Germany; emigrated from Bremen; arrived at

Baltimore, 11 August 1841; Declaration of Intention, 2 November 1843; Proof of Residence, District Court, 5 June 1848, witness, Charly Schussler; naturalization granted 5 June 1848.

Hagarty, William; Declaration of Intention, Kings County, N. Y., 4 November 1835; Proof of Residence, Washington, D. C., 17 November 1847, witness, Patrick McGee; naturalization granted 17 November 1847.

Hager, Christopher; age 23 in 1840; nativity, Germany; emigrated f r o m Havre de Grasse; arrived at Baltimore, August 1828; Declaration of Intention, 3 August 1840; Proof of Residence, same, witnesses, Augusta Schnieder and John Heny; naturalization granted 3 August 1840.

Hager, Frederick; age 25 in 1835; nativity, Germany; emigrated from Havre de Grasse: arrived at Baltimore, 30 August 1829; Declaration of Intention, 26 March 1835; Proof of Residence, 2 April 1839, witnesses, Geo. M. Stepper and Jacob Frank; naturalization granted 2 April 1839.

Hager, Godfrey (Gottfried); age 23 in 1840; nativity, Germany; emigrated from Havre; arrived at New York, 15 August 1837; Declaration of Intention, 14 January 1840; Proof of Residence, 30 December 1843, witnesses, J. H. T. Werner and John Bolayer; naturalization granted 30 December 1843.

Hammont, James; age 32 in 1841; nativity, England; emigrated from London; arrived at New York, June 1834; Declaration of Intention, 27 April 1841; Proof of Residence, 11 April 1849, witness, George Topham; naturalization granted 11 April 1849.

Hanagan, Peter B. O.; age 28 in 1835; nativity, Ireland; emigrated from Belfast: arrived at Baltimore, 4 July 1833; Declaration of Intention, 15 December 1835; Proof of Residence, 13 December 1841, witnesses, Rev. Thomas Lilley and Mr. Charles Kin (King?); naturalization granted 13 December 1841.

Handley, James; age 23 in 1827; nativity, County of Galway, Ireland; emigrated from Galway; arrived at Baltimore year of 1817; Declaration of Intention, 24 December 1827; Proof of Residence, 24 December 1827, witnesses, John Dowling and Arthur Thompson; naturalization granted 24 December 1834.

Haney, Hugh; age 49 in 1845; nativity, Ireland; emigrated from Belfast; arrived at New York, 3 August 1828; Declaration of Intention, 3 April 1845; Proof of Residence, 29 May 1850, witness, William Feeny, naturalization granted 29 May 1850.

Hanna, Francis; age 26 in 1831; nativity, Ireland; emigrated from Ireland; arrived at New York in 1816; Declaration of Intention, 15 October 1831; the Proof of Residence is undated but apparently was same date as the Declaration of Intention, witnesses, George Phillips and Daniel Homans; naturalization granted 15 October 1831.

Hardy, Henry; age 29 in 1842; nativity, England; emigrated from Bristol; arrived at New York, May 1834; Declaration of Intention, 26 March 1842; Proof of Residence, 7 April 1845, witness, William R. Woodward, Esq.; naturalization granted 7 April 1845.

Harlihy (Horlihy), Daniel; age 24 in 1831; nativity, Ireland; emigrated from Cork; arrived at New York, 8 September 1827; Declaration of Intention, 8 June 1831; Proof of Residence, 12 June 1834, witnesses, Gregory Ennis and Philip Ennis; naturalization granted 12 June 1834.

Harper, Andrew; age 26 in 1822; nativity, Ireland; emigrated from Londonderry; arrived at Ogdensburg, N. Y., 16 July 1821; Declaration of Intention, 22 December 1822; Proof of Residence, 24 December 1827, witnesses, Thomas Magnier and Thomas Murray; naturalization granted 24 December 1827.

Harrison, Richard; age 28 in 1826; nativity, County of Thorn, England; emigrated from London; arrived at Norfolk, Virginia, 1818; Declaration of Intention, 27 May 1826; Proof of Residence, 2 April 1839, witnesses, Samuel H. Taylor and Ignatius N. Clements; naturalization granted 2 April 1839.

Harvey, William; age 45 in 1823; nativity, England; emigrated from Island of Guernsey; arrived at Baltimore, 30 September 1818; Declaration of Intention, 16 September 1823; Proof of Residence, 1 June 1824, witnesses, Joriah Bonooitte (Bonooith) and Charles Bill; naturalization granted 1 June 1829.

ABSTRACTS OF NATURALIZATION RECORDS, CIRCUIT COURT, DISTRICT OF COLUMBIA

PETITIONS RECEIVED, 1817-1850

Compiled by VIVIAN HOLLAND JEWETT, San Diego, California

Heider, John Frederick; age 34 in 1848; nativity, Germany; emigrated from Bremen; arrived at Baltimore, 29 June 1841; Declaration of Intention, 14 February 1848; Proof of Residence, 3 June 1850, witness, Henry Horbskarut; naturalization granted 3 June 1850.

Hefferen, Patrick; age 30 in 1824; nativity, Ireland; emigrated from City of Cork; arrived at Alexandria, District of Columbna, 1 November 1817; Declaration of Intention, 4 June 1824; Proof of Residence, 13 July 1829, witnesses, Patrick Delaney and James Sweeney; naturalization granted 13 July 1829.

Heill, Joseph; age 35 in 1843; nativity, Germany; emigrated from Bremen; arrived at Baltimore, 14 October 1837; Declaration of Intention, 28 October 1843; Proof of Residence, 23 March 1846, witness, William Hughes; naturalization granted 26 March 1846.

Hein, Samuel; nativity, Prussia, Declaration of Intention, New York, 14 September 1841; Proof of Residence, District Court, Washington, D. C., 4 June 1849, witness, Thomas McDonnell; naturalization granted, 4 June 1849.

Heitmuller, Alfred; age 31 in 1842; nativity, Germany; emigrated from Bremen; arrived at Baltimore, 8 August 1837; Declaration of Intention, 9 July 1842; Proof of Residence, 5 June 1846, witness, Benjamin K. Morsell, Esq.; naturalization granted 5 June 1846.

Heitmuller, Charles A. T.; age 32 in 1846; nativity, Germany; emigrated from Breman; arrived at Baltimore, 7 September 1840; Declaration of Intention, 1 June 1846; Proof of Residence, 20 May 1850, witness, Alfred Heitmuller; naturalization granted 20 May 1850.

Helfrick, John; age 45 in 1845; nativity, Germany; emigrated from Bremen; arrived at Baltimore, August 1834; Declaration of Intention, 6 June 1845; Proof of Residence, 3 April 1849, witness, Joseph Eckloff; naturalization granted 3 April 1849.

Henry, Christian Frederick; age 34 in 1844; nativity, Germany; emigrated from Bremen; arrived at New York, 5 January 1841; Declaration of Intention, 5 November 1844; Proof of Residence, 3 May 1847, witness, Nathan Edmonston; naturalization granted 3 May 1847.

Henry, John; nativity, Wurtemburg, Germany; emigrated from Havre de Grasse; arrived at Baltimore, 25 September 1829; Declaration of Intention, 2 March 18——; Proof of Residence, 3 August 1840, witnesses, John Taylor and Augustus Snider; naturalization granted 3 August 1840.

Hercus, George; age 30 in 1822; nativity, Haddington, Scotland; emigrated from Leith; arrived at Philadelphia, 12 September 1817; Declaration of Intention, 3 June 1822; Proof of Residence, 26 May 1828, witnesses, William Fitzhugh and J. F. Caldwell; naturalization granted 26 May 1828.

Hess, Jacob; age 23 in 1837; nativity, Germany; emigrated from Bremen; arrived at Baltimoore, 15 October 1832; Declaration of Intention, 26 December 1837; Proof of Residence, 1 December 1840, witnesses, Francis Mohun and Joseph Weber; naturalization granted 3 December 1840.

Hess, William; nativity, Germany; Declaration of Intention, 3 June 1850; Proof of Residence, same, witness, George Kaufmann; naturalization granted 3 June 1850.

Hibbs, Charles; age 29 in 1832; nativity, England; emigrated from Liverpool; arrived at Alexandria, D. C., 22 September 1830; Declaration of Intention, 29 March 1832; Proof of Residence, 19 A p r i l 1836, witnesses, Thomas Woodward a n d Nicholas Hedges; naturalization granted 19 April 1836.

Higgins, Patrick; age 32 in 1837; nativity; Ireland; emigrated from Cork; arrived at New York, May 1834; Declaration of Intention, 14 August 1837; Proof of Residence, 12 December 1844, witness, Charles McNamee; naturalization granted 12 December 1844.

Hine, William; nativity, Germany; Declaration of Intention, 27 May 1850; Proof of Residence, same, witness, Henry Ebeling; naturalization granted 27 May 1850.

Hitz, Florian; age 33 in 1841; nativity, Switzerland; emigrated from Havre; arrived at New York, 14 September 1835; Declaration of Intention, 30 December 1841; Proof of Residence, 10 November 1847, witness, Charles McNamee; naturalization granted 10 November 1847.

Hitz, John; age 62 in 1834; nativity, Switzerland; emigrated from Havre de Grasse; arrived at New York, 20 July 1831; Declaration of Intention, 23 May 1834; Proof of Residence, 5 April 1838, witnesses, D. A. Hall and Thos. P. Jones; naturalization granted 5 April 1838.

Hitz, John, Jr.; age 36 in 1834; nativity, Canton of Grison, Switzerland; emigrated from Canton of Grison, Switzerland; arrived at New York, July 1831; Declaration of Intention, 23 May 1834; Proof of Residence, 5 April 1838, witnesses, D. A. Hall and Thos. P. Jones; naturalization granted 5 April 1838.

Hoffman, George; age 31 in 1838; nativity, Germany; emigrated from Bremen; arrived at Baltimore, 30 July 1833 Declaration of Intention, 3 January 1838; Proof of Residence, 24 May 1843, witnesses, Gottfried Bitner and J. H. D. Werner; naturalization granted 24 May 1843.

Hoffman, George; age 29 in 1848; nativity, Germany; emigrated from Bremen; arrived at Baltimore, 7 July

1832; Declaration of Intention, District Court, 5 June 1848; Proof of Residence, same, witness, Charles Schussler; naturalization granted 5 June 1848.

Hollidge, James (John); age 48 in 1835; nativity, Lincolnshire, England; emigrated from Liverpool; arrived at Norfolk, Va., 28 December 1833; Declaration of Intention, 7 December 1835; Proof of Residence, 16 January 1841, witnesses, Charles Bell and William J o h n s o n; naturalization granted 14 (?) January 1841.

Holohan, John; age "about" 28 in 1818; nativity, Ireland; emigrated from Dublin; arrived at Boston, 18 June 1812; Declaration of Intention, 28 December 1818; Proof of Residence, 9 November 1822, witnesses, Joshua Couch and Asa L. Bassett; naturalization granted 9 November 1822.

Hopp, Nicholas; age 29 in 1842; nativity, Germany; emigrated from Bremen; arrived at B a l t i m o r e, 10 October 1838; Declaration of Intention, 12 September 1842; Proof of Residence, 26 March 1845, witness, Henry Horstkamp; naturalization g r a n t e d 26 March 1845.

Horning, John; age 48 in 1845; nativity, Germany; emigrated from Amsterdam; arrived at Baltimore, 18 August 1827; Declaration of Intention, 2 October 1845; Proof of Residence, 12 May 1848, witness, Charles McNamee; naturalization granted 12 May 1848.

Hughes, Hugh; age 34 in 1842; nativity, Wales; emigrated from Liverpool; arrived at Alexandria, 1 November 1829; Declaration of Intention, 9 April 1842; Proof of Residence, District Court, 5 June 1848, witness, John Fay; naturalization granted 5 June 1848.

Hughes, John; nativity, Monaghan, Ireland; emigrated from Dublin; arrived at Philadelphia, 15 September 18—; Declaration of Intention, 27 May 1837 (?); Proof of Residence, 30 May 1840, witnesses, James ——ity and John Leach; naturalization granted 1 June 1840. (Only two fragments, the left half of a printed Declaration of Intention were in the envelope.)

Hurstcamp, Henry; age 25 in 1840; nativity, Hanover, Germany; emigrated from Bremen; arrived at Baltimore, 2 May 1836; Declaration of Intention, 10 November 1840; Proof of Residence, 10 December 1844, witnesses, Gregory Ennis and John B. Gray; naturalization granted 10 December 1844.

Iddins, Frederick; age 25 in 1839; nativity, England; emigrated from Liverpool; arrived at Philadelphia, 4 September 1837; Declaration of Intention, 8 October 1839; Proof of Residence, 31 March 1845, witness, Henry Truman; naturalization granted 31 March 1845.

Iddins, Samuel; age 38 in 1842; nativity, England; emigrated from Liverpool; arrived at Baltimore, 28 July 1840; Declaration of Intention, 21 February 1842; Proof of Residence, District Court, 5 June 1848, witness, Edmund F. Brown; naturalization granted 5 June 1848.

Indermaur, Jeremiah; nativity, Switzerland; emigrated from Amsterdam; arrived at Philadelphia, November 1817; Declaration of Intention, 13 January 1830; Proof of Residence, 6 April 1835 (?), witnesses, Andrew Noer and Godfrey Eckloff; naturalization granted 6 May 1835.

Iost, Benedict; age 31 in 1839; nativity, Switzerland; emigrated from Havre; arrived at New York, 19 October 1837; Declaration of Intention, 26 March 1839; Proof of Residence, 11 December 1844, witness, John Peabody; naturalization granted 11 December 1844. (This name might be Jost though it is listed in the Index as Iost.)

Ivey, William Henry; age 30 in 1842; nativity, England; emigrated from Liverpool; arrived at New York, 29 September 1834; Declaration of Intention, 13 August 1842; Proof of Residence, 31 May 1845, witness, Charles McNamee; naturalization granted 31 May 1845.

Jacobi, William; age 38 in 1835; nativity, Germany; emigrated from Bremen; arrived at Baltimore, 2 May 1832;

Declaration of Intention, 11 December 1835; Proof of Residence, District Court, 5 June 1848, witness, Thomas Goodall; naturalization granted 5 June 1848.

Jaeger, Benedict; born 1788; nativity, Vienna, Austria; emigrated from Hamburg, Germany in 1827; arrived at New York, November 1831; Declaration of Intention, Princeton, Middlesex County, New Jersey; Proof of Residence, 30 August 1845 in Washington, D. C., witness, John Hitz; naturalization granted 30 August 1845.

Jirdinston, Peter William; age 44 in 1837; nativity, Germany; Declaration of Intention, 20 May 1837; Proof of Residence, same, witnesses, William Stewart and James Gettys; naturalization granted 20 May 1837.

Joice, Richard; age 26 in 1824; nativity, County Cork, Ireland; emigrated from Cork; arrived at Norfolk, Va., July 1818; Declaration of Intention, 2 June 1824; Proof of Residence, 29 May 1832, witnesses, Jeremiah Sullivan and John C. Remely; naturalization granted 29 May 1832.

Jordan, Thomas; merchant; "late of Great Britain and Ireland"; Declaration of Intention, New York, 20 December 1817; Proof of Residence, Washington, D. C., 2 July 1836, witnesses, James Gooch and Thomas Harrison; naturalization granted 2 July 1836.

Jost, Benedict; age 31 in 1839; nativity, Switzerland; emigrated from Havre; arrived at New York, 19 October 1837; Declaration of Intention, 26 March 1839; Proof of Residence, 11 December 1844, witness, John Peabody; naturalization granted 11 December 1844. (This name is listed in the Index as Iost but may be Jost.)

Joyce, John J.; age 30 in 1848; nativity, Ireland; emigrated from Cork; arrived at Norfolk, Va., May 1820; Declaration of Intention, District Court, 5 June 1848; Proof of Residence, same, witness, Michael Joyce; naturalization granted 5 June 1848.

Joyce, Michael; age 28 in 1844; nativity, Ireland; emigrated from Cork; arrived at New York, 28 August 1825; Declaration of Intention, 10 September 1844; Proof of Residence, same, witnesses, Patrick Byrne and Charles McNamee; naturalization granted 10 September 1844.

Judge, John; age "about" 28 in 1818; nativity, County of Mayo, Ireland; emigrated from Portsmouth, England; arrived at Alexandria, 5 November 1817; Declaration of Intention, 29 December 1818; Proof of Residence, 16 April 1823, witnesses, John B. Forrest and Edward Semmes; naturalization granted 16 April 1823.

Kohling (Kahling), John Michael; age 26 in 1842; nativity, Germany; emigrated from Bremen; arrived at New York, 28 August 1839; Declaration of Intention, 3 January 1842; Proof of Residence, 8 April 1845, witness, Joseph Nock; naturalization granted 8 April 1845.

Kaisser, Herm; age 24 in 1843; nativity, Germany; emigrated from Bremen; arrived at Philadelphia, 19 July 1839; Declaration of Intention, 8 March 1843; Proof of Residence, 12 April 1845, witness, Cornelius Andrar; naturalization granted 12 April 1845.

Kane, Patrick; age 26 in 1846; nativity, Ireland; emigrated from Cork; arrived at New York, 8 June 1842; Declaration o f Intention, District Court, 5 June 1848, witness, Jeremiah Sullivan; naturalization granted 5 June 1848. 3 January 1846; Proof of Residence.

Kaufmann, George; age 39 in 1840; nativity, Germany; emigrated from Bremen; arrived at Baltimore, 25 October 1832; Declaration of Intention, 16 October 1840; Proof of Residence, 3 June 1850, witness, Augustus E. S. Keise; naturalization granted 3 June 1850.

Kavanaugh, John; age 35 in 1834; nativity, Ireland; emigrated from Liverpool; arrived at New York, July 1819; Declaration of Intention, 19 April 1834; Proof of Residence, same,

witnesses Wm. C. Easton and Charles G. Wilcox; naturalization granted 19 April 1834.

Keane, John Stephen; age 28 in 1824; nativity, Ireland; emigrated f r o m Limerick; arrived at New York, May 1816; Declaration of Intention, 21 May 1824; Proof of Residence, 2 June 1834, witnesses, Gregory Ennis and Thomas M a g n i e r; naturalization granted 2 June 1834.

Kearnan, Patrick; age "about" 26 in 1816; nativity, County Kerry, Ireland; emigrated from Ireland; arrived at New York, 26 September 1812; Declaration of Intention, 4 April 1817; Proof of Residence, 4 June 1827, witnesses, Joseph Etter and Nicholas Callan; naturalization granted 4 June 1822.(?)

Kedglie, John; age 29 in 1821; nativity, East Lothian, Scotland; emigrated from Liverpool; arrived at New York, 17 December 1807; Declaration of Intention, 23 April 1821; Proof of Residence, 26 April 1839, witnesses, George Creniella (?) and George Lowry; naturalization granted 26 April 1839.

Kehl, John V.; age 25 in 1845; nativity, Germany; emigrated from Bremen; arrived at Baltimore, 26 July 1842; Declaration of Intention, 31 January 1845; Proof of Residence, 11 March 1850; witness, Rezin ((?) Stephens; naturalization g r a n t e d 11 March 1850.

Keily, Rev. Jeremiah; occupation, Minister; age "about" 20 in 1818; nativity, County Cork, Ireland; emigrated from Cork; arrived at Boston, 24 May 1818; Declaration of Intention, 26 June 1818; Proof of Residence, 5 December 1823, witnesses, Hezekiah Langley and Samuel Newton, and for reference, Rev. John Smith; naturalization granted 5 December 1823.

Keiser, Henry; age 21 in 1841; nativity, Germany; Declaration of Intention, Philadelphia, 8 October 1841; Proof of Residence, 19 February 1849 in Washington, D. C., witness, Charles Coleman; naturalization granted 31 May 1854 (?).

Keith (Keitch), John; age 25 in 1820; nativity, England; emigrated from London; arrived at New York, October 1817; Declaration of Intention, 10 June 1820; Proof of Residence, 11 June 1832, witnesses, John H. Houston and John Williams; naturalization granted 11 June 1832.

Keleher, James; age 23 in 1836; nativity, Ireland; emigrated from Cork; arrived at Boston, 7 July 1832; Declaration of Intention, 12 December 1836; Proof of Residence, 31 December 1840, witnesses, John Fleming and John Lynch; naturalization granted 31 December 1840.

Keller, Jonas; age 55 in 1824; nativity, Switzerland; emigrated from Bordeaux; arrived at New York, 6 May 1816; Declaration of Intention, 11 June 1824; Proof of Residence, 23 June 1829; naturalization granted 23 June 1829.

Keller, Jonas P.; age 23 in 1831; nativity, France; emigrated from Bordeaux; arrived at New York, August 1816; Declaration of Intention, 1 June 1831; Proof of Residence, same witnesses, William Stewart and Jacob Hilbus; naturalization granted 1 June 1831.

Keller, Michael; age 43 in 1839; emigrated from Havre de Grasse; arrived at Baltimore, 25 October 1831; Declaration of Intention, 3 June 1839; Proof of Residence, 4 April 1844, witnesses, Charles Schusster and Henry (Harry) M. T. Werner; naturalization granted 4 April 1844.

Kelly, Bernard; age 25 in 1824; nativity, County Donegal, Ireland; emigrated from Liverpool; arrived at Alexandria, D. C., 15 July 1819; Declaration of Intention, 10 August 1824; Proof of Residence, 15 April 1840, witnesses, John H. Goddard (?) and James C. Deasale (?); naturalization granted 15 April 1840.

Keobel, Jacob; age 24 in 1841; nativity, Kingdom of Bavaria; emigrated from Havre; arrived at Baltimore, August 1832; Declaration of Intention, 18 May 1841; Proof of Residence, same, witnesses, Christian Ammach and James Crossfield; naturalization granted 18 May 1841.

Keppler, Henry; age 42 in 1845; nativity, Germany; emigrated from Bremen; arrived at Baltimore, 27 July 1832; Declaration of Intention, 2 June 1845; Proof of Residence, 3 June 1847, witness, Gustavus A. Clarke; naturalization granted 3 June 1847.

Kiernan, Charles; age 35 in 1845; nativity, Ireland; emigrated from Liverpool; arrived at New York, 18 October 1830; Declaration of Intention, 22 May 1845; Proof of Residence, 3 June 1850, witness, James Maguire; naturalization granted 3 June 1850.

Kinney, Jeremiah; age 28 in 1845; nativity, Ireland; emigrated from London; arrived at New York, 8 June 1842; Declaration of Intention, 20 January 1845; Proof of Residence, 30 March 1848, witness, Gustavus A. Clarke; naturalization granted 30 March 1848.

Kinsley, Benjamin; age 33 in 1822; nativity, Lincolnshire, England; emigrated from Liverpool; arrived at Philadelphia, 19 July 1817; Declaration of Intention, 18 April 1822; Proof of Residence, 27 May 1828, witnesses, Charly Vanable and Jeremiah Perkins; naturalization granted 27 May 1828.

Kirkwood, Jonathan; age 33 in 1842; nativity, Edinburgh, "North Britain"; emigrated from Greenock, Scotland; arrived at New York, 1 April 1834; Declaration of Intention, 10 January 1842; Proof of Residence, 15 April 1844, witnesses, William S. Colquhoun and James Clephane; naturalization granted 15 April 1844.

Kleindienst, John P.; nativity, Germany; Declaration of Intention, 30 May 1850; Proof of Residence, same, witness, Thomas Parker; naturalization granted 30 May 1850.

Kleindienst, Sebastian; age 45 in 1834; nativity, Württemburg; emigrated from Amsterdam; arrived at Baltimore, 16 October 1832; Declaration of Intention, 26 November 1834; Proof of Residence, 7 December 1837, witnesses, G. C. Grammer and William Wise; naturalization granted 7 December 1837.

Klotz, George; age 27 in 1837; nativity, Germany; emigrated from Bremen; arrived at Baltimore, 14 A u g u s t 1833; Declaration of Intention, 27 December 1837; Proof of Residence, 1 June 1843, witnesses, William Lovel and Gustavus Hill; naturalization granted 1 June 1843.

Korff, John; age 38 in 1838; nativity, Germany; Declaration of Intention, Baltimore, 17 September 1838; Proof of Residence, District Court, Washington, D. C., 5 June 1848, witness, S a m u e l Devaughn; naturalization granted 5 June 1848.

Krafft, George; age 27 in 1832; nativity, Germany; emigrated from London; arrived at New York, July 1825; Declaration of Intention, 17 May 1832; Proof of Residence, 16 June 1836, witnesses, William Waters and John Bohleyer (Bohleger); naturalization granted 16 June 1836.

Krafft, John; age 31 in 1824; nativity, Württemburg; emigrated from London; arrived at Baltimore, 26 October 1818; Declaration of Intention, 3 June 1824; Proof of Residence, 21 December 1829, witnesses, Frederick C. DeKrafft and Thomas Taylor; naturalization granted 21 December 1829.

Kraft (Kroft), Christopher; age 44 in 1837; nativity, Germany; emigrated from Bremen; arrived at Baltimore, 14 September 1832; Declaration of Intention, 27 December 1837; Proof of Residence, 10 April 1843, witnesses, Jacob Weber and Conrad Hess; naturalization granted 10 April 1843.

Krebs, Charles I.; age 26 in 1837; nativity, Germany; emigrated from Bremen; arrived at Baltimore, 31 August 1832; Declaration of Intention, 1 December 1837; Proof of Residence, 3 January 1840, witnesses, Augustus Snider and John Emmerk; naturalization granted 3 January 1840.

Kroes, Peter Paul; age 35 in 1840; nativity, Holland; emigrated from Antwerk (Antwerp); arrived at New York, 25 October 1832; Declaration of Intention, 10 November 1840;

Proof of Residence, 10 January 1844, witnesses, Revd. Peter O'Flannigan and Lewis Carbery, Esquire; naturalization granted 10 January 1844.

Kuhl, Henry; age 25 in 1848; nativity, Germany; emigrated from Hamburg; arrived at Baltimore, 7 September 1832; Declaration of Intention, 8 May 1848; Proof of Residence, same, witness, John H. Ebarback; naturalization granted 8 May 1848.

Lakemeyer, Frederick; age 33 in 1845; nativity, Germany; emigrated from Rotterdam; arrived at Baltimore, 24 September 1843; Declaration of Intention, 26 May 1845; Proof of Residence, 18 October 1848, witnesses, William Crentzfeldt and C o n r a d Finckman; naturalization granted 18 October 1848.

Lamby, William; age 24 in 1840; nativity, Scotland; emigrated from Scotland; arrived at New York, 13 July 1829; Declaration of Intention, 2 April 1840; Proof of Residence, same, witnesses, William Van Riswick and David J. Ross; naturalization granted 2 April 1840.

Lauchrey (Laukney), Hugh; age 25 in 1839; nativity, Ireland; emigrated from Londonderry; arrived at Philadelphia, 5 June 1831; Declaration of Intention, 10 December 1839; Proof of Residence, 27 May 1842, witnesses, James Duran and Con O'Donnell; naturalization granted 27 May 1842.

Law, John George; age 36 in 1832; nativity, England; emigrated f r o m Spalding, England; arrived at Philadelphia, 19 July 1817; Declaration of Intention, 6 June 1832; Proof of Residence, 5 June 1834, witnesses, Richard Wright and Nicholas Callan; naturalization granted 5 June 1834.

This series of abstracts ends here, apparently incomplete, no further contributions appearing in *NGSQ* subsequent to 1957.

EARLY IRISH EMIGRANTS TO AMERICA
1803–1806

Lists copied from Additional MS 35932. Hardwicke Papers, Vol. DLXXXIV, in the British Museum, of passengers sailing from Ireland to America, with particulars of age, occupation, and place of abode, as sworn to by the masters of the several vessels, 1803–1806:

Passengers who intend going out in the American ship *Eagle*, Andrew Richer, Master, for New York. Burthen per Register, 257 Tons.

Names	Age	Residence
Alexander Radcliffe	23	Ballyroney
John Menter	28	Belfast
William Calvert	33	Killeagh
Ann Calvert	24	Killeagh
James Bryson	27	Kilrock
Peter Leonard	28	Hillsboro'
William Logan	36	Dromoir
Thomas Bain	18	Downpatrick
Joseph Webb	25	Cookstown
William Wilson	22	Derrylea
Margaret Wilson	20	do.
William Kineard	52	do.
Robert Kineard	18	Derrylea
William Hancock	19	do.
Thomas Wilson	23	Armagh
James Drennan	19	Cavehill
John English	40	Tynan
Isabella English	32	do.
William Kerr	18	do.
George Lyster	25	do.
James Lister	20	do.
John Graham	24	do.
Thomas Spratt	50	Clough
John Brown	24	Saintfield
Samuel Campbell	18	Banbridge
Charles Martin	20	Ballynahinch
Robert Halbridge	16	Ballymoney
Robert Eakins	38	Coleraine
William Rafield	23	Ballymena
William Woods	27	Sea Patrick
Archibald Kidd	20	Keady
John Shields	20	do.

Names	Age	Residence
John Cully	24	do.
David Clements	22	do.
Andrew Clements	20	do.
William McAlister	20	Ballycastle

I have no objection to the ship clearing out.

A Copy
C/ Skeffington
Com.

R. Hill
Col. Commg. the Forces
at Belfast
BELFAST, 6th April, 1803

Endorsed
List of Passengers by
the ship *Eagle* for
New York from
Belfast.

Permitted
29 March 1803

———

A List of Passengers to go on board the American Brig *Neptune*, Seth Stephens, Master, for New Castle and Philadelphia. Burthen per admeasurement, 117 Tons at Warrenpoint.

John Grimes	Labourer	aged	28 years
Agnes Grimes	His Wife	"	26 "
James Crummy	Farmer	"	45 "
Agnes "	His Wife	"	30 "
Mary "	Their Daughter	"	15 "
Sarah Crummy	Their Daughter	"	12 "
James "	Their Son	"	6 "
David "	ditto	"	4 "
Susan Dene	Spinster	"	18 "
David Gallon	Farmer	"	40 "
John Henry	ditto	"	40 "
Hanna Henry	His Wife	"	30 "
Nancy Henry	Their Daughter	"	13 "
James Henry	Their Son	"	11 "
William Corenter	Labourer	"	26 "
Mary Corenter	His Wife	"	21 "

Seth Stephens, Master of the Brig *Neptune,* came this day before me and made oath to the truth of the above.

Sworn before me, Custom
House, Newry, 29th March, 1803

SETH STEPHENS.   A. CARLETON
                                        Comr.

(Endorsed—
1803, April 12,—List of 16 Passengers by
the Brig *Neptune* from Warren
Point to Newcastle and Philadelphia.)

List of Passengers on board the Ship *Margaret,* of which Thomas Marsh is Master, burthen 300 Tons, bound for New York in America.

Name	Age	Name	Age
Eliz. Brothers	44	Ann Story	16
Mary "	19	Hugh Alexander	29
Samuel "	12	Jane "	22
James "	10	Jane "	3
William "	7	Sarah "	2
M. Ann Anderson	30	Robert Gooey	20
Mathew Doubly	12	Saml. Douglas	18
James Farrell	30	Thomas Harten	19
Eliz. "	22	John Rolston	27
Wm. "	3	Ann Beard	24
James Harkness	40	Ann Beard	2
Jane "	36	James M'Clean	60
Thos. "	12	Eliz. "	60
Margt. "	10	David "	24
Abigail "	8	John "	22
Sarah "	10	George "	28
Robt. "	6	William Riddle	19
James "	4	Samuel Magil	21
Eliz. Story	47	Samuel Magil	39
Ben "	18	Biddy Enery	35

(Usual oath)   18th April, 1803
THOMAS MARSH   H. HILLAM
(Usual endorsement.)   Comr.
From Newry.

List of Passengers intending to go from Belfast to Philadelphia in the Ship *Edward*; burthen 231-86/95 Tons per Register.

Name	Age	Name	Age
James Greg.	46	James Fox	40
Thomas "	18	Patk. Mooney	16
John "	19	James Tower	22
Thomas Fleming	19	James Burns	20
Hugh Porter	24	Robert Labody	33
John Martin*.	21	Hers. M'Cullough.	27
Alex. M'Meikin	21	Wm. Scott	22
Wm. Dunn	30	James Kirkman	40
Thos. Monks.	60	Wm. Bingham	40
Robt. "	22	James "	14
Joseph "	20	John Norris	16
Thomas "	17	Hugh Murphy	18
John Smith	20	Edwd. Wilson	18
Hu. M'Bride	26	Ardsal Hanlay.	24
W. "	25	James Read	23
W. Dawson.	28	Jos. Haddock	27
Jn. Craven	25		

Usual oath at Belfast

No date—C. SALMON, Cor.

GEORGE CRAIG, Master (Usual endorsement)—Dated 19th April, 1805.

The following lists have been compiled by H. Honiton Ball from MSS. in the British Museum. The MSS. have the title Additional MS., 35,762. F. 101.

List of the passengers who intend going to Newcastle and Philadelphia on board the ship *Brutus* of Philadelphia—George Craig, Master. Burthen, 500 Tons.

Name	Age	Place
Thomas Kennan	25	Stewartstown
Patrick Curley.	20	"
Bennet Boles	22	"
John Wilkinson.	23	Nn. Stewart
Michael Kelley	25	Omagh
Thomas Callaughan	23	Strabane
John Wilson	19	Nn. Conningham
James Clendining.	18	"
Patrick Cue	22	Aughnacloy
James Wilson	20	Nn. Conningham

Wm. Stewart.	25	Coleraine
Alexr. Eakin.	28	"
James Thompson.	25	Donigal
Isaac Cochran	27	Ballynoconey
James Ferrier	24	Bushmills
George Morrow.	28	"
John MacCad	29	"
James Peoples.	23	Latter Kenney
Darby Bayle.	24	" "
Alexander Thompson.	30	" "
Stephen Alley.	24	Derry
John Ewing	20	"
James Smily.	27	"
Thomas Murphy	26	"
Patrick Murphy.	30	"
John Hasson.	24	Cumber
Jean Bayle	21	"
John Johnston	23	"
David King.	29	"

(Note. All of the above put themselves down as labourers except Jean Bayle, who is recorded as "Spinster". As a law of the time forbad the emigration of skilled labour the designation used may or may not be correct.)

There is a sworn document appended to the above list, made by the master, George Craig, in which he makes affidavit that none of the above passengers is an "Artificer, Manufacturer, Seaman" or Seafaring Man, except the crew.

The following list has a similar affidavit appended by the Master George Bray.

A list of Passengers who intend going to New York on Board the Ship *Rover* of New York—George Bray, Master. Burthen 287 65/95 Tons.

Names	Age	Occupation	Residence
Michael Muldoon.	27	Gentleman	Co. Meath
Mrs. Muldoon.	24	Gentlewoman	"
John Jamison	21	Merchant	Dublin
Robt. Greer	38	Chapman	Dungannon
Fras. Ennis.	24	Gentleman	Queen's Co.
Heny. Herron	28	Merchant	Dublin
Elinor Neilson.	22	Spinster	Clones
Francis Evatt	21	Labourer	Co. Cavan
Jno. MacNeill	19	"	"
Mich. Connor	21	Labourer	Wexford
Ben. Hood	30	"	King's Co.

Names	Age	Occupation	Residence
Morris MacNeill.	19	Labourer	King's Co.
Hugh Brady	18	Clerk	Dublin
Stephen Flynn	24	"	"
Pat. Cranning	30	"	Drogheda
Wm. Armstrong.	22	Apothecary	Co. Meath
Petr. Donnolly	18	Clerk	Dublin
David Jones	29	"	"
Margt. Hawthorne	34	Spinster	Britain St., Dublin
Jas. Hawthorne (child) . . .	8		" " "
Kitty Hawthorne " . . .	5		" " "
Sally (servant girl)	19		" " "
Patt Fegan	30	Labourer	Co. Kildare
James Heeran	32	Clerk	"
James Wyland.	20	"	King's Co.
Patk. Lansdown	21	Farmer	Co. Meath
Thos. Fitzgerald	35	"	Co. Dublin
Patt MacNaughly.	27	Labourer	Co. Longford
Matt. Dickson.	20	Clerk	Dublin
Peter Smith	12	"	Co. Cavan
Andrew Murphy	21	Labourer	"

AMERICAN PASSENGER LISTS, 1804-6

[In *Report of the Deputy Keeper of the Records for the Year 1929,* Northern Ireland, Public Record Office (1930), 15, 21-49.]

American Passenger Lists, 1804-6 (British Museum Transcripts).—Masters of vessels leaving Irish ports were, at one time, required to furnish a sworn list of their passengers, probably in order to prevent the escape of offenders against the law and the emigration of seamen or skilled artisans. A collection of these lists is preserved in the British Museum. It covers the years 1803-6. As the great majority of the vessels sailed from Ulster ports, and there were a number of Ulster passengers even in those sailing from other ports, it was thought of interest to make a transcript of the portions not yet published. Between June, 1804, and March, 1806, the lists deal with 47 ships and give the names of some 1,600 passengers. 11 sailed from Belfast, the same number from Dublin, 10 from Londonderry, 9 from Newry, 2 from Sligo, one each from Ballyshannon and Warrenpoint. In two cases the Irish port is not stated. The port of entry in America is in 30 cases New York, in 8 Philadelphia or "Philadelphia and Newcastle," in 4 Boston and 2 each Baltimore and Charleston, 1 New Bedford. The emigrants from counties Antrim, Armagh, Down, Fermanagh, Londonderry and Tyrone have been indexed in Appendix B.

APPENDIX B.

Index to Documents (other than normal increments) deposited in the Public Record office during the year 1929.

Abst.—Abstract ; Acct(s).—Account(s) ; Admon.—Administration ; Afft.—; Affidavit ; Agrmt.—Agreement ; Als.—Alias ; Ans.—Answer ; Arts.—Articles Assgmt.—Assignment ; Atty.—Attorney ; Bp.—Bishop ; Bk.—Book ; C.— Census ; Cert.—Certificate ; Chy.—Chancery ; Conv.—Conveyance ; Ct.— Court ; D.B.N.—De Bonis Non Administratis ; Dft.—Draft ; Dio.—Diocese ; Eq.—Equity ; Exchq.—Exchequer ; Ext.—Extract ; Gt.—Grant ; Haberdashers' Pps.—Papers relating to the lands of the Haberdashers' Company in Co. Londonderry ; I.—Intestate ; Inqn.—Inquisition ; Jugt.—Judgment ; K.B.—King's Bench ; Kilw. Schl. Par.—List of Parents of Pupils at Kilwaughter School, Co. Antrim ; L'derry Address—Address of the Mayor and Citizens of Londonderry to King Will!am III. ; Mge.—Mortgage ; M.L.— Marriage Licence ; N.D.—Undated ; O.D.—Original Document ; P.—Probate ; Par.—Parish ; Pars.—Particulars ; Partn.—Parition ; Pass. to Amer.—List of Passengers from Ireland to America ; Pat.—Patent ; Petn.—Petition ; Pg.— Prerogative ; P.R.—Principal Registry ; Reg.—Register ; Regt.—Regiment ; Retn.—Return ; Settmt.—Settlement ; Solr.—Solicitor ; S.R.O.—Scottish Record Office ; Statmt.—Statement ; T.—Transcript ; T.S.P.I.—Transcripts of State Papers relating to Ireland ; W.—Will ; W/A.—Will Annexed.

Abercorn, Lord. *T.S.P.I.* 1717.
Absentees' Salaries, Estimated Produce of Tax on. *T.S.P.I.* 1717.
Accounts, Public, Report on. *T.S.P.I.* 1717.
Adams, Wm., Glenstall, Co. Ant. *Pass. to Amer.* 1806. (T.)
Addison, Mr. *T.S.P.I.* 1717.
   ,,   Tho., Carrickfergus, Co. Ant. *Pass. to Amer.* 1805. (T.)
   ,,   Ensign Thos. *T.S.P.I.* 1716.
Advowson Bill. *T.S.P.I.* 1719.
Agnew, Edwd. Jones. *Agrmt.* 1790. (O.D.)
   ,,   (or O'Gneeve), John, Ballyhempane, Co. Ant. *Lease. Hill Docts.* 1637. (O.D.)
   ,,   Fras. *Kilw. Schl. Par. Hill Docts.* 1797. (O.D.)
   ,,   Patk., Kilwaughter, Co. Ant. *Assgmt., Convs., etc. Hill Docts.* 1700– 1717. (O.D.) and (T.)
   ,,   Patk., Larne, Co. Ant. *W. Hill Docts.* 1841. (T.)
   ,,   Wm., Kilwaughter, Co. Ant. *Leases, Convs., Pg. W. etc. Hill Docts.* 1737–1776. (O.D.) and (T.)
Akey, Mr., Orbaugh. *Massereene MSS.* 1681. (T.)
Alcorn, Mr., Omagh, Co. Tyr. *Pass. to Amer.* 1806. (T.)
Aldworth, Mr. *T.S.P.I.* 1717.
Alexander, John and Margt., Ballynahinch, Co. Down. *Pass to Amer.* 1805. (T.)
   ,,   Rich., Caledon, Co. Tyr. *Pass. to Amer.* 1805. (T.)
   ,,   Saml. M. and John, Limavady, Co. L'derry. *Chy. Bill; Orders and Petns.* 1866–1871. (T.)
   ,,   Thos. and Sarah, Newtown Hamilton, Co. Arm. *Pass. to Amer.* 1806. (T.)
   ,,   Wm., Co. Tyr. *Pass. to Amer.* 1805. (T.)
Allcock, Mr. *T.S.P.I.* 1717–8.
Allen, Lieut. Col. *T.S.P.I.* 1716–7.
   ,,   John, Lisburn, Co. Ant. *Pass. to Amer.* 1806. (T.)
   ,,   John and Thos.,Gillinahisk (Gilnahirk?), Co. Down. *Pass. to Amer.* 1805. (T.)
   ,,   Joshua. *T.S.P.I.* 1717–9.
   ,,   Patk., Dromore, Co. Down. *Pass. to Amer.* 1806. (T.)
   ,,   Robt., L'derry. *Chy. Orders, Petns, etc.* 1855–6. (T.)
   ,,   Tim., Lands of Moynes, Cregantanvally, Greenland, &c. *Exchq. Order to Sheriff of Co. Ant. Hill Docts.* 1762. (O.D.)
   ,,   Wm., Fintona, Co. Tyr. *Pass. to Amer.* 1805. (T.)
Altham, Lord. *T.S.P.I.* 1719.
Ambrose, Mr. *T.S.P.I.* 1716–7.
Anderson, Alex., Cookstown, Co. Tyr. *Pass. to Amer.* 1805. (T.)
   ,,   Chas., Dav., Mary and Wm., Portaferry, Co. Down. *Pass. to Amer.* 1805. (T.)

Anderson, Jas., Banbridge, Co. Down. *Pass. to Amer.* 1804. (T.)
,, Mary, Omagh, Co. Tyr. *Pass. to Amer.* 1806. (T.)
Andrews, John, Comber, Co. Down. *Downshire MSS.* Jan. 8, 1796. (T.)
,, Saml., Loughbrickland, Co. Down. *Pass. to Amer.* 1805. (T.)
Annesley and Sherlock, Case of. *T.S.P.I.* 1719.
,, Fras. *Downshire MSS.* June 27, 1796. (T.)
,, Maurice. *T.S.P.I.* 1717.
Annour, Mary, Eliza, Marice, Wm. and Saml., Maragall, Co. Ant. *Pass. to Amer.*
1805. (T.)
Anstruther, Capt. *T.S.P.I.* 1718.
,, Ensigns Alex. and Rob. *T.S.P.I.* 1715.
Antrim, Co., Lands in. *Pat. Gt. Massereene MSS.* 1669. (T.)
Antrim, Earl of. *Lease. Hill Docts.* 1637. (O.D.)
,, Alex., Earl of. *Leases; Exchq. Decree. Hill Docts.* 1736-1755. (O.D.)
and (T.)
Aplin, Ensign Rich. *T.S.P.I.* 1716.
Archdall, Hen., Lands of Moynes, Cregantanvally, Greenland, &c. *Exchq. Order to
Sheriff of Co. Ant. Hill Docts.* 1762. (O.D.)
Ardtrea Parish, Co. L'derry. *Vestry Acts. Lenox-Conyngham MSS.* (2). 1730. (T.)
Arthur, Robt., Omagh, Co. Tyr. *Pass. to Amer.* 1805. (T.)
Armagh, Archbp. of. *T.S.P.I.* 1717.
,, Dio. of. *State of.* 1693. (T.)
Armstrong, Chr., Irvinestown, Co. Ferm. *Pass. to Amer.* 1806. (T.)
,, Jasper and Hannah, Enniskillen, Co. Ferm. *Pass. to Amer.* 1805. (T.)
,, Lieut. Mich. *T.S.P.I.* 1717-8.
,, Thos., Enniskillen, Co. Ferm. *Pass. to Amer.* 1804. (T.)
Army, *Commission Registers,* 1737-1760 (T.)
,, in Ireland. *List of Officers,* 1737, *Quarters,* 1739. (T.)
Arnold, Lieut. Hugh, Arnold's Hill, Co. Down. *Election as Volunteer Capt.* 1791. (T.)
Ash, Hen. *L'derry Address.* 1690. (T.)
Ashley, Capt. Wm. *T.S.P.I.* 1720.
Aston, Alex., Mounthill, Co. Arm. *Pass. to Amer.* 1804. (T.)
Atcheson, Sir Arth. *T.S.P.I.* 1716-7.
Atchison, Nanny, Randalstown. Co. Ant. *Pass. to Amer.* 1804. (T.)
Athlowe, Church of. *Haberdashers' Pps.* (*S.R.O.*) Apr. 23, 1617. (T.)
Auld, Wm., Aghaloe, Co. Tyr. *Pass. to Amer.* 1805. (T.)

Babington, —. *Haberdashers' Pps.* (*S.R.O.*). May, 1615. (T.)
,, Capt. Phil. *T.S.P.I.* 1715.
,, Wm., Ardekilley, Co. L'derry. *Rental. Haberdashers' Pps.* (*S.R.O.*)
1616-7. (T.)
Bacon, Robt., Cath. and Mary, Co. Tyr. *Pass. to Amer.* 1805. (T.)
Bagnall, Nichs., Greencastle, Co. Down. *Exchq. Bill Ext.* 1698. (T.)
Bailey, Jas. *Kilw. Schl. Par. Hill Docts.* 1797. (O.D.)
Baill(e)y, Jas. and J., Magherafelt, Co. L'Derry. *Pass. to Amer.* 1805. (T.)
Bailly, Robt. *T.S.P.I.* 1717.
Bailie, Wm., Belfast. *Pass. to Amer.* 1805. (T.)
Baker, Fras. *T.S.P.I.* 1716-7.
Balentine, Wm. *Kilw. Schl. Par. Hill Docts.* 1797. (O.D.)
Ballantine, Wm., Crayhill, Kilwaughter, Co. Ant. *Pg. W. and Gt.* (*P.*) 1893. (T.)
Ballintine, Thos., Newtownstewart, Co. Tyr. *Pass. to Amer.* 1806. (T.)
Ballyleidy Yeomanry. *Letters and Pps. Findlay Colln.* 1825-1831. (O.D.)
Bamber, Margt., Bangor, Co. Down. *Pass. to Amer.* 1805. (T.)
,, Robt., Baughan, Co. Down. *Pass. to Amer.* 1805. (T.)
Bannon, Patk and Ann, Co. Down. *Pass. to Amer.* 1805. (T.)
Barkly, Thos. *Release. Hill Docts.* 1755. (O.D.)
Barlow, Agnes, Lisdillon, Co. L'derry. *Pass. to Amer.* 1805. (T.)
Barnet, Lieut. Wm. *T.S.P.I.* 1715.
Barr, Jane, Ballymoney, Co. Ant. *Pass. to Amer.* 1805. (T.)
Barrell, Col., Regt. of *T.S.P.I.* 1719.
Barry, Mat. *Massereene MSS.* 1680. (T.)
,, Sarah, Elnr. and Ann, L'derry. *Pass. to Amer.* 1806. (T.)
Beatty, Dan. McNeill, Hillmount Co. Ant. *W. Hill Docts.* 1856. (O.D.)
,, Edwd., Fintona, Co. Tyr. *Pass. to Amer.* 1805. (T.)
,, Elizth. Mary, Aughnaskea, Co. Louth. *Pg. W. Ext.* 1844. (T.)
,, John, 'Meaghera' (Maghera, Co. L'derry ?). *Pass. to Amer.* 1806. (T.)

Beatty, Mary, Tullycolrick, Co. Ferm. *Clogher M.L. Bond Ext.* 1752. (T.)
,, Mr. *T.S.P.I.* 1718.
,, Rich. and Margt., Hillsborough, Co. Down. *Pass. to Amer.* 1805. (T.)
,, Wm., Cavenalogh, Co. Ferm. *Clogher M.L. Bond Ext.* 1752 (T.)
Beauford, Capt.-Lieut. Wm. *T.S.P.I.* 1715.
Beaumont, Dr. John, Andw. and Jas., Rathfriland, Co. Down. *Pass. to Amer.* 1805. (T.)
Beer and Ale, Proposed Duty on. *T.S.P.I.* 1717.
Beggs., Alex. and Margt., Ballyroban, Co. Ant. *Pass to Amer.* 1804. (T.)
,, Wm. *Connor W. Hill Docts.* 1834. (T.)
Belfast, Merchants, etc., of. *Petns.* 1766–1800. (T.)
Bell, Alex., Drumlough, Co. Down. *W. Ext.* 1784. (T.)
,, Dav., Patience, Geo. and Thos., Banbridge, Co. Down. *Pass. to Amer.* 1804 (T.)
,, John, Desertmartin, Co. L'derry. *Pass. to Amer.* 1805. (T.)
,, John. *Kilw. Schl. Par. Hill Docts.* 1797. (O.D.)
,, Robt., Killileagh, Co. Down. *Pass. to Amer.* 1805. (T.)
,, Wm., Lurgan, Co. Arm. *Pass. to Amer.* 1805. (T.)
Bellandine, Major Wm. *T.S.P.I.* 1720.
Bennett, Walt. *Acct. Haberdashers' Pps.* (*S.R.O.*) 1617. (T.)
Benson, Wm., Strabane, Co. Tyr. *Pass. to Amer.* 1805. (T.)
Beresford, Tristram, Coleraine, Co. L'derry. *Agrmts. for Leases* ; *Letters Haber-dashers' Pps.* (*S.R.O.*) 30th Mar., 1614 *et seq..* (T.)
Bible, Printing of, in Dublin. *T.S.P.I.* 1717.
Bickford, John. *T.S.P.I.* 1719.
Bigam, Wm., Coleraine, Co. L'derry. *Pass. to Amer.* 1806. (T.)
Bigan, Mores (Moses ?), Rathfryland, Co. Down. *Pass. to Amer.* 1805. (T.)
Bigg, Boleyn. *T.S.P.I.* 1716–7.
Biggem, Wm., Bushmills, Co. Ant. *Pass. to Amer.* 1804. (T.)
Bingham, Chas. *Letter. Massereene MSS.* 1681. (T.)
Birch, Geo., Ballybun, Co. Down. *Deed of Annuity.* 1787. (T.)
Bishop, Saml., Killinchy, Co. Down. *Pass. to Amer.* 1805. (T.)
Bissell, Qr.-Master Wm. *T.S.P.I.* 1715.
Bissett, Lieut.-Gen. Andw., Regt of. *List of Officers.* 1737. (T.)
Black, Edwd., Coleraine, Co. L'derry. *Pass. to Amer.* 1806. (T.)
,, John, Cookstown, Co. Tyr. *Pass. to Amer.* 1804. (T.)
,, Margt., Omagh, Co. Tyr. *Pass. to Amer.* 1805. (T.)
Blackwood, Sir Jas., Bart. *Appointment as Colonel of N. Down Militia. Findlay Colln.* 1800. (O.D.)
Bladen, Col. M. *T.S.P.I.* 1716–7.
Blair, Margt., Larne, Co. Ant. *Pass. to Amer.* 1804. (T.)
,, Randal, Larne, Co. Ant. *Connor W. and Gt.* (*P.*). *Hill Docts.* 1837. (T.)
,, Saml., Ralloo, Co. Ant. *Lease. Hill Docts.* 1747. (T.)
,, Wm. Hen., Cairncastle, Co. Ant. *Lease. Hill Docts.* 1773. (T.)
Blake, Capt. Thos. *T.S.P.I.* 1719.
Blakeney, Col. Wm., Regt. of. *List of Officers.* 1737. (T.)
Bland, Col. Humphry, Regt. of. *List of Officers.* 1737. (T.)
Blayney, Lord. *T.S.P.I.* 1717.
Blundell, Hon. Mrs. *Downshire MSS.* Feb. 4, 1796. (T.)
Bockland, Lieut. Maurice. *T.S.P.I.* 1716.
Bolton, Duke of. *T.S.P.I.* 1717.
Borr, Brig.-Gen. Jacob. *T.S.P.I.* 1716–7.
Bor's Regt. *T.S.P.I.* 1717.
Boswell, Ensign Thos. *T.S.P.I.* 1716.
Bothwell, John, Moneymore, Co. L'derry. *Pass. to Amer.* 1805.(?) (T.)
Bowles, (Brig.-Gen.) *T.S.P.I.* 1719.
,, Brig.-Gen. Pheneas, Regt. of. *List of Officers.* 1737. (T.)
Bowles' Regt. *T.S.P.I.* 1715–8.
Bowyer, Lieut. John. *T.S.P.I.* 1715.
Boyd, John, Antrim. *Pass. to Amer.* 1805. (T.)
,, Capt. Saml. *T.S.P.I.* 1716–7.
,, Wm., Larne, Co. Ant. *W. Hill Docts.* 1842. (T.)
,, Wm., Margt. and Saml., Dungannon, Co. Tyr. *Pass. to Amer.* 1804. (T.)
Boyle, Jas., Co. Down. *Pass. to Amer.* 1805. (T.)
Bracken, Jas., John, Margt. and Robt., Enniskillen, Co. Ferm. *Pass. to Amer.* 1806. (T.)

Bradley, John, Muff, Co. L'derry or Co. Dongl. *Pass. to Amer.* 1806. (T.)
  ,,   Patk. and Cath., Rossgull. *Pass. to Amer.* 1805. (T.)
Bragg, Col. Phil. Regt. of *List of Officers.* 1737. (T.)
Braithwait, 2nd Lieut. John. *T.S.P.I.* 1716.
Branan, Murtaugh, Maghira. *Massereene MSS.* 1681. (T.)
Brandreth, Capt.-Lieut. Mich. *T.S.P.I.* 1715.
Bratten, Jane, Clontibret, Co. Mon. *Clogher M.L. Bond Ext.* 1718. (T.)
Brawnlie, Rich., Keady, Co. Arm. *Pass. to Amer.* 1805. (T.)
Breen, Phil. *Kilw. Schl. Par. Hill Docts.* 1797. (O.D.)
Brennan, Robt. *Kilw. Schl. Par. Hill Docts.* 1797. (O.D.)
Breviter, Rev. Mr. *T.S.P.I.* 1717.
Brice, Brig.-Gen. *T.S.P.I* 1717.
Brice, Edwd., Belfast. *Marr. Arts.* 1712. (T.)
  ,,   Edw., Kilroot, Co. Ant. *Marr. Settmt.* 1751. (T.)
  ,,   Edwd., London. *Release.* 1787. (T.)
Briden, Jas., Strabane, Co. Tyr. *Pass. to Amer.* 1805. (T.)
Bridgman, Capt.-Lieut. Phil. *T.S.P.I.* 1720.
Brissoniere de la, Peter. *T.S.P.I.* 1719.
British Plantations, Export of Linen to. *T.S.P.I.* 1715-6.
Broderick, Mr. Serjt. *T.S.P.I.* 1719.
Broderick, St. John. *T.S.P.I.* 1719.
Brodie, Ensign Alex. *T.S.P.I.* 1716.
Brodrick, Allen. *T.S.P.I.* 1717-8.
  ,,   Lord Chancellor. *T.S.P.I.* 1717.
Brown, Lieut. Gilbert. *T.S.P.I.* 1716.
  ,,   John, Killead, Co. Ant. *Pass. to Amer.* 1805. (T.)
  ,,   Mary. *Renewal of Lease. Hill Docts.* 1768. (O.D.)
  ,,   Nancy, Co. Down. *Pass. to Amer.* 1805. (T.)
  ,,   Saml., Ballymacarrett, Co. Down. *Pass. to Amer.* 1806. (T.)
  ,,   Major Thos. *T.S.P.I.* 1715.
  ,,   Wm. and Cath., Carnmoney, Co. Ant. *Pass. to Amer.* 1805. (T.)
Browne, Thos., " Baley Fatlin " (Ballyfatten, Co. Tyr.?) *Pass. to Amer.* 1806. (T.)
Brownjohn, Lieut. Hen. *T.S.P.I.* 1717.
Brownlow Manor Court, Co. Arm. *Process Forms.* 1800. (O.D.)
Brydal, Capt. Phil. *T.S.P.I.* 1715.
Bubb, Mr. *T.S.P.I.* 1717.
Buchanan, Wm., Moneymore. *Pass. to Amer.* 1805.? (T.)
Budgell, (Eustace). *T.S.P.I.* 1717-8.
Bullick, Isaac, Lurgan, Co. Arm. *W.* 1828. (T.)
Bullock, Ensign John. *T.S.P.I.* 1716.
  ,,   John and Ralph, Aghalee, Co. Ant. *Leases.* 1741. (T.)
  ,,   Ralph, Belynatan, Co. Ant. *Lease.* 1799. (T.)
  ,,   Thos., Bellyceel, Co. Ant. *W.* 1805. (T.)
Burgess, John, Monaghan. *Clogher M.L. Bond Ext.* 1718. (T.)
  ,,   Robt., Aughderig, Co. Down. *Pass. to Amer.* 1805. (T.)
Burgh, Thos. *T.S.P.I.* 1717.
Burleigh, Ruth, Carrickfergus, Co. Ant. *Lease.* 1799. (T.)
Burlington, Rich., Earl of. *T.S.P.I.* 1717.
Burn, Thos., Dromore, Co. Down. *Pass. to Amer.* 1806. (T.)
Burnett, Capt. Alex. *T.S.P.I.* 1715.
Burns, Saml. and Agnes, " Loughgeel " (Loughguile, Co. Ant.?). *Pass. to Amer.*
       1805. (T.)
Burrowes, A. *T.S.P.I.* 1719.
Burston, Geo. *T.S.P.I.* 1716-7.
Busted, Mr. *T.S.P.I.* 1719.
Butle, David, Sovereign of Belfast. *Letter.* July 29, 1704. (T.)
Butler, Mr., Dublin. *Massereene MSS.* 1693. (T.)
  ,,   Mr. *T.S.P.I.* 1718.
  ,,   Theoph. *T.S.P.I.* 1717.
Buttle, Dav., Dublin. *Precipe. Lenox-Conyngham MSS.* (2). N.D. (T.)
  ,,   Geo. Conyngham. *Exchq. Ans. Lenox-Conyngham MSS.* (2), circa 1750.
       (T.)
  ,,   Wm., Coagh, Co. Tyr. *Recovery. Lenox-Conyngham MSS.* (2). 1750. (T.)
Byng, Sir Geo. *T.S.P.I.* 1719.
Byrne, Edmd. *T.S.P.I.* 1719.

Byrne, John and Edwd., Keady, Co. Arm. *Pass. to Amer.* 1804. (T.)
Byrnes, Mat., Newry, Co. Down. *Pass. to Amer.* 1805. (T.)

Cabeen, Robt. *Kilw. Schl. Par. Hill Docts.* 1797. (O.D.)
Cadogan, Bgt. *T.S.P.I.* 1717.
Cahan, John, Cumber. *Massereene MSS.* 1681. (T.)
Cairnes, Dav., L'derry *Release. Lenox-Conyngham MSS.* (2). 1719. (T.)
Calbeck, Wm., Dublin. *Memo. of Reconv. of Mge.* 1796. (T.)
Caldwell, Jas., Killylean, Co. L'derry. *Lease Ext.* 1764. (T.)
  „   John. *T.S.P.I.* 1717.
  „   (or Murphy), Rose. *W. Hill Docts.* 1852. (O.D.)
  „   Widow. *Kilw. Schl. Par. Hill Docts.* 1797. (O.D.)
Calhoun, John, Enniskillen, Co. Ferm. *Pass. to Amer.* 1805(?) (T.)
  „   Saml., Newtownstewart, Co. Tyr. *Pass. to Amer.* 1805. (T.)
  „   Wm. and Jean, Clandy (Claudy, Co. L'derry. ?). *Pass. to Amer.* 1805. (T.)
Calvert, Mr. *Haberdashers' Pps. (S.R.O.)* Apr. 15, 1614. (T.)
Calwell, John, Inver, Co. Ant. *Lease. Hill Docts.* 1769. (T.)
  „   John, Larne, Co. Ant. *Pass. to Amer.* 1806. (T.)
Camden, Earl. *Downshire MSS.* Jan. 26, 1796. (T.)
Campbell, Mr. *T.S.P.I.* 1719.
  „   Andw., Nancy and Mary, Badowney, Co. Tyr. *Pass. to Amer.* 1805. (T.)
  „   Ann and Letitia, Dungiven, Co. L'derry. *Pass. to Amer.* 1806. (T.)
  „   Arth., Ballymagrorty. *Pass. to Amer.* 1805. (T.)
  „   Chas. *Exchq. Bill Ext.* 1717. (T.)
  „   Dan., Castlereagh, Co. Down. *Pass. to Amer.* 1805. (T.)
  „   Jas., Antrim. *Pass. to Amer.* 1806. (T.)
  „   John, Ann, Elr., Sara and Alex., Omagh, Co. Tyr. *Pass. to Amer.* 1805. (T.)
  „   Col. John, Regt. of. *List of Officers.* 1737. (T.)
  „   Col. Josias. *T.S.P.I.* 1716-7.
  „   Saml., Dromore, Co. Down. *Pass. to Amer.* 1805. (T.)
Carabineers, First Regt. of. *List of Officers.* 1737 (T.)
  „   (3rd Regt. of Horse), Tullamore. *List of Officers.* 1770. (T.)
Carew, Hugh, " Carncow " (Carncome, Co. Ant. ?). *Pass. to Amer.* 1805.
Carey, Geo. *Haberdashers' Pps. (S.R.O.)* Apr. 23, 1617. (T.)
Carlisle, Wm., Mary, Wm. and Geo., Malone, Co. Ant. *Pass. to Amer.* 1806. (T.)
Carmichael, Mr. *T.S.P.I.* 1719.
Carpenter, Capt. Jas. *T.S.P.I.* 1717.
Carr, Jos., Killelegh, Co. Arm. *Pass. to Amer.* 1805. (T.)
Carrickbrack, Co. Arm. *Rental.* 1847. (T.)
Carrickfergus, Governorship of. *Letter. Massereene MSS.* 1692. (T.)
Carroll, Elizth., Randalstown, Co. Ant. *Pass. to Amer.* 1804. (T.)
Carron, Leslie, Sarah and Mary, Ross, Co. Down. *Pass. to Amer.* 1805. (T.)
Carrothers, Robt. and Wm., Randalstown, Co. Ant. *Pass. to Amer.* 1804. (T.)
Cars, John, Rathfriland, Co. Down. *Pass. to Amer.* 1804. (T.)
Carson, Jas., Ballygawly, Co. Tyr. *Pass. to Amer.* 1805. (T.)
  „   Dr. Saml., Armagh. *Assgmts.* 1791. (O.D.)
Casement, John M., Ballycastle, Co. Ant. *Pg. W. and Gt. (P.); Eq. Exchq. Report and Decree. Hill Docts.* 1836-1840. (T.)
Cassiday, Chas., Belfast. *Pass. to Amer.* 1805. (T.)
Caswell, Hector. *T.S.P.I.* 1719.
Cateny, Bryan, Magherykilcrany, Co. Arm. *Lease.* 1788. (O.D.)
Cathcart, Jas., Tedavenett, Co. Mon. *Clogher M.L. Bond Ext.* 1718. (T.)
  „   Brig.-Gen. Lord, Regt. of. *List of Officers.* 1737. (T.)
Caulfield, Hon. and Rev. Chas. and Alice, Castlestewart, Co. Tyr. *Exchq. Bill. Lenox-Conyngham MSS.* (2), circa 1750.
  „   Judge W. *T.S.P.I.* 1717.
Cavan Co., Lands in. *Pat. Gt. Massereene MSS.* 1669. (T.)
Cecil, Col. Wm. *Massereene MSS.* 1677. (T.)
Chambers, Alex., Ann, Mary Ann, Sarah, Isa. and Reba., Ballymagrorty. *Pass. to Amer.* 1805. (T.)
  „   Jas., Drumbo, Co. Down. *Pass. to Amer.* 1805. (T.)
  „   Wm., Coleraine, Co. L'derry. *Pass. to Amer.* 1805. (T.)
Cheney, Andw. F. and Mary, Macetown, Co. Meath. *Mge.* 1720. (O.D.)
Cheny, ————. *T.S.P.I.* 1719.
Chetwood, Mr. *T.S.P.I.* 1719.

Chevers, ——. *T.S.P.I.* 1717.
Child, Capt. Robt. *T.S.P.I.* 1716-7.
Chudleigh's Regt. *T.S.P.I.* 1715-6.
Church, Qr.-Master Randal. *T.S.P.I.* 1716.
Churchill's Regt. *T.S.P.I.* 1713-8.
Clare Co., Lands in. *Pat. Gt. Massereene MSS.* 1669. (T.)
Clark, Jas. *T.S.P.I.* 1719.
  ,, John and Elnr., Co. L'derry. *Pass. to Amer.* 1805. (T.)
Clark, Robt., sen. and jun., Antrim. *Agrmt. for Lease. Massereene MSS.* 1695.
    (T.)
  ,, Wm. *Downshire MSS.* Apr. 1, 1796. (T.)
Clogher, Bp of. *T.S.P.I.* 1716-7.
Clokey, Andw. (Spa Volunteers). *Election of Volunteer Capt.* 1791. (T.)
Close, Hen. *Kilw. Schl. Par. Hill Docts.* 1797. (O.D.)
Clotworthy, Sir John and Lady Margt. *Massereene MSS.* 1665. (T.)
  ,, Dame Mary. *Massereene MSS.* 1634. (T.)
  ,, Mary. *Massereene MSS.* 1694. (T.)
Clyde, Thos., Ballyroban, Co. Ant. *Pass. to Amer.* 1804. (T.)
Cobham, Lord. *T.S.P.I.* 1719.
Cochran, Rich., Tubbermore, Co. L'derry. *Pass. to Amer.* 1805(?) (T.)
Cockeran, Family. *Journal, L'pool to New York Voyage.* 1833. (O.D.)
Cockran, Hugh, Gortin, Co. Tyr. *Pass. to Amer.* 1805. (T.).
Coleraine and Londonderry, Governorship of. *Massereene MSS.* 1677. (T.)
Collins, Mr. *T.S.P.I.* 1717.
  ,, Wm., Gilligan (Killagan ?), Co. Ant. *Pass. to Amer.* 1805. (T.)
Collis, Cornet Ray. *T.S.P.I.* 1717-8.
Colvill, Sir Robt., Knt., Newtowne, Co. Down. *Lease. Hill Docts.* 1692. (T.)
Colville, Jos. and Cath., Lough Gele. *Pass. to Amer.* 1804. (T.)
Colvine, Lieut. Ch. *T.S.P.I.* 1715.
Comberback, Capt. *T.S.P.I.* 1717.
Commission Registers Irish. 1737-1760. (T.)
Conelye, Mr. *T.S.P.I.* 1717.
Congreive, Lieut. Wm. *T.S.P.I.* 1716.
Coningham, Hen., Omagh, Co. Tyr. *Pass. to Amer.* 1804. (T.)
  ,, Wm., Springhill. Co. L'derry. *Release. Lenox-Conyngham MSS.* (2).
    1719. (T.)
Connally, Jas., Barony. *Massereene MSS.* 1681. (T.)
Conningham, Hen., Omagh, Co. Tyr. *Pass. to Amer.* 1805. (T.)
Connon, John, Enniskillen. *Pass. to Amer.* 1805. (T.)
Conolly, Kate. *T.S.P.I.* 1718.
  ,, W. *T.S.P.I.* 1716-9.
Conway, Wm., Knockbracken, Co. Down. *Pass. to Amer.* 1804. (T.)
Conyngham, Anne, Springhill, Co. L'derry. *Marr. Arts.; W.* 1745-8. (T.)
  ,, Capt. and Geo. *Case for Counsel. Lenox-Conyngham MSS.* (2).
    1793. (T.)
  ,, Col., Springhill, Co. L'derry. *Letter. Lenox-Conyngham MSS.* (2).
    circa 1750. (T.)
  ,, Dav., Belfast. *Agrmt. Lenox-Conyngham MSS.* (2). 1768. (T.)
  ,, Geo. and (Cornet) Wm., Springhill Co. L'derry. *Mges; Recovery.
    Lenox-Conyngham MSS.* (2.) 1744-6. (T.)
  ,, Geo., Springhill, Co. L'derry. *Lease; Recovery; Marr. Arts. Lenox-
    Conyngham MSS.* (2.) 1731-1755. (T.)
  ,, John, Bath. *Agrmt. Lenox-Conyngham MSS.* (2.) 1768. (T.)
  ,, (Capt.) Wm. *Afft.; Power of Atty. Lenox-Conyngham MSS.* (2.)
    1760-6 (T).
Cooch, Jas., Larne, Co. Ant. *Belfast Gt. (I.). Hill Docts.* 1863. (O.D.)
Cook, Thos. *T.S.P.I.* 1716-7.
Cooke, Ensign, Balle Vickmackin, etc., Co. L'derry. *Rental. Haberdashers' Pps.*
    (S.R.O.) 1616-7. (T.)
  ,,. John, Lymavaddy, Co. L'derry. *Agrmt. for Lease. Haberdashers' Pps.*
    (S.R.O.) May 26, 1615. (T.)
Coot, Mr. *T.S.P.I.* 1719.
Cope, Brig.-Gen. John. *Regt. of. List of Officers.* 1737 (T).
Corn Bill. *T.S.P.I.* 1719.
Corn Bill. *Belfast Petn. against.* Feb. 12, 1784. (T.)
Cornele, John. *T.S.P.I.* 1716-7.

Cornwallis, Col. Steph., Regt. of. *List of Officers.* 1737 (T.)
Corry, Nichs., Co. Down. *Pass. to Amer.* 1805. (T.)
Costerdyne, Geo. *Haberdashers' Pps. (S.R.O.)* • Apr. 29, 1617. (T.)
Cotterel, Ensign John. *T.S.P.I.* 1716.
Coulson, John, Loughbrickland, Co. Down. *Pass. to Amer.* 1805. (T.)
Coult, Capt. *Massereene MSS.* 1681. (T.)
Cox, John, Enniskillen. *Pass. to Amer.* 1805. (T.)
„ Sir Rich. *Lease. Massereene MSS.* 1692. (T.)
Cox, Thos. *Acct. Haberdashers' Pps.(S.R.O.)* 1617(?) (T.)
Coyle, Hugh, Garvagh, Co. L'derry. *Pass. to Amer.* 1805(?) (T.)
Craig, Saml., Larne, Co. Ant. *Pass. to Amer.* 1806. (T.)
„ Saml., Stewartstown, Co. Tyr. *Pass. to Amer.* 1805. (T.)
Craige, Major-Gen. *Downshire MSS.* Jan. 12, 1796. (T.)
Craigmins, Alex., Fintona, Co. Tyr. *Pass. to Amer.* 1805. (T.)
Crammer, John, Enniskillen, Co. Ferm. *Pass. to Amer.* 1805. (T.)
Crawford, Jas., Ballyshavage, Co. Ant. *Marr. Arts.* 1712. (T.)
„ John and Janet, Mounthill, Co. Arm. *Pass. to Amer.* 1804. (T.)
„ Josias, Newtownstewart, Co. Tyr. *Pass. to Amer.* 1805. (T.)
„ Robt. *T.S.P.I.* 1719.
„ Robt., Killeter, Co. Tyr. *Pass. to Amer.* 1805. (T.)
„ Ensign Wm. *T.S.P.I.* 1715.
„ Wm. *Agrmt. Hill Docts.* 1790. (O.D.)
Creighton, Brig.-Gen. (Dav.). *T.S.P.I.* 1717-9.
Cricket, Dav., Drumnashiel (Drumshiel, Co. Tyr.?). *Pass. to Amer.* 1806. (T.)
Crimlisk (or Cunelisk), John and Cath., Antrim. *Pass. to Amer.* 1805. (T.)
Crispin, Wm., Kinsale, Co. Cork. *Pg. Gt. (I.) Ext.* 1682. (T.)
Crofton, Wm. *Chy. Inqn.* 1602. (T.)
Crofts, Brig.-Gen. *T.S.P.I.* 1719.
Crookshanks, John and Wm. *L'derry Address.* 1690. (T.)
Crosbie, Adjt. Cha. *T.S.P.I.* 1717.
Crosier, Jas. and Mary, Co. Tyr. *Pass. to Amer.* 1805. (T.)
Crossan, Patk., Douglass. *Pass. to Amer.* 1805. (T.)
Crothers, Geo., Rathfriland, Co. Down. *Pass. to Amer.* 1805. (T.)
„ John, Laifanny and Jenny, Randalstown, Co. Ant. *Pass. to Amer.* 1804. (T.)
Croyet, Agnes, John, Wilson and Jas., Moneymore, Co. L'derry. *Pass. to Amer.* 1805. (T.)
Crozier, Agnes, Livy and Wm., Armagh. *Pass. to Amer.* 1805. (T.)
Culbutson, Jas. and Sam., Fintona, Co. Tyr. *Pass. to Amer.* 1805. (T.)
Cummin (als Kumming), Jas., Ballywigan, Co. Down. *Lease Ext.* 1727 (T.)
Cumming, Jannett and Elnr., Donegore, Co. Ant. *Pass. to Amer.* 1805. (T.)
Cummyng, Dr. Duncan, Dublin. *Marr. Arts.* 1712. (T.)
Cunelisk (or Crimlisk), John and Cath., Antrim. *Pass. to Amer.* 1805. (T.)
Cunningham, Alex. *L'derry Address.* 1690 (T.)

Dalbine, Sir Gilbert. *T.S.P.I.* 1717.
Daly, Chas., Denis, Domk. and Peter. *Exchq. Decree. Hill Docts.* 1746. (T.)
Dalzell, Lieut.-Gen. Robt., Regt. of. *List of Officers.* 1737. (T.)
Davenport, Major-Gen. (Sherington). *T.S.P.I.* 1717-9.
David, Cornet Peter. *T.S.P.I.* 1715.
Davidson, Robt., Jas. and Eliza, Rathfriland, Co. Down. *Pass. to Amer.* 1804-5. (T.)
„ Wm., Dromore, Co. Down. *Pass. to Amer.* 1806. (T.).
Davis, Wm., Belfast. *Pass. to Amer.* 1805. (T.).
Davison, Jas., Moneyrea, Co. Down. *Pass. to Amer.* 1805. (T.)
„ Robt., Jas. and Eliza, Rathfriland, Co. Down. *Pass. to Amer.* 1805.(T.)
Davys, Hen., Carrickfergus, Co. Ant. *Pg. W. Ext.* 1708. (T.)
Dawson, Mr. *T.S.P.I.* 1719.
Delafaye, Chas., Elizth. and Anne. *T.S.P.I.* 1717-9.
Delaforce, M. *T.S.P.I.* 1716-7.
Denham, Rev. Alex. and Ann, Saintfield, Co. Down. *Pass. to Amer.* 1804. (T.)
„ Lieut. Sir Robt. *T.S.P.I.* 1716.
Derington, Thos., Hillsborough, Co. Down. *Pass. to Amer.* 1806. (T.)
Dermott, Andw., L'derry. *Pass. to Amer.* 1806. (T.)
Derry (als White, als Gough), Cisly, Newry, Co. Down. *Exchq. Bill Ext.* 1698. (T.)
Derry, Dio. of. *State of.* 1693. (T.)
Derry, Dio. of. *Exts. of Visitations.* 1733. (T.)

Derry, Island of. *Chy. Inqn.* 1602. (T.)
Derry, Lawr., Newry, Co. Down. *Exchq. Bill Ext.* 1698. (T.)
Derry, Mayor and Bp. of. *T.S.P.I.* 1717.
Desbrisay, Theoph. *T.S.P.I.* 1716-7.
Desertions from the Army. *T.S.P.I.* 1719.
Dick, Jas., Gillhall, Co. Down. *Pass. to Amer.* 1805. (T.)
„ Saml. and Mary, Scarvagh, Co. Down. *Pass. to Amer.* 1806. (T.)
„ Wm. and Jane, Drumarra, Co. Down. *Pass. to Amer.* 1805. (T.)
Dickey, John, Ballymena, Co. Ant. *Pass. to Amer.* 1805. (T.)
Dickie, Dav., Larne, Co. Ant. *Lease. Hill Docts.* 1769. (T.)
Dickinson, Gordon, Rathfriland, Co. Down. *Pass. to Amer.* 1804. (T.)
Dickson, Wm. *Downshire MSS.* June 27. 1796. (T.)
Dillon, Gerard. *T.S.P.I.* 1719.
„ Mr. and Mrs. *Journal. L'pool. to New York Voyage.* 1833. (O.D.)
Disert, Wm., Dromore, Co. Down. *Pass. to Amer.* 1805. (T.)
Dissenters, Toleration for. *T.S.P.I.* 1719.
Divine, Jas., Donaughkiddy. *Massereene MSS.* 1681. (T.)
Dixon, Saml., Mullabane, Co. Tyr. *Lease.* 1785. (O.D.)
Dobbs, Conway Rich., Fras. and Jane, Castle Dobbs, Co. Ant. *Release.* 1787. (T.)
Doddington, Mr. *T.S.P.I.* 1717.
Dodingby, Capt. *Haberdashers' Pps. (S.R.O.)* May, 1615. (T.)
Dogherty, Cath. and Rose, Newtownstewart, Co. Tyr. *Pass. to Amer.* 1805. (T.)
Doherty, John. *Order for Attachment.* 1867. (T.)
Donachy, Jas. and Cath., Co. Ferm. *Pass. to Amer.* 1805. (T.)
Donahy, Edwd., Killcappell, Co. Arm. *Pass. to Amer.* 1805. (T.)
Donaldson, Hugh, Drumnasole, Co. Ant. *Mge. Hill Docts.* 1750. (O.D.)
„ John, Drumnasole, Co. Ant. *Conr. H.ll Docts.* 1717. (O.D.)
„ Robt., Downpatrick, Co. Down. *Pass. to Amer.* 1805. (T.)
Donegall, Earl of. *Pat. Gt. Massereene MSS.* 1695. (T.)
Donnelly, Jas., *Chy. Cause Petn.* 1855. (T.)
Donnon, Jos. and Jane, Rathfriland, Co. Down. *Pass. to Amer.* 1804. (T.)
Donoly, Jas., Peter, John, Dan., Patk., Margt., Nelly, Susy, Peggy and Reggy, Six-Mile-Cross, Co. Tyr. *Pass. to Amer.* 1805. (T.)
Dorman, Margt., Jas., Jane and Geo., Co. Down. *Pass. to Amer.* 1805. (T.)
Dormer, Lieut.-Gen. Jas., Regt. of. *List of Officers.* 1737. (T.)
Dormer's Regt. *T.S.P.I.* 1716-1720.
Dougherty, Jas., Elizth. and Margt., Muff, Co. L'derry. *Pass. to Amer.* 1804. (T.)
Douglass, Ann, Ballintoy, Co. Ant. *Pass. to Amer.* 1805. (T.)
„ Ensign Arch. *T.S.P.I.* 1715.
Dowglass, Chas., High Sheriff, Co. Down. *Assqmt.* 1760. (T.)
Down, Bp. of. *Downshire MSS.* Jan. 10, 1796. (T.)
Down, Co. *Presentments.* 1841-1894. (T.)
„ Militia. See *"Royal North Down"* and *"Royal South Down."*
Downs, Capt. Hen. *T.S.P.I.* 1715.
Dragoons, 14th Regt. of, Birr. *List of Officers.* 1770. (T.)
„ Royal 5th Regt. of, Athlone. *List of Officers.* 1770. (T.)
Draper, Thos. *T.S.P.I.* 1719.
Drapers' Company. *Calendar of Records.* 1585-1907. (T.)
Drennan and McTier Families, Belfast. *Notes re.* 1672-1879. (T.)
Dromore, Bp. of *Downshire MSS.* Jan. 3, 1796. (T.)
„ Dio. of. *Exts. of Visitations.* 1733. (T.)
Drumorgan, Co. Arm. *Rental.* 1847. (T.)
Dublin, Archbp. of. *T.S.P.I.* 1717.
„ Castle. *T.S.P.I.* 1717.
Dublin's Corn Supply. *Belfast Merchants' Petn. re.* Mar. 17, 1766. (T.)
Dudley, Qr.-Master Thos. *T.S.P.I.* 1720.
Duncan, John. *Kilw. Schl. Par. Hill Docts.* 1797. (O.D.)
Dungannon, Rt. Hon. Arth., Lord Visct. *Lease. Hill Docts.* 1799. (O.D.)
Dunlap, Mich., Tanderagee, Co. Arm. *Pass. to Amer.* 1806. (T.)
Dyer, Ensign John. *T.S.P.I.* 1715.
Dysart, Wm. and Jane, Antrim. *Pass. to Amer.* 1805. (T.)

Eagleason, Wm. and Margt., Killead, Co. Ant. *Pass. to Amer.* 1805. (T.)
Early, John, Ardglass, Co. Down. *Pass. to Amer.* 1804. (T.)
Eaton, Hugh. *Kilw. Schl. Par. Hill Docts.* 1797. (O.D.)
Eccles, 2nd Lieut. John. *T.S.P.I.* 1715.

Eccles, Sir John. *T.S.P.I.* 1717.
,,   Thos. *T.S.P.I.* 1717.
Echlin, Arth., Monaghan, Co. Mon. *Release.* 1737. (O.D.)
Edgar, Dav., Randlestown, Co. Ant. *Pass. to Amer.* 1805. (T.)
Edgcombe, John. *Acct. Haberdashers' Pps. (S.R.O.)* 1617(?) (T.)
Eldred, John. *Haberdashers' Pps. (S.R.O.)* Apr. 23, 1617. (T.)
Eliot, Dav. *Kilw. Schl. Par. Hill Docts.* 1797. (O.D.)
Elliott, John and Margt., Co. Tyr. *Pass. to Amer.* 1805. (T).
Ellis, Alex. and Margt. Ballymena, Co. Ant. *Pass. to Amer.* 1804. (T.)
,,   Fras., Monaghan, Co. Mon. *Release.* 1737. (O.D.)
Enlistments for Pretender. *T.S.P.I.* 1718.
Enniskillen Estates. *Final Notice to Tenants.* 1895. (T.)
Escheated Counties. *General Map of. Cecil MSS., Hatfield.* 1610. (T.)
Eustace, Sir Maurice. *T.S.P.I.* 1719.
,,   Miss. *T.S.P.I.* 1719.
Evans, Rev. Geo., Mullamore, Co. Tyr. *Lease.* 1785. (T.)
Everton, Mr. *Journal. L'pool to New York Voyage.* 1833. (O.D.)
Evett, Ann Jane and Elizth., Daisy Hill. *Pass. to Amer.* 1806. (T.)
Eward, John, Kircubrytt, Scotland. *List of Scottish Freeholders in Ulster.* circa
    1615. (T.)
Exchequer, Court of, Inquiry re. *T.S.P.I.* 1719.

Falkland, Lord. *Settmt. Massereene MSS.* 1684. (T.)
Farrell, Jas., Armagh. *Pass. to Amer.* 1805. (T.)
,,   Jas. Agnew, Larne, Co. Ant. *Lease ; Bond. Hill Docts.* 1799. (O.D.)
Farrer, Ensign John. *T.S.P.I.* 1715.
,,   Cornet Wm. *T.S.P.I.* 1715.
Fausille, Peter de la. *T.S.P.I.* 1715.
Fegan, Ter. and Margt., Ballyroney, Co. Down. *Pass. to Amer.* 1805. (T.)
Femster, Wm., Ballyoran, Co. Arm. *Marr. Settmt.* 1789. (O.D.)
Fenton, Rich. *T.S.P.I.* 1719.
Ferguson, Andw., Omagh, Co. Tyr. *Pass. to Amer.* 1805. (T.)
,,   Jas., Artray, Co. L'derry. *Pass. to Amer.* 1805. (T.)
,,   Jas., Cookstown, Co. Tyr. *Pass. to Amer.* 1805. (T.)
,,   John, Strabane, Co. Tyr. *Assgmt. Lenox-Conyngham MSS.* (2). 1740.
    (T.)
,,   Major and Lieut.-Col. Rob. *T.S.P.I.* 1717–8.
,,   Thos., Armagh. *Pass. to Amer.* 1805. (T.)
,,   Thos., Carnmoney, Co. Ant. *Pass. to Amer.* 1805. (T.)
,,   Capt. Wm. *T.S.P.I.* 1715.
Ferrard, Lord. *T.S.P.I.* 1717.
Ferrers, Brig.-Gen. Thos., *T.S.P.I.* 1716–7.
Ferris, Chas. and Saml., Larne, Co. Ant. *Lease. Hill Docts.* 1769. (T.)
Ffreeman, Raphe. *Haberdashers' Pps. (S.R.O.)* Apr. 29, 1617. (T.)
,,   Wm., London. *Letters. Haberdashers' Pps. (S.R.O.)* Mar.. 30, 1614
    et. seq. (T.)
Filson, Mat., Maughrabar. *Pass. to Amer.* 1806. (T.)
Finlay, Wm., Tullywhickey (Tullywhisker, Co. Tyr.?). *Pass. to Amer.* 1806. (T.)
Fisher, Wm. *T.S.P.I.* 1716–7.
Fitzgerald, Nichs., Waterford. *Memo. re Jacobites. Massereene MSS.* 1693. (T.)
,,   Patk., Capt. of a French Privateer. *Memo. re Jacobites. Massereene
    MSS.* 1693. (T.)
Fitzsimmons, Wm., Rich., Eliza and Anne, Downpatrick, Co. Down. *Pass. to Amer.*
    1805. (T.)
Fitzsymonds, Chr., Dublin. *Memo. re Jacobites. Massereene MSS.* 1693. (T.)
Flaxseed, Imporation of. *Belfast Petn. re.* Nov. 11, 1797. (T.)
Fleck, Geo., Braid, Co. Ant. *Pass. to Amer.* 1805. (T.)
Fleming, John. *Exchq. Bill Ext.* 1698. (T.)
,,   Josias. *Bond. Lenox-Conyngham MSS.* (2). 1720. (T.)
Flemming, Wm., Tubbermore, Co. L'derry. *Pass. to Amer.* 1805. (T.)
Flournois, Peter. *T.S.P.I.* 1717.
Folliott, Lord. *T.S.P.I.* 1718.
Fooks, John and Ellen, Antrim. *Pass. to Amer.* 1805. (T.)
Foot, 50th Regt. of, Cork. *List of Officers.* 1772. (T.)
Forbes, Jos., Ann and John, Omagh, Co. Tyr. *Pass. to Amer.* 1805. (T.)
Forde, Matt., Dublin. *Assgmt. Lenox-Conyngham MSS.* (2). 1769 (T.)

Forde, Talbot. *Decln. of Ejectment. Lenox-Conyngham MSS.* (2). 1765. (T.)
Forester, Edwd., Culdoche, Scotland. *List of Scottish Freeholders in Ulster,* circa 1615. (T.)
Forfar's Regt. *T.S.P.I.* 1715.
Forrester, Ensign John. *T.S.P.I.* 1715.
Forsight, Jas., Co. L'derry. *Pass. to Amer.* 1805. (T.)
Forster, Lord Chief Justice. *T.S..P.I.* 1719.
,, Thos. and Elnr., Co. Ferm. *Pass. to Amer.* 1806. (T.)
Forsythe, Thos., Clough, Co. Down. *Pass. to Amer.* 1805. (T.)
Forth, Mr. *T.S.P.I.* 1719.
Fowler, Robt., Killiman, Co. Tyr. *Pass. to Amer.* 1805. (T.)
Fox, Wm., Dublin. *Pg. M.L. Ext.* 1803. (T.)
Foyle, Lough, Fishery. *Chy. Inqn.* 1602. (T.)
Fraisinet, Peter Granier. de *T.S.P.I.* 1719.
Frankford, Capt. Fra. *T.S.P.I.* 1713.
,, Ensign Hen. *T.S.P.I.* 1713.
Frul, Thos., Enniskillen. Co. Ferm. *Pass. to Amer.* 1805(?) (T.)
Fullerton, Agnes, Armagh. *Pass. to Amer.* 1805. (T.)
,, Lieut. Phil. *T.S.P.I.* 1720.
,, Wm., Kircubrytt, Scotland. *List of Scottish Freeholders in Ulster,* circa 1615. (T.)
Fulton, Jas., Antrim. *Pass. to Amer.* 1805. (T.)
,, Jas. and Mary, Cookstown, Co. Tyr. *Pass. to Amer.* 1805. (T.)
,, John, Agivey, Co. L'derry. *Pass. to Amer.* 1806. (T.)
,, (or Futton), Thos., Ballycastle, Co. Ant. *Pass. to Amer.* 1805. (T.)
Futton, Thos., Killileagh, Co. Down. *Pass. to Amer.* 1805. (T.)

Galbraith, John, Greenland, Co. Ant. *Assgmt. of Lease. Hill Docts.* 1773. (O.D.)
,, Mr., Coleraine, Co. L'derry. *Pass. to Amer.* 1806. (T.)
,, John, " Samullan," Co. Tyr. *Pass. to Amer.* 1806. (T.)
Gale, Hen., Lisburne, Co. Down. *Pass. to Amer.* 1805. (T.)
,, Mr. *Vintners' Co.'s Ct. Bk. Ext.* 1610. (T.)
Gallagher, Edwd. and Owen, Co. Ferm. *Pass. to Amer.* 1805. (T.)
,, Hugh, Strabane, Co. Tyr. *Pass. to Amer.* 1805. (T.)
Gallier, Wm. and Elizth, Banagher. *Pass. to Amer.* 1805. (T.)
Gallway, Lord. *T.S.P.I.* 1716-7.
Gamble, Edwd., Newry, Co. Down. *Pass. to Amer.* 1805. (T.)
Gardnor, Thos., Singleton and Auth., Belfast. *Pass. to Amer.* 1804. (T.)
Gascoyn, Mr. *T.S.P.I.* 1717.
Gawne, Lieut. Rob. *T.S.P.I.* 1716.
General Officers, Warrant for Establishment of. *T.S.P.I.* 1716-7.
George, Robt., Newtown Limavady, Co. L'derry. *Pass. to Amer.* 1806. (T.)
Giddie, Jas., Ballydonnelly, Co. Ant. *Pass. to Amer.* 1805. (T.)
Gillespie, Hugh, Alex. and Margt., Magherally, Co. Down. *Pass. to Amer.* 1804. (T.)
,, Jas., Fintona, Co. Tyr. *Pass. to Amer.* 1805. (T.)
Gillespy, Jane, Co. L'derry. *Pass. to Amer.* 1805. (T.)
Gilling, John. *L'derry Address.* 1690. (T.)
Gillmer, Eliezer Birch, Scion Hill, Dromore, Co. Down. *Lease Ext.* 1799. (T.)
Ginn (or Guin), Jas. and Arth., Irvinestown, Co. Ferm. *Pass. to Amer.* 1806. (T.)
Glasgow, Robt., Ballykeel, Co. Ant. *Lease. Hill Docts.* 1738. (O.D.)
" Glasgow," Ship. *Journal. L'pool to New York Voyage.* 1833. (O.D.)
Gledstanes, Albt., Dublin. *Assgmt. Lenox-Conyngham MSS.* (2). 1740. (T.)
Glen, John, Londonderry. *Lease Ext.* 1764. (T.)
,, Wm., Saml., Jean, Margt., Jennet and Jeany, " Rockbrack." *Pass. to Amer.* 1805. (T.)
Glorney, Benjn., Dublin. *Downshire MSS.* June 24, 1796. (T.)
Glynn, Manor of, Co. Ant. *Rental. Hill Docts.* 1824. (O.D.)
Goddard, J., Newry, Co. Down. *Downshire MSS.* June 28, 1796. (T.)
,, Ensign Thos. *T.S.P.I.* 1715.
Godfrey, Mr. *Letter. Haberdashers' Pps. (S.R.O.)* Apr. 23, 1617. (T.)
Goggin, Jas. and Wm. *T.S.P.I.* 1718.
Gonele, Wm., Garvagh, Co. L'derry. *Pass. to Amer.* 1805. (T.)
Goorley, Eliza, L'derry. *Pass. to Amer.* 1806. (T.)
Gorden, Sir Robt. *Haberdashers' Pps. (S.R.O.)* Aug. 9, 1616. (T.)
Gordon, Geo., Armagh. *Pass. to Amer.* 1805. (T.)

Gordon, J., Loughbrickland, Co. Down. *Downshire MSS.* June 30, 1796. (T.)
„ Lieut. Js. *T.S.P.I.* 1715.
„ John, Fintona, Co. Tyr. *Pass. to Amer.* 1805. (T.)
„ Thos. and Elizth., Mounthill, Co. Arm. *Pass. to Amer.* 1805. (T.)
Gore, Sir Ralph. *T.S.P.I.* 1717–9.
Gough (als White, als. Derry), Cisly, Newry, Co. Down. *Exchq. Bill Ext.* 1698. (T.)
Gourley, Wm. and Jane, Cookstown, Co. Tyr. *Pass. to Amer.* 1804. (T.)
Gracy, Phil. and Jane, Mountnorris, Co. Arm. *Pass. to Amer.* 1805. (T.)
Grafton, Duke of. *T.S.P.I.* 1717.
Graham, Arth., Ballyheriland, Co. Arm. *Renewal of Lease.* 1774. (T.)
„ Arth., Hockley Lodge, Co. Arm. *Renewal of Lease.* 1783. (T.)
„ Capt.-Lieut. Fra. *T.S.P.I.* 1715.
„ Jas. *Downshire MSS.* Feb. 8, 1796. (T.)
Graham, Jas., Badowney, Co. Tyr. *Pass. to Amer.* 1805. (T.)
„ Jas., Ballycastle, Co. Ant. *Pass. to Amer.* 1805. (T.)
„ John, Lurgan, Co. Arm. *Pass. to Amer.* 1806. (T.)
„ Mary Ann, Outlack, Co. Arm. *Marr. Settmt.* 1789. (O.D.)
„ Rich., Tiralas als Islandamuck, Co. Down. *Lease Ext.* 1727. (T.)
Grant, Ensign Alex. *T.S.P.I.* 1715.
Gray, Wm., Edwd. and Nancy, Donaghedy, Co. Tyr. *Pass. to Amer.* 1805. (T.)
Green, Lieut. Nat. *T.S.P.I.* 1720.
Gribbin, Roger, Dublin. *Lease. Hill Docts.* 1740. (T.)
Grier, Jos., Co. L'derry. *Pass. to Amer.* 1805. (T.)
Grimes, Jas., Rossgull. *Pass. to Amer.* 1805. (T.)
Groves, Col., Regt. of. *T.S.P.I.* 1717–9.
Guin (or Ginn), Jas. and Arth., Irvinestown, Co. Ferm. *Pass. to Amer.* 1806. (T.)
Guy, Hen. *Agrmt. Massereene MSS.* 1693. (T.)
Guyle, Lieut. Peter. *T.S.P.I.* 1720.

Haberdashers' Company. *"Buttall" of Lands of. Haberdashers' Pps. (S.R.O.)* circa 1615–6. (T.)
„ Company. *List of Townlands. Haberdashers' Pps. (S.R.O.)* (T.)
„ Company. *Survey of Lands of. Haberdashers' Pps. (S.R.O.)*, circa 1614. (T.)
„ Proportion. *Acct. of Money disbursed upon. Haberdashers' Pps. (S.R.O.)* 1617(?) (T.)
Haddock, Hen., Richhill, Co. Arm. *Pass. to Amer.* 1805. (T.)
„ Jas., Armagh. *Pass. to Amer.* 1805. (T.)
Hagan, Edwd. and Agnes, Carrickfergus, Co. Ant. *Pass. to Amer.* 1805. (T.)
„ Hugh, Co. Tyr. *Pass to Amer.* 1805. (T.)
Haghen, Patk., Tanderagee, Co. Arm. *Pass. to Amer.* 1806. (T.)
Half-Pay Officers in Ireland. *List of.* 1715. (T.)
„ Lists. (4). 1748–9 (T.)
Halket, Capt. Peter. *T.S.P.I.* 1717.
Hall, Albt. *L'derry Address.* 1690. (T.)
„ Alex. and John, Latmacollum, Co. Arm. *Memo. of Marr. Settmt.* 1783. (T.)
„ Roger. *Exchq. Bill Ext.* 1698. (T.)
„ Roger, Narrow-Water, Co. Down. *Marr. Settmt.* 1751. (T.)
„ Saml., Conohan. *Pass. to Amer.* 1806. (T.)
„ Savage, Narrow-Water, Co. Down. *Downshire MSS.* Jan. 5, 1796. (T.)
„ Lieut.-Col. Thos. *T.S.P.I.* 1720.
Hamilton, Mr. *T.S.P.I.* 1719.
„ Abr. *Letter. Lenox-Conyngham MSS.* (2)., circa 1750. (T.)
„ Dr. Andw., Archdcn. of Raphoe. *Assgmt. Lenox-Conyngham MSS.* (2) 1740. (T.)
„ Col. Archd., Regt. of. *List of Officers.* 1737. (T.)
„ Cloud, Monterlony. *Massereene MSS.* 1681. (T.)
„ Darcy, Mary and Patk. *Exchq. Decree. Hill Docts.* 1746. (T.)
„ Capt. Gust. *T.S.P.I.* 1715.
„ Jas., Garvagh, Co. L'derry. *Pass. to Amer.* 1805. (T.)
„ John, Cookstown, Co. Tyr. *Pass. to Amer.* 1805. (T.)
„ Rich., Coleraine, Co. L'derry. *Marr. Settmt.* 1724. (T.)
„ Robt. Killeard (Killead ?), Co. Ant. *Pass. to Amer.* 1805. (T.)
„ Dr. Wm., Dublin. *Mge.; Conv. Hill Docts.* 1750–2. (O.D.)
Hammand, Ensign Hector. *T.S.P.I.* 1715.

Hammon, Capt. Isaac. *T.S.P.I.* 1715.
Handasyd, Col. Wm., Regt. of. *List of Officers.* 1737. (T.)
Handesyde's Regt. *T.S.P.I* 1719.
Hankwitz, Ensign John Godfrey. *T.S.P.I.* 1716.
Hanna, Saml., Newry, Co. Arm. *Fine; Pg. W.* 1797-8. (T.)
Harden, Elnr., Dungiven, Co. L'derry. *Pass. to Amer.* 1805. (T.)
Hare, Wm., Larne, Co. Ant. *Lease. Hill Docts.* 1779. (T.)
Harper, Robt., Isa , Jane, Mary, Wm. and Jas., Lisnaskea, Co. Ferm. *Pass. to Amer.* 1805. (T.)
Harris, Ensign John. *T.S.P.I.* 1715.
   „   Saml., Moneymore, Co. L'derry. *Pass. to Amer.* 1805. (T.)
Harrison, [Francis]. *T.S.P.I.* 1717–9.
Harrison, Lieut. Jas. *Downshire MSS.* Jan. 1, 1796. (T.)
Harrison's Regt. *T.S.P.I.* 1711-1722.
Harvey, Mrs. *T.S.P.I.* 1717.
   „   Robt. and Jon. *L'derry Address.* 1690. (T.)
Haselwood, Ensign John. *T.S.P.I.* 1720.
Hatch, Hen., Lands of Moynes, Cregantanvally, Greenland, &c. *Exchq. Order to Sheriff of Co. Antrim. Hill Docts.* 1762. (O.D.)
   „   John. *Downshire MSS.* Feb. 4, 1796. (T.)
Haveron, Agnes, Larne, Co. Ant. *Pass. to Amer.* 1805. (T.)
Hawkshaw, Rev. Benjn., Ballymackey, Co. Tipp. *Lease Ext.* 1727. (T.)
   „   Dr. *T.S.P.I.* 1719.
   „   John, Dublin. *Lease Ext.* 1727. (T.)
Hawley, Brig.-Gen. Hen., Regt. of. *List of Officers.* 1737. (T.)
Hawley's Regt. *T.S.P.I.* 1719.
Hawthorn, Geo. and Mary, " Aughderig " (Aghaderg ?), Co. Down. *Pass. to Amer.* 1805. (T.)
Hayes, Sir Jas. *Marr. Settmt. Massereene MSS.* 1684. (T.)
Hayward, Edmd. *Haterdashers' Pps. (S.R.O.)* Apr. 29, 1617. (T.)
Heffernan, John, Dairypark, Co. Ant. *Lease. Hill Docts.* 1830. (O.D.)
Hegertye, Patk., Friar, Tawlaught O Crolly. *Massereene MSS.* 1681. (T.).
Henderson, Archd., Elizth, Jane and Wm., Lowtherstown, Co. Ferm. *Pass. to Amer.* 1805. (T.)
Henry, John, Banbridge, Co. Down. *Pass. to Amer.* 1804. (T.)
Hesketh, Rev. Thos. *T.S.P.I.* 1717.
Hewitt, Gen. *Downshire MSS.* Jan. 12, 1796. (T.)
Hewson, Jas. *Exchq. Bill Ext.* 1698. (T.)
   „   Wm. *L'derry Address.* 1690. (T.)
Hicks, Lieut. Thos. *T.S.P.I.* 1720.
Hill, Arth. *T.S.P.I.* 1717–8.
   „   Arth., Belvoir, Co. Down. *Bond.* 1737. (O.D.)
   „   Hugh and Cath., Londonderry. *Marr. Settmt.* 1751. (T.)
Hill's Regt. *T.S.P.I.* 1715.
Hithrington, Js., Newtownstewart, Co. Tyr. *Pass. to Amer.* 1805. (T.)
Hobson, Jas. *L'derry Address.* 1690. (T.)
Holborn, Ensign John. *T.S.P.I.* 1715.
Holden, S. *Downshire MSS.* Apr. 15, 1796. (T.)
Holland, Arms from. *T.S.P.I.* 1716–7.
Holmes, Robt., Crumlin, Co. Ant. *Pass. to Amer.* 1806. (T.)
Honywood, Cornet Rd. *T.S.P.I.* 1718.
Hopkins, John, Abr., Ann, Jane, Jenny and Ruth, " N. L. Vady," Co. L'derry. *Pass. to Amer.* 1805. (T.)
   „   Thos. *T.S.P.I.* 1717–8.
Houghton, Sir Hen. *Letter. Massereene MSS.* 1713. (T.)
Hounahane, Hen. *T.S.P.I.* 1719.
How, Capt. John. *T.S.P.I.* 1716.
Howard's Regt. *T.S.P.I.* 1719.
Hoy, Mr. *T.S.P.I.* 1719.
Hudson, Jas., Rathfriland, Co. Down. *Belf. Gt. (I.)* 1893. (T.)
Hughes, Andw. and Jane, Co. Tyr. *Pass. to Amer.* 1805. (T.)
   „   Patk., Fintona, Co. Tyr. *Pass. to Amer.* 1805. (T.)
Hull, E., Donaghadee, Co. Down. *Downshire MSS.* Mar. 29, 1796. (T.)
   „   Jas. W., Belvidere, Co. Down. *Deed of Annuity.* 1787. (T.)
   „   Wm., Randalstown, Co. Ant. *Pass. to Amer.* 1805. (T.)

Hume Thos., Larne, Co. Ant. *Pass. to Amer.* 1805. (T.)
„ W. *Downshire MSS.* Feb. 6, 1796. (T.)
Humphreys, Chr., jun., Co. Ferm. *Commission in Lurg True Blue Infantry.* 1808.
   (T.)
Hungerford, Anth. and Sir Edwd. *Marr. Settmt. Massereene MSS.* 1684. (T.)
Hunter, Hen. *Exchq. Bill Ext.* 1698. (T.)
„ John. *T.S.P.I.* 1717.
Hunter, Jos., Ballynur, Co. Ant. *Pass. to Amer.* 1804. (T.)
Hutchison, Dav. and Nancy, Co. Down. *Pass. to Amer.* 1805. (T.)
Hutton, Matt. *Agrmt. Massereene MSS.* 1693. (T.)
Hyndman, Hugh, Antrim. *Pass. to Amer.* 1806. (T.)

Innes-Cross, Sarah Jane, Estate of. *Final Notice to Tenants.* 1899. (T.)
Invasion, Fears of. *T.S.P.I.* 1719.
Irish Commission Registers. 1727-1760. (T.)
„ Privy Council. *Cert. Annexed to Irish Parliament Bill.* 1758. (O.D.)
„ Society v. Commrs. of Public Works. *Queen's Bench Order.* 1867. (T.)
„ Society, Governor of. *Letter. Lenox-Conyngham MSS.* (2). 1731. (T.)
Irvine, Chas. and Robt., Loughgeel (Loughguile, Co. Ant.?). *Pass. to Amer.* 1805.
   (T.)
„ Gerard, Newtownstewart, Co. Tyr. *Pass. to Amer.* 1805. (T.)
„ Rich. and Ann, Templecarn, Co. Dongl. *Clogher M.L. Bond Ext.* 1749. (T.)
Irwin, Col. Alex., Regt. of. *List of Officers.* 1737. (T.)
„ Estate, Co. Arm. *Acct.* 1796-1821. (O.D.)
„ Estate, Co. Arm. *Acct. Book.* 1799-1829. (O.D.)
„ Wm., Mount Irwin, Co. Arm. *Release.* 1737. (O.D.)
„ Wm. *Memo. of Agrmt.* 1780. (O.D.)
Irwine, Jas., Moy, Co. Tyr. *Pass. to Amer.* 1806. (T.)
„ John, Trisna. *Pass. to Amer.* 1805. (T.)
„ Wm., Killigarvan, Co. Tyr. *Pass. to Amer.* 1805. (T)
Isaac, Wm. *T.S.P.I.* 1719.

Jackson, Jane, Larne, Co. Ant. *Lease. Hill Docts.* 1791. (T.)
„ Trooper. *T.S.P.I.* 1719.
Jameson, Dav., Braid, Co. Ant. *Pass. to Amer.* 1805. (T.)
„ Wm., Lisburn, Co. Ant. *Pass. to Amer.* 1805. (T.)
„ Wm., Loughbrickland, Co. Down. *Pass. to Amer.* 1806. (T.)
Jasson, Ensign Sebastian. *T.S.P.I.* 1720.
Jebb, Rach., Fintona, Co. Tyr. *Pass. to Amer.* 1805. (T.)
Jelfe, Thos. *T.S.P.I.* 1719.
Jellett, Mary, Moira, Co. Down. *Lease.* 1799. (T.)
Jemmett, Warham. *T.S.P.I.* 1717.
Johnson, Lieut. Alex. *T.S.P.I.* 1717.
„ Robt. and Mary, Co. Arm. *Pass. to Amer.* 1805. (T.)
Johnston, Andw., Geanagh, Co. Ferm. *Clogher M.L. Bond Ext.* 1727. (T.)
„ Andw., Keelin, Co. Dongl. *Clogher M.L. Bond Ext.* 1752. (T.)
„ Arth., Cashelenny, Co. Dongl. *Clogher M.L. Bond Ext.* 1749. (T.)
„ Geo., Scarvagh, Co. Down. *Pass. to Amer.* 1806. (T.)
„ Jas., Ahoghill, Co. Ant. *Pass. to Amer.* 1805. (T.)
„ Jas., Donagh, Co. Mon. *Clogher M.L. Bond Ext.* 1718. (T.)
„ Jas., Cornamucklagh, Co. Ferm. *Clogher M.L. Bond. Ext.* 1753. (T.)
„ . Jas. and Bgt., Glenavy, Co. Ant. *Pass. to Amer.* 1806. (T.)
„ John Moore, Spa Volunteers. *Address.* 1791. (T.)
„ Stephen, Outlack, Co. Arm. *Leases; Marr. Settmt.* 1763-1789. (O.D.)
„ Thos., Ballymoney, Co. Ant. *Pass. to Amer.* 1806. (T.)
„ Walt., Shancho, Co. Ferm. *Clogher M.L. Bond Ext.* 1727 (T.)
Jones, Margt. *Eq. Exchq. Report and Final Decree. Hill Docts.* 1836. (T.)
Jordan, John, Newry, Co. Down. *Pass. to Amer.* 1805. (T.)
Jurisdiction of English House of Lords in Irish Appeals. *T.S.P.I.* 1719.

Kain (or Kane), Col., Regt. of. *T.S.P.I.* 1717.
„ Robt., Jane, John, Anth. and Elizth., Omagh, Co. Tyr. *Pass. to Amer.* 1805.
   (T.)
Kane (or Kain), Col., Regt. of. *T.S.P.I.* 1717.
„ Margt., Isa., Margt., Wm. and Andw., Strabane, Co. Tyr. *Pass. to Amer.*
   1805. (T.)

Kearny, Larry and Mary, Hamiltonbawn, Co. Arm. *Pass. to Amer.* 1806. (T.)
Keenan, Pat and Mary, Markethill, Co. Arm. *Pass. to Amer.* 1804. (T.)
Keer, Wm., Peggy and Robt., Enniskillen, Co. Ferm. *Pass. to Amer.* 1806. (T.)
Keith, Mr. *T.S.P.I.* 1719.
Kellum, Major-Gen. Geo. *T.S.P.I.* 1716-7.
Kellum's Regt. *T.S.P.I.* 1715-1721.
Kelly, —*T.S.P.I.* 1717.
   ,, Jas., Ardstragh. *Massereene MSS.* 1681. (T.)
Kelly, John. *Memo. of Agrmt.* 1780. (O.D.)
   ,, Wm., Jane and Anne, Rathfryland, Co. Down. *Pass. to Amer.* 1805. (T.)
Kenedy, Geo., Garvagh, Co. L'derry. *Pass. to Amer.* 1805. (T.)
Kennedy, Dav. and John, Dublin. *Acquittances. Hill Docts.* 1715-6. (O.D.)
   ,, Hen., Derry. *Pass. to Amer.* 1805. (T.)
   ,, Jas. *Pass. to Amer.* 1805. (T.)
   ,, Saml., Glenavy, Co. Ant. *Pass. to Amer.* 1804. (T.)
Kenney, Wm. *Chy. Inqn.* 1602. (T.)
Kent, Kath., Macetown, Co. Meath. *Mge.* 1720. (O.D.)
Kernan, Fras., Jas. and Manus, Co. Ferm. *Pass. to Amer.* 1805. (T.)
Kerr, Ann, Enniskillen, Co. Ferm. *Pass. to Amer.* 1806. (T.)
   ,, Jas., Ann, Elizth., Alex., Jos., Anne and Jane, Co. Tyr. *Pass. to Amer.* 1805. (T.)
   ,, Brig.Gen. Lord Mark. *T.S.P.I.* 1716-7.
   ,, Mark (Maik? or Muck?), Enniskillen. *Pass. to Amer.* 1805(?) (T.)
Keswett, Rich. *Acct. Haberdashers' Pps. (S.R.O.)* 1617(?) (T.)
Killen, Jenkins, " Corbilly," Co. Down. *Pass. to Amer.* 1805. (T.)
Killigrew, Guildford. *T.S.P.I.* 1717.
Killinchy Yeomanry. *Letters and Papers. Findlay Colln.* 1825-1831. (O.D.)
Killyleagh Yeomanry. *Letters and Papers. Findlay Colln.* 1825-1831. (O.D.)
Kilmore, Bp. of. *T.S.P.I.* 1717.
   ,, Parish, Co. Arm. *Vestry Bk. Exts. C. Rtn.* 1732-1779 ; 1821. (T.)
Kilwaughter, Proposed School at. Co. Ant. *List of Parents of Pupils; Plan and Estimate. Hill Docts.* 1797. (O.D.)
Kinaston, Mr. *Vintners' Co.'s Ct. Bk. Ext.* 1610. (T.)
King, Robt., Margt. and Cath., Lands of Moynes, Cregantanvally, Greenland, &c. *Exchq. Order to Sheriff of Co. Antrim. Hill Docts.* 1762. (O.D.)
   ,, Wm., Archbp. of Dublin. *T.S.P.I.* 1717.
King William's Quarters in Ireland. *Photographic Reproduction.* 1690. (T.)
Kingston, Lord. *T.S.P.I.* 1718-9.
Kinkade, Mary, Gortin, Co. Tyr. *Pass. to Amer.* 1805. (T.)
   ,, Wm., Strabane, Co. Tyr. *Pass. to Amer.* 1805 (?) (T.)
Kinsley, Jas., Glenevy, Co. Ant. *Pass. to Amer.* 1805. (T.)
Knox, Hen. W., Titness Park, Berkshire. *W.* 1802. (T.)
   ,, Hen. W., Waringsford, Co. Down. *Memo. of Reconv. of Mge.;Lease Ext.; Lease.* 1796-1802. (T.)
   ,, John, Waringsford, Co. Down. *Cert. of Burial.* 1791.
   ,, Capt. John, Waringsford Castle, Co. Down. *Muster-Roll of Volunteers Ext.; Pg. Gt. (I.) Ext.* 1779-1802. (T.)
   ,, Thos., Clifton. *Downshire MSS.* June 28, 1796. (T.)
   ,, Thos., Dungannon, Co. Tyr. *W. Ext.* 1769. (T.)
   ,, Wm., Ballysheagh. *Pass. to Amer.* 1806. (T.)
Kumming (als Cummin), Jas., Ballywigan, Co. Down. *Lease Ext.* 1727 (T.)

Lager, John. *T.S.P.I.* 1718-9.
Lambert, Geo., Downpatrick. *Pg. W.* 1723. (T.)
   ,, Montague, Dublin. *Pg. W. Ext.* 1740. (T.)
   ,, Ralph, Dublin. *Pg. W. Ext.* 1762. (T.)
   ,, Robt., Castledawson, Co. L'derry. *Pass. to Amer.* 1806. (T.)
   ,, Robt., Dunlady, Co. Down. *Pg. W. Ext.* 1751. (T.)
Lane, Thos., Hillsborough, Co. Down. *Downshire MSS.* Jan. 27, 1796, *et seq.* (T.)
Langford, Roger. *Pat. Gt. Massereene MSS.* 1621. (T.)
   ,, Sir Roger. *Chy. Bill. Massereene MSS.* circa 1686. (T.)
Lanoe, Col. Chas., Regt. of *List of Officers.* 1737. (T.)
Larwood, Capt. Ben. *T.S.P.I.* 1715.
Latmacollum, Co. Arm. *Rental.* 1847. (T.)
La Touche, Dav., jun., Dublin. *Assgmt. Lenox-Conyngham MSS.* (2). 1769 (T.)

Laughlin, Adam, Coleraine, Co. L'derry. *Pass. to Amer.* 1805. (T.)
Law, E. *Downshire MSS.* Jan. 4, 1796. (T.)
Lawson, John, Cairncastle, Co. Ant. *Fee Farm Gt. Hill Docts.* 1763. (T.)
Lecky, Alex., *L'derry Address.* 1690. (T.)
Lee, Mr. *T.S.P.I.* 1719.
Leeson, Saml. *L'derry Address.* 1690. (T.)
Lennan, Edwd., Castledawson, Co. L'derry. *Pass. to Amer.* 1806. (T.)
Lennox, Anne. *Pg. Gt. (I.) Lenox-Conyngham MSS.* (2). 1778. (T.)
    ., Clotworthy, Londonderry. *Lease. Lenox-Conyngham MSS.* (2). 1746. (T.)
    ,, Clotworthy and Anne, Londonderry. *Agrmt. Lenox-Conyngham MSS.* (2). 1768. (T.)
    ,, John and Clotworthy, Londonderry. *Marr. Arts. Lenox-Conyngham MSS.* (2). 1745. (T.)
    ,, Wm., Dublin. *Marr. Arts. Lenox-Conyngham MSS.* (2). 1745. (T.)
Lenox, John. *Letter Bk. Lenox-Conyngham MSS.* (2). 1738-1745. (T.)
    ,, Wm., Lands of Moynes, Cregantanvally, Greenland, &c. *Exchq. Order to Sheriff of Co. Antrim. Hill Docts.* 1762. (O.D.)
Leslie, Hen. *Downshire MSS.* Jan. 5, 1796. (T.)
    ,, Jas. and Saml. *Downshire MSS.* Jan. 14, 1796. (T.)
    ,, Ensign Tho. *T.S.P.I.* 1717.
Leverall, Bernd., Cookstown, Co. Tyr. *Pass. to Amer.* 1804. (T.)
Levet, Lieut. and Capt. Tho. *T.S.P.I.* 1715-1720.
Lewis, Wm. *T.S.P.I.* 1716-7.
Liddy, Hu., Randalstown, Co. Ant. *Pass. to Amer.* 1804. (T.)
Liggot, Alex., Templepatrick, Co. Ant. *Pass. to Amer.* 1804. (T.)
Light Dragoons, 17th Regt. of, Belturbet. *List of Officers.* 1770. (T.)
Ligonier, Gen. John, Regt. of. *List of Officers.* 1737. (T.)
Limerick, Bp of. *T.S.P.I.* 1717.
    ,, Lord. *T.S.P.I.* 1719.
Lindsay, Thos. See " Armagh, Archbishop of."
Linen Drapers, etc., Belfast. *Petn.* Feb., 1780. (T.)
Linen Export Bill. *T.S.P.I.* 1717.
Lingen, Wm. *T.S.P.I.* 1718.
Linster, Mary, Drumgarla, Co. Ferm. *Clogher M.L. Bond Ext.* 1727. (T.)
Lipsett, Anth. *Acct. Haberdashers' Pps. (S.R.O.)* 1617(?) (T.)
Little, Archd., Douglass. *Pass. to Amer.* 1805. (T.)
    ,, Jas. and Reba., Co. L'derry. *Pass. to Amer.* 1805. (T.)
    ,, Wm., Anne, Sarah and Jane, Co. Arm. *Pass. to Amer.* 1805. (T.)
Livingston, Robt., Armagh. *Marr. Settmt.* 1789. (O.D.)
Loftus, Lieut. Simon. *T.S.P.I.* 1716.
Logan, Hans, Belfast. *Pass. to Amer.* 1804. (T.)
Logie, Dan. *Repeal Association Membership Card.* 1843. (O.D.)
Londonderry and Coleraine, Governorship of. *Massereene MSS.* 1677. (T.)
Longe, John. *Acct. Haberdashers' Pps. (S.R.O.)* 1617(?) (T.)
Longford, Countess of. *Lease. Massereene MSS.* 1692. (T.)
Longwill, Dav. *Chy. Cause Petn.* 1866. (T.)
Lords, Irish House of, appelate jurisdiction. *T.S.P.I.* 1719.
Lough Foyle Fishery. *Chy. Inqn.* 1602. (T.)
    ,, Neagh, Baroue and Boats on. *Pat. Gt. Massereene MSS.* 1680. (T.)
Louth Co., Lands in. *Pat. Gt. Massereene MSS.* 1669. (T.)
Loury, Edwd., Killinchy, Co. Down. *Pass. to Amer.* 1805. (T.)
Love, M., Anne and Mary, Omagh, Co. Tyr. *Pass. to Amer.* 1805. (T.)
Lowrey, John and Elnr., Stewartstown, Co. Tyr. *Pass. to Amer.* 1805. (T.)
Lumly, John. *T.S.P.I.* 1716-7.
Lyle, Hugh, Coleraine, Co. L'derry. *Mge. Exemption Agrmt. Hill Docts.* 1763. (O.D.)
Lym, Mr. *T.S.P.I.* 1717.
Lynch, Dan. *Chy. Cause Petns.* 1866. (T.)
    ,, Wm., Ann and Martha, Tully. *Pass. to Amer.* 1805. (T.)
Lynn, Robt. and Reba., Leek. *Pass. to Amer.* 1805. (T.)
    ,, Wm. and Reba., " Loughgeel " (Loughguile, Co. Ant.?) *Pass. to Amer.* 1805. (T.)
Lyttle, Eliza and Peggy, Leek. *Pass. to Amer.* 1805. (T.)

McAdam, Geo. and Elizth., Aghaderg, Co. Down. *Pass. to Amer.* 1804. (T.)
  ,,   Geo. and Elijah, Drummara. Co. Down. *Pass. to Amer.* 1805. (T.)
McAlexander, John, Doagh, Co. Ant. *Lease. Hill Dorts.* 1760. (O.D.)
McAlice, Jas., Agivy, Co. L'derry. *Pass. to Amer.* 1806. (T.)
McAllin, Dowilloge, Glanylly. *Chy. Inqn.* 1602. (T.)
Macartney, — *T.S.P.I.* 1719.
  ,,   (Gen.) Geo. *T.S.P.I.* 1717-9.
  ,,   Jas. *T.S.P.I.* 1717.
McAuley, Saml., Rathfryland, Co. Down. *Pass. to Amer.* 1805. (T.)
McBrian, Eueny., Derry Orkey, Co. L'derry. *Rental. Haberdashers' Pps. (S.R.O.)* 1616-7. (T.)
McBrian, Gilduf, Crott, Co. L'derry. *Rental. Haberdashers' Pps. (S.R.O.)* 1616-7. (T.)
McBride, Jas., Killileagh, Co. Down. *Pass. to Amer.* 1804. (T.)
  ,,   Jas., Magheramourne, Co. Ant *Lease. Hill Docts.* 1769. (T.)
  ,,   Mary, Moneymore, Co. I.'derry. *Pass. to Amer.* 1805. (T.)
McCabe, Edwd., " Mourene," Co. Down. *Pass. to Amer.* 1805. (T.)
McCafferty, Wm., Strabane, Co. Tyr. *Pass. to Amer.* 1805. (T.)
McCaffry, Bernd., Enniskillen, Co. Ferm. *Pass. to Amer.* 1805. (T.)
McCaherty, Bernd. and Mary, Larne, Co. Ant. *Pass. to Amer.* 1805. (T.)
McCalester, John. *Kilw. Schl. Par. Hill Docts.* 1797 (O.D.)
McCall, Robt., Co. Arm. *Pass. to Amer.* 1806. (T.)
McCalla, Saml., Cornave, Co. L'derry. *Lease. Lenox-Conyngham MSS.* (2). 1746 (T.)
McCalline, John, Magilligan. *Massereene MSS.* 1681. (T.)
McCammon, Jas. and Rose, Aghaderg, Co. Down. *Pass. to Amer.* 1804. (T.)
McCamon, John, Derrycughan, Co. Arm. *Pq. W. Ext.* 1788. (T.)
  ,,   Thos., " Aughderig " (Aghaderg ?), Co. Down. *Pass. to Amer.* 1805. (T.)
McCan, Jas., jun. and sen. *Kilw. Schl. Par. Hill Docts.* 1797. (O.D.)
  ,,   John, Judith and Mary, Tandragee, Co. Arm. *Pass. to Amer.* 1805. (T.)
McCanna, Patk., Omagh, Co. Tyr. *Pass. to Amer.* 1805. (T.)
McCappeny, —— *Exchq. Bill Ext.* 1698. (T.)
McCarry, John and Jas., Ballycastle, Co. Ant. *Pass. to Amer.* 1805. (T.)
McCarthy, Thos., Co. L'derry. *Pass. to Amer.* 1805. (T.)
McCartney, Jas., Belfast *Lease. Massereene MSS.* 1692. (T.)
McCaul, Wm. *Kilw. Schl. Par. Hill Docts.* 1797. (O.D.)
McCausland, Connolly. *Release.* 1787. (T.)
  ,,   Conolly, Culmore, Co. L'derry. *Pass. to Amer.* 1804. (T.)
McClanaghan, John, Antrim. *Pass. to Amer.* 1805. (T.)
McClean, Archd., Ballykelly. *Pass. to Amer.* 1805. (T.
McClelland, Wm., Islandmagee, Co. Ant. *Lease. Hill Docts.* 1769. (T.)
McClilland, Wm., Mary, John, Robt. and Jane, Keady, Co. Arm. *Pass. to Amer.* 1805. (T.)
McClintock, Alex., Dublin. *Assgmt. Lenox-Conyngham MSS.* (2). 1740. (T.)
McCloskey, Patt., Cookstown, Co. Tyr. *Pass. to Amer.* 1805. (T.)
McClosky, Rory, Aughiduffye. *Massereene MSS.* 1681. (T.)
McCloskye, Donaughy Oge, Beanchirr. *Massereene MSS.* 1681. (T.)
McClure, Jane, Ballymoney, Co. Ant. *Pass. to Amer.* 1805. (T.)
  ,,   Wm., Outlack, Co. Arm. *Marr. Settmt.; Lease.* 1789-1799. (O.D.)
McClurg, Robt., Magheradroll, Co. Down. *Pass. to Amer.* 1804. (T.)
McCollum, Angus, Bangor, Co. Down. *Pass. to Amer.* 1805. (T.)
McComb, Jas., Dromore, Co. Down. *Pass. to Amer.* 1805. (T.)
  ,,   Thos., Lurgan, Co. Arm. *Pass. to Amer.* 1805. (T.)
McConally, John, Barony. *Massereene MSS.* 1681. (T.)
McConmee, Art., Ballynascriny. *Massereene MSS.* 1681. (T.)
McConnell, Alex. " Ballymane " (Ballymave, Co. Ant.?) *Pass to Amer.* 1806. (T.)
McCook, Neill, Ballymoney, Co. Ant. *Lease. Hill Docts.* 1776. (O.D.)
McCormac, Dan, Ballintoy, Co. Ant. *Pass. to Amer.* 1805. (T.)
McCrachan, Hugh, Newtown Limavady, Co. L'derry. *Pass. to Amer.* 1806. (T.)
McCrea, Eliza, Kilrea, Co. L'derry. *Pass. to Amer.* 1805. (T.)   ..
McCrory, Robt., Randalstown, Co. Ant. *Pass. to Amer.* 1804. (T.)
  ,,   Torlaugh, Errigall. *Massereene MSS.* 1681. (T.)
McCrossan, Jas., Cammus. *Pass. to Amer.* 1805. (T.)
McCruin, Jas. and Sarah, Tynan, Co. Arm. *Pass. to Amer.* 1804. (T.)
McCullagh, Robt., Latmacollum, Co. Arm. *Memo. of Agrmt.* 1794. (T.)

McCullagh, Wm. and Robt., Co. Down. *Pass. to Amer.* 1805. (O.D.)
McCulloch, Rev. Jas., Moneyrea, Co. Down. *Deed Poll and Memo. Hill Docts.* 1738. (T.)
  ,,   Wm. *Memo. of Agrmt. Hill Docts.* 1790. (T.)
  ,,   Wm., Ballygally, Co. Ant. *Lease. Hill Docts.* 1787. (O.D.)
  ,,   Wm. Ballymena, Co. Ant. *Connor Gt. (I.). Hill Docts.* 1815. (O.D.)
McCullough, Jas., " Ballynine," Co. Ant. *Pass. to Amer.* 1805. (T.)
McCully, Wm., Killileagh, Co. Down. *Pass. to Amer.* 1805. (T.)
McCully, Wm. and Robt., Armagh. *Pass. to Amer.* 1805. (T.)
McCurry, Dan. *Attachment Orders.* 1867. (T.)
McDavid, Edmond Groome, Carrick McCowlin. *Chy. Inqn.* 1602. (T.)
McDavy, Connor, Malon, Co. Dongl. *Chy. Inqn.* 1602. (T.)
McDermott, Hen., Omagh, Co. Tyr. *Pass. to Amer.* 1806. (T.)
McDonald, Thos. and Wm., Portadown, Co. Arm. *Pass. to Amer.* 1806. (T.)
McDonnell, Alex. *Lease. Hill Docts.* 1637. (O.D.)
McDowell, John, Kilwaughter, Co. Ant. *Lease. Hill Docts.* 1769. (O.D.)
  ,,   John. *Kilw. Schl. Par. Hill Docts.* 1797. (O.D.)
McElgorm, Alex., Magherygorah, Co. Ant. *Lease. Hill Docts.* 1772. (O.D.)
McFarland, John, Elizth, Sarah and Jane, Moy, Co. Tyr. *Pass. to Amer.* 1806. (T.)
  ,,   Robt., Ballykelly, Co. L'derry. *Pass. to Amer.* 1806. (T.)
McFarlin, John, Rathfriland, Co. Down. *Pass. to Amer.* 1804. (T.)
McFarnan, Robt., Dungannon, Co. Tyr. *Pass. to Amer.* 1806. (T.)
McGenalty, Edwd. *Massereene MSS.* 1680. (T.)
McGerrald, Connor, Buncrannagh, Co. Dongl. *Chy. Inqn.* 1602. (T.)
McGillegan, Brian bane, Balle McGilgin, Co. L'derry. *Rental. Haberdashers' Pps.* (*S.R.O.*) 1616–7. (T.)
McGilly, Thos., Omagh, Co. Tyr. *Pass. to Amer.* 1805. (T.)
McGin, Wm., Eliza, Saml. and Mary, Clogher, Co. Tyr. *Pass. to Amer.* 1805. (T.)
McGlavey, John, Hillsborough, Co. Down. *Pass. to Amer.* 1805. (T.)
McGoirke, Bryan, Vicar-Gen. of the Dio. of Derry. *Massereene MSS.* 1681. (T.)
  ,,   Hugh Roe, Termond McGoirke. *Massereene MSS.* 1681. (T.)
McGoun, Ensign Alex. *T.S.P.I.* 1715.
McGowan, Bern., Downpatrick. *Pass. to Amer.* 1805. (T.)
  ,,   John and Margt., Armagh. *Pass. to Amer.* 1806. (T.)
  ,,   Peter, Clough, Co. Down. *Pass. to Amer.* 1805. (T.)
McGra, John and Nancy, Co. Tyr. *Pass. to Amer.* 1805. (T.)
McGuire, Lucia. *Letters.* 1786 and N.D. (O.D.)
  ,,   Wm., Clough, Co. Down. *Letters.* 1785–6 and N.D. (O.D.)
McHaig, John, Comber, Co. Down. *Pass. to Amer.* 1805. (T.)
McHenry, Aran, Newry, Co. Down. *Pass. to Amer.* 1805. (T.)
  ,,   Dan. and Elnr., " Callagan " (Killagan, Co. Ant.?) *Pass. to Amer.* 1805. (T.)
McIlgorm, Alex., Greenland, Co. Ant. *Lease and Surrender. Hill Docts.* 1754–9. (O.D.)
  ,,   Alex. and John, Magherageeragh, Co. Ant. *Lease. Hill Docts.* 1762. (O.D.)
McKane, John, Coleraine, Co. L'derry. *Pass. to Amer.* 1806. (T.)
Mackay, Ensign Hugh. *T.S.P.I.* 1719.
McKay, Jas., Ahoghill, Co. Ant. *Pass. to Amer.* 1804. (T.)
McKee, John and Agnes, Aghaderg, Co. Down. *Pass. to Amer.* 1804. (T.)
  ,,   Robt., Rathfriland, Co. Down. *Pass. to Amer.* 1805. (T.)
McKelvy, Jas., Derrnyneal, Co. Down. *Pass. to Amer.* 1805. (T.)
  ,,   John, Ballycroon, Co. Down. *Pass. to Amer.* 1805. (T.)
Mackenzie, John Portpatrick. *Downshire MSS.* Feb. 15, 1796. (T.)
McKeown, Dan., Antrim. *Pass. to Amer.* 1806. (T.)
  ,,   Edwd., Larne, Co. Ant. *W. Hill Docts.* 1856. (O.D.)
Mackey, Saml., Antrim. *Pass. to Amer.* 1806. (T.)
Mackie, Wm. *L'derry Address.* 1690. (T.)
McKinley, John and Mary, Antrim. *Pass. to Amer.* 1805. (T.)
Macklelland, John, Bocbe(?), Scotland. *List of Scottish Freeholders in Ulster.* circa 1615. (T.)
  ,,   John, The Orchard, Scotland. *List of Scottish Freeholders in Ulster.* circa 1615. (T.)
  ,,   Sir Robt., Bombee, Scotland. *List of Scottish Freeholders in Ulster.* circa 1615. (T.)

Macklelland, Wm., Molock, Scotland.   *List of Scottish Freeholders in Ulster.*   circa 1615.   (T.)
,,   Wm., Ouerlawe.   *Haberdashers' Pps.*   *(S.R.O.)*   Apr. 23, 1617.   (T.)
Macklellane, Sir Robt., Bomby, Scotland.   *Haberdashers' Pps.*   *(S.R.O.)*   May, 1615 *et. seq.*   (T.)
,,   Wm., Overlawe, Scotland.   *List of Scottish Freeholders in Ulster.*   circa 1615.   (T.)
Macklin, Wm., Dinnamany, Co. Tyr.(?)   *Pass. to Amer.*   1805   (T.)
McKnown, Wm., Mary, John and Robt., Ardglass, Co. Down.   *Pass. to Amer.*   1804.   (T.)
McKy, Abr.   *Kilw. Schl. Par.   Hill Docts.*   1797.   (O.D.)
McLaghlin, Hugh Carragh, Bullibrack.   *Chy. Inqn.*   1602.   (T.)
McLain, Hugh, Saintfield, Co. Down.   *Pass. to Amer.*   1804.   (T.)
McLashin, Dennis, Ballykinlar, Co. Down.   *Downshire MSS.*   June 25, 1796.   (T.)
McLoughlin, Bernd., Lisburn, Co. Ant.   *Pass. to Amer.*   1805.   (T.)
,,   John and Martha, Ballintoy, Co. Ant.   *Pass. to Amer.*   1805.   (T.)
McMahon, Alex. and Grizzy, Killcappell, Co. Arm.   *Pass. to Amer.*   1805.   (T.)
McManus, Wm., Moy, Co. Tyr.   *Pass. to Amer.*   1806.   (T.)
McManny, Saml., Armagh.   *Pass. to Amer.*   1805.   (T.)
McMast, Jas., Ballymoney, Co. Ant.   *Pass. to Amer.*   1805.   (T.)
McMillan, Sarah, Jas., Sarah, Robt. and Fras., Dungannon, Co. Tyr.   *Pass. to Amer.*   1805.   (T.)
McMorrow, Hen., Co. Ferm.   *Pass. to Amer.*   1805.   (T.)
McMullan, Corns., Elnr. and Eliza, Loughinisland, Co. Down.   *Pass. to Amer.*   1804.   (T.)
McMullen, Dav., Geo., Sarah, Jane, Mary, Margt. and Ann, Ballydonnelly, Co. Ant.   *Pass. to Amer.*   1805.   (T.)
,,   Jas., Donaghmore, Co. Down.   *Pass. to Amer.*   1805.   (T.)
,,   Robt., Martha, Margt., John and Jas., Coleraine, Co. L'derry.   *Pass. to Amer.*   1805.   (T.)
,,   Thos. and Sarah, Dungannon, Co. Tyr.   *Pass. to Amer.*   1805.   (T.)
McMurray, Hugh, Randalstown, Co. Ant.   *Pass. to Amer.*   1805.   (T.)
McMurry, Owen Duff, Mallen, Co. Dongl.   *Chy. Inqn.*   1602.   (T.)
McNalty, Hugh, Bangor, Co. Down.   *Pass. to Amer.*   1806.   (T.)
McNaghten, Bart., Carnglass, Co. Ant.   *Mge.   Hill Docts.*   1762.   (O.D.)
McNaughten, Malcolm and Martha, Broughshane, Co. Ant.   *Pass. to Amer.*   1806.   (T.)
McNeight, Robt., Glenavy, Co. Ant.   *Pass. to Amer.*   1804.   (T.)
McNeill, Archd., Mary and Thos., Killileagh, Co. Down.   *Pass. to Amer.*   1805.   (T.)
McNemee, Frances, Dissirtmartine.   *Massereene MSS.*   1681.   (T.)
Macnevin, Andw., Carrickfergus, Co. Ant.   *Downshire MSS.*   Mar. 25, 1796.   (T.)
McQuade, Jas., Co. Tyr.   *Pass. to Amer.*   1805.   (T.)
,,   Phelemy, Rose and Bgt., Markethill, Co. Arm.   *Pass. to Amer.*   1806.   (T.)
McQueon, Wm. and Jane, Bangor, Co. Down.   *Pass. to Amer.*   1804.   (T.)
McQuillon, Jas., Agivy, Co. L'derry.   *Pass. to Amer.*   1806.   (T.)
McQuoin, Owen, "Mourene," Co. Down.   *Pass. to Amer.*   1805.   (T.)
McReady, Dav., Co. Down.   *Pass. to Amer.*   1805.   (T.)
McRegan, Jas., Ballycastle, Co. Ant.   *Pass. to Amer.*   1805.   (T.)
McRoberts, Jas., Ballygowan, Co. Ant.   *W. Hill Docts.*   1857.   (O.D.)
,,   Wm., Ballygowan, Co. Ant.   *W. Hill Docts.*   1857.   (O.D.)
McShane boy, Brian, Lislane, etc., Co. L'derry.   *Rental.   Haberdashers' Pps.*   *(S.R.O.)*   1616-7.   (T.)
,,   boy, Jas., Dromgawne, Co. L'derry.   *Rental.   Haberdashers' Pps. (S.R.O.)*   1616-7.   (T.)
,,   Michl., Armagh.   *Pass. to Amer.*   1806.   (T.)
McTier and Drennan Families, Belfast.   *Notes re.*   1672-1879.   (T.)
McWhinney, Isa. and John, Saintfield, Co. Down.   *Pass. to Amer.*   1805.   (T.)
Madocks, Mr.   *T.S.P.I.*   1718.
Maffat, Robt., Wm. and Cath., Killigarvan, Co. Tyr.   *Pass. to Amer.*   1805.   (T.)
Magee, John and Bgt., Tandragee, Co. Arm.   *Pass. to Amer.*   1805.   (T.)
Magenis, Glasney.   *Exchq. Bill Ext.*   1698.   (T.)
Magennis, Rich., Dublin.   *Marr. Settmt.*   1751.   (T.)
Magghee, Wm., Kircubrytt, Scotland.   *List of Scottish Freeholders in Ulster.*   circa 1615.   (T.)
Magill, Bernd., Dallagh, Co. Ant.   *Belfast Gt. (P.)*   1888.   (T.)

Magill, John, Ballycastle, Co. Ant. *Pass. to Amer.* 1805. (T.)
Maginis, Jos., Ballymacbrennan, Co. Down. *Lease.* 1799. (T.)
Maginnis, Patk. *Orders for Attachment.* 1867–1870. (T.)
Magorian, M., Ballykinlar, Co. Down. *Downshire MSS.* June 12, 1796. (T.)
Maguire, Jas., Killeter, Co. Tyr. *Pass. to Amer.* 1805. (T.)
　,,　Patt and Bgt., Co. Ferm. *Pass. to Amer.* 1805. (T.)
Main, Thos., Co. Tyr. *Pass. to Amer.* 1806. (T.)
Malcolmson, Js., " Tanarague " (Tandragee ?), Co. Arm. *Pass. to Amer.* 1805. (T.)
Mallet, Capt. John. *T.S.P.I.* 1716.
Mallon, Michl., Dungannon, Co. Tyr. *Pass. to Amer.* 1804. (T.)
Mallows, Mr. *Vintners' Co.'s Ct. Bk. Ext.* 1610. (T.)
Manley, Isaac. *T.S.P.I.* 1717.
　,,　Mr. and Mrs. *T.S.P.I.* 1718–9.
Mann, Lucia. *Letter.* 1785. (O.D.)
Maps, Ancient, relating to Ireland, Memo. of. (T.)
Marks, John, Armagh. *Pass. to Amer.* 1805. (T.)
Marley, Mr. *T.S.P.I.* 1719.
Marshall, Betty, Keady, Co. Arm. *Pass. to Amer.* 1805. (T.)
Martin, Corns. *T.S.P.I.* 1718.
　,,　Capt. Geo. *T.S.P.I.* 1720.
　,,　Margt., Dromore, Co. Down. *Pass. to Amer.* 1805. (T.)
　,,　Moses, Banbridge, Co. Down. *Pass. to Amer.* 1805. (T.)
　,,　Robt., Badowney, Co. Tyr. *Pass. to Amer.* 1805. (T.)
　,,　Wm. *Exchq. Bill Ext.* 1698. (T.)
Masham, Ensign Fra. *T.S.P.I.* 1722.
Massereene MSS. 1605–1713. (T.)
　,,　Lord Visct. *Pat. Gt.; Lease ; Petns.; Massereene MSS.* 1666–1683. (T.)
　,,　Lord Visct. *Memo. of Deeds of Lease and Release.* *Hill Docts.* 1755. (T.)
　,,　Lord Visct., Visctess and Dowager Visctess. *Marr. Settmt.* *Massereene MSS.* 1684. (T.)
Mathewes, John. *Acct. Haberdashers' Pps. (S.R.O.)* 1617(?) (T.)
Mathews, Chas. *T.S.P.I.* 1716–7.
Matthews, Andw. *Exchq. Bill Ext.* 1698. (T.)
　,,　Major. *Downshire MSS.* May 9, 1796. (T.)
Maule, Capt. Wm. *T.S.P.I.* 1715.
Maxwell, Rt. Hon. Barry, Dublin. *Lease.* 1763. (O.D.)
　,,　Hon. Harry and Margt., Lands of Moynes, Cregantanvally, Greenland, &c. *Exchq. Order to Sheriff of Co. Antrim.* *Hill Docts.* 1762. (O.D.)
　,,　Harbert. *Haberdashers' Pps. (S.R.O.)* Apr. 23, 1617. (T.)
　,,　Herbert, Kurkennell, Scotland. *List of Scottish Freeholders in Ulster.* circa 1615. (T.)
　,,　John. *Presentation to Living, Slane, Co. Meath.* *Hill Docts.* 1721. (O.D.)
Maxwell, John. *Pass. to Amer.* 1805. (T.)
　,,　Sir Wm., Gribton, Scotland. *List of Scottish Freeholders in Ireland.* circa 1615. (T.)
Maynard, Mr. *T.S.P.I.* 1719.
　,,　Lieut. Rob. *T.S.P.I.* 1715.
　,,　Wm. *T.S.P.I.* 1718.
Mayne, Thos., Fintona, Co. Tyr. *Pass. to Amer.* 1806. (T.)
Mayo, Ensign John. *T.S.P.I.* 1715.
Meade, Ensign Courthope. *T.S.P.I.* 1715.
Meredyth, Hen., Dublin. *Memo. of Deeds of Lease and Release.* *Hill Docts.* 1755. (T.)
Merrill, John. *T.S.P.I.* 1716–7.
Methuen (Rt. Hon. Paul). *T.S.P.I.* 1716–7.
Michell, Ensign Nat. *T.S.P.I.* 1714.
Mikell, Alex., Kircubryt, Scotland. *List of Scottish Freeholders in Ulster.* circa 1615. (T.)
Military Accounts Memoranda, etc. *T.S.P.I.* 1709–1718.
Militia Bill. *T.S.P.I.* 1719.
　,,　in Ireland. *Official Circulars.* 1854–1863. (O.D.)
Miller, Ensign John. *T.S.P.I.* 1712.
　,,　Lieut. Rd. *T.S.P.I.* 1715.

Millin, Adam, Gordonall, Co. Down. *Oath of Allegiance.* 1797. (T.)
Minnis, Dav., Rathfryland, Co. Down. *Pass. to Amer.* 1805. (T.)
Mitchell, Hen., Dublin. *Warrant of Atty. Lenox-Conyngham MSS.* (2). 1760. (T.)
,, Hen. and Elizth. Sarah (the younger and the elder), Lands of Moynes, Cregantanvally, Greenland, &c. *Exchq. Order to Sheriff of Co. Antrim. Hill Docts.* 1762. (O.D.)
., Hugh, Dublin. *Leases, W., etc. Hill Docts.* 1753-7. (O.D.) and (T.)
., Jane, Magheragall, Co. Ant. *Pass. to Amer.* 1804. (T.)
.. John, Ballymena, Co. Ant. *Pass. to Amer.* 1805. (T.)
., John, Omagh, Co. Tyr. *Pass. to Amer.* 1805. (T.)
.. Randle and Alex., Philadelphia, Penn., U.S.A. *Discharge. Hill Docts.* 1755. (O.D.)
Mitchell, Wm., Dickstown, Co. Ant. *Discharge. Hill Docts.* 1755. (O.D.)
Mogridge, Jo. *L'derry Address.* 1690. (T.)
Molsworth, Lord Visct., Regt. of. *List of Officers.* 1737. (T.)
Molyneux, Dr. *T.S.P.I.* 1719.
Momby, Lieut. *T.S.P.I.* 1716.
Monaghan Co., Lands in. *Pat. Gt. Massereene MSS.* 1669. (T.)
Moncriffe, Tho. *L'derry Address.* 1690. (T.)
Moneypenny, Wm. and M., Tandragee, Co. Arm. *Pass. to Amer.* 1805. (T.)
Montague's Regt. *T.S.P.I.* 1720.
Montandras, Marquis of, Regt. of. *T.S.P.I.* 1717.
Montgomery, John, Larne. *Assgmt. of Lease. Hill Docts.* 1773. (O.D.)
., Sir Hugh. *Haberdashers' Pps. (S.R.O.)* May, 1615. (T.)
., Hugh, Larne, Co. Ant. *Connor W. and Gt. (P.). Hill Docts.* 1778. (O.D.)
., W., Hillsborough, Co. Down. *Downshire MSS.* June 28, 1796. (T.)
., Lieut. Wm. *T.S.P.I.* 1719.
Montrath. Lord. *T.S.P.I.* 1717.
Moore, Adrian, London. *Letters. Haberdashers' Pps. (S.R.O.)* Mar. 30, 1614 *et. seq.* (T.)
,, Alex., Rossgull. *Pass. to Amer.* 1805. (T.)
., Alex. and Isaac, Badowney, Co. Tyr. *Pass. to Amer.* 1805. (T.)
,, Andw., Armagh. *Pass. to Amer.* 1805. (T.)
,, Sir Geo., Lieutenant of the Tower. *Haberdashers' Pps. (S.R.O.)* Aug. 9, 1616 *et seq.* (T.)
., John, Larne, Co. Ant. *Lease. Hill Docts.* 1736. (O.D.)
,, John, Co. Tyr. *Pass. to Amer.* 1805. (T.)
., John, Archd. and Jas., Tamock, Co. Ant. *Lease. Hill Docts.* 1757. (O.D.)
., John, Robt., Jean and Margt., Carncastle, Co. Ant. *Lease. Hill Docts.* 1789. (O.D.)
,, Jos. and Elizth., Drummara, Co. Down. *Pass. to Amer.* 1805. (T.)
,, Tho. *L'derry Address.* 1690. (T.)
Morgan, Jas., Hamiltonbawn, Co. Arm. *Pass. to Amer.* 1806. (T.)
,, Michl., Moy, Co. Tyr. *Pass. to Amer.* 1806. (T.)
Morley, John. *T.S.P.I.* 1719.
Morris, Ann, Newtownards, Co. Down. *Pass. to Amer.* 1805. (T.)
,, Lieut. Fras. *T.S.P.I.* 1715.
,, Quarter-Master-Gen. *T.S.P.I.* 1716-7.
Morrison, Brig.-Gen. *T.S.P.I.* 1719.
,, Wm. *L'derry Address.* 1690. (T.)
,, Wm., Port (Mount?) Norris, Co. Arm. *Pass. to Amer.* 1806. (T.)
Morrow, Andw. and Agnes, Newtownards, Co. Down. *Pass. to Amer.* 1805. (T.)
Moss, Chas., Bryan and Rose, Omagh, Co. Tyr. *Pass. to Amer.* 1806. (T.)
Mountjoy, Lord. *T.S.P.I.* 1719.
Moxon, Mordecai. *T.S.P.I.* 1717.
Moynan, Owen, Co. Tyr. *Pass. to Amer.* 1805. (T.)
Muckamore Priory. *Inqn.; Pat. Gt. Massereene MSS.* 1605 and 1621. (T.)
Mulhallon, Collow. *Massereene MSS.* circa 1619. (T.)
,, (Capt.) Cormack, Corbally, Co. Ant. *Leases and Assgmt. Massereene MSS.* 1673. (T.)
,, Jas., Ann, Cormack and Arthur, Ballycorbally, Co. Ant. *Leases. Massereene MSS.* 1666. (T.)
Mullan, Michl., Leek. *Pass. to Amer.* 1805. (T.)
Mullin, Wm., Jas., Jane and Susan, Armagh. *Pass. to Amer.* 1806. (T.)
Munden, Brig.-Gen. Rich. *T.S.P.I.* 1716-7.

Munden's Regt. *T.S.P.I.* 1720.
Mundoch (?Murdock), Robt., Margt., and Sarah, " Ahadign," Co. Down. *Pass. to Amer.* 1805. (T.)
Munduch (?Murdoch), Sarah, Alex. and Saml., " Ahadign," Co. Down. *Pass. to Amer.* 1805. (T.)
Murdoch, John, Thos. and Jas., " Ahadign," Co. Down. *Pass. to Amer.* 1805. (T.)
Murphy, Mary, Lurgan, Co. Arm. *Pass. to Amer.* 1804. (T.)
,, (or Caldwell), Rose. *W. Hill Docts.* 1852. (O.D.)
Murray, Geo., Co. Down. *Pass. to Amer.* 1805. (T.)
,, Wm., Little Rath, Co. Kild. *Assgmt. Lenox-Conyngham MSS.* (2). 1740. (T.)
,, Wm. and Thos., Glassdrummon, Co. Down. *Pass. to Amer.* 1805 (T.)
Murrell, John, sen. and jun., N. Limavady, Co. L'derry. *Pass. to Amer.* 1805. (T.)
Murry, Jas., Newtown Limavady, Co. L'derry. *Pass. to Amer.* 1806. (T.)
Mutinies in Various Regiments. *T.S.P.I.* 1717.

Naper, Lieut.-Gen. Robt., Regt. of. *List of Officers.* 1737. (T.)
Napier, Brig.-Gen. Robt. *T.S.P.I.* 1716-7.
Neagh, Lough, Barque and Boats on. *Pat. Gt. Massereene MSS.* 1680. (T.)
Needham, Capt. Sam. *T.S.P.I.* 1715.
Neilson, Alex. and Josias. *Kilw. Schl. Par. Hill Docts.* 1797. (O.D.)
,, Hall, " Ahadign," Co. Down. *Pass. to Amer.* 1805. (T.)
Nelson, Corns. and John. *Exchq. Bill Ext.* 1698. (T.)
Nevil, Brig.-Gen. Clement, Regt. of. *List of Officers.* 1737. (T.)
Nevill, Fran. *L'derry Address.* 1690. (T.)
Newton, Rev. Edmd., Umrigan, Co. Wick. *Assgmt. Lenox-Conyngham MSS.* (2). 1740. (T.)
,, Rev. Thos., Dunluce, Co. Ant. *Marr. Settmt.* 1724. (T.)
Nightingall, John. *L'derry Address.* 1690. (T.)
Nixon, Robt. and Elnr., Co. Ferm. *Clogher M.L. Bond Ext.* 1753. (T.)
Norman, Robt. *T.S.P.I.* 1717-8.
Norris, John, Martha, Jas., John and Mary, Maghera, Co. L'derry. *Pass. to Amer.* 1805. (T.)
,, Thos., Belfast. *Pass. to Amer.* 1804. (T.)
North British Fuziliers. *List of Officers.* 1737. (T.)
Northey, Sir Ed. *T.S.P.I.* 1719.
Nugent, Jas. and Cath., Lands of Moynes, Cregantanvally, Greenland, &c. *Exchq Order to Sheriff of Co. Antrim. Hill Docts.* 1762. (O.D.)
Nugin, Rach., Rathfriland, Co. Down. *Pass. to Amer.* 1804. (T.)

O'Brien, Ann, L'derry. *Pass. to Amer.* 1806. (T.)
,, Jas., Carnmoney, Co. Ant. *Pass. to Amer.* 1805. (T.)
O'Cahan, Sir Donnell and Lady. *Haberdashers' Pps.* (*S.R.O.*) Apr. 29, 1617. (T.)
,, Donnohey oge, Drom Drean, Co. L'derry. *Rental. Haberdashers' Pps.* (*S.R.O.*) 1616-7. (T.)
O'Cahane, Brian oge, Camnish, Co. L'derry. *Rental. Haberdashers' Pps.* (*S.R.O.*) 1616-7. (T.)
,, Coy, Gort Carne, Co. L'derry. *Rental. Haberdashers' Pps.* (*S.R.O.*) 1616-7. (T.)
,, Shane, Enish Connohor, etc., Co. L'derry. *Rental. Haberdashers' Pps.* (*S.R.O.*) 1616-7. (T.)
O'Cassady, Brian, Parish Priest of Ballyscullen, Co. L'derry. *Massereene MSS.* 1681. (T.)
O'Dogh, Bryan McTirlagh Chy., Mallen, Co. Dongl. *Chy. Inqn.* 1602. (T.)
,, Dwaltagh McHugh and Neale Crone, Buncrannagh, Co. Dongl. *Chy. Inqn.* 1602. (T.)
,, fferdorogh McCalire, Tormona. *Chy. Inqn.* 1602. (T.)
O'Dogherty, Averkagh McShan, Con McDonell and Hugh Boy McCahyir, Greenecastle, Co. Dongl. *Chy. Inqn.* 1602. (T.)
,, Neale oge McPhelim Brassill, Carrickbragly. *Chy. Inqn.* 1602. (T.)
,, Shan McDwalty, Glannily. *Chy. Inqn.* 1602. (T.)
,, Shane, Glannoganell. *Chy. Inqn.* 1602. (T.)
O'Duffy, Hugh. *Chy. Inqn.* 1602. (T.)
O'Dyri, Patr als. Vickar, Killeigh. *Chy. Inqn.* 1602. (T.)
Officers' Widows. *T.S.P.I.* 1717.
Offices, Sale of. *T.S.P.I.* 1717.

Ogelby, John. *Kilw. Schl. Par. Hill Docts.* 1797. (O.D.)
O'Gneeve (or Agnew), John, Ballyhempane, Co. Ant. *Lease. Hill Docts.* 1637. (O.D.)
O'Hagan, John. *Afft. Lenox-Conyngham MSS.* (2). 1766. (T.)
O'Hanlon, Phelix, Moy, Co. Tyr. *Pass. to Amer.* 1806. (T.)
O'Hara, Col., Regt. of. *T.S.P.I.* 1717.
O'Haro, John, Town Major of Galway. *T.S.P.I.* 1716-7.
O'Hassan, Turlough, Lena More, etc., Co. L'derry. *Rental. Haberdashers' Pps.* (*S.R.O.*) 1616-7. (T.)
„ Hugh, Gort Crosse, Co. L'derry. *Rental. Haberdashers' Pps.* (*S.R.O.*) 1616-7. (T.)
O'Heale, Patk., BallyMcWilliam, Co. Ant. *Lease. Hill Docts.* 1637. (O.D.)
O'Hear, Felix, Banbridge, Co. Down. *Pass. to Amer.* 1804. (T.)
O'Hegarty, Gillechrist. *Chy. Inqn.* 1602. (T.)
O'Kerrelane, Brian, Taugh McVardell, Co. L'derry. *Rental. Haberdashers' Pps.* (*S.R.O.*) 1616-7. (T.)
O'Lavarty, Owen als. Vickar, Moyvilly, Co. Dongl. *Chy. Inqn.* 1602. (T.)
Oliver, Robt., Cloghenodfoy, Co. Lim. *Marr. Arts.* 1712. (T.)
O'Lymbrick, Gilroagh, Kilkell, Co. L'derry. *Rental. Haberdashers' Pps.* (*S.R.O.*) 1616-7. (T.)
O'Lynne, Patk., Balle Hannon, etc., Co. L'derry. *Rental. Haberdashers' Pps.* (*S.R.O.*) 1616-7. (T.)
O'Mulhallan (or Mulhallan), Sheely and Cormuck. *Assgmt. Massereene MSS.* 1686. (T.)
O'Mulhallen, Brian Boy, Prior of Muckamore. *Inqn. Massereene MSS.* 1605. (T).
O'Mullan, Brian, Stradreagh, etc., Co. L'derry. *Rental. Haberdashers' Pps.* (*S.R.O.*) 1616-7. (T.)
„ Carmocke. *Letter. Haberdashers' Pps.* (*S.R.O.*) Apr. 29, 1617. (T.)
„ Donnell, Larginreagh, etc., Co. L'derry. *Rental. Haberdashers' Pps.* (*S.R.O.*) 1616-7. (T.)
„ Edmunde grome, Tawneyherrin beg, etc., Co. L'derry. *Rental. Haberdashers' Pps.* (*S.R.O.*) 1616-7. (T.)
„ Tomlin, Turhurrin, etc., Co. L'derry. *Rental. Haberdashers' Pps.* (*S.R.O.*) 1616-7. (T.)
O'Morish, Manus, Longfield. *Massereene MSS.* 1681. (T.)
O'Neil, Hugh, Cormac and Major. *Massereene MSS.* 1680. (T.)
O'Neile, Sir Hen. and Naile oge. *Abst. of Title. Massereene MSS.* 1641. (T.)
O'Neille, Laughline, Cappy. *Massereene MSS.* 1681. (T.)
Orfeur, Lieut.-Col. John. *T.S.P.I.* 1715.
Orkney's Regt. *T.S.P.I.* 1715-6.
Ormand, Lieut. Ch. *T.S.P.I.* 1715.
Ormsby, Jane, Alacka, Co. Lim. *Marr. Arts.* 1712. (T.)
„ John, Dublin. *Marr. Arts.* 1712. (T.)
Orr, Robt., Killileagh, Co. Down. *Pass. to Amer.* 1805. (T.)
„ Thos., Richhill, Co. Arm. *Pass. to Amer.* 1804. (T.)
O'Scullen, Edmd. *Massereene MSS.* 1681. (T.)
O'Sheale, Bryan, Derry. *Chy. Inqn.* 1602.
„ Hugh boy, Gort carberry, etc., Co. L'derry. *Rental. Haberdashers' Pps.* (*S.R.O.*) 1616-7. (T.)
Otway, Brig.-Gen. Chas., Regt. of. *List of Officers.* 1737. (T.)
Owens, Thos. and Margt., Dryn. *Pass. to Amer.* 1805. (T.)

Pagett, Col. Thos., Regt. of. *List of Officers.* 1737. (T.)
Pagez, Col. de. *T.S.P.I.* 1716-7.
Palmer, Geo. *Acct. Haberdashers' Pps.* (*S.R.O.*) 1617(?) (T.)
Park, Mary, Larne, Co. Ant. *Pass. to Amer.* 1805. (T.)
„ Maxwell, Larne, Co. Ant. *Pass. to Amer.* 1805. (T.)
„ Wm., Coleraine, Co. L'derry. *Pass. to Amer.* 1804. (T.)
Parker, Coll. *Massereene MSS.* 1693. (T.)
„ Phil. *T.S.P.I.* 1719.
Parks, Jas., Belfast. *Pass. to Amer.* 1805. (T.)
Parnell, Thos. *Marr. Settmt. Massereene MSS.* 1684. (T.)
Parry, Benjn. *T.S.P.I.* 1719.
Pary, Mr. *T.S.P.I.* 1717-8.
Paterson, Lieut. Jos. *T.S.P.I.* 1716.
Patterson, Alex., Randalstown, Co. Ant. *Pass. to Amer.* 1806. (T.)

Patterson, Jas., Antrim. *Pass. to Amer.* 1805. (T.)
,,   John, Corn Castle, Co. Ant. *Pass. to Amer.* 1805. (T.)
Paul, Capt. Dan. *T.S.P.I.* 1715.
,,   Saml. and Ann, Co. Arm. *Pass. to Amer.* 1805. (T.)
Payments and Receipts. *T.S.P.I.* 1717.
Paynton, Capt. *Haberdashers' Pps.* (*S.R.O.*) Apr. 15, 1614. (T.)
Payzant, Jas. and L. *T.S.P.I.* 1718.
Peacock, Jas. and Elizth., Newry, Co. Down. *Pass. to Amer.* 1805. (T.)
Pearce, Lieut.-Gen., Regt. of. *List of Officers.* 1737. (T.)
,,   (or Pierce), Major-Gen. *T.S.P.I.* 1716-7.
Peden, Dan. *Lease. Hill Docts.* 1773. (T.)
Pepper, John. *T.S.P.I.* 1717-8.
Perro, Chas. and Anne. *Exchq. Bill Ext.* 1717. (T.)
Perry, John and Saml., Armagh. *Pass. to Amer.* 1805. (T.)
Philips, Squire. *Massereene MSS.* 1681. (T.)
Phillips, Sir Thos., Moneygogey, etc., Co. L'derry. *Rental. Haberdashers' Pps.* (*S.R.O.*) 1616-7. (T.)
Phips, Sir Constantine. *T.S.P.I.* 1717.
Phœnix Park, Dublin. *Massereene MSS.* 1693. (T.)
Pitt's Commercial Propositions. *Belfast Petn. against.* 1785. (T.)
Plunkett, Mr. *T.S.P.I.* 1719.
,,   Oliver. *Massereene MSS.* 1681. (T.)
,,   Thos. *T.S.P.I.* 1717-8.
Poke, Wm., Newtown Limavady, Co. L'derry. *Pass. to Amer.* 1806. (T.)
Pole, Capt. Edwd. *T.S.P.I.* 1715.
Polewheele, Mr. *Memo. re Jacobites.* *Massereene MSS.* 1693. (T.)
Pollard, Dillon, Castle Pollard, Co. W'meath. *Lease.* 1799. (O.D.)
Pollock, Jas. and Jane, Co. Arm. *Pass. to Amer.* 1805. (T.)
Ponsonby, Col. Hen., Regt. of. *List of Officers.* 1737. (T.)
Popery Bill. *T.S.P.I.* 1719.
Portarlington School. *T.S.P.I.* 1717.
Porter, Saml., Leek. *Pass. to Amer.* 1805. (T.)
,,   Vere, Elnr. and Margt., Rathfryland, Co. Down. *Pass. to Amer.* 1805. (T.)
Potts, Wm., Hans and Dav., Co. Down. *Pass. to Amer.* 1805. (T.)
Pratt, John. *T.S.P.I.* 1717-9.
,,   Mr. *T.S.P.I.* 1719.
Prendergast, Lady. *T.S.P.I.* 1717.
Prescot, Cornet and Lieut. Rd. *T.S.P.I.* 1715.
Preston's Regt. *T.S.P.I.* 1715-8.
Pretender, Enlistments for. *T.S.P.I.* 1718.
Primrose's Regt. *T.S.P.I.* 1714-6.
Proclamations. *Pardon on Swearing Allegiance.* May 17 and June 22, 1797. (T.)
Public Accounts, Report on. *T.S.P.I.* 1717.
Pulteney, John. *T.S.P.I.* 1717.
Purvis, Jas. and Jane, Cookstown, Co. Tyr. *Pass. to Amer.* 1805. (T.)
Quarters of the Army in Ireland. 1739. (T.)
Queen's Ware. *Belfast Petn. re manufacture of.* circa 1793. (T.)
Quin, Manus, Drumran. *Pass. to Amer.* 1804. (T.)
,,   Terence, " Mourene," Co. Down. *Pass. to Amer.* 1805. (T.)
Quit Rents Bill. *T.S.P.I.* 1717.

Raferty, Wm., Six Mile Cross, Co. Tyr. *Pass. to Amer.* 1805. (T.)
Raftor, F. *T.S.P.I.* 1716-7.
Ram, Mr. *T.S.P.I.* 1719.
Ramsay, Wm. Fintona, Co. Tyr. *Pass. to Amer.* 1805. (T.)
Ranken, Dr. John, Kirkcubbin, Co. Down. *Pass. to Amer.* 1805. (T.)
Raphoe, Archdcn. of (v. Hamilton, Dr. Andw.)
,,   Dio. of. *Exts. of Visitations.* 1733. (T.)
Raven, Mr. *Haberdashers' Pps.* (*S.R.O.*) Aug. 9, 1616 *et seq.* (T.)
,,   Mr., Moy Keeragh, Co. L'derry. *Rental. Haberdashers' Pps.* (*S.R.O.*) 1616-7. (T.)
,,   Thos. *Haberdashers' Pps.* (*S.R.O.*) Apr. 29, 1617. (T.)
Rawdon, Sir John, Moira, Co. Down. *Lease.* 1742. (T.)
Ray, Wm. and Mary, Co. Arm. *Pass. to Amer.* 1805. (T.)
Read, Jas., Latmacollum, Co. Arm. *Memo. of Agrmt.* 1794. (O.D.)
,,   John, *Lisnadill, Co. Arm.* Lease. 1792. (O.D.)

Reade, John. *Acct. Haberdashers' Pps. (S.R.O.)* 1617(?) (T.)
Receipts and Payments. *T.S.P.I.* 1717.
Redmond, —, Brookhill, Co. Ant. *Deed of Annuity.* 1787. (T.)
Reed, Clement, Ballymakeonan, Co. Down. *Dromore W.* 1720. (T.)
„ or Read, Clement and Jas., Latmacollum, Co. Arm. *Leases.* 1792. (O.D.)
„ Jas., Latmacollum, Co. Arm. *Lease ; Assgmt. ; Dft. Lease ; Exchq. Bill, etc.* 1788–1791. (O.D.) and (T.)
„ Thos., Latmacollum, Co. Arm. *Renewal of Lease.* 1774. (T.)
„ Thos., Monage, Co. Mon. *Leases.* 1783–1790. (O.D.) and (T.)
„ Wm. Ardmore, Co. Arm. *Dromore W.* 1773. (T.)
„ Wm., Latmacollum, Co. Arm. *Afft.; Lease.* 1790. (O.D.)
Reid, Jas. C., Hillsborough, Co. Down. *Pass. to Amer.* 1805. (T.)
„ Rev. Robt., John and Jane, Armagh. *Pass. to Amer.* 1805. (T.)
Reilly, Marlow, Carrickfergus, Co. Ant. *Pass. to Amer.* 1805. (T.)
Reversionary Leases (Clause in Popery Bill). *T.S.P.I* 1719.
Reynel, Mr. *T.S.P.I.* 1719.
Rice, Ter. and Eliza, Pointspass, Co. Arm. *Pass. to Amer.* 1806. (T.)
Richardson, Ensign Leming. *T.S.P.I.* 1715.
Riddall, Hugh, Crumlin, Co.Ant. *Pass. to Amer.* 1805. (T.)
Riddle, Chr., Newtownstewart, Co. Tyr. *Pass. to Amer.* 1805. (T.)
Ritchie, John. *Kilw. Schl. Par. Hill Docts.* 1797. (O.D.)
Roane, Geo. *T.S.P.I.* 1718.
Robb, Cornet Jas., Machrytimpany, Co. Down. *Lease Ext.* 1781. (T.)
Robinson, Alex., Foxhall, Co. Ant. *Connor W. and Gt. (P.). Hill Docts.* 1841. (T.)
„ Jas., Donaghedy, Co. Tyr. *Pass. to Amer.* 1805. (T.)
„ Jane, Belfast. *Pass. to Amer.* 1804. (T.)
„ John, Portavogey, Co. Down. *Pass. to Amer.* 1805. (T.)
„ John and Mary, Ardmore, Co. Arm. *Deed of Sale.* 1788. (O.D.)
„ John and Reba., Newtownstewart, Co. Tyr. *Pass. to Amer.* 1805. (T.)
„ Wm. *Journal. L'pool to New York Voyage.* 1833. (O.D.)
Rochfort, Robt. *Agrmt. Massereene MSS.* 1693. (T.)
Roe, John. *Acct. Haberdashers' Pps. (S.R.O.)* 1617(?) (T.)
Rogan, Michl., Pomeroy, Co. Tyr. *Pass. to Amer.* 1805. (T.)
Rogers, Elizth., Omagh, Co. Tyr. *Pass. to Amer.* 1806. (T.)
„ Jas., Elizth, Wm. and Mary, Carnmoney, Co. Ant. *Pass. to Amer.* 1805 (T.)
„ John, Maghera, Co. L'derry. *Pass. to Amer.* 1805(?) (T.)
„ Matilda, Alex. and Wm., Omagh, Co. Tyr. *Pass. to Amer.* 1805(?) (T.)
Roney, Danl., Loughbrickland, Co. Down. *Pass. to Amer.* 1805. (T.)
Ross, Lieut.-Col. Alex. *T.S.P.I.* 1715.
„ Danl., Magilligan, Co. L'derry. *Pass. to Amer.* 1804. (T.)
„ Jas., Belfast. *Pg. Gt. (W.A.). Hill Docts.* 1796. (O.D.)
„ Lieut. Rob. *T.S.P.I.* 1715.
„ R., Dublin. *Downshire MSS.* Mar. 8 and June 29, 1796. (T.)
Rosse, John, Balle Castlane, Co. L'derry. *Rental. Haberdashers' Pps. (S.R.O.)* 1616–7. (T.)
Ross's Regt. *T.S.P.I.* 1715.
Rousby, Ensign Wm. *T.S.P.I.* 1715.
Rowan, Jas., Saintfield, Co. Down. *Pass. to Amer.* 1805. (T.)
„ R. R. *Downshire MSS.* Jan. 14, 1796. (T.)
Rowley, Hercules, Dublin. *Marr. Arts.* 1712. (T.)
„ Hercules, Summerhill, Co. Meath. *Mge.* 1721. (O.D.)
„ Hercules Langford, Summerhill, Co. Meath. *Marr. Arts. Lenox-Conyngham MSS.* (2). 1745. (T.)
Rowly, Mr. *Letter. Haberdashers' Pps. (S.R.O.)* Apr. 15, 1614. (T.)
Rowlye, Hugh. *Massereene MSS.* 1681. (T.)
Royal North Down Militia. *Courtmartial Bk. Retns. ; Order Bks., etc. Findlay Colln.* 1802–1863. (O.D.)
„ Regt. of Horse. *List of Officers.* 1737. (T.)
„ South Down Militia. *Letters and Papers ; Appts. of Officers and Non-Coms. Findlay Colln.* 1862–3. (O.D.)
Russell, G. *Downshire MSS.* Apr. 7, 1796. (T.)
„ Hen., Newtownstewart, Co. Tyr. *Pass. to Amer.* 1805. (T.)
„ Isaac, Omagh, Co. Tyr. *Pass. to Amer.* 1805. (T.)
„ Wm., Jane, Robt. and Jas., Moneymore, Co. L'derry. *Pass. to Amer.* 1805. (T.)

Ryan, Jas. and Peter, Banbridge, Co. Down.   *Pass. to Amer.*   1804.   (T.)
,,   Michl., Moy, Co. Tyr.   *Pass. to Amer.*   1806.   (T.)
Rycant, Lieut. Paul.   *T.S.P.I.*   1715.

Sabine's Regt.   *T.S.P.I.*   1715–1721.
St. Clair, Col. Jas., Regt. of.   *List of Officers.*   1737.   (T.)
St. George, Mr.   *T.S.P.I.*   1719.
,,   Col. Rich., Regt. of.   *List of Officers.*   1737.   (T.)
St. Leger, Mrs. Baron.   *T.S.P.I.*   1717.
Salaries and Pensions, Proposed Tax on.   *T.S.P.I.*   1717.
Sana, Laird of.   *T.S.P.I.*   1719.
Sandford, Col.   *T.S.P.I.*   1719.
Savage, Pat., Portaferry, Co. Down.   *Downshire MSS.*   Jan. 4, 1796.   (T.)
Scandret, Jas., Hillsborough, Co. Down.   *Pass. to Amer.*   1805.   (T.)
Scott, Wm., Kilsorrell, Co. Down.   *Dromore W.*   1789.   (T.)
Scottish Freeholders in Ulster, List of.   circa 1615.   (T.)
Scravenmore, Mrs.   *T.S.P.I.*   1717–8.
Seaforth, Earl of.   *T.S.P.I.*   1719.
Searight, John and Jane, Banbridge, Co. Down.   *Pass. to Amer.*   1804.   (T.)
Seeds, Jas., Lisburn, Co. Ant.   *Pass. to Amer.*   1806.   (T.)
Seliock, Capt. John.   *T.S.P.I.*   1713.
Semple, Major Hugh.   *T.S.P.I.*   1718.
Shannon, Lord.   *T.S.P.I.*   1716–7.
Sharland, Robt., Hillsborough, Co. Down.   *Downshire MSS.*   Apr. 18, 1796, *et seq.*
    (T.)
Sharman, Wm.   *Downshire MSS.*   Jan. 7, 1796.   (T.)
Shannon, Robt.   *L'derry Address.*   1690.   (T.)
Sharpeless, Lieut. Geo.   *T.S.P.I.*   1720.
Shaw, Hen.   *Memo. of Agrmt.*   *Hill Docts.*   1790.   (T.)
,,   Jas., Clough (Co. Down).   *Pass. to Amer.*   1805.   (T.)
,,   John and Wm., Cairncastle, Co. Ant.   *Fee Farm Gt.*   *Hill Docts.*   1763   (T.)
,,   Sidney, Dublin.   *Warrant of Atty.*   *Lenox-Conyngham MSS.* (2).   1765.   (T.)
,,   Wm., Bush, Co. Ant.   *Assgmt.*   *Hill Docts.*   1700.   (O.D.)
Sheriff, Wm., Ballywillen, Co. Ant.   *Connor W. and Gt.* (P.)   1812.   (T.)
Sherlock and Aneesley, Case of.   *T.S.P.I.*   1719.
Sherrigley, Cornet John.   *T.S.P.I.*   1716.
Shuckburgh, Ensign.   *T.S.P.I.*   1715.
Shute, Barrington.   *T.S.P.I.*   1719.
Sibourg's Regt.   *T.S.P.I.*   1715–6.
Simple, Saml., "Glinlush" (Glenglush, Co. Tyr.?).   *Pass. to Amer.*   1806.   (T.)
Simpson, Thos., Ballyards, Co. Arm.   *Assgmts.*   1791.   (O.D.)
Sinclair, John, Kirkcubbin, Co. Down.   *Pass. to Amer.*   1805.   (T.)
,,   Rev. Robt., Larne.   *Assgmt. of Lease.*   *Hill Docts.*   1759.   (O.D.)
Sinclaire, Robt., Dungannon, Co. Tyr.   *Pass. to Amer.*   1804.   (T.)
Sinot, Ensign Tho.   *T.S.P.I.*   1715.
Skeffington, Clotworthy and Rach.   *Marr. Settmt.*   *Massereene MSS.*   1684.   (T.)
,,   I. C.   *Downshire MSS.*   June 23, 1796.   (T.)
,,   Sir Rich. and Ann.   *Meml. Tablet Inscription.*   *Massereene   MSS.*
    1647.   (T.)
Skelly, Jas., Tullinisky, Co. Down.   *Lease.*   1802.   (T.)
Slade, Mr.   *Downshire MSS.*   June 29, 1796.   (T.)
Sloan, Saml., Ballymacbrennan, Co. Down.   *Down W. and Gt.* (P.)   1852.   (O.D.)
Smart, John, Armagh.   *Pass. to Amer.*   1805.   (T.)
Smiley, Domk., Tanderagee, Co. Arm.   *Pass. to Amer.*   1806.   (T.)
,,   Saml., Inver, Co. Ant.   *Lease.*   *Hill Docts.*   1769.   (T.)
Smith, Alderman.   *Haberdashers' Pps.* (S.R.O.)   Apr. 15, 1614.   (T.)
,,   Edwd. and Mary Anne, Armagh.   *Pass. to Amer.*   1805.   (T.)
,,   Edwd.   See "Down, Bp. of."
,,   Hugh. Co. Ferm.   *Pass. to Amer.*   1806.   (T.)
,,   Hugh.   Newtownards, Co. Down.   *Pass. to Amer.*   1806.   (T.)
,,   Jane.   *T.S.P.I.*   1717.
,,   Matt., Clandy (Claudy, Co. L'derry ?).   *Pass. to Amer.*   1805.   (T.)
,,   Nancy, Co. Down.   *Pass. to Amer.*   1805.   (T.)
,,   Thos.   *Memo. re Jacobites.*   *Massereene MSS.*   1693.   (T.)
,,   Thos.   See " Limerick, Bp. of."
Smyth, Jas., Dublin.   *Memo. of Deeds of Lease and Release.*   *Hill Docts.*   1755   (T.)

Smyth, Jas., L'derry. *Pass. to Amer.* 1805. (T.)
„ John and Mary, Omagh, Co. Tyr. *Pass. to Amer.* 1805. (T.)
„ R. J., Lisburn, Co. Ant. *Downshire MSS.* June 28, 1796. (T.)
„ Robt., Dinnamany, Co. Tyr. (?) *Pass. to Amer.* 1805. (T.)
„ Robt., Limavady, Co. L'derry. *Pass. to Amer.* 1805. (T.)
Snedgrass, Mary, Rich., Eliz., Mary and John, Miltown. *Pass. to Amer.* 1805. (T.)
Sotherby, John, Dublin. *Mge.* 1720. (O.D.)
Southwell, Col. *T.S.P.I.* 1719.
„ Mr. *T.S.P.I.* 1717.
Spaight, Jas. *T.S.P.I.* 1719.
Span, Wm. *Release.* 1787. (T.)
Spencer, Conway, Trumry, Co. Ant. *Lease.* 1749. (T.)
Spirits, Proposed Duty on. *T.S.P.I.* 1717.
Springham, Mr. *Haberdashers' Pps.* (*S.R.O.*) May, 1615. (T.)
Springhill Corps. *Names of Members. Lenox-Conyngham MSS.* (2). 1852. (T.)
Sproul, Mary and Jane, Omagh, Co. Tyr. Pass. to Amer. 1806. (T.)
Squire, Ger., Mayor of Londonderry. *L'derry Address.* 1690. (T.)
Stackallen, Lord. *T.S.P.I.* 1716–7.
Stanhope, Lord. *T.S.P.I.* 1719.
Stanyan, Mr. *T.S.P.I.* 1717–9.
Staples, Sir Robt. *Massereene MSS.* 1681. (T.)
„ Rev. Thos. and Grace, Derryloran, Co. Tyr. *Exchq. Bill. Lenox-Conyngham MSS.* (2) circa 1750. (T.)
Starr, Jas. and Patk., Fintona, Co. Tyr. *Pass. to Amer.* 1805. (T.)
Steel, Mary, Mary, Martha, and Saml., Co. Derry. *Pass. to Amer.* 1805. (T.)
„ Sir Rich. *T.S.P.I.* 1716–7.
Steele, Sarah, Dublin. *Mge. Hill Docts.* 1762. (O.D.)
Stephens, Mary, Armagh. *Pass. to Amer.* 1805. (T.)
Steuart, Capt. Arth. *T.S.P.I.* 1715.
Stewart, Alex., Ballylough, Co. Ant. *Pg. W. and Gt.* (*P.*). 1742 (T.)
„ Alex., Acton, Co. Arm. *Marr. Settmt.* 1751. (T.)
„ Alex. T., Acton, Co. Arm. *Deed of Annuity; Release; Fine, etc.* 1787–1797. (T.)
„ Dr. Archd., Ballintoy, Co. Ant. *Marr. Settmt.; Pg. W and Gt.* (*P.*). 1751–1760. (T.)
„ Dr. Archd. and Alex., Ballintoy, Co. Ant. *Marr. Settmt.* 1724. (T.)
„ G. *Downshire MSS.* Feb. 11, 1796. (T.)
„ Hugh, Middle Temple, London. *Marr. Settmt.* 1724. (T.)
„ Jas., Billy, Co. Ant. *Marr. Settmt.* 1751. (T.)
„ Jas., Jane, Alex., Jas., Jane, Sarah, Eliza., Saml. and Geo., Gilford, Co. Down. *Pass. to Amer.* 1805. (T.)
„ John and Ann, Jamaica. *Marr. Settmt.* 1724. (T.)
„ Moses. *Chy. Bill ; Rolls Ct. Order.* 1871. (T.)
„ Saml., Ballycastle, Co. Ant. *Pass. to Amer.* 1805. (T.)
„ Wm., Newtownstewart, Co. Tyr. *Pass. to Amer.* 1806. (T.)
„ Wm., Ballyhacket, Co. Ant. *Connor W. Hill Docts.* 1848. (T.)
Stitt, Wm., Antrim. *Pass. to Amer.* 1805. (T.)
Stone, Mr. *Haberdashers' Pps.* (*S.R.O.*). Apr. 15, 1614, and Apr. 23, 1617. (T.)
Stothard, Adam, Drumbane, Co. Down. *Lease.* 1742. (T.)
Strain, Wm., Mary, John, Jas., Wm., Jane and Hugh, Armagh. *Pass. to Amer.* 1805. (T.)
Strangford, Lord. *T.S.P.I.* 1717.
Stratford, Edwd., Belan, Co. Kildare. *Memo. of Deeds of Lease and Relase. Hill Docts.* 1755. (T.)
Streeter, Ensign Robt. *T.S.P.I.* 1717.
Strenaghan, Thos. and Elizth., Dehymeet, Co. Down. *Pass. to Amer.* 1805. (T.)
Stuart, Sarah Ann and Elizth., Co. Ferm. *Pass. to Amer.* 1805. (T.)
Sunderland, Lord. *T.S.P.I.* 1717.
Sutton, Lieut.-Gen., Regt. of. *List of Officers.* 1737. (T.)
Sutton's Regt. *T.S.P.I.* 1715.
Swedish Invasion, Rumour of. *T.S.P.I.* 1716–7.
Swift, Capt. (Abr.) *T.S.P.I.* 1717.
„ Cornet Michl. *T.S.P.I.* 1715.
Symes, Lieut. Rd. *T.S.P.I.* 1716.
Synge, Edward. See " Tuam, Archbishop of."

Tattin, Victor, Douglass. *Pass. to Amer.* 1805. (T.)
Taylor, Cath., Dublin. *Memo. of Deeds of Lease and Release. Hill Docts.* 1755. (T.)
  „ Walt., Jas. and Ann, Cookstown, Co. Tyr. *Pass. to Amer.* 1804. (T.)
Teir, Jas., Downpatrick, Co. Down. *Pass. to Amer.* 1805. (T.)
Tempest, Lieut. Rd. *T.S.P.I.* 1715.
Tennison, Cornet Thos. *T.S.P.I.* 1715.
Teyrill (Tyrell ?), Rev. Mr. *T.S.P.I.* 1717.
Thome, Robt., Greenland, Co. Ant. *Lease and Release. Hill Docts.* 1753–5. (O.D.)
Thompson, Ann, L'derry. *Pass. to Amer.* 1806. (T.)
  „ Archd., Six-Mile-Cross, Co. Tyr. *Pass. to Amer.* 1805. (T.)
  „ Hector, Benjn., Jas., Jane, John, Mary, Elizth., and Rosan, Bally-mooney. *Pass. to Amer.* 1804. (T.)
  „ Hugh, Antrim. *Pass. to Amer.* 1805. (T.)
  „ Jas., Craigs, Co. Ant. *Pass. to Amer.* 1805. (T.)
  „ Jas., Co. L'derry. *Pass. to Amer.* 1806. (T.)
Thompson, Jane, Jas., Mary, Rose, Martha and Margt., Newtown Limavady, Co. L'derry. *Pass. to Amer.* 1806. (T.)
  „ John, Omagh, Co. Tyr. *Pass. to Amer.* 1805. (T.)
  „ Robt. *Exchq. Bill Ext.* 1698. (T.)
  „ Robt., Jane and Mary, Co. Down. *Pass. to Amer.* 1805. (T.)
  „ Wm., Killetre. *Pass. to Amer.* 1805. (T.)
Thomson, Robt., Bangor, Co. Down. *Pass. to Amer.* 1806. (T.)
Thornborough, Adjt. Geo. *T.S.P.I.* 1717.
Thornbury, Js. and Mary, Tandragee, Co. Arm. *Pass. to Amer.* 1805. (T.)
Tillage Bill. *T.S.P.I.* 1717–9.
Tilson, George and Thos., Sen. and Jun. *T.S.P.I.* 1717.
Tipperary Co., Lands in. *Pat. Gt. Massereene MSS.* 1669. (T.)
Tirawley's Regt., Mutiny of. *T.S.P.I.* 1717.
Tobine, Ensign Fra. *T.S.P.I.* 1716.
Toleration Bill. *T.S.P.I.* 1719.
Tomlinson, Jos., Drogheda. *Mge.* 1720. (O.D.)
Tomm, Lieut. Fras. *T.S.P.I.* 1719.
Tories, Suppression of. *Letters. Massereene MSS.* 1676–1680. (T.)
Townsend, Col. *T.S.P.I.* 1719.
Townshend, Lord. *T.S.P.I.* 1717.
Tracey, Capt. Wm. *T.S.P.I.* 1717.
Tracy, Capt. Richd. *T.S.P.I.* 1715.
Trainer, Thos., Mary and Jas., Tullylish, Co. Down. *Pass. to Amer.* 1804. (T.)
Tuam. Archbp. of. *T.S.P.I.* 1717.
Tuite, Jas., Fennor, Co. Meath. *Pg. W. Ext.* 1741. (T.)
Tullamore, Lord. *T.S.P.I.* 1717–9.
Tullus, Jas., Corkermaine, Co. Ant. *Deed Poll and Memo. Hill Docts.* 1738. (T.)
  „ Rev. Jas. McCulloch, Kirkcolm, Wigtownshire. *W. Hill Docts.* 1792. (O.D.)
  „ Jas., Wm., Jane and Margt., Corkermain, Co. Ant. *Case for Counsel and Counsel's Opinion. Hill Docts.* 1724–1761. (O.D.)
Turner, J. *Downshire MSS.* Feb. 12, 1796. (T.)
Turtle, Lancelot, Aghagallon, Co. Ant. *Belfast W. and Gt.* (P.) 1861. (T.)
Tweedy, Dav., Rathfriland, Co. Down. *Pass. to Amer.* 1804. (T.)
Twine and Cordage, Proposed Duty on. *T.S.P.I.* 1717.
Tyrawly, Lord, Lieut.-Gen. *T.S.P.I.* 1716–7.

Union, Act of. *Belfast Signatures to Petn. against.* 1799–1800. (T.)
Upton, Clotworthy, Castle Upton, Co. Ant. *Marr. Arts.* 1712. (T.)
  „ Mr. *T.S.P.I.* 1719.
  „ Thos. and Sarah, Dublin. *Mge.* 1721. (O.D.)
Ure, Margt., Jane, Margt., and Jane, Drumbo, Co. Down. *Pass. to Amer.* 1805. (T.)

Valentia, Lord. *T.S.P.I.* 1717.
Veasy, Mr. *T.S.P.I.* 1717.
Vere, Lieut. John. *T.S.P.I.* 1715.
Vesey, Miss. *T.S.P.I.* 1719.
Vigo, Capture of. *T.S.P.I.* 1719.
Vincent, Rev. Rich., Castlecaulfield, Co. Tyr. *Assgmt. Lenox-Conyngham MSS.* (2). 1769. (T.)
Vintners' Company, London. *Ext. from Ct. Bk.* 1610. (T.)

Vogan, Rich., Armagh. *Letters.* 1845–1858. (O.D.)
  ,, Thos., Australia and California. *Letters.* 1845–1858. (O.D.)
Volunteer Orders. 1782. (T.)

Waddell, Jas. *Downshire MSS.* Jan. 7, 1796. (T.)
  ,, Robt., Island-derry, Co. Down. *Lease Ext.* 1759. (T.)
Wade, Cornet Wm. *T.S.P.I.* 1717–8.
Wade's Regt. *T.S.P.I.* 1715–1720.
Wakline, Walt. *Acct. Haberdashers' Pps. (S.R.O.)* 1617(?) (T.)
Walker, Geo., Co. Tyr. *Pass. to Amer.* 1805. (T.)
  ,, Dr. Geo., family of. *T.S.P.I.* 1717.
  ,, John. *T.S.P.I.* 1717.
  ,, Thos., Bangor, Co. Down. *Pass. to Amer.* 1805. (T.)
Wall, Thos. *Letter.* 1785. (O.D.)
Wallace, Widow. *Kilw. Schl. Par. Hill Docts.* 1797. (O.D.)
  ,, Wm. *Exchq. Bill Ext.* 1698. (T.)
Wallas, Robt. *Kilw. Schl. Par. Hill Docts.* 1797. (O.D.)
Waller, Capt. John. *T.S.P.I.* 1715.
Walpole, Robt. *T.S.P.I.* 1717.
Walton, John, Tawneyherrin, Co. L'derry. *Rental. Haberdashers' Pps. (S.R.O.)* 1616–7. (T.)
  ,, Qr.-Master Thos. *T.S.P.I.* 1715.
Wansborough, Capt. Wm. *T.S.P.I.* 1721.
Ward, Mr. *T.S.P.I.* 1717–9.
  ,, Robt. *Volunteer Orders.* 1782. (T.)
  ,, Thos., Nelly and Ch., Glenward. *Pass. to Amer.* 1806. (T.)
Warden, Jas. and Jos., Randalstown, Co. Ant. *Pass. to Amer.* 1804. (T.)
  ,, Jas., Randlestown, Co. Ant. *Pass. to Amer.* 1805. (T.)
Waring, Hen., Waringsford and Bangor, Co. Down. *Dromore W.; Lease Ext.* 1715–1759. (T.)
Waringsford Estate, Co. Down. *Rental.* 1828. (T.)
Warren, Ensign Abel. *T.S.P.I.* 1714.
  ,, Edwd., Limmavaddy, Co. L'derry. *Agrmt. for Lease. Haberdashers' Pps. (S.R.O.)* May 26, 1615. (T.)
  ,, Edwd., Grenan, etc., Co. L'derry. *Rental. Haberdashers' Pps. (S.R.O.)* 1616–7. (T.)
Watson, Hugh, Mary, Mary and Martha, Killcapell, Co. Arm. *Pass. to Amer.* 1805. (T.)
Watt, Jas., Ruskey, Co. L'derry. *W. Lenox-Conyngham MSS.* (2). 1785. (T.)
  ,, Wm., Margt. Wm., Thos. and John B., Randlestown, Co. Ant. *Pass. to Amer.* 1805. (T.)
Webster, E. *T.S.P.I.* 1717–9.
  ,, Sir Thos. Copthall, Essex. *Lease. Lenox-Conyngham MSS.* (2). 1732. (T.)
Weir, Geo., " Ballynine," Co. Ant. *Pass. to Amer.* 1805. (T.)
  ,, Jas. and Mary, Cookstown, Co. Tyr. *Pass. to Amer.* 1804. (T.)
Welch, Patk. *T.S.P.I.* 1719.
Wentworth, Lieut.-Col. Tho. *T.S.P.I.* 1717.
  ,, Col. Thos., Regt. of. *List of Officers.* 1737. (T.)
West, Cornet Rd. *T.S.P.I.* 1720.
Westmeath Co., Lands in. *Pat. Gt. Massereene MSS.* 1669.(T.)
Whaplett, Mr. *Vintners' Co.'s Ct. Bk. Ext.* 1610. (T.)
Whichcote, P. *T.S.P.I.* 1719.
Whiston, Capt. Js. *T.S.P.I.* 1717.
Whit, John. *Abst. of Title. Massereene MSS.* 1637. (T.)
White, Anne. *Exchq. Bill Ext.* 1717. (T.)
  ,, (als Derry als Gough), Cisly, Newry, Co. Down. *Exchq. Bill Ext.* 1698. (T.)
  ,, Saml. and Wm., Newtown Hamilton, Co. Arm. *Pass. to Amer.* 1806. (T.)
  ,, Wm., Belfast. *Pass. to Amer.* 1805. (T.)
Whitfield, Hen. *Marr. Settmt. Massereene MSS.* 1684. (T.)
Whitshed, Lord Chief Justice. *T.S.P.I.* 1719.
Whitworth, Major. *T.S.P.I.* 1716–7.
Wickens, Mr. and Mrs. *Journal. L'pool to New York Voyage.* 1833. (O.D.)
Widdrington, Ensign Chas. *T.S.P.I.* 1714.
Wiley, Jos., Donaghmore, Co. Down. *Pass. to Amer.* 1804. (T.)
William III, King, Quarters in Ireland. *Photographic Reproduction.* 1690. (T.)
Williams, John. *Acct. Haberdashers' Pps. (S.R.O.)* 1616–7. (T.)

Williams, Rich., John, Wm. and Eliza, Strabane, Co. Tyr. *Pass. to Amer.* 1805. (T.)
,, Wm., Banbridge, Co. Down. *Assgmt.* 1760. (O.D.)
Williamson, Major Fra. *T.S.P.I.* 1715.
Willson, Jas., Ballygally, Co. Ant. *Lease. Hill Docts.* 1787. (O.D.)
Wilson, Ann, Carrickfergus, Co. Ant. *Bond. Hill Docts.* 1799. (O.D.)
,, Dav., Ann. and Margt., Lough Gele. *Pass. to Amer.* 1804. (T.)
,, Jane, Randalstown, Co. Ant. *Pass. to Amer.* 1804. (T.)
,, Capt. John. *T.S.P.I.* 1718.
,, John and Jannett, " Kilmander " (Kilmandil, Co. Ant. ?) *Pass. to Amer.* 1805. (T.)
,, Josh. and Mary, Drummarah, Co. Down. *Pass. to Amer.* 1805. (T.)
,, Robt., Newry, Co. Down. *Pass. to Amer.* 1805. (T.)
Wingate, Lieut. Chas. *T.S.P.I.* 1713.
Winnart, Dav. *Kilw. Schl. Par. Hill Docts.* 1797. (O.D.)
Winning, Wm., Fort Gibson, Louisiana, U.S.A. *W. Lenox-Conyngham MSS.* (2). 1843. (T.)
Winter and Kaye, Messrs. *Downshire MSS.* Jan. 4, 1796. (T.)
Withered, Robt., Glenwherry, Co. Ant. *W. Hill Docts.* 1857. (O.D.)
Witherspoon, Jas., Margt., John, Eliza and Hen.. Knockbracken, Co. Down. *Pass. to Amer.* 1804. (T.)
Woods, Saml., Banbridge, Co. Down. *Belfast Gt.* (*D.B.N.*) 1870. (T.)
Workman, Robt., Jas., Saml., Geo., Jane, Margt., Wm. and Agnes, Lisburn, Co. Ant. *Pass. to Amer.* 1805. (T.)
Worthington, Mr. *T.S.P.I.* 1716–7.
Wren, Ensign Jordan. *T.S.P.I.* 1720.
Wright, Jas., Rathfryland, Co. Down. *Pass. to Amer.* 1805. (T.)
,, Jenny, Bangor, Co. Down. *Pass. to Amer.* 1805. (T.)
,, Reedy and Mary, Monage, Co. Mon. *Deed of Sale.* 1788. (O.D.)
,, Robt., Larne, Co. Ant. *W. Hill Docts.* 1856. (O.D.)
Wynn(e), (Major)-Gen. (Owen). *T.S.P.I.* 1717–9.
Young, Jas., Symon and Matt., Dublin. *Exchq. Bill Ext.* 1717. (T.)
,, Martha, Dublin. *Py. M.L. Ext.* 1803. (T.)

LIST OF GERMAN PASSENGERS ARRIVED IN THE PORT

PHILADELPHIA IN THE SHIP MARGARET,

FROM AMSTERDAM

C. E. GARDNER, MASTER

SEPTEMBER 19th, 1804

As taken from the Original Immigrant List on File in the

Division of Public Records, Harrisburg, Pa.

Names	Age	Place of Nativity	County from where they came	Nationality	Occupation	Ht.	Color of Hair
1 Kirn, 2 children	29	Wirtemberg	Wirtemberg	German	Blacksmith	5½	Dark Brown
G. Reichard and wife	27	Ashberg	Wirtemberg	German	Farmer	5¼	Dark Brown
Lewis Weiss, wife, 1 child	26	Naihingen	Wirtemberg	German	Butcher	5½	Dark Brown
John Winter and wife	43	Naihingen	Wirtemberg	German	Weaver	5½	Dark Brown
Israel Bader, wife, 2 children	27	Oberhausen	Wirtemberg	German	Weaver	6	Dark Brown
Caspar Humel, wife, 4 children	36	Elmingen	Wirtemberg	German	Distiller	6	Dark Brown
John Shirtler, wife, 3 children	54	Marhgroninger	Wirtemberg	German	Farmer	6	Grey
Jacob Benzehofer, wife, 2 children	34	Shondorf	Wirtemberg	German	Farmer	6	Black
Michael Conradt, wife, 7 children	50	Ludwigsburg	Wirtemberg	German	Weaver & Dyer	6	Brown
David Ruckenbrodt, wife, 2 children	30	Malmsheim	Wirtemberg	German	Weaver	5½	Flaxen

Names	Age	Place of Nativity	County from where they came	Nationality	Occupation	Ht.	Color of Hair
Henry Lenz, wife, 4 children	43	Bentelspach	Wirtemberg	German	Farmer	5½	Dark Brown
Wm. Geissendorfer, wife, 1 child	24	Stuttgard	Wirtemberg	German	Musician	6	Flaxen
Frederic Emhard, wife, 1 child	35	Mohringen	Wirtemberg	German	Taylor	6	Flaxen
Charles Kuhnle, wife, 1 son	61	Engenhausen	Wirtemberg	German	Giometer	5½	Dark Brown
Conrad Grabenstein, wife, 4 children	55	Wallheim	Wirtemberg	German	Farmer	6	Flaxen
Christoph Epting, wife, 1 child	25	Bissingheim	Wirtemberg	German	Cooper & Brewer	6	Flaxen
Godfrey Villinger and wife	27	Beningheim	Wirtemberg	German	Soap Boiler	5¼	Flaxen
Wm. Hartstein, wife, 2 children	40	Unterhausen	Wirtemberg	German	Stone Cutter	5¼	Dark Brown
Geo. Lenz, wife, 2 children, mothin-in-law	39	Elmingen	Wirtemberg	German	Farmer	5½	Black
Godleib Kaiser, wife, 1 child	26	Beilstein	Wirtemberg	German	Merchant	5½	Dark Brown
Jacob Eheman, wife, 5 children	40	Shornbach	Wirtemberg	German	Farmer	6	Flaxen
David Humel, wife, 7 children	43	Elmingen	Wirtemberg	German	Tobacco Box Maker	6	Dark Brown
Peter Hafelen. wife, 1 child	34	Nordheim	Wirtemberg	German	Shoemaker	5½	Red Brown
Jacob Herman, 6 children	44	Genkengen	Wirtemberg	German	Farmer	5½	Black
Martin, 3 children	43	Genkengen	Wirtemberg	German	Shoemaker	6	Dark Brown
George Brughard, wife, 7 children, maid	43	Oberaichen	Wirtemberg	German	Farmer	5½	Yellow
George Kiess, 5 children	52	Mohringen	Wirtemberg	German	Farmer	5½	Dark Brown
Christian Kiesh, wife, 2 children	31	Heimerdingen	Wirtemberg	German	Shoemaker	5½	Brown
Joshua Vaihinger, wife, 7 children	52	Feldbach	Wirtemberg	German	Farmer	6	Black
Frederic Gross, wife, 6 children	40	Oberaichen	Wirtemberg	German	Farmer	6	Brown
Christoph Mohl, wife, 5 children	58	Phullingen	Wirtemberg	German	Farmer	5½	Grey
Leonard Ulmer, wife, 5 children, maid	40	Mohringen	Wirtemberg	German	Farmer	5½	Black
George Biechtler, wife, 5 children	42	Groenbach	Wirtemberg	German	Stocking Weaver	5	Black
Leonard Staiger, wife, 4 children, maid	39	Mohringen	Wirtemberg	German	Weaver	5½	Black
Thomas Ulmer, wife and child	28	Mohringen	Wirtemberg	German	Shoemaker	5	Grey
George Bertsh, wife, 5 children	45	Unterhausen	Wirtemberg	German	Cooper	5¼	Yellow
George Walz, wife, 1 child	28	Mohringen	Wirtemberg	German	Farmer	6	Black

Names	Age	Place of Nativity	County from where they came	Nationality	Occupation	Ht.	Color of Hair
Wm. Klermundt and wife	41	Caln	Wirtemberg	German	Farmer	5	Brown
Michael Uhl, wife, 4 childn. mother, sister	44	Mussberg	Wirtemberg	German	Farmer	6	Dark Brown
George Keppeler, wife, 4 children	55	Pfullingen	Wirtemberg	German	Farmer	5½	Grey
Frederic Wolfer, wife, 5 children	35	Markgronigen	Wirtemberg	German	Farmer	5½	Brown
Jacob Lullich, wife, 1 child.	25	Reilingshausen	Preussen	German	Farmer	5	Flaxen
Jacob Hohenstein and wife	35	Lowehausen	Holland	Sweden	Miller	6	Brown
John DeYoung	30	Medembleck	Waldeck	Holland	Military Off.	6	Lt. Complxn.
Dedric Heydorn	19	Pyrmont	Wirtemberg	German	Printer	5½	Brown
Frederic Stroh	22	Sachsenheim	Wirtemberg	German	Taylor	5	Flaxen
Christoph Shell	22	Graben	Wirtemberg	German	Taylor	5	Flaxen
Michael Bassler	21	Strempfelbach	Wirtemberg	German	Farmer	6	Dark Brown
I. Jacob Geiger	54	Bissingen	Wirtemberg	German	Carpenter	6	Dark Brown
Frederic Henninger	29	Ludwigsburg	Wirtemberg	German	Stone Cutter	5½	Dark Brown
Frederic Friz	18	Rielingshausen	Wirtemberg	German	Weaver	5	Dark Brown
J. G. Hansberg	28	Halle	Wirtemberg	German	Stocking Weaver	5½	Brown
Ernst Lewis Gaier	34	Markgroninger	Wirtemberg	German	Shepherd	6	Brown
Daniel Trippel	31	Markgroninger	Wirtemberg	German	Butcher	5½	Dark Brown
Daniel Brenner	25	Beutelspach	Wirtemberg	German	Farmer	5	Dark Brown
Lewis Gruis	28	Heilbrunn	Wirtemberg	German	Clerk	4	Flaxen
Lewis Burkhard	21	Ludwigsburg	Wirtemberg	German	Weaver	5	Flaxen
Jacob Renk	21	Enzweihengen	Wirtemberg	German	Carpenter	5½	Flaxen
C. Adam Belz	18	Ludwigsburg	Wirtemberg	German	Taylor	5½	Flaxen
Frederic Jooss	18	Ludwigsburg	Wirtemberg	German	Ropemaker	5	Yellow
G. Godlob Zimmerman	23	Ludwigsburg	Wirtemberg	German	Shoemaker	5	Flaxen
G. Frederic Buchalter	20	Ludwigsburg	Wirtemberg	German	Baker	5½	Brown
J. Frederic Schafer	25	Shornbach	Wirtemberg	German	Weaver	6	Flaxen
J. George Kurz	20	Grossahsbach	Wirtemberg	German	Cooper	5	Black

Names	Age	Place of Nativity	County from where they came	Nationality	Occupation	Ht.	Color of Hair
G. Adam Trefz	19	Grossashbach	Wirtemberg	German	Baker	5½	Brown
John Klein	24	Westhof	Hessen	German	Architect	5½	Flaxen
Gottlieb Lillich	20	Rielingshausen	Wirtemberg	German	Weaver	5½	Yellow
J. Gottlieb Gotz	20	Grossachsenheim	Wirtemberg	German	Glass Maker	5½	Brown
Christian Ernst	22	Fellbach	Wirtemberg	German	Farmer	5½	Black
John Heim	34	Mohringen	Wirtemberg	German	Weaver	5½	Yelow
Jacob Hoffmeister	21	Fellbach	Wirtemberg	German	Farmer	6	Black
J. Michael Reisch	24	Heimerdingen	Wirtemberg	German	Farmer	6	Black
C. Godfrey Phaler	18	Ludwigsburg	Wirtemberg	German	Turner	5½	Brown
Felix Trumpeter	60	Braunau	Bayerland	German	Clerk	5½	Grey
Anton Mozel	18	Hamburg	Zweybruck	German	Bookbinder	5½	Brown
Juda Bair Levy	16	Kreuznach	Wirtemberg	German	Clerk	5½	Flaxen
Regina Shallinn	48	Enaith	Wirtemberg	German		4½	Black
Catherine Kramerinn	40	Mohringen	Wirtemberg	German		5	Black
Charlotte Neuferinn	34	Mohringen	Wirtemberg	German		5½	Brown
Elizabeth Schwaglerinn	50	Gerhardstadten	Wirtemberg	German		5	Black
Frederica Dobelmann	20	Ludwigsburg	Wirtemberg	German		4½	Dark Brown
Godlieb Heim	37	Mohringen	Hambro	German	Weaver	5½	Yellow
Anna Mary Armstrong	28	Gotenborg	Hambro	Sweden		5	Flaxen
Mary Armstrong	12	Gottenborg	Holland	German		4	Flaxen
Wm. Vander Veen	20	Breukelen	Holland	Holland	Doctor	4½	Brown
Tobias Jacob Ezechiel	18	Amsterdam	Holland	Holland		4½	Brown
John Lehl	33	Markgroningen	Wirtemberg	German	Butcher	6	Black
David Jung	24	Johringen	Wirtemberg	German	Joiner	6	Flaxen
David Vinninger and wife	27	Beningheim	Wirtemberg	German	Soap Boiler	5	Flaxen
John Armbrust, 2 children	2	Benosen	Wirtemberg	German	School Master	5	Brown
Burkhard, widow, 3 children	50	Grossachen	Wirtemberg	German		5	Black

PASSENGER LISTS PUBLISHED IN
"THE SHAMROCK OR IRISH CHRONICLE," 1811

J. Dominick Hackett

The date of arrival of early immigrant ancestors from Ireland in America must always be a matter of interest to descendants. The evidence of this lies in the frequent searches of such records.

Official passenger lists may be found at the port of entry. Those in New York date only from 1820 and have to be consulted, if at all, at the Custom House. These lists, which are numerous even in early days, are chronologically arranged and it is almost impossible to find an individual name unless the exact date of arrival is known because the surnames are not alphabetically arranged. The lists are incomplete even after 1820. Alphabetical lists of names of passengers previous to that time are scarce and those which have been compiled form an important source of information.

Early periodicals, such as "The Shamrock" of New York, have published lists of passengers arriving in New York and other American ports of entry from time to time and some of them have been published by our Society in "The Recorder." On account of their unique character, it has been thought desirable to publish the surnames of those who arrived in 1811 in a single alphabetical list. Unfortunately one issue of the Shamrock, July 27, is missing but it may not have contained a Passenger List. Each surname in this consolidated list is preceded by a number which identifies the ship in which the passenger arrived. "List of Ships" shows the name of each ship with its corresponding number, together with attendant particulars such as sailing and/or arrival date, place of departure and/or port of entry; thus, the number 18 preceding the entry "18 Doherty, Henry" refers to the ship, particulars about which will be found in the "List of Ships" following the list of names.

All surnames have been copied exactly as they have originally appeared except in a few cases where the facts have been ascertained or where there is an obvious typographical error. There are indications that names were taken orally from passengers by persons indifferently acquainted with the Irish names or their usual anglicized form, hence the spelling is sometimes unusual; Coil for Coyle, Ceyrin for Kieran. Some of the names are rare, such as Vimmo, Amberson, Turkenton, M'Knott, Charbowell, Cobine, Clothard, Coslarder, Dettart. Others are well known in America today such as Glass, Copeland, Roulstone, Robert Service, Crothers, and Harding. As usual Doherty is spelled in a variety of ways and we find Camble, Cambell and Campbell. Moreover, certain spellings tend to be stereotyped. With a few exceptions the "M'" affix is used rather than the correct form "Mac" or its abbreviation, "Mc". All names in the alphabetical list with the "M'" prefix are arranged as if they had a "Mac" prefix.

The passenger lists already published in "The Recorder" have excited interest. Several persons have been enabled to find the time when their ancestors came to America, the place of departure and the port of entry. For instance, Mr. John R. Morron, President of the Atlas Cement Company, has found that his ancestor, John Morron of Ballybay, Co. Monaghan, departed from Belfast, Ireland, on the "Protection" and arrived in New York in 1811. Further, it has been possible to supply Mr. J. Keresey, New York, with the names of his grand-parents and their kin who came from Lismore, Co. Waterford, and sailed from Cork on the ship "Radius" which arrived in New York May, 1811; the names, however, were written "Kearcey."

The descendants of the 2,000 individuals listed in 1811 probably number no less than 150,000 persons today. It is evident, therefore, that the publication of the list should be of wide interest.

The small proportion of South of Ireland surnames is explained by an interesting historical circumstance. The "Belisarius," sailing from Dublin in 1811, was met by the British ship of war "Atalanta" on the west border of George's Bank, and sixty-two men, women and children, were taken off, it being alleged they had not passed the customs. A passenger, however, claimed that the lists were correct. He further said that those taken off were addressed by the sailors of the British ship, "Come along; you shan't go into that damned Republican country; we are going to have a slap at them one of these days and you shan't be there to fight against us."

Thus, 1811 could not be accounted a normal year of Irish immigration. In any case it is impossible to say whether all the ships

which arrived in that year are included. Moreover, some of the
entries specify children, the number of which is not mentioned. It
is also known that some Irish came from English ports. For instance, of 117 passengers leaving London between Dec. 11 and
December 18th, 1773, Patrick Reiley, William Morgan, William
Boyle, Arch. O'Brian and Thomas Gorman are all mentioned as
having an Irish residence, while Terence MacDonald, James Demsay and Thomas McKoin are mentioned as having a London residence. Thus, about 7 per cent of these passengers were Irish.

In 1802 Robert Slade, secretary of the Irish Society, made a
report to the governors entitled "Narrative of a Journey to the
North of Ireland in the year 1802," from which the following
is extracted:

> "The road from Down Hill to Coleraine goes through the best
> part of the Clothworker's portion, which was held by the Right
> Honorable Richard Jackson, who was the Society's general agent.
> It is commonly reported in the country that, having been obliged
> to raise the rents of his tenants very considerably in consequence
> of the large fine he had to pay, it produced an almost total emigra-
> tion among them to America, and that they formed a principal
> part of the undisciplined body which brought about the surrender
> of the British Army at Saratoga. I think it right to add that Mr.
> Jackson was considered a man of the greatest honour and integrity,
> and that his memory is highly respected by all who knew him."

Long before this period, however, passengers were coming
from Ireland in large numbers. Cheesman A. Herrick, in his
valuable book, *White Servitude in Pennsylvania,* says that, in
1729, there was received in the colony a total immigration of
6,208, of whom 267 were English and Welsh passengers and servants, 43 were Scotch servants, 1,155 were Irish, 4,500 chiefly
Irish were landed at New Castle and 243 were Palatine passengers.
Out of the known emigrants from Great Britain and Ireland it will
be seen that over 75 per cent were Irish at this early period!

The report of the American Historical Association, 1896, quotes
Phineas Bond as saying, in 1788, "I have not yet been able to ob-
tain any account of the number of Irish passengers brought hither
for any given series of years before the war—but from my own
recollection I know the number was great and I have been told
that in one year above 6,000 Irish were landed at Philadelphia,
Wilmington and New Castle upon Delaware."

A LIST OF PASSENGERS FROM IRELAND, ARRIVING IN AMERICAN PORTS, 1811

Transcribed from the "Shamrock" and
Alphabetically Arranged

Note: The number preceding the surname indicates the name of the ship; see "List of Ships" following.

A

21 Adams, Charles.
12 Aiken, Anne; Dromore.
12 Aiken, Jane; Dromore.
14 Aikens, John.
14 Akin, Joseph.
14 Akin, Margaret.
14 Akin, Mary.
14 Akin, William.
19 Alchorn, Michael, Philadelphia.
26 Alcorn, Francis and wife.
26 Alcorn, James.
26 Alcorn, John and family.
26 Alcorn, Joseph.
13 Alexander, Marg.
30 Alges, John.
3 Alsop, Nathaniel and wife; Seafield.
7 Amberson, James; Hill Hall.
31 Anderson, Ann.
9 Anderson, Catherine; Banbridge.
2 Anderson, George, Newtownards.
31 Anderson, Hugh.
10 Anderson, James.
26 Anderson, James.
31 Anderson, James.
2 Anderson, Jennet; Newtownards.
2 Anderson, Samuel; Newtownards.
2 Anderson, T.; Newtownards.
9 Anderson, William; Banbridge.
21 Anderson, William.
16 Andrews, Gabriel.
5 Andrews, John; Cumber.
32 Androhan, John; Wexford.
21 Anthony, William.
30 Arenner, Bernard.
18 Armitage, John; Tipperary.
25 Armstrong, Alex.
12 Armstrong, Arabella; Down.
25 Armstrong, Arm.
34 Armstrong, Eliz.
7 Armstrong, Eliza; Co. Down.
11 Armstrong, Isaac.
20 Armstrong, John.
11 Armstrong, Marg. and child.
34 Armstrong, R.
7 Armstrong, Wm.; Co. Down.
12 Armstrong, Wm.; Down.
12 Armstrong, Wm.; Down.
26 Arthur, James.
2 Aslein, John; Belfast.
30 Atcheson, Hugh and wife.
13 Atkins, Mary.
28 Atkinson, Eliza; Dromore.
28 Atkinson, Henry; Dromore.
28 Atkinson, Henry; Dromore.
28 Atkinson, James; Dromore.
28 Atkinson, Jane; Dromore.
2 Auld, James; Grange, Antrim.
2 Auld Mary; Grange, Antrim.
34, Auld, Margaret.

B

29 Bacon, John and family.
26 Bailey, Esther.
17 Baimbrick, Martin and family.
11 Ballah, William.
5 Banecan, Christopher; Ballytrea.
11 Barker, John.
34 Barklie, L., and family.
21 Barns, William.
13 Barney Patrick.
27 Barr, John and family; Ballinahinch.
28 Barron, John P.; New York.
6 Barry, James; Watergrasshill.
6 Barry, James; Youghal.
1 Barry, John; Co. Louth.
7 Beatty, Alex., and family; Hillsboro.
16 Beatty, George.
16 Beatty, Jane.
30 Beatty, Oliver.
16 Beatty, Wm.
2 Bell, David; Loughgall, Armagh.
5 Bell, David; Lisburn.
13 Bell, Jacob.
11 Bell, James.
5 Bell, James; Lisburn.
35 Bell, John.
5 Bell, Margaret; Lisburn.
13 Bell, Mary.
35 Bell, William.
27 Bennet, James; Co. Armagh.
37 Bennet, Patrick, and family.
16 Bennett, Z.
9 Best, George; Banbridge.
22 Best, John and family.
9 Best, Seragh; Banbridge.
17 Bird, Mary.
17 Bird, Thomas.
17 Birk, Eliza.
17 Birk, John.
21 Birns, Barney.
1 Bishop, John and wife; Co. Dublin.
33 Black, Donaldson, and family; Co. Tyrone.
35 Black, George.
34 Blair, Ann.

31 Blair, Catherine.
31 Blair, Eliza.
28 Blair, Eliza; Cullybackey.
31 Blair, George.
31 Blair, James.
31 Blair, Jane.
31 Blair, John.
34 Blair, Richard.
28 Blair, Samuel; Cullybackey.
31 Blair, Wm.
6 Blake, John; Emly.
12 Blany, Eleanor; Down.
1 Bleakly, William; Dublin.
20 Blythe, Keziah.
12 Bodd, James; Loughbrickland.
33 Boggs, Paul; New York.
7 Bonnel, John; Queens Co.
28 Booney, Harriet; Greencastle.
28 Booney, Samuel; Greencastle.
28 Booney, Sarah; Greencastle.
27 Bowen, Miss Susanna; Belfast.
1 Bowles, Mrs. H.; Co. Sligo.
31 Boyd, Ellen.
14 Boyd, John.
9 Boyd, John; Down.
31 Boyd, Mary-Ann.
31 Boyd, Samuel.
11 Boyd, William and family.
28 Boyd, William; Killeybegs.
21 Boyle, Catherine.
13 Boyle, Dennis.
21 Boyle, John.
30 Boyle, John.
22 Boyle, Neil and family.
21 Boyle, Terance.
36 Bradley, Cath.
36 Bradley, Francis.
19 Bradley, John; Tipperary.
10 Brady, James, and family.
18 Branigan, Thomas; Co. Louth.
28 Bridge, Anthony; Bedford, Pa.
12 Bridget, Joseph, and family, Beleek.
21 Brogan, John.
33 Brown, Alex., and family; Aughan-
   werry.
16 Brown, Ann.
20 Brown, David, and family.
2 Brown, Francis; Kelbroughts, Antrim.
3 Brown, Geo., wife and 7 children;
   Banbridge.
5 Brown, Henry; Lisburn.
8 Brown, James.
2 Brown, John; Loughgall, Antrim.
35 Brown, John, and family.
5 Brown, Rachel; Lisburn.
8 Brown, William.
31 Browne, Bridget.
31 Browne, Mary.
31 Browne, Patrick.
30 Bryan, Anne.
30 Bryan, James, and wife.
5 Bryans, Sarah; Moy.
27 Bryson, Mrs.; Belfast.
25 Buchanan, Wm.
12 Buchanon, John; Carrickfergus.
6 Buckley, Catherine; Cloinmel.
36 Buden, James, and family
6 Bull, John; Kilkenny.
31 Bull, Mary.
6 Bullen, Henry; Clonakilty.
6 Bullen, Mary; Clonakilty.
5 Bunham, Ann; Newry.
12 Burk, Robert; Down.
13 Burnes, James.
13 Burns, Catherine.
13 Burns, Darby.
10 Burns, Elizabeth.

13 Burns, Henry.
13 Burns, James.
13 Burns, Murphy
7 Burns, Samuel; Halls Mill.
13 Burns, John, and family.
13 Burns, Thomas, and family.
10 Burns, William.
35 Burns, William, and family
17 Burton, Ally.
1 Butler, Mary; Co. Wexford.
1 Butler, Michael; Co. Wexford.
18 Byrne, James; Wicklow.
19 Byrne, Miles, and family; Dublin.
1 Byrnes, Bridget; Co. Louth.
1 Byrnes, C. Jr.; Co. Louth.
1 Byrnes, John; Co. Louth.
1 Byrnes, Nicholas; Co. Louth.

C

19 Caffray, Edward; Queens Co.
13 Caldwell, John, and family.
36 Caldwell, Joseph.
23 Callaghan, Michael; Killarney.
6 Callihan, John; Tallow.
12 Calvin, Thomas; Rathfriland.
28 Cambell, Robert; Kilinchy.
9 Camble, Joseph; Duncannon.
16 Campbell, Antho.
25 Campbell, Jane.
28 Campbell, Jemimah; Belfast.
8 Campbell, John.
28 Campbell, Mary; Belfast.
36 Campbell, Patrick, and family.
2 Campbell, Mrs. W.; Blaris, Co. Down.
35 Campbell, Wm., and family.
30 Cane, Charles, and family.
29 Cannon, —, and family.
10 Cannon, John.
13 Cannon, John.
14 Cannon, Patrick.
18 Carden, N., and family; Tipperary.
6 Carey, Richard; Cork.
15 Carney, Richard; Downpatrick.
13 Carling, Philip.
7 Carlton, A.; Hillsboro.
26 Carolan, Rose.
30 Carr, Alexander.
3 Carr, John; Hillsboro
22 Carr, Joseph.
27 Carrall, Dennis; Co. Tyrone.
19 Carrall, John; Tipperary.
8 Carrigan, James.
8 Carrigan, Wm.
5 Carse, William; Killinchy.
14 Carson, George.
14 Carson, James.
14 Carson, John.
33 Cartan, Patrick, and family; Claudy.
11 Carver, Agnes.
6 Casey, John; Emly.
35 Casey, Peter.
22 Cassely, Patrick.
21 Cassidy, Francis.
33 Catherwood, Hugh; Coleraine.
6 Cavanagh, Michael; Cappoquin.
16 Ceyrin, Wm.
9 Chaley, William; Antrim.
17 Charowell, James.
31 Chestnut, Samuel.
36 Child, Alexander.
8 Christie, Margaret, and child.
12 Clagher, Jane; Armagh.
16 Clark, Ann.
16 Clark, David.
18 Clark, Edward; Cavan.

9 Clark, John; Lurgan.
14 Clark, Mary.
14 Clark, Nancy.
11 Clark, William.
16 Clark, William.
16 Clary, John.
35 Class, John, and family.
12 Cleland, John; Lisburn.
9 Cleland, Samuel; Dunleery.
5 Clement, William; Ballybay.
28 Clothard, Anthony; Killinchy.
2 Coal, Alley; Drumbo, Down.
34 Coal, Catherine, and family.
2 Coal, James; Drumbo, Down.
14 Cobine, George.
14 Cobine, Robert.
7 Coborn, Wm., and family; Kilwarlin.
20 Cochlin, James.
33 Cochran, Mr., Ballymoney.
31 Cochran, John.
3 Cochrane, Henry; Co. Mayo.
3 Cochrane, Robert; Co. Mayo.
3 Cochrane, William; Co. Mayo.
29 Coe,—, and sister.
2 Coil, Peter; Derryloran.
2 Coil, Rosa; Derryloran.
2 Coil, Sarah, Derryloran.
2 Coil, William, Derryloran.
7 Coin, Ann and children; Belfast.
19 Colin, Henry; Co. Louth.
14 Collins, Andrew.
36 Collins, James.
31 Colvin, James.
31 Colvin, John.
9 Conaghy, Barnard; Banbridge.
5 Conaghy, Thomas; Antrim.
18 Concannon, Patrick; Kilkenny.
35 Conden, Hannah, and family.
21 Conn, Jane.
21 Conn, Robert.
21 Conn, Samuel.
21 Conn, Sarah.
21 Connel, Stephen.
16 Connelly, Patrick.
17 Connor, Jane, and family.
3 Connor, James; Lisburn.
6 Connor, Jeremiah; Cork.
6 Connor, Mary; Cork.
34 Conolly, Polly, and family.
9 Cook, Henry; Armagh.
31 Cooney, Bryan.
32 Cooper, Mrs.; Dublin.
11 Copeland, James.
11 Copeland, Thomas.
7 Copeland, Wm., and family; Co. Down.
19 Corcoran, Thomas; Dublin.
19 Corcoran, Wm.; Dublin.
15 Corney, Richard; Downpatrick.
30 Corrins, James.
14 Coslarger, James.
17 Costagan, James.
35 Couden, Hannah, and family.
33 Coulter, Ann; Derry.
33 Coulter, Hugh; Pettigo.
33 Coulter, Sarah; Co. Derry.
2 Couples, Elizabeth; Aghaderg.
2 Couples, James; Aghaderg.
17 Courtney, Peter.
12 Cowser, Eliza; Armagh.
12 Cowser, James; Monaghan.
12 Cowser, Sophia, Armagh.
31 Coyle, Daniel.
31 Coyle, John.
18 Craig, Chas., and family; Dublin.
18 Craig, John.
18 Craig, Jos., and family; Dublin.
16 Craig, Wm.
33 Crampsier, John; Magilligar.

37 Cranfin, Mary, and family.
11 Crary, Samuel.
8 Crawford, Rebecca.
26 Crocket, George.
26 Crocket, Samuel.
26 Crockett, George.
26 Crockett, John.
26 Crockett, Robert.
13 Crone, William.
6 Cronin, Stephen; Castlemartyr.
21 Crosier, Eliza.
26 Cross, Elizabeth.
16 Crossen, Cornelius.
16 Crosson, Patrick.
35 Crothers, Hugh.
25 Crow, Jane.
25 Crow, Margaret.
25 Crow, William.
30 Crozier, Eliza.
30 Crozier, Richard.
21 Crummer, Ann.
21 Crummer, Cathar.
21 Crummer, Letitia.
21 Crummer, Mary.
21 Crummer, Nathl.
21 Crummer, Saml.
28 Cubbert, Isaac; Armagh.
26 Culbert, George.
18 Cullin, John; Kilkenny.
31 Cullin, James.
16 Cummings, John.
33 Cummings, John; Ballymoney.
13 Cunningham, C.
13 Cunningham, Coudy.
13 Cunningham, Dan.
6 Cunningham, Frances; Cappoquin.
12 Cunningham, Hugh; Rathfriland.
1 Cunningham, J; Sligo.
13 Cunningham, J.
6 Cunningham, John; Cappoquin.
35 Cunningham, Robert, and family.
16 Curragan, Sarah.
17 Current, Lawrence.
8 Curry, Conell.
22 Curry, John.
20 Currie, Josias.
7 Curry, Mary; Hillsboro.

D

7 Dail, Edward and family, Rathfriland.
37 Dander, Sarah.
4 Danwoody, John; Belfast.
4 Danwoody, Wm.; Belfast.
2 Davidson, John; Loughgall, Armagh.
35 Davidson, John, and family.
16 Davis, Barnard.
3 Davis, Charles; Armagh.
2 Davis, William; Blaris, Down.
15 Davis, William; Coleraine.
2 Davis, William; Hillsboro, Down.
10 Davison, John, and family.
18 Davis, Thomas; Wicklow.
28 Davis, Thomas; Armagh.
19 Daye, Andrew; Queens Co.
18 Dealy, John; Wexford.
7 Deek, Agnes; Ballynahinch.
7 Deek, James, Ballynahinch.
11 De Hart, Edward.
19 Delany, Thomas; Wexford.
8 Denvant, Michael.
9 Deolin, Arthur; Cullsalag.
9 Deolin, Daniel; Banbridge.
24 Derragh, Eliza; Kilrea.
24 Derragh, Ellen (child); Kilrea.
24 Derragh, John; Kilrea.
11 Devan, Francis.

11 Devan, Francis.
30 Dever, Edward, and family.
31 Devilt, James.
31 Devilt, Thomas.
18 Devine, Michael; Co. Louth.
36 Devlin, Sally.
20 Dick, John.
26 Dickey, James.
26 Dickey, Nathaniel.
26 Dickey, Samuel.
20 Dickson, J., and family.
22 Dickson, John.
33 Divin, Patrick; Ballyshannon.
6 Divine, William; Tallow.
14 Dixon, Mary Ann.
9 Dixon, Joanna; Dungannon.
9 Dixon, Thomas; Dungannon.
14 Dixon, Thomas.
33 Doak, David; Fannit.
2 Dobbin, Mrs.; Killeman, Down.
2 Dobbin, Leonard; Killeman, Down.
21 Dogherty, Biddy.
21 Dogherty, Cathar.
21 Dogherty, Dennis.
21 Dogherty, Edward; Carrowkeel.
21 Dogherty, George.
21 Dogherty, Isaac.
21 Dogherty, Mary.
21 Dogherty, Mary.
21 Dogherty, Philip.
14 Doholy, Edward.
14 Dolonson, Hugh, and family.
33 Donaghey, Ann; Roeman.
21 Donaghey, Barney.
21 Donaghey, Pat.
8 Donaghy, Ar.
33 Donaghy, John; Rushey.
13 Donald, Barney.
13 Donald, Eleanor.
13 Donald, Michael.
4 Donaldson, Thomas; Cupar.
8 Donell, Jane.
15 Donnell, Elizabeth; Armagh.
4 Donnelly, William; Belfast.
34 Doorish, Bernard.
16 Dougherty, Abigail.
31 Dougherty, Anthy.
31 Dougherty, Cath.
13 Dougherty, Dudly.
31 Dougherty, Henry.
8 Dougherty, James.
8 Dougherty, John.
21 Dougherty, John.
14 Dougherty, Neal.
14 Dougherty, Philip.
16 Dougherty, Thos.
14 Dougherty, William.
11 Douglass, Joseph.
16 Douglass, Joseph.
33 Douglass, Joseph; Kilrea.
5 Douglass, Robert; Ballymena.
17 Dove, Edward.
16 Doyle; Catherine.
32 Doyle, David; Dublin.
32 Doyle, Dennis; Dublin.
18 Doyle, John; Wexford.
18 Doyle, Michael; Wexford.
3 Drain, John; Co. Armagh.
3 Drain, Henry; Co. Armagh.
10 Drake, Henry.
10 Dreison; Anah.
21 Duddy, Henry.
21 Duddy, William.
1 Duffy, James; Co. Cavan.
13 Duffey, John.
1 Duffy, Fargus; Co. Monaghan.
1 Duffy, Owen; Co. Monaghan.
1 Duffy, Francis; Co. Monaghan.

17 Dunn, John.
16 Duncan, Margaret.
6 Dunnahough, Thomas; Narragh.
19 Durham, James; Dublin.
19 Durham, Margaret; Dublin.
21 Dury, John.
21 Duvas, Terance.

E

25 Eakens, Sarah.
25 Eakins, Margaret.
25 Eakins, Margaret, Jr.
25 Eakins, Rosannah.
18 Echard, George.
16 Edmondson, James.
19 Edwards, G., and family, Dublin.
22 Egar, Jane.
14 Elliot, William.
30 Elliott, Archibald, and family.
20 Emerson, Mrs., and family.
15 English, James; Downpatrick.
3 English, Robert; Scotland.
37 English, Thomas, and family.
19 Erraty, M., and family; Kilkenny.
21 Espy, Sarah.
35 Evans, Samuel.
9 Evart, David; Cullsalag.
9 Ewart, John; Moreyrea.

F

9 Fair, Ann; Saint Clair.
9 Fair, James; Saint Clair.
9 Fair, Thomas; Saint Clair.
13 Fanan, John.
13 Fanen, John.
13 Faren, Thomas.
25 Farland, Margaret.
1 Farley, Terrence; Co. Cavan.
12 Farren, Felix; Dungannon.
12 Farren, James; Dungannon.
12 Farren, Sally; Dungannon.
16 Fee, James.
16 Fee, Patrick.
3 Fendlay, Napshall; Lisburn.
15 Ferguson —; Belfast.
20 Ferguson, Hugh.
3 Ferris, Charles; Armagh.
5 Ferris, James; Banbridge.
35 Ferris, Margaret, and family.
30 Ferry, Maurice.
18 Field, John; Dublin.
16 Fife, James.
12 Finlay, John; Monaghan.
21 Finnegan, Ann.
18 Finney, Matthew; Wexford.
18 Finney, Patrick; Wexford.
1 Fitzgerald, John; Dublin.
19 Fitzgerald, Morris; Dublin.
22 Fitzimmons, Andrew.
22 Fitzsimons, John.
19 Fitzpatrick, T., and family; Cavan.
19 Fitzpatrick, Wm.; Queens Co.
16 Flanagan, Patrick.
18 Flanery, M., and family; Tipp.
35 Flanigan, John.
35 Flanigan, Patrick.
11 Fleman, Betsy.
11 Fleman, Joseph.
20 Flemming, Wm.
13 Fletcher, John.
1 Floughsby, Wm.; Dublin.
21 Floyd, John.
33 Flyn, Luke; Co. Cavan.
6 Foaley, Patrick; Lismore.

6 Fogerty, James; Dungarvan.
16 Folhall, Laurin.
17 Folly, Peter.
12 Forcade, William, and family; Belfast.
18 Forley, Patrick; Cavan.
5 Forsyth, John; Banbridge.
5 Forsyth, Mary; Banbridge.
5 Forsyth, Robert; Banbridge.
5 Forsyth, Robert; Banbridge.
5 Forsyth, Sarah; Banbridge.
5 Forsyth, Valentine; Banbridge.
14 Foster, James.
14 Foster, John.
14 Foster, John.
14 Foster, Margaret.
14 Foster, Mary.
6 Fowey, Thomas; Castlelyons.
2 Francis, Martha; Drumaul.
2 Francis, Wm.; Drumaul.
10 Frasier, James.
10 Frasier, Robert.
8 Freeborn, Thomas, and family.
34 Freeland, Wm.
6 Freeman, Samuel; Waterford.
33 Froster, Patrick; Strabane.
24 Fullam, Ann; Magherafelt.
24 Fullam, James; Magherafelt.
12 Fullan, Eliza; Lisburn.
12 Fullan, Sealton; Lisburn.
35 Fuller, Lucy.
11 Fulton, John, and family.
12 Fulton, John; Lisburn.
21 Fulton, Thomas.
8 Funston, Andrew.
1 Furlong, Edward; Co. Wexford.

G

34 Gaffin, James.
31 Gallaugher, Cath.
31 Gallaugher, Chas.
31 Gallaugher, Hugh.
31 Gallaugher, Mary.
31 Gallaugher, Mich.
31 Gallaugher, Patk.
31 Gallen, Biddy.
31 Gallen, Catherine.
31 Gallen, Hugh.
31 Gallen, James.
31 Gallen, Mary.
31 Gallen, Mary.
31 Gallen, Margaret.
31 Gallen, Owen.
31 Gallen, Owen.
31 Gallen, Sally.
9 Gallery, Eliza; Moreyrea.
9 Gallery, James; Moreyrea.
6 Gallivan, Bridget; Cappoquin.
5 Gamble, Bell; Ballybay.
5 Gamble, Eliza; Ballybay.
5 Gamble, George; Ballybay.
5 Gamble, James; Ballybay.
7 Gamble, James; Ballinahinch.
5 Gamble, John; Ballybay.
5 Gamble, Joseph; Ballybay.
9 Gamble, Samuel; Ballinahinch.
5 Gamble, William; Ballybay.
3 Garvin, Patrick; Lisburn.
21 Gatt, James.
12 Gatt, William; Dungannon.
7 Gelison, Samuel, and family; Down.
9 Gelston, James; Cumber.
16 Genagal, Mary.
31 George, Adam.
20 George, Alexander,
9 George, Andrew; Killead.

20 George, Eliza.
26 George, John.
14 George, John, and family.
35 George, John, and family.
20 George, M.
9 George, Martha; Killead.
9 George, William; Killead.
14 George, William, and family.
18 Gerighaty, Owen; Meath.
34 Getty, James.
32 Gibbons, William; of Ohio.
16 Gibson, Andrew.
22 Gibson, David.
22 Gibson, Robert.
22 Gibson, William, and family.
17 Gilbert, Ann.
17 Gilbert, John.
17 Gilbert, Joseph.
17 Gilbert, Mary Ann.
1 Giles, John; Baillieboro.
16 Gillaspie, James.
13 Giller, Jacob.
14 Gillespie, Fanny.
33 Gillespie, Francis; Ballyshannon.
14 Gillespie, Michael.
8 Gilmer, Samuel.
22 Gilloe, Alexander.
31 Gilmour, John.
14 Given, James.
14 Given, John.
14 Given, Margaret.
36 Givun, John.
22 Glasgau, John.
13 Glass, Alex.
13 Glass, Isabella.
5 Glass, James; Belfast.
9 Glass, John; Grable.
16 Glen, Samuel.
24 Glenfuld, Edward; Lisburn.
21 Glinchy, John.
13 Golley, Dominick.
5 Gordon, Easter; Banbridge.
20 Gordon, James, and family.
31 Gordon, John.
5 Gordon, William; Banbridge.
15 Gorman, Thomas, and family; Castleblaney.
11 Grabbin, Peter.
34 Grady, George, and niece.
8 Graham, Cath., and family.
17 Graham, James.
33 Graham, John; Kilrea.
28 Gray, Elizabeth; Armagh.
28 Gray, George; Armagh.
27 Gray, James; Co. Antrim.
28 Gray, Jane.
28 Gray, Jane; Armagh.
25 Gray, John.
28 Gray, John; Armagh.
28 Gray, Samuel; Armagh.
28 Gray, Walter; Armagh.
28 Gray, William; Armagh.
7 Green, Sally; Lurgan.
18 Gregory, John; Co. Louth.
18 Gregory, M., and family; Meath.
2 Grendle, Robert; Kilmore; Armagh.
2 Grendle, Sarah; Kilmore, Armagh.
8 Grey, James.
31 Griffeth, Biddy.
31 Griffeth, Rose.
31 Griffin, Daw; Fannit.
21 Griffith, Jane.
21 Griffith, Mary.
21 Griffith, Robert.
26 Grimes, James.
12 Gruir, John, and family; Belfast.
6 Guess, James; Borrisokane.

20 Guiy, Margaret.
20 Guiy, Mary.
18 Gunea, Susan; Dublin.
6 Gunn, John; Castlereagh.
7 Gurley, John, and family; Co. Down.
24 Gurry, John, and wife; nigh Downpatrick.

H

13 Hagerty, Daniel.
13 Hagerty, Michael.
13 Haggerty, Mary.
1 Hales, Thomas; Glasstown.
30 Hall, Alexander.
7 Hall, Hobert, and family; Belfast.
14 Hall, John.
30 Hall, Robert.
20 Hall, Samuel.
19 Hallugan, Richard; Co. Louth.
8 Hamard, Michael.
8 Hamill, John.
31 Hamill, John.
16 Hamilton, Charles.
9 Hamilton, Conway; Molany.
16 Hamilton, Daniel.
8 Hamilton, Edw.
9 Hamilton, Elizabeth; Molany.
8 Hamilton, John.
7 Hamilton, John; Hillsboro.
9 Hamilton, Margaret; Molany.
7 Hamilton, Mary; Hillsboro.
31 Hamilton, Robert.
5 Hamilton, Robert; Cumber.
5 Hamilton, Thomas; Antrim.
28 Hamilton, Thomas; Connors.
16 Hamilton, Wm.
8 Hanagan, Denis
31 Hanlan, John.
8 Hanlan, Margaret, and family.
29 Hannah, James, and family.
14 Hanshaw, David.
23 Harding, Charles; Cork.
17 Harding, William, and wife.
14 Harkin, Hugh.
18 Harman, Bridget; Co. Louth.
20 Harper, Catherine.
20 Harper, Jane.
20 Harper, Joseph.
20 Harper, Richard.
35 Harpur, James.
20 Harris, Mary.
20 Harris, Samuel.
28 Harris, Thomas; Banbridge.
9 Harrison, Jane; Cairn.
2 Harrison, John; Aghaderg.
2 Harrison, Mary; Aghaderg.
9 Harrison, Thomas; Cairn.
32 Harrold, James; Dublin.
21 Harshaw, John.
11 Harshaw, John, and family.
21 Harshaw, Margaret.
21 Harshaw, William.
9 Harshaw, William; Down.
20 Hartley, Wm.
14 Harver, Edward.
16 Harvey, David.
2 Harvey, Robert; Blaris, Down.
2 Harvey, Mrs.; Blaris, Down.
7 Hasby, Robert; Maze.
6 Haskett, Massy; Borrisokane.
6 Haskett, Richard; Borrisokane.
21 Haslam, Margaret.
21 Haslam, William.
33 Hasting, Elizabeth; Co. Cavan.
13 Haughey, Benjamin.
13 Haughey, Peter.

12 Hawthorn, Agnes; Ballikeel.
34 Hawthorn, David, and family.
12 Hawthorn, John; Ballikeel.
20 Hayson, Susanna.
12 Hazleton, Edward; Down.
13 Hazleton, John.
1 Hearn, Thomas; New York.
26 Hector, Robert.
33 Hemphill, John and family; Dugh Bridge.
10 Henderson, James, and family.
30 Henderson, John.
21 Henderson, Marg.
21 Henderson, Robert.
30 Henderson, S.
21 Henderson, William.
11 Henrietta, Frances.
11 Henrietta, Francis.
20 Henry, Augustus.
5 Henry, John; Rathfriland.
22 Henry, Michael, and family.
33 Henry, Robert; Coleraine.
13 Henry, William.
12 Heran, Martha; Loughbrickland.
12 Herker, James; Belfast.
12 Heson, William; Carmery.
11 Hetherton, Betsy.
13 Hickings, Patrick.
13 Hickings, William.
33 Hilton, John; Gawagh.
14 Hinds, John.
7 Hinds, Richard, and family; Dromore.
12 Hodgsdon, John; Down.
22 Hodgson, Thomas.
35 Holland, Henry, and family.
18 Horan, John; Kings Co.
18 Horan, John; Tipperary.
1 Horan, Simon; Mullicash.
14 Huges, John.
24 Hughes, Arthur; Belfast.
3 Hughes, Jas.; Dublin.
11 Hughes, John.
28 Hughes, John; Bangor.
3 Hughes, Peter; Ballybay.
10 Hughes, Richard, and family.
17 Huges, Robert, and family.
10 Hun, Rachel.
14 Hunter, Ann.
33 Hunter, David; Omagh.
16 Hunter, Eleanor.
31 Hunter, Gerard.
16 Hunter, James.
11 Hunter, John.
31 Hunter, John.
33 Hunter, John; Newtownlimavaddy.
31 Hunter, Martha.
31 Hunter, Mary.
26 Hunter, Moses.
14 Hunter, Robert.
33 Hunter, Robert; New York.
11 Hunter Samuel, and family.
30 Hunter, Thomas.
16 Hunter, Wm.
20 Hurley, J.
20 Hurley, Wm.
14 Hutchin, John, Jr.
33 Hutchinson, Thomas; Kilrea.
20 Hutchison, Wm.
8 Hutton, John.

I

31 Irvine, Andrew.
31 Irvine, John.
12 Irvine, Samuel and family; Dungannon.
5 Irwine, George; Waringstown.
5 Irwine, George; Waringstown.
5 Irwine, Rachel; Waringstown.

J

33 Janga, Neal; Castlefin.
33 Jack, John; Co. Antrim.
22 Jackson, Mary.
25 Jackson, John.
20 Jameson, John.
9 Jamison, Agnes; Killinchy.
9 Jamison, Samuel; Killinchy.
35 Jeffrys, John, and family.
34 Jackson, Luke.
2 Jenkinson, Mrs.; Loughwall.
2 Jenkinson, Ann; Loughgall.
2 Jenkinson, Elizabeth; Loughgall.
2 Jenkinson, Isaac; Loughgall.
2 Jenkinson, Isaac; Loughgall.
2 Jenkinson, James; Loughgall.
9 Johnson, David; Antrim.
9 Johnson, Elizabeth, Antrim.
9 Johnson, Elizabeth; Hillsboro.
9 Johnson, Elnor; Antrim.
9 Johnson, Hugh; Hillsboro.
10 Johnson, James.
9 Johnson, John; Antrim.
13 Johnson, Samuel.
33 Johnston, Francis; Pettigo.
10 Johnston, Henry, and family.
25 Johnston, John.
33 Johnston, Robert; Pettigo.
8 Jolly, Patterson.
34 Jones, John.
18 Justin, Martin; Queens Co.

K

36 Kain, Percival.
30 Kane, Charles, and family.
21 Kane, Eliza.
20 Kane, Francis, and family.
1 Keally, Patrick; Dublin.
6 Keane, Margaret; Cork.
6 Kearceay, John; Lismore.
6 Kearceay, Margaret; Lismore.
6 Kearceay, Thomas; Lismore.
9 Kearns, Elizabeth; Aghada.
9 Kearns, James; Aghada.
6 Kearney, Francis; Birr.
6 Kearney, Michael; Borrisokane.
8 Kearny, Patrick.
11 Keating, Abraham.
18 Keating, John; Dublin.
18 Keating, Mary, Dublin.
20 Keenan, Dennis.
20 Keenan, Hugh.
11 Kell, John.
33 Kelly, Catherine; Fennit.
33 Kelley, Daw; Ballintrea.
33 Kelley, John; Ballybofey.
36 Kelley, Philip.
1 Kelly, Darby; Co. Meath.
19 Kelly, Michael; Drogheda.
12 Kelly, Molly; Dungannon.
14 Kelly, Neal.
27 Kelly, Patrick; Dublin.
14 Kelly, Robert.
12 Kelly, Thomas; Dungannon.
37 Kench, Richard.
4 Kenmaer, Andrew; Broomhedge.
2 Kennedy, Mrs. J.; Donaghmore, Tyrone.
7 Kennedy, James; Halls Mill.
7 Kennedy, Rachel; Banford.
7 Kennedy, Robert; Banford.
10 Kennedy, Thomas.
29 Kennedy, William, and wife.
18 Kenney, Catherine; Dublin.
18 Kenney, Peter; Dublin.
6 Kent, Redmond; Lismore.

10 Ker, James.
31 Kerr, Allen.
8 Kerr, Catherine, and family.
13 Kirr, Daniel.
35 Kerr, James.
13 Kerr, John.
26 Kerr, John.
24 Kerr, John; nigh Kilrea.
26 Kerr, Matthew.
24 Kerr, Rachel (wife) and 4 children, nigh Kilrea.
19 Kerwan, James; Castlepollard.
19 Ketly, Matthew; Kilkenny.
31 Kevenagh, James.
16 Key, Wm.
11 Kill, John.
14 Killy, Daniel.
18 Kinch, James; Wexford.
18 Kinch, T., and family; Wexford.
17 King, James.
17 King, Jane.
17 King, Jane, and 5 children.
17 King, Mary.
17 King, Richard.
6 Kirby, Cornelius; Cork.
6 Kirby, Eliza; Cork.
6 Kirby, Mary Ann; Cork.
33 Kirk, George; Mountcharles.
25 Kirk, P.
35 Kirk, Samuel, and family.
31 Kirkpatrick, John.
8 Kirkpatrick, Math.
31 Kirkpatrick, Wm.
13 Kirr, Daniel.
36 Knox, Dean.
30 Knox, James, and family.
28 Knox, Jane; Broughshane.
28 Knox, Jane; Broughshane.
3 Knox, Joseph; Ballybay.
28 Knox, Thomas; Broughshane.
31 Knox, Wm.
28 Knox, William; Broughshane.

L

17 Lacy, Edward.
7 Lamb, John; Maze.
8 Lambert, John.
6 Lane, Ellen; Clonmel.
6 Lane, John; Clonmel.
6 Lane, Mary, Clonmel.
17 Langer, Richard.
18 Lanigan, George; Longford.
19 Laplin, John; Kilkenny.
34 Lapsy, Nicholas.
16 Larkie, Alex.
16 Larkie, Mary.
1 Larkin, Miss W.; Co. Wexford.
16 Laverty, James.
28 Laverty, Jane; Newtownards.
28 Laverty, Hugh; Newtownards.
24 Law, Wm.; Belfast.
2 Law, William; Killinchy.
18 Lawler, Patrick; Wexford.
6 Leaky, John; Glanmire.
19 Leary, Michael; Castlepollard.
34 Leman, James.
34 Leman, Margaret.
11 Lemman, George.
11 Lemman, Mary.
8 Lenon, Henry.
1 Leonard, Francis; Glasstown.
20 Leviston, Charles.
20 Leviston, James, and family.
20 Leviston, Mary.
2 Lictson, Mary; Larne, Antrim.
2 Lictson, Thomas; Larne, Antrim.

14 Lindsay, Andrew.
30 Lindsay, David.
14 Lindsay, Isabella.
30 Lindsay, James.
6 Linnen, Luke; Cappoquin.
11 Lister, Eliza, and child.
2 Liston, Eliza; Kilmore, Armagh.
2 Liston, John; Kilmore, Armagh.
10 Little, James.
14 Little, John, and family.
10 Little, Martha.
12 Lockat, John; Down.
20 Lockery, James.
20 Lockery, Margaret.
8 Logan, Charles.
12 Logan, John; Bellikiel.
10 Logan, Mary.
31 Logan, Mary.
31 Logue, Biddy.
31 Logue, James.
31 Logue, Mary.
31 Logue, Wm.
30 Long, Thomas, and family.
31 Loughead, Cath.
31 Loughead, Edward.
33 Love, James; Donaghadee.
33 Love, Robert; Donaghadee.
7 Lowry, Robert, and family; Charlemont.
18 Lucas, Betsy; Queens Co.
28 Luke, James; Antrim.
16 Lurkie, Jane.
32 Lynch, John; Navan.
20 Lynn, Daniel, and family.
8 Lyons, Cornelius.
21 Lyons, Eliza.
21 Lyons, James.
21 Lyons, John.
21 Lyons, Joseph.
21 Lyons, Mary.
8 Lyons, Peter.
13 Lyons, Robert.
21 Lyons, Samuel.

M

10 MacAllisted, Felix.
10 MacAllisted, James.
20 MacAllister, R.
20 MacAllister, Rose.
9 MacAlpin, Hugh; Molany.
9 MacAlpin, James; Molany.
9 MacAlpin, Jane; Molany.
33 MacAlvin, Alex., & family; Co. Antrim.
14 MacAnnulty, James.
12 MacAnorney, Michael; Rathfriland.
26 MacArthur, John.
26 MacArthur, Robert.
30 MacAskin, John.
9 MacAtter, Betty; Blaris.
9 MacAtter, Mark; Blaris.
9 MacAttur, Ann; Killead.
9 MacAttur, James; Killead.
27 MacBride, James, wife and family; Co. Down.
1 MacBrien, John; Glasstown.
16 MacBrine, Jane.
22 MacBurney, Mrs.
11 MacCabe, Betsy.
11 MacCabe, James.
1 MacCabe, Patrick; Co. Dublin.
31 MacCafferty, Edw.
8 MacCafferty, Susan.
8 MacCaghy, Nath., and family.
12 MacCaird, William; Monaghan.
2 MacCance, James; Newtownards.
10 MacCane, Robert.

5 MacCartney, Eliza; Banbridge.
5 MacCartney, Ellen; Banbridge.
5 MacCartney, Hannah; Banbridge.
12 MacCartney, John; Loughbrickland.
12 MacCartney, Nancy; Loughbrickland.
5 MacCartney, Patrick; Banbridge.
5 MacCartney, Samuel; Banbridge.
5 MacCawley, Hugh; Crumlin.
9 MacCarton, Charles; Ballinahinch.
9 MacCarton, James; Ballinahinch.
8 MacCaughall, Geo.
21 MacCaughan, Alex.
19 MacClane, John; Co. Cavan.
19 MacClane, Mary; Cavan.
34 MacClean, David, and family.
22 MacClenaghan, James.
26 MacCloskey, James.
20 MacCloy, Thomas, and family.
36 MacClure, Anne.
28 MacClure, Thomas; Saintfield.
30 MacColgin, John.
13 MacColley, John.
5 MacComb, Ann; Keady.
5 MacComb, Henry; Keady.
5 MacComb, Margaret; Keady.
20 MacComb, Robert, and family.
5 MacComb, Thomas; Keady.
20 MacConaghy, Alex.
13 MacConley, John.
20 MacConnaghy, Jas.
26 MacConnell, James.
7 MacConnell, James; Hill Hall.
35 MacConnell, John.
20 MacConnell, P., and family.
7 MacConnell, Sarah; Hill Hall.
35 MacConnell, John.
20 MacConnell, P., and family.
7 MacConnell, Sarah; Hill Hall.
21 MacConstand, Esther.
13 MacConway, Edw.
18 MacCormick, Thomas; Longford.
33 MacCosker, Bernard; Omagh.
9 MacCoskery, John; Down.
31 MacCoun, Charles.
21 MacCousland, Ann.
21 MacCousland, Mar.
21 MacCousland, Mary.
33 MacCoy, Joseph, and family; Florence court.
5 MacCracken, Robert; Ballymacarret.
33 MacCready, Elinor; Gortward.
8 MacCready, John.
33 MacCready, Wm.; Gortward.
20 MacCrecan, James.
21 MacCreery, John.
31 MacCue, Daniel.
31 MacCue, Michael.
21 MacCue, Thomas.
12 MacCullaugh, John, & family; Carmery.
21 MacCulloch, Geo.
20 MacCulloch, Mary.
20 MacCulloch, Wm.
34 MacCullough, Alex.
7 MacCullough, Hamilton; Co. Tyrone.
25 MacCully, Mathew; Crumlin.
22 MacCune, Clem.
16 MacCurdy, Morgan.
16 MacCurdy, William.
7 MacCurry, Henry; Hillsboro.
12 MacCurtney, James; Loughbrickland.
33 MacDermot, Susana, & family; Derry.
36 MacDevitt, P.
11 MacDonald, Moore.
28 MacDonald, Robert; Portaferry.
17 MacDonald, William.
20 MacDonnell, James, and family.
9 MacDowl, Alexander; Ilandery.
9 MacDowl, Alexander; Saint Clair.

9 MacDowl, Elizabeth; Saint Clair.
9 MacDowl, Ezibella; Ilandery.
9 MacDowl, John; Saint Clair.
9 MacDowl, Mary Ann; Saint Clair.
9 MacDowl, Rachel; Saint Clair.
9 MacDowl, Thomas; Saint Clair.
33 MacEliver, George; Donaghdee.
8 MacElkeney, Robert
26 MacElroy, Arch., and family.
33 MacElwin, Hugh; Dromore.
3 MacElwrath, Rob't, wife and child; Hollywood.
21 MacEver, William.
19 MacEvory, John; Dublin.
30 MacEwen, John.
31 MacFaddin, Eleanor.
31 MacFaddin, Manus.
12 MacFade, Jane; Hillsboro.
13 MacFaden, John.
3 MacFall, John; Portglenone.
25 MacFarland, John, wife and family.
31 MacFarland, Wm.
30 MacFarland, Wm., and family.
14 MacFaul, Daniel.
14 MacFeely, Charles.
13 MacGanty, Edward.
33 MacGaughrin, Farguis; Donegal.
34 MacGaw, John, and family.
28 MacGaw, Robert; Stewardstown.
28 MacGaw, Thomas, Stewardstown.
16 MacGellaghan, Pat.
21 MacGill, Anthony.
8 MacGinley, Corn.
22 MacGinnis, Bernard.
13 MacGinness, D'anl.
11 MacGleeve, James.
24 MacGlonan, Ann, wife; Ballymoney.
24 MacGlonan, James; Ballymoney.
24 MacGlonan, Mary; Ballymoney.
24 MacGlonan, Nathaniel; Ballymoney.
8 MacGohey, Mary.
31 MacGowan, Philip.
16 MacGrath, James.
16 MacGrath, Marg.
30 MacGrath, Patrick.
16 MacGrath, Thos.
19 MacGrath, Wm.; Drogheda.
13 MacGrave, Marg.
13 MacGreedy, John.
1 MacGuinness, Edw.; Co. Meath.
8 MacGuire, Roger.
11 MacGurrah, John, and family.
17 MacHolland, Mich.
20 MacIldoon, Hugh.
21 MacIlroy, Charles.
35 MacIndoo, Robert and wife.
16 MacIntire, Abrm.
33 MacKagh, Nancy, Castlefin.
6 MacKardy, David; Dungannon.
31 MacKay, Charles.
33 MacKee, George; Mountcharles.
20 Mackee, James.
9 MacKee, Jane; Magradill.
9 MacKee, John; Ballynahinch.
9 MacKee, John; Magradill.
5 MacKee, Margaret, Newtownards.
5 MacKee, Patrick; Armagh.
5 MacKee, Robert; Newtownards.
5 MacKee, Thomas; Newtownards.
9 MacKelery, Jane; Moneyrea.
9 MacKelery, William; Moneyrea.
35 MacKenney, Alice.
5 MacKenny, Alexander; Bangor.
2 MacKenzie, Alex., Loughgall, Armagh.
2 MacKenzie, John: Newtownards.
2 MacKenzie, Philip; Loughgall.
2 MacKenzie, Ralph; Loughgall.

34 MacKever, Edward, and family.
35 MacKey, Daniel, and family.
6 MacKey, Ellen; Fermoy.
19 MacKey, James; Tipperary.
6 MacKey, Thomas; Fermoy.
9 MacKey, Thomas; Dunleary.
8 MacKinlay, George.
8 MacKinlay, John.
26 MacKinley, Hugh.
36 MacKinney, Eliza.
36 MacKinney, George.
16 MacKnight, Andrew.
16 MacKnight, Daniel.
16 MacKnight, David.
16 MacKnight, Jane.
16 MacKnight, Mary.
16 MacKnight, Thomas.
30 MacKnott, Robert, and family.
14 MacKosker, Hugh.
2 MacLanna, John; Derrylonan.
8 MacLary, Benjamin.
8 MacLaughlin, Ann.
8 MacLaughlin, Benj.
31 MacLaughlin, Biddy.
31 MacLaughlin, Elea.
11 MacLaughlin, P., and family.
31 MacLaughlin, Fran.
26 MacLaughlin, H.
8 MacLaughlin, Philip.
16 MacLeon, Patrick.
14 MacLoran, Neal.
14 MacLoran, Patrick.
16 MacLorten, Cather.
16 MacLorten, Terrence.
9 MacMagan, Agnes; Banbridge.
9 MacMagan, David; Banbridge.
9 MacMagan, Seragh; Banbridge.
7 MacMahan, Sarah; Dromore.
25 MacMahin, Rebecca.
10 MacMahon, Henry.
36 MacMalin, Wm.
1 MacMally, James; Co. Meath.
13 MacMannyman, John.
36 MacManus, Francis, and wife.
29 MacManus, Mary.
8 MacMenamy, Jos.
8 MacMennamy, Mgt.
33 MacMennomy, Edward; Ballybofey.
8 MacMenamy, Thos.
8 MacMenamy, Wm.
33 MacMinimim, Edward; Castlefin.
4 MacMullan, Hugh; Co. Down.
5 MacMullen, Eliza; Larne.
9 MacMullen, Eliza; Tyrone.
9 MacMullen, James; Tyrone.
35 MacMullen, John, and family.
9 Macmullen, Robert; Tyrone.
2 MacMurray, Alex; Kilmore, Armagh.
2 MacMurray, Hannah; Kilmore; Down.
24 MacMurray, Nancy, 2 children; nigh Kilrea.
24 MacMurray, Wm.; nigh Kilrea.
37 MacMurray, Wm.
4 MacMurrey, Mathew; Belfast.
11 MacMurry, Samuel, and tamily.
21 MacNeal, Frank.
31 MacNeal, Roger.
24 MacNeill, Neal; Belfast.
34 MacNeilly, John.
21 MacNought; James.
3 MacPeak, Owen; Portglenone.
30 MacPharland, widow and 2 children.
30 MacPharland, P.
35 MacQuaid, Edward.
15 MacQuillan, H., and family; Down-Patrick.
31 MacShane, Thomas.

11 MacSleeve, James.
26 MacTogert, Mrs., and family.
20 MacVay, M., and family.
33 MacVeagh, Patrick; Campsey.
5 MacWhatey, Jane; Armagh.
5 MacWhaty, John; Armagh.
5 MacWherter, Jane; Newry.
8 Madden, John.
20 Maffett, James.
16 Mages, Joseph.
5 Magell, Ekiza; Banbridge.
5 Magell, John; Banbridge.
5 Magell, Samuel; Banbridge.
16 Magis, Joseph.
7 Maguinis, Isabella; Co. Down.
7 Maguinis, John; Co. Down.
22 Mahaffy, James, and family.
7 Maharg, James; Co. Down.
36 Maitland, Wm.
24 Malcomson, John, Portadown.
6 Maloney, Margaret; Aglish.
6 Malowney, Jerry; Aglish.
6 Malowney, John; Aglish.
1 Malvin, William, wife, 5 sons and 4
     daughters; Co. Cavan.
13 Manely, Henry.
1 Manly, Joseph; New York.
13 Manely, Michael,
12 Maney, Patrick; Rathfriland.
14 Mansfield, Robert.
31 Manson, John.
7 Mark, Joseph; Dromore.
15 Marks, John, and family; Armagh.
5 Maron, Owen; Ballytrea.
8 Marshall, Eliza.
8 Marshall, Jeorge.
8 Marshall, Joseph.
8 Marshall, W., and family.
29 Martin, —, and family.
12 Martin, Andrew; Kilmore.
28 Martin, Anna; Antrim.
26 Martin, James.
4 Martin, James; Bangor.
33 Martin, James; Newtownlimivaddy.
28 Martin, Jane; Charlemont.
33 Martin, John; Newtownlimivaddy.
26 Martin, Martha.
28 Martin, Nancy; Antrim.
26 Martin, Samuel.
20 Martin, Thomas, and family.
33 Martin, Thomas; Kilrea.
33 Masterson, Ann; Co. Cavan.
33 Masterson, Edward; Co. Cavan.
30 Mathew, Patrick.
17 Mathews; Stephen, and wife.
34 Mathews, Thomas, and family.
14 Mathewson, Wil.
10 Maxwell, Wm.
16 Maze, Francis.
14 Meehan, Catherine.
14 Meehan, Owen.
20 Meckin, Jos.
18 Meeghan, Patrick; Tipperary.
17 Menieur, Dennis.
9 Mention, Agnes; Blaris.
9 Mention, Alexander; Blaris.
9 Metchon, John; Killead.
14 Michel, Joseph.
8 Miligan, Elizabeth.
36 Miller, Anne.
14 Miller, Elizabeth.
24 Miller, Matty; Dungannon.
14 Miller, Robert.
24 Miller, Robert; Dungannon.
2 Miller, Mrs. William; Ahahill, Antrim.
16 Mills, Andrew.
13 Minetes, Biddy.

13 Minetes, Francis.
30 Moffit, John.
12 Moffit, Margaret; Armagh.
20 Molineau, James.
3 Mollin, Patrick, wife and 4 children;
     Armagh.
13 Mollony, John.
16 Monegan, Francis.
30 Monoghan, Torry.
2 Montgomery, J.; Counmoney, Antrim.
22 Montgomery, Joseph, and family.
4 Montgomery, Moses, wife and 3 chil-
     dren; Killele.
22 Montgomery, Wm., and family.
12 Moore, Eliza, Dungannon.
12 Moore, Henry; Rathfriland.
11 Moore, James.
2 Moore, James; Donaghmore, Tyrone.
35 Moore, John.
11 Moore, Margaret.
12 Moore, Mary; Rathfriland.
24 Moore, Mathew, wife and 3 children;
     Strabane.
36 Moore, Robert.
12 Moore, Robert; Dungannon.
12 Moore, Thomas, and family; Rathfri-
     land.
31 Moore, William.
33 Moorhead, Samuel; Co. Antrim.
29 Moran, —, and family.
12 Morgan, James; and family; Down.
11 Morgan, Luke.
27 Morran, Andrew, and wife; Co. Down.
16 Morrison, Elizabeth.
7 Morrison, James, and family; Armagh.
7 Morrison, John; Magheragall.
16 Morrison, Martha.
5 Morron, John; Ballybay.
12 Morrow, Ellen; Monaghan.
10 Morrow, James, and family.
10 Morrow, Jane.
12 Morrow, Jane; Monaghan.
12 Morrow, Jane; Monaghan.
7 Morrow, John; Banford.
2 Mubrea, H., Newtownards.
16 Mulden, Anthony.
20 Mulholland, George.
30 Mullay, James, and family.
29 Mulony, James.
10 Munn, William, and family.
21 Murdock, M. Anne.
21 Murdock, Esther.
21 Murdock, John.
21 Murdock, John.
9 Murdough, Matthew; Moira.
1 Murphy, James; Co. Louth.
35 Murphy, John.
18 Murphy, John; Wexford.
12 Murphy, Mary; Monagher.
30 Murphy, M., and wife.
19 Murphy, Matthew; Dublin.
17 Murphy, Michael, and family.
6 Murphy, Timothy; Castlelyons.
19 Murphy, Timothy; Kings Co.
12 Murphy, William; Monagher.
6 Murry, Edmund; Aglish.
14 Murry, James.
22 Murry, James, and family.
13 Murry, Rodger.
19 Murtagh, Thomas; Drogheda.

N

17 Nailor, Wm., and family.
31 Nanson, Mathew.
1 Neall, Mathew, and wife; Co. Meath.

17 Needham, Catherine.
17 Needham, Eliza.
17 Needham, Valient.
28 Neil, Hugh; Crumlin.
32 Neil, Thomas; Dublin.
4 Neilson, Eliza'h, and 1 child; Dromore.
26 Neilson, James.
4 Neilson, James; Dromore.
7 Neilson, John, and family; Co. Down.
14 Neilson, Thomas.
14 Neilson, William.
14 Neilson, Gerard.
14 Nelson, Gerard.
14 Nelson, John.
15 Nelson, John, and family; Drumduff.
14 Nelson, William.
15 Nelson, William, & family; Drumduff.
17 Newan, Thomas.
23 Nicholas, John, and family; Doneraile.
7 Nixon, George, and family; Kilwarlin.
7 Nixon, Mary, Kilwarlin.
16 Norris, Mary.
31 Norris, Mary.
16 Norris, Robert.
29 O'Brien, Dennis.
6 O'Brien, Henry; Clonmel.
1 O'Brien, James; Co. Meath.
21 O'Brien, Margaret.
21 O'Brien, Owen.
33 O'Donnell, James; Rushey.
14 O'Neal, Felix.
8 O'Neill, John.
33 O'Neill, John; Co. Cavan.
33 O'Neill, Robert, & family; Co. Antrim.
12 O'Ray, Hugh; Belfast.
7 Orr, John, and family; Hill Hall.
26 Orr, Joshua.
35 Orr, Mary.
25 Orr, Mathew.
26 Orr, Robert.
25 Orr, William.
7 Orr, William, and family; Hill Hall.
10 Owens, John.
21 Owins, James.
21 Owins, Margaret.

P

20 Paine, Wm., and family.
4 Park, David; Belfast.
5 Parker, Catherine; Banbridge.
6 Parker, Hugh; Cork.
10 Patterson, Ann.
12 Patterson, David, and family; Down.
5 Patterson, Eliza; Bangor.
12 Patterson, George; Down.
12 Patterson, John; Ballykeel.
12 Patterson, Joseph; Down.
12 Patterson, Mary; Down.
31 Patterson, Samuel.
5 Patterson, Wm.; Bangor.
9 Patton, Edward; Grable.
9 Patrick, Robert; Belfast.
33 Paul, Eliza; Omagh.
34 Peadon, Robert.
7 Pepper, Edward, and family; Moyallen.
9 Perry, Hugh; Cullsallag.
9 Perry, Margaret; Cullsallag.
18 Phelan, Margaret; Tipperary.
17 Phelan, Patrick.
19 Phelan, Thomas; Kilkenny.
17 Phelan, William.
19 Philar, Peter; Queens Co.
9 Phillips, Eliza; Glenary.
9 Phillips, Thomas; Glenary.
13 Philson, Robert.

8 Piden, James.
17 Pierce, Patrick.
12 Pierson, Jacob; Armagh.
12 Pierson, Jane; Armagh.
19 Pigott, Mark; Carlow.
6 Pigott, Robin; Castlehyde.
5 Pinkerton, James; Killinchy.
4 Piper, Samuel; Menneyre.
1 Plaus, Isabell; Co. Longtord.
19 Platt, John; Youghal.
21 Pollock, Hamill.
13 Pollock, Samuel.
13 Pollock, William.
24 Pooler, John; Armagh.
21 Porter, Ann.
21 Porter, Bell.
21 Porter, Elizabeth.
21 Porter, John.
12 Porter, John; Billamegary.
21 Porter, Thomas.
8 Porter, William.
14 Potts, Robert, and family.
28 Preston, Thomas; Armagh.

Q

12 Quail, William, and family; Downpatrick.
27 Quale, William; Downpatrick.
26 Quigley, Martha.
34 Quin, Daniel.
28 Quin, Henry; Antrim.
34 Quin, Hugh.
28 Quin, Jane; Antrim.
28 Quin, John; Antrim.
10 Quin, John, and family.
28 Quin, Margaret; Antrim.
34 Quin, P.
14 Quin, Patrick.
26 Quinn, Charles.

R

30 Rafferty, John.
33 Rafferty, William; Garvagh.
6 Ranighan, John; Cork.
31 Rankin, Robert.
16 Raulstone, Arch.
10 Ray, Thomas, W.
1 Ray, William; Co. Cavan.
31 Rea, John.
36 Rea, William, and family.
20 Reed, David.
26 Reed, James.
30 Reed, Hugh.
20 Reed, Margaret.
20 Reid, Patrick.
9 Reid, William; Cumber.
19 Reilly, Brien; Castlepollard.
34 Reilly, Mary.
34 Reilly, Thomas.
16 Rein, John.
30 Reynolds, Wm.
19 Reynolds, Wm.; Kings Co.
9 Rhea, David; Killead.
9 Rhea, Seragh; Killead.
6 Rian, Thomas; Borrisokane.
30 Rice, Aily.
8 Rice, Edward.
6 Rice, Thomas; Cork.
1 Rigan, Bridget; Co. Wexford.
32 Riley, Mrs.; Co. Wexford.
22 Riley, Margaret.
22 Riley, Nancy.
4 Ritchie, Alx.; Bangor.

36 Ritchie, Eliz.
35 Roark, Mary.
 1 Roberts, John; Dublin.
34 Roberts, George.
12 Roberts, George; Armagh.
20 Robeson, John.
28 Robinson, Jane; Willsborough.
28 Robinson, John; Willsborough.
28 Robinson, Mary; Willsborough.
32 Robinson, Thomas, & Mrs.; Queens Co.
28 Robinson, Thomas; Willsborough.
14 Robison, Andrew, and family.
14 Robston, James.
12 Rock, James; Armagh.
12 Rock, Mary; Armagh.
31 Rodder, Michael.
13 Rodgers, John.
13 Rodgers, Mary.
27 Rodgers, Miss Mary; Belfast.
26 Rodgers, Samuel.
16 Rogers, Nathan.
36 Rogers, Thomas, and family.
19 Rorke, Patrick; Tipperary.
16 Ross, Eleanor.
 5 Ross, James; Killinchy.
16 Ross, Joseph.
30 Ross, Mary.
16 Ross, William.
 3 Ross, William, wife and 4 children; Vernersbridge.
37 Rochford, John.
16 Roulstone, Harvey.
16 Roulstone, James.
16 Roulstone, Martha.
13 Rudder, John.
13 Rudder, Patrick.
21 Russel, John.
 8 Russell, James.
10 Russell, Mary.
 8 Russell, Thomas.
26 Rutherford, John.
26 Rutherford, Mary.
26 Rutherford, Sarah.
19 Ryan, David; Tipperary.
19 Ryan, James; Dublin.
19 Ryan, James; Queens Co.
 1 Ryan, Mary; New Ross.
 1 Ryan, Patrick; Co. Wexford.
17 Ryan, Rev. Mr.
19 Ryan, Thomas; Tipperary.
19 Ryan, William; Dublin.
18 Ryan, William; Tipperary.
35 Ryers, James, and wife.

S

 6 Sadler, Hugh; Cork.
 6 Sadler, Frances; Cork.
 6 Sanders, James; Glanmire.
19 Scully, John; Borrisokane.
30 Scanlon, John.
20 Scott, A.
 8 Scott, Alexander.
12 Scott, David; Ballikeel.
 4 Scott, Henry; Cupar.
21 Scott, James.
30 Scott, James.
22 Scott, James, and family.
14 Scott, John.
12 Scott, Margaret; Ballikeel.
13 Scott, Thomas.
30 Scott, William.
19 Scully, John; Borrisokane.
11 Seave, John, and family.
 5 See, Nevin; Ballybay.
15 Seed, William; Downpatrick.

11 Seeman, Thomas.
20 Service, Robert.
11 Sewere, John.
20 Shaw, John.
12 Shaw, Margaret; Billamegary.
12 Shaw, William; Billamegary.
21 Shaw, William.
13 Shawkling, James.
12 Shee, Arthur; Rathfriland.
34 Shepherd, James.
19 Sherlock, Patrick; Dublin.
10 Sherran Thomas.
22 Shields, George.
19 Shinluig, J., and family; Antrim.
36 Sieven, Tully, and family.
26 Simon, Jane.
 2 Simpson, William; Loughgall.
 5 Sinclaire, Ame; Banbridge.
 5 Sinclaire, John; Banbridge.
 5 Sinclaire, Mary; Banbridge.
19 Sinnot, Nicholas; Wicklow.
 7 Sinton, Mary, and family; Moyallen.
31 Size, Bernard.
31 Size, Hannah.
 6 Slattery, John; Lismore.
 6 Slattery, Margaret; Cappoquin.
 6 Slattery, Peter; Cappoquin.
11 Sleeman, Jane.
28 Sloan, Jane; Doagh.
 8 Sloane, Martha.
13 Smiley, Alex.
13 Smiley, James.
 8 Smiley, John.
31 Smiley, John.
32 Smith, Mr. Cornelius; Manoch.
11 Smith, Eliza, and family.
 7 Smith, John; Ballynahinch.
 7 Smith, Susan; Ballynahinch.
14 Smith, William.
26 Smyth, George.
14 Smyth, James.
 5 Smyth, John; Downpatrick.
 2 Spiers, Mrs. John; Donegore.
 2 Spiers, James; Donegore.
24 Spratt, Hugh; Belfast.
12 Spratt, Mary; Carmery.
12 Spratt, William; Carmery.
33 Sproul, James C.; Stranorlar.
21 Sproul, John.
17 Stanhope, Henry, and wife.
19 Stanley, Wm., and family; Dublin.
10 Stark, Thomas.
13 Starr, Jeremiah.
31 Steel, Elizabeth.
 8 Steel, James.
31 Steel, Joseph.
31 Steel, Sally.
 9 Stephans, Elnor; Cumber.
 9 Stephans, Thomas; Cumber.
 9 Stephanson, John; Armagh.
19 Stephenson, Henry; Dublin.
 9 Stephenson, Samuel; Killead.
33 Stevenson, Hugh; Donegal.
14 Stevenson, John.
21 Stevenson, John.
21 Stevenson, Martha.
14 Stevenson, William.
 5 Sterling, James; Doagh.
 5 Sterling, Robert; Doagh.
 4 Stewart, Alexan.; Dunsmurry.
 4 Stewart, Andrew, wife & child; Stewarts- town.
34 Stewart, Benj.
13 Stewart, David.
34 Stewart, H.
14 Stewart, James.
 4 Stewart, Jane, Jr.; Dunsmurry.

4 Stewart, Jane, Sr.; Dunsmurry.
1 Stewart, William; Belfast.
4 Stewart, William; Dunsmurry.
34 Stewart, William.
31 Stirling, Martha.
31 Stirling, Thomas.
12 Stockdale, Jane; Downpatrick.
19 Stockdale, John; Dublin.
12 Stockdale, William; Downpatrick.
18 Stout, John; Wexford.
24 Strean, John; nigh Dromore.
8 Strong, Chr.
8 Strong, Hugh.
18 Sutliff, Edward; Queens Co.
18 Sutliff, Henry; Queens Co.
17 Sutton, William.
36 Swan, Thomas.
15 Sweeney, James; Londonderry.
8 Sweeny, Connel.
9 Sweeny, Prudence; Ballynahinch.
9 Swenny, Patrick; Ballinahinch.
9 Sweeny, William; Ballinahinch.
26 Syllyman, Billy; Killywaller.
28 Syllyman, John; Killywaller.

T

16 Tagart, Joseph.
7 Tate, James; Maze.
5 Taylor, James; Armagh.
13 Taylor, James.
5 Taylor, Louisa; Armagh.
5 Teas, Easter; Belfast.
7 Tetterton, Ellen; Banford.
7 Tetterton, Robert, & family; Banford.
1 Thomas, John; Ballyhayes.
33 Thompson, Alex, and family; Lenck.
12 Thompson, Eliza; Down.
7 Thompson, George; Belfast.
12 Thompson, George; Down.
10 Thompson, James.
16 Thompson, James.
12 Thompson, James; Down.
36 Thompson, John.
11 Thompson, John, and family.
20 Thompson, John, and family.
12 Thompson, John; Down.
12 Thompson, Joseph; Down.
10 Thompson, Marg't.
12 Thompson, Maria; Down.
4 Thompson, Robert, and wife; Belfast.
8 Thompson, Rob't.
21 Thompson, Rob't.
31 Thompson, Robert.
12 Thompson, Sarah; Down.
8 Thompson, Wm.
34 Thompson, Wm.
36 Thompson, Wm.
19 Thompson, Wm.; Philadelphia.
33 Thompson, William; Carrick.
28 Thomson, James; Lisburn.
28 Thomson, Jane.
16 Thorne, John.
30 Timmory, Edward.
13 Timons, Isabella.
13 Timons, Timothy.
21 Tonner, Catherine.
1 Toole, Emanuel; Dublin.
18 Toole, Peter; Dublin.
26 Torrers, Ann.
26 Torrers, Ruth.
26 Torrers, Samuel.
26 Torrers, Samuel.
20 Tracy, Hugh.
13 Traner, Bany.
19 Tranar, James; Queens Co.

19 Trevar, Patrick; Queens Co.
24 Trimble, William; nigh Armagh.
35 Triven, John, and wife.
17 Tuckerbury, Benj., and family.
9 Turkenton, James; Dungannon.
9 Turkenton, Jane; Dungannon.
9 Turkenton, John; Dungannon.
17 Turner, Bartlett.
17 Turner, William.
28 Tweedy, Effy; Dromore.
22 Tweedy, Patrick, and family.

V

25 Vale, John.
25 Vale, Margaret.
8 Vance, D.
8 Vance, Isaac.
14 Vimmo, Charles.
14 Vimmo, Eliza.
30 Virtue, David, and family.

W

13 Waddel, Ralph.
21 Walker, Armstrong.
20 Walker, James, and family.
11 Walker, John, and family.
28 Walker, Robert J.; Galway.
23 Wall, Mr.; Clonmel.
7 Wall, Easter, Banbridge.
7 Wall, John, and family; Banbridge.
4 Wallace, George; town of Antrim.
36 Wallace, Hugh.
28 Wallace, John; Bangor.
16 Wallace, Sam'l.
1 Walsh, Miss F.; Co. Wexford.
1 Walsh, John, (child); Co. Galway.
27 Walsh, John, and wife; Dublin.
1 Walsh, Mary; Co. Galway.
17 Walsh, Thomas.
19 Walsh, William; Kilkenny.
8 Ward, James.
33 Wardlaw, Elizabeth; Co. Cavan.
12 Warren, Hugh; Belfast.
12 Warren, Jane; Belfast.
16 Wason, Archer.
25 Wason, George
16 Wason, Jane.
25 Wason, Margaret.
33 Wason, Nancy; Ray.
1 Waters, Andrew; Co. Wexford.
21 Watson, James.
5 Watt, James; Lisburn.
28 Watt, Jane; Castlewellan.
22 Watt, John, and family.
5 Watt, Margaret; Banbridge.
28 Wattsher, John; Tyrone.
33 Wamb, John; Castlefin.
1 Weapher, Ann; Rathfarnham.
2 Welsh, John; Newtownards.
2 Welsh, Louisa; Newtownards.
25 Weltch, H.
30 West, David.
1 West, James; Glasstown.
30 West, William.
22 Wharton, Joseph, and family.
22 Wharton, Robert.
4 White, Alexander; Dromore.
12 White, James; Down.
33 White, James; N'limavaddy.
13 White, John.
35 Wilkins, George.
16 Williams, George.
30 Williams, Henry.

16 Williams, Wm.
28 Williamson, Elizabeth; Saintfield.
28 Williamson, Henry; Saintfield.
28 Williamson, Jane; Saintfield.
34 Willikin, Mary, and family.
12 Willis, Margaret; Dungannon.
28 Willis, Mary Ann; Stewartstown.
28 Willis, Mathew; Stewartstown.
12 Willis, William; Down.
12 Willis, William; Dungannon.
19 Wilson, Benjamin; New York.
 4 Wilson, Elizabeth; Dunmurry.
21 Wilson, James.
26 Wilson, John.
 4 Wilson, Robert, wife and 3 children;
     Dunmurry.
21 Wilson, Thomas.
24 Winters, Edward; Portadown.
24 Winters, Mary; Portadown.
16 Wishat, Mary.
16 Wishat, Robert.
16 Wishat, Ruth.
16 Wishat, Sarah.

16 Wishat, Sarah.
 8 Witherington, A.
19 Withers, Henry; Dublin.
 1 Wogan, Christian; Co. Dublin.
16 Woods, Adam.
16 Woods, James.
21 Woods, James.
34 Wright, Ann.
19 Wright, Catherine; Cavan.
19 Wright, Eliza; Dublin.
36 Wright, James, and wife.
19 Wright, John; Dublin.
20 Wylie, Rachel.

Y

24 Young, David; nigh Charlemont.
14 Young, Fanny.
21 Young, James.
31 Young, John.
31 Young, Mary.
14 Young, William.

LIST OF SHIPS

ARRIVING IN AMERICAN PORTS, 1811

Code No.	Port of Departure	Date of Arrival 1811	Port of Entry	Name of Ship	Master	Days on Voyage	Passengers	Point of Origin
1.	Dublin		New York	Erin	Murphy		64	Residence
2.	Belfast		New York	Harvey Hide	Thos. Parker	77	61	Parish and county
3.	Belfast		New York	Hannibal	Crawford		43	Where from
4.	Belfast		New York	Perseverance			40	Where from
5.	Belfast		New York	Protection	Bearns	40	78	Residence
6.	Cork		New York	Radius	Clark	29	63	Nativity
7.	Belfast		New York	Algernon	Clark	36	55	Residence (?)
8.	Londonderry		New York	Westpoint	Boggs		79	
9.	Belfast	May 19	New York	Jupiter	Wm. H. Hitchins		97	Residence
10.	....	May 23	New York	Orlando	Josiah Cromwell	35	37	
11.	Newry	Jun. 9	New York	Aeolus	Charles Henry		49	
12.	Belfast		New York	Africa	John E. Scott		96	Nativity
13.	Londonderry	Jun. 12	New York	Golconda			84	
14.	Londonderry	Jun. 16	New York	Alexandria	Edmund Fanning		85	
15.	Newry	Jun. 17	Philadelphia	Patty	Sawer		11	Residence (?)
16.	Londonderry		Philadelphia	Mary	Wallington	42	95	
17.	Dublin		New York	Belisarius	Morgan		58	
18.	Dublin	Jun. 2	New York	Huntress	Thomas Ronson		47	Residence
19.	Dublin		New York	Shamrock	M'Keon	34	60	Late residence
20.	Belfast		New York	Hibernia	Graham		70	Nativity
21.	Londonderry	Jly 4	Baltimore	Joseph and Phoebe	Plympton		102	
22.	Newry	Jly 8	Philadelphia	Rising State	Stilwell	60	33	
23.	Cork	Jly 14	Philadelphia	Isaac	Delano	56	4	
24.	Belfast		New York	Juno	Thompson	40	44	Residence
25.	Londonderry	Aug. 31	New York	Ann	Alex. Howland	63	27	Town
26.	Londonderry		New York	Fame	William Pollock	54	53	
27.	Belfast		Philadelphia	Maria Duplex		44	15	
28.	....		New York	Protection	Bearns		71	Residence (?)
29.	Dublin		New York	White Oak		48	12	Residence (?)
30.	Londonderry	Oct. 21	New London	Mariner	Hookirk	70	57	
31.	Londonderry	Oct. 31	Philadelphia	Harmony			104	
32.	Dublin		New York	Erin	T. Holden		12	
33.	Londonderry		New York	Westpoint	Graham		73	Residence (?)
34.	Belfast		New York	Hibernia	Fanning		37	Residence
35.	Newry		New York	Aeolus			42	
36.	Londonderry		New York	Alexander	Fanning	47	31	
37.	Belfast		New York	Raleigh			7	

PASSENGER LISTS

From "The Shamrock or Irish Chronicle," 1815-1816

Charles Montague Early

This Passenger List is a further installment of the series published in our annual volume XXVIII and from the same source, "The Shamrock or Irish Chronicle" (new series) for 1815-16. The first list proved to be of such wide interest that the present publication seems justified. Copies of the periodical are exceedingly rare and that in our possession is not in good condition. Official records of the sort were not kept till some years later and the names are not alphabetically arranged. This list forms a chapter in a book that has yet to be written on the extent of Irish immigration from the earliest time. In this circumstance the accumulation of evidence is highly desirable.

The Passenger List following covers about a year beginning September, 1815, and it includes about 3,150 names of persons from whom are descended perhaps 230,000 people living today.

The manner of presentation is the same as in the last list. Each name is preceded by a number which is also to be found in the "List of Ships" following the alphabetically arranged names. This number indicates the name of the ship, the date and place of departure and arrival for each individual wherever such particulars were obtainable from the periodical.

No less than seventy-two vessels are mentioned as having arrived at various American ports, mainly New York; from certain foreign ports, mainly Irish, with passengers having Irish names. The following list shows particulars:

EMBARKATION POINTS AND NUMBERS OF SAILINGS, 1815–1816.

Belfast	16	Galway	2	Londonderry	11
Cork	1	Halifax	2	Newry	7
Demerara	1	Lisbon	1	Sligo	5
Dublin	23	Liverpool	3	Total	72

This list does not include all Irish persons who came to America in the specified period. The list of arrivals from Irish ports is possibly incomplete and, moreover, some Irish must have come by way of Canada and also from such ports as London, England.

Many names, not generally identified as Irish, are found in the list; some are rare even in Ireland. Curred, for instance, is an unusual Sligo name. Rochford is an old Norman name frequently found in Ireland. Strean is better known as Strawn, Stratton or Strahan; it is the name of an old Tyrconnell family. Tigut may be Tuite; Wacum, Sithgon and Wantya are unidentifiable. Record is possibly the same derivation as Ricard. Burr and Strawbridge are not uncommon in Ireland. As a contribution to family nomenclature the list presents many points of interest.

A LIST OF PASSENGERS MAINLY FROM IRELAND, ARRIVING IN AMERICAN PORTS
September 1815 to August 1816
Transcribed from "The Shamrock" and alphabetically arranged

NOTE: The number preceding the surname indicates the name of the ship as shown in the "List of Ships" following the alphabetical list.

A

32 Abercromby, James.
32 Abercromby, Robert.
23 Abbott, Thomas; Lisburn.
30 Acheson, Daniel, Sen.; Letterkenny.
30 Acheson, David, Jun., Letterkenny.
30 Acheson, Mary; Letterkenny;
40 Adair, A; Kilkeel, Co. Down.
52 Adair, Wm.
53 Adams, John.
62 Aeggs, Hugh.
8 Agnew, Deckey; Ballynuse.
68 Aikin, John; Londonderry.
27 Aldwell, Samuel.
45 Alexander, Anne.
64 Alexander, Anne Jane; Co. Armagh.
52 Alexander, E.
64 Alexander, George; Co. Armagh.
64 Alexander, Harriet; Co. Armagh.
13 Alexander, Isabella.
64 Alexander, Jane; Co. Armagh.
64 Alexander, Margaret; Co. Armagh.
64 Alexander, Mary Small; Co. Armagh.
64 Alexander, Thomas; Co. Armagh.
64 Alexander, Hugh Small; Co. Armagh.
45 Alexander, James.
64 Alexander, Robert; Co. Armagh
45 Alexander, Sarah Jane.
61 Allen, Agnes.
32 Allen, Eliz.
32 Allen, George.
51 Allen, Hannah.
51 Allen, Henry S.

32 Allen, James.
70 Allen, Jane.
32 Allen, Joseph.
32 Allen, Mary.
18 Allen, Mr,; Ireland.
51 Allen, Peter.
51 Allen, Peter H.
61 Allen, Samuel.
22 Allen,Thomas; Kings Co.
40 Amact, John; Kilkeel, Co. Down.
8 Anderson, A; Coleraine.
20 Anderson, Alexander; Lettermuck.
20 Anderson, Eliza; Lettermuck.
68 Anderson, Eliza; Londonderry.
53 Anderson, James.
20 Anderson, Jane; Lettermuck.
8 Anderson, John; Coleraine.
37 Anderson, Joseph.
30 Anderson, Margaret; Derry.
8 Anderson, Mrs.; Coleraine.
48 Anderson, William.
20 Anderson, William; Lettermuck.
20 Anderson, William; Lettermuck.
68 Anderson, William; Londonderry.
37 Anderson, William, mother & brother.
22 Andoe, James; Dublin.
25 Andrews, George.
21 Andrews, Robert.
21 Andrews, Robt. Jun.
21 Andrews, Thomas.
21 Andrews, Wm. Jun.
21 Andrews, Wm. Sen.
59 Annis, Mrs,; Dublin.
71 Arcy, Patrick D.; Ballmiobe.

23 Ardis, Alexander; Antrim.
66 Armstrong, Fanny & 4 children; Cavan.
7 Armstrong, Hugh; Drumgolen.
13 Armstrong, James.
13 Armstrong, James.
33 Armstrong, James; Port Norris.
49 Armstrong, John.
16 Armstrong, Mr. & family; Ballynahinch.
52 Armstrong, Samuel.
39 Arnold, J.
22 Arnold, James; Cavan.
2 Arnold, James; Cloghen, Co. Tipperary.
22 Arnold, William; Dublin.
68 Arthur, Joseph; Antrim.
68 Arthur, Rebecca; Antrim.
28 Ash, Cath., Castleblaney, Co. Monoghan.
22 Ashley, Daniel; Manchester, England.
26 Asple, Pierce; Dublin.
61 Atcheson, Adam.
24 Atkinson, David.
16 Atkinson, Francis; Loughgall.
24 Atkinson, Jas.
33 Auchanan, John; Port Norris.
40 Austin, Rebecca; Kilkeel, Co. Down.
40 Austin, Thomas; Kilkeel, Co. Down.

B

39 Bacon, Thomas.
50 Bailie, David.
50 Bailie, Isabella.
50 Bailie, James.
50 Bailie, John.
50 Bailie, John.
50 Bailie, Mary Anne.
50 Bailie, Robert.
54 Bailie, Thomas; Ballymote.
50 Bailie, William.
48 Baird, George.
45 Baird, Samuel.
41 Baird, Washington.
55 Baland, Thomas; Sligo.
16 Ball, James; Ballynahinch.
28 Ballagh, James; Ballybay, Co. Monoghan.
28 Ballagh, Robert; Ballybay, Co. Monaghan.
28 Ballagh, Robert E., Ballybay, Co. Monaghan.
43 Bambrick, Thomas; Kilkenny.
29 Bannin, John; Co. Killkenny.
53 Bankhead, —.
48 Banks, Thomas.
2 Bannan, Peter; Drogheda.
22 Barbadge, Thomas; Dublin.
54 Barbour, Matthew; Carney.
27 Bare, Samuel.
62 Barker, Thomas.
16 Barnett, James; Ballyagherty.
16 Barnett, James R.; Belfast.
27 Barry, James Casey.
48 Barr, John.
18 Barrow, Mr.; Dublin.
2 Barry, Edward.
48 Bayley, John.
54 Beattie, Andrew; Scotland.
62 Beatty, David.
62 Beatty, Eliza.
62 Beatty, Jas.
34 Beatty, William; Co. Fernanagh.
48 Bednard, William.
59 Beerman, Thomas; Queen's County.
16 Beggs, James; Tullyleck.

2 Behan, James; Co. Tipperary.
28 Bell, Abraham; New York.
16 Bell, David; Belfast.
7 Bell, George; Castlereagh.
50 Bell, H.
68 Bell, John; Londonderry.
28 Bell, Mary C.; Stramore, Co. Down.
28 Bell, Rebecca H.; Stramore, Co. Down.
62 Bell, Samuel.
62 Bell, Thomas.
28 Bell, Thomas C.; Stramore, Co. Down.
62 Bell, Wm.
59 Bennett, Thomas; Wexford.
72 Benningham, Eliza; Dublin.
72 Benningham, Thomas; Dublin.
22 Benton, Sam'l; Mountrath.
66 Bergin, Daniel; Queens County.
56 Bernard, Richard.
26 Berney, Ellen; Cavan.
26 Berney, Thomas; Cavan.
56 Berry, Francis.
56 Berry, Michael.
53 Beverly, Eliza; Scotland.
26 Binne, Thomas; Carlow.
14 Birk, John.
16 Black, Archibald; Rathlin.
67 Black, John; Rathlin.
44 Black, Moses.
31 Black, Peter; Ballybay, Co. Monaghan.
41 Blair, James.
13 Blair, Samuel.
50 Blair, Thomas.
8 Blame, William; Ballymena.
5 Blanchfield, Stephen; Waterford.
8 Bleakley, Jane; Drumbo.
8 Bleakley, John; Drumbo.
8 Bleakley, William; Drumbo.
6 Blood, David R.
28 Bloomfield, Saml; Belfast.
7 Boden, Hugh; Ballykeel.
45 Boggs, Alexander.
13 Bogle, Isabella.
13 Bogle, John.
13 Bogle, Samuel.
24 Bohan, Matthew.
68 Boke, Sohn; Londonderry.
39 Bolton, Margaret.
68 Bond, Alexander; Londonderry.
51 Borlridge, Josiah.
40 Borr, James; Portadown, Co. Armagh.
48 Borskin, George.
68 Botham, Isabella; Tyrone.
68 Botham, Robert; Tyrone.
66 Boyce, Anne; Wexford.
33 Boyd, Andrew; Camlagh, Co. Armagh.
62 Boyd, David.
50 Boyd, P.
27 Boyd, Robert.
62 Boyd, Samuel.
42 Boyd, Thomas; Co. Antrim.
53 Boyd, W.
30 Boyle, Chr.; Armagh.
14 Boyle, John, wife & 3 children.
13 Boyle, Robert.
49 Boyle, Samuel.
62 Bradford, James.
35 Bradley, James; Liverpool.
62 Bradley, John.
59 Bradley, John; Navan.
49 Bradley, Peter.
51 Bradley, Philip.
48 Bradley, William.
62 Bradley, Wm.
22 Brady, Anne; Cavan.
25 Brady, Hugh.
71 Brady, Hugh; Currefin, Co. Galway.

6 Brady, James.
22 Brady, John; Cavan.
29 Brady, John; Co. Cavan.
3 Brady, Maurice.
14 Brady, Patrick.
2 Brady, Patrick; Killeshandra.
22 Brady, Susan; Cavan.
56 Brady, Thomas.
70 Braineid, Charles.
4 Braith, William; Co. Antrim.
66 Branick, Jane & child; Dublin.
32 Brankin, Thomas.
70 Branley, Margaret.
68 Brawley, Isabella; Londonderry.
68 Brawley, William, Jr.; Londonderry.
68 Brawley, William, Sr.; Londonderry.
66 Breman, Patrick; Kilkenny.
66 Bremen, Ellen & 2 children; Kilkenny.
56 Brenan, James.
66 Brennan, Bridget; Kilkenny.
48 Brennan, Unity.
55 Brennan, Patrick; Sligo.
55 Bride, Catherine.
22 Bridges, Anne; Dublin.
22 Bridges, James; Dublin.
72 Briggs, Maria; New York.
13 Britton, William.
19 Brogan, Patrick.
13 Brooks, James.
51 Brophy, Jeremiah.
26 Brophy, Michael; Carlow.
17 Bropigan, Thomas; Ireland.
19 Brown, Andrew.
46 Brown, Ann; Tyrone.
48 Brown, Anne.
49 Brown, Bernard.
60 Brown, Edw., Dublin.
13 Brown, James.
8 Brown, James; Augnacloy.
66 Brown, James; Cavan.
33 Brown, James; Co. Down.
20 Brown, Jane; Belfast.
48 Brown, John.
15 Brown, John; Cavan.
8 Brown, John; Dennyroign.
19 Brown, Joshua.
20 Brown, Julia; Belfast.
15 Brown, Margaret & Child; Cavan.
48 Brown, Mary.
48 Brown, Mathew.
38 Brown, Patrick; Kilkenny.
48 Brown, Samuel.
20 Brown, Seth; Boston.
14 Brown, Thomas.
48 Brown, William.
48 Brown, William.
35 Browne, John; Dublin.
13 Bruce, William.
53 Bryd, James.
67 Buchan, George; Rambleton.
13 Buchanan, Samuel.
38 Budden, Nathaniel; Cavan.
50 Buher, John.
47 Burchill, William.
71 Burk, Michael; Ballina, Co. Mayo.
70 Burk, Sibby.
48 Burk, William.
35 Burke, Anne; Dublin.
24 Burke, Edwd.
71 Burke, Francis; St. Nicholas, Galway.
59 Burke, John; Dublin.
26 Burn, James; Carlow.
19 Burns, Andrew B.
13 Burns, Hugh.
54 Burns, John; Mount Temple.
41 Burns, Patrick.
13 Burns, William.

53 Burnside, Joseph & wife.
48 Burnside, Samuel.
44 Burr, John.
48 Butler, Andrew.
48 Butler, Eliza.
48 Butler, George.
48 Butler, Mary.
59 Buttersley, John; Dublin.
59 Buttersley, Mary; Dublin.
9 Butterworth, A.; Naas.
56 Buttle, Margaret.
56 Buttle, Samuel.
53 Byers, David.
52 Byers, Robert.
39 Byrne, Edward.
15 Byrne, George; Dublin.
2 Byrne, James.
27 Byrne, John.
24 Byrne, John.
35 Byrne, John; Dublin.
2 Byrne, John; Co. Tipperary.
22 Byrne, Mary & 3 children; Kildare.
43 Byrne, Michael; Carlow.
24 Byrne, Patk.
39 Byrnes, Hugh.
39 Byrnes, Mary.

C

48 Cafferty, Girzy.
48 Cafferty, Mary.
2 Caffry, Nicholas; Co. Tipperary.
48 Cain, Charles.
48 Cain, Patrick.
61 Cairns, Mary.
61 Cairns, Samuel.
20 Caldwell, Ezekiel; Derry.
29 Caldwell, Joseph; Dublin.
41 Calgan, Catherine.
41 Calgan, Mary .
20 Calhoun, James; Ballymena.
20 Calhoun, William; Ballymena.
58 Callagan, James; Kilkenny City.
48 Callaghan, Edward.
60 Callaghan, James; Balbuggan.
22 Callaghan, Margaret & 2 children; Dublin.
3 Callaghan, Patrick.
28 Calney, Mat; Ballyshannon, Co. Donegal.
22 Calshan, Catherine; Queens Co.
60 Cam, Christopher, wife & son; Balbriggan.
68 Camble, John; Tyrone.
23 Campbell, Archibald; Antrim.
61 Campbell, David.
50 Campbell, Duncan.
41 Campbell, Francis.
62 Campbell, George.
46 Campbell, James; Philadelphia.
54 Campbell, John.
53 Campbell, John.
4 Campbell, John; Co. Antrim.
8 Campbell, John; Co. Antrim.
67 Campbell, John; Enniskillen.
53 Campbell, Matthew.
60 Campbell, Thomas; Co. Tyrone.
14 Campbell, William.
41 Canigan, Michael.
54 Cannelan, John; Sligo.
71 Cannon, Bridget; Athlone, Co. Westmeath.
13 Cannon, Hugh.
44 Cannon, Moses.
71 Cannon, Robert; Athlone, Co. Westmeath.
71 Cannoughton, Patrick; Longford.

54 Canway, Catherine; Mount Temple.
54 Canway, Mary; Mount Temple.
54 Canway, Owen; Mount Temple.
68 Carabine, Catherine; Londonderry.
68 Carabine, Thomas; Londonderry.
46 Carey, Michael; Donegal.
68 Carlan, Patrick; Londonderry.
68 Carlan, Sarah; Londonderry.
26 Carle, John W., Limerick.
26 Carle, Michael; Limerick.
50 Carleton, J.
50 Carleton, J.
50 Carleton, M.
48 Carlin, James.
48 Carlin, John.
8 Carlin, Thomas; Co. Down.
16 Carlisle, James; Balinahinch.
16 Carlisle, John; Balinahinch.
68 Carmachy, Robert; Tyrone.
68 Carmeran, Allen; Londonderry.
68 Carmeran, Anne; Londonderry.
68 Carmeran, Elizabeth; Londonderry.
68 Carmeran, William; Londonderry.
4 Carmichael, Daniel; New York.
26 Carney, Anne; Wexford.
26 Carney, Eliza; Wexford.
48 Carney, John.
44 Carney, John.
26 Carney, John; Wexford.
26 Carney, Mary; Wexford.
26 Carney, Michael; Wexford.
26 Carney, Moses; Wexford.
26 Carney, Patrick; Wexford.
26 Carney, Philip; Wexford.
41 Carr, Elizabeth.
72 Carr, Isaac; Waterford.
53 Carr, John.
20 Carr, Nathaniel; Ballybuny.
61 Carr, Robert.
48 Carrigan, Andrew.
44 Carrigan, Patk.
55 Carroll, Mary.
2 Carroll, Rev. Michael; City of Kilkenny.
55 Carroll, Patrick.
65 Carroll, William; Co. Antrim.
55 Carroll, Tererce.
42 Carslile, Hugh; Co. Down.
49 Carson, George.
23 Carson, James; Belfast.
13 Carter, Robert.
50 Caruthers. Archibald.
50 Caruthers, Jane.
50 Caruthers, John.
50 Caruthers, M.
72 Caselly, Patrick; Armagh.
18 Casey, Mr.; Dublin.
57 Casher, Anne; Wexford.
57 Casher, Bartholomew; Wexford.
57 Casher, M.; Wexford.
57 Casher, Margaret; Wexford.
28 Cassady, Anthony; Ballyshannon, Co. Donegal.
3 Cassady, James.
67 Cassell, Patrick; Armagh.
70 Castello, John.
54 Castello, Michael; Magheraw.
54 Castello, Thomas; Magheraw.
66 Castigan, Thomas; Meath.
53 Castlewood, Hugh.
48 Cathcart, Alexander.
48 Cathcart, Catherine.
39 Catherwood, Thomas.
31 Caughey, Mary; Dramore, Co. Down.
68 Causland, William; Tyrone.
1 Cavanagh, John; Dublin.
36 Cay, James.

36 Cay, Michael.
67 Chambers, Agnes; Danaghdee.
50 Chambers, Eliza.
67 Chambers, Eliza; Danaghdee.
50 Chambers, Charles.
67 Chambers, James; Danaghdee.
67 Chambers, Margaret; Danaghdee.
67 Chambers, Margaret; Danaghdee.
67 Chambers, Mary; Danaghdee.
67 Chambers, Mathew; Danaghdee.
67 Chambers, Robert; Danaghdee.
67 Chambers, Robert; Danaghdee.
67 Chambers, Sarah; Danaghdee.
20 Chambers, Thomas II; Aughterm.
67 Chambers, William; Danaghdee.
61 Chapman, William.
42 Charters, Arthur; Co. Down.
7 Charters, John; Antrim.
50 Chestnut, C.
50 Chestnut, M.
50 Chestnut, S.
16 Chestnut, William; Coleraine.
20 Christa, Adam; Ballymena.
55 Christian, John.
61 Christy, David.
32 Christy, Elizabeth.
32 Christy, Jane.
32 Christy, John.
32 Christy, Adam.
32 Christy, Robert.
32 Christy, Robert.
43 Clancey, James; Co. Wexford.
55 Clancey, John.
72 Clancy, Robert; Athlone.
2 Clark, Charles; King's Court, Co. Cavan.
42 Clark, Hugh; Co. Down.
61 Clark, Jane.
19 Clark, John.
4 Clark, John; Co. Armagh.
33 Clark, John; Aughnamulin, Ballyhay.
61 Clark, Margaret.
61 Clark, Matthew.
68 Clark, Neil; Tyrone.
5 Clark, Richard & wife; Waterford.
47 Clark, William.
16 Clark, William; Stonyford.
21 Clarke, James.
64 Claughey, —; Co. Armagh.
64 Claughey, James; Co. Armagh.
64 Claughey, John; Co. Armagh.
64 Claughey, Mary; Co. Armagh.
64 Claughey, Sarah; Co. Armagh.
72 Clear, Mary; Kilkenny.
57 Cleary, Andrew; Wexford.
6 Clebborn, Samuel.
24 Clegg, Joseph.
41 Clements, James.
41 Clements, Margaret.
2 Clinch, James; Bailiborough.
54 Clinton, Bartholomew; Grange.
50 Cloane, W.
25 Clock, Mathw. & wife.
44 Coach, Isabella.
44 Coach, John.
44 Coach, William.
8 Cochran, Agnes; Grange.
8 Cochran, Isaac; Grange.
8 Cochran, Jane; Grange.
8 Cochran, Mary Ann; Grange.
8 Cochran, Richard; Grange.
68 Cochran, Robert; Londonderry.
41 Cochran, Samuel.
15 Codd, Edward; Wexford.
15 Codd, James; Wexford.
36 Coghlan, Bridget.
36 Coghlan, Catherine.

36 Coghlan, Catherine.
36 Coghlan, Eliza.
36 Coghlan, Mary.
36 Coghlan, Patrick.
2 Cogly, Martin; Wexford.
27 Cole, John.
14 Coleman, Robert, wife & child.
48 Colhoun, John.
67 Coling, Peter; Morrill.
48 Coll, Dennis.
13 Collins, William.
13 Collins, William.
36 Concannon, John.
36 Concannon, William.
48 Coneghan, Patrick.
47 Conerry, John.
36 Connell, Patrick.
55 Connellin, James.
70 Connelly, Mary.
5 Connelly, Peter; Waterford.
14 Conner, Edward.
6 Conner, Jeremiah.
14 Conner, John.
3 Connolan, Thomas.
19 Connoly, Right Rev. Dr.
62 Connolly, Henry & wife.
48 Connor, John.
48 Connor, Hugh.
24 Connor, John.
43 Connor, Joseph; Wexford.
24 Connor, Michl.
24 Connor, Philip.
48 Connor, Richard.
15 Conolan, Charles; Ballybay.
15 Conolan, James; Ballybay.
44 Conolly, James.
55 Conolly, John.
55 Conolly, M.
54 Conolly, Thomas; Carrick on Shannon.
54 Conolly, Thomas; Darby.
55 Conolly, William.
50 Conolly, William J.
72 Conry, Catherine; Kilkenny.
59 Conry, James; Waterford.
72 Conry, Judith; Kilkenny.
72 Conry, Mary; Kilkenny.
72 Conry, Michael; Kilkenny.
3 Conway, Hugh.
68 Cook, Jos.; Tyrone.
55 Cook, Thomas.
63 Cook, Thomas; Co. Carlow.
68 Cooke, David; Londonderry.
68 Cooke, Hugh; Londonderry.
43 Corish, James; Wexford.
56 Corkoran, Michael.
61 Cornwell, John.
8 Corry, Hugh; Cookstown.
49 Corry, James.
43 Cosgrave, James; Wexford.
62 Cosgrove, Thomas.
3 Costello, Thomas.
72 Costigan, James; Dublin.
62 Cotter, Arthur.
5 Coughlan, James; Waterford.
49 Coulta, James.
68 Coulter, John; Tyrone.
67 Covenagh, Robert; Donegal.
13 Cowan, Charles.
29 Coyle, Francis; Co. Fermanagh.
68 Craig, Andrew, Tyrone.
49 Craig, Samuel.
4 Crany, John; Co. Down.
36 Craven, John.
37 Crawford, Anne & 3 children.
48 Crawford, David.
61 Crawford, English.
50 Crawford, J.

46 Crawford, James; Donegal.
68 Crawford, James; Londonderry.
49 Crawford, John.
68 Crawford, John; Londonderry.
50 Crawford, M.
46 Crawford, Mary; Donegal.
13 Crawford, William.
8 Crawford, William; Belfast.
23 Crawley, Lewis; Dublin.
23 Crawley, Michael; Dublin.
39 Crawlon, Patrick.
50 Creighton, James.
13 Crocket, James
13 Crocket, John.
33 Crooks, James; Moneymore, Co. Derry.
68 Crosby, Robert; Tyrone.
62 Crosby, Thomas.
6 Cross, Margaret.
3 Crossan, Michael.
65 Crossen, Francis; Philadelphia.
37 Crumley, Eleanor & sister.
54 Cryan, Bridget; Aughnasare, Co. Roscommon.
54 Cryan, Catharine; Aughnasare, Co. Roscommon.
54 Cryan, James; Aughnasare, Co. Roscommon.
54 Cryan, Martin, Aughnasare, Co. Roscommon
54 Cryan, Mary; Aughnasare, Co. Roscommon.
54 Cryan, Mary; Aughnasare, Co. Roscommon.
54 Cryan, Michael; Aughnasare, Co. Roscommon.
54 Cryan, Patrick; Aughnasare, Co. Roscommon.
54 Cryan, Timothy; Aughnasare, Co. Roscommon.
70 Cullen, Allen.
7 Cullen, Mary; Mays.
4 Cumming, Hans; Co. Down.
4 Cumming, Tho.; Co. Down.
24 Cummins, Catherine.
36 Cummins, Thomas.
44 Cunnay, Thomas.
20 Cunningham, Alexander; Aughnacloy.
44 Cunningham, James.
14 Cunningham, John.
62 Curran, Peter.
48 Currant, Patrick.
54 Curred, Bartholomew; Grange.
54 Curred, Bryan; Grange.
54 Curred, Dominick; Grange.
62 Currell, Elizah.
62 Currell, Susannah.
41 Curry, Alexander.
70 Curry, Michael.
41 Curry, William.
66 Cusack, Patrick; Coothill.

D

68 Daily, Henry; Tyrone.
47 Dale, Daniel.
4 Dale, George; Co. Antrim.
47 Dale, John.
47 Dale, Samuel.
47 Dale, William.
16 Dallas, Alexander; Coleraine.
48 Dally, Edward.
3 Dalton, Henry.
5 Daly, Anthony; Waterford.
66 Daly, Bryan; Kilkenny.
66 Daly, Ellen and 3 children; Kilkenny.
71 Daly, Ellen, Parish of Kildare, Kings County.

71 Daly, Martin; Parish of Kildare, Kings County.
71 Daly, Michael; Parish of Kildare, Kings County.
68 Daly, P.; Tyrone.
71 Daly, William; Ballina, Co. Mayo.
1 Daly, Wm. George; Cavan.
19 Danaho, Patrick.
67 Danford, James; Caldatt.
67 Danford, Ralph; Letterkenny.
36 Daniel, James.
71 Dannan, John; Athlone, Co. Westmeath.
12 Darcey, Thos.; Goery.
66 Daren, Anne; Meath.
66 Davenport, Catherine; Dublin.
37 Davenport, James.
71 Davey, Cornelius; Curreigh, Co. Galway.
61 Davidson, John.
8 Davidson, William; Ballybanden.
68 Davies, John; Tyrone.
49 Davis, Henry.
39 Davis, Mary.
21 Davis, Owen.
28 Davison, Christ.; Stramore, Co. Down.
28 Davison, John; Stramore, Co. Down.
28 Davison, Sarah; Gilford, Co. Down.
28 Dawson, Hugh; Carnmoney, Co. Antrim.
52 Dawson, Robert.
28 Dawson, Sarah; Carnmoney, Co. Antrim.
7 Dawson, Washington; Belfast.
2 Deale, Francis; Granard.
48 Deary, James.
28 Deavlin, Danl., Derry.
28 Deavlin, Neil; Derry.
54 Deighan, Joseph; Dublin.
2 Delahunt, Thomas; Drogheda.
59 Delany, Nicholas, Kilkenny.
66 Dempsey, Catherine; Dublin.
7 Dempsey, John; Aghadowy.
63 Dempsey, John; Portarlington.
27 Dennisson, Richard.
48 Derlin, Anne.
2 Deroy, Edward; Dublin.
2 Deroy, James; Dublin.
67 Deulin, Wm.; Londonderry.
57 Devereaux, James; Wexford.
53 Devlin, John.
24 Devlin, Michl.
36 Dew, Thomas.
8 Deymour, William; Drumbo.
17 Deyr, John; Ireland.
50 Diamere, J.
62 Diamond, John.
53 Dickey, Samuel.
8 Dickson, David; Co. Derry.
62 Dickson, Eliza.
62 Dickson, Hugh.
62 Dickson, Jane.
53 Dickson, John.
62 Dickson, Mary Ann.
62 Dickson, Sally.
62 Dickson, Samuel.
71 Dillan, David; Ballywaslee, Co. Galway.
24 Dillon, Ellen.
24 Dillon, James.
15 Dillon, John; Dublin.
38 Dillon, Patrick; Balbrigan.
24 Dillon, Richard.
70 Discord, J.
46 Diver, Edward; Donegal.
48 Diver, George.
48 Diver, Mary.

41 Diver, Patrick.
48 Diver, Sidney.
48 Diver, Susan.
48 Diver, William.
43 Dixon, Catherine; Co. Wexford.
37 Dixon. John.
13 Doak, Margaret.
13 Doak, Michael.
7 Dobson, Fanny; Moy.
7 Dobson, James; Moy.
7 Dobson, John; Moy.
7 Dobson, Mary; Moy.
7 Dobson, Susan; Moy.
7 Dobson, William; Moy.
52 Doffin, Wm.
41 Dogherty, Anne.
48 Dogherty, Michael.
48 Doherty, Anne.
61 Doherty, Anthony.
41 Doherty, Bryan.
8 Doherty, Catherine; Belfast.
8 Doherty, Catherine; Belfast.
54 Doherty, Charles; Coothall, Co. Roscommon.
48 Doherty, David.
48 Doherty, Daniel.
8 Doherty, Daniel; Belfast.
48 Doherty, Hugh.
48 Doherty, John.
68 Doherty, Maria; Londonderry.
8 Doherty, Mary; Belfast.
48 Doherty, Michael.
48 Doherty, Philip.
48 Doherty, William.
51 Doly, Arthur.
51 Doly, Altha.
51 Doly, Jane.
51 Doly, Henrietta.
51 Doly, Henrietta.
51 Doly, Maria.
48 Donaghe, Henry,
13 Donaghy, Anne.
13 Donaghy, Anne.
13 Donaghy, John.
49 Donnell, Daniel.
48 Donnell, James.
48 Donnelly, James.
28 Donnelly, John; Stuartstown, Co. Tyrone.
48 Donnelly, Patrick.
48 Donnelly, Robert.
63 Donoher, Simon; Co. Kildare.
1 Donohoo, James, Co. Meath.
68 Doogan, John; Tyrone.
5 Dooling, Michael; Waterford.
56 Dooney, John.
22 Doran, Paul; Wexford.
20 Dougherty, Bridget; Derry.
20 Dougherty, James; Derry.
46 Dougherty, John; Donegal.
37 Dougherty, William.
7 Douglass, Andrew; Belfast.
20 Douglass, James, Derry.
20 Dowe, Thomas; Aughterm.
72 Dowling, Michael; Kilkenny.
15 Downey, Michael; Dublin.
22 Doyle, Eliza and child; Dublin.
35 Doyle, John; Co. Wexford.
35 Doyle, Margaret; Co. Wexford.
35 Doyle, Martin; Strabane.
22 Doyle, Moses; Wexford.
42 Doyle, Patrick; Co. Down.
22 Doyle, Patrick; Wexford.
15 Doyne, Charles; Dublin.
62 Drain, John.
62 Drain, Richard.
16 Dripps, James; Maghera.

12 Dudley, Margaret; Roscrea.
4 Duff, Eliza; Co. Tyrone.
43 Duff, Jane; Dublin.
43 Duff, John; Dublin.
43 Duff, Margaret; Dublin.
8 Duff, Samuel; Co. Tyrone.
43 Duff, Thomas; Dublin.
37 Duffin, Anne.
71 Duffy, Charles; Coldaragh.
48 Duffy, Fanny.
71 Duffy, John; Parish of Kildare, Kings County.
72 Duffy, Mary and child; Carrickmacross.
48 Duffy, Patrick
48 Duffy, Patrick.
35 Duffy, Peter; Dundalk.
24 Duigan, Anne.
24 Duigan, Bridget.
24 Duigan, Eliza.
24 Duigan, Wm.
27 Duncan, Richard.
8 Duncan, William; Magherafelt.
27 Duneen, Daniel.
63 Duney, Robert; Co. Carlow.
57 Dunn, Elizabeth; Kings County.
57 Dunn, Mary; Kings County.
57 Dunn, Mathew; Kings County.
57 Dunn, Peter; Kings County.
57 Dunn, William; Kings County.
72 Dwyer, John; Kilkenny.
21 Dycle, John.
21 Dycle, Robert.

E

70 Eagan, Patrick.
68 Eager, Robert; Tyrone.
70 Earrie, Edward.
55 Edwards, Richard; Drimshambo.
5 Egan, Thomas; Waterford.
41 Elder, James.
48 Elder, John.
9 Elliot, J.; Dublin.
31 Elliot, Rev. Robert.
59 Ellis, Bartholomew; Dublin.
59 Ellis, Joseph; Dublin.
4 Ellison, John; Belfast.
46 Elliston, Robert; Donegal.
63 Elms, James; Co. Carlow.
60 Ennis, George; Enniscorthy.
6 Ennis, Mark.
28 Erwin, James; Ballybay, Co. Monaghan.
19 Erwin, John.
19 Erwin, Mary.
19 Erwin, Mary.
25 Evans, Wm.
7 Everitt, William; Belfast.
56 Evins, Samuel.
10 Ewing, Alexander D.; Londonderry.

F

15 Fagan, Michael; Dublin.
36 Fahey, Garrit.
36 Fahey, Mary.
36 Fahey, Tim. T.
71 Fahy, Andrew; Leitrim.
23 Fair, Alexander; Dublin.
3 Faley, Thomas.
66 Faley, William; Queens County.
70 Falin, Mary.
70 Fallan, William.
56 Farley, Owen.
28 Farmer, John; Belfast.
19 Farms, Ellen.
19 Farms, Mary.

19 Farms, Robert.
71 Farrel, Anne; Athlone, Co. Westmeath.
66 Farrel, Edward; Dublin.
35 Farrell,—; Philadelphia.
2 Farrell, Miss; Drogheda.
23 Farrell, Ellen; Tyrone.
56 Farrell, Peter.
9 Farrell, Richard; Co. Meath.
72 Farrell, William James; Dublin.
44 Faulkender, Patk.
19 Fax, Peter.
28 Fay, James; Castleblaney, Co. Monaghan.
1 Fay, Luke; Navan.
49 Fay, Patrick.
42 Fearis, Catherine; Co. Down.
42 Fearis, John; Co. Down.
42 Fearis, John; Co. Down.
42 Fearis, Margaret; Co. Down.
42 Fearis, Margaret; Co. Down.
42 Fearis, Mary; Co. Down.
46 Fee, Hugh; Donegal.
70 Feeney, Martin.
54 Feeny, Michael; Magheraw.
2 Fegan, Nich. & wife; Castle Pollard.
24 Fegan, Richd.
58 Fennely, Patrick; Kilkenny City.
25 Fenton, Geo.
46 Fergue, Eliza; Donegal.
46 Fergue, James; Donegal.
3 Ferguson, Charles.
54 Ferguson, Eleanor; Drumcliff.
62 Ferguson, Eliza.
54 Ferguson, Edward; Drumcliff.
67 Ferguson, James; Londonderry.
4 Ferguson, John; Co. Down.
54 Ferguson, John; Drumcliff.
62 Ferguson, Mary Ann.
13 Ferguson, Mathew.
62 Ferguson, Sally.
62 Ferguson, Susannah.
62 Ferguson, William & wife.
40 Ferris, David; Newry.
62 Ferris, James.
13 Fevry, Hugh.
15 Field, John; Dublin.
61 Fife, John.
61 Fife, Mary.
6 Finegan, Thomas.
4 Fingusin, Michael; Co. Tyrone.
33 Finigan, Hugh.
59 Finigan, James; Dublin.
40 Finigan, Matthew; Drogheda.
54 Finlan, Bridget; Mount Temple.
54 Finlan, James; Mount Temple.
54 Finlan, John; Mount Temple.
54 Finlan, Mary; Mount Temple.
54 Finlan, Mary; Mount Temple.
54 Finlan, Owen; Mount Temple.
54 Finlan, Patrick; Mount Temple.
48 Finlay, Charles.
38 Finn, James; Dublin.
41 Fisher, Hugh.
53 Fisher, James, wife & 5 children.
41 Fisher, Margaret.
41 Fisher, Michael.
19 Fitzgerald, John.
19 Fitzgerald, Mary.
16 Fitzgerald, Matthew; Larne.
14 Fitzgerald, Thomas.
26 Fitzgerald, Thomas; Queens County.
25 Fitzpatrick, Bernd.
56 Fitzpatrick, Daniel.
26 Fitzpatrick, Dennis; Queens County.
26 Fitzpatrick, Edmund; Kilkenny.
26 Fitzpatrick, James; Dublin.
26 Fitzpatrick, Mary Ann; Queens Co.

26 Fitzpatrick, Sally; Queens County.
26 Fitzpatrick, Terence; Cavan.
26 Fitzpatrick, Thomas; Queens County.
38 Flaherty, Margaret; Dublin.
13 Flaherty, Patrick.
54 Flanagan, Dominick; Mullaghmore.
24 Flanagan, Patrick.
39 Flanagan, Patrick.
71 Flanagan, Samuel; Parish of Kildare, Kings County.
56 Flemming, William.
51 Flinn, James.
30 Flinn, William; Banbridge.
5 Flood, Daniel; Waterford.
4 Flood, Samuel; Derry.
29 Flurn, Pack; Dublin.
59 Flushing, Eleanor; Carlow.
59 Flushing, George; Carlow.
59 Flushing, John; Carlow.
27 Flyn, James.
55 Flynn, Hugh; Ballifarnan.
38 Flynn, John; Balbrigan.
38 Flynn, John, Jun.; Balbrigan.
54 Flynn, Joseph; Drumahare.
38 Flynn, Mary; Balbrigan.
55 Foley, Anne; Sligo.
54 Foley, William; Mount Temple.
70 Folin, Bryan.
68 Forbes, Fanny; Tyrone.
68 Forbes, Jane; Tyrone.
68 Forbes, John; Tyrone.
68 Forbes, William, Junr.; Tyrone.
68 Forbes, William, Senr.; Tyrone.
27 Forest, John.
8 Forsyth, George; Magherafelt.
13 Forsyth, James.
35 Fortune, Patrick; Co. Wexford.
8 Foster, —; Belfast.
9 Foster, John; Co. Tyrone.
13 Frame, John.
23 Francis, Miss Day; Liverpool.
23 Francis, Joseph Day; Bath, England.
23 Francis, Redmond Day; Liverpool.
15 Frayne, James; Dublin.
15 Frayne, William; Dublin.
7 Frazer, Eliza; Belfast.
7 Frazer, Jane; Belfast.
7 Frazer, John; Belfast.
7 Frazer, Joseph; Belfast.
7 Frazer, Margaret; Belfast.
7 Frazer, Sarah; Belfast.
54 Freal, Honor; Mount Temple.
54 Freal, Owen; Mount Temple.
70 Froheley, Daniel.
70 Fuman, Michael.
13 Funston, Anne.
13 Funston, Francis.
13 Funston, John.
13 Funston, Joseph.
13 Funston, Robert.
43 Furlong, John; Wexford.
57 Furlong, Mathew; Wexford.
41 Fulton, —.
41 Fulton, Catherine.
41 Fulton, Kearns.

G

6 Gafney, James.
67 Galangher, James; Letterkenny.
19 Galbraith, Anne.
13 Galbraith, Charles.
19 Galbraith, Eliza.
13 Galbraith, William.
19 Galbraith, William.
19 Galbreath, James.
19 Galbreath, Rachael.

55 Galey, Anne; Sligo.
55 Galey, Eliza; Sligo.
46 Galey, William; Tyrone
46 Galey, Wister; Tyrone.
49 Gallager, Bridget.
49 Gallager, Peter.
45 Gallagher, Betsey.
45 Gallagher, Hugh.
13 Gallagher, Hugh.
13 Gallagher, John.
45 Gallagher, Michael.
20 Gallagher, Patrick; Bellybeggs.
54 Gallagher, Patrick; Teeling, Co. Donegal.
20 Gallagher, Roger; Derry.
34 Gallagher, Thomas; Co. Sligo.
20 Gallagher, William; Strabane.
41 Gamble, James.
3 Gamel, Andrew.
29 Ganly, John; Co. Antrim.
29 Ganly, Thomas; Co. Antrim.
71 Ganner, Dennis; Asker, Co. Galway.
29 Gannan, Hugh; Dublin.
71 Gannon, William; Parish of Kildare, Kings County.
68 Ganway, Bernard; Tyrone.
7 Gardner, Arthur; Belfast.
7 Gardner, Arthur, jun.; Belfast.
7 Gardner, Debarah; Belfast.
7 Gardner, Eleanor; Belfast.
7 Gardner, Elizabeth; Belfast.
7 Gardner, Elizabeth; Belfast.
53 Gardner, James.
29 Garelan, William; Co. Cavan.
39 Garney, Michel.
7 Garrett, Hugh; Saintfield.
48 Garven, William.
13 Gault, G.
49 Gault, George.
20 Gault, Robert; Coleraine.
20 Gault, Thompson; Coleraine.
52 Gausley, Jno.
27 Geary, Patrick.
63 Geohegan, Christopher; Co. Dublin.
14 Geoghegan, Henry.
14 Geoghegan, Murtoch.
39 George, John.
54 Gereghy, Paul; Mount Temple.
67 German, Patrick; Morrill.
50 Gibbons, H.
50 Gibbons, J.
50 Gibbons, M.
69 Gibbs, John; Co. Cavan.
69 Gibbs, John; Sligo.
69 Gibbs, Mary; Sligo.
69 Gibbs, Ruth; Sligo.
46 Gibson, Ann; Tyrone.
61 Gibson, Hugh.
62 Gibson, James.
61 Gibson, James.
32 Gibson, John.
61 Gibson, Margaret.
21 Gibson, Robert.
45 Gilfillin, John.
3 Gillan, Darby.
3 Gillan, Sally.
4 Gillen, Henry; Co. Antrim.
70 Gillen, John.
54 Gillen, Patrick; Magheraw.
50 Gillespie, Eliza.
13 Gillespie, Isabella.
50 Gillespie, James.
50 Gillespie, Mary.
50 Gillespie, Mary Anne.
13 Gillilan, William.
19 Gillin, Francis.
19 Gillin, James.

19 Gillin, Margaret.
70 Gillown, Anne.
70 Gillown, Owen.
61 Gilmore, Christopher.
65 Gilmore, James; Co. Tyrone.
19 Gilmore, John.
61 Gilmore, John.
61 Gilmore, John.
40 Gilmore, Margaret; Portadown, Co. Armagh.
61 Gilmore, Mary.
61 Gilmore, Matthew.
40 Gilmore, William; Portadown, Co. Armagh.
40 Gilmore, William jun.; Portadown, Co. Armagh.
16 Gilmour, Felix; Randlestown.
48 Gilmour, Joseph.
16 Gilmour, Michael; Randlestown.
59 Gilson, John; Carlow.
53 Gitty, James.
53 Gitty, John.
17 Given, John; Ireland.
41 Given, Joseph.
61 Given, Samuel.
52 Glass, Robert.
41 Glassey, Matthew.
41 Glassey, Robert.
72 Glynn, Joseph; Co. Tipperary.
5 Godfrey, Thomas; Waterford.
5 Godkin, Henry; Waterford.
54 Golrich, Martin; Sligo.
3 Golrick, Terence.
59 Gonry, Eleanor; Waterford.
13 Goodman, Catherine.
13 Goodman, Richard.
23 Gordon, Elizabeth; Dumfries, Scotland.
23 Gordon, John; Dumfries, Scotland.
23 Gordon, John; Dumfries, Scotland.
72 Gordon, Thomas; Co. Cavan.
40 Gordon, William; Kilkeel, Co. Down.
54 Gore, Luke.
67 Gorman, Hugh; Morrill.
68 Gorman, Hugh; Tyrone.
67 Gorman, Mary; Morrill.
26 Gorman, Rev. Michael; Kilkenny.
61 Gorman, William.
68 Gormley, Bernard; Tyrone.
54 Gormley, Martin; Boyle.
69 Gorvorn, Michael; Sligo.
54 Goveran, Peter.
5 Gowan, Henry; Waterford.
37 Gowan, James.
9 Gowran, John; Dublin.
5 Grace, Francis; Waterford.
42 Gracey, William; Co. Down.
24 Grady, Wm.
31 Graham, Alexander & wife.
28 Graham, James; Carnmoney, Co. Antrim.
22 Graham, James; Westmeath.
21 Graham, John.
45 Graham, Martin.
71 Graham, Mary; Ballyfair, Co. Kildare.
13 Graham, Patrick.
71 Graham, Thomas; Ballyfair, Co. Kildare.
50 Granthorn, Henry I.
46 Gray, Ann; Strabane.
21 Gray, Henry.
49 Gray, Samuel.
8 Gray, William; Edinburg.
42 Green, Henry; Co. Down.
45 Green, James.
68 Green, James chls.; Donegal.
28 Greene, Hugh; Belfast.

66 Greenham, Mary; Meath.
66 Gregory, Bridget & 2 children; Cavan.
32 Grey, Isaac.
20 Grier, Alexander; Derry.
45 Griffiths, Henry.
48 Griswell, John.
48 Griswell, Mary.
48 Griswell, Robert.
48 Griswell, William.
51 Guirson, Robert.
70 Gunigle, James.
56 Gunn, Patrick.
62 Gurroll, Charles.
48 Guthrey, John.

H

35 Haaff, James; Co. Westmeath.
48 Hagan, Edward.
60 Hagan, James; Enniscorthy.
8 Hagan, John; Co. Tyrone.
52 Hair, John.
21 Hale, Robert.
49 Hall, William.
59 Halle, Thomas; Wexford.
57 Halpen, James; Kilkenny.
30 Halpin, Bernard; Drogheda.
52 Hamilton, Eliza.
50 Hamilton, W.
52 Hamilton, Wm.
46 Hamilton, William; Donegal.
33 Hammill, Patrick; Portadown.
49 Hammond, Hugh.
48 Hammond, Hugh.
59 Hanley, James; Tipperary.
59 Hanley, Mary; Tipperary.
22 Hanlon, John O.; Longford.
40 Hanna, Robert; Kilkeel, Co. Down.
70 Haran, Mary.
46 Harbison, Henry; Maherafelt.
7 Harbison, Samuel; Philadelphia.
20 Harcourt, Anne; Bushill.
20 Harcourt, Richard; Bushill.
56 Harding, John.
71 Hardman, Darby; Tyapien, Co. Galway.
54 Hargaden, Patrick; Grange.
68 Hargon, William; Londonderry.
48 Harkin, John.
66 Harkin, Laurence; Kildare.
66 Harkin, Mary & 3 children; Kildare.
54 Harkin, Patrick; Mount Temple.
33 Harper, Alexander; Shea Bridge, Co. Down.
32 Harper, William.
43 Harpur, William; Co. Wexford.
8 Harris, Mary; Richhill.
39 Harrison, James.
39 Harrison, Thomas.
55 Hart, Bridget.
69 Hart, Hugh; Grange.
69 Hart, Hugh; Sligo.
54 Hart, John.
9 Hart, John; Dublin.
55 Hart, Margaret.
55 Hart, Mark; Sligo.
68 Hartness, George; Tyrone.
48 Harvey, Anne.
48 Harvey, Catherine.
28 Harvey, Jacob; Limerick.
16 Haslett, Fortescue; Belfast.
68 Hassan, Alexander; Londonderry.
68 Hassan, John; Londonderry.
68 Hassen, Bryan; Londonderry.
43 Hatch, Thomas; Dublin.
41 Hawkins, Thomas.
56 Hawthorn, Bill.

43 Hawthorn, Ellen; Dublin.
56 Hawthorn, Esther.
56 Hawthorn, John.
56 Hawthorn, Thomas.
70 Hay, John.
69 Hay, John; Sligo.
49 Hay, Robert.
52 Hay, Robert.
28 Hay, William; Carrickfergus, Co. Antrim.
5 Hayden, Bridget; Waterford.
5 Hayden, Bridget, jun; Waterford.
35 Hayden, Patrick; Co. Wexford.
61 Hays, Thomas.
54 Healy, Bryan; Magheraw.
22 Healy, John; Dublin.
54 Healy, John; Grange.
70 Healy, Margaret.
54 Healy, Mary; Grange.
54 Healy, Michael; Grange.
54 Healy, Patrick; Grange.
56 Heany, Francis.
37 Heely, Mary.
13 Henderson, Anne.
13 Henderson, Catherine.
13 Henderson, Christopher.
50 Henderson, Eleanor.
13 Henderson, Francis.
47 Henderson, George.
13 Henderson, George.
50 Henderson, James.
17 Henderson, James; Ireland.
13 Henderson, Jane.
33 Henderson, John.
13 Henderson, John.
13 Henderson, John.
13 Henderson, Joseph.
70 Henderson, Robert.
13 Henderson, Robert.
47 Henderson, Thomas.
50 Henderson, William.
3 Henderson, William.
15 Henderson, William; Belfast.
13 Henderson. Williams.
27 Hendrick, Eliza.
27 Hendrick, John.
55 Henegan, James.
6 Henney, Peter.
63 Henry —, & daughter; Co. Meath.
70 Henry, Anne.
69 Henry, David; Sligo.
69 Henry, George; Sligo.
70 Henry, James W.
28 Henry, John; Cookstown, Co. Derry.
69 Henry, John; Sligo.
70 Henry, Samuel.
69 Henry, Samuel; Sligo.
69 Henry, Samuel; Sligo.
7 Henry, William; Belfast.
42 Herran, George; Co. Down.
4 Herrin, Thomas; Co. Down.
53 Hetherington, John.
53 Hetherington, Sarah & 5 children.
2 Hewett James; Killeschandra.
34 Hewit, David; Co. Antrim.
7 Hice, Eleanor; Drumgolen.
38 Hicks, Maurice; Kilkenny.
55 Higgins, John; Ballifarnan.
36 Higgins, Martin.
53 Hill, Adam.
48 Hill, Anne.
54 Hill, George; Scotland.
53 Hill, John.
40 Hill, John; Liverpool.
70 Hill, Martin.
48 Hill, Matilda.
39 Hill, Samuel.

48 Hill, Samuel.
7 Hill, Samuel; Ballycastle.
53 Hill, Thos.
25 Hobbart, Edward.
24 Hogan, Patk.
57 Holden, Edward; Wexford.
13 Holmes, George.
13 Holmes, James.
20 Holmes, John; Raphoe.
31 Holmes, Joseph; Dramore, Co. Down.
51 Hopkins, Mathew.
23 Hopkins, Samuel; Ballycastle.
20 Houston, James; Strabane.
66 Howell, John; Landaff.
15 Hoye, Patrick; Dublin.
45 Huey, Betty.
45 Huey, James.
63 Hugh, —.
59 Hughes, Charles; Dublin.
25 Hughes, Hugh.
50 Hughes, J.
45 Hughes, John.
61 Hughes, Patrick.
53 Hughes, Peter.
50 Hughes, S.
48 Hulton, Patrick.
51 Humphreys, Francis.
38 Hunt, Wilson A.; Dublin.
50 Hunter, Catherine.
50 Hunter, Charles.
68 Hunter, James; Londonderry.
68 Hunter, John; Londonderry.
68 Hunter, Mary; Londonderry.
68 Hunter, William; Londonderry.
49 Husson, James.
68 Hutton, James; Londonderry.
68 Hutton, Patrick; Londonderry.
71 Hynes, Edward; Melick, Co. Galway.

I

66 Ingraham, Thomas, wife & 9 children; Dublin.
51 Ingram, Farmer.
51 Ingram, Florena.
51 Ingram, Florena.
51 Ingram, John.
51 Ingram, Mary.
51 Ingram, Mary.
51 Ingram, Sally.
13 Irvine, Dary.
13 Irvine, Mr.
7 Irvine, James; Markethill.
13 Irvine, John.
20 Irvine, Robert; Ballindrate.
13 Irvine, William.
7 Irvine, William; Markethill.
66 Irwin, James; Coothill.
59 Ivers, Anne; Carlow.
59 Ivers, Catherine; Carlow.
59 Ivers, John; Catlow.
59 Ivers, R.; Carlow.
59 Ivers, Samuel G.; Carlow.
59 Ivers, William; Carlow.
1 Ivory, Chr., wife & child; Co. Limerick.

J

21 Jack, Robert.
68 Jackson, James; Londonderry.
64 James, Elizabeth; Castle Canfield.
32 James, Elizh.
32 James, Elizh.
32 James, Jane.
32 James, John.
32 James, John.
32 James, Joseph.

32 James, Mary.
32 James, Robert.
72 James, Thomas; New York.
32 James, William.
 8 Jameson, Andrew; Grey Abbey.
50 Jameson, B.
 4 Jameson, Hugh; Co. Antrim.
53 Jameson, J. & brother.
69 Janes, Roger; Sligo.
69 Janes, William; Sligo.
40 Jacques, John J.; Monmouth, New Jersey.
 5 Jeffers, Anthony; Waterford.
57 Johnson, Catherine; Wexford.
 5 Johnson, George; Waterford.
 5 Johnson, Henry; Waterford.
72 Johnson, James; near Sheffield.
62 Johnson, Joseph.
 5 Johnson, Martha, (a child); Waterford.
 1 Johnson, Robert; Wicklow.
72 Johnson, Samuel; near Sheffield.
 5 Johnson, Sarah; Waterford.
68 Johnson, William; Londonderry.
55 Johnston, —; Sligo.
39 Johnston, Anne.
68 Johnston, Archibald; Tyrone.
55 Johnston, Elizabeth; Sligo.
55 Johnston, Francis.
44 Johnston, Gera.
55 Johnston, Jane; Sligo.
44 Johnston, Mary.
44 Johnston, Oliver.
 8 Johnston, Patrick; Ballymena.
15 Johnston, Robert; Cavan.
68 Johnston, Samuel; Tyrone.
44 Johnston, William.
13 Johnston, William.
55 Johnston, William; Sligo.
39 Jolly, Margaret.
39 Jolly, Robert.
69 Jones, Catherine; Sligo.
 9 Jones, Henry; Dublin.
22 Jones, James; Dublin.
51 Jordain, Thomas.
57 Jordan, Dennis; Wexford.
26 Jordan, Richard; Dublin.
50 Jugant, James.

K

59 Kananak, Langn, Longford.
68 Kane, John; Londonderry.
56 Kane, Patrick.
66 Kane, Robert; Leitrim.
 8 Keanen, Patrick; Richhill.
52 Kearney, Henry.
59 Kearney, James; Kildare.
59 Kearney, John; Kildare.
33 Kearney, Johnston; Armagh.
52 Kearney, Jno.
 2 Kearns, Patrick; Dublin.
66 Keating, Anne & child; Kilkenny.
66 Keating, Edward; Kilkenny
60 Keating, Hugh; Kings County.
20 Keen, Samuel; Augher.
66 Keenan, Daniel; Upperwood.
66 Keenan, Ellen & child; Meath.
66 Keenan, Thomas; Meath.
69 Keeny, John; Sligo.
67 Keer, Alexander; Newtown Stewart.
24 Kehoe, Mary.
63 Kehoe, Michael; Co. Carlow.
43 Kehoe, Thomas; Co. Wexford.
56 Keirnan, James.
28 Keith, Rebecca; Belfast.
59 Kelly, Adam; Carlow.

54 Kelly, Charles; Carrick on Shannon.
15 Kelly, Anne & child; Dublin.
48 Kelly, Dudley.
59 Kelly, Edward; Carlow.
 2 Kelly, Hugh; Banbridge.
 2 Kelly, Hugh; Cavan.
59 Kelly, Hugh; Carlow.
35 Kelly, James; Co. Wexford.
24 Kelly, Jas.
59 Kelly, John; Carlow.
59 Kelly, John; Carlow.
54 Kelly, John; Drumahare.
 2 Kelly, John; Dublin.
59 Kelly, Margaret; Carlow.
59 Kelly, Margaret; Carlow.
 2 Kelly, Margaret; Cavan.
42 Kelly, Margaret; Co. Down.
29 Kelly, Margaret; Mount Melick.
66 Kelly, Mary; Carlow.
66 Kelly, Michael; Carlow.
54 Kelly, Michael; Drumahare.
63 Kelly, Michael; Co. Carlow.
 9 Kelly, Miss; Dublin.
48 Kelly, Patrick.
59 Kelly, Richard; Carlow.
40 Kelly, Robert; Banbridge.
35 Kelly, Robert; Dublin.
57 Kelly, Thomas; Carlow.
59 Kelly, William; Carlow.
 6 Kemple, John.
66 Kenedy, Bridget; Dublin.
66 Kenedy, John; Dublin.
51 Kennady, Val.
52 Kennedy, Alexander.
48 Kennedy, Alexander.
62 Kennedy, Andrew.
54 Kennedy, Anne; Grange
14 Kennedy, Edward.
54 Kennedy, John; Grange.
62 Kennedy, John & wife.
59 Kennedy, Joseph; Carlow.
19 Kennedy, Margaret.
26 Kennedy, Margaret; Dublin.
14 Kennedy, William.
62 Kennedy, William.
26 Kenny, Michael; Cavan.
13 Kernaghan, Robert.
14 Keown, James R.
27 Kerby, Mich.
13 Kerr, Alexander.
13 Kerr, Catherine.
 3 Kerr, George.
45 Kerr, Henry.
13 Kerr, Isabella.
13 Kerr, James.
45 Kerr, John.
13 Kerr, John.
13 Kerr, Matilda.
45 Kerr, Nancy.
31 Kerr, Patrick; Monaghan.
45 Kerr, Robert.
 8 Kerr, Robert; Ballymena.
45 Kerr, Thomas.
63 Kervan, Thos.; Phillipstown.
71 Kerrvan, Henry; St. Nicholas Galway.
46 Keys, Elizabeth; Donegal.
46 Keys, Samuel; Donegal.
39 Kidd, J.
23 Kield, Isaac; Dublin.
71 Kilfoyle, Peter; Parish of Kildare, Kings County.
 6 Killen, Thomas.
70 Kilmartin, Charles.
54 Kilmartin, Hugh; Mount Temple.
54 Kilmartin, Hugh; Mullaghmore.
54 Kilmartin, John; Mount Temple.
54 Kilmartin, Mary; Mullaghmore.

54 Kilmartin, Patrick; Mullaghmore.
59 Kinanak, Matthew; Meath.
32 King, Thomas.
9 King, Thomas; Balbriggan.
61 Kingsland, John.
43 Kinshela, William; Co. Wexford.
20 Kirk, William; Buncrana.
48 Kirkpatrick, Alexander.
48 Kirkpatrick, And.
28 Kirkpatrick, Anne; Belfast.
48 Kirkpatrick, Crissey.
48 Kirkpatrick, Eliza.
46 Kirkpatrick, George; N. S. Stewart.
20 Kirkpatrick, George; Ringsend.
48 Kirkpatrick, Jane.
28 Kirkpatrick, John; Belfast.
28 Kirkpatrick, Margt.; Belfast.
28 Kirkpatrick, Mary; Belfast.
28 Kirkpatrick, Rob.; Belfast.
13 Knox, James.
13 Kyle, Elizabeth.
13 Kyle, Robert.
27 Kynn, John.

L

36 Laffey, James.
35 Lain, David; Dublin.
13 Laird, Andrew.
60 Lalor, Danl.; Queens County.
71 Lally, Michael; Buttersbridge, Co. Cavan.
15 Lambert, Anne; Birr.
72 Lambert, Margaret; Kilkenny.
71 Lambert, William; Lambert-Ledge, Co. Galway.
66 Lane, Mary Anne; Almerita.
15 Langley, Michael; Dublin.
43 Langton, Daniel; Kilkenny.
48 Laperty, Michael.
72 Laphen, Philip; Armagh.
60 Larkin, Patrick; Balbriggan.
9 Latham, Elias; Dublin.
60 Latham, Hannah; Queens County.
9 Latham, Henry; Dublin.
7 Latham, Hugh; Crumlin.
9 Latham, Martha; Dublin.
9 Latham, Nathaniel; Dublin.
9 Latham, Thomas & wife; Dublin.
9 Latham, William; Dublin.
48 Laughery, Isabella.
48 Laughlin, George.
52 Laughlin, Wm.
52 Laughran, Jas.
64 Laughton, Robert; Laughgall.
53 Law, John; Scotland.
34 Law, William; Co. Down.
63 Lawler, John, wife & child; Co. Kildare.
48 Lawn, Edward.
14 Lea, Robert.
60 Leahy, Henry; Dublin.
1 Lear, John; Dublin.
55 Leary, Matthew.
48 Leckey, Thomas.
56 Leddy, Michael.
25 Leddy, Mrs. & 2 children.
8 Lee, Alexander; Co. Cavan.
8 Lee, Anne; Co. Cavan.
8 Lee, Edward; Co. Cavan.
7 Lee, George; Moy.
8 Lee, Jane; Co. Cavan.
7 Lee, John; Moy.
8 Lee, Mary; Co. Cavan.
7 Lee, Sarah; Moy.
7 Lee, Simon; Moy.
7 Lee, Thomas; Moy.

68 Leech, A.; Tyrone.
67 Leech, Andrew; Balbriggan.
68 Leech, Malcolm; Tyrone.
67 Leech, Sarah; Balbrigan.
38 Left, Adam; Dublin.
20 Lester, Anne; Strabane.
20 Lester, John; Strabane.
68 Lighton, William; Londonderry.
71 Lilly, John; Buttersbridge, Co. Cavan.
41 Limerick, Alexander.
65 Linchey, James; Philadelphia.
55 Lingan, Bridget.
55 Lingan, John.
3 Lindsay, George.
55 Lindsay, Isabella; Sligo.
3 Lindsay, Richard.
3 Lindsay, Robert.
62 Lindsay, Susan.
4 Linn, Daniel; Co. Antrim.
72 Linnan, John; Dublin.
54 Little, Thomas; Carney.
13 Lockhart, John.
13 Lockhart, Margaret.
66 Lockwood, John; Leister.
13 Logan, Daniel.
30 Logan, John; Monaghan.
13 Logan, Thomas.
66 Long, Joseph; Cavan.
27 Long, William.
8 Longman, Robert; Rushmills.
20 Loony, Anne; Bushill.
26 Loughnan, Martin; Queens County.
48 Love, Alexander.
13 Love, Anne.
13 Love, Samuel.
8 Low, John; Co. Antrim.
13 Lowden, Robert.
64 Lowry, Samuel; Co. Tyrone.
64 Lowry, Thomas; Co. Tyrone.
59 Lucas, Eleanor; Dublin.
23 Luke, Samuel; Belfast.
2 Lynch, Bryan; King's Court, Co. Cavan.
48 Lynch, John.
18 Lynch, Mr.; Dublin.
19 Lynch, Patrick.
69 Lynch, Peter; Sligo.
48 Lynch, Susan.
19 Lynch, Thomas.
38 Lyndon, James; Dublin.
38 Lyndon, Mary.
35 Lynes, Peter; New York.
40 Lyons, William; Armagh.

M

61 MacAffer, Andrew.
61 MacAlister, Anthony; Antrim.
28 MacAlister, Daniel; Donegal; Co. Antrim.
53 MacAllignon, Rich.
48 MacAloo, Daniel.
69 MacAnalty, Patrick; Sligo.
37 MacArand, Patrick.
39 MacArdle, Anne.
39 MacArdle, John.
39 MacArdle, Mary Anne.
39 MacArdle, Owen.
39 MacArdle, Peter.
6 MacArnon, Mary.
7 MacAtier, James; Aghadowy.
26 MacAuley, James; Castleblaney.
44 MacBraty, Chs.
62 MacBride, Bernard.
4 MacBride, James; Co. Antrim.
48 MacBride, John.

46 MacBride, Patrick; Donegal.
42 MacBride, William; Co. Armagh.
2 MacCabe, John; Cavan.
31 MacCabe, Pat.; Ballybay, Co. Monaghan.
56 MacCabe, Terrence.
32 MacCall, Alex.
32 MacCall, Alice.
68 MacCallan, James; Londonderry.
42 MacCam, Felix; Co. Antrim.
8 MacCambridge, Alexander; Cushendun.
53 MacCambridge, Jas.
61 MacCanaghty, James.
68 MacCanaghy, David; Tyrone.
68 MacCanaghy, Mary; Tyrone.
34 MacCanbrey, Rich.; Co. Antrim.
22 MacCarfin, T.; Longford.
11 MacCarter, James; Ireland.
34 MacCanly, Robert; Co. Down.
39 MacCann, Bernard.
4 MacCann, Daniel; Derry.
45 MacCann, John.
39 MacCann, Owen.
14 MacCann, William.
31 MacCannell, Carry; Clare, Co. Armagh.
31 MacCannell, Samuel; Clare, Co. Armagh.
4 MacCarden, Edward; Co. Down.
61 MacCarker, Patrick.
66 MacCarthy, Bryan; Cavan.
62 MacCartney, Patrick.
4 MacCarty, Rose; Co. Armagh.
30 MacCaskey, Eliza; Aughnacloy.
30 MacCaskey, John; Aughnacloy.
14 MacCasle, Thomas.
26 MacCathen, Adam; Dublin.
46 MacCauley, Eliza; N. S. Stewart.
46 MacCauley, Elizabeth; N. S. Stewart.
37 MacCauley, Robert & brother.
30 MacCauly, Jane; Lurgan.
62 MacCauly, John.
30 MacCauly, John; Lurgan.
53 MacCausland, Andrew.
52 MacCawley, James.
48 MacClaskey, Dennis.
48 MacClaskey, Henry.
49 MacClaskey, Hugh.
50 MacClean, James.
50 MacClean, M.
4 MacCleary, Sam.; Co. Tyrone.
8 MacClelland, Mr.; Co. Down.
8 MacClelland, Mrs.; Co. Down.
8 MacClelland, James; Richhill.
8 MacClelland, Mary; Co. Down.
8 MacClelland, Samuel; Richhill.
8 MacClellon, William; Ballymena.
67 MacCloud, Anne; Londonderry.
67 MacCloud, Daniel; Londonderry.
67 MacCloud, James; Londonderry.
67 MacCloud, John; Londonderry.
67 MacCloud, Mary Anne; Londonderry.
67 MacCloud, Neile; Londonderry.
42 MacClushey, Matilda.
42 MacClushey, Martha.
41 MacCoal, Charles.
41 MacCoal, Patrick.
48 MacColgan, George.
46 MacColgan, John; Donegal.
13 MacColim, Daniel.
13 MacColim, Margaret.
39 MacColley, John.
13 MacCollison, David.
13 MacCollison, Thomas.
52 MacCollough, Wm.
68 MacComb, Daniel; Donegal.
48 MacComb, John.

61 MacConley, George.
66 MacConnell, James; Monaghan.
68 MacCool, James; Donegal.
3 MacCormack, B.
66 MacCormick, Esther; Leitrim.
53 MacCormick, James.
36 MacCormick, John.
52 MacCormick, Jno.
66 MacCormick, Patrick; Leitrim.
41 MacCoy, Alexander.
23 MacCracken, Alexander; Belfast.
23 MacCracken, Alexander, Jr.; Belfast.
23 MacCracken, Joseph; Belfast.
49 MacCrea, John.
49 MacCrea, John.
67 MacCrossin, John; Danaghdee.
1 MacCullagh, Michael; Dublin.
53 MacCulloch, James.
34 MacCullum, Joseph; Co. Antrim.
8 MacCurdy, James; Coleraine.
8 MacCurdy, Jane; Coleraine.
16 MacCurdy, John; Ballycastle.
16 MacCurdy, Neil; Ballycastle.
8 MacCurdy, William; Coleraine.
68 MacCusker, Terence; Tyrone.
41 MacDaid, John.
22 MacDaniel, Mrs. & child; Kildare.
22 MacDaniel, And'w; Kilkenny.
62 MacDaniel, John.
66 MacDaniel, Less; Kilkenny.
6 MacDaniel, Mary.
6 MacDaniel, Michael.
66 MacDaniel, Owen; Kilkenny.
22 MacDaniel, T.; Kildare.
22 MacDaniel, Tho.; Kilkenny.
51 MacDemiott, Peter.
66 MacDermot, John; Meath.
41 MacDermott, Charles.
47 MacDermott, Daniel.
63 MacDermott, John.
41 MacDermott, Mary.
63 MacDermott, Owen.
43 MacDermott, Owen; New York.
24 MacDermott, Patk.
41 MacDermott, Patrick.
41 MacDermott, Rose.
41 MacDermott, Susannah.
41 MacDermott, William.
41 MacDermott, William.
53 MacDill, John; Scotland.
69 MacDonagh, James; Sligo.
70 MacDonald, Thos.
66 MacDonel, James; Queens County.
63 MacDonnel, —; Co. Meath.
72 MacDonnell, Judith; Thurles.
72 MacDonnell, Margaret; Thurles.
72 MacDonnell, Michael; Thurles.
61 MacDonnell, Robert.
61 MacDonnell, Thomas.
3 MacDougal, John.
3 MacDougal, Mary.
67 MacDougal, Mary; Letterkenny.
67 MacDougall, John; Letterkenny.
50 MacDowel, C.
50 MacDowel, C.
50 MacDowel, John.
50 MacDowel, M.
50 MacDowel, W.
16 MacDowell, Alexander; Dromore.
42 MacDowell, John; Co. Down.
65 MacEvoy, Edward; Co. Tyrone.
39 MacEvoy, Owen.
48 MacFadden, Charles.
13 MacFadden, Samuel.
41 MacFarland, Robert.
46 MacFarlane, John; Maherafelt.
53 MacGaragher, J., wife & 5 children.

54 MacGaraghy, Bryan; Mount Temple.
44 MacGattiger, Daniel.
44 MacGavaran, John.
28 MacGeoch, Ellen; Ballybay, Co. Monaghan.
28 MacGeoch, Grace; Glymluse, Wigtonshire.
28 MacGeoch, Sam.; Newtown Stewart.
62 MacGibbon, Samuel.
28 MacGill, Robert; Cookstown, Co. Derry.
68 MacGinn, Rose; Tyrone.
48 MacGinnis, Daniel.
34 MacGinnis, Daniel; Co. Antrim.
48 MacGinnis, Ellen.
48 MacGinnis, Henry.
47 MacGinnis, John.
48 MacGinnis, Owen.
48 MacGinnis, Thomas.
16 MacGladery, Samuel; Stillwater.
55 MacGlam, John.
55 MacGlam, Patrick.
13 MacGlaughlin, Robert.
48 MacGloin, Edward.
55 MacGloin, Henry.
55 MacGloin, John.
54 MacGloin, Margaret; Tauly.
55 MacGloin, Mary & child.
13 MacGloughlin, Dennis.
13 MacGloughlin, Mary.
13 MacGloughlin, Patrick.
68 MacGlyn, Catherine; Tyrone.
48 MacGongle, Henry.
7 MacGouran, Samuel; Comber.
6 MacGovern, Charles.
61 MacGowan, Andrew.
48 MacGowan, Dennis.
68 MacGowan, Dennis; Tyrone.
13 MacGowan, James.
4 MacGowan, James; Co. Antrim.
54 MacGowan, John; Dunally.
61 MacGowan, Mary.
55 MacGowan, Patrick.
48 MacGowan, Patrick.
20 MacGowan, Bernard; Newtown Stewart.
69 MacGown, Andrew; Sligo.
50 MacGra, John.
48 MacGranahan, Thomas.
19 MacGrath, James.
37 MacGrath, William.
68 MacGreevy, Patrick; Tyrone.
61 MacGrery, James.
61 MacGrery, Margaret.
20 MacGrier, Robert; Armagh.
60 MacGrim, Bryan; Drogheda.
55 MacGuire, Bridget.
31 MacGuire, Ellen; Mullingar, Co. Westmeath.
55 MacGuire, Mary.
68 MacGum, Patrick; Tyrone.
68 MacGuragle, Robert; Londonderry.
62 MacGuskin, A.
48 MacHale, Thomas.
70 MacHugh, Andrew.
49 MacIlhames, John.
67 MacIlheny, Robert; Letterkenny.
8 MacIlrath, King; Co. Antrim.
23 MacIlroy, Charles; Down.
62 MacIlroy, Patrick.
23 MacIlroy, Mrs.; Down.
13 MacIntire, James.
13 MacIntire, Robert.
62 MacIntire, Robt.
13 MacIntire, Samuel.
67 MacIntosh, Jane; Danaghdee.
67 MacIntosh, William; Danaghdee.

4 MacKay, Alexander; Co. Antrim.
43 MacKay, Eliza; Co. Dublin.
14 MacKay, Francis.
43 MacKay, James; Co. Dublin.
50 MacKay, P.
50 MacKay, S.
43 MacKay, William; Co. Dublin.
39 MacKee, Robert.
4 MacKee, Robert & wife; Co. Antrim.
40 MacKee, William; Kilkeel, Co. Down.
23 MacKell, Thomas; New York.
50 MacKeene, Peter.
53 MacKeighan, —.
16 MacKennan, Bernart; Monaghan.
16 MacKennan, Patrick; Monaghan.
16 Mackeon, Isabella; Ballymena.
65 MacKeon, Robt.; Co. Tyrone.
16 MacKeon, Rose; Randlestown.
16 Mackeon, William; Ballymena.
68 MacKeown, Anne; Tyrone.
68 MacKeown, John, Junr.; Tyrone.
68 MacKeown, John Senr.; Tyrone.
68 MacKeown, Margaret; Tyrone.
68 MacKeown, Mary; Tyrone.
68 MacKeown, Mary; Tyrone.
68 MacKeown, Saml.; Tyrone.
68 MacKeown, Samuel; Tyrone.
68 MacKeown, Sarah; Tyrone.
68 MacKeown, William; Tyrone.
61 Mackerill, James.
61 Mackerill, Jane.
61 Mackerill, Thomas.
9 MacKernan, Edward; Co. Leitrim.
9 MacKernan, Patrick; Co. Leitrim.
25 Mackeson, James.
35 MacKevers, Peter; Co. Louth.
37 MacKey, Eleanor.
61 MacKill, Thos.
53 MacKinne, John.
33 MacKinstry, John.
54 MacKninon, Hannah; Mullaghmore.
20 MacLachling, John; Derry.
60 MacLain, John; Drogheda.
45 MacLaughlin, Cornelius.
48 MacLaughlin, Dennis.
67 MacLaughlin, Dennis.
72 MacLaughlin, Edward; Kilkenny.
61 MacLaughlin, Hugh.
39 MacLaughlin, James.
54 MacLaughlin, James; Drumahare.
71 MacLaughlin, James; Somerset, Co. Galway.
48 MacLaughlin, John.
71 MacLaughlin, John; Somerset, Co. Galway.
61 MacLaughlin, Margaret.
68 MacLaughlin, Mary; Londonderry.
41 MacLaughlin, Peter.
48 MacLaughlin, Philip.
48 MacLaughlin, Sarah.
3 MacLean, Bridget.
3 MacLean, Owen.
8 MacLean, Peter; Co. Derry.
25 MacLean, Thomas.
61 MacLorran, William.
19 MacMahon, Bridget.
61 MacMail, Hugh.
70 MacMarrow, Mary.
70 MacMarrow, Owen.
70 MacManus, Bernard.
40 MacManus, Bernard; Cavan.
2 MacManus, Michael; Killeshandra.
25 MacManus, Nathl., wife & 2 children.
56 MacManus, Patrick.
3 MacManus, Patrick.
41 MacMenamy, John.

41 MacMenamy, Peter.
67 MacMenomy, Elizabeth; Letterkenny.
67 MacMenomy, Elizabeth; Letterkenny.
48 MacNenomy, Hugh.
67 MacMenomy, Hugh; Letterkenny.
68 MacMenomy, John; Donegal.
67 MacMenomy, Robt., Letterkenny.
67 MacMenomy, Thomas; Letterkenny.
67 MacMenomy, William; Letterkenny.
13 MacMiller, Gideon.
4 MacMullen, Alexander; Co. Antrim.
28 MacMullen, Catherine; Lurgan, Co. Armagh.
61 MacMurray, Archibald.
28 MacMurray, David; Ballybay, Co. Monaghan.
28 MacMurray, Jess; Belfast.
68 MacNarna, Wm.; Tyrone.
22 MacNarney, John; Longford.
22 MacNarney, Michael; Longford.
8 MacNaughten, John; Monaghan.
68 MacNemee, Francis; Tyrone.
13 MacNeremon, William.
54 MacNulty, Wm.; Tauly.
68 MacPhilaney, Margaret; Tyrone.
70 MacPhiloron, Dennis.
61 MacQueen, Matthew.
62 MacQuig, William.
39 MacQuinn, Patrick.
16 MacQuoid, James; Clogher.
8 MacRalin, Roger; Ballymena.
41 MacRedden, James.
68 MacSerley, James; Tyrone.
13 MacShane, Daniel.
14 MacSheldon, James.
54 MacSherry, Patrick; Darby.
68 MacSwigon, Mary; Tyrone.
68 MacSwigon, Philip; Tyrone.
62 MacTahan, Henry & wife.
42 MacTea, Arthur; Co. Down.
62 MacTice, Andrew.
68 MacVaid, James; Tyrone.
52 MacVea, Jas.
68 MacVeigh, Henry; Tyrone.
16 MacVicker, Thos.; Larne.
48 MacVoy, Dominick.
9 Madden, James; Kilkenny.
22 Madden, James; Slane.
19 Madigan, Ally.
19 Madigan, Anne.
19 Madigan, Edward.
19 Madigan, James.
19 Madigan, Judy.
19 Madigan, Mary.
19 Madigan, Peggy.
19 Madigan, Walter.
19 Madigan, Walter.
19 Madigan, William.
23 Magee, Bernard; Dublin.
32 Magee, Bernd.
62 Magee, James.
62 Magee, John.
62 Magee, John.
35 Magee, John; Kilkenny.
35 Magee, Patrick; Kilkenny.
62 Magee, William.
53 Magher, —.
23 Magill, Daniel; Dublin.
20 Magill, John; Killetter.
12 Maguire, Henry; Dublin.
50 Mahany, John.
50 Mahany, Mary.
50 Mahany, Mary.
50 Mahany, Mary J.
38 Mahon, Catherine; Kilkenny.
56 Mahon, Charles.
38 Mahon, Joseph; Kilkenny.

2, Mahony, F.
5 Mahony, Jas.; Wexford, a citizen of U. S.
15 Maiben, Mrs. Jane & child; Dublin.
15 Maiben, Richard; New York.
34 Malcomson, Adam; Co. Down.
2 Malone, Francis; Killeshandra.
6 Malone, Henry.
45 Malsey, Mary.
26 Maly, John; Dublin.
42 Manning, William; Co. Antrim.
69 Mara, James; Lurgonboy.
14 March, Charles.
24 Marfelt, John.
28 Markey, James; Ballybay, Co. Monaghan.
8 Marshall, Isabella; Co. Antrim.
8 Marshall, John; Co. Antrim.
8 Marshall, Margaret; Co. Antrim.
8 Marshall, Mary; Co. Antrim.
8 Marshall, Samuel; Co. Antrim.
62 Marshall, William.
65 Martin, Andrew; Co. Antrim.
61 Martin, George.
22 Martin, Hugh; Kildare.
44 Martin, James.
30 Martin, James; Markethill.
46 Martin, James; N. S. Stewart.
62 Martin, John.
53 Martin, John.
3 Martin, John Golrick.
22 Martin, Marcella; Kildare.
8 Martin, Martha; Aughill.
3 Martin, Pat. Golrick.
8 Martin, Rachel; Aughill.
56 Martin, Robert.
61 Martin, Robert.
56 Martin, Thomas.
3 Martin, Thomas.
34 Martin, Thos.; Co. Antrim.
61 Martin, William.
8 Martin, William; Aughill.
30 Martin, William; Markethill.
3 Mason, Daniel.
63 Mason, Thomas & wife.
56 Masterson, Charles.
2 Masterson, Hugh; Granard.
56 Masterson, Patrick.
66 Mathews, Michael; Drogheda.
7 Mathews, Thomas; Dundee.
67 Mathewson, Clark; Strabane.
67 Mathewson, David; Strabane.
62 Maurice, James.
8 Maxwell, Eliza; Rushmills.
33 Maxwell, Isabella; Armagh.
33 Maxwell, James; Armagh.
8 Maxwell, John; Rushmills.
13 Maxwell, Margaret.
8 Maxwell, Margaret; Rushmills.
8 Maxwell, Mrs. T.; Rushmills.
72 Maxwell, Thomas; Kilkenny.
26 Mead, John; Dublin.
13 Mechan, Catherine.
48 Mechan, James.
54 Mechlan, Mary.
54 Mechlan, William.
21 Medile, David.
54 Mein, John; Scotland.
52 Meloy, Jno.
70 Michaw, James.
49 Millar, John.
49 Millar, Robert.
41 Miller, Alexander.
28 Miller, Benjamin; Cothill, Co. Monaghan.
67 Miller, John; Londonderry.
7 Miller, John; Randlestown.

28 Miller, Margaret; Ballybay, Co. Monaghan.
55 Miller, Thomas; Drimkeeran.
49 Miller, William.
16 Millgan, Bernard; Balinahinch.
53 Milliken, W.; Scotland.
32 Minis, Catherine.
28 Minnis, Fras.; Saintfield, Co. Down.
67 Mitchel, James; Letterkenny.
55 Mitchell, Charles.
52 Mitchell, Jas.
69 Mitchell, Martin; Sligo.
68 Mitchell, Samuel; Londonderry.
56 Mite, Samuel.
70 Mochan, Elizabeth.
67 Moffat, Edward; Letterkenny.
19 Moffat, John.
19 Moffat, William.
61 Mollan, Hugh.
22 Molloghan, Patrick; Longford.
3 Molloy, Patrick.
38 Monaghan, Peter; Kings County.
65 Monderson, Isaac; Co. Antrim.
65 Monderson, John; Co. Antrim.
65 Monderson, Margaret; Co. Antrim.
65 Monderson, Sarah; Co. Antrim.
62 Money, Charles.
62 Money, Margaret.
21 Montgomery, John.
29 Moody, James; Armagh.
50 Moone, J.
42 Mooney, Alexander; Co. Antrim.
56 Mooney, John.
42 Mooney, Mary; Co. Antrim.
56 Mooney, Michael.
20 Moore, Alexander; Derry.
45 Moore, Andrew.
16 Moore, James; Donoughmore.
72 Moore, James; Dublin.
20 Moore, Jane; Derry.
19 Moore, John.
28 Moore, John; Belfast.
9 Moore, John; Co. Carlow.
23 Moore, John; Dublin.
20 Moore, Letty; Claugh.
16 Moore, Margaret; Donoughmore.
16 Moore, Robert; Donoughmore.
20 Moore, Samuel; Claugh.
16 Moore, Samuel D.; Carrickfergus.
21 Moore, William.
19 Moore, William.
60 Moore, William; Co. Cavan.
16 Moore, William; Donoughmore.
6 Moran, James.
61 Morer, James.
44 Morgan, Edwd.
5 Morgan, John; Waterford.
66 Morine, John; Kilkenny.
66 Morine, Judith & 2 children; Kilkenny.
1 Morris, John; Boyle, Co. Roscommon.
43 Morris, Mary; Wexford.
50 Morrison. J.
61 Morrison, Matthew.
50 Morrison, R.
33 Morrow, Joseph; Donaghmore, Co. Down.
32 Morrow, Robert.
21 Morrow, Thomas.
25 Morrow, Thos.
40 Morton, Francis; Kilkeel, Co. Down.
60 Muldary, Thomas; Mullingar.
6 Muldawney, Michael.
66 Mulhall, Mary; Kilkenny.
67 Mulheron, John; Letterkenny.
50 Mulholland, Henry.
44 Mulholland, John.

7 Mullan, Arthur; Aghadowy.
48 Mullan, Bridget.
7 Mullan, Cicey; Aghadowy.
33 Mullan, James; Roughforth, Templepatrick.
7 Mullan, John; Aghadowy.
31 Mullan, Richd.; Monaghan.
7 Mullan, William; Aghadowy.
4 Mullay, William; Dublin.
57 Mullen, Edward; Carlow.
57 Mullen, Patrick; Carlow.
57 Mullen, Thomas; Carlow.
65 Mulligan, James C.; Banbridge.
22 Mulligan, Michael; Longford.
57 Mulvany, Patrick; Dublin.
6 Mulvany, Thomas.
56 Mulvey, Isabella.
56 Mulvey, John.
42 Murdoch, John; Co. Down.
4 Murdoch, Obediah; Co. Down.
40 Murney, Patrick; Dublin.
35 Murphy, Bridget; Dublin.
57 Murphy, Bridget; Wexford.
35 Murphy, Catherine; Carlow.
59 Murphy, Cicily; Carlow.
35 Murphy, Dennis; Co. Wexford.
59 Murphy, Eleanor; Carlow.
27 Murphy, Frances.
57 Murphy, Francis; Wexford.
27 Murphy, James.
59 Murphy, James; Carlow.
35 Murphy, James; Dublin.
57 Murphy, Johanna; Wexford.
39 Murphy, John.
1 Murphy, John; Dublin.
9 Murphy, John; Dublin.
57 Murphy, John; Wexford.
57 Murphy, Lawrence; Wexford.
34 Murphy, Marg. & 2 children; Co. Tyrone.
43 Murphy, Martin; Co. Wexford.
57 Murphy, Martin; Wexford.
35 Murphy, Mary; Co. Wexford.
57 Murphy, Mary; Wexford.
35 Murphy, Mary; Co. Wexford.
35 Murphy, Morris; New York.
2 Murphy, Morris; Dublin.
27 Murphy, Patrick.
48 Murphy, Patrick.
21 Murphy, Patrick.
57 Murphy, Simon; Wexford.
43 Murphy, Susan; Co. Wexford.
47 Murray, Bernard.
69 Murray, Bridget; Sligo.
38 Murray, Daniel; Carlow.
61 Murray, James.
24 Murray, Jas.
60 Murray, John, wife & 2 children; Balbriggan.
15 Murray, John; Banbridge.
20 Murray, Patrick; Auchinloe.
34 Murray, William; Co. Armagh.
38 Murray, William; Carlow.
20 Murrin, Thomas; Derry.
2 Murtagh, Mr. & wife; Co. Longford.
66 Murtaugh, John; Westmeath.
69 Murry, Felix; Sligo.

N

36 Nalty, Bridget.
36 Nalty, Margaret.
36 Nalty Mary.
36 Nalty, Patrick.
36 Nalty, Thomas.
22 Narey, Peter; Westmeath.

23 Nasida, Catherine; Dublin.
71 Naughten, Patrick; Athlone, Co. West-
    meath.
38 Neal, Michael; Dublin.
 8 Neil, James; Ballymoney.
 8 Neil, Margaret; Ballymoney.
70 Neill, Henry D.
70 Neill, Madge D.
54 Nesbit, Hugh; Sligo.
38 Nevin, Patrick; Kilkenny.
32 Newberry, Robert.
63 Newlan, Patrick; Co. Carlow.
13 Nickle, Thomas.
48 Nickle, William.
52 Nielson, James.
71 Niven, Patrick; Somerset, Co. Gal-
    way.
36 Nolan, P.
50 Noone, John.
63 Nowlan, Charles; Co. Dublin.
15 Nowlan, Christopher; Dublin.
56 Nowland, James.
14 Nugent, Laurence.

O

 3 O'Beirn, Michael.
44 O'Boyle, Neal.
29 O'Bream, John; Dublin.
19 O'Brien, John.
60 O'Brien, John, wife, & child; Dublin.
36 O'Brien, Lawrence.
19 O'Brien, Margaret.
36 O'Brien, Mary.
19 O'Brien, Michael.
50 O'Cain, Thos. H.
 6 O'Connell, Miss Ann.
60 O'Connor, Thomas; Dublin.
53 O'Donnel, M. & wife.
16 O'Donnell, Isabella; Randlestown.
16 O'Donnell, Mary; Randlestown.
44 O'Donnell, Patk.
 5 O'Donnell, Wm. & wife; Waterford.
59 Ogilby, Frederick; Dublin.
59 Ogilby, John; Dublin.
59 Ogilby, Mrs.; Dublin.
59 Ogilby, Robert; Dublin.
26 O'Hara, William; Dublin.
63 O'Hara, William; Tullamore, Kings
    County.
41 O'Hare, John.
10 O'Leary, James; Dublin.
50 O'Loone, Henry.
38 O'Neal, Anne.
59 O'Neal, John; Carlow.
38 O'Neal, Nicholas; Dublin.
52 O'Neall, Alexander.
 4 O'Neil, Charles; Derry.
50 O'Neil, J.
54 O'Neil, James; Ballymote.
31 O'Neil, John; Rostrevor, Co. Down.
53 O'Neil, John, wife & child.
53 O'Neil, Owen, wife & child.
25 O'Neill, Sarah.
59 O'Reilly, Edward; Carlow.
59 O'Reilly, Eliza; Carlow.
59 O'Reilly, Hugh; Carlow.
59 O'Reilly, Margaret; Carlow.
15 O'Reilly, Miles E.; Dublin.
 3 O'Rorke, Bernard.
 3 O'Rorke, Patrick.
32 Orr, Anne.
32 Orr, Elizabeth.
32 Orr, George.
32 Orr, James.
32 Orr, Jane.

62 Orr, Patrick.
32 Orr, Thomas.
32 Orr, William
20 Osborne, George; Dromore.
45 O'Shaughnessy, Limerick.
45 O'Shaughnessy, Margaret; Limerick.
20 Owens, James; Armagh.

P

68 Paisley, Christopher; Londonderry.
52 Palmer, Esther.
 8 Palmer, Joseph; Magherafelt.
52 Palmer, Margaret.
66 Parcell, Ellen & child; Kilkenny.
45 Park, David.
45 Park, David.
48 Park, Mathew.
31 Parker, John; Dramore, Co. Down.
42 Parker, Moses; Co. Down.
61 Parr, Anne.
61 Parr, Eliza.
61 Parr, John.
61 Parr, Margaret.
61 Parr, Mary.
61 Parr, Thomas.
61 Parr, William.
61 Parr, William, Jun.
13 Patterson, David.
 4 Patterson, David; Co. Antrim.
56 Patterson, Edward.
33 Patterson, John; Port Norris.
 2 Patterson, Joseph; Co. Cavan.
 2 Patterson, William; King's Court, Co.
    Cavan.
32 Peacock, James.
48 Peden, James.
28 Peirie, Hugh; Donaghy, Co. Tyrone.
66 Pendergrass, Michael; Kilkenny.
14 Peppard, Patrick & wife.
 5 Percival, John; Waterford.
35 Perrin, —; Philadelphia.
43 Pether, William; Co. Wexford.
56 Petit, Berrard.
53 Pettigrew, William.
72 Pettit, Bernard; Co. Longford.
57 Pettit, Patrick; Wexford.
26 Phalen, Daniel; Queens County.
72 Phelan, John; Queens County.
21 Phillips, Bernard.
53 Phoenix, John.
63 Picket, Mark; Co. Carlow.
62 Pierce, Alex.
43 Pierce, John; Co. Wexford.
69 Pigeon, Andrew; Sligo.
15 Pilkington, Edward; Dublin.
22 Pitman, Peter; Nova Scotia.
 9 Ploughman, John; Dublin.
72 Pogue, Alexander; Co. Cavan.
62 Poland, Peter.
50 Pole, W.
67 Pollock, John; Londonderry.
49 Pomeroy, James.
22 Poole, Robert; Wexford.
31 Porter, Hugh; wife & 4 children; Dra-
    more, Co. Down.
 5 Power, Maurice; Waterford.
35 Prain, Fanny; Philadelphia.
34 Prey, David; Co. Down.
66 Price, Margaret & 3 children; Kil-
    kenny.
66 Priston, William; Leister.
22 Purcel, Charles; Limerick.
22 Purcel, Sarah; Limerick.
22 Purcell, Fanny; Kildare.
 2 Purdon, Thomas; Dublin.

Q

55 Queenan, Bryan.
70 Queenan, Martin.
41 Quigley, David.
33 Quin, Agnes; Port Norris, Co. Down.
53 Quin, Arthur.
 8 Quin, John; Cookstown.
44 Quince, Thomas.
48 Quinn, Arthur.
68 Quinn, Charles; Donegal.
68 Quinn, Francis; Donegal.
28 Quinn, Henry; Lurgan, Co. Armagh.
68 Quinn, James; Donegal.
68 Quinn, John; Donegal.
37 Quinn, Letita.
13 Quinton, Robert.

R

40 Rafferty, Patrick; Drogheda.
26 Rafferty, Simeon; Dublin.
53 Rafferty, Stewart.
72 Rafter, Dennis; Kilkenny.
71 Raftrey, John; Athlone, Co. West-
      meath.
27 Ragan, T.
 8 Rainey, James; Ballymena.
20 Ramsey, George; Coleraine.
48 Rankin, Sarah.
33 Rea, Patrick.
29 Read, James; Dublin.
47 Read, Thomas.
37 Recard, George.
 5 Recard, John & wife; Waterford.
22 Rechil, Patrick; Longford.
71 Reddington, Patrick; Loughrea, Co.
      Galway.
33 Reed, John.
62 Reed, Martin.
71 Regin, John; St. Nicholas, Galway.
31 Reid, Adam; Clare, Co. Armagh.
50 Reid, George.
50 Reid, James.
 8 Reid, James; Ballymena.
50 Reid, M.
50 Reid, Rachael.
50 Reid, Robert.
50 Reid, Thomas.
 1 Reilly. —; Shercock, Co. Cavan.
59 Reilly, Charles; Meath.
 1 Reilly, Fras; Granard.
 2 Reilly, John; King's Court, Co. Cavan.
 1 Reilly, Michael; Cavan.
 9 Reilly, Patrick; Co. Longford.
38 Reilly, Thomas.
59 Reilly, Thomas; Meath.
14 Reily, Philip.
48 Renenaugh, James.
41 Reynolds, Catherine.
56 Reynolds, Eliza.
56 Reynolds, Joseph.
56 Reynolds, Laurence.
55 Reynolds, Patrick.
63 Reynolds, William; Co. Kildare.
35 Riall, Patrick; Dublin.
31 Rice, Canlan; Ballybay, Co. Monag-
      han.
33 Rice, Patrick; Camlagh, Co. Armagh.
68 Richie, Catherine; Tyrone.
68 Richie, William; Tyrone.
70 Richley, Daniel.
62 Riddle, Samuel.
62 Riddle, William.
71 Rider, William; Aghram, Co. Galway.
48 Ridge, James.
51 Rielly, Eliza.
51 Rielly, Elizabeth.
51 Rielly, Rose.
27 Riordan, Coleman.
62 Ritchie, John.
62 Ritchie, Wm.
70 Roaney, Anne.
70 Roany, Charles.
65 Robb, Charles; Philadelphia.
34 Roberts, John M.; Co. Antrim.
39 Robertson, Catharine.
44 Robertson, D.
44 Robertson, Eleanor.
 8 Robin, William; Banbridge.
66 Robins, Bridget & child; Westmeath.
44 Robinson, John.
 8 Robinson, John; Newtownards.
 8 Robinson, Joseph; Co. Cavan.
68 Robinson, Thomas; Antrim.
11 Robinson, Mrs. & family; Ireland.
43 Roche, David; Co. Wexford.
27 Roche, James.
43 Roche, John; Co. Wexford.
27 Roche, William.
43 Rochford, Francis; Co. Wexford.
57 Rochford, Walter; Wexford.
13 Rodgers, Patrick.
47 Rogan, Charles.
62 Rogers, Alexr.
62 Rogers, Ann.
61 Rogers, Hugh.
48 Rogers, John.
16 Rogers, John; Ballinahinch.
62 Rogers, John & wife.
62 Rogers, Mary.
28 Rogers, Patrick; Derry.
70 Roney, Catherine.
28 Rooney, Hugh; Malenadony, Co. Lei-
      trim.
54 Rooney, Michael.
55 Rooney, Michael.
69 Roony, Charles; Sligo.
54 Roony, John; Tauly.
54 Roony, Sarah; Tauly.
68 Rosborough, John; Londonderry.
24 Rose, Geo.
70 Rosman, Martin.
61 Ross, James.
60 Roundtree, Owen & wife; Dublin.
46 Rowan, James; Belfast.
43 Rowan, John; Mountrath.
53 Rowan, Mary & 4 children.
43 Rowan, Margaret; Mountrath.
 2 Rowland, Mrs. & child.
66 Rudd, Grace; Dublin.
62 Ruddock, James.
14 Russel, Isaac.
46 Russell, Alexander; Donegal.
46 Russell, Francis; Donegal.
46 Russell, James; Donegal.
46 Russell, Jane; Donegal.
44 Russell, John.
46 Russell, John; Donegal.
50 Rutledge, John.
19 Ryan, Ellen.
19 Ryan, James.
66 Ryan, Margaret; Carlow.
66 Ryan, Mary & child; Carlow.

S

66 Salmon, Mathew; Meath.
15 Salter, Thomas; Dublin.
 7 Sampson, David; Dundee.
31 Sampson, John; Ballygalley, Co. Ty-
      rone.
40 Saunderson, Henry; Portadown, Co.
      Armagh.
69 Scandler, Bryan; Sligo.
67 Scanlon, Maney; Letterkenny.

4 Scellan, Thos.; Dublin.
61 Scilly, Jane.
61 Scilly, John.
61 Scilly, Margaret.
69 Scinlon, Bryan; Castleton.
13 Scott, Catherine.
48 Scott, Edward.
61 Scott, Eliza.
13 Scott, Hugh.
13 Scott, Jane.
61 Scott, Jane.
44 Scott, John.
44 Scott, John.
61 Scott, Sarah.
65 Scott, Thomas W.; Philadelphia.
54 Scott, Walter; Scotland.
13 Scott, William.
35 Sculler, James; Co. Wexford.
39 Seeds, William.
68 Segarson, William; Londonderry.
68 Semple, Robert; Londonderry.
7 Semple, Thomas; Aghadowy.
42 Service, Alexander; Co. Antrim.
1 Shales, —; Shercock, Co. Cavan.
16 Shanks, William & wife; Dromore.
48 Shannan, John.
8 Shannon, David; Drumbo.
7 Shannon, Hugh & wife; Belfast.
50 Shannon, M.
4 Shannon, Quinton; Co. Down.
68 Sharkey, William; Donegal.
37 Sharkey, William & sister.
52 Shaw, Ann.
52 Shaw, James.
52 Shaw, John.
8 Shaw, John; Co. Antrim.
52 Shaw, Mary.
52 Shaw, Robert.
52 Shaw, Rose.
52 Shaw, Rose.
52 Shaw, Thomas.
52 Shaw, Wm.
48 Shearer, Mathew.
27 Sheehey, Mary.
42 Shepherd, Jane; Co. Tyrone.
42 Shepherd, Margaret; Co. Armagh.
42 Shepherd, Richard; Co. Armagh.
42 Shepherd, Simpson; Co. Derry.
14 Sheppard, James & wife.
14 Sheppard, Peter & wife.
68 Sheran, Andrew; Tyrone.
2 Sherdon, Jane; Killeshandra.
2 Sherdon, Thomas; Killeshandra.
38 Sherlock, Robert.
18a Shields, Frindley; Ireland.
45 Shields, William Junr.
45 Shields, William Senr.
49 Simpson, —.
61 Simpson, James.
49 Simpson, Robert.
62 Simpson, Wm. & wife.
50 Singer, James.
43 Sinnot, Richard; Wexford.
20 Sinton, Henry; Bushill.
20 Sinton, James; Bushill.
20 Sinton, John; Bushill.
20 Sinton, Joseph; Bushill.
20 Sinton, Rebecca; Bushill.
68 Sithgon, William; Londonderry.
22 Slattery, Patrick; Tipperary.
19 Slavin, Anne.
19 Slavin, Catherine.
19 Slavin, James.
19 Slavin, Michael.
32 Sleith, John.
32 Sleith, Margaret.
61 Slinler, M.
42 Sloan, Catherine; Co. Antrim.

42 Sloan, Catherine; Co. Antrim.
61 Sloan, James.
16 Sloan, William; Armagh.
56 Smith, —.
56 Smith, —.
8 Smith, Abraham; Co. Antrim.
54 Smith, Alexander; Scotland.
2 Smith, Bernard; Cavan.
56 Smith, Catharine.
48 Smith, Eliza.
8 Smith, Hugh; Co. Antrim.
65 Smith, Hugh; Co. Antrim.
62 Smith, James.
48 Smith, John.
2 Smith, John; England.
7 Smith, Joseph; Drimaragh.
14 Smith, Michael.
6 Smith, Peter.
70 Smith, Peter.
14 Smith, Phillip.
35 Smith, Robert; Dublin.
2 Smith, Thomas; Jun.; Cavan.
2 Smith, Thos. & wife; Co. Cavan.
42 Smyth, Jane; Co. Down.
19 Smyth, John.
56 Smyth, Patrick.
20 Smyth, Robert; Dromore.
67 Smyth, Robert; Enniskillen.
13 Smyth, William.
47 Somerville, Jane.
47 Somerville, Mary.
8 Spark, James; Derrock.
53 Sparks, Alexander; Scotland.
53 Sparks, Eliza; Scotland.
22 Spelman, D.; Longford.
8 Spencer, Robert; Co. Antrim.
44 Spencer, Samuel.
5 Spratt, Andrew; Waterford.
42 Spratt, Mary; Co. Down.
42 Spratt, Thomas; Co. Down.
68 Spraule, Armour; Tyrone.
14 Spunner, Thomas.
55 Standford, Edward.
23 Stanley, Peter; Dublin.
51 Stasey, Doritha.
51 Stasey, Eliza.
51 Stasey, John.
51 Stasey, Margaret.
51 Stasey, Sarah.
51 Stasey, Wm.
23 Stavely, Andrew; Antrim.
16 Steel, James; Larne.
4 Steel, William; Co. Antrim.
3 Steen, Robert; Co. Antrim.
3 Stephens, John.
48 Stephens, John.
72 Stephens, John; Dublin.
16 Sterling, Sobert; Derry.
69 Stevens, James; Sligo.
57 Stevens, William; Wexford.
22 Steward, Geo.; Monaghan.
52 Stewart, Alexander.
8 Stewart, Alexander; Belfast.
16 Stewart, Alexander; Drumbridge.
62 Stewart, Allan.
8 Stewart, Charles; Rushmills.
61 Stewart, Daniel.
48 Stewart, David.
8 Stewart, James; Rushmills.
52 Stewart, Jane.
62 Stewart, Jane.
62 Stewart, John.
8 Stewart, John; Rushmills.
62 Stewart, John & wife.
8 Stewart, Mrs. Letitia; Belfast.
52 Stewart, Martha.
8 Stewart, Rebecca; Belfast.
52 Stewart, Robert.

8 Stewart, Rose; Rushmills.
8 Stewart, Sally; Rushmills.
49 Stewart, Samuel.
13 Stewart, Thomas.
48 Stewart, William.
52 Stewart, Wm.
42 Stilt, John; Co. Armagh.
1 Stinton, Daniel; City of Limerick.
13 Stoop, John.
48 Story, Robert.
22 Stram, John; Fernagh.
48 Strawbridge, John.
23 Strean, John; Newtownards.
33 Stuart, James; Hill-Hall, Co. Down.
68 Stuart, William; Londonderry.
68 Stuart, William; Tyrone.
27 Sullivan, Jeremiah.
52 Swan, Alexander.
52 Swan, David.
52 Swan, John.
52 Swan, Margaret.
52 Swan, Margaret.
63 Sweeney, Terence.
63 Sweeney, Terence.
20 Sweeny, Andrew; Burligh.
20 Sweeny, Anne; Burligh.
20 Sweeny, Archibald; Burligh.
61 Sweeny, Catherine.
61 Sweeny, Eleanor.
34 Sweeny, James; Co. Antrim.
54 Sweeny, Jeremiah; Coolerrah.
20 Sweeny, Mary; Burligh.
20 Sweeny, William; Burligh.
66 Sweetman, Catharine; Meath.

T

62 Taggart, William & wife.
53 Tanner, John.
23 Taylor, Michael; Perth, Scotland.
55 Taylor, Richard; Sligo.
15 Templeton, William; Belfast.
61 Temen, Robert.
59 Thomas, William; Wexford.
7 Thompson, Andrew; New York.
3 Thompson, Mr.
40 Thompson, Arthur; Liverpool.
23 Thompson, Geo.; Antrim.
59 Thompson, George; Dublin.
62 Thompson, James.
71 Thompson, James; Stonepark, Co. Roscommon.
21 Thompson, John.
49 Thompson, John.
13 Thompson, Joseph.
8 Thompson, Mary; Dromore.
53 Thompson, Thomas.
8 Thompson, Thomas; Dromore.
49 Thompson, William.
48 Thompson, William.
20 Thornberry, Susan; Bushill.
57 Thornton, John; Dundalk.
57 Thornton, Nicholas; Dundalk.
57 Tierney, Francis; Carlow.
57 Tierney, Joseph; Carlow.
57 Tierney, Margaret; Carlow.
46 Tierny, Hugh; Donegal.
29 Tighe, Michael; Co. Antrim.
44 Tigut, Matthew.
50 Tiney, Thomas.
15 Tindall, William; Dublin.
5 Tobin, Catherine; Waterford.
61 Todd, Samuel.
13 Todd, Stephen.
45 Toland, John.
39 Toner, B.
38 Tonnaly, James; Co. Meath.
71 Toole, Michael; Tram, Co. Galway.

49 Todd, Thomas.
62 Tone, Robert.
6 Tracey, William.
72 Tracy, Catharine; Kilkenny.
72 Tracy, Dennis; Kilkenny:
72 Tracy, Mary; Kilkenny.
72 Tracy, Thomas; Kilkenny.
69 Travers, Patrick; Lurganboy.
70 Trotter, William.
40 Trotter, William; Monmouth, New Jersey.
42 Turley, Anne; Co. Down.
42 Turley, Eliza; Co. Down.
42 Turley, John; Co. Down.
42 Turley, Sarah; Co. Down.
42 Turley, Sarah; Co. Down.
59 Twamley, George; Wicklow.
59 Twamley, Jane; Wicklow.
59 Twamley, Mary; Wicklow.

V

60 Vaharty, Miles; Enniscorthy.
27 Vaughan, James.
27 Vaughan, Thomas.
27 Vaughan, Y.
19 Veatch, James.

W

63 Wacum, Robert, wife & child; Co. Dublin.
43 Wade, James & wife; Dublin.
60 Waldron, Thomas; Balbriggan.
48 Walker, Constantine.
61 Walker, David.
61 Walker, David.
48 Walker, Eliza.
48 Walker, George.
50 Walker, H.
50 Walker, J.
50 Walker, J.
48 Walker, James.
61 Walker, Jane.
16 Walker, John F.; Rich Hill.
48 Walker, Joseph.
50 Walker, M.
61 Walker, Martha.
48 Walker, Mary.
50 Walker, R.
48 Walker, William.
68 Walker, William; Londonderry.
4 Walkinshaw, William; Co. Antrim.
20 Wallace, Hannah; Dromore.
41 Wallace, James.
62 Wallace, Margaret.
53 Wallace, S.
20 Wallace, Thomas; Dromore.
19 Walsh, Bridget.
27 Walsh, Daniel.
19 Walsh, Eliza.
2 Walsh, Hugh; Co. Tipperary.
43 Walsh, James; Co. Wexford.
62 Walsh, John.
38 Walsh, John; Tipperary.
2 Walsh, Lawrence; Co. Tipperary.
22 Walsh, M. R.; Sligo.
1 Walsh, Patrick; Dublin.
48 Wantya, Richmond.
70 Ward, Anne.
70 Ward, Patrick.
26 Ward, William; Carlow.
43 Wardle, Jeremiah; Lancashire.
68 Wardler, Hugh; Tyrone.
13 Ware, James.
50 Warnick, R.
23 Warnock, John; Dublin.

59 Warr, Eliza; England.
59 Warr, George; England.
59 Warr, Samuel; England.
63 Warren, Edward; Co. Carlow.
63 Warren, John; Co. Carlow.
51 Warrier, George.
66 Wass, John; Dublin.
65 Waters, Archibald; Co. Antrim.
55 Waters, John.
55 Waters, Roger.
3 Waters, Winifred.
63 Waters, —; City of Dublin.
15 Waterson, John; Belfast.
61 Watson, Alexander.
28 Watson, James; Newtownards; Co. Down.
8 Watson, William; Co. Tyrone.
67 Watt, James; Templemore.
30 Watts, Charles; Tyrone.
30 Watts, James; Tyrone.
30 Watts, Jane; Tyrone.
30 Watts, Joseph; Tyrone.
30 Watts, Margaret; Tyrone.
30 Watts, Mary; Tyrone.
42 Weathers, Joseph; Co. Down.
4 Webster, Thomas; England.
51 Weeks, Caroline.
14 Weeks, Charles.
51 Weeks, Frances.
51 Weeks, Jane.
51 Weeks, Thos.
5 Wells, Peter; Waterford.
55 West, Anne.
24 West, Jas.
51 West, John.
51 West, Margaret.
51 West, Margaret.
14 West, Thmoas.
55 West, William.
51 West, Wm.
26 Whalen, Thomas; Dublin.
22 Wheelock, Alice; Wexford.
2 Whelan, Nicholas.
5 Whelan, Patrick; Waterford.
5 Whit, John; Waterford.
68 White, Alexander; Tyrone.
68 White, Elizabeth; Tyrone.
68 White, Ellen; Tyrone.
59 White, Francis; Dublin.
70 White, James.
48 White, Jane.
22 White, Richard; Dublin.
68 White, Mathew; Tyrone.
45 Whiteside, William.
34 Whitford, William; Co. Antrim.
30 Wigging, Rachel; Monaghan.
61 Wiggins, Henry.
47 Wiley, Ann.
47 Wiley, Elizabeth.
45 Wiley, John.

47 Wiley, Mary.
47 Wiley, Thomas.
27 Wilis, James.
3 Wilkinson, John.
3 Wilkinson, William.
32 Willes, Joshua.
32 Willes, Mary.
26 William, Mrs. E. W.; Dublin.
27 Willis, Eleanor.
27 Willis, Richard.
30 Wilson, Rev. A.; Jonesborough.
56 Wilson, Charles.
65 Wilson, David; Co. Tyrone.
4 Wilson, James; Co. Antrim.
42 Wilson, James; Co. Armagh.
65 Wilson, James; Co. Tyrone.
70 Wilson, Jane.
13 Wilson, John.
65 Wilson, Joseph; Co. Tyrone.
45 Wilson, Marcus.
65 Wilson, Mary; Co. Tyrone.
62 Wilson, Matthew.
61 Wilson, Robert.
42 Wilson, Sarah; Co. Armagh.
53 Wilson, Thomas.
14 Wilson, Thomas.
12 Wilson, Thomas; Dublin.
29 Wilson, William; Co. Antrim.
43 Winstanley, John; Dublin.
15 Withers, Wm.; Belfast.
20 Wood, Thomas; Auchnalcoy.
61 Woods, Eliza.
61 Woods, James.
8 Woods, Ruth; Richhill.
8 Woods, William; Richhill.
50 Woodside, R.
50 Woodside, Wm.
28 Workman, George; Tamletocrilly, Co. Derry.
68 Worrhington, John; Londonderry.
13 Wray, James.
13 Wray, William.
39 Wright, Henry.
69 Wright, James; Newtown Stewart.
69 Wright, Jane; Sligo.
69 Wright, John; Sligo.
69 Wright, Mariam; Sligo.
32 Wright, Mathan.
21 Wright, Michael.
13 Wright, William.
54 Wynne, Patrick.

Y

55 Young, Alexander.
55 Young, Eliza & child.
62 Young, John.
55 Young, Robert.
68 Young, Susan; Londonderry.
55 Young, Thomas; Drimkeeran.

LIST OF SHIPS

ARRIVING IN AMERICAN PORTS, 1815 AND 1816.

Code No.	Port of Departure	Date of Arrival 1815	Port of Entry	Name of Ship	Passengers	Point of Origin
1	Dublin	......	New York	Nautilus	18	County
2	Dublin	......	New York	Amphion	48	County
3	Sligo	......	New York	Helen	38	......
4	Belfast	Sept. 2	New York	Christopher	37	County
5	Waterford	Sept. 2	New York	Virginia	33	County
6	Dublin	Sept. 24	New York	Mary	23	......
7	Belfast	Oct. 14	New York	George	53	County
8	Belfast	Oct. 26	New York	James Bayley	98	County
9	Dublin	Nov. 10	New York	C. Fawcett	23	County
10	Liverpool	Nov. 14	New York	William	2	County
11	Halifax	Nov. 14	New York	Two Friends	3	County
12	Liverpool	Nov. 14	New York	Mexico	4	County
13	Londonderry	Nov. 14	New York	Marcus Hill	121	......
14	Dublin	Oct. 23	Philadelphia	George & Albert	42	......
15	Dublin	Nov. 18	New York	Orient	35	County
16	Belfast	Nov. 22	New York	Westpoint	47	County
17	Liverpool	......	New York	Minerva	5	County
18	Libson	......	New York	Courier	4	......
18ᵃ	Demarara	......	New York	Favorite	1	......
19	Dublin	Nov. 24	New York	Sally	57	County
20	Londonderry	Nov. 25	New York	Emp. Alexander	64	County
21	Newry	......	New York	Leda	22	......

1816

Code No.	Port of Departure	Date of Arrival	Port of Entry	Name of Ship	Passengers	Point of Origin
22	Dublin	Jan. 19	New York	Ontario	56	County
23	Belfast	Jan. 18	New York	Shannon	32	County
24	Dublin	Mar. 11	New York	Erin	31	......
25	Dublin	Mar. 7	New York	Amphion	20	County
26	Dublin	Apr. 3	New York	Dublin Packet	39	......
27	Cork	Apr. 13	New York	Anne	34	......
28	Belfast	May 2	New York	Lorenzo	53	......
29	Dublin	Apr. 25	New York	Hannah	15	County
30	Newry	May 4	Philadelphia	Nancy	22	County
31	Newry	May 4	Baltimore	Globe	23	County
32	Belfast	May 5	New York	Elizabeth	46	......

LIST OF SHIPS—*Continued*

Code No.	Port of Departure	Date of Arrival 1816	Port of Entry	Name of Ship	Passengers	Point of Origin
33	Newry	May 6	Philadelphia	Dido	22	County
34	Belfast	May 10	New York	John	18	County
35	Dublin	May 12	New York	Ch. Fawcett	31	County
36	Galway	May 12	New York	Hare	30	......
37	Londonderry	May 13	Philadelphia	Active	25	County
38	Dublin	May 17	Philadelphia	Louisa	26	......
39	Newry	......	New York	Aeolus	36	......
40	Newry	Jun. 1	New York	London	24	County
41	Londonderry	Jun. 4	New York	Foster	50	......
42	Belfast	Jun. 5	New York	Westpoint	45	County
43	Dublin	Jun. 10	New York	Wilson	37	County
44	Londonderry	......	New York	Enterprize	33	......
45	Londonderry	......	New York	Falcon	34	......
46	Londonderry	Jun. 14	Philadelphia	Jane	33	County
47	Belfast	Jun. 15	New York	William Hill	20	County
48	Londonderry	Jun. 15	New York	Marcus Hill	155	County
49	Londonderry	Jun. 17	New York	Niagara	34	County
50	Belfast	Jun. 20	New York	Ossian	90	......
51	Dublin	Jun. 22	Philadelphia	Conistoga	45	......
52	Belfast	Jun. 24	Philadelphia	George	46	......
53	Belfast	Jun. 26	New York	Sophia	82	......
54	Sligo	Jun. 30	New York	Foundling	90	Place
55	Sligo	Jly. 1	New York	Orient	57	County
56	Dublin	Jly. 1	New York	Bristol	47	......
57	Dublin	Jly. 2	Philadelphia	Ceres	37	County
58	Halifax	......	New York	Montague	2	County
59	Dublin	Jly. 3	New York	Dibby & Eliza	64	County
60	Dublin	Jly. 6	Philadelphia	Only Son	29	County
61	Belfast	Jly. 8	New York	George	91	......
62	Dublin	Jly. 10	New York	Prince of Brazil	99	......
63	Dublin	Jly. 15	New London	Actress	31	......
64	Newry	Aug. 1	Philadelphia	Boudain	37	Place
65	Belfast	Jly. 22	New York	Alpha	46	County
66	Dublin	Aug. 7	New York	Ontario	97	Place
67	Londonderry	Aug. 14	New York	Barkley	58	County
68	Londonderry	Aug. 12	New York	Mount-Bay	133	County
69	Sligo	Aug. 16	New York	Juno	38	......
70	Sligo	Aug. 8	New York	Margaret	54	......
71	Galway	Aug. 2	New York	John	40	Place
72	Dublin	Aug. 14	New York	Bristol	40	Place

"RESTAURATIONEN," WITH THE FIRST NORSE EMIGRANTS ON BOARD, SAILING OUT OF STAVANGER HARBOR, 1825. PAINTING BY BEN BLESSUM

"Restaurationen"— the Norse Mayflower

By RASMUS B. ANDERSON

ON THE 4th of July, 1825, began the Norwegian emigration to this country. The first emigrants left Stavanger, a quaint old town on the west coast of Norway, on our National day of Independence, in a small sloop named *Restaurationen.* The officers and passengers numbered, counting men, women, and children, fifty-two souls, and when they reached New York on the 9th of October they were fifty-three, a little girl having been born on the 2nd of September in the Mid-Atlantic. The centennial of the departure from Norway of this Norwegian Mayflower is soon to be celebrated, and the event has been fittingly recognized by our government. The Post Office Department is issuing a memorial stamp, and Congress has authorized a silver medal in commemoration of the event.

In connection with this centennial, it is eminently proper to review the history of the movement that began a hundred years ago.

The father and promoter of Norwegian emigration in 1825 was Cleng Peerson, who was born in Norway on May 17th, 1782, and died in Texas on December 16th, 1865. Some years ago I wrote for the AMERICAN-SCANDINAVIAN REVIEW an extended account of Cleng Peerson, to which readers of this article are referred, while I may be permitted to repeat: that he, as the emissary of a Quaker society in

Stavanger and vicinity, went to America in 1821, remained here for three years investigating conditions and prospects for Norwegian immigrants, and returned to Norway in 1824 with a most optimistic report.

The leader of the *Restaurationen* party of emigrants was Lars Larson i Jeilane. He was born in Stavanger, Norway, September 24, 1787. He became a ship-carpenter and served on board a Norwegian merchant ship. During the Napoleonic wars Russia compelled Denmark to make war on England, but was unable to prevent England from sending a fleet to the Sound, where a bloody naval engagement was fought on the 2nd of April, 1801. Six years later, in September, 1807, to cross the plans of Napoleon, England bombarded Copenhagen and captured the Danish fleet. The allies of Denmark afforded her no protection. In the Danish war with England from 1807 to 1814, the commerce and finances of Denmark were ruined, and Denmark, as an ally of France, was put on a war-footing with nearly all of Europe. Denmark lost Norway and other possessions and was left in a bankrupt condition. I mention this here for the reason that down to 1814 Norway had for several hundred years been united with Denmark, so that this war also involved Norway.

In the first year of the war, that is to say, in 1807, the ship in which Lars Larson was employed was captured by the English, and he and the rest of the crew remained prisoners of war in England for seven years. In 1814, immediately after the treaty of peace, he, with the other prisoners, was released, and he thereupon spent a year in London in the employ of a prominent Quaker lady, the widow Margaret Allen, mother of Joseph and William Allen, who at that time held high positions near the English Court. During the period of his imprisonment and during his subsequent sojourn in London, Lars Larson had acquired a pretty thorough speaking knowledge of the English language, and he had also become converted to the Quaker religion. Some of his Norwegian companions in captivity had likewise accepted the Quaker faith. In 1816 Lars Larson returned to Norway, and he and his friends at once began to make propaganda for Quakerism and to organize a little Society of Friends. In Stavanger he and Elias Tastad and Thomas and Metta Hille became the founders of the Society of Friends in Norway. This Society never became large and never spread beyond the limits of Stavanger Amt or County, but it still exists, and to-day numbers about two hundred adult members. The first Quaker meeting in Norway was held in the home of Lars Larson in the year 1816. He was not married at the time, but his deaf and dumb sister, Sara, kept house for him. At Christmas, in 1824, he married Martha Georgiana Peerson, who was born October 10, 1803, on Fogn, a small island near Stavanger. Miss Peerson was in no way related to Cleng Peerson.

During the time we are now discussing, Norway, and particularly the southwest coast districts, contained a large number of semi-dissenters from the established Church—the followers of Hans Nielsen Hauge, a reformer, born in 1771. Though he had only a common peasant education, he began to preach in 1795. He protested against the liberalism and secularization then prevalent among the clergy of Norway. He advocated the right of laymen to preach and laid special stress upon the spiritual priesthood of all believers, while he was, on the other hand, charged with an extravagant undervaluation of an educated ministry, of ordination, and of the ceremonies practised by the State Church.

Hauge's zeal secured him many followers, particularly among the peasants, who did not, however, as did the Quakers, withdraw from the established Church. Still, they were looked upon with disfavor by the governing class, and their leader, Hauge, was sent to prison for seven years. The Haugeans looked upon their leader as a martyr, and this fact intensified the strained relations existing between them and the civil and religious rulers of Norway. It may be stated, without exaggeration, that many of the government officials of that time, not only those who had charge of secular affairs, but also the servants of the Church, were inclined to be arbitrary and overbearing, and all dissenters from the Lutheran Church, which was the State religion, were persecuted by those in authority. The treatment accorded to Hauge is proof of this. Although he was guilty of no crime known to the code of morality, and although he was one of the most sincere Christians in all the land, he, like John Bunyan in England, was made to languish for seven long years within the walls of a prison simply because he held profound religious views and insisted on practising them. All the followers of Hauge were made to feel more or less the keen edge of scorn from their superiors. The persecution of the Quakers is, however, a still darker chapter in the modern ecclesiastical history of Norway. On a complaint of the State priest the Sheriff would come and take the children by force from Quaker families and bring them to the priest to be baptized. People were fined for not going to the Holy Communion. Parents were compelled to have their children confirmed, and even the dead were exhumed from their graves in order that they might be buried in consecrated ground according to the Lutheran ritual.

These cruel facts, I regret to say, are perfectly authenticated, and there is not a shadow of doubt that this disgraceful intolerance on the part of the officials in Norway, as in the case of the Huguenots in France and the Puritans and Independents in England, was one of the main causes of the first large exodus from Norway to the United States of America. The very fact that Norwegian emigration began in Stavanger County, and that the emigrants were dissenters from the established Church, is conclusive proof of the correctness of this view. Here it was that Lars Larson, Elias Tastad, and Thomas and Metta Hille had founded the Quaker Society. In the city of Stavanger and in its vicinity many had been converted to the Quaker doctrine, and there were no Quakers in Norway outside of Stavanger County.

In all lands and climes, the beginning of emigration can often be traced to religious intolerance and persecution. Did not France lose half a million of her most desirable citizens on account of the persecution of the Huguenots? Did not the Huguenots flee to Switzerland, Holland, England, and to America? Wherever they settled they brought with them art and manufacture and the refinement of civilization, and so they enriched their adopted countries. And what of the Pilgrim fathers who landed in Plymouth in 1620 and founded the first settlement in New England? Were they not men of strong minds, good judgment, and sterling character, and did they not rigidly conform their lives to their principles? Persecution led them to emigrate, and in New England they embodied their principles in a framework of government, on which a most stable foundation of our Great American Republic has been built up. History repeats itself in Norway in the early years of the nineteenth century, and the sloop *Restaurationen* left Norway in 1825 because Quakers were not permitted to worship God according to the dictates of their own conscience. The story of William Penn is repeated in Norway.

Of course, there were economic reasons also, and the emigrants hoped to better their material as well as their religious conditions. It should also be remembered that there was a widespread feeling of suspicion and distrust among the common folk of Norway against the office-holding class. There were many unprincipled officials who exacted exorbitant and even unlawful fees for their services, and with such officials ordinary politeness to the common man was out of the question. Thus, poverty, oppression on the part of the officials, and religious persecution co-operated in turning the minds of the people in Stavanger city and county toward the land of freedom and abundance in the far West.

While I am compelled to present these gloomy pictures of conditions in Norway in the early part of the last century, I am happy to be able to state that things have changed radically since then. A broad religious tolerance now exists there and has accelerated the tendency which since 1840 has been steadily toward more freedom and toward more opportunities for all classes of citizens.

The emigration from Stavanger afterwards inspired the people in other parts of Norway to leave the Fatherland and seek homes in America. In each succeeding group there was a pioneer, a leader, and these leaders will not be forgotten in connection with the centennial celebration.

The "Selen," a Sister Ship to the Sloop "Restaurationen," Built by the Same Firm in Hardanger and Said to Resemble It Exactly. No Picture of "Restaurationen" Is in Existence

Cleng Peerson, from the Farm Hesthammer, in Tysver Parish, Skjold District, Stavanger County, was the man who gave the first impetus to the emigration of Norwegians to America. As already stated, in the year 1821, he and a comrade, by name Knud Olson Eide, from the small island, Fogn, near Stavanger, left Norway and went by the way of Gothenburg, Sweden, from Norway to make an investigation of conditions and opportunities in America. Cleng and Knud were practically sent on this mission by the Quakers of Stavanger County. Cleng and Knud were not themselves Quakers, but they were dissenters from the established church. Cleng was strongly attached to the Quakers and sympathized with their religious views, so far as he gave religion any thought, but neither of them had at this time any very pronounced religious convictions. While they dissented from the State Church, they had not accepted the tenets of any other. They appear to have lacked, to a certain extent, the religious temperament.

After a sojourn of three years in America, all that time spent in and around New York City, where they did such work as they could find, Cleng Peerson being a carpenter by trade, they returned to Norway in 1824. Here their reports of social, political, and religious conditions in America and their discussion of opportunities in the

New World awakened the greatest interest, and culminated in a resolution to emigrate.

Lars Larson, the same man at whose house the first Quaker meeting had been held in 1816, at once undertook to organize a party of emigrants, being successful in finding a number of people who were ready and willing to join him. Six heads of families converted their scanty worldly possessions into money and purchased a sloop which had been built in the Hardanger Fjord, and which they loaded with a cargo of iron. For this sloop of forty-five tons burden and cargo they paid the sum of 1800 Norwegian dollars. While six of the party owned some stock in this vessel, the largest share was held by Lars Larson, who was in all respects the leader of the enterprise. He had acquired a pretty thorough knowledge of the English language during his eight years' sojourn in England, and the general supervision of the preparations and of the voyage naturally fell into his intelligent hands. The captain, Lars Olson Helland, and the mate, Erikson, were engaged by him.

This little Norwegian Mayflower of the nineteenth century received the name *Restaurationen* (The Restoration) and on the Ameri-

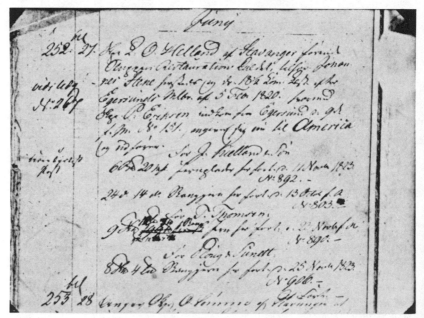

RECORD OF CLEARANCE FOUND IN THE STAVANGER CUSTOMS' BOOK FOR JUNE 27, 1825, STATING THAT CAPTAIN L. O. HELLAND IS SAILING FOR AMERICA WITH THE SLOOP "RESTAURATIONEN," THE CARGO BEING IRON

can day of Independence, July 4, 1825, the brave little company of emigrants sailed out of the harbor of the ancient city of Stavanger. The company consisted of fifty-two persons, including the two officers mentioned, chiefly from Stavanger city and Tysver Parish, north of Stavanger. There were also a few from other parts of Stavanger County. They were fifty-two when they left Stavanger, but when they reached New York on the second Sunday of October (October 9th) they numbered fifty-three, Mrs. Martha Georgiana Larson, the wife of the leader, having given birth to a beautiful girl baby on the 2nd of September.

Their fourteen weeks' journey across the Atlantic Ocean was a romantic and perilous one. The stories of that voyage, told to me by one of the party, were the delight of my childhood. They passed through the British Channel, and a few days later they anchored in a small harbor named "The Lizzard" on the coast of England, where they remained until the next day. Here they began to sell liquor to the residents, which was against the law, and when they perceived the danger in which they had thus placed themselves, they made haste to steer the little craft out on the boundless ocean. They either must have lost their reckoning by looking for the trade winds, or the captain must have been somewhat deficient in his knowledge of navigation, or, to take a more charitable view of the case, the wind must have been against them, for when we next hear of them we find them drifting into the harbor of Funchal in the Island of Madeira. Near the Madeira Islands they found a pipe of wine floating on the water. It must have been very old wine, for the cask in which it was contained was entirely covered with barnacles. Lars Larson got out in a yawl-boat to fish it up, and while he was putting a rope around the pipe, a shark came near biting his hand off. To celebrate this piece of good fortune, both the officers and passengers had to taste of the delicious contents of the pipe of wine, and the result was that most of them got more or less under its influence. In consequence they neglected their duties. They came drifting into the Harbor of Funchal without colors and without command. Here it was feared they had some kind of contagious disease on board, and one of the officers of the *Bremen,* a vessel anchored in the harbor, shouted to them that if they did not wish to be greeted by the cannon already aimed at them by the fortress, they had better hoist their colors at once. Thorstein Olson Bjaadland, who was for many years our neighbor in Wisconsin, never grew weary of telling us this story, and he always added that it was he who hunted up the Norwegian flag which was stored away with other baggage, and ran it up the mast, thus averting the danger. A couple of custom-house officers then came on board the ship and made an investigation, finding everything in good order. Much attention was shown to the party at Funchal. The American Consul increased their store of provisions, giving them also an abundance of grapes, and before their departure he invited the whole sloop party to a magnificent dinner. They arrived in Funchal on Thursday, July 28th, and left the following Sunday, July 31st, and as they sailed out of the harbor the fortress fired a salute in their honor.

Four weeks had passed since they left Stavanger, and for ten more weary weeks the sloop had to contend with the angry waves of the rough Atlantic. It may be added here that only the captain and mate were seamen in the strict sense of the word, but Lars Larson was by trade a ship-carpenter, and most of the adult men on board, having been reared on the coast of Norway as fishermen, were naturally familiar with the sea.

In New York quite a sensation was awakened by the fact that these Norwegians had ventured across the ocean in so small a craft. Such a thing had not been heard of before. Here they also got into trouble with the authorities, on account of having a larger cargo and a larger number of passengers than the American laws permitted a ship the size of the sloop to carry, and in consequence of this violation of Uncle Sam's laws, Captain Lars Olson Helland was arrested, and the ship with its cargo was seized by the custom-house authorities of New York.

Cleng Peerson was in New York when the sloop arrived there. He had again gone by the way of Gothenburg, Sweden, and was in New York ready to receive his friends and to give them such assistance as he was able. He had found Quakers in New York, who were prepared to give our Norwegian Pilgrims a welcome and such help as they most needed. I suppose the authorities in New York, partly in consideration of the ignorant and childish conduct of the sloop immigrants and partly influenced by the powerful intercession of Quaker Friends, decided to be merciful. The fact is, at all events, that the captain was released from captivity, and the sloop and its cargo were restored to their owners.

I have it from the lips of passengers who came in the sloop that the Quakers in New York took a deep interest in these Norwegian newcomers, who were well-nigh destitute of food, clothing, and money. These Friends gave many of them shelter under their own roofs and supplied them with money to relieve their most pressing needs. The Quakers showed themselves in this case, as everywhere in history, to be friends indeed. Mrs. Atwater, the lady who was born on the sloop, has told me, on the authority of her parents, how kind the Quakers in New York were to all the sloop people. Enough money was raised by the Quakers to pay the expenses of the immigrants, $6.00 for each, from New York City to the town of Kendall in Orleans County, New York, where farms were secured by them.

Here, then, was formed the first Norwegian settlement in America in modern times.

The captain and the mate remained in New York. The leader of the party, Lars Larson, sent his wife and daughter on with the rest of the sloop party to Kendall, but he himself remained for several weeks in New York City to dispose of the sloop and its cargo. He finally succeeded in selling both for the paltry sum of $400. By this time winter had set in, and it was in the early days of December that he started out to join his family. The canal was frozen, and he had to skate from Albany to Holley in Orleans County, twenty-three miles beyond Rochester. He did not remain with the colony in Kendall, but went with his family back to Rochester, where he soon obtained employment from a canal-boat builder. He prospered, and in a short time he was able to go into business for himself as a canal-boat builder. It will be remembered that he had been a ship-carpenter in Norway, and both by his knowledge of English and by his trade he was equipped for his new occupation.

Lars Larson is described as a rather small man with a smooth, intelligent face, with dark hair which turned gray very early. He was a kind husband and a good father, in short, a man of good habits and large-hearted. His home in Rochester was hospitality itself. In the years from 1836 to 1845 he received visits from thousands of Norwegians who were on their way from Norway to Illinois and Wisconsin. They brought him fresh news from Norway, and from him they received valuable information and advice concerning America. His canal-boat business prospered, and already in 1827 he was able to build for himself and family a very substantial house in Rochester, a house which still stands on the original site and which is the oldest house now in existence built in America by a Norwegian Argonaut of the nineteenth century. The house was occupied until recently by Georgiana Larson, the youngest and only surviving child of Martha and Lars Larson. At present time she rents it to tenants, living herself in a smaller house near by. She will be 87 years old June

LARS LARSON, THE LEADER OF THE SLOOP EXPEDITION. FROM A PHOTOGRAPH TAKEN AFTER HIS DEATH

MARTHA LARSON, WIFE OF LARS LARSON,
THE LEADER OF THE SLOOP-FOLK

19, this year. She never married.

Lars Larson lost his life by an accident November 13, 1845, while on his way to New York with a canalboat which he intended to sell. He died from a fall from the boat into the canal. He had given his children a good education, and on his death left them, not a fortune, but a competency for maintaining the old home. His widow, Martha Georgiana, a woman of great intelligence and force of character, lived to a ripe old age. The writer met her in 1875 and was struck with her stateliness and womanly dignity. She had become entirely Americanized, but still spoke her old Stavanger dialect with ease and fluency. Her death occurred in Rochester, October 17, 1887.

Mr. and Mrs. Larson left eight children, six girls and two boys. Their oldest child, born on the sloop in the middle of the Atlantic Ocean, was a girl whom they named Margaret Allen, after the Quaker widow with whom her father had lived for a year or more in London, and through whose influence he had embraced the Quaker faith. Margaret Allen married, in 1857, John Atwater of Rochester, who later became a prominent publisher in Chicago. She died December 12, 1916, in her home at Western Springs, near Chicago, Illinois, and is survived by a son and two daughters. Another daughter, Martha Jane, born July 30, 1832, married an inventor of New York, Elias C. Patterson, who died in Rochester, New York, in 1879. She has the honor of being one of the first two persons of the Norwegian group of our population to have taught in our public schools. She began teaching in Rochester during vacation in 1844, when she was only twelve years old and had about twenty scholars, who paid her ten cents a week each. She then attended a ladies' seminary and became assistant teacher in it in 1848. In the spring of 1850 she taught a public country school in Kendall, Orleans County. In the spring of 1851 she taught at Lockport, New York, and in the

THE HOUSE OF LARS LARSON BUILT IN 1827,
STILL STANDING AT 41 ATKINSON ST., ROCHESTER

autumn of the same year she was given a position in one of the public schools of Rochester, New York. She came west in 1857 and entered the public schools of Chicago as a teacher. Her name deserves to be remembered on that account. Many a Miss Larson or Miss Olson has given instruction in our American common schools, but Martha Jane Larson was one of the first two. The very first of the Norwegian group in this country to teach in our public schools was a niece of Cleng Peerson, a daughter of the slooper, Cornelius Nelson Hersdal. She married Canute Peterson and in 1849 moved to Utah, where her husband became a prominent Mormon bishop; but before go-

An Old Picture of Georgiana Larson, Only Surviving Daughter of Lars Larson (to the Left), with Her Cousin, Mrs. Anna Parker, of Kendall

ing to Utah, she taught in the public schools in the Fox River settlement in Illinois, beginning in 1845, four years earlier than Martha Jane Larson.

The sloop *Restaurationen* attracted the notice of the press in New York on its arrival from Norway. There were extended notices in the *Commercial Advertiser* for October 10, in the *New York Daily Advertiser* of October 12, in the *New York American* of October 10; and on October 22 the *New York American* contained a long clipping from the *Baltimore American*. As our space is limited, we are unable to reproduce here the very interesting notices found in the New York papers of October, 1825, and we will have to limit ourselves to a notice found in the *Albany Patriot* October 24. Here it is:

"On Saturday, as we are informed, the Norwegian immigrants that lately arrived in a small vessel in New York, passed through this city on their way to their place of destination. They appeared to be quite pleased with what they see in this country, if we may judge from their good-humored countenances. Success attend their efforts in this asylum of the oppressed."

In Kendall land was sold to the Norwegians by Joseph Fellows at $5.00 an acre, but as they had no money to pay for it, Mr. Fellows agreed to let them redeem it in ten annual installments. Each head of a family and adult person purchased forty acres. During the first year they suffered great privations. The land was heavily wooded, and the clearing of the forests required hard work. The emigrants longed to get back to old Norway, but like Xerxes of old they had

burned the bridges behind them, and a return would be not only
humiliating but well-nigh impossible. Joseph Fellows and other
benevolent neighbors helped them, and in the course of time their in-
dustry brought its reward.

As they did not reach New York before the 9th of October, it
was November before they got settled in Kendall, and the cold weather
soon set in. The country thereabouts was but sparsely settled in 1825,
and there was not much opportunity for getting employment or shelter. Twenty-four of them, including their children, combined and
put up a log house, 12 by 12 feet with a garret. Crowded together
in this little hut, their patience must have been taxed to the utmost,
and only the hope of a brighter future could support them under such
circumstances.

In those days threshing machines were not known, and these
Norwegian settlers made their first little earnings by threshing out
grain for the older settlers with a flail. For this kind of work they got
every eleventh bushel.

The next year, 1826, they cleared on an average two acres on
each of their farms. On this piece of ground they raised wheat, which
gave them bread for their next winter's support.

In the pioneer history of Orleans County, New York, written by
Arad Thomas and published in 1871, we find the following interesting notice of this first Norwegian settlement in America:

"About the year 1825 a company of Norwegians, about fifty-two in number,
settled on the lake shore in the northeast part of the town. They came from Norway
together and took up land in a body. They were an industrious, prudent, and worthy
people, held in good repute by people in that vicinity. After a few years they began
to move away to join their countrymen who had settled in Illinois, and but a few of
that colony are still in Kendall. They thought it very important that each family
should have land and a home of their own. A neighbor once asked a little Norwegian
boy, whose father had happened to be too poor to own land, where his father lived,
and was answered, 'Oh, we don't live nowhere; we hain't got no home.'"

This is touchingly prophetic of the fact that so large a percentage
of the Norwegian immigrants have settled on farms and become
owners of land. In this manner then began the great Scandinavian
exodus of the nineteenth century, which has brought 1,250,000 immigrants, and thus was founded the first settlement which has been followed by so many large and thrifty ones throughout the United States.

As this sloop party will always be of the greatest interest to all
Norwegians and their descendants in this country, I have taken all
possible pains to ascertain definitely who the fifty-three persons were
who came in it. By the aid of the survivors and various others who
knew them, I think I am able to present a well nigh perfect list of the
adult members, with the number of children in each family. Here it is:

(1 to 3) Lars Larson (i Jeilane), wife and daughter; (4 to 9) Cornelius Nelson Hersdal, wife and four children; (10 to 13) Johannes Stene, wife and two children; (14 to 18) Oyen Thompson (Thorson), wife and three children; (19 to 25) Daniel Stenson Rossadal, wife and five children; (26 to 30) Thomas Marland, wife and three children. These six families were the owners of the sloop, of which Lars Larson owned the largest share. (31 to 35) Simon Lima, wife and three children; (36 and 37) Nels Nelson Hersdal and wife, Bertha; (38) Jacob Anderson (Slogvig); (39) Knud Anderson (Slogvig); (40) Sara Larson, deaf and dumb sister of Lars Larson; (41 and 42) Henrick Christofferson Hervig and wife; (43) Ole Johnson; (44) Gudmund Haugaas; (45) Thorstein Olson Bjaadland; (46) George Johnson; (47) Andrew (Endre) Dahl, the cook; (48) Halvor Iverson; (49) Nels Thompson, a brother of Oyen Thompson; (50) Ole Olson Hetletvedt; (51) Andrew Stangeland; (52) Lars Olson Helland, the captain; (53) Erikson, the mate.

The writer has himself seen and talked with eight of the sloop passengers, viz.: Thorstein Olson Bjaadland; Mrs. Lars Larson and her daughter, Mrs. Atwater; Nels Nelson Hersdal and his wife; Mrs. Hulda Olson, a daughter of Daniel Stenson Rossadal; Mrs. Martha Fellows and Mrs. Inger Mitchell, the last two daughters of Cornelius Nelson Hersdal; and he has had a considerable correspondence with three others: Mrs. Sara T. Ritchie, a daughter of Oyen Thompson; Mrs. Jacob Anderson (Slogvig), the daughter of Thomas Madland; and Mrs. Sara A. Peterson, the daughter of Cornelius Nelson Hersdal.

In 1833, Cleng Peerson made a journey on foot from Kendall, New York, to LaSalle County, Illinois, and there selected the location of the second Norwegian settlement in America. He returned at once to Kendall, New York, and in 1834 and 1835 a large number of the settlers in Kendall moved west to LaSalle County, Illinois, where they secured land at the government price, and in the course of time they were joined by immigrants coming from Norway in 1836 and the following years. This first settlement of Norwegians in the West became very large and prosperous. The parents of the writer lived there from 1837 to 1840.

The large body of Norwegian immigrants become Americanized fully as rapidly as any other class of immigrants from the European continent. They acquire the English language easily and make most loyal citizens. They are by nature industrious and thrifty, and pay much attention to the proper education of their children. It is universally admitted that the Norwegians are among the most desirable immigrants to this country from Europe. While the Norwegians have filled a considerable number of offices, national, state, and county, and as a rule with great credit to themselves, they are not an office-seeking class. The Norwegian press is as a rule enlightened, of high ideals, and is exceedingly loyal to America and its institutions.

FOUR IMMIGRANT SHIPLOADS OF 1836
AND 1837

By Henry J. Cadbury

There will always be a special interest in the first groups of Norwegians that came as immigrants to America in the third and fourth decades of the nineteenth century. The premier place is held by the brave band of fifty-two, counting crew and children, who came on the sloop " Restaurationen " in 1825. Next to them the principal large contingents were those who came nearly a dozen years later in four vessels, the Køhler brigs " Norden " and " Den Norske Klippe " in 1836 and the barks " Ægir " and " Enigheden " in the following year. The uncertainty as to the personnel of these parties, especially of the famous sloop party, led the author to inquire from the federal authorities whether there were some records at New York Harbor concerning the vessels that brought them. The immigration records there prior to June 15, 1897, were destroyed in the Ellis Island fire of that date and they probably did not extend back before 1845. At the Customs House, however, the records of vessels arriving from foreign ports date back to 1795, and it was there that the lists and other data of arrivals given below were obtained. The passenger list of " Restaurationen " is missing, but one entry yields the following information: Sloop: Restoration, 60 tons; Master: Kelland; Port: Stavanger, Norway; Date: October 14, 1825.[1]

[1] It was through the courtesy of Mr. H. C. Stewart, assistant collector of the port of New York, that the writer came into possession of the lists and other data. In his first letter Mr. Stewart sent the entry for " Restaurationen " and added, " The passenger list is missing and there is no record of any seizure at this port." Later he wrote that the indexes show the entries for the vessels " Norden," " Ægir," and " Enigheden," but not for " Den Norske Klippe." The item of greatest interest, however, was his statement that the office had on file passenger

These lists should be of great interest not only for the thousands of descendants of the pioneers whose names they include, but also for all who appreciate the historical importance of the journeys. The lists are probably not quite infallible, but they are far more complete and accurate than the records based upon oral tradition, as some comparison will easily show. Several of the individual immigrants on the four boats were important figures in the early Norwegian migration and settlement.

In size and influence no other group of immigrants in the first generation of Norwegian immigration can compare with the 343 passengers of these four ships that constituted the bulk of the exodus of 1836 and 1837. The general information conveyed by the lists may be summarized as follows:

Name	Date of Manifest	Master	No. of Pas.	Tons
Brig "Norden"	July 20, 1836	Tønnes Willemsen	110	290
Brig "Den Norske Klippe"	August 15, 1836	Peter Rolfsen	57	150
Bark "Ægir"	June 11, 1837	Christian K. Behrens	84	21-?
Brig "Enigheden"	September 14, 1837	Jens Pedersen	91	—

The total number of passengers would thus be 342, but one birth and five deaths on "Norden" on the voyage would change it to 338.[2] All the passengers but one ("Ægir" 73) were Norwegians.

lists of "Norden" and the "Ægir." The author accordingly arranged to have these lists copied by Miss Dikka Bothne of the American-Scandinavian Foundation. Subsequently he verified and corrected the copies by the originals and prepared them for the press. This was already completed when he had another opportunity to visit the record department at the Customs House and he determined to search for the lists of the other two ships, which the custodians had reported that they were unable to find. To his great delight he was rewarded by finding the complete passenger lists for "Enigheden" and "Den Norske Klippe," and he is therefore now able to offer all four for the use of students of early Norwegian immigration.

[2] Olaf M. Norlie, in his *History of the Norwegian People in America*, 138 (Minneapolis, 1925) gives 337 as the total number on the four ships. This work will be referred to hereafter by the author's surname.

Each of the lists has the following printed headings: "Names," "Age," "Sex," "Occupation," "The Country to which they severally belong," "The Country in which they intend to become inhabitants," and "Died on the voyage." Not all the columns have been copied in the case of every ship. Only "Norden" has entries under "Died on the voyage." The native country is indicated as Norway for all the passengers except one, A. C. Stange from Germany ("Ægir" 73). The destination is marked as United States for all on "Norden" and the "Ægir" and as Illinois for all on "Den Norske Klippe" and "Enigheden." The occupation list has not always been filled out with care; the entries under "Occupation" are very incomplete for the two vessels last named and even the entries under "Sex" are often obscure and carelessly written. For convenience of reference, numbers have been prefixed to the names; indeed, this had already been done on the manifest of "Enigheden." It will be observed that the lists differ in the way names and kinship are designated, but fortunately the names appear to be arranged by families.

The lists are given in chronological order. No attempt has been made to give full or elaborate discussion, but each list is followed by brief notes, with references to a few standard works. No doubt those who are more conversant with Norwegian-American lore will find many other points of interest in the simple contemporary data here offered for study.

"NORDEN"

According to an interesting letter from Captain Tønnes Willemsen to Elias Tastad, written in Bremerhaven on November 18, 1836, the voyage of "Norden," though comparatively brief, was cold, wet, and stormy, though no hurricane was encountered.[3] Many of the passengers caught severe colds,

[3] Willemsen's letter was published by Gunnar J. Malmin in *Decorah-Posten*, December 5, 1924.

probably from lack of sufficient clothing, especially for the legs; at least, that is the explanation of the captain, who blames them for not heeding his advice in that regard and recommends that future immigrants provide themselves with wooden shoes. He refers also to the illness of nursing infants, incurred from their mothers, but, strangely enough, he makes no mention of the five deaths on the voyage noted in the manifest. On the contrary, he repeatedly speaks of the voyage as having gone very well.

Except for " Restaurationen," which made the voyage eleven years before, " Norden " was the first immigrant ship from Norway to reach America. As on the earlier occasion, the bright colors displayed as the immigrants landed in their best clothes made some impression at the harbor. This the captain mentions, as well as the admiration that the Americans felt for their quietness when compared with the Irish and the Germans.

Evidently Knud Anderson Slogvig was the leader of this party, as he was of the exodus in general. Rasmus B. Anderson gives the date of departure from Stavanger as the first Wednesday after Pentecost and that of arrival at New York as July 12, 1836.[4] The later date of the ship's manifest is no real contradiction. The number of passengers on the brig, 110, approached very near the legal limit. It will be remembered that the American law permitted only two passengers for every five tons and that on that account "Restaurationen," with fifty-two passengers and forty-six tons, met trouble on its arrival in New York in 1825. Probably because

[4] *The First Chapter of Norwegian Immigration (1821-1840); Its Causes and Results,* 43 ff. (Madison, Wisconsin, 1895). On page 156 Anderson gives the first Sunday after Pentecost as the date of departure. He makes no attempt to give all the names of the passengers of " Norden " and apparently he did not know their total number. Anderson's book will be referred to hereafter by his surname. *The Shipping and Commercial List* (New York), July 20, 1836, gives the arrival in its marine list as of July 16, 17: " Nor. brig Nordon, Williamson, Stephanda [*sic*], Norway."

Willemsen and Tastad knew of this difficulty with the authorities, Willemsen added in a postscript to his letter: " The ship was measured in New York 280½ tons and so I can take 112 persons."

<DISTRICT OF NEW-YORK — PORT OF NEW-YORK.>

<I,> Tonnes Willemsin <do solemnly, sincerely and truly> Swear <that the following List or Manifest of Passengers, subscribed with my name, and now delivered by me to the Collector of the Customs for the District of New-York, contains, to the best of my knowledge and belief, a just and true account of all the Passengers received on board the> Brig. Norden <whereof I am Master, from> Stavanger

<*Sworn to, the*> 20 July <183>6<,> <So help me God.> <*before me,* >JAS CAMPBELL Dy Coll TÖNNES WELLEMSIN

<List or Manifest of all the Passengers taken on board the> Brig. Norden (Norwegian) <whereof> Tonnes Willemsin <is Master, from> Stavanger <Burthen> 290 [*Portion crossed out*].

NAMES		AGE		SEX	OCCUPA-TION	DIED ON VOYAGE
		YRS.	MOS.			
1	Knud Olsen Hetleved	43		Male	Countryman	
2	Sigrid	his wife	43		Female	
3	Ole	" Son	12		Male	
4	Johannes	" Do	6		Do	
5	Sören	" Do	—	6	Do	
6	Ellen Sophia	" daughter	15		Female	
7	Malene	" Do	8		Do	
8	Birthe Serina	" Do	3		Do	
9	Jacob Jacobsen		25	6	Male	Countryman	
10	Christine	his wife	22		Female	
11	Lars Nielsen Hellen		27		Male	Countryman	
12	Martha	his wife	22	6	Female	
13	Samuel Enersen		49		Male	Countryman	
14	Birtha	his wife	51		Female	
15	Kirstina	his daughter	13		Do	
16	Bertha Serina	Do	8		Do	
17	Halvar Bergersen		32		Male	Countryman	

	NAMES	AGE YRS. MOS.		SEX	OCCUPA-TION	DIED ON VOYAGE
18	Martha Olsdatter his wife	31		Female		
19	Peder Ornmundsen	32		Male	Countryman	
20	Bertha Karina " wife	20		Female		
21	Hendrick Erichsen	44		Male	Countryman	
22	Magle his Wife	36		Female		
23	Johnas " Son	10		male		
24	Erich " Do	7		Do		
25	Peder " Do	—	6	Do		
26	Bertha " daughter	14		Female		Dead
27	Walbarg " Do	3		Do		
28	Anton Osmundsen	24		Male	Joiner	
29	Johannes Berecssen (?) Hetland	30		Do	Countryman	
30	Bertha his wife	27		Female		
31	Lars " Son	1		Male		
32	Osmund (?) Endresen Tretland (?)	38		Male	Countryman	
33	Maria his Wife	33		Female		
34	Endre " Son	11		male		
35	Reier " Do	7		Do		
36	Osmund " Do	4		Do		
37	Endre " Do	1		Do		Dead
38	Peder Ormsen	33		Do	Countryman	
39	John Jacobsen Hallen	55		Do	Countryman	
40	Kirsten his wife	50		Female		
41	Hanna " daughter	24		Do		
42	Gurri " Do	20		Do		
43	Kirsten . Do	14		Do		
44	Helge . do	7		Do		
45	Jacob . Son	18		male		
46	Marcus " Do	10		Do		
47	Isack Jacob Gudmunsen	20		Do	Countryman	Dead
48	Anna Olsdatter " Sister	18		Female		
49	Ole Marcussen	46		Male	Carpenter	
50	Anna Cathrina wife	44		Female		
51	Kleng Klensen	27		Male	Carpenter	
52	Inger his Wife	24		Female		
53	Marthe daughter	3		Do		
54	Gurri do		3	Do		Dead
55	Ole Kleppe	25		male	Carpenter	
56	Karen " Sister	36		Female		
57	Djorn Andressen Eike	34		male	Carpenter	

Names		Age Yrs. Mos.		Sex	Occupation	Died on Voyage
58	Abel Catharina " Wife	26		Female		
59	Arenhaldus Andreas " Son	4		male		
60	Augustinus Meldal Drun Do	2		Do		
61	Baar Hansen Boe	48		Do	Carpenter	
62	Helge his Wife	41		Female		
63	Hans " Son	12		male		
64	Birtha " Daughter	15		Female		
65	Boel " Do	10		Do		
66	Anna Dorthea do	8		Do		
67	Anna do	6		Female		
68	Karen do	5		Do		
69	Holger Hansen Natvig (?)	35	6	Male	Smith	
70	Andreas Sigbjornsen	26		Do	Countryman	
71	Marthe Govertsdatter	26		Female	Maid Servant	
72	Ole Tensen	25	6	male	Countryman	
73	Anders Enersen	45		Do	Countryman	
74	Oline his Wife	47		Female		
75	Ener " Son	15	6	male		
76	Anderes " Do	9		Do		
77	Susanna " daughter	14		Female		
78	Lisbeth " Do	11		Do		
79	Iver R. Walde	35		male	Countryman	
80	Anna his Wife	26		Female		
81	Bertha " daughter	7		Do		
82	Cecille " do	5		Do		
83	Reier " Son	1	6	male		Dead
84	Karen Christophersdatter	24		Do		
85	Johan Gieruldsen	21		Do	Shopman	
86	D. Anæstatter widow	40		Female		
87	Aad her Son	15		male		
88	Gudmund " Do	9		Do		
89	Anna " Daughter	15		Female		
90	Ellen Sophia Do	13		Do		
91	Bertha Serina Do	6		Do		
92	Knud A. Slogvig	38		male	Countryman	
93	Anderes A. Oskeland	34		Do	Countryman	
94	Malene his Wife	30		Female		
95	Andereas " Son	3		male		
96	Anna Larsdatter	18		Female	Maid Servant	
97	T. Jacobsdatter	18		Do	Maid Servant	

NAMES		AGE YRS. MOS.	SEX	OCCUPA- TION	DIED ON VOYAGE
98 Lars Larsen Brimsoe		24	Male	Joiner	
99 Jacob K. Djerke		47	Do	Countryman	
100 Magle	his Wife	44	Female		
101 Gjertrud	" daughter	12	Do		
102 Britha	" Do	9	Do		
103 Bagnhild	" Do	5	Do		
104 Knud	" Son	3 6	male		
105 Jacob	" do	10	male		
106 John A. Kalleftad		34	Do	Countryman	
107 Lars L. Narrevig		—	Do	Countryman	
108 Ole C. L. Lomme		56	Do	Countryman	
109 Ana Olsdatter		29	Female	Maid Servant	
110 Mette Troelsdatter		30	Do	Maid Servant	
BORN ON THE PASSAGE					
————Anderson			Female		
				TINNES WILLEMSIN	

The Hetletvedt (Hetleved) family (1-8) is dealt with by Anderson on pages 110-112 and 151.[5] Knud, the father, had two brothers, the slooper Ole Olson Hetletvedt and Lars Olson Hetletvedt. The ages given by Ole Olson (Olsen) the younger (3) agree with the manifest. Two of the children died in September, 1836, on their journey west. The parents died in the cholera epidemic in La Salle County, Illinois, in 1849. The names and dates given by Anderson are: (1) Knud Olson Hetletvedt, born in Stavanger *Amt* on April 21, 1793, died in Mission, Illinois, on August 12, 1849; (2) Siri (Sigrid) — not "Serina" as Anderson gives it on page 151 — born on January 13, 1793, died at Mission, Illinois, on August 3, 1849; (3) Ole Olson Hetlevedt, born in Ombo, Stavanger *Amt,* on April 23, 1824;[6] (4) John, born on April 8, 1830,

---

[5] In cases where names used in the notes differ in spelling from those in the lists, the spellings used in the lists are given in parentheses. The numbers following names refer to those prefixed to the names in the lists.

[6] On page 151 Anderson says that Ole Olson Hetlevedt was born in Skjold Parish on April 24, 1824.

died at Rochester, New York, on September 5, 1836; (5) Soren, born on December 30, 1835; (6) Sophia, born on July 18, 1821; (7) Malinda, born on May 12, 1827, died on Lake Michigan, September 10, 1836; and (8) Bertha, born on December 30, 1832. Norlie states on page 134 that an account of Knud and of his brother, the slooper, written by Knud's granddaughter, Mrs. C. J. Eastvold, was published in *Visergutten* (Canton, South Dakota), May 7, 1925.

Hellen (11), from which this surname is taken, is in Stavanger *Amt*. Anderson on page 135 quotes a letter written at Hellen on May 14, 1836, which says: " A considerable number of people are now getting ready to go to America from this Amt. Two brigs are to depart from Stavanger in about eight days from now, and will carry these people to America, and if good reports come from them, the number of emigrants will doubtless be still larger next year."

Anderson on page 152 refers to a Henrik Erikson Sebbe (Hendrick Erichsen, 21), who " came to America in 1836 with his two sons. They first settled in the Fox River settlement, but in 1848, they went to Salt Lake City, and there joined the Mormons." A daughter, Anna Hendrikson Sebbe, came from Norway in 1848 and married Lars Larson (Larsen) Brimsoe (98).

" Osmund Tutland from Hjelmeland in Ryfylke and wife Malinda from Aardal in Ryfylle [*sic*] and two children had come to Mission Township, La Salle County in 1836. . . . Tutland became in 1854 the founder of the Norwegian colony at Norway, Benton County, Iowa." So says Flom on page 356, but Tutland's identification with Osmund Endresen Tretland (32), whose wife was named Maria and who had three children when he arrived in America, can hardly be regarded as certain.[7] Does this name become the " Osmund Tuttle " who Anderson, on page 111, says was born in 1797,

[7] George T. Flom, *A History of Norwegian Immigration to the United States* (Iowa City, 1909). The author's surname will be used for further references to this work.

came from Hjelmeland in Stavanger *Amt* in 1836, and died
in 1880? The list at New York shows that the copyist started
to write the last name with " He " and changed to " Tre " or
possibly " Tu." It is notable that a second son was named
Endre. It is usual to name one son, the oldest, for the father's
father.

Information about " Kleppe " (55) and " Klep," which are
Stavanger *Amt* place names, may be found in Norwegian
works.

Bjørn Anderson Kvelve (Djorn Andressen Eike) and his
wife and two sons (57-60) are the parents and brothers of
Rasmus B. Anderson. He gives their names and ages on
pages 155-170; Bjørn Anderson Kvelve, born in Vigedal
parish, Stavanger *Amt,* on June 3, 1801, died at Lake Koshkonong, Wisconsin, on August 10, 1850; Abel Catharine von
Krogh, born in Sandeid parish on October 8, 1809, died in
Worth County, Iowa, on October 31, 1885; Arnold Andrew,
born on April 9, 1832; Augustinus Meldahl Bruun, born in
1834, died in Wisconsin on August 6, 1850. The fact that
twice in the names of this family and not elsewhere in the
list the letter " B " was misread as " D " suggests that the
copy at the Customs House, written in a uniform hand, was
derived from an original list in which the names of each family were entered in different handwriting, presumably that of
the literate member of the family.

Anderson on page 150 says that Andrew Anderson Aasen
(Anders Enersen, 73), his wife Olena (Oline, 74), a son
Einar (Ener, 75), and two other sons and two daughters
came with his, Anderson's, parents on " Norden." Olena,
he says, was the sister of Nels Nelson Hersdal, the slooper.
The family lived two years with the latter at Kendall and
then went to Illinois. Anderson mentions five children at
Kendall; the manifest, which spells the name " Enerson " and
gives no final name, lists only four children. It seems probable, however, that the families are the same. It is possible,

though doubtful, that the infant born on the voyage (111) was a fifth child.[8] There is a picture of Einar (Ener, 75) Anderson Aasen in Anderson opposite page 150. Flom on page 93 says : " John Hidle from Stavanger County, Norway, also emigrated in 1836, coming direct to La Salle County '[*Illinois*]. In 1838 he settled at Lisbon, Kendall County. . . . Hidle, who wrote his name Hill in this country, married Susanna Anderson [77], daughter of Andrew Anderson; she was fourteen years old when her parents came to America, and is still living [*1909*], at Morris, Illinois, with her daughter Mrs. Austin Osmond." The name " John Hidle " or " Hill " does not appear on any of the four manifests here presented.

The name " Walde " (79) may have come from " the farm Vælde in Vats Parish, Stavanger Amt," mentioned by Anderson on page 219. As a personal name it is also spelled " Valder." " Enigheden " carried several passengers named Walde and one named Velde.[9]

Knud A. Slogvig (92) is said to have been one of the sloopers, though there are reasons to doubt this. In any case, he had been in America for some years and had returned to Norway not before 1835. It is said that he spread the " America fever " and was thus responsible for the exodus of 1836. Because he and Anders Askeland (93) stayed in New York after the arrival of " Norden," the rest of the party proceeded without leadership to Rochester. To other problems concerning Slogvig this list, which represents him as traveling to America without a wife, adds another, since tradition implied that when he returned to Norway he married a sister of the brothers Olson Hetletvedt.[10]

[8] See the note on p. 31, *post,* in regard to this child (111).

[9] See numbers 5, 33, and 38 in the list for " Enigheden," p. 411, *post.*

[10] See the note on Ana Olsdatter (109), p. 31, *post.* Slogvig's earlier history, taken from Quaker records in New York and Oslo, is given by the writer in " De første norske Kvækere i Amerika," in *Decorah-Posten* (Decorah, Iowa), November 20, 1925, and " De første Kvækere i Stavanger," in the same paper, June 11, 1926.

In footnotes 8 and 10 above, for p. 31 read p. 395

The juxtaposition in the list of the Askeland (Oskeland) family (93-95) to Knud Anderson Slogvig (92) is no accident. Captain Willemsen's letter tells that three weeks before the arrival of " Norden," Anders Askeland's wife gave birth to a baby girl, probably the infant given in the list as born on the passage (111), and that Knud remained with them in New York instead of going forward with the main party.[11] This family is to be distinguished from Anders Enersen's family (73-78). Anderson on page 186 also mentions Anders Askeland as one of those who in 1837 went with Kleng Peerson to found a colony in Shelby County, Missouri, and later returned to La Salle County, Illinois. Flom on page 125 and Norlie on page 156 also mention Anders, or Andrew, Askeland as among the first of the Shelby County settlers.

Lars Larsen Brimsoe (98) is named by Anderson on pages 151-153 as among those who migrated in 1836. Among other information, Anderson says that Brimsoe was born on October 14, 1812, that on January 1, 1849, he married Anna Hendrikson Sebbe from Hjelmeland, a daughter of Hendrick Erichsen (21), and that he died on September 26, 1873. Anderson gives his picture opposite page 151.

Lars L(arsen) Narrevig (107) was perhaps a brother of Ingebret Larson Narvig, whom Anderson on page 179 refers to as a Quaker from Tysver, who came from Norway to Boston in 1831, thence went to Kendall, and later to Michigan, where, it is said, he had two brothers. The passenger list of the " Ægir," however, includes a K. H. Nordviig (68), and that of " Enigheden " has a Lars Larsen Narrwig (4).[12]

If Knud Anderson Slogvig (92) married a sister of the Olson Hetletvedt brothers, not in Norway but in America, Ana Olsdatter (109) may have been the woman he married. Another younger woman of the same name is given in the list (48) as a sister (?) of Isack Jacob Gudmunsen.

[11] *Decorah-Posten,* December 5, 1924.

[12] See the note on Lars Larson Narrwig (" Enigheden " 4), p. 413, *post.*

Metha (Metta, Mette) Trulsdatter (Troelsdatter) Hille (Hill) (110) was an early convert to Quakerism mentioned in the records at Oslo and in the Larson correspondence.[13]

The Anderson infant (111) is probably the girl " Pige " mentioned by Captain Tønnes Willemsen as born to the Anders Askeland family (93-95) three weeks before the arrival in New York.[14] The infant died in a hospital in New York.

" DEN NORSKE KLIPPE "

" Den Norske Klippe " was the smallest of the four vessels and had the shortest list of passengers. It is said to have been, like " Norden," a Køhler brig and to have belonged to the Kielland Company, a noted house of merchants at Stavanger. It seems probable, however, that the Køhler firm really owned the vessel and arranged for the transportation of passengers, while the Kiellands at most consigned freight upon it. Lars Larsen, writing the next summer to adjust some money matters connected with " Norden," asked Elias Tastad to go to Køhler about them.[15] Though the master's name is given three times on the manifest and five times in the indexes of arrivals at New York, it is difficult to make sure of the surname. The New York shipping news published his name as " Rolfsen," which is probably right, though the other data in its notice do not commend themselves as reliable.[16] The columns under " Sex " and " Occupation " are

---

[13] Information about Metha Trulsdatter Hille is given by the writer in " De første Kvækere i Stavanger," in *Decorah-Posten,* June 4, 1926.

[14] *Decorah-Posten,* December 5, 1924.

[15] Lars Larson's letter is in *Decorah-Posten,* December 5, 1924.

[16] In *The Shipping and Commercial List,* August 15, 1836, is this entry: " Ar. August 13, 14 Swe. brig Norske Klippe, Rolfson, Stavanger, Norway "; and in the *United States Gazette* (Philadelphia), August 16, 1836, is the following: " New York, Aug. 15, Ar. Swe. brig Norska, Klipde, from Rolfsen, Norway." The historians give neither the length of the voyage nor the date of sailing.

marked collectively " male " and " countryman," with the exception of 1, " shoemaker," 2, " farmer," and 49, " Turner." A few of the passengers are mentioned by historians as having arrived in 1836, but apparently no one has previously been identified as a passenger on " Den Norske Klippe," nor has the total number of passengers been known.

<DISTRICT OF NEW-YORK — PORT OF NEW-YORK>

<I,> Peter Rolfsen <do solemnly, sincerely, and truly> swear <that the following List or Manifest of Passengers, subscribed with my name, and now delivered by me to the Collector of the Customs for the District of New-York, contains, to the best of my knowledge and belief, a just and true account of all the Passengers received on board the> Brig Nortske Klippe <whereof I am Master, from> Stavanger
Sworn <to the> 15 Augu[s]t <18> 36 <,>
    <before me,> J H BLEECKER [?]   Dy Coll
<List or Manifest of all the Passengers taken on board the> Nortske Klippe <whereof> Peter Rolofsen <is Master, from> Stavanger <burthen> 150 <tons.>

PEDER ROLFSEN

NAMES	AGE YRS. MOS.		SEX	OCCUPATION
1 Martin Pobetz (?) Mohn (?)	27		male	shoemaker
2 Johnas Nielson	33		do	farmer
3 Erich Johannessen Haase	33			
4 Ingebord Haase	27			
5 Ommund Endressen Hodnefield	30			
6 Lars Olsen Boe	29			
7 Cecilia Hallingstad	27			
8 Tjerran O Hallingstad	30			
9 Lars Larsen Sandenæs	41			Countryman
10 Martha Sandenæs	38			
11 Lars Sandenæs	11			
12 Fosten Sandenæs	08			
13 Johannes Sandenæs	4	6		
14 Fosten J Sandenæs	67			
15 Bixgitha Sandenæs	67			

	NAMES	AGE YRS. MOS.		SEX	OCCUPATION
16	Swent K. Lothe	39			
17	Ragnhild Lothe	41			
18	Knud Lothe	04			
19	Johanness Lothe	01	6		
20	John J. Age	41			
21	Torbjore Age	43			
22	Halstein Age	11			
23	Herborg Age	4			
24	Helge Watnem	42			
25	Kari Watnem	32			
26	Lars Watnem	7			
27	Ole Watnem	5			
28	Peder Watnem	2			
29	Thormond Watnem	2			
30	Sophia Watnem	4			
31	Britha K Watnem		8 days		Countryman
32	Jacob J Gesmaroig	45			
33	Malina Gesmaroig	50			
34	Rasmus Gesmaroig	12			
35	Jacob Gesmaroig	10			
36	Peder A Fesen	24			
37	Ansten E Maage	24			
38	Halstein T Meehas	32			
39	Gurri Mehaas	29	6		
40	Rasmus Mehaas	2			
41	Sidseller Mehaas	4			
42	Ole T. Gismerierz	50			
43	Sigtreed Gismerierz	50			
44	Elizabeth do	19			
45	Neils do	14			
46	Hannah do	14			
47	Saml P Custod	25			
48	Lars H Aadland	20			
49	Edward A Koben	44			Turner
50	Toleff J Grodem	33			
51	Thorbjen T Honde (?)	22			
52	Thorbjen N Klonning (?)	22			
53	Osmund Olsen	19			Countryman
54	Ole A Hille	27	6		
55	Tormes Tollevson (?)	30			
56	Sikke Svensdatter	18 (?)			
57	Oline Johndatter	20			

Erich Johannessen Haase (3) and Ingebord Haase (4) are almost certainly the Erik and Ingeborg Johnson Sævig mentioned by Anderson on pages 149 and 169. According to Anderson, Erik Johnson Sævig was born in 1803 and came to America in 1836 from Kvinhered Parish in Norway. He died in the Fox River settlement in 1840, leaving two children, John, who later lived in Wyoming, and Anna Bertha (Betsy Ann), who became the wife of John J. Naset in Christiana, Dane County, Wisconsin. Flom on pages 175-179 gives a fuller account of him under the name " Erick Johanneson Savik." His widow married Amund Anderson Hornefjeld (Ommund Endressen Hodnefield, 5). She was born on November 22, 1802, and died on November 7, 1884.

Ommund Endressen Hodnefield (5) is most probably the Amund Anderson Hornefjeld of whom Anderson gives much information. He was born on the island of Moster near Stavanger on February 16, 1806. He married Ingeborg Johnson (Ingebord Haase, 4) in La Salle County, Illinois, in 1841 and settled with her and her two children at Albion, Dane County, Wisconsin, where he died on March 18, 1886. Portraits of Amund Anderson and his wife are given by Anderson opposite page 167. The parish registers printed by Flom contain the entry, on page 315, " Amund Anderson [came from] Stavanger 1836 [wife] Ingeborg."

Lars Olsen Boe (6) may be Lars B. Olson, who Anderson on page 153 says came to America in 1836, settled in La Salle County, Illinois, and later moved to Iowa, where he died. Flom on page 93 says that a Lars Bø, who came to America in 1836, lived and died in La Salle County. A letter of Margaret Larson, written in July, 1838, refers to a Lars Boe, who apparently was then about to return to Stavanger.[17]

[17] This letter is in *Decorah-Posten,* December 12, 1924. A letter of about the same date from Lars Larsen to Elias Tastad refers to a woman named Sissel (?), who, he says, lived about twenty-five miles west of Rochester, New York, and spoke the English language very well. The single obscure name stands, perhaps, for Cecilia, whether Cecilia Hallingstad (7) or some other.

It is natural to suppose that the name " Fosten " (12, 14) should be " Tosten."

Flom on page 95 says that " Svein Knutson Lothe [*Swent K. Lothe, 16*], who emigrated with wife and two children from Hardanger in 1836, was from the Parish of Ullensvang." As Svein Knutson Lothe he is listed as a resident of Chicago in the directory of 1839, the first directory published there, according to Flom on page 231.

Flom on page 95 refers to a Jon Jonson Aga (John J. Age, 20) and his wife and two children as having come from the same province and Parish, Ullensvang, from which Lothe (16) came. But the three other persons whom Flom names as having come from Hardanger that year do not appear to have come on either of the Køhler brigs.

In speaking of the arrival at Chicago in 1837 of the passengers on " Enigheden," Malinda Nelson, according to a statement by Anderson on page 229, said that the new immigrants engaged Helge Vatname (Watnem, 24) and Samuel Peerson (47?) to take them to Norway, Illinois. Evidently the two were Norwegians who had already established themselves at Norway and had acquired " Hoosier wagons," which they used for this journey.

There is no reason why Halstein Mehaas (Meehas, 38) may not be another of the few Norwegians mentioned by historians as living in America before 1837. Flom on page 94, following Anderson and Knud Langeland, speaks of a Halstein Torison (Torrison or Tørison) as the first Norwegian resident of Chicago. " He was from Fjeldberg in Söndhordland," says Flom, " and he came to Chicago with wife and children in October, 1836."

It seems reasonable to identify Samuel P. Custod (47) with Samuel Peerson mentioned in connection with Helge Vatname (Watnem, 24).

At first glance number 55 on the manuscript list appears to be " Tormes Tollerson," but it should doubtless be read as " Tonnes Tollevson." Anderson on page 166 says, " This

Tønnes Tollefson came from Klep Parish, Stavanger *Amt,* in one of the Köhler brigs in 1836." Flom on page 204 says that Tønnes Tolleivson, or Tollefson, came from Jæderen to America in 1839. Both historians locate him after that date in the Jefferson Prairie settlement, Boone County, Illinois, and refer to his wife, Anna ("Ægir" 43). He died in 1893.

"ÆGIR" [18]

There is some disagreement in the dates of departure and arrival of the "Ægir" given by historians. Anderson on page 198 says: "'Ægir' was eight weeks in crossing the Atlantic. In mid-ocean it collided with an American packet, but no damage was done"; and of Mons Adland (Aadland, 24), one of the passengers, he says on page 285, "He left Bergen, Norway, April 7, 1837, arriving in New York about June 12." Norlie on page 137 follows the mistaken tradition that the "Ægir" sailed on July 4, suggested, probably, by the traditional sailing date of "Restaurationen," which is also questioned.[19] O. N. Nelson gives April 7, 1837, as the sailing date, but for the arrival he gives June 9, a date supported by a notice in the marine news of the New York *Evening Star,* June 10, 1837.[20]

It is interesting to compare the list with the partial lists of passengers on the "Ægir" given by Anderson on pages 197 and 198 and Flom on pages 100 and 101. Following Knud

[18] An account of the voyage of the "Ægir" is given by Theodore C. Blegen, in "Ole Rynning's True Account of America," in *Minnesota History Bulletin,* 2 : 221 ff. (November, 1917). Rynning's account has recently been more fully edited by Mr. Blegen and published under the same title, *Ole Rynning's True Account of America (Publications of the Norwegian-American Historical Association, Travel and Description Series,* vol. 1 — Minneapolis, 1926).

[19] See an article by the writer, "The Norwegian Quakers of 1925," in Norwegian-American Historical Association, STUDIES AND RECORDS, 1 : 63, note 5 (Minneapolis, 1926).

[20] *History of the Scandinavians and Successful Scandinavians in the United States,* 224 (Minneapolis, 1900).

Langeland's account, Anderson mentions the following heads of families: N. P. Langeland (77), Mons Aadland (24), Nils Frøland (33), Anders Nordvig (15), Anders Rosseland (41?), Thomas Bauge (7), Ingebrigt Brudvig (1), and Thorbjørn Veste; and the following unmarried men: Døvig (12?), Rosseland (46), Bauge, Frøland (38), Nordvig (68), Hisdal (32), Tøsseland (39), and Ole Rynning (72). Flom repeats all these except the two Rosselands and adds the following names: Nils L. Jørdre and his wife and six children and Peder J. Maurset and his wife and child from Hardanger; Amund Rosseland and his wife and three children (41–45), Lars G. Skeie and his wife and two children (48–51), Sjur E. Rosseland (46), and Svein L. Midthus (47) from Vikør; and Halle Væte and his wife and grown daughter, Odd J. Himle, Kolbein O. Saue, Styrk O. Saue, Nils L. Bolstad (13), Baard Haugen, John H. Bjørgo (14), and Ole Dyvik (12).

It will be seen that, while there is a variety of spelling, the primary list used by Anderson and Flom is generally accurate, but that, while the additions by Flom contain two groups in agreement with the passenger list, 41–51 and 12–14, he wrongly infers that all these persons were married when they crossed and he includes several names that do not belong in this party at all. The latter part of Flom's list is identical with the list of names that Anderson, on pages 328 and 329, gives of emigrants from Voss in 1837, but Anderson does not claim, as does Flom, that they came on the " Ægir " or that they were all married when they came. He says that Stark Olson Saue was married in America.

<DISTRICT OF NEW-YORK — PORT OF NEW-YORK.>

<I,> Christian K Beherns <do solemnly, sincerely, and truly> swear <that the following List or Manifest of Passengers, subscribed with my name, and now delivered by me to the Collector of the Customs for the District of New-York, contains, to the best of my knowledge and belief, a just and true account

of all the Passengers received on board the [*blank in MS*] where-
of I am Master, from> Bergen
Sworn <to the> 10th June <18> 37 <,> <*So help me God.*>
  <Before me,> J H BLEECKER [*?*] D Col C. K. BEHRENS.
<List or Manifest of all the Passengers taken on board the>
Barque Aegier <whereof> C K Beherns <is Master, from>
Bergen <burthen> 210 8/95 <tons.>

	NAMES	AGE YRS. MOS.		SEX	OCCUPATION
1	Ingebrigt Nielsen Brudwig	48	"	Male	Farmer
2	S Monsdatter	40	"	Female	"
3	J J Dahle	40	"	Male	"
4	A Sjursdatter	33	"	Female	"
5	A Dahle	7	"	"	"
6	J J Dahle	4	"	Male	"
7	T N Buge	61	"	"	"
8	S. Johannesdatter	61	"	Female	"
9	N Thomassson	27	"	Male	"
10	S Johannasdatter	52	"	Female	"
11	H N Dahlseider	36	"	Male	"
12	O A Dyvigen	33	"	"	"
13	N L Rolstad	36	"	"	"
14	J H Biorge	32	"	"	"
15	A H Nordvig (?)	45	"	"	"
16	M. Knudsdatter	38	"	Female	"
17	H. Andersdatter	19	"	"	"
18	M Andersdatter	15	6	"	"
19	S Andersdatter	12	6	"	"
20	M Andersdatter	10	"	"	"
21	K Andersdatter	6	"	"	"
22	H Anderson	3	"	Male	"
23	K Anderson	1	"	"	"
24	M K Aadland	44	"	"	"
25	E Knudsdatter	39	"	Female	"
26	M Monsdatta	13	"	"	"
27	B do	11	6	"	"
28	K Monsen	10	"	Male	"
29	T do	7	"	"	"
30	S Monsdatter	5	"	Female	"
31	P Monsen	2	"	Male	"

	Names	Age Yrs. Mos.		Sex	Occupation
32	O H Hisdahe	25	"	"	"
33	N L Froland	41	"	"	"
34	A Vilhelmsdatter	39	"	Female	"
35	B Nielsdatter	9	"	"	"
36	L Nielson	5	"	Male	"
37	V Nielson	2	"	"	"
38	P L Froland	34	"	"	"
39	K V Tysland	28	"	"	"
40	L Shudalsness	27	"	"	"
41	A E Rosseland	46	"	"	"
42	G Ellingsdatter	40	"	Female	"
43	A Amands	18	"	"	"
44	E Amundsen	13	"	Male	"
45	E Amundsen	5	"	"	"
46	S E Rosseland	31	"	"	"
47	S L Mithus	34	"	"	"
48	L G Scheie	38	"	"	"
49	K Ellingsdatter	30	"	Female	"
50	G Larsdatter	5	"	"	"
51	A Larsdatter	3	"	"	"
52	V L Schultz	23	"	Male	"
53	S E Trangereide	27	"	"	"
54	S Andersdatter	23	"	Female	"
55	E Samuelsen	1	6	Male	"
56	M B Bystolen	29	"	"	"
57	H A Saboe	45	"	"	"
58	T Johannesdatter	46	"	Female	"
59	A M Halvorsdatter	19	"	"	"
60	A do	16	"	"	"
61	B do	12	"	"	"
62	T do	9	"	"	"
63	H Halvorsen	4	"	Male	"
64	A Halvorsen	21	"	"	"
65	N O Nordhienes	34	"	"	"
66	T A Ovrevieg	21	"	"	"
67	T A Birkeland	25	"	"	"
68	K H Nordviig (?)	20	6	"	"
69	N K Vettesloe	30	"	"	"
70	B Aamundsdatter	28	"	Female	"
71	E Nielsdatter	1	6	"	"

Names	Age Yrs. Mos.		Sex	Occupation
72 O Rynning	27	"	Male	"
73 A C Stange	33	"	"	
74 J J Skoerping (?)	38	"	"	"
75 J F Voltziem	15	"	"	"
76 K J Alne	26	"	Female	"
77 N P Langeland	41	"	Male	"
78 M Nielsdatter	39	"	Female	"
79 N Nielsen	12	"	Male	"
80 P Nielsen	5	"	"	"
81 A Nielsdatter	14	"	Female	"
82 B Nielsdatter	10	"	"	"
83 A Nielsdatter	8		"	"
84 M Nielsdatter		6	"	"

C. K BEHRENS.

Ingebrigt Brudvig (Brudwig, 1), according to Anderson on pages 199–201, was one of the explorers and founders of the ill-fated settlement at Beaver Creek, Iroquois County, Illinois.

Anderson on page 295 writes: " One of the oldest settlers in Muskego [*Waukesha County, Wisconsin*] was John J. Dale [*J. J. Dahle, 3*]. He was born in Bergen Stift, Norway, in August, 1795, and came to America in the same ship with Ole Rynning in 1837. He first settled in the Fox River settlement, and came to Muskego in 1842, where he died in 1882. Anna, his wife, died in Illinois in 1839."

Ole Dyvik (O. A. Dyvigen, 12), is mentioned by Anderson on pages 328 and 329 as having migrated from Voss, but he did not know what became of him. It is probably he who appears in Anderson's list for the " Ægir " as a bachelor named Døvig.[21]

Presumably N. L. Rolstad (13) is Nils Larsen Bolstad, a Vossing frequently mentioned by Anderson and Flom as one of the first settlers in Koshkonong, or Deerfield, Wisconsin.

[21] See *ante*, p. 402

According to Anderson on pages 336 and 345, he married Anna, a sister of Gunnul Vindeg. The church register given by Flom contains the following entry on page 319: " Niels Larsen Bolstad [came from] Vos [in] 1837 [wife] Anne [children] Lars, Ingeborg."

Probably I. H. Biorge (14) is John Haldorson Bjørgo, frequently mentioned by Anderson with Bolstad (Rolstad, 13) as one of the first settlers in Koshkonong. Svein Nilsson also mentions John Haldorson Bjørgo as an early settler in Koshkonong.[22]

Anderson, on page 284, says that Anders Nordvig (15) settled in Beaver Creek and died there.[23]

According to Anderson on pages 227 and 284, Magdalena Nordvig (M. Knudsdatter, 16), the wife of Anders Nordvig (15), was a sister of Knud Langeland, the journalist, and of Mons Aadland (24). After her husband's death she " moved to the Fox River settlement, where she died about the year 1892, over 90 years old."

One of the daughters of Anders Nordvig (15) with the initial " M " (18 or 20) is presumably the daughter Malinda, who Anderson on page 285 says was the wife of Iver Lawson, " who was a prominent Norwegian real estate owner in Chicago, and the mother of [the late] Victor F[reemont] Lawson, the well known owner of the Chicago *Record* and *News*." Norlie on page 139 and Flom on page 112 also mention Malinda Nordvig as the wife of Larson and the mother of Victor F. Lawson.

Flom on page 113 says, " Another daughter [*of Anders Nordvig, 15*], Sarah [*S. Andersdatter, 19*] (born 1824), married a Mr. Darnell, a pioneer of Benton County, Iowa, in 1854." Anderson on page 227 mentions " Mrs. Sarah Darnell, of Sandwich, Ill.," as a daughter of Anders Nordvig.

[22] " De skandinaviske Setlementer i Amerika," in *Billed-Magazin*, 1: 387 (1869).

[23] See, however, the note on Lars Larsen Narrwig (" Enigheden " 4) p. 413, *post*.

Evidently M. K. Aadland's (24) full name was Mons Knudson Aadland. Flom on page 162 says he was a nephew of Nils P. Langeland (77). His family is discussed at length by Anderson on pages 225 and 284–290, and his photograph faces page 287. Anderson states that he was born on April 14, 1793, left Bergen on April 7, 1837, and arrived in New York about June 12 and in Chicago a month later. He then went to Beaver Creek and finally to Racine County, Wisconsin, where he died on April 25, 1869. These data suggest comparison with the entry of the manifest.

E. Knudsdatter (25) is given by Anderson on page 286 as " Ellen (Thompson) Adland," and she is said to have died two years before her husband (24). Six of their children grew to maturity and three were living in 1895 (?) — Knud (28), Thomas (29), and Martha (26?).

According to Anderson on page 225, " A daughter [*of Mons Aadland, 24*] Martha [*M. Monsdatta, 26*] . . . married the Lutheran minister, Rev. A. C. Preus, who succeeded Rev. Dietrichson on Koshkonong in Wisconsin, and later returned to Norway, where he died. The widow, Mrs. Preus, is still living [*1895*] at Horten in Norway."

Anderson on pages 285–290 quotes a sketch of Thomas, son of Mons Aadland (24), who must be T. Monsen (29), though the sketch says that he was born on August 12, 1831.

For O. H. Hisdahe (32), Anderson on page 198 gives " Hisdal," with no initials.

The later history of Nils Frøland (33) is given by Anderson on page 223. He died in 1873.

Anderson on page 223, writing of a visit he paid near Norway, La Salle County, Illinois, in August, 1894, says: " I found Nils Fröland's widow, Anna [*A. Vilhelmsdatter, 34*], still living. She was then 95 years old, being born March 24, 1798."

According to Anderson on page 178, " Lars Fruland [*L. Nielson, 36*] came with his father, Nels Fruland, in 1837 " to La Salle County. Norlie on page 139 says, " Lars Fruland, born March 15, 1831, is still alive [*1925*] and resides at Newark, Illinois, spry as a man of 60, in spite of his 96 years of hard labor."

Flom on page 336, writing of the settlement in Spring Prairie, Dane County, Wisconsin, says: " In the spring of 1846 Peder Fröland [*P. L. Froland, 38*] who had come to America in 1837 came up there from La Salle County "; and on page 334 he says, " In 1847 Peder Fröland . . . and Ole Jone, both from Hardanger, became the founders of the Hardanger Settlement there."

K. V. Tysland (39) may be the unmarried man on the " Ægir " named Tösseland, whose initials historians do not give. Or perhaps it is Knut W. Tysland, who, according to Flom on page 355, located at Newark, Illinois, in 1838, or the Knut Tysland of Beaver Creek mentioned by Anderson on page 368.

Flom on page 100 refers to the eleven persons numbered 41 to 51 on the list and implies that they came from Vikør. He gives some of the names more fully than does the manifest.

Anderson on pages 197 and 342–345 correctly speaks of Amund (Anderson) Rossaland, as well as Anders Rosseland. On 166 and following pages he gives an account of Amund Rossaland, his wife (G. Ellingsdatter, 42), his sons Elling and Endre (E. Amundsen, 44, 45), and his daughter Anna (A. Amands, 43). Anna married Tönnes Tollefson (" Den Norske Klippe " 55).

Sjur E. Rosseland (46) and Svein L. Midthus (Mithus, 47) are mentioned by Flom on page 100 as emigrants from Vikør.

Anderson on pages 166 and 343 mentions Lars Scheie (48) and his family (49-51) in connection with Amund Anderson, with Rossaland (41) and his family, and with Bjørn Anderson (" Norden " 57) and his family. On page 344 he gives the daughters' names as " Gyri " and " Anna." On page 175

Flom, following Anderson, gives " Lars Scheie," but on page 100 he writes " Lars G. Skeie."

Anderson mentions frequently Magne Bottolfson Byställ(en) (M. B. Byställen, 56). The land records quoted by Anderson on page 354 spell the name " Magany Buttelson." He settled in Wisconsin.

In the case of K. H. Nordviig (68) we find again a name mentioned by the historians, though they give no initial for this unmarried Nordvig.

Ole Rynning (72) from Trondhjem *Amt*, a college graduate, was one of the more influential members of the party.[24]

A. C. Stange (73) from Germany was the only passenger not from Norway.

Nils P. Langeland (77) settled with his family in Detroit, according to Anderson on page 224. Flom on pages 97 and 99 speaks of him as a school teacher from Samnanger, already an elderly man, whose work for popular education had been thwarted by the clergy. It is said that he was influenced to emigrate by a visit to Knud Slogvig (" Norden " 92) and that he was largely influential in leading his own neighbors to migrate in 1837.

" ENIGHEDEN "

The name of this bark is spelled " Enigheten " in the mani· fest, dated September 14, 1837. The tonnage is not given Its ninety-one passengers are numbered on the left margin of the manifest. Flom on page 96 and Norlie on page 137 give ninety-three as the number of passengers. Of the voyage and of the first part of the passengers' experience in America some information is available. Anderson gives an account on page 196, and on 229 and following pages he quotes an account from the lips of Malinda Nelson (*née* Danielson, 86), who came over in the ship at the age of ten. The voyage, she

---

[24] For accounts of Rynning see Anderson, 202-218; Blegen, in *Minnesota History Bulletin,* 2: 221 ff. (November, 1917); and Blegen, *Rynning's True Account.*

says, occupied eleven weeks and three days.[25]   From New York the immigrants went up the Hudson to Albany, thence by the canal to Rochester, where they stopped several days, thence to Buffalo, and then on by the lakes to Chicago. From Chicago many of them went immediately to Norway, Illinois. Of their stay at Rochester a few sentences from a letter of Martha Larson, dated October 11, 1837, give a clear picture: " About two weeks ago there arrived from ninety to a hundred people. They stayed at our house and my brother's [*Ole Johnson Eie's*] house about a week, and we furnished meals for nearly all of them. Most of them have now gone to Illinois. Knud Eye [*Knud Olsen Eie, 23*] with family and Endre Aragebo [*Endré Osmunden Aagagerh, 69?*] were the last to leave." [26]

Of the following list several persons have already been definitely known by historians as passengers on " Enigheden." Flom, for example, following Anderson, on page 96 mentions as among its passengers the persons numbered on the list 1, 5, 23, 38, 43, 84, and their families. But, though assigned to " Enigheden," neither Thomas A. Thompson, mentioned by Anderson on page 227 and by Flom on page 114, nor Hans Barlien, whom Flom names on page 108 and Norlie on page 138, can be identified with names on the manifest, not to mention other immigrants assigned to this year. On page 96 Flom speaks of the passengers as " for the most part from Tysvær and Hjelmeland, and Aardal in Ryfylke, from the city of Stavanger, and from Egersund."

<DISTRICT OF NEW-YORK — PORT OF NEW-YORK.>

<I,> Jens Pedersen <do solemnly, sincerely, and truly> swear <that the following List or Manifest of Passengers, sub-

[25] The voyage lasted seventy-three days, according to the marine notice published in the *United States Gazette,* September 16, 1837, which gives the following: " New York, September 15, Ar. Norwegian barque, Enegheden, Pedersen, Norway, 73 days."

[26] Martha Larson's letter is in *Decorah-Posten,* December 12, 1924, and a translation of part of it may be found in the *American Scandinavian Review,* 13 : 361 ff. (June, 1925).

scribed with my name, and now delivered by me to the Collector of the Customs for the District of New-York, contains, to the best of my knowledge and belief, a just and true account of all the Passengers received on board the> Barque Enigheden <whereof I am Master, from> Stavanger
[*blank in MS*] <to the> 14 Sept <18> 37 <,> J. PEDERSEN
 Before me, <JAS CAMPBELL> Dy Col
<List or Manifest of all the Passengers taken on board the> Brig Enigheten <whereof> Jens Pederson <is Master, from> Stavanger <burthen> [*blank in MS*] <tons.>

	NAMES		AGE YRS. MOS.		SEX	OCCUPATION
1	Osten Knudsen Espeland		22		male	farmer
2	Siri Houlsdatter		18		female	
3	Swent Ostensen		½		male	
4	Lars Larsen Narrwig		21		male	do
5	Hans Olsen Velde		23		male	do
6	Berthe Olddatter	do	22		female	
7	Ole Hansen	do	¼		————	
8	Jacob Pertersen Eike		33		male	do
9	Siri Jonas Datter	do	39		do	do
10	Bertha Christendatter		14			do
11	Karin Christendatter		12		do	do
12	Forber Christen Datter		8			
13	Peder Jacobsen Datter		1		"	do
14	Niels Olsen Osterlen (?)		50		male	do
15	Elisabeth Beerdatter		40		male	do
16	Elen Neilsdatter	do	18		female	
17	Berthe	do	16		do	do
18	Oele Nielsen		13(?)		male	do
19	Enig	do	9		"	do
20	Neils Tobias	do	7		"	do
21	Berent Elias	do	4			
22	Magreth Meve Nielsdatter		1		female	do
23	Knud Olsen Eie		50		male	Seaman
24	Merthe Eie		(?)		female	do
25	John Knudsen		9		male	
26	Ole	do	6		male	
27	Andreas	do	3		male	
28	Elen Knudsdatter		1	½	female	
29	Samuel Thoralsen Tjiel		22		male	farmer

Names	Age Yrs. Mos.		Sex	Occupation
30 Aadne Biornsdatte Bratted	20		female	do
31 Borgilde Petterdatter	48		male	do
32 Raier Olsen Oserhaus	60		male	do
33 Osmund Danielsen Walde	39		male	do
34 Inger Reier Datter do	26		"	do
35 Danielsen Walde	3	½	"	do
36 Peter Jacobsen do	17			
37 Siri Osmund Datter	6			do
38 Christen Danielsen Walde	42		male	do
39 Merthe Thordatter do	29		female	do
40 Daniel Christian do	14		"	"
41 Jacob do	11		———	
42 Christen do	2	½	"	do
43 Ole Thorbiorns	17		male	farmer
44 Osmund Guterensen (?) Ahling	49		male	do
45 Berthe Mathias do	39		female	do
46 Erik Osmond do	11		male	
47 Guttorn do	10		do	
48 Osmundir (?) do	6		do	
49 Merye Osmund' Datter	9		female	
50 Anne	3			
51 Guttron (?) Erichsen Overz-land (?)	24		male	do
52 Thorborn Torsen Magreth	28		female	do
53 Bion Jorgensen Hellestad	45			
54 Ragnilde Olsdatter	35			
55 Ane				
56 Ane Lovdatter Shenbove (?)	40		male	
57 Halvor Halversen	9		female	do
58 Elen Halvordatter	12		do	do
59 J. J Johanisen	28		male	Portrait-painter
60 Hewis (?) Ostedahl	20			blacksmith
61 Rasmus Dahl (?)	20		male	shoemaker
62 Even Johansen Me(sk?)eeveg	49		male	farmer
63 Malene Johndatter	30		do	do
64 Johannes Evenson	5	½	do	do
65 Jane do	4			do
66 Even do	1	¾	do	do
67 Siri Evendatter	15		do	do
68 Inger Evensdatter	13		do	do
69 Endré Osmunden Aagagerh	33		male	Glazier

NAMES		AGE YRS. MOS.		SEX	OCCUPATION
70	Stine Olsdatter	40		female	do
71	Ase do	44		do	do
72	Siri do	33		male	
73	Magdale Knudsdatter	30		do	do
74	Ole Endersen	3	½		do
75	Bolte Randine Endersedatter	5			
76	Herman Osmunde Auga(s?)	20		male	do
77	Barbro Halverdatter Breth	28		male	
78	Ole Pierson	33		do	do
79	Ane Baersen	31		do	do
80	Soren Oelsen	6			
81	Atleethe Oldendatter	3		do	do
82	Rachel do	1			
83	Lars Pedar Reierssoen	24		do	porter
84	Knud Danielson Wallen	36		do	farmer
85	Siri Oldatter	33		do	do
86	Malene Daniel datter	10		do	do
87	Daniel Knudzen	6		do	do
88	Aase Knuds datter	4		do	do
89	Ane do	1		do	do
90	Bergethe Merie Cederberg	29		do	servant
91	Matheas Osmund	1		do	do

J. PEDERSEN

According to Anderson on page 219, Osten Espeland (1) came from Hjelmeland in Norway. At Detroit he left most of the other immigrants, went by rail to Adrian, Michigan, and settled near there in Lenawee County. Later he moved to the Fox River settlement. After his death his widow remarried and was still living in 1895.

Lars Larsen Narvig (Narrwig, 4) was perhaps a brother of Ingebrigt Larsen (Ingebret Larson) Narvig, a Quaker who came from Tysvær in 1831 and who is frequently mentioned by Anderson. Two of Ingebrigt's brothers, according to Anderson on page 220, were for a time with him, Osten Espeland (1) and Hans Valder (Hans Olsen Velde, 5), at the settlement in Lenawee County, Michigan. It is possible that A. H. Nordvig (" Ægir " 15) was the other brother in spite of the initial " H." There is also another Nordvig on the lists, K. H. Nordviig (" Ægir " 68). Flom on page 101 gives Ingebrigt's surname as " Nordvig." But there is another Lars L. Narrevig (" Norden " 107), unless we suppose that he was the same individual and had returned to Norway.

Anderson gives a biographical sketch of Hans (Olsen) Valder (Vælde, Velde, 5) on pages 219-222, with a photograph opposite page 219. He was born at Vælde in Vats Parish, October 18, 1813, and taught school at Tysver. He, like Espeland (1) and Narvig (4), did not accompany the bulk of the passengers to Chicago, but went from Detroit to Lenawee County, Michigan.

The names 9 to 13 were probably those of a man and his wife accompanied by three children of her deceased husband (Christen) and one child of her present husband (Jacob, 8).

The last syllable of the name " Osterlen " (14) is very doubtful. It may possibly be " Osterboe."

Knud Olson (Olsen) Eie (23) had the same name as that of an early companion of Cleng Peerson, though it may be doubtful that the voyagers of 1821 and 1837 were the same, according to Anderson on page 62. The one of 1821 came from Eide on the island of Fogn, near Stavanger, from which also at least two of the sloopers came, as well as Ole Thorbiorns (Eie, 43) of the present list. Little is known of his later life.

Christopher Danielson (Valle) (Christen Danielsen Walde, 38) came from Aarland in Stavanger *Amt,* settled in Mission Township, La Salle County, Illinois, and died of cholera in 1849. Apparently Merthe Thordatter (39) was his second wife and after her death he married the widow of Knud Danielsen Wallen (85). His age on the manifest does not agree with the date of his birth, 1780, given by Anderson on page 222.

Christopher (Christen) Danielsen (42) is apparently the correspondent whom Anderson mentions on pages 151 and

223. Anderson's index does not distinguish the son from his father, who had the same name (38). In 1895, according to Anderson, he was residing at Sheridan, Illinois. He had come in " Enigheden " as a small boy and he later married Ann, a daughter of Osmund Thomasen, who had come to America with her father in 1836.

Ole Thorbiorns (43) must be Ole Thompson (Thorbjørnson) Eide, named by Anderson on pages 60, 176, and 196 as a passenger on " Enigheden." He was living at Sheridan, Illinois, in 1895. Mrs. Larson in the letter quoted above wrote: " Ole Torbiornson Eye staid with us as long as he was in Rochester. It gave me great joy to do good to him whose father treated me and my old mother so ill, which I can never forget as long as I live. But I wish that he might be converted. I am willing to forgive him if God is." [27]

Anderson on page 398 speaks of a Bjørn Hatlestad (Bion Jorgensen Hellestad, 53?) who came to America about 1836, held religious services for a time after his arrival in the Kendall settlement, and died in Dane County, Wisconsin, about 1880. It is not at all certain that Hatlestad was the passenger Hellestad (53).

It is tempting to identify the Me(sk?)ewig family (62-68) with " Even Askvig," who, according to Flom on page 115, came to America in 1837 from Hjelmeland Parish with his wife and family and lived successively in Indiana, Illinois, Texas, and Iowa. The spelling on the manifest is not quite clear.

---

[27] *Decorah-Posten*, December 12, 1924. The next sentence, accidentally omitted in the publication of the letter, reads: " Hans Ladegaard also staid with us." This name it is natural to regard as belonging to one of the same set of immigrants passing through Rochester, but it is not to be found on our lists. Besides the Norwegians arriving in 1836 and 1837 on these four vessels, there was probably the usual scattered migration through other channels, especially on Swedish ships from Gothenburg. By the route last named a group of Norwegians reached New York in August, 1836.

In spite of the difference in spelling of the surname, Endré Osmunden Aagagerh (69) must be the Endre Aragebo to whom Martha Larson in her letter refers definitely as a member of this contingent.[28]   Likewise Anderson on page 410 mentions Endre and Herman Osmundson Aaragerbö as Lutheran laymen who preached in America before 1843.

Possibly Herman Osmunde Auga(s?) (76) is the Herman Osmundson Aaragerbö' mentioned in the preceding note. Flom on page 94 says that Herman Aarag Osmond, born near Stavanger, 1818, also came to America in 1836, and tells of his subsequent history and settlement at Newark, Illinois.   The dates do not quite fit this passenger (76).   On page 355 Flom refers to Herman Osmonson and Knut W. Tysland (" Ægir " 39) as settling in Newark in 1838.

Ole Pierson's (78) name is too common to identify him without further information.   An Ole Peerson is mentioned by Anderson on page 394 among the first settlers in Bosque County, Texas.

A statement of Malinda Danielson (Malene Danieldatter, 86) is given in substance by Anderson on page 229.   The family came from Aurdal, Norway.   Her mother's (Siri Oldatter's, 85) maiden name was Sara Olson.   Knud Danielson (Knud Danielson Wallen, 84) died in 1838, and his widow married Christopher Danielson (38).   Malinda was born on September 29, 1827.   Anderson gives her photograph opposite page 228.

[28] *Decorah-Posten,* December 12, 1924.

PASSENGER LIST OF THE "SARAH SHEAFFE", MAY, 1836

Contributed by Louis C. Cramton
Lapeer, Michigan

Note:—Judge Cramton swears that the following is a true copy of the list attached to a letter from Robert Taylor of Philadelphia to Messrs. Abraham Bell & Co., New York and postmarked Phila 8 Jul. The letter is in his possession.

LIST OF PASSENGERS ENGAGED BY ROBERT TAYLOR PHILA-
DELPHIA AND ARRIVED PER SHIP SARAH SHEAFFE FROM
BELFAST VIA NEW YORK, MAY, 1836

No.								
1	David McBride	20		Amount brot forward	$570		
2	Mary A do	20		32	Benjamin Wray	20	
3	Eliza do	20		33	Ann Robinson	20	
4	Agnes do	10		34	Ann do	20	
5	Mary Welsh	20		35	Peggy do	17	50
6	Anne do	20		36	Rose do	10	
7	John do	20		37	Robert Armstrong	20	
8	Wm McQuade	20		38	Charles Miller	20	
9	John Morris	20		39	William Gilles	20	
10	Richard Finlay	20		40	Catherine do	20	
11	Martha do	20		41	Eliza do	20	
12	Sarah do	20		42	Robert Martin	20	
13	Mary do	10		43	Jane do	20	
14	Margt. do	10		44	John Martin	20	
15	Martha do	10		45	Jane do	20	
16	Eliza do	20		46	Jane Kerr	20	
17	Eliza Ann McKeown	20		47	Elizabeth do	20	
18	Patrick Murray	20		48	Thomas McIlroy	20	
19	John Flynn	20		49	Jane McLernan	20	
20	John Cairne	20		50	Maybel do	20	
21	Terence Fagan	20		51	James do	10	
22	Mary do	20		52	Mary Ann Beatty	20	
23	Biddy Cannon	20		53	Elizabeth do	20	
24	Alex McCalmont	20		54	David Dickson	20	
25	Sarah do	20		55	Amelia McGargle	20	
26	Mary do	20		56	Elizabeth Wray	20	
27	Jane do	20		57	Ally McKenna	20	
28	Robert do	20		58	Ann do	20	
29	Eliza do	10		59	Patrick do	10	
30	Jane Williams	20		60	James do	10	
31	Martha Wray	20				$1107	50
	Carried forward	$570					

CHARGES

To cash paid Freight for Fagan Baggage	$ 2.14	
To Advertising 6.00 Postages 2.00	8.00	
To Commission on 1107.50 @ 5 pr ct	55.37	65.51
	Nett proceeds	$1041.99

E E

Philadelphia 8th July 1836

ROBERT TAYLOR

AN IMMIGRANT SHIPLOAD OF 1840

BY C. A. CLAUSEN

Stavanger on the west coast of Norway was the point of departure for the earliest Norwegian emigrant ships. From that port the famous "Restoration" carried the first group of settlers in 1825; and eleven years later the two brigs "Norden" and "Den Norske Klippe," which ushered in almost a century of steady Norwegian immigrant traffic, also sailed from Stavanger. The next year, 1837, two more ships loaded with homeseekers set out for the New World, "Enigheden" from Stavanger and "Ægir" from Bergen.[1] Not until 1839 did an emigrant ship leave from an east Norwegian port. On June 12 of that year the bark "Emilie," commanded by Captain Thomas Anchersen, set sail from Drammen for Göteborg en route to New York, where it arrived on August 26.[2]

Not much is known about this first emigrant ship from eastern Norway or her captain, but a few shreds of information can be patched together. According to one of the passengers who came across with the "Emilie" in 1840, Captain Anchersen had declared that the bottom of his ship was 150 years old; and the narrator, A. A. Vinje, probably suspected that the vessel had passed its prime, for he continued by saying that when they were in mid-ocean they encountered a severe storm which gave the old bark such a severe shaking that "the timbers sustaining the upper berths gave way,

---

[1] For information concerning "Norden," "Den Norske Klippe," "Enigheden," and "Ægir" see an article by H. J. Cadbury, "Four Immigrant Shiploads of 1836 and 1837," in *Studies and Records*, 2:20–52 (Northfield, 1927). Life aboard the early immigrant ships is interestingly discussed by Theodore C. Blegen in *Norwegian Migration to America: The American Transition*, ch. 1 (Northfield, 1940), and by Ingrid Semmingsen in *Veien mot vest*, 96–151 (Oslo, Norway, 1941).

[2] Blegen, *Norwegian Migration to America, 1825–1860*, 121, note 25 (Northfield, 1931). From June 13 to June 22 the "Emilie" remained at Göteborg where it took on a cargo of iron.

precipitating them upon the lower ones, and the screams and cries of the frightened passengers added to the fury of the storm."[3] We do not know how large a ship the "Emilie" was, but her size can probably be estimated with some degree of accuracy from the fact that American law in those years stipulated that the ratio between passengers and tonnage could not exceed two to five. Ansten Nattestad, who came with the "Emilie" on his return trip to America in 1839, remarked that Captain Anchersen had to turn away some prospective emigrants because his ship could carry only one hundred passengers.[4] But this figure evidently referred to the capacity of the ship as viewed by the Norwegian owners rather than to its legal capacity under American law, for one of Nattestad's fellow travelers, Mrs. Myhre, related that as there were too many passengers on board, Anchersen had to resort to a little ruse. "Just before arriving in New York, he had some of the passengers put on sailors' clothes, and in this way he avoided all trouble with the custom house officers."[5] In 1840 the "Emilie" left Göteborg, apparently with ninety emigrants, and, as far as we know, this time the captain was able to land without resorting to any sailor's tricks. If we assume that he took aboard as many passengers as the law allowed, we can fix the size of his ship at 225 tons.[6]

Thomas Anchersen probably sailed an old bark and he

[3] Quoted in G. T. Flom, *Norwegian Migration to the United States,* 200 (Iowa City, Iowa, 1909).

[4] Quoted in C. C. Qualey, *Norwegian Settlement in the United States,* 43 (Northfield, 1938).

[5] Quoted in R. B. Anderson, *First Chapter of Norwegian Immigration (1821–1840): Its Causes and Results,* 257 (Madison, Wisconsin, 1906).

[6] A. A. Vinje, whose account was written many years later, places the number of passengers in 1840 at ninety. The ship's list enumerates eighty-nine passengers, and of these one (number 77) was probably born en route to New York. It is possible, however, that one or two of the passengers may have died during the trip without any record being made of the fact. The name of a man 30 years old was entered between numbers 43 and 44 of our list but later struck out.

According to Blegen, *Norwegian Migration to America,* 1:133, Anchersen brought over a party of 90 in 1841 and still another of 115 in 1842, but it is not stated that these trips were made with the "Emilie." If the trip of 1842 was made with the "Emilie," it must have been a ship of at least 287.5 tons, unless Anchersen appeared in New York with a still larger force of "sailors" than he did in 1839.

seems to have resorted to questionable ruses in order to elude the American shipping laws, but the few facts we are able to gather about him nevertheless assure him an honorable place among those captains who pioneered in the Norwegian emigrant traffic a hundred years ago. To reassure those who may be uneasy about this skipper's ways with the law, we can relate that whereas captains usually conducted religious services for their emigrant passengers only on Sundays, Thomas Anchersen had prayers and religious singing on deck every evening.[7] He seems to have been equally concerned about the physical welfare of his passengers. In those days emigrant ships rarely carried doctors, nor was it usual for the passengers to be given physical examinations before embarking. As far as we know, Captain Anchersen never took a doctor along on his ship, but it is reported that before setting out on his first trip he consulted a medical authority and laid in supplies of remedies for the most common diseases,[8] while in 1842 he saw to it that all the emigrants were duly examined before embarking. In this respect he seems to have been a pioneer among Norwegian captains. It would also appear that he realized the importance of fresh foods for seafaring people. When he took his first group of emigrants over in 1839 he treated all of them to fresh meat in Göteborg, to fresh fish in Udøefjord and again twice in the English channel as well as on the Newfoundland banks.[9] Nor did his concern for the inexperienced travelers cease as soon as he got them safely ashore in America. Like many other Norwegian captains he won the gratitude of his passengers by the solicitude he showed for them after they had landed, bewildered, on the shores of the New World. In 1839 he accompanied the newcomers up the Hudson to Albany, where the whole group were his guests for a meal at a large hotel. This was undoubtedly a memorable occasion

[7] Semmingsen, *Veien mot vest,* 119.
[8] Gunnar Malmin, " Norsk landnåm i U. S.," in *Decorah-posten,* March 6, 1925.
[9] Blegen, *Norwegian Migration to America,* 2: 27, note 72.

for many a Norwegian immigrant. The captain stayed with
them until they reached Schenectady, where he made certain
that they would have comfortable accommodations for the
trip into the interior. Captain Anchersen believed that the
immigrants ought to travel somewhat decently even if it cost
a bit more to do so. Evidently there was some disagreement
with this idea, for he later published a letter in the Drammen
newspaper *Tiden* in which he defended himself against criti-
cism.[10] At Schenectady the party took a heartfelt farewell
of their beloved captain. In a letter later published both in
an American and in a Norwegian newspaper the spokesmen
for the immigrants declared that it was as touching to say
goodbye to their captain as it was to leave their fatherland.
He had been a wise and kindly commander: "For our own
benefit we were always held to cleanliness and good order,
and we could always depend upon our captain for sound advice and helpful actions," said the letter writers.[11]

Captain Anchersen made two or three trips to America
with emigrant ships after 1840. Serving with him was Hans
Friis, who deserves mention in connection with early Norwegian emigrant voyages. Friis was employed aboard the
"Enigheden" when it made its trip to America in 1837. "In
1839 we find him a sailor in Captain Anchersen's ship
'Emilie.' . . . He sailed several years with Captain Anchersen, the last year as second mate. After some years Captain
Anchersen quit sailing, and Friis hired in another ship from
Drammen."[12] During the years 1837–47, Friis made nine
trips to New York with emigrant ships. In the latter year
he decided to remain in America. For a while he sailed on
the Great Lakes and later tried unsuccessfully to enter the
service of the United States Navy. When the Civil War

[10] Blegen, *Norwegian Migration to America,* 2:27, note 72.

[11] Cited in Blegen, *Norwegian Migration,* 2:27; and quoted in Semmingsen,
Veien mot vest, 123. The letter, written by Knud Knudsen and Claus Stabæk,
appeared in the *New Yorker Stats-Zeitung,* September 4, 1839, and was reprinted
in *Tiden,* December 31, 1839.

[12] Anderson, *First Chapter,* 361.

broke out he joined the Union army, was wounded, and re-
tired on a pension. His last years were spent on a farm
which he had bought in the Muskego neighborhood. There
he died in 1886.

In commenting on the emigrants who sailed with Anchersen in 1839, the newspaper *Tiden* of Drammen spoke of them
as representing the best youth of the land. "As a whole
they were vigorous and well appearing people; there were
no old people, few children, and sixteen young unmarried
girls." [13] Much the same could have been said about the
emigrant group of 1840. There were no aged people among
them, the oldest individual being only fifty-five. Only four
of them were beyond forty-five years of age. If we break
down the ages into different categories we get the following
results: individuals over forty-five, 4; individuals between
eighteen and forty-five inclusive, 56; and individuals under eighteen, 29. There were forty-eight males and forty-one
females in the group. All the men, with only two exceptions,
were either farmers or artisans. The exceptions were the
two young men who head the list, one a clerk, the other a
student. The farmers, some twenty-two in number, were
in the majority.[14] In the group were also a shoemaker, a
blacksmith, a tailor, a carpenter, and a baker. A boy fourteen years old and three young men nineteen years of age
were classified as servants. Of the adult women fourteen
were listed as wives, while an equal number of maidservants,
ranging in age from sixteen to thirty-five, were going to try
their chances in the New World. One woman forty-eight
years old was entered on the list (number 63) with no occupation given.

The largest family in the " Emilie " list included only five
children. The great majority of the emigrants were unmar-

---

[13] Quoted by Blegen in *Norwegian Migration*, 1:120.
[14] Actually only twenty-one are listed as farmers, but I have included A. A.
Vinje (number 84) in that group, since he was the son of a farmer and became a
farmer in America. On the list his occupation is not given. Even Hansen Heg

ried, and most of the married couples were young, with their best years ahead. Transplantation to the New World did not hamper their fecundity, because, as will be seen below, some members of the group were to become the parents of nine, ten, twelve, or even fifteen children. In the light of these figures one can understand the Yankee who conceded to a pioneer Norwegian editor that the Scandinavians, the Germans, and notably the Irish so far outstripped the native American stock in reproductive capacity that the future in this country belonged to those races of Europeans who had immigrated since the beginning of the nineteenth century.[15] But a counterpoise to the high birth rate was an alarmingly high mortality rate. A large percentage of this party and their children died young. Cholera was one of the worst scourges; it carried many of them away to an untimely grave.

An easy generalization runs to the effect that the immigrants were a poverty-striken lot, harried out of their country by want and misery. Certainly the urge for better economic conditions was the main force behind the whole Norwegian migration of the nineteenth century. But that does not mean that all the migrants had been brought up in poverty at home and came to America penniless. Most of the passengers who left for America with the "Emilie" in 1839 were described by a contemporary newspaper as being "in good circumstances" and a couple of them owned several thousand specie dollars.[16] As will become evident below, at least a fair proportion of the emigrants of 1840 also were comparatively well-to-do, many of them having enough ready cash to buy fairly extensive land holdings soon after their arrival in America.

In 1839 practically all of Captain Anchersen's passengers came from Numedal, while two years later most of them

(number 3) was an innkeeper in Norway, but he became a farmer in America. Ole K. Trovatten was a schoolteacher, *klokker,* and farmer.

[15] *Billed-magazin,* 2:282 (September 3, 1870).

[16] Malmin, in *Decorah-posten,* March 6, 1925.

were from Telemarken. These two valleys also contributed some recruits to the group of 1840, but that year the largest contingents came from the Drammen area and from Voss, about thirty and twenty people respectively.[17] According to Ole Knudsen Trovatten " the price for transportation was $33 apiece for himself and his wife and $25 each for his children; for board during the voyage he paid $12 apiece for himself and his wife. The contract for the journey from New York to the interior called for $13 for adults, half that amount for children under twelve, and nothing for children under two." [18] The "Emilie" did not carry passengers only. Both in 1839 and 1840 it picked up cargoes of Swedish iron at Göteborg. In 1840 the ship left Drammen on May 17 and, after remaining in Göteborg about two weeks, set sail for New York. After a stormy trip it arrived there on or shortly before August 12. The immigrants took the usual route up the Hudson River, the Erie Canal, and the Great Lakes to the interior. Even Heg and his party disembarked at Milwaukee in order to join their friends Søren Bache and Johannes Johansen at Muskego, where they arrived safely on Sunday evening, August 28.[19] The Vossings continued on to Chicago, where a small group from their home community had already settled.[20]

[17] Blegen places the number from Drammen at about thirty; *Norwegian Migration to America*, 1:126. According to A. A. Vinje there were twenty from Voss. This party boarded the "Emilie" at Göteborg. They left Voss on April 16 for Bergen, where they secured passage to the Swedish port. There they had to wait several weeks before they were fortunate enough to be picked up by Captain Anchersen. See K. A. Rene, *Historie om udvandringen fra Voss og vossingerne i America*, 172 (Madison, Wisconsin, 1930).

[18] Quoted from Trovatten's unpublished journal, in Blegen, *Norwegian Migration to America*, 1:127.

[19] Entry in Søren Bache's diary for that day. Bache's manuscript diary is in the library of St. Olaf College.

[20] On the list as drawn up by the New York immigration official the two first passengers, the clerk and the student, were going to New York while all the others were destined for Missouri. As far as I have been able to find none of them ever went to the latter state. A Norwegian settlement had been started by the indomitable Cleng Peerson in Shelby County, Missouri, in 1837, but the venture proved to be a failure. By 1840 the settlement was breaking up and most of the people were moving into Iowa. For a brief account of the Shelby County settlement see Blegen, *Norwegian Migration to America*, 1:112–114.

II

The original passenger list of the "Emilie" for 1840 was drawn up by an American immigration official in New York on August 12 of that year,[21] and we are including a transcript of this list.[22]

N. B. Schubarth (1) was one of the 280 subscribers to *Nordlyset,* the first Norwegian newspaper in America.[23]   At the time when it appeared, 1847–49, he was living in Providence, Rhode Island; in the directory for that city (volumes for 1856 and 1858) [24] Nils B. Schubarth is listed as a civil engineer.   It would appear, therefore, that he was one of the earliest, if not the very first, of that great number of Norwegian civil engineers who have found employment for their talents and training in the New World.

No further trace has been found of E. Warloe (2) who appears as a student on the list.   In those days it was unusual for people with much formal education to emigrate, and it caused something of a sensation in 1837 when the student Ole Rynning left for the New World.   Like Schubarth, Warloe probably remained in the East; these two alone among the passengers stated that New York was their destination.

Even Hansen (3), better known as Even Hansen Heg, became one of the outstanding leaders in the Muskego settlement.   He was influential in organizing the famous Norwegian Lutheran congregation there and in founding the newspaper *Nordlyset.*   His spacious barn played a prominent part in the early history of the settlement, both as an

[21] This passenger list was found by Dr. Blegen in the archives of the New York Customs House.   The early passenger lists that were long preserved there have been transferred to the National Archives in Washington.

[22] Numbers have been prefixed to the names on the transcript that is given here to clarify the author's references that follow it. In the manifest form there is a final column headed " Died on the voyage," but there are no entries for this list. From item 32 to the end of the list in the original, wavy lines extend the ditto marks under the two final headings.

[23] Knud Langeland, *Nordmœndene i Amerika: nogle optegnelser om de norskes udvandring til Amerika,* 106 (Chicago, 1888).

[24] These were the only volumes from the period that were available for examination.

assembly place and as a "hotel" for Norwegian immigrants trekking farther into the West. In Drammen, Heg had been the owner of a hotel, but in Wisconsin he became a farmer. He died in 1850.[25] S. Olsdatter (4), Siri, the wife of Even Heg, died in 1842. Hans Evensen (5) is the well-known Colonel Hans Christian Heg, leader of the Fifteenth Wisconsin Regiment (the "Norwegian Regiment") during the Civil War. As a youth he took an active part in the life of the Muskego settlement, and in 1849 the gold rush carried him to California. After his father's death, he returned to Muskego, took charge of the family farm, and soon marred Gunild Einong, who lived in the settlement. In 1859 he entered business in Waterford and, the same year, was elected prison commissioner for Wisconsin, thus becoming the first Norwegian elected to a state position in America.[26] When the war broke out he gave up his promising business and political career to become organizer and leader of the above-mentioned regiment. He was mortally wounded at the battle of Chickamauga and died the next day, September 20, 1863. Ole Evensen (6) was the younger son of Even Heg. As a boy he was one of the two typesetters for *Nordlyset* during its short span of life. In the early part of the Civil War he served as quartermaster for the Fifteenth Wisconsin, thus being one of the one hundred and fifteen men named "Ole" who saw service in that regiment. Later in life he seems to have been engaged in various business and political activities. He died at Burlington, Wisconsin, in 1911.[27] Andrea Evansdatter (7) was the elder daughter of Even Heg. From Anderson we learn that she was "one of the first Norwegians

[25] Full information about Heg and his family can be found in all the standard works on Norwegian immigration.

[26] Waldemar Ager, *Oberst Heg og hans gutter*, 247 (Eau Claire, Wisconsin, 1916). For information about Colonel Heg see especially T. C. Blegen, *The Civil War Letters of Colonel Hans Christian Heg* (Northfield, 1936).

[27] Ella Stratton Colbo, *Historic Heg Memorial Park*, 27 (Racine, Wisconsin, 1940). Pictures of Ole Heg and his two sisters can be found on p. 19 of this pamphlet.

DISTRICT OF NEW-YORK — PORT OF NEW-YORK

I, *Thomas Ancherson* do solemnly, sincerely, and truly *swear* that the following List or Manifest of Passengers, subscribed with my name, and now delivered by me to the Collector of the Customs for the District of New-York, contains, to the best of my knowledge and belief, a just and true account of all the Passengers received on board the *Norw Bark Emilie* whereof I am Master, from *Gothenburg*

Thomas Anchersen

to the *Aug. 12th 1840*
Before me, *G. W. Daus* [?]

LIST OR MANIFEST of all the PASSENGERS taken on board the *Norw Bark Emilie* whereof *Ancherson* is Master, from *Gothenburg* burthen_____ tons.

NAMES	AGE Years	Months	SEX	OCCU-PATION	The Country to which they severally belong	The Country in which they intend to become inhabitants
1 N B Schubarth	22		Male	Clerk	Norway	New York
2 E Warloe	21		"	Student	Do	Do
3 Even Hansen	50		"	Farmer	Do	Missouiri
4 S Olsdatter	40		Wife			
5 Hans Evensen	10		boy			
6 Ole Do	9		"		Do	Do
7 Andrea Evansdatter	5		"			
8 Sophie Do	3		Girl			
9 Johannes Evensen	45		Male	Do	Do	Do
10 B Olsdatter	35		Wife			
11 O Johansen	5		boy			
12 Even "	3		"			
13 Anthon "	..	9	"			
14 S Engebrethsen	30		Male	Shoemaker	Do	Do
15 G Halvordatter	35		Wife			
16 S Syvertson		6	child			
17 S Christensdatter	23		female	Maid servant	Do	Do
18 B Gulliksdatter	35		"	"	Do	Do
19 Olaus Olsen	18	6	Male	Servant	Do	Do
20 Hans Christensen	14		"	"	Do	Do
21 I H Olsdatter	16		female	Maid "	Do	Do
22 Elen Helgesdatter	33		Do	" "	Do	Do
23 Jorgen Larsen	24		Male	Blacksmith	Do	Do
24 Ole Danielsen	19		Do	Servant	Do	Do
25 G Larsdatter	24		female	Maid "	Do	Do
26 K Hendriksdatter	16		"	" "	Do	Do
27 R G Nubberied	38		Male	Farmer		
28 K Knudsdatter	27		Wife		Do	Do
29 A Renersdatter	4	3	child			

30	O H Gronhoft	25		Male	farmer ⎫
31	K Christophersdatter	20		Wife	⎭
32	O A Gravmeng	36		Male	Taylor ⎫
33	I Haagensdatter	27		Wife	
34	A Olsdatter	4	..	Girl	
35	Anders Olsen	2	9	boy	⎬
36	I Olsdatter	1	..	Girl	⎭
37	O A Myran	26		Male	Farmer
38	K H Bruhnsdahl	21		Do	"
39	G O Langerud	19		female	Maid servant
40	H G Haugen	55		Male	farmer ⎫
41	S Persdatter	38		Wife	
42	G Hansen xx	13		Boy	⎬
43	G Hansen	3	6	Do	⎭
	H J Thune [1]	30		Male	
44	Anne O Windag	29		female	Maid servant
45	I Liveried	28		"	
46	P. Jonassen	27		Male	Carpenter
47	H H Overn	22		"	farmer
48	I Olsen	39		"	Baker
49	O Knudzon	32	6	"	farmer ⎫
50	B Aslaksdatter	32	6	Wife	
51	I Olsdatter	7		Girl	⎬
52	A Olsen	4		Boy	
53	I Olsen		8	"	⎭
54	H I Taane	30		Male	farmer ⎫
55	S Gjermundsdatter	26		Wife	⎬
56	I Helgesdatter	2		Girl	
57	A Do		8	"	⎭
58	O I Lovingen	28		Male	Do ⎫
59	M Kittilsdatter	30		Wife	⎬
60	I Olsdatter	6		Girl	
61	K Olsen	4	6	Boy	⎭
62	I Aanunasen	17		female	Maid Servant
63	H Jacobsdatter	48		"	⎱
64	G Stenersen	7		boy	⎰
65	E Helgesen	33		Male	farmer
66	M Olsdatter	20		female	Maid servant
67	L. Baarsen	42		Male	farmer ⎫
68	G Gullaksdatter	43		Wife	⎬
69	M Larsdatter	18		Girl	⎭
70	M Torstensdatter	23		female	Maid servant
71	T Olsen	49		Male	farmer ⎫
72	A Guliksdatter	45		Wife	⎬
73	G Torstenssen	20		Male	⎭
74	C G Grimestad	28		Male	farmer ⎫
75	R Olsdatter	21		Wife	
76	B Clausdatter	1	9	Girl	⎬
77	G Do		1	"	⎭
78	K Ercksen	19		male	Servant
79	L I [?] Rothe	21		Male	farmer
80	K J Hylle	22		Do	Do
81	M Torstendatter	23		female	Maid servant
82	B Godskalksen	26		Male	farmer
83	B L Bolt	20		"	" ⎫
84	A A Windge	20		"	
85	M Gulliksdatter	24		Wife	⎬
86	A Arnsen	2		Boy	⎭
87	M N Sondve	33		Male	Do
88	O S Gilderhuus	26		"	Do
89	E N Berslien	20		Girl	Maid servant

[1] A line is drawn through this name in the manifest.

to teach English district school in Wisconsin. She taught school in the Muskego settlement during the winter of 1855 and 1856. She afterwards married Dr. Stephen Himoe (Høimo) . . . who was surgeon of the fifteenth regiment, Wisconsin volunteers; and after the war she settled with her husband in Kansas and died there." [28] Sophie Evansdatter (8) was the younger daughter of Even Heg. She later married a man named Halsted.

Johannes Evensen (9) Skofstad was related to Even Heg.[29] Like his relative he must have been fairly well-to-do because shortly after his arrival in the Muskego settlement he bought 250 acres of land, and by 1842 he was able to write to friends in Norway and impress them with the fact that "We have built a house of oak, thirty feet long and twenty feet wide." In this letter we also catch a glimpse of the newcomer's naïve surprise at the American way of life. "The native-born Americans are called Yankees," wrote Skofstad. "They have such cold houses that the snow blows into them. They eat three times a day, always at a decked table. No matter how simple a workingman they may have with them, all eat at the same table, without distinction as to persons. These people work daily at their various tasks even though they are merchants or officials." [30] Together with Even Heg and six other men, Johannes Evensen Skofstad served on the first board of the Muskego congregation.[31] B. Olsdatter (10) was the wife of Johannes Evensen Skofstad, and O. Johansen (11), Even Johansen (12), and Anthon Johansen (13), were their sons.

S. Engebrethsen (14), better known as Syvert Engebrethsen Narverud, came from Eker in Norway and settled at Muskego. He seems to have played a prominent part in the church life of the settlement, since in one of the numerous

[28] Anderson, *First Chapter*, 283.
[29] *Billed-magazin*, 1:13 (November 14, 1868).
[30] Quoted by Blegen in *Norwegian Migration to America*, 1:204.
[31] Bache Diary, December 24, 1843.

theological disputes of this community, he served on a commission to determine whether the Muskego congregation should adopt the Danish-Norwegian church ritual of 1685, as Clausen and Dietrichson desired.[32] Engebrethsen and his wife Gunhild (G. Halvor[s]datter — 15) became very close friends of the Reverend and Mrs. H. A. Stub, who served the Muskego parish from 1848 to 1855.

R. G. Nubberied (27) was probably the Nubberud from Milwaukee County who, according to Søren Bache,[33] was one of the eight men to serve on the board of the Muskego congregation when it was organized late in 1843. According to the passenger list, " Nubberied's " first name was Rener, for his daughter's name is entered as A. Renersdatter (29), but Bache gives Nubberud's first name as Reier. It is probable, however, that either the immigration official or the diarist made a mistake in recording the name.

O. A. Gravmeng (32) is undoubtedly the Ole Anderson who is mentioned as coming to Muskego with the Heg party in 1840,[34] because the initials and the ages of the Gravmeng group as given on the list agree with those of the Anderson family. Furthermore, a great-granddaughter of Ole Anderson, Ella Stratton Colbo, has informed me that he was a tailor, the occupation which is ascribed to O. A. Gravmeng in the list. Both Ole Anderson Gravmeng and his wife, Ingeborg (I. Haagensdatter, number 33 on the list), spent the rest of their lives at Muskego and are buried in the Norway Hill cemetery of that settlement. A. Olsdatter (34), the four-year-old daughter of the above-mentioned couple, was no doubt the person later known as Anna Anderson. I can do no better than let her granddaughter summarize the events of her life:

"Anna Anderson was born in Norway, June 15, 1836.

[32] N. N. Rønning, *The Saga of Old Muskego*, 28 (Waterford, Wisconsin, 1943).
[33] Bache Diary, December 14, 1843.
[34] Colbo, *Historic Heg Memorial Park*, 10, 62.

With her parents in 1840, she made the 13-week trip across the Atlantic as a member of the party of immigrants led by Even Hansen Heg. As a small child she helped, with the other children of the community, to carry shingles to the top of Indian Hill (now called Norway Hill) during the building of their first church. She attended Sunday school classes in the Even Heg barn, and later in the first church. She was a member of the first class confirmed by Rev. Stub in the old church. During her early teens, she was one of the survivors of the terrible visitations of cholera which caused Muskego to be known for a time as The Region of Death." [35] She married Halvor Benedickson, by whom she had seven children. For a number of years the Benedickson family occupied the old pioneer cabin which is now one of the most interesting features of Heg Memorial Park.

From R. B. Anderson [36] we learn the following about H. G. Haugen (40) and S. Persdatter (41): "The first Norwegian to be buried in Rock County or in Wisconsin soil, so far as I have been able to learn, was Hans Gjermundson Haugen, who came from Vægli in Numedal in 1840. His wife's name was Sigrid Persdatter Valle. Hans Gjermundson was born in 1785 and died on Jefferson Prairie in the latter part of October, 1840. Sigrid was born January 30, 1803, and died in Beloit, January 21, 1885." G. Hansen (42) was the son of H. G. Haugen. Anderson [37] says that his first name was Gunnel, that he was born in Numedal in 1827 and died in Canby, Minnesota, in January, 1893. We are also told that he taught the first English school in the town of Primrose, Wisconsin, in the winter of 1849–50, that he took part in the Pike's Peak gold rush, and that he served in the Civil War. G. Hansen (43) was also a son of H. G. Haugen. Anderson quotes at length from a letter which he received from Hansen when, as an old man, he was living in Beloit, Wisconsin, un-

[35] Colbo, *Historic Heg Memorial Park*, 62.
[36] *First Chapter*, 260.
[37] *First Chapter*, 260.

der the Americanized name of George Jackson. Among
other things the letter explains how this strange metamor-
phosis of a name took place. "Among the passengers across
the sea was a man by name Ludvig. He had spent some
time in England and was pretty well versed in the English
language. He acted as interpreter for the emigrants. He
told my father that his name, Hans, translated into English,
would be Jack and Hanson would accordingly be Jackson,
and as my name was Gjermund Hanson, it was turned into
George Jackson. The whole family adopted the name Jackson."[38] From the letter we also learn that during the Civil
War Gjermund Hansen (George Jackson) recruited a company in the vicinity of Primrose, Dane County, and that he
was commissioned a captain in the Forty-third Regiment of
Wisconsin Volunteers.

Anne O. Windag (44) came from Numedal. Her brother,
Gunnel Olsen Vindeg, who came to America in 1839, is well
known in Norwegian immigrant history as a writer of boast-
ful, but influential America letters.[39] Another brother,
Helleik, gained fame, or rather notoriety, along another line
of endeavor. Together with two companions he decided to
try a quick and easy way to riches. "During the winter of
1841 these three unmarried men, all from Numedal, spent
their time partly at Koshkonong and partly in Whitewater,
making Norwegian money. . . . They wore the money as
soles in their boots in order to make the bills look old and
worn."[40] In the spring of 1842 or 1843 they returned to
Norway to cash in on their cunning but landed in prison for
long terms instead. Anna Vindeg married the Vossing, Nils
Larson Bolstad, in 1841; he was one of the pioneers in the
famous Koshkonong settlement. They settled in the town

[38] *First Chapter*, 263.
[39] Blegen, *Norwegian Migration*, 1:143; "Koshkonong og Vindeg-slegten," in
Numedalslagets årbog, no. 2, p. 91–101 (1916).
[40] Anderson, *First Chapter*, 344. See also "Falskmyntnerne," in *Numedalslagets årbog*, no. 8, p. 53 (1922).

of Deerfield, Dane County, Wisconsin, where they remained until Bolstad died in 1865. Shortly afterwards Anna Vindeg Bolstad sold the farm and moved to North Dakota, where she died in 1912. She had three daughters and three sons, one of whom joined the Fifteenth Wisconsin Regiment and died in battle, June 28, 1864.[41]

H. H. Overn (47) is presumably the Helge H. Øvern whom Søren Bache mentions [42] as living close to Silver Lake, not far from the Muskego settlement.

O. Knudzon (49) Trovatten is a well-known figure in early Norwegian immigrant history. In his native Lardal he was both schoolteacher and *klokker,* and in the parishes round about he had gained great respect among the peasantry as a man of learning " who could silence both minister and judge when he so desired." From far and near they came to seek his advice on knotty points. But there was evidently a serious flaw in his make-up, since he left Norway under the suspicion of forgery, and later, in America, was ruined completely by excessive drinking.[43] During his first years in this country he sent back a series of letters which apparently precipitated something like a class struggle in his home valleys. We quote the following from Gunder Mandt, who had himself fallen under the spell of Trovatten's letters and emigrated in 1843:

The *klokker's* praise of America exerted a tremendous influence among the masses of the people in Upper Telemarken, and now for several years rich people and poor, the great as well as the humble, talked about Ole Trovatten, some to blame and defame him, others to praise and extol him. The opponents of emigration avowed that he was a dangerous person who sought to lead people to ruin, while others took a different view of the matter and declared that they were ready to place their hand on the Holy Bible and, under oath, testify that in his home community Ole was known to be a reliable man. I shall not try to pass

[41] Rene, *Historie om udvandringen,* 241.
[42] Bache Diary, April 8 and 12, 1843.
[43] *Billed-magazin,* 2:283 (September 3, 1870).

judgment upon his honesty, but by the common people he was generally regarded as an angel of peace, who had gone beforehand to the New World, whence he sent back home to his countrymen, so burdened with economic sorrows, the olive-branch of promise, with assurance of a happier life in America. . . . " Ole Trovatten has said so " became the refrain in all accounts of the land of wonders, and in a few years he was the most talked of man in Upper Telemarken. His letters from America gave a powerful impulse to emigration, and it is probable that hundreds of those who are now plowing the soil of Wisconsin and Minnesota would still be living in their ancestors' domains in the land of Harald Hairfair, if they had not been induced to bid old Norway farewell through Trovatten's glittering accounts of conditions on this side of the ocean.[44]

While Trovatten was in Drammen waiting for passage to America, he was roundly abused by some of the citizens for wanting to quit his native land. One old woman declared " with cursing and swearing " that he was taking his wife and children to a harsh new land merely to get rid of them. Ole Trovatten reasoned that he could afford to ignore the first part of the charge, but it seemed to him that she carried things too far when she accused him of wanting to kill innocent children. If Trovatten had been of a superstitious turn of mind, he might have believed that the cursing old woman had cast a spell upon his family, for his wife, B. Aslaksdatter (50), died of cholera a few years after her arrival in America and their children, I. Olsdatter (51), A. Olsen (52), and I. Olsen (53) seem to have been carried away by the same epidemic.

E. Helgesen (65) is evidently the Erik Helgesen who is mentioned as coming from Gjerpen or Slembdal and settling

---

[44] *Billed-magazin,* 2:38. The latter part of this quotation is taken from Flom's translation in *Norwegian Immigration,* 82. All the principal works on early Norwegian emigration make mention of Trovatten's great influence upon his fellow Telemarkings. Besides these references see especially Blegen, *Norwegian Migration to America,* 1:197–200; Semmingsen, *Veien mot vest,* 75; and H. R. Holand, *De norske settlementers historie,* 146 (Ephraim, Wisconsin, 1909). Two of Trovatten's letters are published in *Telesoga* no. 5, p. 2–9 (September, 1910). A brief article about Trovatten, together with a translation of one of his letters, is given by Theodore C. Blegen in *North Star,* 2:76 (Minneapolis, March, 1920).

near Pine Lake, Wisconsin. According to Holand, he established himself there in 1843.[45]

All the persons on the list from numbers 67 to 89 inclusive
came from Voss and went to Chicago, where a small Vossing
colony had grown up during the preceding few years. From
Chicago most of them went north into the new lands of northern Illinois and southern Wisconsin.[46]

L. Baarsen's (67) full name was Lars Baardsen Saude.
Shortly after their arrival in Chicago, he and Claus Grimestad bought land in Boone County, Illinois, immediately
south of the Wisconsin line and thus became founders of the
great Vossing settlement on Jefferson Prairie. Later Lars
Baardsen also bought a couple of farms on the Wisconsin side
of the line. He is reported to have been an able farmer and
a typical "handy man" who became a natural leader in the
settlement during the early years. He was also influential in
inducing others to emigrate from Voss. He died on the old
homestead in 1881. G. Gullaksdatter (68) was Gudve, the
wife of Lars Baardsen Saude. Both of them were born in
Voss in 1798. She was a widow when she married him. By
her first husband she had a daughter Ranveig of whom we
will hear more later. Gudve died in 1879. M. Larsdatter
(69) was evidently the daughter of Lars and Gudve Baardsen
although Rene says that no child came of their union. If M.
Larsdatter was their child, as our list indicates, she must have
died early because after their deaths the lands of Lars and
Gudve passed into the hands of more distant relatives.

M. Torstensdatter's (70) full name was Martha Torstensdatter Saude. A few years after her arrival in America,
probably in 1843, she married Peder Davidson Skjerveim,
who had come from Voss in 1837. The Reverend C. L. Clau-

---

[45] Holand, *De norske settlementers historie*, 170; Bache Diary, April 8 and 12, 1845.

[46] Much information about this party of Vossings is presented in Rene, *His-torie om udvandringen*, which I have consulted in preparing the material on this group that follows.

sen is reported to have officiated at the ceremony. Peder
Davidson Skjerveim is noted as one of the founders of the
large Vossing settlement in Wiota, Wisconsin. Together
with two friends he had bought land there in 1841. He fell
a victim to cholera in 1850, and the next year Martha married Ole Munson from Land, Norway. They settled on a
farm near Gratiot, Wisconsin. Both Martha and her husband Ole were very active in religious work. She even wrote
some religious songs which were printed after her death in
1882 and distributed among her relatives. Martha had two
daughters by each marriage.

T. Olsen (71), Torsten Olsen Saude, evidently came to
America with the intention of buying land because he took
a trip to Jefferson Prairie shortly after his arrival but soon
returned to Chicago where he died a year or two later. A.
Guliksdatter (72), who was the wife of Torsten Olsen Saude,
died about the same time as her husband. G. Torstenssen
(73), Gullick Torstensen Saude, was the son of the couple
just mentioned. Gullick was less than twenty years old
when he emigrated, but the "America fever" seems to have
gripped him while he was in his teens; it was to satisfy him,
it is said, that the parents also decided to leave the old home.
They must have been fairly well-to-do because, on their
death, they left him $1,000. Armed with this inheritance
the aggressive young man went to Koshkonong in 1843, and
the next year he could write to friends in Voss that he had
bought 248½ acres, of which 35 were under cultivation. In
1845 he married the sister of Lars Røthe (number 79 below),
and in 1850 he went to California in search of gold, whence
he returned to Koshkonong by way of Panama and New
York, $1,500 richer. He seems to have invested all his
money in land, for he ultimately became the largest land-
holder in Koshkonong. On his death in 1895 his wide holdings passed to his son, Torger Thompson, the only one of nine
children to survive him. Torger Thompson played a promi-

nent part in community and state affairs and is noted for his liberal gifts to charitable and educational institutions both in Voss and Wisconsin. His lively interest in the land of his fathers is evidenced by his many visits to Norway and especially by the fact that after his death most of his wealth went to the University of Wisconsin as the Torger Thompson Fund for the encouragement of Scandinavian studies.

C. G. Grimestad's (74) full name was Claus Isakson Grimestad. He was married three times, twice in Norway and once in America. By his first wife he had a daughter who was left with foster parents in Voss. As already mentioned, he was one of the founders of the Vossing settlement on Jefferson Prairie where he bought 160 acres of land immediately after his arrival in this country and 40 acres some time later. His second wife died about 1846, and in 1849 he married Guri Kolbe from Sigdal, Norway. By his last marriage he had eight children, all of whom took the name Isaacs. Claus Grimestad died in 1892. R. Olsdatter (75) has already been referred to as Ranveig, the daughter of Gudve Gullaksdatter (number 68 above). She was the second wife of Claus Grimestad (number 74), and, as already mentioned, she died about 1846. According to Rene (p. 176), Ranveig and Claus Grimestad had three children: Lars, Isak (born in 1844), and Britha (born about 1846), while on page 174 he mentions that they had a daughter Brita when they left Norway. From our list it would appear that they had two daughters when they arrived in New York: B. Clausdatter (76), one year and nine months old, and G. Clausdatter (77), one month old. If the latter girl was one month old on arrival in New York she must have been born aboard the ship. Perhaps both of these girls died in infancy and the parents had another daughter shortly before the mother's death in 1846 who was also called Britha. The son Lars (Louis) Isaacs died in battle during the Civil War.

K. Ercksen (78), Knut Eriksen Rokne, first bought land

on Koshkonong, near Cambridge, Wisconsin, but in 1853 he sold his farm and, as the first known Vossing to settle in what later became the state of Minnesota, laid foundations for the extensive Vossing settlement in Dodge, Olmsted, and Goodhue counties. He lived there the rest of his life. He was married to Arnbjørg Torstensdatter from Numedal, by whom he had two sons.

L. I. [?] Rothe (79), Lars Torgerson Røthe, worked aboard the lake steamer " G. W. Dole " until he returned to Voss in 1843. In the spring of 1844 he married Ingeborg Davidsdatter Mølster and returned to America. Like so many other Vossings he found his way to Koshkonong where he finally acquired a farm of 264 acres. Røthe played a prominent part in local political and church affairs until his death in 1898.

K. J. Hylle (80), Knut Johnson Hylle, seems to have had much in common with Lars Røthe. They came to America together; together they returned to Voss in 1843, where they staged a double wedding in Vossevangen's old church on May 8, 1844. After this the two couples returned to America, settled on Koshkonong, and brought into the world families of twelve children. It appears that Knut Hylle was a pioneer in more respects than one, for he helped organize the Methodist church in Cambridge, Wisconsin, which is said to have been the first Norwegian church of that denomination ever to be founded.

M. Torstendatter (81) has already been listed as number 70 above. Evidently the emigration official made a slip, because he failed to enter the name of Martha Tormodsdatter Ringheim, an unmarried woman twenty-eight years old who also came across with this party from Voss. All we know of her is that later she accompanied the group to Chicago, where she secured work.

B. Godskalksen (82), Brynjulv Godskalksen Ronve, soon returned to Norway where he lived the rest of his life. As far as we know he was the only member of the entire group of immigrants who did not remain in this country. His American venture could not have been too discouraging, however, because a brother and a sister of his later settled in Wisconsin.

The entry B. L. Bolt (83) is evidently a clerical error for Baard Larson Bøe, who was one of the party of Vossings emigrating in 1840, while no Bolt is mentioned by the contemporary accounts. B. L. Bøe bought 160 acres of land on Koshkonong, where he died, probably in 1847. He was unmarried.

The entry A. A. Windge (84) is another clerical error. It is evidently an American attempt to put on paper the sound of the Vossing name Arne Anderson Vinje. He was the son of a *Stortingsmand* and as such probably received a better education than did the average Norwegian boy of those days. Be that as it may, at any rate he wrote a brief account of his early experiences in America, and from him we learn much about the emigrants from Voss in 1840.[47] "Knudt Hylle and myself began our first work in Chicago upon the streets of what was then Chicago's west side," says Vinje. "My work was handling a heavy plank scraper, drawn by a yoke of oxen and used to scrape the sod from the sides of the road into the center. This was such heavy work that the Americans avowed they would not do it for $8.00 per day while I got only $16.00 per month, board not included." The heavy work, the hot weather, and the unclean water got the better of even Vinje's strong constitution and he was bedridden for a while.

"At that time, and while I was still in bed, the election of General Harrison to the presidency took place. Inspired by the excitement of the occasion, and supported by two men, I went to the booth and cast my first vote for president, tho

[47] Rene has included much of this report in his volume, while Flom has turned parts of it into English in *Norwegian Immigration*, 200–202. A. A. Vinje is also referred to at times as A. A. Urland.

I did not understand a word of the language used. Then, quite exhausted, I was assisted back to bed. The candidate was the people's favorite, and from my bed I saw a log cabin, such as he lived in, mounted upon wheels and drawn through the streets to show that he was a man of the people. That was effective campaigning!" After Christmas he had recovered sufficiently to join his fellow Vossings on Sundays in attending an English school conducted by a Swede in a barracks at Fort Dearborn. "But this school came to a sudden stop since some of the pupils thought they were just as wise as the teacher."

In July, 1841, Vinje was one of three Vossings who laid the foundations of the Wiota settlement in Wisconsin. His first wife died in 1863, and in 1868 he married Ragnild Nilsdatter Karavold from Sogn. He continued to take a lively interest in American politics after his early introduction to it in Chicago. Being an especially earnest abolitionist, he is said to have aided many a slave to escape to Canada. He died in 1903. He had seven children by his first wife, M. Gulliksdatter (85), or Martha Gulliksdatter Kinne, and two by his second wife. A. Arnsen (86), Anders Arnesen Vinje, was the oldest son of A. A. Vinje and Martha Gulliksdatter. He went to Minnesota, where he died in 1861.

M. N. Sondve (87), Mads Nilsen Sonve, remained in Chicago a short while, then moved to Wiota where he died in 1842.

O. S. Gilderhuus (88), Ole Sjurson Gilderhus, bought land on Koshkonong in 1840 and in 1842 returned to Chicago where he married E. N. Berslien (89) whose full name was Eli Nilsdatter Bergslien. Gilderhus soon returned with his wife to Koshkonong where they lived the rest of their lives. They had two children. He died in 1882, and his wife died in 1885.

We are thus brought to the end of the passenger list. In spite of careful examination of all available material a fairly large number still remain unidentified.[48] The unmarried women have proved especially elusive, partly, no doubt, because they usually arrived in this country under some name ending in "datter," which in the course of time would be changed either through marriage or Americanization. As we have seen, a large percentage of the male passengers also changed their names after arriving in the United States. A surprisingly large number of patronymics ending in "sen" or "son" were dropped in favor of Norwegian place names, while a few tried to ease the process of Americanization by assuming such surnames as Thompson, Isaacs, or Jackson. This confusion of names, so characteristic of early Norwegian-American history, is one of the many obstacles thrown in the way of those who try to follow the fortunes of their immigrant forefathers in the New World.

[48] According to H. R. Holand in "Muskego," in *Symra*, 3:191, and A. O. Barton in "Muskego, the Most Historic Norwegian Colony," in *Scandinavia*, 1:23, two men named Helge Thompson and Ole Haagensen and their families accompanied the Heg party to Muskego. I have been unable to find these families on the ship's list; but Ole Haagenson may be O. H. Gronhoft (30) and Helge Thompson may be H. I [?] Taane (54). Taane's first name is Helge; his daughters are listed as Helgesdatter. Among the eighty signers of the famous Muskego manifesto of January 6, 1845, as enumerated in the Bache Diary, are Ole Aslesen Myren and Jorgen Larsen. It is possible that these men are the O. A. Myran (37) and Jorgen Larsen (23) who appear on the ship's list. In Mrs. Colbo's *Historic Heg Memorial Park* and Rønning's *The Saga of Old Muskego,* one Tosten Kleven is mentioned as coming with the Heg party. But after the appearance of her book, Mrs. Colbo was informed by Miss Emma Cleven of St. Paul, Minnesota, a granddaughter of Tosten Kleven, that he did not emigrate until 1842. Through the kindness of Mrs. Colbo, I was able to examine the unpublished history of the Cleven family, written by Miss Emma Cleven. It makes it clear that Tosten Kleven did not immigrate until 1842. This also agrees with an entry in a book of reminiscences shown me by Mrs. F. C. Henderson of Stoughton, Wisconsin, which her mother, a daughter of Tosten Kleven, had kept.

SHIP LIST OF THE *ORIENT,* 19 MAY 1842

Contributed by Lucy Mary Kellogg
Brighton, Michigan

"Ship list . . . sworn to this 19th day of May 1842, contains a true and just account of all the Passengers received on board the 'ship "Orient"' whereof I am Master, from Falmouth, England. So help me God." /s/ JOHN LEUTY. This ship list, giving passengers' names, ages and occupations, is in the records of the Port of New York, at The National Archives in Washington, D.C.

VINCENT,	Elizabeth	30	
	Elizabeth	7	
	Saml	5	
	Mary	2	
ROWE,	George	48	miner
	John	1	
	George	17	
	James	14	
KNEEBONE,	John	23	miner
HOCKING,	James	36	farmer
	James	8	
EDWARDS,	William	36	farmer
BASKETT,	James	28	
	Mary	26	
	James	7	
	Wm.	3	
	Rich^d	7 months	
[?A] BLECOCK,	Elizabeth	26	
	Elizabeth	4	
CUNDY,	Solomon	29	miner
	Maria	27	
	Emma	6	
	Elizabeth	4	
	Mary	1	
RICHARDS, Thos		22	miner
FANNYDE, Thos		21	
THOMAS,	Richard	30	
	Mary	4----------died	
	Mary	36	
	Ann	2	
	Louisa	8 months	
OATEY,	Peter	35	miner
	Louisa	30	

LITTLEWIN,	Elizabeth	25	
	Elizabeth	3	
	John	2	
KASKAT,	John	3	
	Jane	3 months	
MARTIN,	John	35	publican
	Mary	36	
	John	13	
	Eliza	11	
	Wm	7	
	Mary	5	
	Elizabeth	3	
	Jane	1	
	Caroline	2 months	
MARTIN,	Robert	25	miner
ROBBIN,	John	39	
	Jane	36	
	Elizabeth	13	
	John	11	
	Wm	9	
THOMAS,	Rich^d	19	
TIPPET,	Reginald	60	
	Hannah	19	
	Charles	10	
WALLIS,	James	23	
MATHEWS,	Rich^d	23	
	Susan	22	
	Emma	2	
STEPHENS, Saml		28	farmer
TREWARTHA, Edwd		25	miner
WILLEY, Edwd		23	do
BENNETT, George		32	do
BARQUILL, Wm		25	do
HOLMAN, John		25	do
CORY [or LONG], John		24	do
CUNDY,	John	25	do
	Ann	50	
	Eliza	11	
ROBERTS, Rich^d		26	miner
LINCOCK, W^m		36	miner
	Amelia	36	
	do	14	
	Saml	11	
	Wm	9	
	Thomas	15	
	Ann	5	

LINCOCK, John	2	
Benjamin	2	
(torn) [Might be Thomas Ford]		
Elizabeth	47	
Richard	13	
Thomas	11	
Wm	10	
Francis	6	
KASKAT, John	30	miner
Jane	30	
EDWARDS, Thomas	10	
STEPHENS, Ann	28	
FOXALL, William**	33	carpenter
GOLDSWORTHY, Rich^d	48	farmer
Johanna	48	
Mary	22	
Jane	20	
Elizabeth	18	
Rich^d	14	
Thos	11	
Harritt	8	
Caroline	4	
RUSSELL, James	24	miner
RICHARDS, Richard	22	
Mary	22	
HARRIS, James	11	
GOLDSWORTHY, John	22	miner
MOYLE, Thomas*	29	
Susan	34	
John	1	
HODGE, James	20	miner
GEORGE, William*	30	miner
Jane*	30	
Thomas*	1	
ROBERTS, James	24	miner
Henry	48	miner
Catharine	25	
Phillippa	20	
Saml	18	
Joseph	15	
Grace	13	
Elizabeth	11	
Thos	11	
John	8	
James	3	
JONES[?JOSE], William	20	miner

ROBERTS, James	25	miner
John	22	miner
COOD[?COAD], W^m	28	miner
COOD, Henry	30	miner
RANDALL, Jeremiah	32	miner
ABRAHAM, John	20	miner
STEPHENS, Edward	30	do
ANDREWS, Solomon	33	do
Grace	33	
DAVIS, Saml	43	farmer
do	16	
PAUL, John	36	miner
Eleanor	39	
Richard	10	
Jane	4	
Harriette	1	
EDWARDS, Richard	53	miner
Ann	53	
Mary	19	
Rich^d	17	
Grace	14	
Edwin	11	
RANDALL, Mary	30	
HANCOCK, John	42	miner
Elizabeth	41	
John	12	
Rich^d	10	
Saml	8	
W^m	6	
Thomas	5	
Elizabeth	21	
THOMAS, W^m	18	miner
Ann	21	
GEORGE, Saml	18	miner
TONKIN, Caroline	15	
WILLIAMS, John	36	miner
Elizabeth	32	
Elizabeth	7	
Thos	6	
Eliza	3	
IVY[?HAY], John	33	farmer
TARNLANE, Thos	20	miner
HANY[?], James	47	miner
Tamlane	49	
Mary Ann	11	
James	8	

HANY[?], Matthias	6	
DALE, John	25	miner
W^m	24	miner
Thos	14	
JAMES, Ann Maria**	34	
FOXALL, Ann**	60	
JAMES, Thos**	3	
John**	1	
RULE, Jane	11	
HICKS, Henry	24	
Elizabeth	20	
DAVIS, Charles	40	miner
ROWE, Wm.	27	miner
KNEEBONE, Elizabeth	20	
PAINTER, Rich^d	21	farmer
HICKS, Elizabeth	24	
CUNDY, Solomon	born on passage	

---

* In "The American Descendants of John Moyle, Farrier, ..." this issue of *DSGR Magazine*, p. 59

** Same as above, p. 60

STATE-AIDED EMIGRATION SCHEMES
FROM CROWN ESTATES IN IRELAND
c. 1850

Presented by

EILISH ELLIS, M.A.

By resolution of the Irish Manuscripts Commission of 19 June 1945, it was decided to publish in *Analecta Hibernica* a set of documents illustrative of state-aided emigration schemes from crown estates in Ireland, c. 1850.

Attention had been directed to these documents by Dr. R. C. Simington of the Commission. Already, in 1927, at the request of the late James F. Kenney of the Public Archives of Canada, an investigation was made into documents in the Quit Rent Office, Dublin, which contained information relating to persons assisted to emigrate to North America from crown estates in Ireland. This investigation revealed the existence of a collection of material relating to the estates of Ballykilcline, Co. Roscommon; Irvilloughter and Boughill, Co. Galway; Kilconcouse, Offaly; Kingwilliamstown, Co. Cork, and Castlemaine, Co. Kerry. (By the courtesy of the then Superintendant of the Quit Rent Office, the late G. H. Burnett, copies of portions of this material were sent to Dr. Kenney).[1]

The emigration schemes had been carried out under the direction of the Commissioners of Woods, Forests and Land Revenues of the Crown,[2] whose office was in London, and under whom the Quit Rent Office, Dublin, functioned from 1827.[3] Some material relating to the schemes had been sent to the Quit Rent Office from the Office of Woods after the transfer of the land revenues of the Crown to the Irish Free State from 31 March 1923.

The Quit Rent Office collection of books and papers was removed to the Public Record Office, Dublin, in 1943, on the transfer of the Quit Rent Office to the Land Commission, and a MS index to it has been compiled by Miss Margaret Griffith, Deputy-keeper, and other

---

[1] A typescript copy of the material sent to Canada is preserved in the Q.R.O. file 11821.

[2] Hereinafter referred to as Commissioners of Woods or Office of Woods.

[3] The Commissioners of Woods were then of quite recent origin having been appointed in 1810, (50 Geo. III. c. 65), for the purpose of the management of the revenues derived from Crown lands in England ; they succeeded the 'Court of General Surveyors' one of whom was a surveyor-general of the land revenues and the other of woods and forests. In 1832 it was considered expedient to unite the department of the Surveyor-General of Works and Public Buildings with that of the Commissioners of Woods. Under the title, Commissioners of Woods, Forests, Land Revenues, Works and Buildings, this union lasted until 1851 when they were again divided, (14 & 15 Vic. c. 42).
The Quit Rent Office derived its title from one of the hereditary revenues of the Crown, viz. quit rents which arose mainly from grants of land after the

members of the staff. The documents in the Public Record Office dealing specifically with emigration from the crown estates are found in the bundles of loose papers, indexed under the name of each particular estate, (*e.g.*, Correspondence relating to Kingwilliamstown), as well as in the letter books of the Quit Rent Office and the Office of Woods, London, and in the files of the Forfeiture Office.

This collection provides much material which would be of interest to the student of social and economic conditions in 19th century Ireland. There are references to trades and occupations, farming methods, the rundale system, the evils of the land system and proposed remedies. Several excellent maps and tracings of estates, as well as plans of houses to be erected as part of crown improvements, are readily available. There is information too on the erection of schools under the Commissioners of National Education, on the erection of churches and rectories, bridges and roads, railways and canals. Eye-witnesses' accounts of the progress of the famine are available in the petitions for relief and in the letters from local relief committees. There is also material relating to the working of the Poor Law.

The present report consists of :—

I. A note on the emigration scheme and a list of the emigrants from each estate. These as here presented are compiled from :—

(a) Preliminary lists of potential emigrants from each estate, compiled at the request of the clerk of the Quit Rent Office, Dublin, or the Commissioners of Woods in London, by a local crown official, giving details of name, age, with, in some cases, additional information as to occupancy of land and occupation.

(b) Shipping-agents' receipted accounts containing the names to whom sailing tickets were issued, the ticket numbers and the family groupings; the number of adults and children with

---

Restoration of Charles II. These rents, of a confirmatory nature from the Commonwealth period and earlier, were regulated by the Acts of Settlement and Explanation. In 1669 hereditary revenues (including customs and excise), were set to farm. When this procedure ended shortly before 1688, the system of collection (including the office of Clerk of the Quit Rents) established by the farmers was adopted by government and entrusted to the Commissioners of Revenue.

Some lands forfeited in 1641 and not disposed of by the Crown at the Restoration were subsequently leased subject to rents; likewise lands forfeited in 1688 which had remained undisposed of after the sales by the Trustees of Forfeited Estates in 1703, were leased by the Commissioners of Revenue. Prior to the transfer to the Commissioners of Woods in 1827, the collection of the Irish land revenues had been entrusted to the Commissioners of Excise in succession to the General Board of Revenue abolished in 1806.

the appropriate fare; the cost of provisions, tins and cooking utensils supplied, and the amount of 'landing money' and commission payable at the port of disembarkation.

(c)   Receipted accounts of 'landing-money' paid by agents of the shipping companies in New York and Quebec.

(d)   Returns and clearance papers from emigration officers at the port of embarkation.

(e)   Expense accounts of the local official in charge of travel arrangements to the port of embarkation.

(f)   Inter-departmental letters between the offices of the Commissioners of Woods, Emigration, the Quit Rent Office and the Treasury.

(g)   Miscellaneous letters and memorials from tenants, local landlords and agents.

II. A collection of four letters from emigrants written shortly after their arrival in the United States. These are printed verbatim with spelling and punctuation as in the originals.

The manuscripts, letter-books and papers, which are used, are cited according to the MS index to the Quit Rent Office collection in the Public Record Office, Dublin.

When available, the names of emigrants from each estate are presented in alphabetical order under the following headings :—

(a)   Name : In this column the heads of the family are placed first; then come the male members of the family with christian names in alphabetical order, followed by females. A relative of the same surname is placed last in the family group.

(b)   Details of age.

(c)   Additional information : This column is used to indicate family relationships and any other information available. (The letters in section II supply information as to where some of the emigrants settled in America.)

(d)   Date of departure from port of embarkation.

(e)   Date of arrival in North America.

(f)   Name of ship.

EVENTS LEADING TO THE ADOPTION OF STATE-AIDED
EMIGRATION SCHEMES

The estates from which state-aided emigration took place were
part of crown property in Ireland the management of which was
one of the functions of the Quit Rent Office. They had been let on
various long term leases which expired or were terminated in the
early 1830's when it was discovered that a considerable population
dependent on uneconomic holdings had accumulated on the estates,
e.g., Ballykilcline. A survey of this estate made in 1836 revealed
that there were 463 subdivisions and a population of just over
500 on a farm of approximately 602 acres. The impossibility of
instituting improvements under these conditions of over-population
is apparent, and, with the possible exception of the model farm
experiment at Kingwilliamstown, little was done under the Commissioners of Woods in the years before the famine to solve the
problems arising from the dependence of an ever-increasing population on an over-worked and worn-out soil.

That emigration would provide an outlet was recognised at least
as early as 1836, when a census of the population of Irvilloughter
was made by order of the Commissioners of Woods, with this end
in view. The tenants refused the offer to help them emigrate and
twelve years were to elapse before they themselves petitioned the
Commissioners to be sent to America.

The immediate cause of the inauguration of the state-aided
emigration scheme was the necessity for providing some relief for
a group of Ballykilcline tenants evicted after protracted court
proceedings for non-payment of rent. They petitioned the Commissioners of Woods on 28 May 1847, asking either that they be
allowed to re-occupy their holdings, or, that 'the means of emigration
on a scale similar to that lately practised by the landlords in this
vicinity' be provided for them. The Commissioners almost immediately authorised the clerk of the Quit Rents to make arrangements
for the departure, not only of those willing to emigrate, but of those
who had lately been evicted. The failure of the potato crop, 1845-7,
was the reason for the extension of the scheme to the estates of
Irvilloughter and Boughill. Between 1847 and 1852, while state-
aided emigration was in progress, just over eleven hundred people
left these five crown estates in Ireland to settle in Canada and the
United States.

The implementation of the scheme for the estates of Ballykilcline,
Boughill, Irvilloughter and Kilconcouse was entrusted to John
Burke, clerk of the Quit Rents, who was assisted by the crown agent

or collector of excise for the district in which the particular estate was situated. Michael Boyan, superintendent of Kingwilliamstown model farm, was responsible for the scheme for that estate and for Castlemaine, under the direct control of the Commissioners. It may be noted that more complete details are available for those estates for which Burke was responsible.

Two separate lists of names were compiled by the supervisor of the emigration scheme for each particular estate. The first, consisting of those who had signified their intention of emigrating or who had been compulsorily ejected, was necessary for assessing the amount of money required from the Treasury. It sometimes differed from the second list which gave the names of those who actually left, and which was compiled on or shortly before the day of departure for the port of embarkation. Both lists were sent either direct to the office of the Commissioners of Woods in London, or to the clerk of the Quit Rents in Dublin who forwarded copies to the Commissioners. The second list was checked later with the returns from the shipping agents and the emigration officials at New York and Quebec. It is thus possible to arrive at an almost exact figure of the number of emigrants and be assured of reasonable accuracy in the lists of names.

NOTE ON THE EMIGRATION SCHEME FROM BALLYKILCLINE

The crown estate of Ballykilcline was situated in the parish of Kilglass in the barony of Ballintubber, Co. Roscommon. It contained about 602 acres sub-divided into very minute holdings occupied by 'cottier labourers', and was almost completely over-tilled and worn out when the lease to the tenant, Lord Hartland, fell in in April, 1834. Before the expiration of the lease, terms for the sale of the property had been proposed to Lord Hartland who did not accept them, and the rents, which appeared to have been paid regularly to his agent, were placed in charge with the agents of the Commissioners of Woods, from 1 May 1834.[4] Though the annual amount payable by the under-tenants, of whom there were 74, amounted to £411 19s. 11d., less than £350 had been collected when the payment of all rents ceased from 1836. Notices to quit were served and possession demanded from the tenants, and by 1 May 1837, 56 holdings had been surrendered. The remainder however, refused, and in the spring of 1842, John Burke, clerk of the Quit Rent Office, proposed their eviction after a visit to the estate.[5]

There was considerable opposition to the attempts made by crown officials to enter the estate; the assistance of the police was necessary on several occasions;[6] houses were re-occupied and bailiffs attacked when serving eviction notices.[7] However, those charged with assaulting the bailiffs were acquitted by a jury, who, in the opinion of the crown agent, 'were a set of the *lamest* and most ignorant men could be impanelled, and a disgrace to any Court of Justice'.[8] The establishment of a police barracks on the estate was considered at one stage, so determined was the resistance.[9]

It was not until it became evident that there was organised opposition among the tenantry that the Commissioners of Woods

---

4 Q.R.O., O.W. Land Revenue Series Letter Books, memo of James Weale, surveyor for Commissioners of Woods, 2 April 1834. Mr. Weale was a zealous collector of papers relating to Ireland. His MS purchases at the sale of Lord de Clifford's library in 1834 included "The History of the Survey of Ireland commonly called the Down Survey by Doctor William Petty", which was later edited by Larcom for the Irish Archaeological Society (1851). Mr. Weale died in 1838.

5 *Ibid.* Burke to Commissioners of Woods, 28 February 1842. In a letter of 23 December 1841 to the Commissioners, Burke vehemently opposed the letting of the land to a middleman who might be compelled to resort to eviction of an 'immense population'.

6 *Ibid.*, R. Hamilton & Co., crown solicitors, to Burke, 27 April 1842.

7 *Ibid.*, Michael Ryan, Quit Rent driver, to John Tuck, collector of excise, Athlone, 13 March 1844; George Knox, crown agent, to Burke, 10 May 1844.

8 *Ibid.*, George Knox to Burke, 9 July 1844.

9 *Ibid.*, Commissioners of Woods to Burke, 29 May 1844.

grew impatient. It was reported that the tenants had employed a lawyer named Hugh O'Farrell, whom they were paying at the rate of five shillings per acre each, to prevent their being evicted. A party of 'Molly Maguires' also visited the estate.[10]

A decree in favour of the Crown was obtained in April, 1846,[11] and on May 12, petitions were received from the tenants through their agent, Hugh O'Farrell, and the O'Conor Don, asking for leases under the Crown. The Lord Lieutenant, Lord Bessborough, also pleaded for a year's grace, and on 19 June 1846, the Commissioners of Woods expressed their willingness to grant tenancies on condition that two years rent be paid beforehand by those against whom decrees were obtained. The year's grace expired and steps were taken to execute the writ of possession. An army of 60 police, 25 cavalry, 30 infantry and a stipendiary magistrate were deemed necessary as an escort for the sheriff, and on 27 May 1847, fourteen houses were occupied; two were thrown down; the doors and windows were taken out of others and 12 policemen were left on the premises.[12]

The tenants next petitioned the Commissioners of Woods seeking either permission to re-occupy their holdings, or 'the means of emigration on a scale similar to that which has been lately practised by the landlords in this vicinity'.[13] The Commissioners of Woods gave their approval for assisting the evicted parties and any others who wished to emigrate, and sought the advice of the Colonial Land and Emigration Commissioners as to where they should be sent and the most efficient manner of travelling. The latter suggested that Quebec would be the best destination as there was a Government Emigration Agent there who could give advice as to the districts where employment was readily available and pay a small sum to each emigrant on arrival.[14]

The approval of the Commissioners of the Treasury was given on 12 August 1847, and on September 8, the first group of emigrants arrived in Dublin en route for Liverpool where they were to embark for New York. This party of 55, under the care of a special agent, was detained in Liverpool for several days due to the winds being contrary but sailed on the packet ship *Roscius* on 19 September 1847. A complaint from the emigrants that food was scarce was investigated and it was shown that the captain of the vessel did not issue the provisions for the voyage until she had sailed. This was the established procedure.

---

[10] *Ibid.*, 14 February 1846; Burke to Commissioners of Woods, 16 April 1846.

[11] *Ibid.*, R. Hamilton & Co., to Burke, 21 April 1846.

[12] *Ibid.*, R. Hamilton & Co., to Burke, 12 May 1847, Thomas Conry Knox, crown agent, to R. Hamilton & Co., 27 May 1847.

[13] *Ibid.*, Petition to Commissioners of Woods, 28 May 1847.

[14] *Ibid.*, Stephen Walcott, secretary Emigration Commissioners, to Charles Gore, Commissioner of Woods, 26 July 1847.

w

The shipping agents in charge of the arrangements were Henry and William Scott, Eden Quay, Dublin, and the charge was £4 for an adult and £2 15s. for a child under fourteen years. Provisions, tins and cooking utensils at the rate of thirty shillings each for an adult and fifteen shillings each for a child were provided, as well as landing money at the usual rate of a pound per adult and ten shillings per child, to be paid in American currency.

Between 19 September 1847 and 25 April 1848, when the last party sailed, a total of 366 persons from Ballykilcline had left Liverpool for New York, having sailed in seven different vessels. A certain consideration for the well-being of the travellers is noticeable throughout the arrangements made. Clothing was provided where necessary; a passenger too ill to sail was sent with her husband by a later vessel;[15] another 'not allowed to proceed in consequence of his great age' was transferred to Dublin and sent to New York from there.[16] By order of the Lord Lieutenant and at the request of the parish priest of Kilglass, a prisoner in the gaol of Roscommon, father of an emigrating family, was released in time to join them on the way to Liverpool.[17]

There was an increase in fares in 1848–from £4 to £4 5s. and £4 10s. (for the last party to leave) in the case of an adult, and from £2 15s. to £3 15s. for a child, with the same charge for provisions and utensils. The expenses for the emigration scheme from Ballykilcline, by far the most comprehensive of the state-aided schemes, amounted to £2,459 14s. 3d.[18] Thus, with the exception of six families or twenty-two individuals who declined the offer to help them emigrate, and who were evicted from their holdings within a month of the departure of the last party, the entire tenantry of this estate had emigrated to America. On 17 May 1848 it was reported that the lands 'are perfectly untenanted'.

The estate was sold the following year to William George Downing Nesbitt for £5,500.[19]

---

[15] *Ibid.*, Burke to Commissioners of Woods, 28 September 1847; 20 November 1847.

[16] *Ibid.*, T. E. Hodder, emigration officer, Liverpool, emigration certificate; Burke to Commissioners of Woods, 21 March 1848.

[17] *Ibid.*, Very Rev. Henry Brennan to Burke, 12 April 1848; Burke to Conry Knox, 15 April 1848.

[18] 26*th Report of Commissioners of Woods, Forests and Land Revenues*, pp. 7-8; app. no. 82, p. 104.

[19] Q.R.O., Particulars of Sales of Crown Property since the year 1824, p.30. The date of the conveyance was 13 October 1849.

EMIGRANTS from BALLYKILCLINE

Itinerary : Dublin—Liverpool—New York

Name		Age	Personal Details	Date of Departure Liverpool	Date of Arrival New York	Ship
Brennan,	William	70		18 Oct. 1847	22 Nov. 1847	*Creole*
or	Andrew	20	son			
Brannon	Daniel	24	son			
	Gilbert	7	son			
	Roger	28	son			
	William	26	son			
	Jane	18	daughter			
Carlon	John	30		19 Sept. 1847	21 Oct. 1847	*Roscius*
or	Honor	40	wife			
Carlin	Bridget	18 ⎱	no relationship			
	Ellen	9 ⎰ specified				
	Mary	7				
Carrington,	John	14	with family group of James Hanly, q.v.	18 Oct. 1847	22 Nov. 1847	*Creole*
Caveney,	Luke [20]	46		25 April 1848		*Progress*
	Mary	40	wife			
	Edward	12	son			
	Luke	10	son			
	Patrick	17	son			
	Thomas	15	son			
	Anne	7	daughter			
	Catherine	1	daughter			
	Mary	19	daughter			
Cline,	William	58	father-in-law of Pat Kelly, q.v.; occupied holding	13 Mar. 1848	17 Apr. 1848	*Channing*
Colgan,	Margaret	66	occupied cabin on estate	13 Mar. 1848	17 April 1848	*Channing*
	Honor	30	daughter			
	Mary	28	daughter			
Colgan,	Patrick	44		26 Sept. 1847	30 Oct. 1847	*Metoka*
	Anne	40	wife			
	Bernard	8	son			
	Michael	4	son			
	William	1	son			
	Anne	12	daughter			
	Betty	6	daughter			
	Mary	15	daughter			
Colgan,	Patrick	36	evicted	19 Sept. 1847	21 Oct. 1847	*Roscius*
	Mary	40	wife			
	Michael	19	son			
	Patrick	8	son			
	Anne	7	daughter			
	Bridget	12	daughter			
	Margaret	16	daughter			

[20] Q.R.O., Correspondence—Ballykilcline. Released from Roscommon Jail by order of the Lord Lieutenant, 14 April 1848, at the request of the parish priest, Very Rev. H. Brennan.

NAME		AGE	PERSONAL DETAILS	DATE OF DEPARTURE LIVERPOOL	DATE OF ARRIVAL NEW YORK	SHIP
Connor,	James	45	occupied holding	25 April		*Progress*
	Honor	44	wife	1848		
	Martin	22	son			
Connor,	John	37	evicted; did not sail with party in *Metoka* due to wife's illness; died at sea. [21]	30 Sept. 1847	19 Nov. 1847	*Jane* *Classon*
	Catherine	27	wife			
Connor,	Terence	50	evicted	19 Sept.	21 Oct.	*Roscius*
	Mary	35	wife	1847	1847	
	Thomas	20	son			
	Mary	11	daughter			
Costello,	Ellen	55		18 Oct.	22 Nov.	*Creole*
	John	8	son	1847	1847	
	Bridget	16	daughter			
	Mary	18	daughter			
Costello,	Thomas	46	occupied holding	13 Mar.	17 April	*Channing*
	Mary	45	wife	1848	1848	
	Martin	12	son			
	Michael	14	son			
	Pat	17	son			
	Thomas	6	son			
	Anne	16	daughter			
Croghan,	Patrick	28	evicted	19 Sept.	21 Oct.	*Roscius*
	John	24	brother	1847	1847	
	Margaret	26	sister			
Deffely, or Deffley	Mary, George, James	60, 26, 20	no relationship specified	18 Oct. 1847	22 Nov. 1847	*Creole*
Deffely, or Deffley	Patrick	60		18 Oct.	22 Nov.	*Creole*
	Mary	55	wife	1847	1847	
	Bridget	14	daughter			
Donlan, or Donnellan	Martin	32	not evicted; no family relationship specified.	19 Sept. 1847	21 Oct. 1847	*Roscius*
Donlon,	Patrick	28		18 Oct.	22 Nov.	*Creole*
	Anne	27	wife	1847	1847	
Donlan,	Patrick	60		18 Oct.	22 Nov.	*Creole*
	Edward	25	son	1847	1847	
	John	36	son			
	Patrick	27	son			
	William	16	son			
	Margaret	14	daughter			
Fallon,	Garret	32		18 Oct.	22 Nov.	*Creole*
	Eliza	26	wife	1847	1847	
	Bridget	20	sister			

[21] Q.R.O., O.W. Land Revenue Series Letter Books, Burke to Commissioners of Woods, 28 March 1848.

NAME		AGE	PERSONAL DETAILS	DATE OF DEPART- URE LIVER- POOL	DATE OF ARRIVAL NEW YORK	SHIP
Fallon,	Thomas	33		18 Oct.	22 Nov.	*Creole*
	Anne	32	wife	1847	1847	
	Martin	5	son			
	Ellen	8	daughter			
	Mary	1	daughter			
	Patrick	16	brother of Thomas			
	Bridget	25	sister of Thomas			
Falion,	Thomas	43		18 Oct.	22 Nov.	*Creole*
	Mary	18	wife	1847	1847	
Farrell,	Bridget	36	no relationship specified	13 Mar. 1848	17 April 1848	*Channing*
Farrell,	Pat	55	occupied cabin on estate; another son John, stayed in Liverpool with his grandmother.[22]	13 Mar. 1848	17 April 1848	*Channing*
	Mary	50	wife			
	William	18	son			
	Bridget	14	daughter			
	Mary	16	daughter			
Finne, or Finn	Patrick	35		26 Sept. 1847	30 Oct. 1847	*Metoka*
	Margaret	24	wife			
	Michael	22	brother of Patrick			
	Bridget	20	sister of Patrick			
	Margaret	9	sister of Patrick			
Fox,	Francis	35	lived in cabin on estate, no land	13 Mar. 1848	17 April 1848	*Channing*
	Mary	33				
	Francis	4	son			
	Pat	7	son			
	Thomas	26	brother of Francis			
	Catherine	16	sister of Francis			
Gallagher,	Michael	24		26 Sept. 1847	30 Oct. 1847	*Metoka*
	Margaret	20	sister			
Geenty, or Ginty	Margaret or Mary	60		26 Sept. 1847	30 Oct. 1847	*Metoka*
	Bernard	14	son			
	Bridget	16	daughter			
Gill,	Bernard	30	occupied cabin on estate	13 Mar. 1848	17 April 1848	*Channing*
	Catherine	25	wife			
	Andrew	3	son			
	Pat	2	son			
Hanly, or Hanley	James	64		26 Sept. 1847	30 Oct. 1847	*Metoka*
	Betty	54	wife			
	James	14	son			
	John	18	son			
	Martin	22	son			
	Patrick	20	son			
	Roger	12	son			
	Mary	17	son			

[22] Q.R.O., O.W. Land Revenue Series Letter Books, Burke to Commissioners of Woods, 21 March 1848.

Name	Age	Personal Details	Date of Departure Liverpool	Date of Arrival New York	Ship
Hanly, or Hanley	James 30		18 Oct. 1847	22 Nov. 1847	*Creole*
	Susan 30	wife			
	John 7	son			
	Peter 5	son			
Hanly, or Hanley	Thomas 60		18 Oct. 1847	22 Nov. 1847	*Creole*
	Mary 50	wife			
	Darby 16	son			
	Edward 18	son			
	Michael 13	son			
	Patrick 24	son			
	Honor 22	daughter			
	Mary 20	daughter			
Hoare,	Michael 35	occupied holding	13 Mar. 1848	17 April 1848	*Channing*
	Mary 30	wife			
	James 5	son			
	John 7	son			
	Thomas 2	son			
	Bridget 8	daughter			
	Mary 11	daughter			
Kelly,	James 45	occupied holding	13 Mar. 1848	17 April 1848	*Channing*
	Mary 40	wife			
	Edward 18	son			
	James 16	son			
	John 2	son			
	Anne 12	daughter			
	Catherine 14	daughter			
	Eliza 10	daughter			
	Ellen 7	daughter			
	Mary 20	daughter			
Kelly,	Pat 40	occupied holding; son-in-law of William Cline who sailed in *Channing*.	25 April 1848		*Progress*
	Eliza 36	wife			
	Thomas 12	son			
	William 8	son			
	Anne 10	daughter			
	Bridget 1	daughter			
	Maria 14	daughter			
McCormack, or McCormick	Catherine 55	was ill in quarantine hospital, but recovered.	26 Sept. 1847	30 Oct. 1847	*Metoka*
	Patrick 22	son			
	Peter 15	son			
	Anne 9	daughter			
	Ellen 30	daughter			
McCormick,	Edward 40		26 Sept. 1847	30 Oct. 1847	*Metoka*
	Margaret 32	wife			
	Edward 4	son			
	James 1	son			
	Thomas 8	son			
	Anne 14	} no relationship specified			
	Catherine 6				
	Mary 18				
McCormick, or McCormack	Mary 26		26 Sept. 1847	30 Oct. 1847	*Metoka*
	Anne 20	sister			
	Bridget 24	sister			

NAME	AGE	PERSONAL DETAILS	DATE OF DEPARTURE LIVERPOOL	DATE OF ARRIVAL NEW YORK	SHIP
McCormick, Michael	19		18 Oct. 1847	22 Nov. 1847	*Crecle*
Honor	17	sister			
Margaret	19	sister			
Sally	16	sister			
McCormick, Pat	32	occupied holding	13 Mar. 1848	17 Apr. 1848	*Channing*
Catherine	28	wife			
Michael	4	son			
Pat	6	son			
Anne	8	daughter			
Mary	20	sister of Pat			
McDermott, Hugh	50	evicted	19 Sept. 1847	21 Oct. 1847	*Roscius*
Eliza	48	wife			
Bernard	28	son			
Hugh	12	son			
James	26	son			
John	24	son			
William	18	son			
Anne	25	daughter			
Bessy	20	daughter			
Ellen	13	daughter			
Rosanna	14	daughter			
Susan	22	daughter			
McDermott, Mary	44		26 Sept. 1847	30 Oct. 1847	*Metoka*
John	13	son			
Thomas	15	son			
Bridget	11	daughter			
Ellen	20	daughter			
Mary	17	daughter			
McDermott, Michael	44		26 Sept. 1847	30 Oct. 1847	*Metoka*
Ellen	40	wife			
Michael	16	son			
Anne	8	daughter			
Betty	14	daughter			
Ellen	10	daughter			
Maria	12	daughter			
McDonnell, Andrew	18		13 Mar. 1848	17 Apr. 1848	*Channing*
Anne	22	sister			
Ellen	16	sister			
McDonnell, Michael	50	occupied cabin on estate	13 Mar. 1848	17 Apr. 1848	*Channing*
Michael	21	son			
Catherine	24	daughter			
Mary	18	daughter			
McDonnell, Patrick	24	no family relationship specified	26 Sept. 1847	30 Oct. 1847	*Metoka*
McGann, John	24	occupied holding	13 Mar. 1848	17 Apr. 1848	*Channing*
or Atty	19	brother			
McGanne Luke	20	brother			
Anne	26	sister			
Mary	15	sister			
John	1	no relationship specified			

NAME		AGE	PERSONAL DETAILS	DATE OF DEPART-URE LIVER-POOL	DATE OF ARRIVAL NEW YORK	SHIP
McGann, or McGanne	Mary	40	occupied holding	13 Mar. 1848	17 Apr. 1848	*Channing*
	James	18	son			
	John	5	son			
	Thomas	8	son			
	Anne	1	daughter			
	Bridget	10	daughter			
	Eliza	14	daughetr			
McManus,	Thomas	29	occupied holding	13 Mar. 1848	17 Apr. 1848	*Channing*
	James	20	brother			
McManus,	Thomas	24	occupied holding	13 Mar. 1848	17 Apr. 1848	*Channing*
	Andrew	21	brother			
	Pat	23	brother			
	Mary	18	brothor			
Madden,	Mary	46	occupied cabin on estate	13 Mar. 1848	17 Apr. 1848	*Channing*
	Thomas	13	son			
	Catherine	16	daughter			
Magan,	John	34		18 Oct. 1847	22 Nov. 1847	*Creole*
	Patrick	22	brother			
	Anne	28	sister			
	Ellen	26	sister			
	Catherine	24	sister			
Maguire,	John	30		18 Oct. 1847	22 Nov. 1847	*Creole*
	Mary	30	wife			
	Patrick	5	son			
	Mary	3	daughter			
Moran,	John	56		26 Sept. 1847	30 Oct. 1847	*Metoka*
	Winifred	44	wife			
	Francis	7	son			
	John	15	son			
	Catherine	10	daughter			
Mullera,	Anne	25	occupied holding; listed as head of family but on separate sailing ticket from Pat.	13 Mar. 1848	17 Apr. 1848	*Channing*
	Pat	29	no relationship specified.			
Mullera, Mullerea or Mulere	Catherine	30	occupied holding; surrendered possession.	19 Sept. 1847	21 Oct. 1847	*Roscius*
Mullera,	James	50		18 Oct. 1847	22 Nov. 1847	*Creole*
	Bridget	50	wife			
	Denis	12	son			
	Anne	9	daughter			
	Bridget	10	daughter			
Mullera, or Mulera	James	22		26 Sept. 1847	30 Oct. 1847	*Metoka*
	Thomas	20	brother			

NAME	AGE	PERSONAL DETAILS	DATE OF DEPART-URE LIVER-POOL	DATE OF ARRIVAL NEW YORK	SHIP
Mullera, John	35	lived in cabin on	13 Mar.	17 Apr.	*Channing*
Sarah	30	wife estate	1848	1848	
Francis	6	son			
James	4	son			
John	8	son			
Patrick	12	son			
Thomas	10	son			
Pat	25	brother of John			
Mullera, Thomas	36	occupied holding	13 Mar.	17 Apr.	*Channing*
Mary	30	wife	1848	1848	
Thomas	6	son			
Anne	2	daughter			
Bridget	55	mother of Thomas			
Narry, Bartholomew	45	occupied holding;	13 Mar.	17 Apr.	*Channing*
or Bartley		brother of Pat Narry who sailed in *Roscius*	1848	1848	
Michael	26	son			
William	36	brother			
Narry, Patrick	40	evicted	19 Sept.	21 Oct.	*Roscius*
or Mary	28	wife	1847	1847	
Neary Bridget	1	daughter			
Neary, Mary	35		18 Oct.	22 Nov.	*Creole*
James	3	son	1847	1847	
Anne	7	daughter			
John	16	brother-in-law			
Bridget	14	sister-in-law			
Catherine	24	sister-in-law			
O'Neal, Bernard	45		26 Sept.	30 Oct.	*Metoka*
or Betty	40	wife	1847	1847	
O'Neill Bernard	13	son			
John	16	son			
Anne	20	daughter			
Padian, Richard	32		19 Sept.	21 Oct.	*Roscius*
Mary	30	wife	1847	1847	
James	9	son			
William	12	son			
Bridget	10	daughter			
Maria	6	daughter			
Quinn, Catherine	30	ill in hospital after arrival but recovered. [23]	18 Oct. 1847	22 Nov. 1847	*Creole*
Hugh	6	son			
James	8	son			
John	1	son			
Anne	3	daughter			
Catherine	17	no relationship specified.			

[23] Q.R.O., O.W. Land Revenue Series Letter Books, Burke to Commissioners of Woods, 24 February 1848; 28 March 1848.

NAME	AGE	PERSONAL DETAILS	DATE OF DEPARTURE LIVERPOOL	DATE OF ARRIVAL NEW YORK	SHIP
Reynolds, James	28	evicted ; listed as head of family	19 Sept. 1847	21 Oct. 1847	*Roscius*
Bridget	60	mother			
John	24	son of Bridget			
Joseph	22	son of Bridget			
Thomas	40 ⎫				
Bridget	14 ⎬ no relationship specified.				
Catherine	2 ⎭				
Reynolds, Michael	9	listed with family of Mary McGann, but no relationship specified.	13 Mar. 1848	17 Apr. 1848	*Channing*
Reynolds, Thomas	33		26 Sept. 1848	30 Oct. 1848	*Metoka*
Mary	30	wife			
Andrew	5	son			
James	8	son			
John	6	son			
Thomas	2	son			
Mary		infant daughter			
Andrew	27	brother of Thomas			
Bridget	60	mother of Thomas			
Stewart, Bridget	35	no land ; lived in cabin on estate	13 Mar. 1848	17 Apr. 1848	*Channing*
James	17	son			
Michael	5	son			
Bridget	14	daughter			
Stewart, Francis	56	occupied cabin on estate; sailed from Dublin [24]	16 Mar. 1848		*Laconic*
Anne	50	wife	13 Mar. 1848	17 Apr. 1848	*Channing*
John	30	son			
Stuart, George	40		18 Oct. 1847	22 Nov. 1847	*Creole*
Bridget	32	wife			
Charles	6	son			
John	4	son			
Mary	10	daughter			
Stuart, James	63	evicted	19 Sept. 1847	21 Oct. 1847	*Roscius*
Ellen	60	wife			
George	20	son			
Ellen	18	daughter			
Stuart, John	21	not listed as head of family; possibly did not occupy holding.	18 Oct. 1847	22 Nov. 1847	*Creole*
Bridget	17	sister			
Catherine	15	sister			
Stuart, or Stewart Patrick	18	evicted	19 Sept. 1847	21 Oct. 1847	*Roscius*
Catherine	25	sister			

[24] *Ibid.*, 21 March 1848. Burke states that due to his 'aged appearance' he was not accepted as a passenger in Liverpool and was sent from Dublin instead. A. & W. Scott to Burke, 4 July 1848, who reported that he was ill in hospital in New York. His 'landing money' was not claimed.

Name		Age	Personal Details	Date of Departure Liverpool	Date of Arrival New York	Ship
Stuart,	William	47	ill in hospital after arrival, but recovered [25]	18 Oct. 1847	22 Nov. 1847	*Creole*
	Bridget	43	wife			
	Charles	14	son			
	Michael	12	son			
	William	8	son			
	Eliza	10	daughter			
Winters, or Winter	Honor	60		26 Sept. 1847	30 Oct. 1847	*Metoka*
	Thomas	30	son			
	Honor	18	daughter			
	Margaret	24	daughter			
	Catherine	1	no relationship specified.			
Wynne,	Bridget	30	her family had gone in *Metoka*; she had been in England at the time. [26]	13 Mar. 1848	17 Apr. 1848	*Channing*
Wynne, or Winn	John	52		26 Sept. 1847	30 Oct. 1847	*Metoka*
	Patrick	22	son			
	Mary	13	daughter			
Wynne,	Michael	60	occupied cabin on estate.	13 Mar. 1848	17 Apr. 1848	*Channing*
	Bell	55	wife			
	James	16	son			
	Catherine	13	daughter			
	Mary	18	daughter			

---

[25] See note 23.
[26] Q.R.O., O.W. Land Revenue Series Letter Books, Burke to George Knox, 17 February 1848.

NOTE.—The dates of arrival have been verified in files of *The Mercantile Gazette* in the British Museum Newspaper Library, which also supplied the names of the ships' masters. Eldridge commanded the *Roscius*; McGuire, the *Metoka*; Huttleston, the *Channing* and Rattoone, the *Creole*.

NOTE ON THE EMIGRATION SCHEME FROM
IRVILLOUGHTER AND BOUGHILL

The crown estates of Irvilloughter and Boughill were situated
within a few miles of one another near Ahascragh in Co. Galway.
Irvilloughter was in the parish of Ahascragh, barony of Clonmac-
nowen, while Boughill was in the parish of Taghboy, one mile from
Ballyforan village and five miles from Ahascragh itself, in the
barony of Killian. The emigrants from the two estates travelled
together to Galway and thence to Quebec. The official in
charge of the scheme was Golding Bird, collector of excise in
Galway.

Boughill was the smaller of the two estates and was an island of
arable and pasture land containing 111 statute acres almost completely
surrounded by 320 acres of bog. According to a survey made in 1821,
the arable land was exhausted by the numbers of poor people 'who
hold it in small lots at an exorbitant rent'.[1] The bog was 'an
inducement to a number of petty linen manufacturers to settle
thereon, inasmuch as the great abundance of turbary enables them
to carry on their manufacture, by which means they pay their rents'.[2]
At that time 92 individuals were resident on the estate. The immediate lessee under the Crown was Nicholas D'Arcy who was the assignee
of Edward Kelly, a descendant of Hugh Kelly who had forfeited
the lands after 1688. He paid an annual rent of £4 12s. 3d. and
received a sum of £56 17s. 4d. and 56 days labour of men and horses
per annum from John Killelea and his nine 'partners'. This estate
provides one of the best examples of the working of the rundale
system—the 'co-partnership or holding in joint occupation' of the
land, with all its attendant difficulties of cultivation and maintenance.
The Commissioners of Woods resumed possession of the estate from
4 September 1830, and granted a lease for seven years from 1831
at £50 a year to John Killelea and 'partners'.[3]

The Boughill tenants enjoyed the reputation of being 'a happy
contented people', ready to pay their rent at the appointed time

[1] Q.R.O., Files of Forfeiture Office and Miscellaneous Papers, File No. 10,
Valuation of lands of Boughill, 13 June 1821; Correspondence—Irvilloughter
and Boughill, Report of Commissioners appointed to inquire into the crown's
title, 23 September 1822.

[2] *Ibid.*

[3] Q.R.O., Correspondence—Irvilloughter and Boughill, Commisioners of
Woods to Nicholas D'Arcy, 4 September 1830; *Ibid.* to John Killelea, 19 April
1831.

and anxious for separate leases for 21 years.[4] In a memorial for relief after 'the failure of the potatoe crop in Ireland', they asked that drainage works be started and that a passage from the public road to the estate be repaired. Michael Boyan, superintendant of Kingwilliamstown model farm, sent by the Commissioners of Woods to survey the estate, reported that their potatoes were all gone—the report was dated 28 October 1846—and that they were living on oatmeal made from the oats with which they used to pay their rents. There were 111 persons then living on the estate and he recommended that relief works to the value of £192 be started to provide food for the tenants for six months and then that 'the property should be divided into new allotments'.[5] Another survey was made of the estate in October, 1847, when, unlike most other relief schemes, it was found that careful drainage had made a considerable improvement in land hitherto unproductive. State-aided emigration was recommended for those anxious to leave as this would enable the Commissioners of Woods to enlarge the farms of those who remained behind. Furthermore, the estate would be improved fully 'to the extent of the outlay necessary' for such a scheme, 'unlike the Irvilloughter estate'.[6] In 1846 the estate was held in common between seventeen families. Each partner held between three and seven acres in several lots in different parts of the property. It may be noted that the tenants of Boughill thanked the Commissioners of Woods for the public works to which they attributed 'their exemption from the awful fate of so many of their countrymen'.[7]

The estate of Irvilloughter had been let on a sixty-one year lease from 1 May 1773 to Ross Mahon of Castlegar, Co. Galway.[8] Under the provisions of the Land Revenue Act of 1827,[9] an order of 30 October 1830, addressed to Sir Ross, determined the existing lease and the crown resumed possession. It was found that a 'numerous tenantry' was resident on the estate and the suggestion was made by James Weale, agent of the Commissioners of Woods, that a vessel be chartered to send them to America. The tenants refused the offer to help them emigrate.[10]

Sir Ross Mahon was a resident and improving landlord who had given extensive employment to the labourers of the district on his estate ; he had 'set out Irvilloughter several years since in lots

[4] Q.R.O., O.W. Land Revenue Series Letter Books, Norman Ashe, collector of excise, to Burke, 26 May 1845; Memorial of Boughill Tenants, 20 May 1845.
[5] *Ibid.*, Boyan to Commissioners of Woods, 28 October 1846.
[6] *Ibid.*, C.P. Brassington, surveyor, to Burke, 19 October 1847.
[7] Q.R.O., Files of Forfeiture Office and Miscellaneous Papers, File No. 12.
[8] Later Sir Ross Mahon, 1st Baronet.
[9] 7 and 8 Geo IV, c.68.
[10] Q.R.O., O.W. Land Revenue Series Letter Books, Boyan to Commissioners of Woods, 23 March 1846.

to his labourers'; (some of these lots were held in common by 6 or 8 families to each lot), and he accepted labour in lieu of rent.[11] After his death in 1835 the living conditions of the tenantry deteriorated, and by 1843 large arrears of rent due to the Commissioners of Woods had accumulated 'in consequence of extreme poverty—particularly as the prices for what small farmers have to dispose of, namely, pigs, corn and potatoes being particularly low'.[12] The tenants considered that the rent of twenty-five shillings per acre was excessive —the usual rent on adjoining properties of superior land was only fourteen shillings and four pence half-penny—and in June, 1843, they asked the Commissioners of Woods to reduce it. A temporary reduction of ten per cent. was allowed.[13] In 1846 there were 408 persons living on Irvilloughter ; the estate of 694 acres was parcelled into nearly 300 separate divisions, held by a 100 tenants, and, in the opinion of the clerk of the Quit Rents, 'the holdings cannot be enlarged' until a considerable number of persons be removed.[14]

The tenants on Irvilloughter seem to have suffered more from the destitution arising from the famine than those on any of the other estates under review. The collector of excise from Galway who attended in November, 1845, to receive the rents, reported that at least a quarter of the potato crop was very seriously damaged. The oats lay out in the haggards unthreshed so he recommended that they should first of all attend to separating the good from the damaged potatoes, then that they should thresh the oats, hold a supply for seed and a reasonable amount to make good the deficiency of the potato crop, and sell the remainder at the high prices prevailing in order to pay the rent.[15] In March, 1846, Michael Boyan, who came to survey the conditions on the estate for the Commissioners of Woods, reported that the disease was increasing. 'I have been looking at the children on the estate employed peeling the *raw potatoes* when preparing them for dinner. They first peel off the skin, then they scoop out the black or diseased spots on all sides, as the disease inters (sic) into the potato at different depths, it has rather a curious appearance when cleared of all the black spots, and even it looks much worse boiled than raw. The people prefer to use them poun[d]ed or mashed up with salt, and milk when the milk can be procured, this dish they call "canny" or "calcannon" '. He referred to the gloomy pensive manner of the tenants and recommended that certain useful relief works be started :—(a) that an extensive tract of 100 acres of wet land be drained ; (b) that farm roads be

---

11 *Ibid.*

12 *Ibid.*, Norman Ashe to Burke, 12 May 1843.

13 *Ibid.*, Commissioners of Woods to Burke, 4 September 1843.

14 *Ibid.*, Burke to Commissioners of Woods, 11 December 1847.

15 *Ibid.*, Ashe to Burke, 15 November 1845.

made, and (c) that the level of a neighbouring river be lowered. He also reported that the population of the estate in March, 1846, was 208 males and 200 females and the number of men fit to work was 114. In fulfilment of a promise to pay their rent on the guarantee that public works would be started, the tenants paid £80 6s. 8d. out of a possible £96 16s. 5d. on 13 April 1846.

By the end of October, 1846, just over £59 was spent on these relief works. The wages of each man was 5s. per week. At least 70 men were totally dependent on the crown for employment so it was recommended that during the winter months old ditches be levelled and drains made.[16]   A memorial from the tenants in March, 1847, told of their miserable plight and their inability to pay their rents. Relief works continued and between June 21 and September 13 1847, a total sum of £221 5s. 10d. was spent on this estate and on Boughill, which was administered jointly with it.

In July, 1847, Charles Gore, one of the Commissioners of Woods, asked whether aided emigration from Irvilloughter and Boughill 'might not enhance the value of the lands to an extent commensurate with the expense that would be incurred'. That, replied Burke, was now purely a secondary consideration in view of the poverty and destitution existing on the estates, and he urged that four tenants with twelve children from Boughill, and twelve tenants with twenty-nine children from Irvilloughter, be provided with their passage money without delay.[17] No ultimate destination was specified ; getting the tenants away was for him the main consideration.

Instructions to proceed with the scheme did not come from the Commissioners of Woods until 15 December 1847, when Golding Bird was appointed to carry it out. He reported that so many of the tenants were in abject poverty that it would be necessary to supply clothing for them. The cost, estimated at £1,837 12s. 6d. for removing 223 persons, (136 adults and 87 children), was considered excessive by the Commissioners of Woods in view of the fact that upwards of £600 had been spent already on relief works on the estates. The sanction of the Treasury was not forthcoming until 29 March 1848, when £1,850 was advanced.

It was proposed by Golding Bird that the emigrants from these estates be sent from Galway. There was, he said, an 'emigrant officer' at that port as laid down by act of parliament, whose duty it was to inspect the vessels, and he guaranteed that the ships would sail punctually.   Arthur Ireland, shipping agent, Galway, quoted

---

[16] *Ibid.*, Boyan to Commissioners of Woods, 29 October 1846.
[17] *Ibid.*, Burke to Commissioners of Woods, 15 July 1847.

£5 6s. as the fare for an adult passenger from Galway to Quebec, and £2 15s. 6d., the fare for a child. He would supply :

2 lbs. of meal or biscuit each per day.
2 lbs. of beef or pork each per week.
1 lb. of butter each per week.
1 lb. of tea each per voyage.
9 lbs. of sugar each per voyage.

Cooking utensils also would be provided. Children under 14 would receive half the above amounts with the exception of meal when they were to receive 1½ pounds.[18] On 25 April 1848, Burke authorised the immediate start of the project. Landing money was to be paid to the emigrants in Quebec by the emigration agent there.

The first party of 253 emigrants left Galway on 10 June 1848 on board the *Sea Bird* under Captain McDonagh, Galway, and arrived in Quebec on 23 July 1848. There were only two deaths on the voyage, (one adult and one child), a fact which was considered worthy of favourable comment by the organiser of the project.[19]   According to a report from the emigration department in Quebec, they 'all proceeded to Upper Canada with the exception of 2 families who had friends in the States'.[20]   It may be noted that in the event of the death of a passenger at sea, landing money was paid to the deceased's relatives.

The cost of the project was £1,646 9s. 11d., almost £200 less than the estimate. The population of Irvilloughter in June, 1848, was 463, so that about 220 still remained on the estate, while 73 but of a total of 104 remained in Boughill. A further scheme was expected during the spring of 1849 and petitions from the tenants praying to be sent to Canada were numerous.

On 14 July 1849, the Treasury authorised a further grant of £1,400 and Golding Bird was appointed once more to carry out the scheme. On 17 August 1849, the *Northumberland* sailed from Galway carrying 114 adults and 44 children. The shipping agents were Messrs. Evans and Sons, Galway. Their rates were £5 7s. 6d. for an adult and £2 17s. 6d. for a child. Arrangements were made in this instance for the captain of the ship to pay head money to the port authorities at Quebec at the rate of 7s. 6d. per adult, and 5s. per child between the age of five and fifteen years. A doctor was summoned to examine the emigrants before they sailed.[21]   The *Northumberland* arrived in Quebec on 2 October 1849, after which the emigrants went by steamer to Montreal, at a reduced rate of a shilling sterling each.[22]

---

18 *Ibid.*, Arthur Ireland to Golding Bird, 11 April 1848.
19 *Ibid.*, Bird to Burke, 24 August 1848.
20 Q.R.O., Files of Forfeiture Office and Miscellaneous Papers, File No. 16., A.C. Buchanan, Emigration Dept., Quebec, to Stephen Walcott, secretary, Colonial Land & Emigration Commissioners, London, 26 August 1848.
21 *Ibid.*, File No. 18, Bird to Burke, 11 December, 1849.
22 *Ibid.*, Buchanan to Walcott, 5 October 1849.

Four deaths occurred on the sea voyage.

The expenses amounted to £1,168 8s. 5d., making a total of £2,814 18s. 4d., for the entire project.

In 1851, about 180 persons were living on the lands but no further emigration schemes were mooted. Finally, in July, 1855, the estates were sold when Boughill realized £1,500 and Irvilloughter, £6,325.[23]

[The rentals, census and other documents to be found in Files 10 to 23 of the Files of the Forfeiture Office and Miscellaneous Papers, have been used to supplement the biographical details in the compilation of the list of emigrants from Irvilloughter and Boughill.]

---

[23] Q.R.O., Particulars of Sales of Crown Property since the year 1824, p. 23.

IRVILLOUGHTER and BOUGHILL

NAME	AGE	PERSONAL DETAILS	DATE OF DEPARTURE GALWAY	DATE of ARRIVAL QUEBEC	SHIP
Brien, Michael Byrne or Bryne [24]	22	of Boughill; occupied cabin and rood of land ; single man ; very poor.	15 June 1848	23 July 1848	*Sea Bird,* Galway
Byrne, Anne	20	of Boughill; grouped with John Killalea but no relationship specified.	15 June 1848	23 July 1848	*Sea Bird,* Galway
Byrne, Mary	20	of Irvilloughter ; grouped with Catherine Kelly and Mary Kennedy.	17 Aug. 1849	2 Oct. 1849	*Northumberland,* Galway
Byrne, Michael or Birne	41	of Boughill; weaver; son of Thady, 'in a dying state' aged 90.	17 Aug. 1849	2 Oct. 1849	*Northumberland,* Galway.
Bridget	38	wife			
John	8	son			
Michael	11	son			
Timothy	4	son			
Ellen	18	daughter			
Byrne, Pat	15	of Boughill	17 Aug. 1849	2 Oct. 1849	*Northumberland,* Galway
Bridget	26	sister			
Byrne, Thomas [25]	21	of Boughill; occupied cabin only; very poor.	17 Aug. 1849	2 Oct. 1849	*Northumberland,*
Ellen	20	sister			
Mary	19	sister			Galway.
Carney, Anne [26]	20	of Irvilloughter; niece of John White (Red); cousin of Pat White, q.v.	15 June 1848	23 July 1848	*Sea Bird,* Galway
Carroll, Thomas	31	of Irvilloughter; son of Patrick and Bridget.	17 Aug. 1894	2 Oct. 1849	*Northumberland,* Galway.
Bridget	23	wife			
John	22	brother of Thomas			
Michael	24	brother of Thomas			
Bridget	15	sister of Thomas			
Mary Ann	18	sister of Thomas			
Ann Rafferty	20	no relationship specified			
Mary	½				

[24] Writer of letter No. 4.
[25] Q.R.O., Files of Forfeiture Office and Miscellaneous Papers, File No. 15. A list in this file states that the family group of Thomas Byrne consisted of Catherine and Judith Hamberry and Mary Byrne, and stated that this family, 'Brother and Sisters, and Sister-in-law, holds only a Cabin, all wretchedly poor'. In File No. 11 it is stated that Mary Byrne was Thomas's sister and Catherine 'Amberry' his aunt.
[26] Q.R.O., Correspondence—Irvilloughter and Boughill, Census of 1836.

Name		Age	Personal Details	Date of Departure Liverpool	Date of Arrival New York	Ship
Carty, or McCarthy	John	60	of Irvilloughter; occupied cottage and 3 acres; very poor.	15 June 1848	23 July 1848	*Sea Bird. Galway.*
	Bridget	55	wife			
	Edward	12	son			
	Martin	15	son			
	Peter	10	son			
	Thomas	14	son			
	Mary	25	daughter [27]			
	Peggy	21	daughter			
	Ann	2	no relationship specified			
Carty,	Owen	22	of Irvilloughter	17 Aug. 1849	2 Oct. 1849	*Northumberland, Galway.*
	Catherine	20	sister			
Casey,	John	16	of Irvilloughter; two orphans included in Denis Grady's family group.	15 June 1848	23 July 1848	*Sea Bird, Galway.*
	Pat	15				
Coffey,	Michael	20	of Irvilloughter; included in family group of Catherine Donnellan but no relationship specified	15 June 1848	23 July 1848	*Sea Bird, Galway.*
Conway,	Bridget	42	of Irvilloughter	15 June 1848	23 July 1848	*Sea Bird, Galway.*
	Pat	16	son			
	Mary	12	daughter			
Conway,	James	27	of Irvilloughter; occupied cabin and 1 acre; very poor.	15 June 1848	23 July 1848	*Sea Bird, Galway.*
	Margaret or Mary	24	wife, daughter of Pat Lynskey, decd.; sister of Bridget, q.v.			
	Thomas	7	son			
	Pat	2	son			
	Margaret	3	daughter			
Conway,	John	31	of Irvilloughter	17 Aug. 1849	2 Oct. 1849	*Northumberland, Galway.*
	Biddy	20	sister			
	Catherine	36	sister			
	Mary	25	sister			
	Mary Ann	41	sister			
Cosgrave,	Bridget	50	of Irvilloughter; widow of John; occupied cottage and 4 acres; very poor.	15 June 1848	23 July 1848	*Sea Bird, Galway.*
	James	13	son			
	John	26	son			
	Michael	16	son			
	Pat	7	son			
	Peter	29	son			
	Thomas	20	son			
	Anne	18	daughter			
	Margaret	17	daughter			
	Mary	10	daughter			

[27]   Q.R.O., Files of Forfeiture Office and Miscellaneous Papers, File No. 14. Mary is described here as a step-daughter of John Carty.

Name		Age	Personal Details	Date of Departure Liverpool	Date of Arrival New York	Ship
Cosgrave, Ellen		24	of Irvilloughter; niece of Michael Kennedy who did not emigrate; [28] in family group of John Guinnessy but no relationship specified.	17 Aug. 1849	2 Oct. 1849	*Northumberland,* Galway.
Cosgrave, James		41	of Irvilloughter; son of Thomas, a thatcher, and Mary Cosgrave; occupied cabin and 1½ acres; very poor.	15 June 1848	23 July 1848	*Sea Bird,* Galway.
	Mary	37	wife			
	Pat	6	son			
	Thomas	3	son			
	William	2½	son			
	Catherine	2	daughter			
	Maria	8	daughter			
	Anne	12	sister of James.			
	Bridget	22	sister of James.			
Cosgrave, John [29]		24	of Irvilloughter; occupied a cottage and 1½ acres; very poor.	15 June 1848	23 July 1848	*Sea Bird.* Galway.
	Francis	20	brother			
	Ann	34	sister			
	James	1	son of Ann			
	John	4	son of Ann			
	Thomas	11	son of Ann			
	Bridget	12	daughter of Ann			
Cosgrave, Julia		22	of Irvilloughter; occupied house and 1 acre with Catherine Jennings [30] and Mary Dowd.	15 June 1848	23 July 1848	*Sea Bird,* Galway.
Cosgrave, Pat		35	of Irvilloughter; mason; son of Peter and Catherine; occupied a cabin and rood; very poor.	15 June 1848	23 July 1848	*Sea Bird,* Galway.
	Mary	32	wife			
	John	4	son			
	Bridget	3	daughter			
Cosgrave, Thomas		38	of Irvilloughter; 'taylor'; occupied a cabin and rood; very poor.	15 June 1848	23 July 1848	*Sea Bird,* Galway.
	Hannah	23	wife			
	Hannah	1½	daughter			

[28] Q.R.O., Correspondence—Irvilloughter and Boughill, Census of 1836.

[29] Q.R.O., Files of Forfeiture Office and Miscellaneous Papers, File No. 14.

[30] In the Census of 1836, Catherine is described as a visitor to house of Thomas Cosgrave, father of James, q.v. and Judy.

NAME		AGE	PERSONAL DETAILS	DATE OF DEPARTURE LIVERPOOL	DATE OF ARRIVAL NEW YORK	SHIP
Cosgrave,	William	21	of Irvilloughter;	17 Aug.	2 Oct.	*Northumberland,* Galway.
	Ellen	19	sister	1849	1849	
Craughwell, or Croghell	Michael	20	of Irvilloughter; son of Matt & Bridget	17 Aug. 1849	2 Oct. 1849	*Northumberland,* Galway.
	Ann	22	sister			
	Ellen	16	sister			
Craughwell,	Nancy	41	of Irvilloughter; widow of Pat.	17 Aug. 1849	2 Oct. 1849	*Northumberland,* Galway.
	Pat	20	son			
	Margaret Peggy	17	daughter			
	Kenedy	40	sister of Nancy			
	John	15	son of Peggy			
	Thomas	7	son of Peggy			
Craughwell,	Peter	40	of Irvilloughter; son of Rosy; occupied cabin and 1½ acres; very poor.	15 June 1848	23 July 1848	*Sea Bird,* Galway.
	Winifred	36	wife			
	John	4	son			
	Patrick	6	son			
	Bridget	14	daughter			
	Catherine	18	daughter			
	Ellen	11	daughter			
	Kitty	20	daughter			
	Mary	16	daughter			
	Rose	13	daughter			
Craughwell,	Thomas	20	of Irvilloughter; son of Pat, decd.	15 June 1848	23 July 1848	*Sea Bird,* Galway.
	Pat	15	brother			
	Honoria	18	sister			
	Mary	16	sister			
Curley,	Margaret	30	of Irvilloughter; widow of John, son of Margaret.	17 Aug. 1849	2 Oct. 1849	*Northumberland,* Galway.
	Biddy	5	daughter			
Daw, or Dawe	Thomas	32	of Irvilloughter; occupied a cabin only; very poor.	15 June 1848	23 July 1848	*Sea Bird,* Galway.
	Bridget	28	wife			
	Pat	2	son			
	Biddy	4	daughter			
	Mary Ann	½	daughter			
	James	20	brother of Thomas			
	John	18	brother of Thomas			
	Anne	20	sister of Thomas			
	Mary	16	sister of Thomas			

NAME	AGE	PERSONAL DETAILS	DATE OF DEPARTURE LIVERPOOL	DATE OF ARRIVAL NEW YORK	SHIP
Dempsey, Henry	50	of Irvilloughter; labourer, occupied a cabin and ½ acre. 'In a horrid state of poverty'.	15 June 1848	23 July 1848	*Sea Bird,* Galway.
Catherine	47	wife			
Henry	4	son			
John	13	son			
Michael	10	son			
Patrick	21	son			
Anne	13	daughter			
Catherine	1½	daughter			
Margaret	18	daughter			
Mary	15	daughter			
Dempsey, John	57	of Irvilloughter; occupied cottage and 1½ acres; very poor. 'An industrious quiet man'. [31]	15 June 1848	23 July 1848	*Sea Bird,* Galway
Bridget	55	wife			
John	30	son			
Biddy	30	wife of John Jr.			
Ann	5	daughter of John Jr.			
Catherine	1	daughter of John Jr.			
Margaret	6	daughter of John Jr.			
Dempsey, Michael	32	of Irvilloughter; occupied cabin and 4 acres; very poor.	15 June 1848	23 July 1848	*Sea Bird,* Galway.
Catherine	31	wife			
Pat	5	son			
Bridget	8	daughter			
Dolan, Bryan	17	of Irvilloughter; orphans, nephews of, and reared by family of John Dempsey, q.v.[32]	15 June 1848	23 July 1848	*Sea Bird,* Galway.
John	15				
Dolan, Thomas	15	of Irvilloughter: in Denis Grady's family group, but no relationship specified.	15 June 1848	23 July 1848	*Sea Bird,* Galway.
Donnellan, Donolan or Donlon Catherine	55	of Irvilloughter; widow of Patrick, labourer; occupied cabin and rood; very poor.	15 June 1848	23 July 1848	*Sea Bird,* Galway.
John	26	son			
Pat	20	son			
Thomas	30	son			
Bridget	17	daughter			
Catherine	33	daughter			
Dooley, Thomas	1	of Irvilloughter; orphan grandchild of Catherine Donnellan	15 June 1848	23 July 1848	*Sea Bird,* Galway.

---

[31] Q.R.O., Correspondence—Irvilloughter and Boughill, Census of 1836.
[32] Q.R.O., Files of Forfeiture Office and Miscellaneous Papers, File No. 15.

NAME		AGE	PERSONAL DETAILS	DATE OF DEPARTURE LIVERPOOL	DATE OF ARRIVAL NEW YORK	SHIP
Dowd,	Mary	20	of Irvilloughter; occupied house with Julia Cosgrave and Catherine Jennings.	15 June 1848	23 July 1848	*Sea Bird,* Galway.
Egan,	Bridget	51	of Irvilloughter;. widow of John Egan; occupied cabin and 3 acres; very poor.	17 Aug. 1849	2 Oct. 1849	*Northumberland,* Galway.
	John	18	son			
	Michael	10	son			
	Pat	14	son; died at sea. [33]			
Egan,	Mary	20	of Irvilloughter; daughter of Bridget above.	15 June 1849	23 July 1848	*Sea Bird* Galway.
Flannery, or Flanary	Nicholas	40	of Irvilloughter; son of Catherine; occupied a cottage and 6 acres; very poor.	15 June 1848	23 July 1848	*Sea Bird* Galway.
	Nancy	38	wife			
	John	½	son; died at sea. [34]			
	Michael	12	son			
	Pat	13	son			
	Catherine	8	daughter			
	Ellen	5	daughter			
	Margaret	7	daughter			
	Mary	10	daughter			
	Winifred	4	daughter			
Foster,	John	20	of Irvilloughter; an orphan reared by family of Michael Lynskey, q.v.	15 June 1848	23 July 1848	*Sea Bird* Galway.
Glynn,	Michael	55	of Irvilloughter;	17 Aug. 1489	2 Oct. 1849	*Northumerland,* Galway.
	Julia	53	wife			
	Michael	21	son			
	Pat	16	son			
	Timothy	8	son			
	Bridget	26	daughter			
	Margaret	19	daughter			
	Mary	24	daughter			
	Peggy Leonard	23	no relationship specified to Glynns, but niece of Patrick Leonard who did not emigrate.			
Golden,	Michael	24	of Irvilloughter; brother-in-law of Denis Grady.	15 June 1848	23 July 1848	*Sea Bird,* Galway.
	Hannah	24	wife, nee Grady			
	Thomas	1	son			
	Mary	3	daughter			

---

[33] *Ibid.*, File No. 18, Burke to Bird, 1 November 1849.
[34] Q.R.O., O.W. Land Revenue Series Letter Books, 10, ii, 153, Immigrant List from Quebec.

NAME		AGE	PERSONAL DETAILS	DATE OF DEPART- URE LIVER- POOL	DATE OF ARRIVAL NEW YORK	SHIP
Gormally,	Margaret	37	of Boughill; daughter of Catherine and sister-in-law of Mary Gormally, q.v.	15 June 1848	23 July 1848	*Sea Bird,* Galway.
Gormally or Gormley	Mary	36	of Boughill; wife of Thady; occupied cabin and 1½ acres; labourers. 'Almost naked'.	15 June 1848	23 July 1848	*Sea Bird,* Galway.
	John	13	son			
	Thady	4	son			
	Bridget	11	daughter			
	Catherine	9	daughter			
Grady, or Gready	Denis	30	of Irvilloughter; son of John; occupied a cottage and 8 acres; very poor; brother-in-law of Michael Golden.	15 June 1848	23 July 1848	*Sea Bird.* Galway.
	John	21	brother			
	Honoria	20	sister			
Grady, or Gready	Peter	31	of Irvilloughter; son of Peter and Bridget; brother of Thomas, q.v. [35]	17 Aug. 1849	2 Oct. 1849	*Northum- erland,* Galway.
	Mary	27	wife; daughter of John White 'Red', and sister of Pat q.v.			
	Thomas	½	son; died at sea. [36]			
	Catherine	2	daughter; died at sea.			
Grady, or Gready	Thomas	41	of Irvilloughter; son of Peter and Bridget.	17 Aug. 1849	2 Oct. 1849	*Northum- berland,* Galway.
	Catherine	36	wife			
	John	14	son			
	Michael	3 mths.	son			
	Pat	6	son			
	Thomas	2	son			
	Ann	11	daughter			
	Bridget	4	daughter			
Gready,	Mary	18	of Irvilloughter; included in Denis Grady's family group q.v., but no relationship specified.	15 June 1848	23 July 1848	*Sea Bird,* Galway.
Guinnessy,	John	27	of Irvilloughter	17 Aug. 1849	2 Oct. 1849	*Northum- berland,* Galway.
	Hanora	25	wife			
	John	2	son			
	Thomas	3 mths.	son			

35 See Pat Mannion, p. 365. Families of Peter and Thomas shared house.
36 Q.R.O., Files of Forfeiture Office and Miscellaneous papers, File No. 18.

NAME		AGE	PERSONAL DETAILS	DATE OF DEPART- URE LIVER- POOL	DATE OF ARRIVAL NEW YORK	SHIP
Guinnessy,	Pat	55	of Irvilloughter; carpenter.	17 Aug. 1849	2 Oct. 1849	Northum- berland, Galway.
	Mary	51	wife; daughter of Lackey or Laughlin Looby or Luby.			
	James	20	son			
	Malachy	16	son			
	Pat	13	son			
	Ann	14	daughter			
	Catherine	3	daughter			
Guinnessy,	Thomas	22	of Irvilloughter	15 June 1848	23 July 1848	Sea Bird, Galway.
	Bridget	20	sister			
Hanbury, Hambury or Hamberry	Catherine	36	of Boughill	17 Aug. 1849	2 Oct. 1949	Northum berland, Galway.
Hambury, or Hansbury	Judy	23	of Boughill; wife of Thomas; sister of Thomas Byrne, q.v. Travelled in family group of Darby Killalea.	15 June 1848	23 July 1848	Sea Bird, Galway.
Hart,	Michael	36	of Irvilloughter ; son of John and Catherine, decd.	17 Aug. 1849	2 Oct. 1849	Northum- berland, Galway.
	Pat	2	son			
	Mary	8	daughter			
	Catherine	32	widowed sister			
	James	23	⎫			
	John	1	⎪ no relationship specified.			
	Michael	17	⎬			
	Thomas	16	⎪			
	Catherine	14	⎭			
Horan,	Michael	38	of Irvilloughter	15 June 1848	23 July 1848	Sea Bird, Galway.
	Anne	34	wife			
	Michael	6	son			
	Thomas	2	son			
	Catherine	4	daughter			
	Eliza	16	no relationship specified			
Jennings,	Catherine	19	of Irvilloughter; grand-daughter of Thomas and Mary Cosgrave ; occupied house with Julia Cosgrave and Mary Dowd.	15 June 1848	23 July 1848	Sea Bird, Galway.
Kelly,	Bryan	21	of Irvilloughter; in family group of John Rafferty, q.v.	15 June 1848	23 July 1848	Sea Bird, Galway.
Kelly,	Catherine	21	of Irvilloughter; with Mary Byrne and Mary Kennedy	17 Aug. 1849	2 Oct. 1849	Northum- berland, Galway.

NAME	AGE	PERSONAL DETAILS	DATE OF DEPARTURE LIVERPOOL	DATE OF ARRIVAL NEW YORK	SHIP
Kelly,	John (Sen.) 52	of Irvilloughter; husband of Ellen, decd.	17 Aug. 1849	2 Oct. 1849	*Northumberland.* Galway.
	Barney 21	son			
	John (Jnr.) 24	son			
	Michael 18	son			
	Thomas 19	son			
	Ann 17	daughter			
	Bridget 8	daughter			
	Mary 11	daughter			
Kelly,	Margaret 35	of Irvilloughter; widow of Pat.	17 Aug. 1849	2 Oct. 1849	*Northumberland,* Galway.
	Catherine 9	daughter			
	Margaret 7	daughter			
	Mary Connolly 18	no relationship specified.			
Kennedy, Mary	24	of Irvilloughter; with Catherine Kelly and Mary Byrne.	17 Aug. 1849	2 Oct. 1849	*Northumberland,* Galway.
Kennedy, Pat	28	of Irvilloughter; died on voyage; [37] son-in-law of John Carty, q.v.	15 June 1848	23 July 1848	*Sea Bird,* Galway.
	Anne 24	wife			
	Bridget 24	sister			
	Catherine 19	sister			
	Pat 10	no relationship specified.			
Kennedy, Pat (John)	48	of Irvilloughter; son of John, decd.; occupied cottage and 3 acres; very poor.	15 June 1848	23 July 1848	*Sea Bird,* Galway.
	Mary 40	wife			
	John 16	son			
	Thomas 6	son			
	Ann 14	daughter			
	Biddy 16	daughter			
	Bridget 20	daughter			
	Catherine 18	daughter			
	Hannah 12	daughter			
	Mary 10	daughter			
	Peggy 4	daughter			
Kennedy, Thomas	30	of Irvilloughter; son of Patrick (Marks) and Mary.	17 Aug. 1849	2 Oct. 1849	*Northumberland,* Galway.
	Biddy 20	sister			
	Honoria 18	sister			
	Peggy 17	sister			
	Ellen 3	no relationship specified.			

---

[37] Q.R.O., O.W. Land Revenue Series Letter Books, Commissioners of Woods to Burke, 9 October 1848.

NAME		AGE	PERSONAL DETAILS	DATE OF DEPART-URE LIVER-POOL	DATE OF ARRIVAL NEW YORK	SHIP
Kennedy,		33	of Irvilloughter; widow of Andrew.	17 Aug. 1849	2 Oct. 1949	*Northum-berland,* *Galway.*
	Daniel	18	no relationship			
	Michael	17	specified.			
	Pat	12	do.			
	Ann	15	do.			
	Bridget	9	do.			
	Catherine	9	do.			
	Mary Ann	6	do.			
Kilcannon,	Anthony	17	of Boughill; in family group of Bridget Killalea, q.v.	15 June 1848	23 July 1848	*Sea Bird.* *Galway.*
Killalea,	Abegail	27	of Boughill; occupied cabin and 2½ acres; very poor.	17 Aug. 1849	2 Oct. 1849	*Northum-berland,* *Galway.*
	Biddy	25	sister			
	Catherine	20	sister			
	Ellen	17	sister			
Killalea,	Bridget	35	of Boughill ; widow of Thomas; occupied cabin and 2½ acres; very poor.	15 June 1848	23 July 1848	*Sea Bird,* *Galway.*
	John	8	son			
	Mark	1	son			
	Margaret	7	daughter			
	Mary	11	daughter			
Killalea,	Bridget	16	born and reared on Boughill; 38 cousin of Bridget Killalea, q.v.	15 June 1848	23 July 1848	*Sea Bird,* *Galway.*
Killalea,	Catherine	45	of Boughill	17 Aug. 1849	2 Oct. 1849	*Northum-berland,* *Galway.*
	Ann	20	daughter			
	Catherine	7	daughter			
	Margaret	15	daughter			
Killalea,	Darby	46	of Boughill; labourer.	15 June 1848	23 July 1848	*Sea Bird,* *Galway.*
	Margaret	44	wife			
	John	15	son			
	Bridget	9	daughter			
	Mary	16	daughter			
Killalea,	John	19	of Boughill ; grouped with Anne Byrne.	15 June 1848	23 July 1848	*Sea Bird,* *Galway.*
Killalea,	Mathias	45	of Boughill; labourer.	15 June 1848	23 July 1848	*Sea Bird,* *Galway.*
	Sally	40	wife			
	Lawrence	8	son			
	Mathias	10	son			
	Michael	19	son			
	Thomas	14	son			
	Peggy	16	daughter			
Killalea,	Patrick Senior	42	of Boughill; labourer in family group of Darby Killalea, q.v.	15 June 1848	23 July 1848	*Sea Bird,* *Galway.*
	Patrick	17	son			

38 Q.R.O., Files of Forfeiture Office and Miscellaneous Papers, File No. 15.

Name		Age	Personal Details	Date of Departure Liverpool	Date of Arrival New York	Ship
Loftus,	Biddy	40	of Irvilloughter; wife of Thomas; occupied a cabin only. Distress ' beggars descriptions'.	15 June 1848	23 July 1848	*Sea Bird,* Galway.
	John	15	son			
	Michael	15	son			
	Thomas	6	son			
	Biddy	9	daughter			
	Ellen	3	daughter			
	Mary	22	daughter			
	Mary Ann	16	daughter			
Looby, Luby or Lubey	John	15	of Irvilloughter; grandson of Lackey, woodcutter and wife Mary; son of Tom and Peggy; first cousin of John Guinnessy. [39]	17 Aug. 1849	2 Oct. 1849	*Northumberland,* Galway.
Lynskey,	Bridget	25	of Irvilloughter; sister-in-law of James Conway, q.v. Her father was the original tenant of the holding. [40]	15 June 1848	23 July 1848	*Sea Bird,* Galway.
Lynskey,	Michael	50	of Irvilloughter; occupied cabin and 1½ acres; very poor; labourer.	15 June 1848	23 July 1848	*Sea Bird,* Galway.
	Judy	40	wife			
	John	16	son			
	Thomas	21	son			
	Catherine	10	daughter			
	Mary	12	daughter			
	Timothy	40	brother			
Lynskey,	Margaret or Mary	61	of Irvilloughter; widow of John; in family group of Thomas McLoughlin, her son-in-law.	17 Aug. 1849	2 Oct. 1849	*Northumberland* Galway.
	Mary	20	daughter			
McLoughlin,	Thomas	37	of Irvilloughter; wife; daughter of Margaret or Mary Lynskey.	17 Aug. 1849	2 Oct. 1849	*Northumberland,* Galway.
	Ellen	35				
	Bridget	4	daughter			
	Catherine	1	daughter			

---

[39] Q.R.O., Correspondence—Irvilloughter and Boughill, Census of 1836.
[40] Q.R.O., Files of Forfeiture Office and Miscellaneous Papers, Files Nos. 14, 15.

Name		Age	Personal Details	Date of Departure Liverpool	Date of Arrival New York	Ship
Manahan, or Monaghan	Anthony	20	of Irvilloughter; in family group of Owen Carty but no relationship specified; nephew of Patrick Crosby, stone cutter. [41]	17 Aug. 1849	2 Oct. 1849	*Northumberland,* Galway.
Manly,	Richard	48	of Irvilloughter; occupied cabin only; very poor.	15 June 1848	23 July 1848	*Sea Bird,* Galway.
	Bridget	40	wife			
	James	9	son			
	John	12	son			
	Richard	3	son			
	Bridget	16	daughter			
	Ellen	18	daughter			
	Mary	14	daughter			
Mannion,	Pat	38	of Irvilloughter; with family group of Peter Grady, q.v.	17 Aug. 1849	2 Oct. 1849	*Northumberland* Galway.
	Peggy	40	wife; sister of Peter and Thomas Grady.			
	John	17	son			
	Malachy	10	son			
	Pat	13	son			
	Thomas	8	son			
	Mary	5	daughter			
Morrissey,	John	40	of Irvilloughter; occupied cabin and ½ acre; very poor.	15 June 1848	23 July 1848	*Sea Bird,* Galway.
	Hannah	33	wife			
	Pat	3	son			
	Bridget	2	daughter			
	Catherine	4	daughter			
	Ellen	11	daughter			
	Maria	10	daughter			
Morrissey,	Thomas (Roger)	37	of Irvilloughter; occupied cabin and 1 acre; very poor.	15 June 1848	23 July 1848	*Sea Bird,* Galway.
	Peggy	36	wife			
	John	12	son			
	Bridget	6	daughter			
	Mary	8	daughter			
Mullen, or Mullin	Mary	45	of Irvilloughter; widow; occupied cabin only; very poor and almost naked.	15 June 1848	23 July 1848	*Sea Bird,* Galway.
	John	14	son			
Naughton,	Catherine	26	of Irvilloughter; in family group of Pat Cosgrave but no relationship specified.	15 June 1848	23 July 1848	*Sea Bird,* Galway.

---

[41] Q.R.O., Files of Forfeiture Office and Miscellaneous Papers, File No. 15.

NAME	AGE	PERSONAL DETAILS	DATE OF DEPARTURE LIVERPOOL	DATE OF ARRIVAL NEW YORK	SHIP
Rafferty, Ellen	24	of Irvilloughter	17 Aug. 1849	2 Oct. 1849	*Northumberland,* Galway.
Catherine	15	sister			
Mary	20	sister			
Rafferty, Ellen C.	22	of Irvilloughter; in family group of Catherine Donnellan but no relationship specified.	15 June 1848	23 July 1848	*Sea Bird,* Galway.
Rafferty, John	50	of Irvilloughter; ' fish tramper to and from Galway'; occupied cottage and 1½ acres; very poor. [42]	15 June 1848	23 July 1848	*Sea Bird,* Galway.
Mary Ann	50	wife			
John	15	son			
Pat	18	son			
Bridget	24	daughter			
Catherine	20	daughter			
Mary Ann	22	daughter			
Rafferty, Mary	40	of Irvilloughter; widow of John; occupied cabin and 1½ acres; very poor.[43]	15 June 1848	23 July 1848	*Sea Bird,* Galway.
John Jun.	20	son			
Pat	16	son			
Thomas	12	son			
Catherine	15	daughter			
Spencer, Mary	13	of Irvilloughter; an orphan reared in family of Michael Lynskey, q.v.	15 June 1848	23 July 1848	*Sea Bird,* Galway.
White, Anne	16	of Irvilloughter	15 June 1848	23 July 1848	*Sea Bird* Galway.,
White, Bridget	36	of Irvilloughter; widow of Pat, son of Edward and Peggy; labourer.	17 Aug. 1849	2 Oct. 1849	*Northumberland,* Galway.
John	6	son			
Pat	16	son			
Bridget	8	daughter			
Margaret	10	daughter			
Mary	16	daughter			
White, Bridget	39	of Irvilloughter; widow of Thomas; occupied cabin and 1½ acres; very poor.	17 Aug. 1849	2 Oct. 1849	*Northumberland,* Galway.
Ann	14	daughter			
Catherine	6	daughter			
Mary	15	daughter			
Sally	19	daughter, died at sea.[44]			

[42] Q.R.O., Correspondence—Irvilloughter and Boughill, Census of 1836.
[43] Q.R.O., Files of Forfeiture Office and Miscellaneous Papers, File No. 12.
[44] *Ibid.*, File No. 18.

Name	Age	Personal Details	Date of Departure Liverpool	Date of Arrival New York	Ship
White, John 'Black'	50	of Irvilloughter; occupied cottage and 6 acres; very poor and half naked.	15 June 1848	23 July 1848	*Sea Bird*, Galway.
Bridget	41	wife			
John	16	son			
Martin	12	son			
Michael	6	son			
Pat	14	son			
Biddy	15	daughter			
Jane	3	daughter			
Mary	20	daughter			
Nancy	18	daughter			
White, Michael	21	of Irvilloughter	17 Aug. 1849	2 Oct. 1849	*Northumberland.* Galway.
Margaret	22	sister			
White, Pat	26	of Irvilloughter; son of John (Red) and Catherine.	15 June 1848	23 July 1848	*Sea Bird*, Galway.
John	18	brother			
White, Thomas	26	of Irvilloughter	17 Aug. 1849	2 Oct. 1849	*Northumberland*, Galway.
Honor or Harriet	28	wife; daughter of James Finnerty or Ferraghty.[45]			
Michael	6	son			
Bridget	3	daughter			
Margaret	7	daughter			

---

[45] Q.R.O., Files of Forfeiture Office and Miscellaneous Papers, File No. 11.

NOTE ON THE EMIGRATION SCHEME FROM
KINGWILLIAMSTOWN

The crown estate of Kingwilliamstown was situated in the parish
of Nohaval Daly, barony of Duhallow, near Kanturk and the Cork-
Kerry border, in Co. Cork. The decision to promote a state-aided
emigration scheme for the estate was taken by the Commissioners
of Woods some time after 11 April 1849, when a report from Richard
Griffith recommended such a scheme for the removal of the 'surplus
population'.[1] The crown agent on the estate, Michael Boyan, who
also had charge of the model farm experiment at Kingwilliamstown,
was instructed to prepare lists of those who would emigrate willingly,
or whose compulsory removal was necessary for the 'improvements'
on the estate.

A Treasury warrant of 6 August 1849 authorised the expenditure
of £1,500 for removing 238 persons, 158 adults and 80 children, from
Kingwilliamstown to New York, at an estimated cost of £6. 15s.
for each adult and £5. 3s. for each child. A first instalment of £800
was sent to Boyan, with instructions to proceed with the implementation of the scheme.[2]

The first party, consisting of 119 persons, left Kingwilliamstown
for Cork on 30 August 1849. They sailed for Liverpool aboard the
'*Nimrod*', and embarked for New York on 7 September 1849.
Kennelly and Company, of 23 Maylor Street, Cork, agents of the
Liverpool firm of Harnden and Company, had charge of the travel
arrangements. The fare for an adult was three pounds and for a
child, two pounds five shillings. Food or 'sea stores' was provided,
and each adult was to receive one pound and each child ten shillings
in American currency on landing in New York.[3]

Complaints by some of the Kingwilliamstown emigrants, that
sufficient food was not forthcoming on the journey from Cork, were
investigated by Boyan on instructions from the Commissioners of
Woods. He reported that the scarcity of food was caused by the
refusal of the captain of the '*Nimrod*' to delay departure while
supplies were being loaded.[4] Three persons died at sea between

---

[1] Q.R.O., Correspondence—Kingwilliamstown, Richard Griffith to Commissioners of Woods, 11 April 1849. Griffith was then compiling the Ordinance
Survey.
[2] Ibid., Boyan to Commissioners of Woods, 17 August 1849 ; O.W. Letter,
Account, Sales, etc. entry books, Ireland, no. I 2, Commissioners of Woods to
Commissioners of Treasury, 20 July 1849 ; Commissioners of Woods to Boyan,
13 August 1849.
[3] The exchange rate was $4.80 to the pound sterling. Passenger lists, invoices
and receipts are to be found in Correspondence—Kingwilliamstown.
[4] Q.R.O., Correspondence—Kingwilliamstown, Boyan to Commissioners of
Woods, 25 September 1849 ; T. E. Hodder, Government emigration officer,
Liverpool, to Stephen Walcott, secretary Emigration Commissioners, 7 September
1849.

Cork and Liverpool and two sisters were sent home, so that only 114 persons sailed from Liverpool.[5]   The total cost of this movement of emigrants was £498. 3s. 6d.[6]

In February, 1850 a letter was delivered to the Office of Woods, having been sent from America by John Galivan or Galvin, who complained that neither he nor his family had received any provisions while in Liverpool or during the voyage to America. Reports from the emigration officer at Liverpool insisted that all the travellers had adequate supplies of food.[7]

Nevertheless, when arrangements for the departure of the second group of emigrants were being made, a copy of the tender from the shipping agents was sent by the Commissioners of Woods to the Emigration Commissioners [8] for their opinion on the amount of food to be allocated to each individual for the voyage. The fare in this instance was four pounds for an adult, three pounds ten shillings for a child under fourteen, and a pound for an infant under one year. According to the tender the food to be supplied to each adult was as follows :—

> 3 quarts of water daily,
>
> 2½ lbs bread or biscuit weekly,
>
> 2 lbs rice   ,,
>
> 1 ,, wheat flour   ,,
>
> 3 ,, oatmeal   ,,
>
> ½ ,, sugar   ,,
>
> ½ ,, molasses   ,,
>
> 2 ozs tea   ,,

Children under fourteen would receive half of the above quantities.[9]

In their report, the Emigration Commissioners suggested that, in order to comply with the requirements of the Passengers' Act 1849,[10] that the allowance of oatmeal be raised to five lbs weekly per person. The shipping agents should be responsible for maintaining the party in Liverpool should any delay occur before sailing.[11]

---

[5] Ibid.

[6] *27th Report of Commissioners of Woods, Forests, and Land Revenues*, app. p. 81.

[7] Q.R.O., O.W. Letter, Account, Sale, etc. entry books, Ireland, no. J 2, Commissioners of Woods to Hodder, 21 February 1850 ; ibid. to Boyan, 4 March 1850.

[8] Their full title was the Colonial Land and Emigration Commissioners whose chief work at this period was the regulation of emigration.

[9] Q.R.O., O.W. Letter, Account, Sale, etc. entry books, Ireland, no. K 2, Commissioners of Woods to Emigration Commissioners, 29 May 1850.

[10] 12 & 13 *Vic. c.* 33, *sec.* 24. For an account of the emigration traffic see article by O. McDonagh in I.H.S., No. 34, pp. 162—189.

[11] Q.R.O., O.W. Letter, Account, Sale, etc. entry books, Ireland, no. K 2, Commissioners of Woods to Boyan, 1 June 1850 ; Boyan to Commissioners of Woods, 25 May 1850.

The all-in charge of six guineas for an adult was made up of the following items :—

	£	s.	d.
Travelling expenses from Kingwilliamstown to Cork		4	0
Clothes supplied		12	0
Extra 'sea-stores'		10	0
Landing money	1	0	0
Fare and supplies		4	0	0

The all-in cost for a child was £4 16. 0. On the acceptance of the amended tender, thirty-six persons left Cork for Liverpool on 15 June 1850, and arrived at New York shortly before 29 July 1950.[12] Several of this group settled in Buffalo.

A third party of seventeen left Cork on 5 October 1850.[13] The cost of the emigration of this and the second party was £313 8s. 7d.[14]

Arrangements for the departure of the fourth and last organised party of nineteen were sanctioned by the Commissioners on 10 September 1851 and they sailed from Cork for Liverpool on 20 September.[15] Expenses amounted to £92. 19s. 3d.[16]

Thus in the three years, 1849-50-51, a total of 191 persons left Kingwilliamstown at a cost of £904. 1s. 4d., almost £600 less that the amount originally allocated for the scheme.

The population of the crown estate of Kingwilliamstown ,which was returned as 656, (344 males and 312 females) in the crown agent's report of 16 May 1849, had declined to 479 persons by 24 November 1852.[17] Accordingly, a scheme to send a further 100 persons to America was proposed,[18] but nothing appears to have been done and the last reference to such schemes concerns the eldest daughter of Daniel Sullivan who had been caretaker of the estate. Six pounds was advanced for her fare to America on 25 April 1855.[19]

The crown estate of more than 5000 acres which was referred to

---

[12] Q.R.O., Correspondence—Kingwilliamstown, Register of Population, 1 November 1850; Return of Expenses of Emigration for 1850, 11 December 1850.
[13] Q.R.O., *Reports on Kingwilliamstown improvements*, Richard Griffith, 5 June 1851, in Par. Paper, No. 612, Session 1854.
[14] *28th Report of Commissioners of Woods, Forests and Lands Revenue*, app. p. 141.
[15] Q.R.O., O.W. Letter, Account, Sale, etc. entry books, Ireland, no. 1 2, Commissioners of Woods to Boyan, 10 September 1851 ; Correspondence—Kingwillaimstown, Boyan to Commissioners of Woods, 17 February 1852.
[16] *29th Report of Commissioners of Woods, Forests, and Land Revenues*, app. p. 115.
[17] Q.R.O., Register of population of Kingswilliamtown, Boyan to Commissioners of Woods, 16 May 1849 ; Correspondence—Kingwilliamstown, ibid., 24 November 1852.
[18] Q.R.O., MSS reports on Kingwilliamstown, Report of S.G. MacCulloch, 31 December 1852.
[19] Q.R.O., Correspondence—Kingwilliamstown, Commissioners of Woods to Boyan, 25 April 1855.

as the 'mountain pasture of Pobble O'Keefe' in older surveys, was sold by auction in five lots in April 1855 for a total sum of £14,520.[20] The village which has grown on part of the estate has within the last few years been renamed Ballydesmond.

---

[20] Q.R.O., Particulars of Sales of Crown Property since the year 1824, pp. 32–3.

EMIGRANTS FROM KINGWILLIAMSTOWN ESTATE

Itinerary : Cork—Liverpool—New York

NAME	AGE	PERSONAL DETAILS	DATE OF DEPART- URE LIVER- POOL	DATE OF ARRIVAL NEW YORK	SHIP
Buckley, Darby	51	of Tooreenclassagh; farmer.[21]	Sept. 1851		
Mary	39	wife			
John	2	son			
Michael	16	son			
Tade	18	son			
Johanna	9	daughter			
Margaret	5	daughter			
Mary	12	daughter			
Casey, John	56	of the Town Farm; wife named Rosian;[22] two of his daughters were sent back from Liverpool. One had not 'use of one leg'.[23] Mary Sullivan was of this family group.	7 Sept. 1849	22 Oct. 1849	*Columbus*
Michael	13	son			
Bab or Barbara	19	daughter			
Johanna	18	daughter			
Rosean	16	daughter			
Collins, Mary	27	niece of Mary Guiney; left with Guiney family and probably went to Buffalo with them.[24]	June 1850		
Connell, David	45	of Glencollins; probably stayed in New York	7 Sept. 1849	22 Oct. 1849	*Columbus*
Margaret	35	wife			
Dan	15	son			
Jerry	10	son			
John	13	son			
Pat	3	son			
Eileen	½	daughter			
Johanna	8	daughter			
Margaret	9	daughter			
Mary	5	daughter			

[21] *Census of Ireland*, 1901, *General Topographical Index*. With the exception of the townland Tooreenkeagh, which is mentioned in the censuses of 1834, 1836/7, available in Q.R.O., Correspondence—Kingwilliamstown, all the townlands mentioned are listed in above. The crown lands of Pobble O'Keefe contained in addition to the village of Kingwilliamstown the following townlands: Meenganine, Carriganes, Tooreenkeagh, Glencollins, Tooreenglanahee and Tooreenclassagh.
[22] Q.R.O., Correspondence—Kingwilliamstown, Return of Population for Kingwilliamstown, April, 1849, gives Rosian's age as 54.
[23] Ibid., Michael Boyan to Commissioners of Woods, 25 September 1849.
[24] See letters herewith pp. 386-94 for this and other probable destinations of emigrants.

Name		Age	Personal Details	Date of Departure Liverpool	Date of Arrival New York	Ship
Connell,	Patrick	50	of Town Farm; farmer.	7 Sept. 1849	22 Oct. 1849	*Columbus*
	Ellen	44	wife			
	Dan	16	son			
	John	13	son			
	Philip	19	son			
	Johanna	4	daughter			
	Judy	15	duaghter			
	Margaret	7	daughter			
	Mary	22	daughter			
Cremin,	John	28	brother of Timothy, farmer, who did not emigrate.	7 Sept. 1849	22 Oct. 1849	*Columbus*
	Kitty	25	wife			
	Timothy	3 mths.	son			
Cronin,	Betty	17	daughter of Mary Cronin, widow of John of Glencollins, who did not emigrate; went to Norfolk.	June 1850		
Daly,	Daniel	50	of Glencollins; labourer, native of Kerry; died on the way to America.[25]	7 Sept. 1849	22 Oct. 1849	*Columbus*
	Margaret	50	wife			
	John	26	son; went to Norfolk leaving family at New York.			
	Bessy	25	daughter			
	Judy	20	daughter			
	Margaret	19	daughter			
Danihy,	Denis (Daniel)	40	of Tooreenclassagh; farmer, native of Kerry; died on the way to Liverpool from Cork;[26] wife and family went to Buffalo.	7 Sept. 1849	22 Oct. 1849	*Columbus*
	Johanna	40	wife			
	Con	15	son			
	Dan	17	son			
	Denis	7	son			
	Matt	5	son			
	Michael	13	son			
	Mary	19	daughter			
	Mary	13	niece; daughter of Michael, brother of Denis (Daniel) Sen.			

[25] Q.R.O., Correspondence—Kingwilliamstown, Michael Boyan to Commissioners of Woods, 25 September 1849.
[26] Ibid.

NAME		AGE	PERSONAL DETAILS	DATE OF DEPART- URE LIVER- POOL	DATE OF ARRIVAL NEW YORK	SHIP
Danihy,	Denis (Matt)	60	of Tooreenclassagh; farmer, native of Kerry; settled with all his family in Buffalo.	7 Sept. 1849	22 Oct. 1849	*Columbus*
	Johanna	50	wife			
	Daniel	19	son			
	Denis	7	son			
	John	17	son			
	Matt	21	son			
	Michael	11	son			
	Tade	3	son			
	Bridget	15	daughter			
	Eileen	10	daughter			
	Mary	23	daughter			
Danihy,	John	25	of Tooreenglanahee; son of Ellen, aged 65 in 1850; brother Daniel did not emigrate; stayed in New York.	June 1850		
	James	21	brother, who went to Orange County, N.Y.			
	Eileen (or Ellen)	27	sister, who went to Orange County, N.Y.			
	Kitty	30	sister, who stayed in New York.			
Danihy,	Tim	40	of Glencollins; lab-ourer.	7 Sept. 1849	22 Oct. 1849	*Columbus*
	Mary	42	wife			
	Con	3	son			
	Dan	13	son			
	Michael	8	son			
	Tade	5	son			
	Nelly	10	daughter			
Dillon,	Pat	47	overseer of labourers at Kingwilliamstown; had already sent out two daughters at own expense.[27]	June 1850		
	Judy	51	wife			
	Margaret	23	daughter			
Duggan,	Denis	27	farmer, son of Daniel of Tooreen-glanahee and Mary, his wife who did not emigrate; writer of letter No. 3, p. 393; settled in Buffalo.	June 1850		

---

[27] Q.R.O., Correspondence—Kingwilliamstown, List of emigrants.

NAME		AGE	PERSONAL DETAILS	DATE OF DEPART- URE LIVER- POOL	DATE OF ARRIVAL NEW YORK	SHIP
Duggan,	Margaret or Madge	29	daughter of Harry Duggan, farmer, of Tooreenglanahee, a blind man, and Norry, his wife who did not emigrate; went to New Jersey.	June 1850		
	Eileen or Helen	25	sister; went to Buffalo.			
Fenigan,	Daniel	55	labourer	7 Sept. 1849	22 Oct. 1849	*Columbus*
	Johanna	48	wife			
	Johanna	20	daughter			
	Judy	7	daughter			
	Kitty	10	daughter			
	Mary	22	daughter			
Foley, or Fowley	John	52	of Carriganes; farmer; native of Kerry.	7 Sept. 1849	22 Oct. 1849	*Columbus*
	Eileen	50	wife			
	Dan	18	son			
	John	21	son			
	Pat	16	son			
	Eileen	28	daughter			
	Johanna	11	daughter			
	Julea	8	daughter			
	Mary	24	daughter; died in Liverpool.[28]			
Galvin,	John	32	mason	7 Sept. 1849	22 Oct. 1849	*Columbus*
	Margaret	30	wife			
	Patrick	2	son			
	Tade	4	son			
	Biddy	6	daughter			
Galvin,	Tade	30	brother of John above.	7 Sept. 1849	22 Oct. 1849	*Columbus*
Guiney,	Darby	45	of Glencollins; lab- ourer.	Oct. 1850		
	Kitty	37	wife			
	Ben	5	son			
	Dan	17	son			
	Darby	3	son			
	Tade	5	son; twin of Ben.			
	Biddy	9	daughter			
	Eileen	11	daughter			
	Joney	13	daughter			

[28] Q.R.O., Correspondence—Kingwilliamstown, Michael Boyan to Commissioners of Woods, 25 September 1849.

NAME		AGE	PERSONAL DETAILS	DATE OF DEPART- URE LIVER- POOL	DATE OF ARRIVAL NEW YORK	SHIP
Guiney,	Mary	50	widow of Benjamin Guiney, farmer, of Glencollins; daughter of 'Big' Daniel Leary of Tooreenglanahy and Johanna, his wife; aunt of Mary Collins above; settled in Buffalo with family.	June 1850		
	Ben	8	son			
	Dan	23	son			
	Tade	14	son			
	Gubby	11	daughter			
Keeffe,	John	25	son of John Keeffe, farmer, of Tooreen-classagh and Mary his wife, who did not emigrate; settled in Buffalo.	June 1850		
	Hanora or Norry	19	sister			
Keeffe, or O'Keeffe	Margaret	50	listed among labourers	7 Sept. 1849	22 Oct. 1849	*Columbus*
	Eugene	17	son			
	Jeane	13	daughter			
	Johanna	21	daughter			
	Nano	23	daughter			
Kelleher,	Daniel	69	of Tooreenglanahee	7 Sept. 1849	22 Oct. 1849	*Columbus*
	Dan	29	son			
	Kitty	26	wife of Daniel, junior			
	Tade	2	son of Daniel, junior			
	Kitty	3	daughter of Daniel, junior			
	Mary	21	daughter of Daniel, senior			
	John	36	nephew of Daniel, senior			
Leary,	Catherine	22	daughter of Timothy Leary of Tooreen-keagh, a farmer, who did not emigrate and his late wife, Peg.	June 1850		
Leary,	Connor or Daniel	55	labourer, later farmer of Glencollins; died in hospital probably in Buffalo, shortly after landing; family settled in Buffalo.	7 Sept. 1849	22 Oct. 1849	*Columbus*
	Ellen	50	wife; widow by 9 Aug. 1850.			
	Jerry	11	son			
	John	18	son			
	Eileen	16	daughter			
	Johanna	20	daughter			
	Mary	13	daughter			
	Peggy	5	daughter			

Name		Age	Personal Details	Date of Departure Liverpool	Date of Arrival New York	Ship
Leary,	John	19	son of late John 'Bawn' Leary, farmer, and Kate, his wife; brother of Pat who did not emigrate; settled in Norfolk.	June 1850		
Leary,	Mary	22	daughter of Daniel Leary, labourer and Ellen or Peg his wife; went out to Tade Houlihan with Betty Murphy and Davy Connell.	June 1850		
Leary	Matthew	50	of Tooreenglanahee; labourer, settled in Buffalo with his family.	7 Sept. 1849	22 Oct. 1849	*Columbus*
	Mary	45	wife			
	Dan	6	son			
	Darby	18	son			
	John	16	son			
	Matt	1	son			
	Pat	13	son			
	Johanna	4	daughter			
	Judy	20	daughter			
McAuliffe,	Denis	28	of Carriganes; son of Robert, farmer, native of Newmarket.	7 Sept. 1849	22 Oct. 1849	*Columbus*
	Michael	22	brother			
	Robert	17	brother			
	Johanna	24	sister			
McCarthy,	Margaret	22	daughter of Sandy McCarthy, carpenter to the Crown estate, native of Boherboy, and Nell his wife; wrote letter of date 22 Sept. 1850, pp. 390-3; settled in New York.	7 Sept. 1849	22 Oct. 1849	*Columbus*
Minehan, or Moynihan	Biddy	41	widow, daughter of Johanna aged 74 in 1849.	Sept 1851		
	John	15	son			
	Patrick	12	son			
Moynihan, or Moynehan	Denis	33	labourer, who 'took a house in New York'.[29]	June 1850		
	Johanna	28	wife			
	John	2	son			
	Johanna	5	daughter			

[29] See p. 389.

NAME		AGE	PERSONAL DETAILS	DATE OF DEPART- URE LIVER- POOL	DATE OF ARRIVAL NEW YORK	SHIP
Mahony, or Moynehan	Mary	55	widow, included among labourers.	June 1850		
	Dan	18	son			
	Tade	14	son			
	Ellen	26	daughter			
	Johanna	21	daughter			
	Norry	12	daughter			
Murphy,	Jane	20	daughter of Michael Murphy, farmer, of Tooreenclassagh, and Mary his wife, who did not emigrate; settled in Norfolk.	June 1850		
Murphy,	Johanna	20	daughter of Timothy Murphy, farmer, of Tooreenclassagh, and Margaret or Mary, his wife, who did not emigrate; settled in New York.	June 1850		
Reen,	Darby	51	(oge) of Tooreen-glanahee.[30]	Sept. 1851		
	Bridget	41	wife			
	Jerry	9	son			
	John	12	son			
	Michael	15	son			
	Tade	19	son			
	Ellen	5	daughter			
	Mary	6	daughter			
Reen,	Denis	25	son of late Darby Reen, farmer, of Tooreenglanahee, [31] and Biddy his wife; brother of John who did not emigrate; settled in Buffalo.	June 1850		
	Tade	22	brother			
Sullivan,			eldest daughter of Daniel Sullivan, care-taker of Kingswil-liamstown Model Farm, also describe-ed as woodranger; six pounds advanced by the Treasury, 25 April 1855.[32]	Summer 1855		

[30] Return of Tenants of Kingwilliamstown, c. May 1849, describes him as farmer.
[31] Later census gives Tooreenclassagh.
[32] Q.R.O., Correspondence—Kingswilliamstown, Commissioners of Woods to Michael Boyan, 25 April 1855. In return of population of Kingwilliamstown, April 1849, Daniel Sullivan's family consists of: Peggy, wife, 41, Denis, son, 8, Madge, daughter, 14, Judy, daughter, 11, John, son, 4.

NAME	AGE	PERSONAL DETAILS	DATE OF DEPARTURE LIVERPOOL	DATE OF ARRIVAL NEW YORK	SHIP
Sullivan, John	35	labourer, also called Pat in survey of Kingwilliamstown.	7 Sept. 1849	22 Oct. 1849	*Columbus*
Ellen	30	wife			
John	½	son			
Sullivan, Mary	25	step-daughter o f John Casey, q.v.	7 Sept. 1849	22 Oct. 1849	*Columbus*
Sullivan, Pat	50	of Carriganes, farmer.	Oct. 1850		
Judy	43	wife			
Dan	4	son			
John	12	son			
Michael	8	son			
Pat	7	son			
Judy	1	daughter			
May	14	daughter			

NOTE ON THE EMIGRATION SCHEME
FROM CASTLEMAINE.

The crown estate of Castlemaine was situated in the parish of Kiltallagh, Co. Kerry, on the river Maine, a short distance inland from the bay of Castlemaine. The estate, known as the Constable's Acres, was one of the perquisites of the sinecure post of governor of the fort of Castlemaine, and was placed under the management of the Commissioners of Woods when the governorship was abolished from 12 August 1835, on the death of the last holder of the office.[1] Despite several searches made by orders of the Commissioners, no records could be found as to how or when the lands became attached or annexed to the office of governor,[2] and the estate, (which in 1839 consisted of about nine acres, a fishing weir and a village of thirty-one 'thatched Cabbins of the poorest description', and one small slate house),[3] was usually leased by the governor for the term of his interest in the office. In 1839 three of the houses were occupied by publicans, two by tradesmen and the rest by labourers. The village was in a 'reduced state', and no rent had been paid by the tenants from 1835, when the lease expired, to 25 March 1840.[4]

Arrangements were made about 1839 for the erection of a quay, and Michael Boyan, superintendant of the model farm experiment in Kingwilliamstown, was appointed overseer of the improvements. It was not until this time that possession of the premises was sought for the Crown, and by 31 March 1841, all but three of the properties had been recovered.

But in spite of the erection of the quay, and a new schoolhouse and dwelling houses in the village, the tenants' lot did not improve due to the lack of employment and scarcity of food, and when the Commissioners of Woods adopted a policy of state-aided emigration, Castlemaine was included in its scope.

There were at least three separate group departures from this estate, but despite an intensive search, the list for the second and largest party to leave has not been found among the papers in the Quit Rent Office collection.

The first party of emigrants left in the autumn of 1848 on a date subsequent to 4 September 1848.[5] Their departure is recorded in

---

1 Q.R.O., Land Revenue Series Letter Books, Commissioners of Woods to Burke, 2 March 1841.
2 Ibid., Paymaster of Civil Services to Burke, 25 March 1841; R. Hamilton & Co., Crown Solicitors, to Burke, 31 March 1841.
3 Ibid., Boyan to Commissioners of Woods, 26 November 1839.
4 Ibid., 11 July 1840.
5 Q.R.O., O.W., Letter, Account, Sale, etc. Entry Books, no. G 2, Commissioners of Woods to Boyan, 4 September 1848.

a report of 21 December 1848, but the names of heads of families only are given, when it would appear that twelve persons emigrated at a cost of £72 3s. 11d.[6]

A further scheme was proposed in June 1849, and the expenditure of £500 was authorised for removing forty-three adults and twenty-four children from Castlemaine to New York.[7] As far as can be discovered, in the absence of the official list, at least thirteen families, or sixty-three individuals, left at a cost of £279 7s. 1d. on or before 20 September 1849.[8] From a brief reference in a letter written at the time, it is evident that this party joined the emigrants from Kingwilliamstown who sailed on the *Columbus* from Liverpool for New York on 7 September 1849, 'at the same rate of charge' as those from Kingwilliamstown.[9] The names of Patrick O'Brien and John Coffey have been included in the list. According to a note made in the 'House Book' for that area, Coffey is described as 'having gone to America leaving his holding in the hands of the Crown'.[10]

The third party of eight left Cork on 20 September 1851, on the same day as nineteen emigrants from Kingwilliamstown, at a total cost of £42 3s. 2d.[11]

There are therefore only twenty-two names in the accompanying list which, with the group of sixty-three for which no names or details are available, (with the possible exceptions of John Coffey and Patrick O'Brien), gives a total of eighty-five emigrants. The total cost of the entire emigration project for Castlemaine was £393 4s. 2d.

The town, lands, tolls of two fairs and fishing rights in the river Maine, were sold for £1,120 in August 1855.[12]

[6] Ibid., no. I 2, Commissioners of Woods to Commissioners of Treasury, 21 December 1848 ; 29 June 1849; 28*th Report of Commissioners of Woods*, app. p. 141. No explanation is offered for the delay in returning this figure.
[7] Ibid., no. I 2, Commissioners of Treasury to Commissioners of Woods, 23 July 1849.
[8] Ibid., no. J 2, Commissioners of Woods to Boyan, 14 August 1849; 4 October 1849; no. K 2, 21 December 1850; Files of Forfeiture Office, Crown Lands—General, Rental for Castlemaine, 1853; 27*th Report of Commissioners of Woods*, app. p. 81.
[9] Q.R.O., Correspondence—Kingwilliamstown, Boyan to Commissioners of Woods, 25 September 1849.
[10] Q.R.O., Valuation Office Collection, House Book for Kiltallagh parish, Co. Kerry. These books were compiled c. 1826-51, in the course of work on the general valuation. See article by Margaret Griffith in *I.H.S.*, viii, No. 29.
[11] Q.R.O., Rental for Kingwilliamstown, Castlemaine and Kinsale estates, 1851-2 ; Correspondence—Kingwilliamstown, Boyan to Commissioners of Woods, 17 February 1952; O.W. Letter, Account, Sale, etc. Entry Books, no. L 2, Commissioners of Woods to Boyan, 10 September 1851; 29*th Report of Commissioners of Woods*, app. p. 115.
[12] Q.R.O., Particulars of Sales of Crown Property since the year 1824, p. 34.

EMIGRANTS FROM CASTLEMAINE

NAME	AGE	PERSONAL DETAILS	DATE OF DEPART-URE LIVER-POOL	DATE OF ARRIVAL NEW YORK	SHIP
Coffey,	John[13]				
Daly,	Mary		24 Sept. 1851		
	?	daughter of Mary			
	?	mother of Mary			
Griffin,	Daniel		Sept. 1848		
	?	wife			
	?	son			
	?	son			
	?	son			
Hanifen,	Ulick[14]	30	son-in-law of Margaret Sullivan	24 Sept. 1851	
	Mary	31	wife		
	Dan	2	son		
	Mary	6	daughter		
McCarthy,	John		undertenant of Daniel Griffin	Sept. 1848	
	?		mother		
	?		sister		
Shea,	John[15]		son of Thomas who died 1848	Sept. 1848	
	?		brother		
	?		brother		
	?		sister		
O'Brien,	Patrick[16]		Prior to 4 Aug. 1851		
Sullivan,	Margaret	67	mother-in-law of Ulick Hanifen, above.	24 Sept. 1851	

TOTAL   ....   23 individuals

---

[13] See introduction.
[14] Rental for Kingwilliamstown, Castlemaine and Kinsale estate, 1851-52. Q.R.O., Correspondence—Kingwilliamstown, Return of Population for Castlemaine estate, 4 August 1851.
[15] Q.R.O., O.W. Letter, Account, Sale, etc. Entry books, no. I 2, Commissioners of Woods to Commissioners of Treasury, 21 December 1848. The immediate reason of the emigration of the Griffin, McCarthy and Shea families was that their dwellings had been acquired and demolished preparatory to the erection of a National School in Castlemaine.
[16] Q.R.O., Correspondence—Kingwilliamstown, Return of Population on Castlemaine Estate, 4 August 1851.

NOTE ON THE EMIGRATION SCHEME
FROM KILCONCOUSE

The crown estate of Kilconcouse was situated in the parish of Kinnity, King's Co., and comprised 871 acres. This estate differed from Ballykilcline, Irvilloughter and Boughill in that in this case, from 1829 onwards, leases had been granted to the tenants for a twenty-one year term. The rents appeared to have been paid fairly regularly until the year 1846 when the famine intervened. In a report from the secretary of the Kinnity District relief committee, it was stated that twelve families of 68 persons were without any provisions and 'in a most precarious state'. Forty individuals were unable to work.[1] Subscriptions amounting to £35 were contributed by the Commissioners of Woods.

In April, 1847, the Commissioners authorised the collector of excise, Parsonstown, 'to give such indulgence in payment to each tenant as their circumstances may appear to require',[2] when a number of the tenants appealed for lenience.

The leases for twenty-one years expired in 1850 when an arrear of rent of £1,531 14s. 9d. had accumulated. It was then decided to remove the 'surplus population'; to redivide the land among those selected from the remaining tenants and to abandon the collection of arrears. The friction and unrest which arose from this redivision was the cause of an inquiry by a select Committee of the House of Lords into the management of the estate.[3]

Fifty-six persons left Kilconcouse at a cost of £363 19s. 8d.

---

[1] Q.R.O., O.W. Land Revenue Series Letter Books, Report of H. Tyrrell on Distress, c. 21 May 1846.

[2] Ibid., Commissioners of Woods to Burke, 8 April 1847.

[3] *Report from the Select Committee of the House of Lords . . . into the Management . . . of Kilconcouse, etc.*, 1854, xxi, 3.

EMIGRANTS FROM KILCONCOUSE

Itinerary Dublin—Liverpool—New York.

Name		Age	Personal Details	Date of Departure Liverpool	Date of Arrival New York	Ship
Blake,	Edward	50	} no relationship specified.	11 June 1852[4]		
	James	3				
	Ann	25				
	Sarah	20				
	Sarah	1				
Dunn,	William	45				
	Ann	43	wife			
	James	8	son			
	William	6	son			
	Biddy	19	daughter			
Fitzgerald,	James	55				
	Margaret	58	wife			
	James	16	son			
	Hanoria	18	daughter			
	Margaret	19	daughter			
Fitzgerald,	John	42				
	Ellen	30	wife			
	Denis	12	son			
	Thomas	8	son			
	Margaret	10	daughter			
Horan,	Patrick	30				
	Catherine	29	wife			
	John	3	son			
	Ann	7	daughter			
	Catherine	5	daughter			
	Margaret	12	daughter			
	Mary	10	daughter			
Karney or Kearney	Patrick	45				
	Ann	37	wife			
	Joseph	11	son			
	Pat	18	son			
	Thomas	16	son			
	William	8	son			
	Ann	14	daughter			
	Mary	21	daughter			
Kenehan,	John	45				
	Mary	37	wife			
	Jeremiah	16	son			
	John	12	son			
	Matthew	18	son			
	William	6	son			
	Ann	8	daughter			

4 All the emigrants from Kilconcouse sailed from Liverpool on 11 June 1852 with one exception, Patrick Lowry. It is therefore unnecessary to repeat date of departure with each family group.

NAME		AGE	PERSONAL DETAILS	DATE OF DEPART- URE LIVER- POOL	DATE OF ARRIVAL NEW YORK	SHIP
Kennedy,	Peter	63				
	Mary	50	wife			
Lowry[5]	Patrick	40				
	Ann	43	wife			
	John	20	son			
	Ann	12	daughter			
	Sarah	17	daughter			
Spain,	Biddy	30				
	Catherine	25	sister			
White,	Mary	38				
	James	13	son			
	John	8	son			
	Bridget	16	daughter			
	Mary	5	daughter			

---

[5] Q.R.O., Files of Forfeiture Office and Miscellaneous Papers, File No. 5, Burke to Commissioners of Woods, 3 September 1852, states that as Patrick Lowry has only one eye he was judged 'unfit for New York' and was sent to Philadelphia instead.

LETTERS HOME FROM EMIGRANTS WHO SETTLED IN
THE UNITED STATES

Three of the following letters were sent with a report dated 11 December 1850, by Michael Boyan to Charles Gore, one of the Commissioners of Woods. He reported on the latest group departure from the crown lands of Kingwilliamstown and observed :—'I am happy to state that those persons who emigrated in June and October last were all contented and well pleased, and several letters have been received from them and in general they are all employed and doing well, and some of them have remitted money to assist their parents. I send herewith some of the letters received from them, to show the Board that they are well employed at the same time this Estate is benefited by being relieved from their support'.[1] Two years later Boyan reported that £150 in letters of credit had been received by relatives in Kingwilliamstown.[2]

The fourth letter was written by an emigrant from Boughill, Co. Galway, to the crown agent in Galway who was in charge of the emigration scheme from that estate.

---

[1] Q.R.O., Correspondence—Kingwilliamstown, Boyan to Gore, 11 December 1850.

[2] Ibid., 24 November 1852.

1

Exchange Street Buffalo August 9th 1850.

Dear Mother and Brothers

We Embrace the opportunites of writing these few lines to you hoping that this Silent Messenger may find you and all our Dear friends and Beloved Neighbours in as good a state of health as this leaves us at present thanks be to God for his benefits to us all. Therefore we mean to let you know our Situation at present

We left New York 29th of July and Sailed out for Buffalo and arrived the following day in albany   we left albany the same day and Came out on the Canal Boat which was dravon By horses it took us Eight days to come to Buffalo which was very expensive to us   Bread and Milk was very Dear along the Canal   we Could walk out any time we pleased and walk 2 or three miles and Could eat plenty apples when we had any Desire   this place is full of Orchards and Woods   this is a very fine Country you may be Sure that we had a fine prospect Comming out here and according as we were Coming out the Country was getting Better   as for the Crops here the indian Meal is growing here like woods and the finest fields of Clover that ever wer seen   and as to the Stock they are like the Cows to Home and horses and sheep are Just the same   We could see fine large Stock of Cattle 40 and 50 Cows together and so on from that down to ten and twelve and 5 or six   We could see six and 7 score of Sheep and 12 or 14 horses togather you may be sure that we seen great many wonders

the Yankees are the wisest Men in the world in respect of doing business we arrived here abot 5 o clock in the afternoon of yesterday 14 of us together where we were received with the greatest Kindness and respectibility By Mathew Leary and Denis Danihy as soon as we came in we made them off at once   Matt Denis Danihy went and Brought a horse and took Dan Guineys luggage to the house and paid for it himself   we had no other one but his   But when we came to the house we could not state to you how we were treated we had Potatoes Meat Butter Bread and tea for Dinner and you

may be sure we had Drink after in Mathew Learys house   the whole
of Denis Danihys family and Denis Daniels wife and family   Connor
Learys wife and Daughter   But the poor woman is left a widow
Connor Died in hospital

I mean to let you know that we had a pleasant night they went
to the Store and brought 2 Dozen of Bottles of Small beer and
a Gallon of Gin otherwise whiskey   So that we were drinking untill
morning   if you were to see Denis Reen when Daniel Danihy Matt
Dressed him with clothes suitable for this Country you would think
him to be a Boss or Steward   so that we have scarcely words to
state to you how happy we felt at present

Dear friends if you were to see old Denis Danihy he never was
as Good in health and looks better than ever he did at home   Ye
would not beleive how fat and strong he is—And you may be Sure
he Can have plenty tobacco and told me to mention it to Tim
Murphy—and as to the girls that used to be troting on the bogs
at home to hear them talk English would be of great astonishment
to you

Dear friends we mean to let you know them that came out here
Denis and Tade Reen Tade Leary Dan Guiney and family Paddy
Sheehan John Keeffe and Sister Denis and Ellen Duggan   we have
plenty work at Six Shillings a day thats equal to 3 shillings of your
Money   we would get a Dollor a day in Diffirent places but we
would Sooner be all together   But if Dan Guiney got to Detroit
and that he might get a better Chance he will acquaint us of it

we left John and James Danihy after us in New York they would
be out with us But James had to go out to Ellen to Orange County
in York state She Being the first person that was Employed Kate
is in New York with her Brothers Madge Duggan is out in Jersey
Mary Reen went to Boston   Betty Murphy and Mary Leary went
out to Tade Houlihan with Davy Connell   Jonoah Murphy in New
York.[3]

Daniel Guiney means to forward a few lines to Patsey Leary
Patrick My Dear friend i am sorry to say that i had to part with
Johnny but still i am Glad to let you know that he is to be received
by his Cousins   when we Came to New York I wrote a letter to
John Dailey   But he wrote Back to me directly and wanted me to
go out to him   But he told me that there was no place fit for my
family but i could not go to him at present but I Expect to see him
in a short time   then Sir he stated to Me that Thomas Gnaw[?]
rote to him and stated to him if Johnny Came to his place to write

---

3 Almost two lines are crossed out here, but of these the words 'You all know
the reason why'—are decipherable. 'Jonoah Murphy in New York' is in
the same ink as that used for crossing out the two lines.

to him and that he would send him plenty money to fetch him out
and said that it was Jerry that wrote to him about it   Now Dear
Patrick I went with him to the train to see him Secured for Norfolk
Betsey Cronin and Jane Murphy were with him for Jack Daly
wrote to me to have Betty Cronin go out to him if she had not got a
place   So this is how we all are Scattered in the Country   Denis
Moynahan has taken a house in New York

Dear Patrick and Uncles   I Cannot say more at present until
I get to Detroit   But I hope you will let me know in the answer
of this letter how my Grandfather and Tim Murphy and family
are   No more from me at present.

John Keeffe Means to have his Brother write to him as soon as
posible and to let Know if his sister went to her husband to England
and also to have his father and Mother Make themself easy and that
as soon as he would have any thing earned that he would send them
some assistance

Ellen Duggan is in good health and wishes to know from her father
and Mother also

Denis Duggan wishes to know how his Dear Mother and family
are and Daniel Keliher and wife   Timothy Leary is all right   he
is in as good a health as ever he was and wishes to have his Mother
make her mind easy and he would wish to know if John Reen and
daughter got Married   Dear Mother you well know how I proved to
you at home and I expect to act so hereafter

Denis and Tade Reen   Dear Mother You may be sure that we
wont forget you we are in good health and with the help of God
we expect do something for you after a time   and John keep the
children to School and tell the Scannells if they wer here that they
would do first rate   Dear Uncles let me know if my Sister was
Delivered of a child and Likewise wher is My aunt Jude and also
if ther be any person in our house and what about Dan Danihy
and let us know all about the Crops

No More But remains your truly untill Death   one Letter will
do for us all

                              Daniel Guiny

(There were two postscripts.)

Mary Keeffe got two Dresses one from Mary Danihy & the other
from Biddy Matt

let ye write as soon as possible and Direct your letter to Jeremiah
Keliher Exchange Street Buffalo for Denis Danihy.

2

Envelope addressed

Michael Boyan Esqre., Kingwilliamstown Kanturk post office
County of Cork Ireland.
to be forwarded to Mr. Alexander MCarthy, of same place.

New York September 22nd. 1850.

My Dr. Father and Mother Brothers and Sisters

I write these few lines to you hopeing That these few lines may find
you all in as good State of health as I am in at present thank God
I Received your welcome letter To me Dated 22nd. of May which
was A Credit to me for the Stile and Elligence of its Fluent Language
but I must Say Rather Flattering My Dr. Father I must only say
that this a good place and A good Country for if one place does not
Suit A man he can go to Another and can very easy please himself
But there is one thing thats Ruining this place Especially the
Frontirs towns and Cities where the Flow of Emmigration is most
the Emmigrants has not money Enough to Take them to the Interior
of the Country which oblidges them to Remain here in York and
the like places for which Reason Causes the less demand for Labour
and also the great Reduction in wages for this Reason I would
advise no one to Come to America that would not have Some Money
after landing here that [would] Enable them to go west in case they
would get no work to do here but any man or woman without a
family are fools that would not venture and Come to this plentyful
Country where no man or woman ever Hungerd or ever will and
where you will not be Seen Naked, but I can asure you there are
Dangers upon Dangers Attending Comeing here but my Friends
nothing Venture nothing have Fortune will favour the brave have
Courage and prepare yourself for the next time that, that worthy
man Mr. Boyen is Sending out the next lot, and Come you all Together Couragiously and bid adiu to that lovely place the land of
our Birth. that place where the young and old joined Together
in one Common Union, both night and day Engaged in Innocent
Amusement, But alas. I am now Told its the Gulf of Miserary
oppression Degradetion and Ruin of evry Discription which I am
Sorry to hear of so Doleful a History to Be told of our Dr. Country
This my Dr. Father Induces me to Remit to you in this Letter 20

Dollars that is four Pounds thinking it might be Some Acquisiton to
you untill you might Be Clearing away from that place all together
and the Sooner the Better for Beleive me I could not Express how
great would be my joy at our seeing you all here Together where you
would never want or be at a loss for a good Breakfast and Dinner. So
prepare as soon as possible for this will be my last Remittince untill
I see you all here. Bring with you as much Tools as you can as it
will cost you nothing to Bring them And as for your Clothing you
need not care much But that I would like that yourself would Bring
one good Shoot of Cloth that you would spare until you come here
And as for Mary She need not mind much as I will have for her A
Silk Dress A Bonnet and Viel according and Ellen I need not mention
what I will have for her I can fit her well you are to Bring Enough
    Flannels and do not form it at home as the way the wear Flannel
at home and here is quiet different for which reason I would Rather
that you would not form any of it untill you Come, with the Exception of whatever Quantity of Drawers you may have you can
make tham at home But make them Roomly Enough But Make No
Jackets
    My Dr Father I am Still in the Same place but do not Intend to
Stop there for the winter. I mean to Come in to New York and there
Spend the winter   Thade Houlehan wrote to me Saying that if I
wished to go up the Country that he would send me money but I
declined so doing untill you Come and then after you Coming if you
thing it may be Better for us to Remain here or go west it will be for
you to judge but untill then I will Remain here   Dan Keliher
Tells me that you Knew more of the House Carpentery than he did
himself and he can earn from twelve to fourteen Shilling a day
that is seven Shilling British and he also Tells me that Florence
will do very well and that Michl can get a place Right off as you
will not be In the Second day when you can Bind him to any Trade
you wish And as for John he will Be Very Shortly able to Be Bound
two So that I have Every Reason to Believe that we will all do will
Together So as that I am sure its not for Slavery I want you to
Come here no its for affording My Brothers and Sisters And I an
oppertunity of Showing our Kindness and Gratitude and Comeing on
your Seniour days that we would be placed in that possision that
you my Dr. Father and Mother could walk about Lesuirly and
Indepenly without Requireing your Labour an object which I am
Sure will not fail even by Myself if I was oblidged to do it without
the assistance of Brother or Sister for my Dr. Father and Mother
    I am proud and happy to Be away from where the County Charges
man or the poor Rates man or any other Rates man would have the
Satisfaction of once Inpounding my cow or any other article of mine
Oh how happy I feel and am sure to have look as The Lord had not
it destined for [hole in paper probably obliterating 'me'] to get

married to Some Loammun or another at home that after a few months he and I may be an Incumberance upon you or perhaps in the poor house by this, So my Dr. Father according as I had Stated to you I hope that whilst you are at home I hope that you will give my Sister Mary that privelage of Injoying herself Innocently on any occation that She pleases so far as I have said Innocently and as for my Dr. Ellen I am in Raptures of joy when I think of one day Seeing her and you all at the dock in New York and if I do not have a good Bottle of Brandy for you Awaiting your arrival its a Causion.

Well I have only to tell My Dr. Mother to Bring all her bed Close and also to bring the Kittle and an oven and have handles to them and do not forget the Smoothing Irons and Beware when you are on board to Bring some good floor and Ingage with the Captain Cook and he will do it Better for you for very little and also Bring some whiskey and give them the Cook and Some Sailors that you may think would do you any good to give them a Glass once in a time and it may be no harm

And Dr. Father when you are Comeing here if you Possiblely can Bring My Uncle Con I would Be glad that you would and I am sure he would be of the greatest acquisision to you on board and also Tell Mary Keeffe that if her Child died that I will pay her passage very Shortly and when you are Comeing do not be frightened Take Courage and be Determined and bold in your Undertaking as the first two or three days will be the worst to you and mind whatever happens on board Keep your own temper do not speak angry to any or hasty the Mildest Man has the best chance on board So you make your way with evey one and further you are to speak to Mr. Boyan and he I am sure will get one Request for you Mr. Boyan wil [l d]o it for me, when you are to Come ask Mr. Boyan [to g]ive you a few lines to the Agent or Berth Master of the Ship that will Secure to you the Second Cabin which I am sure Mr. Boyan will do and as soon as you Receive this letter write to me and let me know about every thing when you are to come and what time and state Particulars of evry thing to me and Direct as before. And if you are to come Shortly when you come to Liberpool wright to me also and let me know when you are to sail and the name of the Ship you sail in as I will be uneasy untill I get an answer

No more at present But that you will give Mr. and Mrs Boyan my best love and respect And let me know how they and family are as they would or will not Be ever Better than I would wish them to be also Mrs. Milton and Charles Mr. and Mrs. Roche and family Mr. and Mrs. day and family Mr. Walsh and as for his family I sure are all well Mr. and Mrs. Sullivan and family Mrs. O Brien Con Sheehan wife and family all the Hearlihys and familys Tim Leahy and family own Sullivan of Cariganes and family Darby Guinee and family John Calleghan and family Timothy Calleghan and family Timothy Sheehan and Mother   So no more at present form your Ever Dear and Loveing Child

Margaret MCarthy.

3

[The following letter has no address, date or formal salutation.]

Daniel Duginn of Buffalo
I Should like to Know how is Johanna Dugin and familey Honnorah Murphy and familey if Denis Towmey Comes to America I will Garintee to him to have him and us be one in table Bed and work Patrick Cronin the Same Coreneles Coffee the same that is if they make up there minds to Come and if Timothy Murphy Sends his Dater I would recommend him to Sind her I want you to Mention to me how is Dinis Murpey and familey Offer hickey and familey
    No More at Present Wee remain your True and Affectinate friends untill Deth and after if Posible

Direct youre Letter to Mr. Denis O'Danihey of Buffalo City
Ery · [?] County State of New York
America

Write to us as quick as Posible in haiste

Buffalo City.

4

Michael Byrne from Boughill to Golding Bird Collector of Excise, Galway.

Sept. 13th 1848.

Hon. Sir,

Sir With submission I take the liberty of writing those few lines to you hoping to find your Honour in Good Health which leaves me and all the Emigrants at present I am to inform you of our safe arrival at Quebeck and we were recived most kindly at the Goverment office. Every promises that ever your Honour made to us was performed & Sir I have to let your Honour know that we had a safe and speedy passage which is A Consolation to you and which I am Bound to pray for you during my Days. I have to let you know in Conformity that we got A free passage to Monthreal I took the steamer from Monthreal to the lands of liberty And which I am to Inform your Honour that I am Employed in the rail road line earning 5s. a day of your Irish money And instead of being chained with poverty in Boughill I am crowned with glory and so I bless the day that you had come to Boughill And when I cannot return you no other thanks I write theese few lines of pleasure to you in Adoption to you and Family And I am better pleased to come to this country than if you bestowed me five Acres of land in Boughill.

I have to let your Honour know that all the Emigrants of Boughill has send you their best respect and blessing And we are in hopes that we will never die intil we see you once more And as this is A letter of pleasure to you I hope you will let the tenants of Boughill know of our safe arrival in America.

And as it is my first writing to you I am to let you know that I am Employed in Section 35 rail road lines Middlebury post office state of Vermounth.

No more at present but we all join in sending our loving friendship to you untill Death

I remain your most respectfully Micke [?] Byrne And I am your Humble and obedient Servient Michael Byrne.

This is Michael Killelea his hand writing Matheis[?] Killelea his son

To Golding Bird Esqure
    Galway

PASSENGER LIST OF SHIP "CATHERINE"
(August 14 – September 19, 1850)

(From a letter to L. Hensen & Co., Amsterdam, by Paulus den Bleyker, in "Paulus den Bleyker: Type and Prototype," by Timothy Rey, *Michigan Heritage*, II (1960), 15-16.)

Names	Age-Year	Month	Birthplace	Occupation	List
Paulus den Bleyker	45	8	Ouddorp of South Holland	Land owner	
Neeltjee Dogger Bleyker	39	4	Texel, N. Holland	None	
John den Bleyker	10	11	Texel, N. Holland	None	
Maartje den Bleyker	9	9			
Peter den Bleyker	2	6			
Diemmen den Bleyker		9			
Martje Bakker	21	8	Niewkerk, Groningen	Servant	7 persons
Jacob Dogger	37	4	Texel	Tailor	
Miss Groot	42	5	Texel	None	
Peter Dogger	2	11	Texel	None	3 persons
Albert Siersema	36	8	Ulrum, Groningen	Farm laborer	
Tryntje Dogger	28	7	Texel	None	
Katarina Maria Siersema	3	11	Texel	None	
Deuwertje Siersema	1		Texel	None	4 persons
Sakum Dogger	26	7	Texel	Farm laborer	
Fytje Kuiper	28	1	Texel	None	2 persons
Tonnes Van huise	25	10	Bedum, Groningen	Farm laborer	
Pietertje Kuiper	30		Texel	None	2 persons

Names	Age-Year	Month	Birthplace	Occupation	List
Jan Hoek	49	4	Ouddorp, South Holland	Day laborer	
Maartje Hameetman	40	5	Ouddorp	None	
Wouter Hoek	13	9	Ouddorp	Laborer	
Johanna Hoek	12	9	Ouddorp	None	
Jannetje Hoek	9	10	Sevenhuize, South Holland	None	
Job Hoek	7	10	Texel	None	
Pieternella Hoek	4	7	Texel	None	
Aagge Hoek	3	8	Texel	None	
Leendert Hoek	2	4	Texel	None	9 persons
H Groot	31	7	Besterhout, North Holland	Day laborer	1 person
Pieter Bakker					1 person
				Total	29 persons

A PASSENGER LIST OF MENNONITE IMMIGRANTS FROM RUSSIA IN 1878

Published from the Original Printed List

Among the documents in the Mennonite Historical Library at Goshen College is an original passenger list of the North German Lloyd steamer, "Strassburg," from Bremen to New York, sailing June 18, 1878. It came into the possession of the Library as part of the papers of the late John F. Funk of Elkhart, Indiana, who was most active in assisting the Russian Mennonite immigrants on their way to their new homes in the prairie states. As indicated at the head of the list, all Mennonites were steerage passengers, the customary passage used by poorer immigrants. The list is here reproduced in the original German form exactly as printed in the official passenger list in 1878. It may be of interest to note that among the passengers was Maria Wall, writer of the autobiographical sketch published in the REVIEW for April, 1941, under the title, "Childhood Reminiscences of a Russian Mennonite Immigrant Mother." —H. S. Bender.

Passagiere Liste

des

Post-Dampfschiffes, "Strassburg"

Capitain O. Heimbruch

von

BREMEN nach NEW YORK

am

16. Juni 1878.

ZWISCHENDECKS-PASSAGIERE

Johann Röpp	aus Kleefeld	nach Mountain Lake, Minn.
Suzanne Röpp	"	"
Johann Röpp	"	"
Susanne Röpp	"	"
Anna Röpp	"	"
Jakob Röpp	"	"
Peter Röpp	"	"
Jakob Harms	"	"
Anna Harms	"	"
Johann Harms	"	"
Margar. Harms	"	"
Peter Harms	"	"
Elisah. Voth	"	"
Benjamin Ratzlaff	"	nach Sutton, Neb.
Helene Ratzlaff	"	"
Justina Ratzlaff	"	"
Abraham Ratzlaff	"	"

Peter Ratzlaff	„	„
Johann Ratzlaff	„	„
Sara Ratzlaff	„	„
Bernhard Ratzlaff	„	„
Maria Ratzlaff	„	„
Peter Ratzlaff	„	„
Maria Wall	aus Alexanderthal	nach Halstead, Kans.
Kornelius Wall	„	„
Justina Wall	„	„
Margar. Wall	„	„
Heinrich Balzer	„	nach Mountain Lake, Minn.
Katharina Balzer	„	„
Katharina Balzer	„	„
Jakob Balzer	„	„
Susanne Balzer	„	„
Peter Balzer	„	„
Aron Pukkau	„	„
Margaretha Pukkau	„	„
Aron Pukkau	„	„
Simeon Pukkau	„	„
Anna Pukkau	„	„
Gerhard Pukkau	„	„
Jakob Hildebrand	„	nach Burton, Kans.
Aganeta Hildebrand	„	„
Jacob Hildebrand	„	„
Anna Hildebrand	„	„
Heinrich Hildebrand	„	„
Katharina Hildebrand	„	„
Aganeta Hildebrand	„	„
Peter Hildebrand	„	„
Jakob Schmidt	„	„
Elisabeth Schmidt	„	„
Jakob Schmidt	„	„
Elisabeth Schmidt	„	„
Peter Schmidt	„	„
Sara Schmidt	„	„
Johann Schmidt	„	„
Gerhard Friesen	aus Fürstenwerder	nach Newton, Kans.
Maria Friesen	„	„
Johann Friesen	„	„
Johann Hooge	„	nach Sutton, Neb.
Anna Hooge	„	„
Gertrude Hooge	„	„
Johann Harder	„	„
Helene Harder	„	„
Maria Harder	„	„
Helene Harder	„	„
Kornelius Wiens	„	nach Mountain Lake, Minn.
Helene Wiens	„	„
Kornelius Wiens	„	„
Johann Wiens	„	„

Peter Wiens	„	„
Helene Wiens	„	„
Franz Wiens	„	„
Diedrich Thiessen	„	„
Anna Thiessen	„	„
Anna Thiessen	„	„
Johann Wall	aus Alexanderthal	nach Halstead, Kans.
Margaretha Wall	„	„
Johann Wall	„	„
Maria Wall	„	„
Johann Wall	„	„
Peter Wall	„	„
Maria Wall	„	„
Peter Wall	„	„
Johann Wall	„	„
Anna Wall	„	„
Kornelius Neufeld	aus Lichtfelde	nach Mountain Lake, Minn.
Margaretha Neufeld	„	„
Kornelius Neufeld	„	„
Margaretha Neufeld	„	„
Peter Regier	aus Neukirch	nach Newton, Kans.
Anna Regier	„	„
Jacob Penner	aus Prangenau	nach Peabody, Kans.
Anna Penner	„	„
Anna Penner	„	„
Elisab. Penner	„	„
Helena Penner	„	„
Jacob Penner	„	„
Heinrich Penner	„	„
Peter Penner	„	„
Franz Heinrich	„	„
Kornelius Penner	„	nach Burton, Kans.
Elisabeth Penner	„	„
Nikolai Penner	„	„
Kornelius Braun	aus Elisabeththal	„
Frau Braun	„	„
Johann Franz	aus Alexanderthal	nach Mountain Lake, Minn.
Susanne Franz	„	„
Martin Franz	„	„
Susanne Franz	„	„
Anna Franz	„	„
Kornelius Franz	„	„
Peter Franz	„	„
Johann Franz	„	„
Wittwe Janzen	„	„
Isaak Wall	aus Pordenau	nach Sutton, Neb.
Elisab. Wall	„	„
Isaak Wall	„	„
Anna Wall	„	„
Gerhard Lohrenz	aus Marienthal	„
Helena Lohrenz	„	„

Gerhard Lohrenz	„	„
David Lohrenz	„	„
Maria Lohrenz	„	„
Helena Lohrenz	„	„
Anna Lohrenz	„	„
Peter Lohrenz	„	„
Abraham Regehr	„	„
Sara Regehr	„	„
Abraham Regehr	„	„
Isaak Regehr	„	„
Gerhard Regehr	„	„
Theodor Nickel	aus Rudnerweide	nach Mountain Lake, Minn.
Anna Nickel	„	„
Theodor Nickel	„	„
Helena Nickel	„	„
Peter Nickel	„	„
Anna Nickel	„	„
Wilhelm Nickel	„	„
David Nickel	„	„
Anna Nickel	„	„
Gertrude Nickel	„	„
Johann Becker	„	„
Aganeta Becker	„	„
Aganeta Becker	„	„
Maria Becker	„	„
Helena Becker	„	„
Johann Becker	„	„
David Becker	„	„
Jakob Becker	„	„
Abraham Becker	„	„
Peter Becker	„	„
Peter Kliewer	„	„
Frau Kliewer	„	„
Anna Kliewer	„	„
Susanna Kliewer	„	„
Helena Kliewer	„	„
Johann Sudermann	„	nach Burton, Kans.
Elisabeth Sudermann	„	„
Jakob Sudermann	„	„
Leonhard Sudermann	„	„
Bernhard Gerbrand	aus Grossweide	„
Katharina Gerbrand	„	„
Anna Gerbrand	„	„
Bernhard Gerbrand	„	„
Jakob Friesen	„	nach Sutton, Neb.
Sarah Friesen	„	„
Sarah Friesen	„	„
Gerhard Friesen	„	„
Peter Friesen	„	„
Jakob Friesen	„	„
Franz Friesen	„	„

Wittwe Ewert	„	nach Mountain Lake, Minn.
Jakob Ewert	„	„
Aganeta Ewert	„	„
Helena Ewert	„	„
Wilhelm Ewert	„	„
David Ewert	„	„
Abraham Ewert	„	„
Elisab. Ewert	„	„
Heinrich Schröder	aus Sparrau	nach Halstead, Kans.
Katharina Schröder	„	„
Peter Schröder	„	„
Susanna Schröder	„	„
Sahra Schröder	„	„
Katharina Schröder	„	„
Abraham Unruh	„	„
Eva Unruh	„	„
Peter Unruh	„	„
Julia Unruh	„	„
Cornelius Wall	aus Konteniusfeld	nach Grafton, Neb.
Aganeta Wall	„	„
Kornelius Wall	„	„
Elisabeth Wall	„	„
Aganeta Wall	„	„
Johann Wall	„	„
Gerhard Wall	„	„
Kornelius Unruh	aus Mariawohl	nach Yankton, Dak.
Sarah Unruh	„	„
Jakob Unruh	„	„
Katharina Unruh	„	„
Johann Regeln	„	„
Jakob Pauls	„	„
Anna Unruh	„	„
Kornelius Unruh	„	„
Peter Dück	„	„
Katharina Dück	„	„
Peter Dück	„	„
Susanna Dück	„	„
Heinrich Dück	„	„
Isaak Dück	„	„
Johann Peters	aus Nikolaidorf	nach Sutton, Neb.
Helena Peters	„	„
Jakob Peters	„	„
Diedrich Peters	„	„
Helena Peters	„	„
Aganeta Peters	„	„
Johann Peters	„	„
Helena Peters	„	„
Maria Peters	„	„
Johann Peters	„	„
Helena Peters	„	„
Elisabeth Peters	„	„

Aron Reimer	„	nach Mountain Lake, Minn.
Maria Reimer	„	„
Helena Reimer	„	„
Susanna Reimer	„	„
Johann Reimer	„	„
Heinrich Reimer	„	„
Justina Reimer	„	„
Cornelius Dück	aus Margenau	nach Sutton, Neb.
Justina Dück	„	„
Justina Dück	„	„
Franz Dück	„	„
Elisabeth Dück	„	„
Cornelius Dück	„	„
Johann Dück	„	„
Helene Dück	„	„
Helene Dück	„	„
Franz Dück	„	„
Anna Dück	„	„
Margaretha Dück	„	„
Johann Dück	„	„
Bernhd. Kröker	„	„
Katharina Kröker	„	„
Helene Kröker	„	„
Maria Kröker	„	„
Wittwe Quapp	„	„
Heinrich Ott	„	„
Heinrich Harms	„	nach Peabody, Kans.
Katharina Harms	„	„
Maria Harms	„	„
Johann Harms	„	„
Katharina Harms	„	„
Jakob Görzen	aus Fürstenwerder	nach Mountain Lake, Minn.
Maria Görzen	„	„
Johann Görzen	„	„
Abraham Görzen	„	„
Justina Görzen	„	„
Kornelius Görzen	„	„
Isaak Görzen	„	„
Franz Görzen	„	„
Diedrich Görzen	„	„
Diedrich Peters	„	nach Sutton, Neb.
Helena Peters	„	„
Helena Peters	„	„
Diedrich Peters	„	„
Kornelius Peters	„	„
Margaretha Peters	„	„
Jakob Peters	„	„
Johann Peters	„	„
Isaak Peters	„	„
Abraham Peters	„	„
Isaak Bärgen	„	„

Sahra Bärgen	,,	,,
Gerhard Fast	,,	,,
Sarah Fast	,,	,,
Isaak Fast	,,	,,
Katharina Fast	,,	,,
Abraham Fast	,,	,,
Kornelius Fast	,,	,,
Jakob Fast	,,	,,
Gerhard Fast	,,	,,
Johann Fast	,,	,,
Klaas Fast	,,	,,
Peter Dück	,,	nach Burton, Kans.
Maria Dück	,,	,,
Maria Dück	,,	,,
Peter Duck	,,	,,
Wilhelm Schirling	,,	nach Newton, Kans.
Anna Schirling	,,	,,
Abraham Schirling	,,	,,
Elisab. Schirling	,,	,,
Aganeta Schirling	,,	,,
Heinrich Pauls	,,	nach Burton, Kans.
Elisabeth Pauls	,,	,,
Heinrich Pauls	,,	,,
Henriette Pauls	,,	,,
Helena Pauls	,,	,,
Franz Pauls	,,	,,
David Pauls	,,	,,
Justina Pauls	,,	,,
Susanna Pauls	,,	,,
Peter Kröker	,,	,,
Helena Kröker	,,	,,
Klaas Kröker	,,	,,
Anna Kröker	,,	,,
Peter Kröker	,,	,,
Heinrich Kröker	,,	,,
Helena Kröker	,,	,,
Katharina Kröker	,,	,,
Gerhard Neufeld	aus Alexanderwohl	nach Mountain Lake, Minn.
Justina Neufeld	,,	,,
Gerhard Neufeld	,,	,,
Isaak Neufeld	,,	,,
Johann Neufeld	,,	,,
Peter Neufeld	,,	,,
Jacob Neufeld	,,	,,
Heinrich Neufeld	,,	,,
Jacob Mierau	aus Gnadenheim	nach Sutton, Neb.
Elisabeth Mierau	,,	,,
Jacob Mierau	,,	,,
Peter Mierau	,,	,,
Abraham Mierau	,,	,,
Katharina Mierau	,,	,,

Susanne Mierau	„	„
Johann Mierau	„	„
Heinrich Mierau	„	„
Gerhard Janzen	„	„
Helena Janzen	„	„
Maria Janzen	„	„
Katharina Janzen	„	„
Gerhard Janzen	„	„
Johann Janzen	„	„
Helena Janzen	„	„
Jakob Janzen	„	„
Peter Janzen	„	„
Franz Wiens	„	„
Frau Wiens	„	„
Franz Wiens	„	„
Maria Wiens	„	„
Susanna Wiens	„	„
Klaas Wiens	„	„
Jakob Wiens	„	„
Johann Pankratz	„	nach Newton, Kans.
Margaretha Pankratz	„	„
Gerhard Pankratz	„	„
Johann Pankratz	„	„
Heinrich Pankratz	„	„
Maria Pankratz	„	„
Johann Friesen	„	„
Isaak Schulz	aus Friedensdorf	nach Mountain Lake, Minn.
Frau Schulz	„	„
Isaak Schulz	„	„
Maria Schulz	„	„
Wilhelm Schulz	„	„
Sahra Schulz	„	„
Abraham Willms	„	nach Newton, Kans.
Elisabeth Willms	„	„
Margaretha Willms	„	„
Abraham Willms	„	„
Aganeta Willms	„	„
Elisabeth Willms	„	„
Peter Warkentin	„	nach Beatrice, Neb.
Wilhelmine Warkentin	„	„
Wilhelmine Warkentin	„	„
Peter Warkentin	„	„
Helena Warkentin	„	„
Justina Warkentin	„	„
Gerhard Warkentin	„	„
Elisabeth Warkentin	„	„
Peter Kliewer	aus Hierschau	nach Burton, Kans.
Eva Kliewer	„	„
Peter Kliewer	„	„
Heinrich Kliewer	„	„
Elisabeth Kliewer	„	„

Wittwe Susanne Kliewer	„	„
Friederike Kliewer	„	„
Wilhelmine Kliewer	„	„
Isaak Töws	„	nach Sutton, Neb.
Elisabeth Töws	„	„
Gerhard Töws	„	„
Isaak Töws	„	„
Peter Voth	aus Liebenau	nach Mountain Lake, Minn.
Katharina Voth	„	„
Abraham Voth	„	„
Katharina Voth	„	„
Diedrich Voth	„	„
Maria Voth	„	„
Sussanna Voth	„	„
Peter Voth	„	„
Elisabeth Voth	„	„
Heinrich Balzer	„	nach Newton, Kans.
Frau Balzer	„	„
Johann Regehr	aus Fürstenau	nach Mountain Lake, Minn.
Anna Regehr	„	„
Katharina Regehr	„	„
Johann Regehr	„	„
Peter Sawatzki	„	„
Frau Sawatzki	„	„
Elisabeth Sawatzki	„	„
Gerhard Sawatzki	„	„
Justina Sawatzki	„	„
Wilhelm Nickel	„	„
Maria Nickel	„	„
Maria Nickel	„	„
Peter Teichgröb	„	„
Anna Teichgröb	„	„
Hermann Teichgröb	„	„
Susanna Teichgröb	„	„
Peter Teichgröb	„	„
Anna Teichgröb	„	„
Katharina Teichgröb	„	„
Maria Teichgröb	„	„
Justina Teichgröb	„	„
David Janzen	aus Fischau	nach Sutton, Neb.
Anna Janzen	„	„
Johann Janzen	„	„
David Janzen	„	„
Heinrich Janzen	„	„
Agatha Janzen	„	„
Anna Janzen	„	„
Elisabeth Janzen	„	„
Aganeta Janzen	„	„
Wittwe Kornelsen	„	„
Jakob Schierling	„	„
Jakob Schierling	„	„
Anna Schierling	„	„

Elisabeth Schierling	,,	,,
Aganeta Schierling	,,	,,
Johann Schierling	,,	,,
Diedrich Schierling	,,	,,
Sarah Dörksen	,,	,,
Johann Enns	,,	,,
Agatha Enns	,,	,,
Agatha Enns	,,	,,
Abraham Nickel	aus Lichtenau	nach Newton, Kans.
Frau Nickel	,,	,,
Abraham Nickel	,,	,,
Katharina Nickel	,,	,,
Jakob Nickel	,,	,,
Anna Nickel	,,	,,
Justina Nickel	,,	,,
Aron Warkentin	aus Blumstein	nach Burton, Kans.
Helena Warkentin	,,	,,
Abraham Warkentin	,,	,,
Katharina Warkentin	,,	,,
Jakob Friesen	,,	,,
Frau Friesen	,,	,,
Katharina Friesen	,,	,,
Jakob Friesen	,,	,,
Helena Friesen	,,	,,
Johann Friesen	,,	,,
Gerhard Friesen	,,	,,
Sarah Friesen	,,	,,
Hermann Friesen	,,	
Franz Günther	,,	nach Yankton, Dak.
Frau Günther	,,	,,
Franz Günther	,,	,,
Maria Günther	,,	,,
Gerhard Günther	,,	,,
Anna Günther	,,	,,
Franz Kröker	,,	,,
Katharina Kröker	,,	,,
Franz Kröker	,,	,,
Jacob Kröker	,,	,,
Johann Kröker	,,	,,
Heinrich Kröker	,,	,,
Jacob Peters	aus Nikolaithal	nach Sutton, Neb.
Elisabeth Peters	,,	,,
Daniel Peters	,,	,,
Jacob Peters	,,	,,
Peter Peters	,,	,,
Elisabeth Peters	,,	,,
Kornelius Peters	,,	,,
Heinrich Peters	,,	,,
Johann Peters	,,	,,
Peter Dalke	aus Tiegerweide	,,
Sarah Dalke	,,	,,
Abraham Dalke	,,	,,

Heinrich Dalke	„	„
Johann Dalke	„	„
Kornelius Dalke	„	„
Franz Dalke	„	„
Sarah Dalke	„	„
Katharina Dalke	„	„
Peter Dalke	„	„
Peter Warkentin	aus Altonau	nach Newton, Kans.
Frau Warkentin	„	„
Susanna Warkentin	„	„
Johann Warkentin	„	„
Frau Warkentin	„	„
Johann Warkentin	„	„
Helena Warkentin	„	„
Abraham Willms	aus Rückenau	nach Yankton, Dak.
Agatha Willms	„	„
Abraham Willms	„	„
Maria Willms	„	„
Anna Willms	„	„
Johann Willms	„	„
Helena Willms	„	„
Jakob Willms	„	„
Katharina Willms	„	„
Johann Dörksen	aus Gnadenthal	nach Newton, Kans.
Aganeta Dörksen	„	„
Maria Dörksen	„	„
Johann Dörksen	„	„
Heinrich Dörksen	„	„
Helena Dörksen	„	„
Peter Dörksen	„	„
Katharina Dörksen	„	„
Cornelius Dörksen	„	„
Aganeta Dörksen	„	„
Gerhard Dörksen	„	„
Eva Dörksen	„	„
Anna Dörksen	„	„
Susanna Dörksen	„	„
David Dörksen	„	„
Gerhard Neufeld	„	nach Burton, Kans.
Margaretha Neufeld	„	„
Susanna Neufeld	„	„
Gerhard Neufeld	„	„
Peter Neufeld	„	„
David Neufeld	„	„
Jakob Neufeld	„	„
Gerhard Dörksen	„	„
Benjamin Wedel	aus Wernersdorf	nach Newton, Kans.
Benjamin Wedel	„	„
Elisabeth Wedel	„	„
Peter Wedel	„	„
Abraham Wedel	„	„
Anna Wedel	„	„

Elisabeth Wedel	„	„
Peter Görzen	aus Fürstenwerder	nach Mountain Lake, Minn.
Susanna Görzen	„	„
Peter Görzen	„	„
Susanna Görzen	„	„
Helena Görzen	„	„
Kornelius Görzen	„	„
Elisabeth Görzen	„	„
Maria Görzen	„	„
Johann Nickel	aus Grossweide	nach Yankton, Dak.
Frau Nickel	„	„
Jacob Nickel	„	„
Johann Nickel	„	„
Abraham Nickel	„	„
Diedr. Friesen	aus Taschenak	nach Mountain Lake, Minn.
Anna Friesen	„	„
Katharina Friesen	„	„
Bernhard Friesen	„	„
Diedrich Friesen	„	„
Anna Friesen	„	„
Jakob Vogt	aus Pastwa	„
Anna Vogt	„	„
Aganeta Vogt	„	„
Agatha Vogt	„	„
Kornelius Janzen	aus Franzthal	„
Sarah Janzen	„	„
David Janzen	„	„
Sarah Janzen	„	„
Aganeta Janzen	„	„
Aganeta Friesen	„	„
Jakob Köhn	aus Waldheim	nach Newton, Kans.
Frau Köhn	„	„
Johann Köhn	„	„
Jakob Köhn	„	„
Peter Köhn	„	„
Anna Köhn	„	„
Elisabeth Köhn	„	„
Katharina Köhn	„	„
Klaas Regehr	aus Klippenfeld	nach Sutton, Neb.
Maria Regehr	„	„
Maria Regehr	„	„
Gerhard Fast	„	„
Elisabeth Fast	„	„
Susanna Fast	„	„
Elisabeth Fast	„	„
Helena Fast	„	„
Gerhard Fast	„	„
Johann Fast	„	„
Jakob Wurms	aus Ladekopp	„
Katharina Wurms	„	„
Anna Wurms	„	„
Katharina Wurms	„	„

Helena Wurms	"	"
Jakob Wurms	"	"
Johann Penner	aus Schunuk	nach Yankton, Dak.
Margaretha Penner	"	"
Jakob Penner	"	"
Margaretha Penner	"	"
Johann Penner	"	"
Katharina Penner	"	"
Peter Penner	"	"
Maria Penner	"	"
Elisabeth Penner	"	"
Helena Penner	"	"
Heinrich Penner	"	"
Peter Engelbrecht	"	"
Anna Engelbrecht	"	"
Maria Engelbrecht	"	"
Jacob Engelbrecht	"	"
Anna Engelbrecht	"	"
Peter Engelbrecht	"	"
Elisabeth Engelbrecht	"	"
Helena Engelbrecht	"	"
Peter Dück	aus Rudnerweide	"
Johann Unruh	aus Elisabeththal	nach Peabody, Kans.
Maria Unruh	"	"
Heinrich Unruh	"	"
Adelgunde Unruh	"	"
Johann Unruh	"	"
Susanna Unruh	"	"
Klaas Unruh	"	"
Peter Unruh	"	"
Helena Unruh	"	"
Maria Unruh	"	"
Katharina Unruh	"	"
Kornelius Wall	aus Konteniusfeld	nach Grafton, Neb.
Sarah Wall	"	"
Katharina Wall	"	"
Helena Wall	"	"
Anna Wall	"	"
Aganeta Wall	"	"
Gerhard Enns	"	"
Johann Regehr	aus Wernersdorf	nach Mountain Lake, Minn.
Maria Regehr	"	"
Katharina Regehr	"	"
Anna Regehr	"	"
Margaretha Regehr	"	"
Sarah Regehr	"	"
Justina Regehr	"	"
Eva Regehr	"	"
Kornelius Regehr	"	"
Heinr. Kröker	aus Fürstenwerder	nach Sutton, Neb.
Sarah Kröker	"	"
Heinrich Kröker	"	"

Peter Friesen	aus Hierschau	„
Anna Friesen	„	„
Peter Friesen	„	„
Jacob Friesen	„	„
Helena Friesen	„	„
Katharina Friesen	„	„
Franz Friesen	„	„
Anna Friesen	„	„
Gerhard Friesen	„	„
Susanna Friesen	„	„
Diedrich Löwen	aus Kleefeld	nach Mountain Lake, Minn.
Frau Löwen	„	„
Heinrich Löwen	„	„
Diedrich Löwen	„	„
Elisabeth Löwen	„	„
Katharina Löwen	„	„
Peter Löwen	„	„
Sarah Löwen	„	„
David Schmidt	aus Waldheim	nach Sutton, Neb.
Eva Schmidt	„	„
Heinrich Schmidt	„	„
Maria Schmidt	„	„

SCRAPS & SPLINTERS

MARRIAGES OF EMIGRANTS TO VIRGINIA

The following marriages taken from Volume XIV of the Hampshire, England, marriages, p. 32, may be of interest:

Newport, Isle of Wight, Parish Registers begin 1541: p. 32, 11 Feb. 1620-21, Henry Bushell & Alice Crocker, Christopher Cradocke & Alice Cooke, Edward Marshall & Mary Michell, Walter Beare & Ann Greene, Robert Gullever & Joan Pie. "All which last fyve coupple were for virgenia".

Winifred Lovering Holman,
39 Winston Ave., Watertown, Mass.

PASSENGERS ON THE *GRIFFIN,* JUNE 23, 1675

[Excerpted from "Fenwick, Adams, Hedge, and Champneys, of Salem, N.J.," by Lewis D. Cook, in *The Genealogical Magazine of New Jersey,* XXXV (1960), 108.]

The Shipp called the Griffin arrived in Dellaware River, in wᶜʰ sᵈ shipp Came the p[er]sons hereafter named, being the first English Shipp yᵗ was bound to this part of ye p[ro]vince. Imprms John ffenwick, Esqr., of the County of Berks late p[ro]prietʳ of Salem Tenth in the p[ro]vince of New West Jersey, deceased. with him 3 Daughters Elizabeth, Anna & Presilia. Alsoo John Adams husband to the sᵈ Elizabᵗʰ, of Redding in the County of Berks, Weavor & 3 Childʳⁿ Elizabeth Aged 11 yrs ffenwick aged 9 yeares, & Mary Adams aged 4 years. Edward Champneys, husband to the sᵈ Pres[illa] of Thornbury in the Countie of Gloster Joyner & 2 Childʳⁿᵉ John aged about [*blank*] years & Mary [*blank*] years ould . . .

PASSENGERS ON THE *GRIFFIN,* JUNE 23, 1675

[Excerpted from "Memoir of John Fenwicke, Chief Proprietor of Salem Tenth, New Jersey," by Robert G. Johnson, in *Proceedings of the New Jersey Historical Society,* IV (1849-1850), 61.]

I now for the present, take leave of Fenwicke and his difficulties and concernments while in England, to speak of his embarking and landing at Salem in West Jersey. Having all things in readiness he went on board the ship with his family, consisting of his three daughters, by his first wife, Elizabeth, Anna, and Priscilla, and his housekeeper Mary White; also, John Adams, the husband of Elizabeth, with their three children—Elizabeth Fenwicke and Priscilla; also, Edward Champneys, the husband of Priscilla, with two children—John and Mary, with their servants, viz: Robert Turner, Gervas Bywater, William Wilkenson, Joseph Worth, Michael Eaton, Eleanor Geere, Ruth Geere, Zachariah Geere, Sarah Hutchins—these were the servants of Fenwicke—and Mark Reeve, Edward Webb, and Elizabeth Waits, the servants of Champneys. Anna Fenwicke, his daughter, some short time after their arrival married Samuel Hedge. They all arrived at Salem on the 23d of June, 1675, in the ship called the Griffin, Capt. Robert Griffith.

PASSENGERS FOR NEW ENGLAND.

" Wee vnderwritten being now bound
from London to New England doe attest
that on this day ye Date hereof wee
together with Nicholas Hayward Notary
Publique of this Citty were prefent and
did See mr John Chamberlain & Robert
Willfey and Thomafin Jenney Make
Oath in due form vpon ye holy Evange-
lists to ye Tenour of ye aforegoing depo-
fitions by them Signed before the Right
Honourable Sr John Peake Knight Lord
Mayor of ye City of London and this wee
will Seueraly affirm upon Our Oathes
when it shall pleafe God wee ariue in
New England if thereunto Required wit-
nefs Our hands in London ye 31 of May
1687.   John Balston
                              John Herring
                              Sarah Brickenate
                              Samuel Hayward "
—*Essex Registry of Deeds, book* 11, *leaf* 28.

PASSENGERS FROM THE RHINELAND TO
PENNSYLVANIA

PASSENGERS FROM THE RHINELAND TO PENNSYLVANIA. *The Pennsylvania Gazette* of March 22, 1732-3, thus called the attention of fifteen derelict passengers to the stern rule of life and the sea, in German as well as English: " Those Palatines who came Passengers from Rotterdam, in the Ship John and William, Constable Tymberton, Commander, and have not yet paid their Passages, nor given Security, are hereby required to make speedy Payment, or to give good Security to Mr. George McCall, Merchant in Philadelphia; otherwise they may expect to be prosecuted as the Law directs. Their names are as follows: Hans Emich, Stephen Matts, Frederich Kooler, Michael Bloemhower, Hans Peter Brechbill, Hans Brechbill, Philip Melchoir, Nicholas Pashon, George Adam Stees, Abraham Diebo, Matthais Manser, Hans Riel, Caspar Willaar, Philip Melchoir Meyer, John George Wahnzodel." In those days, according to an old opera, No Song, No Supper.—H. E. G.

LIST OF CONVICTS FROM BRISTOL TO
SOUTH CAROLINA [1728]

[Excerpted from "The White Indentured Servants of South Carolina," by Theodore D. Jervey, in *The South Carolina Historical and Genealogical Magazine*, XII (1911), 171.]

List of Convicts Imported from Bristol to the province of S°. Carolina on board the Ship called the Expedition John McKenzie was.

Edward Bond............... Convicted 4ᵗʰ. October 1726 Com. Wilts
                    Felony 7 Years.

Mary Walter
Henry Cooper
Eliz: Ends   }........Convicted 16ᵗʰ. March 1727. Com Wilts
Solomon Grar   Felony 7 Years.
John Moore
Wᵐ. Purnell Eod. Die...............Com Wilts...............petty Larceny.
John Dudson   }........Convicted 16 March 1727 Worcester
Thos. Oliver   Felony 7 Years.
Wᵐ. Thompson
Thoˢ. Smith   }........Convicted 24 Augˢᵗ.....................Worcester
Mary Deeley   Felony 7 Years.
Jane Lewis
Mary Robertson
Wᵐ. Vaughn
Sam: Foster   }........Convicted 14 Sepᵗ. 1728...............at Bristol
Robᵗ. Kates   Felony 7 Years.
Wᵐ. Fitchut
Wᵐ. Richardson ....Convicted 8 Janry 1728 ....at Bristol
                    Felony 7 Years.
John Evans
Joseph Ashton   }........Convicted 22ᵈ July 1728........at Gloucester
Ralph Phillips   Felony 14 Years.
Caleb Stowell   }........D°...................Felony 7 Years.
Mary Hillier

PHILADELPHIA ARRIVALS, 1738

PHILADELPHIA ARRIVALS, 1738.—In the Reynell Papers, recently acquired by The Historical Society of Pennsylvania, is an Invoice of goods shipped from London, July, 1738, on board the *Elizabeth*, Edward Kervell Master, for account of Daniel Flaxney and consigned to John Reynell, a Philadelphia merchant, the following indentured passengers: Listed as "7 Servants"—

> Jno. Cox, a Boy, 5 years
> John Richards, Gardner, 4 years
> Edw. Hancock, Butcher, 4 years
> Nth. Manton, Surgeon, 4 years
> Geo. Goodman, Butcher, 4 years
> Jno. West, Wool-comber, 4 years
> Jno. Kamb, Shoemaker, 4 years.

The passages, at £5. each, were charged on invoice at £35.0.0 and the "Clothes &c." at £3. each, or £21.0.0, making a total of £56.

This is the first instance which has come to my attention where servants were entered on an Invoice; and I have examined hundreds of such papers for the early eighteenth century.

HARROLD E. GILLINGHAM.

NATURALIZATION OF MARYLAND SETTLERS IN PENNSYLVANIA.

The reports of the Pennsylvania authorities to the British Board of Trade, copies of which are contained in the Pennsylvania Historical Library, show that the following Marylanders went to Pennsylvania for naturalization in the latter days of the Province, most of them being naturalized at York: 1767—Jacob Werryfield, Jacob Bowman, Christian Whitmore, John Yeager, Henry Inkle, Samuel Wolgamode and Paul Werkslagen, all affirmed; 1768—Frederick Cramer, Stephen Wink, Michael Miller, Conrad Fox, Jacob Snyder, Simon Schicky, and Jacob Miller, all affirmed; 1769—George Pooderbach, affirmed; 1770—Lawrence Shook, took oath; 1771—George Yerkardt and Peter Naffager, both affirmed; 1772—Michael Huber, Christopher Miller, and Philip Fishbourne, all took oath; and John Erdman Doritz and Henry Worman, both affirmed.

Those who affirmed were probably Dunkers or Mennonites.

LIST OF PASSENGERS AND CREW ON BOARD THE BRIGANTINE *MATTY*, FROM SCOTLAND TO NEW YORK, MAY 19–JULY 22, 1774

[Excerpted from "Journal of Colonel Alexander Harvey of Scotland and Barnet, Vermont," in *Proceedings of the Vermont Historical Society* (1921-1923), 204.]

I Alexander Harvie Entred aboard the Brigantin | Matty Captain Thomas Chochran master Robert | Buchannan / ,Mate. Alex^r Thomson, Alex^r Robertson | James Currel James forest Walter Mcfarlan | John [Peblor, in pencil, in another hand] Daniel Petter Craford John poke | Sailours: Ninian Scot Alexander Mciver Cab. | William Stirling His wife and two Childeren James | Mcgoun His wife and two Children James Wh | etlay Robert paul Marg^t paul M^{rs} paul | William Mcalpine John Mitchel John Clerk | John Graham Daniel Murray his wife and 3 | Childeren John Armstrong John Reid John | Waker Alexander Camery William and John | Mathies Rober Bartly James Fergueson J | Alexander Conie John Galbreath Arch^d Nesbet | James fergueson Robert Anderson Thomas Clerk | James Bryson William Aiken Charles Burt— | James Laird John Murdock Daniel ferguson | William Gelespie James Watson and wife John | Louden and wife William Bell and wife and | 2 childeren Robert Robertson wife and 1 | child. All pasangers William Watersone | Cook William Steell Margrat Robertson | John Reed Alexr Young Charles Burt. |

INDEX OF NAMES

---, Archibald 120
  Cecilia 399
  Con 509
  Ellen 505, 508, 509
  Florence 508
  Gustavus S. 121
  Jerry 506
  John 259, 260, 506, 508
  Johnny 505
  Jude 506
  Kate 505
  Mariane 104
  Mary 508
  Michl 508
  Patrick 505, 506
  Sally 294
  Sissel 399
..., James F. 280
...ity, James 284

-- A --

Aadland, Lars H 398
  M. K. 401, 402, 403, 406, 407
  Martha 407
  Mons 401, 402, 406, 407
  Mons Knudson 407
  Thomas 407
Aagagerh, Endré Osmunden
  410, 412, 416
Aamundsdatter, B 404
Aanunasen, I 429
Aaragerbö, Endre 416
  Herman Osmundson 416
Aasen, Andrew Anderson 393
  Einar 393, 394
  Einar Anderson 394
  Olena 393
Abbot, Joseph 262
Abbott, Martha 139
  Thomas 348
  Thomas M. 274
Abercorn, ---, Lord 296
Abercromby, James 348
  Robert 348
Ablecock, Elizabeth 443
Aboab, Joshua 155
Abraham, John 446
Abrahams, Solomon 154
Abrathar, Joseph 152
Acheson, Daniel, Sen. 348
  David, Jun. 348
  Mary 348
Acker, Henry 8
  Philip Jacob 8
Ackermahnn, Jacob 172
Ackerman, Geo. 165
Ackermann, Jacob 172
Adair, A 348
  Agnes 217
  Ann 217
  Jean 217
  Patrick 217
  William 115, 217

Wm. 348
Adam, Henry 240
Adams, Benedict L. 254
  Charles 332
  Elizabeth 530
  Elizabth. 530
  Fenwick 530
  Fenwicke 530
  John 249, 348, 530
  Mary 530
  Priscilla 530
  Thomas 262
  Wm. 296
Addison, --- 296
  Tho. 296
  Thos., Ensign 296
Addy, Solomon 165
Ade, Solomon 165
Adie, James 262
Adkins, David 192
Adland, Ellen Thompson 407
  Knud 407
  Martha 407
  Mons 401
  Thomas 407
Adler, Morris 262, 275
  Moses 262
Adolphus, Isaac 161, 163
Advowson, Bill 296
Adworth, --- 296
Aeggs, Hugh 348
Affray, Baletis 166
Aga, Jon Jonson 400
Age, Halstein 398
  Herborg 398
  John J. 398, 400
  Torbjore 398
Ageron, Anthony 106
Agg, John 262
Agnew, Alexander 217
  Deckey 348
  Edwd. Jones 296
  Forbes 217
  Fras. 296
  Janet 217
  John 296, 317
  Patk. 296
  William 217
  Wm. Kilwaughter 296
Agster, Jacob 239
Aguilar, Moses 154
Ahling, Anne 412
  Berthe Mathias 412
  Erik Osmond 412
  Guttorn 412
  Osmund Guterensen 412
  Osmundir 412
Ahmey, Frederick 262
Aigler, Jacob 262, 275
Aiken, Anne 332
  Jane 332
  William 534
Aikens, John 332
Aikin, John 348
Ailer, George 262
Aker, David 279

Akey, --- 296
Akin, Joseph 332
  Margaret 332
  Mary 332
  William 332
Alberthal, Balthasar 34
  Elisabeth Catharina 34
  Franz Nikolaus 34
  Johann Nickel 34
  Johann Nicklaus 34
  Nickellas 34
Albertthal, Franz Niclaus 34
  Johann Niclaus
Albrecht, Daniel 238
Albright, Daniel 238
  Joseph 3
Albuquerques, Daniel 155
Alchorn, Michael 332
Alcorn, --- 296
  Francis 332
  James 332
  John 332
  Joseph 332
Aldwell, Samuel 348
Alexander, Agnes 217
  Alexander 217
  Ann 217
  Anne 348
  Anne Jane 348
  Charles P. 263
  E. 348
  George 348
  Harriet 348
  Hugh 217, 291
  Hugh Small 348
  Isabella 348
  James 217, 348
  Jane 291, 348
  John 217, 296
  Marg. 332
  Margaret 348
  Margt. 296
  Mary Small 348
  Rich. 296
  Robert 217, 348
  Saml. M. 296
  Sarah 291, 296
  Sarah Jane 348
  Thomas 348
  Thos. 296
  William 263
  Wm. 296
Alferino, Phineas 156
Alges, John 332
Allan, Alexr. 200
Allcock, --- 296
Allen, --- 348
  ---, Lieut. Col. 296
  Agnes 348
  David 220
  Eliz. 348
  Erskine 269
  Ezekiel 269
  George 348
  Hannah 348
  Henry S. 348

James 348
Jane 348
Janet Stewart 220
John 296
Joseph 348, 372
Joshua 296
Margaret 372
Mary 348
Patk. 296
Peter 348
Peter H. 348
Robt. 296
Samuel 348
Thomas 348
Thos. 296
Tim. 296
William 372
Wm. 296
Alley, Stephen 293
Allman, Henrich 56
Allmann, Anna Elisabetha 55
   Anna Margretha 55
   Henrich 55
   Johann Henrich 55
   Johann Nicol 55
   Maria Barbara 55
   Maria Catharina 55
   Maria Elisabetha 55
   Maria Sara 55
Almeyda, Isaac Campos 153
   Rica Campos 154
Alne, K J 405
Alsop, Nathaniel 332
Altham, ---, Lord 296
Altschuh, Maria Catharina 47
Alvares, Moses 153
Alvaringa, Esther Da Costa 153
   Rachael 153
   Rachael Da Costa 153
Amact, John 348
Amatis, Nicholas 76
   Paul 76
Amberry, Catherine 471
Amberson, --- 330
   James 332
Ambrose, --- 296
Ammach, Christian 287
Amstutz, David 165
Amundsen, E. 404, 408
Anaestatter, Aad 390
   Anna 390
   Bertha Serina 390
   D. 390
   Ellen Sophia 390
   Gudmund 390
Anchersen, Thomas, Capt. 419,
   420, 421, 422, 423, 424,
   425, 428
Ancherson, Thomas 428
Anderras, Michael 62
Andersdatter, H. 403
   K 403
   M 403, 406
   Malinda 406
   S. 403, 404, 406
   Sarah 406
Anderson, --- 391, 395, 396
   ---, Mrs. 348
   A 348
   Alex. 296
   Alexander 348
   Amund 399, 408
   Andrew 394
   Ann 332
   Anna 431
   Anne 117
   Bjorn 408
   Chas. 296

Catherine 115, 332
Eliza 348
Elizabeth 133, 134
Frances 133, 134
George 133, 332
H 403
Hugh 332
Ingeborg 399
Jacob 383
James 139, 332, 348
Jane 348
Janet 221
Jas. 297
Jennet 332
John 133, 134, 139, 348
Joseph 348
K 403
Knud Anderson 383, 387
M. Ann 291
Malcolm 121
Margaret 133, 134, 348
Mary 115, 297
Ole 431
Patrick 115
Pige 396
Rasmus B. 393
Robert 534
Samuel 332
Susanna 394
T. 332
William 133, 134, 332, 348
Andoe, James 348
Andrar, Cornelius 286
Andrei, John (William) 250
Andres, Georg Michell 62
   Hanss Michell 62
   Maria Juditha 62
Andrews, Gabriel 332
   George 260, 348
   Grace 446
   John 297, 332
   Robert 348
   Robt., Jun. 348
   Saml. 297
   Solomon 446
   Thomas 192, 348
   William 191
   Wm., Jun. 348
   Wm., Sen. 348
Androhan, John 332
Aneesley, --- 320
Angus, William 217
Annesley, --- 297
   Fras. 297
   Maurice 297
Annis, ---, Mrs. 348
Annour, Eliza 297
   Marice 297
   Mary 297
   Saml. 297
   Wm. 297
Anstruther, ---, Capt. 297
   Alex., Ensign 297
   Rob., Ensign 297
Anthony, John 192
   William 332
Antrim, Alex., Earl of 297
Apel, Jonas 34
Apfel, Anna Catharina 42
   Georg 42
   Margaretha 42
Aplin, Rich., Ensign 297
Appeal, Barbary 165
   Magdalen 165
Appel, John 13
Applen, David 257
Appler, David 257, 275
Apples, David 257

Aragebo, Endre 410, 416
Archdall, Hen. 297
Archer, William 263, 265
Arcy, Patrick D. 348
Ardis, Alexander 349
Arenner, Bernard 332
Armbrust, John 328
Armbruster, Jacob 178
Armitage, John 332
Armstrong, --- 349
   Alex. 332
   Anna Mary 328
   Arabella 332
   Arm. 332
   Chr. 297
   Eliz. 332
   Eliza 332
   Fanny 349
   Hannah 297
   Hugh 349
   Isaac 332
   James 349
   Jasper 297
   John 332, 349, 534
   John French 248
   Marg. 332
   Mary 328
   Mich., Lieut. 297
   R. 332
   Robert 417
   Samuel 349
   Thos. 297
   Wm. 294, 332
Arner, Ulrich 12
Arney, Joseph 250
Arnold, Ansel 236
   Hugh, Lieut. 297
   J. 349
   James 349
   Johann Georg 20
   William 349
Arnott, John 250
Arnsen, A. 429, 436, 441
Arrie, Elisabeth 231
Arteser, John 263
Arthur, James 332
   Joseph 349
   Rebecca 349
   Robt. 297
Ash, ---, General 102
   Cath. 349
   Hen. 297
Ashe, Norman 466, 467
Ashley, Daniel 349
   Wm., Capt. 297
Ashton, Joseph 532
   Leonard 273
Askeland, --- 395
   Anders 394, 395, 396
   Andrew 395
   Pige 396
Askvig, Even 415
Aslaksdatter, B. 429, 435
Aslein, John 332
Asple, Pierce 349
Aston, Alex. 297
Atcheson, Adam 349
   Arth., Sir 297
   Hugh 332
Atchison, Nanny 297
Atkins, Mary 332
Atkinson, David 349
   Eliza 332
   Francis 349
   Henry 332
   James 332
   Jane 332
   Jas. 349

Atwater, John 380
Margaret Allen 378, 380, 383
Auchanan, John 349
Augas, Herman Osmunde 413, 416
Augenstein, Abraham 177
  Anna Maria 177
  Caspar 177
  Christian 177
  Hannss Georg 177
Augspourger, Samuel 113
Auld, James 332
  Margaret 332
  Mary 332
  Wm. 297
Auldjo, Alexr. 193
  John 193
Austin, Rebecca 349
  Thomas 349
Aylward, Pierce 246

-- B --

Baardsen, Lars 436
Baarsen, L. 429, 436
Babington, Phil., Capt. 297
  Wm. 297
Bac, Ulric 104
Bach, Albrecht, Sr. 43
  Johann Niclaus 43
  Juliana 43
  Nickel 43
  Niclaus 43
  Sebastian 43
Bache, Soren 425, 431, 434
  Uhrich 106
Bachelois, Batiste 104
  Francois 104
  Madeleine 101
  Marie 104
Bachelor, Francis 112
Bachman, Ulrick 165
Bachus, John 250
Bacon, Anthony, Capt. 137,
  138, 140
  Cath. 297
  John 332
  Mary 297
  Robt. 297
  Thomas 349
Bader, Israel 325
Baer, Caspar 51
  Maria Catharina 51
Baersen, Ane 413
Baertges, Georg 47
  Johann Georg 47
  Matthias 47
  Michael 47
Bagnall, Nichs. 297
Bahl, John 237
  Tobias 9
Bailey, Esther 332
  Jas. 297
Bailie, David 349
  Isabella 349
  James 349
  John 245, 349
  Mary Anne 349
  Robert 349
  Thomas 349
  William 349
  Wm. 297
Bailley, Jas. 297
Baillie, William 203
Bailly, J. 297
  Jas. 297
  Robt. 297

Baimbrick, Martin 332
Bain, Thomas 289
  William 208
Baird, George 349
  Samuel 349
  Washington 249
Baker, Conrad 263
  Fras. 297
  John 262
  John H. 278
Bakker, Martje 512
  Pieter 513
Baland, Thomas 349
Balbierer, Henrich 57
  Maria Barbara 57
  Philipp Nickel 57
Balbirer, Philliebs 57
Bald, Anna Elisabetha 46
  Anna Maria 46
  Niclaus 46
Balentine, Wm. 297
Ball, James 349
  Robert 275
Ballagh, James 349
  Robert 349
  Robert E. 349
Ballah, William 332
Ballantine, Wm. 297
Ballintine, Thos. 297
Balston, John 531
Balzer, ---, Frau 522
  Heinrich 515, 522
  Jakob 515
  Katharina 515
  Peter 515
  Susanne 515
Bamber, Margt. 297
  Robt. 297
Bambrick, Thomas 349
Banaki, Joseph 108
Banaquier, Joseph 108
Bands, Mary 190
Banecan, Christopher 332
Bankhead, --- 349
Banks, Thomas 349
Bannan, Peter 349
Bannin, John 349
Bannon, Ann 297
  Patk 297
Banz, Catharina 40
  Georg Michel 40
Barbadge, Thomas 349
Barbour, Matthew 349
Barcroft, John 263, 273
Bardier, Adam 44
  Carl Ludwig 44
  Sibilla 44
Bare, Samuel 349
Bares, Joseph 156
  Solomon 159
Bärgen, Isaak 519
  Sahra 520
Barker, Jacob 263, 271
  John 332
  Thomas 349
Barklie, L. 332
Barkly, Thos. 297
Barlien, Hans 410
Barlow, Agnes 297
Barnard, Robert 251, 275
Barnet, Wm., Lieut. 297
Barnett, James 349
  James R. 349
Barney, Patrick 332
Barns, William 332
Barquill, Wm 444
Barr, Jane 297
  John 332, 349

  Thomas 263
Barrell, ---, Col. 297
Barrios, Daniel Lopes 155
Barron, John P. 332
Barrow, --- 349
Barry, Ann 297
  Edward 349
  Elnr. 297
  Francis 263
  James 263, 332
  James Casey 349
  James D. 257
  John 332
  Mat. 297
  Richard 263
  Robert T. 263
  Sarah 297
Bartges, Johann Georg 29
  Matthias 29
  Michael 29
Barth, Anna Christina 124
  Anna Maria 124
  Johann Nikolaus 124
  Johannes 124
Bartjes, Michael 29, 47
Bartley, James 139
Bartly, Rober 534
Bartoun, Augustus 107
Bartsch, Hubertus 6
  John 6
Baskem, Silvain 230
Baskett, James 443
  Mary 443
  Richd. 443
  Wm. 443
Bassett, Asa L. 284
Bassler, Michael 327
Bastrop, --- 227
Bates, Thomas 263
Battefeldt, Johannes 170
Batteiger, Anna Eva 73
  Johann Peter 73
  Johann Valentin 58, 73
  Maria Eva 58, 73
  Peter 58
  Valentin 58, 73
Battenfeld, Johann 170
Batty, Eliza. 192
Baudemont, Andre 54
Bauer, Hans 33
Bauersachs, --- 62, 63
  Anna Elisabetha 72
  Anna Maria 57, 71, 72
  David 57
  Elisabetha 71
  Hans 72
  Hans David 72
  Hans Nichol 71
  Hans Nickel 71
  Johann 71, 72
  Johann David 71
  Johan Nickel 72
  Johann Nikolaus 72, 73
  Johann Valentin 72
  Johannes 72, 73
  Jöog Adam 72
  Magdalena 72
  Maria Barbara 72
  Maria Elisabeth 72
  Maria Elisabetha 71
  Nichel 71
  Paul 57, 71, 73
  Paulus 57, 71, 73
Bauersax, --- 71
Bauge, --- 402
  Thomas 402
Bauman, John Dieter 3
Baumann, Frantz Xaver 224

Baumgart, Anna 165
Baur, Anna Catharina 42
　Georg 42
　Jacob 42
Baussman, Johann Michel 36
　Michel 36
Baussmann, Michel 36
Baxter, Roger, Revd. 263
Bayer, Adam 32
　Andres 64
　Catharina 32
　Johann Matthias 47
　Johann Nikolaus 64
　Johann Philip 64
　Johann Philipp 61
　Marie 32
　Matthias 30, 47
　Matthias, Sr. 30
Bayle, Darby 293
　Jean 293
Bayley, John 349
Beall, Thomas 251
Bealton, Mary 115
Bean, Timothy 257
Bear, John 110
Beard, Ann 291
　Michael 240
Beardsley, Joseph 264
　Joseph, Jr. 264
Beare, Ann 529
　Walter 529
Bearns, --- 346
Beasley, George 264
Beaton, David 200
　Flora 201
Beattie, Andrew 349
Beatty, --- 298
　Agnes 217
　Alex. 332
　Dan. McNeill 297
　David 349
　Edwd. 297
　Elisa 349
　Elizabeth 417
　Elizth. Mary 297
　George 332
　Jane 332
　Jas. 349
　John 297
　Margt. 298
　Mary 217, 298
　Mary Ann 417
　Oliver 332
　Rich. 298
　William 217, 349
　Wm. 298, 332
Beauford, Wm., Capt.-Lieut.
　298
Beaumont, Andw. 298
　Jas. 298
　John, Dr. 298
Beblor, John 534
Beck, Anna Margaretha 20
　Conrad 167
　Heinrich 20
　Johan Loretz 54
　Johann Joerg 20
　Lorentz 54
Beckenbach, ---, widow 20
　Casper 21
　Georg Adam 21
　Georg Leonhardt 21
Beckenhaub, Adam 54
　Anna 54
　Hans Adam 54
　Jacob 54
Becker, Abraham 517
　Aganeta 517

Anna Margarethe 125
　David 517
　Helena 517
　Jacob 36
　Jakob 517
　Johann 517
　Maria 517
　Nikolaus 125
　Peter 517
Bede, George 264
Bednard, William 349
Beeler, Lewis 264
　Louis 277
Beelers, Lewis 275
Bccr, --- 7
Beerdatter, Elisabeth 411
Beerman, Thomas 349
Beesely, Moses 139
Beggs, Alex. 298
　James 349
　Margt. 298
　Wm. 298
Behan, James 349
Beherns, C K 403
　Christian K 402
Behn, --- 7
Behr, Jacob 170
　Johann Jacob 170
Behrens, C. K. 403
　Christian K. 385
Beier, Andres 64
　Anna Elisabeth 124
　Anna Maria 124
　Johann Andreas 124
　Johann Friedrich 124
　Johann Kasimir 124
　Johann Nikolaus 124
　Johann Wilhelm 124
Beil, Balthazar 13
Beir, Andres 64
Beisel, Peter 10
Belert, Anna 62
　Anna Margaretha 62
　Eva Margaretha 63
　Johann Adam 63
　Johann Christoph 63
　Johann Friderich 62
　Johann Michael 63
　Philipp Jacob 62
Bell, Abraham 349
　Alex. 298
　Charles 284
　Dav. 298
　David 332, 349
　Elizabeth 134
　Geo. 298
　George 349
　H. 349
　Jacob 332
　James 134, 332
　John 134, 298, 332, 349
　Margaret 134, 332
　Mary 332
　Mary C. 349
　Patience 298
　Rebecca H. 349
　Robt. 298
　Samuel 349
　Thomas 349
　Thomas C. 349
　Thos. 298
　William 332, 534
　Wm. 298, 349
Bellandine, Wm., Major 298
Bellgrove, Benjamin 140
Belt, Benjamin M. 251, 257
Belton, Janet 190
Belz, C. Adam 327

Benckle, Michael 50
Bendeker, Christian 166
Bender, Jacob 170, 263
Bene, John Rinehard 15
Benedickson, Halvor 432
Bennet, James 332
　Patrick 332
Bennett, George 444
　Thomas 349
　Walt. 298
　Z. 332
Benninger, Peter 20
Benningham, Eliza 349
　Thomas 349
Benson, Wm. 298
Benton, Sam'l 349
Benzehofer, Jacob 325
Ber, Caspar 51
Berecssen, Bertha 389
　Johannes 389
　Lars 389
Beresford, Tristram 298
Berg, Anna Margaretha 39
　Jacob 39
Bergemann, Henry 264
Berger, William 264
Bergersen, Halvar 388
　Martha 389
Bergin, Daniel 349
Bergman, J. H. C. 264
Bergslien, Eli Nilsdatter 441
Bernard, Elias 110
　Henry 255
　John, Sir 148
　Richard 349
Berney, Ellen 349
　Thomas 349
Beroth, Franz Ludwig 32, 33
　Susanna 32
Berry, Anna Elisabeth 64
　Anna Eva 64
　Anna Margaretha 64
　Edward 252
　Eva Christina 64
　Francis 349
　Isaak 64
　Johann Ludwig 64
　Maria Barbara 64
　Michael 349
　William 139
Berslien, E. N. 429, 436, 441
Berst, Anthony 264
Bertsch, Georg 178
Bertsh, George 326
Besch, Whilhelm 170
Besnard, Jno. 188, 191
Bessborough, ---, Lord 454
Best, Anthony 281
　George 332
　John 332
　Seragh 332
Bettle, Michel 17
Bettner, Godfrey 264
Betts, Margaret 139
Beverly, Eliza 349
Bey, --- 7
Beyer, Andres 64
　Anna Apollonia 64
　Anna Barbara 64
　Christoph 64
　Clara Elisabeth 64
　Eva Elisabeth 64
　Georg Jakob 64
　Johann Andreas 64
　Johann Martin 64
　Johann Nickel 29, 47
　Johann Nikolaus 64
　Johann Philipp 64

Johann Wendell 64
Kunigunde 64
Maria Elisabeth 64
Maria Magdalena 64
Martin 64
Matthias 29, 47
Thomas 64
Beyerle, Anna Barbara 50
Anna Catharina 46, 50
Anna Maria 46
Dieter 46
Frederick 46
Friedrich 46
Georg 50
Johann Diether 46
Johannes 46
Simon 46
Bibighausen, George 15
Bickford, John 298
Bickle, Adam 20
Biechtler, George 326
Biery, Joseph 15
Bietighoffer, Philipp 178
Bigam, Wm. 298
Bigan, Mores 298
Moses 298
Bigg, Boleyn 298
Biggam, Andrew 217
Hamilton 246
Jean 217
Mary 217
Thomas 217
William 218
Biggem, Wm. 298
Bigler, Paul Linsen 7
Bignell, Jane 192
Bignion, Joseph 92
Joseph, Revd. 101
Bignoll, Marmaduke 139
Bigsby, Nathl. 252
Bill, A. T. F. 251, 255
Charles 282
Binckle, Michael 50
Dincldi, Hanoo 50
Binder, Jacob 177
Bingham, Chas. 298
James 292
Wm. 292
Bingio, --- 87
Bingley, Hans Michel 50
Binion, Joseph, Revd. 101
Binne, Thomas 349
Biondi, Antonio 264
Biorge, I. H. 406
J H 402, 403, 406
Birch, Geo. 298
Bird, Golding 465, 468, 469, 511
Mary 332
Thomas 332
Birk, Eliza 332
John 332, 349
Birme, Anna Barbara 182
Anna Maria 182
Christian 182
Maria Sara 182
Birne, Bridget 471
Ellen 471
John 471
Michael 471
Thady 471
Timothy 471
Birns, Barney 332
Birth, James 252
Bischoff, Johann 26
Bishop, Henry 264
John 332
Saml. 298
Bissell, Wm., Qr.-Master 298

Bissett, Andw., Lieut.-Gen. 298
Bitner, Gottfried 284
William G. 278
Bittner, (Johann) Casper 32
Bjaadland, Thorstein Olson
  377, 383
Bjorgo, John H. 402
John Haldorson 406
Black, Ann 214
Archibald 349
Christian 214
Donald 214
Donaldson 332
Duncan 214
Edwd. 298
Ewen 214
George 332
James 254
Jannet 214
John 213, 298, 349
Margt. 298
Mary 213
Moses 349
Peter 349
Blackburn, Benjamin 188
John 244
Robt. 264
Blackett, Joshua 139
Tobiah 190
Blackwood, Jas., Sir 298
Bladen, M., Col. 298
Blaess, Lorentz 25
Blagden, George 258
Blagsen, George 258
Blair, Ann 332
Catherine 333
Eliza 333
George 333
James 333, 349
Jane 333
John 134, 333
Margt. 298
Randal 298
Richard 333
Saml. 298
Samuel 333, 349
Thomas 349
Wm. 333
Wm. Hen. 298
Blake, Ann 501
Edward 501
James 501
John 139, 333
Sarah 501
Thos., Capt. 298
Blakeney, Wm., Col. 298
Blakswik, James 189
Blame, William 349
Blanchard, William 251
Blanchfield, Stephen 349
Bland, Edward 257
Humphry, Col. 298
Blane, Eliza 218
Jean 218
Jenny 218
Patrick 218
Blany, Eleanor 333
Blasdell, Nicholas 254
Blayney, ---, Lord 298
Bleakley, Jane 349
John 349
William 349
Bleakly, William 333
Bleecker, J. H. 397, 403
Bleutlingers, Conrad 240
Blewer, Jno. 165
Bley, Adam 55
Elisabeth 27

Elisabetha 38
Hanss Werner 27
Margaretha Catharina 55
Philipp 27, 38
William 38
Bleyker, Neeltjee Dogger 512
Bloemhower, Michael 531
Blood, David R. 349
Bloomfield, Saml 349
Blum, Eva Elisabetha 57
Valentin 57
Blundell, ---, Hon. Mrs. 298
Blythe, John 194
Keziah 333
Bo, Lars 399
Bocke, Abraham 66
Elisabeth 66
Matheus 66
Rachell 66
Rahel 66
Rosina (Barbara) 67
Bockland, Maurice, Lieut. 298
Bodd, James 333
Boden, Hugh 349
Boe, Anna 390
Anna Dorthea 390
Baar Hansen 390
Baard Larson 440
Birtha 390
Boel 390
Hans 390
Helge 390
Karen 390
Lars Olsen 397, 399
Boeckel, Christiana 183
Friedrich 183
Johann Nicolaus 183
Johannes 183
Magdalena 183
Maria 183
Tobias 183
Boehm, Anthony Wilhelm 5
Catharina 53
Johanna Felicitas 5
John Philip, Rev. 5
Boelert, Philipp Jacob 62
Boën, Joseph 230
Boerstler, Johann Georg 40
Jorg 40
Boettle, Michel 17
Boggs, --- 346
Alexander 349
Paul 333
Bogle, Isabella 349
John 349
Samuel 349
Bohan, Matthew 349
Bohlander, Anna Barbara 50
Johann Adam 50
Johannes 50
Bohlayer, John C. 264
Bohleger, John 288
Böhlert, Maria Barbara 62
Philipp Jacob 62
Bohleyer, John 265, 288
Böhm, Catharina 70
Bohn, --- 7
Henrich Thielemann 142
Bohr, Friedrich 26
Boke, Sohn 349
Bokman, Jno. 166
Bolayer, John 281
Boles, Bennet 292
Bollmann, Jacob 168
Bolstad, Anna Vindeg 434
Anne 406
Ingeborg 406
Lars 406

Niels Larsen 406
Nils L. 402
Nils Larsen 405, 406, 433
Bolt, B. L. 429, 436, 440
Bolton, Elianor 139
  Margaret 349
Bond, Alexander 349
  Edward 532
  Isaac 251
  Samuel 251
  William 278
Bonn, Solomon Heim 157
Bonnel, John 333
Bonninger, Abraham 108
Bonooith, Joriah 282
Bonooitte, Joriah 282
Bonyoe, Isaac 109
Boone, Igni. 252
Booney, Harriet 333
  Samuel 333
  Sarah 333
Bopp, Frederick 251
Boquet, --- 135
Borland, Alexander 265
Borlridge, Josiah 349
Born, Anna Catharina 181
  Anna Maria 181
  Anna Marie 181
  Christina Margaretha 181
  Johann Daniel 181
  Johannes 181
  Ludwig 181
  Maria Barbara 181
  Samuel 181
Bornheker, John Gerlach 23
Bornhuetter, Johann Gerlach 23
Borr, Jacob, Brig.-Gen. 298
  James 349
Borskin, George 349
Borst, Michael 5
Bortner, Baltzer 8
  Jacob 8
Bossert, Johannes 46
  Margaretha 46
  Michael 177
Boston, Robert 247
Boswell, Thos., Ensign 298
Bosworth, Jonah 262
Boteler, Charles W. 262
Botham, Isabella 349
  Robert 349
Bothen, Hans 166
Bother, Hans 166
Bothwell, John 298
Boudmond, Andreas 54
  Philipp 54
Boulanger, Jean Joseph Paschale 265
Boume, Henry 164
Bouquet, Abraham 67
  Barbara 67
  Elisabetha 67
  Matheus 50, 66, 67
  Rachell 50, 66
  Rahel 66
  Rosina 50, 67
Bourquin, Benedict 109
  Henry 109, 112
  Henry Francois 107
  Jean Baptist 107
  Jean Baptiste 100, 109
  Mary 110
Bouthron, John 265
Bovey, Margaret 80
  Mrt. 80
Bowen, Leonidas 277
  Susanna 333
Bowersox, --- 63

Christian 72
Georg Adam 72
Paul 71
Bowie, Ann 192
Bowles, H., Mrs. 333
  Pheneas, Brig.-Gen. 298
Bowling, Timothy 76
Bowman, Jacob 533
  John George 3
Bowser, Henry 240
Bowyer, John, Lieut. 298
  Michael 134
  Thomas 134
  Thos. 134
Box, ---, Widow 81
Boyan, Michael 452, 466, 467,
  468, 485, 486, 487, 488,
  489, 490, 492, 495, 497,
  498, 503, 507, 509
Boyce, Anne 349
  Terance 333
Boyd, Alexander 134
  Andrew 349
  David 349
  Ellen 333
  James 217
  Jean 218
  John 298, 333
  Margt. 298
  Mary-Ann 333
  P. 349
  Robert 349
  Saml. 298
  Saml., Capt. 298
  Samuel 333, 349
  Thomas 349
  W. 349
  William 333
  Wm. 298
Boyle, Catherine 333
  Chr. 349
  Christopher 265
  Dennis 333
  Jas. 298
  John 333, 349
  Neil 333
  Robert 349
  Samuel 349
  William 331
Braband, Daniel, Dr. 111
Brabant, Daniel, Dr. 100
  John, Dr. 111
Brace, John Peter 107
Brach, Nickel 37
Bracken, Jas. 298
  John 298
  Lawrence 246
  Margt. 298
  Robt. 298
Bradford, James 349
Bradish, Wheaton 246
Bradley, Cath. 299, 333
  Francis 333
  James 349
  John 299, 333, 349
  Joseph H. 269
  Patk. 299
  Peter 349
  Philip 349
  William 80, 349
  Wm. 349
Brady, Anne 349
  Hugh 115, 294, 349
  James 333, 350
  John 115, 350
  Maurice 350
  Patrick 350
  Peter 251, 272

Susan 350
Thomas 265, 350
Bragg, Phil., Col. 299
Braineid, Charles 350
Braith, William 350
Braithwait, John, 2nd Lieut. 299
Branan, Murtaugh 299
Brandon, Esther Pinto 154
  Jacob 152
  Jacob Pinto 152
Brandreth, Mich., Capt.-Lieut. 299
Branick, Jane 350
Branigan, Thomas 333
Brankin, Thomas 350
Branley, Margaret 350
Brannan, John 251
  Luke 246
Brannon, Andrew 456
  Daniel 456
  Gilbert 456
  Jane 456
  Roger 456
  William 456
Brassington, C. P. 466
Bratted, Aadne 412
Bratten, Jane 299
Braun, ---, Frau 516
  Christoph 32, 173
  Jacob 180
  Kornelius 516
Bravo, Benjamin 151
  David 152
Brawley, Isabella 350
  William, Jr. 350
  William, Sr. 350
Brawnlie, Rich. 299
Bray, George 293
Brechbill, Hans 531
  Hans Peter 531
Brecht, Johann 17
  Stephan 17
Breckenridge, --- 133
  Alexander 133, 134
  George Robert 133
  John 133
  Letitia 133
  Lettice 134
  Robt., Sr., Col. 134
  Smith 133
Breckinridge, William Dunlop 265
Breen, Phil. 299
Breiner, George 8
Breitenbach, Friedrich 224
  Johann Heinrich 224
Breman, Patrick 350
Bremen, Ellen 350
Brenan, James 350
Brendel, Anna Maria 183
  Elisabeth 183
  Eva Catharina 183
  George 183
  Heinrich 183
  Johann Georg 183
  Johannes 183
  Maria Barbara 183
Brener, Peter 34
Brengel, Anna Catharina 58
  Christian 58
  Georg 58
  Jacob 58
  Juliana 58
  Kilian 58
Brennan, Andrew 456
  Bridget 350
  Daniel 456
  Gilbert 456

H., Rev. 456
Henry, Rev. 455
Jane 456
John 246
Patrick 350
Robt. 299
Roger 456
Unity 350
William 456
Brenner, Daniel 327
Frantz Peter 34
Hans Philipp 170
Philipp 170
Brerton, Samuel 251
Breth, Barbro Halverdatter 413
Breton, ---, widow 104
Francoise 112
Jean Pierre 104
Breviter, ---, Rev. 299
Brice, ---, Brig.-Gen. 299
Edw. 299
Edwd. 299
Brickell, Christopher 109
Brickenate, Sarah 531
Bricker, Jacob 172, 225
Brickert, Jacob 172
Mathias 172
Bride, Catherine 350
Chirst 200
Flora 201
Briden, Jas. 299
Bridge, Anthony 333
Bridges, Anne 350
James 350
Bridget, Joseph 333
Bridgman, Phil., Capt.-Lieut. 299
Brien, Bernard 267
Michael 471
Briggs, Maria 350
Brimsoe, Anna Hendrikson 395
Lars Larsen 391, 392, 395
Lars Larson 392
Brit, James 265
Britton, William 350
Broadback, Jacob 251
Brobst, Michael 10
Brockwell, James 139
Brodback, Jacob 251
Brodbeck, Jacob 265
Broderick, St. John 299
Serjt 299
Thomas 265
Brodie, Alex., Ensign 299
Brodrick, Allen 299
Brogan, John 333
Patrick 350
Brook, Sam 256
Brooke, W.J. 274
Brooks, Francis 251
James 350
Brophy, Jeremiah 350
Michael 350
Bropigan, Thomas 350
Brothers, Eliz. 291
James 291
Mary 291
Samuel 291
William 291
Brouer, Frederick 251
Broughton, ---, Lieut. Governor 114
Brown, Alex. 333
Andrew 350
Ann 333, 350
Anne 350
Bernard 350
Cath. 299

Charles 228
Christian 115
Daniel 264
David 265, 333
Duncan 120
Edmund F. 285
Edmund J. 264
Edw. 350
Elisabeth 228
Francis 333
Geo. 333
Gilbert, Lieut. 299
Henry 333
Hugh 133
James 134, 333, 350
Jane 350
John 139, 190, 289, 299, 333, 350
Joshua 350
Julia 350
Katrine 199
Margaret 133, 350
Mary 133, 299, 350
Mathew 350
Merrian 121
Nancy 299
Patrick 350
Phebe 264
Rachel 228, 333
Robert 133, 262, 265
Sali 228
Saml. 299
Samuel 211, 228, 350
Seth 350
Thomas 266, 350
Thos., Major 299
William 133, 139, 247, 266, 333, 350
Wm. 299
Browne, Bridget 333
John 350
Mary 333
Patrick 333
Thos. 299
Brownjohn, Hen., Lieut. 299
Brubacher, Abraham 39
Jacob 39
Bruce, Robert 218
William 350
Bruch, Heinrich 225
Brückert, Matthäus 172
Brückner, Susanna Christina 69
Brudvig, Ingebrigt 402, 405
Brudwig, Ingebrigt Nielsen 402, 403, 405
Brueckner, Christina 53
Brughard, George 326
Bruhnsdahl, K H 429
Brulott, Guillo. 107
Bruning, John H. 267
Brunnemer, Anna Margaretha 57, 73
Johann Peter 73
Johannes 57, 73
Peter 57
Brunner, Catharina 40
Felix 9
Johann Peter 40
Johannes 48
Peter 40
Bryan, Anne 333
Benjamin 258
Bernard 266
Hugh 114
James 333
Bryans, Sarah 333
Bryd, James 350
Brydal, Phil., Capt. 299

Bryne, Michael 471
Bryson, ---, Mrs. 333
James 289, 534
Bubb, --- 299
Bubigkoffer, Josef 22
Joseph 22
Buch, Ulrich 113
Buchalter, G. Frederic 327
Buchan, George 350
Buchanan, A. C. 469
Archd. 202
Archibald 202
John 217
Samuel 350
Wm. 299, 333
Buchannan, Robert 534
Buchanon, John 333
Buche, Abram 103
Danl. Henry 103
Francis 108
Francois 103
Jean Pierre 103
Margarette 103
Susanne 103
Buches, David 108
Buchter, Rudolph 164
Buck, Andrew 165
Buckheart, Jno. Geo. 167
Buckle, Adam 20
Buckley, Catherine 333
Christian 251
Darby 489
Johanna 489
John 489
Margaret 489
Mary 489
Michael 489
Tade 489
Timothy K. 267
Bucks, Michael 168
Budden, Nathaniel 350
Buden, James 333
Budgell, Eustace 299
Buech, Francis 108
Buettner, Caspar 31, 32
Johann 32
Maria Elisabetha 32
Buge, T N 402, 403
Buges, James 197
Bugnion, Joseph, Revd. 101, 112
Buher, John 350
Buist, David 267
William 267
Bulger, Patrick 267
Bull, John 333
Mary 333
William, Col. 114
William, Esqr. 91
Wm., Col. 91, 92, 95
Bullen, Henry 333
Mary 333
Bullett, Thomas, Capt. 134
Bullick, Isaac 299
Bullitt, Thomas, Capt. 135
Bullock, John, Ensign 299
Ralph 299
Thos. 299
Bunham, Ann 333
Bunyan, John 373
Burch, William S. 274
Burchill, William 350
Burchland, Jacob 166
Burchmore, William 139
Burg, Apollonia 46
Elisabetha Margaretha 46
Jacob 46
Johann Georg 47
Maria Catharina 47

Maria Elisabetha 46
Maria Margaretha 47
Philipp Jacob 46
Burgess, John 299
Robt. 299
Burgh, Thos. 299
Burk, Michael 350
Robert 333
Sibby 350
William 350
Burke, Anne 350
Edwd. 350
Francis 350
John 350, 451, 452, 453, 454,
455, 457, 458, 462, 463,
464, 466, 467, 468, 469,
497, 500, 501
William 134
Burkhalter, Ulrich 11
Burkhard, --- 328
Lewis 327
Burki, Jacob 11
Burkmayer, Marg't 167
Burkmeier, Conrad 167
Burleigh, Ruth 299
Burlington, Rich., Earl of 299
Burn, James 350
Thos. 299
Burnes, Charles 252
James 333
Burnett, Alex., Capt. 299
Burney, --- 231
Gillaume 231
Jacques 231
Jean 231
William 231
Burns, Agnes 299
Andrew B. 350
Catherine 333
Charles 252
Darby 333
Elizabeth 333
Henry 333
Hugh 350
James 292, 333
John 252, 333, 350
Murphy 333
Patrick 350
Samuel 299, 333
Thomas 333
William 333, 350
Burnside, Joseph 350
Samuel 350
Burr, --- 348
John 350
Nichlas 276
Burrowes, A. 299
Burrows, John 267
Burston, Geo. 299
Burt, Charles 534
Burton, Ally 333
Charles 252
John 134
Bush, Mathias 157
Bushell, Alice 529
Henry 529
Buss, Hans 164
Busted, --- 299
Buthmann, John H. 267
Butle, David 299
Butler, --- 299
Abraham 267, 277
Andrew 350
Ann 191
Eliza 350
George 350
John 191
Mary 333, 350

Michael 333
Theoph. 299
Buttal, --- 104
Buttelson, Magany 409
Buttersley, John 350
Mary 350
Butterworth, A. 350
Buttle, Dav. 299
Geo. 299
Margaret 350
Samuel 350
Wm. 299
Büttner, Peter 32
Butz, Peter 15
Byers, David 350
Robert 350
Byng, Geo., Sir 299
Byrd, ---, Col. 134
Byrne, Anne 471, 480
Bridget 471
Charles 256
Edmd. 299
Edward 350
Edwd. 300
Ellen 471
George 350
James 267, 333, 350
John 300, 350, 471
Judy 478
Mary 350, 471, 478, 479
Michael 350, 471, 511
Micke 511
Miles 333
Pat 471
Patrick 286
Patk. 350
Thady 471
Thomas 471, 478
Timothy 471
Byrnes, Bridget 333
C., Jr. 333
Hugh 350
John 333
Mary 350
Mat. 300
Nicholas 333
ByStöl, Magne Bottolfson 409
Bystolen, M B 404, 409
Bystölen, Magne Bottolfson 409
Bywater, Gervas 530

-- C --

Cabeen, Robt. 300
Caden, James 267
Cadogan, Bgt. 300
Cafferty, Girzy 350
Mary 350
Caffray, Edward 333
Caffry, Nicholas 350
Cahan, John 300
Cain, Charles 350
Patrick 350
Cairne, John 417
Cairnes, Dav. 300
Cairns, Mary 350
Samuel 350
Calam, Henry 247
Calame, Jacob 104
Calbeck, Wm. 300
Calder, James 257
Caldwell, ---, Widow 300
Agnes 133
Alexander 115
Ezekiel 350
J. F. 283

James 115, 133
Jas. 300
Jean 133
John 115, 133, 300, 333
Joseph 333, 350
Mary 115, 133
Rose 300, 316
Samuel 133
Sarah 133
Calewell, Danl. 200
Calfiel, Mich'l 167
Calgan, Catherine 350
Mary 350
Calhoun, James 350
Jean 300
John 300
Saml. 300
William 350
Wm. 300
Calis, Benjamin 107
Callagan, James 350
Callaghan, Edward 350
James 350
Margaret 350
Michael 333
Patrick 350
Callan, John F. 279
Nicholas 252, 256, 265, 267,
268, 270, 273, 286, 288
Nicholas, Jr. 268
Nicholas, Sr. 268
Patrick 252, 268
Callaughan, Thomas 292
Calleghan, John 510
Timothy 510
Callihan, John 333
Callon, Nicholas 253
Calloway, Arthur 248
Jacob 248
Calney, Mat 350
Calshan, Catherine 350
Calvert, --- 300
Ann 289
Charles 268
Mary 76
William 289
Wm 76
Calvin, Thomas 333
Calwell, John 300
Cam, Christopher 350
Cambell, --- 330
Robert 333
Camble, --- 330
John 350
Joseph 333
Camden, ---, Earl 300
Cameron, Alexander 221
Allan 201
Angus 201, 220
Duncan 221
James 115
John 80, 221
Katherine McDonald 220
Katrine 201
Mary 220
Richard 80
Camery, Alexander 534
Cammack, Christopher 268
William 268
Cammerer, Joseph 178
Campbell, ---, Capt. 116, 118
Agnes 218
Alex 201
Alex. 300
Alexander 115
Alexr. 206, 216
Andrew 218
Andw. 300

Ann 116, 200, 300
Anna 115, 116, 118
Anne 115
Antho. 333
Archibald 115, 116, 215, 350
Arth. 300
Catharine 115, 118
Cathn. 200
Charles 134
Chas. 300
Colin 188, 221
Dan 252, 300
Danl. 200
David 350
Donald 115, 210
Dugald 115
Duncan 115, 116, 211, 215, 350
Edward 248
Elisabeth 116
Eliz. 120
Elizabeth 134
Elr. 300
Esther 134
Francis 350
Gennet 134
George 116, 350
Girzie 215
Hector 206
Hugh 134
Isbell 115
James 115, 116, 350
Jane 333
Janet 116
Jas 388, 411
Jas. 300
Jean 197, 198, 218
Jemimah 333
John 115, 116, 134, 218, 300, 333, 350
John, Col. 300
Josias, Col. 300
Katherine 211
Lachlan 215
Lauchlin 116
Lauchlin, Capt. 115
Lauglan, Capt. 116
Letitia 300
Malcolm 116
Margaret 115, 118
Mary 115, 116, 118, 134, 215, 300, 333
Mary Ann 116, 218
Matthew 350
Merran 115
Nancy 300
Neil 116, 215
Nicholas 248
Patrick 134, 333
Patrick, Jr. 134
Peggy 115
Robert 115, 116, 211
Ronald 116, 202
Saml. 300
Samuel 289
Sarah 300
Sarah 115, 134
Thomas 350
W., Mrs. 333
William 116, 134, 211, 350
Wm. 333
Campos, Isaac Henriques 152
Judith Henriques 155
Cane, Charles 333
Canigan, Michael 350
Cannelan, John 350
Cannon, --- 333
Biddy 417
Bridget 350

Clementine 76
Hugh 350
James 76
John 333
Marmaduke 76
Mary 76
Moses 350
Patrick 333
Richard 76
Robert 350
Cannoughton, Patrick 350
Canway, Catherine 351
Mary 351
Owen 351
Carabine, Catherine 351
Thomas 351
Carberry, Joseph 257
Lewis 272
Carbery, Lewis 267, 272
Lewis, Esquire 288
Thomas 255, 259
Cardell, William 137, 139
Carden, N. 333
Cardonnel, M 202
Cardosa, Rachaell 152
Cardozo, Abm. Roiz 154
Daniel 153
Leah 153
Sarah 153
Carew, Hugh 300
Carey, Geo. 300
Mathew 254
Michael 351
Richard 333
Cargill, David 116
Elizabeth 116
James 116
Jean 116
John 116
Margaret 116
Carille, Abraham 155
Carlan, Patrick 351
Sarah 351
Carle, John W. 351
Michael 351
Carleton, A. 291
J. 351
M. 351
Carlin, Bridget 456
Ellen 456
Honor 456
James 351
John 351, 456
Mary 456
Thomas 351
Carling, Philip 333
Carlisle, Geo. 300
James 351
John 351
Mary 300
Wm. 300
Carlisles, ---, Col. 256
Carlon, Bridget 456
Ellen 456
Honor 456
John 456
Mary 456
Carlton, A. 333
Carlyle, John 134
Carmachy, Robert 351
Carmack, Christopher 268
William 268
Carmeran, Allen 351
Anne 351
Elizabeth 351
William 351
Carmichael, --- 300
Alexander 116

Allan 213
Archibald 213, 214
Catharine 116
Catherine 214
Christian 213
Daniel 351
Donald 116
Dugald 116, 213
Elizabeth 116
Evan 213
Jennat 116
John 116
Katherine 213
Margaret 213
Mary 116, 213, 214
Neil 116
Carmichail, Donald 212
Carney, Anne 351, 471
Eliza 351
John 351
Mary 351
Michael 351
Moses 351
Patrick 351
Philip 351
Richard 333
Carolan, Rose 333
Carondelet, ---, governor 226
Carpenter, Jas., Capt. 300
Carr, Alexander 333
Elizabeth 351
Isaac 351
John 133, 333, 351
Jos. 300
Joseph 134, 333
Lucey 133
Margaret 133
Nathaniel 351
Robert 351
Carrall, Dennis 333
John 333
Carrigan, Andrew 351
James 333
Patk. 351
Wm. 333
Carrington, John 456
Carroll, Ann Rafferty 471
Bridget 471
Charles 137, 138
Daniel 252
Danl. 260
Elizth. 300
John 265, 268, 271
Mary 351, 471
Mary Ann 471
Michael, Rev. 351
Patrick 351, 471
Terence 351
Thomas 471
William 351
Carron, Leslie 300
Mary 300
Sarah 300
Carrothers, Robt. 300
Wm. 300
Cars, John 300
Carse, William 333
Carslile, Hugh 351
Carson, George 333, 351
James 333, 351
Jas. 300
John 333
Saml., Dr. 300
Cartan, Patrick 333
Carter, James 268
Robert 351
Carty, Ann 472
Bridget 472

Catherine 472
Edward 472
John 472, 479
Martin 472
Mary 472
Owen 472, 482
Peggy 472
Peter 472
Thomas 472
Carusi, Augustus 268
Gaetano 252
Lewis 268
Caruso, Gaetano 252
Caruthers, Archibald 351
Jane 351
John 351
M. 351
Carver, Agnes 333
Carwell, James 76
Margaret 76
Caselly, Patrick 351
Casement, John M. 300
Casey, --- 351
Bab 489
Barbara 489
Johanna 489
John 333, 472, 489, 496
Michael 489
Pat 472
Peter 333
Rosean (Rosian) 489
Cashell, Randell 252
Casher, Anne 351
Bartholomew 351
M. 351
Margaret 351
Caske, Isaac C. 254
Casparis, James 268
Cassaday, Nicholas 252
Cassady, Anthony 351
James 351
Cassaway, Hania 251
Cassell, Patrick 351
Cassely, Patrick 333
Cassiday, Chas. 300
Francis 333
Nicholas 275
Castello, John 351
Michael 351
Thomas 351
Castigan, Thomas 351
Castle, Mary 139
Castlewood, Hugh 351
Caswell, Hector 300
Catalano, Antonio 264
Salvadore 269
Catanoch, John 204, 205, 208
Cateny, Bryan 300
Cathcart, ---, Brig.-Gen. Lord 300
Alexander 351
Catherine 351
Jas. 300
Catherwood, Hugh 333
Thomas 351
Caton, John 252, 257
Caughey, Mary 351
Caulfield, Alice 300
Chas., Hon. & Rev. 300
W., Judge 300
Causland, William 351
Causton, Tho. 78
Thomas 76, 77
Cavanagh, John 351
Michael 333
Caveney, Anne 456
Catherine 456
Edward 456

Luke 456
Mary 456
Patrick 456
Thomas 456
Cay, James 351
Michael 351
Cecil, Wm., Col. 300
Cederberg, Bergethe Merie 413
Cellier, Jo. 80
Mary 80
Ceyrin, --- 330
Wm. 333
Chaley, William 333
Chalmers, James 198
Chamberlain, John 531
Chambers, Agnes 351
Alex. 300
Ann 300
Charles 245, 351
Eliza 351
Isa. 300
James 351
Jas. 300
John 245
Margaret 351
Mary 300, 351
Mathew 351
Reba. 300
Robert 351
Sarah 300, 351
Thomas, II 351
William 351
Wm. 300
Champneys, Edward 530
John 530
Mary 530
Presilla 530
Priscilla 530
Chapman, Henry 139, 188
William 351
Charbowell, --- 330
Chardonet, Abraham 109
Charles, ---, Mrs. 510
Charmason, Peter 106
Charowell, James 333
Charters, Arthur 351
John 351
Chefeille, Henry 112
Cheney, Andw. F. 300
Mary 300
Cheny, --- 300
Chestnut, C. 351
M. 351
S. 351
Samuel 333
William 351
Chetwood, --- 300
Chevelis, John 108
Chevers, --- 301
Chiefelle, --- 96
Chiffelle, --- 97
Henry, Rev. 101, 102
Child, Alexander 333
Robt., Capt. 301
Chivillet, John 107
Choppin, William 269
Choupart, Daniel 109
Chown, George 248
Christa, Adam 351
Christendatter, Bertha 411, 414
Karin 411, 414
Christen Datter, Forber 411, 414
Christensdatter, S 428
Christensen, Hans 428
Christian, Anna Barbara 124
Elizabeth 134
Fillip 36
Gilbert 134

Israel 134
Johann Georg 124
Johann Peter 124
Johann Valentin 124
John 351
John, Capt. 135
Maria Elisabeth 124
Philip Jacob 36
Philipp Jakob 124
Christians, David 110
Christie, Margaret 333
Thomas 77, 78
Christophersdatter, K 429
Karen 390
Christy, Adam 351
Alexander 116
David 351
Elizabeth 351
Jane 351
John 351
Robert 351
Church, Randal, Qr.-Master 301
Chutkowski, Ignatius 269
Cimbers, George 230
Circus, Joh. 167
Claas, Johann Matthaeus 225
Clagher, Jane 333
Clancey, James 351
John 351
Clancy, Robert 351
Clark, Angus 116
Ann 333
Catharine 116
Charles 77, 351
Cristy 120
David 333
Edward 333
Elnr. 301
Hugh 351
James 77, 190
James A. 269
Jane 351
Jas. 301
John 135, 301, 334, 351
Joseph 252
Joseph S. 277
Judith 77
Margaret 351
Mary 116, 334
Matthew 351
Nancy 334
Neil 351
Peter 77
Richard 351
Robert 77
Robt., jun. 301
Robt., sen. 301
William 116, 270, 334, 351
Wm. 301
Clarke, Edward W. 272
Francis 252
Gustavus A. 280, 287
James 218, 351
John 247, 270
Jos. 252
Joseph S. 275
Robert 77
Robt. 252
Walter 252, 260
William 252, 270
Clary, John 334
Class, John 334
Claudius, Augustus 245
Claughey, --- 351
James 351
John 351
Mary 351
Sarah 351

Clausdatter, B. 429, 436, 438
  Britha (Brita) 438
  G. 420, 429, 436, 438
Clausen, --- 431
  C. L., Rev. 436
  Isak 438
  Lars 438
Claveloux, Mark 270
Claxton, John 139
  Thomas 279
  John C. 254
Clear, Mary 351
Cleary, Andrew 351
Clebborn, Samuel 351
Clegg, Joseph 351
Cleland, John 334
  Samuel 334
Clemens, Christian 269
Clement, William 334
Clements, Andrew 290
  David 290
  Ignatius N. 282
  James 351
  Margaret 351
Clementz, Anna Maria 45
  Georg 45
  Johann Adam 45
  Johann Valentin 45
  Juliana 45
  Sebastian 45
  Valentine 45
Clendining, James 292
Clephane, James 270, 287
Clerk, Jo 201, 216
  John 534
  Thomas 534
Cless, Maria Dorothea 125
  Philipp Heinrich 125
Cleven, --- 442
Clinch, Frederick 240
  James 351
Cline, Daniel 240
  Henry 240
  William 456, 459
Clinton, Bartholomew 351
  Dewitt, Esq. 261
Clitsh, Henry Christian Frederick 270
Cloane, W. 351
Clock, Mathw. 351
Clokey, Andw. 301
Close, Ann 77
  Hannah 77
  Hen. 301
  Henry 77
Clothard, --- 330
  Anthony 334
Clotworthy, John, Sir 301
  Margt., Lady 301
  Mary 301
  Mary, Dame 301
Clugston, John 197
Clyde, Thos. 301
Coach, Isabella 351
  John 351
  William 351
Coad, Wm. 446
Coal, Alley 334
  Catherine 334
  James 334
Cobham, ---, Lord 301
Cobine, --- 330
  George 334
  Robert 334
Cobley, Jemmett, Esqr. 107
Coborn, Wm. 334
Cochlin, James 334
Cochran, --- 334

Agnes 351
Isaac 293, 351
Jane 351
John 334
Mary Ann 351
Rich. 301
Richard 351
Robert 351
Samuel 351
Thomas, Capt. 534
William J. 281
Cochrane, Basil 198, 202, 203
  Henry 334
  Robert 334
  William 334
Cockeran, --- 301
Cocking, William 251
Cockran, Hugh 301
Codd, Edward 351
  James 351
Coe, --- 334
Coffee, Coreneles 510
Coffey, John 498, 499
  Michael 472
Coghlan, Bridget 351
  Catherine 351, 352
  Eliza 352
  James 248
  Mary 352
  Patrick 352
Cogly, Martin 352
Cohen, Abraham Myers 156, 163
  Samuel Myers 163
  Samuel Myers 156
Coil, --- 330
  Peter 334
  Rosa 334
  Sarah 334
  William 334
Coin, Ann 334
Colbo, Ella Stratton 431
Colder, Jenet 119
Cole, Diana 139
  John 352
Coleman, Charles 270, 274, 286
  Robert 352
Coles, Anna 77
  Joseph 77
Colgan, Anne 456
  Bernard 456
  Betty 456
  Bridget 456
  Honor 456
  Margaret 456
  Mary 456
  Michael 456
  Patrick 456
  William 456
Colhoun, John 352
Colin, Henry 334
Coling, Peter 352
Coll, Dennis 352
Collins, --- 301
  Andrew 334
  Cornelius 116
  George C. 270
  James 334
  Mary 489, 493
  Thomas 270
  William 352
  Wm. 301
Collis, Ray, Cornet 301
Collume, Jacob 107
Colquhoun, Ann 213
  Archibald 213
  William S. 287
Columbus, Charles 270
Colvill, Robt., Sir Knt. 301

Colville, Jos. 301
  Cath. 301
Colvin, James 334
  John 334
Colvine, Ch., Lieut. 301
Comberback, ---, Capt. 301
Combs, Wm. 189
Conaghy, Barnard 334
  Thomas 334
Concannon, John 352
  Patrick 334
  William 352
Conden, Hannah 334
Coneghan, Patrick 352
Conelye, --- 301
Conerry, John 352
Congreive, Wm., Lieut. 301
Conie, Alexander 534
Coningham, Hen. 301
  Wm. 301
Conlon, Peter 270
Conly, Francis 278
  Thomas Y. 270
Conn, Jane 334
  Robert 334
  Samuel 334
  Sarah 334
Connally, Jas. 301
Connel, Robert 278
  Stephen 334
Connell, Dan 489, 490
  David 489
  Davy 494, 505
  Eileen 489
  Ellen 490
  Jerry 489
  Johanna 489, 490
  John 489, 490
  Judy 490
  Margaret 489, 490
  Mary 489, 490
  Pat 489
  Patrick 352, 490
  Philip 490
Connellin, James 352
Connelly, Francis 253
  Mary 352
  Michl. 277
  Owen 270, 272, 279
  Patrick 334
  Peter 352
  Thomas Y. 270
Conner, Edward 352
  Jeremiah 352
  John 352
  Thomas 273
Conningham, Hen. 301
Connolan, Thomas 352
Connolly, Henry 352
  Thomas 280
Connoly, ---, Right Rev. Dr. 352
Connon, John 301
Connor, Catherine 457
  Honor 457
  Hugh 352
  James 334, 457
  Jane 334
  John 352, 457
  Jeremiah 334
  Joseph 352
  Martin 457
  Mary 334, 457
  Mich. 293
  Michl. 352
  Philip 352
  Richard 352
  Thomas 457
  Torence 457

Conolan, Charles 352
  James 352
Conolly, James 352
  John 352
  Kate 301
  M. 352
  Polly 334
  Thomas 352
  William 352
  William J. 352
  W. 301
Conrad, Christian 183
  Jacob 183
  Johan Jacob 183
  Johannes 183
  Maria Catharina 183
Conrade, Jacob, Jr. 142
Conradt, Anna Maria 124, 126
  Georg 142
  Johann Konrad 124
  Johann Nikolaus 124, 126
  Michael 325
Conrath, Connrad 124
Conroy, Dennis James 245
  Dominick 271
Conry, Catherine 352
  James 352
  Judith 352
  Mary 352
  Michael 352
Conway, Biddy 472
  Bridget 472
  Catherine 472
  Hugh 352
  James 271, 472, 481
  John 472
  Margaret 472
  Mary 472
  Mary Ann 472
  Pat 472
  Thomas 472
  Wm. 301
Conyngham, ---, Capt. 301
  ---, Col. 301
  Anne 301
  Dav. 301
  Geo. 301
  John 301
  Wm., Capt. 301
  Wm., Cornet 301
Cooch, Jas. 301
Cood, Henry 446
  Wm. 446
Cook, David 253
  Elizabeth 76
  Henry 334
  J.H. 268
  Jos. 352
  Lawrence 76
  Thomas 251, 352
  Thos. 301
  Will., Major 78
Cooke, ---, Ensign 301
  Alice 529
  David 352
  George 146
  Hugh 352
  John 139, 301
Coombe, Lowry Griffith 251
Cooney, Bryan 334
Cooper, ---, Mrs. 334
  Daniel 235
  Henry 532
  Joseph 77, 271
  William 259
  William, Jr. 271
Coot, --- 301
Coote, Clement 278

Clement T. 268, 271, 272
Cope, John, Brig.-Gen. 301
Copeland, --- 330
  James 334
  Thomas 334
  Wm. 334
Coplinger, --- 7
Corche, Elias Fernandes 152
  Joseph Alvares 153
  Moses Alvares 152
Corcoran, Thomas 334
  Thomas, Jr. 253
  Thos., Jr. 251
  Wm. 334
Cordoso, Jacob 153
  Rachael 153
Corenter, Mary 290
  William 290
Corish, James 352
Corkoran, Michael 352
Corme, William 256
Cormock, Mary 79
Cornele, John 301
Corney, Richard 334
Corning, Zipporah 259
Cornish, ---, Capt. 96
  Joseph 88
Cornwallis, Steph., Col. 302
Cornwell, John 352
Corr, Barbara 181
  Casper 181
  Christian 181
Correa, Moses Alvares 153
Corrins, James 334
Corry, Hugh 352
  James 352
  Nichs. 302
Cory, John 444
Cosgrave, Ann 473
  Anne 472, 473
  Bridget 472, 473
  Catherine 473
  Ellen 473, 474
  Francis 473
  Hannah 473
  James 352, 472, 473
  John 472, 473
  Judy 473
  Julia 473, 476, 478
  Margaret 472
  Maria 473
  Mary 472, 473, 478
  Michael 472
  Pat 472, 473, 482
  Peter 472, 473
  Thomas 472, 473, 478
  William 473, 474
Cosgrove, Thomas 352
Coslarder, --- 330
Coslarger, James 334
Costagan, James 334
Coste, Isaac 108
Costello, Anne 457
  Bridget 457
  Ellen 457
  John 457
  Martin 457
  Mary 457
  Michael 457
  Pat 457
  Thomas 352, 457
Costerdyne, Geo. 302
Costigan, James 352
  Joseph 253
Cotter, Arthur 352
Cotterel, John, Ensign 302
Cottler, Anthony 165
Couch, Joshua 284

Couden, Hannah 334
Coughlan, James 352
Coulan, Peter 278
Coulson, John 302
Coult, ---, Capt. 302
Coulta, James 352
Coulter, Ann 334
  Hugh 334
  John 352
  Sarah 334
Coumba, William 253
Couples, Elizabeth 334
  James 334
Courtenay, John 253
Courtney, Peter 334
Coussins, John 264
Covenagh, Robert 352
Cover, George 254
Cowan, Charles 352
  Hugh 271
Cowman, Thos. 193
Cowser, Eliza 334
  James 334
  Sophia 334
Cox, Eunice 77
  Frances 77
  Jane 134
  Jno. 533
  John 302
  Rich., Sir 302
  Thos. 302
  William 77
  Wm 77
  Wm. 77
Coxe, Richard 262
Coyle, --- 330
  Andrew 272
  Daniel 334
  Francis 352
  Hugh 302
  John 334
Cradocke, Alice 529
  Christopher 529
Craford, Daniel Petter 534
Craft, Mich'l 165
Craig, Andrew 352
  Chas. 334
  George 292, 293
  John 334
  Jos. 334
  Saml. 302
  Samuel 352
  Wm. 334
Craige, ---, Major-Gen. 302
Craigmins, Alex. 302
Cramer, Frederick 533
  Johann Friedrich 36
Crammer, John 302
Crampsier, John 334
Cranch, Wm 260
Cranfin, Mary 334
Cranmer, Andreas 167
Cranning, Pat. 294
Crany, John 352
Crary, Samuel 334
Crauch, Wm 260
Craughwell, Ann 474
  Bridget 474
  Catherine 474
  Ellen 474
  Honoria 474
  John 474
  Kenedy 474
  Kitty 474
  Margaret 474
  Mary 474
  Matt 474
  Michael 474

Nancy 474
Pat 474
Patrick 474
Peggy 474
Peter 474
Rose 474
Rosy 474
Thomas 474
Winifred 474
Craven, Jn. 292
John 352
Crawford, --- 346
Ann 134
Anne 352
David 352
English 352
George 134
J. 352
James 134, 352
Janet 302
Jas. 302
John 302, 352
Josias 302
M. 352
Margaret 134
Mary 134, 352
Patrick 134
Rebecca 334
Robt. 302
Samuel 134
William 352
Wm. 302
Wm., Ensign 302
Crawley, Lewis 352
Michael 352
Crawlon, Patrick 352
Creager, George 240
Creaser, Thomas 271
Creasor, Thomas 271
Credy, Julius 164
Crefeld, --- 1
Creighton, Dav., Brig.-Gen. 302
James 352
Rebecca 121
Creiner, Andreas 47
Cremer, Johann Friedrich 36
Cremin, John 490
Kitty 490
Timothy 490
Creniella, George 286
Crentzfeldt, William 288
Creutzfeldt, William 271
Crewer, Philip 262
Cricket, Dav. 302
Crimlisk, Cath. 302
John 302
Crisman, George 241
Crispin, Wm. 302
Cristy, Hannah 116
Isbell 116
John 116
Mary 116
Crocker, Alice 529
Crocket, George 334
James 352
John 352
Samuel 334
Crockett, George 334
John 334
Robert 334
Crody, Henry 166
Croft, Catherine 165
Mich'l 165
Crofton, Wm. 302
Crofts, ---, Brig.-Gen. 302
Alexander 246
Croggan, Henry B. 271
Croggon, Henry B. 271

Croghan, Patrick 457
John 457
Margaret 457
Croghell, Ann 474
Ellen 474
Michael 474
Croissant, Anna Catharina 42
Jacob 42
Johann Georg 42
Cromery, James 221
Cromwell, Josiah 346
Cron, Anna Christina 125
Anna Magdalena 124
Anna Margarethe 125
Anna Maria 125
David 124
Hans Simon 130
Johann David 125
Johann Konrad 125
Johann Philipp 125
Sabine 130
Simon Jacob 125
Simon Jakob 124
Susanna Martha 125
Crone, William 334
Cronenberger, Anna Catharina 105
Elizabeht 105
Gertrues 105
Henrich 105
Nicolas 105
Cronin, Betsey 506
Betty 490
John 490
Mary 490
Patrick 510
Stephen 334
Crooks, James 352
Crookshanks, John 302
Wm. 302
Croon, Simon Jacob 125
Cropley, Edward S. 271
George 253
Richard 253
Crosbie, Cha., Adjt. 302
Crosby, Patrick 482
Robert 352
Thomas 352
Crosier, Eliza 334
Jas. 302
Mary 302
Cross, Judith 77
Margaret 352
Tho. 77
Crossan, Michael 352
Patk. 302
Crossen, Francis 352
Crossfield, James 287
Crothers, --- 330
Geo. 302
Jenny 302
John 302
Laifanny 302
Crotty, Patrick 271
Crowley, Timothy 253
Crown, Hendk. 24
Croyet, Agnes 302
Jas. 302
John 302
Wilson 302
Crozier, Agnes 302
Livy 302
Richard 334
Wm. 302
Cruit, Robert 271
Crumley, Eleanor 352
Crummer, Ann 334
Cathar. 334

Letitia 334
Mary 334
Nathl. 334
Saml. 334
Crummy, Agnes 290
David 290
James 290
Mary 290
Sarah 290
Cryan, Bridget 352
Catharine 352
James 352
Martin 352
Mary 352
Michael 352
Patrick 352
Timothy 352
Cubbert, Isaac 334
Cue, Patrick 292
Cuillat, Adam 111
Cuillatt, Wallier 107
Culbert, George 334
Culbreth, Merran 116
Culbutson, Jas. 302
Sam. 302
Cull, John 272
Cullen, Allen 352
Mary 352
Cullet, Adam 108
Cullin, James 334
John 334
Cully, John 290
Cumings, George 244
Cummin, Jas. 302, 309
Cumming, Elnr. 302
Hans 352
Jannett 302
Tho. 352
Cummings, James 272
John 218, 334
Patrick 272
Cummins, Catherine 352
Christopher 253
Thomas 352
Cummyng, Duncan, Dr. 302
Cuna, Isaac Henriques 153
Cundy, Ann 444
Eliza 444
Elizabeth 443
Emma 443
John 444
Maria 443
Mary 443
Solomon 443, 447
Cunelisk, Cath. 302
John 302
Cunha, Isaac Mendes 153
Rachel Henriques 155
Cunnay, Thomas 352
Cunningham, Alex. 302
Alexander 352
C. 334
Coudy 334
Dan. 334
Frances 334
Hugh 334
J. 334
James 352
John 334, 352
Robert 198, 281, 334
Samuel 272
Cunnington, Michael 272
Cuntz, Johann Nickel 37
Nickel 37
Cuntzer, Nickel 31
Cunz, Johann Jacob 17
Curiel, Solomon 152
Curley, Biddy 474

James 272
John 474
Margaret 474
Patrick 292
Curling, --- 192, 193
Curner, Joh. 167
Curragan, Sarah 334
Curran, Peter 352
Currant, Patrick 352
Curred, --- 348
  Bartholomew 352
  Bryan 352
  Dominick 352
Currel, James 534
Currell, Elizah. 352
  Susannah 352
Current, Lawrence 334
Currie, Catharine 216
  Josias 334
Curry, Alexander 352
  Conell 334
  John 334
  Mary 334
  Michael 352
  William 352
Curswel, Jeanne 228
  Mathiew 228
  Robert 228
  Samüel 228
Curtis, Jacob 280
Cusack, Patrick 352
Custis, Eliza 250
Custod, Saml P 298, 400
  Samuel P. 400
Cuthbert, Joseph 244
Cuvillier, Joseph 272

-- D --

Dabzall, Willson 193
da Costa, Moses Nunez 153
Da Costa, Abraham Nunez 153
  Del. Mz. 152
  Isaac Nunez 152
  Jacob Nunez 152
  Moses Pera. 155
Dahl, Andrew 383
  Endre 383
  Rasmus 412
Dahle, A 403
  J. J. 403, 405
Dahlinger, Caspar 178
Dahlseider, H N 403
Dail, Edward 334
Dailey, John 505
Daily, Henry 352
  John 272
Dalbine, Gilbert, Sir 302
Dale, Anna 405
  Daniel 352
  George 352
  John 352, 447
  John J. 405
  Samuel 352
  Thos. 447
  William 352
  Wm. 447
Dalescale, Vincent 111
Daley, James 134
  Jesse 134
Dalke, Abraham 523
  Franz 524
  Heinrich 524
  Johann 524
  Katharina 524
  Kornelius 524

Peter 523, 524
Sarah 523
Dallas, Alexander 352
Dally, Edward 352
Dalrymple, Ann 196
  Archd. 196
  Janet 196
  Jas. 196
  Jean 196
  Jn. 196
  Jno. 196
  Wm. 196
Dalton, Henry 352
Daly, Anthony 352
  Arthur 247
  Bessy 490
  Bryan 352
  Chas. 302
  Daniel 490
  Denis 302
  Domk. 302
  Ellen 352
  Jack 506
  John 490
  Judy 490
  Margaret 490
  Martin 353
  Mary 499
  Michael 353
  P. 353
  Peter 302
  William 353
  Wm. 353
Dalzell, Robt., Lieut.-Gen. 302
Damgen, Anna Christina 131
  Christian 131
Damian, Anna Maria 57, 71, 72
Danaho, Patrick 353
Dander, Sarah 334
Danford, James 353
  Ralph 353
Daniel, James 353
Danieldatter, Malene 416
Daniel datter, Malene 409, 413,
  416
Danielsen, Ann 415
  Christen 414
  Christopher 414
  Ole 428
Danielson, Christopher 414, 416
  Knud 416
  Malinda 409, 416
  Sara (Siri) 416
Danihy, Bridget 491
  Con 490, 491
  Dan 490, 491, 506
  Daniel 490, 491
  Denis 490, 491, 504, 505, 506
  Denis, Sen. 490
  Denis Daniel 505
  Eileen 491
  Ellen 491
  James 491, 505
  Johanna 490, 491
  John 491, 505
  Kitty 491
  Mary 490, 491, 506
  Matt 490, 491
  Matt Denis 504
  Michael 490, 491
  Nelly 491
  Tade 491
  Tim 491
Dannan, John 353
Danner, Dieter 18, 35, 36
  Dietrich 18
  Michael 18
  Michel 35, 36

Dantroon, --- 115
Danwoody, John 334
  Wm. 334
Darby, John 191
Darcey, Thos. 353
D'Arcy, Nicholas 465
Daren, Anne 353
Darnell, Sarah 406
Dashwood, James, Sir 147
Da Silva, Daniel 153
  Jacob 152
  Judica 154
  Rica 155
Datis, --- 231
Daub, Anna Maria 46, 48
  Ludwig 67
  Nicklaus 67, 68
  Nisklaus 67
Dauber, Wilhelm 58
Daum, Johannes 25
Dauwer, Wilhelm 58
Davenport, ---, Major Gen. 302
  Catherine 353
  James 353
Davey, Cornelius 353
David, Daniel Abraham 112
  Peter, Cornet 302
Davidson, Eliza 302
  Jas. 302
  John 272, 334, 353
  Robt. 302
  William 353
  Wm. 302
Davies, John 353
Davis, Ann 80
  Barnard 334
  Charles 334, 447
  Charles A. 273
  David 135
  Edward 253
  Henry 134, 353
  James 134
  John 140
  Mary 134, 353
  Morgan 80
  Owen 353
  Richard 270
  Saml. 446
  Samuel 134
  Thomas 139, 334
  William 134, 334
  Wm. 302
Davison, Christ. 353
  Eliza 302
  George 134
  James 134
  Jas. 302
  John 134, 334, 353
  Robt. 302
  Samuel 134
  Sarah 353
  Thomas 134
  William 134
Davys, Hen. 302
Daw, Anne 474
  Biddy 474
  Bridget 474
  James 474
  John 474
  Mary 474
  Mary Ann 474
  Pat 474
  Thomas 474
Dawe, Anne 474
  Biddy 474
  Bridget 474
  James 474
  John 474

Mary 474
Mary Ann 474
Pat 474
Thomas 474
Dawes, Charlotte Maria 272
Frederick Dawes 272
Dawson, --- 302
Hugh 353
Robert 353
Sarah 353
W. 292
Washington 353
Day, --- 510
Daye, Andrew 334
Deacon, John 139
Deale, Francis 353
Dealy, John 334
Deane, Thomas 139
Deary, James 353
Deasale, James C. 287
Deavlin, Danl. 353
Neil 353
de Bastrop, ---, Baron 226,
227, 228, 230
de Beaufain, Berenger 101
Hector Berenger 100
De Beaufin, Hector Berenger
107
de Breard, ---, Baron 226
de Bréard, --- 230
De Campos, Abram, Senr. 154
de Carondelet, ---, Baron 226
de Casa-Calvo, ---, Marquis
227
Dechant, Jacob William 234
Jakob Wilhelm 234
Jk. Wm. 235
Decker, Anna Barbara 44
Georg 44
Johann Jacob 177
Johann Joerg 44
De Crasto, Jacob Lopez 152
Dee, Robert 193
Deek, Agnes 334
James 334
Deeley, Mary 532
Deffely, Bridget 457
George 457
James 457
Mary 457
Patrick 457
Deffley, Bridget 457
George 457
James 457
Mary 457
Patrick 457
de Fraisinet, Peter Granier 305
de Gallier, Jean Henry Pierre 112
De Gallin, Jean Pierre 107
Degreiff, Anna Margaretha 40
Jacob 40
de Hart, Abraham 228
Jacob 228
Jean 228
Jeannette 228
Winton 228
De Hart, Edward 334
Deighan, Joseph 353
DeJeau, ---, Capt 113
De Krafft, Frederick C. 288
de la Brissoniere, Peter 299
de la Fausille, Peter 304
Delafaye, Anne 302
Chas. 302
Elizth. 302
Delaforce, M. 302
Delagaye, John 112
Delahunt, Thomas 353

Delancy, Michael 192
Delane, John 139
Sam 113
Delaney, Patrick 274, 283
Delano, --- 346
Delany, Nicholas 353
Patrick 258
Thomas 334
de la Penha, Isl. 152
De la Penha, Jacob 152
De Lara, Jacob Nunez 155
Delarha, Moses Cohen 152
De Las, James 107
Delater, Anna Elisabetha 41
David 41, 42
De Leas, Abraham 157, 163
Delessert, Adrian Stephen 248
Armand John James 245
Deller, Georg 43
Johann Georg 43
Delman, Henry 240
Delpont, Jean 106
Del Vecchio, Charles 247
De Mon Clar, Andre Albatestier
108
Dempsey, Ann 475
Anne 475
Biddy 475
Bridget 475
Catherine 353, 475
Edward 247
Francis 247
Henry 475
John 353, 475
John, Jr. 475
Margaret 475
Mary 247, 475
Michael 475
Pat 475
Patrick 475
Demsay, James 331
den Bleyker, Diemmen 512
John 512
Maartje 512
Paulus 512
Peter 512
Dene, Susan 290
Denham, Alex, Rev. 302
Elkansh 271
Robt., Lieut. Sir 302
Dennison, Daniel 135
Dennisson, Richard 353
Denvant, Michael 334
Deolin, Arthur 334
Daniel 334
de Pagez, ---, Col. 317
Depais, Rachel Lopez 155
De Pia, Peter 111
Derick, John Henry 111
Derington, Thos. 302
De Rivera, Abm. Rodrigues 163
de Rivieres, Abrm. Rodrigues 156
Derlin, Anne 353
Dermott, Andw. 302
De Roch, John Henry 111
De Roche, Henry 106
Deroy, Edward 353
James 353
Derragh, Ellen 334
Eliza 334
John 334
Derry, Anne 323
Cisly 302, 306
Lawr. 303
Valentine 245
de Saussure, Henry 100
Desaussure, Henry 109
Desbrisay, Theoph. 303

Desch, Johann Philipp 131
Deshler, David 10
Dessaure, Henry 111
Detlaf, John 191
Sarah 191
Detmestre, Peter 111
Detrevis, Godfrey 113
Detrivirs, Godfrey 113
Detscher, Peter 111
Dettart, --- 330
Detweiler, Henry 237
Detwiller, Henry, Dr. 237
Deulin, Wm. 353
Devall, Louis 113
Devalle, Isaac 152
Devan, Francis 334, 335
Devaughn, Samuel 288
Develin, John S. 272
Dever, Edward 335
Deveraux, William 272
Devereaux, James 353
Devill, Lewis 109
Devilt, James 335
Thomas 335
Devine, Michael 335
Devision, Peter Abraham 108
Devlin, John 253, 353
Michl. 353
Sally 335
Dew, Thomas 353
Dewdney, John 273
Deymour, William 353
DeYoung, John 327
Deyr, John 353
Diamere, J. 353
Diamond, John 353
Dick, Jane 303
Jas. 303
John 335
Mary 303
Nicholas 234
Saml. 303
Wm. 303
Dickes, Johannes 56
Maria Magdalena 56
Dickey, James 335
John 303
Nathaniel 335
Samuel 335, 353
Dickie, Dav. 303
Dickinson, Gordon 303
Jonathan 2
Dickson, David 353, 417
Eliza 353
Hugh 353
J. 335
Jane 353
John 273, 335, 353
Mary Ann 353
Matt. 294
Sally 353
Samuel 353
Wm. 303
Diebendoerfer, Johann Alexander
17
Diebo, Abraham 531
Diefenderfer, Alexander 3
Diel, Michael 2
Michel 17
Dielboen, Henrich 142
Dierwaechter, Anna Catharina
42
Georg 42
Johann Erhard 42
Peter 42
Dieterich, Anna Margretha 49
Johann 29
Johann Nicol 49

Maria Catharina 29
Susanna Elisabetha 29, 49
Dietrich, Isaac 142
Dietrichson, --- 431
---, Rev. 407
Dietz, Johann Jacob 125
Johann Jakob 125
Johann Michel 125
Maria Dorothea 125
Maria Barbara 126
Nikolaus 125
Diffenderfer, Frank Ried 3
John 3
John Michael 3
Dillan, David 353
Dillinger, Henrich Wilhelm 4
Dillmann, Georg 177
Dillon, --- 303
Ellen 353
Gerard 303
James 353
John 270, 353
Judy 491
Pat 491
Margaret 491
Patrick 353
Pierce N 247
Richard 353
William 273
Dirr, Nich. 167
Discord, J. 353
Disert, Wm. 303
Ditmastre, Peter 111
Ditts, Johann Jacob 125
Diver, Edward 353
George 353
Mary 353
Patrick 353
Sidney 353
Susan 353
William 353
Divin, Patrick 335
Divine, Jas. 303
William 335
Dix, John 254
Dixon, Catherine 353
Henry 194
Jacob 254
James 273
Joanna 335
John 353
Mary Ann 335
Saml. 303
Thomas 335
Djerke, Bagnhild 391
Britha 391
Gjertrud 391
Jacob 391
Jacob K. 391
Knud 391
Magle 391
Doak, David 335
John 135
Margaret 353
Michael 353
Dobbin, ---, Mrs. 335
Leonard 335
Dobbs, Conway Rich. 303
Fras. 303
Jane 303
Dobelmann, Frederica 328
Dobson, Fanny 353
James 353
John 353
Mary 353
Susan 353
William 353
Docherdy, Rose 118

Doddington, --- 303
Dodds, James 273
Dodingby, ---, Capt. 303
Doermer, Charles 273
Doerner, Bernhard 45
Catharina 45
Jacob 46
Margaretha 45
Maria Catharine 45
Doerr, Adam 26
Jacob 46
Johann Heinrich 25
Maria Catharina 46
Maria Margaretha 58
Nicolaus 25
Peter 58
Sebastian 46
Doerter, Johann Anton 37
Doffin, Wm. 353
Dogger, Jacob 512
Neeltjee 512
Peter 512
Sakum 512
Tryntje 512
Dogherty, Anne 353
Biddy 335
Cath. 303
Cathar. 335
Dennis 335
Edward 335
George 335
Isaac 335
Mary 335
Michael 353
Philip 335
Doherty, --- 330
Anne 353
Anthony 353
Bryan 353
Catherine 353
Charles 353
Daniel 353
David 353
Henry 329
Hugh 353
John 303, 353
Maria 353
Mary 353
Michael 353
Philip 353
William 353
Doholy, Edward 335
Dolan, Barney 260
Bryan 475
John 475
Thomas 475
Doll, Anna Elisabetha 53, 70
Anna Margaretha 54
Casper 15
Conrad 54
Friedrich 53, 70
Georg 54
Dolonson, Hugh 335
Doly, Altha 353
Arthur 353
Henrietta 353
Jane 353
Maria 353
Domie, Johannes 25
Dominick, John 109
Donachy, Cath. 303
Jas. 303
Donaghe, Henry 353
Donaghey, Ann 335
Barney 335
Pat. 335
Donaghy, Anne 353
Ar. 335

John 335, 353
Donahy, Edwd. 303
Donald, Barney 335
Eleanor 335
Michael 335
Donaldson, Hugh 303
John 303
Robt. 303
Ronald 262
Thomas 335
Donavan, Michael 274
Donell, Jane 335
Donelly, William 335
Donivan, James 274
Donlan, Edward 457
John 457
Margaret 457
Martin 457
Patrick 457
William 457
Donlin, John A. 275
Donlon, Anne 457
Bridget 475
Catherine 475
John 475
Pat 475
Patrick 457, 475
Thomas 475
Donnatt, Abraham 111
Donnell, Daniel 353
Elizabeth 335
James 353
Donnellan, Bridget 475
Catherine 472, 475, 483
John 475
Martin 457
Pat 475
Patrick 475
Thomas 475
Donnelly, James 353
Jas. 303
John 353
Patrick 353
Robert 353
Donnoghue, John 274
Donnolly, Petr. 294
Donnon, Jane 303
Jos. 303
Donoher, Simon 353
Donohoo, James 353
Donolan, Bridget 475
Catherine 475
John 475
Pat 475
Patrick 475
Thomas 475
Donoly, Dan. 303
Jas. 303
John 303
Margt. 303
Nelly 303
Patk. 303
Peggy 303
Peter 303
Reggy 303
Susy 303
Donoughua, Patrick 254
Donovan, James 274
John 274
Michael 274
Doogan, John 353
Dooley, Michael 274
Thomas 475
Dooling, Michael 353
Dooney, John 353
Doorish, Bernard 335
Dorah, Samuel 266
Doran, Paul 353

Dorff, George Minguers 107
Doritz, John Erdman 533
Dörksen, Aganeta 524
    Anna 524
    Cornelius 524
    David 524
    Eva 524
    Gerhard 524
    Heinrich 524
    Helena 524
    Johann 524
    Katharina 524
    Maria 524
    Peter 524
    Sarah 523
    Susanna 524
Dorman, Geo. 303
    Jane 303
    Jas. 303
    Margt. 303
Dormer, Ja. 76
    Jas., Lieut.-Cor. 303
Dorner, Jacob 46
Dornin, Bernard 246
Dorst, Maria Catharina 54
    Peter 54
Dorten, Johann Anton 37
Dorth, Johann Jakob 124
    Maria Elisabeth 124
Doubly, Mathew 291
Dougherty, Abigail 335
    Anthy. 335
    Bridget 353
    Cath. 335
    Dudly 335
    Elizth 303
    Henry 335
    James 335, 353
    Jas. 303
    John 335, 353
    Joseph 254
    Margt. 303
    Neal 335
    Philip 335
    Thos. 335
    William 335, 353
Douglas, Alexander 194
    John 195, 262
    Saml. 291
Douglass, Andrew 353
    Ann 303
    Arch., Ensign 303
    James 353
    John 274
    Joseph 335
    Robert 335
    William 281
Dovalle, Daniel 152
Dove, Edward 335
    John 275
Dovig, O A 402
    Ole 405
Dowd, Mary 473, 476, 478
Dowe, Thomas 353
Dowglass, Chas. 303
Dowling, John 282
    Michael 353
    William 274, 280
Downes, James 139
Downey, Michael 353
Downie, Christn. 199
    Joseph 212
    Mary 199, 212
Downs, Hen., Capt. 303
    John H. 265
Downy, Christian 212
Doyle, Catherine 335
    David 335

Dennis 335
Eliza 353
John 270, 274, 335, 353
    Margaret 353
    Martin 353
    Michael 274, 335
    Moses 353
    Patrick 353
Doyne, Charles 353
Drach, Anna Maria 41
    Rudolph 6, 41
Drafts, Jacob 165
Drain, Henry 335
    John 335, 353
    Richard 353
Draine, Charles 274
Drake, Henry 335
Draper, Thos. 303
Drautman, Hans George 48
Dreher, Godfrey 165
Dreibelbiss, Johann Jacob 44
Dreisch, Michael 274
Dreison, Anah. 335
Drennan, --- 303, 313
    James 289
Drew, Solomon 253, 254, 257,
    260
Drexler, David 234
Dripps, James 353
Drumphey, Thomas 275
Dubant, Marc 274
Dubbs, Joseph H., Rev. Dr. 9
Duberdosser, Henry 111
Duboisson, Stephen, Revd. 274
Dubs, Jacob 9
Dubuisson, Stephen, Revd. 274
Duck, Peter 520
Dück, Anna 519
    Cornelius 519
    Elisabeth 519
    Franz 519
    Heinrich 518
    Helena 519
    Isaak 518
    Johann 519
    Justina 519
    Margaretha 519
    Maria 520
    Peter 518, 520, 526
    Susanna 518
Duckworth, John 251
Duddy, Henry 335
    William 335
Dudenhöfer, Anna Barbara 67
Dudley, Henry 244
    Margaret 354
    Thos., Qr.-Master 303
Dudson, John 532
Duebendorffer, John 3
Duebinger, Bernhart 19
Duff, Anthony D. 245
    Eliza 354
    Jane 354
    John 197, 354
    Margaret 354
    Samuel 354
    Thomas 354
Duffey, James 274
    John 335
Duffief, Cheruibin 254
Duffin, Anne 354
Duffy, Charles 354
    Fanny 354
    Fargus 335
    Francis 335
    James 335
    John 354
    Mary 354

Owen 335
Patrick 354
Peter 248, 354
Dufief, Cheruibin 254
Duggan, Daniel 491
    Denis 491, 505, 506
    Eileen 492
    Ellen 505, 506
    Harry 492
    Helen 492
    Madge 492, 505
    Margaret 492
    Mary 491
    Norry 492
Duggen, John 139
Dugin, Johanna 510
Duginn, Daniel 510
Duigan, Anne 354
    Bridget 354
    Eliza 354
    Wm. 354
Dulany, Patrick 254
Dumph, John 254
Dumphey, John 251, 254
Duncan, James 205
    John 303
    Margaret 335
    Richard 354
    William 354
Duneen, Daniel 354
Duney, Robert 354
Dungannon, Arth., Rt. Hon. 303
Dunkelberger, Clement 4
    John 4
Dunkersly, Benjamin 139
Dunlap, James 135
    Mich. 303
Dunlop, John 198, 201
Dunn, --- 115
    Ann 501
    Biddy 501
    Catherine 221
    Elizabeth 354
    James 221, 501
    John 221, 275, 335
    Mary 354
    Mathew 354
    Peter 354
    Thomas 254
    William 354, 501
    Wm. 292
Dunnahough, Thomas 335
Dupplin, ---, Lord 146
Duran, James 288
Durham, James 335
    Margaret 335
Durmmond, John 195
Durr, Johann Georg 177
Dury, John 335
Duvas, Terance 335
Dwyer, John 354
Dycle, John 354
    Robert 354
Dyer, Edward 268
    Edwd. 268
    John, Ensign 303
    Joseph 193
Dysart, Jane 303
    Wm. 303
Dyvigen, O. A. 402, 403, 405
Dyvik, Ole 402, 405
Dzierozynski, Francis 275

-- E --

Eagan, Patrick 354

Eager, Robert 354
Eagleason, Margt. 303
  Wm. 303
Eakens, Sarah 335
Eakin, Alexr. 293
Eakins, James 139
  Margaret 335
  Margaret, Jr. 335
  Robert 289
  Rosannah 335
Earl, Robert 275
Early, John 303
Earrie, Edward 354
Easton, Wm. C. 286
Eastwood, Sarah 193
Eaton, Hugh 303
  Michael 530
Ebarback, John H. 288
Ebehrth, Andereas 59
Ebeleng, Henry 275
Ebeling, Frederick 275
  Henry 263, 264, 275, 284
Eberback, Henry 275
Eberhard, Frederick 12
  Joseph 3
  Michael 4
Eberhardt, Andreas 59
  Elisabetha 59
  Friderich 59
Eberle, Adam 170
  Johann Adam 170
  Leon[h]ard 169
Ebert, Anna Elisabeth 124
  Johann George 124
Eccles, John, 2nd Lieut. 303
  John, Sir 304
  Thos. 304
Echard, George 335
Echlin, Arth. 304
Eckardt, Henry 275
Eckel, Anna Catharina 43
  Georg Peter 43
  Johann Georg 43
  Juliana 43
  Michael 43
Eckert, Conrad 224
Eckles, John 197
  Wm. 197
Eckloff, Christian 254, 275
  Godfrey 275, 277, 278, 285
  Joseph 283
Ecloff, Christian 254
Ecolier, David 107
Edes, William H. 263
Edgar, Dav. 304
Edgcombe, John 304
Edmiston, David 134
  Isabella 134
  Jesse 134
  John 134
  Moses 134
  Rachel 134
  William 134
Edmondson, James 335
Edmonston, Nathan 283
Edmunds, Jacob 139
Edward, Jane 190
  John 190
Edwards, Ann 446
  Edwin 446
  G. 335
  Grace 446
  John 88
  Mary 446
  Richard 354, 446
  Richd. 446
  Thomas 445
  William 443

Egan, Bridget 476
  John 476
  Mary 476
  Michael 476
  Pat 476
  Thomas 354
  William 275
Egar, Jane 335
Egert, Anna Barbara 67
  Peter 67
Eglin, Stephen 193
Egnia, Ann Marie 111
Eheman, Jacob 326
Ehret, Peter 170
Ehrhard, Anna Barbara 126
  Anna Margarethe 125, 130
  Anna Maria 126
  Elisabeth Dorothea 125
  Johann Heinrich 125
  Johann Henrich 125
  Johann Peter 125
  Johann Philipp 125
  Johannes 125, 126
  Maria Elisabeth 125
  Maria Christina 125
Ehrhardt, Johannes 126
Eichert, Christian 32
Eichler, Abraham 165
Eide, Knud Olson 375
  Ole Thompson 415
  Ole Thorbjornson 415
Eie, Knud Olsen 410, 411, 414
  Knud Olson 414
  Merthe 411
  Ole Johnson 410
  Ole Thorbiorns 414
Eigender, John 6
Eigler, Jacob 275, 278
Eike, Abel Catharina 390
  Arenhaldus Andreas 390
  Augustinus Meldal Drun 390
  Djorn Andressen 389, 393, 408
  Jacob Pertersen 411, 414
  Siri Jonas Datter 411, 414
Einbroet, John David 275
Einong, Gunild 427
Einsel, Anna Catharina 46
  Apollonia 46
  Johann Ludwig 46
  Ludwig 46
Eisenhauer, Adam 21
Elbert, Sarah 76
  Will 76
Elder, James 354
  John 354
Eldred, John 304
Eldridge, --- 464
Eliot, Dav. 304
  Samuel, Jr. 260
Elizar, Isaac 162
Elizard, Abraham 107
Elizer, Isaac 161, 163
Ell, John 218
  William 218
Ellingsdatter, G. 404, 408
  K 404, 408
Elliot, Alfred 268
  J. 354
  Johnathan 254
  Robert, Rev. 354
  Samuel A. 270
  William 335
Elliott, Archibald 335
  John 304
  Johnathan 254
  Margt. 304
  Mary 140

Ellis, Alex. 304
  Bartholomew 354
  Fras. 304
  Harry 270
  Henry 275, 277
  Joseph 354
  Margaret 139
  Margt. 304
  Thomas 79
Ellison, John 354
Elliston, Robert 354
Elms, James 354
Elvans, Richard 275
Emerson, ---, Mrs. 335
Emhard, Frederic 326
Emich, Hans 531
Emmerick, John 276
Emmerk, John 288
Emmert, Henry 277
  William 277
Emmesk, Andreas 167
Emmet, Thomas Addis 244
Enderlin, Henry 108
Endersedatter, Bolte Randine 413
Endersen, Ole 413
Ends, Eliz. 532
Enersen, Anderes 390
  Anders 390, 393, 395
  Bertha Serina 388
  Birtha 388
  Ener 390, 393, 394
  Kirstina 388
  Lisbeth 390
  Oline 390, 393
  Samuel 388
  Susanna 390, 394
Enery, Biddy 291
Engebrethsen, S. 428, 430, 431
Engel, Maria 55
Engelbrecht, Anna 526
  Elisabeth 526
  Helena 526
  Jacob 526
  Maria 526
  Peter 526
English, Isabella 289
  James 335
  John 289
  Robert 335
  Thomas 335
Ennis, Fras. 293
  George 354
  Gregory 264, 265, 267, 272, 277, 278, 279, 280, 282, 285, 286
  John F. 280
  Mark 354
  Philip 277, 278, 279, 282
  Phillip 279
Enns, Agatha 523
  Gerhard 526
  Johann 523
Eno, Richard 271
  Thomas 271
Epex, Josiah 258
Epinette, Peter, Rev. 254
Epting, Christoph 326
  Jno. Adam 167
Erb, Charles 277
Ercksen, K. 429, 436, 438
Erdman, John 12
Erhard, Wilhelm 126
Erhart, Johann Henrich 125
  Johannes 126
Erichsen, Bertha 389
  Erich 389
  Hendrick 389, 392, 395
  Johnas 389

Magle 389
Peder 389
Walbarg 389
Erikson, --- 376, 383
Erle, Jacob 225
Ernst, Christian 328
  Johann Georg 20
Erraty, M. 335
Erskine, John 254
Erwin, James 354
  John 354
  Mary 354
Esbey, John 264
Eschback, John 254
Eschelman, Christian 11
  Peter 11
Esenwein, Johannes 23
Esewein, Johannes 23
Esling, Johann Georg 142
Espeland, Osten Knudsen 410,
  411, 413, 414
Espey, John 264
Espy, Sarah 335
Essex, Jonah 262
Essig, Christoph Heinrich 225
Etter, Joseph 286
Euler, Johannes 169
Eulers, Johannes 169
Eurich, Hanss (Georg) 178
Eustace, ---, Miss 304
  Maurice, Sir 304
Evans, --- 469
  ---, Capt 85
  Benjamin 192
  Cadwallader 274
  Evan 277
  Geo., Rev. 304
  James 138
  John 532
  Mark 246
  Samuel 335
  Wm. 354
Evansdatter, Andrea 427, 428
  Sophie 428, 430
Evart, David 335
Evatt, Francis 293
Evendatter, Siri 412, 415
Evensdatter, Inger 412, 415
Evensen, Hans 427, 428
  Johannes 428, 430
  Ole 427, 428
Evenson, Johannes 412, 415
Everitt, William 354
Everton, --- 304
Evett, Ann Jane 304
  Elizth. 304
Evins, Samuel 354
Eward, John 304
Ewart, John 335
  Wittwe 518
Ewell, James 265
Ewert, Abraham 518
  Aganeta 518
  David 518
  Elisab. 518
  Helena 518
  Jakob 518
  Wilhelm 518
Ewig, Christian 20
Ewing, Alexander D. 354
  John 293
Eye, Knud 410
  Ole Torbiornson 415
Ezechiel, Tobias Jacob 328

-- F --

Fabian, Joseph 18
Fagan, --- 418
  Mary 417
  Michael 354
  Terence 417
Fahey, Garrit 354
  Mary 354
  Tim. T. 354
Fahy, Andrew 354
Fair, Alexander 354
  Ann 335
  James 335
  Thomas 335
Faley, Thomas 354
  William 354
Falin, Mary 354
Falkland, ---, Lord 304
Falkner, Daniel 1
Fallan, William 354
Fallet, Abraham 108
Fallon, Anne 458
  Bridget 457, 458
  Edward 255
  Eliza 457
  Ellen 458
  Garret 457
  Martin 458
  Mary 458
  Patrick 458
  Thomas 458
Fanan, John 335
Fanen, John 335
Fanning, --- 346
  Edmund 346
Fannyde, Thos. 443
Faren, Thomas 335
Farland, Margaret 335
Farley, Owen 354
  Terrence 335
Farmer, John 354
Farms, Ellen 354
  Mary 354
  Robert 354
Farrar, John Morgan 277
Farrel, Anne 354
  Edward 354
Farrell, --- 354
  ---, Miss 354
  Bridget 458
  Eliz. 291
  Ellen 354
  Francis 248
  James 291
  Jas. 304
  Jas. Agnew 304
  Mary 458
  Pat 458
  Peter 354
  Richard 354
  William 354, 458
  Wm. 291
Farren, Felix 335
  James 335
  Sally 335
Farrer, John, Ensign 304
  Wm., Cornet 304
Fass, Maria Catharine 45
  Nickel 46
  Niclaus 45
Fast, Abraham 520
  Elisabeth 525
  Gerhard 520, 525
  Helena 525
  Isaak 520
  Jakob 520

  Johann 520, 525
  Katharina 520
  Klaas 520
  Kornelius 520
  Sarah 520
  Susanna 525
Fath, Eva Catharina 23
  Georg 23
Faubell, Anna Elisabetha 46
  Johannes 46
Faucounet, David 110
Faulkender, Patk. 354
Faulkner, Alice 139
Faure, Francois 112
Faut, Jacob 53, 69
Fauth, Bernhard 53, 68
  Jacob 53, 69
  Johann Jacob 68, 69
  Johann Jakob 53, 69
  Katharina 53
  Katharine 68
  Louisa 53, 68
Fax, Peter 354
Fay, James 354
  Johann Nikolaus 126
  John 284
  Luke 354
  Patrick 354
Fearis, Catherine 354
  John 354
  Margaret 354
  Mary 354
  Robert 135
Federolf, Peter 31
Federolff, Niclaus 22
Fee, Hugh 354
  James 335
  Patrick 335
Feeney, Martin 354
  William 277
Feeny, Michael 354
  William 282
Fegan, Margt. 304
  Nich. 354
  Patt 294
  Richd. 354
  Ter. 304
Fegley, Bernard 11
  Henrich 11
  Mathias 11
Fehlten, Conrad 29
  Johann Peter 29
  Johann Petter 47
Feiner, William 277
Felber, Hans Jerg 22
Felder, John Perry, Capt 113
Fellows, Joseph 381, 382
  Martha 383
Felte, Peter 30, 47
Femster, Wm. 304
Fendlay, Napshall 335
Fenigan, Daniel 492
  Johanna 492
  Judy 492
  Kitty 492
  Mary 492
Fennely, Patrick 354
Fenstermacher, --- 33
  Mathias 13
  Philip 12
Fenton, Geo. 354
  Rich. 304
Fenwick, Anna 530
  Benedict, Rev. 257
  Elizabeth 530
  Enoch, Revd. 263
  John, Esqr. 530
  Presilia 530

Priscilla 530
Fenwicke, Anna 530
  Elizabeth 530
  John 530
  Priscilla 530
Fergeson, Anna 116
  Catharin 116
  Donald 116
  Florence 116
Fergue, Eliza 354
  James 354
Fergueson, James 534
  James, J 534
Ferguson, --- 335
  Andw. 304
  Ann 221
  Charles 354
  Daniel 534
  Edward 354
  Eleanor 354
  Eliza 354
  Helen 221
  Hugh 335
  James 221, 354
  Jas. 304
  Jean McGregor 221
  John 200, 304, 354
  Mary 221
  Mary Ann 354
  Matthew 354
  Rob., Major & Lieut.-Col. 304
  Robert 221
  Sally 354
  Susannah 354
  Thos. 304
  William 277, 354
  Wm., Capt. 304
Fernandes, Aron Dias 152
  Ben. Dias 155
  Daniel Alves 152
  David 153
  Ester Dias 155
  Isaac 152
  Moses Dias 155
Fernandez, Abigail 154
Ferraghty, Harriet 484
  Honor 484
  James 484
Ferrand, Benjamin F. 248
Ferrard, ---, Lord 304
Ferrers, Thos., Brig.-Gen. 304
Ferrier, James 293
Ferris, Charles 335
  Chas. 304
  David 354
  James 335, 354
  Margaret 335
  Saml. 304
Ferrity, Nicholas 277
Ferro, Jacob, Junr. 156
  Jacob, Jur. 163
Ferry, Maurice 335
Fesen, Peder A 398
Fetherolff, Jacob 224
  Johann Georg 224
Fetsch, Barbara 50
  Christian 50
  Joseph 50
Fetterolf, Peter 6
Fevry, Hugh 354
Fey, Anna Barbara 126
  Anna Katharina 126
  Anna Margarethe 126
  Anna Maria 124, 126, 131
  Johann Ludwig 126
  Johann Michael 126
  Johann Nikolaus 126, 130

Johann Michel 126
Johann Peter 126
Johann Simon 126
Johann Tobias 126
Johann Wilhelm 126
Johannes 126, 131
Maria Barbara 126
Maria Christina 126
Maria Magdalena 126
Peter 126
Sabine 130
Simon Jakob 124, 126
Susanna Barbara 216
Tobias 216
Fhiny, Benjamin 253
Field, John 335, 354
Fiesler, Henry 165
Fife, James 335
  John 354
  Mary 354
Fightig, Christian 240
Filbrick, Henry 135
Fill, John 277
Filson, Mat. 304
Finch, Geo. Ludovick 167
Finck, Anna Maria 126
  Friedrich 178
  Hans Georg 126
  Heinrich 126
  Johann Nickel 127
  Johann Nikolaus 127
Finckman, Conrad 288
Fine, Magdalena 51
Finegan, Thomas 354
Fingusin, Michael 354
Finigan, Hugh 354
  James 354
  Matthew 354
Finkenauer, Anna Eva 35
Finkman, Conrad 278
Finlan, Bridget 354
  James 354
  John 354
  Mary 354
  Owen 354
  Patrick 354
Finlay, Charles 354
  Eliza 417
  John 335
  Margt. 417
  Martha 417
  Mary 417
  Richard 417
  Sarah 417
  Wm. 304
Finn, Bridget 458
  James 354
  Margaret 458
  Michael 458
  Patrick 458
Finne, Bridget 458
  Margaret 458
  Michael 458
  Patrick 458
Finnegan, Ann 335
Finnerty, Harriet 484
  Honor 484
  James 484
Finney, Matthew 335
  Patrick 335
Fischer, Anna Barbara 48
  Anna Maria 183
  Anna Sybilla 183
  Catharina 27, 38
  Catharina Barbara 183
  Georg 48
  George Andrew 278
  Johann Philipp 225

Johannes 183
  Philipp 48
Fishbourne, Philip 533
Fisher, Hugh 354
  James 354
  Margaret 354
  Michael 354
  Wm. 304
Fister, John 278
Fitchut, Wm. 532
Fitzgerald, David 278
  Denis 501
  Ellen 501
  Hanoria 501
  James 274, 278, 501
  John 278, 335, 354, 501
  Margaret 501
  Mary 354
  Matthew 354
  Morris 335
  Nichs. 304
  Patk., Capt. 304
  Thomas 354, 501
  Thos. 294
Fitzhugh, William 283
Fitzimmons, Andrew 335
Fitzpatrick, Bernd. 354
  Daniel 354
  Dennis 354
  Edmund 354
  James 278, 354
  Mary Ann 354
  Sally 355
  T. 335
  Terence 355
  Thomas 355
  Wm. 335
Fitzsimmons, Anne 304
  Eliza 304
  Rich. 304
  Wm. 304
Fitzsimons, John 335
Fitzsymonds, Chr. 304
Fitzwalter, Joseph 78, 81
  Molly 78
  Penelope 81
Flack, Francis 140
Flaherty, John 278
  Margaret 355
  Patrick 355
  William 278
Flanagan, Dominick 355
  Patrick 335, 355
  Samuel 355
Flanary, Catherine 476
  Ellen 476
  John 476
  Margaret 476
  Mary 476
  Michael 476
  Nancy 476
  Nicholas 476
  Pat 476
  Winifred 476
Flanery, M. 335
Flanigan, John 335
  Patrick 335
Flannery, Catherine 476
  Ellen 476
  John 476
  Margaret 476
  Mary 476
  Michael 476
  Nancy 476
  Nicholas 476
  Pat 476
  Winifred 476
Flannigan, Michael 278

Flar, --- 104
Flatt, James 194
Flaxney, Daniel 533
Fleck, Geo. 304
Fleman, Betsy 335
  Joseph 335
Fleming, John 278, 287, 304
  Josias 304
  Thomas 292
Flemming, William 355
  Wm. 304, 335
Fles, David Da Silva 154
Fletcher, Angus 199
  Euphame 199
  John 335
  Katrine 199
  Mary 199
  Nancy 199
  Wm 259
Flickinger, Ulrich 10
Flinn, James 355
  Lawrence 255
  William 355
Flood, Daniel 355
  Samuel 355
Floughsby, Wm. 335
Flournois, Peter 304
Flower, Joseph Edward, Lieut.
  Col. 92
  Joseph Edwd., Esqr. 107
Flowers, Joseph Edward, Capt.
  90
Floyd, John 335
Flurn, Pack 355
Flusing, Eleanor 355
  George 355
  John 355
Flyn, James 355
  Luke 335
Flynn, Hugh 355
  John 355, 417
  Joseph 355
  Mary 355
  Stephen 294
Foaley, Patrick 335
Foetsch, Joseph 50
Fogerty, James 336
Foley, Anne 355
  Dan 492
  Eileen 492
  Johanna 492
  John 492
  Julea 492
  Mary 492
  Pat 492
  William 355
Folhall, Laurin 336
Folin, Bryan 355
Folliott, ---, Lord 304
Follmer, George Jacob 14
  Jacob 14
Folly, Peter 336
Folmer, Jacob 14
  Michael 14
Foltz, Andreas 183
  Eva Elisabeth 183
  Johann Peter 183
  Johann Stephan 183
  Peter 183
Fooks, Ellen 304
  John 304
Forbes, Ann 304
  Fanny 355
  Jane 355
  John 304, 355
  Jos. 304
  William, Junr. 355
  William, Senr. 355

Forcade, William
Ford, Elizabeth 445
  Francis 445
  Joseph B. 271
  Richard 139, 445
  Thomas 445
  Wm 445
Forde, Matt. 304
  Talbot 305
Forest, James 534
  John 355
Forester, Edwd. 305
Forgison, Jannet 117
  Jennett 117
Forley, Patrick 336
Forrest, Andrew 260
  John B. 286
Forrestel, James 278
Forrester, John, Ensign 305
Forrestil, James 278
Forsight, Jas.
Forster, ---, Lord Chief Justice
  305
  Anna Juditha 51
  Benedict 51
  Elnr. 305
  John 191
  Ludwig 51
  Thos. 305
Forsyth, Bezabeer 193
  George 355
  James 355
  John 336
  Mary 336
  Robert 336
  Sarah 336
  Valentine 336
Forsythe, Thos. 305
Forth, --- 305
Fortune, Patrick 355
Fosselman, Ludwig 50, 67
  Maria Margaretha 50, 67
Fosselmann, Elisabetha Mar-
  garetha 67
  Erhard 50
  Hans Erhard 67
  Hanss Erhard 50, 67
  (Johann) Ludwig 67
  Maria Elisabetha 50, 67
  Maria Margaretha 50, 67, 68
Foster, --- 355
  James 336
  John 336, 355, 476
  Margaret 336
  Mary 336
  Sam. 532
Fountain, John 107
Fowey, Thomas 336
Fowler, Charles 251
  Henry W., Capt. 269
  Robt. 305
Fowles, Elizabeth 139
Fowley, Dan 492
  Eileen 492
  Johanna 492
  John 294
  Julea 492
  Mary 492
  Pat 492
Fox, Catherine 458
  Conrad 533
  Francis 458
  James 292
  Jesse 254
  Mary 458
  Pat 458
  Thomas 458
  Walter 78

Wm. 305
Foxall, Ann 447
  William 445
Foy, John 265, 270, 279
  Mordecai 279
Foyle, Lough 305
Frame, John 355
Francis, Day, Miss 355
  John 279
  Joseph Day 355
  Martha 336
  Redmond Day 355
  Richard 279
  Wm. 336
Franck, Anna Catharina 52
  Anna Maria 52
  Anna Susana 105
  Danl 105
  Gertrud 52
  Johannes 52
  Leonhards 105
  Peter 172
Frank, Anna Barbara 107, 175
  Jacob 156, 281
  Leonard 112
  Maria Catharina 175
  Maria Elisabetha 175
Frankford, Fra., Capt. 305
  Hen., Ensign 305
Franklin, Cesar 139
  William 279
Franks, H.B. 157
  Moses Benjamin 163
  Moses Benjn. 157
Frantz, Anna Elisabetha 29, 49
  Jacob 177
  Johann Nicol 29, 49
  Maria Elisabetha 29, 49
Franz, Anna 516
  Hans Geo. 168
  Johann 516
  Kornelius 516
  Martin 516
  Peter 516
  Susanne 516
Fraser, James 279
Frasher, John 164
Frasier, James 336
  Robert 336
Frayne, James 355
  William 355
Frazer, Catherine 117
  Charles 117
  Colin 117
  Eliza 355
  Elizabeth 117
  Isbell 117
  Jane 355
  Jean 117
  John 355
  Joseph 355
  Margaret 355
  Mary 117
  Robert 117
  Sarah 115, 117, 355
Freal, Honor 355
  Owen 355
Freeborn, Thomas 336
Freeland, Wm. 336
Freeman, Raphe 304
  Samuel 336
  Wm. 304
Frere, Barrow 279
  James B. 279
Freund, Anna Margarethe 128
  Philipp 128
Frey, Anna Barbara 183
  Anna Eva 183

Anna Maria 183
Casper 164
Christian 183
Jacob 170
Johann Georg 183
Johann Peter 183
Johann Valentin 183
Juliana 183
Maria Margaretha 183
Peter 183
Freyer, Joh. 167
Friday, John 165
Martin 164
Fridig, J. J. 165
Martin 164
Fried, Paul 54
Friesen, ---, Frau 523
Aganeta 525
Anna 525, 527
Bernhard 525
Diedr. 525
Diedrich 525
Franz 517, 527
Gerhard 515, 517, 523, 527
Helena 523, 527
Hermann 523
Jacob 527
Jakob 517, 523
Johann 515, 521, 523
Katharina 523, 525, 527
Maria 515
Peter 517, 527
Sarah 517, 523
Susanna 527
Friis, Hans 422
Friz, Frederic 327
Froellich, Anna Margaretha 49
Apolonia 49
Johann Henrich 49
Valentin 49
Froheley, Daniel 355
Frohnhaeuser, Andreas 47
Maria Catharina 47
Mathes 47
Froland, N L 402, 404, 407
Nils 402, 407
P. L. 402, 404, 408
Fröland, Anna 407
Nils 407
Peder 408
Fromm, Clemens 167
Froster, Patrick 336
Frul, Thos. 305
Fruland, Lars 407, 408
Nels 407
Frutschy, Anna Regina 46
Elisabeth 46
Peter 46
Frutzuy, Johann Peter 46
Fry, Casper 164, 165
John 274, 275
Joseph 88
Fuchs, Anna Katharina 127
Anna Margarethe 127
Anna Maria 58
Elisabeth Katharina 127
Friedrich 127
Georg Henrich 54
Johann Jacob 54, 127
Johann Nikolaus 127
Johann Peter 127
Maria Magdalena 127
Maria Margaretha 58
Maria Margarethe 127
Fuertado, Isaac 151
Fullalove, James 279
Fullam, Ann 336
James 336

Fullan, Eliza 336
Sealton 336
Fuller, Lucy 336
Fullerton, Agnes 305
Phil., Lieut. 305
Wm. 305
Fulton, --- 355
Catherine 355
Jas. 305
John 305, 336
Kearns 355
Mary 305
Thomas 336
Thos. 305
Fuman, Michael 355
Funston, Andrew 336
Anne 355
Francis 355
John 355
Joseph 355
Robert 355
Furlong, Edward 336
John 355
Mathew 355
Furtado, Ester Henriques 155
Isaac Henriques 155
Rachael Oroibo 155
Furtudo, Judith Orobio 154
Furzend, Chetwyn 81
Furzer, Chetwin 81
Futton, Thos. 305
Fuus, Christian 105

-- G --

Gable, John 166
Gabriel, Benjn. Rodrigues 152
Gaddis, Adam 279
Gadsen, Tho. 89
Gaffin, James 336
Gafney, James 355
Gage, ---, General 215
Gahan, William 279
Gaier, Ernst Lewis 327
Gail, Georg Ludwig 225
Gaither, Greenberry 252
Galabrun, Louis Jean 280
Galache, Pierre 112
Galangher, James 355
Galbraith, --- 305
Anne 355
Charles 355
Eliza 355
John 305
William 355
Galbreath, Angus 199
James 355
John 534
Katrine 199
Rachael 355
Gale, --- 305
Hen. 305
Gales, Joseph, Jr. 260
Galey, Anne 355
Eliza 355
William 355
Wister 355
Galivan, John 486
Gallager, Bridget 355
Peter 355
Gallagher, Betsey 355
Edwd. 305
Hugh 305, 355
John 355
Margaret 458
Michael 355, 458

Owen 305
Patrick 355
Roger 355
Thomas 355
William 355
Gallant, William 280
Gallasper, John 164
Gallaugher, Cath. 336
Chas. 336
Hugh 336
Mary 336
Mich. 336
Patk. 336
Gallen, Biddy 336
Catherine 336
Hugh 336
James 336
Margaret 336
Mary 336
Owen 336
Sally 336
Gallery, Eliza 336
James 336
Gallibrun, Louis Jean 280
Gallier, Elizth 305
Wm. 305
Gallivan, Bridget 336
Gallon, David 290
Galloway, John 218
Sarah 218
Gallway, ---, Lord 305
Galvin, Biddy 492
John 486, 492
Margaret 492
Patrick 492
Tade 492
Gamble, Bell 336
Edwd. 305
Eliza 336
George 336
James 336, 355
John 336
Joseph 336
Samuel 336
William 336
Gamel, Andrew 355
Ganley, Jean 218
Ganly, John 355
Thomas 355
Gannan, Hugh 355
Ganner, Dennis 355
Gannon, James 255
William 355
Ganshorn, Hans Jörg 170
Gansshorn, Johann Georg 170
Gantier, David 106
Ganway, Bernard 355
Gardiner, George A. 280
Gardner, Arthur 355
Arthur, jun. 355
C. E. 325
Debarah 355
Eleanor 355
Elizabeth 355
James 355
Gardnor, Thos. 305
Garelan, William 355
Garmyer, Francis 240
Garney, Michel 355
Garrett, Hugh 355
Garven, William 355
Garvin, Patrick 336
Gascoyn, --- 305
Gasman, Henry 109
Gassmann, Philipp 172
Philipp Rheinhard 172
Gatt, James 336
William 336

Gauger, George Nicholas 12
John Wilhelm 12
Gault, G. 355
George 355
Robert 355
Thompson 355
Gausley, Jno. 355
Gautier, Charles 280
Gawne, Rob., Lieut. 305
Gaytes, Isaac 139
Geary, Patrick 355
Geenty, Bernard 458
Bridget 458
Margaret 458
Mary 458
Geere, Eleanor 530
Ruth 530
Zachariah 530
Geffers, William Joseph 280
Geger, Jno. 165
Gehman, Benedict 6
Christian 6
Geib, Conrad 35
Johann Conrad 35
Johann Henrich 142
Geiger, Abram 164
Hans Jac. 164
Herman 164
I. Jacob 327
Geis, Philipp Jacob 59
Geisemer, Johann Daniel 225
Geiser, Christof 18, 35
Christoph 18, 35
Geiss, Agatha 59
Anna Appolonia 59
Anna Catharina 73
Anna Rosina 73
Henrich 59, 73
Johann Georg 59
Maria Barbara 59
Philipp Jacob 59, 73
Geissendorfer, Wm. 326
Geister, Christoph 18
Geizler, Hans Adam 65
Gelberth, Anna Rosina 73
Henrich 73
Geldermersher, Charles A. 248
Gelespie, William 534
Gelison, Samuel 336
Gelston, James 336
Genagal, Mary 336
Genbretz, John 110
Gender, Andrew 113
Gentes, Anna Appolonia 28, 41
Nickel 28, 41
Gentess, Christina Margareta 28
Christina Margaretha 41
Gentil, Pierre Francois 246
Geoghegan, Henry 355
Murtoch 355
Geohegan, Christopher 355
George, Adam 336
Alexander 336
Andrew 336
Eliza 336
Jane 445
John 336, 355
M. 336
Martha 336
Robt. 305
Saml. 446
Thomas 445
William 336, 445
Gerard, William G. 255
Gerbrand, Anna 517
Bernhard 517
Katharina 517

Gerdes, Ferdinand H. 280
Gereghy, Paul 355
Gerhard, Dieter 36
Johann 35
Johann Henrich 125
Lenhart 142
Gerhardt, Anna Maria 184
Barbara 184
Conrad 184
Elisabeth 184
Friedrich 184
Jacob 184
Johann Dietrich 36
Johannes 184
Peter 184
Gerighaty, Owen 336
Gerlinger, Maria Catharina 47
Philipp Jacob 47
German, Patrick 355
Gerner, Johan Matthes 170
Johann Mathias 170
Geroud, David 107
Gesler, Hans Adam 65
Gesmaroig, Jacob 398
Jacob J 398
Malina 398
Rasmus 398
Getty, James 336
Gettys, James 260, 279, 285
Gibbons, H. 355
J. 355
M. 355
William 336
Gibbs, John 355
John H. 274
Mary 355
Ruth 355
Gibson, Andrew 336
Ann 355
David 336
Hugh 355
James 355
John 218, 355
Margaret 355
Robert 336, 355
William 336
Giddie, Jas. 305
Gieruldsen, Johan 390
Giesler, Anna Catharina 65
Johann Adam 64
Johann Michel 65
Maria Christina 64
Maria Magdalena 64
Giger, Abram 164
Gilbert, Ann 336
John 336
Joseph 336
Mary Ann 336
Gilchrist, Angus 200
Arch'd 121
John 201
Marion 201
Gilderhus, Ole Sjurson 441
Gilderhuus, O. S. 429, 436, 441
Giles, John 336
Gilfillin, John 355
Gilkeson, Archibald 135
Robert 135
Sarah 135
Gilks, Edward 191
Gill, Andrew 458
Bernard 458
Catherine 458
Pat 458
Gillan, Darby 355
Sally 355
Gillaspie, James 336
Gillchrist, Alexander 117

Duncan 117
Florance 117
John 117
Margaret 117
Mary 117
Gillen, Henry 355
John 355
Patrick 355
Giller, Jacob 336
Gilles, Catherine 417
Eliza 417
William 417
Gillespie, Alex. 305
Angus 117
Eliza 355
Fanny 336
Francis 336
Gilbert 117
Hugh 305
Isabella 355
James 355
Jas. 305
Margt. 305
Mary 117, 355
Mary Anne 355
Michael 336
Neil 117
Gillespy, Jane 305
Gillich, Jacob 234
Gillilan, William 355
Gillin, Francis 355
James 355
Margaret 356
Gilling, John 305
Gillis, Alexander 121
Catharine 117
Duncan 121
Elizabeth 121
James 121
Jenet 120
Margaret 121
Mary 121
Gillmer, Eliezer 305
Gilloe, Alexander 336
Gillott, Joseph 280
Gillown, Anne 356
Owen 356
Gilmer, Samuel 336
Gilmore, Christopher 356
James 356
John 356
Margaret 356
Mary 356
Matthew 356
William 356
William, jun. 356
Gilmour, Felix 356
John 356
Joseph 356
Michael 356
Gilson, John 356
Gim, Charles 229
Jean 229
Ginger, David 111
Ginn, Arth. 305
Jas. 305, 306
Ginnings, --- 191
Ginty, Bernard 458
Bridget 458
Margaret 458
Mary 458
Girardin, Anne 104
David 103
Henry 103, 106
Jean Henry 106
Joseph 107
Marguerite 103
Giroud, David 104

558

Gismerierz, Elizabeth 398
  Hannah 398
  Neils 398
  Ole T. 298
  Sigtreed 398
Gissler, Hans Adam 65
Gitty, James 356
  John 356
Given, James 336
  John 336, 356
  Joseph 356
  Margaret 336
  Samuel 356
Givens, Samuel 133
Giveny, Bernard 280
Givun, John 336
Gjermundsdatter, S 429
Glasgau, John 336
Glasgow, Robt. 305
Glaspey, Margaret 133
  Matthew 133
Glass, --- 330
  Alex. 336
  Isabella 336
  James 336
  John 336
  Robert 356
Glassey, Matthew 356
  Robert 356
Glat, Anna Maria 184
  Elisabeth 184
  Georg 184
  Maria Catharina 184
  Nicolaus 184
Glatz, Henrich 32
Gledstanes, Albt. 305
Gleich, Anna Catharina 42
  Henrich 42
Glen, Jean 305
  Jeany 305
  Jennet 305
  John 305
  Margt. 305
  Saml. 305
  Samuel 336
  Wm. 305
Glenfuld, Edward 336
Glenn, David 280
Glinchy, John 336
Glorney, Benjn. 305
Glover, Charles 252, 255
Glynn, Bridget 476
  Joseph 356
  Julia 476
  Leonard 476
  Margaret 476
  Mary 476
  Michael 476
  Pat 476
  Peggy 476
  Timothy 476
Gnaw, Thomas 505
Gochnaur, Jacob 7
Goddard, Elizabeth 78
  J. 305
  James 78
  John 78
  John H. 287
  William C. 270
Godfrey, --- 305
  Thomas 356
Godkin, Henry 356
Godskalksen, B. 429, 436, 439
Goetschy, Anna 11
  John Henry 11
  Maurice, Rev. 11
Goetz, Friedrich Sebastian 224
  George Michael 225

Goggin, Jas. 305
  Wm. 305
Goinor, John 280
Gölbert, Henrich 73
  Maria Catharina 73
Golden, Hannah 476
  Mary 476
  Michael 476, 477
  Thomas 476
Goldsworthy, Caroline 445
  Elizabeth 445
  Harritt 445
  Jane 445
  Johanna 445
  John 445
  Mary 445
  Richd. 445
  Thos. 445
Goliere, Anthony 110
Goll, John 241
Golley, Dominick 336
Golrich, Martin 356
Golrick, Terence 356
Gombze, Michael 110
Gomez, Daniel 156, 163
  David 156, 163
  Mordecai 156, 163
Gonele, Wm. 305
Gonry, Eleanor 356
Gonzalez, Ambrozio L. 280
Gooch, James 285
Goodal, Thomas 270
Goodall, Thomas 255, 270, 285
Goodman, Catherine 356
  Geo. 533
  Richard 356
Gooey, Robert 291
Goorley, Eliza 305
Gorden, Robt., Sir 305
Gordon, Alexander 203
  Charles 204
  Easter 336
  Elizabeth 356
  Elizth. 306
  Geo. 305
  George 208
  J. 306
  James 280, 336
  John 203, 306, 336, 356
  Js., Lieut. 306
  Katherine 78
  Marg. 196
  Peter 78
  Thomas 336, 356
  Thos. 306
  William 203, 336, 356
Gore, Charles 454, 468, 503
  Luke 356
  Ralph, Sir 306
Gormally, Bridget 477
  Catherine 477
  John 477
  Margaret 477
  Mary 477
  Thady 477
Gorman, Hugh 356
  John B. 255, 278
  Mary 356
  Michael, Rev. 356
  Thomas 331
  William 356
Gormans, John B. 268
Gormlay, Philip 280
Gormley, Bernard 356
  Bridget 477
  Catherine 477
  John 477
  Martin 356

  Mary 477
  Thady 477
Gorvorn, Michael 356
Görzen, Abraham 519
  Diedrich 519
  Elisabeth 525
  Franz 519
  Helena 525
  Isak 519
  Jakob 519
  Johann 519
  Justina 519
  Kornelius 519, 525
  Maria 519, 525
  Peter 525
  Susanna 525
Goss, Francis 279
Gothe, Eva Elisabeth 71
  Maria Elisabetha 71
  Velten 71
Gottlieb, Geo. 167
Gotz, J. Gottlieb 328
Gough, Anne 323
  Cisly 302, 306
  Stephen H. 263
Gould, John 280
Gouldsborough, Charles W. 265
Gourley, Wm. 306
Goveran, Peter 356
Govertsdatter, Marthe 390
Gowan, Henry 356
  James 356
Gowran, John 356
Grabbin, Peter 336
Grabenstein, Conrad 326
Grabs, John 108
Grace, Francis 356
  William 255
Gracey, William 356
Gracy, Jane 306
  Phil. 306
Grady, Ann 477
  Bridget 477
  Catherine 477
  Denis 472, 475, 476, 477
  George 336
  Hannah 476
  Honoria 477
  John 477
  Mary 477
  Michael 477
  Pat 477
  Peggy 482
  Peter 477, 482
  Thomas 477, 482
  Wm. 356
Graeber, Emanuel 178
Graebner, Emanuel 178
Graf, Barbara 177
Graff, Anna Katharina 126
  Franz 25
  Kaspar 126
Graffert, Anna Eva 35
  Christoffel 35
  Christoph 35
  Philipp Peter 35
Grafton, John 190
Graham, --- 346
  Alexander 117, 356
  Angus 117
  Archibald 117
  Arth. 306
  Cath. 336
  Catharin 118
  Catharine 117
  David 248
  Edward 117
  Eliz. 118

Fra., Capt.-Lieut. 306
James 336, 356
Jas. 306
Jean 117
John 289, 306, 336, 356, 534
Malcom 120
Martin 356
Mary 117, 356
Mary Ann 306
Patrick 356
Rich. 306
Thomas 356
Grammer, G. C. 287
Gottlieb Christopher 255
Grand, John Rodolph 112
Grant, Alex., Ensign 306
George 207
Grantham, Peter 245
Granthorn, Henry I. 356
Grar, Solomon 532
Grassi, John, Rev. 255
Gratzmann, Anna Margarethe 128
Peter 128
Grauss, Jacob 169
Graves, William 139
Gravin, Barbara 177
Gravmeng, O. A. 429
Ole Anderson 431
Gray, Ann 356
Edwd. 306
Eliz. 80
Elizabeth 336
George 336
Henry 356
James 336
Jane 336
John 336
John B. 265, 272, 285
Nancy 306
Nicholas 246
Samuel 336, 356
Walter 336
William 336, 356
Wm. 306
Gready, Ann 477
Bridget 477
Catherine 477
Denis 477
Honorie 477
John 78, 477
Mary 477
Michael 477
Pat 477
Peter 477
Thomas 477
Greason, William 267, 280
Green, Elizabeth 139
Henry 356
James 280, 356
Nat., Lieut. 306
Owen 280, 281
Patrick 281
Peter 117
Sally 336
William 139
Greene, Ann 529
Hugh 356
Greenfield, Charles 76
Sarah 76
Wm 76
Greenham, Mary 356
Greenlees, John 200
Mary 200
Greenock, Pt. 201
Greer, James 255
Robt. 293
Greeves, Thomas 255
Greg, James 292

John 292
Thomas 292
Gregory, Bridget 356
John 336
M. 336
Grehl, Margaretha 62
Maria Barbara 62
Philipp 62
Greiner, Andreas 47
Maria Catharina 47
Grendle, Robert 336
Sarah 336
Grenier, John 108, 109
Grey, Cyril Vernon 281
Isaac 356
James 336
Saml. 81
Samuel 81
Gribbin, Roger 306
Grier, Alexander 356
Jos. 306
Griesheimer, Valentine 6
Velde (Velten) 31
Griffeth, Biddy 336
Rose 336
Griffin, Daniel 499
Daw 336
Griffith, Jane 336
Mary 336
Richard 485, 487
Robert 336
Robert, Capt. 530
Griffiths, Henry 356
Grill, Johann Georg 56
Maria Dorothea 56
Grim, Egidius 4
Grimes, Agnes 290
Guy 281
James 336
Jas. 306
John 290
Grimestad, Britha 438
C. G. 429, 436, 438
Claus 436
Claus Isakson 438
Isak 438
Lars 438
Ranveig 438
Grimm, Anna Elisabetha 56
Anna Katharina 130
Anna Margarethe 127
Friderich Jacob 56
Johann David 127
Johann Jakob 127
Johann Nicol 56
Johann Peter 127
Johann Philipp 127
Johann Simon 130
Maria Dorothea 56
Maria Elisabeth 127
Maria Magdalena 56
Valentin 142
Grintor, Wm. 251
Grisimer, Velde (Velten) 31
Griswell, John 356
Mary 356
Robert 356
William 356
Grob, Andelheith 108
Elizabeth 108
Grober, George Schonman 109
Grodem, Toleff J 398
Groeter, Abraham 184
Barbara 184
Jacob 184
Johann Georg 184
Groh, Catharina 52, 68
Groner, Jacob 177

Gronhoft, O. H. 429, 442
Groom, Ann 139
Charles 139
Groot, ---, Miss 512
H 513
Groscost, Philipp 31
Gross, Anna Maria 50, 67
Eva Barbara 67
Frantz 50, 67
Frederic 326
Georg Michael 50, 67
Peter 238
Susanna 67
Grossi, John, Rev. 255
Grosskasten, Philipp 31
Grove, Frantz 26
Franz 25
Grovenemberg, Henry 107
Groves, ---, Col. 306
Edward 139
Gruber, Anna Catharina 42
Gruir, John 336
Gruis, Lewis 327
Grün, Martin 175
Grupe, William 281
Gudmunsen, Isack Jacob 389, 395
Guegan, Louis Henry 255
Guelich, Jacob 234
Guenter, Andreas 59
Anna Appolonia 59
Guess, James 336
Guilder, Gilbert 166
Guildner, Frantz 13
Guin, Arth. 306
Jas. 305, 306
Guinee, Darby 510
Guiney, Ben 492, 493
Benjamin 493
Biddy 492
Dan 492, 493, 504, 505
Daniel 505
Darby 492
Eileen 492
Gubby 493
Joney 492
Kitty 492
Mary 489, 493
Tade 492, 493
Guinness, Ann 478
Bridget 478
Catherine 478
Hanora 477
James 478
John 473, 477, 481
Malachy 478
Mary 478
Pat 478
Thomas 477, 478
Guiny, Daniel 506
Guirson, Robert 356
Guiy, Margaret 337
Mary 337
Guliksdatter, A. 429, 436, 437
Gullaksdatter, G. 429, 436
Gudve 436, 438
Gullerin, Nicholas 225
Gullever, Joan 529
Robert 529
Gulliksdatter, B 428
M. 429, 436, 441
Martha 441
Gun, Donald 208
Gunea, Susan 337
Gunn, John 337
Patrick 356
Gunnell, James L. 267
Günther, ---, Frau 523
Anna 523

Franz 523
Gerhard 523
Maria 523
Gunton, Thomas, Junior 281
  William 281
Guntor, Wm. 251
Gurley, John 337
Gurroll, Charles 356
Gurry, John 337
Guschwa, Johannes 172
Guth, Helena 73
  Johannes 59, 73
  Lorentz 14
  Maria Helena 59, 73
  Magdalena 73
Gutheil, Anna Katharina 130
  Konrad 130
Guthrey, John 356
Guttensohn, John 281
Gutteres, Jacob Mendes 151
Guttschlick, E. 264, 276
  Ernest 255
Guttschride, Ernest 255
Guttslick, Ernest 255
Guy, Hen. 306
Guyle, Peter, Lieut. 306
Gyder, Herman 164
Gyger, Hans Jac. 164

-- H --

Haaff, James 356
Haagensdatter, I 429, 431
  Ingeborg 431
Haagensen, Ole 442
Haas, Johann Abraham 142
  Johann Georg 41
  Philipp 41
  Philipp Carel 41
Haase, Erich Johannessen 397, 399
  Ingebord 397, 399
Haber, Philipp 26
Haddock, Benjamin F. 264
  Hen. 306
  Jas. 306
  Jos. 292
Hadfield, George 250, 255
Haehn, (Johann) Jacob 67
Haen, Anna Barbara 67
  Jacob 50, 67
  Johann 67
Haf, Katharina 53
  Katharine 68
Hafelen, Peter 326
Haffner, Maria Magdalena 59
Hagan, Agnes 306
  Edward 356
  Edwd. 306
  Hugh 306
  James 356
  John 356
Hagarty, William 281
Hager, Christopher 281
  Frederick 281
  Godfrey 281
  Gottfried 281
Hagerty, Daniel 337
  Michael 337
Haghen, Patk. 306
Hahn, Adam 45
  Anna Catharina 45
  Conrad 42
  Jacob 42
  Johann 42
  Johann Jacob 42

Johann Niclaus 45
Hair, John 356
Halbach, John F. 239
Halbridge, Robert 289
Hale, Robert 356
Hales, Thomas 337
Halket, Peter, Capt. 306
Hall, Albt. 306
  Alex. 306
  Alexander 337
  D.A. 284
  Hobert 337
  John 264, 306, 337
  Robert 337
  Roger 306
  Saml. 306
  Samuel 337
  Savage 306
  Thos., Lieut.-Col. 306
  William 356
Halle, Thomas 356
Hallen, Gurri 389
  Hanna 389
  Helge 389
  Jacob 389
  John Jacobsen 389
  Kirsten 389
  Marcus 389
Haller, Elisabeth 27
  Elisabetha 57
  George W. 253
  Heinrich 27, 28, 57
  Henrich 57
  Jacob 27, 57
Halliday, James F. 274
Hallingstad, Cecilia 397, 399
  Tjerran O 397
Hallohan, John 260
Hallugan, Richard 337
Halpen, James 356
Halpin, Bernard 356
Halsted, Sophie 430
Halversen, Halvor 412
Halvordatter, G 428, 431
  Ellen 412
Halvorsdatter, A 404
  A M 404
  B 404
  Gunhild 431
  T 404
Halvorsen, A 404
  H 404
Halzapfel, Johann Martin 129
Hamard, Michael 337
Hamberry, Catherine 478
  Judith 471
Hambery, Catherine 471
Hambury, Catherine 478
  Judy 478
  Thomas 478
Hameetman, Maartje 513
Hamell, Archibald 117
  Mary 117
  Murdoch 117
Hamill, John 337
Hamilton, --- 306
  Abr. 306
  Andw., Dr. 306
  Archd., Col. 306
  Charles 337
  Cloud 306
  Conway 337
  Daniel 337
  Darcy 306
  Edw. 337
  Eliza 356
  Elizabeth 337
  Gust., Capt. 306

Jas. 306
John 306, 337
Margaret 337
Mary 337
R. 453, 454, 497
Rich. 306
Robert 337
Robt. 306
Thomas 337
W. 356
William 356
Wm. 337, 356
Wm., Dr. 306
Hammand, Hector, Ensign 306
Hammann, Elisabetha 48
  Maria Catharina 48
  Maria Catharine 173
  Peter 48
Hammel, Bernhard 54
  Christian 54
Hammell, Merran 117
Hammer, Friedrich 26
Hammill, Patrick 356
Hammon, Isaac, Capt. 307
Hammond, Hugh 356
Hammont, James 281
Hanagan, Denis 337
  Peter B.O. 281
Hanbury, Catherine 478
Hancock, Edw. 533
  Elizabeth 446
  John 446
  Richd. 446
  Saml. 446
  Thomas 446
  William 289
  Wm. 446
Handasyd, Wm., Col. 307
Handesyde, --- 307
Handley, James 281
Haney, Hugh 282
Hanifen, Dan 499
  Mary 499
  Ulick 499
Hankwitz, John Godfrey, Ensign 307
Hanlan, John 337
  Margaret 337
Hanlay, Ardsal 292
Hanley, Betty 458
  Darby 459
  Edward 459
  Honor 459
  James 356, 458, 459
  John 458, 459
  Martin 458
  Mary 356, 458, 459
  Michael 459
  Patrick 458, 459
  Peter 459
  Roger 458
  Susan 459
  Thomas 459
Hanlon, John O. 356
Hanly, Betty 458
  Darby 459
  Edmund 265
  Edward 459
  Honor 459
  James 456, 458, 459
  John 458, 459
  Martin 458
  Mary 458, 459
  Michael 459
  Patrick 458, 459
  Peter 459
  Roger 458
  Susan 459

Thomas 459
Hanna, Francis 282
  Robert 356
  Saml. 307
Hannah, James 337
Hansberg, J. G. 327
Hansbury, Judy 478
  Thomas 478
Hansen, Even 423, 426, 428
  G. 429, 432
  Gunnel 432
Hanshaw, David 337
Hanson, Gjermund 433
Hanstear, Gasper 164
Hany, James 446
  Mary Ann 446
  Matthias 447
  Tamlane 446
Happes, George 21, 180
  Joerg 21, 180
Haran, Mary 356
Harbaugh, Leonard 270
  Valentine 272
Harbison, Henry 356
  Samuel 356
Harcourt, Anne 356
  Richard 356
Hardcastle, Mary 139
Harden, Elnr. 307
Harder, Helene 515
  Johann 515
  Maria 515
Harding, --- 330
  Charles 337
  John 356
  William 337
Hardman, Darby 356
Hardt, Philip 25
Hardy, Henriette 229
  Henry 282
Hare, Jarvis 137, 139
  Wm. 307
Hargaden, Patrick 356
Hargon, William 356
Harkin, Hugh 337
  John 356
  Laurence 356
  Mary 356
  Patrick 356
Harkness, Abigail 291
  James 291
  Jane 291
  Margt. 291
  Robt. 291
  Sarah 291
  Thos. 291
Harley, ---, Lord 147
Harlihy, Daniel 282
Harman, Bridget 337
Harms, Anna 514
  Heinrich 519
  Jakob 514
  Johann 514, 519
  Katharina 519
  Margar. 514
  Maria 519
  Peter 514
Harnden, --- 485
Harper, Alexander 356
  Andrew 282
  Catherine 337
  Isa. 307
  Jane 307, 337
  Jas. 307
  Joseph 337
  Mary 307
  Richard 337
  Robt. 307

Walter 256
William 356
Wm. 307
Harpur, James 337
  William 356
Harrington, Robert 256
Harris, James 445
  John, Ensign 307
  Mary 337, 356
  Saml. 307
  Samuel 337
  Thomas 337
Harrison, Benjamin 440
  Francis 307
  James 356
  Jane 337
  Jas., Lieut. 307
  John 337
  Mary 337
  Richard 282
  Thomas 285, 337, 356
Harrold, James 337
Harshaw, John 337
  Margaret 337
  William 337
Hart, Bridget 356
  Catherine 478
  Hugh 356
  James 478
  John 256, 356, 478
  Levy 161, 163
  Margaret 356
  Mark 356
  Mary 478
  Michael 478
  Pat 478
  Solomon, Jur. 163
  Solon., Junr. 156
  Thomas 478
Harten, Thomas 291
Hartland, ---, Lord 453
Hartley, Wm. 337
Hartmann, Johann Adam 175
  Ulrich 142
Hartness, George 356
Hartstein, Wm. 326
Harver, Edward 337
Harvey, ---, Mrs. 307, 337
  Anne 356
  Catherine 356
  David 337
  Jacob 356
  Jon. 307
  Robert 337
  Robt. 307
  William 282
Harvie, Alexander 534
Hasby, Robert 337
Haselwood, John, Ensign 307
Haskett, Massy 337
  Richard 337
Haslam, Margaret 337
  William 337
Haslett, Fortescue 356
Haspelhorn, Anna Barbara 127
  Anna Sara 127
  Hans Michael 127
  Johann Ludwig 127
  Johann Peter 127
  Ludwig 127
  Sabina Katherina 127
Hass, Johann Abraham 142
Hassan, Alexander 356
  John 356
Hassemager, Martin 165
Hassen, Bryan 356
Hasson, John 293
Hasting, Elizabeth 337

Hastings, John 139
Hatch, Hen. 307
  John 307
  Thomas 356
Hatfield, George 255
Hatlestad, Bjorn 415
Hauck, Anna Maria 48
  Caspar 18
Hauer, Bernhardt 177
  Christoph 177
Haugaas, Gudmund 383
Hauge, Hans Nielsen 373
Haugen, Baard 402
  H. G. 429, 432
  Hans Gjermundson 432
Haughey, Benjamin 337
  Peter 337
Hauser, Jno. Christian 165
Haushalter, Anna Margaretha 69
  Anna Maria 69
  Christian 69
  Eva Maria 69
  Georg Simon 69, 70
  Johann Jörg 69
  Jörg Simon 69
  Lorentz 178
  Maria Eva 69
Hauss, Johannes 177
  Michael 177
Hauswirth, Barbara 51
  Christian 51
Haveron, Agnes 307
Hawkshaw, ---, Dr. 307
  Benjn., Rev. 307
  John 307
Hawley, Hen., Brig.-Gen. 307
Hawthorn, Agnes 337
  Bill 356
  David 337
  Ellen 356
  Esther 357
  Geo. 307
  John 337, 357
  Mary 307
  Thomas 357
Hawthorne, Jas. 294
  Kitty 294
  Margt. 294
Haxel, Johann Adam 225
  Johann Friedrich 225
  Philipp Heinrich 225
Hay, David 163
  John 357, 446
  Judah 163
  Robert 357
  William 357
Hayatt, Seth 255
Hayden, Bridget 357
  Bridget, jun 357
  Patrick 357
Hayes, Jas., Sir 307
  Judah 156
Hayre, John 256
Hays, Andrew 134
  Barbara 134
  Catherine 134
  Charles 134
  Frances 134
  Isaac 157, 161, 163
  Jane 134
  Jean 134
  John 134
  Margaret 134
  Patrick 134
  Rebecca 134
  Robert 134
  Ruth 134
  Thomas 357

William 134
Hayson, Susanna 337
Hayward, Edmd. 307
  Nicholas 531
  Samuel 531
Hazleton, Edward 337
  John 337
Healy, Bryan 357
  John 357
  Margaret 357
  Mary 357
  Michael 357
  Patrick 357
Heany, Francis 357
Hearlihy, --- 510
Hearn, Thomas 337
Heart, John 281
Heb, Anna Catharina 45
Heblich, Anna Christina 128
  Anna Elisabeth 128
  Anna Margarethe 128
  Christmann 128
Heckman, Anna Maria 73
  Mary 140
Heckmann, Caspar 21
Hector, Robert 337
Hedge, Anna 530
  Samuel 530
Hedges, Nicholas 267, 284
Heely, Mary 357
Heeran, James 294
Hefferen, Patrick 283
Heffernan, John 307
Heg, Andrea 427
  Even Hansen 423, 425, 426,
    427, 430, 431, 432, 442
  Gunild 427
  Hans Christian 427
  Ole 427
  Siri 427
Heger, Jonathan 28, 41
Hegertye, Patk. 307
Hehn, Johann Peter 30, 44
  Nicol 30, 44
Heider, John Frederick 283
Heill, Johannes 56
  Joseph 283
  Maria Catharina 56
  Michael 56
Heilner, Samuel 234
Heim, Godlieb 328
  John 328
Heimbruch, O., Capt. 514
Hein, Samuel 283
Heine, Heinrich, Rev. 236
Heinen, Henry, Rev. 236
Heinrich, Franz 516
Heintz, Catharina 53
  Eva Barbara 67
  Georg Jakob 53, 69
  Johann Michael 67
  Johanna 67
  Maria Catharina 69
  Michael 67
  Wendel 67
  Wendell 67
Heinz, Susanna 48
Heitmuller, Alfred 283
  Charles A. T. 283
Held, Anna Maria 42
Helfrich, John 6
Helfrick, John 283
Helgesdatter, A 429
  Elen 428
  I 429
Helgesen, E. 429, 435
  Erik 435
Helland, Lars Olson, Capt.

376, 378, 383
Hellen, Lars Nielsen 388
  Martha 388
Heller, Christopher 13
  Simon 13
Hellestad, Ane 412
  Bion Jorgensen 412, 415
Hemperl, Elisabetha 177
Hemphill, John 337
Henderson, Anne 357
  Archd. 307
  Catherine 357
  Christopher 357
  Eleanor 357
  Elizth 307
  Francis 357
  George 258, 357
  Hugh 246
  Jam:_ 337, 357
  Jane 307, 357
  John 337, 357
  Joseph 357
  Marg. 337
  Robert 337, 357
  S. 337
  Thomas 357
  William 337, 357
  Williams 357
  Wm. 307
Hendrick, Eliza 357
  John 357
Hendriksdatter, K 428
Hendry, Catherine 215
  Neil 216
Henegan, James 357
Henge, Catharina 27, 38
  Georg 27, 38
  Philipp 27, 38
Henn, Johann Peter 30, 44
Henney, Peter 357
Henning, Thomas 137, 139
Henninger, Frederic 327
Henrie, Mary 110
Henrietta, Frances 337
  Francis 337
Henriond, Benjamin 106
Henriques, Abraham Lopez 152
  Isaac Nunes 157, 163
  Jacob Lopes 153
  Jacob Nunes 154
  Moses Lopes 152
  Moses Nunes 154
  Rachel 153, 154
  Rachael Lopes 154
  Sarah Lopes 154
Henry, --- 357
  Anne 357
  Augustus 337
  Charles 346
  Christian Frederick 283
  David 357
  George 357
  Hanna 290
  James 290
  James W. 357
  John 283, 290, 307, 337, 357
  John Francis 111, 112
  Michael 337
  Nancy 290
  Robert 337
  Samuel 357
  William 337, 357
Hensen, L. 512
Heny, John 281
Heran, Martha 337
Herchnecht, George 110
Hercus, George 283
Hergedt, Johann Peter 32

Herget, Johann Peter 32, 33
  Peter 172
Herker, James 337
Herlein, Michael 234
Herman, Jacob 326
  Joh 168
Hermann, Michel 42
Herr, Hans Martin 23
  Peter 168
Herran, George 357
Herre, Anna Maria 23
  Hans 23
  Hanss Martin 23
  Simon 23
Herrin, Thomas 357
Herring, John 531
Herrman, Margaretha 42
  Michael 42
Herron, Heny. 293
Herschberger, Henrich 180
Hersdal, Bertha 383
  Cornelius Nelson 381, 383
  Inger 383
  Martha 383
  Nels Nelson 383, 393
  Olena 393
  Sara A. 383
Herter, Andreas 22
Hervig, Henrick Christofferson
  383
Hes, Jeremias 31
Hesketh, Thos., Rev. 307
Heson, William 337
Hess, Conrad 288
  Jacob 283
  William 283
Hetherington, John 357
  Sarah 357
Hetherton, Betsy 337
Hetletvedt, --- 391
  Bertha 392
  John 391
  Knud Olson 391
  Lars Olson 391
  Malinda 392
  Ole Olsen 391
  Ole Olson 383, 391, 392
  Olson 394, 395
  Serina 391
  Sigrid 391
  Siri 391
  Sophia 392
  Soren 392
Hetleved, --- 391
  Birthe Serina 388
  Ellen Sophia 388
  Johannes 388
  Knud Olsen 388, 391, 392
  Malene 388
  Ole 388
  Sigrid 388
  Sören 388
  Ole Olson 391
Hewett, James 357
Hewit, David 357
Hewitt, ---, Gen. 307
  Wm. 307
Hewson, Jas. 307
Heyd, Jacob 177
Heydorn, Dedric 327
Heyl, Elisabetha Catharina 29, 45
  Johann Peter 45
  Susanna Catharina 45
Heylmann, Anna Maria (Regina)
  19
Heyman, Moses 156
Heyworth, Robert 260
Hezel, Jacob 18

Hibbs, Charles 283
Hice, Eleanor 357
Hickey, Offer 510
Hickings, Patrick 337
    William 337
Hickroat, Henry 241
Hicks, Elizabeth 447
    Henry 447
    Maurice 357
    Mary 76
    Thos., Lieut. 307
Hidle, John 394
Higgins, John 357
    Martin 357
    Patrick 284
    William 244
Hilb, Catharina 43
Hilbus, Jacob 287
Hild, Elisabeth 21
Hildebrand, Aganeta 515
    Anna 515
    Heinrich 515
    Jacob 515
    Jakob 515
    Katharina 515
    Peter 515
Hill, Adam 357
    Anne 357
    Arth. 307
    Cath. 307
    George 357
    Gustavus 288
    Hugh 307
    Johann Andreas 18
    John 357, 394
    Martin 357
    Matilda 357
    Metha Trulsdatter 396
    R. 289
    Samuel 357
    Thomas 195
    Thos. 357
Hillam, H. 291
Hille, Metha Trulsdatter 396
    Metta 372, 374
    Ole A 398
    Thomas 372, 374
Hillegs, John Frederick 2
Hillier, Mary 532
Hillman, Jno. Hendrich 166
Hilton, John 337
Himle, Odd J. 402
Himmler, Barbara 50
Himoe, Andrea 430
    Stephen, Dr. 430
Hind, Geo. 166
Hindman, Mary 200
Hinds, John 337
    Richard 337
Hine, William 284
Hipp, Geo. 167
Hirschberger, Henrich 180
Hirschfeld, Friedrich 55
    Johann Friedrich 55
    Johann Henrich 56
    Johann Philipp 55
    Maria Elisabetha 56
    Maria Margaretha 56
    Maria Margretha 55
Hirschfeldt, Friedrich 56
    Johann Friedrich 55
Hisdahe, O.H. 402, 404, 407
Hisdal, --- 407
    O H 402
Hitchins, Wm. H. 346
Hithrington, Js. 307
Hitz, Florian 284
    John 268, 284, 285

John, Jr. 284
Hoare, Bridget 459
    James 459
    John 459
    Mary 459
    Michael 459
    Thomas 459
Hobbart, Edward 357
Hobson, Jas. 307
Hochlaender, Johann Michael 65
    Juliana 65
Hochlander, Hans Michael 65
Höchlander, Johann Adam 65
Hochländer, Johannes 65
Hochstraser, Catharina 27, 39
    Elisabetha 27, 39
    Jacob 27
    Paul 27, 39
    Samuel 27, 39
Hochstrasser, Jacob 39
    Paulus 39
Hock, Maria Margaretha 41
Hocking, James 443
Hodder, T.E. 455, 485, 486
Hodge, James 445
Hodges, Elizabeth 78
    Mary 78
    Richard 78
    Sarah 78
Hodgsdon, John 337
Hodgson, Thomas 337
Hodnefield, Ommund Endressen
    397, 399
Hoek, Aagge 513
    Jan 513
    Jannetje 513
    Job 513
    Johanna 513
    Leendert 513
    Pieternella 513
    Wouter 513
Hoenich, Jacob 48
Hoenick, Jacob 48
Hoff, Anna Elisabetha 49
    Frantz 49
    Lorentz 31
    Maria Catharina 29, 49
Hoffman, Barbara 67
    Christina 53
    Daniel 53
    George 284
    Hanss Georg 50, 66, 67
    Jacob 53
    Konrad 126
    Lorentz 67
    Rosina 50, 67
    Susanna Christina 69
Hoffmann, Adam Heinrich 21
    Anna Maria 52, 126
    Daniel 53, 69
    Georg Bernhardt 54
    Hans Georg 54
    Hanss Georg 54
    Hanss Peter 54
    Jacob 18
    Johann Jacob 69
    Margaretha 54
    Maria Elisabetha 54
    Valentin 52
Hoffmeister, Jacob 328
Hoffner, Jac. 168
Hoffstaetter, Georg 19
Hofman, Johann Petter 55
Hog, Marg. 197
Hogan, Patk. 357
Hogg, ---, Capt. 134, 135
Hogheim, Hans Jacob 168
Hoglander, Hans Michael 65

Hohenstein, Jacob 327
Hoimo, Stephen, Dr. 430
Holborn, John, Ensign 307
Holbrick, Charles 241
Holden, Edward 357
    S. 307
    T. 346
Holdzendorf, John, Capt 107
Holiday, Thomas 255, 256
Holland, Henry 337
Hollaran, William 256
Holliday, James F. 274
    Thomas 251
Hollidge, James 284
    John 284
Hollihorn, John 256
Hollmann, John T. 238
Hollohon, John 260
Holman, John 444
Holmead, Anthony 254
Holmeade, Anthony 275
Holmes, George 357
    James 357
    John 270, 357
    Joseph 357
    Robt. 307
    Sylvanus 270, 272
Holohan, John 260, 284
Holroyd, Joseph 256
Holtzapfel, --- 128
Holzapiel, Johann Nikolaus 129
    Maria Katharina 128
Holzendorf, John Frederick 93,
    100, 111
Homans, Daniel 282
Honde, Thorbjen T 398
Honywood, Rd., Cornet 307
Hood, Ben. 293
    Elizabeth 80
    Jonathan 80
Hooge, Anna 515
    Gertrude 515
    Johann 515
Hook, J.H. 268
Hookirk, --- 346
Hoolhand, John 259
Hoover, John 253
    Michael 253
Hopkins, ---, Col. 134
    ---, Governor 161
    Abr. 307
    Ann 307
    Jane 307
    Jenny 307
    John 307
    Mathew 357
    Ruth 307
    Samuel 357
    Thos. 307
Hopp, Nicholas 263, 284
Hopper, Richard 193
Hoppold, Chris'r Henry 167
Horan, Ann 501
    Anne 478
    Catherine 478, 501
    Eliza 478
    John 337, 501
    Margaret 501
    Mary 501
    Michael 478
    Patrick 501
    Simon 337
    Thomas 478
Horbskarut, Henry 283
Horlihy, Daniel 282
Hornefjeld, Amund Anderson 399
Horner, John 253
Horning, John 284

564

Horrica, James 246
Horsey, Saml., Col 95
Horstkamp, Henry 284
Horter, Agnes 53, 69
  Anna Barbara 69, 70
  Anna Maria 70
  Barbara 53, 69
  Georg 53, 69, 70
  Georg Adam 53, 69
  Georg Jacob 53, 70
  Georg Jakob 70
  Jacob 53, 69
  Johann Valentin 70
  Johann Valtin 53, 70
  Maria 69
  Velten 53, 69, 70
Hostermann, --- 25
Hostetter, Oswald 7
Houghton, Hen., Sir 307
Houlehan, Thade 508
Houlihan, Tade 505
Houlsdatter, Siri 411
Hounahane, Hen. 307
Houseman, Henry 193
Houston, James 357
  John H. 287
How, John, Capt. 307
Howard, Peter 251
  Thomas 259
Howe, William, Sir 10
Howell, John 357
Howie, Mary 200
  Robt. 199
Howland, Alex. 346
Hoy, --- 307
Hoye, Patrick 357
Hubbard, Ephraim 139
Huber, Anna Barbara 42
  Caspar 42
  Elisabeth 27
  Elisabetha 38
  Johann Caspar 42
  Michael 42, 533
Hubin, Anna Maria 72
Hubner, John F. 233
Huddleston, Joseph 252
Hudson, Jas. 307
Huebener, Joh Frid 233
  Johann Friedrich 233
Huey, Betty 357
  James 357
Huges, John 337
  Robert 337
Hugh, --- 357
Hughes, --- 77
  Andw. 307
  Arthur 337
  Charles 357
  Eliz. 81
  Elizabeth 78
  Hugh 284, 357
  J. 357
  Jane 307
  Jas. 337
  John 284, 337, 357
  Joseph 78
  Lucy 139
  Patk. 307
  Patrick 357
  Peter 337, 357
  Richard 337
  S. 357
  Thomas 257
  William 270, 283
Huginier, David 113
Huguenin, Abraham 103
  Danl. 103
  David 103

  Marguerite 103
Huguenium, Margaret 112
Huie, Jean 200
  Martha 199
Hull, E. 307
  Jas. W. 307
  Wm. 307
Hulton, Patrick 357
Humber, David Pierre 112
Hume, Thos. 308
  W. 308
Humel, Caspar 325
  David 326
Hummel, Anna Catharina 42
  Peter 168
Humphreys, Chr., jun. 308
  Francis 357
Hun, Rachel 337
Hungerford, Anth. 308
  Edwd., Sir 308
Hunold, Matthäus 176
Hunt, Wilson A. 357
Hunter, Abram 198
  Alexander 117
  Ann 337
  Catherine 357
  Charles 357
  David 337
  Eleanor 337
  Gerard 337
  Hen. 308
  James 337, 357
  Jenat 117
  John 308, 337, 357
  Jos. 308
  Martha 337
  Mary 337, 357
  Moses 337
  Robert 244, 337
  Samuel 337
  Thomas 337
  William 357
  William Alexander 117
  Wm. 337
Huquin, David 110
Hurley, J. 337
  Wm. 337
Hurstcamp, Henry 285
Husar, Barbary 166
Husson, James 357
Husted, Caleb 232
Hutcheson, Eleanor 134
  George 134
  Jennitt 134
  John, Jr. 134
  John, Sr. 134
  Margaret 134
  Mary 134
  William 134
Hutchin, John, Jr. 337
Hutchins, Sarah 530
Hutchinson, Samuel 256
  Thomas 337
Hutchison, Dav. 308
  Nancy 308
  Robert 247
  Wm. 337
Huth, Elisabeth 23
  Jacob 23
  John 2
Hutmacher, Maria Margaretha 40
Hutter, Charles L. 236
Huttleston, --- 464
Hutton, James 357
  John 337
  Matt. 308
  Patrick 357

Huy, David 156
Hyde, Thomas 262, 264, 274
Hylle, K. J. 429, 436, 439
  Knudt 440
  Knut Johnson 439
Hyman, Margaret 121
Hyndman, Andw. 200
  Cathn. 200
  Hugh 308
  Margt. 200
Hynes, Edward 357
Hype, (Johann) Henrich 142

-- I --

Ibach, Gideon 238
  Gustavus 238
Iddins, Frederick 285
  Samuel 285
Imes, Abraham, Rev. 102
Imhaeusser, Adam 25
Immenhauser, Adam 25
Indermaur, Jeremiah 285
Ingler, Anna 113
Inglerine, Anna 109
Ingraham, Thomas 357
Ingram, Farmer 357
  Florena 357
  John 357
  Mary 357
  Sally 357
Inkle, Henry 533
Innes-Cross, Sarah Jane 308
Iost, Benedict 285
Ireland, Arthur 468, 469
Irvine, --- 357
  Andrew 337
  Ann 308
  Chas. 308
  Dary 357
  Gerard 308
  James 357
  John 337, 357
  Rich. 308
  Robert 357
  Robt. 308
  Samuel 337
  William 357
Irving, John 139
Irwin, Alex., Col. 308
  James 357
  Wm. 308
Irwine, George 337
  Jas. 308
  John 308
  Rachel 337
  Wm. 308
Isaac, Jacob 157
  Wm. 308
Isaacs, --- 438, 442
  Abraham 156, 163
  Isak 438
  Lars 438
  Louis 438
Ising, George 237
Isoug, Hans Ulrick 111
Israel, Henriq. 152
  Mildrach 157
Israells, Ansel 156
Ivers, Anne 357
  Catherine 357
  John 357
  R. 357
  Samuel 357
  William 357
Iverson, Halvor 383

Ivey, William Henry 285
Ivory, Chr. 357
Ivy, John 446

-- J --

Jabez, ---, Brother 6
Jack, John 338
    Robert 357
Jackson, --- 442
    Benjamin 266
    Elizabeth 139
    George 433
    James 248, 357
    Jane 308
    John 338
    Luke 338
    Mary 338
    Richard 331
    Trooper 308
Jacob, Abraham 56
    Anna Margretha 56
    Georg Abraham 56
    Johann Georg 56
    Johann Peter 56
    Maria Dorothea 56
    Maria Magdalena Elisabetha
        56
Jacobi, Anna Catharina 53
    Anna Maria 224
    Catharina 54
    Eva Rosina 54
    Martin 54
    William 285
Jacobsdatter, H 423, 429
    T. 390
Jacobsen, Christine 388
    Jacob 388
Jacobsen Datter, Peder 411, 414
Jacot, Susanne 103
Jacques, John J. 358
Jaeger, Andreas 48
    Benedict 285
Jahraus, Andreas 53, 70
    Anna 70
    Margaretha 53, 70
    Catharina 53, 70
    Georg Adam 53, 70
Jamaison, James 195
James, Ann Maria 447
    Charles H. 277
    Elizabeth 357
    Elizh. 357
    Gabriel 134
    Jane 357
    John 357, 447
    Joseph 357
    Mary 358
    Robert 358
    Thomas 358
    Thos. 447
    William 358
Jameson, Andrew 358
    B. 358
    Dav. 308
    Hugh 358
    J. 358
    John 338
    Wm. 308
Jamison, Agnes 338
    John 293
    Samuel 246, 338
Janes, Roger 358
    William 358
Janga, Neal 338
Jannet, Jacob 113

Janson, Anna Barbara 127
    Johann Michael 127
Janzen, Aganeta 522, 525
    Agatha 522
    Anna 522
    David 522, 525
    Elisabeth 522
    Gerhard 521
    Heinrich 522
    Helena 521
    Jakob 521
    Johann 521, 522
    Katharina 521
    Kornelius 525
    Maria 521
    Peter 521
    Sarah 525
    Wittwe 516
Jarrett, Henry 239
Jasson, Sebastian, Ensign 308
Jaton, Anthony 111, 112
Jeanneret, Henry 103
    Jacques Abram 103
    Jean Pierre 103
    Marie 103
    Pierre 103
    Rose Marie 103
Jebb, Rach. 308
Jeckel, Adam 56
    Anna Elisabetha 56
    Anna Maria 56
    Johann Christoph 56
    Johann Jacob 56
Jeffers, Anthony 358
Jefferson, Henry 217
    Thomas 249
Jeffrys, John 338
Jelfe, Thos. 308
Jellett, Mary 308
Jemmett, Warham 308
Jenbuck, John 113
Jenkinson, ---, Mrs. 338
    Ann 338
    Elizabeth 338
    Isaac 338
    James 338
Jenneret, Anne 106
Jenney, Thomasin 531
Jennings, Catherine 473, 476,
        478
Jindra, Abraham 110
Jirdinston, Peter William 285
Joachim, Friedrich 33
Jochs, Bernard 230
Johanisen, J.J 412
Johannasdatter, S 403
Johannesdatter, S. 403
    T 404
Johansen, Anthon 428, 430
    Even 428, 430
    Johannes 425
    O. 428, 430
Johndatter, Malene 412, 415
    Oline 398
Johnson, Alex., Lieut. 308
    Anne 77
    Catherine 358
    David 338
    Elizabeth 338
    Elnor 338
    George 358, 383
    Henry 358
    Hugh 338
    Ingeborg 399
    James 338, 358
    John 241, 338
    Joseph 253, 255, 258, 358
    Lewis 259

    Martha 358
    Mary 139, 308
    Ole 383
    Robert 77, 358
    Robert, Governor 83, 84, 85,
        87, 89, 90, 91, 92, 93, 94,
        95, 96, 97, 98, 103
    Robt. 80, 308
    Samuel 338, 358
    Sarah 358
    William 284, 358
Johnston, --- 358
    Andw. 308
    Ann 80, 134
    Anna 119
    Anne 358
    Arch'd 117
    Archibald 358
    Arth. 308
    Elizabeth 134, 358
    Francis 338, 358
    Geo. 308
    Gera 358
    Henry 338
    James 256
    Jane 358
    Jas. 308
    John 134, 293, 338
    John Moore 308
    Kirstine 117
    Mary 358
    Oliver 358
    Patrick 358
    Robert 77, 338, 358
    Robt. 80
    Samuel 358
    Stephen 308
    Thos. 308
    Walt. 308
    William 134, 358
Joice, George 255, 256
    Richard 285
    William 255, 256
Jolly, Margaret 358
    Patterson 358
    Robert 358
Jonas Datter, Siri 411, 414
Jonassen, P. 429
Joncherez, Alexr. L. 254
    Louis F. 267
Jone, Ole 408
Jones, Catherine 358
    Cornelius 81
    David 294
    Henry 358
    James 358
    John 338
    Margt. 308
    Mary 79
    Noble 78
    Sarah 78, 139
    Thos. P. 284
    William 139, 265, 445
Jooss, Anna Maria 46
    Frederic 327
Jopp, Anna 63
    Maria Margaretha 43, 63
    Michel 43, 63
Jordain, Thomas 358
Jordan, Dennis 358
    John 308
    Richard 358
    Thomas 285
    Ulrich 26
Jordre, Nils L. 402
Jordte, Ulrich 26
Jose, William 445
Joseph, Tobias 156

Jost, Benedict 285
Joyce, George 256
  John J. 285
  Michael 285, 286
  William 256
Judge, John 279, 286
Juengst, Johannes 23
Jugant, James 358
Jung, Anna Margaretha 42
  David 328
  Elisabeth Dorothea 125
  Hermann 42
  Jacob 164
  Johann Adam 51
  Johann Georg 42
  Johann Jacob 51
  Johannes 125
  Magdalena 51
  Maria Catharina 51
  Peter 51
  Valentin 51
Jungker, Johann Nicklas 37
Justin, Martin 338

-- K --

Kaercher, Agnes 47
  Nickel 47
Kaeufer, --- 51
  Catharina 51
  Catharina Elisabetha 44
  Georg Jacob 44
  Johannes 44
Kahling, John Michael 286
Kaill, Ludovick 110
Kain, ---, Col. 308
  Anth. 308
  Elizth. 308
  Jane 308
  John 308
  Percival 338
  Robt. 308
Kaiser, Godleib 326
  Joseph 225
Kaisser, Herm 286
Kalleftad, John A. 391
Kamb, Jno. 533
Kananak, Langn 358
Kane, ---, Col. 308
  Andw. 308
  Charles 338
  Eliza 338
  Francis 338
  Isa. 308
  John 358
  Margt. 308
  Patrick 286, 358
  Robert 358
  Wm. 308
Kansler, Chas. 164
Kanster, Chas. 164
Karavold, Ragnild Nilsdatter 441
Kargher, John Nicklas 47
Karner, Jacob 173
Karney, Ann 501
  Joseph 501
  Mary 501
  Pat 501
  Patrick 501
  Thomas 501
  William 501
Kaskat, Jane 444, 445
  John 444, 445
Kast, Hans Georg 45
  Hans Jerg 45

Hanss Georg 45
  Margaretha 45
Kates, Robt. 532
Kaucher, Jacob 177
  Michael 177
Kauffman, Johannes 68
  Johannes, Jr. 68
Kauffmann, Anna Apollonia 68
  Anna Maria 68
  Catharina Elisabetha 68
  Christoph 68
  Johann Georg 68
  Johann Jacob 68
  Johanna 68
  Johannes 50, 67, 68
  Juliana 67
  Maria Apollonia 68
  Maria Elisabetha 50, 67
  Maria Magdelena 68
  Maria Margaretha 68
  Matheus 67
Kaufmann, George 283, 286
Kaul, Anna Barbara 124
  Anna Maria 128
  Johann Peter 128
  Johannes 124
Kavanaugh, John 286
Kay, Alexander 221
Kaye, --- 324
Keally, Patrick 338
Keane, John Stephen 286
  Margaret 338
Keanen, Patrick 358
Kearceay, John 338
  Margaret 338
  Thomas 338
Kearcey, --- 330
Kearnan, Patrick 286
Kearney, Ann 501
  Francis 338
  Henry 358
  James 358
  Jno. 358
  John 358
  Johnston 358
  Joseph 501
  Mary 501
  Michael 338
  Pat 501
  Patrick 501
  Thomas 501
  William 501
Kearns, Elizabeth 338
  James 338
  Patrick 358
Kearny, Larry 309
  Mary 309
  Patrick 338
Keating, Abraham 338
  Anne 358
  Edward 358
  Hugh 358
  John 358
  Mary 338
Keck, Henry 9
Kedglie, John 286
Keefe, Hanora 493
  Mary 493, 509
Keeffe, Eugene 493
  Jeane 493
  Johanna 493
  John 493, 505, 506
  Margaret 493
  Mary 506
  Nano 493
  Norry 493
Keegan, Michael 248
Keen, Samuel 358

Keenan, Daniel 358
  Dennis 338
  Ellen 358
  Hugh 338
  Mary 309
  Pat 309
  Thomas 358
Keeny, John 358
Keer, Alexander 358
  Peggy 309
  Robt. 309
  Wm. 309
Kehl, John V. 286
  Lewis 113
Kehoe, Mary 358
  Michael 358
  Thomas 358
Keily, Jeremiah, Rev. 286
Keirnan, James 358
Keise, Augustus E. S. 286
Keiser, Henry 286
Keitch, John 287
Keith, --- 309
  Effie 117
  John 287
  Rebecca 358
Keleher, James 287
Keliher, Dan 508
  Daniel 506
  Jeremiah 506
Kell, John 338
Kelland, --- 384
Kelleher, Dan 493
  Daniel 493
  Danile, junior 493
  Daniel, senior 493
  John 493
  Kitty 493
  Tade 493
  Mary 493
Keller, Anna Catharina 43
  Anthony 142
  Daniel 28, 40
  Elisabetha 184
  Gertraud 57
  Johannes 28, 40, 184
  John F. 258
  Jonas 287
  Jonas P. 263, 280, 287
  Maria Margaretha 49
  Michael 287
  Nicolaus 25
Kelleway, Eliz. 81
  Will. 78, 81
Kelley, Alexander 218
  Daw 338
  Elizabeth 218
  James 218
  Jean 218
  John 338
  Margaret 218
  Mary 218
  Michael 292
  Peter 218
  Philip 338
  Robert 218
Kellum, Geo., Major-Gen. 309
Kelly, ---, Miss 358
  Adam 358
  Ann 479
  Anne 309, 358, 459
  Barney 479
  Bernard 287
  Bridget 459, 479
  Bryan 478
  Catherine 338, 459, 471, 478, 479
  Charles 358

Darby 338
Dudley 358
Edward 358, 459, 465
Eliza 459
Ellen 459, 479
Hugh 358, 465
James 358, 459
Jane 309
Jas. 309, 358
John 309, 358, 459
John, Jnr. 479
John, Sen. 479
Margaret 358, 479
Maria 459
Mary 358, 459, 479
Mary Connolly 479
Michael 338, 358, 479
Molly 338
Neal 338
Pat 456, 459, 479
Patrick 338, 358
Richard 358
Robert 338, 358
Thomas 338, 358, 359, 479
William 358, 459
Wm. 309
Kelpius, Johannes 1
Kelso, Elizabeth 216
Kemmerer, George 238
Kempff, Gregorius 241
Kemple, John 358
Kench, Richard 338
Kenedy, Bridget 358
Geo. 309
John 358
Kenehan, Ann 501
Jeremiah 501
John 501
Mary 501
Matthew 501
William 501
Kengla, Jacob 278
Kenmaer, Andrew 338
Kennady, Val. 358
Kennan, Thomas 292
Kennburgh, James 197
John 197
Kenneday, Mary 190
William 193
Kennedy, Alexander 358
Andrew 358, 480
Angus 221
Ann 479, 480
Anne 358, 479
Biddy 479
Bridget 479, 480
Catherine 479, 480
Daniel 480
Dav. 309
Edward 358
Ellen 479
Hannah 479
Hen. 309
Honoria 479
J., Mrs. 338
James 338
Jas. 309
John 220, 309, 358, 479
Joseph 358
Margaret 358
Mary 471, 478, 479, 502
Mary Ann 480
Michael 473, 480
Pat 479, 480
Patrick 479
Peggy 479
Peter 502
Rachel 338

Robert 338
Saml. 309
Thomas 338, 479
William 338, 358
Kennelly, --- 485
Kenney, Catherine 338
Peter 338
Wm. 309
Kenny, Michael 358
Kent, Kath. 309
Redmond 338
Keobel, Jacob 287
Keogh, Mathew 256
Mathias 256
Keogle, Mathias 256
Keown, James R. 358
Keplinger, --- 7
Keppeler, George 327
Keppler, Henry 287
Simon 33
Ker, James 338
Kerby, Mich. 358
Kercher, Catharina 48
Kern, Anna 63
Anna Elisabeth 43, 63
George 13
Johann Christoph 43, 63
Johann Jost 63, 71
Johann Justus 63
Johann Thomas 43, 63
John Jost 63
Jost 63
Maria Margaretha 43, 63
Peter 43, 63
Philipp Jacob 63
Sophie Margarethe 63
Kernaghan, Robert 358
Kernan, Francis 247
Fras. 309
Jas. 309
Manus 309
William 244
Kerr, Alex. 309
Alexander 255, 358
Allen 338
Ann 309
Anne 309
Catherine 338, 358
Elizabeth 417
Elizth. 309
George 358
Henry 358
Isabella 358
James 338, 358
Jane 309, 417
Jas. 309
John 338, 358
Jos. 309
Maik 309
Mark 309
Mark, Brig.-Gen. Lord 309
Matilda 358
Matthew 338
Muck 309
Nancy 358
Patrick 358
Rachel 338
Robert 358
Thomas 358
William 289
Kerrvan, Henry 358
Kervan, Thos. 358
Kervell, Edward 533
Kerwan, James 338
Kesseler, Anna Maria 52
Kessler, Margaretha 51
Keswett, Rich. 309
Ketly, Matthew 338

Kevenagh, James 338
Keveny, Owen 245
Key, Wm. 338
Keys, Elizabeth 358
Samuel 358
Keyworth, Robert 253
Khell, Loudwick 110
Kickler, Joseph 142
Kidd, Archibald 289
J. 358
Kiel, Johann 25
Kield, Isaac 358
Kieran, --- 330
Kiernan, Charles 281, 287
Hugh 257
Kiesh, Christian 326
Kiess, George 326
Kiessinger, Jacob 17
Kilcannon, Anthony 480
Kilfoyle, Peter 358
Kill, John 338
Killalea, Abegail 480
Ann 480
Biddy 480
Bridget 480
Catherine 480
Darby 478, 480
Ellen 480
John 471, 480
Lawrence 480
Margaret 480
Mark 480
Mary 480
Mathias 480
Michael 480
Patrick 480
Patrick, Senior 480
Peggy 480
Sally 480
Thomas 480
Killelea, John 465
Matheis 511
Michael 511
Killen, Jenkins 309
Thomas 358
Killigrew, Guildford 309
Killy, Daniel 338
Kilmartin, Charles 358
Hugh 358
John 358
Mary 358
Patrick 359
Kin, Charles 281
Kinanak, Matthew 359
Kinaston, --- 309
Kincaid, James 257
Kinch, James 338
T. 338
Kinchey, Paul 257
Kineard, Robert 289
William 289
King, Benjamin 260
Cath. 309
Charles 258, 281
David 293
George 255, 272
James 338
James C. 252
Jane 338
Margt. 309
Mary 338
Richard 338
Robt. 309
Thomas 359
Wm. 309
Kingman, Sarah 137, 139
Kingsland, John 359
Kingston, ---, Lord 309

Kinkade, Mary 309
    Wm. 309
Kinne, Martha Gulliksdatter 441
Kinney, Charles 287
    Jeremiah 287
Kinshela, William 359
Kinsley, Benjamin 287
    Jas. 309
Kipps, William 140
Kirby, Cornelius 338
    Eliza 338
    Mary Ann 338
Kircher, Catharina 48
Kirk, George 338
    P. 338
    Samuel 338
    William 359
Kirkham, Watson 267
Kirkman, James 292
Kirkpatrick, Alexander 359
    And. 359
    Anne 359
    Crissey 359
    Eliza 359
    George 359
    Jane 359
    John 338, 359
    Margt. 359
    Mary 359
    Math. 338
    Rob. 359
    Wm. 338
Kirkwood, Jonathan 287
Kirn, I. 325
Kirr, Daniel 338
Kirsch, Conrad 19
    Georg 19
    Johann Jacob 19
Kistner, Anna Elisabeth 128
    Johann Peter 128
    Johann Simon 128
    Simon Jakob 128
Kittilsdatter, M 429
Klein, Anna Catharina 42
    Anna Magdalena 128
    Anna Margarethe 128
    Anna Maria 128
    Jacob 128
    Johann David 128
    Johann Georg 128
    Johann Heinrich 36
    Johann Hennerich 36
    Johann Jakob 128
    Johann Peter 128
    John 328
    Maria Margarethe 128
    Peter 128
Kleindienst, John P. 287
    Sebastian 287
Kleinduist, Sebastian 277
Kleinhantz, John George 7
Klensen, Gurri 389
    Inger 389
    Kleng 389
    Marthe 389
Klep, --- 393
Kleppe, --- 393
    Karen 389
    Ole 389
Klermundt, Wm. 327
Kleven, Tosten 442
Kleyn, Jacob 128
Kliewer, ---, Frau 517
    Anna 517
    Elisabeth 521
    Eva 521
    Friederike 522
    Heinrich 521

Peter 517, 521
    Susanna 517
    Helena 517
    Wilhelmine 522
    Wittwe Susanne 522
Klingler, Debalt 73
    Maria Catharina 73
    Theobald 73
Klonning, Thorbjen N 398
Klotz, George 288
Klund, Anna Barbara 45
    Johann Adam 45
Kneebone, Elizabeth 447
    John 443
Kneller, George 257
Kney, Bernhard 40
    Maria Margaretha 40
    Philipp 40
Knight, Robt. 188
Knoblock, John 251
Knoll, Evea 167
Knox, Dean 338
    George 453, 464
    Hen. W. 309
    James 338, 359
    Jane 338
    John 309
    John, Capt. 309
    Joseph 338
    Thomas 338, 454
    Thos. 309
    William 338
    Wm. 309, 338
Knudsdatter, E. 403, 407
    Elen 411
    K 428
    M. 403, 406
    Magdale 413
Knuds datter, Aase 413
    Ane 413
Knudsen, Andreas 411
    John 411
    Knud 422
    Ole 411
Knudzen, Daniel 413
Knudzon, O. 429, 434
Koben, Edward A 398
Koberstein, Anna Catharina 171
    Hans Gorg 171
    Johann Georg 170
Koch, Christian 36
    Georg Friedrich 49
    Johann Christian 36
    Philipp Carl 49
Kocher, Martin 13
Kocherthal, --- 1
Koebel, Philipp 225
Koehler, Andreas 51
    Anna Catharine 51
    Jacob 52
    Johann Jacob 51
Koenig, Abraham 68
    Abrahamb 50
    Anna Maria 68
    Balthasar 21, 108
    Balzar 21
    Frantz 50
    Maria 50
    Maria Magdalena 68
Koerner, Jacob 173
Kohl, Anna Barbara 105
    Anna Marill 105
    Gertrud 52
    Henrich 52
    Jaquer 105
    Luis 105
    Margaritha 105
    Maria Margaritha 105

Nicolas 105
Kohla, Christian 165
Köhler, Anna Elisabetha 72
Kohling, John Michael 286
Köhn, ---, Frau 525
    Anna 525
    Elisabeth 525
    Jakob 525
    Johann 525
    Katharina 525
    Peter 525
Kolman, Anthony, Rev. 257
Konig, Balzer 180
König, Anna Maria 67
    Frantz 67, 68
    Rahel 67, 68
Kooler, Frederick 531
Kopp, Samuel Eberhard 15
Korest, Janet 223
    Mary 221
Korff, John 288
Kornelsen, Wittwe 522
Körner, Jacob 174
Kotiler, Anthony 165
    Christian 165
Kraemer, Bartel 25
    Johann Peter 36
Krafft, George 288
    John 288
Kraft, Catherine 165
    Christopher 288
Kramerinn, Catherine 328
Kratzmann, Johann Nikolaus 126
    Maria Christina 126
Krauss, George 174
    Jacob 169
    Johannes 22
Krebs, Charles I. 288
Kreeps, John 107
Krehebuehl, Johann Adam 19
Kremer, George 2
Kreutzer, Friedrich 225
Krieg, Anna Barbara 65
    Anna Maria 66
    Johann Philipp 65
    Margaretha Dorothea 65
Krimm, Jacob 142
    Valentin 142
Kroes, Peter Paul 288
Kroft, Christopher 288
Kröker, Bernhd. 519
    Franz 523
    Heinr. 526
    Heinrich 520, 523, 526
    Helena 520
    Helene 519
    Jacob 523
    Johann 523
    Katharina 519, 520, 523
    Klaas 520
    Maria 519
    Peter 520
    Sarah 526
Kron, Henrich 23
Kroner, Jacob 177
Kuechler, Joseph 142
Kueffer, Devall 110
    Theobald 109
Kuehl, Johannes 25
Kueller, George 257
Küffer, Anna Margarita 104
    Barbara 105
    Elissabeth Margaritt 104
    Elizabeht Catarina 105
    Jaque 104
    Margaritt 104
    Maria Ottillia 105
    Theobald 104

Kugel, Elisie 230
    Jean 230
    Marthe 230
Kuhl, Henry 288
Kuhn, Elisabetha 40
    Georg 54
    Margretha 40
    Nicklaus 40
    Nicolaus 225
    Valentin 54
Kuhnle, Charles 326
Kuiffer, David 112
Kuiper, Fytje 512
    Pietertje 512
Kuller, Joh. 167
Kumming, Jas. 302, 309
Kumpff, Georg 170
Kuntz, Bernhard 15
    John Jacob 15
    Margaretha 45
Kunz, Franz 57
    Heinrich 28
    Henrich 41
    Maria Margaretha 41
Kuse, E. L. 264
Kurter, Abraham 231
    Catherine 231
    Hamilton 229
    Henry 231
    Jean 229
    Jeannette 229
    Joseph 231
    Mathieu 229
    William 229
Kurz, J. George 327
Kvelve, Abel Catharine 393
    Arnold Andrew 393
    Augustinus Meldahl Bruun 393
    Bjorn Anderson 393
Kyle, Elizabeth 359
    Robert 359
Kyne, Mathias 252, 257
Kynn, John 359

-- L --

Laam, Peter 30, 52
Labody, Robert 292
Labord, John 110, 111
Labrille, Louis 263
Lackey, Mary 478
La Croix, Alexander 106
Lacy, Edward 338
Ladegaard, Hans 415
Ladesma, Moses 153
Laer, Henrich 181
    Joseph 181
    Margaretha 181
    Robert 181
    Thomas 181
Laffey, James 359
Laffite, Peter 108
    Peter, Capt 110
Lagayes, John 109
Lager, John 309
Laguna, Abm. 152
    Jacob, Junr. 153
    Rebecca 154
Lahm, Johan Petter 52
    Johann Conrad 30, 47
    Johann Konradt 30, 47
    Johann Nicklaus 30, 52
    Johann Peter 30
    Maria Catharina 30, 52
    Matthias 30, 52

Nickel 30, 52
    Peter 30, 47
Lain, David 359
Laird, Andrew 359
    James 534
    John 257
Lake, George 257
Lakemeyer, Frederick 288
Lally, Michael 359
Lalor, Danl. 359
Lamb, John 338
Lambert, Anne 359
    Geo. 309
    John 338
    Margaret 359
    Montague 309
    Ralph 309
    Robt. 309
    William 359
Lambright, Geo. 262
    George 257
Lamby, William 288
Lamera, Aaron 152
Land, Richard 139
Lander, Jonas 244
Landriker, Jno. 164
Lane, Ellen 338
    John 338
    Mary 338
    Mary Anne 359
    Thos. 309
Lang, Anna Catharina 53
    Anna Eva 132
    Conrad 19
    Eva Elisabetha 57
    Johann Nikolaus 132
    Johannes 53
    Nickel 53, 54, 57
Lange, Ferben 246
Langeland, Anderson 400
    Knud 400, 406
    N. P. 402, 404, 407, 409
    Nils P. 407, 409
Langer, Richard 338
Langerud, G O 429
Langford, Roger 309
    Roger, Sir 309
Langley, Hezekiah 286
    Michael 359
Langton, Daniel 359
Lanigan, George 338
Lanoe, Chas., Col. 309
Lanphier, Robert G. ,279
Lansdown, Patk. 294
Laperty, Michael 359
Lapham, Oliver 267
Laphen, Philip 359
La Pierre, Matthew 108
Laplin, John 338
Lapp, Jno. Geo. 167
Lapsy, Nicholas 338
Larkie, Alex. 338
    Mary 338
Larkin, Patrick 359
    W., Miss 338
Larner, Martin 278
Larsdatter, A 404, 408
    Anna 390, 408
    G 404, 408, 428
    Gyri 408
    M. 429, 436
Larsen, Jorgen 428, 442
    Lars 399
Larson, ---, Miss 381
    Georgiana 379, 381
    Lars 372,374,376,377,378,
        379,380,381,383,396
    Malinda 406

Margaret 399
    Margaret Allen 380
    Martha 410, 415, 416
    Martha Georgiana 372,377,
        380
    Martha Jane 380, 381
    Sara 372, 383
Larwood, Ben., Capt. 309
La Sama, --- 105
Lasman, John Martin 111
Latfitte, Peter 112
Latham, Elias 359
    Hannah 359
    Henry 359
    Hugh 359
    Martha 359
    Nathaniel 359
    Thomas 359
    William 359
La Touche, Dav., jun. 309
Laubach, Christian 14
    Reinhard 14
Lauchrey, Hugh 288
Laudenback, Johann David 129
Lauer, Anna Barbara 57
    Michel 57
Lauffer, Johann Christian 57
    Lorentz 57
Laughery, Isabella 359
Laughlin, Adam 310
    George 359
    Mary 478
    Wm. 359
Laughran, Jas. 359
Laughton, Robert 359
Laukney, Hugh 288
Laurie, James 257
Lautenbach, Anna Margarethe
    128
    Anna Maria 124
    Friedrich 124
    Johann David 129
    Johannes 128, 219
    Maria Katharina 128
Laverty, Hugh 338
    James 338
    Jane 338
Law, E. 310
    John 359
    John George 288
    Thomas 250
    Thomas, Esqr. 257
    William 338, 359
    Wm. 338
Lawler, John 359
    Patrick 338
Lawn, Edward 359
Lawrence, James 267
Lawson, Iver 406
    John 310
    Malinda 406
    Victor F. 406
    Victor Freemont 406
Laxgang, Lorentz 173
Laye, Joseph 111
Laymeister, Wilhelm 25
Lazares, Elias 154
Lea, Robert 359
Leach, John 284
Leahy, Henry 359
    Tim 510
Leaky, John 338
Lear, John 359
Leary, Bawn 494
    Catherine 493
    Connor 493, 505
    Dan 494
    Daniel 493, 494

Darby 494
Eileen 493
Ellen 493, 494
Jerry 493
Johanna 493, 494
John 493, 494
Judy 494
Kate 494
Mary 493, 494, 505
Mathew 504, 505
Matt 494
Matthew 359, 494
Michael 338
Pat 494
Patsey 505
Peg 493, 494
Peggy 493
Tade 505
Timothy 493, 506
Lebkucher, Henrich 54
Lebkuecher, Henrich 54
Johann Adam 54
Lebray, Fanshaw 110
Jane 110
Twinet 110
Leckey, Thomas 359
Lecky, Alex. 310
Leddy, ---, Mrs. 359
Michael 359
Ledgerwood, Agnes 133
Elener 133
James 133
Jane 133
Martha 133
William 133
Lee, --- 310
Alexander 359
Anne 359
Archo 252
Edward 359
George 359
Jane 359
John 359
Mary 359
Sarah 359
Simon 359
Thomas 359
William, Senior 281
Leech, A. 359
Andrew 359
Malcolm 359
Sarah 359
Leeson, Saml. 310
Left, Adam 359
Legare, John 110
Lehl, John 328
Lehn, Johann 25
Leibrock, Jacob 49
Johann Georg 49
Leidick, Francis 257
Leidicks, Francis 257
Leight, John 241
Leiner, Georg 27
Ludwig 27, 38
Leitzeit, Joh. Jac 167
Leman, James 338
Margaret 338
Lemman, George 338
Mary 338
Lenglay, Hezekiah 252
Lennan, Edwd. 310
Lennox, Anne 310
Clotworthy 310
John 310
Wm. 310
Lenon, Henry 338
Lenox, Ann 116
John 310

Peter 255, 265
Wm. 310
Lenz, Geo. 326
Henry 326
Leonard, Francis 338
Gilberto 227
Patrick 476
Peter 289
Leonhard, Niclas 174
Wilhelm 174
Lerch, Andreas 14
Anthony 14
Pancratius 14
Peter 14
Le Roy, Abraham 112
Leslie, Hen. 310
Jas. 310
Saml. 310
Tho., Ensign 310
Lesslie, Catherine 117
Lester, Anne 359
John 359
Leuty, John 443
Levan, Daniel 3
Le Vent, Daniel 17
Lever, Jno. 164
Leverall, Bernd. 310
Levet, Tho., Lieut. & Capt. 310
Leviston, Charles 338
James 338
Mary 338
Levy, Henry 154
Isaac 156, 163
Juda Bair 328
Moses 153, 157, 163
Samuel 163
Simon Isaak 225
Lewis, Israel H. 246
Jane 532
Wm. 310
Leyer, Peter 21
Philipp 22
Leymeister, Johann Wilhelm 26
L'Fabuere, Rachael 192
Lichtenwalner, John 9
Lichter, Anna Dorothea 19
Georg 19
Lichtner, Anna Dorothea 19
Georg 19
Licker, Georg 21
George 180
Lictson, Mary 338
Thomas 338
Liddiard, Sarah 139
Liddy, Hu. 310
Liech, Duncan 115
Mary 115
Lier, John Rodolff 109
Liggot, Alex. 310
Lighton, William 359
Ligonier, John, Gen. 310
Lilley, Thomas, Rev. 281
Lillich, Gottlieb 328
Lilly, John 359
Lima, Simon 383
Limerick, ---, Lord 310
Alexander 359
Linchey, James 359
Lincock, Amelia 444
Ann 444
Benjamin 445
John 445
Saml. 444
Thomas 444
Wm. 444
Lincoln, ---, General 102
Lindemann, Henrich 142
Jacob 142

Justus 142
Linder, John 108
Lindesay, Christian 117
Donald 117
Duncan 117
Effie 117
Richard 117
Lindsay, Andrew 339
David 339
George 359
Isabella 339, 359
James 339
Richard 359
Robert 359
Susan 359
Thos. 310
Ling, Georg 170
Lingan, Bridget 359
John 359
Lingen, Wm. 310
Lingenfelder, Johannes 56
Peter 56
Linn, Daniel 359
William 218
Linnan, John 359
Linnen, Luke 339
Linster, Mary 310
Lintz, Jerg 170
Linz, George 170
Lipsett, Anth. 310
Lischy, --- 184
Lister, Eliza 339
James 289
Liston, Eliza 339
John 339
Litle, Charles 263
Littel, Will. 79
Wm 79
Littell, Elizabeth 79
Mary 79
Wm. 79
Little, Anne 310
Archd. 310
Eliz. 81
James 339
Jane 310
Jas. 310
John 339
Martha 339
Reba. 310
Robert 257
Sarah 310
Thomas 359
Wm. 310
Littlejohn, Duncan 221
Littlewin, Elizabeth 444
John 443
Litzenburger, Maria Barbara 129
Maria Christina 129
Philipp 129
Theobald 129
Liver, Jno. 164
Liveried, I 429
Livingston, Donald 117
Duncan 117
Isabell 117
James 117
John 117
Robt. 310
Lloyd, Henry 77
Phobe 77
Thomas 268, 270
Lobb, Ri. 78
Richard 78
Loble, Georg 176
Lochiell, --- 115
Lockat, John 339
Lockery, James 339

Margaret 339
Lockhart, John 359
Margaret 359
Lockwood, John 359
Loeffel, Balthasar 33, 173
Loeffler, Balthasar 33
Löffel, Balthasar 33
Loffler, Dieterich 177
Löffler, Balsazar 173
Balthasar 33
Loftus, Biddy 481
Ellen 481
John 481
Mary 481
Mary Ann 481
Michael 481
Simon, Lieut. 310
Thomas 481
Logan, Charles 339
Daniel 359
David 134
Hans 310
John 257, 339, 359
John, Dr. 250
John A. 250
Mary 134, 339
Thomas 359
William 134, 289
Logie, Dan. 310
Logue, Biddy 339
James 339
Mary 339
Wm. 339
Lohr, Philipp 224
Lohrenz, Anna 517
David 517
Gerhard 516, 517
Helena 516, 517
Maria 517
Peter 517
Lomme, Ole C. L. 391
Lonagere, Jacob 11
Ulrich 11
Ulrich, Jr. 11
Long, Henry 218
John 444
Joseph 359
Michael 164
Thomas 339
William 359
Longacre, --- 11
Longe, John 310
Longemon, John 241
Longman, Robert 359
Longwill, Dav. 310
Looby, John 481
Lackey 481
Mary 478, 481
Peggy 481
Tom 481
Loony, Anne 359
Looser, Mich'l 167
Lopez, Aaron 162
Abigail 155
Moses 156, 163
López, Ramón 227, 228
Lorentz, Johann Peter 30, 52
Peter 30, 52
Lothe, Johanness 398
Knud 398
Ragnhild 398
Svein Knutson 400
Swent K. 398
Louden, John 534
Loudinback, Johann David 129
Loughead, Cath. 339
Edward 339
Lougheed, James 244

Loughnan, Martin 359
Loury, Edwd. 310
Love, Alexander 359
Anne 310, 359
James 339
M. 310
Mary 310
Robert 339
Samuel 359
Lovel, William 288
Lovingen, O I 429
Low, John 359
Lowden, Robert 359
Löwen, ---, Frau 527
Diedrich 527
Elisabeth 527
Heinrich 527
Katharina 527
Peter 527
Sarah 527
Lowrey, Elnr. 310
John 310
Lowry, Ann 502
George 286
John 502
Patrick 501, 502
Robert 339
Samuel 359
Sarah 502
Thomas 359
Loyd, Henry 77
Luber, Anna Maria 72
Lubey, John 481
Lackey 481
Mary 481
Peggy 481
Tom 481
Luby, John 481
Lacky 481
Mary 478, 481
Peggy 481
Tom 481
Lucas, Betsy 339
Eleanor 359
Lucius, --- 225
Ludvig, --- 433
Ludwig, Adam 170
Hans Adam 170
Johan George 171
Johann Georg 170
Maria Margaretha 171
Luecker, Joerg 21, 180
Luetz, Elisabetha Cahtarina 29, 49
Johann Willhelm 49
Matthes 29
Matthess 49
Lugenbiehl, Peter 43
Lugenbuehl, Kilian 43
Peter 43
Luke, James 339
Samuel 359
Lullich, Jacob 327
Lumly, John 310
Lundie, --- 115
Lurkie, Jane 339
Lusk, James 97
Lutie, Peter 111
Lutz, Johann Wilhelm 29
John 253
Margaret 52
Margaretha 68
Luwer, Anna Maria 73
Lyle, Hugh 310
Lym, --- 310
Lynch, --- 359
Abraham 258
Ann 310

Bryan 359
Dan. 310
John 270, 274, 277, 287, 339, 359
Martha 310
Patrick 359
Peter 359
Susan 359
Thomas 359
Wm. 310
Lyndon, James 359
Mary 359
Lynes, Peter 359
Lynn, Daniel 339
Reba. 310
Robt. 310
Lynskey, Bridget 472, 481
Catherine 481
John 481
Judy 481
Margaret 472, 481
Mary 472, 481
Michael 476, 481, 483
Pat 472
Thomas 481
Timothy 481
Lyon, Jacob 152
James 197
Mary 197
Math. 197
Lyons, Cornelius 339
Eliza 339
James 339
John 339
Joseph 339
Mary 339
Peter 339
Robert 339
Samuel 339
William 359
Lyster, George 289
Lyttle, Eliza 310
Peggy 310

-- M --

Maage, Ansten E 398
MacAffer, Andrew 359
MacAlister, Anthony 359
Daniel 359
MacAllignon, Rich. 359
MacAllisted, Felix 339
James 339
MacAllister, R. 339
Rose 339
MacAloo, Daniel 359
MacAlpin, Hugh 339
James 339
Jane 339
MacAlvin, Alex. 339
MacAnnulty, Patrick 359
MacAnorney, James 339
MacAnorney, Michael 339
MacArand, Patrick 359
MacArdle, Anne 359
John 359
Mary Anne 359
Owen 359
Peter 359
MacArnon, Mary 359
MacArthur, John 339
Robert 339
Macartney, --- 311
Geo., Gen. 311
Jas. 311
MacAskin, John 339

572

MacAtier, James 359
MacAtter, Betty 339
   Mark 339
MacAttur, Ann 339
   James 339
MacAuley, James 359
MacBraty, Chs. 359
MacBride, Bernard 359
   James 339, 359
   John 359
   Patrick 360
   William 360
MacBrien, John 339
MacBrine, Jane 339
MacBurney, ---, Mrs. 339
MacCabe, Betsy 339
   James 339
   John 360
   Pat. 360
   Patrick 339
   Terrence 360
MacCad, John 293
MacCafferty, Edw. 339
   Susan 339
MacCaghy, Nath. 339
MacCaird, William 339
MacCalester, Elisabeth 229
   Jacques 229
MacCall, Alex 360
   Alice 360
MacCallan, James 360
MacCam, Felix 360
MacCambridge, Alexander 360
   Jas. 360
MacCammar, Samuel 339
MacCanaghty, James 360
MacCanaghy, David 360
   Mary 360
MacCanbrey, Rich. 360
MacCance, James 339
MacCanly, Robert 360
MacCann, Bernard 360
   Daniel 360
   John 360
   Owen 360
   William 360
MacCannell, Carry 360
   Samuel 360
MacCarden, Edward 360
MacCarfin, T. 360
MacCarker, Patrick 360
MacCarter, James 360
MacCarthy, Bryan 360
MacCartney, Eliza 339
   Ellen 339
   Hannah 339
   John 339
   Nancy 339
   Patrick 339, 360
   Samuel 339
MacCarton, Charles 339
   James 339
MacCarty, Rose 360
MacCaskey, Eliza 360
   John 360
MacCasle, Thomas 360
MacCathen, Adam 360
MacCaughall, Geo. 339
MacCaughan, Alex. 339
MacCauley, Eliza 360
   Elizabeth 360
   Robert 360
MacCauly, Jane 360
   John 360
MacCausland, Andrew 360
MacCawley, James 360
MacCawlley, Hugh 339
MacClane, John 339

Mary 339
MacClaskey, Dennis 360
   Henry 360
   Hugh 360
MacClean, David 339
   James 360
   M. 360
MacCleary, Sam. 360
MacClelland, --- 360
   James 360
   Mary 360
   Samuel 360
MacClellon, William 360
MacClenaghan, James 339
MacCloskey, James 339
MacCloud, Anne 360
   Daniel 360
   James 360
   John 360
   Mary Anne 360
   Neile 360
MacCloy, Thomas 339
MacClure, Anne 339
   Thomas 339
MacClushey, Martha 360
   Matilda 360
MacCoal, Charles 360
   Patrick 360
MacColgan, George 360
   John 360
MacColgin, John 339
MacColim, Daniel 360
   Margaret 360
MacColley, John 339, 360
MacCollison, David 360
   Thomas 360
MacCollough, Wm. 360
MacComb, Ann 339
   Daniel 360
   Henry 339
   John 360
   Margaret 339
   Robert 339
   Thomas 339
MacConaghy, Alex. 339
MacConley, George 360
   John 339
MacConnaghy, Jas. 339
MacConnell, James 339, 360
   John 339
   P. 339
   Sarah 339
MacConstand, Esther 339
MacConway, Edw. 339
MacCool, James 360
MacCormack, B. 360
MacCormick, Esther 360
   James 360
   Jno. 360
   John 360
   Patrick 360
   Thomas 339
MacCosker, Bernard 339
MacCoskery, John 339
MacCoun, Charles 339
MacCousland, Ann 339
   Mar. 339
   Mary 339
MacCoy, Alexander 360
   Joseph 339
MacCracken, Alexander 360
   Joseph 339
   Robert 339
MacCrea, John 360
MacCready, Elinor 339
   John 339
   Wm. 339
MacCrecan, James 339

MacCreery, John 339
MacCrossin, John 360
MacCue, Daniel 339
   Michael 339
   Thomas 339
MacCullagh, Michael 360
MacCullaugh, John 339
MacCulloch, Geo. 339
   James 360
   Mary 339
   S. G. 487
   Wm. 339
MacCullough, Alex. 339
   Hamilton 339
MacCullum, Joseph 360
MacCully, Mathew 339
MacCune, Clem. 339
MacCurdy, James 360
   Jane 360
   John 360
   Morgan 339
   Neil 360
   William 339, 360
MacCurry, Henry 339
MacCurtney, James 339
MacCusker, Terence 360
MacDaid, John 360
MacDaniel, ---, Mrs. 360
   And'w 360
   John 360
   Less 360
   Mary 360
   Michael 360
   Owen 360
   T. 360
   Tho. 360
MacDemiott, Peter 360
MacDermot, John 360
   Susana 339
MacDermott, Charles 360
   Daniel 360
   John 360
   Mary 360
   Owen 360
   Patk. 360
   Patrick 360
   Rose 360
   Susannah 360
   William 360
MacDevitt, P. 339
MacDill, John 360
MacDonagh, James 360
MacDonald, Moore 339
   Robert 339
   Terence 331
   Thos. 360
   William 339
MacDonel, James 360
MacDonnel, --- 360
MacDonnell, James 339
   Judith 360
   Margaret 360
   Michael 360
   Robert 360
   Thomas 360
MacDougal, John 360
   Mary 360
MacDougall, John 360
MacDowel, C. 360
   John 360
   M. 360
   W. 360
MacDowell, Alexander 360
   John 360
MacDowl, Alexander 339
   Elizabeth 340
   Ezibella 340
   John 340

Mary Ann 340
Rachel 340
Thomas 340
MacEliver, George 340
MacElkeney, Robert 340
MacElroy, Arch. 340
MacElwin, Hugh 340
MacElwrath, Rob't 340
MacEver, William 340
MacEvory, John 340
MacEvoy, Edward 360
Owen 360
MacEwen, John 340
MacFadden, Charles 360
Samuel 360
MacFaddin, Eleanor 340
Manus 340
MacFade, Jane 340
MacFaden, John 340
MacFall, John 340
MacFarland, John 340
Robert 360
Wm. 340
MacFarlane, John 360
MacFaul, Daniel 340
MacFeely, Charles 340
MacGanty, Edward 340
MacGaragher, J. 360
MacGaraghy, Bryan 361
MacGattiger, Daniel 361
MacGaughrin, Farguis 340
MacGavaran, John 361
MacGaw, John 340
Robert 340
Thomas 340
MacGellaghan, Pat. 340
MacGeoch, Ellen 361
Grace 361
Sam. 361
MacGibbon, Samuel 361
MacGill, Anthony 340
Robert 361
MacGinley, Corn. 340
MacGinn, Rose 361
MacGinness, Danl. 340
MacGinnis, Bernard 340
Daniel 361
Ellen 361
Henry 361
John 361
Owen 361
Thomas 361
MacGladery, Samuel 361
MacGlam, John 361
Patrick 361
MacGlaughlin, Robert 361
MacGleeve, James 340
MacGloin, Edward 361
Henry 361
John 361
Margaret 361
Mary 361
MacGlonan, Ann 340
James 340
Mary 340
Nathaniel 340
MacGloughlin, Dennis 361
Mary 361
Patrick 361
MacGlyn, Catherine 361
MacGohey, Mary 340
MacGongle, Henry 361
MacGouran, Samuel 361
MacGovern, Charles 361
MacGowan, Andrew 361
Bernard 361
Dennis 361
James 361

John 361
Mary 361
Patrick 361
Philip 340
MacGown, Andrew 361
MacGra, John 361
MacGranahan, Thomas 361
MacGrath, James 340, 361
Marg. 340
Patrick 340
Thos. 340
William 361
Wm. 340
MacGrave, Marg. 340
MacGreedy, John 340
MacGreevy, Patrick 361
MacGregor, Peter 247
MacGrery, James 361
Margaret 361
MacGrier, Robert 361
MacGrim, Bryan 361
MacGuinness, Edw. 340
MacGuire, Bridget 361
Ellen 361
Mary 361
Roger 340
MacGum, Patrick 361
MacGuragle, Robert 361
MacGurrah, John 340
MacGuskin, A. 361
MacHale, Thomas 361
Machen, Thomas 259
MacHolland, Mich. 340
MacHugh, Andrew 361
MacIldoon, Hugh 340
MacIlhames, John 361
MacIlheny, Robert 361
MacIlrath, King 361
MacIlroy, ---, Mrs. 361
Charles 340, 361
Patrick 361
MacIndoo, Robert 340
MacIntire, Abrm. 340
Donald 211
James 361
Katherine 211
Margaret 211
Mary 211
Robert 361
Robt. 361
Samuel 361
MacIntosh, Jane 361
William 361
Mack, Fred'k 167
MacKagh, Nancy 340
MacKardy, David 340
Mackay, Aeneas 209
Hugh, Ensign 312
John 80
Will. 79
MacKay, Alexander 361
Charles 340
Eliza 361
Francis 361
James 361
P. 361
S. 361
William 361
Mackee, James 340
MacKee, George 340
Jane 340
John 340
Margaret 340
Patrick 340
Robert 340, 361
Thomas 340
William 361
MacKeene, Peter 361

MacKeighan, --- 361
MacKelery, Jane 340
William 340
MacKell, Thomas 361
MacKennan, Bernart 361
Patrick 361
MacKenney, Alice 340
MacKenny, Alexander 340
Mackenzie, John 194
John Portpatrick 312
MacKenzie, Alex. 340
John 340
Philip 340
Ralph 340
Mackeon, Isabella 361
William 361
MacKeon, Robt. 361
Rose 361
MacKeown, Anne 361
John, Junr. 361
John, Senr. 361
Margaret 361
Mary 361
Saml. 361
Samuel 361
Sarah 361
William 361
Mackerill, James 361
Jane 361
Thomas 361
MacKernan, Edward 361
Patrick 361
Mackeson, James 361
MacKever, Edward 340
MacKevers, Peter 361
Mackey, Saml. 312
MacKey, Daniel 340
Eleanor 361
Ellen 340
James 340
Thomas 340
Mackie, Wm. 312
MacKill, Thos. 361
MacKinlay, George 340
John 340
MacKinley, Hugh 340
MacKinne, John 361
MacKinney, Eliza 340
George 340
MacKinstry, John 361
Macklelland, John 312
Robt., Sir 312
Wm. 313
Macklellane, Robt., Sir 313
Wm. 313
Macklin, John 189
Wm. 313
Mary 189
Mackloud, Richard 139
MacKnight, Andrew 340
Daniel 340
David 340
Jane 340
Mary 340
Thomas 340
MacKninon, Hannah 361
MacKnott, Robert 340
MacKosker, Hugh 340
Mackoy, John 80
MacLachling, John 361
MacLain, John 361
MacLanna, John 340
MacLary, Benjamin 340
MacLaughlin, Ann 340
Benj. 340
Biddy 340
Cornelius 361
Dennis 361

Edward 361
Elea 340
F. 340
Fran. 340
H. 340
Hugh 361
James 361
John 361
Margaret 361
Mary 361
Peter 361
Philip 340, 361
Sarah 361
MacLean, Bridget 361
Owen 361
Peter 361
Thomas 361
MacLeon, Patrick 340
MacLoran, Neal 340
Patrick 340
MacLorran, William 361
MacLorten, Cather. 340
Terrence 340
MacMagan, Agnes 340
David 340
Seragh 340
MacMahan, Elisabeth 229
Jacques 229
Maria 229
Sarah 340
MacMahin, Rebecca 340
MacMahon, Bridget 361
Henry 340
MacMail, Hugh 361
MacMalin, Wm. 340
MacMally, James 340
MacMannyman, John 340
MacManus, Bernard 361
Francis 340
Mary 340
Michael 361
Nathl. 361
Patrick 361
MacMarrow, Mary 361
Owen 361
MacMenamy, John 361
Jos. 340
Peter 362
Thos. 340
Wm. 340
MacMennamy, Mgt. 340
MacMenomy, Elizabeth 362
Hugh 362
John 362
Robt. 362
Thomas 362
William 362
MacMiller, Gideon 362
MacMinimim, Edward 340
MacMullan, Hugh 340
Macmullen, Robert 340
MacMullen, Alexander 362
Catherine 362
Eliza 340
James 340
John 340
MacMurray, Alex 340
Archibald 362
David 362
Hannah 340
Jess 362
Nancy 340
Wm. 340
MacMurrey, Mathew 340
MacMurry, Samuel 340
MacNarna, Wm. 362
MacNarney, John 362
Michael 362

MacNaughly, Patt 294
MacNaughten, John 362
MacNeal, Frank 340
Roger 340
MacNeill, Jno. 293
Morris 294
Neal 340
MacNeilly, John 340
MacNemee, Francis 362
MacNenomy, Hugh 362
MacNeremon, William 362
Macnevin, Andw. 313
Mac Nichol, Donald 211
Katherine 212
MacNought, James 340
MacNulty, Wm. 362
MacPeak, Owen 340
MacPharland, ---, widow 340
P. 340
MacPhilaney, Margaret 362
MacPhiloron, Dennis 362
MacQuaid, Edward 340
MacQueen, Matthew 362
MacQuig, William 362
MacQuillan, H. 340
MacQuinn, Patrick
MacQuoid, James 362
MacRalin, Roger 362
MacRedden, James 362
MacSerley, James 362
MacShane, Daniel 362
Thomas 340
MacSheldon, James 362
MacSherry, Patrick 362
MacSleeve, James 341
MacSwigon, Mary 362
Philip 362
MacTahan, Henry 362
MacTea, Arthur 362
MacTice, Andrew 362
MacTogert, ---, Mrs. 341
MacVaid, James 362
MacVay, M. 341
MacVea, Jas. 362
MacVeagh, Patrick 341
MacVeigh, Henry 362
MacVicker, Thos. 362
MacVoy, Dominick 362
MacWhatey, Jane 341
MacWhaty, John 341
MacWherter, Jane 341
Madden, Catherine 461
James 362
John 341
Mary 461
Thomas 461
Madigan, Ally 362
Anne 362
Edward 362
James 362
Judy 362
Mary 362
Peggy 362
Walter 362
William 362
Madison, James 249
Madland, Thomas 383
Madocks, --- 313
Maeurer, Philipp (Jacob) 35
Maffat, Cath. 313
Robt. 313
Wm. 313
Maffett, James 341
Magan, Anne 461
Catherine 461
Ellen 461
John 461
Patrick 461

Magee, Bernard 362
Bernd. 362
Bgt. 313
James 362
John 313, 362
Patrick 362
William 362
Magell, Ekiza 341
John 341
Samuel 341
Magenis, Glasney 313
Magennis, Rich. 313
Mages, Joseph 341
Magghee, Wm. 313
Magher, --- 362
Magil, Samuel 291
Magill, Bernd. 313
Daniel 362
John 314, 362
Maginis, Jos. 314
Maginnis, Patk. 314
Magis, Joseph 341
Magnier, Thomas 257, 273, 278,
282, 286
Thos. 263
Magorian, M. 314
Magrath, Thomas 258
Magreth, Thorborn Torsen 412
Magruder, James A. 259
Lewis 255
Maguinis, Isabella 341
John 341
Maguire, Bgt. 314
Henry 362
James 287
Jas. 314
John 265, 461
Mary 461
Patrick 461
Patt 314
Thos. 263
Mahaffy, James 341
Mahany, John 362
Mary 362
Mary J. 362
Mahar, James 279
Maharg, James 341
Maher, James 274, 275
Mahon, Catherine 362
Charles 248, 362
Joseph 362
Ross, Sir 466
Mahony, Dan 495
Ellen 495
F. 362
Jas. 362
Johanna 495
Mary 495
Norry 495
Tade 495
Maiben, Jane, Mrs. 362
Richard 362
Maillier, Peter 112
Main, Thos. 314
Maitland, Rd. 190
Wm. 341
Malcolmson, Js. 314
Malcomson, Adam 362
John 341
Malkey, Abraham 109
Mallet, John, Capt. 314
Mallett, Gideon 110
Malliet, Pierre 113
Mallon, Michl. 314
Mallows, --- 314
Malone, Francis 362
Henry 362
Maloney, Margaret 341

Malowney, Jerry 341
John 341
Malsey, Mary 362
Malvin, William 341
Maly, John 362
Man, --- 140
Manahan, Anthony 482
Mandt, Gunder 434
Manely, Henry 341
Michael 341
Maney, Patrick 341
Mankin, James 271
Manley, --- 314
Isaac 314
Manly, Bridget 482
Ellen 482
James 482
John 482
Joseph 341
Mary 482
Richard 482
Mann, Lucia 314
Manning, William 362
Mannion, John 482
Malachy 482
Mary 482
Pat 482
Peggy 482
Thomas 482
Manro, Philip 263
Mans, Eva 51
Margaretha 51
Matheis 51
Manser, Matthais 531
Mansfield, Robert 341
Manson, John 341
Manton, Nth. 533
Mara, James 362
March, Charles 362
Morris 265, 277
Marck, John 236
Marcussen, Anna Cathrina 389
Ole 389
Marfelt, John 362
Mark, Joseph 341
Markey, James 362
Marks, John 314, 341
Patrick 479
Marland, Thomas 383
Marlborough, --- 100
Marley, --- 314
Maron, Owen 341
Marsh, Morris D.C. 279
Thomas 291
Marshal, David 189
Marshall, Betty 314
Edward 529
Eliza 341
Isabella 362
Jeorge 341
John 195, 362
Joseph 341
Margaret 362
Mary 362, 529
Samuel 362
W. 341
William 362
Marsteller, Frederick Ludwig 5
Philip, Col. 5
Martain, ---, Capt. 135
Marte, Abram 104
Marthe, Abraham 106
Marthin, Hans Steffan 22
Joerg 21
Martin, --- 147, 150, 326, 341
Andrew 341, 362
Anna 341
Caroline 444

Charles 289
Corns. 314
Eliza 444
Elizabeth 444
Geo., Capt. 314
Georg 21
George 362
Hugh 362
James 251, 255, 256, 341, 362
Jane 341, 417, 444
Johann Stephan 22
John 292, 341, 362, 417, 444
John Golrick 362
Marcella 362
Margt. 314
Martha 341, 362
Mary 444
Moses 314
Nancy 341
Pat. Golrick 362
Rachel 362
Robert 362, 417, 444
Robt. 314
Samuel 341
Thomas 341, 362
Thos. 362
William 362
Wm. 314, 444
Martine, Donald 121
Florence 121
Malcolm 121
Mary 121
Martins, Leah 153
Martius, Moses 151
Marx, John 236
Masham, Fra., Ensign 314
Maskal, Henry 188
Mason, Daniel 362
Thomas 362
Massereene, ---, Lord Visct. 314
Masson, Mary 108
Peter 109
Masterson, Ann 341
Charles 362
Edward 341
Hugh 362
Patrick 362
Matheis, Andres 180
Matheson, Hugh 206
Jas. 196
Kathrine 206
Margt. 196
Mathew, Patrick 341
Mathewes, John 314
Mathews, Chas. 314
Emma 444
Michael 362
Richd. 444
Stephen 341
Susan 444
Thomas 341, 362
Mathewson, Clark 362
David 362
John, Jr. 258
John, Sr. 258
Wil. 341
Mathias, Berthe 412
John 164
Mathies, John 534
William 534
Mathys, John 164
Matt, Biddy 506
Daniel Danihy 505
Mattern, Peter 8
Mattey, Abraham 109
Matthews, ---, Major 314
Andw. 314

John 139, 140
Mattock, Isobel 222
Mattos, Phinelias 152
Matts, Stephen 531
Maule, Wm., Capt. 314
Maurer, Adam 142
Anna Elisabeth 129
Anna Eva 129
Jacob 129
Johann Jacob 43
Johann Jakob 129
Katharina 129
Paul 129
Phielib Jacob 35
Maurice, James 362
Maurset, Peder J. 402
Maus, Franz Carl 34
Friderich 38
Friedrich 44
Georg Jacob 34
Jacob 34
Maria Margaretha 38
Samuel 38, 44
Susanna 38, 44
Mauss, Friedrich 27
Maria Margaretha 27
Samuel 27
Susanna 27
Maxwell, Alexander 134
Barry, Rt. Hon. 314
David 219
Eliza 362
George Clerk 198, 202, 203
George P. 254
Harbert 314
Harry, Hon. 314
Herbert 314
Isabella 362
James 362
Jean 219
John 134, 219, 314, 362
John, Jr. 134
Margaret 134, 362
Margt. 314
Marion 219
Mary 134
Robt. 193
T., Mrs. 362
Thomas 134, 362
William 139
Wm. 341
Wm., Sir 314
Mayer, Caspar 237
Michael 177
Mayerhoffer, John Henry 109
Mayhew, Robert 244
Maylaender, Anna Appolonia 59
Conrad 59
Maynard, --- 314
Rob., Lieut. 314
Wm. 314
Mayne, Thos. 314
Mayo, John, Ensign 314
Mayorholser, John Henry 111
Mayorhotser, John Henry 111
Maze, Francis 341
M'Bride, Hu. 292
W. 292
McAdam, Elijah 311
Elizth. 311
Geo. 311
McAlegant, Jane 134
McAlester, Cathn. 200
Coll 216
Mary 200, 216
McAlexander, John 311
McAlice, Jas. 311
McAlister, Angus 117

Catharine 117
Charles 117
Duncan 117
Effie 117
Elizabeth 116
John 117
Margaret 117
William 290
McAllin, Dowilloge 311
McAllister, Florance 117
Margaret 117
McAllum, Cathn. 200
Duncan 200
Mcalpine, William 534
McAlpine, Robert 117
McArthur, Alexander 117, 118
Ann 200
Anna 118
Archibald 222
Catharine 117, 118
Catherine 222
Cathn. 200
Charles 118
Chirst. 200
Christian 118
Colin 118
Donald 118, 221, 222
Duncan 117, 118, 221, 222
Eliza McEwen 221
Florence 118
Flory 117
Isbell 116
Jean 200
Jennet 118
John 118, 200, 221, 222
Katherine 222
Margaret 118
Mary 118, 120
Neil 118
Patrick 118
Peter 200, 221
MCarthy, Alexander 507
Margaret 510
Mary 509
McAuley, Saml. 311
McAuliffe, Denis 494
Johanna 494
Michael 494
Robert 494
McAulla, Christian 118
McAwan, Agnes 219
McBeath, John 205
McBrian, Eueny 311
Gilduf 311
McBride, Agnes 417
Alexr. 197
Archd. 196
David 417
Eliz. 196
Eliza 417
George 245
Jas. 196, 311
Jenny 196
Mary 311
Mary A 417
McCabe, Edwd. 311
McCadden, Patrick 133
McCafferty, Wm. 311
McCaffry, Bernd. 311
McCaherty, Bernd. 311
Mary 311
McCalester, John 311
McCall, George 531
James 248
John 248
Robt. 311
McCalla, Saml. 311
McCalline, John 311

McCallum, Duncan 214
Mary 116
McCalmont, Alex 417
Eliza 417
Jane 417
Mary 417
Robert 417
Sarah 417
McCammon, Jas. 311
Rose 311
McCamon, John 311
Thos. 311
McCan, Jas., jun. 311
Jas., sen. 311
John 311
Judith 311
Mary 311
McCane, Robert 339
McCanlon, Elizabeth 134
William 134
McCann, Janet 220
Jean 220
John 220
Sarah 220
William 220
McCanna, Patk. 311
McCapine, Donald 118
Dugald 118
Mary 118
McCappeny, --- 311
McCarry, Jas. 311
John 311
McCarthy, Ann 472
Bridget 472
Edward 472
Florence 256
John 472, 499
Margaret 494
Martin 472
Mary 472
Nell 494
Peggy 472
Peter 472
Sandy 494
Thomas 472
Thos. 311
McCarthys, Sarah 256
McCartney, Jas. 311
McCarty, Michael 278
McCaul, Wm. 311
McCausland, Con(n)olly 311
McChristian, Alexander 118
McClanaghan, John 311
McClean, Archd. 311
McClelland, John 251
John M. 251
Wm. 311
McClilland, Jane 311
John 311
Mary 311
Robt. 311
Wm. 311
McClintock, Alex. 311
McCloskey, Patt. 311
McClosky, Rory 311
McCloskye, Donaughy Oge 311
McCloud, Catharin 118
Donald 118
Duncan 118
John 118
McClumpha, Jean 219
John 219
Thomas 219
McClure, Agnes 134
Andrew 134
Eleanor 134
James 134
James, Jr. 134

Jane 134, 311
John 134
Wm. 311
McClurg, Robt. 311
McCole, Alexander 212
Ann 212, 214
Christian 213, 214
David 214
Donald 212, 213
Dougald 212
Dugal 212
Dugald 213
Duncan 213, 214
Evan 213
John 212
Katherine 213
Marget 212
Mary 212, 214
Mildred 212, 214
Samuel 212
Sarah 212, 214
McColl, John 118
McCollum, Allan 118
Angus 311
Anne 118
Arch'd 118
Archibald 118
Donald 118
Duncan 118
Flory 118
Hugh 118
John 118
Margaret 118
Mary 118
Merran 118
Merrian 118
McComb, Alexander 219
Jas. 311
Thos. 311
McConmee, Art. 311
McConnally, John 311
McConnell, Alex. 311
McCook, Neill 311
McCore, Archibald 118
John 118
McCormac, Dan. 311
McCormack, Anne 459
Bridget 459
Catherine 459
Ellen 459
Patrick 459
Peter 459
Mary 459
McCormick, Alexander 265
Anne 459, 460
Bridget 459
Catherine 459, 460
Edward 459
Ellen 459
George 278
Honor 460
James 459
Margaret 459, 460
Mary 459, 460
Michael 258, 460
Pat 460
Patrick 459
Peter 459
Sally 460
Thomas 459
McCowen, Elizabeth 134
Francis 134
Markham 134
Mary 134
McCrachan, Hugh 311
McCrae, Hugh 219
Eliza 311
McCrory, Robt. 311

Torlaugh 311
McCrossan, Jas. 311
McCruin, Jas. 311
Sarah 311
McCuag, Isabell 117
McCuaige, Anna 119
McCullagh, Robt. 312
Wm. 312
McCulloch, Jas., Rev. 312
Wm. 312
McCullough, Jas. 312
McCullum, Flory 120
Peter 222
McCully, Robt. 312
Wm. 312
McCurry, Dan. 312
McCutchen, Thomas 262
McDavid, Edmond Groome 312
McDavy, Connor 312
McDermott, Anne 460
Bernard 460
Bessy 460
Betty 460
Bridget 460
Eliza 460
Ellen 460
Hen. 312
Hugh 460
James 460
John 460
Maria 460
Mary 460
Michael 279 460
Michl 280
Rosanna 460
Susan 460
Thomas 460
William 274, 460
McDiarmed, Eliza 222
Jean 222
John 222
Katherine 222
Mary 222
McDiarmid, Mary 120
McDonagh, ---, Capt. 469
Mcdonald, Alexander 206
George 206
Hector 206
John 206
McDonald, Alexander 117
Anne 118, 119
Archibald 118
Catharine 118, 119
Christy 214
Donald 118, 205
Eliz. 205
Jean 119
Jessy 215
John 117, 118, 258
Katherine 220
Mary 117, 215
Neil 118
Thos. 312
William 206, 215
Wm. 312
McDonall, Alexander 220
McDonnell, Alex. 312
Andrew 460
Anne 460
Ellen 460
Catherine 460
James Joseph 244
Mary 460
Michael 460
Patrick 460
Thomas 283
McDougal, Alexander 219
Margaret 221

McDougald, Allan 118
Anna 116, 118
Eliz. 118
Hanna 118
Margaret 118
McDowall, Edward 220
Robert 220
McDowell, Jane 133
John 133, 312
Magdalene 133
Margaret 133
Martha 133
Robert 133, 134
Samuel 133
William 133
McDuffie, Alexander 115, 118
Anna 115
Anne 118
Arch'd 118
Archibald 118
Catherina 118
Dudly 118
Duncan 118
Isbell 118
James 118
Jenny 118
John 118
Malcom 118
Margaret 118, 121
Mary 118
Rose 118
McDuffy, Dudly 119
Dugald 119
Margaret 119
Mary 119
McDugald, Alexander 119
Angus 119
Arch'd 119
Betty 119
Christian 119
Dugald 119
Duncan 119
Hugh 119
Jenet 119
Jennat 119
John 119
Margaret 119
Ronald 119
Ronold 119
McDugall, John 119
Mary 118, 120
McEachern, Anne 119
Arch'd 119
Catharine 119
Donald 119
Florence 120
Jean 119
Mary 119, 120
Patrick 119
McEachoin, Flory 118
McElgorm, Alex. 312
McElroy, John, Rev. 258
McEuen, Alexander 120
Anne 120
Archibald 119
Catharine 116
Duncan 119
Hugh 119, 120
James 119
Janet 119
Jennat 119
John 119
Malcom 119
Mary 119, 120
Merran 119
McEwen, Anna 119
Eliza 221
John 119

Malcolm 119
Mcfarlan, Walter 534
McFarland, Elizth 312
Jane 312
John 312
Robt. 312
Sarah 312
Mcfarlane, Walter 198
McFarlane, Dond. 199
McFarlin, John 312
McFarnan, Robt. 312
McGann, Anne 460, 461
Atty 460
Bridget 461
Eliza 461
James 461
John 460, 461
Luke 460
Mary 460, 461, 463
Thomas 461
McGanne, Anne 460, 461
Atty 460
Bridget 461
Eliza 461
James 461
John 460, 461
Luke 460
Mary 460, 461
Thomas 461
McGargle, Amelia 417
McGarvin, Jean 219
McGee, Patrick 281
McGenalty, Edwd. 312
McGerrald, Connor 312
McGibbion, John 119
McGie, William 119
McGillchrist, Margaret 119
McGillegan, Brian bane 312
McGilly, Thos. 312
McGin, Eliza 312
Saml. 312
Mary 312
Wm. 312
McGlavey, John 312
McGlue, George T. 265
McGoirke, Bryan 312
Hugh Roe 312
Mcgoun, James 534
McGoun, Alex., Ensign 312
McGowan, Bern. 312
John 312
Margt. 312
Peter 312
McGown, Angus 119
Anna 119
Archibald 119
Duncan 119
Eachern 119
Hector 119
John 119
Malcom 119
Margaret 119
Patrick 119
McGra, John 312
Nancy 312
McGrath, Thomas 258
McGregor, Donald 222
Hugh 222
Isabel 223
Jean 221
Jean McNaughton 222
Katherine 222
McGuary, Anne 120
McGuire, --- 464
Lucia 312
Wm. 312
McHaig, Ann 218
Grizzel 218

John 218, 312
Margaret 218
McHenry, Aran 312
Dan. 312
Elnr. 312
McIlgorm, Alex. 312
John 312
McIllfeder, Archibald 119
Catharine 119
Effie 120
Mary 117
McIlroy, Thomas 417
McIlwrey, Bridget 119
Catharine 119
Donald 119
Hugh 119
John 119
Mary 119
McIlwry, Effie 119
McIndiore, Merran 119
McInish, Ann 213
Archibald 213
Catherine 213
Donald 213
Jannet 213
John 213
Malcolm 213
McInnish, Anne 119
Archibald 119
Catharine 117, 119
Florence 119
Merran 119, 121
Murdoch 119
Neil 119
McIntagert, John 119
McIntaylor, Donald 119
John 119
McIntire, Alexander 271
Angus 119
Ann 212, 213
Archibald 212
Catharine 120
Charles 213
Christian 119, 121
Dan'l 121
Donald 120, 213
Duncan 211, 214
Elizabeth 214
Gilbert 213
John 120, 211, 212, 213
Katherine 213, 214
Malcolm 213
Margaret 120, 212, 213
May 214
Nicolas 120
Polk 197
McIntosh, Angus 120
Thomas 256, 258, 259
McIntyre, Alexander 222
Ann Walker 221
Archibald 221
Catherine 221
Christy 199
Donald 199, 221
Dond. 199
Duncan 199, 222
Evan 213
Helen McNab 222
Isobel 199
John 199, 222
Katrine 199
Margaret 222
Margt. 199
Mary 199
Nancy 199
McIsaac, Malcom 221
Mciver, Alexander 534
McKackey, John 219

McKane, John 312
McKay, ---, Colonel 204
Dond. 200
Duncan 120
George 208
James 211
Jas. 312
William 203
Willm. 207
McKeay, Duncan 120
Florrance 122
Mary 115
Merran 119
McKee, Agnes 312
John 312
Robt. 312
McKellar, Archibald 120
Catharine 120
Charles 120
Florence 120
Janet 120
Margaret 120
Mary 120
McKelvy, Jas. 312
John 312
McKendrick, Janet 200
McKenna, Ally 417
Ann 417
Hugh 246
James 417
Patrick 417
McKenzie, Archibald 120
Catharin 120
Collin 120
Donald 120
Florence 120
George 120
Gilbert 216
John 120, 532
Martha 197
Mary 120, 216
McKeown, Dan. 312
Edwd. 312
Eliza Ann 417
McKichan, Janet 200
Neil 200
Rob 200
McKie, Margaret 220
Samuel 220
McKine, John 218
McKinley, Jean 219
John 312
Mary 312
Michael 219
McKinven, Duncan 120
McKissack, Janet 219
Thomas 220
McKnown, John 313
Mary 313
Robt. 313
Wm. 313
McKoin, Thomas 331
McKorest, Mary 221
McKy, Abr. 313
McLaghlin, Hugh 313
McLain, Hugh 313
McLaren, Donald 214
Duncan 214
Hugh 221
James 222
Lachlan 214
McLarine, Lawrine 214
McLashin, Dennis 313
McLauchlin, Florence 121
McLaughlin, John 252
M'Clean, David 291
Eliz. 291
George 291

James 291
John 291
McLean, Alexander 120
Catharine 115
John 120
Lauchlin 120
Mary 117
Merran 118
McLeod, Aeneas 209
Willm. 210
McLeran, Hugh 221
McLernan, James 417
Jane 417
Maybel 417
McLoughlin, Bernd. 313
Bridget 481
Catherine 481
Ellen 481
John 313
Martha 313
Thomas 481
McMahon, Alex. 313
Grizzy 313
McManny, Saml. 313
McManus, Andrew 461
James 461
Mary 461
Pat 461
Thomas 461
Wm. 313
McMartin, Peter 222
McMartine, Donald 223
Duncan 223
Hugh 223
Isabel McGregor 223
Margaret 223
McMast, Jas. 313
McMasters, Elianora 220
Eliza 220
John 219
Robert 219
McMicken, Alexander 219
James 219
Janet 220
William 219, 220
Janet 196
McMiking, James 220
John 219
Thomas 219
McMillan, Alexander 120
Arcd. 199, 200, 216
Barbara 199
Daniel 200
Donald 120
Fras. 313
Gelbt. 200
Iver 200
Jas. 313
Jean 200
Jenet 120
Margaret 219
Mary 120, 199
Robt. 313
Sarah 313
McMorrow, Hen. 313
McMullan, Cathn. 200
Corns. 313
Eliza 313
Elnr. 313
Malm. 200
McMullen, Ann 313
Dav. 313
Geo. 313
Jane 313
Jas. 313
John 313
Margt. 313
Martha 313

Mary 313
Robt. 313
Sarah 313
Thos. 313
McMurchie, Archd. 216
 Elizabeth 216
 Hugh 216
 Mary 216
 Patrick 216
 Robert 216
McMurchy, Archd. 215
 Barbara 216
 Charles 215
 Elizabeth 216
 Neil 215
McMurray, Hugh 313
McMurry, Owen Duff 313
McNab, Helen 222
McNabb, John 197
 Tebby 197
McNaghten, Bart. 313
McNalty, Hugh 313
McNamee, Charles 264, 267,
 270, 271, 277, 278, 284,
 285, 286
 Charles M. 274
 W. 273
McNaney, Thomas 281
McNantz, Neil 265
McNaugh, James 120
McNaught, Alexander 120
 Florence 120
 Jennat 120
 John 120
 Mary 120
 Moses 120
McNaughten, Malcolm 313
 Martha 313
McNaughton, Angus 222
 Christian 221, 222
 Daniel 222
 Donald 222
 Duncan 222
 Elizabeth 222
 Janet Anderson 221
 Jean 222, 223
 John 221, 222
 Katherine 222, 223
 Katherine Robinson 223
 Peter 222
McNauty, Neil 265
McNeight, Robt. 313
McNeil, Anne 120
 Danl. 201
 Hector 201
 Isobel 201
 Jean 120, 215
 John 120
 Malcolm 202
 Margaret 120
 Mary 121, 201
 Neil 201
 Peter 201
 Roger 120
 Willm. 201
McNeill, Archd. 313
 Barbara 120
 Betty 120
 Catharine 120
 Eliz. 120
 John 120
 Mary 313
 Neil 120
 Peggy 120
 Thos. 313
McNemee, Frances 313
McNevan, William James 244
McNicol, Angus 212

Ann 212
Annapel 198
Archibald 212
Jean 198
John 198, 212
Mary 212
Nicol 212
Robet. 198
McNiven, Catharin 120
 Elizabeth 120
 John 120
 Mary 120
 Merran 120
 Rachel 120
McPhaden, Dirvorgill 120
 Donald 120
 Duncan 120
 Flory 120
 John 120
 Margaret 120
 Mary 118, 120
 Neil 120
McPhail, Cristy 120
 Flory 120
 Gilbert 120
 John 120
 Margaret 120
McPherson, Christn. 199
 Janet 199
 John 250
 Malcolm 199
 Willm. 199
McQuade, Bgt. 313
 Jas. 313
 Phelemy 313
 Rose 313
 Wm 417
McQuary, Anne 120
 John 120
 Mary 119
McQueen, William 219
McQueon, Jane 313
 Wm. 313
McQuestion, Anthony 220
McQuillon, Jas. 313
McQuin, Anna 118
McQuiston, Joan 196
 Jno. 196
McQuoin, Owen 313
McQuore, Christian 120
 Donald 120
 Duncan 120
 Effie 120
 Gilbert 120
 John 120
 Mary 117
McRay, George 207, 209, 210
 Wm. 210
McReady, Dav. 313
McRegan, Jas. 313
McRob, Duncan 216
McRoberts, Jas. 313
 Wm. 313
McShane, Brian 313
 Jas. 313
 Michl. 313
McTaggart, James 219
McTier, --- 303, 313
M'Cullough, Hers. 292
McVain, Mary 222
 Sarah 222
McVane, Katherine 212
McVey, Doug. 197
McVicar, John 197, 198, 216
McVurah, Peter 222
McVurich, Archibald 121
 Florence 121
 Lauchlin 121

Mary 120
 Merran 121
McWhinney, Isa. 313
 John 313
McWilliams, Alex 279
 Alexdr. 257
 Elizabeth 220
 George 220
 James 219
 Janet 219
Mead, John 362
Meade, Courthope 314
 Thomas 272
Mean, William 220
Mechan, Catherine 362
 James 362
Mechlan, Mary 362
 William 362
Mechling, Jacob 4
 Theobald 4
Meckel, Christian 26
Meckin, Jos. 341
Medart, Carl 45
 Catharina 45
 Johann Adam 45
 Valentin 45
Medile, David 362
Meeghan, Patrick 341
Meehan, Catherine 341
 Owen 341
Meehas, Halstein T 398, 400
Mehaas, Gurri 398
 Halstein 400
 Rasmus 398
 Sidseller 398
Mein, John 362
Meinzer, Johannes 177
 Martin 177
Meister, Anna Elisabetha 52
 Anna Maria 52
 Georg Bernhard 19, 24
 Peter 52
 Veit 19, 24
Melchier, Johannes 129
Melchior, Johannes 129
 Maria Katharina 129
Melchoir, Philip 531
Meloy, Jno. 362
Melvin, James 257
Mendes, Abigail 153
 Abraham 155
 Abraham Pereira 155
 Benjamin Pereira 155
 Esther 154, 155
 Esther Pereira 153
 Gabriel 155
 Jacob Pereira 153
 Judith 155
 Rachel 155
 Rapl. 152
 Saml. Pra. 155
 Sime 154
 Solomon 152
Mendez, David 153
Mengel, Friederich 25
 Frietz 25
Mengersdorff, Anna Sibilla 105
 Elizabeht 105
 Hendrick 105
 Sorg 105
Menieur, Dennis 341
Menter, John 289
Mention, Agnes 341
 Alexander 341
Menzies, Archd. 198, 203
 Mary 198
Mercer, Jane 79
 Sml. 79

Mercle, Jno. David 167
Meredith, James 139
Meredyth, Hen. 314
Merkam, Conrad 15
Merret, Daniel 109
  John Philip 109
Merrill, John 314
Merring, Richard 138
Merschheimer, Henrich 180
Merz, Philipp 26
Meskeeveg, Even 412, 415
  Even Johansen 412, 415
  Jane 412, 415
Mesquita, Moses, Senr. 155
  Jacob Fernandes 152
Messerschmid, Elizabeth Mar-
  garetha 36
  Joerg Emich 36
Messinger, Michael 7
Metchon, John 341
Methuen, Paul, Rt. Hon. 314
Metsger, Jacob 111
Metz, Henry 166
Metzgar, Sara 8
Meuron, Abraham 87
  Jacob Henry 104
Meyer, --- 224
  Anna Catharina 184
  Anna Maria 184
  Christina 184
  Hanss Jerg 177
  Henry 258
  Johann Philipp 184
  Johannes 184
  Jos. 168
  Maria Margaretha 184
  Philip Melchoir 531
  Thomas 237
  Tobias 184
Meyers, Napthaly Hart 163
Michael, Wilhelm 46
Michall, John 111, 112
Michaw, James 362
Michel, Joseph 341
  Levis 108
Michell, Mary 529
  Nat., Ensign 314
Muckum, Samuel 262
Midthus, Svein L. 402, 408
Mierau, Abraham 520
  Elisabeth 520
  Heinrich 521
  Jacob 520
  Johann 521
  Katharina 520
  Peter 520
  Susanne 521
Mies, Anna Barbara 181
  Casper 181
  Christiana 181
  Johann Georg 181
  Louisa 181
  Philip 181
  Philippus 181
Mikell, Alex. 314
Mikine, Agnes 218
  Jean 218
  John 218
  Mary 218
  Nanny 219
  Rosanna 218
  Rosina 218
Milborn, Andrew 194
  Christopher 194
Miligan, Elizabeth 341
Millar, John 362
  Robert 362
  Joohue 275

Joshua 277
Miller, Alexander 362
  Anne 341
  Benjamin 362
  Charles 275, 417
  Christian 17
  Christopher 533
  Christyan 17
  Elizabeth 341
  George 274
  Grover 254
  Guill. 232
  Jacob 533
  John 241, 362
  John, Ensign 314
  John Jacob 110
  Margaret 363
  Matty 341
  Michael 18, 533
  Peter 5
  Rd., Lieut. 314
  Robert 253, 254, 341
  Thomas 363
  William 363
  William, Mrs. 341
Millgan, Bernard 363
Millidge, Elizabeth 79
  Frances 79
  James 79
  John 79
  Richard 79
  Sarah 79
  Thomas 79
Milliken, W. 363
Millin, Adam 315
Millner, Mary Magdalen 166
Millroy, Agnes 219
  Anthony 219
  Eliza 219
  Janet 219
  John 219
  Mary 219
  Sarah 219
Mills, Andrew 341
  Elizabeth 195
  George 245
  John 195
Millwane, Mary 220
  Thomas 219
Milton, ---, Mrs. 510
Minch, Simon 43
Minech, Peter 63
  Simon 65
Minehan, Biddy 494
  Johanna 494
  John 494
  Patrick 494
Miner, Philip H. 270
Minetes, Biddy 341
  Francis 341
Mingersdorffe, George 111
Minich, Catharina 65
  John Simon 65
Minigh, Hans 31, 32
Minis, Catherine 363
Minnich, --- 65
Minnig, --- 65
Minnis, Dav. 315
  Fras. 363
Minor, Philip H. 270
Minors, Philip H. 270
Miranda, Isaac Rodriques 154
Miss, Anna Juliana 182
  Catharina 182
  Georg 182
  Johann Georg 182
  Johann Gerhard 182
  Johann Heinrich 182

  Maria Christina 182
Mitchel, James 363
  John 534
Mitchell, Alex. 315
  Ann 200
  Charles 363
  Elizth. Sarah 315
  Hen. 315
  Hugh 315
  Inger 383
  Jane 315
  Jas. 363
  John 139, 315
  Martin 363
  Randle 315
  Robt. 200
  Samuel 363
  William 195
  Wm. 315
Mite, Samuel 363
Mithus, S L 402, 404, 408
Mittelberger, Gottlieb 22
M'Keon, --- 346
M'Knott, --- 330
M'Meikin, Alex. 292
Mochan, Elizabeth 363
Mockabee, John 279
Moeda, Rodriques 153
Moerschheimer, Henrich 180
Moessinger, John 7
Moffat, Edward 363
  John 363
  William 363
Moffet, John 258
Moffit, John 258, 341
  Margaret 341
  Mary 258
  Robert 258
Mog, John 109
Mogridge, Jo. 315
Mohl, Christoph 326
Mohn, Martin Pobetz 397
Mohnn, Michael P. 264
Mohr, Johann Peter 142
Mohun, Francis 283
  Philip 278
Molineau, James 341
Mollan, Hugh 363
Molley, ---, Mrs. 191
Mollin, Patrick 341
Molloghan, Patrick 363
Mollony, John 341
Molloy, Patrick 363
Molster, Ingeborg Davidsatter 439
Molsworth, ---, Lord Visct. 315
Molyneux, ---, Dr. 315
Momby, ---, Lieut. 315
Monaghan, Anthony 482
  Peter 363
Moncriffe, Tho. 315
Monderson, Isaac 363
  John 363
  Margaret 363
  Sarah 363
Monegan, Francis 341
Money, Charles 363
  Margaret 363
Moneypenny, M. 315
  Wm. 315
Mongin, Daniel 107
  Francis 107
Monheimer, Jacob 237
Monks, Joseph 292
  Robt. 292
  Thomas 292
  Thos. 292
Monoghan, Torry 341

Monro, Hugh 206, 210
　Willm. 208
Monsdatta, B 403
　M 403, 407
Monsdatter, S 403
Monsen, K 403, 407
　P 403
　T. 403, 407
Montague, Samuel 107
　Samuel, Colo. 107
Montgomery, Alexander 116, 121
　Anna 121
　Catherine 117
　Hugh 121, 315
　Hugh, Sir 315
　J. 341
　John 315, 363
　John B. 247
　Joseph 341
　Moses 341
　W. 315
　William 247
　Wm. 341
　Wm., Lieut. 315
Montrath, ---, Lord 315
Moody, James 363
Moone, J. 363
Mooney, Alexander 363
　John 363
　Mary 363
　Michael 363
　Patk. 292
Moony, Charles 246
Moore, Adrian 315
　Alex. 315
　Alexander 363
　Andrew 363
　Andw. 315
　Archd. 315
　Eliza 341
　Elizth. 315
　Geo., Sir 315
　Henry 341
　Isaac 315
　James 258, 341, 363
　Jane 363
　Jas. 315
　Jean 315
　John 315, 341, 363, 532
　Jos. 315
　Letty 363
　Margaret 341, 363
　Margt. 315
　Mary 341
　Mathew 341
　Matthew 110
　Mildred 81
　Robert 341, 363
　Robt. 81, 315
　Samuel 363
　Samuel D. 363
　Tho. 315
　Thomas 341
　William 341, 363
　Wm. 252
Moorhead, Samuel 341
Moran, --- 341
　Catherine 461
　Francis 461
　James 363
　John 461
　Patrick 280
　Winifred 461
Morehouse, Abraham 227, 228
Morer, James 363
Morgan, --- 228, 346
　Edwd. 363
　George 208

James 341
Jas. 315
John 139, 363
Luke 341
Michl. 315
William 248, 331
Morgenstern, Johann Engel 39
　Johann Engelbert 39
　Johann Philipp 39
　Maria Rosina 39
Moriarty, Ambrose 256
Moriatta, Ambrose 259
Morine, John 363
　Judith 363
Morison, Alexr. 208
Morley, John 315
Morr, John James 109
Morran, Andrew 341
Morris, ---, Quarter-Master-
　Gen. 315
　Ann 315
　Fras., Lieut. 315
　James 196
　John 244, 363, 417
　Mary 363
Morrison, ---, Brig.-Gen. 315
　Edward 198
　Elizabeth 341
　J. 363
　James 341
　John 341
　Martha 341
　Matthew 363
　R. 363
　Wm. 315
Morrissey, Bridget 482
　Catherine 482
　Ellen 482
　Hannah 482
　John 482
　Maria 482
　Mary 482
　Pat 482
　Peggy 482
　Roger 482
　Thomas 482
Morron, John 330, 341
Morrow, Agnes 315
　Andw. 315
　Ellen 341
　George 293
　James 341
　Jane 341
　John 341
　Joseph 363
　Robert 363
　Thomas 363
　William 280
Morschheimer, Henrich 180
Morsell, Benjamin K., Esq. 283
Morton, Francis 363
Moser, Elisabeth 27
　Elisabetha 57
　Martin 4
　Tobias 8
Moss, Bryan 315
　Chas. 315
　Rose 315
Moultrie, ---, General 102
Mount, Thomas 267
Mountjoy, ---, Lord 315
Mower, Jacob 129
Moxon, Mordecai 315
Moyle, John 445, 447
　Susan 445
　Thomas 445
Moynahan, Denis 506
Moynan, Owen 315

Moynehan, Dan 495
　Denis 494
　Ellen 495
　Johanna 494, 495
　John 494
　Mary 495
　Norry 495
　Tade 495
Moynihan, Biddy 494
　Denis 494
　Johanna 494
　John 494
　Patrick 494
Mozel, Anton 328
Mubrea, H. 341
Mudd, Jerh. 252
Mueller, Anna Elisabeth 184
　Catharina 27, 38, 184
　David 22
　Dietrich 18
　Friedrich 184
　Jacob 18, 184
　Johann Friedrich 171
　Johann Michael 169
　Johannes 184
　Joseph 184
　Maria Margaretha 27, 38
　Peter 31
　Philipp Georg 169
　Salome 184
　Samuel 27, 28
　Susanna 27, 38, 44
Muench, (Anna) Maria Katharina
　65
　Christina 43
　Jacob Peter 43
　Johann Georg 43
　Johann Peter 63
　Johann Simon 65
　Maria Christina 63
　Peter 43
　Philipp Simon 43
Muenig, Hans Georg 43
Mugridge, Francis 79
Muhlberger, Anna Christina 129
　George 129
Muhlenberg, Henry Melchior,
　Rev. 5
Mühlenberg, H. M, Pastor 71
Mühlschlägel, Johann Andreas
　173
Muir, Ellen 79
　James 79
　John 79
　Mary 79
Muldary, Thomas 363
Muldawney, Michael 363
Mulden, Anthony 341
Muldoon, ---, Mrs. 293
　Michael 293
Mulera, James 461
　Thomas 461
Mulere, Catherine 461
Mulhall, Mary 363
Mulhallan, Sheely 317
Mulhallon, Ann 315
　Arthur 315
　Collow 315
　Cormack 315
　Cormack, Capt. 315
　Jas. 315
Mulheron, John 363
Mulholland, George 341
　Henry 363
　John 363
Mulhollen, John 134
Mullan, Arthur 363
　Bridget 363

Cicey 363
James 363
John 363
Michl. 315
Richd. 363
William 363
Mullay, James 341
William 363
Mulledy, Thomas 258
Mullen, Edward 363
John 482
Mary 482
Patrick 363
Thomas 363
Müller, Anna 62
Christian 17
Christoph 175
Johann Michael 170
Michael 18
Pips Georg 169
Mullera, Anne 461, 462
Bridget 461, 462
Catherine 461
Denis 461
Francis 462
James 461, 462
John 462
Mary 462
Pat 461, 462
Patrick 462
Sarah 462
Thomas 461
Mullerea, Catherine 461
Mullidy, Thomas 258
Mulligan, James C. 363
Michael 363
Mullin, Jane 315
Jas. 315
John 482
Mary 482
Susan 315
Wm. 315
Mulony, James 341
Mulvany, Patrick 363
Thomas 363
Mulvey, Isabella 363
John 363
Munch, Johann Peter 65
Johannes 32
Münch, Jacob Peter 63
Jean Noe 32
Johann Christoph 65
Johann Georg 63
Johann Nikolaus 65
Johann Peter 63
Johann Philipp 65
Johann Simon 63
Johanna 32
Maria Apollonia 65
Maria Barbara 65
Maria Catharina 65
Maria Elisabetha 32
Philipp Simon 63
Munden, Rich., Brig.-Gen. 315
Mundoch, Margt. 316
Robt. 316
Sarah 316
Munduch, Alex. 316
Saml. 316
Sarah 316
Munn, Christian 121
William 341
Munro, Philip 259, 263
Munroe, Thomas 271
Munson, Ole 437
Murchie, Finlay 215
Murdoch, Jas. 316
John 257, 316, 363

Obediah 363
Sarah 316
Thos. 316
Murdock, Esther 341
John 341, 534
M. Anne 341
Robt. 316
Murdough, Matthew 341
Murney, Patrick 363
Muron, Abraham 107
Murpey, Dinis 510
Murphy, --- 346
Andrew 294
Anthony 121
Betty 494, 505
Bridget 363
Catherine 363
Cicily 363
Dennis 363
Edward 258
Eleanor 363
Frances 363
Francis 363
Honnorah 510
Hugh 292
James 341, 363
Jane 495, 506
Johanna 363, 495
John 341, 363
Jonoah 505
Lawrence 363
M. 341
Marg. 363
Margaret 495
Martin 363
Mary 316, 341, 363, 495
Matthew 341
Michael 341, 495
Morris 363
Patrick 293, 363
Rose 300, 316
Simon 363
Susan 363
Thomas 293
Tim 505, 506
Timothy 341, 495, 510
William 341
Murray, Alexander 221
Archibald 221
Bernard 363
Bridget 363
Christian 221
Daniel 363, 534
Geo. 316
James 221, 363
Jas. 363
John 221, 363
Katherine 221
Little Rath 316
Margaret McDougal 221
Michael 258
Patrick 363, 417
Thomas 251, 256, 258, 259,
  282
Thos. 316
William 221, 363
Wm. 316
Murrell, John, jun. 316
John, sen. 316
Murrin, Thomas 363
Murry, Edmund 341
Felix 363
James 341
Jas. 316
Roger 341
Murtagh, --- 363
Thomas 341
Murtaugh, John 363

Musselmann, Hans 21
Johannes 21
Mussgnug, Jacob 179
Mussgnung, David 177
Myer, Donrade 166
Gasper 108
Myers, Hyam 161, 163
John 139
Manuel 161, 163
Samuel 138
Solomon 156, 163
Myhre, ---, Mrs. 420
Myran, O.A. 429, 442
Myren, Ole Aslesen 442

-- N --

Naffager, Peter 533
Nagel, Frederick Wilhelm 15
Joachim 177
Sebastian 177
Mailor, Wm. 341
Nalty, Bridget 363
Margaret 363
Mary 363
Patrick 363
Thomas 363
Nanson, Mathew 341
Naper, Robt., Lieut.-Gen. 316
Napier, Robt., Brig.-Gen. 316
Nare, Solomon 160, 163
Narey, Peter 363
Narrevig, Lars L. 391, 395, 414
Lars Larsen 395
Narrwig, Lars Larsen 395, 406,
  411, 413, 414
Narry, Bartholomew 462
Bartley 462
Bridget 462
Mary 462
Michael 462
Pat 462
Patrick 462
William 462
Narverud, Syvert Engebrethsen
  430
Narvig, Ingebret Larson 395, 413
Ingebrigt Larsen 413
Lars Larsen 413, 414
Naset, Anna Bertha 399
John J. 399
Nasida, Catherine 364
Nathane, Alexander 155
Nattestad, Ansten 420
Natvig, Holger Hansen 390
Naughten, Patrick 364
Naughton, Catherine 482
Neagh, Lough 316
Neal, Michael 364
Neale, Francis, Rev. 254, 259
James 275, 277
Neall, Mathew 341
Neals, Henry C. 254
Neary, Anne 462
Bridget 462
Catherine 462
James 462
John 462
Mary 462
Patrick 462
Nedin, William 263
Needham, Cahterine 342
Eliza 342
Sam., Capt. 316
Valient 342
Neef, John 113

Neff, Jacob 40
   Peter 40
   Veronika 40
Neil, Hugh 342
   James 364
   Margaret 364
   Thomas 342
Neill, Henry D. 364
   Madge D. 364
Neilson, Alex. 316
   Elinor 293
   Eliza'h 342
   Gerard 342
   Hall 316
   James 342
   John 342
   Josias 316
   Thomas 342
   William 342
Neitzell, John 241
Nelson, Corns. 316
   Gerard 342
   John 316, 342
   Malinda 400, 409
   William 342
Nesbet, Archd. 534
Nesbit, Hugh 364
Nesbitt, William George Downing
   455
Netman, Jean Rudolph 107
   John Redolph 108
Netterville, John Thomas 244
Neu, Anna Margaretha 41
   Catharina 54
   Christina Margareta 28
   Christina Margaretha 41
   Christoffel 29, 47
   Fallendin 54
   Georg 28, 41
   Johann Jacob 55
   Johann Michel 30, 47
   Johann Nickel 29, 47
   Johann Otto 41
   Johann Simon 41
   John Michel 30
   Joseph 28, 41
   Maria Elisabetha 55
   Maria Margretha 55
   Peter 28, 41
   Philipp 30
   Philps 47
   Valentin 54
   Wilhelm 41
Neufeld, David 524
   Gerhard 520, 524
   Heinrich 520
   Isaak 520
   Jacob 520
   Jakob 524
   Johann 520
   Justina 520
   Kornelius 516
   Margaretha 516, 524
   Peter 520, 524
   Susanna 524
Neuferinn, Charlotte 328
Neuhard, Anna Barbara 55
   Jacob 55
   Margaretha Catharina 55
   Susanna Catharina 55
Neustadt, Oberamt 7
Nevil, Clement, Brig.-Gen. 316
Nevill, Fran. 316
Nevin, Patrick 364
Newall, Thomas 106
Newan, Thomas 342
Newberry, Robert 364
Newdigate, Roger, Sir 147, 151

Newhard, George 13
   George Frederick 12
   Michael 13
Newlan, Patrick 364
Newport, George 248
Newton, Clemt. 252
   Edmd., Rev. 316
   Samuel 286
   Thos., Rev. 316
Neymeyer, Conrad 239
Nice, --- 232
Nicholas, John 342
Nicholls, Jno 140
Nichols, David 110
   James 192
Nick, Anna Regina 33
Nickel, ---, Frau 523, 525
   Abraham 523, 525
   Anna 517, 523
   David 517
   Gertrude 517
   Helena 517
   Jacob 525
   Jakob 523
   Johann 525
   Justina 523
   Katharina 523
   Maria 522
   Peter 517
   Theodor 517
   Wilhelm 517, 522
Nickle, Thomas 364
   William 364
Nickler, Elisabetha 40
Nicolson, Alexr. 204, 205, 208
Niecke, Anna Regina 33
Niederauer, Jost Fritz 56
   Michel 56
Nielsdatter, A 405
   B 404, 405
   E 404
   M 405
   Magreth Meve 411
Nielsen, N 405
   Oele 411
   P 405
Nielson, James 364
   Johnas 397
   L. 404, 407
   V 404
Nightingall, John 316
Niven, Patrick 364
Nixon, Elnr. 316
   George 342
   Mary 342
   Robt. 316
Nock, Joseph 286
Noer, Andrew 285
Nolan, P. 364
Noone, John 364
Nordhienes, N O 404
Nordvig, --- 409
   A.H. 402, 403, 406, 413
   Anders 402, 406
   Ingebrigt 414
   K H 402
   Magdalena 406
   Malinda 406
   Sarah 406
Nordviig, K. H. 395, 402, 404,
   409, 414
Norman, Robt. 316
Norris, Jas. 316
   John 292, 316
   Martha 316
   Mary 316, 342
   Robert 342
   Thos. 316

Northey, Ed., Sir 316
Notz, Johann Leonhard 20
   Lenhart 20
Nourse, Joseph 257, 260
Nowlan, Charles 364
   Christopher 364
Nowland, James 364
Noyes, Jacob 251
Nubberied, R.G. 428, 431
   Rener 431
Nubberud, Reier 431
Nugent, --- 147
   Cath. 316
   Jas. 316
   Laurence 364
Nugin, Rach. 316
Null, Conrad 241
Nunes, Isaac Rodriques 156
Nunez, Joshua 153
   Sarah 153
Nutt, Elizabeth 121
   James 121
   John 121
   Mary 115
   Rebecca 121
   Robert 121

-- O --

Oatey, Louisa 443
   Peter 443
O'Beirn, Michael 364
Oberbeck, Andreas 7
Oberkircher, Henrich 49
   Johann Henrich 49
   Maria Margaretha 49
Obert, Anna Regina 46
O'Boyle, Neal 364
O'Bream, John 364
O'Brian, Arch. 331
O'Brien, ---, Mrs. 510
   Ann 316
   Dennis 342
   James 342
   Jas. 316
   John 364
   Lawrence 364
   Margaret 342, 364
   Mary 364
   Michael 364
   Owen 342
   Patrick 498, 499
O'Cahan, ---, Lady 316
   Donnell, Sir 316
   Donnohey oge 316
O'Cahane, Brian oge 316
   Coy 316
   Shane 316
O'Cain, Thos. H. 364
O'Cassady, Brian 316
Och, Isaac 230
O'Connell, Ann, Miss 364
O Connor, Dennis 245
O'Connor, Thomas 364
O'Danihey, Denis 510
Odernheimer, Jahannes 25
   Philip 25
O'Dogh, Bryan McTirlagh 316
   Dwaltagh McHugh 316
   Ferdorogh McCalire 316
   Neale Crone 316
O'Dogherty, Averkagh McShan
   316
   Neale oge McPhelim Brassill
   316
   Shan McDwalty 316

Shane 316
O'Donnel, M. 364
O Donnell, James Delaney 247
O'Donnell, Con 288
  Isabella 364
  James 342
  Mary 364
  Patk. 364
  Wm. 364
O'Donoghue, Peter 265
O'Duffy, Hugh 316
O'Dyri, Patr_als 316
Oelsen, Soren 413
O'Farrell, Hugh 454
Offen, Christoffer 232
  Jean 232
  Joseph 232
  Margareite 232
  Maria 232
Offutt, Zachariah M. 274
O'Flannigan, Peter, Revd. 288
O'Freiel, Catherine 134
  Morris 134
Ogelby, John 317
Ogier, Catherine 189
  Charlotte 189
  George 188
  John 189
  Lewis 189
  Lucy 189
  Mary 189
  Peter 189
  Thomas 189
Ogilby, ---, Mrs. 364
  Frederick 364
  John 364
  Robert 364
Ogleby, David 258
Oglethorpe, --- 75, 76, 78
  James, Esqr. 96
O'Gneeve, John 296, 317
O'Hagan, John 317
O'Hanlon, Phelix 317
O'Hara, ---, Col. 317
  William 364
O'Hare, John 364
O'Haro, John 317
O'Hassan, Hugh 317
  Turlough 317
O'Heale, Patk. 317
O'Hear, Felix 317
O'Hegarty, Gillechrist 317
Ohrendorf, Anna Margaretha 182
  Barbara 182
  Christian 182
  Johann Christian 182
  Johann Heinrich 182
  Louisa 182
  Magdalena 182
O'Keeffe, Eugene 493
  Jeane 493
  Johanna 493
  Margaret 493
  Nano 493
O'Kerrelane, Brian 317
O'Lavarty, Owen 317
  Vickar 317
Oldatter, Siri 413, 414, 416
Olddatter, Berthe 411
Oldendatter, Atleethe 413
  Rachel 413
O'Leary, James 364
Oliphant, John 270
Oliver, Robt. 317
  Thos. 532
O'Loone, Henry 364
Olsdatter, A. 429, 431
  Ana 391, 394, 395

Anna 389, 395
Ase 413
B. 428, 430
I. 429, 435
I H 428
Martha 389
R. 429, 436, 438
Ragnilde 412
Ranveig 436, 438
M 429
S. 427, 428
Siri 413, 427
Stine 413
Olsen, A. 429, 435
  Anders 429
  I. 429, 435
  K 429
  Olaus 428
  Osmund 398
  T. 429, 436, 437
Olson, ---, Miss 381
  Hulda 383
  Lars B. 399
  Sara 416
O'Lymbrick, Gilreagh 317
O'Lynne, Patk. 317
O'Morish, Manus 317
O'Mulhallan, Cormuck 317
  Sheely 317
O'Mullan, Brian 317
  Carmocke 317
  Donnell 317
  Edmunde grome 317
  Tomlin 317
O'Neal, Anne 364, 462
  Bernard 462
  Betty 462
  Felix 342
  John 364, 462
  Nicholas 364
O'Neale, James 270
O'Neall, Alexander 364
O Neil, Hugh 245
O'Neil, ---, Major 317
  Charles 364
  Cormac 317
  Hugh 317
  J. 364
  James 364
  John 364
  Owen 364
O'Neile, Hen., Sir 317
  Naile oge 317
O'Neill, Anne 462
  Bernard 462
  Betty 462
  John 342, 462
  Robert 342
  Sarah 364
O'Neille, Laughline 317
Onil, Charles 232
Onne, William 270
O'Ray, Hugh 342
O'Reilly, Edward 364
  Eliza 364
  Hugh 364
  Margaret 364
  Miles E. 364
Orfeur, John, Lieut.-Col. 317
Ormand, Ch., Lieut. 317
Orme, Thomas 274
  William 270
Ormsby, Jane 317
  John 317
Ormsen, Peder 389
Ormston, Ralph 241
Ornmundsen, Bertha Karina 389
  Peder 389

O'Rorke, Bernard 364
  Patrick 364
Orr, Alexander 244
  Anne 364
  Elizabeth 364
  George 364
  James 364
  Jane 364
  John 259, 342
  Joshua 342
  Mary 342
  Mathew 342
  Patrick 364
  Robert 342
  Robt. 317
  Thomas 364
  Thos. 317
  William 342, 364
Ortellier, Daniel Jacob 111
Osborne, George 364
O'Scullen, Edmd. 317
Oserhaus, Raier Olsen 412
O'Shaughnessy, Limerick 364
  Margaret 364
O'Sheale, Bryan 317
  Hugh 317
Oskeland, --- 395
  Andereas 390
  Anderes A. 390, 394
  Malene 390
Osmond, Austin, Mrs. 394
  Herman Aarag 416
Osmonson, Herman 416
Osmund, Matheas 413
Osmund Datter, Siri 412
Osmund' Datter, Meye 412
Osmundsen, Anton 389
Ospeland, Osten 413
Ostedahl, Hewis 412
Ostensen, Swent 411
Oster, Anton 26
  Leonard 63
  Maria Christina 63
Osterboe, Niels Olsen 414
Osterlen, Berent Elias 411
  Berthe 411
  Elen Neilsdatter 411
  Enig 411
  Niels Olsen 411, 414
  Neils Tobias 411
Ostermann, Hans Jacob 26
Osterstock, Georg Thomas 24
  Johann Philipp 24
  Maria Barbara 24
  Thomas 24
Oth, Maria Margaretha 50, 68
  Michael 50
  Niclaus 50, 68
Ott, Andreas 52, 68
  Catharina 52, 68
  Georg 52
  Heinrich 519
  Johann Andreas 68
  Johann Georg 68
  Johann Michael 68
  Johann Nickolaus 50, 68
  Niclaus 68
Otto, Anna Katharina 129
  Johann Friedrich 129
  Johann Tobias 129
  Maria Katharina 129
Ottridge, William 253, 259
Otway, Chas., Brig.-Gen. 317
Ould, Henry 259
Overend, Joshua 79
Overn, H.H. 429, 434
  Helge H. 434
Overy, Isaac 112

Overzland, Guttron Erichsen 412
Ovrevieg, T A 404
Owens, James 364
　John 342
　Margt. 317
　Thos. 317
Owins, James 342
　Margaret 342
Oyer, Vendel 241

-- P --

Padian, Bridget 462
　James 462
　Maria 462
　Mary 462
　Richard 462
　William 462
Pagett, Thos., Col. 317
Paine, Wm. 342
Painter, Richd. 447
Pairo, Thomas W. 259
Paisley, Christopher 364
Pallons, Anthony 109
Palmer, Esther 364
　Geo. 317
　Joseph 364
　Margaret 364
Pancoast, William 259
Pankratz, Gerhard 521
　Heinrich 521
　Johann 521
　Margaretha 521
　Maria 521
Parcell, Ellen 364
Park, David 342, 364
　Mary 317
　Mathew 364
　Maxwell 317
　Wm. 317
Parker, --- 224
　Anna 381
　Catherine 342
　Coll. 317
　Hen. 77
　Hugh 342
　Jane 79
　John 364
　Moses 364
　Phil. 317
　Samuel 79
　Thomas 79, 287
　Thos. 346
Parks, Jas. 317
Parnell, Thos. 317
Parr, Anne 364
　Eliza 364
　John 364
　Margaret 364
　Mary 364
　Thomas 364
　William 364
　William, Jun. 364
Parris, ---, Col 89
Parry, Benjn. 317
Parsons, Thomas 254, 257
Pary, --- 317
Pashon, Nicholas 531
Pastorius, --- 1
Paterson, Jos., Lieut. 317
Paton, Philip 195
Patrick, Robert 342
Patterson, Alex. 317
　Ann 342
　David 342, 364
　Edward 364

Elias C. 380
Eliza 342
Elizabeth 133, 134
George 342
Grace 133
Jas. 318
John 139, 318, 342, 364
Joseph 342, 364
Margaret 120
Martha Jane 380
Mary 133, 134, 342
Robert 133, 134
Samuel 342
Thomas 133, 134
William 364
Wm. 342
Patton, Edward 342
Paul, ---, Mrs. 534
　Ann 318
　Anna Barbara 48
　Dan., Capt. 318
　Eleanor 446
　Eliza 342
　Harriette 446
　Jane 446
　John 446
　Margt. 534
　Richard 446
　Robert 534
　Saml. 318
Pauls, David 520
　Elisabeth 520
　Franz 520
　Heinrich 520
　Helena 520
　Henriette 520
　Jakob 518
　Justina 520
　Susanna 520
Paynton, ---, Capt. 318
Payzant, Jas. 318
　L. 318
Peabody, John 285
Peacock, Elizth. 318
　James 364
　Jas. 318
Peadon, Robert 342
Peake, John, Sr. Knight 531
　Rebecca 139
　William 139
Pearce, ---, Lieut.-Gen. 318
　---, Major-Gen. 318
Peartree, Samuel 139
Peden, Dan. 318
　James 364
Pedersen, J. 411, 413
　Jens 385, 410, 411
Peerson, Cleng 371, 372, 375,
　　378, 380, 383, 414, 425
　Kleng 395
　Martha Georgiana 372
　Ole 416
　Samuel 400
Peirie, Hugh 364
Pelham, --- 145, 148
Pelow, Jonas 109
Pendergrass, Michael 364
Penha, Jacob Gutteres 152
Penman, Ed. 197
　Edward 198
Penn, William 374
Pennea, Rebecca 152
Penner, Anna 516
　Elisab. 516
　Elisabeth 516, 526
　Heinrich 516, 526
　Helena 516, 526
　Jacob 516

Jakob 526
Johann 526
Katharina 526
Kornelius 516
Margaretha 526
Maria 526
Nikolai 516
Peter 516, 526
Penrose, Elizabeth 79
　John 79
Peoples, James 293
Peppard, Patrick 364
Pepper, Edward 342
　John 318
Percival, John 75, 364
Pereira, Esther Lopes 154
　Rachel Fernandes 155
Perkins, Jeremiah 252, 287
Perrin, --- 364
Perro, Anne 318
　Chas. 318
Perrotet, John Peter 110
Perrottet, John Peter 109
Perry, Hugh 342
　John 318
　John, Capt 113
　Margaret 342
　Saml. 318
Persdatter, S. 429, 432
Peter, Casper 6
Peters, --- 6
　Abraham 519
　Aganeta 518
　Daniel 523
　Diedrich 518, 519
　Elisabeth 518, 523
　Heinrich 523
　Helena 518
　Isaak 519
　Jacob 523
　Jakob 518, 519
　Johann 518, 519, 523
　Kornelius 519, 523
　Margaretha 519
　Maria 518
　Peter 523
Peterson, Canute 381
　Kirstin 121
　Sara A. 383
Pether, William 364
Petit, Berrard 364
Petterdatter, Borgilde 412
Pettigrew, William 364
Pettit, Bernard 364
　Patrick 364
Petzer, Samuel 21
Pfaff, Theobald 27, 38
　Theobalt 38
Pfeiffer, Catharina 26
　John Caspar 237
Pfeil, Friedrich 25
Pflining, Abraham 168
Pfuster, Catharina 45
Phalen, Daniel 364
Phaler, C. Godfrey 328
Phelan, John 364
　Margaret 342
　Patrick 342
　Thomas 342
　William 342
Philar, Peter 342
Philips, ---, Squire 318
　George 259
　R. E. 195, 197, 198
Phillips, Bernard 364
　Eliza 342
　George 282
　Ralph 532

Thomas 342
Thos., Sir 318
William 271
Philson, Robert 342
Phips, Constantine, Sir 318
Phoebus, Thomas 252
Phoenix, John 364
Piarsh, Hugett 112
Pichard, Charles Jacob 109
Picken, Martha 199
Willm. 199
Picket, Mark 364
Piden, James 342
Pie, Joan 529
Pierce, ---, Major-Gen. 318
Alex. 364
John 364
Patrick 342
Pierson, Jacob 342
Jane 342
Ole 413, 416
Pigeon, Andrew 364
Pigott, Mark 342
Robin 342
Pilkington, Edward 364
Pillet, Daniel 110
Pindar, Charles 248
Pinkerton, James 342
Pinnell, Abell 108
Pinto, Joseph Jesurum 161, 163
Piper, Samuel 342
Pitman, Peter 364
Pitt, --- 148
Place, Lorentz 25
Platt, John 342
Platz, Friedrich 25
Plaus, Isabell 342
Pleir, John Rodolph 110
Plotz, Friedrich 25
Ploughman, John 364
Plummer, John 139
Plumpsell, Thomas 263
Plunkett, --- 318
Oliver 318
Robt., Rev'd 259
Thos. 318
Plympton, --- 346
Poague, Elizabeth 134
George 134
John 134
Margaret 134
Martha 134
Mary 134
Robert 134
Sarah 134
William 134
Pogue, Alexander 364
Poke, John 534
Wm. 318
Poland, Peter 364
Pole, Edwd., Capt. 318
W. 364
Polewheele, --- 318
Pollard, Dillon 318
Pollock, Hamill 342
Jane 318
Jas. 318
John 364
Samuel 342
William 342, 346
Pomeroy, James 364
Pond, ---, Capt. 188
Ponsonby, Hen., Col. 318
Pontius, Andreas 34
Anna Marie 34
Johann David 34
Johann Philipp 34
John 13

Pontzius, David 34
Pooderbach, George 533
Pool, Philip 164
Poole, Robert 364
Pooler, John 342
Poor, Moses 251, 268
Nathaniel P. 260
Valentine 166
Porter, Ann 342
Bell 342
Elizabeth 342
Elnr. 318
Hugh 292, 364
John 342
Margt. 318
Robert 234
Saml. 318
Thomas 342
Vere 318
William 342
Potter, John 140
Potts, Dav. 318
Hans 318
James B. 252
Robert 342
Wm. 318
Powell, Samuel 139
Power, ---, Latrie 231
Catherine 231
Folli 231
Margareite 231
Martha 231
Maurice 364
Nancy 231
Thomas 231
Powers, William 274
Poyas, John Lewis 107
Prain, Fanny 364
Pratt, --- 318
John 318
Thomas 80
Prendergast, ---, Lady 318
Prescot, ---, Cornet & Lieut. 318
Prester, Nich. 167
Preston, Daniel 76
John 133
Lettice 134
Thomas 342
William 259
Prette, Isaac Lopes 152
Preus, A.C., Rev. 407
Martha 407
Prevost, ---, General 102
Danl. 78
Prey, David 364
Price, Ann (Johanna) 138
Elizabeth 139
Margaret 364
Rice 107
Prime, William 258, 259
Priston, William 364
Probst, Christoph 67
Elisabetha Margaretha 67
Pukkau, Anna 515
Aron 515
Gerhard 515
Margaretha 515
Simeon 515
Pulitizi, V. 272
Pulizzi, Felice 252
Venenando (Genenando) 252
Venerando 272
Purcel, Charles 364
Sarah 364
Purcell, Fanny 364
Purdon, Thomas 364
Purnell, Wm. 532
Purry, --- 104

Charles 92, 94, 98, 100, 101,
108
Jean Pierre 82, 83, 84, 85, 87
John Peter 85, 86, 87, 88, 89,
90, 91, 92, 93, 94, 95, 96,
97, 98, 99, 100, 103, 106
John Rodolph 100
Rodolff 108
Purvis, Jane 318
Jas. 318

-- Q --

Qacharie, Yve. [Vve.] 232
Quail, William 342
Quale, William 342
Quap, Wittwe 519
Quast, Joh. 58
Johannes 58
Quay, Eden 454
Queen, John 260
Queenan, Bryan 365
Martin 365
Quigley, David 365
Martha 342
Quin, Agnes 365
Anne 462
Arthur 365
Daniel 342
Henry 342
Hugh 342
James 462
Jane 342
John 342, 365, 462
Manus 318
Margaret 342
P. 342
Patrick 342
Terence 318
Quince, Thomas 365
Quinch, Lewis 108
Quinn, Arthur 365
Charles 342, 365
Catherine 462
Francis 365
Henry 365
Hugh 462
James 365
John 365
Letita 365
Quinton, Robert 365

-- R --

Rachie, Urich 112
Radcliffe, Alexander 289
Raddin, George W. 264
Rae, ---, Lord 208, 209, 210, 211
Raferty, Wm. 318
Rafferty, Bridget 483
Catherine 483
Ellen 483
Ellen C. 483
John 342, 478, 483
John, Jun. 483
Mary 483
Mary Ann 483
Pat 483
Patrick 365
Simeon 365
Stewart 365
Thomas 483
William 342
Rafield, William 289

Rafter, Dennis 365
Raftor, F. 318
Raftrey, John 365
Ragan, T. 365
Rainey, James 365
Ram, --- 318
Ramage, Alexr. 211
Ramalho, Isaac 152
  Leah 153
Ramb, Christian 26
Ramenstein, Chris'r 167
Ramsay, Wm. 318
Ramsey, George 365
Randall, Jeremiah 446
  Mary 446
Ranighan, John 342
Ranken, John, Dr. 318
Rankin, Robert 342
  Sarah 365
Rapp, Apolonia 49
Ras, H. L. 225
Rattoone, --- 464
Ratzlaff, Abraham 514
  Benjamin 514
  Bernhard 515
  Helene 514
  Johann 515
  Justina 514
  Maria 515
  Peter 515
  Sara 515
Rauenzaner, Magdalena 72
Raulstone, Arch. 342
Rausch, --- 7
Raven, --- 318
  Thos. 318
Rawdon, John, Sir 318
Ray, Mary 318
  Thomas W. 342
  William 342
  Wm. 318
Raymond, Henry 87
Rea, John 342
  Patrick 365
  William 342
Read, Clement 319
  James 292, 365
  Jas. 318, 319
  John 318
  Thomas 365
  William 244
Reade, John 319
Reais, Mich'l 165
Recard, George 365
  John 365
Rech, Anna Margreth 29
  Anna Margretha 45
  Johann Conrad 29, 45
  Johann Michael 29
  Johann Michel 45
Rechil, Patrick 365
Record, --- 348
Recorder, Francis Lewis 111
Recordon, Pierre Louis 106
Reck, Jacob 109
Reddington, Patrick 365
Redin, Wm. 270
Redmond, --- 319
  Bernard 245
Reed, Agnes 134
  Clement 319
  David 342
  Hugh 342
  James 342
  Jas. 319
  John 365, 534
  Margaret 342
  Martin 365

Thos. 319
Wm. 319
Reen, Biddy 495
  Bridget 495
  Darby 495
  Denis 495, 505, 506
  Ellen 495
  Jerry 495
  John 495, 506
  Mary 495, 505
  Michael 495
  Tade 495, 505, 506
Reeve, Mark 530
Regehr, Abraham 517
  Anna 522, 526
  Eva 526
  Gerhard 517
  Isaak 517
  Johann 522, 526
  Justina 526
  Katharina 522, 526
  Klaas 525
  Kornelius 526
  Margaretha 526
  Maria 525, 526
  Sara 517
  Sarah 526
Regeln, Johann 518
Regier, Anna 516
  Peter 516
Regin, John 365
Rehrer, Johann Gottfried 20
Reiber, Abraham 33
  Anna Margaretha 33
Reich, Mattheus 177
Reichard, G. 325
Reichert, Jacob 21
Reid, Adam 365
  Alexander 121
  Andrew 136, 137, 138, 140
  Angus 121
  Donald 121
  Duncan 121
  George 365
  James 365
  Jane 319
  Janet 120
  Jas. 319
  Jeannie 121
  John 121, 319, 534
  M. 365
  Margaret 121
  Mary 121
  Nicklies 121
  Patrick 342
  Peter 121
  Rachael 365
  Robert 365
  Robt. 319
  Roger 121
  Thomas 365
  William 365
Reidebach, Michel 57
Reidenbach, Johann Michel 57
  Johann Nickel 57
  Johann Nicolaus 57
  Michel 57
Reier Datter, Inger 412
Reierssoen, Lars Pedar 413
Reiley, Patrick 331
Reilly, --- 365
  Brien 342
  Charles 365
  Fras 365
  John 365
  Marlow 319
  Mary 342
  Michael 365

Patrick 365
  Thomas 342, 365
Reily, John H. 271
  Philip 365
Reimer, Aron 519
  Balthaser 52
  Heinrich 519
  Helena 519
  Johann 519
  Justina 519
  Maria 519
  Susanna 519
Rein, John 342
Reiner, Anna Maria 24
  Christian 24
  Eberhardt 24
  Eberharst Friedrich 24
  Friedrich 24
  Georg Philipp 24
  Johan Dietrich 24
  Johann Christian 24
  Johann Dietrich 24
  Johannes 24
  Margaretha 24
  Maria Magdalena 24
  Maria Margaretha 24
  Maria Sara 24
  Sara 24
Reinhard, Nicklas 21
Reisch, J. Michael 328
Reiser, Jacob 179
Reisinger, Nicolaus 26
Reister, Jacob 179
Reitenbach, Anna Barbara 57
  Gertraud 57
  Jacob 57
Reitzel, Anna 28
  Anna Maria 28
  Johann Georg 28, 37
  Johann Peter 29, 37
  Maria Wilhelmina 28, 37
  Sybilla 28, 37
Rellie, Hugh 197
Remely, John C. 285
Remensperger, Jac. 164
Remond, Jeremiah 111
Renenaugh, James 365
Renersdatter, A 428, 431
Renk, Jacob 327
Renner, Jacob 180
  Johann Jacob 180
Rennoi, Damie 259
Rester, John 165
Rettich, Christoph Gottlieb 237
Reuter, Johann Lorentz 36
Reuther, Anna Juditha 51
  Anna Margaretha 33
  Catharina 33
  Hans Jacob 33
  Hans Jakob 33
  Hans Stefan 33
  Mathes 33
  Susanne 33
Reutzel, Johann Georg 28, 29, 38
Reutzele, Anna Maria 44
  Anna Sybilla 44
  Johann Georg 44
Revera, Jacob Rodrigues 157
Revout, Gabriel Francois 107
Reymer, Balthasar 52
Reymond, Joseph 106
Reyn, Maria 166
Reynel, --- 319
Reynell, John 533
Reynolds, Andrew 463
  Arnold 139
  Bridget 463
  Catherine 365, 463

Eliza 365
James 247, 463
John 463
Joseph 365, 463
Laurence 365
Mary 463
Michael 463
Patrick 365
Tho. 252
Thomas 463
William 365
Wm. 342
Rezer, Anna Maria 42
Michel 42
Theobald 42
Rham, Henry Casimar 244
Rhea, David 342
Seragh 342
Rheinberger, Anna Catharina 52
Rhoads, Peter, Hon. 10
Rhodes, Thomas 247
Riall, Patrick 365
Rian, Thomas 342
Ribas, Monashe 152
Ribiero, Abraham 152
Ricard, --- 348
Rice, Aily 342
Canlan 365
Edward 342
Eliza 319
Patrick 365
Ter. 319
Thomas 342
Rich, Joh. 167
Richard, Andriane 104
James 87, 89
James, Major 106
Richards, James, Major 88, 110
John 533
Mary 445
Richard 445
Thos. 443
Richardson, Leming, Ensign 319
Ralph 193
Wm. 532
Richer, Andrew 289
Richie, Catherine 365
William 365
Richley, Daniel 365
Rickard, Stephen 245
Riddall, Hugh 319
Riddle, Chr. 319
Samuel 365
William 291, 365
Rider, William 259, 365
Ridge, James 365
Ried, Anna Margareth 184
Casper 184
Christina 184
Elisabetha Catharina 184
Friedrich 184
Johann Casper 184
Johann Georg 184
Johann Michael 184
Johann Philip 184
Maria Barbara 184
Maria Margaretha 184
Riegel, George 8
Mathias 8
Rieger, --- 184
Johannes Barthalomay 6
Riel, Hans 531
Rielly, Eliza 365
Elizabeth 365
Rose 365
Riemensperger, Jac. 164
Rieser, Ulrich 3
Rift, Andreas 167

Rigan, Bridget 342
Riger, Anna Barbara 105
Catarina Barbara 105
Janett Ottallia 105
Michael 105
Nicolas 105
Riguer, Nicholas 108
Riley, ---, Mrs. 342
Margaret 342
Nancy 342
Ring, John 111
Ringgold, Tench 251, 257, 263, 269
Ringheim, Martha Tormods-datter 438
Riordan, Coleman 365
Ripley, William 194
Ritchie, Abner 256
Alx. 342
Eliz. 343
John 319, 365
Sara T. 383
Wm. 365
Ritter, Casper 7
Henry 7
Johann Heinrich 129
Johann Michael 129
Johann Peter 129
Johannes 129
Maria Elisabeth 129
Matthias 129
Paul 7
Rivera, Jacob Rodrigues 163
Rixon, John 192
Riz, Hannah Lopes 153
Roane, Geo. 319
Roaney, Anne 365
Roany, Charles 365
Roark, Mary 343
Robb, Charles 365
Jas., Cornet 319
Robbin, Elizabeth 444
Jane 444
John 444
Wm 444
Robert, Josué 103
Marie Madeleine 103
Roberts, Catharine 445
David 110
Elizabeth 445
George 343
Grace 445
Henry 445
James 445, 446
John 343, 445, 446
John M. 365
Joseph 445
Josua 112
Phillippa 445
Richd. 444
Saml. 445
Thos. 445
Robertson, Alexr. 534
Catharine 365
D. 365
Eleanor 365
Henry B. 268, 272, 279
Katherine 223
Margrat 534
Mary 532
Patrick 121
Peter 121
Robert 534
Robeson, John 343
Robins, Bridget 365
Robinson, ---, Mrs. 343, 365
Alex. 319
Ann 417

George 134
James 134
Jas. 319
Jane 319, 343
John 186, 197, 198, 202, 203, 319, 343, 365
Joseph 365
Mary 319, 343
Peggy 417
Reba. 319
Rose 417
Thomas 254, 343, 365
William 134
Wm. 319
Robison, Andrew 343
Robston, James 343
Roch, Anna 68
Friedrich 52
Johann Peter 52, 68
John Jacob 110
Margaret 52
Margaretha 68
Maria Barbara 52, 68
Peter 52, 68
Roche, --- 510
David 365
James 365
John 365
William 365
Rochford, --- 348
Francis 365
John 343
Walter 365
Rochfort, Robt. 319
Rock, James 343
Mary 343
Rodder, Michael 343
Rodelsperger, Christian 166
Roderiques, Moses 154
Rodgers, John 343
Mary 343
Mary, Miss 343
Patrick 365
Samuel 343
Rodrigues, Moses 152
Roe, John 319
Roedel, Anna Apollonia 46
Georg Friedrich 46
Georg Simon 46
Johann Dieter 46
Roehmell, Catharina 44
Georg 44
Martin 44
Michael 44
Roehrer, Johannes 20
Roeller, Maria Catharina 51
Roesch, Johann Michael 21
Veronika 40
Rogan, Charles 365
Michl. 319
Rogers, Alex. 319
Alexr. 365
Ann 365
Elizth. 319
Hugh 365
Jas. 319
John 319, 365
Mary 319, 365
Matilda 319
Nathan 343
Patrick 365
Thomas 343
Wm. 319
Rokne, Knut Eriksen 438
Rolfsen, Peter 385, 396, 397
Rolfson, --- 396
Rollar, Johann Peter 130
Rollard, Anna Christina 129

Johann Peter 129, 130
Ludwig 129
Rollauer, Anna Magdalena 124
Ludwig 124
Roller, Johann Peter 130
Rolofsen, Peter 397
Rolstad, Anna 406
N. L. 402, 403, 405, 406
Rolston, John 291
Rometsch, Anna Margaretha 65
Caspar 65
Johann Caspar 65
Romich, John Adam 9
Rommigh, G. Michael 44
Hans George 44
Roney, Catherine 365
Danl. 319
Ronson, Thomas 346
Ronve, Brynjulv Godskalksen 439
Rooney, Hugh 365
Michael 365
Roony, Charles 365
John 365
Sarah 365
Rooss, Johann 26
Röpp, Anna 514
Jakob 514
Johann 514
Peter 514
Susanne 514
Suzanne 514
Rorke, Patrick 343
Rosborough, John 365
Rose, Geo. 365
Hugh 107, 112
Robert 188
Rosman, Martin 365
Ross, Alex., Lieut.-Col. 319
Alexander 220
Danl. 319
David J. 288
Eleanor 343
Isaac 271
Isabella 220
James 343, 365
Jas. 319
Jean 121, 220
John 209
Joseph 343
Margaret 220
Mary 121, 343
Patrick 208
R. 319
Rob., Lieut. 319
Samuel 241
William 343
Rossadal, Daniel Stenson 383
Hulda 383
Rossaland, Amund Anderson 408
Anna 408
Elling 408
Endre 408
Rosse, John 319
Rosseland, A E 402, 404, 408
Amund 402
Anders 402, 408
S E 402, 404, 408
Sjur E. 402, 408
Rossle, Gabriel 177
Rosynkowski, Julian K. 269
Roth, Anna Catharina 50
Daniel 10
Henry 10
Rothe, L. I. 429, 436, 439
Lars Torgerson 437, 439
Rothmayer, Johannes 64
Maria Magdalena 64

Rotscher, Michel 230
Rottlesperger, Christian 166
Roulstone, --- 330
Harvey 343
James 343
Martha 343
Roundtree, Owen 365
Rousby, Wm., Ensign 319
Rouse, --- 7
Routzan, Magdalena 72
Rouyter, Lorents 36
Rowan, James 365
Jas. 319
John 365
Margaret 365
Mary 365
R. R. 319
Rowe, George 443
James 443
John 443
Wm. 447
Rowland, ---, Mrs. 365
Rowley, Hercules 319
Hercules Langford 319
Rowly, --- 319
Rowlye, Hugh 319
Ruch, George, Senior 9
Ruckenbrodt, David 325
Rudd, Grace 365
Rudder, John 343
Patrick 343
Ruddock, James 365
Ruff, Anna Maria 168
Ruffin, Anna Maria 168
Rule, Jane 447
Rumetsch, Johann Caspar 65
Rumy, Samuel 274
Runckel, Johann Jacob 26
Nicolaus 25
Wendel 26
Rupp, Christian 19
Rupperter, Johann Leonhard 35
Leonhard 35
Rury, Samuel 274
Russel, Isaac 365
John 343
Russell, Alexander 365
Francis 365
G. 319
Hen. 319
Isaac 319
James 343, 365, 445
Jane 319, 365
Jas. 319
John 365
Mary 343
Robt. 319
Thomas 343
Wm. 319
Rutherford, John 343
Mary 343
Sarah 343
Ruthven, Dugald 215
Rutledge, John 365
Rutter, John 133
Ryan, ---, Rev. Mr. 343
David 343
Ellen 365
James 343, 365
Jas. 320
Margaret 365
Mary 343, 365
Michael 453
Michl. 320
Patrick 343
Thomas 343
William 343
Rycant, Paul, Lieut. 320

Ryers, James 343
Rynning, O 402, 405, 409
Ole 402, 405, 409

-- S --

Saboe, H A 404
Sacheverel, --- 146
Sachs, Daniel 33
Sadler, Frances 343
Hugh 343
Saeger, John Nicholas 11
Saevig, Anna Bertha 399
Betsy Ann 399
Erik Johnson 399
Ingeborg Johnson 399
John 399
Sager, Jacob 70
Sahner, Anna Maria 58
St. Clair, George 252
Jas., Col. 320
St. George, --- 320
Rich., Col. 320
St. John, --- 90, 114
St. Leger, Baron, Mrs. 320
Saldana, Abraham Dovall 154
Solomon 154
Salmon, C. 292
Mathew 365
Salom, David 152
Esther 154
Salter, Anna 77
Tho. 77
Thomas 365
Saltzer, Chris'r 167
Sammes, John 80
Samms, John 80
Sampson, Catharine Anne 247
David 365
Grace 247
John 365
John Curran 247
William 245
Samuel, Levy 156, 163
Myers 138
Samuelsen, E 404
Sanches, Abraham 154
Benjamin 155
Sarah 153
Sandenaes, Bixgitha 397
Fosten 397, 399
Fosten J 397, 399
Johannes 397
Lars 397
Lars Larsen 397
Martha 397
Sanders, James 343
Sanderson, John 194
Sandford, ---, Col. 320
Sansober, --- 112
Sassler, Anna Maria 23
Satchfield, Elizabeth 79
Sauce, David 109
Saude, Gullick Torstensen 437
Lars Baardsen 436
Martha Torstensdatter 436, 437
Torsten Olsen 437
Saue, Kolbein O. 402
Stark Olson 402
Styrk O. 402
Sauer, Melchior 165
Sauerheber, Jacob 48
Johann Jacob 48
Maria Catharina 48
Saunderson, Henry 365

Saussy, David 112
Savage, Pat. 320
Savik, Erick Johanneson 399
Savy, John, Lieut. 90
Sawatzki,---, Frau 522
  Elisabeth 522
  Gerhard 522
  Justina 522
  Peter 522
Sawer, --- 346
Saxby, Geo. 89
  Wm., Jur. 89
Scallam, James 259
Scallan, Robert 259
Scallion, James 252
Scallon, James 275
  Robert 259
Scallun, James 262
Scandler, Bryan 365
Scandret, Jas. 320
Scanlon, John 343
  Maney 365
Scannell, --- 506
Scellan, Thos. 366
Schaeffer, Anna Maria 55
  Elisabetha 27, 38
  Georg Michael 55
  Heinrich 55
  Maria Catharina 56
  Maria Dorothea 55
  Maria Margaretha 50, 67
Schaeffle, Carl Friedrich 237
Schaeffter, George Frederich
  260
Schaefter, George Frederich 260
Schafer, J. Frederic 327
Schäffer, Maria Margaretha 67
  Susanna 67
Schalter, Elisabeth 40
  Frantz Baltzer 40
  Franz Balthasar 40
  Johann Georg 40
Schapbert, Filb 130
Schapperdt, Nicolaus 130
Schappert, Anna Barbara 130
  Anna Christina 131
  Anna Katharina 130
  Johann Michael 130
  Johann Nikolaus 130
  Johann Philipp 130
  Johannes 128, 130, 131
  Maria Margarethe 128
Schaub, Balthasar 55
  Heinrich 55
  Henry 55
  Maria Dorothea 55
  Susanna Catharina 55
Schaus, John Adam 12
Schedla, Johann Christian 36
  Johann Heinrich 36
Schedler, Henrich 36
Scheffer, Hans Eric 165
Scheid, Leonhardt 21
Scheie, L G 402, 404, 408
  Lars 408, 409
Scheis, Conrad 165
Schenk(Anna) Maria Katharina 65
  Johann Jacob 65
Schenkel, Heinrich 175
  Jacob 175
  Johann Philipp 175
  Philipp Carl 175
Schetfley, John Lewis 111
Schickle, Georg 176
Schicky, Simon 533
Schierling, Aganeta 523
  Anna 522
  Diedrich 523

  Elisabeth 523
  Jakob 522
  Johann 523
Schifferdecker, Jacob 22
Schilling, Johannes 21
Schirling, Abraham 520
  Aganeta 520
  Anna 520
  Elisab. 520
  Wilhelm 520
Schleicher, Maria Margaretha
  24
Schley, Thomas 40
Schlickers, Ludwig 177
Schlindwein, Anna Eva 62
Schlosser, Leonard 9
Schmebile, Frederick 168
Schmelzle, Rudolph 177
Schmid, Anna 70
  Margaretha 53, 70
Schmidt, Abraham 28, 41
  Anna Katharina 129
  Anna Magdalena 124
  David 527
  Elisabeth 515
  Eva 527
  Georg 28, 41
  Heinrich 527
  Jakob 515
  Johann 515
  Johann Jacob 58
  Johann Thielmann 129
  Johannes 124
  Johannes J. 238
  John William 246
  Maria 527
  Matheis 28
  Matheiss 41
  Peter 515
  Sara 515
  Sebastian 58
Schmit, Anna Maria 185
  Balthasar 185
  Heinrich 185
  Johann Friedrich 185
  Johann Jacob 185
  Maria Dorothea 185
  Maria Eva 185
Schmitt, Andreas 53
  Andres 70
  Anna Elisabetha 53, 70
  Anna Maria 73
  Catharina 53, 70
  David 173
  Helena 73
  Johan Henrich 31
  Johann Henrich 58
  Johann Jacob 59
  Lorentz 59, 73, 74
  Lorenz 73
  Magdalena 53
  Maria Henena 59
  Maria Helena 73, 74
  Maria Magdalena 73, 74
  Mathes 59
  Matthes 73
  Philipp Peter 59
Schnee, Catharina Elisabetha
  29, 49
  Johannes 29, 49
  Maria Margretha 29, 49
Schneebele, Rudolph 11
Scheidemann, Georg Friedrich
  179
Schneider, Anna Barbara 130
  Anna Margarethe 125, 130
  Anna Maria 55
  Frederick 266

  Heinrich 130
  Johann Karl 125, 130
  Johannes 130
  John Nicholas 13
Schneller, Joseph 259
Schneyder, Carl 130
Schnieder, Augusta 281
Scholl, Frederick 5
Schopping, Anna Barbara 66
  Johann Adam 66
  Magdalena 66
Schrader, Henry 241
Schramm, Johann Theobald 39
  Theobald 39
Schreiber, John Jacob 10
Schreiner, Anna Margaretha 66
  Anna Maria 66
  Hans Adam 66
  Johann Adam 66
  Johann Friedrich 66
  Johann Georg Heinrich 66
  Johann Michael 66
  Johann Philipp 66
  Johann Valentin 66
  Martin 66
Schreyner, Hans Adam 66
Schröder, Heinrich 518
  Katharina 518
  Peter 518
  Sahra 518
  Susanna 518
Schubarth, N. B. 426, 428
  Nils B. 426
Schuchart, Anna Catharina 184
  Anna Elisabeth 185
  Anna Maria 184
  Carl 185
  Heinrich 184
  Johan Heinrich 185
  Johann Jost 184
  Johannes 184
  Margaretha 185
  Maria Christina 185
  Tobias 185
Schuller, Phil. Jac. 168
Schultz, David 3
  V L 404
Schulz, ---, Frau 521
  Isaak 521
  Maria 521
  Sahra 521
  Wilhelm 521
Schunk, Catharina 28, 39
  Elisabeth 28, 39
  Johannes 28, 39
  Maria 28, 39
  Simon 28, 39
  Wilhelm 28, 39
Schussler, Charles 267, 275, 284
  Charley 262
  Charly 281
Schusster, Charles 287
Schuster, Jacob 175
  Maria Elisabetha 48
Schwab, Andreas 58, 73
  Georg Adam 58, 73
  John George 3
  Rosina Barbara 58, 73
Schwachlerback, Andreas 167
Schwaglerinn, Elizabeth 328
Schwann, Abraham 18
Schwartz, Anna Elisabeth 64
  Catharina 28
  Maria Francisca 64
  Wendel 64
Schwarz, Catharina 39
  Conrad 259
  Matthias 177

Schweickart, Abraham 26
Schweigert, Samuel 21
Schweikert, Samuel 21
Schwenkfelder, --- 11
Schwerdafeger, Jno. Abraham 165
Scilly, Jane 366
  John 366
  Margaret 366
Scinlon, Bryan 366
Scot, Ninian 534
Scott, A. 343, 463
  Alexander 343
  Catherine 366
  Edward 366
  Eliza 366
  Francis 80
  David 343
  Henry 343, 455
  Hugh 366
  James 343
  Jane 134, 366
  John 134, 343, 366
  John E. 346
  Margaret 189, 343
  Samuel 134
  Sarah 366
  Thomas 343
  Thomas W. 366
  W. 463
  Walter 366
  William 189, 343, 366, 455
  Wm. 292, 320
Scouler, Jasper 193
Scravenmore, --- 320
Sculler, James 366
Scully, John 343
Seagler, William 241
Seale, William 140
Seaman, Mary Ann 166
Searight, Jane 320
  John 320
Seave, John 343
Sebbe, Anna Hendrikson 392, 395
  Henrik Erikson 392
See, Nevin 343
Seed, William 343
Seeds, Jas. 320
  William 366
Seeman, Thomas 343
Segarson, William 366
Seger, Philip 13
Seggers, Elisabeth 229
  Faderie 229
  Jean 229
  Joseph 229
  Marie 229
  Sali 229
Sehm, John George 8
Seiberlein, Hans Konrad 129
  Maria Barbara 129
Seider, Michael 15
Seiss, Anna Barbara 130
  Anna Elisabeth 130
  Anna Eva 132
  Anna Maria 124
  Antonius 130
  Johann Adam 131
  Johann Andreas 130
  Johann Jakob 130
  Johannes 130
  Johannetta 130
  Maria Barbara 130
  Matthias 130
  Michael 124
  Michel 132
  Sabine 130
Seixas, Isaac 163
  Jacob Mendes 156

Seiz, Johannes 179
Seliock, John, Capt. 320
Sell, Johann Nikolaus 142
Seller, Jacob 5
  Philip Henry 4
Seltenreich, Leonard 3
Seltzer, Charles 241
Semmes, Edward 277, 286
Semple, Hugh, Major 320
  Mary 121
  Robert 366
  Thomas 366
Senderling, Johann Niclaus 36
  Johann Nicolas 36
Sequira, Abraham Henriques 152
  Isaac Henriques 152
Serren, Wm. 264
Service, Alexander 366
  Robert 330, 343
  Wm. 264
Sessford, John 250, 259
Sewere, John 343
Seyffert, Anna Elisabetha 41
  Johann Gottfried 41
Seysen, Joh. Andreas 130
  Johann Adam 131
Shaeffter, George Frederich 260
Shafer, Conrad 241
Shaffele, Henry 108
Shales, --- 366
Shallinn, Regina 328
Shane, Conrad 241
Shanks, William 366
Shannan, John 366
Shannon, ---, Lord 320
  David 366
  Hugh 366
  M. 366
  Quinton 366
  Robt. 320
Sharkey, William 366
Sharland, Robt. 320
Sharman, Wm. 320
Sharpeless, Geo., Lieut. 320
Shaules, Michael 260
Shaw, Ann 366
  Catharine 121
  Donald 121
  Duncan 121
  Florence 116, 121
  Gustavus 121
  Hen. 320
  James 366
  Jas. 320
  John 121, 220, 320, 343, 366
  Margaret 343
  Mary 121, 366
  Merran 121
  Merrian 121
  Neil 121
  Robert 366
  Rose 366
  Sidney 320
  Thomas 366
  William 139, 343
  Wm. 320, 366
Shawkling, James 343
Shea, John 499
  Thomas 499
Shearer, Mathew 366
Shee, Arthur 343
Sheehan, Con 510
  Paddy 505
  Timothy 510
Sheehey, Mary 366
Shell, Christoph 327
Shenbove, Ane Lovdatter 412
Shepherd, James 343

  Jane 366
  Margaret 366
  Richard 366
  Simpson 366
Sheppard, James 366
  Peter 366
Sheran, Andrew 366
Sherdon, Jane 366
  Thomas 366
Sheriff, Wm. 320
Sherlock, --- 297, 320
  Patrick 343
  Robert 366
Sherran, Thomas 343
Sherrigley, John, Cornet 320
Shever, Elisabeth 27
  Elizabeth 38
Shields, Frindley 366
  George 343
  John 289
  William, Junr. 366
  William, Senr. 366
Shiffle, ---, Revd. 113
Shifle, John Louis 113
Shiker, William 241
Shillig, Jno. 164
  Ulrich 164
Shinluig, J. 343
Shipard, Daniel 112
Shirer, Conrad 168
Shirtler, John 325
Shold, Matthias 241
Shook, Lawrence 533
Shuckburgh, ---, Ensign 320
Shudalsness, L 404
Shute, Barrington 320
Sibley, William I. 266
Siegerist, Martin 70
Sien, Samuel 74
Siersema, Albert 512
  Deuwertje 512
  Katarina Maria 512
Sieven, Tully 343
Sigbjornsen, Andreas 390
Sigrist, Anna Apollonia 70
  Anna Apolonia 53
  Catharina 53, 70
  Martin 53, 70
Sillar, Catharine 216
  Hugh 216
  Mary 216
Silva, Isaac Gomes 153
  Joshua Gomez 153
Silvain, Michel 232
Sim, Jane 189
  William 189
Simmes, Edward 277
Simms, Edward 265, 275
Simon, Jane 343
  John 274
  Jos. 157
Simple, ---, Saml. 320
Simpson, --- 366
  Isobel 201
  James 366
  Robert 366
  Thos. 320
  William 343
  Wm. 366
Simson, Joseph 156, 163
Sinclair, Alex. 207
  Ann 212
  Duncan 199
  Isobel 199
  James 209
  John 199, 320
  John, Sir 207
  Margarit 212

Mary 199
Robt., Rev. 320
Sinclaire, Ame 343
John 343
Mary 343
Robt. 320
Singer, James 366
Sinn, Anna Agatha 74
Anna Barbara 59
Johann Friedrich 60
Johann Peter 74
Peter 59
Samuel 59, 74
Sinnot, Nicholas 343
Richard 366
Sinot, Tho., Ensign 320
Sinton, Henry 366
James 366
John 366
Joseph 366
Mary 343
Rebecca 366
Siousa, John 260
Sithgon, --- 348
William 366
Size, Bernard 343
Hannah 343
Sjursdatter, A 403
Skeffington, Ann 320
C/ 290
Clotworthy 320
I. C. 320
Rach. 320
Rich., Sir 320
Skeie, Lars G. 402, 409
Skelly, Jas. 320
Skjerveim, Peder Davidson 436, 437
Skoerping, J J 405
Skofstad, Johannes Evensen 430
Slade, --- 320
Robert 331
Slattery, John 343
Margaret 343
Patrick 366
Peter 343
Slavin, Anne 366
Catherine 366
James 366
Michael 366
Sleeman, Jane 343
Sleith, John 366
Margaret 366
Slinler, M. 366
Sloan, Catherine 366
James 366
Jane 343
Saml. 320
William 366
Sloane, Martha 343
Slogvig, Jacob Anderson 383
Knud 383, 409
Knud A. 390, 394, 395, 409
Knud Anderson 395
Slotsunder, Hans Michael 65
Smart, John 320
Smeisser, Matthias 6
Smiley, Alex 343
Domk. 320
James 343
John 343
Saml. 320
Smily, James 293
Smissaert, Gilbert 248
Smith, --- 366
---, Alderman 320
Abraham 134, 366
Alexander 366

Bernard 366
Catharine 366
Christopher 194
Cornelius 343
Daniel 134
David 173
Duncan 121
Edwd. 320
Eliza 343, 366
Elizabeth 139
Esther 194
Francis 139
Geo. 78
Hannah 77
Henry 134, 251, 257
Hugh 320, 366
Ja. 77
James 192, 366
Jane 320
Johannes 238
John 134, 139, 190, 191, 192, 241, 260, 292, 343, 366
John, Rev. 286
John A. 265
Joseph 134, 366
Malm. 200
Margaret 134
Mary 200
Mary Anne 320
Matt. 320
Michael 139, 366
Nancy 320
Peter 200, 294, 366
Phillip 366
Robert 366
Sebastian 3
Susan 343
Thomas 195, 246
Thomas, Jun. 366
Thos. 320, 366, 532
William 260, 343
Smoot, Sam'l 259
Walter 263
Smotz, Adam 241
Smyter, ---, Capt 81
Smyth, George 343
James 343
Jane 366
Jas. 321
John 321, 343, 366
Mary 321
Patrick 366
R. J. 321
Robert 366
Robt. 321
William 366
Snabley, John 11
Snedgrass, Eliz. 320
John 320
Mary 321
Rich. 320
Snider, Augustus 283, 288
Snowd, William 137, 140
Snyder, Carl 130
Henry 241
Jacob 533
Simon 14
Soares, Joseph 152
Leah 152
Soffel, Bernhardt 55
Maria 55
Maria Barbara 55
Sohland, Agnes 53, 69
Maria 69
Solomon, Joseph 157
Solomons, Jonas 161, 163
Somerville, Jane 366
Mary 366

Sondve, M. N. 429, 436, 441
Sonntag, Abraham 175
Sonve, Mads Nilsen 441
Sotherby, John 321
Southwell, --- 321
---, Col. 321
Sower, Melchior 165
Spach, Jonas 106
Spaight, Jas. 321
Spain, Biddy 502
Catherine 502
Spalding, Randolph 272
Richard 252, 253
Span, Wm. 321
Spark, James 366
Sparks, Alexander 366
Eliza 366
Spatz, Georg Michael 179
Spaulding, Richard 269
Speir, Alexander 216
Spelman, D. 366
Spencer, Conway 321
Mary 483
Robert 366
Samuel 366
Spenler, Jac. 164
Spieden, William 263
Spiers, James 343
John, Mrs. 343
Spiess, Maria Magdalena 126
Spittler, Barbara 181
Catharina 181
Jacob 181
Johannes 181
Verona 181
Spohn, Peter 170
Sponheimer, Anna Christina 131
Anna Margarethe 131
Anna Maria 131
Johann Nikolaus 131
Johann Peter 131
Johann Wilhelm 125, 131
Susanna Martha 125
Spratt, Andrew 366
Hugh 343
Mary 343, 366
Thomas 260, 289, 366
William 343
Spraule, Armour 366
Springham, --- 321
Sproul, James C. 343
Jane 321
John 343
Mary 321
Sproull, Joseph 244
Spunner, Thomas 366
Squire, Ger. 321
St---ger, Frederick 253
St---ges, Frederick 253
Stabaek, Claus 422
Stackallen, ---, Lord 321
Stackley, Jac. 165
Stadler, Anna 68
Maria Barbara 52, 68
Stahler, John Nicholas 15
Staiger, Leonard 326
Standford, Edward 366
Stange, A. C. 386, 405, 408
Stangeland, Andrew 383
Stanhope, ---, Lord 321
Henry 343
Stanley, Joseph 80
Peter 366
Sarah 139
Wm. 343
Stanly, Elizabeth 80
Joseph 80
Stanyan, --- 321

Staples, Grace 321
   Robt., Sir 321
   Thos., Rev. 321
   William 113
Stark, Elizabeth 134
   Thomas 343
Starr, Jas. 321
   Jeremiah 343
   Patk. 321
Stasey, Doritha 366
   Eliza 366
   John 366
   Margaret 366
   Sarah 366
   Wm. 366
Stavely, Andrew 366
Stead, Thomas 193
Steckel, Daniel 15
   Peter 15
Steel, Elizabeth 343
   James 343, 366
   Joseph 343
   Martha 321
   Mary 321
   Rich., Sir 321
   Sally 343
   Saml. 321
   William 366
Steele, Sarah 321
Steell, William 534
Steen, Robert 366
Stees, George Adam 531
Steffinger, Eva Rosina 54
   Friedrich 54
Steiman, John 8
Stein, Johann Esaias 19
Steinbrech, Johann Vallentin 36
Steinbrecher, Johann Valentin 36
Steininger, Leonard 6
Steinman, John George 8
   Peter 8
   Sara 8
Steinwender, Daniel 179
Stemple, Christian 241
Stene, Johannes 383
Stenersen, G 429
Stephans, Elnor 343
   Thomas 343
Stephanson, John 343
Stephen, Ulrich 3
Stephens, Ann 445
   Edward 246, 260, 445
   John 366
   Mary 321
   Rezin 286
   Saml. 444
   Seth 290, 291
Stephenson, Clotworthy 254,
   255, 258
   Henry 343
   John 134
   Mary 134
   Samuel 343
   Sarah 134
Stepper, Geo. M. 281
Sterchis, James 109
Sterchy, Peter 111
Sterling, James 343
   Robert 343
   Sobert 366
Stern, Jacob 156
Stettinius, Samuel 256, 257
Steuart, Arth., Capt. 321
Steven, Chrn. 196
   Jas. 196
   Sarah 196
   Thos. 196
Stevens, James 366

   William 366
Stevenson, Catherine 117
   Hugh 343
   John 343
   Martha 343
   William 343
Stewa, William 139
Steward, Geo. 366
Stewart, Alex. 321
   Alex. T. 321
   Alexan. 343
   Alexander 212, 213, 366
   Allan 212, 366
   Allan, Capt. 215
   Andrew 343
   Ann 321
   Anne 463
   Archd., Dr. 321
   Archibald 212
   Banco 213
   Benj. 343
   Billy 321
   Bridget 463
   Catherine 463
   Charles 212, 366
   Christian 213
   Daniel 366
   David 343, 366
   Dougald 212
   Eliza. 321
   Elizabeth 211
   Francis 463
   G. 321
   Geo. 321
   H. 343
   Hugh 321
   Isobel 213
   James 121, 212, 343, 366, 463
   Jane 321, 366
   Jane, Jr. 343
   Jane, Sr. 344
   Janet 211, 220
   Jas. 321
   John 211, 212, 213, 321, 366,
   463
   Kenneth 213
   Letitia, Mrs. 366
   Lilly 212
   Margaret 211
   Martha 366
   Michael 463
   Moses 321
   Patrick 211, 463
   Rebecca 366
   Robert 366
   Rose 367
   Sally 367
   Saml. 321
   Samuel 367
   Sarah 321
   Thomas 212, 367
   William 213, 220, 285, 287,
   344, 367
   Wm. 293, 321, 367
   Wm. H. 258
Stiehl, Abraham 37
   Johann Abraham 37
Stiles, James 139
Stilt, John 367
Stilwell, --- 346
Stinebrenner, Christian 241
Stinton, Daniel 367
Stirling, Martha 344
   Thomas 344
   William 534
Stitt, Wm. 321
Stockdale, Jane 344
   John 344

   William 344
Stocker, Michael 6
Stoehr, Anna Elisabeth 185
   Anna Margaretha 185
   Anna Maria 185
   Heinrich 185
   Johannes 185
   Maria Barbara 185
   Maria Magdalena 185
   Philip 185
Stoever, John Caspar, Jr., Rev. 4
   John Caspar, Sr., Rev. 4
Stolea, Hanna Maria 164
Stoll, Anna Maria 46
Stolze, Anna Maria 224
Stone, --- 321
Stoneby, Henry 251
Stoop, John 367
Story, Ann 291
   Ben 291
   Eliz. 291
   Robert 367
Stothard, Adam 321
Stout, John 344
Stowell, Caleb 532
Strahan, --- 348
Strain, Hugh 321
   Jane 321
   Jas. 321
   John 321
   Mary 321
   Wm. 321
Stram, John 367
Stranblar, John 110
Strangford, ---, Lord 321
Strassburger, Johann Andreas 25
   Ulrich 25
Stratford, Edwd. 321
Stratton, --- 348
Strawbridge, --- 348
   John 367
Strawn, --- 348
Strean, --- 348
   John 344, 367
Strebeck, Christian 27, 38
   Jerich 27, 38
Street, Thomas 140
Streeter, Robt. 321
Strenaghan, Elizth. 321
   Thos. 321
Stribeck, Christian 27, 38
   Conrad 27, 38
   Elisabetha 27, 38
   Johann Georg 27, 38
Stringer, Ann 139
   Frederick 275
Stroh, Frederic 327
Strohm, Benedict 3
Strohschneider, Anna Barbara 44
   Philipp 44
Strong, Chr. 344
   Hugh 344
Strouse, Henry 241
Struck, John 166
   John, Jr. 166
Strunck, Johann Wilhelm 23
Stuart, Bridget 463, 464
   Catherine 463
   Charles 463, 464
   David 230
   Eliza 464
   Elizth. 321
   Ellen 463
   George 230, 463
   Guillaume 230
   James 139, 367, 463
   John 463
   Mary 230, 463

594

Michael 464
Michel 230
Patrick 463
Rachel 230
Salli 230
Sarah Ann 321
William 367, 464
Stub, H. A., Rev. 431, 432
Stubbs, Edward 245
William 245
Stuebinger, Andreas 48
Michel 48
Stuiger, George 251
Stuly, Jacob 113
Stump, Johann Michel 36
Johann Nickel 36
Stuotz, Frederick 275
Sudermann, Elisabeth 517
Jakob 517
Johann 517
Leonhard 517
Suess, Cyriacus 35
Sullivan, --- 510
Dan 496
Daniel 138, 487, 495
Denis 495
Jeremiah 260, 272, 277, 279, 285, 286, 367
John 495, 496
Judy 495, 496
Madge 495
Margaret 499
Mary 489, 496
May 496
Michael 496
Own 510
Pat 496
Peggy 495
Sumners, Sarah 139
Sunderland, ---, Lord 321
Surzedas, Abraham 155
Rachael 155
Sutherland, Anna 121
Elisbie 121
John 210
Thomas J. 260
Willm. 210
Wm. 204
Worthington 260
Sutliff, Edward 344
Henry 344
Sutton, ---, Lieut.-Gen. 321
William 344
Svensdatter, Sikke 398
Swagert, Hans Mich'l 167
Swan, Alexander 367
David 367
John 367
Margaret 367
Thomas 344
William 245
Swanton, John 247
Swart, Margaret 166
Sweeney, George 251
James 283, 344
Terence 367
Sweeny, Andrew 367
Anne 367
Archibald 367
Catherine 367
Connel 344
Eleanor 367
George 262, 277
James 367
Jeremiah 367
Mary 367
Prudence 344
William 344, 367

Sweetman, Catharine 367
John 245
Swenny, Patrick 344
Swift, Abr., Capt. 321
Michl., Cornet 321
Swiney, John 245
Swope, Christopher 241
Syce, Johann Adam 131
Syllyman, Billy 344
John 344
Symes, Ann 80
Anne 80
Eliz. 80
George 80
Rd., Lieut. 321
Sarah 80
Syms, Anne 77
Geo. 77
Synge, Edward 321
Syvertson, S 428

-- T --

Taane, H. I. 429, 442
Helge 442
Tagart, Joseph 344
Taggart, William 367
Talebach, George 107
Tanner, Jacob 108
John 367
Tarnlane, Thos. 446
Tash, Johann Philipp 131
Tastad, Elias 372, 374, 386, 388, 396, 399
Tastel, Nicholas 260
Tastet, Nicholas 260
Tate, James 344
Tattin, Victor 322
Taverner, George 190
Taylor, Ann 322
Cath. 322
Duncan 121
James 344
Jas. 322
John 283
Louisa 344
Marion 201
Mary 121, 199
Michael 367
Richard 367
Robert 417, 418
Samuel H. 282
Thomas 263, 288
Walt. 322
Teas, Easter 344
Teichgröb, Anna 522
Hermann 522
Justina 522
Katharina 522
Maria 522
Peter 522
Susanna 522
Teir, Jas. 322
Teis, Georg Adam 70
Te Kamp, John 245
Teleback, George 112
Teller, Jno. 165
Temen, Robert 367
Tempest, Rd., Lieut. 322
Templeman, William 192
Templeton, William 367
Tennison, Thos., Cornet 322
Tensen, Ole 390
Tesch, Anna Christina 131
Johann Michel 131
Johann Peter 131

Johann Philipp 125, 131
Maria Dorothea 125, 131
Paul 131
Simon Philipp 131
Tetterton, Ellen 344
Robert 344
Textor, Anna Margarethe 131
Christina Elisabeth 131
Hieronymus 131
Textur, Hieronimus 131
Teyrill, ---, Rev. 322
Theiler, Jac. 164
Theiss, Andreas 70
Catharina 53
Johann Adam 53, 69
Jörg Adam 70
Louisa 53, 68
Magdalena 53, 69, 70
Maria Catharine 69
Theobald, Johannes 48
Maria Catharina 48
Theobaldt, Johann Jacob 142
Thermin, Anthoine 106
Theyler, Jno. 164
Thibaut, Daniel 80
Diana 80
James 80
Mary 80
Thielbon, Henrich 142
Thiessen, Anna 516
Diedrich 516
Thim, David 234
Thomas, ---, Capt. 76
Ann 443, 446
Edward Augustus 241
John 344
Louisa 443
Mary 443
Richard 443
Richd. 444
William 367
Wm. 446
Thomasen, Ann 415
Osmund 415
Thomasson, N 403
Thome, Robt. 322
Thommas, Michel 31
Thompson, --- 346, 367, 442
---, Capt. 77, 97
Alex 344
Alexander 293
Andrew 367
Ann 322
Archd. 322
Archibald 272
Arthur 282, 367
Benjn. 322
Eliza 344
Ellen 407
Elizth. 322
Geo. 367
George 223, 256, 344, 367
Hannah 139
Hector 322
Helge 442
Hugh 322
Isaac 193
James 293, 344, 367
Jane 134, 322
Janet Wilson 223
Jas. 322
John 322, 344, 367
Joseph 344, 367
Margt. 322
Marg't 344
Maria 344
Martha 322
Mary 121, 322, 367

Moses 134
Nels 383
Oyen 383
Peter 223
Pishey 260
Pishie 250
Richard Whyte 244
Robert 134, 344
Robt. 322
Rob't 344
Rosan 322
Rose 322
Sara T. 383
Sarah 344
Thomas 367
Thomas A. 410
Torger 437, 438
William 134, 344, 367
Wm. 322, 344, 532
Thomson, Alexander 223
Alexr. 534
Allan 121
Archibald 121
Betty 223
Catharine 121
Cristie 121
Dugald 121
Duncan 121
Elisbie 121
Henry 223
James 344
Jane 344
Janet Korest 223
Katherine 223
Margaret 121
Neil 200
Robt. 322
Rodger 121
William 223
Thorbiorns, Ole 410, 412, 414, 415
Thordatter, Merthe 412, 414
Thornberry, Susan 367
Thornborough, Geo., Adjt. 322
Thornbury, Js. 322
Mary 322
Thorne, John 344
Thornton, John 367
Nicholas 367
Thorpe, Robert 95
Thorson, Oyen 383
Thuerwaechter, Ehrhardt 42
Thune, II J 420, 429
Tiebinger, Bernhard 19
Tiefenbach, Caspar 179
Tierney, Francis 367
Joseph 367
Margaret 367
Tierny, Hugh 367
Tighe, Michael 367
Tigut, --- 348
Matthew 367
Tilson, George 322
Thos., Jun. 322
Thos., Sen. 322
Timmory, Edward 344
Timons, Isabella 344
Timothy 344
Tims, Henry 256
Tindall, William 367
Tiney, Thomas 367
Tippet, Charles 444
Hannah 444
Reginald 444
Titerly, Jno. 167
Tizzard, John 139
Tjiel, Samuel Thoralsen 411
Tobin, Catherine 367
Tobine, Fra., Ensign 322

Todd, Samuel 367
Stephen 367
Thomas 367
Toland, John 367
Tollefson, Anna 401
Tonnes 401
Tönnes 408
Tolleivson, Anna 401
Tonnes 401
Tollerson, Tormes 400
Tollevson, Tonnes 400
Tormes 398, 400, 408
Tomkyns, Jno. 188, 189, 190,
191, 192, 193, 194
Tomlinson, Jos. 322
Tomm, Fras., Lieut. 322
Ton, Henry 165
Tone, Robert 367
Toner, B. 367
Tong, ---, Miss 191
Tonkin, Caroline 446
Tonnaly, James 367
Tonner, Catherine 344
Toole, Emanuel 344
Michael 367
Peter 344
Topham, George 281
Torborn, Andrew 220
Torison, Halstein 400
Torrers, Ann 344
Ruth 344
Samuel 344
Torres, David 152
Rema 154
Torrison, Halstein 400
Torry, Catharine 122
Florrance 122
George 122
James 122
Mary 122
Torstendatter, M. 429, 436, 439
Torstensdatter, Arnbjorg 439
M. 429, 436, 438
Torstensen, G. 429, 436, 437
Tosseland, K V 402
Tösseland, --- 408
Towor, James 292
Towmey, Denis 510
Townsend, ---, Col. 322
Edwd. 78
Mary 78
Townshend, ---, Lord 322
Töws, Gerhard 522
Isaak 522
Tracey, William 367
Wm., Capt. 322
Tracy, Catharine 367
Dennis 367
Hugh 344
Mary 367
Richd., Capt. 322
Thomas 367
Trainer, Jas. 322
Mary 322
Thos. 322
Tranar, James 344
Traner, Bany 344
Trangereide, S E 404
Transu, Abraham 31
Transue, Abraham 6
Traub, Heinrich 51
J. Adam 51
Jacob 51
Johann Adam 51
Trauth, Anna Barbara 60
Johann Georg 60
Trautman, Georg Adam 224
Trautmann, Georg 48

Henrich 48
Hieronimus 18
Johannes 19
Maria Eva 48
Susanna 48
Trauttmann, Hyronimus 19
Travers, John 258
Patrick 367
Trawiener, Peter 31
Trayor, Godfrey 165
Trefz, G. Adam 328
Treibel, Martin 170
Treibelbiss, Anna Margaretha 44
Jacob 44
Johann Jacob 44
Trenham, James 194
Tretland, Endre 389, 392
Maria 389, 392
Osmund 389
Osmund Endresen 389, 392
Reier 389
Trevar, Patrick 344
Trewartha, Edwd. 444
Trexler, David 234
Trimble, Ann 134
John 134
Margaret 134
Mary 134
William 344
Trippel, Daniel 327
Trist, --- 226
Triven, John 344
Troelsdatter, Mette 391, 396
Trois, David Nunes 155
Ester Nunes 155
Trotter, William 367
Trovatte, Ole K. 424
Trovatten, O. Knudzon 434
Ole 434, 435
Ole Knudsen 425
Troxell, John 12
John Peter 12
Peter 9
Truckenmiller, Sebastian 9
Trueb, Anna Barbara 48
Catharina Elisabetha 48
David 48
Jacob 48
Trulsdatter, Metha (Metta, Mette)
396
Truman, Henry 285
Trumpeter, Felix 328
Trunnel, Henry 269
Tschiffely, Frederick 260
Frederick D. 250
Tuck, John 453
Tucker, Amaziah 265
James 260
Tuckerbury, Benj. 344
Tuckfield, Wm. H. P. 256, 260
Tuebinger, Bernhard 19
Tuite, --- 348
Jas. 322
Tukance, ---, Capt. 78
Molly 78
Tullamore, ---, Lord 322
Tullus, Jane 322
Jas. 322
Jas. McCulloch, Rev. 322
Margt. 322
Wm. 322
Turkenton, --- 330
James 344
Jane 344
John 344
Turley, Anne 367
Eliza 367
John 367

596

Sarah 367
Turner, --- 77
  Bartlett 344
  J. 191, 322
  James 113
  Robert 530
  William 139, 344
Turtle, Lancelot 322
Tuscanee, ---, Capt. 78
Tutland, Malinda 392
  Osmund 392
Tuttle, Osmund 392
Twamley, George 367
  Jane 367
  Mary 367
Tweedy, Dav. 322
  Effy 344
  Patrick 344
Twiggs, D. E., Col. 269
Tyler, Truman 251
Tymberton, Constable 531
Tyrawly, ---, Lord, Lieut.-Gen. 322
Tyrell, ---, Rev. 322
Tyrrell, H. 500
Tysland, K. V. 402, 404, 408, 416
  Knut 408
  Knut W. 408, 416
Tzatt, Saml. 189

-- U --

Uhl, Michael 327
Uhler, Anastasius 7
Ullm, Anna Barbara 67
  Johann Michael 67
Ullrich, Catharina 44
Ulm, Johanna 67
Ulmer, Leonard 326
  Thomas 326
  Verner 167
Underwood, Richard 139
Ungerer, Anna Maria 58
  Johann Michel 58
  Stephan 58
Unruh, Abraham 518
  Adelgunde 526
  Anna 518
  Eva 518
  Heinrich 526
  Helena 526
  Jakob 518
  Johann 526
  Julia 518
  Katharina 518, 526
  Klaas 526
  Kornelius 518
  Maria 526
  Peter 518, 526
  Sarah 518
  Susanna 526
Upton, --- 322
  Clotworthy 322
  Sarah 322
  Thos. 322
Ure, Jane 322
  Margt. 322
Urland, A. A. 440
Urquhart, Alexr. 190, 194
Uttermuhle, William 271

-- V --

Vaelde, Hans Olsen 414

Vaete, Halle 402
Vaharty, Miles 367
Vaihinger, Joshua 326
Valder, --- 394
  Hans 413, 414
  Hans Olsen 414
Vale, John 344
  Margaret 344
Valentia, ---, Lord 322
  Abigall 154
  David 154
Valle, Christopher Danielson 414
  Sigrid Persdatter 432
Valleton, Anne 103
Valours, Jaques 110
Vanable, Charly 287
Vanay, John Francis 111
Vance, D. 344
  Isaac 344
Vanderheyd, --- 113
Vanderplank, John 81
Vander Veen, Wm. 328
Vandle, Jacob 117
Van huise, Tonnes 512
Van Lengerke, Harmann Fredrich 247
Vannerheid, Peter Janett 113
Van Riswick, William 288
Varela, Pedro 227
Varnod, ---, Madame 104
  Abram 104
  Francois 104
  Frantions 104
Vas, Antony 246
Vatname, Helge 400
Vatt, Jean 83
Vaughan, George 140
  James 367
  Thomas 367
  Y. 367
Vaughn, Wm. 532
Veasy, --- 322
Veatch, James 367
Vega, Rice 154
Velde, --- 394
  Berthe Olddatter 411
  Hans Olsen 410, 411, 413, 414
  Ole Hansen 411
Velten, Conrad 47
  Johann Peter 29
  Johann Petter 47
Verdier, Andre 108
Vere, John, Lieut. 322
Vernan, Thomas 188
Vernays, Francis 108
Vernezobre, Daniel 98, 100, 107
Vernezohre, Daniel 98
Vesey, ---, Miss 322
Veste, Thorbjorn 402
Vetter, Adam 179
Vettesloe, N K 404
Viel, Anna Margaretha 45
  Anna Maria 29
  Johann Jacob 44
  Maria 45
  Theobald 44, 45
Vieller, Frederick 250
Vigneu, Stephen 108
Vilhelmsdatter, A. 404, 407
Viller, Anna Eunets 109
  Anna Maria 109
  Anne Mary 109
Villinger, Godfrey 326
Vimmo, --- 330
  Charles 344
  Eliza 344
Vincent, Elizabeth 443
  Mary 443

Rich., Rev. 322
Saml. 443
Vindeg, Anna 406, 433
  Gunnel Olsen 433
  Gunnul 406
  Helleik 433
Vinera, Dall. Rodrigues 163
  Danll. Rodrigues 156
Vinje, A. A. 419, 420, 425
  Anders Arnesen 441
  Arne Anderson 440, 441
Vinninger, David 328
Virtue, David 344
Vizea, Rebecca Nunez 155
Vogan, Rich. 323
  Thos. 323
Vogelgesang, Anna Appolonia 41
  Georg 28, 41
  Georg, Jr. 41
Vogelsang, Anna Appolonia 28
  Georg 28
Vogt, Aganeta 525
  Agatha 525
  Anna 525
  Jakob 525
Voltziem, J F 405
von Diebendorf, Cuno, Knight 3
von Krogh, Abel Catharine 393
Vorsner, Jos. 167
Vosselmann, Hans Erhart 50
Vosselmann, Ludwig 68
  Maria Margaretha 68
Voth, Abraham 522
  Diedrich 522
  Elisabeth 522
  Elisah. 514
  Katharina 522
  Maria 522
  Peter 522
  Sussanna 522
Voucher, Alles 113
Voyer, Jeanne Urbaine 106

-- W --

Wacum, --- 348
  Robert 367
Waddel, Ralph 344
Waddell, Jas. 323
  Robt. 323
Wade, James 367
  Wm., Cornet 323
Wagenor, John 241
Wagner, Anna Margaretha 39
  Anna Maria 124
  Barbara 48
  Johanes 21, 180
  Johann 180
  Johann Adam 48
  Johann Sebastian 124
  Johannes 21
  Mathias 8
  Theobald 48
Wahnzodel, John George 531
Waits, Elizabeth 530
Waker, John 534
Wakline, Walt 323
Walcott, Stephen 454, 469, 485
Walde, --- 394
  Anna 390
  Bertha 390
  Cecille 390
  Christen 412, 414
  Christen Danielsen 410, 412, 414, 415
  Daniel Christian 412

Danielsen 412
Inger Reier Datter 412
Iver R. 390, 394
Jacob 412
Merthe Thordatter 412, 414
Osmund Danielsen 412
Peter Jacobsen 412
Reier 390
Walder, Jno. 166
Johann Jacob 66
Waldron, Thomas 367
Walker, Ann 221
Armstrong 344
Cathr. 196
Constantine 367
David 223, 260, 367
Donald 223
Eliza 223, 367
Geo. 323
Geo., Dr. 323
George 367
H. 367
J. 367
James 344, 367
Jane 367
John 323, 344
John F. 367
Joseph 367
M. 367
Martha 367
Mary 367
R. 367
Robert J. 344
Samuel 277
Thos. 323
William 190, 260, 367
Walkinshaw, William 367
Wall, --- 344
Aganeta 518, 526
Anna 516, 526
Cornelius 518
Easter 344
Elisab. 516
Elisabeth 518
Gerhard 518
Helena 526
Isaak 516
Johann 516, 518
John 344
Justina 515
Katharina 526
Kornelius 515, 518, 526
Margar. 515
Margaretha 516
Maria 514, 515, 516
Peter 516
Sarah 526
Thos. 323
Wallace, ---, Widow 323
George 344
Hannah 367
Hugh 344
James 246, 255, 367
James, Rev. 261
John 344
Jonathan 254
Margaret 367
S. 367
Sam'l 344
Thomas 367
Wm. 323
Wallach, Richard 257, 270, 281
Richard, Esq. 255
Wallack, Richard 254, 262
Wallas, Robt. 323
Wallen, Knud Danielsen 414
Knud Danielson 410, 413, 414, 416

Siri 413, 414
Waller, John, Capt. 323
Nicholas 64
Wallington, --- 346
Wallis, Elizabeth 76
James 444
Walpole, Robt. 323
Walsh, --- 510
Bridget 367
Daniel 367
Eliza 367
F., Miss 344
Hugh 367
James 367
John 344, 367
Lawrence 367
M. R. 367
Mary 344
Patrick 367
Thomas 344
William 344
Walter, Hans 66
Johan Jakob 66
Johannes 66
Mary 532
Nicholas 64
Walther, Anna Apollonia 64
Anna Elisabeth 64
Anna Maria 66
Christoph 18
Christopher 18
Johann Jacob 66
Johann Jakob 66
Nicolaus 64
Walton, John 323
Thos., Qr. Master 323
Walz, George 326
Wamb, John 344
Wander, Anna Christina 131
Anna Eva 132
Anna Maria 131
Heinrich 131
Johann Heinrich 132
Johann Philipp 131
Johann Tobias 131
Simon Jakob 131
Wansborough, Wm., Capt. 323
Wantya, --- 348
Richmond 367
Ward, --- 323
---, Chief Justice 162
Anne 367
Ch. 323
Elizabeth 138
James 344
John 270
Nelly 344
Patrick 367
Robt. 323
Thomas 139
Thos. 323
William 367
Warden, Jas. 323
Jos. 323
Wardlaw, Elizabeth 344
Wardle, Jeremiah 367
Wardler, Hugh 367
Ware, James 367
Waring, Hen. 323
Warkentin, ---, Frau 524
Abraham 523
Aron 523
Elisabeth 521
Gerhard 521
Helena 521, 523, 524
Johann 524
Justina 521
Katharina 523

Peter 521, 524
Susanna 524
Wilhelmine 521
Warle, Jacob 166
Warloe, E. 426, 428
Warnick, R. 367
Warnock, John 367
Warr, Eliza 368
George 368
Samuel 368
Warren, Abel, Ensign 323
Edward 368
Edwd. 323
Hugh 344
Jane 344
John 139, 368
Warrier, George 368
Warrin, Elizabeth 80
John 80
Wm. 80
Wart, Bernhard 34
Warth, Bern 34
Wasenberger, Peter 25
Washbourn, Levi 264
Washburn, Levi 264
Washington, ---, President 10
George 249
Martha 250
Wason, Archer 344
George 344
Jane 344
Margaret 344
Nancy 344
Wass, John 368
Watchter, Jno. Geo. 167
Waterland, ---, Dr. 81
Wm 81
Waters, --- 368
Andrew 344
Archibald 368
John 251, 254, 368
Roger 368
Thos. G. 251
William 288
Winifred 368
Wm. 251
Waterson, John 368
Watersone, William 534
Watnem, Britha K 398
Helge 398, 400
Kari 398
Lars 398
Ole 398
Peder 398
Sophia 398
Thormond 398
Watson, Alexander 368
Hugh 323
James 344, 368, 534
Martha 323
Mary 323
Thomas 139
William 368
Watt, James 344, 368
Jane 344
Jas. 323
John 344
John B. 323
Margaret 344
Margt. 323
Thos. 323
Wm. 323
Watts, Charles 368
Frances 77
Ja., Lieut. 77
James 368
Jane 368
Joseph 368

Margaret 368
Mary 368
Wattsher, John 344
Weale, James 453, 466
Weapher, Ann 344
Weathers, Joseph 368
Weaver, Jacob 165
Webb, Edward 530
Joseph 289
Weber, Anna Margarethe 127
Daniel 49
Georg 49
Jacob 49, 241, 288
Johann Daniel 49
Johann Peter 224
Johanna Felicitas 5
Joseph 283
Michael 5
Philipp 49
Phillis 5
Sebastian Jakob 127
Webster, E. 323
Thomas 368
Thos., Sir 323
Wedel, Abraham 524
Anna 524
Benjamin 524
Caspar 20
Elisabeth 524, 525
Michel 17
Peter 524
Weeks, Caroline 368
Charles 368
Frances 368
Jane 368
Thos. 368
Weffs, John 110
Weibel, Friedrich 225
Weiber, Henry 164
Weidel, George Adam 5
Weilbrenner, Catharina 43
Georg Daniel 43
Johann Peter 43
Weinheimer, Anna Margaretha 54
Weir, Geo. 323
Jas. 323
Mary 323
Weis, Daniel 51
Johann Peter 51
Margaretha 51
Weiser, Anna 185
Anna Catharina 181
Benjamin 185
Christoph 185
Conrad 14
Elisabeth 185
Friedrich 181
Georg Friedrich 185
Jabez 185
Jacob 181, 185
Johann Conrad 185
Margaretha 185
Philippus 181
Rebecca 181
Weiskob, Johan Esaias 36
Weiss, --- 44
Abraham 51
Adam 25
Catharina 51
Conrad 179
Daniel 51
Frantz 51
George Michael, Rev. 2
Hanss Peter 51
Jacob 51
Johann Adam 26
Lewis 325

Margaretha 51
Maria Odilia 46
Weisskopff, Esaias 36
Weitzel, Peter 25
Welch, Patk. 323
Welcker, Georg 19
Jacob 41
John George 2
Wilhelm 28
Welde, Jacob 175
Welker, Jacob 28, 41
Wilhelm 41
Wellecker, Rudolf 2
Wellemsin, Tönnes 388
Wellen, Elias Ann 77
Weller, Adam 241
Henrich 2
Wells, Cornelius 279
John 137
Joseph 140
Peter 368
Welsh, Anne 417
John 344, 417
Louisa 344
Mary 417
Weltch, H. 344
Went, James 137, 139
Wentworth, Tho., Lieut.-Col. 323
Thos., Col. 323
Wentzell, Johann Adam 173
Werkslagen, Paul 533
Werner, Debalt 58
Harry M. T. 287
Henry M. T. 287
J. H. D. 284
J. H. T. 281
John Jacob 241
Werns, Jacob 180
Wernz, Jacob 180
Werryfield, Jacob 533
Wescott, Philip 192
Wessener, --- 179
Wessingher, Jno. 164
West, Anne 368
David 344
Eliz. 81
Elizabeth 78, 79, 81
James 344
Jas. 368
Jno. 533
Jo. 78
John 78, 79, 81, 193, 368
Margaret 368
Rd., Cornet 323
Richard 81
Thmoas 368
William 344, 368
Wm. 368
Westerberger, Peter 25
Weston, Ann 192
Wetzel, Catharina 32
Conrad 32
Johann Adam 173
Lawrence 165
Wetzstein, Andreas 21
Weytzel, Johann Paul 25
Whalen, Thomas 368
Whaplett, --- 323
Wharton, James 252, 253
Jas. 251
Joseph 344
Robert 344
Wheelock, Alice 368
Whelan, Nicholas 368
Patrick 368
Whetlay, James 534
Whichcote, P. 323

Whiston, Js., Capt. 323
Whit, John 323, 368
White, Alexander 344, 368
Ann 483
Anne 323, 483
Biddy 484
Bridget 483, 484, 502
Catherine 483, 484
Cisly 302, 306
Edward 483
Elizabeth 368
Ellen 368
Francis 368
Harriet 484
Honor 484
James 344, 368, 502
Jane 368, 484
John 191, 192, 344, 471, 477, 483, 484, 502
Margaret 483, 484
Martin 484
Mary 477, 483, 484, 502, 503
Mathew 368
Michael 484
Nancy 484
Pat 471, 477, 483, 484
Peggy 483
Richard 368
Sally 483
Saml. 323
Sarah 191
Thomas 483, 484
Wm. 323
Whiteside, William 368
Whitfield, Hen. 323
Whitford, William 368
Whitmore, Christian 533
Whitshed, ---, Lord 323
Whitworth, ---, Major 323
Whyt, Robert 195
Wickens, --- 323
---, Mrs. 323
Wicks, Fra. 76
John 139
Mary 76
Widdrington, Chas., Ensign 323
Widron, Jean 122
Wieand, Wendel 5
Wiedtemann, Maria Juditha 62
Wiens, ---, Frau 521
Franz 516, 521
Helene 515, 516
Jakob 521
Johann 515
Klaas 521
Kornelius 515
Maria 521
Peter 516
Susanna 521
Wigging, Rachel 368
Wiggins, Henry 368
Wilcox, Charles G. 268, 286
Wild, Anna Maria 27
Conrad 27
Nickel 27
Philipp 27
Wildemann, Jacob 177
Wildfang, Jacob 11
Wiley, Ann 368
Elizabeth 368
John 259, 368
Jos. 323
Mary 368
Thomas 368
Wilhe, André 230
Wilis, James 368
Wilkenson, William 530
Wilkins, George 344

599

Wilkinson, John 292, 368
  Samuel 264
  William 368
Will, Anna Eva 62
  Anna Marie 17
  Isaac 62
  Wilhelm 62
Willaar, Caspar 531
Willberger, Charles 264
  Charles H. 263
Wille, Isaac 62
Willemsen, Tonnes 385, 386,
  388, 395, 396
Willemsin, Tonnes 388
Willes, Joshua 368
  Mary 368
Willey, Edwd. 444
Willfey, Robert 531
William, E. W., Mrs. 368
Williams, Ann 139
  Eliza 324, 446
  Elizabeth 446
  George 344
  Henry 344
  James 275
  Jane 417
  John 188, 287, 323, 324, 446
  Michael P. 279
  Rich. 324
  Robert 110
  Thomas 262
  Thomas Hollaway 262
  Thos. 446
  William R. 244
  Wm. 324, 345
Williamson, --- 387
  Andrew 195
  Elizabeth 345
  Fra., Major 324
  Henry 345
  Jane 345
Willikin, Mary 345
Willis, Eleanor 368
  Margaret 345
  Mary Ann 345
  Mathew 345
  Richard 368
  William 345
Willmott, Samuel Devonshire
  262
Willms, Abraham 521, 524
  Aganeta 521
  Agatha 524
  Anna 524
  Elisabeth 521
  Helena 524
  Jakob 524
  Johann 524
  Katharina 524
  Margaretha 521
  Maria 524
Willner, George 262, 275
Willson, Jas. 324
Wilmott, Samuel Devonshire 262
Wilson, A., Rev. 368
  Ann 139, 324
  Benjamin 345
  Charles 368
  Charity 134
  Dav. 324
  David 134, 189, 368
  Edwd. 292
  Elizabeth 134, 345
  Gilbert 193
  James 81, 134, 190, 197, 241,
    292, 345, 368
  Jane 324, 368
  Janet 223

Jannett 324
John 134, 292, 324, 345, 368
John, Capt. 324
Joseph 368
Josh. 324
Marcus 368
Margaret 289
Margt. 324
Martha 134
Mary 324, 368
Matthew 134, 368
Mildred 81
Robert 345, 368
Robt. 324
(S) L. M. 270
Sarah 134, 368
Thomas 289, 345, 368
William 134, 188, 289, 368
Wiltberger, Charles 264
  Charles H. 263
Wimsett, John 253
Winckler, Andrew 105
  Anna Susan 105
  Eve Elizabeth 104
  Frederick 104
  Luis 104
Windag, Anne O. 429, 433
Windge, A. A. 423, 429, 436, 440
Wingate, Chas., Lieut. 324
Wingerter, Anna Barbara 66
  Anna Margaretha 66
  Anna Maria 66
  David 66
  Johann Daniel 66
  Johann Jakob 66
  Maria Christina 66
Wink, Stephen 533
Winkler, Andrew 106, 109
  Anna Catarina 104
  Jacob 106
  Jaque 104
  Nicholas 104
Winnart, Dav. 324
Winning, Wm. 324
Winship, Thomas 191
Winstanley, John 368
Winter, --- 324
  Catherine 464
  Honor 464
  John 325
  Margaret 464
  Samuel 262
  Thomas 139, 192, 464
Winters, Catherine 464
  Edward 345
  Honor 464
  Margaret 464
  Mary 345
  Thomas 464
Winther, Samuel 176
Wintz, Georg 39
  Margretha 39
  Sibilla 39
Wirt, John L. 280
Wirth, Anna Christina 129
  Johann Philipp 129
  Matthias 129
Wirthsbacher, Friedrich 40
Wise, William 287
Wiseman, John 259
Wishat, Mary 345
  Robert 345
  Ruth 345
  Sarah 345
Withered, Robt. 324
Witherington, A. 345
Withers, Henry 345
  Sarah 139

Wm. 368
Witherspoon, Eliza 324
  Hen. 324
  Jas. 324
  John 324
  Margt. 324
Witmer, --- 11
  Michale 10
  Peter 10
  Ulrich 10
Woessinger, Mattheus 179
Wogan, Christian 345
Wolf, Hayman 238
  Henry 238
  Wolfgang 25
Wolfart, Johann Adam 171
Wolfer, Frederic 327
Wolff, Johannes 142
Wolffskehl, Anna Margretha 29, 37
  Anna Maria 29, 37
  Elisabetha 29, 37
  Johan Jacob 29
  Johannes 29, 37, 45
  Maria 29, 37
  Maria Agnes 29, 37
Wolgamode, Samuel 533
Wollfarth, Johann Adam 171
Wood, James 138
  Mary 138
  Thomas 368
Woodhouse, ---, Capt. 257
Woodman, Mary 79
Woods, Adam 345
  Eliza 368
  James 345, 368
  Ruth 368
  Saml. 324
  William 289, 368
Woodside, R. 368
  Wm. 368
Woodward, Thomas 271, 272, 284
  William 271
  William R. 282
Woolf, Henrich 238
  Heyman 238
Woolff, Hayman 238
  Heyman 238
Worker, Nathaniel 190
Workman, Agnes 324
  Geo. 324
  George 368
  Jane 324
  Jas. 324
  Margt. 324
  Robt. 324
  Saml. 324
  Wm. 324
Worlich, Michael 177
Worman, Henry 533
Worner, Phillipp Jacob 177
Worrington, John 368
Worth, Joseph 530
Worthington, --- 324
Wray, Benjamin 417
  Elizabeth 417
  James 368
  Martha 417
  William 368
Wren, Jordan, Ensign 324
Wright, Ann 345
  Catherine 345
  Daniel 267
  Eliza 345
  Elizabeth 81
  Henry 368
  Isobel 215
  James 345, 368
  Jane 368

600

Jas. 324
Jenny 324
John 81, 345, 368
Mariam 368
Mary 324
Mathan 368
Mathew 272
Michael 368
Penelope 81
Reedy 324
Richard 264, 267, 288
Robt. 324
Thomas C. 253
William 368
Wuertenbecher, Anna Maria 45
  Bernhard 45
  Johann Adam 45
  Johannes 45
Wuerthsbacher, Friedrich 40
  Margretha 40
Wuertz, Anna 11
  John Conrad 11
Wulff, Wolfgang 26
Wunder, Andreas 71
  Anna Maria 70
  Catharina 71
  Christian 69, 71
  Christoph 70
  Jacob 70, 71
  Jakob 70
  Johann Jacob 70
  Johann Jakob 69, 70
  Jörg Adam 70
  Maria Barbara 70
  Maria Eva 71
  Sebastian 70
  Valentin 70
Wunderlick, John 109
Wurms, Anna 525
  Helena 526
  Jakob 525, 526
  Katharina 525
Wurtzbacher, Friderich 40
Wyandt, Wendel 5
Wyland, James 294
Wylie, David 248
  Rachel 345

Wynn, John 464
  Mary 464
  Owen, Major-Gen. 324
  Patrick 464
Wynne, Bell 464
  Bridget 464
  Catherine 464
  James 464
  John 464
  Mary 464
  Michael 464
  Owen, Major-Gen. 324
  Patrick 368, 464

-- X --

Xander, David 179

-- Y --

Yanam, Francis 113
Yeager, John 533
Yerkardt, George 533
Yost, Benedict 277
Young, Agada 134
  Alexander 368
  Alexr 534
  David 345
  Eliza 368
  Fanny 345
  Jacob 164
  James 134, 345
  Jas. 324
  John 345, 368
  Julia 134
  Martha 324
  Mary 345
  Matt. 324
  Robert 134, 368
  Samuel 134
  Susan 368
  Symon 324
  Thomas 81, 198, 368

Valantine 51
William 252, 345

-- Z --

Zacharias, Daniel 236
Zachelmeyer, Margaretha 62
Zaenglein, Johann Christoph 234
Zagelmejer, Margaretha 62
Zahneissen, Juliana 45
  Valentin 45
Zaneichel, Vallentin 45
Zcisloff, George 12
Zell, Johann Mikolaus 142
Zilling, Michel 170
Zimmer, Anna Catharine 51
Zimmerman, G. Godlob 327
  Michael 3
Zimmermann, Andreas 18
  Catharina 22
  David 179
  Niclas 21
Zimpelmann, Adam 51
Zoller, Geo. Leonard 46
  Georg Leonard 46
  Leonard 46
  Maria Odilia 46
Zouberbukber, Savastian 112
Zublier, David 111
Zutter, Balthasar 27, 38
  Benedict Baltzer 38
  Benedikt Balthasar 27
  Daniel 27, 38
Zweisig, Valdin 18, 35
  Valentin 18
  Valentine 35
Zweissig, Valentin 18
Zwicker, Georg Melchior 59
  Johann Georg 59
  Johann Peter 59, 74
  Magdalena 59
  Maria Barbara 59
  Maria Magdalena 59
  Samuel 74
  Susanna Barbara 74

INDEX OF SHIPS

Active 370
Actress 370
Adventure 43
Adventurer 3, 8
Aegier 403
AEgir 384, 385, 386, 395, 401,
    402, 405, 408, 413, 416, 419
Aeolus 346, 370
Africa 346
Ajax 198
Albany 40
Alexander 346
Alexandria 346
Algernon 346
Alpha 370
Amphion 369
Anderson 51, 172, 177
Ann 81, 346
Anne 76, 369
Atalanta 330

Bachelor 203
Bannister 59
Barclay 45, 51
Barkley 370
Batchelor 211
Belisarius 330, 346
Betsey 57, 71
Betsy 27, 38, 40
Beulah 58
Bilander Thistle 15
Boston 175
Boudain 370
Bremen 377
Bristol 370
Britannia 33, 48, 53, 70, 180
Brittania 6
Briton 190, 194
Brotherhood 43, 172
Brothers 22, 52, 68, 170, 171, 177
Brutus 292

C. Fawcett 369
Carolina 188, 191
Carolina Packet 191, 192, 202
Catherine 512
Ceres 370
Ch. Fawcett 370
Chance 27, 38, 42, 130
Channing 456, 457, 458, 459, 460,
    461, 462, 463, 464
Charming Nancy 15, 51
Chesterfield 169
Christopher 369
Christy 197
Columbus 489, 490, 491, 492, 493,
    494, 496, 498
Commerce 195
Conistoga 370
Courier 369
Crawford 28, 41, 46, 58, 180
Creole 456, 457, 458, 459, 460,
    461, 462, 463, 464

Den Norske Klippe 384, 385, 386,
    396, 408, 419
Den Nortske Klippe 397
Diana 215
Dibby & Eliza 370
Dido 370
Dolphin 97
Dragon 8, 26, 33, 55, 126, 127, 169,
    170
Dublin Packet 369
Duke of Bedford 46
Duke of Wirtenberg 177

Eagle 289
Edinburg 38, 39, 44
Edinburgh 21, 23, 26, 27, 40, 45,
    57, 130, 131, 180
Edward 292
Elisabeth 20, 22
Elizabeth 369, 533
Emilie 419, 420, 422, 423, 424,
    425, 426, 428
Emp. Alexander 369
Enigheden 384, 385, 386, 394, 395,
    399, 409, 410, 411, 414, 415, 419,
    422
Enigheten 409, 411
Enterprize 370
Erin 346, 369
Europa 30, 47
Expedition 532

Falcon 370
Fame 346
Fane 23
Favorite 369
Foster 370
Foundling 370
Francis & Elizabeth 35
Friendship 3, 14, 73, 125, 126, 129,
    130, 131, 190, 191

Gale 217
George 369, 370
George & Albert 369
Glasgow 13
Globe 369
Golconda 346
Good Intent 50
Griffin 530

Hamilton 46, 67
Hampshire 24, 25, 26
Hannah 369
Hannibal 346
Hare 370
Harle 12, 54
Harmony 346
Harvey Hide 346
Helen 369
Henrietta 22
Hero 40, 48, 54

Hibernia 346
Hope 10
Huntress 346

Isaac 26, 36, 49, 346

Jackie 196
Jacob 43, 170
Jamaica Packet 195
James 193
James Bayley 369
James Goodwill 4, 17
Jane 370
Jane Classon 457
Janet 21, 42
Jenneffer 180
John 370
John & Elizabeth 51
John & William 9, 50, 531
Johnson 7
Joseph & Phoebe 346
Judith 36
Juno 346, 370
Jupiter 211, 346

Ketty 50
Kitty 177

Laconic 463
Laurel 2
Le De Spencer 188
Leda 369
London 192, 193, 370
Lorenzo 369
Louisa 370
Lowther 6, 193
Loyal Judith 8, 15, 23, 25, 29, 34,
    35, 36, 37, 142
Lydia 30, 52, 54, 57, 124

Magna Charta 190
Marcus Hill 369, 370
Margaret 291, 325, 370
Margaret & Mary 189
Maria Duplex 346
Mariner 346
Marlborough 125
Mary 346, 369
Mary & Hannah 194
Mary of London 44
Matty 534
Mayflower 371, 376
Mercury 11, 25
Metoka 456, 457, 458, 459, 460,
    461, 462, 463, 464
Mexico 369
Minerva 28, 39, 41, 58, 73, 369
Molly 17, 18, 35, 38, 126, 131
Monimia 198
Montague 370
Mortonhouse 4, 5

602

Mount-Bay 370

Nancy 33, 369
Natchez 226, 230
Nautilus 369
Neptune 45, 46, 53, 124, 290, 291
Newmarket 193
Niagara 370
Nimrod 485
Nlle. Madrid 226, 230
Norden 384, 385, 386, 387, 388,
    393, 394, 395, 396, 419
Norris 62
Northumberland 469, 471, 472,
    473, 474, 476, 477, 478, 479,
    480, 481, 482, 483, 484

Oliver 50
Only Son 370
Ontario 369, 370
Orient 369, 370, 443
Orlando 346
Osgood 22, 54, 171
Ossian 370

Pallas 191
Patience 21, 23, 35, 37, 41, 49,
    169, 170, 173
Patty 346
Peggy 65, 66
Pennsylvania Merchant 27
Pennsylvania Packet 34
Pensilvania Merchant 38
Perseverance 346
Peter & James 88
Phoenix 21, 35, 36, 46, 47, 50, 52,
    58, 59, 62, 68, 177
Polly 53, 69, 70, 71, 190
Prince of Brazil 370

Prince of Wales 58
Princess Augusta 12, 48
Progress 456, 457, 459
Protection 346
Purrysburgh 88, 90

Queen Elizabeth 14
Queen of Denmark 21, 180

Radius 330, 346
Raleigh 346
Restauration 19
Restaurationen 371, 372, 374,
    375, 376, 381, 384, 387, 401
Restoration 376, 384, 419
Richard & Elizabeth 11
Richard & Mary 42, 43, 47, 130
Richmond 56, 57
Rising State 346
Robert & Alice 13, 18, 20, 36, 53,
    65
Rockingham 193
Rosannah 18
Roscius 454, 456, 457, 460, 461,
    462, 463
Rover 293
Rowand 52
Royal Union 46, 71, 173

St. Andrew 11, 12, 19, 24, 26, 28,
    39, 42, 57, 128
Saint Andrew 15, 36
Sally 34, 49, 55, 369
Samuel 6, 9, 12, 15, 43, 63, 65,
    125, 127, 129
Sandwich 35, 172
Sarah Sheaffe 417
Sea Bird 469, 471, 472, 473, 474,
    475, 476, 477, 478, 479, 480,

481, 482, 483, 484
Selen 375
Shamrock 346
Shannon 369
Shirley 19, 22, 24, 177
Shoreham 88
Simmon 96
Snow Squirrel 28, 41
Sophia 370
Speedwell 170
Squirrel 28, 41
Strassburg 514

Thistle 5, 14
Thistle of Glasgow 31, 32
Townshend 20
Tryal 34
Two Brothers 29, 30, 32, 33, 35,
    44, 47, 51, 46, 170, 173, 176, 177
Two Friends 369
Two Sisters 20

Ulysses 197, 198
Union 46, 50, 189

Virginia 369
Volant 81

Westpoint 346, 369, 370
White Oak 346
William 192, 369, 370
William & John 257
William & Sarah 2, 17, 18
Wilson 370
Winter Galley 13, 32, 64, 65, 66

York 138